THE INTERNATIONAL ENCYCLOPEDIA OF FILM

GENERAL EDITOR: **Dr Roger Manvell**

AMERICAN ADVISORY EDITOR: **Professor Lewis Jacobs**

ASSOCIATE EDITORS: **John Gillett**
Margaret Hinxman
David Robinson

ASSISTANT EDITOR (TEXT): **Enid Audus**

ASSISTANT EDITOR (PICTURES): **Louise F. Manvell**

ADDITIONAL CONTRIBUTORS: **Roy Armes**
Brian Coe
Jan Dawson
Gillian Hartnoll
Jack King
John Francis Lane
Jay Leyda
Kenneth Thompson

Michael Joseph

THE INTERNATIONAL ENCYCLOPEDIA OF FILM

This book was designed and produced by
Rainbird Reference Books Limited,
Marble Arch House,
44 Edgware Road, London, W2,
for Michael Joseph Limited,
52 Bedford Square, London, WC1.

House Editor: Mark Amory

Assistant House Editor: Caroline Benwell

Designer: Judith Allan

SBN 7181 1016 1

The text was set in Monophoto Bembo by
Jolly & Barber Limited, Rugby, England.
The book was printed and bound by
Dai Nippon Printing Company Limited,
Tokyo, Japan.

CONTENTS

THE CONTRIBUTORS

Roger Manvell is the author of many well-known books on the film, as well as being a biographer and historian. He was for 12 years Director of the British Film Academy, and is currently Consultant to the Society of Film and Television Arts, into which the Academy was merged in 1959, and editor of its Journal. He is Head of the Department of Film History at the London Film School, and a Visiting Fellow of the University of Sussex. He has scripted many informational and animated films, working with the Halas and Batchelor animation studios in London for several years. He has scripted documentaries and plays for television, and has lectured on the film in some 40 countries in Europe, North America, the Caribbean and Asia. He is a Doctor of Philosophy of London University and in 1971 was made the first non-honorary Doctor of Letters of the University of Sussex for his work in film studies.

Lewis Jacobs trained initially as a painter, but gave his primary attention to the cinema, both as a film-maker and as a critic. After founding 'Experimental Cinema', the first American magazine to be devoted to film as an art and a social force, he became a screenwriter in Hollywood and directed a workshop at Columbia Pictures Corporation for professional writers who wanted to learn about the medium. Since 1950 he has concentrated on directing short films, among them *The Raven, The Stylist, World That Nature Forgot, Ages of Time, The Hutterites.* He also lectures in film study courses at university level. His book 'The Rise of the American Film' (1939) set new standards in the writing of film history. Among later works he has edited are 'Introduction to the Art of the Movies' (1960), 'The Emergence of Film Art' (1968), 'The Movies as Medium' (1970) and 'The Documentary Tradition' (1971).

John Gillett, critic and film researcher, was born in Acton, London and entered films in 1948 after a period as a journalist. He spent 3 years as information assistant with the British Film Academy and then joined the British Film Institute, where he has worked in various departments including Information, National Film Theatre and Distribution. He is a regular contributor to BFI publications including 'Sight and Sound' and 'Monthly Film Bulletin' and contributes articles and festival reviews to the 'Sunday Telegraph', 'The Scotsman', 'The Guardian', etc, as well as overseas journals. He has taken part in various radio and television discussions on film matters and is Secretary of the British Branch of FIPRESCI *(Fédération Internationale de la Presse Cinématographique).* His special interests are the American, French and Japanese cinemas.

Margaret Hinxman, film critic of the 'Sunday Telegraph', is also a feature writer, interviewer, and television and radio broadcaster on the film industry. She was educated at Haberdashers' Aske's Hatcham Girls' School and in most of the local cinemas of South East London, where she was born. After an apprenticeship as an editorial dogsbody on 'Time and Tide' and a brief period as its film critic, she joined the staff of the film weekly 'Picturegoer' where she remained until its demise in 1960. Thereafter she was film reviewer successively for the 'Daily Herald', 'The Daily Cinema' and 'Queen'; scriptwriter for the television programme *Close-Up*; contributor on film subjects to many varied publications including 'Sight and Sound' and 'Woman'. She has published a number of short stories in 'Woman's Realm' and serves on the committees of several bodies attached to the British Film Institute, the Central Office of Information and the Critics' Circle.

David Robinson has been the film critic of 'The Financial Times' since 1958. Before that time he was Associate Editor of 'Sight and Sound' and programme planner of the National Film Theatre. He was also editor of 'Contrast', the only public journal in Britain to be devoted to the aesthetic and technical problems of television (predictably, it was short-lived). He is a specialist in the prehistory of the cinema, Soviet cinema and film comedy, in its relation to vaudeville and music-hall. Books: 'Buster Keaton', 'Hollywood in the Twenties', 'The Great Funnies', 'Cinema in Revolution' (translation), 'Concise History of the Cinema', 'The Cinema Poster'.

Roy Armes, author of 'The Cinema of Alain Resnais' (1968), 'French Cinema Since 1946' (1966, 1970), 'Patterns of Realism' (1971).

Enid Audus, assistant editor and researcher.

Brian Coe, Curator of the Kodak Museum.

Jan Dawson, Editor of the 'Monthly Film Bulletin' and Staff Contributor to 'Sight and Sound', British Film Institute.

Gillian Hartnoll, Librarian of the Book Library, British Film Institute.

Jack King, Executive Producer of Halas and Batchelor Animation Ltd.

John Francis Lane, Rome-based freelance film critic and correspondent.

Jay Leyda, film historian, specializing in the Soviet cinema.

Kenneth Thompson, former trade critic, now a freelance writer and researcher.

LIST OF COLOUR PLATES

ACKNOWLEDGMENTS

The Editors wish to thank for help with the illustrations:

The Companies:
Academy Cinema, Allied Artists, Anglo-Amalgamated, Associated British Pathé, Bargate Films, British Lion, Bryanstone, Columbia Pictures, Connoisseur Films, Contemporary, Curzon Film Distributors, Eros, Gala Film Distributors, Lion International, London Independent Productions, Lopert, Metro-Goldwyn-Mayer, Paramount, the Rank Organisation, Republic, RKO Radio, Sebricon, Twentieth Century-Fox, Universal International, United Artists, Warner Brothers, Warner-Pathé.

Organisations:
National Film Archive, London; Cinemathèque Française, Paris; Swedish Film Institute; Sovexport, London; UniFrance; Unitalia; UniJapan; Hungarofilm; Children's Film Foundation, London; the press departments of the film festivals at Berlin, Cannes, Cracow, Edinburgh, London, Mar del Plata, Moscow, Venice, Osaka, Sorrento, etc.

Individuals:
Michelangelo Antonioni, Rome; John Halas; Tom Hodge, Singapore; John Francis Lane, Rome; Mrinal Sen, Calcutta; Kenneth Thompson; Tony Rayns; John Kobal; Carmen d'Avino, New York.

The Editors would like to express their special gratitude to the officers of the Information Department of the British Film Institute for their constant help during the preparation of this volume, to the Society of Film and Television Arts and to the London Film School. It will be appreciated that, as several of the colour plates are taken from actual frames, the quality of reproduction is inevitably uneven.

FOREWORD

How to Use the Book

This book attempts to cover the international history of the film, mainly as an art, but also as an industry which forms a significant part of the social development of our century. This Encyclopedia takes primarily an alphabetic form with over a thousand entries (biographies; national film histories; general topics; technical terms), and some thousand illustrations, supplemented by:

a chronological outline of film history, indicating selected events year by year;

a selected bibliography from past and present historical and critical writing on the film.

This Encyclopedia does not attempt to enter into the complex technology of film production and of the equipment involved, or into the sciences of cinematography, sound recording, and so forth.

THE TEXT The alphabetic part of the Encyclopedia contains the following general items, in addition to the biographies and definitions to a selection of technical terms:

Special Subjects:
Archives and Film Preservation
Animation
Avant-garde and Underground Film
Censorship of Film
Children's Entertainment Films
Cinematography
Colour Cinematography
Design and Art Direction
Documentary
Editing Film
Journalism for Film
Music and Film
News and Record Film
Posters
Publicity for Film
Screenwriting

National Cinemas:
Arab Film (including Egypt)
Asian Film (see also China, India, Japan)
Australia
Belgium
Bulgaria
Canada
China, People's Republic of
Cuba
Czechoslovakia
France
Germany (West and East)
Great Britain
Greece
Hungary
India
Israel
Italy
Japan
Latin America (Argentina, Brazil, Mexico)
Netherlands
Poland
Portugal
Romania
Russia and the USSR
Scandinavia (Denmark, Finland, Norway, Sweden)
Spain
Switzerland
Turkey
USA
Yugoslavia

Finally, since the alphabetic form of an encyclopedia fragments the subject, the prefatory article on the seventy-five years of the film shows the organic nature of the growth of the film internationally as an art, an industry, a technology, and a social force at once reflecting and influencing the very various societies it serves.

ILLUSTRATIONS The vast majority of the illustrations are either portraits of key personalities or action stills from outstanding, or otherwise significant films. Wherever possible the date or the period of all portraits is given.

The illustrations are inevitably spread to match individual entries and articles. For example, while the illustrations accompanying the article on Italian cinema present important examples, historically-speaking, of that nation's films, further illustrations will appear alongside Italian directors, stars, etc, throughout the volume, and must also be taken into account in the total illustration of Italian film-making. Readers are reminded, therefore, that the Index interlinks the illustrations, wherever they may occur.

Our readers will no doubt have their own ideas about the film-makers and stars they would themselves include in any selection approaching one thousand names, which is what our space allowed. Our own list was arrived at after initial discussion spread over many weeks, and much subsequent revision. Some relatively well-known names will not be found while, on the contrary, many names not so well-known as we think they should be are included. The biographies in any case supplement the national film articles and the specialized articles, and enable a fuller filmography to be given than would be possible in a general context.

Our final choice of biographical subjects was affected by many considerations, such as:

the degree to which the selected film-maker or player has contributed, or is contributing to the film, either through sheer individuality of style, or because he or she represents a trend in either the contemporary cinema or that of the past – including trends which may represent a 'fashion' rather than anything of deep significance;

a desire especially to reflect contemporary activity in film-making, and its representatives among directors, players, etc;

a desire to include representative names of screenwriters, directors of photography, designers, editors, composers and choreographers, animation directors, and others who have contributed notably to film-making.

It should be realized also that very many film-makers and players not represented by a biography find a place in either the national or the specialized articles, or both.

It is inevitable that there must be some degree of overlap between the general articles and the biographical entries; however, the general articles have all been written with the additional information in the biographies in mind, and readers are invited to regard each as supplementary to the other. Because of this, the names of all those who have biographical entries are normally set in SMALL CAPITALS when they first occur in any general article (or in someone else's biography), and occasionally from time to time subsequently, to act as a reminder.

Once again, the Index is of key importance in binding together the various relevant sections where information is given on each individual.

INTRODUCTION

Seventy-five Years of the Film

Most countries, however small or newly established, make films. The number of productions may be restricted, and virtually confined to newsreels recording the coming and going of local potentates; this is the position in the emergent states in Africa, or in the smaller Caribbean communities with only one or two reasonably qualified cameramen. There are highly-developed countries, such as Canada, Holland or Belgium, which have a considerable output of sophisticated, internationally-acclaimed documentary and informational films, but a restricted output of feature films. There are considerable local, or regional developments in production – in the principal Latin American countries for instance, in Egypt (for the Arabic-speaking world) and in Hong Kong (for Chinese-speaking audiences). Hong Kong, indeed, has become one of the most highly productive centres of film-making in the world in post-war years, though with the costs of their films rigidly pegged to ensure a profit from their relatively limited outlets.

This is one way to achieve some perspective in relation to the complexities of the contemporary film world. Another involves studying film economics and politics. The world is, broadly speaking, divided into two main areas: first, the capitalist countries which undertake the production of entertainment films primarily for profit, and second, the areas which, professing varied forms of socialism and communism, produce films mainly for social, artistic, or propagandist reasons – apart from the desire to use films for export in order to achieve hard currency credits outside the communist world. Productions in both areas, communist and non-communist, involve considerable expense, at its top level, for example, in the American *Cleopatra* or the Russian *War and Peace*, but ideally such films, whatever their economic background, should recoup their costs, and much more than this if possible, through the combined distribution of the home and foreign markets. Economically speaking, only the profit motive of the private company is absent in the economy of film production in the communist countries, while ideologically, films form a most important part of the social-artistic-propaganda network of communist-humanist culture.

In addition, note should be made of the increasing output of films which are in one way or another sponsored by governments, industry, enterprise and organizations needing 'public relations', by special interests (such as education and the entertainment of children), and, above all in quantity, by television. The films which result from these varied forms of sponsorship are either factual films of all kinds, or entertainment films – the latter virtually confined to the television series produced in quantity in the USA, and to a lesser, but still notable, degree in Britain. Sponsored films (apart from those made for television) for the most part do not look for direct profit; rather their costs represent expenditure undertaken in order to provide information, influence opinion, or afford educational or technological instruction. The world-wide output in these various fields is enormous and ever-increasing. In quantity it has come greatly to exceed the output (in footage) of the far more prominent feature films, and the television series in particular plays an important part in exports, particularly for Britain and the USA.

ORIGINS The vast, highly international enterprise of motion pictures represents something quite new in our rapidly expanding 20th-century cultural development. There has been nothing resembling it in past centuries since it is wholly dependent for its existence on technological invention, originating in primitive form towards the end of the 19th century and subject to constant improvement and expansion ever since. It forms a very important part of the great communications network (press, telephone – with its potential video developments – wireless telegraphy, gramophone, film, sound radio, television, sound tape-recording and videotape, and, most recently, cassette film and videotape) which is characteristic of our century; collectively this communications network has completely changed human relationships in 'advanced' countries at every level – international, national, regional, local, and personal. It is one of the sadder aspects of our times that this rapid development in communications facilities has only served to widen the dangerous cultural gap between the so-called privileged and under-privileged nations.

The interdependence of the various forms of communication is evident – each has increasingly come to rely on other media for common subject matter and for mutual promotion with the public. The film specifically depends on the press and broadcasting for its public relations, and on television for an increasing degree of sponsorship, while videotape (already so important in production for television) will evidently become equally so for film in the next ten years or so. The film industry represents the annual investment of thousands of millions of dollars in production, while the world's 200,000 or so motion-picture theatres cater for an estimated audience of some 375 million weekly (UNESCO figures in 1964). International audiences watching films of every kind on television, including regular revivals of older cinema films, are by now incalculable. Those countries with a widespread television service have made the audiences for which they cater virtually film-saturated. But, as in other even more important considerations, there are the 'have' and 'have not' regions as far as regular film entertainment is concerned.

Motion pictures, achieved by means of cinematography and projection on to a screen, came comparatively early to the network of modern communications – through developments culminating in 1895–6 in Germany, France, Britain and the USA, all of which originated their own equipment, for the most part independently of each other. Other countries also lay claim to the technological invention of silent movie. The silent film arrived after mass-production printing, the telephone and gramophone – all in effect developments achieved by the 1870s – but three decades before sound broadcasting. Television as a mass-medium is essentially a development which followed the Second World War, just as sound broadcasting was established in the years following the First World War.

The instinct to create pictures which offered an illusion of movement, which in effect possessed the magic attributes of life, is manifest in the earliest of art forms: the cave paintings of Altamira and Lascaux, with their multiple-limbed animals running, leaping and galloping to avoid the hunters' missiles. The casting of moving shadows on to a wall surface, and the more sophisticated Asian shadow-theatres, forecast the cinema in pre-photographic forms. Certain toys (such as the zoetrope) predate photographic film, depending on persistence of vision when creating the illusion of a single mobile image from the rotation before the eye of a recurrent series of phased static images. But motion pictures as we know them depended on the prior existence of, first, still photography; secondly, primitive motion-picture cameras which could pass a length of coated celluloid before the lens to record a series of pictures at the requisite speed, becoming in the 1890s 16 frames a second; and thirdly, the reel of transparent celluloid providing a base on which the images could be successively recorded. All this finally came to fruition in 1895, together with the means to project the finished film on to a screen. Many of the early cameras could in fact be converted into projectors, and the first audiences for motion pictures saw them projected in cafés, fairground tents, empty shops and the like, as well as in the music-halls which were still numerous at the turn of the century and which introduced the short films of the period (news items, vaudeville turns, visual sketches, and the like) as items in their programmes.

Every country which took part in originating motion pictures as an industry during the 1890s – notably France, Britain and the USA – passed through the initial period of establishing films with the public on the level of the popular show. It begun as an adjunct to other kinds of show business, and was promoted into a full-scale entertainment in its own right with the development of theatres and other public buildings specially adapted for motion picture exhibition in the early years of the century, and the production of longer films of greater substance as stories and spectacles – promoted largely by the Italians, the French, the Americans, the British, and the Germans in the years preceding the First World War. By this time many other countries were sponsoring film production – among them Denmark, Sweden, Russia and Japan.

A WORLD INDUSTRY ESTABLISHED: THE INFLUENCE OF THE USA Film-making began on an amateur-craftsman level before developing into a relatively small-scale international industry in the period before 1914. The first film-makers were pioneers, as much, if not more interested in developing and exploiting their apparatus (often made with their own hands) than in the kind of films they made. The first-generation artist-directors – Méliès and Feuillade in France, Porter and Griffith in the USA, Hepworth in Britain – were concerned with the quality of the films they made, and took the first elementary steps needed to discover the nature of the medium. Griffith, indeed, was to become the first master of the art of the film.

The silent film was easy to internationalize; its action was visual, its printed titles could easily be translated and the films released in different language versions. Soon distribution companies were established to market British, French, American and Italian films in other countries; as the films grew longer the prints were rented, not – as was the case initially – sold outright to the exhibitors and shown for limited runs in the newly-established movie theatres. The familiar triangle of the industry – producer, distributor, exhibitor – was in full-scale existence by 1910, and famous companies with international roots, such as Gaumont and Pathé, had been founded.

The growing resources of American production began to tell in Europe before the First World War. American production companies were, for a period, established in Britain. The economic dislocation in Europe caused by war enabled the American distribution companies to entrench themselves as the primary source of film entertainment in world markets. The range and quality of the better American product grew rapidly, and the main genres of popular entertainment began to be laid down in forms which everyone, whatever his nationality or cultural background, could readily appreciate. Drama and comedy, the one-reel and two-reel slapstick burlesques stemming from successful vaudeville acts developed in film form by Mack Sennett, the Western, the war film, the serials with their 'cliff-hanger' break-points (first developed effectively in France), and the film spectacle (first developed as a genre in Italy), all became hall-marked as standard American screen entertainment. The first movement of top European talent to the USA began – for example, Chaplin from vaudeville in England, von Stroheim as an immigrant from Germany seeking a career in films. But the greatest take-over of talent was to come after the war, in the 1920s, the era of the major boom in motion pictures and its foundation as an international industry of considerable importance – socially, artistically, and financially.

The industry which stood to suffer most from American competition was the British film, which lacked the popular flair and drive of the thrusting American industry, and ran down almost to nothing in the mid 1920s. Nevertheless the 1920s saw the first films of Hitchcock and Asquith to be made in England. In any case, the interchange between the American and British of English-speaking talent had already begun. The Swedish film, too, after a brilliant if small-scale flowering at the turn of the 1920s, died back with the departure of their principal directors, Sjöström and Stiller, to the USA. Other small-scale European industries were also developing, in Poland, in Czechoslovakia, in Hungary – while Italy, though productive enough, had to wait until the 1930s for the boost she was to receive from Mussolini, and somewhat later for the emergence of her major talents. During the 1920s, the more important Asian industries of Japan and India put down roots in the popular market of their territories.

The popularity of films depended increasingly on the star system, which operated on two distinct levels: the local or purely national level, and the international level, represented primarily by the American industry's promotion of stars in world-distributed product. Stars could become established as such in their own country, but remain virtually unknown internationally. On the other hand, they could start their careers in their native country and then 'graduate' by being offered contracts in Hollywood, when this finally became the centre for American production. Notable examples were both Greta Garbo from Sweden and Marlene Dietrich from Germany. American-born players, on the other hand, had to rise to prominence within their own industry, sometimes with, sometimes without stage experience behind them, as Mary Pickford, Douglas Fairbanks Senior, Tom Mix, William S. Hart and numerous others were fortunate enough to do.

However, the predominance of Hollywood in film production remained undisputed. It emerged during the 1920s as an industry which seemed able to draw on almost limitless resources, creating in quantity films, both elaborate and less elaborate, featuring stars it made world-renowned through its universal system of distribution and its incessant stream of publicity. Nevertheless, other industries of some significance were developing elsewhere, often in a somewhat freer position to experiment with more varied kinds of film-making than was possible in Hollywood (whose very success enforced the production of films in established moulds which had been, with their appropriate stars, time and again proved popular at the world's box-offices). This was particularly true of the more unusual films produced by the French, German, and Russian industries of the 1920s, the last, of course, the product of a nationalized cinema.

THE 1920s – A GOLDEN AGE FOR SILENT FILM ART The 1920s saw the golden age of the silent cinema, which ended with the coming of sound during the period 1928–9. It was a golden age in the USA, seeing, for example, fine work from such directors as Chaplin, Keaton, von Stroheim, and Ford. It was a golden age in Germany, with the best of the expressionist films, and the emergence of such directors as Lubitsch (soon to go to the USA), Lang, Murnau, Pabst and possibly the greatest individual scenarist of the silent period, Carl Mayer. It was a golden age in France, with the establishment of directors as varied as Clair, Gance, Feyder, and Renoir, as well as the extraordinary work of the French avant-garde directors. It was a golden age too, in the newly-founded Soviet industry, with the films of such directors as Eisenstein, Pudovkin, Dovzhenko, and Dziga Vertov. In Scandinavia the careers of Sjöström, Stiller and Dreyer were established. It is difficult to think of a richer period of production at any time in the history of the cinema than that which occurred in the comparatively brief span of years between 1922 and 1928. Everywhere the film seemed to be developing as an art – an art revealing strong national roots and characteristics, like literature and the theatre, and at the same time an art of such flexibility that highly individual personalities (such as Dreyer or von Stroheim, Clair or Pabst, Eisenstein or Chaplin) could make it the medium for their personal expression as artists. By the close of the 1920s there could be no doubt whatsoever that a new art form of great potentiality had developed, and that at the same time a new industry of equal pretension was in process of evolving. In keeping with the 20th century, the film was essentially an art form which overstepped national barriers with greater ease than literature or the drama because its basic form was visual.

Film as an art had achieved various and divergent levels of sophistication. The central core of box-office films, the more or less serious drama and melodrama, was in general the weakest branch of motion pictures, scripted and performed on the level of the novelette. Acting stemmed, even as late as the 1920s, from theatrical melodrama, its mime and use of facial expression both exaggerated and emotionally over-simplified. The rarer films which began to introduce true screen-acting, with psychologically detailed rather than bravura performances, were the work of directors such as von Stroheim, Clair, Lubitsch and Murnau (who both developed the German *Kammerspiel*, or intimate film drama of the early 1920s), Pudovkin, Feyder or Dreyer, and of a few exceptional stars, such as Asta Nielsen, who understood fully the intimate nature of screen acting. The work of Emil Jannings, certainly one of the outstanding performers of the 1920s, was nevertheless seldom free from melodramatic touches, in spite of the care and detail he brought to his characterizations; while the sole extraordinary performance of Falconetti in Dreyer's *The Passion of Joan of Arc* (1928) seems to have evolved from the near-hypnotic influence of the director upon the artist. But for the most part, the material of screen drama was at this stage artificial, elementary and melodramatic in plot and situation, and rarely calling for qualities which might lead to highly creative screen acting.

The popular silent film achieved its peak most consistently in the two opposite poles of the burlesque and the epic. The burlesque began with the sharply conceived and rigorously cut one- and two-reeler slapstick farces for which Mack Sennett assembled his celebrated team of clowns. Many great or very talented artists, directors and writers developing in his studio were to create later the high burlesque comedies of the 1920s, with their scrupulously controlled chaos. These films of the 1910s and 1920s still entertain audiences today much more readily than all but the very best of the serious screen dramas. The art these great creative comedians developed from stage vaudeville became a *commedia dell' arte* of the screen in its own right.

On the other hand, the screen developed its own panoramic films of action.

Inspired by Italian epics such as *Cabiria* (1914) Griffith showed the way with the historical spectacles of *The Birth of a Nation* (1915) and *Intolerance* (1916) and in turn inspired the Russian masters, Eisenstein and Pudovkin, to create their large-scale propaganda histories, from *Battleship Potemkin* (1925) and *The End of St Petersburg* (1927) to *October* (1927). In the USA the Western developed into the panoramic studies of pioneer history, in such films as *The Covered Wagon* (1923) and *The Iron Horse* (1924).

Finally there were during the silent period the developments, unique to the film, of documentary, cartoon animation, and experimental avant-garde production, notably in France and Germany. The English cinematographer Herbert Ponting's coverage of Scott's expedition to the Antarctic (ending 1913), the work much later of Flaherty, both in the Hudson Bay and in the South Seas, the ethnographical films of the French, of Schoedsack and Cooper of the USA, and of Turin of the USSR, opened up entirely new and popular forms of human documentation. The secrets of plant growth and flower movement were first revealed by Percy Smith of Britain before 1910, and photomicroscopy, showing the movements of minute organisms, was developed in particular by the Frenchman Painlevé. Dr R. G. Canti of London was among the first to use film for medical diagnosis in the 1920s and 1930s. Science had gained a new tool of observation and record, while in the world of the artist's imagination the mobility of film gave the exponents of surrealism and Dada a new and fascinating outlet. The manifestations of the subconscious and the imagery of dreams found their counterpart in the dream-like continuity of silent movie. Clair, Germaine Dulac, and above all Buñuel developed this aspect of the film, and so created another, unique branch of this multifarious and expanding art. Finally, the animated cartoon film, so popular with audiences and creating its own stars – such as Felix the Cat – out of a few active, graphic outlines or silhouettes, opened up the limitless possibilities of the moving image to the artist. This was a form of film-making which would come into its own with sound.

It must not, of course, be overlooked that the silent film was seldom silent in the sense that it was presented to audiences in silence. It was accompanied by music and even effects (such as gunshots) performed 'live' or, in certain Asian countries, notably Japan, by the voice of a narrator, or story-teller. But certain directors, in particular Griffith, initiated the use of fully-orchestrated scores, the band parts of which circulated with their films to be played by such orchestras as the theatres could provide. This became a regular practice for the more important films of the 1920s; otherwise the music as well as the sound effects were improvised either by pianists playing solo or by the music directors who conducted the orchestras in the movie theatres. With the coming of sound, however, the need for live accompaniment passed, and directors were able to synchronize the music with their films as they desired.

THE COMING OF SOUND: THE 1930s This was how the film had appeared up to 1928 to the growing number of people conscious of its powers. Books and journals seriously dedicated to the medium began to appear, as distinct from the trade and (later) the fan journals almost as old as the industry itself. So long as it remained silent nations could exchange great stars like Jannings or Garbo, both among the many who went to Hollywood only to be faced in 1928 with the disconcerting arrival of the sound film. Major stars of the silent era disappeared completely within a year or so because their voices proved incompatible with their established images, or because, like Jannings, they were incapable of mastering the English language or unwilling to try. Many European stars were forced to abandon hope of further work in Hollywood, and valuable talents were lost to the film altogether. The arrival of the sound film undoubtedly introduced a considerable measure of insularity into an art which had known few such boundaries up to 1928, although its benefits to the art of films were to prove immeasurable. The pattern of world cinema in 1930 was based on division rather than on fusion.

The medium had to move from silent mime to the spoken word, from the summary indication of speech in printed captions and mouthed phrases to the full delivery of dialogue as on the stage. This involved a considerable period of adjustment for directors, writers and actors. There were those (notably Pagnol in France) who thought the sound film should involve the photographic recording of stage plays, and Pagnol was indeed to achieve this with adroitness, featuring skilful players and fine locations. But the whole development of silent film art – the significant selection and continuity of images to offer detailed observation of character, situation and story – seemed threatened with total loss because sound in the form of dialogue, music and effects appeared to be paramount. The earliest sound films in 1929 resembled for the most part bad television drama in the 1950s: talking heads and talking groups functioning in front of stagey studio sets. The more perceptive film-makers of the time (Hitchcock, Milestone, Clair, Mamoulian and Pabst among them) understood that the various phenomena of sound must in some way be integrated with the art of the film as it had been so finely developed before 1928. Speech and sound must not suddenly become totally dominant, but be absorbed in order to increase the powerful illusion of the image for the audience, and also to give (where relevant) an entirely new dimension of actuality to the moving picture. The unreal, dreamlike quality of the silent image was replaced by an image of almost stark, immediate actuality as the films of Pabst, for example, were among the first to show, as well as (in a totally different vein) the initial gangster films in the USA, and yet again, the early work of the British documentary film-makers. Film seemed fully capable at last of projecting scenes from real life with complete authenticity. On the other hand, the close integration of music and sound effects in the wholly artificial world of the American musical, involving elaborate and spectacular cine-choreography, seemed to be in itself a new art form, while René Clair's early musicals created the opposite effect – charm and wit unhurriedly presented in the simplest manner.

The relationship of the scriptwriter (with his special command of characterized dialogue) to the primarily visual medium of film had also to be resolved. While directors such as Clair created their own scripts with minimal dialogue, the old story-scenarists of the silent period gave way to the professional screenwriters of the sound film, such as Dudley Nichols in the USA or Charles Spaak in France. Similarly the new stars and actors for sound film had to learn how to handle dialogue effectively in the circumstances of the close proximity of camera and microphone. A whole new generation of stars was born during the 1930s, stars whose voices as well as their appearance formed a significant part of their personalities: Edward G. Robinson, Bette Davis, Humphrey Bogart, for example, in Hollywood; Jean Gabin, Michel Simon, Françoise Rosay, or Raimu in France; Charles Laughton in Britain; Nicolai Cherkassov in Russia; and so forth. Among the stars to survive effectively the transfer to sound were Chaplin (with some initial pain and dislocation) and Laurel and Hardy, while among the new clowns in the early days of sound were the Marx Brothers.

Out of this situation arose the second phase of naturalism in the cinema. Spoken dialogue obviously emphasized the purely national quality in sound films, and erected the language barrier between the industries. Various devices were introduced to overcome this: recording the dialogue in two or more languages at the time of shooting; the subsequent dubbing of new sound tracks as the films were introduced into foreign language areas; sub-titling, which printed capsulated versions of the dialogue in the form of a series of captions superimposed at the base of the cineframe. The latter was the best compromise, since it left the original voice of the foreign artist on the sound track, retaining therefore the *total* performance of the actor as first created, and not merely a truncated one, with some alien voice endeavouring to ape in another language that of the original performer. Dubbing mattered least in the kind of films in which character mattered least, but its use in pictures of high quality, in which subtleties of characterization were of the first importance, offered a grave threat to the integrity of the original work. One of the film's greatest gifts to international culture was its capacity to give world circulation to the work of leading film-makers and performers without the inevitable dilution of quality which comes with translation, as in literature, or transmutation from one culture to another, as in the performance of translated plays by actors with a different cultural background.

From this new language situation a variety of unforeseen problems arose – the fact that the English and American accents proved at first mutually incomprehensible, especially during the early, rather indistinct period of speech recording, or the subsidiary fact that the more marked dialects of different regions within a single language territory could be incomprehensible in other regions of the same territory when used in a film. Recording quality was soon to improve, but emphasis on clarity led to somewhat wooden performances in many early sound films, as well as compromises in the handling of accent and dialect. The last thing Hollywood wanted to do was talk themselves out of their impregnable world market, both in the regions where English, in various forms, was spoken and where it was not. A new branch of the industry grew up for the dubbing and sub-titling of films for the foreign markets, and audiences, particularly in non-English-speaking areas, had to acquire a new skill – glance-reading sub-titles while at the same time watching the action taking place above.

The more marked national divergences in the film industry soon appeared during the 1930s. The American industry, ruled now by the major companies with their competitive entertainment policies and carefully controlled contract stars, continued to dominate the world market and set its own unique pace in more or less standardized movie. The other industries operated peripherally to Hollywood, their strongest card being their cultural uniqueness – films in specific languages reflecting the life of specific areas and desired therefore by audiences alongside the imported, dubbed or titled American product, with its sharp and sometimes deliberately shocking reflection of what was, or purported to be, life as it was lived in the richest and largest nation representative of Western culture. The 1930s was a very good period for American films, with the work of such directors as Ford, Capra, Wellman, Wyler, Lubitsch, Dieterle, Chaplin, Hawks and many others setting their individual standards. In between the non-English-speaking film industries and the all-powerful American industry hovered uneasily the British film industry, with a culture of its own to reflect but fighting a David-and-Goliath action against Hollywood, which sought always to engulf this modest competitor. With the assistance of a protective Quota Act British films, so weak in the 1920s, sought to recover lost ground in the 1930s, and to a limited extent were successful in doing so – though their better artists (such as Hitchcock the director and Laughton the actor) were almost inevitably lured at some stage to Hollywood. But under such quality producers as Alexander Korda and Michael Balcon, the better British films began to prevail over the great mass of mere quota product, and to be appreciated abroad when they achieved export, even in the hard market of the USA. Further reputation for British films was won internationally by a considerable output of good documentary films, many with a strong social message reflecting the problems of the difficult 1930s.

Apart from American production, the industry of the 1930s with the strongest national image in the eyes of those who appreciated good films was probably the French. A strong school of film-makers was working in France, led by Renoir, Feyder, Duvivier and, later, Carné. It was, in general, a 'literate' cinema, deriving from novels or from the work of such dialogue-conscious scriptwriters as Spaak and Prévert. It was a cinema of intelligent and sensitive direction and acting. It was also strongly marked by the fatalistic mood of the period, but France was not to have so outstanding and unified a school of film-making again until the 1960s, the period of the French New Wave.

The 1930s was the period with the fullest development so far of ideological film-making. Goebbels's deliberate policy as propaganda Minister in Nazi Germany was to keep the feature film as light and escapist as possible, concentrating his propaganda into a comparatively few 'prestige' features and full-length documentaries. Over and above the films he sponsored, Leni Riefenstahl, on direct orders from Hitler, made what is probably the most famous Nazi propaganda film, *Triumph of the Will* (1934). The Italian cinema was less distinctive at this period, though certain of the greater talents of the future were during the later years of the Mussolini régime acquiring their initial skills – De Sica, Rossellini and Visconti among them. The Japanese cinema was also harnessed to the intense form of imperialism characteristic of the time, although their major directors still produced wholly personal work as far as possible. The Russian cinema was forced by Stalin's mandates to abandon the 'bourgeois formalism' of the 1920s (most marked in the films of Eisenstein) and adopt the policy of 'socialist realism'. This meant that both contemporary life and the reinterpretation of history should be presented in ideologically acceptable terms, and in a form which at the worst became plain and pedestrian in style, but at the best achieved a directness and humanity which made, for example, Donskoi's Maxim Gorki trilogy distinctive. Eisenstein, for the most part frustrated in his attempts at film-making by the authorities, produced only one completed film in Russia during the pre-war decade, *Alexander Nevsky* (1938).

Documentary, the recording and 'creative interpretation' of real life in all its forms and processes, which was probably Britain's most distinctive contribution to world cinema in the 1930s, also developed effectively elsewhere – sometimes, as in the case of Belgium and Holland, where feature production scarcely existed. Documentary, supplementing the brief and grossly over-simplified newsreels, offered our civilization its first living form of self-portraiture, and is of permanent value in the record and study of history. The 1930s began to recognize the importance of the film not only as an art but as a unique documentary record of the times, and official film preservation in special archives began, for example, in Britain and the USA. Indeed the USA, as part of its system of copyright, had for a while preserved film records in the form of paper prints early in the century; what mattered now was to preserve valuable films in such a way that their nature and content could be registered and indexed, and their perishable image cared for and reproduced in more permanent form and made available for screening.

Compilation documentaries, summarizing the history of past periods which had been recorded on film, had already been successfully developed, especially in the USSR. The film was expanding its frontiers, not least in that special art of animation, with its various branches. Cartoon shorts, such as the work of Cohl and Winsor McKay, had existed before the First World War, and been perfected as a popular art by Max Fleischer and Pat Sullivan during the silent period; now animation came into its own, with sound enabling exact synchronization or counterpoint of picture, music, voice and sound effects to be achieved. The great name of the 1930s and 1940s in animation was, of course, Walt Disney, but his inventive genius in comic entertainment, developed eventually at feature length, must not obscure the very different achievements in Europe of such notable artists as Lotte Reiniger in silhouette animation, Hans Richter, Oskar Fischinger and Len Lye in abstract animation, and George Pal and Alexander Ptushko in puppet animation. Animation for instruction was also developed, for example by Fleischer in the 1920s and by the Shell Film Unit in Britain during the 1930s, in the latter case by specialists in devising mobile technological diagrams.

THE WAR YEARS The rapid development of the sound film was not halted by the occurrence of the Second World War; it was rather suddenly deflected from its normal paths into others appropriate to war conditions at varying times for different countries between 1939 and 1941. The British, French and American films of the late 1930s were relatively slow to come into the open against Hitler, though the American magazine film, the *March of Time*, did so well before 1939. Russian anti-Nazism was silenced by the German-Russian pact of August 1939 until the invasion of Russia in 1941. Goebbels during the war years kept to his policy that the film industry was primarily concerned with the production of escapist entertainment, with propaganda confined to a relatively few state-financed feature films, feature-length documentaries, war shorts and newsreels of ever-increasing length. German combat photography, like that of the Russians, Americans and British, was of a high order, many cameramen losing their lives in the effort to secure front line action on film, with the result that the international archives are filled with spectacular material of land, sea and air warfare. The fiction film was not slow to adopt war subjects, mostly at first in forms which may appear ludicrously unreal today, but which moved gradually in the direction of a closer approximation to actuality as the conduct and circumstances of the war came more directly within the range of experience of civilians as well as service men and women. Broadly speaking, war films began as somewhat sentimental, jingoistic exercises, then turned in the direction of more or less realistic accounts of war action, and finally, in the more interesting cases, placed greater emphasis on the reactions of individual characters to war at home or on active service, and to psychological problems arising from war conditions. Films became of major importance for entertainment, for propaganda, and for news and information. Production, though reduced in quantity through the loss of technicians and artists to the Services and the scarcity of raw materials in the studios, was nevertheless given a high priority alike in Britain, the USA, the USSR, Japan and Nazi Germany, while the Germans maintained controlled forms of production in the occupied countries, particularly France. The showing of films was not confined to movie theatres; various forms of mobile projection took films wherever it was felt they were needed.

POST-WAR ADJUSTMENT: THE ARRIVAL OF TELEVISION The film industry emerged from the war with soaring attendances and a boom in both production and exhibition. In some countries this was to be short-lived. The impact of television was to begin to be felt at the turn of the decade, and theatre attendance began to fall sharply in the 1950s.

During this brief period of the film's ascendancy a new, documentary-style technique was manifest, not only in post-war films about the war, but in certain kinds of entertainment films, including the Italian social films and American crime films and films presenting social problems. The post-war Italian style known as neo-realism, as revealed in the films of Rossellini and De Sica which were widely shown internationally, found its counterpart in the post-war 'rubble' films of East and West Germany, and in the endless films reconstructing the war made in the communist countries, as well as in Britain and France. The world trend was towards a greater sense of actuality in both subject and treatment, and a desire to take the camera outside the studio into the open world of streets and landscape. The people on the screen, and the artists who impersonated them, became during the 1950s more and more the counterparts to the people in the auditorium. Stars almost entirely lost their pre-war 'dream' quality and became, like the characters they played in the more serious films, at least credible as human beings. This represented a distinct phase in the gradual maturing of subject and treatment in the popular cinema.

But this more realistic treatment matching the documentary style in which the better war films had been and were still being made was not in itself sufficient to keep audiences in the theatres when the full impact of television was felt. It came far more slowly in the Western European countries (Italy, France, West Germany, etc) and in Japan than it did in Britain and North America because of their comparatively slow recovery from the aftermath of war. Public Service television was re-introduced by the BBC in 1946, and developed rapidly, especially when reinforced by the establishment of commercial television in 1955; in the USA sponsored television developed with a rush on a multiplicity of channels during the early 1950s. The effect on attendances in the motion picture theatres (especially in Britain) and on production (especially in the USA) was almost catastrophic, as the following figures show:

Great Britain:	No. of TV Receivers:	No. of Admissions Weekly to Theatres:
1950	0·34 million	26·8 million
1955	4·55 million	22·7 million
1960	10·04 million	10·0 million
1965	13·56 million	6·3 million

United States:	No. of TV Receivers:	No. of Feature Films Produced:
1949	1·5 million	363
1952	18·0 million	278
1960	60·0 million	211
1962	60·0 million	138

Apart from Canada, no effects on attendances at motion picture theatres in any way comparable to the above were experienced elsewhere until the 1960s.

The industry's reply to the competitive small-screen was the simple one of going big. Widescreen in various forms was rushed into front-line theatres, principally in the form of Cinerama (using initially a deeply curved, triptych screen filled by three synchronized images from three aligned projectors) and, much more commonly, CinemaScope (adapted from Henri Chrétien's anamorphic lens system developed during the later 1920s). The standard-sized screens were also increased in height and width, so that in all cinemas during the 1950s audiences were faced by a greatly enlarged, more dominating image of varying ratio (width to height) according to whether it was a standard or CinemaScope picture which was being shown. Widescreen came to stay; the less fortunate attempts at commercializing various three-dimensional (3D) systems failed, except in Soviet Russia where Semyon Ivanov developed a system giving excellent 3D illusion without the audience being required to wear spectacles, especially designed to feed appropriate images to the left and right eye. The effect of all these changes in the motion picture theatres' battle to retain their audiences against the insidious televiewing habit was to break up the former universal standardization of the size and shape of the screen image, as various countries introduced their own forms corresponding to CinemaScope and Cinerama. In order to produce a more satisfactory, grain-free colour image on the very largest screens, an enlarged form of film, 70 mm, double the standard 35 mm width, was introduced during the 1960s, while multiple magnetic tracks, replacing optical tracks, fed sound to speakers placed strategically around the auditorium. Other more extreme forms of technical diversification were introduced experimentally, mostly during the 1960s, including synchronizing a series of films which collectively made up a complete circle, a 360° image completely surrounding a standing spectator, and the combination of the live performer with a screen image, sometimes of himself. The introduction in the 1950s of the magnetic recording of sound in the studios and into key motion picture theatres added immeasurably to the quality of sound.

More important than these technical changes were the changes, apparent already in the 1950s and consolidated in the 1960s, which led to a further maturing of the film in subject and treatment. Contrary to what is commonly thought, the film seldom leads society in the establishment of new values or habits; rather it takes its cue from society in its more 'advanced' sections, as well as from the values already suggested in the other narrative arts, fiction and drama. Different societies and different countries have exercised differing moral, religious and ideological controls over films which are shown to the public – these can be very strict indeed, for divergent reasons, for example in India and Communist China, whereas Japanese censorship, especially more recently, has become noticeably relaxed. Certain broadly 'puritan' restrictions have exercised control over the British and American film (both countries possessing unofficial censorship systems established originally as self-protection by the film industry), but with major relaxations taking place during the 1960s for the handling of sexual relationships on the screen. There has been divergence, however, between the two countries in the censor's attitude to the introduction of 'gratuitous' violence, the Americans being less restrictive than the British in this respect. In Britain scenes of extreme violence have remained highly suspect by the censor unless deeply involved in the dramatic motivation. Sweden has long been in the van in placing little restraint on sexual activity on the screen, and the 1960s has seen the total abolition of film censorship (other than for children) in a number of countries. West Germany, like Japan, has indulged freely and prolifically in the so-called 'sexploitation' films. In the European communist countries the treatment of sex relations has during the 1960s become very free, although Russia is much more prudish than, for example, Czechoslovakia, Poland, or Yugoslavia. On the other hand, Communist China has, for a while at least, abandoned the fiction film entirely in order to concentrate on the production of ideologically inspired documentaries and other subjects with political themes (such as filmed ballet and opera).

For a variety of reasons, therefore – the moral 'liberation' in many societies, the revolt of the younger generation against the stuffier, more bourgeois values of the past, the progressive influence of the new literature in the USA and the new drama in Britain, the rising wages of the young which have enabled them to become influential patrons of 'pop' culture good and bad, progressive trends in the more advanced forms of television (both documentary and drama, more especially in Britain) – the tone of the film has changed. It has entered the 1970s with treatments of certain subjects, and of sexual relations in particular, which would have been unbelievable even ten years before. The 1960s did, however, initiate a new freedom of dialogue in such English-language productions as the British *Saturday Night and Sunday Morning* (1960) and the American *Anatomy of a Murder* (1959), while Ingmar Bergman leant hard upon the censorship with his scenes of rape in *The Virgin Spring* (1959) and masturbation in *The Silence* (1963). Censorship controls relaxed at an uneven pace, relatively quickly in Britain and the USA, more slowly in, for example, Australia, and scarcely at all in India and Ceylon. On the other hand, they have disappeared altogether (except for children) in Sweden and Denmark. Italy has remained for ever a censorship battleground, causing continuous embarrassment to the more advanced film-makers; any individual or organization can demand that a film be banned or suppressed, and so cause the producers and distributors trouble.

It is impossible to understand how the cinema has reached its present level of maturity without taking certain important influences into account; a film is shaped by the varying cultural backgrounds of the societies which produce it, though it can, as in the case of *Easy Rider*, help considerably to popularize trends already established, on which it draws for its subjects. It is in turn moulded by the other arts, and indeed now by television, which in Britain, in particular in the 1960s, was broadly-speaking well ahead of the cinema as a liberating force, causing continuous controversy because of its so-called permissiveness. The authorities in territories with less developed communities who patronize the cinema – the Caribbean islands, for example, India, Ceylon, the African countries, Singapore, and so forth – are in general greatly concerned to ensure that imported films do as little as possible to disturb traditional morality and religious belief in their communities. It is probably in the long run a vain hope, especially now that television is being established in country after country, with the public display of screens in those communities too impoverished to allow for much individual purchase of receiving sets.

ECONOMICS OF FILM-MAKING The first films, as we have seen, were very short, and sold direct to the travelling showmen who wore the prints out replaying them during months of exhibition. The development of distributors or renters in the early years of the century coincided with the gradual lengthening of films and the need to change programmes frequently in the growing number of centres, the first motion picture theatres, which were exhibiting films continually to audiences whom they hoped to establish as regular patrons. By 1910 the basic pattern of international motion picture production, distribution and exhibition was emerging, with considerable cross-fertilization between the three branches of the industry. There was also a rapidly expanding internationalization in distribution, for example by the Gaumont and Pathé companies, who established their own offices in many countries, such as Britain and Germany, while the highly productive American companies set-up a world-wide network of distribution for their films. American producers were already attempting to establish studios in Britain at the time of the First World War.

It was the First World War which gave the USA an opportunity to consolidate her hold on the international market in preparation for the boom period which followed. The financing of production related directly to the feed-back of money to the producers through the distribution of their films, and it was obvious that American producers could afford to invest far greater sums in their productions, and establish high-paid contract stars with a world-wide reputation. A few stars, notably Fairbanks, Chaplin and Keaton, became producers with companies of their own. Production in the USA passed largely into the hands of wealthy combines with a considerable annual turnover of films and a roster of contract directors, writers and senior executives as well as stars on their payroll. The large-scale industry in Japan followed a similar monolithic pattern, while on the other hand the industries in the Western European countries were less consolidated. The largest of these was in Germany, with the UFA combine established as the richest and most prolific centre of production; one of the smaller industries at this time was the British, the industry least protected from intrusion by the American colossus. To save British production from virtual extinction, a protective Quota Act was introduced in 1927. Various forms of protective quota were eventually to be introduced by other countries whose industries were threatened by the mass importation of American films, with exhibitors committed blindly in advance to showing product over the selection of which they had little or no control. The average British film at this time, with a budget perhaps of some £25,000 to £30,000, had small chance of success in competition with the best of the imported American product, offering stars of world fame and far more lavish production.

With the coming of sound, as we have seen, films became segregated through language. Sound films cost on average some 25% to 30% more than their silent equivalents had done, and during the 1930s, after the industry's recovery from the effects of the Wall Street crash and its repercussions in Europe, the market for American films became larger than ever before. Those American companies, such as Warners, which had been for some while in financial difficulties, found their position greatly strengthened by the mid-1930s. Costs, however, were rising all the time, especially for films with spectacular sets and casts. But American pictures were well placed, since they were able to recoup their high costs in the USA before reaping the profits which came from additional distribution in the many foreign markets open to them.

In Nazi Germany, Goebbels gradually assumed ever greater economic control of the means of production, though the industry was not actually nationalized until the war years. In the Soviet Union, film production had been nationalized in 1919, the State promoting whatever films it was felt were needed, and absorbing the box-office takings as revenue from which to finance the state-owned studios and pay the state-employed film workers.

The post-war film situation began with a brief, pre-television boom, during which it was discovered that the public was at least prepared to patronize a certain number of films which had social content and meaning, and did not necessarily cost large sums to make or carry the names of big stars. These were popular in the USA – the first films of many highly talented directors such as Kazan and Zinnemann were in this style. Many were made largely outside the studios, on interesting locations. In Britain this kind of production was represented by the Ealing films, both the comedies and more serious subjects, and in Italy by the neo-realist films. But when the motion-picture theatres began their long-drawn battle with television in the 1950s, the sheer size and scale of the pictures shown began to increase. Films became longer and far more costly. The break-up of the great Hollywood companies through the American anti-Trust laws, the exile of many talented people with leftist-liberal views at the time of the Un-American Activities investigations, the search abroad by enterprising American independent producers for less costly places than Hollywood in which to make their films, together with the instinct to compete with the enclosed images of television by presenting theatre audiences with ever-more exotic locations in many different parts of the world, all gave American films in the 1950s and 1960s a much wider range of visual appeal. But the costs were often astronomical; budgets of $10 million and more were frequent. Italy was followed by Spain and Spain by Yugoslavia as centres for American production; costs rose in each country as it became popular with producers, while in Britain, always a tempting area for American film-makers, costs were second only to those of Hollywood, though the technical facilities and skills available were correspondingly high. Gradually during the 1960s American finance penetrated deeper into British production itself until, at the close of the decade, it represented some 90% of the capital invested in current production. However, this form of investment was to recede sharply in the early 1970s when the dollar came under increasing pressure and American investment in film production abroad declined.

British production, like that in the other European countries, had to devise methods for raising finance in order to continue active. Governments, more or less reluctantly and suspiciously, found themselves supporting this difficult industry in Britain, France, Italy, West Germany and elsewhere with loans, subsidies, financial awards, tax reliefs, and the like. Government-financed film festivals kept individual countries in Western Europe – notably France (Cannes), West Germany (Berlin) and Italy (Venice and other centres) – in the forefront as nations interested in the art of the film, as well as in its commercial exploitation and international distribution. International agreements for co-production between various Western European countries were signed during the 1960s so that quota barriers could be relaxed, with the result, for example, that a high proportion of Italian production was sponsored in conjunction with producers in West Germany, Spain or France. The more powerful Italian producers eventually came to co-produce English-language films in association with American producers. The European communist countries (which have their own annual international festival alternating between Moscow and Karlovy-Vary in Czechoslovakia) have followed suit, not only by setting up co-productions between themselves, but also by working with the West, a notable example being the Russian-Italian co-production *Waterloo* (1970).

The general picture of the world's film industries became even more complex in the 1960s than it had been hitherto. Broadly speaking it might be divided as follows:

(i) The small, or local industries, appealing to ethnic or specific language groups with outlets on a modest scale in European countries (for example, Greece, Denmark, or Finland), and elsewhere (for example, the smaller Asian communities or the Philippines).

(ii) The larger regional industries appealing to a widespread ethnic community – for example, Hong Kong's production in Mandarin Chinese, Egypt's production in the Arabic tongue, and the Indian industry's production in such languages as Hindi, Tamil, and Bengali.

(iii) The more important industries producing films in French, Italian, German, Swedish, Spanish and other languages in Western Europe and Latin America, of which certain industries (notably France, Italy, Germany and Sweden) have proved over the years to be prime contributors not only to the world film industry but to the development of the film as an art.

(iv) The state-owned and ideologically-controlled industries of the communist countries. These can be divided into three categories: first, the small, independent industries in Asia, in Cuba, Albania and (most important of all) Yugoslavia; second, the more or less closely-grouped East European industries of Poland, Czechoslovakia, East Germany, Hungary, Romania, Bulgaria, together with Russia and, outside Europe, the constituent republics of the USSR; and third, China.

(v) The English-language industries, of which the American is the primary and the British the secondary source – with further contributions, notably in documentary, from Canada and Australia. The American and British industries, too, have been in the forefront in their contribution both to the art and the industry of film-making. The position of the USA could be said to have been unique throughout the total development of the medium.

The most recent development in film finance has been the intrusion of television into feature production, sponsoring films initially for the motion picture theatres, and later for exhibition on the television screen. This arose out of the very high rentals being charged to the television companies by the film industry for the replay of old feature films on television, especially in the USA. The sponsorship of feature film production by the television interests is not confined to the USA; for example RAI-Television in Italy has sponsored feature-length films by such directors as Rossellini, Castellani, Fellini, Jancsó, Olmi, Bertolucci and Pasolini, though the nature of these productions may not always make them suitable for widespread screening in motion-picture theatres, other than art houses. In Britain film records have been made of outstanding theatre productions, largely with outlets on television in mind. In various ways television and feature film production draw closer, especially as major talents, such as Schlesinger in Britain or Lumet and Frankenheimer in the USA, came to feature production through television. Economically, technologically and artistically, the two media are coinciding to an increasing extent, while ahead lies a third potential form of sponsorship in distribution of films through video-cassettes designed for use with the television receiver in the home.

PRESENT FORM The whole bias of creative film-making turned during the 1950s and especially the 1960s in the direction of the individual master-director, away from the impersonal, hall-marked entertainment produced by the monolithic companies through their roster of contract film-makers. It was these independent producer-directors who set the pace for American film-making, some of them in an expatriate situation (such as Losey or Kubrick), but most working internally within the USA, such as Wilder or Kazan. In Britain the independent-minded directors are represented very variously, by Reisz, Lindsay Anderson, Schlesinger or Russell. On the European Continent the turn of the 1950s and 1960s was the period of the French New Wave and of the individualistic directors who followed, as well as of other film *auteurs* of the quality of Antonioni, Fellini or Rosi in Italy, Bergman in Sweden, and so forth. Buñuel in Mexico, Kurosawa, Ozu, Mizoguchi and Oshima in Japan and Satyajit Ray in Bengal all broke away from the hard moulds of screen entertainment. This independence furthered immeasurably the mature diversification of style and viewpoint in the film of the 1960s, and even in the communist countries the individualist appeared and shone out against the background of sober film-making which characterized Eastern Europe: Wajda, Polanski, Němec, Forman, Jancsó, Makavejev. The much freer, more flexible style of direction which characterized the 1960s was aided by the use of much lighter film equipment, especially the hand-held or harness camera and highly mobile recording facilities. Improvisation, created directly through the camera, became fashionable, and was used in varying degrees by directors according to the nature of the control (or in some cases lack of control) they felt they had over the medium. With a few directors pre-scripting gave way to direct, 'plastic' creation: certain sympathetic players who enjoyed improvisation were gathered together on location and the situation allowed to develop.

But in general this independent approach (only a relative independence, since these directors still had for the most part to obtain their finance from orthodox sources) could only be to the great advantage of the film, even if it did not satisfy the great body of mainly young film-makers of the 1960s who wanted to break altogether with the established film industry and do work which was as divorced as possible from the production, distribution and exhibition machine against which they were for many reasons in revolt. As it were through a collective need, they founded primarily in the USA, but also in Britain and elsewhere, what became a second industry based on club exhibition. Their revolt was in most cases total – against bourgeois society and its morality, against censorship, against established principles of film technique. The conventions of pre-scripted, narrative and plot structures fell before their policy of everyone 'doing his thing' with camera and microphone. Often, from the more orthodox film-makers' point of view, this achieved only a chaos of improvised images which appeared to do little but emphasize the 'director's' political or social protests or his urge towards sexual exhibitionism. All accepted forms of film-making collapsed in the drive to record instinctual, irrational behaviour. The vast output of underground films made in Europe and the USA, and exhibited in countless clubs interested only in this branch of the film far outstrips any previous production or exhibition of the comparatively rare avant-garde or experimental film. The underground reveals an entirely new formula of self-made, self-serve cinema, and forms a part of the wider revolution of our time against the more gradual evolution of society. Some of it has represented a 'drop-out' culture which is a negation of culture as it has been previously understood, though it is quite often the product of well-educated and fundamentally well-meaning people. Their deeply-felt protest against war and racial intolerance is the subject of much of their film-making, notably in the USA.

A factor in all these changes is the general refusal of film-makers to be tied to the purely realistic approach characteristic of most films in the past other than the wholly experimental. Many leading film-makers, among them Fellini, Buñuel, Bergman, Wajda, and Oshima have turned away from direct narrative and adopted an allusive or imagistic approach. Indeed, the more advanced films of the 1960s have to a considerable extent drawn away from plotted action and story-telling to examine the psychological condition of their characters and present some significant phase in their experience. As the expressionist and avant-garde film-makers of the 1920s discovered, the film is well-adapted to present illusion and hallucination, blending the 'real' with the 'non-real', so that it becomes difficult to distinguish between what is actual and what imagined by the human mind under stress. Certain films have been made under the influence of drugs, while others have sought to present the experience of the mentally disturbed. It is obvious that the devising of images of the psychedelic type can develop into a fashionable cult, and the excesses which have occurred in certain films are no more than a kind of psycho-aesthetic indulgence, first of all by the film-makers and later by their audiences.

If the film of our time, the late 1960s and early 1970s, has a besetting fault, this is the tendency to dwell on violence, prolonged sadistic scenes, and what amounts to incessant sexual voyeurism. The explanation offered is that this has become an increasingly violent age, with terrorism a universal experience in warfare, political persecution, and the legacy of sadism and genocide in the concentration camps. This is undeniable, but it is a wholly insufficient reason to turn the screen into a shambles, as distinct from examining and exposing the roots of violence in human nature which have been manifest in recent history.

As the restraints of censorship were withdrawn the film, as we have seen, gained a new freedom to rank alongside literature and drama (both now at least technically free of censorship in many countries) in the responsible presentation of human experience, including sexual relations of every kind. But at the same time it gained a corresponding freedom to indulge in what might be termed the 'new voyeurism' of behaviour of a degraded kind. It is, perhaps, the price which has to be paid in order to gain the other, more positive aspects of a liberated screen, but it could only too easily aid those who advocate a reversion to the older, more repressive forms of censorship, characteristic of an immature society. It would seem in the end best to continue to rely on the good sense of present and future generations in this matter, in the hope that they can be relied upon to bring a sufficiently mature *average* judgment to bear on the nature and circumstances of what is being presented. This might enable us to abandon censorship altogether, other than in underdeveloped countries, where progress in this direction must of necessity be slower. To admit otherwise is also to admit that our own, so-called advanced society is still underdeveloped. If indeed it is, then presumably some form of film censorship must continue to protect immature adult minds, just as it almost universally protects children.

Whether or not the film is to be regarded as the greatest single art-form so far created – and many admittedly interested parties argue it is so, pointing out that it combines the powers and potentialities of many other, longer-established art forms – its rapid rise from the infant stage of 70 years ago to its present-day diversification and mature achievement cannot be denied. But little point is gained by trying to prove it 'superior' to literature, drama, music, or the fine arts. It certainly borrows from all of these, as they have so often borrowed from each other. But the film can never supplant them, nor is it its function to do so. Each art possesses its own uniquely developed powers, including the art of the film.

Good films have long since ceased to be limited to a few, hand-picked productions a year. The film has become, on the one hand, a universal art designed to entertain, to excite, to reveal, to disturb – and on the other, a powerful narcotic inducing the standardization throughout our various societies of many ill-conceived values. It forms an inescapable part of the expression of every advanced society and acts as an influence for good or bad on both the advanced and the less advanced among the world's communities. Its range and flexibility increase with every decade, and each generation lays claim to the powers of this new art as something uniquely their own.

ROGER MANVELL

The Development of Colour Cinematography

A black-and-white photograph is one in which the colours of the original are reproduced in varying shades of grey. A correct record would reproduce objects of the same brightness, but different colours, in the same density. To do this, the photographic negative material must have a uniform sensitivity to all colours of the spectrum. The earliest photographic materials were sensitive only to blue and ultra-violet radiation. Thus, in the picture, all colours other than blue would be rendered much darker than the visual impression. In 1873 H. W. Vogel discovered that, by treating photographic materials with dyes, the sensitivity of the emulsion could be extended to record green light – making possible the ORTHOCHROMATIC plate. Further improvements followed, and in 1903 A. Meithe and A. Traube described a method of sensitizing plates to red light. As a result, in 1906 the English firm of Wratten and Wainwright were able to introduce the first commercially produced true PANCHROMATIC plates, sensitive to all colours.

The first motion-picture materials were of 'ordinary' sensitivity, recording ultra-violet, violet and blue light only; this inevitably gave a false tone rendering of many colours. Flesh tones, warm in colour, were often recorded in a harsh way. Although such negative materials could be treated by the user to improve colour sensitivity, this method was not very satisfactory, but it was not until 1913 that a commercially produced panchromatic negative motion-picture film was introduced. Made by the Eastman Kodak Company, it was intended for the Gaumont colour process, Chronochrome, but later this material was made available to the motion-picture trade for experimental purposes, and by 1919 it had been so used by, among others, cameraman Charles Rosher. In 1922 Ned Van Buren filmed a feature, *The Headless Horse-man*, on panchromatic negative, and by 1923 the material was in regular production. Initially more expensive than 'ordinary' negative, in 1926 the panchromatic negative film was reduced to the same price, and went into widespread use. One of the earliest productions to make effective use of the new material was ROBERT FLAHERTY's *Moana* (see footnote page 133); it made a considerable impact with the fine tonal quality it achieved. Although the ordinary material continued to be available for many years, the use of panchromatic materials rapidly became standard practice in studio production. An important effect of this widespread use of fully colour-sensitive film was to alter studio lighting requirements. Ordinary film required light rich in blue content; if daylight was insufficient or unavailable, arc lamps were required for successful results. The incandescent lamp, with high red output, only became fully practical with the advent of panchromatic film, but then rapidly replaced the arc lamp as the basic studio light source.

Coloured motion-picture films were first seen almost at the beginning of the film itself. Many of the earliest public presentations of film in 1896 included subjects in colour. These early productions were coloured by hand, frame by frame, as many as six colours being applied to a black-and-white print. The operation was carried out in factories employing a number of girls, each of whom applied a single colour. This method, widely used in the first decade of the cinema, became impractical as the length of films increased and the number of copies of each production required became greater. The illustrations page **33A&B** show examples produced before 1900. An important production making spectacular use of hand-colouring was GEORGE MÉLIÈS's *Voyage Across the Impossible* (1904, **33C**). Although hand-colouring ceased to be widely used after the early years of this century, the technique was occasionally revived for special effects. A notable example is found in original prints of *The Battleship Potemkin* (EISENSTEIN, 1925), where dramatic effect was given to the scene of the raising of the revolutionary flag by hand-colouring it red (**33D**).

Around 1905 PATHÉ Frères introduced the Pathécolor process, in which stencils were prepared by cutting, from each frame of a print, areas corresponding to the same colour (**33E**). A maximum of six stencils, for as many colours, might be prepared. These were run in succession through staining machines in register with the final print, to which the colours were applied through the stencils with dye-charged rollers or brushes. Since it was expensive, this process was largely confined to shorts or inserted colour sequences in feature films. It was in operation until the 1930s, and was capable of beautiful results.

The earliest examples of stencil colouring illustrated here are from a series of epic Italian films on the life of Christ, (*c.* 1909, **33F&G**). Other examples are: from newsreel fashion sequences (*c.* 1912, **34A&B**); *c.* 1914, **34C&D**; *c.* 1925, **34E&F**; *The Last Days of Pompeii* (1926, **34G**); and an advertising film *4711* (*c.* 1930, **34H**).

Hand and stencil colouring processes were relatively expensive, and more general methods of producing colour effects were available. One process involved tinting the film with a uniform wash of colour – illustrations page **35A&B** are from Herbert Ponting's film of Scott's Antarctic expedition (1912), while example **35C** is from *The Gnomes* (a Nordisk film, 1908). The colours were chosen to suit subject and mood; colour changes from shot to shot could give a crude but effective result. Example **35D** (c. 1910) shows an arsonist at work. He enters a factory at night – blue tint – to set fire to it; as the flames flare up the shot is tinted red. The sudden transition of colour adds to the drama of the scene. In example **35E** (*c.* 1920) the transition from blue-tinted night exterior to yellow-tinted lamplit interior has a similar effect. Tinting was much used in the 1920s, when a film entirely in black-and-white was a relative rarity (**35F,G&H**, 1924–5). A variation on the process used coloured film base, especially after the coming of sound made it necessary to develop tinting methods which did not interfere with the sound track. Illustrations page **36A-N** show the tinted bases available from the Eastman Kodak Company in the Sonochrome range (*c.* 1930). The tints were given exotic names: Peach-blow (**36A**), Inferno (**36B**), Rose Dorée (**36C**), Candle Flame (**36D**), Sunshine (**36E**), Firelight (**36F**), Purple Haze (**36G**), Fleur de Lis (**36H**), Azure (**36I**), Nocturne (**36J**), Verdante (**36K**), Aqua Green (**36L**), Argent (**36M**), Caprice (**36N**).

An alternative method of colouring used chemical toning, in which the black-and-white image was converted to a coloured image by suitable treatment. Example **35I** is again from the Ponting Antarctic film (1912), while examples **35J** and **35K** date from *c.* 1924.

The two techniques of tinting and toning could be combined to produce more elaborate colour effects (**35L,M&N**, *c.* 1924).

The principles of the photographic reproduction of colours had been described by Clerk Maxwell in 1855 and demonstrated by him at the Royal Society in 1861. He showed that if three negatives are taken through, respectively, red, green and blue filters, these negatives will yield positives which, if projected through their appropriate red, green and blue filters and superimposed on a screen, will give a picture in natural colours.

Many attempts were made to produce colour motion pictures on the basis of this additive mixture of red, green and blue images, notably by Lee and Turner in 1899, but the difficulties of recording and registering the three images on the screen were such that the system was not practical. G. A. Smith, in his patent of 1906, and in the two-colour process commercialized in 1908 as Kinemacolor, was the first to resolve the difficulty. The Kinemacolor process employed a camera (**37A**) running at 32 frames per second, twice the normal speed, taking alternative pictures (**37B**) through red and blue-green sections of a rotating filter disc. The black-and-white prints (**37D**) were projected at the same speed by a projector (**37C**) also having a rotating filter disc. The two successively projected coloured images (**37E**) were merged in the eye by persistence of vision – the principle on which the motion-picture itself is based – to give a picture in colour. The pictures suffered from lack of a complete colour range due to the use of only two colours, and some fringing occurred on moving objects, but for many subjects the results were remarkably good. The process enjoyed some commercial success; the most notable production being *The Delhi Durbar* (1912), a colour record of the Indian celebrations of the coronation of King George V (**37B,D&E**). A rival process, Biocolour, (**37F**), employed red and green staining of the alternate frames, avoiding the need for a modified projector, but introducing problems of unevenness of colour.

Other two-colour additive processes appeared, using simultaneous recording and projection of the two colour records. Most of these processes, such as Colcim colour (1916, **37G&H**), the Busch system (1930, **37I**) and Raycol (1928–33, **37J**), used two small images occupying the normal frame area. Three-colour processes employing Maxwell's principles also appeared. The first to be demonstrated commercially was the Gaumont Chronochrome system (1913) using three almost full-size frames (**38A**). It suffered in consequence from mechanical troubles and was not commercially exploited. Most subsequent systems recorded the three separation images within a standard frame area – e.g. Horst process (1930, **38B**), Franchita-Realita (Opticolor; 1935, **38C**). All these two- and three-colour processes suffered from defects such as colour fringing due to lack of registration of the component images projected through multiple lenses, and poor definition. The Keller-Dorian/Berthon process avoided these problems by using film with a lenticular base which enabled three images to be simultaneously recorded on a single film through a colour filter of three red, green and blue strips placed before the camera lens. No other modification to the camera was needed. A similar filter was placed over the projection lens, and, in combination with the lenticular structure of the film, allowed the three component images to be projected through a single lens, thus avoiding registration difficulties. Problems of duplication of the original film restricted its professional use; however, it enjoyed some success as an amateur process from 1928 to 1935, marketed under the name Kodacolor in 16 mm form. A similar process was introduced by the Agfa Company in 1930.

The most successful additive systems were those using a mosaic of minute filter elements – red, green and blue applied, at about 1 million to the square inch, to the film base (**38D**). This was then coated with panchromatic emulsion which, in the camera, was exposed through the base and filter mosaic. The image thus recorded the proportions of red, green and blue present in the scene. The black-and-white image, separated from the filter grid and highly magnified, is seen in **38E**. This image, in combination with the filter mosaic, gave a colour image directly, without additional optical or mechanical devices (**38F**). By building into the film the necessary taking and projection filters the process required no modification to apparatus and no special operating techniques. The earliest such process in still photography appeared in the last century; the first successful motion picture system was Dufaycolor. This process appeared in 1934 in 16 mm and 9·5 mm form for amateur use, and in 35 mm form for studio work. At first a reversal process (**38G,H&I**), it yielded a direct positive from the film exposed in the camera. Later, in 1937, a negative-positive version (**38J&K**) was introduced as a more effective solution to the problems of professional production (**38L-O**). The negative-positive process was used for Humphrey Jennings's first film *Design for Spring* (1938, **38P,Q&R**). It was not revived for motion-picture use after the Second World War.

All additive methods suffer from a serious drawback, however: projection must take place through filters which, by their very nature, transmit less than one-third of the total light available. The most successful colour film processes have therefore been those based on the principles of subtractive colour reproduction, which had been described by Ducos du Hauron in the last century.

In principle, most subtractive colour processes employ a film bearing three superimposed coloured images, each of which controls the amount of either red, green or blue light passing through it to the screen. These three images are cyan (blue-green), magenta and yellow respectively. Original exposures are made either through red, green and blue filters on separate films in a beam-splitting camera, or on a tripack material of which the three layers are sensitive to red, green and blue light. Printing and processing is arranged so that the red record is printed as a cyan image, the green record as a magenta image and the blue record as a yellow image. Thus, black is given by a maximum concentration of all three colours; white when no dyes at all are present. Red is formed by the presence of yellow and magenta, and absence of cyan; green by the presence of yellow and cyan and absence of magenta; and so on. The result is a full-colour positive of great transparency, needing no special projection apparatus.

The earliest subtractive motion picture process was introduced by Eastman Kodak in 1915, as a result of the work of J. G. Capstaff of the Kodak Research Laboratories. Marketed as Kodachrome (old form) it involved a two-colour analysis only. A beam-splitting camera was used to obtain two negatives recording the red and blue-green content of the scene (**39A**). These were printed on to opposite sides of double-coated print film, bearing an emulsion on both sides of the film base. Suitable chemical treatment converted the black-and-white images to red-orange and blue-green (**39B**). The resulting combined image (**39C**) had a restricted but adequate range of colours. Examples **39D-L** are from the period 1920–30.

Subsequently other similar two-colour processes appeared. W. Van Doren Kelly in the USA developed the Prizma process in 1919 (**40A**) which directly or indirectly gave rise to a number of two-colour processes, among them Multicolor (**40B**), Magnacolor, Trucolor and Cinecolor (**40H**). The last-named was one of the most successful commercial processes using two-colour reproduction, surviving until the early 1950s. Other processes, using similar principles, were in use in Europe between the two World Wars – among them Ufacolor (**40G**), Sirius Colour, and Chemicolor, used in 1937 for *Pagliacci* (**40E&F**). The Polychromide process, devised by Aaron Hamburger, enjoyed some commercial success in Great Britain in the 1920s and 1930s (**40C&D**).

The formation of the Technicolor Motion Picture Corporation by KALMUS, Westcott and Comstock took place in 1915. After first attempting a two-colour additive process, in 1919 they commenced work on a two-colour subtractive process, using a beam-splitting camera. The two negative records from this camera were printed on to two positive films, which, after being processed to give subtractively dyed relief images, were finally cemented back to back. The first film so made was *Toll of the Sea*, later followed by *Cytheria*, *Ben-Hur* (1924, **41A**) and many other productions, including, in 1926, *The Black Pirate*.

The cemented positive prints proved unsatisfactory, and in 1928 the process was changed to one of imbibition printing, in which dye images were transferred from a matrix film bearing a relief image to a final print film. Although requiring exceedingly accurate registration, this method was successful, and has formed the basis of the Technicolor printing process to the present day.

The first major production to use the two-colour imbibition printing method was *On With the Show* (1928, **41B**), followed by *Show* *of Shows* (1928, **41C**), and many other productions (**41D&E**). Later a three-colour printing method was introduced for the WALT DISNEY Silly Symphony *Flowers and Trees* (**41F**), where separation negatives recording red, green and blue were made from the original. Illustrations **42A,B&C** show this process applied to one of the drawings from the cartoon film *Three Little Pigs* (1933). From these negatives the three matrix films were made, bearing the positive relief images (**42D,E&F**). These were used to transfer dye images in cyan, magenta and yellow (**42G,H&I**) to the final print film, which carried a black-and-white 'key' image and the sound track (**42J**). This combination produced the final full-colour print (**42K**). The Technicolor process remained in this form until the early 1950s.

To produce live-action film, the two-colour camera was redesigned to record three negative films simultaneously. The first complete production in the new process using the three-strip camera was *La Cucaracha* (1935), followed in that year by the feature *Becky Sharp* (**43A&B**). The first English Technicolor production was *Wings of the Morning* (1936, **43C**). In that same year *The Trail of the Lonesome Pine* was the first Technicolor feature to be shot entirely on location (**43D**). Other early Technicolor productions were *The Garden of Allah* (1936, **43E**) and two years later *Vogues of 1938* (**43F**), *The Mikado* (**43G**) and *The Divorce of Lady X* (**43H**). Later productions included the Academy Award-winning *Black Narcissus* (1947, **44A&B**), *Henry V* (1944, **44C**), *London Town* (1947, **44E**), *Colour* (1948, **44F**), and *The Coronation of Queen Elizabeth* (1953, **44G**).

A large number of cartoon films have been made in the Technicolor process since Disney first employed it for *Flowers and Trees* (**41F**). His other cartoons in Technicolor include *Snow White and the Seven Dwarfs* (**45A**), *The Pied Piper of Hamelin* (**45B**), *Hiawatha* (**45C**), *Pluto's Birthday Party* (**45D**) and *Fantasia* (**45E&F**). NORMAN MCLAREN's *Now is the Time...* (1951, **45G**) and HALAS and BATCHELOR's *The Magic Canvas* (1947, **45H**) also used this process.

The Technicolor process subsequently underwent further change with the introduction of new processes based upon the tripack construction. Such materials, first described in theory by Ducos du Hauron and others in the last century, employ three light-sensitive layers independently recording red, green and blue components of the scenes. Processing produces dye images of complementary, subtractive colours in the three layers, in proportion to the original exposure. It was not until the 1930s that the practical problems of manufacturing such materials were solved. The Gasparcolor process was the first to appear for motion picture use (**46A-D**). Different from most modern processes in employing a dye-destruction principle, it first appeared in 1934 and was used until 1940, principally for animated films (**46E-F**). The first of the modern tripack processes to use the current principles was Kodachrome (**46G-J**) in 1935. Introduced in 16 mm and 8 mm form, primarily for amateur use, it was subsequently used on occasion to provide master material for printing up to 35 mm by the Technicolor process. A 35 mm version under the name of Technicolor Monopack was introduced in the 1940s to provide location material for printing by the Technicolor process: *Thunderhead, Son of Flicka* (1944, **44D**) was the first feature to be shot entirely on Monopack.

The introduction of a 16 mm reversal tripack process by the Agfa Company in 1936 was followed by the development of an Agfacolor negative-positive system (**47A**) for professional motion-picture use. Introduced during the Second World War in Germany for films such as *Die Goldene Stadt* (1944, **47B**), the Agfacolor patents and manufacturing details were released in 1945 for general use; many systems based upon the Agfa process appeared subsequently, among them Gevacolor (Belgium), Ferraniacolor (Italy) and Fujicolor (Japan, **47E**).

Other Agfacolor-derived processes to have some application were Anscocolor (USA), used for a number of productions in the 1950s including *The Wild North* (1952, **47D**), and the Russian Sovcolor process, illustrated by *Othello* (1955, **47C**).

The introduction of Eastman Colour materials in 1952 led to a dramatic increase in the number of colour productions. The Eastman Colour negative film incorporated a method of 'masking' – a technique designed to improve colour rendering in the final print (**47H**). Among the early productions using the Eastman Colour materials was *Gate of Hell* (Japan, 1953, **47F**); it created a sensation with its sensitive and dramatic use of colour. The process continued to evolve: *Circus of Horrors* (1960, **47G**) was shot on an improved version of the Eastman Colour negative material.

The modern Technicolor process now makes use of such materials to provide the masters for printing; the three-strip camera was rendered obsolete almost overnight by their appearance.

The Evolution of Colour Processes

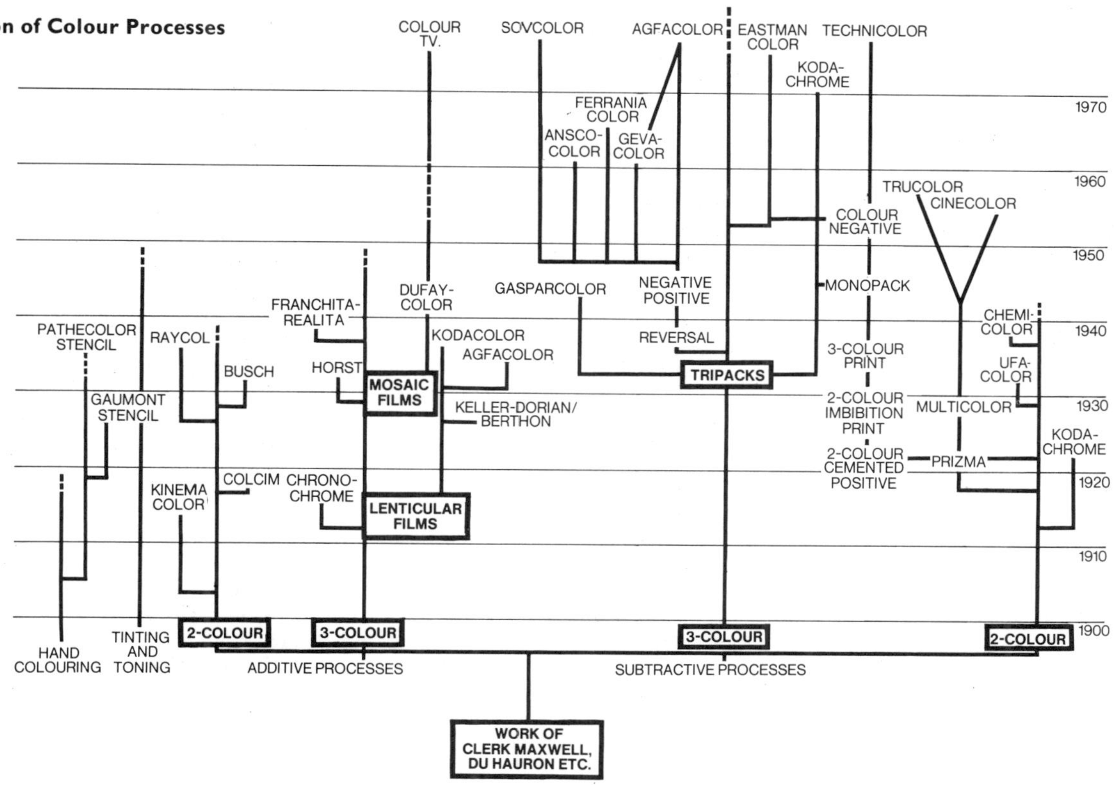

The dye-transfer imbibition printing method continues in use, although the cost of preparation of the matrices is only justified if large numbers of prints will be made; the contracting market makes the use of this printing system less economic. The nature of the imbibition printing process makes possible the development of special colour effects; from time to time 'special' Technicolor productions have been made. The most notable example is *Moby Dick* (1956, **44H**), for which a special low-colour saturation printing process was developed, combined with the use of a monochrome image of a type similar to the 'key' image used in the earlier Technicolor process (see above and page **42A-K**) but discarded for normal production around 1950.

The appearance of materials such as Eastman Colour negative film has greatly facilitated the development of widescreen and wide-film processes, most of which would not have been practical with earlier, more complex colour systems. The earliest widescreen colour system to reach the public was Cinerama, in which three films were shown combining on the screen to produce a panoramic image. A fourth magnetic film carried multi-track stereophonic sound. The first production was *This is Cinerama* (1952, **48A,B&C**).

The demand for widescreen projection of conventional films led to some loss of quality through over-enlargement of the image. For a time, it became the practice to use larger area negatives, printed by reduction to conventional image sizes for projection; the resulting prints could be shown on wide screens with improved image quality. The most widely used process of this type was VistaVision, in which a double-sized negative image (**48D**) was recorded on a horizontally-running film in the camera. The negative was usually printed by reduction to give a conventional release print (**48E**). The two illustrations shown are both taken from *The Black Tent* (1956). Occasionally, contact prints from the original negative were shown in specially equipped theatres with very large screens; as with this example from *The Battle of the River Plate* (1956, **48F**).

The use of an ANAMORPHIC LENS to 'squeeze' the image laterally in the camera enabled a wider than normal panoramic image to be recorded in the standard format. The distorted image is restored to its original proportions on the wide screen by projection though a lens similar to that used on the camera. The CinemaScope process appeared in 1953; similar systems are still in use. Among films using the 'squeeze' process are *The Bridge Over the River Kwai* (1957, **48G**), *Ferry to Hong Kong* (1959, **48H**) and *The Man Who Never Was* (1956, **48I**).

Other wide-screen processes use wide film for both negative and print. The Todd-AO process (**48J**) employed 65 mm Eastman Color negative film printed on to 70 mm wide colour print stock. Other processes have employed 70 mm prints made from conventional negatives by enlargement; the Technirama process employed a double-size horizontally disposed negative similar to that of VistaVision, reduced to conventional size or enlarged to 70 mm print, as in *Solomon and Sheba* (1959, **48K**). BC

Pages 33–48

- **33 Hand-colouring**
  - **A (c. 1898)**
  - **B (c. 1900)**
  - **C (1904)**
  - **D (1925)**
  - **Pathécolor**
  - **E,**
  - **F, G (c. 1909)**
- **34 A, B (c. 1912)**
  - **C, D (c. 1914)**
  - **E, F (c. 1925)**
  - **G (1926)**
  - **H (c. 1930)**
- **35 Tinting**
  - **A, B (1912)**
  - **C (1908)**
  - **D (c. 1910)**
  - **E (c. 1920)**
  - **F (c. 1925)**
  - **G, H (c. 1924)**
  - **Toning**
  - **I (1912)**
  - **J, K (c. 1924)**
  - **Tinting and Toning combined**
  - **L–N (c. 1924)**
- **36 Sonochrome tints**
  - **A–N (c. 1930)**
- **37 Kinemacolor**
  - **A Camera**
  - **B (1912)**
  - **C Projector**
  - **D, E (1912)**
  - **Biocolor**
  - **F (c. 1912)**
  - **Colcim colour**
  - **G, H (c. 1916)**
  - **Busch process**
  - **I (c. 1930)**
  - **Raycol**
  - **J (1933)**
- **38 Chronochrome**
  - **A (1919)**
  - **Horst colour process**
  - **B (c. 1930)**
  - **Franchita-Realita**
  - **C (1937)**
  - **Dufaycolor**
  - **D–F (c. 1933)**
  - **Dufaycolor reversal process**
  - **G-I (c. 1935)**
  - **Dufaycolor negative**
  - **J (1937)**
  - **Dufaycolor positive**
  - **K (1937)**
  - **L–O (c. 1938)**
  - **P–R (1938)**
- **39 Kodachrome**
  - **A–C (1916)**
  - **D–I (1920–8)**
  - **J–L (c. 1930)**
- **40 Prizma colour**
  - **A (c. 1920)**
  - **Multicolor**
  - **B (c. 1930)**
  - **Polychromide**
  - **C, D (c. 1930)**
  - **Chemicolor**
  - **E, F (1937)**
  - **Ufacolor**
  - **G (c. 1933)**
  - **Cinecolor**
  - **H (c. 1949)**
- **41 Technicolor**
  - **A (1924)**
  - **B, C (1928)**
  - **D, E (c. 1929)**
  - **F (1933)**
- **42 Technicolor process**
  - **A–K (1933)**
- **43 Technicolor**
  - **A, B (1935)**
  - **C–E (1936)**
  - **F–H (1938)**
- **44 A, B (1947)**
  - **C, D (1944)**
  - **E (1947)**
  - **F (1948)**
  - **G (1953)**
  - **H (1956)**
- **45 A-F (1937-44)**
  - **G (1951)**
  - **H (1947)**
- **46 Gasparcolor**
  - **A–F (c. 1937)**
  - **Kodachrome**
  - **G–J (c. 1937)**
- **47 Agfacolor**
  - **A, B (c. 1944)**
  - **Sovcolor**
  - **C (1955)**
  - **Anscocolor**
  - **D (1952)**
  - **Fujicolor**
  - **E (c. 1959)**
  - **Eastman color**
  - **F (1953)**
  - **G (1960)**
  - **Eastman color negative and positive**
  - **H**
- **48 Cinerama/Eastman color**
  - **A-C (1952)**
  - **VistaVision**
  - **D–F**
  - **Cinemascope**
  - **G (1957)**
  - **H (1959)**
  - **I (1956)**
  - **Todd-AO**
  - **J**
  - **Technirama**
  - **K (1959)**

The following frames are by courtesy of the Kodak Museum, London.

A

B

C

D

E

F

G

A

B

C

D

E

F

G

H

A

B

C

D

E

F

G

H

I

J

K

L

M

N

A B C D E F G H I J K L M N

A

B

C

D

E

F

G

H

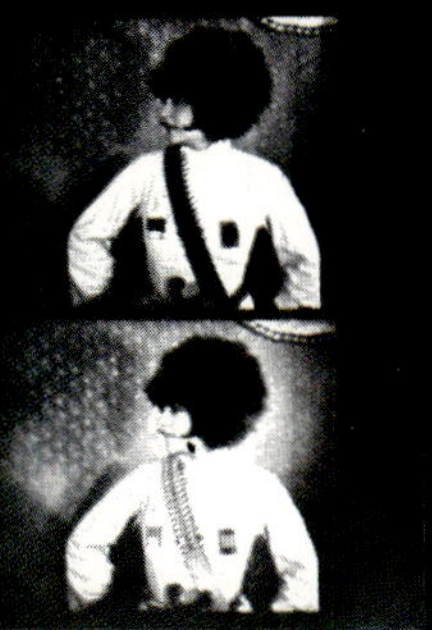

I

J

A

B

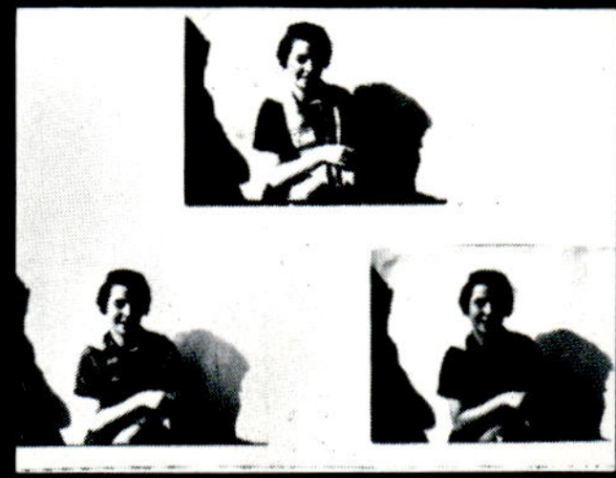

C

D

E

G

H

I

J

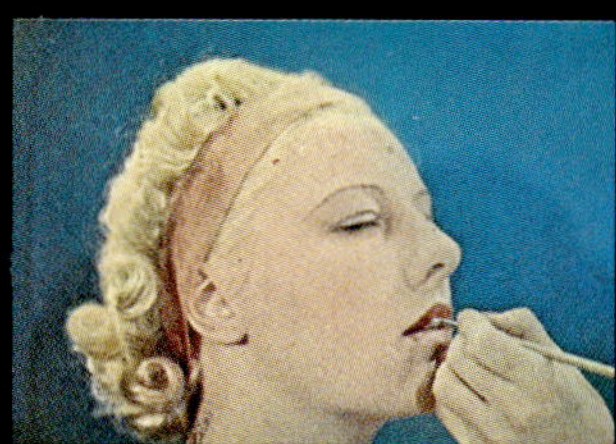

K

L

M

N

O

P

Q

R

A

B

C

D

E

F

G

H

I

J

K

L

A

B

C

D

E

F

G

H

A

F

A

B

D

E

G

H

J

A

B

C

D

E

F

G

H

A

B

C

D

E

F

G

H

A

B

C

D

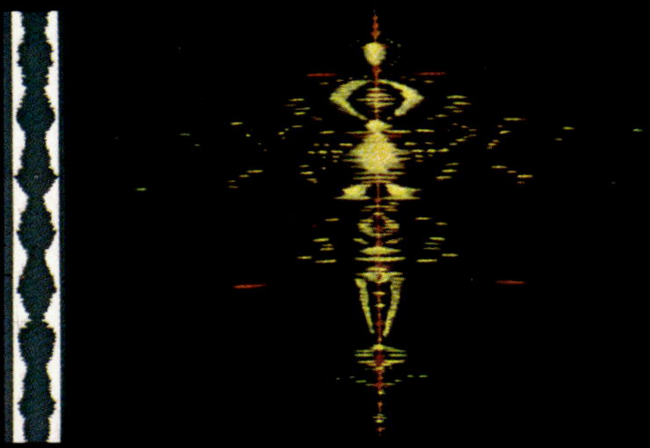

E

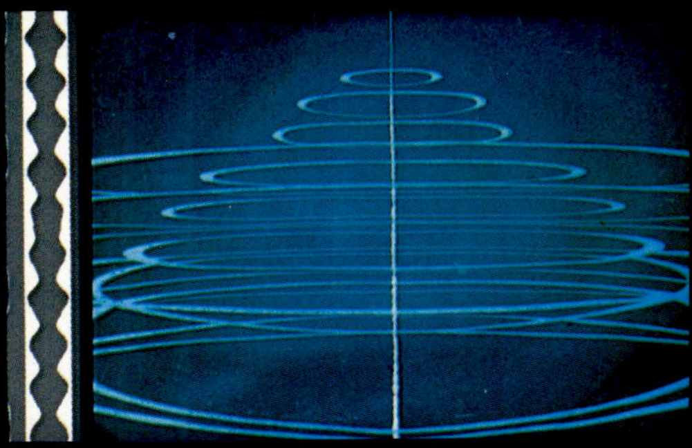

F

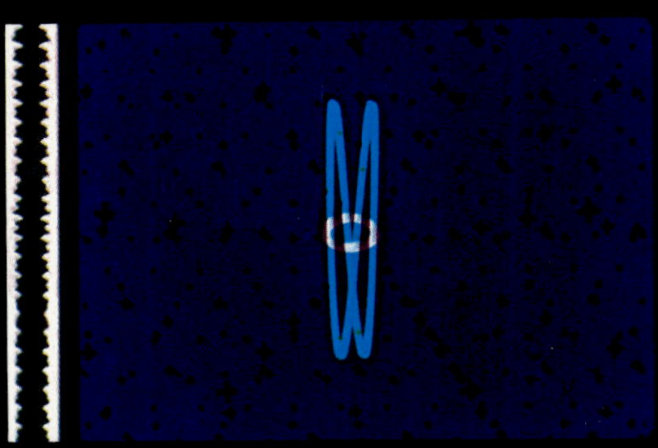

G

H

A

B

C

D

E

F

G

H

I

A

B

C

D

E

F

G

H

A

B

C

D

E

G

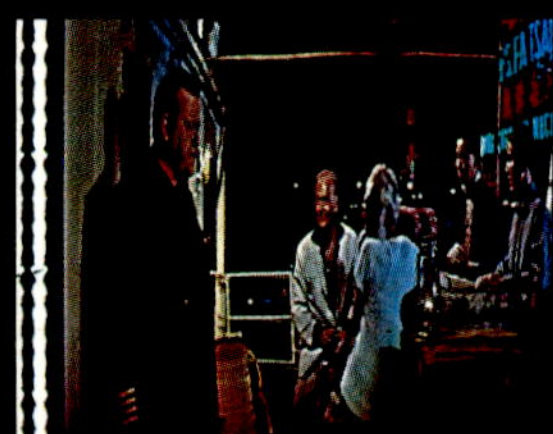

H

I

J

K

THE DEVELOPMENT OF THE FILM

The Prehistory of Cinema Includes

—the shadow theatres of the Far East
—optical illusions using lights or mirrors, dating back to the earliest recorded times
—a growing passion for optical entertainments (Barker's Panorama, c.1780; De Loutherbourg's Eidophusikon, 1781; Daguerre's Diorama, 1822) throughout the second half of the 18th and the 19th centuries.

A.D.

130 Ptolemy of Alexandria in his study of optics wrote on the laws of reflection and touched on the phenomenon of 'the persistence of vision'.

1250 Leone Battista Alberti, an Italian priest, invented a light and shadow device, a forerunner of the *camera obscura*, for use by artists copying from nature.

1267 Roger Bacon, an English monk, described the use of mirrors and lenses.

1500 Leonardo Da Vinci described the *camera obscura*, the 'dark room' inside which viewers can see a projected image of the sunlit world outside, received through a small aperture. Later (1568) the *camera obscura* was improved by substituting a lens for a plain aperture. The *camera obscura* is the starting point both for photography and projection.

1671 Athanasius Kircher, a Jesuit priest, described the Magic Lantern in the second edition of his 'Ars Magna Lucis et Umbrae'. The magic lantern was, however, already apparently widely known, since Pepys bought one some years before this date.

1770–80s Great vogue for Chinese-style shadow theatres in France, Germany and England.

1814 Nicéphore Niepce (France) began work on photography, working in association with Louis-Jacques-Mandé Daguerre after 1829. Earlier a number of scientists had applied themselves without great success to the problems of fixing the image received in the *camera obscura*.

1824–31 Peter Mark Roget, Michael Faraday and other scientists studied the phenomenon of 'the persistence of vision'.

1826 The Thaumatrope, a scientific toy, first practically demonstrated the principle of 'the persistence of vision'.

1833 Plateau (Belgium) and Stampfer (Austria) developed the so-called Magic Disc (alias Phantascope, Stroboscope, Phénakistiscope).

1834 William Horner patented the Zoetrope, or Wheel of Life, an improvement on the Magic Disc, which similarly produced an illusion of movement in little comic drawings.

1835–9 Fox-Talbot (Britain) and Daguerre succeeded in the chemical fixing of images received through a lens in a *camera obscura*, thus achieving photography.

1839 Wheatstone (British) studied binocular vision, proposed a stereoscopic device and suggested the possibility of making stereoscopic daguerreotypes.

1850 Photography introduced to magic lantern slides.

1853–4 Uchatius (Austria), Sequin (France), Duboscq (France) and others experimented with projection of photographic moving pictures, employing individually posed photographs and a Magic Disc device.

1873 Muybridge (British, working in California) began his experiments in photographing successive phases of human and animal locomotion.

1877 Reynaud's Praxinoscope; developed as a projector of successive images on a screen in 1879 in France.

1878–95 Marey, a French physiologist, developed various forms of camera for recording human and animal movements.

1884 Eastman (USA) manufactured the first roll-paper films for use with the Kodak camera.

1887 EDISON, having developed the phonograph, took the first steps with his assistant, Dickson, in the realization of a motion-picture recording and reproducing device to accompany recorded sound.

1888 Le Prince (Britain) patented a design for a camera-projector, probably impractical. He disappeared in 1890.

1889 Eastman applied to patent his 'Flexible photographic film'. (Following disputes, patent only issued in 1898.) Friese-Greene (British) patented his design for a projector. Reynaud experimented with perforated film.

1890–1 Edison, using perforated film, developed his Kinetograph camera and Kinetoscope individual viewer, a form of peepshow. (Promoted commercially in New York, London and Paris in 1894.)

1892 Reynaud opened his Théâtre Optique in Paris, the first movie theatre, but projected only hand-drawn images.

1895–6 The LUMIÈRES promoted the Cinématographe commercially in Paris (December, 1895) and subsequently abroad. PAUL in England, Armat and others in the USA, Skladanowski in Germany, demonstrated the projection of motion picture photography on to a screen.

Raymond Spottiswoode has summed up the history of the invention of cinema as follows:

The Basic Elements

The basic elements of cinematography are generally held to be the following (their originators or discoverers are given in parenthesis):

1 The application of the principle of persistence of vision to the fusion of discontinuous phases of action into a seemingly continuous movement (Plateau, Roget, Wheatstone, and Faraday).

2 The use of a narrow, flexible band of celluloid film carrying a sensitive emulsion on which the phases of action can be recorded photographically (Marey, EDISON and Eastman).

3 The establishment of a system of registration by regular perforations punched prior to use in the flexible band, so that all the images are of identical size and evenly spaced in the camera, and are moved forward an equal distance in the projector (Edison, partially anticipated by Reynaud).

4 Means for taking the images in rapid succession, the film being held stationary while each image is photographed, and obscured while the film is moved on to the next image space (Marey, Le Prince, Friese-Greene, and Edison). This is the essence of a film camera of the normal intermittent type.

5 Means for projecting the images so taken, the film being held stationary while each image is projected and obscured while the film is moved on to the next image (Le Prince and Friese-Greene). This is the essence of a film projector.

The Invention

The invention of the cinema (setting aside its shadowy antecedents in antiquity) occupied a period of about 65 years, dating from the investigation of the phenomenon of persistence of vision and the invention of the phénakistiscope by Plateau around 1833 to the first successful projections of film by modern methods in Paris and New York in 1895, and slightly later in London. So long and complex a chain of inventions could not possibly have been the achievements of one man. After Plateau and others had established the basic principles, it was necessary to arrive at a satisfactory photographic process (Fox-Talbot, Niepce, Daguerre). Then the system of movement analysis by 'successive poses' had to be investigated – Duboscq, Wheatstone, Sequin. Methods of projecting these still pictures in rapid sequence followed – Rudge, who later became the partner of Friese-Greene and Heyl. Successive photography reached its pinnacle in Muybridge's work which stimulated renewed efforts all over the world to solve the final problems of the film camera, the projector, and the photographic material itself. In France in 1882, Marey produced a workable camera in the form of a gun; and by using glass plates, he successfully analysed the flight of birds. Then, with the invention of ways to make continuous bands of celluloid film – Hyatt and Eastman – camera inventions came thick and fast – Marey in 1887–8; Friese-Greene, Le Prince, Edison, and Dickson in 1888; with greater success by the same inventors in the following year. In June 1889, Friese-Greene took out his patent for a camera; Reynaud used preperforated film in the same year: and in 1890–1 Edison perfected the system of perforation which remains the standard to this day. The projection of film, which had been accomplished experimentally by Friese-Greene, Edison, Dickson, and Le Prince, was not satisfactorily achieved until 1895–6 – Armat, Jenkins, and LeRoy in the USA; LUMIÈRE in France – and then only by quite different mechanical means.

1896–1906 The first LUMIÈRE programme includes several 'record' sequences, showing street and railway scenes of the day. Lumière's Agents travel the world. Films are rapidly established as an entertainment in fairgrounds and as items in vaudeville performances. GEORGES MÉLIÈS begins to make trick films and fantasies in France and R. W. PAUL short films in Britain.

Establishment of G. A. Smith, James Williamson and CECIL HEPWORTH as film-makers in Britain, the Pathé Company and FERDINAND ZECCA in France and STUART BLACKTON in the USA. Film-making also begins in Spain, Denmark, Bohemia (Czechoslovakia) and Japan.

Development of short 'interest' films (topicals, actualities and travelogues, news-films). Examples: G. A. Smith's *Waves and Spray* (1898); C. Hepworth's *Express Trains* (1898) and *Views from an Engine Front* (1900); R. W. PAUL's *Monorail* (1898); J. Williamson's *Seed-Threshing* (1899); Hepworth's *Day with the Hop-pickers* (1903) and *The Alien's Invasion* (1906) and *Henley Regatta* (1906). News subjects: *Queen Victoria's Funeral* (1901); and coverage of the South African War (1899–1902) and the Russo-Japanese War (1904). Travelogues included the Paris Exhibition (1900). Hepworth's cameraman and agents covered subjects in Japan, India, China, North Africa and Germany, similar to the Lumières' cinematographers. Hales' Tours began early in the 20th century, showing travelogues in mock-ups of railway coaches which swayed the audience about.

1902 *Le Voyage dans la Lune* (MÉLIÈS).

1903 In USA: The first Western, a six-minute film called *The Great Train Robbery*, filmed by EDWIN S. PORTER.

1905 In France: MAX LINDER, the comedian who influenced CHARLES CHAPLIN, begins work. In USA: *Rescued by Rover* (HEPWORTH) reveals advanced film-continuity for the period.

1906 In Britain: George Albert Smith patents the first true cinematograph colour system, called Kinemacolor. Biograph Studios established in New York City.

1907 In USA: D. W. GRIFFITH enters American films as an actor, directing his first film the next year. The Italians begin to produce spectacular classical Roman subjects.

1908 In Britain: PERCY SMITH begins his researches into filming nature, later using variant-speed filming and photo-micrography (linking the camera and the microscope).

1908–11 In USA: MACK SENNETT appears as actor in GRIFFITH's films. In France: ÉMILE COHL experiments in film animation, using hand-drawn match-stick figures. PATHÉ starts the first regular newsreel. Film-making begins in Russia.

1909 In USA: Winsor McKay makes *Gertie the Trained Dinosaur*, using some 10,000 drawings. Shackleton records on film his expedition to the South Pole. Production begins in Sweden.

1910–2 Establishment of an international star system, originating mainly in America with such players as Florence Lawrence, MARY PICKFORD and TOM MIX the cowboy star. These years saw the beginning of the feature-length film, a new distribution system which replaced film buying with film renting by exhibitors, and the popularity of the nickelodeon, the picture palace, or cinema as a centre for a full afternoon's or evening's entertainment. First regular movie theatre probably the Electric Theatre, Los Angeles, 1902. In Britain: PERCY SMITH makes *Birth of a Flower*. In Italy: newsreel cameras cover the eruption of Etna.

1911 In USA: MACK SENNETT produces the first Keystone comedy.

1912 In USA: LILLIAN GISH appears in Griffith's *An Unseen Enemy*. In France: film serials begin. Sarah Bernhardt, the great actress of the French theatre, appears in an historical spectacle film, *Queen Elizabeth*. Films of this kind help to lift cinema out of the fairground and make it respectable entertainment for 'ladies and gentlemen'; they also rob it of its original liveliness and vulgarity. In Italy: production exceeds 700 films. In Britain: the Board of Film Censors is established by the film industry itself to avoid the imposition of official censorship. Mr and Mrs Martin Johnson begin their celebrated series of travelogues exploring the less civilized world.

1913 *Quo Vadis?* and then *Cabiria*, the first outstanding Italian spectacular productions, inspire GRIFFITH to plan an 'epic'. In France: LOUIS FEUILLADE enters the film industry. In USA: Hollywood founded as a suburb of Los Angeles. CECIL B. DE MILLE and SAM GOLDWYN enter films. GRIFFITH makes his first spectacular, *Judith of Bethulia*. In Germany: the first version of *The Student of Prague* made by PAUL WEGENER. In Sweden: VICTOR SJÖSTRÖM directs *Ingeborg Holm*. In Denmark: August Blom advances film technique with *Atlantis* and BENJAMIN CHRISTENSEN makes *The Mysterious X*.

Documentary: Herbert Ponting covers Scott's expedition to the Antarctic, making one of the first major documentary films recording exploration.

Animation: in USA, Ben Harrison and Manny Gould produce *Krazy Kat* cartoons. 1913–7 sees the development of cell animation.

1914 In USA: CHAPLIN makes his first Keystone comedy. The first famous American cliff-hanger-serial, *The Perils of Pauline*, begins. WILLIAM S. HART, a Shakespearean actor who became the first great hero of Westerns, begins his screen career. In France: LOUIS FEUILLADE makes *Fantômas*, a five-part serial.

1914–8 Full newsreel coverage of First World War.

1915 In USA: *The Birth of a Nation*, GRIFFITH's three-hour epic on the American Civil War, demonstrates the greatness of the cinema as a medium for the dramatic presentation of history. DOUGLAS FAIRBANKS makes his first film. CECIL B. DE MILLE directs *Carmen*. CARL LAEMMLE founds Universal City in San Fernando Valley, California. In France: FEUILLADE makes *Les Vampires*, a 12-part serial.

1916 In USA: *Intolerance*, GRIFFITH's second three-hour epic, involves the simultaneous projection of four periods in human history. *Civilisation* (THOMAS INCE). HAROLD LLOYD appears as Lonesome Luke.

Documentary: in Britain, *The Battle of the Somme*.

1917 In USA: *Easy Street* (CHAPLIN). *Poor Little Rich Girl* features MARY PICKFORD.

JOHN FORD starts directing. BUSTER KEATON begins acting in films.

Animation: in USA, PAT SULLIVAN ensures the popularity of the cartoon by developing his Felix the Cat series.

1918 CHAPLIN, after many brilliant one- and two-reel comedies, makes his first short feature comedy, *Shoulder Arms. Hearts of the World* (GRIFFITH). In Germany: ERNST LUBITSCH makes his first film. In France: ABEL GANCE makes *J'accuse*.

Animation: the first feature-length animated film, *The Sinking of the Lusitania* made by Winsor McKay in USA.

1919 In Germany: *The Cabinet of Dr Caligari*, the famous macabre film of ROBERT WIENE. FRITZ LANG directs his first film. In USA: VON STROHEIM makes his first film *(Blind Husbands). Male and Female* (CECIL B. DE MILLE). *Broken Blossoms* (GRIFFITH). In Britain: the *Secrets of Nature* series begins, produced by H. Bruce Woolfe; PERCY SMITH joins unit in 1921.

Film industry nationalised in the USSR.

1920 LON CHANEY begins his long career as an actor in American horror films. CARL DREYER makes *Leaves From Satan's Book*. In USA: *Way Down East* (GRIFFITH). DOUGLAS FAIRBANKS features in *The Three Musketeers. The Kid* (CHAPLIN). BUSTER KEATON begins directing.

1921 In USA: RUDOLPH VALENTINO first makes an impression on the public in *The Four Horsemen of the Apocalypse. Foolish Wives* (VON STROHEIM). In Sweden: SJÖSTRÖM makes *Thy Soul Shall Bear Witness*. In Denmark: *Häxan* (CHRISTENSEN) and *The Parson's Widow* (DREYER).

Documentary: FLAHERTY finishes his great documentary of Eskimo life, *Nanook of the North* (shown with great success in 1922). In Britain: H. Bruce Woolfe produces *Zeebrugge*, a strategic war film using animated models.

Animation: in Germany, HANS RICHTER and Viking Eggeling develop abstract film-making. MAX FLEISCHER produces the *Out of the Inkwell – Koko the Clown* series.

1922 In USA: *Robin Hood* (DOUGLAS FAIRBANKS). In Germany: *Doctor Mabuse* FRITZ LANG); *Nosferatu* (MURNAU). In France: *La Roue* (GANCE).

1923 In USA: JAMES CRUZE directs *The Covered Wagon*, one of the first films to show the life of the American pioneer. HAROLD LLOYD stars in *Safety Last*, and LON CHANEY in *The Hunchback of Notre Dame*. In *Greed*, VON STROHEIM to some extent anticipates modern forms of realism. *A Woman of Paris* (CHAPLIN with ADOLPHE MENJOU). *Our Hospitality* (KEATON). In Sweden: quality of GRETA GARBO first realized in STILLER's *The Saga of Gösta Berling*.

Animation: in USA, an instructional film using animated diagrams is produced by MAX FLEISCHER to illustrate *Einstein's Theory of Relativity*. WALT DISNEY founds his first studio.

1924 In USA: CECIL B. DE MILLE makes his first version of *The Ten Commandments*, with RAMON NOVARRO. JOHN FORD makes *The Iron Horse*, about the Union Pacific, and LUBITSCH the sophisticated comedy, *The Marriage Circle*. MGM founded. In Germany: *The Nibelung Saga* (LANG); *The Last Laugh* (MURNAU). In USSR: *Strike* (SERGEI EISENSTEIN). In France: RENÉ CLAIR makes *Entr'acte* and, along with other directors, including LUIS BUÑUEL and JEAN RENOIR, helps found an experimental (avant-garde) movement. The artist Fernand Léger makes *Le Ballet Mécanique*.

Documentary: JOHN GRIERSON leaves Britain for the USA to study films and other forms of communication on a Rockefeller Research Fellowship in Social Science. In USA: Paul Strand is co-director of *Mannahatta*. In USSR: DZIGA VERTOV establishes the Kino-eye movement.

1925 In USSR: EISENSTEIN makes one of his most influential films, *Battleship Potemkin*. In Germany: G. W. PABST begins his series of 'dark' social and psychological films with *The Joyless Street*. In USA: KING VIDOR makes an outstanding retrospective war film, *The Big Parade. Seven Chances* (KEATON); *The Gold Rush* (CHAPLIN).

Documentary: the feature-length documentaries develop: in USA, *Grass* by Cooper and Schoedsack; in France *La Croisière Noire*, by LÉON POIRIER. FLAHERTY finishes *Moana* in the South Seas.

1926 In USA: BUSTER KEATON stars in one of the best silent comedies, *The General*. LAUREL and HARDY start their partnership. FRED NIBLO makes the most spectacular silent film of all in *Ben Hur*. Warner Brothers show a film with synchronised music on disc, *Don Juan*. JOAN CRAWFORD begins her long career as a star. In USSR: PUDOVKIN finishes *Mother*. In Germany: *Metropolis* (LANG). In Britain: ALFRED HITCHCOCK directs his first thriller, *The Lodger*.

Animation: in Germany, LOTTE REINIGER makes her silhouette film, *The Adventures of Prince Achmed*.

Founding of the London Film Society.

1927 In USA: FRANK CAPRA directs the comedian HARRY LANGDON in *Long Pants*. CECIL B. DE MILLE makes his first version of *King of Kings*. GRETA GARBO and JOHN GILBERT appear together for the first time in *The Flesh and the Devil*. HAROLD LLOYD in *Kid Brother*. Warner Brothers demonstrate sound with film in *The Jazz Singer*, starring AL JOLSON. CLARA BOW stars in *It* (C. BADGER). *The Wedding March* (VON STROHEIM. In France: ABEL GANCE experiments with triple screen projection for *Napoléon. The Italian Straw Hat* (CLAIR). In Germany: *The Love of Jeanne Ney* (G. W. PABST)

Documentary: in France, *Verdun* (LÉON POIRIER), *Rien que les Heures* (CAVALCANTI). In Germany: *Berlin-Symphony of a Great City* (RUTTMAN). In USA: Schoedsack and Cooper make *Chang*. The Academy Awards are instituted.

1928 Silent films continue with *The Crowd* (KING VIDOR), *The Docks of New York* (VON STERNBERG), *The Circus* (CHAPLIN), *October* (EISENSTEIN), *The Passion of Joan of Arc* (DREYER), *The Wind* (SJÖSTRÖM), *The Cameraman, Steamboat Bill Junior* (KEATON). In Britain: the first Quota Act establishes protection for home production in the face of American competition. In Japan: *Crossways* (KINUGASA). OZU continues to make silent films until 1936.

Documentary: in France, JEAN EPSTEIN makes *Finis Terrae* and LUIS BUÑUEL, *Un Chien Andalou*, a film using surrealist techniques. In USA: VORKAPICH and FLOREY make *Life of a Hollywood Extra* in the expressionist manner. In USSR: DZIGA VERTOV and MIKHAIL KAUFMAN make *Man with a Movie Camera*. In Britain: JOHN GRIERSON, returned from the USA, becomes Film Officer of the Empire Marketing Board.

Animation: in USA, WALT DISNEY waits for sound before releasing his first Mickey Mouse cartoon, *Steamboat Willie*.

1929 In Britain: HITCHCOCK makes *Blackmail*, a silent film which was remade to become the first British sound film with dialogue. ANTHONY ASQUITH's first film, *Shooting Stars*, is silent. In USA: *Broadway Melody* sets the standard for the early American musicals. *Applause* (MAMOULIAN). In Germany: MARLENE DIETRICH appears in the first sound film.

Documentary: In Britain, JOHN GRIERSON starts a new school of social documentary with his silent film *Drifters*. In Holland: JORIS IVENS makes *Rain*. In Germany: METZNER makes the psychological study *Überfall*. In the USSR: TURIN makes *Turksib*, and EISENSTEIN *The General Line*. Canti develops X-ray cinematography in Britain to diagnose his cases, including cancer.

1930 In USA: *All Quiet on the Western Front* (LEWIS MILESTONE); *Hell's Angels* (HOWARD HUGHES). The Motion Picture Association of America establishes the Censorship Code as an act of self-protection by the film industry. In France: RENÉ CLAIR directs the first French sound film, *Sous les Toits de Paris. Le Sang d'un Poète* (JEAN COCTEAU). In Germany: MARLENE DIETRICH appears in *The Blue Angel* (JOSEPH VON STERNBERG); *Westfront 1918* (PABST). In USSR: *Earth* (DOVZHENKO's last silent film).

Documentary: in France, JEAN VIGO makes his satiric film *À Propos de Nice*. In USA: LEWIS JACOBS makes *Mobile Composition*.

Animation: in USA, DISNEY produces the first Silly Symphony *Skeleton Dance*.

1931 In USA: *City Lights* (CHAPLIN); *Public Enemy* (WILLIAM WELLMAN with JAMES CAGNEY); *Little Caesar* (MERVYN LE ROY with EDWARD G. ROBINSON); BING CROSBY makes his first appearance as a crooner in a MACK SENNETT comedy. *Dracula*, with BELA LUGOSI, and *Frankenstein*, with BORIS KARLOFF, set the pattern for horror films. *The Front Page* (LEWIS MILESTONE with ADOLPHE MENJOU) exposes the American newspaper world. In Germany: *Kameradschaft* (PABST), *M* (LANG). In France: *La Chienne* (RENOIR) and *A Nous la Liberté* (CLAIR). In Britain: *Tell England* (ASQUITH).

Avant-Garde: in France, *L'Age d'Or* (BUÑUEL).

Documentary: *Tabu* (MURNAU and FLAHERTY).

Animation: in Germany, *Brahms' Hungarian Dance* (OSKAR FISCHINGER). In Britain: LEN LYE begins his experiments with images hand-drawn on the celluloid.

1932 In USA *Scarface* (HOWARD HUGHES with PAUL MUNI); *Love Me Tonight* (MAMOULIAN); *Trouble in Paradise* (LUBITSCH); *The Sign of the Cross* (CECIL B. DE MILLE); *Animal Crackers* (1930) and *Horse Feathers* (1932) established the screen reputation of the MARX BROTHERS. CLAUDE RAINS appears in *The Invisible Man*. In USSR: *Ivan* (DOVZHENKO). In Britain: ALEXANDER KORDA founds London Film Productions, and MICHAEL BALCON takes charge of Gaumont-British Picture Corporation after some ten years as a producer.

Documentary: in Britain, FLAHERTY comes to make *Industrial Britain* for GRIERSON. F. S. Smythe covers a feat of mountaineering in *Kamet Conquered*. In Spain: BUÑUEL makes *Land Without Bread*, an uncompromising study of mental deficiency, starvation and inbreeding among Spanish peasants.

Foundation of Venice Film Festival.

1933 In USSR: PUDOVKIN experiments with sound in *Deserter*. In Britain: *The Private Life of Henry VIII* (KORDA, with CHARLES LAUGHTON) creates an international success. In USA: GRETA GARBO in *Queen Christina* (MAMOULIAN). KATHARINE HEPBURN stars in the American film *Little Women* (GEORGE CUKOR). FRED ASTAIRE begins his film career with GINGER ROGERS in *Flying Down to Rio*. *42nd Street* (BACON); *King Kong* (Schoedsack and Cooper). In Germany: Goebbels takes control of the film industry on behalf of the Nazi régime, and bans *The Testament of Dr Mabuse* (LANG). *Liebelei* (OPHÜLS). In France: JEAN VIGO makes *Zéro de Conduite*.

Documentary: in Britain, PAUL ROTHA makes *Contact*. With closure of the Empire Marketing Board, for which GRIERSON has produced over a hundred documentaries, the General Post Office founds its own film unit to give continuity to this work; GRIERSON is appointed Producer.

Animation: in Germany, LOTTE REINIGER makes *Carmen*. In USA: MAX FLEISCHER begins his *Popeye* series. DISNEY uses the new three-colour Technicolor system for Silly Symphonies.

Foundation of the British Film Institute.

1934 In USA: *It Happened One Night* (FRANK CAPRA with CLARK GABLE and CLAUDETTE COLBERT) popularizes American 'screwball' comedy. *The Scarlet Empress* (VON STERNBERG). In Britain: *The Man Who Knew Too Much* (HITCHCOCK). In France: *L'Atalante* (VIGO). In USSR: *Chapayev* (VASILIEV BROTHERS) and *Happiness* (MEDVEDKIN's silent parody).

Documentary: in Britain, FLAHERTY completes *Man of Aran* for MICHAEL BALCON. ARTHUR ELTON, specialist in scientific and engineering subjects, makes *Aero-engine*. RICHARD MASSINGHAM, specialist in off-beat humour, makes *Tell Me If it Hurts*. In Holland: IVENS makes *New Earth*. In USA: *The Wave* (Paul Strand). In Germany: LENI RIEFENSTAHL makes *Triumph of the Will* as a tribute to Hitler. In France: Jean Painlevé, scientist and film-poet, makes *L'Hippocampe (Seahorse)*. In USSR: DZIGA VERTOV produces *Three Songs of Lenin*, the last of his major compilation films.

Animation: in France, experimentation with *Joie de Vivre* (Hoppin and Anthony Gross) using graphic stylization quite different from normal cartoon film-making. *L'Ideé*, Berthold Bartosch's idealistic propaganda film with designs based on woodcuts, and Alexeieff and Parker's pin-screen animation in *Night on a Bare Mountain*.

1934–9 Founding of many documentary film units in Britain, including the Shell Film Unit (1934), Strand (1936) and Realist (1937). Foundation of the National Film Library (now Archive) by British Film Institute.

1935 In USA: *The Informer* (FORD). *Mutiny on the Bounty* stars CHARLES LAUGHTON and CLARK GABLE. W. C. FIELDS appears as Micawber in the American *David Copperfield*. *Top Hat* stars FRED ASTAIRE and GINGER ROGERS. *The Story of Louis Pasteur* (WILLIAM DIETERLE with PAUL MUNI) establishes the popularity of screen biography. *The Devil is a Woman* (VON STERNBERG). *The 39 Steps* (ALFRED HITCHCOCK). In France: RENOIR continues his fine films of the 1930s with *Toni* and *Le Crime de M Lange* (1936), etc. *La Kermesse Héroïque* (FEYDER).

Documentary: in USA, *The March of Time*, a social and political magazine series, produced by LOUIS DE ROCHEMONT. In Britain: documentary productions include *Coalface*, *Housing Problems* (with on-the-spot interviews in London slums), *Night Mail*, *Shipyard*, *Song of Ceylon* (the finest lyrical film of the period), and *BBC, the Voice of Britain*.

Animation: in USSR, Ptushko's *A New Gulliver*, a puppet feature. In Germany: REINIGER's silhouette film *Papageno*. In Britain: LEN LYE's *Colour Box*, an abstract film with colour patterns painted direct on the film.

1936 In USA: *Mr Deeds Goes to Town* (CAPRA, with GARY COOPER); *Modern Times* (CHAPLIN). *Fury* (FRITZ LANG) deals with the American social problem of lynching; *Black Legion*, with HUMPHREY BOGART, faces mass terrorism in modern society. *Romeo and Juliet* (GEORGE CUKOR), one of the more successful pre-war attempts to screen Shakespeare, stars NORMA SHEARER and LESLIE HOWARD. In England: H. G. Wells's *Things to Come* (WILLIAM CAMERON MENZIES).

Documentary: in Britain, EDGAR ANSTEY makes *Enough to Eat?* on malnutrition. In USA: PARE LORENTZ makes *The Plow That Broke the Plains* on the dustbowl problem.

Animation: in Britain, LEN LYE's *Rainbow Dance*. In USSR: specialized studios in Moscow produce work mainly in folklore tradition. In USA: DISNEY is at the height of his art, with such films as *Mickey's Moving Day*, *Band Concert*, *Clock-Cleaners*, *The Three Little Pigs*, all made during the mid-1930s.

Regular television service started by BBC; abandoned in 1939 on outbreak of war. Cinémathèque Française founded in Paris.

1937 In France: *La Grande Illusion*, JEAN RENOIR's great anti-war film. In USA: *Dead End*, with HUMPHREY BOGART, deals with juvenile delinquency and violence. *The Life of Emile Zola* (DIETERLE with PAUL MUNI). DEANNA DURBIN, aged 15, becomes a teenage singing star in *One Hundred Men and a Girl*. In USSR: *Lenin in October* (ROMM); *Peter the Great* (PETROV). Cinecittà Studios opened in Rome.

Documentary: IVENS makes *Spanish Earth* with Ernest Hemingway. *The River* (LORENTZ).

Animation: in Britain, Hoppin and Gross make *Foxhunt* for KORDA.

1938 In USSR: *Alexander Nevsky* (EISENSTEIN); *Childhood of Maxim Gorki* (DONSKOI). In Britain: MICHAEL BALCON take over production at Ealing Studios. *The Lady Vanishes* (HITCHCOCK).

Documentary: in Germany, LENI RIEFENSTAHL completes *Olympiad* on 1936 Olympic Games. In Britain: HARRY WATT makes *North Sea*, a new development towards individual characterization in British documentary.

Animation: in USA, *Snow White and the Seven Dwarfs* (DISNEY).

1939 In France: *Le Jour se Lève* (CARNÉ); *La Règle du Jeu* (RENOIR). In USA: *Stagecoach* (FORD) and *Destry Rides Again*, (MARSHALL, with JAMES STEWART and MARLENE DIETRICH), help develop the unusual Western. *Only Angels Have Wings* (HAWKS). *Wuthering Heights* (WILLIAM WYLER, produced by SAM GOLDWYN with LAURENCE OLIVIER and Merle Oberon). *Gone With the Wind* (VICTOR FLEMING with VIVIEN LEIGH); JUDY GARLAND in *The Wizard of Oz* (FLEMING); *Confessions of a Nazi Spy* (ANATOLE LITVAK), one of the first American anti-Nazi films, featuring EDWARD G. ROBINSON and GEORGE SANDERS; *Ninotchka* (LUBITSCH, with GARBO). In Britain: *The Stars Look Down*, CAROL REED's first major film. In USSR: *Shchors* (DOVZHENKO).

Documentary: in USA, *The City* (Ralph Steiner and WILLARD VAN DYKE). In Canada: GRIERSON takes charge of the newly-founded National Film Board of Canada, which becomes the greatest single centre for the production of documentary so far established in the world. In Britain: GPO unit becomes Crown Film Unit.

1940 In USA: *The Great Dictator* (CHAPLIN); *The Grapes of Wrath* (FORD), with HENRY FONDA; *The Philadelphia Story* (CUKOR). In Britain: *Gaslight* (THOROLD DICKINSON).

Documentary: in Britain, *London Can Take it*, HARRY WATT with Quentin Reynolds. The Ministry of Information re-organizes its production and distribution system, and founds its mobile film units to take programmes of films to every audience in need of information or training.

Animation: in USA, DISNEY's *Fantasia* and *Pinocchio*. In Italy: EMMER and Gras make *Paradise Lost* (Bosch), the first of a series of short films on art.

1941 In USA: *Citizen Kane* reveals the talent and technical innovation of ORSON WELLES. *The Little Foxes* (WILLIAM WYLER with BETTE DAVIS). *The Maltese Falcon* shows the ability of director JOHN HUSTON. In Britain: *49th Parallel*, MICHAEL POWELL's most important film so far.

Documentary: in Britain, *Merchant Seamen; Listen to Britain* (one of HUMPHREY JENNING's finest films); *Target for Tonight* (HARRY WATT). In Italy: *La Nave Bianca*, ROBERTO ROSSELLINI's first film as director.

Animation: in Canada, NORMAN MCLAREN begins his career producing individual, experimental films for the National Film Board. In USA: DISNEY makes *Dumbo*. *Forgotten Village* (Herbert Kline). In Britain: HALAS and BATCHELOR Cartoon Film Unit established.

1942 In Britain: NOËL COWARD's *In Which We Serve* establishes DAVID LEAN. In Italy: LUCHINO VISCONTI anticipates the post-war realist movement with *Ossessione*. In USA: *The Road to Morocco*, with BOB HOPE and BING CROSBY.

Documentary: in USA, *Why We Fight* series made by FRANK CAPRA for the American armed services. *The Land* (FLAHERTY).

1943 In USA: *For Whom the Bell Tolls* (SAM WOOD); *The Oxbox Incident* (WELLMAN). In Britain: *The Way Ahead* (REED); *San Demetrio – London* (CHARLES FREND). In France: *Le Corbeau* (CLOUZOT). In Denmark: *Day of Wrath* (CARL DREYER).

Documentary: in Britain, *Fires Were Started* (HUMPHREY JENNINGS), one of the most imaginative of the hundreds of documentaries made in Britain during the war, which include in the same year PAUL ROTHA's controversial film on food *World of Plenty*, the Army documentary *Desert Victory* and *The Silent Village* (JENNINGS). In USSR: *Stalingrad*, one of their finest action war-films. In USA: MAYA DEREN makes *Meshes of the Afternoon*, a lyrical experimental film featuring herself.

1944 In USSR: *Ivan the Terrible* (parts 1 and 2, 1944–6), EISENSTEIN's last films. In USA: *Meet me in St Louis* reveals the talent of VINCENT MINNELLI as a director of musicals, with JUDY GARLAND as star. *A Tree Grows in Brooklyn* (ELIA KAZAN); *Hail the Conquering Hero* and *The Miracle of Morgan's Creek* (PRESTON STURGES); *Double Indemnity* (WILDER); *Laura*, OTTO PREMINGER's first major American film. In Britain: *Henry V*, OLIVIER's first experiment in projecting Shakespeare on the screen. In Sweden: *Hets* ('Torment', titled in English *Frenzy*), with script by INGMAR BERGMAN, directed by SJÖBERG.

Documentary: in Britain, *Western Approaches* (Pat Jackson), a feature shot at sea with non-professional actors about merchantmen whose vessel is torpedoed. In USA: *The Fighting Lady* (LOUIS DE ROCHEMONT for US Navy), *The Battle of San Pietro* (HUSTON).

Rank Organization establishes Children's Entertainment Films in Britain (1944–50) under the direction of MARY FIELD.

1945 In Britain: *The Way to the Stars* (ASQUITH); *Brief Encounter* (LEAN with CELIA JOHNSON and TREVOR HOWARD). In USA: *The Southerner*, JEAN RENOIR's principal production in America; *The Story of G.I. Joe* (WELLMAN), a film that epitomizes the American attitude to the war; *The Lost Weekend* (WILDER); *A Walk in the Sun* (MILESTONE). LOUIS DE ROCHEMONT's *House on 92nd Street* is one of the first films to use the contemporary, documentary approach to the drama of crime and espionage. In Italy: *Rome, Open City* (ROBERTO ROSSELLINI with ANNA MAGNANI) is one of the first Italian post-war realist films. In France: *Les Enfants du Paradis* (CARNÉ).

Documentary: in Britain, *Our Country* (commentary by Dylan Thomas); *Land of Promise* (ROTHA); *Burma Victory*; *The True Glory* (Anglo-American production by KANIN and CAROL REED: subject, the relief of Europe).

Animation: in Czechoslovakia, JIŘÍ TRNKA makes satiric, anti-Hitler cartoon, *Spring-Heeled Jack*. In USA: UPA Unit founded by Stephen Bosustow and other break-away animators from DISNEY studios.

1946 In USA: *The Best Years of our Lives* (GOLDWYN and WYLER); *My Darling Clementine* (FORD). In Italy: *Paisà* (ROSSELLINI); *Shoeshine* (DE SICA). In France: *La Belle et la Bête*, JEAN COCTEAU's first important feature film. In Australia: *The Overlanders* (HARRY WATT) made for BALCON. In Britain: *Great Expectations*, DAVID LEAN's first adaptation from Dickens. *A Matter of Life and Death* (MICHAEL POWELL and EMERIC PRESSBURGER). In Germany: WOLFGANG STAUDTE's Russian-sponsored *Die Mörder sind unter Uns* (*The Murderers are Among Us*) launches the post-war revival of the cinema.

Documentary: in France, Roger Leenhardt makes *Naissance du Cinéma*. COUSTEAU makes his first important undersea production, *Paysages du Silence*. NICOLE VÉDRÈS makes *Paris 1900*, an outstanding archive compilation film, edited by ALAIN RESNAIS. In USA: a new avant-garde movement develops with such directors as KENNETH ANGER, CURTIS HARRINGTON, James Broughton, SIDNEY PETERSEN, MAYA DEREN, LEWIS JACOBS and Theodore Huff making candid-camera films, such as *Sunday Beach*. In Britain: new development of instructional films with, for example, *Instruments of the Orchestra* (music by Benjamin Britten), *Longitude and Latitude* (with animation).

Animation: in Czechoslovakia, TRNKA develops his post-war work in puppet films.

BBC Television service recommences. Cannes Film Festival founded.

1947 In USA: *Monsieur Verdoux* (CHAPLIN); *Macbeth* (WELLES); *The Treasure of Sierra Madre* (JOHN HUSTON with HUMPHREY BOGART). In Britain: *Oliver Twist* (LEAN); *Odd Man Out* (REED with JAMES MASON). In France: *Le Diable au Corps* (AUTANT-

LARA); *Le Silence est d'Or* (CLAIR); *Jour de Fête* (JAQUES TATI).

Documentary: in USA, HANS RICHTER makes *Dreams that Money can Buy*, with Max Ernst, Fernand Léger, Marcel Duchamp, Man Ray and Alexander Calder. In Sweden: *Rhythm of a City* (SUCKSDORFF). In France: *Farrebique* (ROUQUIER).

Animation: in France, *Le Petit Soldat* (GRIMAULT and Sarrut).

Actor's Studio formed by LEE STRASBERG in New York. British Film Academy founded.

1948 In USA: ANATOLE LITVAK's *The Snakepit*, with OLIVIA DE HAVILLAND, creates a sensation through its presentation of a case of mental illness. *Louisiana Story* (FLAHERTY); *The Naked City* (DASSIN); *Easter Parade* with FRED ASTAIRE and JUDY GARLAND; *Letter from an Unknown Woman* (OPHÜLS). In Britain: *Scott of the Antarctic* (CHARLES FREND with JOHN MILLS); *The Queen of Spades* (THOROLD DICKINSON with EDITH EVANS); MICHAEL POWELL's ballet *The Red Shoes*; *Hamlet* (OLIVIER). In Poland: *The Last Stage* (WANDA JAKUBOWSKA), depicting life in a concentration camp, sets the pace for the high level of post-war production in Poland. In Italy: *La Terra Trema*, VISCONTI's study of life in Sicily; *Bicycle Thieves* (DE SICA).

Documentary: in Britain, *The World is Rich* (ROTHA); *Daybreak in Udi; They Travel by Air* (MASSINGHAM). In Italy: *Nettezza Urbana* (ANTONIONI). In USA: *The Quiet One* (Sidney Meyers); *Muscle Beach* (LERNER and STRICK). In France: *Van Gogh* (RESNAIS).

1949 In USA: *Intruder in the Dust* (CLARENCE BROWN), one of the more successful attempts to deal with racial tension in USA. STANLEY KRAMER's new production company establishes a reputation for making timely, low-budget films such as *Champion, Home of the Brave*, etc. *All the King's Men* (ROBERT ROSSEN, with BRODERICK CRAWFORD) is based on the life of Huey Long. *On the Town*, the first STANLEY DONEN and GENE KELLY musical. In Britain: *Kind Hearts and Coronets* (ROBERT HAMER with ALEC GUINNESS) represents the school of comedy film developed by MICHAEL BALCON at Ealing Studios. *The Third Man* (CAROL REED with ORSON WELLES, TREVOR HOWARD and JOSEPH COTTEN). In France: *Le Silence de la Mer* (MELVILLE).

Documentary: in France, *Le Sang des Bêtes* (GEORGES FRANJU).

Animation: in USA, *Ragtime Bear*, first Magoo film by UPA. In Czechoslovakia: *The Emperor's Nightingale* (TRNKA). In Canada: *Begone Dull Care* (MCLAREN).

1950 In USA: in *Sunset Boulevard* (BILLY WILDER, with GLORIA SWANSON) Hollywood looks back on its past. *Born Yesterday* (CUKOR); *All About Eve* (MANKIEWICZ). *Destination Moon* helps create a new wave in American science fiction. In *The Asphalt Jungle* (HUSTON) MARILYN MONROE has a small part. *The Men* (FRED ZINNEMANN) introduces MARLON BRANDO. In Japan: AKIRA KUROSAWA's film *Rashomon* initiates a worldwide reputation for the best post-war Japanese films. In Sweden: *Summer Interlude* (INGMAR BERGMAN). In France: *Journal d'un Curé de Campagne* (ROBERT BRESSON); *La Ronde* (MAX OPHÜLS); *Justice est Faite* (CAYATTE); *Orphée* (COCTEAU). In Mexico: *Los Olividados* (BUÑUEL).

Documentary: in Holland, *Mirror of Holland* (BERT HAANSTRA). In France: *Guernica* (ALAIN RESNAIS). In USA: *Beaver Valley* (WALT DISNEY's début in live action documentary).

Animation: in USA, *Gerald McBoing-Boing* (Robert Cannon for UPA). In Britain: *As Old as the Hills* (HALAS and BATCHELOR).

1951 In USA: *An American in Paris* (VINCENT MINNELLI with GENE KELLY). *A Streetcar Named Desire* (ELIA KAZAN, with MARLON BRANDO and VIVIEN LEIGH) starts the vogue for films about the American South, mostly associated with Tennessee Williams. *Death of a Salesman* (LASLO BENEDEK). *A Place in the Sun* (STEVENS). In Britain: *The Lavender Hill Mob* (CRICHTON); *The Man in the White Suit* (MACKENDRICK). In Sweden: *Miss Julie* (SJÖBERG).

Documentary: in Britain, *Henry Moore* (John Read for BBC-Television); beginning of series of films on art, sponsored by BBC. JOHN HALAS: *Poet and Painter* series.

Animation: in Canada, NORMAN MCLAREN's experimental film in 3–D, *Around is Around* for Festival of Britain.

Festival cinema on South Bank, London, established under British Film Institute; predecessor to present National Film Theatre.

1952 In USA: Giant-screen Cinerama launched in New York. *Singin' in the Rain* (KELLY and DONEN); *High Noon* (FRED ZINNEMANN) produced by STANLEY KRAMER and written by CARL FOREMAN, with GARY COOPER and GRACE KELLY; CHAPLIN stars CLAIRE BLOOM in *Limelight; Othello* (WELLES); *Viva Zapata!* (KAZAN). In France: *Casque d'Or* (JAQUES BECKER) reveals the talent of SIMONE SIGNORET. *Les Belles de Nuit* (CLAIR with GINA LOLLOBRIGIDA); *Wages of Fear* (CLOUZOT); *Les Vacances de Monsieur Hulot* (TATI); *Jeux Inderdits* (CLÉMENT). In Italy: *Umberto D*, DE SICA's finest Italian social film. In Japan: *Living* (KUROSAWA), *The Life of O-Haru* (MIZOGUCHI).

Documentary: in France, *Hôtel des Invalides* (FRANJU), *Les Statues Meurent Aussi* (RESNAIS, MARKER), *Crin Blanc* (LAMORISSE).

Animation: in USA, key period for UPA with such films as *Madeleine*. In Britain: Joan and Peter Foldes make *Animated Genesis*.

1953 In USA: *Julius Caesar* (JOSEPH L. MANKIEWICZ), Hollywood's most successful screen adaptation of Shakespeare; *Rear Window* (HITCHCOCK); *Shane* (GEORGE STEVENS). In Britain: *Genevieve* (HENRY CORNELIUS) the comedy that established KENNETH MORE. In Japan: *Gate of Hell* (KINUGASA); *Ugetsu Monogatari* (MIZOGUCHI); *Tokyo Story* (OZU). In Sweden: *Sawdust and Tinsel* (*The Naked Light*, BERGMAN).

Commercial 3–D (the three-dimensional cinema) and wide-screen Cinema Scope launched in the USA: *The Robe*, the first feature production in Cinema Scope.

Documentary: in Britain, *Powered Flight* (Shell), *The Conquest of Everest* (Tom Stobart and George Lowe), *World Without End* (WRIGHT and ROTHA). In Sweden: *The Great Adventure* (SUCKSDORFF). In Holland: *Houen Zo* (Herman van der Horst). In Australia: *Back of Beyond* (John Heyer). In USA: *Victory at Sea* series for NBC Television. STAN BRAKHAGE, American avant-garde director, makes *Desist film*.

Animation: *Neighbours* (MCLAREN). In USA: *The Unicorn in the Garden* (UPA). In France: *La Bergère et le Ramoneur* (GRIMAULT and Sarrut). In Britain: *O Dreamland* (LINDSAY ANDERSON).

1954 In USA: *On the Waterfront* (ELIA KAZAN, produced by SAM SPIEGEL) and *The Wild One* (BENEDEK) both with MARLON BRANDO; *The Divided Heart* (CRICHTON). In Italy: *La Strada*, with ANTHONY QUINN and GIULIETTA MASINA, makes an international reputation for the director FEDERICO FELLINI. *Senso* (VISCONTI). In France: *Rififi* (DASSIN). In Poland: *A Generation* (ANDRZEJ WAJDA). In Japan: *Sansho Dayu* (MIZOGUCHI).

Documentary: in Britain, *Thursday's Children* (ANDERSON and Guy Brenton). In USA: *Time Out of War* (Denis Sanders); *On the Bowery* (LIONEL ROGOSIN).

Animation: in Britain, *Animal Farm* (JOHN HALAS and JOY BATCHELOR), the first British feature-length entertainment cartoon, a serious dramatic fable based on George Orwell's book.

1955 In USA: JAMES DEAN begins his brief stardom, appearing in three films during 1955–6: *East of Eden* (ELIA KAZAN), *Rebel Without a Cause* (NICHOLAS RAY) and *Giant* (GEORGE STEVENS). In Italy: ANTONIONI establishes his style with *Le Amiche*. In USSR: *Othello* (SERGEI YUTKEVICH). In France: *Gervaise* (CLÉMENT);

Lola Montès (MAX OPHÜLS's last film). In Sweden: *Smiles of a Summer Night* (BERGMAN). In Britain: *Richard III*, LAURENCE OLIVIER's third experiment in Shakespearean screen presentation. *The Dam Busters* (MICHAEL ANDERSON). In India: *Pather Panchali* establishes the reputation of the director SATYAJIT RAY. In Spain: *Death of a Cyclist* (BARDEM).

Documentary: in Britain, *The Rival World* (HAANSTRA for Shell); *Momma Don't Allow* (TONY RICHARDSON and KAREL REISZ). In France: *Nuit et Brouillard* (ALAIN RESNAIS).

Animation: *A Short Vision* (Joan and Peter Foldes).

ITV (commercial television) starts in Britain: ITV News founded. Denis Mitchell begins to apply wild-track 'Think-tapes' to his television films.

1956 In USA: *War and Peace* (KING VIDOR). *Around the World in Eighty Days* (produced by MICHAEL TODD) and *The Ten Commandments* (DE MILLE) inaugurate a new era in ever larger and longer films. *The Searchers* (FORD). The prolific ROGER CORMAN makes *The Day the World Ended. The Man with the Golden Arm* (OTTO PREMINGER). In Sweden: The *Seventh Seal* establishes the name of director INGMAR BERGMAN. In Spain: BARDEM makes *High Street*. In India: *Aparajito* (SATYAJIT RAY). In France: *Et Dieu Créa la Femme* (VADIM, with BARDOT). In Japan: *The Burmese Harp* (KON ICHIKAWA).

Documentary: in France, *Le Mystère Picasso* (CLOUZOT with Picasso). *The Silent World* (COUSTEAU).

Animation: *To Your Health* (HALAS and Philip Stapp). In USA: ERNEST PINTOFF begins independent cartoon film-making (*Flebus, The Interview*, etc.). In Yugoslavia: the Zagreb studio of cartoon film-making becomes centre for work of VLADO KRISTL, Mladen Feman, Ivo Urbanic, B. Kolar, DUŠAN VUKOTIĆ etc.

1957 In USSR: *The Cranes are Flying* (MIKHAIL KALATOZOV) shows a revival of deeper characterization and a recession of propaganda in Soviet Russian films. In Poland: *Kanal* (WAJDA); *Eroica* (MUNK). In Britain: *Bridge on the River Kwai* (DAVID LEAN, with ALEC GUINNESS, produced by SAM SPIEGEL). In Japan: *Throne of Blood* (KUROSAWA). In Sweden: *Wild Strawberries* (BERGMAN). In USA: *Will Success Spoil Rock Hunter?* (FRANK TASHLIN); *Twelve Angry Men* (LUMET); *3.10 to Yuma* (DELMER DAVES). In Argentina: *The House of the Angel* (TORRE NILSSON).

Documentary: in Britain, *Every Day Except Christmas* (LINDSAY ANDERSON). In Poland: *Dom* (Kadr Group), one of the earlier films revealing the experimental work developed in short film-making in Poland, more especially in the Film Training School at Lodz. In France: *Les Mistons* (TRUFFAUT).

1958 In Britain: *Room at the Top* (JACK CLAYTON) brings a new realism into British films; *Carry on Sergeant* (Gerald Thomas) the first of over 20 'Carry on . . .' films. In USA: *Paths of Glory* (KUBRICK). JOHN CASSAVETES introduces full-scale improvisation in *Shadows*. In Poland: *Ashes and Diamonds* reveals the full talent of WAJDA. In France: *Le Beau Serge* (CLAUDE CHABROL). In India: *The World of Apu* (SATYAJIT RAY).

Documentary: in Belgium, *Volcano* (HAROUN TAZIEFF). In Holland: *Glass* (HAANSTRA). In Poland: *Two Men and a Wardrobe* (ROMAN POLANSKI). In USA: *Come Back, Africa* (ROGOSIN).

Animation: In Britain, *The Little Island* (RICHARD WILLIAMS). In France: *La Joconde* (Henri Gruel).

1959 In Britain: *I'm All Right Jack, Carlton Browne of the F.O.* and *The Mouse that Roared* combine to project the talent of PETER SELLERS. *The Angry Silence* (Guy Green) is a forerunner of the tougher, more socially aware British cinema which emerged in the 1960s. In America: *Ben Hur* (WYLER); *On the Beach* (KRAMER); *Some Like it Hot* (WILDER). In Italy: *L'Avventura* makes an international reputation for MICHELANGELO ANTONIONI. *La Dolce Vita* (FELLINI). In USSR: *The Lady with the Little Dog* (HEIFITZ); *Ballad of a Soldier* (GRIGORI CHUKHRAI). In France: *Hiroshima Mon Amour, Les Quatre Cents Coups* and *À Bout de Souffle* (*Breathless*) represent the work of the three most discussed directors of the French New Wave, ALAIN RESNAIS, FRANCOIS TRUFFAUT and JEAN-LUC GODARD.

Documentary: in USA, *The Savage Eye* (JOSEPH STRICK, with Ben Maddow and Sidney Meyers).

Animation: in USA, *The Violinist* (ERNEST PINTOFF).

1960 In Britain: *Saturday Night and Sunday Morning* (KAREL REISZ, with ALBERT FINNEY) gives Britain her first major working-class picture. *The Criminal* (*The Concrete Jungle*) made by JOSEPH LOSEY. *The Entertainer* (RICHARDSON, with LAURENCE OLIVIER). In USA: *Psycho* (HITCHCOCK); *Inherit the Wind* (KRAMER). In Italy: *La Notte* (ANTONIONI).

Documentary: in Britain, *Terminus* (JOHN SCHLESINGER, coming from BBC Television); *This is the BBC* (Richard Cawston, the future head of the BBC's documentary film department). In USA: *Primary* (RICHARD LEACOCK and others cover Kennedy's Primary tours in connection with his nomination for President).

Animation: in USA, *Moonbird* (JOHN HUBLEY). In Canada: *Universe* (National Film Board of Canada). In Britain: the main work of GEORGE DUNNING (*The Wardrobe, The Apple, The Flying Man*, etc.) and of BOB GODFREY (*Polygamous Polonius, Do-It-Yourself Cartoon Kit*, etc.) begins.

1961 In Britain: by this year, cinema attendances have fallen to one-third their level in 1948, and 1,700 cinemas have closed since that year. *A Taste of Honey* (RICHARDSON); *The Innocents* (JACK CLAYTON). In USA: *West Side Story* (WISE and Robbins); *The Hustler* (ROSSEN); *The Misfits* (HUSTON), MARILYN MONROE's last completed film; *One-Eyed Jacks*, MARLON BRANDO's first personal production; *El Cid* (ANTHONY MANN). In Spain: *Viridiana* (BUÑUEL). In Italy: *Il Posto* (OLMI); *Salvatore Giuliano* (ROSI). In USSR: *Clear Skies* (GRIGORI CHUKRAI) is the first anti-Stalinist feature film. In France: *Last Year in Marienbad* (RESNAIS); *Jules et Jim* (TRUFFAUT); *Cleo de Cinq à Sept* (VARDA); *Paris Nous Appartient* (RIVETTE).

Documentary: in France, JEAN ROUCH establishes *cinéma-vérité* with *Chronique d'un Été*.

Animation: in USA, *One Hundred and One Dalmations* (DISNEY).

1962 USA produces only 138 feature films, British exhibitors spend £1·4m (1959–62) in attempt to keep old films off television screens. Cinemas in Britain drop to 2,600. In Britain: *A Kind of Loving* (SCHLESINGER); *Lawrence of Arabia* (LEAN). *Dr No* (Terence Young) starts the boom in Bond films. *Lord of the Flies* (BROOK). In USA: *Long Day's Journey Into Night* (LUMET); *The Manchurian Candidate* (FRANKENHEIMER); *The Balcony* (JOSEPH STRICK); *Freud – The Secret Passion* (HUSTON); *Lolita* (KUBRICK). In Poland: *Knife in the Water* (POLANSKI). In France: *Le Joli Mai* (MARKER); *Vivre Sa Vie* (GODARD). In Japan: *An Autumn Afternoon* (OZU's last film).

Documentary: in Germany, *The Life of Adolf Hitler* (ROTHA). In Canada: *Lonely Boy* (National Film Board of Canada). In USA: JONAS MEKAS, leader of the New York school, makes the experimental *Guns of the Trees. The Chair* (RICHARD LEACOCK) uses *cinéma-vérité*. In Sweden: *The War Game* (MAI ZETTERLING).

Animation: in Britain, *Love Me, Love Me, Love Me* (WILLIAMS). In USA: *The Critic* (PINTOFF). In France: *Labyrinth* (LENICA).

1963 Italian production exceeds that of USA: 230 feature films. In USA: *Cleopatra* (MANKIEWICZ with ELIZABETH TAYLOR) costs £13,000,000 – reputedly the most expensive film ever made. *The Fall of the Roman Empire* (ANTHONY MANN); *Hud* (MARTIN RITT). In Britain: *Dr Strangelove* (KUBRICK); *This Sporting Life* (ANDERSON);

Tom Jones (RICHARDSON); *The Servant* (LOSEY); *Billy Liar* (SCHLESINGER); *Nothing but the Best* (DONNER); *The Leather Boys* (FURIE); *The Pumpkin Eater* (CLAYTON). In Italy: *Le Mani Sulla Città* (ROSI); *The Leopard* (VISCONTI); *8½* (FELLINI). In France: *Muriel* (RESNAIS); *Le Feu Follet* (MALLE). International censorship set a problem by *The Silence* (BERGMAN). Experimental film: in USA, *Hallelujah the Hills* (ADOLFAS MEKAS).

Animation: *Automania 2000* (HALAS); *La Jetée* (MARKER) uses primarily still pictures.

1964 American films still occupy two-thirds of the screentime of 70 principal countries open to take them; some revival in USA production. British attendances 7·2 million weekly, half those of 1957. Japanese audiences halve between 1960 and 1963. In USA: *My Fair Lady* (CUKOR); *The Pawnbroker* (LUMET). In USSR: first two parts of BONDARCHUK's *War and Peace; Hamlet* (KOZINTSEV). In France: *Une Femme Mariée* (GODARD). In Italy: *The Red Desert* (ANTONIONI); *The Gospel According to St Matthew* (PASOLINI). In Denmark: *Gertrud* (DREYER's last film). In Britain: *King and Country* (LOSEY). In Japan: *Woman of the Dunes* (TESHIGAHARA). In Czechoslovakia: *Diamonds of the Night* (NĚMEC).

Documentary: in Britain, Tony Essex produces *The Great War* series of television films using archive material from First World War.

1965 In USA: attendances show signs of increase. *The Group* (LUMET) reveals a more liberal approach to censorship. In Britain: attendances drop to 6·1 million weekly, but rise at specialized cinemas. The two circuits (Rank and Associated British Picture Corporation) now control a third of Britain's cinemas, which now total less than 2,000. RICHARD LESTER's *The Knack* wins Grand Prix at Cannes. *Repulsion* (POLANSKI). *Darling* (SCHLESINGER) wins JULIE CHRISTIE an Oscar and BFA Award. DAVID LEAN completes *Doctor Zhivago* (an American-sponsored film). In France: *Alphaville* (GODARD). In Italy: *Juliet of the Spirits* (FELLINI). In Japan: *Tokyo Olympiad* (ICHIKAWA). In Hungary: *The Round-Up* (MIKLÓS JANCSÓ). In Czechoslovakia: *A Blonde in Love* (MILOŠ FORMAN).

Documentary: for British television, *Debussy* (KEN RUSSELL), *Culloden* and *The War Game* (PETER WATKINS).

Animation: Hoffnung series (HALAS); in France, *Un Garçon Plein d'Avenir* and *Appétit d'Oiseau* (Peter Foldes).

1966 In Britain: *A Man for All Seasons* (ZINNEMANN); *Morgan – a Suitable Case for Treatment* (REISZ); *Fahrenheit 451* (TRUFFAUT). Jonathan Miller's BBC film of *Alice in Wonderland* causes questions in Parliament. *It Happened Here* (Brownlow and Mollo) achieves a season in one of London's principal cinemas. In Sweden: *Persona* (BERGMAN). In Italy: the DINO DE LAURENTIIS production *The Bible* (HUSTON) is finally completed. Italy becomes the most prolific producer (and co-producer with France, Spain and West Germany) in Europe, making 270 films. *Fists in the Pocket* (BELLOCCHIO). GILLO PONTECORVO makes *Battle of Algiers* (a Franco-Algerian co-production). In Spain: WELLES makes *Chimes at Midnight*. In USSR: *Andrei Roublev* (Tarkovsky's controversial allegory). In Czechoslovakia: *The Party and the Guests* (NĚMEC).

1967 Vilgot Sjöman's *I am Curious – Yellow* (Sweden) and JOSEPH STRICK's adaptation of Joyce's *Ulysses* (Britain) challenge world censorship. Films from the American underground begin to penetrate Europe. In Britain: the number of cinemas reduced to some 1,700 with attendances below 6 million weekly. *Far From the Madding Crowd* (SCHLESINGER); *Accident* (LOSEY); *Blow-Up* (ANTONIONI); *Herostratus* (Don Levy); *Dutchman* (ANTHONY HARVEY); *The White Bus* (LINDSAY ANDERSON). KEN LOACH (*Poor Cow*) and PETER WATKINS (*Privilege*) lead a major influx of television directors into cinema work. In Germany: ALEXANDER KLUGE's *Yesterday Girl* hints at a revival of imaginative film-making. In Sweden: *Elvira Madigan* (BO WIDERBERG). In France: *Belle de Jour* (BUÑUEL); *Weekend* (GODARD); TRUFFAUT's homage to HITCHCOCK and RENOIR, *The Bride Wore Black*. In USA: *Bonnie and Clyde* (ARTHUR PENN) causes considerable controversy and sets some fashions.

Animation: in Britain, *Flow Diagram* (HALAS and BATCHELOR) introduces computerized techniques. In Yugoslavia: *The Wall* (Zagreb Film); *The Fly* (Marks and MIMICA, Zagreb Film).

1968 In Britain: *Oliver!* (REED) and *2001 – A Space Odyssey* (KUBRICK), examples of growing American-sponsored production and co-production; *The Bofors Gun* (JACK GOLD); *If...* (LINDSAY ANDERSON); *Charlie Bubbles* (ALBERT FINNEY); *Isadora* (KAREL REISZ); *Kes* (KEN LOACH). Italian-British co-production *Romeo and Juliet* (FRANCO ZEFFIRELLI). In USA: *Rachel, Rachel* (PAUL NEWMAN's first film as director); *Rosemary's Baby* (POLANSKI); *The Secret Life of an American Wife* (AXELROD). In France: *La Voie Lactée* (BUÑUEL), *Z* (COSTA-GAVRAS, Franco-Algerian). In Italy: *Theorem* (PASOLINI). In Sweden: *The Shame* (BERGMAN).

In USA and Europe the underground cinema develops an ever-increasing public at clubs, festivals, etc. *Flesh* (WARHOL).

Documentary: *Consider Science* (Peter de Normanville); *Bridges of Holland* (HAANSTRA); *Great Barrier Reef* (Australian Commonwealth Film Unit); *Drawing With Light* (H. Niebeling).

Animation: *Pas de Deux* (MCLAREN). In USA, *Windy Day* (JOHN HUBLEY), *Man Creates* (Saul Bass). *Fluid Water Flow Dynamics* represents computerized animation at Los Alamos Scientific Laboratory. In Britain: *The Yellow Submarine* (GEORGE DUNNING for The Beatles), Britain's first feature-length cartoon since *Animal Farm; The Question* (HALAS and BATCHELOR).

1969 In Britain: investment of American capital in British feature production reaches its peak of some 90%. *Oh! What a Lovely War* (RICHARD ATTENBOROUGH's first film as director); *Women in Love* (KEN RUSSELL). In USA: DENNIS HOPPER and PETER FONDA's *Easy Rider* (cost £150,000, box-office takings estimated at £20 million) sets new sights for American production in a year when the big companies face losses estimated around £50 million. *The Wild Bunch* (SAM PECKINPAH); *Midnight Cowboy* (SCHLESINGER); *Butch Cassidy and the Sundance Kid* (GEORGE ROY HILL); *M★A★S★H* (ROBERT ALTMAN); *Zabriskie Point* (ANTONIONI). In Canada: *Prologue* (Robin Spry). In Sweden: *Adalen '31* (BO WIDERBERG). In Italy: *Porcile* (PASOLINI), *Fellini-Satyricon* (FELLINI). In Brazil: *Antonio das Mortes* (GLAUBER ROCHA). In Japan: *Double Suicide* (Shinoda).

Documentary: *Apollo 11* (NASA), *Test of Violence – the Paintings of Juan Genoves* (Stuart Cooper); *The Henry Miller Odyssey* (Robert Synder).

Animation: *The Intellectual* (Giersz); *Adam II* (LENICA); *Walking* (Larkin); *Good Friends* (Murakami); *Dissent Illusion* (Goldscholl); *Universe* (Otero); *Goldframe* (Servais); *Film, Film, Film!* (Khitruk and Zuikov). *Everything is Number, Wind, Drought* and *Stairs* (Stefan Schabenbeck) represent a variety of animation techniques.

1970 In Britain: the partial withdrawal of American investment in production reduces output sharply. *Ryan's Daughter* (LEAN); *Cromwell* (KEN HUGHES); *Leo the Last* (JOHN BOORMAN); *The Private Life of Sherlock Holmes* (WILDER). Younger film-makers aim for low-budget production, such as *Bronco Bullfrog* (PLATTS-MILLS). In USA: *Catch 22* (MIKE NICHOLS); *Tora! Tora! Tora!* (FLEISCHER). In Spain: *Tristana* (BUÑUEL); *Waterloo* (BONDARCHUK's USSR-Italy co-production). In Italy: *The Conformist* (BERTOLUCCI).

Documentary: *The Tribe That Hides From Man* (Adrian Cowell, for television); *Oisin* (Patrick Carey); *Woodstock* (Michael Wadleigh).

Animation: *Henry 9 till 5* (GODFREY); *The Wall* (Carmen d'Avino); *Archy and Mehitabel* (John Wilson, feature-length).

1971 Further decline in British and American cinema attendances is attributed to the proliferation of 'sexploitation' films. A move back to family entertainment is evidenced by the success of Britain's *The Railway Children* (Lionel Jeffries) and *The Tales of Beatrix Potter* (Arthur Hiller), and the phenomenal popularity of America's *Love Story*. Student protest and 'road' pictures modelled on *Easy Rider* (HOPPER) prove to be passing fashions. In Britain: *The Go-Between* (LOSEY); *Sunday, Bloody Sunday* (SCHLESINGER); *Walkabout* (Nicholas Roeg); *The Devils* and *The Boy Friend* (RUSSELL). A number of films based on television series reveal the extent of the industry's nervous play-safe policy. In USA: *Little Big Man* (ARTHUR PENN); *Klute* (Alan J. Pakula); *Carnal Knowledge* (MIKE NICHOLS); *Taking Off* (MILOŠ FORMAN's first American film). In USSR: *King Lear* (KOZINTSEV). In Italy: *Durante l'Estate* (OLMI). In France: *Quatre Nuits d'un Rêveur* (BRESSON).

Historical Background to the development of Sound with Film and Sound on Film

1889 First unauthenticated 'Kinetophonograph' demonstration: 'Good morning, Mr Edison'. (Combined cylinder-gramophone and Kinetoscope: synch viewer.)

1893 Kinetophonograph demonstrated on peep-show basis for the single viewer at the Chicago World Exposition.

1896 Pathé introduces the Berliner gramophone, using discs, in quasi synchronization with film. Oscar Messter gives a similar demonstration in Berlin. Lack of amplification makes these multi-viewer performances ineffective.

1899 EDISON tries to gain amplification by using banks of phonographs.

1900 Attempts to synchronize film and disc by GAUMONT in France and Goldschmidt in Germany, leading later to the American Vitaphone and the German Lignose-Brousing systems.

Pineaud in France among those who attempt development of a 'relief' process with the edge of the film notched to control the reproduction of sound after the manner of a pianola. Other systems parallel to this development in Germany and the USA.

1912 Eugene Lauste designs experimental 'sound on film' system in Britain.

1918–9 A system known as Tri-Ergon begun in Germany by Vogt, Engel and Massolle, which leads to sound being *recorded on film* photographically. Behind their work lie pioneer experiments in Britain and elsewhere as early as 1880 for the recording of sound in terms of light. This system proves preferable to the developments of Blattner based on the magnetization of steel wire. The photography of sound was also developed by Lee De Forrest in his Phono-film system.

1923 Phonofilm shown as special demonstration shorts in public.

6 August 1926 Première of the silent film *Don Juan* with synchronized discs developed by WARNERS in association with the Bell Telegraph Co and Western Electric. The records were 16″ diameter and 33⅓ rpm. The film, recorded by the New York Philharmonic Orchestra, was preceded by a spoken short recorded by Will H. Hayes. The reproduction of sound was synchronized mechanically with the camera and projector, but the reproduction was still crude, and normal film editing impossible.

FOX acquires the rights to the German Tri-Ergon system and the rights to a derivative of De Forrest's Phonofilm system. Begins release of shorts with sound and puts scores to otherwise silent feature films: first feature to be given this form of track, *What Price Glory?*

April 1927 Fox Movietone News begins. First major success for sound. Lindberg, Mussolini, Shaw filmed talking.

6 October 1927 Warners present AL JOLSON in *The Jazz Singer*, a silent picture with musical accompaniment on disc, but with four talking or singing sequences. This, the first part-talking picture, establishes the popularity of sound for the public as far as features were concerned.

July 1928 First all-talking picture *The Lights of New York* (Warners) recorded with sound on disc.

The Terror had Conrad Nagel actually speaking the credits.

1,300 of USA's 20,500 theatres wired for sound by the end of the year.

1928–9 Other sound on disc part-talking, part-singing pictures followed: including *The Singing Fool* (Warner's), *Showboat* (Universal), D. W. GRIFFITH's *Lady of the Pavements* and Fairbanks's *The Iron Mask* (United Artists). *Hallelujah* (VIDOR).

Films initially made with disc accompaniment were later re-issued with a sound-track during the dual period when both systems were in circulation.

Steamboat Willie (DISNEY's first Mickey Mouse cartoon, 1928) was recorded sound on film.

1929 *The Taming of the Shrew* with PICKFORD and FAIRBANKS, and with additional dialogue by the director, Sam Taylor.

Broadway Melody. First of the MGM Musicals.

9,000 American cinemas wired for sound. In consequence of sound, admissions to the cinema rose from 60 million weekly in 1927 to 110 million in 1929.

The last important silent film was *The Kiss* (November 1929), with GARBO. MGM was uncertain about the effect of Garbo's accent. Garbo talked successfully, however, in *Anna Christie* (1930). CHAPLIN alone hung on to the silent techniques: *City Lights* (1931) and *Modern Times* (1936) were still essentially silent films with synchronized sound effects and music.

A

Abbas, Khwaja Ahmed

Born 1914 in Panipat India. Screenwriter, director, producer, as well as lifelong journalist. Educated at Alighar University, he went to Bombay and worked as journalist and astringent film critic on the Bombay *Chronicle*; meanwhile he was presenting scripts to Bombay Talkies. His first script, *Naya Sansar* (*The New World*, 1941), concerning a journalist resisting pressure from business men, was made into a successful film. During the war he wrote an anti-Japanese film, *The Journey of Dr Kotnis*, using his acute political sense to satisfy both the Indian progressives and the British. After Independence he wrote socially-conscious films against the mainstream in Indian cinema – *Children of the Earth* (1949), about the chronic indebtedness of the Indian peasant, and *The Lost Child* (1954), about an orphan child wandering in Bombay, which he produced as well as wrote. This was followed by more commercial films featuring the socially-conscious star, Raj Kapoor – *The Vagabond* (1951) and *Shri 420* (1955). Both films achieved success abroad in the Soviet Union, and this led to Abbas co-directing with V. M. Pronin the Indian-Soviet co-production, *Pardesi (The Traveller)* in 1956–7. Always controversial and left-wing, Abbas has argued in favour of the nationalization of the Indian film industry. A more recent production, *Saat Hindustani* (1970), concerns the liberation of Goa. RM

Academy Mask

The introduction of the optical sound frame printed at the side of a 35 mm frame reduced the width of the picture. To restore the rectangularity of the screen proportions a mask was adopted which, by reducing the height of the camera image as well as cutting off the sound track area, restored the original proportions of the frame. This was later standardized by the Academy of Motion Picture Arts and Sciences to frame an image 0·631 inches high by 0·868 inches wide, a proportion of approximately 3 : 4. The area enclosed by the mask is known as an Academy Aperture.

Accelerated Motion

The illusion of the action in a scene taking place at a greater speed than in reality by photographing with a camera running at a slower speed than that at which the film is later projected.

Opposite: Anouk Aimée in 'La Dolce Vita' (Federico Fellini, Italy, 1959)

Acetate Base

The plastic support on which a film is coated, and which, being slow burning, is known also as Safety Base.

Actuality

The recording of an event as it actually occurs. i.e. without being reconstructed and without the use of actors.

Additive Process

A colour cinematographic process in which two or more basic colours are juxtaposed on the film in such a way that when projected they mingle in differing proportions on the screen.

Adrian (1903–1959)

Born in Connecticut, USA. Leading American film costume designer at MGM during the influential 1930s and 1940s when his wardrobes for GRETA GARBO, JEAN HARLOW, NORMA SHEARER, JOAN CRAWFORD and many other female contract stars were imitated by fans all over the world. His first film credit was for *Love* (1928). In keeping with the MGM star grooming formula, he blended good taste with striking original design especially created to fit the individual personalities – and physical idiosyncracies – of the stars. His first name was Gilbert, but he was always known simply as Adrian. He was married for some years to actress Janet Gaynor.

Africa (North)

See ARAB FILM

Aimée, Anouk

Born 1932 in Paris, France. Actress. Studied in France and England (both as a dancer and actress) and made her film début in 1946. She first came to attention as the romantic, love-struck girl in CAYATTE's *Les Amants de Verone* (1948), and created the sensual, slightly mysterious, figure (which she was to develop in later films) in ASTRUC's *Le Rideau Cramoisi* (1952). FELLINI developed these characteristics in *La Dolce Vita* (1959) and *8½* (1962), but her most memorable creations are probably JACQUES DEMY's *Lola* (1961), and its American sequel, *Model Shop* (1968), and the saddened, vulnerable heroine of LELOUCH's *Un Homme et une Femme* (1966). She has appeared in several English language films including *Justine* (1969), but her European films seem to reveal more completely her individual charm and seriousness. JG

Albers, Hans (1892–1960)

Born Hamburg, Germany. Actor. Early career in circus, vaudeville, the theatre. Initially a romantic lead and man of action, he appeared in a vast output of silent films throughout the 1920s, and later during the sound period appeared in such films as *The Blue Angel* (1930), and, during the Nazi period, the propaganda films *Flüchtlinge* (1933), which was anti-Russian, and the anti-British *Carl Peters* (1941). However, he mixed as little as possible in politics, retaining his romantic image throughout his extensive career, though turning to character parts as he grew older. He appeared also in *Münchhausen* (1943) and the remake of *The Last Laugh (Der Letzte Mann)* (1955).

Aldo, G. R. (1902–1953)

Born in Scorge, Italy. Cinematographer. Learned much about the cinema while working as stills photographer in various Paris studios. After a period as camera operator, he became lighting cameraman on L'HERBIER's *Les Derniers Jours de Pompeii* (1949) and Genina's *Cielo Sulla Palude* (1949). But it was his work with LUCHINO VISCONTI on *La Terra Trema* (1948) which revealed the full richness of his lighting style, with its heavily contrasted blacks-and-whites, and almost stereoscopic depth of focus. His collaboration with VITTORIO DE SICA also produced some fine work, ranging from the fantasy world of *Miracolo a Milano* (1951) to the neo-realist drama of *Umberto D* (1952). He also worked on ORSON WELLES's *Othello* (1952), remarkable for its brilliant exteriors and close-up work. Aldo was killed in a car accident while working on VISCONTI's *Senso* (1954), which was completed by ROBERT KRASKER. Other notable films include: *Tre Storie Proibite* (1952), *Stazione Termini* (1953), *La Provinciale* (1953). JG

Aldrich, Robert

Born 1918 in Evanston, USA. American director who first made his mark during the influential late 1940s and early 1950s in Hollywood, as assistant and production manager to JOSEPH LOSEY, WILLIAM WELLMAN, CHARLES CHAPLIN, ABRAHAM POLONSKY, and ROBERT ROSSEN. Although he did not suffer professionally from the subsequent communist witch-hunts, as did Polonsky, Losey, and Chaplin, the early films he directed – *Apache* (1954), *The Big Knife* (1955), *Attack!* (1957) – were liberal, hard-hitting indictments of the treatment of Indians, the Hollywood scene, the brutalizing effect of war. Starting out as a production clerk at RKO in 1941, he directed his first film *The Big Leaguer* in 1953. His version of Mickey Spillane's *Kiss Me Deadly* (1955) is considered a classic of its kind. Latterly his style has coarsened as his productions have grown in size and budget, alternating between grotesque, feminine shockers – *Whatever Happened to Baby Jane?* (1962), *Hush, Hush, Sweet Charlotte* (1964), *The Killing of Sister George* (1968) – and masculine toughies – *The Flight of the Phoenix* (1965), *The Dirty Dozen* (1966), *Too Late the Hero* (1969), *The Grissom Gang* (1971). MH

Alekan, Henri

Born 1909 in Paris, France. Cinematographer. After studying at L'Institut d'Optique, he was an assistant operator (1929–1937), camera operator (1937–1940) and a director of photography since 1941. Alekan is a leading member of the elder French photographic school who has specialized both in documentary realism (*La Bataille du Rail,* 1945) and in lush costume pieces (*La Belle et la Bête*, 1946). He is particularly adept in rendering bare atmospheric locations (the cold, deserted beach and resort in *Une si Jolie Petite Plage*, 1948) and his subsequent collaborations with directors like CARNÉ, YVES ALLÉGRET and CAYATTE reveal an all-round professionalism and a sharp feeling for dark-toned, often exotic, settings. Recently, he has photographed several Comédie Française productions and directed some art documentaries. JG

Alexandrov, Grigori Vassilievitch

Born 1903 in Ekaterinburg, USSR. Beginning his professional life as wardrobe assistant, scene-painter and electrician at the Ekaterinburg Opera House, Alexandrov joined the production course of the Workers' and Peasants' Theatre in 1918, and three years later arrived in Moscow where he became an actor at the First Proletkult Theatre. Here he met EISENSTEIN, and played in Eisenstein's first brief film, *Glumov's Diary,* made as an interlude in his production of 'Enough Simplicity in Every Wise Man'. Eisenstein used him as an actor and assistant director on *Strike* and *Potemkin,* and on *October* (1927) and *The General Line* (1929), Alexandrov was credited as co-director. He was associated with Eisenstein and PUDOVKIN on their celebrated manifesto on sound in films; and went with Eisenstein and TISSE on their ill-fated tour of Europe, America and Mexico. In Paris Alexandrov directed an experimental

Above: Madeleine Robinson and Gérard Philipe in 'Une si Jolie Petite Plage' (Yves Allégret, cameraman Henri Alekan, France, 1948)
Below: Hans Albers and Annabella in 'Variété' (Nicolas Farkas, Germany, 1935)

musical short, *Romance Sentimentale*; in America he collaborated on abortive scripts for Paramount and in Mexico he was Eisenstein's co-director on the unfinished *Que Viva Mexico!*

Later Alexandrov and Eisenstein seemed to draw apart. Of Alexandrov's own films, the most successful have been his musical comedies, *Jazz Comedy* (1934), *Circus* (1936) and *Volga-Volga* (1938), his favourite musical star being his wife, Lyuba Orlova. Subsequent films have included: *Parade of Athletes* (1938), *Bright Road* (1940), *Springtime* (1947), *Meeting on the Elbe* (1949), *Glinka* (1952), *From Man to Man* (1958), *Russian Souvenir* (1960), *Lenin in Switzerland* (1966). DR

Algeria

See ARAB FILM

Allégret, Marc

Born 1900 in Basle, Switzerland. French director who made a notable début with a collaboration with André Gide: *Voyage au Congo* (1926). During the first decade of sound, Allégret assumed a place among the best French directors of the period, with *Mam'zelle Nitouche* (1931), *Fanny* (1932), *Lac aux Dames* (1934), *Les Beaux Jours* (1935), and two films which adopted the pessimistic, 'poetic realist' mood of the late 1930s: *Gribouille* (1937) and *Orage* (1938). After the war Allégret inclined to glossy commercial production, including *Blanche Fury* (1948) in Britain, *Maria Chapdelaine* (The Naked Heart, 1950) in Austria and Canada and *L'amante di Paride* (1953) and *Femmina* (1954), both made in Italy with HEDY LAMARR. Allégret was reputed for his discovery of new stars, among them MICHÈLE MORGAN, Simone Simon, Jean-Pierre Aumont and BRIGITTE BARDOT. DR

Allégret, Yves

Born 1907 in Paris, France. Brother of MARC. Yves Allégret directed a number of shorts before the war, and collaborated with Léon Joannon on *Vous n'avez rien à déclarer?* (1936); but it was only in the post-war period that he established a reputation with a group of excellent films in the currently popular 'black' vein: *Dédée d'Anvers* (1947), *Une si Jolie Petite Plage* (1948), *Manèges* (1949). Later films include: *Les Miracles n'ont Lieu qu'une Fois* (1951), *Les Orgueilleux* (1953), *Mam'zelle Nitouche* (1954), *La Meilleure Part* (1956), *Méfiez-vous Fillettes* (1957), *Germinal* (1963) in Hungary.

Altman, Robert

Born 1925 in Kansas City, USA. Trendsetting

contemporary American director who won a reputation and *carte blanche* for future films with his savagely unorthodox, bawdy anti-war film *M.A.S.H.* (1970). Prior to that he could claim a history of bad relations with studio tycoons – including JACK WARNER – and television executives who took exception to his outspoken episodes in the *Bus Stop* and *Combat* American television series. After war service as a pilot in the Second World War, he went into the industrial-film business, graduated to television where he learned his trade and made the feature film *That Cold Day In The Park* (1969) in Canada. Following the sudden success of *M.A.S.H.* he has directed *Brewster McCloud* (1971), 'an adult fairy tale'. Latest film: *McCabe and Mrs Miller* (1971). MH

Alwyn, William
Born 1905 in Northampton, England. Composer, who studied at the Royal Academy of Music, where he was later to be a professor. He has created scores for over a hundred British features and documentaries, as well as being primarily a distinguished composer for the concert-hall. As a professional musician in London, he had experience playing in the orchestra accompanying silent films, and his compositions for sound films date back to 1936. His concept of film music is that it should be an integral part of the dramatic and atmospheric nature of the film; the composer should see himself as a member of the creative team, working on the film in its formative stage. He was much sought after by British directors who understood the part music could play in the art of film-making; he developed motifs associated with individual characters, phrasing integrated with action and dialogue, and he had a capacity for imaginative pastiche, as in his score for *The Rake's Progress* and the BBC Television film history of cartoon, *Black on White*. In feature film he has worked frequently with CAROL REED and in documentary with PAUL ROTHA. His scores for documentaries include those for *Fires were Started* (1942), *World of Plenty* and *Desert Victory* (1943), *Our Country* (1944), *The True Glory* (1945), *Henry Moore* (1951). His vast range of feature film scores include those for *The Way Ahead* (1944), *Odd Man Out* (1946) and *The Fallen Idol* (1948). William Alwyn's views were very influential, and are represented in 'The Technique of Film Music' (Manvell and Huntley, 1957), a book sponsored by the British Film Academy and supervised by a committee of composers and film-makers of which Alwyn was chairman. RM

Ambrosio, Arturo (1869–1960)
Born in Turin, Italy. The true founder of the Italian cinema, Ambrosio was running a small photographic business when he began to interest himself in cinematography in the early years of the century. In 1904, with Roberto Omegna he made the first Italian documentaries, which he developed in his own laboratory. Soon after he built a little studio in his garden, and in 1906 started the production of story films. He achieved his greatest importance in the international film industry in the era of the first spectacle films, making the phenomenally successful *The Last Days of Pompeii* (1908), *Nero* (1909) and *The Slave of Carthage* (1910), and obtaining, in 1911, exclusive rights on film adaptations of the work of D'Annunzio. Although his company never fully recovered from the commandeering of its studio during the First World War, or from the general eclipse of the Italian cinema after it, Ambrosio continued to be active in the industry until 1943. DR

Rod Steiger and Jack Palance in 'The Big Knife' (Robert Aldrich, USA, 1955)

America
See UNITED STATES OF AMERICA

Amidei, Sergio
Born 1904 in Trieste, Italy. Screenwriter. Influential in establishing neo-realism, he was closely associated with ROBERTO ROSSELLINI in planning *Rome, Open City* (1945) before the German army had left Rome. His work, like that of many leading Italian scriptwriters, has often been consultative and collaborative with others, and he has worked with many notable directors, including DE SICA, CASTELLANI, EMMER, and CARLO LIZZANI. His principal credits include the films *Rome, Open City*, *Paisa* and *Sciuscia* (1946), *Anni Difficili* and *Sotto il Sole di Roma* (1948), *Stromboli* (1949), *Domenica d'Agosto* (1950), *Ragazze di Piazza di Spagna* (1952), *Angst* (1955), *Il Generale della Rovere* (1959), *Il Processo di Verona* (1962).

Anamorphic
A lens system which in shooting squeezes laterally a wide screen image within the width of a standard film frame and which extends this compressed image to its original proportions on projection (as in the case of CinemaScope).

Anderson, Lindsay
Born 1923 in Bangalore, South India. The most richly gifted director and the most significant progressive force at work in the British cinema between the 1950s and 1970s, Anderson first made his voice heard as an editor of the magazine 'Sequence' (1946–1952), which vigorously attacked the outworn conventions and establishment of a 'metropolitan based, class-bound cinema'. Anderson began to put his ideas into practice with a series of documentaries. *Meet the Pioneers* (1948), *Idlers That Work* (1949), *Three Installations* (1952) and *Trunk Conveyor* (1954) were made with tiny budgets for a Yorkshire mining engineering firm; *Wakefield Express* (1952) was made on 16 mm for a local newspaper organization. In 1954 *Thursday's Children*, a film about deaf children made in collaboration with Guy Brenton, was awarded an Oscar. Concurrently with this film Anderson had made *O Dreamland*, a bitter and scathing commentary on the poverty of contemporary popular culture. Anderson continued to work on sponsored documentaries and television serial episodes. In 1956–59 he was the inspiration behind a series of programmes of new, independently made films, *Free Cinema*, which, together with a belligerent article by Anderson on the current state of film criticism, 'Stand Up, Stand Up', did much to focus the new spirit that was stirring in the British cinema. Anderson's documentary on Covent Garden Market, *Every Day Except Christmas* (1957) and his first feature film, the tragic *This Sporting*

Life (1963) were significant contributions to the new cinema. From 1957 Anderson worked increasingly, and with great success, as a theatre director, using the stage as an extension of many of his film ideas. Returning to the cinema, he directed *The White Bus* (1967), intended as part of an episode film, but released separately as a short. The following year he made a short, *The Singing Lesson*, in Poland and in 1968 his second feature film, *If . . . .* DR

Anderson, Michael
Born 1920 in London, England. British director. Son of actor Lawrence Anderson. Entered the film industry in 1935 as a bit player and office boy at Elstree Studios. Edged his way up to assistant director and unit manager, often working with ANTHONY ASQUITH. Served with the British Army Film Unit during Second World War. In 1949 he co-directed *Private Angelo* with PETER USTINOV; was sole director on *Waterfront* (1950). At his best in handling suspense – *The Dam Busters* (1955), *Chase a Crooked Shadow* (1957), *The Wreck of the Mary Deare* (1959), *The Quiller Memorandum* (1966) – though his chief claim to fame is as MIKE TODD's choice of director on the star-studded period spectacular, *Around the World in Eighty Days* (1956). Other notable films: *Shake Hands with the Devil* (1959), *Operation Crossbow* (1965), *Shoes of The Fisherman* (1968), *Pope John* (1971).

Andersson, Bibi
Born 1935 in Stockholm, Sweden. One of INGMAR BERGMAN's distinguished film leading ladies, she studied at the Royal Theatre School. First met Bergman at the age of 16, when she appeared in a soap commercial. As a resident Bergman heroine, she acted in his *Smiles of a Summer Night* (1955), *The Seventh Seal* (1956), *Wild Strawberries* (1957), *The Face* (1958), *So Close to Life* (1960), *The Devil's Eye* (1961), *Persona* (1966), *A Passion* (1970) and *The Touch* (1971). She went to Hollywood to star not too successfully in the Western *Duel at Diablo* in 1965. Other notable films: *My Sister, My Love* (1965), *The Girls* (1968), *Story of a Woman* and *The Kremlin Letter* (1969). Her richly expressive style is particularly suited to the modern, sexually complex women created by Bergman.

Above: Malcolm McDowell and Christine Noonan in 'If . . .' (Lindsay Anderson, GB, 1968)
Below: Ursula Andress in 'Dr No' (Terence Young, GB, 1962)

Andersson, Harriet
Born 1932 in Stockholm, Sweden. Highly individual member of INGMAR BERGMAN's celebrated film repertory company, she left school to work as a lift girl, then studied drama for three years. Moulded, but not subjugated, as an actress by Bergman, she made her first film for him as the sensual *ingénue* in *Summer with Monika* in 1952, followed by *Sawdust and Tinsel* (1953), *A Lesson in Love* (1954), *Smiles of a Summer Night* (1955), *Through a Glass Darkly* (1962), and *Now about these Women* (1965). She came to Britain for *The Deadly Affair* in 1966. Other notable films: *To Love* (1964), *People Meet* and *The Girls* (1968). Lively and spontaneous, her characterizations mix humour with a sly sexuality.

Andress, Ursula
Born 1936 in Berne, Switzerland. Statuesque European beauty who, after several casual appearances in continental films, became an international success in the first of the James Bond adventures, *Dr No* (1962). As the voluptuous *She* (1964), she was widely touted as the new screen sex symbol though the role fitted her less well than that of sex-comedienne. Hardly a memorable actress, she has nevertheless revealed a distinct gift for inconsequential comedy in *What's New, Pussycat?* and *The Tenth Victim* (1965), *Perfect Friday* (1970).

Andrews, Dana
Born 1912 in Mississippi, USA. Attractive Hollywood 'crusading hero' star of the 1940s who achieved his peak in *Laura* (1944), *A Walk in the Sun* (1945), *The Best Years of our Lives* (1946) and *Boomerang* (1947). Theatre-trained, he went to Hollywood in the 1930s under contract to SAMUEL GOLDWYN, making his screen début in *The Westerner* (1939). After a series of romantic leading man roles, he has since become an excellent character actor. Main films include: *Tobacco Road* (1941), *Berlin Correspondent* (1942), *The Purple Heart* (1943), *Fallen Angel* (1945), *Elephant Walk* (1953), *Duel in The Jungle* (1954), *Madison Avenue* (1960), *The Satan Bug*, *In Harm's Way* and *The Loved One* (1965), *The Devil's Brigade* (1969).

Andrews, Julie
Born 1935 in Surrey, England. Ladylike British musical comedy artist whose well-trained voice, unexpected astringency and professional expertise made her the leading screen musical star of the 1960s. A show business family background conditioned a career which achieved its peak in the theatre in 'My Fair Lady'. Losing the film version to AUDREY HEPBURN, she played the lead in DISNEY's *Mary Poppins* (1964), for which she won an Academy Award. She consolidated her success in *The Sound of Music* (1965) and *Thoroughly Modern Millie* (1967). Her attempts at drama, however, notably in HITCHCOCK's *Torn Curtain* (1966), were poorly received and her game performance as Gertrude Lawrence in *Star!* (1968) could not rescue the film from box-office failure.

Other films: *The Americanization of Emily* (1964), *Hawaii* (1966), *Darling Lili* (1969). DR

Above: Mary Tyler Moore and Julie Andrews in 'Thoroughly Modern Millie' (George Roy Hill, USA, 1967)
Right: 'La Retapeur de Cervelles' (Émile Cohl, France, 1910–1)

Anger, Kenneth

Born 1932 in Santa Monica, California, USA. Underground film-maker. Began film-making at the age of nine, including science-fiction, 'psycho dramas', and a film about incest, all completed before he was 12. His first psycho-drama to be exhibited was *Escape Episode* (1944–6). His interests include ritual, magic, the occult (as practised by Aleister Crowley, who died in 1947), and the montage theories and practice of EISENSTEIN. Many of his films were to remain incomplete through various kinds of frustration or prohibition. His more celebrated films include: *Fireworks* (1947), *Le Jeune Homme et la Mort* (made in Paris and based on COCTEAU's ballet, 1953), *Eaux d'Artifice* (made in the Villa d'Este gardens, 1953), *Inauguration of the Pleasure Dome* (1954, recut 1966), *Thelma Abbey* (a study of Crowley's original headquarters in Sicily, with its erotic paintings, 1955), *Histoire d'O* (1959–61) with the subject of sexual sadism, made in France and never exported, and, made in the USA, *Scorpio Rising* (1962–4), on demonic forces in modern youth inspired by Nazism. He has been involved recently in a feature, called *Lucifer Rising*. RM

Animation

Animation is the application of motion picture technique to graphic or plastic art. In the case of the drawn image, pictures have to be prepared in series with minute progressive variations in the positioning of the figures – the arrested phases of movement. When this succession of pictures is photographed by a cine-camera frame by frame and projected the illusion of movement is created on the screen, just as the succession of single still photographs in a live-action film create the illusion of movement when projected at 24 frames a second for sound film, or 16 for silent film. In the case of plastic figures or objects, such as three-dimensional puppets, animation means minute adjustments of the pose and expression of the figure which are recorded successively frame by frame by means of stop-motion cinematography, the camera being stopped after each frame is exposed. There is no end to the variety of graphic images which can be given movement by means of animation. It can be as naturalistic in appearance as a photograph, or as highly stylized as a drawing by Picasso. Animation is a technique which brings life and movement and developing character to any images the graphic artist cares to imagine, however extreme, provided the necessary technical disciplines are observed by means of which a film is made.

The History of Animation:
from the beginning to about 1940

It would seem on the face of it that anyone looking at one of the earliest LUMIÈRE prints of 1895–6 would have realized that photographed drawings could have been substituted for the live-action photography of normal film-making. But it is usual to regard ÉMILE COHL as the first established animator; his earliest films – very short, and using jerky little matchstick figures, often outlined in white on a black background – did not appear until 1908–9: *Fantasmagorie*, *Le Cauchemar de Fantôche*, *Drame Chez les Fantôches*, and so forth. Fantôche, a kind of comic everyman, ill-fated but resilient, became his standard character. But prior to Cohl, as part of the story of the pre-history of the cinema, came many forms of art, as well as different forms of visual toy, which anticipated certain of the principles of animation. The multi-limbed, leaping animals of the cave-paintings in Altmira and Lascaux anticipate the kind of images animators would favour. The Chinese shadow theatre, imported into Europe as a favourite form of entertainment in the 18th century, is the direct ancestor of silhouette animation – created in the past by placing jointed flat-figures close to a translucent screen illuminated from behind by means of candles.

An extraordinary artist in the prehistory of motion pictures is Emile Reynaud. His apparatus, the praxinoscope, developed in the late 19th century, was an elaboration of the optical toy known as the zoetrope – the peepshow device which, when rotated, allowed the eye to see in rapid succession a series of 12 or so drawings which completed in phases a single action, such as a skipping child, in a cycle lasting a second or so which would be endlessly repeated. Reynaud drew long sequences of coloured pictures which, when projected in his *Théâtre Optique* in 1892, threw reflected images on a screen in a manner unique to this apparatus – but more closely related to the

Above: The Praxinoscope of Émile Reynaud (France, 1882)
Below: 'Gertie the Trained Dinosaur' (Winsor McKay, USA, 1909)

magic lantern than the cinematograph, since photography did not enter into his work. He cranked the pictures through by hand; they were painted onto reels of celluloid. Another highly inventive and imaginative artist who might well have taken advantage of animation was MÉLIÈS, but he preferred to create his fantasies in the live-action settings of his theatre and studio. He was, however, as his drawings prove, a remarkably fine draughtsman.

Emile Cohl's matchstick figures were followed by the work in the USA of Winsor McKay, who created the short cartoon, *Gertie the Trained Dinosaur* (1909), and much later, after other work, the notable serious cartoon, *The Sinking of the Lusitania* (1918). For his first film, McKay drew every frame at the silent film speed of 16 frames per second. No wonder the early cartoonists adopted the simple outlines of the artists who drew strips for the popular press – the backgrounds a matter of a few lines, and the figures themselves, which had to move, the barest configuration suggesting the body and the expression on the face. In any case, most of them, like Winsor McKay, had drawn strips for the press.

What stood in the way of the development of the cartoon film was, on the one hand, the immense labour involved in producing a few minutes of action, and on the other, the very low rentals these films earned in the cinemas, even allowing for international distribution, which was from 1914 curtailed through the divisions caused by the war. Nevertheless, the cartoons were popular with audiences, their simple, basic humour turning for the most part on animal characters, and also to a lesser extent on caricatures of human beings. Sheer public demand kept the cartoonists at work, creating their films in series round a succession of popular characters such as, during the 1920s, Betty Boop, the cartoon vamp, and Koko the Clown (both created by MAX FLEISCHER), Krazy Kat, Mutt and Jeff, and above all at this time, PAT SULLIVAN's Felix the Cat, a character originated as early as 1914, but coming into his own in the 1920s. Sullivan, an emigré from Australia to the USA, was a press cartoonist. Few movie theatre programmes were complete without a cartoon; Felix had his own signature tune 'Felix kept on Walking' which made the audience cheer in anticipation. The cartoon was often enough the best film in the programme, even though it only lasted a few minutes.

The cartoonists in the USA had during the early war years devised the brilliant short cut of cel-animation, which, with other devices, greatly reduced the labour of producing cartoons, making them more viable economically. Cel-animation involved the superimposition of a set of transparent celluloid sheets over the background drawing, with whatever character or object was moving inked in (either as outline or, like Felix, as black silhouette) on one sheet, while other cels carried whatever figures or objects were, for the moment, static. Thus, the area of the pictures which was in motion could be separated from that which remained still, and the single drawing of the background could be re-used throughout the shot or sequence. The total picture on which the camera was exposed frame by frame consisted, therefore, of a background with successive sets of cels superimposed on it in careful register. As each character sprang into action, so the cel-layer carrying that character became the animated segment of the picture. Further than this, cels in series covering cyclic movements could be used and re-used for standard characters like Felix in sequence after sequence and in film after film. Felix's characteristic walk, up and down, 'hands' behind his back, with the fixed rotation of his foot-movements and the twist of his head, could be drawn on a series of cels which were used repeatedly. Thus the choreography of a Felix cartoon of the 1920s alternated movement with stillness, now one character, now another taking over the movement which, whenever possible, was repetitious, involving the re-use of established cel-cycles.

Above: Felix the Cat (Pat Sullivan, USA)
Below: Bimbo and Betty Boop (Max Fleischer, USA)

Far from detracting from the cartoons, it brought them a delightful formalization, a kind of visual music with repeated tunes.

Magnificent as pop-art though many of the early, silent cartoons were, they depended too much on the whole-hearted, well-timed and witty co-operation of the music-makers in the movie theatres. The cartoon came into its own with the arrival of the optical track in 1928. The cartoonist then gained complete control not only over musical synchronization with the movements of his characters, but the elaborate use of sound and vocal effects. The animator who took full advantage of this was first of all WALT DISNEY.

Disney had developed his cartoon technique during the 1920s, and finally settled for an astute mouse character, Mickey, a rewarding and fertile creature, whom Disney held back in readiness for the optical track. *Steamboat Willie*, the first Mickey Mouse cartoon with its improvisations on 'Turkey in the Straw', appeared in September 1928. Parallel with his series of Mickey Mouse cartoons, which soon gained world-wide recognition for their quality, Disney produced his series of Silly Symphonies, beginning with *Skeleton Dance* (1930), which

Above: Mickey Mouse (Walt Disney, USA)
Below: 'Skeleton Dance' (Walt Disney, USA, 1930)

was set up to Saint-Saëns's 'Danse Macabre'. Disney developed a whole range of special subjects, such as *The Three Little Pigs* (1933), whose lyric 'Who's Afraid of the Big Bad Wolf?' became one of the theme songs challenging the economic depression. Disney added to his group of special characters in the Mickey series – Minnie, Mickey's girl-friend, and the splendid trio, stars in their own right, Pluto, Goofy, and above all, Donald Duck, whose wild vituperations against the stupidities of the world, recalcitrant machines and life in general were always a tonic.

Although he himself stopped drawing in 1928, delegating his graphics to others, Disney was wise to develop along a number of parallel lines in animation. His best creative period was to be the first fifteen years of sound, from the first, primitive but imaginative films like *Steamboat Willie* to the colourful elaborations of *Fantasia*, *Pinocchio*, or *Dumbo*. By now, his style had settled into a mould; he had created his own choreographic clichés of animal movement, reaction and sentiment. His strange, child-like predilections for sentimentality, innocence, violence and horror declined into a kind of tastelessness, which reached its nadir in the visual travesties of such films as *Alice in Wonderland*. The drawing became gross and vulgar, and the huge studio complex he headed led to loss of personal touch. His mixtures of paternalism and authoritarianism led several of his more sensitive artists to stage a 'strike' in 1941, and eventually break away from him. But he should be remembered for the greatness of his creative work of the 1930s and early 1940s, during which time his name was virtually synonymous with the animated cartoon.

Disney developed more and more what one critic, Ralph Stephenson, has called the 'cosy, nursery anthropomorphism' of his animal characters, which modern, advanced animation has virtually discarded, but which survives in a brutalized form in the outrageous violences, for example, of the traditional Tom and Jerry series of TEX AVERY, the Cat and Mouse characters originated in the late 1940s.

The anthropomorphism of cartoon animals, fully established by Felix the Cat, originated in ancient times when mankind tried in this way to relate himself to the other species, and either make them sacred or endow them with his own characteristics and motives. PAT SULLIVAN's Felix possessed considerable human resource in facing his dilemmas. Disney's anthropomorphism was at its best in the astute, astringent characterization of Mickey and Donald, while his Big, Bad Wolf harked back to the sharp observation of Aesop or La Fontaine.

It was the difficult economics of short-film animation which finally drove Disney into the wider field of the cartoon feature. The more subtle the choreography of colour cartooning became – Disney first introduced Technicolor into his Silly Symphonies as early as 1931 in *Hearts and Flowers* – the more elaborate and prolonged were the technical stages through which it had to pass, and the more skilled the staff artists had to become to fulfil Disney's exacting demands. This inflated costs, which were not matched by short-film rentals. Walt's brother Roy, his business manager, set up Disney Enterprises to develop money-making sidelines in press-strips and advertising. The average costs for a short film in the 1940s have been given as $43,000; those for features, which involved much greater organization and delegation of responsibility: *Snow White and the Seven Dwarfs* $1,700,000; *Pinocchio* $2,600,000; *Fantasia* $2,200,000. Although *Snow White* is said to have earned Disney $15,000,000 in all over the years, not all the features were so successful, and he was gradually to change over to live-action features and

Above: Donald Duck in 'Dumbell of the Yukon' (Walt Disney, USA, 1946)
Below: The Seven Dwarfs in 'Snow White and the Seven Dwarfs' (Walt Disney, USA, 1938)

Above: Popeye (Max Fleischer, USA)
Below: 'The New Gulliver' (Alexander Ptushko, USSR, 1935)

other enterprises, such as the popular Disneyland, to maintain his fortune.

Parallel to Disney, and in competition with him, the various major studios attempted either to set up their own series or distribute those acquired from independent animators – Columbia under Charles B. Mintz redeveloped Krazy Kat, 20th Century Fox distributed Paul Terry's Terrytoons, Universal adopted Walter Lantz's Oswald the Rabbit series. MGM set up their own animation studios, where several animators worked who were later to become celebrated in their own right – TEX AVERY, creator of Tom and Jerry, and William Hanna and Joseph Barbera, later the creators of Huckleberry Hound. Ub Iwerks, Disney's early colleague, developed Flip the Frog. Paramount distributed the work of MAX FLEISCHER, animator of the Popeye series (starting 1933); Fleischer became Disney's closest rival in popularity. Popeye the Sailor began originally as a comic-strip character by Segar. Popeye's humour, of course, came from his transformation into a superman by eating spinach. Fleischer, like Disney, tried his luck in features, but ultimately failed.

In contrast to the USA, Europe was significant pre-war not so much for the quantity of its animation (Anson Dyer, for example, produced very conventional cartoons with relative success in Britain), but for the stimulating development of a number of experimental forms which were collectively to break the dominant graphic style of Disney, Fleischer and the rest who held the screen. Working outside the mainstream of commercial cinema during the 1920s and 1930s, artists-animators such as HANS RICHTER, LOTTE REINIGER, Berthold Bartosch, Alex Alexeieff and Claire Parker, OSKAR FISCHINGER, LEN LYE, Hector Hoppin and Anthony Gross, and the puppeteers GEORGE PAL, W. Starewicz and Alexander Ptushko, were all experimenting with new forms. Richter, with his friend Viking Eggeling, began early in the 1920s in Germany tracing abstract designs onto short rolls of 35 mm film, thus creating the first mobile patterns projected on the screen without the intermediate use of photography. Also working in Germany from 1921 LOTTE REINIGER developed flat-figure, silhouette animation inspired by the Chinese shadow-theatres. Using black, cut-out figures with jointed limbs and heads laid on a translucent glass plate illuminated from underneath, she adjusted their poses by hand between each single-frame take by the camera. In France, one of her former assistants, Berthold Bartosch, produced the serious, left-wing political film, *L'Idée*, with music by Arthur Honegger, which exploited to extraordinary dramatic and emotional effect one of the early electronic instruments, the Ondes Martenot. This film was doubly important – it was the first time that humour and charm were put aside from an animated film (except for the early cartoon, *The Sinking of the Lusitania*), and a dramatic allegory presented in such a way as to inspire a powerful emotional response. The figures were partly silhouette, partly bold outline with simple, stylized expressions like the woodcuts by Frans Masereel on which they were based. The theme was revolution – a proletarian artist trying to lead the workers against the machinations of Church and State and Capital, inspired by the Eternal Idea which is represented by a nude woman, his muse, who is Truth and Beauty. *L'Idée*, a landmark in animation, was banned and little seen.

Another German artist, OSKAR FISCHINGER, created a series of mobile abstract patterns corresponding to the rhythm and 'weight' of music, and this in turn led to the experiments of Len Lye, working in Britain. Lye painted his musical patterns direct on the celluloid reel, anticipating the greatest artist in this field, NORMAN MCLAREN, whose key work was to be achieved from the 1940s; Lye worked with abstract colour patterns set to jazz and other forms of popular music. A further advance was made by Hector Hoppin and Anthony Gross in France; their charming film *Joie de Vivre* (1934) was conceived in a contemporary graphic style in total contrast to the work of Disney – the figures were drawn in light, highly stylized outline, and the settings, as well as the theme, were figments of fantasy drawn with the delicate touch of an etching. Another experimental form in France was pin-screen animation devised by Alex Alexeieff and his wife, Claire Parker, resulting in a shadowy image like an engraving achieved by lateral lighting cast on an area covered by close-set pin-heads which could be raised and lowered to create an irregular surface with highlights and shadows. Their early, macabre film *Night on a Bare Mountain* (1934) was set to Moussorgsky's music: very few films were ever to be made by this means, but Alexeieff was to work later for certain sponsors, including the National Film Board of Canada. In one way or another, European graphic animation contributed successfully to the creation of a much wider conception of what animation could mean, including the abstract film – which could, of course, be created by other means, such as the play of moving light on cut-out shapes, as in certain of the films of the artist Moholy-Nagy.

The work of Lotte Reiniger and Berthold Bartosch linked graphic animation to three-dimensional puppet animation. This developed in Europe with various forms of stylized dolls and settings. The Hungarian GEORGE PAL, working in Holland, began his puppet advertising films using wooden figures with jointed limbs. Wladyslaw Starewicz, a Russian emigré in France, made *The Mascot* (1934), in which the heads of his puppets were of wood, the rest being largely made of bendable wire covered with doll's clothes. The most elaborate puppet film made in pre-war Europe was the feature-length Russian production, *The New Gulliver* (1935), Ptushko's remarkable ideological adaptation from Swift, in which the live figure of

Above: 'The Adventures of Prince Achmed' (Lotte Reiniger, Germany, 1926)
Right: Working drawings for animation of jointed figures (Lotte Reiniger, early 1930s)
Below: 'L'Idée' (Berthold Bartosch, France, 1934)

a man played alongside the moulded wax puppets representing the Lilliputians. Gulliver brings left-wing enlightenment to the oppressed workers of Lilliput.

Traditional Techniques of Animation

We have seen that the traditional techniques of animation were based on frame-by-frame exposure by the rostrum camera on the successive layers of cels, placed over the separate succession of backgrounds, which usually remained unchanged throughout the scene. With puppet animation, the initial principle remained the same, frame by frame exposure of the camera following frame by frame adjustment of the puppets. In puppet films the action is three-dimensional, the dolls performing in miniature sets built to scale. Changes in their expression were achieved either by adjustment of the plastic material of their faces, or by using a succession of masks. The essence of animation lies in frame by frame exposure, or some modification of it. This is also called 'stop frame' or 'stop motion' cinematography, and is a technique which can be applied to any object capable of adjustment before the camera. The animation of packaged goods, for example, is familiar in television commercials.

Production procedure is almost entirely different from that of live-action film-making, although there are parallels here and there. The vast majority of animated films are short, lasting from the few seconds of the briefest commercial to, say, ten minutes or so. Nevertheless, if a cartoon is very fully animated one second of action requires 24 cel sets, plus background, one minute 1,440 cel sets, plus background, and ten minutes 14,400 cel sets, plus the necessary number of backgrounds. Thus a feature cartoon lasting, say, one hundred minutes requires some 1·4 million set-ups of cels and backgrounds for 1·4 million exposures. How many within this number of cel layers are either momentarily static (and therefore usable for many exposures) depends on the degrees of refinement in the animation. Staccato forms of animation, for example, emphasizing jerky movements, can be animated every other frame or even every third frame, saving a great deal of labour, if carefully and wittingly devised.

All the artistic potential in the medium should be at the back of the mind of anyone preparing a 'treatment', or advance script for a cartoon film, or any other form of animation. If the animator is his own scriptwriter, his partly verbal preparations before the advance sketches begin to pour out may seem very slight – he is thinking *visually* from the start, and the span of action in a short cartoon may consist of little more than the elaboration of half a dozen quick action 'gags' – such as the wild succession of

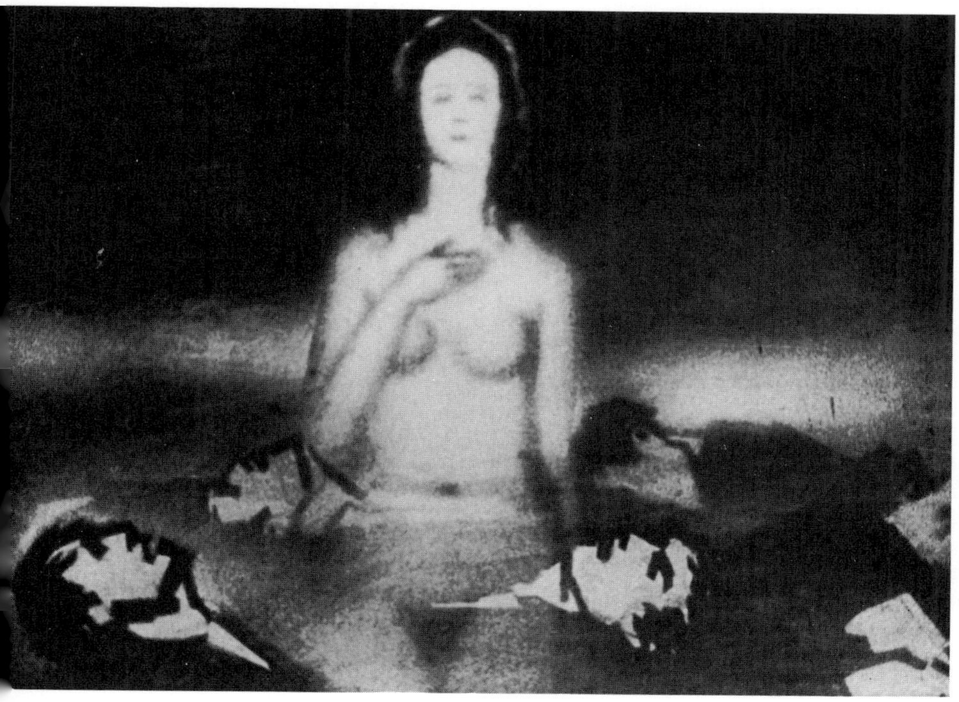

battles between Tom and Jerry. But a film with any plot elaboration or, in the case of a documentary-type animated instructional film, complex exposition, the line of development needs to be set down on paper, and the total balance and shape of the action studied in terms of its detailed suitability for animation. If gags are included, they need to be worked out and timed, and this may be most easily achieved in words rather than sketches, especially if the characters are standard ones already well-known to the animators, the principal of whom is probably the director of the film.

The treatment, and the more detailed verbal script which follows, breaking the action down more precisely, may be accompanied by sketches which begin to foresee the film in visual terms. If the characters are new ones, then their graphic nature must be defined in order to fit and justify their actions, and their appearance as conceived by the director (as controller of the graphics of the film) firmly established. For drawn figures or puppets are not human; they have their own, essentially graphic or plastic character, which has been well described by an animator himself in contrasting the graphic nature of Disney-like characters with that of the UPA group which broke away from him: 'In Disney's cartoon films . . . the rich, even sugary colouring and bulbous forms are matched by movements that resemble a bladder of water moving floppily and sensuously. The sentimentality of mood is matched with cute, coy, easy movement and sadism, by excessive distortion and squashing. UPA artists favour simplicity of form and simplicity of movement, the essence without the frills. Acid colours and sharp forms are matched by movement the way cane, glass, wire would move, springy, whippy, staccato. The wit and cynicism of these cartoons is acted out in slapstick of a high but blasé kind.' In other words, a great part of the character of an animated figure comes from the way it is drawn or, if a puppet, designed and made. If he is drawn with a few straight lines, he can jerk about like a few straight lines would do. In addition, there are the voices to consider; Mickey's determined little treble was voiced by Disney himself.

Most animated films are next prepared in the form of a 'Storyboard', which presents the action, point by point, in what is really an elaborate cartoon strip. The characters, conceived in a mass of sketches, are now seen in the context of key phases of action set against rough backgrounds – the Storyboard begins to look like a succession of film frames, accompanied by words describing the action. At the same time the director, possibly with the help of his key animators, will be preparing the 'Modelling Drawings' for the principal characters. These establish two all-important aspects of the future film – the nature and temperament of each character, its appearance from all viewpoints, and its relative size in comparison with the other characters. The graphic style of the film and its overall colour scheme is determined: the film must have a unified aesthetic quality. An animation director should have a sense of pastiche, or the command of different graphic styles, like a set designer for the theatre or a book illustrator. Further than this, he should see beyond the *static* sketch the character (and, where needed, its environment) in *motion*. The modelling drawings foresee the character in typical action, typical gesture, typical expression. At the same time, the 'Backgrounds' are being designed, forming the setting for the action – sometimes these involve movement, caused, for example, by wind or storm, or the reaction of seemingly static objects which may also become anthropomorphized – a recalcitrant petrol pump, for instance, which has come to hate thirsty cars.

One could describe the flow of action in an animated film as being choreographed like a ballet, with music very closely integrated, as well as stylized sound effects and voices. The cartoon world is mostly one of extreme stylization, although at one stage the bias of animators such as Disney and the Russian school was towards naturalism in the treatment of 'straight' human characters, like Snow White. Animators have even gone so far as to film a live player and then reproduce in drawings his frame by frame photographed movements. This is quite alien to the genius of animation, which should never lose sight of its non-human, graphic nature. Modern animation, as we shall see, reflects every visual characteristic within the range of contemporary art, as well as expanding graphic invention in its own right, especially in the field of kinetic art.

Above: Tracing (Halas and Batchelor, GB)
Above right: Touching-up (Halas and Batchelor, GB)
Below right: The rostrum camera (Halas and Batchelor, GB)

The detailed visual choreography of animation, carefully timed to given fractions of a second, is eventually 'scored' in a 'Work Book', which controls the action in time-bars, much like the bars in a music score. If the music (either established, as in Disney's *Fantasia*, or specially composed, as in most animated films) has been recorded beforehand, the animation has its timing pre-determined; if the composition of the music succeeds the animation, then the composer devises music, and music effects, to accompany the action he can see on the screen; the director creates for him a 'Time Chart' – giving the salients of the action in terms of detailed time continuity. In either case, a fusion of sight and sound must take place. The 'Work Book' and (if needed) the 'Time Chart' are the ultimate technical controls on the actual execution of the film. A third control is the 'Dope Sheet' (or Camera Exposure Chart), designed to instruct the rostrum cameraman in setting up the cycles of backgrounds and cels for each frame.

When every phase of preparation is concluded, the background artists and animators set to work. If the film is a long or complex one, there may well be more than one 'Key' or 'Senior Animator', each concentrating, probably, on one or more characters in the film, working on the individual cel levels to which their special characters are confined in the break-

down of the graphic scene into its components. Each key animator has his 'Assistant', or 'Junior Animator' who fills in the intermediate drawings between the salient drawings which control the detailed nature of a character's movements or transitional expressions, such as emotional reactions or lip-synchronization to spoken words.

Most animation units are small, and their work very much dominated by one or two directors who are probably also the key animators of their individual work; the larger units may have several films in production at once, with a supervisory director-producer who may well delegate the design and direction of individual films to his established animators. Animation units tend to be relatively flexible. Advanced animation is highly individual work, like painting, associated with the style and talent of an individual artist. There are today some 200 notable animation directors with marked styles working throughout the world. This remarkable expansion of the medium has come largely in the last 20 years.

If the traditional animation technique is followed, the key animators and their assistants pass their cycles of drawings (executed on drawing paper) over to 'Tracers' and 'Painters', who are usually girls with exceptionally keen eyes, who trace the drawings onto cels and paint them with opaque colours. A break in this tradition came with the use of coloured cellgraph pencils which enables the animators themselves to work direct onto the cels, since cellgraph pencil marks can be rubbed out and corrected if any detail goes wrong. Complex movements are in any case 'Line-Tested', that is drawn in pencil-outline only, photographed by the rostrum cameraman, and projected for checking and, if desired, alteration. Key animators are highly skilled, and therefore highly paid, artists. The efficient animation producer naturally cannot afford to waste their work. An animated film should be controlled in such a way as to cut out any form of waste; every picture on the drawing board should ultimately have its momentary place in the visual cycle which reaches the screen. Good organization and careful planning are especially necessary in the large units so that highly-paid artists are kept on continuous productive work. The smaller the unit, the wider the range of work each individual must normally undertake. Animated films can be undertaken by single individuals. A great number of NORMAN MCLAREN's films are the work of himself and a single assistant, Evelyn Lambart.

Choreographing puppet animation is only dissimilar to graphic animation in that three-dimensional figures and objects standing in miniature sets have, as we have seen, to be adjusted between each frame-take. The movements of a wooden, wire or plastic doll is as stylized in its own way as the movements of a drawing. The movements have to be 'pre-scored', timed to music or other forms of sound effect and vocal accompaniment. Silhouette marionettes, or the flat, jointed figures filmed frontally (as in Peter Foldes's *A Short Vision*) are nearer to normal animation, since they are photographed by a rostrum camera, though they are adjusted frame by frame, like puppets.

The final exhibition print of an animated film is obtained by the normal means; the various sound tracks (speech, effects, music) are dubbed together at a recording session, and 'married' to the visuals in their final assembled, or edited form. During the course of this, the sound is transferred from magnetic to optical recording. There is little latitude for normal editing, as in live action, especially if the film has been pre-scored for music. Some trimming may be possible here and there. But in all essentials an animated film is pre-edited on the drawing-board.

Recent Technical Innovations – Automation and Computerization

The high costs of animation stem from the great labour involved by highly skilled staff artists and technicians. Various attempts have been made to automate routine forms of animation with the help of the computer, initially in the field of the mobile diagram film offering, for example, mathematical or technological demonstrations. The computer, in fact, has enabled scientific films demonstrating certain principles to be produced with an exactitude impossible through unaided human calculation and execution. Precision animation achieved through the computer, which once it is programmed, calculates and predetermines the images which are to be filmed off the tube-screen on which they are created, are becoming of increasing importance to scientific record, research and advanced instruction. For more normal forms of animation, automated aids are provided as adjuncts to the modern rostrum camera itself – expensive precision instruments, but with many built-in, labour-saving devices which achieve automatically such special effects as fades, dissolves, superimpositions, and smooth panning, tracking, or zooming, all of which involve elaborate calculation, adjustment and re-focusing if done purely by hand. Another important innovation is the so-called aerial image photography – this enables live action photography to be combined with animation without resort to travelling matter, through a process akin to back projection of the live image. All these devices save time, labour and expensive optical work in the laboratory. The rostrum camera becomes the animator's principal technical aid within his own studio.

The Uses of Animation

Animation has been put to many uses beyond the general field of entertainment. As entertainment it has during the post-war years mostly lost its once honoured place in cinema programmes and been transferred to television in such simple graphic outline as the *Huckleberry Hound* series. The cartoon, however, is much favoured in the cinemas of the communist countries where, astonishingly, advanced forms of stylization have been fostered, for almost two decades in some cases, especially in Yugoslavia, Hungary, and Czechoslovakia, where, in addition to cartoons, the most polished development of puppet animation was developed under the late JIŘÍ TRNKA. All this work has been intended for entertainment, though some serious social moral is often expressed in symbolic form by the animators working in the communist countries.

In the rest of Europe and the USA the entertainment cartoon – apart from the occasional series for television – is usually the individual work of animators who subsidise their art through the profits they make out of television commercials, and other forms of sponsored work. But their often highly inventive, imaginative films seldom result in other than financial loss, though they are familiar to animation lovers through film festivals, film society screenings, occasional exhibition on television, and their occasional inclusion in art house and specialized cinema programmes.

A great proportion of work in animation has moved over to the various forms of sponsored films – especially commercials (which can make advertising points at lightning speed), public relations films, and instructional or informational films. Animators are often called in to create titles for live feature films (Saul Bass, for example, has done outstanding work here), or even, more rarely, insets, such as RICHARD WILLIAMS's animated political cartoons in *The Charge of the Light Brigade* (1968). Just as MAX FLEISCHER had pioneered the animated, or partially animated instructional film with *The Theory of Relativity* (1923), Disney was to continue with similar work for the US government during the Second World War and even venture into popular science for the cinemas, with *The Conquest of Space* (1954).

The use of animation for class and lecture room instruction has been developed during the 1960s in the form of the 8 mm loop loaded in a cassette for instant projection at the instructor's will on special projectors. These films become an integral part of the course, illustrating (with repeats as often as wanted) a single point in scientific or technological subjects, in which the schematized mobile diagram and coloured drawing can readily demonstrate or analyze a simple process (such as the action of the heart), emphasizing by momentary colour heightening and other visual devices now this, now that aspect of the process as the teacher speaks. Textbooks are being published which incorporate the use of such films, and this extends to many different subjects, including, for example, language-teaching. Analytical, schematic drawings, diagrams, maps, statistical material, and so forth, are obviously much clearer (and quicker) than their still equivalents in demonstrating processes, actions, and cumulative information. An animated film was even produced in Britain to explain a company balance sheet.

Animation, therefore, has its distinct and recognized place in entertainment, public relations and advertizing, as well as in instruction and research. It also belongs to the realm of pure art, and artists are responding increasingly to the aesthetic possibilities which movement and sound offer them. Duchamp, Léger and, latterly, Picasso are among the major artists who have turned to cinema – Picasso in CLOUZOT's *Le Mystère Picasso*, creating in this remarkable full-length feature a whole gallery of very different paintings and drawings conceived in time, evolving and dissolving before the eyes of the spectator. Certain of these were achieved by means of stop-motion approximating to animation. The whole range of contemporary animation is to be seen at the various festivals devoted entirely to this branch of film-making, more especially those alternating annually in Annecy in France and Mamaia in Romania.

Above: From a scientific loop film for instruction, showing the wallings of the heart (Halas and Batchelor, GB, 1961)
Below: 'The Charge of the Light Brigade' (Tony Richardson, director of animation Richard Williams, GB, 1968)

Top: 'Windy Day' (John Hubley, USA, 1968)
Above centre: UPA's 'Unicorn in the Garden' (William Hurtz, USA, 1953)
Above: UPA's Mr Magoo in 'Safety Spin' (Pete Burness, USA, 1953)

The Post-War Development of Animation

The industrialization of the cartoon by Disney led to the breakaway of some of his leading talents, such as Stephen Bosustow, JOHN HUBLEY, William Hurtz, and Bob Cannon, who with others formed their own company in 1945 – UPA (United Productions of America) – in which individual talent was encouraged to flower. Totally new kinds of stylization were the rule in such widely appreciated UPA films as *Gerald McBoing Boing*, *Madeleine* (after Bemelman), *Unicorn in the Garden* (after Thurber), *Rooty Toot Toot* (1952), and the Magoo series in which Pete Burness, another Disney secessionist, was to specialize.

The 1950s were to see a proliferation of talent, many animators eventually breaking away from UPA to found their own units, for example, John Hubley (one of the greatest of America's animators), ERNEST PINTOFF, who originated Flebus with Gene Deitch (in 1957), another UPA artist who was later to work in Prague, and, more recently, Carmen D'Avino. Jimmy Murakami and others who wanted to make exceptionally advanced films. Other talents in the USA include STAN VANDERBEEK, Robert Breer, John and James Whitney, Morton and Mildred Goldscholl. Continuing to work on more familiar ground in entertainment were, among others, TEX AVERY and Chuck Jones (identified with Tom and Jerry), Fritz Freleng (identified with Bugs Bunny, and Tweety Pie and Sylvester), Walter Lantz of Woody Woodpecker, and William Hanna and Joseph Barbera (identified with Huckleberry Hound). The violence of much of the work of Avery, Jones, and Hanna and Barbera has often been criticized. Paul Terry of Terrytoons is less conventional in his approach.

UPA has set out entirely to divorce their cartoon characters from any taint of naturalism, which they felt infected and sentimentalized much of Disney's later work, however caricatured his figures might appear to be. Since the UPA animators emphasized the 'drawingness' of a drawing their graphics were often of the simplest, their animation formalized almost to comic abstraction, and great play was made with holding figures static, which was, of course, very economical. UPA lost some of its originality when so many of its key talents left, but its influence during the early 1950s on world animation cannot be over-emphasized. During the 1960s the USA was also to lead the world in applying the computer to animation, starting with experiments at the Bell Telephone Company and developing this later in the work of VANDERBEEK, Bruce Cornwall and John Whitney.

Canada was also to develop its own school of animation over and above the wholly exceptional work of NORMAN MCLAREN, each of whose films represents an extension of animation technique. Colin Low (with *Romance of Transportation*, 1952, and *Universe*, 1960), GEORGE DUNNING (later to work in England), and Gerald Potterton, developed Canadian animation, along with Robert Verrall, Joe Koenig, Wolf Koenig, Maurice Blackburn, and Ryan Larkin.

In Britain the longest established unit is that of JOHN HALAS and JOY BATCHELOR, who founded what became the largest studio in Western Europe in 1940. Specializing in public relations, they made many brilliant informational films

Below: 'Pas de Deux' (Norman McLaren, Canada, 1968)

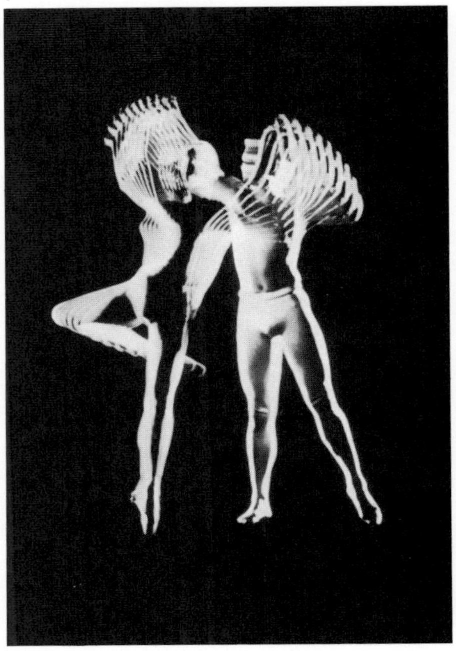

Above: Sniff in 'The Grand Concert' (a paper puppet film for television, Halas and Batchelor, GB, 1960–1)
Below: 'Automania 2000' (Halas and Batchelor, GB, 1963)
Below right: Napoleon in 'Animal Farm' (Halas and Batchelor, GB, 1954)

starting with sponsored wartime subjects; *Dustbin Parade* (1942) used stylization anticipating UPA, while *As Old as the Hills* (1950) among other post-war films made for the oil industry, and *To Your Health* (1956) a study of alcoholism directed by Philip Stapp, were beautifully designed. Latterly specializing in technical educational films, they have not neglected the entertainment film, adapting Orwell's *Animal Farm* (1954) as their first venture into feature-length cartoon. They have ventured into satire with *History of the Cinema* (1956) and *Automania 2,000* (1963), the television series using a paper-cutout technique in *Snip and Snap*, and the Hoffnung series for the BBC. They have frequently pioneered new techniques in Western Europe, especially recently in automation and computerization. Another outstanding unit in the field of specialized cartooning has been the Larkins Studio, whose films by Beryl Stevens on banking are perhaps the best known, but who have also achieved brilliant animation in the scientific field.

Far more zany and biting than the varied but comparatively smooth and serious work of the Larkins and Halas and Batchelor studios has been the work of the three outstanding individualists in British animation – BOB GODFREY of Australia, and George Dunning and DICK WILLIAMS, Canadians who came to Britain in the 1950s. Williams is at heart more a serious than comic film-maker: *The Little Island* (1958) announced his talent, and his sympathetic satire *Love Me Love Me Love Me* (1962) enhanced it. George Dunning is more surrealist in his obsessive films like *The Apple* (1962) or *The Flying Man* (1962), while he adopted pop-art styles brilliantly in the Beatles' feature film, *The Yellow Submarine* (1968). Bob Godfrey's cartoons have a cold, destructive, highly sexed sense of humour, seen in such films as *Polygamous Polonius* (1960) and *Henry Nine till Five* (1970), and the clever satire, *Do-It-Yourself-Cartoon Kit* (1960). The temperaments of these three differ radically, and this is seen in both the nature and the graphics of their art.

Animation in Western Europe is largely concentrated in France. More traditional forms and styles were developed after the war by PAUL GRIMAULT and André Sarrut *(Les Gémeaux)*. The culmination of their work was *Le Petit Soldat* (1947) and the feature *La Bergère et le Ramoneur* (1953), with their strongly stylized graphics and colour. The elaborate nature of their art finally beat them economically.

A whole international school of animators has grown up subsequently in France. The most commercial and prolific was Jean Image, who came from Hungary, as did Peter Foldes, who worked for a while in Britain. France has also attracted important film-makers from Poland – WALERIAN BOROWCZYK, JAN LENICA and Piotr Kamler, as well as the immensely inventive artist-technician Arcady, from Bulgaria, and Manuel Otero from Spain. The painter Peter Foldes's deeply moving British film of a nuclear destruction of the Earth, *A Short Vision* (1955), combining paintings with the animation of flat, jointed figures, has been followed ten years later in France by devastating studies in line-drawing of man's destructiveness, partly sexual, partly the result of sheer aggression in *Un Garçon Plein d'Avenir* and *Appétit d'Oiseau*. While Lenica, Kamler and Borowczyk are surrealists, with great graphic invention, Otero is more a stylized representational artist of satire subjects. Other important animators include Henri Gruel (whose destructively irreverent treatment of the Mona Lisa in *La Joconde*, 1958, was a *reductio ad*

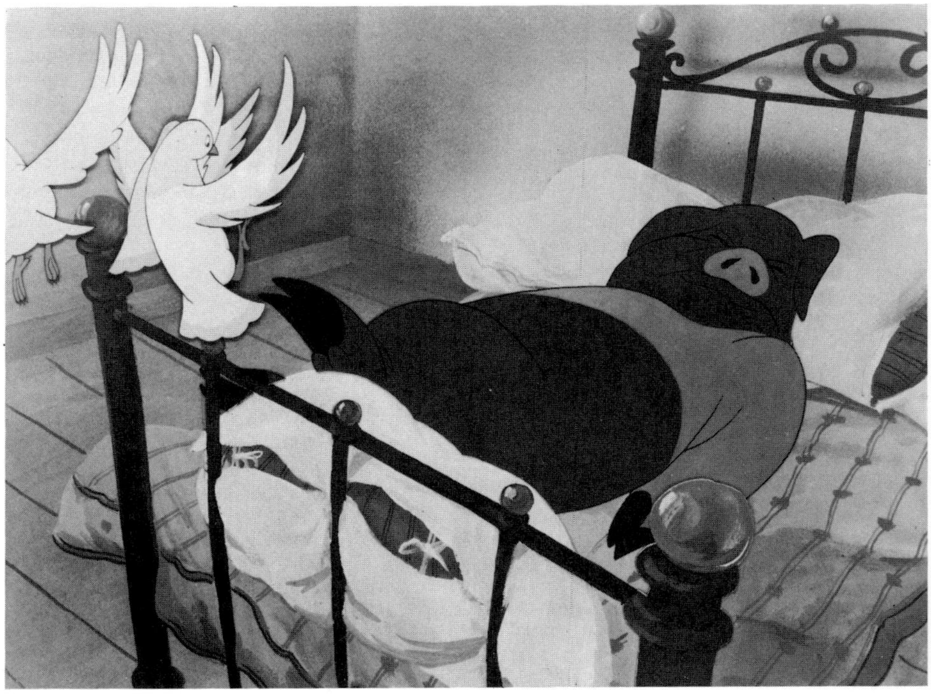

Above: 'The Little Island' (Richard Williams, GB, 1958)
Below: 'Kabal' (Walerian Borowczyk, France, 1967)

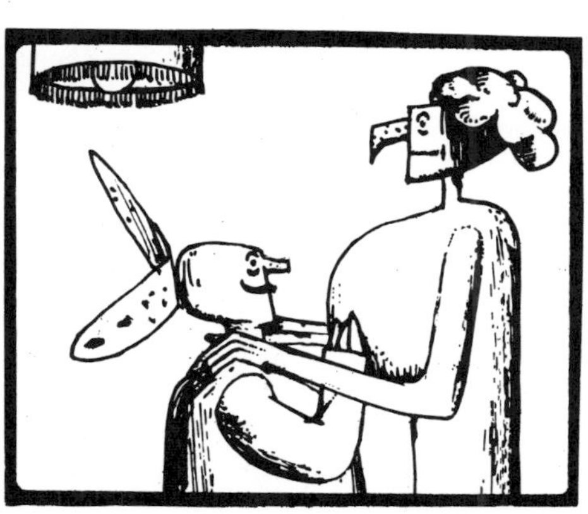

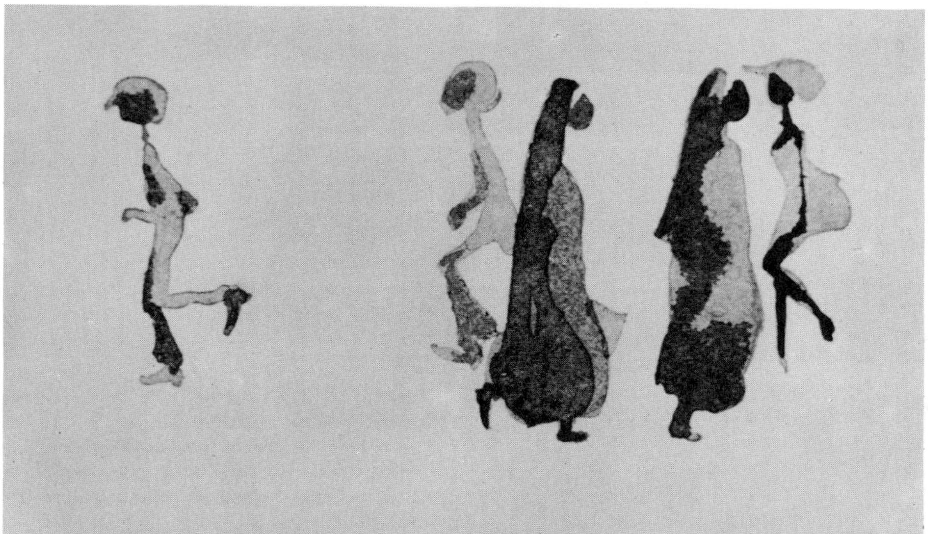

absurdum of cartoon) and Robert Lapoujade (*Prison*, 1962, and *Trois Portraits d'un Oiseau qui n'existe pas*, 1963).

The corruscating talents of Borowczyk and Lenica, first established in Poland, found fruition in France. Both these great artists together with Kamler (*L'Araignéléphant*, 1968) are endeavouring to fulfil their imagination through the images of surrealism. Poland has other distinguished, but essentially lighter talents – Witold Giersz, whose popularity began with the satiric *The Little Western* (1960), and who has more recently been experimenting in thick, hand-painted surfaces with films like *The Intellectual* (1969), Jerzy Kotowski (*The World in Opera* and *Shadow of Time*, 1964), Daniel Szczechura, and Stefan Schabenbeck (*Everything is Number* and *Stairs*, 1969).

Czechoslovakia led Eastern European anima-

Right: 'L'Araignéléphant (Piotr Kamler, France, 1968)
Above: 'Walking' (Ryan Larkin, Canada, 1969)

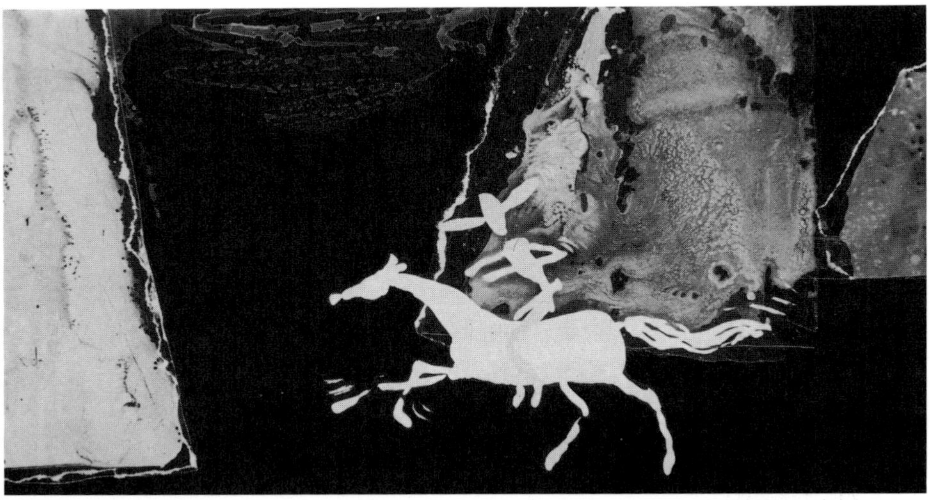

Top left: 'The Little Western' (Witold Giersz, Poland, 1960)
Top right: 'Concerto for Sub-Machine Gun' (Vukotić and Kolar, Yugoslavia, 1959)
Above: 'Stairs' (Stefan Schabenbeck, Poland, 1969)
Left: 'The Intellectual' (Witold Giersz, Poland, 1969)

tion immediately after the war with the work in graphics and above all in puppetry by the late JIŘÍ TRNKA, undoubtedly the finest puppet animator so far. He has been followed by KAREL ZEMAN. Unlike the Poles, the Czechs with few exceptions have concentrated on amusing and lightly satiric subjects rather than dire, dynamic themes. A more surreal approach can be found in the collage films of Josef Kluge and Hana Stepanova.

Possibly Yugoslavia has produced the longest-established, most inventive and sophisticated school of cartoon animation in Eastern Europe; the names of VUKOTIĆ, MIMICA, Kolar, and KRISTL (who later went to West Germany) were synonymous with animation in the 1950s. Such films as Vukotić's *Concerto for Sub-Machine Gun* (1959), Mimica's *At the Photographer's* (1959) and Kristl's *The Great Jewel Robbery* (1961), made with Mladen Feman, set a standard which left the later work of UPA, which had originally inspired them, far behind. The younger generation of Yugoslav animators includes Nedeljiko Dragic, Zlatko Grgic, Zlatko Bourek and Boris Kolar.

The Russians, who have had a great output of conventionally styled cartoon work since the 1930s, in which Ivan Ivanov-Vano was outstanding as the Disney of the Soviet Union, settled to traditional story-telling in the 1950s, often folklore for children. The great animation studio established in Moscow in 1936 has been prolific, and was undoubtedly the largest in Europe. Ivanov-Vano's *The Mechanical Flea* (1964), using cardboard puppets, showed some advance in design, which was maintained in later films, culminating in Fedor Khitruk's lively, excellently designed light satire on film-making; *Film, Film, Film!* (1969).

In the Far East only the phenomenal work of YOJI KURI stands out in a sea of conventional work. In Europe there are other individual animators making a significant contribution to the art. These include Bruno Bozzetto in Italy, Todor Dinov in Bulgaria, Raoul Servais in Belgium, Etien Raik in France, Eino Ruutsalo in Finland, Ernest Ansorge in Switzerland, Lasse Lindberg in Sweden, Wolfgang Urchs in West Germany, and the Moro Studios in Spain. RM

Animation Board

A drawing board into which is set a disc rotatable through 360 degrees. Into the disc is set a translucent glass rectangle and one or more sliding bars with pegs and ruled dividers. The pegs correspond to all other animation registry devices. The dividers are used for computing moves, pans, etc.

Above: Production still from 'Old Czech Legends' (a feature-length puppet film, Jiří Trnka, Czechoslovakia, 1953)
Below: 'Inspiration' (Karel Zeman, Czechoslovakia, 1949)

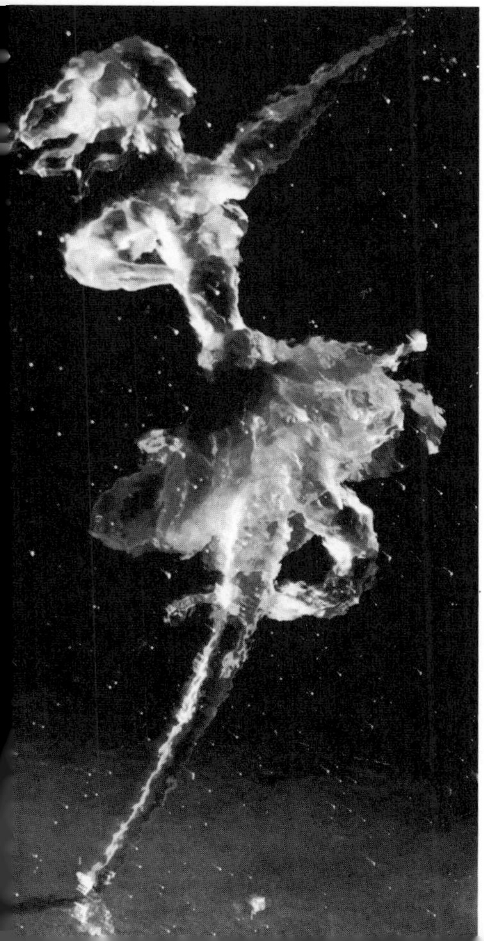

Top: 'Film, Film, Film!' (Khitruk, USSR, 1969)
Above: 'Goldframe' (Raoul Servais, Belgium, 1969)

Animation Camera
A special camera (usually mounted on a post or column) which racks up and down. It is equipped to expose one frame at a time and to keep an accurate count of all frames exposed.

Animator
Artist who produces the series of drawings which when photographed and projected produce the illusion of movement in a cartoon or diagram film.

Annakin, Ken
Born 1914 in Yorkshire, England. British director and former journalist, who came to the feature film via the theatre and the documentary school of film-making. A competent craftsman specializing in neatly turned entertainment films, he directed his first, *Holiday Camp*, in 1946, followed by *Miranda* (1948), *Hotel Sahara* (1951), *The Planter's Wife* (1952). Latterly, he has concentrated on sprawling epics, either action films – *Battle of the Bulge* (1965), *The Long Duel* (1967) – or comedies – *Those Magnificent Men in their Flying Machines* (1965), *Monte Carlo or Bust* (1969). Latest: *The Playroom* (1970).

Anstey, Edgar
Born 1907 in Watford, England. Documentary director and producer: also film critic. Joined JOHN GRIERSON at the Empire Marketing Board Film Unit in 1930, remaining when it became the GPO Film Unit in 1934. In 1934 he set up the Shell Film Unit in Britain. During this period he directed a number of documentaries, including the important sociological films, *Housing Problems* (1935 with ARTHUR ELTON) and *Enough to Eat* (1936). In 1935 he became the production director in London for the American *March of Time* series, and 1937–8 was foreign editor for *March of Time* in New York. In 1940–9 he was on the board of directors of Film Centre in London, and on behalf of the Centre took charge of production at the Shell Film Unit in 1941–5. In 1949 he became Film Officer, British Transport Commission, and producer of many of the best post-war documentaries to be made in Britain. He has travelled widely in the service of documentary films, and occupied positions of influence, including being a member of the Films Council (1948–51), chairman of the British Film Academy, chairman of the Society of Film and Television Arts, President of the Scientific Film Association, and of the International SFA. He has also been a critic on 'The Spectator' and for the BBC. RM

Answer Print
The first combined print of a colour film produced by a laboratory for the acceptance of the producer and which, when approved, becomes the standard for subsequent prints.

Antonioni, Michelangelo

Born 1912 in Ferrara, Italy. Italian director. Graduated in economics and commerce at Bologna University. His interests were higher mathematics, art, the theatre and tennis; he also contributed film criticism to local papers. Eventually he cut himself off financially from his father, a wealthy businessman, and at the age of 27 went to live in Rome and at times almost starved in order to establish his independence. He attended the Centro Sperimentale for film training, but left because he felt he had nothing to learn there. 'The technical side of the cinema in itself has never interested me,' he has said. After working as an assistant to various directors (including CARNÉ on *Les Visiteurs du Soir*, 1943) and helping in screenwriting, he began in 1942 at the age of 30 to make sponsored documentaries. His film, *Gente del Po* (1943, re-edited 1947), was partly destroyed during the German occupation, and he turned to film criticism for a living until after the war. He then made *Nettezza Urbana* (1948) about the street-cleaners of Rome. At the same time he formed his creative association with the composer, GIOVANNI FUSCO, who was to compose the scores for many of his films.

After further short films, Antonioni finally achieved private backing for his first feature, *Cronaca di un Amore* (1950), which has the theme of guilt and reflects his deeply felt melancholy. 'I have only melancholy, a fidelity to my ideas, and lack of money in common with BERGMAN,' he has said. Making films about the middle classes in a style quite opposed to the current fashion of neo-realism, Antonioni climbed to fame slowly and painfully by keeping, like BRESSON and BERGMAN, closely to his own personal themes and to a non-dynamic style in film-making. After *Signora sensa Camelie* (1953), about the decline of a young film star in search of her identity, he had his first marked success with *Le Amiche* (1955), the study of a group of middle-class, provincial women and their inconclusive relations with men, which was followed by *Il Grido* (1957), the story of a man's search through other women for the woman he has lost. The characteristics of much of Antonioni's work – the search for some undefined goal, unease and a sense of guilt, elements of plot or situation unresolved – are most apparent, perhaps, in *Le Amiche*, which won the Golden Lion award at the Venice Film Festival and prepared Antonioni for the trilogy (all prize-winning Italian-French co-productions) – *L'Avventura* (1959) *La Notte* (1960) and *L'Eclisse* (1962) – in all of which the actress most closely associated with his work at this time, MONICA VITTI, starred. These films brought him a world-wide reputation.

Writing of *L'Avventura*, in which a wealthy girl is unaccountably lost on an island off Sicily, while her fiancé falls in love with her girlfriend, Antonioni referred to 'eroticism, the disease of our age', and the need for his vaguely-motivated characters, with their 'emotional sickness', at least to find 'reciprocal compassion'.

La Notte, too, shows the unstable relationship of a celebrated writer and his wife, while in *L'Eclisse*, a girl breaks off her long-established relationship with an intellectual and goes in search of another man. 'I try to *un*dramatize,' Antonioni has said. Deeply hurt by those who persistently denigrate his work as self-indulgently melancholy and boring, Antonioni defends his films as an 'analysis of the emotions', speaking of *Deserto Rosso* (1964), his first colour film, as the study of a woman 'having to reshape herself entirely' through failure to adapt to an alien environment. More recently, in *Blow-Up* (1967) and *Zabriskie Point* (1969), Antonioni has applied his fatalism to themes set in the (for him) unfamiliar environments of Britain and the USA. For comment see 'Antonioni' by Philip Strick (1963), 'Michelangelo Antonioni' by Pierre Leprohon (English translation 1963), John Russell Taylor's 'Cinema Eye, Cinema Ear' (1964), and 'Antonioni' by Ian Cameron and Robin Wood (1968). RM

Aperture

The opening in the iris or shutter of a camera through which light passes to the sensitive negative film.

Arab Film

There is considerable production and exhibition of films in the Arab countries, in spite of the religious tradition that Islam prohibits representational pictures, especially the representation of the human face, and the prohibition of drama until modern times – other than the age-old shadow-theatre, which was possibly even known to the ancient Egyptians. The shadow-show was originally used by priests in temples for religious and moral instruction; they employed figures made of dried leather, projecting their mobile images onto display surfaces using a pair of mirrors. This corresponds to an early form of cinema: alternatively, the cinema could claim to be a modern form of shadow theatre. In fact, the cinema has met with far less opposition in modern times in the Arab World than the live theatre, but the joint arrival of these media during the 20th century has unfortunately led to the death of the once-popular shadow-plays.

Above: Jeanne Moreau and Marcello Mastroianni in 'La Notte' (Michelangelo Antonioni, Italy, 1960)
Below: 'Al-Azima' ('La Volonté', Kamel Selim, Egypt, 1939)

Arab film-going is widespread, though with very varying density according to whether the country concerned is more or less 'developed'. The Arab countries in the Middle East and North Africa have over 1,100 movie theatres, led by the United Arab Republic (Egypt), Algeria, Morocco, Tunisia, Lebanon, Iraq and Syria. Egypt holds the dominant position with feature film production established since 1930, and average output now of some 50 films a year. Feature production has also developed to a limited extent elsewhere, in the Lebanon (some 15 features a year, mainly co-productions with other Arab countries), Morocco (international productions at Rabat studios), Tunisia, Iraq, and Algeria (occasional productions). In addition, there is production of short films and newsreels in these territories and elsewhere, for example in Kuwait.

Egyptian films are shown widely throughout the Arab world; other films shown are, of course, American and, to a lesser extent, films from other countries. French films are shown in Algeria, Morocco and Tunisia; Italian in Libya, and so forth. Indian films find a market where there are Indian populations, as in Morocco.

Egypt, therefore, is the great centre of Arab film production. Other Arab countries with suitable studio facilities tend to seek co-production with Egypt, which has had a relatively prolonged association with the cinema. The LUMIÈRE film programmes reached Alexandria, for instance, as early as 1896. Indigenous feature production, however, did not begin until the 1920s, though prior to this certain Italian film-makers had produced films in Egypt.

The first successful indigenous films included *The Civil Servant* (1923), *Bayoumi* (the love affair of a civil servant and a belly-dancer), *Leila* (1927, the sad story of a pregnant girl, featuring the popular actress, Aziza Amir), the location picture, *Kiss in the Desert* (Ibrahim Lama, 1927–8), Mohammad Karim's *Zeinab* (1930), and the films of the Italian director Stelio Chiarini. The first talkie had to be filmed in Paris by another Italian, Mario Volpi – *The Song of the Heart* (1932). As in Indian films, song and dance (including the belly-dance) became a feature of Egyptian production. Many women became famous at this period not only as actresses but as producers: for example, Fatma Roshdi, Bahiga Hafez, Mary Queeney.

The celebrated Misr Studios were established in 1935, specializing in musicals, melodrama and comedy, as well as producing a newsreel. Techniques, crude until now, began to show signs of maturing: *Al-Azima* (Kamel Selim, 1939) remains the outstanding film of the 1930s for realism in dealing with the lives of the poor in Cairo.

The number of films produced continued to increase both during and after the war, coming from a variety of companies. After the revolution of 1952 the new government established a National Organization for the Cinema (1957). Annual awards were instituted to encourage improvements in the films, and out-and-out bad films were even to some extent banned. A training centre for film technicians was established in Cairo in 1959, while in 1965 a project for building a $14 million Cinema City was only halted by the war with Israel.

Egyptian production is divided between State and private sponsorship; four studios are government-owned. Films on nationalistic and patriotic lines are encouraged, together with films on more contemporary and less laxly box-office subjects. The more mature directors in the contemporary cinema include the 'social-realist' Salah Abu Saif (winner of two awards at Cannes in the 1950s), Youssef Shahin (discoverer of OMAR SHARIF in 1953, and director of the first Egyptian epic, *Saladin*, 1963), and Hussein Kamal, who was trained in France and represents the more modern approach to popular production (*The Impossible*, 1965; *The Porter*, 1967; *A Certain Fear*, 1968; *My Father under the Tree*, 1969).

Although the Egyptian cinema is mainly concerned with providing escapist comedy and drama entertainment for a generally uncritical

Left: 'The Night of Counting the Years' (Shadi Abdelsalam, Egypt, 1970)
Below: 'The Leech' (Salah Abu Seif, Egypt)

'The Battle of Algiers' (Gillo Pontecorvo, Franco-Algerian, 1966)

public, the Venice Festival 1970 introduced a young director, Shadi Abdelsalam, with one short and one feature – *The Night of Counting the Years* – which broke away completely from earlier conventions. Abdelsalam's previous experience as an art director on *Cleopatra* and *Pharaoh* is apparent in his sensitive response to the architecture and desert backgrounds in this mysterious tale of mummy-robbers in the last century. Sensitive colour and a remarkable plastic sense combine to make it a most auspicious début, although it is a little early to prophesy what effect its undoubted success at overseas festivals may have on the future of the Egyptian film.

A few films directed in the Arab countries by foreign, visiting directors have been notable – for example, *Itto* (JEAN BENOÎT-LEVY in Morocco, 1934), *Goha* (Jacques Baratier in Tunisia, 1958), *Marie-Chantal Contre le Docteur Kha* (CLAUDE CHABROL in Morocco, 1965), and *The Battle of Algiers* (GILLO PONTECORVO and Ali Yahya, in Algiers, 1966). Notable films have also been made on location in Egypt, for example *The Ten Commandments, The Bible* and *Khartoum*, while much of *Lawrence of Arabia* was filmed in Jordan. RM

Arbuckle, Roscoe (Fatty) (1881–1933)
Born in Smith Center, Kansas, USA. When he was one of the most popular early American slapstick comedians, Arbuckle's career was abruptly ended by a scandalous manslaughter case occasioned by the death of a girl following a party in his hotel suite. Though he was cleared, the industry and the public never forgave him. Towards the end of his career he directed one or two films under the pseudonym of William B. Goodrich. Originally a monologuist and singer in touring fit-ups and vaudeville companies, he entered films about 1908, subsequently joined SENNETT's Keystone company and eventually formed his own company, Comicque. His best-known films are those in which he worked with CHAPLIN (at Keystone) and KEATON, who began his film career with Arbuckle at Comicque.

Archives and Film Preservation
Archives The preservation of films, like that of books, works of art and the artefacts of our civilization, is of the greatest importance. Films are not only part of the history of art and culture, they offer also a 'living' record of the past, showing it with its natural movement and, since 1928, in movement with recorded sound. The 20th century is the first to be put on intimate, naturalistic record in this way, and the study of factual film records therefore is of the greatest importance to the general historian, as the study of film as an art is to the historian of culture.

Film, however, is difficult and expensive to preserve. Up to 1951 all films were printed on nitro-cellulose stock, which was replaced from 1952 by the present-day acetate stock. Not only was nitrate film highly inflammable, it was also inherently unstable, and subject (according to the conditions in which it was kept) to rapid deterioration and decomposition. The image would fade and the film become sticky, especially in damp or humid conditions. Much precious film from the earlier years of the century has therefore been lost. Acetate film has a far longer life, estimated around three centuries.

It was not until the early 1930s that recognition of the film's importance both as historical record and as art led to the foundation of archives for the collection and preservation of films. The National Film Archive, with Ernest Lindgren as Curator, was set up in Britain in 1935 as a department of the newly-founded British Film Institute – the same year in which Iris Barry and John Abbott established the Film Department of the Museum of Modern Art in New York. At the same time Einar Lauritzen's private film collection in Stockholm was absorbed into the Swedish Technical Museum, and another private collector, Henri Langlois, whose passion was to show old films, became associated with the young GEORGES FRANJU in the founding in 1936 of the Cinémathèque in Paris. These four national collections formed the International Federation of Film Archives (FIAF) in 1938. Today, FIAF has 35 corporate members in 29 countries.

The purpose of a film archive has been defined by Ernest Lindgren as follows: 'to build up and maintain, by continual acquisition and by preservation, a national collection of moving pictures, recorded on film or tape (whether from the cinema or television or any other source) which have lasting value either as works of art or as historical records, so as to ensure that they will always be available to anyone who wants to consult them, now and in the future'. In addition, most archives maintain collections of books about the film, stills, screenplays and other materials related to the history of the film.

Films should be stored in the best conditions for their physical preservation, which means in a well-ventilated vault kept at a comparatively low temperature of around 55° Fahrenheit (13° Centigrade) throughout the year. Nitrate films have to be watched constantly and tested chemically for possible deterioration; normally, if they are of sufficient significance to warrant the expense, nitrate films are copied onto acetate stock, so that the dangerous and unstable original can be discarded. Sometimes copying can be done normally by a commercial laboratory, but for delicate, damaged or otherwise difficult prints it may be necessary to copy slowly, frame by frame, by means of special printing equipment.

Owing to the sheer quantity of professional films produced and shown, and the cost of maintaining suitable vaults for their preservation, most archives operate selectively, especially with films of more recent times. Not every film made and shown is automatically preserved. The primary objective of a national archive is to preserve the films of its own country and, secondly, to preserve films from other nations which are likely to have any kind of importance for students of the film, historians, and others (such as scientists and technologists) who need films of fact as records. Different principles of selection operate for the main branches of film, and different archives maintain different methods of selection. In Britain, for example, special selection committees have been maintained for many years for the art and entertainment film, and for films as historical and scientific record. The preservation of films made specially for television has also become a matter of increasing importance in recent years.

There is not only the question of films for preservation, but the problem of acquisition. There is legal and statutory deposit of films in Italy, Denmark and the Argentine. Such statutory deposit requires producers or distributors to place copies of their films in the national archive if requested to do so, as publishers are required to do in some countries. If necessary, those depositing prints could be refunded the print cost by the archive, which should have money placed at its disposal by the State in order to meet such costs. As things are at present, all countries without statutory deposit depend on the goodwill of distributors to give or loan the archives used prints of the films requested from them when they are no longer wanted for distribution. This is obviously unsatisfactory. It means that in Britain, for example, barely half the British feature films selected and requested are actually deposited, and less than one third of the American features – this in spite of the fact that the archive naturally offers producers and distributors every guarantee they may ask concerning the use to which these loan prints may be put. The copyright in the films remains, of course, with the producers. These problems do not arise in the case of the Communist countries, where all films produced are in any case the property of the State.

One of the most important functions of an archive is to index and catalogue the prints it preserves, which in the case of Britain was by 1970 some 18,000 titles. Indexing and cataloguing films is more difficult than in the case of books. Films are relatively difficult to handle, view, and assess for their content-value. Preservation prints can only properly be viewed by archive staff, students and research workers on an editola; if they are needed for full-screen projection they must be copied, so that the original does not suffer any of the regular dangers of wear and tear, especially scratching. (Reference copies may well be made on videotape in the future, rather than expensively on film.) But an archive is useless if its contents remain unknown, and published catalogues giving broad descriptions of the films, supplemented by card indexes giving more elaborate, detailed information of their content are essential. The records of the films are, of course, supplemented by the stills collections, which in Britain amounted in 1970 to some 700,000 photographs at the National Film Archive.

There are national film archives now in Albania, Australia, Austria, Belgium, Bulgaria, Canada, Cuba, Czechoslovakia, Denmark, Finland, France, West Germany, East Germany, Great Britain, Holland, Hungary, India, Israel, Italy, Norway, Poland, Portugal, Romania, Spain, Sweden, Turkey, USA, USSR and Yugoslavia. In the United States there are a number of film archives: (i) The National Archives and Record Service is confined to a custodial service only; its collection arose out of the need which was felt by the pioneer producers to copyright their work as photographs, and many of the early films (1897–1915) are preserved in Washington in the form of positive paper prints. From 1912 copyright was established by means of verbal description, not the deposition of prints, and the primary collection, therefore, is limited to this early period, supplemented by gifts or purchases of individual collections, such as the MARY PICKFORD collection. (ii) George Eastman House, Rochester, New York, which became a member of FIAF in 1952, was founded as a Museum in 1948, with many international film classics in its collection, though its primary concern is to preserve American film, together with a vast collection of stills, and make the prints available for research students and historians. (iii) The Museum of Modern Art Film Department (founded 1935) is best known to the public for its enterprising screenings, publications and distribution of prints of important films in the history of screen art to film clubs and the like. (iv) In addition, there is the Hollywood Museum, whose curator was the film historian, Arthur Knight.

In 1967 the American Film Institute was established (with a grant from public and foundation funds of some $5 million) to preserve and make available to the interested public an historical collection of American films and, like the British Film Institute in London, to encourage study and appreciation of the film.

Stock Shot Libraries The compilation film, edited from the vast collection of old newsreel and other record material held in the film archives and the 'stock shot' libraries, has been prominent in film production from comparatively early times – many notable films of this kind being produced from the 1930s. (See NEWS AND RECORD FILM.) More recently, the voracious demands of television for lengthy series of compilation films on recent history (such as the two world wars) has led to an increase in the number of commercial stock shot libraries, which grew originally out of the collections of news and documentary material held by the newsreel and news magazine producers. For example, Sherman Grinberg's Libraries in New York and Hollywood have over a million subject cards microfilmed and cross-referenced. But too many important private collections are indexed only in the minds and memories of their owners.

The 'World Directory of Stockshot and Film Production Libraries' (London, the Pergamon Press, 1969) lists numerous libraries in some 58 countries. So great is the quantity of material available that the potential user's problem is not so much concern that his subject, however seemingly remote, does not exist anywhere on film, but concern that he may fail to locate it. Comparatively few libraries have devised satisfactory systems of indexing their possessions, with a detailed breakdown of the subjects of the films they hold down to shot level. With valuable, often unique material scattered all over the world, it often becomes a matter of intuition born of experience in producers specializing in the production of compilation films to sense where they may track down what they want. But inadequately indexed material is almost as bad as material totally lost. Libraries, however, face enormous problems in viewing and indexing their material; the United States Air Force Picture Film Depository, to take one instance, has 100 million feet of film available; the Dance Museum in Sweden, to take another, very different case, 10,000 metres on its special subject dating back to 1920.

Television itself has become a further great producer of stock-shot material, as well as its greatest user. The BBC-TV Archive in London has a weekly intake of over half a million feet of film, both 35 mm and 16 mm; in addition to this, there is a considerable body of videotape picture material to store. It is obvious that not all this can be stored and indexed, and so a carefully controlled policy of evaluation and selection against any potential future need has to be applied. Like the National Film Archive, this archive uses the Universal Decimal Classification Scheme to keep track of the material in its possession. Visnews, producers in London providing an international news film service specially designed for the constant demands of television, creates specially some 12,000 news stories a year, and classifies them for preservation with some 80,000 catalogue cards. In 1970 its vaults held 35 million feet of film, after some 13 years' operation.

Specialists are moving into the archive and stock-shot field who aim to serve producers as consultants by helping them to track down what they need, and supplying it for them. New technology in storing, indexing and supplying news and other film records already involves automation and computerization, not only for 'information retrieval' but, ultimately, for actually locating and setting up immediate screening of wanted shots and sequences for potential users. RAI Television in Rome have been pioneers since 1964 in the field of automating information about availability of film material in Italy. RM

Arc Light

High powered source of illumination used for projectors and studio lights which is produced by a bridge of incandescent vapour which carries an electric current from one electrode to another.

Argentina

See LATIN AMERICA

Arletty

Born 1898 in Paris, France. Real name: Léonie Bathiat. Elegant French actress, equally distinguished on the stage and the screen, who made an indelible impression in the films of MARCEL CARNÉ during the 1930s and, later, in his classic *Les Enfants du Paradis* (1944), produced at the time of the German occupation during the Second World War. Epitomizing French style and sophistication for a generation of filmgoers, Arletty began her working life as a factory hand and typist. When she was 22 she turned to the theatre and then the music hall, where she was discovered for her first film role in *Un Chien qui Rapporte* (1931). Since then she has made over 40 films, returning often to the theatre, which claimed more of her time during the 1950s and 1960s. Other notable films: *Hôtel du Nord* (1938), *Le Jour se Lève* (1939), *Les Visiteurs du Soir* (1942), *Huis Clos* (1954), *Les Petits Matins* (1961), *The Longest Day* (1962). MH

Arliss, George (1868–1946)

Born in London, England. Actor. First stage

appearance in London in 1886 at Elephant and Castle Theatre. Travelled to USA with Mrs Patrick Campbell in 1901; played stage parts there until 1920, when film career began. He became identified with many of his famous roles: Disraeli, Voltaire, Richelieu, Wellington, etc. Films include: *The Green Goddess* (1923 and 1930), *Disraeli* (1930), *The Man who played God* (1931), *Voltaire* (1933), *Cardinal Richelieu* and *The House of Rothschild* (1934), *The Iron Duke* (1935), and *Dr Syn* (1938). His autobiography, 'George Arliss by Himself', was published in 1940.

Above: Arletty and Gaby Sylvia in 'Huis Clos' (Jacqueline Audry, France, 1954)
Below: 'Zoya' (Lev Arnshtam, USSR, 1944)

Arnold, Malcolm
Born 1921 in Northampton, England. Composer. After a successful career as an orchestral trumpet player, he turned to full-time composition after the Second World War, and a sizeable part of his output has been devoted to film music. Like his concert work, these scores are characterized by bold, full-blooded orchestration, witty parody elements and an air of brash enjoyment. Main films include: *The Sound Barrier* (1951), *Hobson's Choice* (1953), *The Bridge on the River Kwai* (with its Oscar winning march arrangements, 1957), *Inn of the Sixth Happiness* and *The Key* (1958), *The Heroes of Telemark* (1965), *David Copperfield* (1969). Has also written music for several television series. JG

Arnshtam, Lev
Born 1905 in Dnepropetrovsk, Ukraine, USSR. Director. Trained at the Leningrad Conservatoire, where he studied pianoforte, Arnshtam joined MEYERHOLD's theatre as a musician (1924–7). Having collaborated on the early sound films *The Golden Mountains* (YUTKEVITCH, 1931) and *Counterplan* (YUTKEVITCH and ERMLER, 1933), Arnshtam became a director in his own right with *Girl Friends* (1936). Subsequent films: *Friends* (1938), *Zoya* (1944), *Glinka* (1947), *Romeo and Juliet* (1955), *The Lesson of History* (1957).

Art Direction
See DESIGN AND ART DIRECTION

Art Director
Person who supplies the designs for the backgrounds to a film (and sometimes the costumes) and is responsible for their being built and decorated.

Arthur, Jean
Born 1908 in New York City, USA. Actress. She did some stage work before entering films in the mid 1920s, playing her first lead in 1928. With her attractive gurgling voice and combination of innocence and resilience, she quickly established herself in the sound era (the office girl in FORD's *The Whole Town's Talking*, 1935) and in a series of films for FRANK CAPRA, who found her an ideal, quick-talking, resourceful heroine in *Mr Deeds Goes to Town* (1936), *You Can't Take It With You* (1938) and *Mr Smith Goes to Washington* (1939). HOWARD HAWKS also developed this quality of tough vulnerability in *Only Angels Have Wings* (1939). Her perfect timing and overall comic sense made her supreme in many other social comedies including *Easy Living* (1937) and *Talk of the Town* (1942). JG

Arzner, Dorothy
Born 1900 in San Francisco, USA. One of Hollywood's rare women directors, Dorothy Arzner was a First World War nurse and subsequently a journalist before starting work in Hollywood as an editor *(Blood and Sand, The Covered Wagon, Old Ironsides)*. She directed her first film *Fashions for Women* in 1927, and the 15 films she made in the next 16 years, though generally strictly commercial assignments, included one of CLARA BOW's better sound films, *Wild Party* (1929). Other films: *Ten Modern Commandments* and *Get Your Man* (1927), *Manhattan Cocktail* (1928), *Sarah and Son, Anybody's War* and *Paramount on Parade* [part] (1930), *Honor Among Lovers* and *Working Girls* (1931), *Merrily We Go To Hell* (1932), *Christopher Strong* (1933), *Nana* (1934), *Craig's Wife* (1936), *The Bride Wore Red* (1937), *Dance, Girl, Dance* (1940), *First Comes Courage* (1943). DR

Asian Film
Apart from the outstanding industries of INDIA, JAPAN and CHINA, the most interesting countries are: (i) *Ceylon*. Film production has existed in Ceylon on a relatively small scale

Above: Thomas Mitchell, Jean Arthur and Charles Lane in 'Mr Smith Goes to Washington' (Frank Capra, USA, 1939)
Below: 'Gamperaliya' (Lester James Peries, Ceylon, 1964)

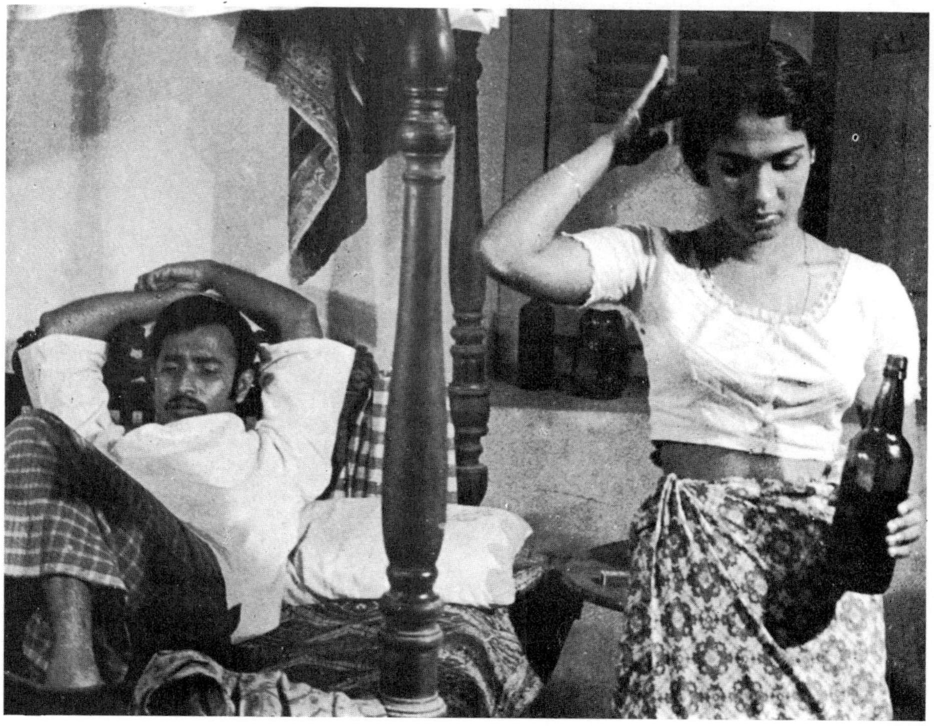

for about a quarter century, and one film-maker of considerable talent, LESTER JAMES PERIES has emerged; he has produced films which, while pushing the standard of Sinhalese production forwards, have also enjoyed limited showing in other countries. A sophisticated attitude to the film exists in Colombo and Kandy and, as in the metropolitan centres of India, the younger film-makers are anxious to create opportunities to produce less conventional films. There is a growing film society movement in Ceylon, and an Institute, financed by government, is to be established to act as a centre for the encouragement of more advanced film production, the training of film-makers, and the establishment of an archive.

Ceylon is a small country – the rapidly rising population is around 15 million. It is predominantly Buddhist, and there is a Tamil speaking minority in the north, who look to Madras for their film entertainment. Commercial film-making in Sinhala exists on a small scale, but stays in a rut from which it is difficult for an industry intent on such profits as it can muster to emerge. The Sinhala film has tried to copy the traditions of the more reactionary South Indian style, or lack of style, based on romanticizing the popular film stars in 'formula' films; most of such films have been made in South India, while Hindi and Tamil films have been dubbed into Sinhala. This has frustrated the growth of a local film industry in a country with great natural advantages and a distinct culture of its own.

An early successful Sinhalese film was K. Gunaratnam's *Sujata* (1953); it was still romantic in tone but inspired equally by Western and Indian influences. It remained for Peries, a journalist who had watched feature film-making in England, to establish the true Sinhala film with *Rekava* (1956), which derived wholly from Sinhalese culture; his later film *Gamperaliya* (1964) won the Grand Prix at the New Delhi Film Festival in 1965. Peries's career has concentrated, not without difficulty, on establishing Sinhalese subjects with the general, film-going public in Ceylon, and, to some extent, with the outside world; for example, *Rekava* was shown at four international film festivals and has been commercially distributed in English, Russian, Czech and German. Peries's patron-producer is Anton Wickremasinghe, a businessman interested in the arts.

Peries is not quite alone in his task; other directors of indigenous films include: Piyasiri Gunaratnam *(Mokada Vune)*, who studied film-making in Prague; Mudalinayake Somaratne (*Binaramalee*, based on a popular radio serial); Amarnath Jayatilake (*Adarawanthayo, The Lovers*, a first film by a young journalist who studied film-making in India. Second film, *Priyanga*); Sugathapala Senarath Yapa (*Miniha saha Kaputa, Man and the Crow*; a short experimental film). Siri Gunasingha *(Sach Samudurz)* and G. D. L. Perera *(Sāmā)*.

However, mainstream Sinhalese films, like mainstream Indian films, belong technically to the past; stories are remote from actuality and the plots are elaborated at length, with the obligatory inclusion of songs. Ceylon, too, is only in the process of establishing professional actors, as there is no indigenous professional theatre, and no television to employ actors. Advanced Sinhalese film, led by the work of Peries, has begun to introduce Western conventions of realism, or near-realism; the films are shorter, the characters and situations nearer to real life. The tendency is to 'spell out' the action, with numerous dialogue scenes; but Peries, like SATYAJIT RAY, can obtain sincere performances from his virtually non-professional casts.

There is also the problem of censorship, of what is permitted in the way of public expression on the screen within the strict conventions of Sinhalese society. Although the Westernized, sophisticated branch of the Sinhalese middle class is prepared to air truths about social and even sexual matters, neither the general public nor the film censors are prepared to go along with too much liberalizing. Few, if any, films are free to deal with 'social problems' in realistic terms. Peries's *Ran Salu* (*The Yellow Robes*, 1961) which to a certain extent does so in that

Above: 'Ran Salu' ('The Yellow Robes', Lester James Peries, Ceylon, 1964)
Below: 'Day Shall Dawn' (Aaejay Kardar, Pakistan, 1959)

the Westernized hero has an illegitimate child by a girl he takes to live with him, is very exceptional, and in any case compensates when the girl decides to become a Buddhist nun.

Distinguished film-makers from abroad have worked in Ceylon; BASIL WRIGHT's lyrical film of the 1930s, *Song of Ceylon*, is highly regarded. Other documentary film-makers from Europe who have worked for a period in Ceylon include RALPH KEENE and Paul Zils, who is now resident there as documentary consultant. Among Western features which have used Ceylon for locations is DAVID LEAN's *Bridge on the River Kwai*.

(ii) *Pakistan* Film-making for the Moslem peoples of India was negligible prior to partition in 1947; a few films were produced, such as *Shakuntala* and *Taqdeer* in the West in 1943, and *Misery is their Lot* (1946) in the East. Dacca became the centre of Moslem culture in that part of Bengal which lay in East Pakistan, and film-making began in the 1950s, with Aaejay Kardar's *Day Shall Dawn* (1959) as the first film of any significance; WALTER LASSALLY from Britain was the cameraman. Although this film won an award at Moscow, it was not a commercial success. Its subject, the lives of the fishermen of East Bengal, helped to establish a modest tradition of 'folk cinema', some films in this style being made in Urdu to win a wider market. Audiences can be classified as (i) the artisan proletariat, (ii) the intelligentsia, and (iii) the rural peasantry. In the East, the problem of combating the influence of Bengali films imported from Calcutta, and in West Pakistan the popular films imported from Bombay was met by the simple expedient of restricting importations, starting with a sharply increased tax on imported film in 1948 and a virtual embargo in 1952.

Production of Pakistani films in the West started in the 1950s, encouraged to some extent by the influx of Moslem talent from India, taking the place of departing Hindu talent. The quality of film-making remains generally low, and the market, which is poorly financed, is essentially local. The emphasis remains on escapist, romantic subjects. The main studios are centred on Dacca in East Pakistan (production some 30 films a year, mainly in Bengali), and at Lahore and Karachi in the West. Films are patronized by some 5% only of the population of approximately 60 million in East Pakistan, and by some 10% in West Pakistan, with its population of approximately 40 million.

(iii) *Hong Kong* A tradition of film-making in Chinese developed first in Shanghai during the 1920s. The key production period, 1921–6, saw up to 100 film studios in operation. The first prominent Chinese star, however, did not emerge until the 1930s in sound film – Hu Tieh (Miss Butterfly), who appeared in *Singing Peony* (1931); she was an actress of marked personality, emotional control, charm and beauty. She was to come out of retirement after the war and re-appear in a Shaw Brothers production, *Back Door*, which on the strength of her acting won the Grand Prix at the Asian Film Festival held in Tokyo in 1960. Like so many others, she had moved to Hong Kong when the revolution in China overtook Shanghai. Her leading man in *Singing Peony*, Wang Yuan-lung, became an outstanding actor, as did Hung Shen, a man of considerable culture who had studied at Pekin University and in the USA, and who became a director. He also carried on his work in Hong Kong, where he died in 1960.

Hong Kong, like Shanghai, had become a centre of production during the 1930s; anti-Japanese films appeared up to the time the Japanese invaders over-ran and occupied (December 1941 to September 1945) this British colony. After recovering from this, by 1949, production began to boom; it was not unknown for cinema proprietors to band together to finance simple films in the Cantonese language to show in their small cinemas. The first Chinese colour film, *The Dream Wedding*, was completed in Shanghai at the very time the revolutionary forces were advancing towards the city. By then most of the studio personnel and the actors had moved to Hong Kong or Taiwan (Formosa).

Production in Hong Kong was initially on a modest basis; films were made in quantity and rapidly on small budgets. But the Chinese Shaw Brothers aimed to raise the standard of their film-making and capture the middle-class market which had hitherto preferred American films. Their production, *The Gates of Hell*, was a commercial success, and their studios, along with those of their rival, Cathay, became the most prominent in Hong Kong during the 1950s. Their stars included Lin Dai; she appeared in such films as *The Kingdom and the Beauty*, which won the Grand Prix at the festival of Kuala Lumpur in 1959. Another outstanding actress was Li Li Hwa, who appeared in *The Long Voyage Home* (1959), a story of Chinese fisherfolk.

Production reached its height in Hong Kong from 1957 to 1963, the number of films made rising to no less than 302 in 1961, 30% in Cantonese and 70% in the more widely understood Mandarin Chinese. Recently, production of films in Cantonese has given way to those in Mandarin, since the export of films in Cantonese had declined sharply. All main production is in colour and widescreen, with the emphasis on violent action pictures set in 'historical' periods, together with modern 'sophisticated' drama and comedy. Although the industry is facing changes (with average costs for each main picture running at over US $100,000), it has been, with its Taiwan co-production added, making on average more than 200 features a year during the 1960s, and

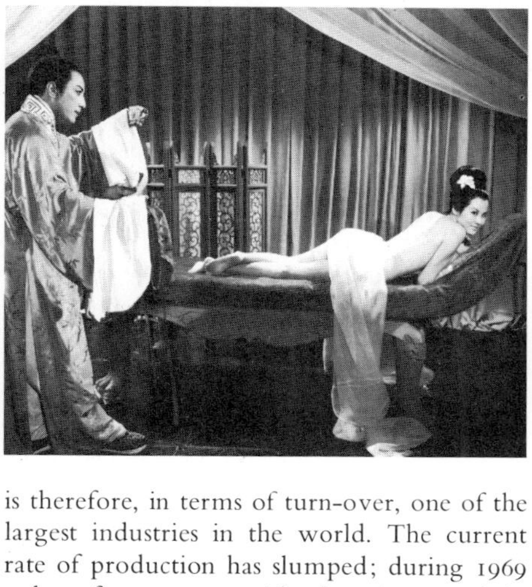

is therefore, in terms of turn-over, one of the largest industries in the world. The current rate of production has slumped; during 1969 only 55 features were said to have been made in Hong Kong itself. There is also a limited amount of communist-inspired film-making, though these films are not normally welcome in Mao's China. Audiences, apart from those in Hong Kong (with its population inflated to some 4 million by the influx of refugees and a prolific birth-rate), are reached through export not only in Taiwan (also a centre of production), but in the Philippines (where further films are made on some scale, but not for the Chinese), and other areas in South-East Asia with Chinese populations.

Foreign films made in Hong Kong include *Ferry to Hong Kong* (LEWIS GILBERT, 1959), and the locally celebrated film *The World of Suzie Wong* (RICHARD QUINE, 1960), which featured a Hong Kong actress, Nancy Kwan. RM

Top left: Fatimah Ahmad in a version of 'Macbeth' (Hong Kong)
Left, below left, above right: 3 stills typical of Hong Kong productions of the late 1960s
Below: Paul Massie in 'Orders to Kill' (Anthony Asquith, GB, 1958)

Aspect Ratio
The relationship between the width and height of a projected image.

Asquith, Anthony (1902–1968)
Born in London, England. British director for 40 years who was influential in raising the tone of British films, particularly just before, during and after the Second World War. His film versions of Terence Rattigan's plays – *French Without Tears* (1939), *While the Sun Shines* (1946), *The Winslow Boy* (1948), *The Browning Version* (1951) – created a market for civilized, literate, well-constructed screen entertainment. Later, his films from Rattigan screenplays – *The VIPs* (1963), *The Yellow Rolls-Royce* (1964), which was also his last – tended to become suffocated with multi-star casts and over-glossy production values. But Asquith's main contribution to the British film industry, an elegance of style and a deep concern for human values, survived. The son of a Prime Minister of England he was nicknamed 'Puffin' and he developed an obstinate passion for films at Oxford, went to Hollywood in 1925 to study film-making and in 1927 he co-directed his first film in England, *Shooting Stars*. Considered a daring innovator in the 1920s, he developed a distinctive technique admirably suited to the sympathetic and gently mocking subjects he chose, which often made admiring fun of the British character – *Quiet Wedding* (1940), *The Demi-Paradise* (1943), *The Final Test* (1953). His film version of *The Importance of Being Earnest* (1951) is the best screen adaptation of an Oscar Wilde play. In 1958, his troubled feeling about individual responsibility in times of war was crystallized in *Orders To Kill*. In 1953 he produced 'Carmen' at Covent Garden. Other notable films: *Pygmalion* (1938), *We Dive at Dawn* (1943), *The Way to the Stars* (1945), *Libel* (1960), *The Millionairess* (1961). See 'Anthony Asquith' by Peter Noble (1951, British Film Institute Index). MH

Assembly
The joining together of the shots of a film in the right order, thus producing what is known as the rough-cut.

Astaire, Fred

Born 1899 in Nebraska, USA. American dancer and actor who, with his partner GINGER ROGERS, established a unique style of film musical comedy in the 1930s, later overtaken by the more identifiably American fantasies of GENE KELLY and the block-buster versions of stage musicals. Christened Frederick Austerlitz, he started dancing at the age of four and was enrolled at a local dancing school with his sister Adele. They made their professional début as a team in vaudeville, went on to star in stage musicals in New York and London. When Adele retired to marry, Fred made his film début in 1933 in *Dancing Lady*. The same year launched his partnership with Ginger Rogers in *Flying Down To Rio*, and began a career which significantly influenced the development of screen choreography. The new team followed this with *The Gay Divorcée* (1934) and went on to make eight more musicals together, ending with *The Barkleys of Broadway* (1949). Astaire continued dancing, but now with a series of partners, notably RITA HAYWORTH, LESLIE CARON, Vera Ellen, Cyd Charisse. In 1959 he played a completely straight role in *On The Beach* and has made only one musical since then, *Finian's Rainbow* (1968). Other notable films: *The Ziegfeld Follies* (1945), *Yolanda and the Thief* (1946), *Easter Parade* (1948), *The Band Wagon* (1953), *Funny Face* (1956), *Silk Stockings* (1957), *The Notorious Landlady* (1962), *A Run On Gold* (1969). In 1960 he published his autobiography 'Steps In Time'. MH

Astor, Mary

Born 1906 in USA. Actress. Won beauty contest in 1920 and in the same year made her film début in *Beggar's Maid*. Acted in radio and on the stage, and in such silent films as *Bright Shawl* (1923), *Beau Brummell* (1923), and *Don Juan* (1926), the first all-synchronized film. Main films: *Red Dust* (1932), *Midnight* (1939), one of the best comedies of that time. In 1941 she appeared in *The Maltese Falcon* with HUMPHREY BOGART and PETER LORRE and in 1944 in *Meet Me in St Louis*. More recently she appeared in *Act of Violence* and *Little Women* (1949) and *Return to Peyton Place* (1961), among other films. Cool and assured in both comedy and drama, she has a potent inner charm and likeable femininity.

Top: George Cole and Richard Attenborough in 'Morning Departure' (Roy Baker, GB, 1949)
Above: Kim Stanley and Richard Attenborough in 'Seance on a Wet Afternoon' (Bryan Forbes, GB, 1964)
Below: Jean-Claude Pascal and Anouk Aimée in 'Le Rideau Cramoisi' (Alexandre Astruc, France, 1952)

Astruc, Alexandre

Born 1923 in Paris, France. Director and writer. A student of law who became a journalist and film critic. His celebrated article on the *caméra-stylo* ('camera-pen') published in 'L'Écran Français' in 1948 claimed that the film should become a totally independent form of expression freed from the tyranny of the purely verbal concepts of the writer, created directly through the camera, its subtleties those of visual creativity. This concept was largely adopted by the new-wave directors who were about to start making feature films; they frequently improvised their work through the camera. Nevertheless, Astruc was himself a novelist and screenwriter as well as a director of short films (*Le Rideau Cramoisi*, 1952, which was stylish and without dialogue) before turning to features in the mid-1950s. His earlier films were visually beautiful and very polished – *Les Mauvaises Rencontres* (1955) and *La Proie pour l'Ombre* (1960), for example – and deal with the intimate problems of women. In spite of his theories, his films remain somewhat literary and old-fashioned in feeling, adapting Maupassant in *Une Vie* (1957) and Flaubert in *L'Éducation Sentimentale* (1961). Latterly he made the war films, *La Longue Marche* (1966), an unusual exposure of certain aspects of the French Revolution, and *Flammes sur L'Adriatique* (1968). RM

Attenborough, Richard

Born 1923 in Leicester, England. British actor, who made a notable début as a director with *Oh! What a Lovely War* (1969). After studying at the Royal Academy of Dramatic Art, he was chosen by NOEL COWARD to play a cowardly seaman in *In Which We Serve* (1942). The role bedevilled his early acting career; though his neurotic hoodlum in *Brighton Rock* (1947) was a typical attempt to step out of character. In 1959, with fellow actor-writer BRYAN FORBES he co-produced and starred in *The Angry Silence* (1959) in the teeth of industry foreboding. The film became a hit and helped establish a vogue for tougher, more realistic British movies and set an example of actor participation in production in Britain. Keenly devoted to the future of British films, he mustered a majestic star cast for *Oh! What a Lovely War*: an imaginative, critical, though not especially a box-office, success. Principal films as actor: *The Guinea Pig* (1949), *Private's Progress* (1955), *Dunkirk* (1958), *The Great Escape* (1963), *Séance on a Wet Afternoon* (1964), *Guns at Batasi* (1964), *The Sand Pebbles* (1966), *The Last Grenade* and *The Magic Christian* (1969), *David Copperfield*, *A Severed Head*, *Loot* and *10 Rillington Place* (1970). In 1972 he directed *Young Winston*. MH

Top: 'Eureka Stockade' (Harry Watt, GB, 1948)
Above: 'The Valley is Ours' (John Heyer, Australia, 1949)
Below: 'Desert People' (Ian Dunlop, Australian Commonwealth Film Unit, Australia, 1967)

Audry, Jacqueline

Born 1908 in Orange, France. Director. Worked in films from 1933, initially as assistant to PABST, DELANNOY, OPHULS, and others. In 1943 she directed the documentary *Les Chevaux des Vercors*. Her first feature was *Les Malheurs de Sophie* (1945). She favours themes of emotional crisis and even abnormal psychology. Among her best-known films are: *Gigi* (1949), *Olivia* (1951), *Huis Clos* (1954), *Les Petits Matins* (1962), *Soledad* (1966).

Aurenche, Jean

Born 1904 in France. Screenwriter. Works largely in association with Pierre Bost. Their highly professional scripts include those for such well-known films as CLAUDE AUTANT-LARA's *Le Diable au Corps* (1947), *Occupe-toi d'Amélie* (1949), *L'Auberge Rouge* (1951), and *Le Blé en Herbe* (1953), and RENÉ CLÉMENT's *Les Jeux Interdits* (1951) and *Le Gervais* (1955). They also scripted JEAN DELANNOY's *Dieu a Besoin des Hommes* (1949). Working on his own, Aurenche has scripted Autant-Lara's *Le Journal d'une Femme en Blanc* (1965).

Australia

Australia (population approximately 12 million) has developed only sporadic film production, and this largely as a result of the investment of foreign capital. In spite of television, Australians remain keen filmgoers and support some 1,100 theatres, including drive-ins. Notable films have been made by visiting film-makers in Australia on Australian subjects (for example, HARRY WATT's *The Overlanders*, 1946, and *Eureka Stockade*, 1948), and more recently the films directed by MICHAEL POWELL, *They're a Weird Mob* and *Age of Consent*, Philip Leacock's *Adam's Woman*, Ted Kotcheff's *Outback*, Nicolas Roeg's *Walkabout*, and TONY RICHARDSON's *Ned Kelly*, with Mick Jagger. Australian films of some note in the past are few and far between, but include Raymond Longford's *The Sentimental Bloke* (1920), Charles Chauvel's *40,000 Horsemen* (1940), Ken Hall's *Dad and Dave* series, and, post-war, John Heyer's award-winning documentaries, *The Valley is Ours* (1949) and *Back of Beyond* (1953).

Documentary production has its central core in the work of the Commonwealth Film Unit (founded as the National Film Board in 1945), a much smaller counterpart to the Canadian National Film Board. Making some 50 subjects a year, it was until 1970 under the leadership of Stanley Hawes, who had worked with JOHN GRIERSON. [See DOCUMENTARY]. Among the more notable Australian films made in recent years are:

- *Desert People* (Ian Dunlop): part of a 3-hour study of people in the Australian Western Desert
- *The Pudding Thieves* (Brian Davies): a Godard-like film about two street photographers in Melbourne
- *Two Thousand Weeks* (Tim Burstall): a Melbourne man, aged 30, with the possibility like his fellows, of 2,000 weeks to live
- *Cardin in Australia* (Peter Thompson): a witty record of the couturier's visit to Australia
- *Great Barrier Reef* (Kit Guyatt): marine life on the Reef
- *After Cook* (Don Murray): a study of Australia and Australians
- *After Proust* and *No Roses for Michael* (Christopher McGill and John Baxter): first short productions of a new company

There is also some activity in underground film-making and exhibition, and hopes have been raised by the establishment of a government grant towards the founding of a national film school and an experimental film fund.

Among Australian actors Chips Rafferty (1909–1971) created a likeable portrait of the tough, reliable frontiersman, first making his reputation in *The Overlanders* (1946). RM

Austria
See GERMANY

Autant-Lara, Claude
Born 1903 in Luzarches, Seine-et-Oise, France. Director. He first came to notice in the 1920s as an inventive, delicate designer on films by L'HERBIER, CAVALCANTI, and others. After several successful short films, he began directing features in the 1930s, but it was not until the war period that he revealed a distinctive style in such period love stories as *Le Mariage de Chiffon* (1942) and *Douce* (1943), and the charming ghost story *Sylvie et le Fantôme* (1945). His varied post-war work includes: *Le Diable au Corps* (1947), a passionate romantic drama from Radiguet's novel; *L'Auberge Rouge* (1951), a fiercely anti-clerical comedy; *Le Blé en Herbe* (1953) another sensitively realized love story. In recent years, he has alternated between elaborate historical extravaganzas and modern dramas, in which his technical skill prevails but which lack the delicacy and gentle humour of the earlier period pieces. Other films: *En Cas de Malheur* (1957), *Le Joueur* (1958), *Le Bois des Amants* (1960), *Tu ne tueras point* (1961), *Le Meurtrier* (1962). JG

Avant-Garde and Underground Film
No comprehensive definition can be given for either the avant-garde or underground film. It represents many aspects of film-making which lie outside the normal channels of commercial entertainment; it is nearer to the personal film, but includes alike the short film using experimental techniques, such as the films of NORMAN MCLAREN, which may well reach a very large public in the theatres or through television, and the type of underground film which represents in one way or another forms of protest (aesthetic, social, political, or sexual) which lead to banning or exclusion from the normal forms of public exhibition, and is therefore confined to the more or less private cine-clubs.

It must, of course, be recognized that much experiment takes place in main-stream film production, in VON STROHEIM's *Greed*, for example, in EISENSTEIN's *Strike* and *Potemkin*, or in the work of such seminal directors since 1950 as BERGMAN, RESNAIS OR FELLINI. But this work is not properly avant-garde, as the term has come to be applied to the film; in film the avant-garde is essentially peripheral to main-stream cinema, a more private kind of work – the film poem, the film essay, the off-beat animated cartoon, or the highly individual work of directors such as BUÑUEL during his early career in France, VIGO, and, much later, in the USA, John and James Whitney, MAYA DEREN, KENNETH ANGER, STAN BRAKHAGE OF ANDY WARHOL.

For convenience, we divide the main output of the avant-garde into the following sections: the European avant-garde mainly of the 1920s; the American experimental film of the 1930s and 1940s; the American underground film from the late 1940s to the present day; and the international underground from the 1950s to the present day.

The Avant-Garde in Europe: the first Phase
The term avant-garde was first applied to the work mainly of European film-makers during the 1920s. The centre for such experiment was France, which had produced the first truly imaginative experiments in the commercial cinema of MÉLIÈS and FEUILLADE, though some work of this kind was also undertaken in Germany and elsewhere. Many of the films which masqueraded as experimental were merely exhibitionist, and as such artistically spurious, like much so-called underground work of the 1960s. It is necessary to distinguish between films which in one way or another, and in varying degree, advance or expand the medium in the enriched presentation of any kind of subject, and those which merely use it (more or less inadequately) to exploit hitherto 'forbidden' subjects, such as intimate scenes of copulation, or for social or political challenge which is merely an act of self-indulgence, however genuine in feeling.

In France during the 1920s many film-makers worked close to artists experimenting in advanced work in painting, theatre or literature. This was the period of the theatre of the 'absurd', of 'cruelty', the period of outstanding expression in abstract art, of dada, and the

Above: Eve Francis in 'La Femme de Nulle Part' (Louis Delluc, France, 1922)
Below: Two stills from 'Entr'acte' (René Clair, France, 1924)

period during which a more profound understanding of psychoanalysis by certain artists stretched the boundaries of art into new fields of surrealistic discovery. It was in this atmosphere that the principal work of the French avant-garde film was created. It was both preceded and paralleled in the early 1920s by informed and imaginative writing by film-makers and critics such as CLAIR, DELLUC, Desnos, Moussinac, Canudo and others, who drew attention to the potentialities of the film as an imagistic medium which possessed innate powers for creating illusions barely yet discovered, but either latent or present in embryo in the work of such accepted film-makers as GRIFFITH, FEUILLADE, GANCE, SENNETT and CHAPLIN. The foundation in France of the influential cine-clubs ('Club des Amis du Septième Art', 'Ciné-club de France', 'Tribune Libre du Cinéma', 'Ursulines', 'Studio 28', 'Agriculteurs', etc) for showing advanced work from any source, together with lectures on film at the Théâtre du Vieux Colombier, further encouraged production, and even supplied a small financial return. The equally influential Film Society was formed in 1925 in London to show advanced forms of film-making.

The main faults of the avant-garde soon became apparent – exhibitionist camerawork exploiting meaningless angles or movements (such as rapid rotations), great play with distortion, superimposition: soft focus paralleled soft-mindedness in the development of story, situation, or subject, as, for example, in MARCEL L'HERBIER's film, *L'Inhumaine* (1923), the study of a love affair between an aged woman and a young man, with sets by Fernand Léger and ALBERTO CAVALCANTI, who also designed L'Herbier's later, much better film, *Feu Mathias Pascal* (1925), adapted from Pirandello. On the borderline between the truly experimental and more conventional forms of film-making with varying degrees of poetic, atmospheric treatment are the films of DELLUC (*Fièvre*, 1921; *La Femme de Nulle Part*, 1922; *L'Inondation*, 1924), the earlier films of GERMAINE DULAC, such as *La Fête Espagnol* (made from a script by Delluc, 1919) and *La Souriante Madame Beudet* (1922), a psychological study of a housewife, CLAUDE AUTANT-LARA's *Fait-Divers* (1924), RENOIR's *Charleston* (1926) and *La Petite Marchande d'Allumettes* (1927), and Cavalcanti's *La P'tite Lili* (1928), which followed his work in design and documentary.

The French avant-garde was to strengthen as it developed. The artists Fernand Léger, Marcel Duchamp, and Man Ray (painter and photographer) all made short films as an extension of their art. Duchamp, pioneer of kinetic art, made the mobile abstract film *Anaemic Cinéma* (1927), and looked forward to the third dimension in the film.

Having fun with the non-rational, the wholly illogical, the absurd, using, of course, the tricks of the camera, reflected the attitude of CLAIR in his delightful burlesque fantasy, *Entr'acte* (1924), made as an interlude for the Swedish Ballet, and of Léger's *Le Ballet Mécanique* (made with the American, Dudley Murphy, 1924–5), in which, like a comic nightmare, a fat woman is forced by the camera to climb and reclimb the same stairs; the interchange in this film of negative and positive images was included merely for the sake of photographic tone and atmosphere. The search was on for a *cinéma pur*, and the influence in Clair's early work was a desire to 'purify' Sennett's gags and produce a kind of lyrical, even surrealist choreography in his fantasies *Paris qui Dort* (1923), *Le Fantôme du Moulin Rouge* (1924) and *Le Voyage Imaginaire* (1925). Writing of film and surrealism in 1925, Clair said: 'Even if the cinema cannot be a perfect medium of expression for surrealism, it remains, in the spectator's mind, an incomparable field for surrealistic activity.' As for

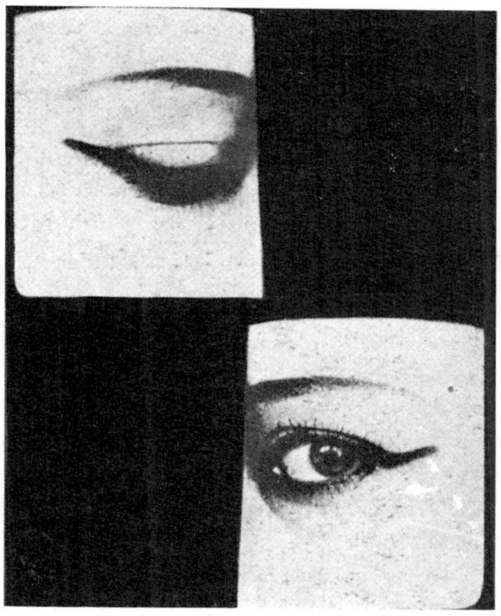

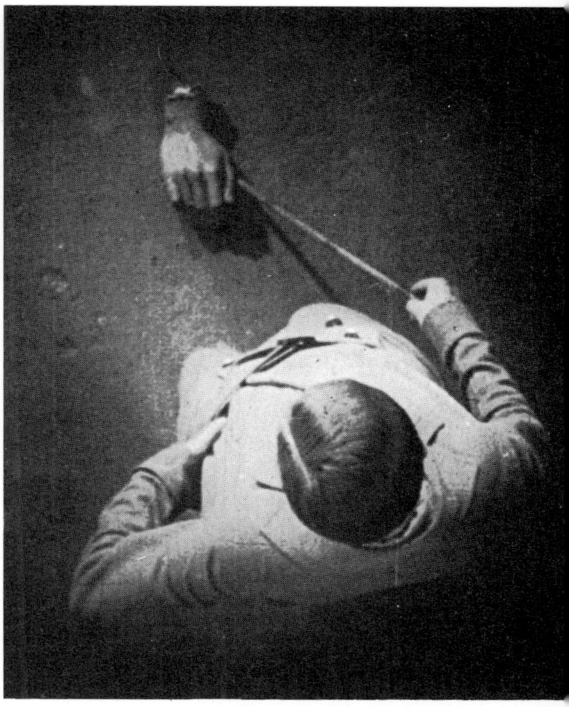

Above left: 'Le Ballet Mécanique' (Fernand Léger, France, 1924–5)
Above right: 'Un Chien Andalou' (Luis Buñuel, France, 1928)
Below: Two stills from 'The Seashell and the Clergyman' (Germaine Dulac, France, 1926)

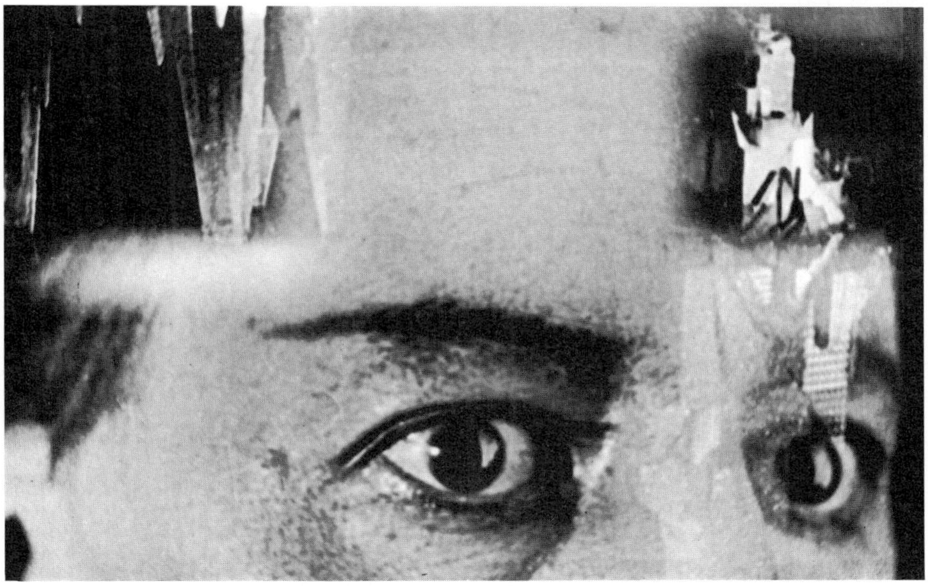

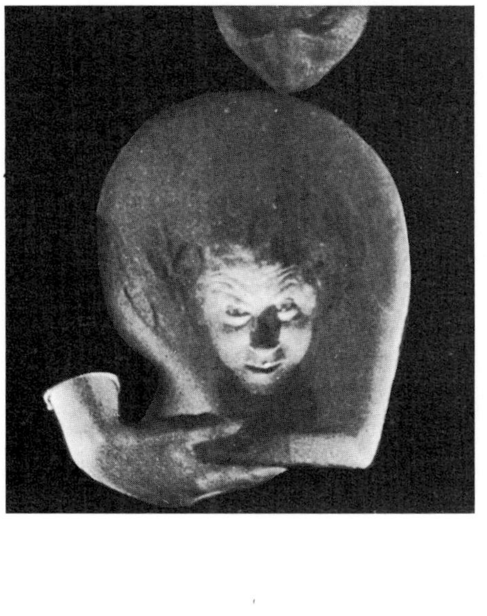

cinéma pur, Clair's brother, Henri Chomette, made *Jeux des Reflets et de la Vitesse* (1925) and *Cinq Minutes du Cinéma Pur* (1926), a montage of rhythmic patterns resulting from the play of light on moving crystals. Man Ray made *Le Retour à la Raison* (1923), using ray-o-gram images combined with natural shots assembled inconsequentially to challenge 'reason'; *Emak Bakia* (1926) – the title is Basque for *Leave me Alone* – a film of light patterns from rotating objects; and later films which projected human and dramatic situations in semi-surrealistic terms, *L'Étoile de Mer* (1928) and *Les Mystères du Château de Dés* (1929), improvised at the château of the Comte de Noailles, who was later to sponsor BUÑUEL's *L'Age d'Or* and COCTEAU's *Le Sang d'un Poète*. The cinema of abstract pattern was created by JEAN EPSTEIN in *Photogénic* (1925), in the Dutchman JORIS IVENS's films made in Hollywood – such as *Rain* (1929) – in Eugene Deslaw's *Marche des Machines* (1928) and *La Nuit Electrique* (1930) and in GERMAINE DULAC's later films *Disque 927* and *Rhythme et Variations* (1930).

Surrealism entered the French cinema on various levels – the deliberately inconsequent work of Duchamp and Léger, the burlesque of Clair, the heavily Freudian imagery in Germaine Dulac's compellingly visual *The Seashell and the Clergyman* (1926), scripted by Antonin Artaud, and possibly anti-surrealist because of its highly conscious use of textbook symbolism in its study of the sexual frustrations of a celibate priest. The strong eidetic possibilities of the cinema – its powerful hallucinatory nature – came to the fore in the most celebrated surrealist work of the period, the Spanish director LUIS BUÑUEL's *Un Chien Andalou* (made with Salvador Dali, 1928), a violent, obsessive film born of anarchic revolt against the traditional frustrations with which society encrusts mankind's sexual needs, both conscious and unconscious. Buñuel followed this with his sound film, *L'Age d'Or* (1930), a further, passionately-felt protest against sexual frustrations especially those imposed by the Catholic Church. Both these films were austerely made from the technical point of view, their cruel, penetrating images undefiled by cinema tricks. They were so disturbing as to be totally banned in their period.

The only true successor to *L'Age d'Or* was JEAN VIGO's *Zéro de Conduite* (1933), its painful and macabre quality tempered by its moments of humour, and even charm. Cocteau's *Le Sang d'un Poète* (1930) was a polished, self-conscious work (wonderfully photographed by GEORGES PÉRINAL) returning to the tricks of the camera rather than to anything like the deeply-felt experiences of Buñuel and Vigo. In effect, this saw the end of the French avant-garde, whose makers had either found the sound film too expensive, or had, like Renoir, Carné, Clair or JACQUES PRÉVERT, for example, found increasing possibilities in the commercial cinema or, like Buñuel, Cavalcanti, Ivens, and such promising factual film-makers as the Belgian HENRI STORCK, turned to the experimental branches of the documentary film or animation. (See ANIMATION; DOCUMENTARY.)

The avant-garde in Germany was on an altogether smaller scale, and less of a conscious movement than in France. The earliest work was in abstract film, which began as a form of animation, with designs painted or inked direct onto the celluloid reel by HANS RICHTER and Viking Eggeling, starting as early as 1919, but shown much later. Abstract design was developed more demonstratively by RUTTMANN in his series of *Opera* (1923–5). Ruttmann was later to make, with a team of expert cameramen, *Berlin – Rhythm of a City* (1927), the first of the many city symphonies, with music by Edmund Meisel which was played 'live' with the film. Richter moved in the direction of surrealism with his brief *Filmstudy* (1926) and *Vormittagsspuk* (*Ghosts before Breakfast*, 1928), which had a score by Hindemith, again played 'live'. Meanwhile in the field of animation LOTTE REINIGER had started her prolonged work on the silhouette film. (See ANIMATION.)

With the coming of sound, Ruttmann began his experiments with sound-film the moment it became available to him, with *Tönende Welle* and *Melody of the World* (1929), on which his pupil and successor in abstract film-making, OSKAR FISCHINGER, worked. Fischinger, who worked in Germany until 1935 and finally settled in the United States, made a succession of abstract pattern-films set to recordings of established music which properly belong to animation. The avant-garde in Germany also found expression in the work of the painter, ERNO METZNER, whose silent short film, *Accident* (*Überfall*, 1929) used distorting lenses and montage in the Russian style to reconstruct the experiences under anaesthetic of the victim of an assault by a thief.

In Britain, avant-garde film-making was on an even smaller scale. Nearest was the work of Kenneth MacPherson, editor of the well-known magazine on film art, 'Close-Up', who made psychoanalytic-styled films, in particular *Foot-*

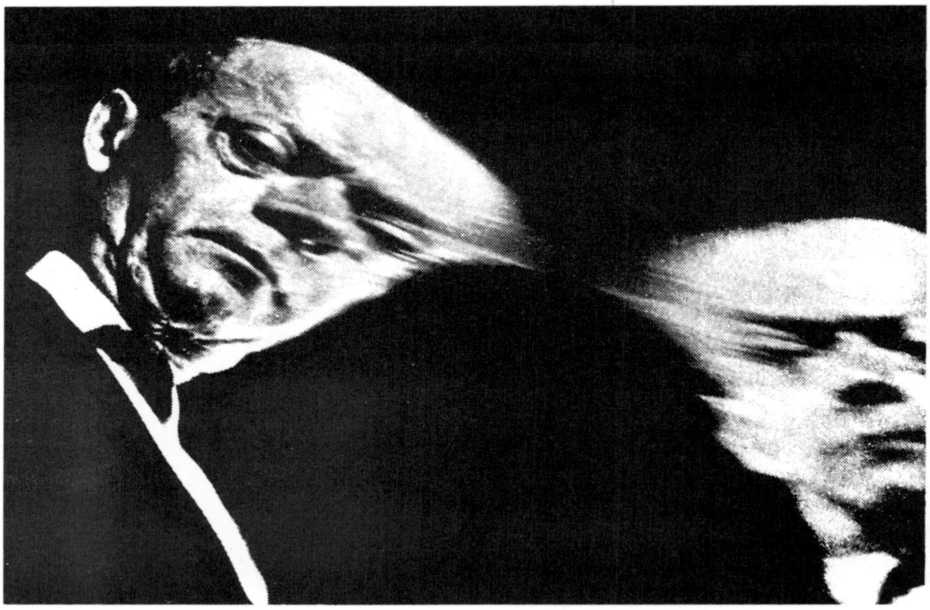

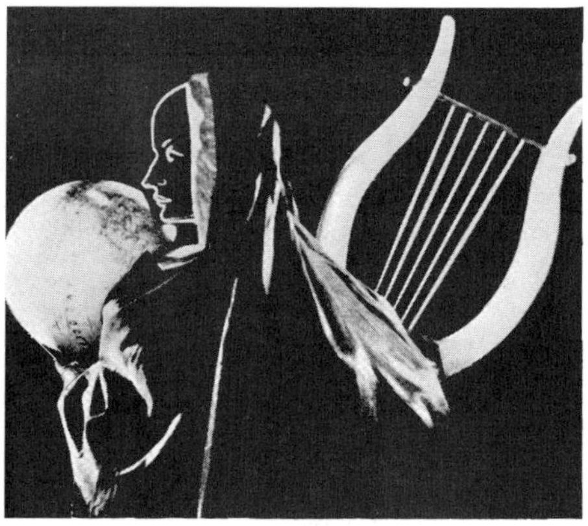

Above: 'Accident' ('Uberfall', Erno Metzner, Germany, 1929)
Below left: 'Zérode Conduite' (Jean Vigo, France, 1933)
Below right: 'Le Sang d'un Poète' (Jean Cocteau, France, 1930)

Opposite: Shima Iwashita in 'An Autumn Afternoon' (Yasujiro Ozu, Japan, 1962)
Overleaf above: Mickey Mouse in 'Fantasia' (Walt Disney, USA, 1940)
Below: Boxer and Benjamin in 'Animal Farm' (Halas and Batchelor, GB, 1954)

THEATRE
press pass

hills (1929) and *Borderline* (1931), which featured PAUL ROBESON. Using the play of light on moving cardboard cut-outs, the Belgian Francis Brugière made the abstract film *Light Rhythms* (1931) with Oswell Blakeston. Ivor Montagu at the close of the silent period made three short comedies with simplified, stylized sets featuring CHARLES LAUGHTON and ELSA LANCHESTER, of which the best was *Bluebottles*. But experiment in Britain was to be largely associated with the documentary movement during the 1930s more especially in such rare films as Benjamin Britten's film-oratorio, *Coalface* (1935), made from stock shots of mining by Britten, W. H. Auden, and the painter, William Coldstream; impressions of the mining scene combined with statistics were conveyed either chorally or in recitative. The New Zealander, LEN LYE, took up the technique of painting direct onto the celluloid reel where Richter and Eggeling had left off, working first in Australia and later in Britain, where his first film, *Tusalava* (1928), involved normally photographed animation. His subsequent work in both Britain and the USA belongs primarily to experimental animation.

Above: 'A Hollywood Extra' (Robert Florey and Slavko Vorkapich, USA, 1928)
Below: 'H_2O' (Ralph Steiner, USA, 1929)
Bottom: 'Lot in Sodom' (J. S. Watson and Melville Webber, USA, 1934)

The American Experimental Film of the 1930s and 1940s

American experimental film-making was to develop mainly during the 1930s, but a not inconsiderable number of avant-garde films were made during the silent period, which in this branch of production lasted some years longer than was the case with the commercial film. *Mannahatta* (Charles Sheeler and Paul Strand, 1924) was an impressionistic short about New York seen in terms of its geometric architecture and the movement patterns of ships, people and so forth, while ROBERT FLAHERTY's *24 Dollar Island* (1925) was, according to Flaherty, a 'camera-poem . . . of skyscrapers', using telephoto lenses. German expressionism influenced ROBERT FLOREY's and Slavko Vorkapich's *Life and Death of 9413 – A Hollywood Extra* (1928), shot for them by GREGG TOLAND; this was a satirical fantasy on the typing of players in Hollywood made largely out of boxes, cans and cardboard cut-outs on which a single strong light was played. Florey also made other films in a similar style, notably *The Loves of Zero* (1929), on the mechanization of industrialized mankind. Also made under the influence of German expressionism was PAUL FEJÖS's feature-length *The Last Moment* (1927), in which the kaleidoscope of a man's life passes through his mind at the moment he is being executed. Shot by LEON SHAMROY, it was by far the most elaborate of America's experimental films of the 1920s, using every camera device, including multiple exposure and split-screen.

Other short films turned to Poe in order to experiment in the macabre – Charles Klein's *The Tell-Tale Heart* (1928) and James Sibley Watson and Melville Webber's *The Fall of the House of Usher* (1928). Ralph Steiner, the photographer, turned to film for other reasons – to use the devices of the camera to look at natural movements with a fresh vision, as in the play of light on water in *H_2O* (1929) and movement in nature in *Surf and Seaweed* (1931). LEWIS JACOBS made *Mobile Composition* (1930) with Joe Gerson acting and Hershell Lewis as assistant cameraman. This was a study of a developing love affair in terms of significant psychological detail. Another attempt at subjectivity by Gerson and Lewis was *The Story of a Nobody* (1930), which used an elaborate sonata form and equally elaborate camerawork.

The influence of German and French avant-garde films was to be replaced by that of Russian realism: camera-tricks became unfashionable. CHARLES VIDOR's *The Spy* (1932), as Lewis Jacobs has pointed out, used a 'flash-forward' technique, showing the wish-fulfilment for escape of a man about to be shot, but ending

Overleaf above: 'Gorilla's Dance' (screenplay by Dušan Vukotić, direction by Milan Blažeković, Yugoslavia, 1969) Below: 'The Wall' (Carmen d'Avino, USA, 1970)
Opposite: 'Yellow Submarine' (George Dunning, GB, 1968)

with his actual death. The new realism took many forms – the impressionistic study of cities in such films as Herman Weinberg's *Autumn Fire*, Jay Leyda's *Bronx Morning*, Jo Berne's *Dawn to Dawn* and LEWIS JACOBS's *Footnotes to Fact*. John Flory and Theodore Huff made *Mr Motorboat's Last Stand* (1933), a satiric film on the successive poverty and wealth of a Negro, while the name of ELIA KAZAN occurs, along with IRVING LERNER and Ralph Steiner, as associated in the making of *Pie in the Sky* (1934), an improvisation based on the odds and ends found in a rubbish dump, with the ironic message that however bad things become during the Depression, all will be well in heaven. Lewis Jacobs satirized Hollywood's exaggerations in a *mélange* of trailers in *Commercial Medley*, and with Joseph Schillinger made *Synchronization*, with drawings by MARY ELLEN BUTE illustrating the principles of rhythm in motion. In *Olivera Street*, Mike Seibert showed the violent aftermath to love-making between two Spanish street vendors.

The avant-garde tended, partly for economic, partly for aesthetic reasons, to approach sound cautiously. The best early sound film of this kind was Watson and Webber's *Lot in Sodom* (1934), which visualized the destruction of the Biblical city in terms of its widespread homosexuality, presented symbolically, with music by Louis Siegel.

Mary Ellen Bute and Ted Nemeth, as camera operator, developed the experimental sound film in abstract 'visual symphonies' set to music, sometimes subtly developing the dual compositions in sight and sound in counterpoint, taking the techniques of Fischinger further than he had done. They worked eventually in tonal depths and colour as well as in black and white, and used three-dimensional shapes and objects filmed with elaborate camera-devices, including prisms, distorting mirrors and long-focus lenses, and the interplay of light and movement based on exact mathematical calculation. Their films include *Rhythm in Light* and *Synchrony No 2* (1936) and *Tarantella* (1941). Other makers of abstract films include Douglas Crockwell in *Fantasmagoria I* (1938) and his film of 'plastic landscapes', as Sheldon Renan describes it, *Glen Falls Sequence* (1946), elaborate mobile paintings using stop-motion photography to record the flow of paints on varying levels of glass. CHARLES EAMES, the architect, made the striking *Blacktop* (1950), recording the strong patterns made as water spreads over an asphalt playground.

Experiment along more familiar lines continued. Fischinger, living in the USA from 1935, continued his work in abstract mobile designs set to music. John and James Whitney however evolved their own special techniques, described as follows by Lewis Jacobs: 'First they compose a thematic design in a black and white sketch. Then by virtue of an optical printer, pantograph and colour filters, they develop the sketch to cinematic proportions in movement and colour. Multiple exposures, magnifications, reduction and inversion enable them to achieve an infinite variety of compositions in time and space. Their sound is entirely synthetic – tone produced by the recorded oscillations of an optical wedge activated by pendulums of varying length connected to the wedge by steel wires. They call their films 'exercises'. Such films as these, like those of Douglas Crockwell, bridge the gap between animation and various contemporary forms of 'kinetic' film-making.

Above: Maya Deren in 'At Land' (Deren, USA, 1944)
Below: Marcel Duchamp in his own sequence from 'Dreams that Money can Buy' (Hans Richter, USA, 1944-7)

Working with the documentary film-maker, Alexander Hammid, MAYA DEREN made *Meshes of the Afternoon* (1943), a short film in which a girl (Maya Deren) dreams her own suicide, which becomes reality at the end of the film; this was followed by the highly symbolistic *At Land* (1944), in which real time and space are displaced to create new relationships between people and events, relating the principal character (played by Maya Deren) to 'a fluid, apparently incoherent, universe'. Maya Deren's next significant film, *Ritual in Transfigured Time* (1946), used cine-choreography in film space and time to represent 'a critical metamorphosis . . . of a widow into a bride'. Another expressionist in cine-choreography was Sara Arledge in her incomplete work, *Introspection* (1947), using distorting lenses to film dancers, parts of whose moving bodies were obscured.

Slavko Vorkapich, who worked in Hollywood on montages for feature films, made in his own right *Forest Murmurs* and *Fingal's Cave*, impressionistic films of nature, and on similar lines Paul Burnford made the beautiful *Storm Warning*, with music by David Raksin. This is the cinema of natural observation, developed in other connections by LEWIS JACOBS in *Tree Trunk to Head*, a study of Chaim Gross, the sculptor, at work, and *Sunday Beach*, an exercise in concealed-camera, 'candid' photography.

HANS RICHTER, who left Germany for the USA in 1940, produced there *Dreams that Money Can Buy* (1944–7), a feature-length surrealistic film made in colour with the combined talents of Max Ernst, Fernand Léger, Marcel Duchamp, Man Ray and Alexander Calder, each of whom was responsible for episodes in the film. James Broughton, working in San Francisco, made the satiric *Mother's Day* (1948), in which adults behave as if they were children; Broughton became a highly individual film-maker who was later to work in Britain. Joseph Vogel, a painter, made *House of Cards* and *All the News* (both 1947), which were psychological films; in *House of Cards*, lithographs were combined with live action. Ian Hugo made semi-abstract films of great visual beauty and technical skill in colour, *Ai-Ye* (1950), and, with his wife Anais Nin, *Bells of Atlantis* (1952), in which he was assisted by LEN LYE, and which had for its subject the city sunk in the ocean.

We approach the threshold of the American underground film with KENNETH ANGER's first notable film, *Fireworks* (1947), an uninhibited study of a homosexual's hallucinations of sadistic persecution by a group of homosexual sailors. The symbols used are powerful and unconcealed, and present a subject which at the time the film was made was a strictly forbidden one on the screen. It started a vogue for films which also dealt with the problems of the homosexual, such as CURTIS HARRINGTON's *Fragment of Seeking* (1946), in which an adolescent homosexual experiences direct revulsion in the arms of a girl; SIDNEY PETERSON's and James Broughton's *The Potted Psalm*, a visually striking but entirely incoherent film, of which the makers said that observation was replaced by intuition; and GREGORY MARKOPOULOS's *Psyche* (1947–8), *Lysis* and *Charmides* (1948). RM LJ

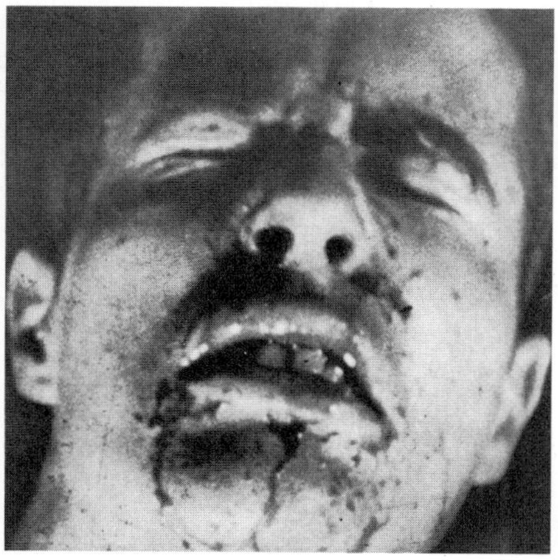

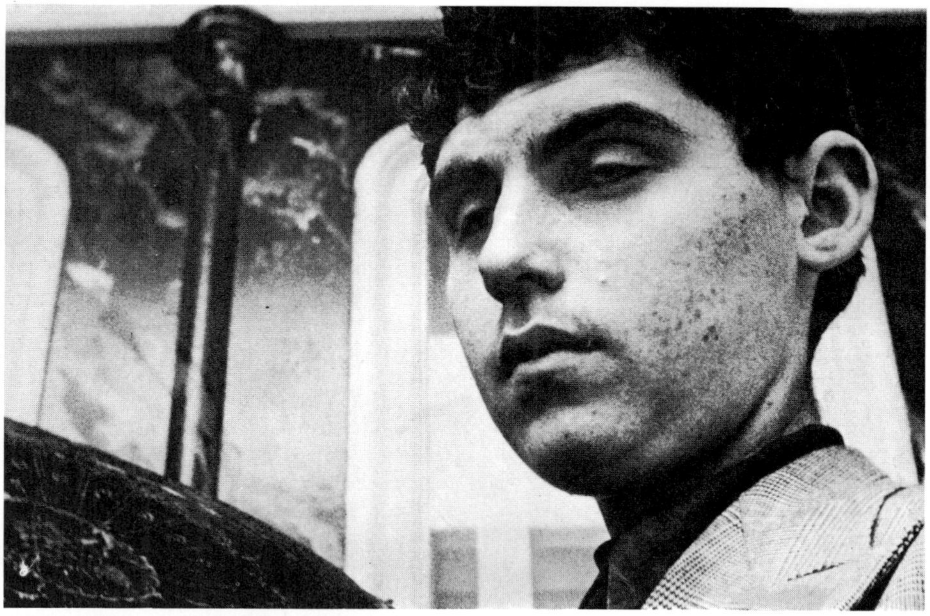

Above left: 'Fireworks' (Kenneth Anger, USA, 1947)
Above right: 'The Potted Psalm' (Sidney Peterson and James Broughton, USA, 1947)
Below: 'House of Cards' (Joe Vogel, USA, 1947)

The American Underground Film from the late-1940s to the present day

The widespread film-making activity on the West Coast declined during the 1950s. SIDNEY PETERSON and James Broughton, two of the 'senior' figures in San Francisco, both abandoned films in the early 1950s. Peterson retired after completing his most interesting work, *The Lead Shoes* (1949), a distorted-lens film in which a mother seeks to communicate with her son, dead inside a diving suit, and presented some of his equipment to the young STAN BRAKHAGE, who began his own films in 1953; Broughton made his 'last' film in Britain, a comic fantasy called *The Pleasure Garden* (1953), though he has since broken his retirement to make *The Bed* (1967), a typically warm and humorous short in which Pan conjures every variant of human sexuality on a bed in the open countryside. In addition Frank Stauffacher died in 1955; himself the director of such poetic

Peter H. Beard and Marty Greenbaum in 'Hallelujah the Hills' (Adolfas Mekas, USA, 1963)

documentaries as *Notes on the Port of St Francis* (1952), between 1947 and his death he had organized seminal 'Art in Cinema' exhibitions on the West Coast.

Also at this time, the three most important young Los Angeles film-makers, ANGER, MARKOPOULOS and CURTIS HARRINGTON, left America for Europe. Frustrated and relatively unrecognized at home, they were attracted by the person of JEAN COCTEAU and encouraged by the unique position he occupied in French culture; but they found their situation equally difficult in France (although Anger did succeed in realizing a version of Cocteau's ballet, *Le Jeune Homme et la Mort* in 1953, now unshowable for copyright reasons) and have since followed erratic paths. Harrington returned to America, and after completing *The Wormwood Star* (1955), in which an alchemist is herself transmuted into gold, renounced the underground film as being 'too much in love with its own pretty effects, too introverted and too lazy', in favour of the commercial film industry, with such films as *Night Tide* (1961) and *Games* (1967). Markopoulos has travelled extensively, making films wherever circumstances permitted, and now works from a base in Zürich. Anger returned to America in 1954 to make his mythological fantasy *Inauguration of the Pleasure Dome* (definitively edited 1966) and again in 1963 to make *Scorpio Rising*, but he is an essentially restless figure, recently based in Britain.

The sporadic film-making that continued on the West Coast during the 1950s consisted mainly of animated and abstract work. Inspired by the RICHTER and FISCHINGER films he had seen at the 'Art in Cinema' programmes, Jordan Belson began his own films in 1947. Alternation of his film work with painting, Belson's interests (manifest in such films as *Bop Scotch*, 1953, using stop-motion animation of objects) led him to work on the *Vortex Concerts* founded by the composer Henry Jacobs: pioneering attempts to use programmed film and light to create a total environment, they were held from 1957 to 1959 in the Morrison Planetarium in San Francisco. Belson's work since 1960 has centred on continuous light-manipulation in film rather than animation; he withholds his films from distribution because he prefers to control the environment in which they are screened. Harry Smith began making 'batiked abstractions' in the early 1940s and gradually evolved complicated projection systems for his films, whose screenings he too likes to control. From the mid-1950s his work has chiefly been animated collage, anticipating in style and method the much-acclaimed work of the Europeans BOROWCZYK and LENICA. His major work, *No 12* (also known as *Heaven and Earth Magic*, 1943/58), explores a world whose 'deity' and motive force is a drug which infuses all the elements in the film: taking his materials from 19th-century trade catalogues, Smith's witty animation created an invented 'cycle of nature'. Of the numerous small animated films that continued to be made, the best-known are those of Francis Lee; in *Le Bijou* (1947), he animated jewelry.

Marie Menken and her husband Willard Maas made their first film, *Geography of the Body*, in New York in 1943: a series of extreme close-ups of parts of the human body with a related commentary by the poet George Barker. This venture led to the formation of the Gryphon Group, which was the first manifestation of the underground as it is known today and which has included, at various times, NORMAN MCLAREN, Ben Moore, STAN BRAKHAGE and GREGORY MARKOPOULOS. Maas and Moore made several films that were not major achievements in their own right, but which were seminal to the New York film-making explosion of the turn of the decade: *Image in the Snow* (1948), a painful psychodrama of an alienated homosexual seeking his mother's grave, and *Mechanics of Love* (1955), which demonstrated sexual intercourse in a stream of Freudian symbols, were prominent amongst these. Marie Menken made a series of films on her own (*Visual Variations on Noguchi*, 1945; *Hurry, Hurry*, 1957; *Dwightiana*, 1959): frequently playful animations dominated by phallic motifs, they established her as a key film-maker of the movement. She has since worked in various styles (diary-film, portrait-film, and time-lapse photography) and is now equally well known in the underground as an actress, having played in ANDY WARHOL films amongst others.

A new and more poetic group of city symphonies were made during the 1950s. After making several dance films, SHIRLEY CLARKE made *Bridges-go-Round* (1959), in which New York's bridges are conjured into motion through the use of superimposition and a continuously mobile camera. Francis Thompson made the classic of the genre with his *N.Y., N.Y.* (1958), in which distorting lenses turn the city's skyscrapers into a kaleidoscopic series of plastic compositions.

At the time they were made, the only outlet for many of these films was Amos Vogel's 'Cinema 16' organization. However, in 1955, JONAS MEKAS and his brother ADOLFAS founded the magazine 'Film Culture', which has – after an early hesitancy – championed the underground and set it in the aesthetic context of figures like VERTOV, EISENSTEIN and VON STROHEIM. In 1962 Mekas founded the New York Film-makers Co-operative, the first attempt to bring together the by-then widespread independent film-makers in America. Besides distributing films, the New York Co-operative also arranged its own regular screenings. These undoubtedly inspired many people to make their own films, while the regular audience they ensured for the films marked a turning point in the development of the underground.

Many of the key figures in the underground's sudden rise to prominence were apparent from the start. JACK SMITH appeared in Ken Jacobs' films (*Little Stabs at Happiness*, 1958–61; *Blonde Cobra*, 1959–62), and subsequently extended the dime-store-myth qualities of these films in his own work, including the classic *Flaming Creatures* (1963). RON RICE was associated with the same group, and made *Chumlum* (1964), a colour 'Arabian Nights vision of a palace brothel' employing multiple superimposition and elaborate costuming and settings, with Smith and members of his entourage. Rice's other remarkable films were *The Flower Thief* (1960), inspired by the poet Taylor Mead, who also plays the leading character; *Senseless* (1962), about a beat community in Mexico and employing a 'stream-of-consciousness' technique; and the unfinished feature *The Queen of Sheba Meets the Atom Man* (begun 1963), which was interrupted by his premature death in 1964. STAN BRAKHAGE began making psychodramas in the vein of ANGER's *Fireworks* in 1953 (*The Way to Shadow Garden*, 1955, for example), but his interest quickly shifted to the proposition that the camera's eye is equivalent to an ideal viewer's eye, and his films correspondingly moved from 'telling' to 'seeing'. His mature work (*Dog Star Man*, 1959–64; *The Art of Vision*, 1965; or *Lovemaking*, 1969, amongst numerous others) synthesizes the domestic and everyday with the universal, and to enrich the vision of his films he has used every technical device available to him in treating the filmed image. The leading New York animator and technical experimenter is STAN VANDERBEEK (a member of the original Black Mountain group), who has constructed a 'Movie-drome' at his home outside New York for complex multiple-projection of his work. His films have been mainly collages, at once satirical, political and slapstick (*Skullduggery*, 1960–1; *A Damn Rib Bed*, 1964–5), and in them he has developed his search for an 'international picture-language'. He has also experimented with distorting lenses (*Spherical Space*, 1967), computer-programmed films (various *Poemfields*), and with videotape (*Panels for the Walls of the World*, 1965). At the other extreme, Mike and George Kuchar started making 8 mm 'home movies' with their friends in the Bronx in the early 1950s; with titles like *Screwball* (1957) and *Pussy on a Hot Tin Roof* (1961) they studiously imitated television soap operas and Hollywood excesses, creating a unique genre of films that blended cut-price fantasy and abortive sex with a genuine humanity and an affection for their characters. Now working in 16 mm, they make films independently, but remain true to their themes and style.

On the West Coast, the equivalent to JONAS MEKAS's organization job was carried out by BRUCE BAILLIE, who founded the Canyon Cinema Co-operative. Baillie's own films synthesize the spirit of West Coast film-making: a kind of picaresque humanism, with a good deal of humour. His major works are the ambitious *Quixote* (1964–5), which attempts to present a cross-section of America's social, political and cultural life in a symbolic journey across the continent; and *Mass for the Dakota Sioux* (1963–4), which movingly places quotations from Sioux chieftains in the context of the sick society that killed them. Baillie has pioneered a style of mixing images within the camera (by blocking off parts of the frame), which is at its best in his poetic portrait, *Castro Street* (1966). Robert Nelson concerns himself with the glossy surface of American life, returning constantly to consumer-images of sex and violence, to television commercials, and to images of city life. *The Great Blondino* (1966–7) is an 'odyssey' through American life in the manner of Baillie's *Quixote*, in which he uses the famous tightrope-walker as a Keaton-like figure. In other films Nelson has satirized American television quiz programmes (*Bleu Shut*, 1965), the myth of Negro sexuality (*Oh, Dem Watermelons*, 1965), and the clichés of the war film (*War is Hell*, 1966). Many of his films are made in collaboration with the painter William Wiley. In a similar vein, Bruce Conner also makes collages of 'found' material: his first film *A Movie* (1958) consists entirely of stock footage of natural and man-made disasters, arranged into a sometimes cosmic, sometimes terrifying narrative of destruction and hopeful rebirth. His equally celebrated *Cosmic Ray* (1961) superimposes fast-motion footage of a nude girl dancing over an explosive wealth of material, creating the effect of a continuously orgasmic flow. In *Report* (1963), he uses similar techniques to a more sombre end, creating a 'documentary' about the first Kennedy assassination. Among the more prominent newcomers to West Coast film-making is Will Hindle: *Billabong* (1968), about a boys' reformatory, and *Chinese Firedrill* (1969), about a young man's confusion and struggle for identity, are both technically accomplished and sufficiently rich in invention to make a basically very personal experience accessible. His next film, *Watersmith*, was made in 1970.

Above: 'Pull My Daisy' (Robert Frank and Alfred Leslie, USA, 1959)
Below: 'The Quiet One' (Sidney Meyers, USA, 1948)

Parallel with this activity is a series of what might be called semi-underground films: usually feature length, made with minimal crews and outside the usual commercial systems of production and exhibition. Like many of the underground films these have frequently focused on the more deprived areas of American society. Sidney Meyers (*The Quiet One*, 1948) and MORRIS ENGEL (*The Little Fugitive*, 1953; *Weddings and Babies*, 1958) pioneered the genre, and it was quickly taken up by LIONEL ROGOSIN in his *On the Bowery* (1954) which staged a simple narrative about alcoholic derelicts with characters cast from life. Alfred Leslie and Robert Frank made *Pull My Daisy* (1959) from a play by the beat writer Jack Kerouac, with rehearsed 'freewheeling' effects used to create a sense of spontaneity. Frank later made the drama *The Sin of Jesus* (1961) in the same manner. In *Shadows* (1958/9), JOHN CASSAVETES used professional lead actors alongside numerous amateurs, and though the result was carefully edited, the majority of the scenes were freely improvized. SHIRLEY CLARKE abandoned her dance and pattern films in favour of *The Connection* (1960), a version of Jack Gelber's play rethought in cinematic rather than theatrical terms. She followed this with *The Cool World* (1963), a study of the underprivileged inhabitants of New York's Harlem district, and *Portrait of Jason* (1967), a two-hour monologue, edited down from a continuous 14-hour session with a black male prostitute. *Echoes of Silence* (1962–5), Peter Goldman's feature film about loneliness in New York and the city's oppressiveness, was clearly autobiographical. More recently, similar films have been made by Sheldon Rochlin: *Dope* (1969) follows the activities of people in a London commune using various hard and soft drugs; *Vali* (1965), shot in France, explores the character of a young witch. Rochlin has also made a video-tape film of the final performance (in Berlin) of the Living Theatre's production *Paradise Now* (1969), itself an experiment in audience involvement. Robert Downey made satirical comedies like *Chafed Elbows* (1967), whose style and humour attest the influence of the more progressive American television comedy shows. Norman Mailer, the novelist, has recently begun making films as well. His *Beyond the Law* (1969–70) presents an evening in a New York police station which suggests a similarity between the behavioural codes of police and criminals; in *Maidstone* (1970), Mailer himself plays a director of sex films who runs for presidency of the USA. However, the single most important film-maker in this group is ANDY WARHOL, the pop painter: in his films he strives to suppress any but the most elementary directorial control and allows his characters complete autonomy.

During the 1960s a new type of underground film has emerged whose form and content are exclusively determined by an interest in the phenomenon of visual perception. Tony Conrad has made films consisting entirely of alternating frames of solid black and solid white (*The Flicker*, 1965; *The Eye of Count Flickerstein*, 1966), in which the stroboscopic effect creates a minimal drama based solely on relative pace and its effect upon the viewer's eyes. George Landow's *Bardo Follies* (1967) is a purely meditative film – inspired by the Tibetan Book of the Dead – whose visuals are restricted to light-patterns. Paul Sharits has made films with nothing but solid frames of pure colour (*Ray Gun Virus*, 1966) in which he aims to destroy the viewer's conscious mind ('mental suicide') in order to bring about 'rebirth as self-projection'. His later films are on Eastern religions of 'the mandala openings to the other side of consciousness': *Razor Blades* (1965–8); *N:O:T:H:I:N:G* (1968), and *T,O,U,C,H,I,N,G,* (1968). The painter and sculptor Michael Snow made the classic *Wavelength* (1967), consisting of a 45-minute continuous zoom shot from one side of an attic to a photograph of waves pinned on to the wall of the other, interrupted only by the four stages of a banal human drama of murder. In this work, Snow attempts to define the limits of cinema as a medium and also to suggest its vast potential. The film's widespread recognition has undoubtedly been instrumental in creating the new genre of what might be called 'structural' cinema, evident in the West Coast work of Scott Bartlett. In *Off-on* (1968) and *Moon* (1969) Bartlett uses electronic distortion of original material to create colour videotape collages in which he attempts to unite Eastern and Western religions in a kind of space age pantheism.

The term underground is becoming increasingly inapposite in the United States, where 'underground' film-makers certainly outnumber mainstream commercial directors. Indeed, their films now represent a major aspect of American culture, whose fragmentation they reflect. JD

Above: Ben Carruthers and Lelia Goldoni in 'Shadows' (John Cassavetes, USA, 1958-9) Below: 'The Connection' (Shirley Clarke, USA, 1961)

The International Underground from the 1950s to the present day

The majority of the experimental films produced in Europe in the 1920s and 1930s were integral to artistic movements like surrealism and dada. The decline of these movements at the start of the Second World War, and the departure of many of their key figures to America, perhaps explain the dearth of underground film-making in Europe in the 1940s and 1950s. Indeed, almost the only underground films made outside America in this period were those made by expatriate Americans. In addition, other countries were slow to follow the American example in establishing film-makers' co-operatives, and although these do now exist in several countries, none has achieved anything like the strength or prominence of its American antecedent. JONAS MEKAS and P. Adams Sitney conducted a travelling exposition of New American Cinema films through many countries during the 1960s, and in many cases this provoked underground film-making where there had previously been none. It is thus difficult to speak of international underground *movements*, and discussion inevitably centres on individual figures rather than groups.

The only major underground film made in Europe in the 1950s was Jean Genet's *Chant d'Amour* (1953), made in France and probably financed by the group of writers who had petitioned for Genet's release from prison in the late 1940s. *Chant d'Amour* deals with the homosexual tensions between prisoners and their sadistic gaoler; Genet interweaves past and present, and the subjective realities and fantasies of his characters, into a complex whole that anticipates similar experiments in mainstream cinema (in the work of RESNAIS, FELLINI, etc.).

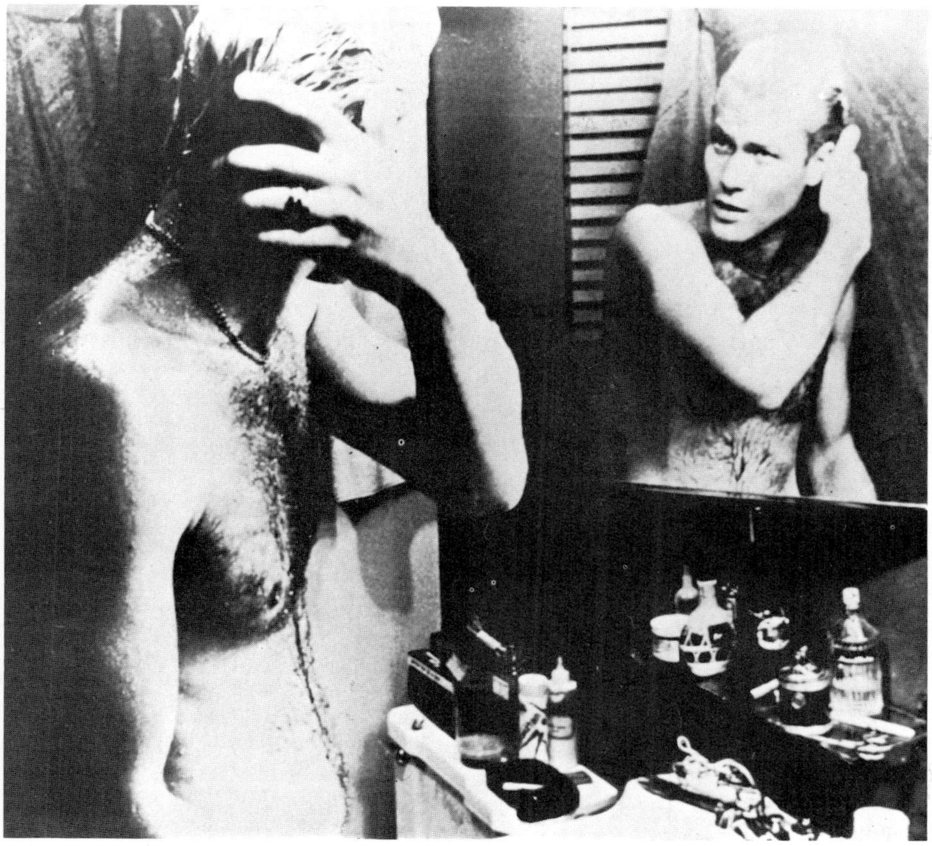

Paul America in 'My Hustler' (Andy Warhol, USA, 1965)

The first country to have organized underground film-making outside America was Holland, where the Scorpio Film Group was founded in the early 1960s. The Dutch film industry has always been oriented towards short film production, and the Scorpio group's work visibly derived from the commercial mainstream, with few innovations in style or technique. The founders were Pim de la Parra, Wim Verstappen, Mattijn Seip and Paul de Mol (later joined by Barbara Meter and Willum Fillum amongst others), all of whom were associated with the Amsterdam 'provo' movement of social revolutionaries. When the Czech film-maker JAN NĚMEC visited Holland briefly in 1967, the Scorpio group was able to finance his *Mother and Son*, a short made at their suggestion. More recently, as this movement has become practically indistinguishable from its commercial counterpart (in films like Niko Paape's horror-film parody *Frankenstein cum Cannabis*), Frans Zwartjes has begun making films. Working very rapidly, he has made numerous very short films in which his characters are reduced to human basics like desire and self-gratification; his method is clearly influenced by the plays and novels of Samuel Beckett.

Italy was one of the countries where the New American Cinema expositions had most effect. Films were made by Roberto Capanna and Giorgio Turi (*Il Fachira*, 1963; *Voyage*, 1964), Mario Masini (*Il Sogno di Anita*, 1963) and Antonio Vergine (*Chronoche*, 1963); their work variously sought to recapture the purity of 'old techniques' and to rebel against 'narrative means of literary origin'. By 1967 the movement was so advanced that a co-op was formed, though political differences dissolved it barely a year after its inception. The painter Mario Schifano began making 'psychedelic' colour films, lyrical in tone and rich in superimpositions; but his *Implosion* (1969) is a two-hour feature, using recognized actors and popular imagery, that has effectively made him a mainstream director. Alfredo Leonardi, mainstay of the short-lived Co-op, began film-making in association with the Living Theatre company in 1964, and in films like *Amore Amore* (1966) and the *Cinegiornale* (1967) he has established his proposition that he prevents the formation of a coherent narrative point of view by shooting 'cinema direct' material and handling it 'according to rhythmic rules, or analogies, or visual or semantic oppositions'. Gianfranco Baruchello made *Verifica Incerta* (1965) with Alberto Grifi, a lengthy stream of collated clichés from Hollywood films, and has gone on to become the most prolific of Italian underground film-makers. Paolo Meusie and Tonino de Bernardi made *Monstro Verde* (1967), a twin-screen 'celebration of the power of invention' that was the country's first work of 'expanded' cinema. After the collapse of the Co-op, a group was organized in Turin, consisting of Mario Ferrero (*Paillard 16*, 1967; *Show*, 1968), Pia Epremian (*Medea* and *Double Suicide*, 1968), Michelangelo Pistoletto (an organizer of street theatre) and the teacher Tonino de Bernardi, whose magnum opus, *Dei* (begun 1968), is currently five hours long, and is to be expanded indefinitely.

A French underground of sorts was established by Jean-Jacques Lebel with his Festival of Free Expression in 1965. A French Canadian living in Paris, Etienne O'Leary, made *Day-tripper* (1965), *Homeo* (1966) and *Chromo Sud* (1967): fast, disorganized films with multiple superimpositions, which encouraged others, including the actor PIERRE CLÉMENTI (*Pontpoint*, 1966) and Michel Auder (*Krylon*, 1967), to make their own films. Senior members of the French *nouvelle vague* GODARD and RESNAIS contributed to the French underground by making a series of anonymous *Cinétracts*, constructed of still photographs and captions, and conceived as political commentaries on the May 1968 revolution in Paris. A post-*nouvelle vague* generation of film-makers has arisen in the past two years, close in spirit to the French youth of the May events: Philippe Garrel (*Le Révélateur*, 1968) is the most prominent, his work analysing patterns of 'civilized' social behaviour in almost anthropological terms.

Other countries have seen even more isolated examples of underground film-making. In Belgium Roland Lethem (*Les Souffrances d'un Oeuf Meurtri*, 1967; *La Fée Sanguinaire*, 1968; and *Bande de Cons*, 1970) has with increasing success outraged bourgeois morality and satirized conventional politics in the surrealist tradition of BUÑUEL's *L'Age d'Or*. In Sweden the playwright Peter Weiss (best known for his Marat/Sade play) has made shorts like *Endligt Lag* (mid-1950s) on the sexual misery of prisoners, and one ambitious feature *The Mirage* (1959) which presents a character alienated from a hostile society in surprisingly Chaplinesque terms. In Japan, Takahiko Iimura has made shorts like *Dance Party in the Kingdom of Lilliput* (1967), which defines its lead character in terms of his physical functions and day-to-day routine, and *Ai* (1968) with music by Yoko Ono, which depicts copulation in huge close-up. In Austria Peter Kubelka has conducted a one-man odyssey into pure cinema: his shorts *Adebar* (1956–7), *Schwechater* (1957–8) and *Arnulf Rainer* (1958–60) are amongst the cinema's few genuinely experimental works, in which Kubelka breaks down shots into constituent frames, and constructs moments of the most powerful expression from near-abstract materials. His longest film, the twelve-minute *Unsere Afrikareise* (1961–6) exploits his discoveries in a film whose documentary subject is an excuse to allow Kubelka an attempt to imbue every second with the maximum expression and emotion.

The German underground was founded during the mid-1960s with films by Werner Nekes, his wife Dore O, and Bazon Brock. In March 1968 'xscreen' was founded in Cologne by Wilhelm and Birgit Hein, who had been intro-

Gabriella Licudi in 'Herostratus' (Don Levy, GB, 1967)

duced to the underground by meeting MARKOPOULOS. 'xscreen' united many of the currently active German film-makers: the Heins themselves (*Rohfilm*, 1968; *625*, 1969; *Work in Progress Teil A*, *Teil B*, 1969–70; and numerous others), whose interest is primarily in the natural properties of the human retina; Peter Weibel and Valie Export (*Electron Ray Tube*, 1969), who perform expanded cinema events including live action in order to destroy 'reality' and 'language'; Otto Mühl (*Sodoma*, 1970), who uses film merely as a despised recording instrument to preserve his 'material actions', live performances with tactile materials and human activity reduced to physical functions; and Hans Peter Kochenrath (*Cyrus*, 1969; *Eruption*, 1970), whose films are more sophisticated versions of the psychodramas of early American underground film. Less radical than these, and more conventionally accomplished filmically, is Fritz-André Kracht, whose *Heroic Landscape* and *It's so Peaceful in the Country* (1969) gently tease out moments of regret and longing.

Of all countries, Britain has had the most widely disparate underground film activity. Jeff Keen, a second-generation surrealist, has made innumerable films (many on 8 mm) celebrating the auto-destructive spirit of old Hollywood B-film fantasies; his *Ray Day Film* (1970) is an expanded cinema event involving live action to the same end. Antony Balch has made *Towers Open Fire* (1963), *The Cut-ups* (1967) and *Who's Who* (1970) in collaboration with the author William Burroughs; the films move progressively towards a purely cinematic presentation of Burroughs's preoccupations. The expatriate Australian Don Levy made a series of sponsored 'scientific' shorts, which used their ostensible subjects as springboards for a dynamic editing style, and employed a wide variety of special photographic effects. His techniques were consolidated in a feature film, *Herostratus* (1967); this attempted an almost metaphysical analysis of the roots of society's decay and pioneered the notion of improvised acting within a rigidly formal filmic structure. Another expatriate, the American Stephen Dwoskin made a series of short portraits of women in private moments of sexuality or boredom, and has recently made a feature (*Times For*, 1970) which synthesizes his previous work into a narrative of a Joycean hero adventuring amongst the women of an illusory cinematic brothel. Peter Gidal experiments with loops and unedited continuous-take films; he considers himself influenced by WARHOL and Beckett. Malcolm LeGrice is the most radical of British film-makers; eschewing direct subject-matter, he makes purely thematic films that employ film-loops, multi-screen, and recently computer-programmed image-patterns. *How to Screw the CIA* (1970) brings together his various techniques in a five-part film that is primarily concerned with the phenomenon of visual perception.

In conclusion, and to some extent instead of a definition, one might observe that the underground film has found a new and different audience from other forms of cinema. Many of its film-makers prefer their work to be shown in small halls or private rooms rather than in conventional cinemas, and accordingly they have made 8 mm prints of their work for sale to individual collectors. It is equally true that many underground films are made with the implicit assumption that they will be viewed many times over. The paradox is that, while avidly experimenting with the latest technological innovations, many of these film-makers seem also to look nostalgically back to the age of the private patron. Though it may of course be a looking forward, since present advances in the field of video-tape cassettes will almost certainly help to promote the distribution of these highly personal films in this, no less personal, way. JD

Avery, Tex

Born 1918 in Dallas, Texas, USA. Animation director. Avery's biography remains mysterious; but his name appeared as director on the credits of many of the best commercial cartoon films made in Hollywood in the 1940s and 1950s. First at MGM and then at Universal, Avery used traditional (post-Disney) graphic styles, but applied them to his own surreal and anarchistic uses. He frequently showed a predilection for stories involving characters of abnormal stature (*Kingsize Canary*; *Half-pint Pigmy*). Among his best-known creations was the penguin Chilly-Willy and the dog Droopy.

Axelrod, George

Born 1922 in New York, USA. Writer, producer and director. He began as an actor, radio writer and novelist and later established himself as a dramatist. Many of his Broadway successes were filmed (sometimes with his script collaboration), including *The Seven Year Itch* (1955) and *Will Success Spoil Rock Hunter?* (1957). Axelrod's best work has a recognisably American vein of dark, sardonic humour, mocking many of the social conventions of the time, expressed through cuttingly abrasive dialogue which transfers very successfully to the screen. In recent years, he has become more involved in production (*The Manchurian Candidate*, 1962) and directed *Lord Love a Duck* (1966) and *The Secret Life of an American Wife* (1968) which deftly satirized the American cults of physical and sexual prowess and the star figure. JG

B

Bacall, Lauren
Born 1924 in New York City, USA. After fashion modelling and stage experience, her first film was *To Have and Have Not* (1944), with HUMPHREY BOGART, in which she played the highly-sexed, sultry but ironic type of girl, a character to which she was for a while tied in her partnership with Bogart (whom she married) in such films as *The Big Sleep* (1946) and *Dark Passage* (1947). Gradually her screen characters grew in sophistication; her later films include: *Key Largo* (1948), *How to Marry a Millionaire* (1953), *Designing Women* (1957), *Northwest Frontier* (1959), *Sex and the Single Girl* (1964), *Harper* (1966).

Background Music
Music played behind dialogue, commentary, or other recorded sound.

Back Lighting
The illumination of a shot from a source behind it. In animation it is used behind either a drawing or celluloid to give a silhouette or transparent effect.

Back Projection
A method of staging live action characters over a pre-photographed image projected behind a translucent screen.

Bacon, Lloyd (1890–1955)
Born California, USA. Versatile American director and one-time actor (notably in a series of CHAPLIN shorts) whose competently made films are most interesting in summing up the Hollywood reaction to the Depression era, although individually few are distinguished: *42nd Street* (1933), *Gold Diggers of 1937*, *A Slight Case of Murder* (1938), *Invisible Stripes* (1940) are among the exceptions. Before the First World War he toured in summer stock and vaudeville, entered films as an actor in 1918. In 1921 he directed his first film for MACK SENNETT, later joining Warners, where he directed the film with AL JOLSON, *The Singing Fool* (1928). He revealed a talent for handling the hard-shell back-stage musicals, swaggering comedies and action melodramas in which the studio specialized. His work after the Second World War was generally pleasant as entertainment but cinematically unexceptional. Other main films: *Boy Meets Girl* (1939), *Brother Orchid* (1940), *Action in the North Atlantic* (1943), *The Sullivans* and *Sunday Dinner for a Soldier* (1944), *Golden Girl* (1951), *The Great Sioux Uprising* (1954). MH

Above: Lauren Bacall in 'Key Largo' (John Huston, USA, 1948)
Below: Damian O'Flynn, Bette Davis and Ben Welden in 'Marked Woman' (Lloyd Bacon, USA, 1936)

Badger, Clarence G.
Born 1880 in San Francisco, USA. One of the most talented directors of comedy of the silent period, Badger was an actor, printer and journalist before trying his hand as a screenwriter. In 1915 he directed his first film for SENNETT at Keystone. Subsequently he worked for GOLDWYN (on a series of WILL ROGERS comedies), First National, Metro, Famous Players and Paramount. He had an unusual sympathy for the comic talent of his artists; and the series of films with Rogers (*Jubilo*, *The Strange Boarder*, *Doubling for Romeo*, etc) were among the comedian's best work. Badger had however a special talent for directing lady comics. At Sennett's he had directed GLORIA SWANSON; and some of Bebe Daniels's most successful films were made by him, notably *Miss Brewster's Millions* (1926), *She's a Sheik*, *A Kiss in the Taxi* and *Senorita* (1927) and *Hot News* (1928). But Badger's greatest screen creation was the 'It' girl: he directed CLARA

BOW in three of her most successful films: *It* (1927) and *Red Hair* and *Three Weekends* (1928). Badger's own masterpiece, however, was *Hands Up!*, with RAYMOND GRIFFITH, a spoof Western that ranks with KEATON for its attack, logic and elegance. Badger continued to direct until 1939 *(Rangle River)*. DR

Baillie, Bruce
Born 1931 in Aberdeen, South Dakota, USA. Underground film-maker. After serving in Korea, touring, and taking film courses in Minnesota and London, England, he settled in San Francisco. Here he began to make local news films, followed by documentaries in which his strong personal style in photography and editing began to show itself – *Mr Hayashi* and *The Gymnasts* (1961), *A Hurrah for Soldiers* (1962–3), and the colour film *To Parsifal* (1963). Bruce is much concerned about the exploitation of the good and the innocent by society. He went on to make *Mass* (1963–4), dedicated to the Sioux, and *Quixote* (1964–5), a highly personal tour of the States, exploring the resources of the camera. His films are meditative and beautiful, concerned with protest, as in *Newsreel* (1966), as well as with film aesthetics.

Baker, Stanley
Born 1928 in Glamorgan, Wales. British actor and producer. Son of a mining family, he made his first film *Undercover*, at the age of 14. After early stage experience, he became a utility 'heavy' in British films and graduated to tough, insecure heroes. He formed his own production company, which had a big popular success with *Zulu* in 1963. He starred in several memorable films for JOSEPH LOSEY, including *The Criminal* (1960), *Eve* (1962) and *Accident* (1967). He is generally credited with helping to establish the actor-producer in Britain in the 1960s as a force to be reckoned with. Other notable films: *A Hill in Korea* (1956), *Yesterday's Enemy* (1960), *Robbery* (co-produced, 1967), *Where's Jack?* (co-produced, 1969), *The Games* and *Perfect Friday* (1970).

Balazs, Bela (1884–1949)
Born Szeged, Hungary. Scriptwriter, director, and influential film theorist, primarily associated with the Hungarian and German cinemas. He is remembered best now for his books on film art, 'Der sichtbare Mensch' (1924, published in Vienna while he was in exile from the Horthy régime), 'Der Geist des Films' (1930) and 'Film: Werden und Wesen einer neuen Kunst' (1948, published in English as 'Theory of the Film', 1952). In Germany he was associated with the avant-garde and collaborated on several scripts including that of *The Threepenny Opera* and *The Blue Light*. With the coming of Hitler he went to work in the Soviet Union. He returned to Hungary after the war and the establishment there of the communist régime, and he became once again an influential writer and teacher, publishing a new book, 'Film Culture', editing a journal on film art, and scripting two films, *Somewhere in Europe* and *Song of the Cornfields*. RM

Balcon, Michael
Born 1896 in Birmingham, England. British executive producer and *entrepreneur* with a rare gift for spotting and utilizing film talent; he discovered ALFRED HITCHCOCK in the 1920s. The high point of an impressive career was his period as production head at Ealing Studios, whose policy of making indigenous British films, from 1938 to 1955, won international as well as national acclaim. Knighted 1948.

Starting out in film distribution during the First World War, he made his début as a producer with *Woman to Woman* in 1922. During the next 16 years, he headed Gainsborough Studios, Gaumont-British, MGM British; was responsible for many important British films, including FLAHERTY's *Man of Aran* (1934), as well as a series of popular frothy comedies featuring Jack Hulbert, Jessie Matthews, Tom Walls and other well known British stars.

But it was at Ealing that he put his individual stamp on the British industry, with war-time documentaries and, after the war, human interest stories resolutely British-based and the celebrated Ealing comedies, some of which – *Whisky Galore* and *Kind Hearts and Coronets* (1949), *The Man in the White Suit* (1951) among them – are now regarded as classics of their kind. The Ealing group of directors and writers – including ALEXANDER MACKENDRICK, ROBERT HAMER, BASIL DEARDEN, T. E. B. CLARKE, CHARLES CRICHTON, CHARLES FREND, HENRY CORNELIUS, Michael Truman – was formed and cherished by Michael Balcon. In time the Ealing strain wore thin and the Studios folded in 1955; their ex-chief helped to launch Bryanston Films, which promoted, through Woodfall, the early films of TONY RICHARDSON and KAREL REISZ. Up to 1971 he was Chairman of the British Film Institute Production Board.

In the 1960s, he became involved less in film production than in behind-the-scenes battles and he has been especially critical of the American financial take-over of and Hollywood influence in British films. An esteemed elder statesman of the British film industry, he published his autobiography 'A Lifetime of Films' in 1969. MH

Opposite: Stanley Baker in 'A Hill in Korea' (Julian Aymes, GB, 1956)
Below: Anne Bancroft in 'The Pumpkin Eater' (Jack Clayton, GB, 1962)

Bancroft, Anne
Born 1931 in New York, USA. Dynamic American stage, screen and television actress whose early career in dire second features – including such choice items as *Gorilla at Large* (1954) – did not prevent her from making a triumphal return to films in *The Miracle Worker* (1962), for which she won an Academy Award after starring in the play on Broadway. Since then she has appeared only rarely in films and then in fastidiously chosen roles – *The Pumpkin Eater* (1962), *Seven Women* (1965), *The Slender Thread* (1966), *The Graduate* (1968) – which have given her ample scope to exercise her flair for portraying intense, liberated modern women. Latest film: *Young Winston* (1971).

Bara, Theda (1890–1955)
Born in Cincinnati, Ohio, USA. Actress. A quiet Cincinnati girl with modest dramatic aspirations, Bara was thrust to stardom by WILLIAM FOX's publicity department, which created a great edifice of myth and mystery about her, giving her a fictitious oriental background, a predatory quality of eroticism and the word 'vamp' (from 'vampire') to define her quality. As the glowering *femme fatale* of more than forty films, starting with the archetypal *A Fool there Was* (Frank Powell, 1914), Bara – whose *nom de guerre* was said to be an anagram of ARAB DEATH – created an entirely new sexual symbolism. Later films included *Carmen* and *The Devil's Daughter* and *Sin* (1915), *The Eternal Sappho* (1916), *The Tiger Woman*, *Du Barry*, *Cleopatra* and *Camille* (1917), *The She-Devil* and *When a Woman Sins* (1918), *When Men Desire* (1919). In 1919, her popularity in films declining, she returned to the stage; and an attempted comeback in 1926 (*The Unchastened Woman*, *Madame Mystery*) showed that her style and era had been eclipsed. DR

Bardem, Juan-Antonio
Born 1922 in Madrid, Spain. Director and screenwriter. His parents were both prominent players in the theatre. In 1947 Bardem qualified at the Film School in Madrid. Initially a film critic, he endeavoured, virtually single-handed along with LUIS BERLANGA, another journalist and screenwriter, to bring a quality of realism and humanity to the backward Spanish cinema of the 1950s. Working with Berlanga, he wrote and directed *Esa Pareja Feliz* (1951), and scripted Berlanga's two films, *Bienvenido, Mister Marshall!* (1952) and *Novio a la vista* (1953). His most notable films in the realist style were *Death of a Cyclist* (1955) and *Calle Major* (1956). His more recent films have turned in the direction of melodrama. They include: *La Venganza* (1957), *Sonatas* (1959), *A las cinco de la tarde* (1960), *Los Innocentes* (1962), *Nunca pasa nada* (1963), *Les pianos mécaniques* (1964), *El Ultimo*

Above: Brigitte Bardot in 'Viva Maria' (Louis Malle, France, 1965)
Below: Fabien Loris, Arletty and Jean-Louis Barrault in 'Les Enfants du Paradis' (Marcel Carné, France, 1944)

Día de la Guerra (*The Last Day of War*, 1969), *Varietés* (1971). RM

Bardot, Brigitte
Born 1934 in Paris, France. Much-imitated French actress who under the guidance of her director husband ROGER VADIM was the reigning European screen sex symbol for over a decade. Starting out as a cover girl model, she was introduced to the film world by MARC ALLÉGRET. Vadim was Allegrét's assistant when they married. A series of small roles and an eye-catching personal success at the Cannes Film Festival in 1953 led to the prototype Bardot starring role in *Et Dieu créa la Femme* (1956). Her pouting, provocative, dishevelled looks, occasional nudity (before it became a film vogue) and free-living heroines made her an idol in France and a tempting example for young women everywhere. The image invariably obliterates the actress, who is generally better than she is given credit for. Principal films: *Vie Privée* (1962), *Le Mépris* (1963), *Viva Maria* (1965), *Two Weeks in September* (1967), *Shalako* (1968), *Les Petroleuses* (1971). MH

Barker, Reginald (1886–1937)
Born in Bothwell, Scotland. Director. Went to America at an early age and became actor and producer. Became involved in the cinema from 1913, working on several short films and then joining the THOMAS H. INCE company as director. His numerous westerns and comedies with WILLIAM S. HART and Charles Ray display a precise visual sense and feeling for landscape, as well as a dramatic flair: *The Coward* (with Charles Ray, 1915) and *The Golden Claw* (1915) and *The Apostle of Vengeance* (1916), the last two with Hart. In the 1920s, he worked with several leading romantic stars such as Renée Adorée – *The Eternal Struggle* (1923), *Women Who Give* (1924), *The Flaming Forest* (1926) – as well as making several adventure dramas which might well bear rediscovery. JG

Barnet, Boris (1902–1965)
Born in Moscow, USSR. Actor and director. A former boxer, Barnet was a founder-member of KULESHOV's famous Studio (1920). Appearing as an actor in Kuleshov's *Strange Adventures of Mr West in the Land of the Bolsheviks* (1924) and OZEP's *The Living Corpse* (1926), he made his début as a director in collaboration with Ozep on *Miss Mend* (1926). His own best films combine lyricism, and a sharply comic human observation. His later films (the last was *Annushka*, 1959) however never equalled the silent *Girl with a Hat Box* (1927) and *The House on Trubnaia Square* (1928) or his first sound film, the masterly *Okraina* (*Suburbs*, with its early use of synthetic sound, 1933).

Barrault, Jean-Louis
Born 1910 in Le Vésinet, France. Leading French stage and screen actor and influential figure in the theatre as a producer and innovator. Although his provocative performances in many films, including *Drôle de Drame* (1937), *Les Enfants du Paradis* (1944), *La Ronde* (1950), *Le Testament du Docteur Cordelier* (1959), have been widely acclaimed and have served as a guide for younger French actors, his principal work has been done for the theatre. He formed his own company at the Théâtre Marigny, was Director of the French National Theatre and with his wife, Madeleine Renaud, has toured widely on the stage throughout the world. Latest films: *The Longest Day* (1962), *Chappaqua* (1968).

Barrymore, Lionel (1878–1954), **Ethel** (1879–1959), **John** (1882–1942)
All born in Philadelphia, USA. Distinguished American stage and screen family (brothers and sister) who were celebrated in the early decades of the 20th century as 'the Royal family of Broadway'. Lionel dedicated much of his career to films, starting in silent films such as *The Copperhead* (1920), but gaining his greatest fame as the resident, crusty, wheelchair-ridden wise man of MGM films, notably the *Dr Kildare* series in which he played the know-all Dr Gillespie. Ethel also made silent films: first *The Divorce* (1909); but it was in the talkies that her stage-trained technique came into its own, principally acting refined, wealthy, sharp old ladies in such films as *The Spiral Staircase* (1945) and *Deadline USA* (1952). John had the greatest talent, was a memorable American Hamlet and was the most careless with his dramatic gifts. He made his silent film début in 1912 to play swashbuckling heroes; notable sound films: *Grand Hotel* and *A Bill of Divorcement* (1932), *Dinner at Eight* (1933), *Romeo and Juliet* (1936), *Midnight* (1939), *The Great Profile* (1940). ERROL FLYNN played the role of John in *Too Much Too Soon* (1957) and in 1944 Gene Fowler published a biography of him, 'Goodnight Sweet Prince'. Lionel, John and Ethel starred together in MGM's trouble-fraught *Rasputin and the Empress* (1932). MH

Barthelmess, Richard (1895–1963)
Born in New York, USA. Actor. The son of a noted actress, Barthelmess was first noticed by ALLA NAZIMOVA (his mother's voice coach), and appeared with her in his second film, *War Brides* (1916). His romantic qualities and extreme sensitivity were most fully developed however in the films he made with D. W. GRIFFITH, notably *Broken Blossoms* (1919) and *Way*

Above: Leslie Howard and John Barrymore in 'Romeo and Juliet' (George Cukor, USA, 1936)
Below: Iya Savina and Alexei Batalov in 'The Lady with the Little Dog' (Yosif Heifitz, USSR, 1959)
Bottom: Harry Baur in 'Un Carnet de Bal' (Julien Duvivier, France, 1937)

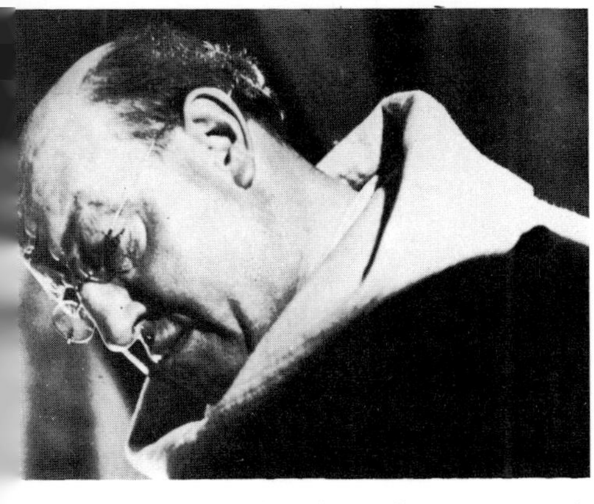

Down East (1920), but above all in HENRY KING's classic *Tol'able David* (1921). His best sound role was probably in WILLIAM DIETERLE's *The Last Flight* (1932). In later years he became an effective character actor (notably in HAWKS's *Only Angels have Wings*, 1939). His last role was in *Desert Fury* (1947).

Batalov, Alexei Vladimirovitch
Born 1928 in Moscow, USSR. Actor. The nephew of Nikolai Batalov (the celebrated leading actor of PUDOVKIN's *Mother*, ROOM's *Bed and Sofa* and EKK's *The Road to Life*), Alexei Batalov is one of the most gifted and sensitive contemporary Soviet actors, his best-known roles being in *A Big Family* (1954), *The Rumyantsev Case* (1956), DONSKOI's remake of *Mother* (1956), *The Cranes are Flying* (1957), *The Lady with the Little Dog* (1959), *Nine Days of One Year* (1962). In 1960 Batalov made his début as a director with an adaptation of Gogol's *The Overcoat*; and subsequently directed *A Day of Happiness* (1964) and *The Light of Distant Stars* (1965).

Batchelor, Joy
See HALAS, JOHN

Bates, Alan
Born 1930 in Allestree, Derbyshire, England. Actor, who has appeared on the London and New York stage and television as well as in films. Main films: *A Kind of Loving* (1961), *Whistle Down the Wind* (1962), *The Caretaker* and *The Running Man* (1963), *Nothing But the Best* (1964), *Zorba the Greek* (1965), *Georgy Girl* (1966), *Far From the Madding Crowd* (1967), *The Fixer* (1968), *Women in Love* (1969), *Three Sisters* (1970), *The Go-Between* (1971).

Baur, Harry (1880–1943)
Born in Paris, France. Distinguished French stage and screen actor in the grand tradition who made his first film *Shylock* in 1910. Subsequent films include *Poil de Carotte* (1932), *Un Carnet de Bal* (1937), *Volpone* (1939), *Symphonie Eines Lebens* (1943).

Bazin, André (1918–1958)
Born in France. Critic and theorist, closely associated with certain important directors in the French *nouvelle vague* cinema. In 1947 he founded 'La Revue du Cinéma', changing its identity in 1950 to 'Cahiers du Cinéma', of which he was co-editor up to the time of his death at the early age of 40. Among the new-wave film-makers who wrote for him were JACQUES DONIOL-VALCROZE (co-founder of the 'Cahiers'), CLAUDE CHABROL, JEAN-LUC GODARD, ERIC ROHMER, JACQUES RIVETTE, and, in particular, FRANÇOIS TRUFFAUT, whom Bazin introduced to the 'Cahiers'. His many influential articles were collected into four volumes, 'Qu'est-ce que le Cinéma?'. He wrote about films as an aesthete, working out his arguments and tracing his reactions to film with great intellectual care. Among the more celebrated of his essays were 'The Evolution of Film Language', and studies of eroticism in the cinema, the Stalin myth in film, neo-realism, the Western, etc., and he also wrote a monograph on ORSON WELLES and was influential in establishing the 'auteur' approach to film criticism. He wrote always as a liberal who was also a convinced Catholic, and he was under constant attack from the Left, particularly in the journal 'Positif', which opposed the policy and thought of the 'Cahiers'. RM

Beatty, Warren
Born 1937 in Virginia, USA. American actor-producer. Brother of actress SHIRLEY MACLAINE, specializing in vogueish mixed-up heroes on screen and an awe-inspiring romantic reputation off-screen. Studied drama under Stella Adler; eventually won small roles on television and in summer stock. After his Broadway success in William Inge's 'A Loss of Roses', ELIA KAZAN brought him to Hollywood in 1960 for *Splendour in the Grass*. His refusal to conform to Hollywood convention handicapped his career at first, but he firmly established himself in 1967 when he produced, starred in and energetically promoted the trend-setting *Bonnie and Clyde*. Other notable films: *The Roman Spring of Mrs Stone* (1961), *All Fall Down* (1962), *Lilith* and *Mickey One* (1965), *The Only Game in Town* (1969), *McCabe and Mrs Miller* (1971).

Becker, Jacques (1906–1960)
Born in Paris, France. Director. Becker was assistant director on most of JEAN RENOIR's films from 1931 to 1937, occasionally taking small parts in his and other directors' films. He began directing himself in the mid-1930s, but it was not until the war years that he began to form his style with the pastoral drama *Goupi mains rouges* (1943). During the war he was a member of the underground Comité de Libération du Cinéma Français. Immediately after the war, he made a trio of films about young lovers – *Antoine et Antoinette* (1946), *Rendezvous de Juillet* (1949), *Edouard et Caroline* (1951) – which revealed a charming tenderness and a vein of ironic humour also evident in an even more mature work like the impeccably designed period love story, *Casque d'or* (1952), which helped to make SIMONE SIGNORET's reputation. After a series of lighter films, including one of the best French gangster dramas, *Touchez pas au grisbi* (1954), he made an atmospheric study of Modigliani's life called *Montparnasse 19* (1957). His final work, *Le Trou* (1960), was a detailed, probing account of a prison escape which summed up the essentially humanistic aspect of his art. Becker was both a brilliant technician and a fastidious artist and his best films communicate an infectious air of enjoyment. JG

Beery, Wallace (1889–1949)
American actor, who first appeared in circus and musical comedy. He entered silent films in 1912 as a female impersonator but became famous and very popular as a rascally character with a lovable personality under the tough and ugly exterior. Main films: *Teddy at the Throttle* (1916), *The Four Horsemen of the Apocalypse* (1921), *Robin Hood* (1924), *The Lost World* and *The Sea Hawk* (1925), *The Last of the Mohicans* (1927), *Min and Bill* (1931), *The Champ* and *Grand Hotel* (1932), *Tugboat Annie* and *The Bowery* (1933), *Viva Villa* and *Treasure Island* (1934), *Barnacle Bill* (1941).

Belgium
Belgium, one of the most densely populated European countries with some 10 million

Above: Jean-Paul Belmondo in 'À Bout de Souffle' (Jean-Luc Godard, France, 1959)
Below: 'Symphonie Paysanne' (Henri Storck, Belgium, 1947)

people, supports about 1,000 cinemas. Not notable until recently for feature production, Belgium has produced directors of documentary, led by HENRI STORCK. [See DOCUMENTARY.] It must be remembered that Belgium is divided into two language areas, French-speaking and Flemish-speaking. During the 1960s some interesting feature films have been produced, of which the following is a selection:

Si le Vent te Fait Peur; *Béatrix*; *Palabre* (Emile Degelin)
Monsieur Hawarden and *Daughters of Darkness* (Harry Kümel; co-productions with the Netherlands)
The Man who had his Hair Cut Short; *Un Soir, un Train* and *Rendezvous à Bray* (ANDRÉ DELVAUX, the latter films French-sponsored)
Le Départ (JERZY SKOLIMOWSKI, from Poland)
Les Gommes (Lucien Deroisy; a Franco-Belgian co-production)
Le Fruit du Paradis (Vera Chytilova, from Czechoslovakia)
Bhakti (Maurice Béjart)
L'Etreinte (Pierre Collet and Pierre Drouot).

Belgium has four major film schools, a very lively Cinémathèque in Brussels, and many young film-makers anxious to begin. RM

Bell, Monta

Born 1891 in Washington, USA. Director. Was theatre actor in the early 1920s, then began a collaboration with CHAPLIN, including assistance on the editing of *A Woman of Paris* (1923). Became director in 1924, making a series of comedies and sophisticated romantic dramas seemingly influenced by LUBITSCH: *The King on Main Street* and *Lady of the Night* (1925), *The Torrent* (GARBO's first American film, 1926), *After Midnight* (with NORMA SHEARER) and *Man, Woman and Sin* (with JOHN GILBERT, 1927). He adapted less easily to sound, although *The Worst Woman in Paris?* (1933) has echoes of the boulevard irony of his earlier work. Later in the 1930s, he turned to production. Bell is another of those relatively forgotten American directors who needs re-assessing. JG

Bellocchio, Marco

Born 1939 in Piacenza, Italy. Director. Following a religious education and upbringing, he made some short films and then emerged suddenly as one of the most forceful directors of the younger generation, with two features *I Pugni in Tasca* (1966) and *La Cina è Vicina* (1967). Both are intricately interwoven with the religious and political fabric of Italian life, and their tough irony and mordant humour owe something to BUÑUEL. *Pugni* shocked audiences with its portrait of a young epileptic who decides to kill off his family, and *Cina* evolves a complex political allegory from the interactions of another family enclave, and its anti-bourgeois satire is often wickedly funny. Bellocchio's talent is a difficult one (which means he has problems in obtaining commercial backing), but his uncompromising temperament has left its mark on the Italian scene. Latest film: *In the Name of the Father* (1971). JG

Belmondo, Jean-Paul

Born 1933 in Neuilly-sur-Seine, France. Leading French actor who, for a time, distilled the essence of the *nouvelle vague* anti-hero, modelled on the HUMPHREY BOGART 'image'; latterly, his performances have become lazier and more dependent on instant personality appeal. Son of the sculptor Paul Belmondo, he studied drama and made his first film, *Sois Belle Et Tais-Toi*, in 1958. But it was not until JEAN-LUC GODARD chose him for the leading male role in *A Bout de Souffle* (1959) that Belmondo distinguished himself. While repeating this amoral, more-or-less outlaw character several times on the screen, he also revealed a genuine dramatic talent in more sensitive roles – in *Moderato Cantabile* (1960), *Léon Morin, Prêtre* and *Two Women* (1961). Other principal films: *A Double Tour* (1959), *Une Femme Est Une Femme* (1961), *Cartouche* (1962), *That Man from Rio* (1964), *Pierrot Le Fou* (1965), *Le Voleur* (1967), *The Brain* (1969), *Borsalino* (1970). MH

Benedek, Laslo

Born 1907 in Budapest, Hungary. Director, working chiefly in America. He entered films as a cameraman, joining a company in Budapest straight from University, where he studied psychiatry. He became an editor and assistant producer to JOE PASTERNAK, with whom he worked on several films in Europe. He also spent some time script-writing in England. He made his début as a director with *The Kissing Bandit* (1948). A sensitive but minor talent, his reputation rests principally on *Death of a Salesman* (1951) and the controversial *The Wild One* (1954). Other notable films: *Moment of Danger*

(1958), *Namu, the Killer Whale* (1966), *Salem come to Supper* (1970). He has also directed for television.

Benoît-Lévy, Jean (1888–1959)
Born in Paris, France. Director and producer. During the silent period he collaborated with JEAN EPSTEIN in making *Pasteur* (1922), an official documentary of considerable quality on the work of Pasteur. Benoît-Lévy was one of the earliest directors in France to develop realistic, near-documentary feature films, particularly studies of childhood. His best-known film was *La Maternelle* (1932), which he made in association with Marie Epstein, Jean Epstein's sister and collaborator. After a number of relatively indifferent features, including *Itto* (1934), made in Morocco, his *La Mort du Cygne* (1938), although a story film, was also a valuable documentary of ballet. During the 1930s he produced and directed many documentary films, including *Le Chant de la Mine et du Feu* (1932). In 1941–6 he was Professor at the New School of Social Research, New York, and from 1946 produced documentary and educational films for UNESCO. He was active in many organizations, both national and international, concerning the cinema in pre-war France, and author of the book, 'The Art of the Motion Picture' (1947). RM

Bérard, Christian (1902–1949)
Born in Paris, France. Designer. Best known as a designer for the stage. Bérard turned to the screen with striking success as art director of *La Belle et la Bête* (1946), *Les Parents Terribles* and *L'Aigle à deux têtes* (1948) and the episode *La Voix Humaine* in ROSSELLINI's *L'Amore* (1947).

Berger, Ludwig (1892–1969)
Born in Mainz, Germany. Director. Began working as theatre and opera producer, at the beginning of the century, often with Max Reinhardt, and entered films in 1922. From the beginning, Berger displayed an elegant, rococo style with a fondness for fantasy and fairy-tale and the world of Strauss and Lehar operettas. *Cinderella* (1923) and *Waltz Dream* (1926) are typical of his early period with their lavish, glowing sets and inventive camerawork. From the late 1920s onwards, he began to move from one country to another (including the USA, France, Britain and Holland), sometimes working as script collaborator, associate director and occasionally cinematographer. Few of the films belonging to the American part of his career (including *The Vagabond King*, 1930, with JEANETTE MACDONALD and *The Playboy of Paris*, 1931, with MAURICE CHEVALIER) have been revived, nor is it possible to assess many of the later sound films made in Europe. In England, he collaborated with MICHAEL POWELL and Tim Whelan on *The Thief of Bagdad* (1940), where he was clearly attracted by the Arabian Nights setting. Berger was essentially a miniaturist, but he brought a welcome touch of civilized charm and wit into the film cultures of several countries. JG

Above: Ingmar Bergman
Right: Max von Sydow and Liv Ullman in 'The Shame' (Ingmar Bergman, Sweden, 1968)
Below: Kevin McCarthy, Fredric March and Claire Carleton in 'Death of a Salesman' (Laslo Benedek, USA, 1951)

Bergman, Ingmar
Born 1918 in Uppsala, Sweden. The dominant influence in Swedish films for twenty years and a key director-writer in the history of world cinema. He has also worked prolifically for

Swedish theatre, radio and television. Persistently and, often, over-analysed, his allegorical obsessions with religious and *Doppelgänger* themes and with conflicts between the soul and the flesh, derive in part from a childhood lived according to the stern dictates of his Lutheran parson father. Although a comparison with Strindberg is far too confining, his films reflect as powerfully the summer fevers and winter darkness of the Swedish character, expressed through a versatile range of moods from the sophisticated comedy of morals (*A Lesson in Love*, 1954) to the doomed vision of an apocalyptic future (*The Shame*, 1968 – the centrepiece of a trilogy which includes *The Hour of the Wolf*, 1968, and *A Passion*, 1970).

He started his career in the theatre in 1938, which eventually led to his appointment as director of the Royal Dramatic Theatre in Stockholm from 1963 to 1966. His first professional screen credit was the screenplay for *Frenzy* (1944). The following year he directed and wrote *Crisis*. Almost immediately he established the working methods and cultural ties which were to become Bergmanian trademarks in more than thirty films. In 1956 he created the film that more than any other was to make him an internationally acclaimed name, the medieval morality, *The Seventh Seal*.

Totally individual in concept his films are very much a part of the Swedish screen tradition, relating to elder directors, STILLER, SJÖBERG, who directed *Frenzy*, and SJÖSTRÖM, who played the lead in possibly Bergman's most popularly sympathetic film, *Wild Strawberries* (1957). The Bergman stock company, including two distinguished actors, MAX VON SYDOW and GUNNAR BJÖRNSTRAND, and a series of remarkable actresses, INGRID THULIN, HARRIET ANDERSSON, EVA DAHLBECK, BIBI ANDERSSON, GUNNEL LINDBLOM, LIV ULLMAN, influence to a large extent the manner in which Bergman develops his themes, adapting the essential qualities and physical attributes of his players to the demands of the script.

Particularly impressive is his feeling for the torments, compulsions and idiosyncrasies of the female sex, especially in *So Close to Life* (1957), *The Silence* (1963) and *Persona* (1966). His flexible style allows him to use a variety of dramatic techniques to suit his over-riding purpose: farce, fantasy, symbolism, drably styled naturalism and opulent period mannerism, sunny romance and the blackest kind of teutonic sadism. His increasingly bleak concern with man's spiritual dilemma has led to a certain revaluation of his contribution to contemporary cinema. One of his recurrent themes is that of the artist's, often ambiguous role in society. But, unwaveringly, Bergman continues to uncover the layers upon layers of that 'reality beyond reality' which is his chosen province.

Other principal films: *Port of Call* (1948), *Summer Interlude* (1950), *Waiting Women* and *Summer with Monika* (1952), *Sawdust and Tinsel* (1953), *Smiles of a Summer Night* (1955), *The Magician* (1958), *The Virgin Spring* (1959), *The Devil's Eye* (1960), *Through a Glass Darkly* (1961), *Winter Light* (1962), *Now About These Women* (1964), *The Rite* (1969), *The Touch* (1971). Books on Ingmar Bergman include Jörn Donner's 'The Personal Vision of Ingmar Bergman', Robin Wood's 'Ingmar Bergman' and Peter Cowie's 'Ingmar Bergman: a Monograph' and a study in 'Sweden 2' (1970). MH

Above: Ingrid Bergman in 'Europa '51' (Roberto Rossellini, Italy, 1952)
Below: Laurence Olivier and Elisabeth Bergner in 'As You Like It' (Paul Czinner, GB, 1936)

Bergman, Ingrid

Born 1915 in Stockholm, Sweden. Swedish actress who became a Hollywood prototype of the healthy, interesting 'good' woman until her escape to Rome and director ROBERTO ROSSELLINI in 1949 aroused the wrath of the women's clubs in the puritan belt of America. A graduate of the Swedish Royal Dramatic School, she appeared in eleven films in two years, but it was the Swedish version of *Escape to Happiness* that brought her to the notice of Hollywood. She remade the film in English with LESLIE HOWARD in 1940, remaining to star in many films of which the most notable were *Dr Jekyll and Mr Hyde* (1941), *Casablanca* (1942), *For whom the Bell Tolls* (1943) and *Joan of Arc* (1948). She won an Academy Award for her performance in *Murder in Thornton Square* (1944) and played in several HITCHCOCK films including *Spellbound* (1945), *Notorious* (1946). After making *Under Capricorn* (1949) in Britain for Hitchcock, she rebelled against the old Hollywood order, went to Italy where she made *Stromboli* (1949) and married its director, Rossellini, whom she later divorced. After several years of working in Europe on some of Rossellini's key films, she was welcomed back to the American fold with *Anastasia* (1956), which won her another Academy Award. Other notable films: *Elena et les Hommes* (1955), *Inn of the Sixth Happiness* (1958), *The Visit* (1964), *Cactus Flower* (1969), *A Walk in the Spring Rain* (1970). MH

Bergner, Elisabeth

Born 1900 in Vienna, Austria. Distinguished European stage and screen actress whose greatest screen successes were produced in England; although her most popular 'waiflike' characterizations in *Dreaming Lips* (1932), *Escape Me Never* (1935), *A Stolen Life* (1939) were a waste of her considerable talents. She worked almost exclusively with her producer husband DR PAUL CZINNER. First film in Germany: *Der Evangelimann*. First British film: *Catherine the Great* (1934). She made the silent *Nju* (1924) and *Fraulein Else* (1929) and later played opposite LAURENCE OLIVIER in *As You Like It* (1936). In 1941 she made *Paris Calling* in America and retired from the screen for nearly 30 years to return in an inferior role in *Cry of the Banshee* (1970).

Berkeley, Busby

Born 1895 in Los Angeles, USA. Choreographer and director. After a period on Broadway, he went to Hollywood as dance director on several Eddie Cantor musicals including *Whoopee* (1931) and *Roman Scandals* (1933). On joining Warner Brothers, he worked on a number of films with 'show business' backgrounds (often directed by LLOYD BACON) and perfected a unique stylistic fusion between camera and dancers, full of surrealist, erotic images and featuring dozens of chorines against exotic backgrounds – often photographed from above – performing routines involving phalanxes of grand pianos, illuminated violins, a jumbo-sized swimming-pool or gigantic hall of mirrors (*42nd Street* and *Footlight Parade*, 1933; *Dames*, 1934; the *Gold Digger* series, 1933–7). On moving to MGM in the late 1930s, he turned to dramatic subjects as well as smaller-scale musicals (with MICKEY ROONEY and JUDY GARLAND) which lacked much of his former zest and extravagance. *The Gang's All Here* (Fox, 1943), with its elaborate settings and mobile camera, marked a return to form; subsequent work including *Take Me Out to the Ball Game* (1948) and *Billy Rose's Jumbo* (1962) were less well sustained. In 1970, after years of inactivity, he supervised an American theatrical revival of 'No, No, Nanette', with Ruby Keeler. JG

Berlanga, Luis Garcia
Born 1921 in Valencia, Spain. Director. Was writer and journalist before turning to films as scenario collaborator and made his first feature *Esa Pareja Feliz* in 1951 with his friend, J. A. BARDEM. From the beginning, he developed a sharp, satirical style – *Bienvenido Mr Marshall* (1952), *Calabuch* (1956) – taking off certain Spanish foibles and lampooning aspects of political and social life which has not endeared him to the Spanish authorities. His best recent work is *El Verdugo* (1963), a bitterly black comedy about a reluctant hangman; after this, he seems to have had difficulty in finding subjects conducive to his ebullient, attacking temperament. JG

Berman, Pandro S.
Born 1905 in Pittsburgh, USA. Discerning American producer for over 30 years whose films are distinguished for their high gloss, technical and literary quality, if not always for their dramatic vitality. Starting out as a script boy at RKO in the early 1920s, he spent the next eight years learning all he could about film-making and produced his first film for the studio in 1931, *The Gay Diplomat*. He went on to produce the first musicals starring ASTAIRE–ROGERS, *The Gay Divorcée* and *Roberta* (1934), *Top Hat* (1935), and several films with KATHARINE HEPBURN, including *Morning Glory* (1932), *The Little Minister* (1934), *Alice Adams* (1935), *Mary of Scotland* (1936), *Stage Door* (1937). In 1940 he joined MGM, where he was responsible for many handsome – if occasionally hollow – class entertainments. Other notable films: *Winterset* (1936), *The Picture of Dorian Gray* (1944), *The Three Musketeers* (1948), *Madame Bovary* (1949), *Father of the Bride* (1950), *Ivanhoe* (1952), *All the Brothers were Valiant* (1954), *The Blackboard Jungle* (1955), *Bhowani Junction* (1956), *The Brothers Karamazov* (1958), *Sweet Bird of Youth* (1962), *A Patch of Blue* (1966). MH

Right: Billy Bitzer and D. W. Griffith on location for 'Way Down East' (Griffith, USA, 1920)
Below: 'Footlight Parade' (Lloyd Bacon, dance director Busby Berkeley, USA, 1933)

Bernard, Raymond
Born 1891 in Paris, France. Director. The son of the playwright Tristran Bernard, Raymond Bernard began his career with adaptations of his father's plays, notably *Le Petit Café* (1919), with MAX LINDER. Later he was best known for his costly and finely staged spectacle films, such as *Le Miracle des Loups* (1924) and *Les Misérables* (1935). Bernard continued to direct until the 1950s, his later films including *La Dame aux camélias* (1953), *Les Fruits de l'été* (1955) and *Le Septième Commandement* (1956).

Bertini, Francesca
Born 1896 in Florence, Italy. In spite of her Tuscan birth, Bertini, whose real name is Elena Vitielle, is from a Neapolitan family. She acted in the Neapolitan dialect theatre as a child with her parents, who had their own company. Her first important film role was in *Rosa di Tebe* (1912), in which she played opposite one of the top stars of the Italian silent screen and stage, Amleto Novelli. The Tiber company borrowed her from Cines, paying her 2,000 lire a month. Yet three years later she signed a contract with Caesar which made her one of the most highly paid stars in the world. Different film companies argued over who had her under contract; this was valuable publicity for Bertini, who went on from success to success, signing a fabulous new contract in 1919. She was to have made eight films but after the third, *La Fanciulla di Amalfi* (1921), she decided to retire and married a Florentine nobleman. Like GARBO, she has never made a comeback.

Bertolucci, Bernardo
Born 1941 in Parma, Italy. Director. One of the most talented of the younger generation of Italian directors, he first came to prominence with *La Commare Secca* (1962) and *Prima della Rivoluzione* (1964), which combined neo-realist elements with a concern for contemporary social values. *Partner* (1968), a bizarre *Doppelgänger* fantasy attempted to absorb Godardian influences with mixed results, but with *The Conformist* (1970) he returned to political and social satire with considerable success, not least in the remarkable settings re-creating the Europe of the 1920s and 1930s, enclosing an atmosphere of intrigue, guilt and retribution. *The Spider's Strategy* (1970), made for Italian television, turns the hero myth upside-down whilst making acknowledgments to RESNAIS and, like the previous film, reveals a masterly feeling for colour, ranging from low-key interiors to sun-drenched country exteriors. The scripts he has written for other directors include collaboration on *Once Upon a Time in the West* (SERGIO LEONE, 1968), with its quirky response to a quite different milieu, that of the American West. He has also made an episode in *Love and Anger* (1967–9). JG

Big Close Up (BCU)
Shot taken nearer to the subject than necessary for a close-up. In relation to a human subject this would be a shot of the face only.

Billington, Kevin
Born 1933 in England. Television and radio trained British director whose reach, so far, has been rather more impressive than his grasp. Main films include: *Interlude* (1968), *The Rise and Rise of Michael Rimmer* (1970), *The Light at the Edge of the World* (1971).

Bitzer, G. William ('Billy') (1874–1944)
Born in Boston, Massachusetts, USA. One of the authentic pioneers of the cinema, Bitzer joined the Biograph Company in 1896 and was property man, electrician and general handyman before he graduated to being the company's cameraman and director. In 1899 he took the first film by artificial light, when he recorded the Jeffreys–Sharkey fight. The most fruitful period of Bitzer's career however was the 16 years in which he collaborated with D. W. GRIFFITH, from Griffith's first film *The Adventures of Dollie* (photographed by Arthur Marvin, but with Bitzer's advice) in 1908 to *America* (1924). Between them Bitzer and

Griffith devised a whole repertoire of camera devices – the iris, the fade, gauzes, masks; but the superb photography of the great Griffith films, such as *Intolerance*, *Birth of a Nation*, *Way Down East*, was Bitzer's own, achieved with inflexible, antiquated equipment, and often under conditions of extreme difficulty – the dust of a battlefield, or arctic cold. After parting with Griffith, who showed a preference for Henrik Sartov as his cameraman after 1924, Bitzer worked for other directors, but without achieving the same extraordinary results that he had enjoyed in the Griffith films. He died in obscurity and straitened circumstances four years before Griffith. DR

Bipack
The running of two films simultaneously through a camera or printer either to expose both or to expose one through the other. In a colour process denotes the location of two colour sensitive emulsions on separate films which are exposed simultaneously.

Björnstrand, Gunnar
Born 1909 in Stockholm, Sweden. Highly accomplished Swedish stage and screen character actor and a valued member of the INGMAR BERGMAN 'repertory' company. His air of quizzical elegance, which he adapts equally convincingly to comedy or tragedy, seems more typically French than Scandinavian. He made his film début in 1931 in *The False Millionaire*. Main films: *Frenzy* (1944) and over a dozen Bergman films, including *Sawdust and Tinsel* (1953), *Smiles of a Summer Night* (1955), *The Seventh Seal* (1956), *Winter Light* (1962), *Persona* (1966), *The Shame* and *The Rite* (1970).

Blackton, James Stuart (1875–1941)
Born in Sheffield, England. Director. Blackton – one of the most neglected figures in the early history of the American cinema – was unique as the only pioneer of the first years of movies who survived in the industry until the end of the silent period. Originally a newspaper cartoonist he was initiated into films when he was filmed at the Edison Studio, in 1896, as *Blackton the Evening World Cartoonist*. The following year, in partnership with Albert E. Smith, Blackton began film production, and established the Vitagraph Company. Many of the innovations which Blackton brought to editing and film acting predated GRIFFITH; and he was also a pioneer of animated films. Few of the vast number of films he directed are now remembered individually, though as a body his work is marked by high standards of craftsmanship and intelligence. Among his films may be specially recalled the highly successful early 'reconstructed actualities' *Tearing Down the Spanish Flag* (1897) and *The Battle of Santiago Bay* (1899), an extensive series of Shakespearean adaptations in 1908–9; and *The Glorious Adventure* (1922) made in Britain in the 'Prizmacolour' process, and starring Lady Diana

Above: Pierre Blanchar in 'Un Carnet de Bal' (Julien Duvivier, France, 1937)
Below: Laurence Olivier and Claire Bloom in 'Richard III' (Olivier, GB, 1954)

Manners. Blackton's last film was *Passionate Quest* (1926). DR

Blaché, Alice Guy
See GUY-BLACHÉ

Blanchar, Pierre (1895–1963)
Born in Philippeville, Algeria. Actor. Celebrated actor alike of the stage and screen, he appeared as early as 1923 in *Jocelyn*, and later in *L'Atlantide* (1931) and *Mademoiselle Docteur* (1936). He became recognized internationally through his outstanding performance as the epileptic doctor in *Un Carnet de Bal* (1937). His other more notable films include Chenal's *Crime and Punishment* (1936), *Pontcarral* (1942) and *La Symphonie Pastorale* (1946). During the occupation of France he was one of the foremost members of the underground Comité de Libération du Cinéma Français.

Blasetti, Alessandro
Born 1900 in Rome, Italy. Director. Began his career as film critic and editor on several Italian papers in the 1920s. With a group of friends, he made a feature film, *Sole* (1929), which began a career spanning the fascist 1930s, the neo-realist 1940s and the more uncertain 1950s and 1960s. Although Blasetti has never developed a really distinctive personal style, he has taken subjects of all kinds, from small-town comedies – *Four Steps in the Clouds* (1942) – to mass epics beloved by directors of his generation – *Fabiola* (1948). The early part of his career was particularly influential: an innovator in the early sound era with such period evocations as *1860* (1933) about Garibaldi's expedition to Sicily, done with much Russian-inspired revolutionary fervour, and continuing later with several enjoyably extravagant costume dramas – *Un'avventura di Salvator Rosa* (1940) and *La Corona di Ferro* (1941). His main neo-realist contribution was the little-known *Un giorno nella vita* (1946); apart from a few pleasant, minor comedies (*Prima Comunione*, 1950) and several sketch films, his post-war output has been relatively undistinguished. But his best work in various historical genres aptly reflects the Italian cinema's obsession with its country's political and social past. JG

Blimp
The soundproof cover used on any apparatus to prevent the sound of its mechanism being heard during sound recording.

Bloom, Claire
Born 1931 in London. Actress, with a cool charm and precise manner on the stage at the Old Vic before becoming a star in films. Main films: *The Blind Goddess* (1948), *Limelight* (1952), *The Man Between* (1953), *Richard III* (1954), *Alexander the Great* (1955), *The Brothers Karamazov* (1958), *Look Back in Anger* (1959), *The Spy who came in from the Cold* (1965), *Three into Two won't Go* and *A Severed Head* (1970).

Blow Up
Colloquial term for the enlargement of a picture, e.g. the production of a 35 mm film from a 16 mm original.

Boetticher, Budd
Born 1916 in Chicago, USA. American director of small-scale but superior Westerns and action melodramas, extravagantly admired by cine-enthusiasts. In Mexico, during his student days, he developed an interest in bull-fighting and became a pupil of a professional matador. He was taken on as technical adviser on a remake of *Blood and Sand* (1941), graduated to assistant director, then co-director. His initial

films as a director – under the name of Oscar Boetticher Jnr – were undistinguished 'quickies'. But his first considerable work – as Budd Boetticher – was *The Bullfighter and the Lady* (1951). His Westerns, especially those with RANDOLPH SCOTT, have a gritty integrity and simplicity much revered by critics of 'Cahiers du Cinéma': notably *Seven Men from Now* (1956) and *Ride Lonesome* (1959). He has also directed for television. Other principal films: *The Man from the Alamo* (1953), *The Magnificent Matador* and *The Killer is Loose* (1955), *The Tall T* and *Decision at Sundown* (1957), *The Rise and Fall of Legs Diamond* (1960), *Arruza* (1968), *A Time for Dying* (1969), the script of *Two Mules for Sister Sara* (1970). MH

Bogarde, Dirk
Born 1921 in London, England. British actor of Dutch descent who dramatically changed direction in mid-career. After Second World War service and a success on the stage in 'Power Without Glory', he was signed to an interminable Rank contract. His first leading role was in *Esther Waters* (1948). Following a run of problem juvenile roles, he became Britain's leading screen matinee idol in the *Doctor in the House* series. After 12 years of bland screen stardom, he played the homosexual hero in *Victim* (1961) and changed his image even more drastically in a number of films with director JOSEPH LOSEY: *The Servant* (1963), *King and Country* (1964), *Modesty Blaise* (1966), *Accident* (1967). Now a highly accomplished and internationally acclaimed character actor, living in Europe. Latest films: *The Fixer* (1968), *Justine* and *The Damned* (1969), *Death in Venice* (1970). MH

Above: Dirk Bogarde in 'Death in Venice' (Luchino Visconti, Italy, 1970)
Below: 'Comanche Station' (Budd Boetticher, USA, 1960)

Bogart, Humphrey (1900–1957)
Born in New York, USA. One of the great Hollywood stars who represented the tough-surfaced, soft-centred lost generation of the 1930s and 1940s for his own and subsequent generations. Years after his death, he and his films became a cult-hobby with the young. Bogart served in the Navy in the First World War and on demobilization worked on the Stock Exchange for a time. He went into the theatre, graduated to acting and made his first Broadway appearance in 'Drifting' in 1922.

The accomplished, surprisingly suave Broadway actor made his first film in 1930, *Devil with Women*, and a few others, but he failed to arouse much interest and returned to the stage until he played the gangster Duke Mantee in *The Petrified Forest* (1936). He became Hollywood's third-string gangster – after JAMES CAGNEY and EDWARD G. ROBINSON – in many films, mostly for Warners, including *Dead End* (1937), *The Amazing Dr Clitterhouse* and *Angels with Dirty Faces* (1938), *The Roaring Twenties* (1939). In *High Sierra* (1941) his gangster was more sympathetic and the same year he made *The Maltese Falcon* for JOHN HUSTON, an association which – with *The Treasure of Sierra Madre* (1947), *Key Largo* (1948) – was to prove a turning point in both careers.

The bitter-sweet tough guy, with his irresistible built-in lisp, full of emotional complexes and moral rectitude, was firmly established with *Casablanca* (1942). But the greater

range of Bogart's dramatic talent was not finally recognized until *The African Queen* (1951), for which he won an Academy Award. In 1945, he married his fourth wife LAUREN BACALL, with whom he starred in several films, including *The Big Sleep* (1946), in which he vividly created Raymond Chandler's private eye Philip Marlowe. Other notable films: *To Have and Have Not* (1944), *Murder Inc* (1951), *Beat the Devil* (1953), *The Caine Mutiny*, *Sabrina Fair* and *The Barefoot Contessa* (1954) and his last *The Harder They Fall* (1956). MH

Bolognini, Mauro
Born 1923 in Pistoia, Italy. Director. Starting his career as assistant to ZAMPA, DELANNOY and ALLÉGRET, Bolognini emerged as a director in his own right with *Ci troviamo in galeria* (1953). Bolognini's best films have been *Giovani mariti* (1957), *Il Bel Antonio* (1960), *La Viaccia* (1961), *Senilità* and *Agostino* (1962), *L'Absolute Naturale* (1969), *Metello* (1970), *Bubu* (1971); his period work in particular shows a great flair for design and colour.

Bolt, Robert
Born 1924 in Manchester, England. Prestigious British playwright and screenwriter whose association with director DAVID LEAN has produced three of the biggest post-war film successes: *Lawrence of Arabia* (1962), *Doctor Zhivago* (1965) and *Ryan's Daughter* (1970). A teacher, then radio script-writer, he survived the rejection of countless plays before 'Flowering Cherry' was accepted and became a hit in 1957. He also wrote the screenplay for the film version of his own play, *A Man for all Seasons* (1967). By comparison with his previous work, his first original screenplay, *Ryan's Daughter*, seems both shallow and too pretentious for its slim, romantic theme. In 1971 he directed his first film *Lady Caroline Lamb*.

Bondarchuk, Sergei
Born 1920 in Belozersk, Ukraine, USSR. Actor and director. Studied to become an actor in Rostov-on-Don, and appeared first in an army theatrical group. Studied again in Moscow after the war, his first film appearance being in GERASSIMOV's *The Young Guard* (1948). His many films as an actor include *Story of a Real Man* (1948), *Cavalier of the Golden Star* (1950), MIKHAIL ROMM's *Admiral Ushakov* (1953), Samson Samsonov's *The Grasshopper* (1955), and YUTKEVITCH's *Othello* (1955). He is best known in heroic character roles, with tragedy or suffering involved, showing his capacity for quiet, intense, serious performance. He played such a part in his first film as director, *Destiny of a Man* (1959), the story of the rehabilitation of a Russian prisoner-of-war, and then showed his taste and capacity to direct one of the great spectaculars of screen history – the 8-hour, 4-part version of Tolstoy's *War and Peace* (1964–7), in which he played Pierre. He also directed the Russo-Italian production, *Waterloo* (1970), in which the battle-scenes on widescreen outflanked to some extent the performances by an outstanding cast, headed by ROD STEIGER. Latest film (as an actor) *Uncle Vanya* (1971). RM

Above: Humphrey Bogart in 'Treasure of Sierra Madre' (John Huston, USA, 1947)

Below: Sergei Bondarchuk in 'Destiny of a Man' (Bondarchuk, USSR, 1959)

Boom
The movable mechanical arm from which a microphone is suspended during shooting.

Boorman, John
Born 1933 in London, England. Leading younger generation British director who came to films via a distinguished career in radio and television documentary. His first feature film *Catch Us if You Can* (1966) was overshadowed by other more successful films, notably RICHARD LESTER's *A Hard Day's Night* (1964) and *Help!* (1965), which sought to capture the essence of the new British pop musical on the screen. But his first American film *Point Blank* (1967) was a powerful reworking of the classic gangster theme that has gained in prestige through the years. Other films: *Hell in the Pacific* (1968), *Leo the Last* (1969).

Borowczyk, Walerian
Born 1923 in Kwilcz, Poland. Animator and director. Studied at the Polish Academy of Fine Arts, and became an established graphic artist 1951–5. Worked initially on films with JAN LENICA, with whom he made the experimental film *Once Upon a Time* (1957) – the metamorphosis of a slightly sinister, undefined furry creature – *Love Requited* (1957) and *Dom* (*House*, 1957), the projection in hallucinatory images of a girl's fears at being left alone in a house. Like Lenica, Borowczyk left Poland to work in France, where he settled in 1959. Working on his own, he made *L'École* (1958), the absurd gyrations of a soldier on manoeuvres, and, using collage and pixillation techniques, *Les Astronautes* (1959), a satiric exposure of competitive space-travel. Borowczyk's work is deeply pessimistic about the state of the world, introducing violence and the absurd with strikingly original visual techniques. Any form of animation may be used as it is felt to be apt. The simplest visual idea, as in *Renaissance* (an almost child-like assembly of toys and other objects which emerge from chaos into order, and then collapse once again into chaos), contains profound disquiet. In *Le Dictionnaire de Joachim* (1966) each letter in the alphabet gives rise to satiric definition of its representative word. *Les Jeux des Anges* (1964) is a nightmare journey into the horrors of the concentration camp. His feature-length film *Le Théâtre de M et Mme Kabal* (1962–7) concerns characters representing cruelty. Meanwhile in *Le Phonographe* (1969) Borowczyk has made a gentler film about the rivalry of two tunes recorded on gramophone cylinders of 1905. In 1968 he scripted and directed his first live-action feature, *Goto, L'Île d'Amour*, the disturbing study of ruthless totalitarianism on an island isolated from the rest of the world, the reference to love being ironic. Latest film: *Blanche* (1971). RM

Borzage, Frank (1893–1962)
Born in Salt Lake City, Utah, USA. Director. Began acting when a teenager, later playing in several important THOMAS INCE films (1914–5). After a period of acting and directing, he became a full-time director in 1917, his first important film being *Humoreske* (1920). His large silent output took in comedies and romantic dramas, the most notable being *Lazybones* (1925), a sensitive, beautifully played piece of rural Americana, and *Seventh Heaven* (1927), a First World War romance whose open-hearted sentimentality and fine atmospheric qualities gained him an Oscar and virtually made his reputation. Other characteristic silent films include *Street Angel* (1928), *Lucky Star* and *The River* (1929). The 1930s was also a rich period including *A Farewell to Arms* (1932), *A Man's Castle* (1933), several sophisticated comedies and satires (*Desire*, 1936), and more lush romantic sagas like *History is Made at Night* (1937) and *Three Comrades* (1938). His work from the mid-1940s was less interesting, except for a strange, somewhat pretentious chase melodrama *Moonrise* (1948). Borzage was a fine technician, with an expert feeling for camerawork and design influenced, occasionally, by German traditions; some of his subjects were excessively maudlin but his best work has the rich, romantic glow redolent of the American 1920s and 1930s. JG

Bost, Pierre
See AURENCHE, JEAN

Boulting, John and Roy
Born 1914 in Buckinghamshire, England. Ambidextrous British film-makers, twin brothers, who have served the film industry in many capacities, usually alternating as producer and director. Starting their film careers separately, they teamed up to found Charter Film Productions in 1937, specialising in thoughtful, hard-hitting films such as *Pastor Hall* (1939), *Thunder Rock* (1942). After the Second World War, they continued in this socially conscious vein with *Fame is the Spur* (1946), *Brighton Rock* (1947), *The Guinea Pig* (1949), *Seven Days to Noon* (1950). The success of the comedy *Private's Progress* (1955) encouraged them to broaden their range with a series of increasingly boisterous satires on various aspects of the British Establishment – *Brothers in Law* (1956), *Lucky Jim* (1957), *I'm All Right Jack* (1959), *Heaven's Above* (1963), *Rotten to the Core* (1965). They are also policy-making directors of British Lion Films. Recent films: *The Family Way* (1966), *Twisted Nerve* (1968), *There's a Girl in my Soup* (1970). MH

Bow, Clara (1905–1965)
Born in Brooklyn, USA. As the 'It'-girl, Clara Bow was one of the archetypal figures of the Roaring Twenties, along with Jack Dempsey, Lindbergh, Aimée MacPherson, Al Capone and AL JOLSON. She was brought to Hollywood as a result of one of the first beauty contests and made her film début in CHRISTIE CABANNE's *Beyond the Rainbow* (1922). She was given con-

Above: James Hall and Clara Bow in 'The Fleet's In' (Malcolm St Clair, USA, 1928)
Below: Margaret Rutherford in 'I'm All Right Jack' (John and Roy Boulting, GB, 1959)

tinual work during the next few years, and gave notable performances in *My Lady of Whims*, *Dancing Mothers*, *Mantrap* and *Kid Boots* (all 1926); but the turning point of her career was when Elinor Glyn selected her for the leading role in *It* (1927). For the next three years Bow's career was at its zenith. She could not however protect herself against scandal; and after her marriage to the cowboy star Rex Bell, she retired from the screen. Two attempts at comebacks in 1931 and 1932 were unsuccessful. Bow's career was deserved: with her radiant looks and inescapable sexuality she combined the gifts of a first-rate comedienne and actress, turning with facility from pathos to high farce. DR

Boyer, Charles
Born 1899 in France. Actor on stage and screen who made his name in Hollywood in the 1930s as a romantic 'great lover' type. Has also worked in French films and in television. Main films: *La Ronde Infernale* (1927), *Liliom* (1933), *Mayerling* (1934), *The Garden of Allah* (1936), *Tovarich* (1937), *Marie Walewska* and *Algiers* (1938), *All This and Heaven Too* (1940), *The Constant Nymph* (1944), *Confidential Agent* (1945), *Fanny* (1961), *How to Steal a Million* (1966), *Barefoot in the Park* (1967), *The Mad Woman of Chaillot* and *The April Fools* (1969).

'B' Picture
Film designed as a second or supporting feature in a commercial cinema programme

Brackett, Charles (1892–1969)
Born in New York State, USA. Astringent American writer and producer whose most distinguished period was during his association with BILLY WILDER at Paramount. A short story writer, drama critic and author, he went to Hollywood in the 1930s and collaborated on the screenplays for *Ninotchka* and *Midnight* (1939), *Arise My Love* (1940) and *Ball of Fire* (1941). His witty, sophisticated style ideally matched the talents of Wilder, and together they made *Five Graves to Cairo* (1943), *Double Indemnity* (1944), *The Lost Weekend* (1945), *A Foreign Affair* (1948) and *Sunset Boulevard* (1950). The partnership was almost too successful to last. Brackett went to Fox as a solo producer, but never achieved the same cinematic harmony again. Other main films: *Titanic* (1953), *The King and I* (1956), *Journey to the Centre of the Earth* (1957), *State Fair* (1961).

Brakhage, Stan
Born 1933 in Kansas City, Missouri, USA. Underground film-maker. Studied film-making in San Francisco, and began his enormous output of films in the early 1950s. Sheldon Renan, historian of the underground cinema, says of him that he is 'the major transitional figure in the turning away of 'experimental' film from literature and surrealist psychodrama and in its subsequent move towards the more purely personal and visual'. His earlier films include *Desistfilm* (1953), *Flesh of the Morning* (1957, a film about masturbation), and *Loving* (1957–8). He became an addict of the camera, experimenting in its capacities to create new vision for him. This vision was seen in *Anticipation of the Night* (1958), *Wedlock House: An Intercourse* (1959), a study of his own marriage, and *Prelude* (1961). His major work is *Dog Star Man* (1959–64). Following the theft of his 16 mm camera, he concentrated on the potentialities of 8 mm film-making. Many of his films have dealt with childhood and the behaviour of very young children. RM

Brando, Marlon
Born 1924 in Nebraska, USA. Pre-eminent post-war American actor whose style, much misunderstood 'Method' and total involvement with his characters produced an army of imitators and revolutionized the concept of acting in American films.

The archetypal Brando performances in his early screen career developed through the animalistic Kowalski in *A Streetcar Named Desire* (1951) and the rampaging 'easy rider' in *The Wild One* (1954) to the still primitive but growingly receptive hero of *On the Waterfront* (1954), for which he won an Academy Award. Obsessed by the box-office type rather than the talent behind it, Hollywood tried to clamp him into the role that had proved so commercial. His battle to stretch his range and branch out as a producer and director – *One-eyed Jacks* (1959) – left him bitter and, in the estimation of some critics, defeated.

In the past ten years he has nothing like fulfilled the apparently endless promise of his early career, though his films – apart from the crass *Candy* (1968) – have not lacked interest. A protégé of dramatic teacher Stella Adler and, later, stage and screen director ELIA KAZAN, he played his first Broadway role at 15 in 'I Remember Mama', following this with several notable stage performances which won him praise and, eventually, acclaim in 'A Streetcar Named Desire'. In 1950 he went to Hollywood, appeared as the paraplegic hero of FRED ZINNEMANN's *The Men*, followed by the film of *Streetcar*. Personally, he was a calculated nonconformist at a time when Hollywood was still conforming to its own past reputation as the glamour factory. Though he played many varied characters – the Mexican revolutionary in *Viva Zapata!* (1952), Mark Antony in *Julius Caesar* (1953), Napoleon in *Désirée* (1954), the Broadway gambler in the musical *Guys and*

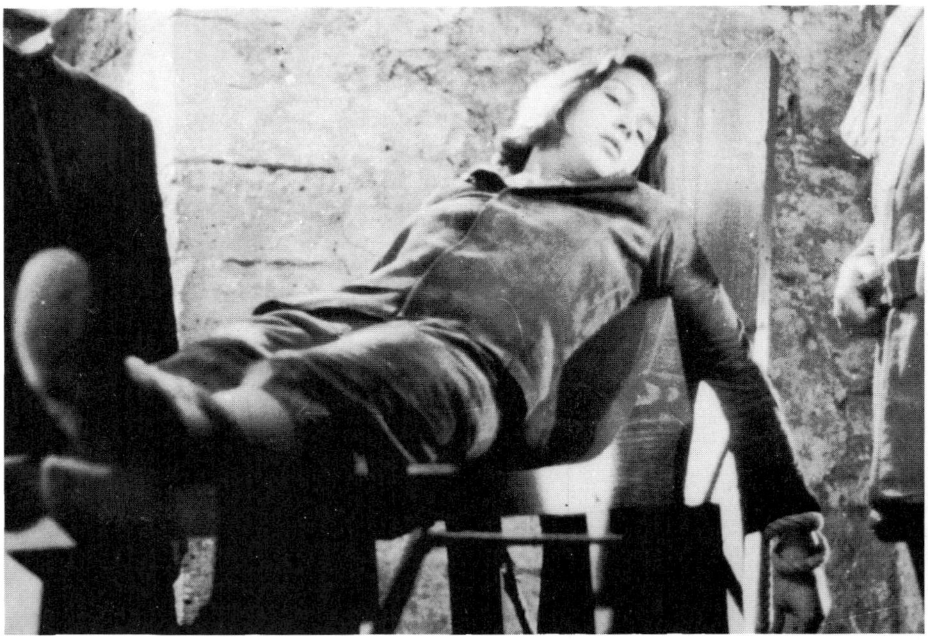

Above: Florence Carrez in 'Procès de Jeanne d'Arc' (Robert Bresson, France, 1962)
Below: Pierre Brasseur in 'Barbe Bleu' (Christian-Jaque, France, 1951)

Dolls (1955) – the popular image of Brando as the mumbling slob persisted.

In the 1960s, he devoted himself to the Civil Rights Movement in America. Other notable films: *The Young Lions* (1958), *Mutiny on the Bounty* (1962), *The Chase* (1966), *A Countess from Hong Kong* (1966, for Chaplin), *Reflections in a Golden Eye* (1967), *¡ Queimada!* (1970), *The Night-Comers* and *The Godfather* (1971). MH

Brasseur, Pierre
Born 1903 in Paris, France. Imposing French stage and screen actor and occasional playwright. His distinguished career in the theatre has been paralleled in films since 1925. An actor with a masterful presence and commanding voice he has appeared most notably in *Quai des Brumes* (1938), *Lumière d'Eté* (1942), *Les Enfants du Paradis* (1944), *Les Portes de la Nuit* (1946), *Julie de Carneilhan* (1950), *Il Bell' Antonio* (1960), *Deux Heures à Tuer* (1965) and in several major films by FRANJU.

Brazil
See LATIN AMERICA

Brenon, Herbert (1880–1958)
Born in Dublin, Ireland. Director. Emigrating to the USA in 1896, Brenon began his career as an actor, but went into the cinema around 1912, directing his first film, *Ivanhoe*, the following year. His first great successes were the films featuring the swimming star Annette Kellerman – *Neptune's Daughter* (1914), *Daughter of the Gods* (1916) – though LEWIS JACOBS considered *War Brides* (1916), which starred NAZIMOVA and was withdrawn from circulation after America's entry into the war, as his best silent film. In the 1920s, specializing in spectacular and prestige productions like *Peter Pan* (1925), *The Great Gatsby*, *A Kiss for Cinderella*, *Beau Geste* (all 1926) and *Laugh, Clown Laugh* (1928), Brenon was reckoned to be 'the X in Fox'. Brenon's star faded with the coming of talkies; and in 1934 he came to England, directing his last film, *The Flying Squad*, in 1940. DR

Bresson, Robert
Born 1907 in Auvergne, France. Director. Studied painting in his youth and was assistant to several French directors in the 1930s. Apart from a comedy short made in 1934, his directing career did not begin until *Les Anges du péché* (1943), a convent drama set in a fairly conventional mould but with above-average characterization. With *Les Dames du Bois de Boulogne* (1945), a Diderot adaptation with COCTEAU dialogue, Bresson's style – with its rigorous paring down and precise character delineation – became consolidated and assured. His next two films, *Journal d'un curé de campagne* (1950) and *Un condamné à mort s'est échappé* (1956) are, for many people, his masterpieces – the first, an intense, interior study of a dying priest taken from Bernanos's novel; the second, an equally unsparing, though more optimistic, account of a French prisoner's escape from the Germans. Here, Bresson takes the audience on a kind of spiritual journey through the dark night of the soul, in which none of the expected dramatic emphases are allowed to intrude; 'all is grace' as the perfectly controlled images dissolve into each other (the great BUREL was Bresson's cameraman for many years), and a meticulous use of natural sounds gives life and depth to the narrative. *Pickpocket* (1959), with its flowing, detailed scenes of pickpockets at work was less successful when making acknowledgments to Dostoievsky; and *Procès de Jeanne d'Arc* (1962) turned the original records into a kind of documentary reportage, hard yet compassionate. With his subsequent work – including *Au Hasard, Balthazar* (1965), *Mouchette* (1967) and *Une Femme Douce* (1969) – the same rigorous principles (including the use of non-professional actors) are applied to a variety of subjects but, despite extraordinary scenes such as Mouchette's suicide by the river, Bresson now seems in danger of becoming a prisoner of his own style. What in earlier work seemed irrevocably correct, tends to appear forced, even calculated, in its effect rather as if the style is being forced on the subject. To understand Bresson fully, of course, one must be aware of the Catholic concepts which run all through his work, with the oft-repeated themes of death and humiliation leading to a spiritual redemption through suffering. Though it is possible to find aspects of this ideology repugnant, Bresson is a great enough artist to involve one completely in his rapt, personal vision, and in his latest work *Quatre Nuits d'un Rêveur* (1971), a great film-maker emerges once again in this typically muted tender reworking of Dostoievsky's 'White Nights'. JG

Bridge
A device or musical phrase to cover the gap between one musical area or mood and another. Also a short piece of animation used primarily in television cartoon shows to close the gap between different segments of a longer show which may be made up of shorter segments which have no natural continuity with each other.

Bridging Shot
Shot used to cover a time jump or a break in continuity

Bronston, Samuel
Born 1908 in Bessarabia, Romania. Independent producer of some taste and a flair for spectacular epics which eventually seized up when he was beset by financial troubles in the middle 1960s. A film distributor in Paris, then executive producer at Columbia, he also spent several years making films for the Vatican. In 1943 he set up his own company, was executive producer on *Jack London* (1943), *A Walk in the Sun* (1946). When large-scale productions became popular, to counteract the impact of television, he produced in ever increasing size *John Paul Jones* (1959), *King of Kings* (1960), *El Cid* (1961), the best of his epics, *55 Days at Peking* (1962), *The Fall of the Roman Empire* and *Circus World* (1964). Then the commercial bubble burst until the formation of his latest project *Isabella of Spain* (1972). MH

Brook, Clive
Born 1891 in London, England. Actor, who made his début in 1918. Educated at Dulwich College. Eventually became a distinguished leading man in Hollywood films, specializing in romantic parts which called for faultless gentlemanly behaviour. His silent films include: *A Debt of Honour* (1919), *Women to Women* (1921), *The Sheik* (1922), *Underworld* (1927), *The Four Feathers* (1928). His sound films include: *The Return of Sherlock Holmes* (1929), *Shanghai Express* (1932), *Cavalcade* (1933), *On Approval* (1944), which he directed. After virtually abandoning films for the stage he made a fleeting return to the screen in *The List of Adrian Messenger* (1963).

Brook, Peter
Born 1925 in London, England. British stage and screen director, whose provocative films have tended to excite respect rather than admiration. He became interested in film-making at Oxford, but started his career in the theatre, where he worked principally. During 1944–5 he wrote and directed instructional short films. After this, he was appointed director of productions at Covent Garden, worked at the Stratford Memorial Theatre, and produced plays for television. In 1952 he directed his first film (apart from an amateur production at Oxford), *The Beggar's Opera*. His most striking film was a fine adaptation of *Lord of the Flies* (1962). But the film versions of his unconventional stage productions – *Marat-Sade* (1966) and *Tell Me Lies* (1967) – were (some thought) pretentiously overwrought. Other films: *Moderato Cantabile* (1960), *King Lear* (1970). MH

Brooks, Louise
Born 1906 in Cherryvale, Kansas, USA. Actress. Trained as a dancer, she appeared with Ruth St Denis from 1921, and in the Ziegfeld Follies in 1925. Her unique good looks got her into films in undistinguished parts, though with distinguished fellow-players, such as ADOLPHE MENJOU in *A Social Celebrity* (1926) and W. C. FIELDS in *It's the Old Army Game*; she also appeared in JAMES CRUZE's film, *The City Gone Wild*. Her opportunity as an artist came when G. W. PABST, after seeing her in WILLIAM WELLMAN's *Beggars of Life* and HOWARD HAWKS's *A Girl in Every Port* (1928), invited her to Germany to star in his *Pandora's Box* (1928) and *The Diary of a Lost Girl* (1929). She had secured her release from Paramount with some difficulty, but in these nymphomaniac parts she realized her full potentiality for suggesting intense sexual passion with tragic implications which sprang from the basic innocence of the women involved. Returning to Hollywood, she became

Above: Louise Brooks in 'Pandora's Box' (G. W. Pabst, Germany, 1928)
Below: 'Freaks' (Tod Browning, USA, 1932)

extremely careful of the parts she chose, refusing far more than she accepted, and finally making herself bankrupt in 1932. Working only intermittently, she was never to reconquer the screen, and eventually shut herself away only to re-emerge in the 1950s to write and talk with great intelligence about the art of the film. But without her brief career in Pabst's silent films her great talents as an actress might never have been known. RM

Brooks, Richard
Born 1912 in Philadelphia, USA. Forceful American writer and director whose toughly idealistic films have latterly hovered uneasily between old-style traditionalism and contemporary trendiness. Starting out as a journalist, broadcaster and short story writer, he has also written several novels. His sinewy screenplays for *Swell Guy* and *Brute Force* (1947) and other hard-hitting films of the 1940s led to his first assignment as writer and director on *Crisis* (1950). Though his style is most distinctive with lean, masculine subjects – *Deadline USA* (1952), *The Blackboard Jungle* and *The Last Hunt* (1955), *The Professionals* (1966) – his adaptations of Tennessee Williams's plays, *Cat on a Hot Tin Roof* (1958) and, especially, *Sweet Bird of Youth* (1961) were strikingly successful and a high-keyed version of Sinclair Lewis's *Elmer Gantry* (1960) was a *tour de force* which won him an Academy Award for the screenplay. Other principal films: *Battle Circus* (1952), *The Last Time I Saw Paris* (1954), *Something of Value* (1957), *The Brothers Karamazov* (1958), *Lord Jim* (1964), *In Cold Blood* (1967), *Happy Ending* (1969). MH

Brown, Clarence
Born 1890 in Clinton, USA. In the course of a long career Brown succeeded uniquely in remaining a 'commercial' director without ever compromising his own artistic integrity and excellence. Trained as an automobile engineer, he entered the cinema as assistant to MAURICE TOURNEUR; and two of his first films, *The Last of the Mohicans* (1920) and *The Foolish Matron* (1921), were directed with Tourneur. Brown's name first appears solo on the credits of *The Great Redeemer* (1920). Brown's mixture of romanticism and delicate satirical humour ideally suited him to be a director of stars: Pauline Frederick in *Smouldering Fires* (1924), VALENTINO in *The Eagle* (1925), Louise Dresser in *The Goose Woman* (1925), Norma Talmadge in *Kiki* (1926); and above all the series of films he made with GRETA GARBO: *Flesh and the Devil* (1927), *A Woman of Affairs* (1928), *Anna Christie* and *Romance* (1930), *Inspiration* (1931), *Anna Karenina* (1935), *Conquest* (1937). Throughout the 1930s, also, Brown was directing prestige vehicles for CLARK GABLE, JOAN CRAWFORD, MYRNA LOY and NORMA SHEARER. Later films included *National Velvet* (1944), *The Yearling* (1946), *Intruder in the Dust* (1949), *When in Rome* (1952) and *Plymouth Adventure* (1953). DR

Brown, Joe E.
Born 1892 in USA. Actor and comedian, famous for his large mouth and wide smile. Has performed in circus and vaudeville and made his film début in 1928 with *Crooks Can't Win*. Main films: *On with the Show* (1929), *Sally* (1930), *The Tenderfoot* (1932), *A Midsummer Night's Dream* (1935), *Shut My Big Mouth* (1941), *Pin-Up Girl* (1943), *The Tender Years* (1949), *Showboat* (1951), *Some Like it Hot* (1959), *A Comedy of Terrors* (1963). See his autobiography 'Laughter is a Wonderful Thing' (1959).

Brown, Rowland (1900–1963)
Born in Ohio, USA. Director and screenwriter. He came to Hollywood in 1928, became a gag man and then scenario contributor. Wrote and directed three crime melodramas, *Quick Millions* (1931), *Hell's Highway* (1932) and *Blood Money* (1934), which revealed an original flair in handling narrative and actors as well as a distinctive visual style and a close knowledge of underworld morality. His individualistic manner did not endear him to producers and his directorial career came to an end in the 1930s, although he continued writing scripts for several years for Warner Brothers, one being for *Angels with Dirty Faces* (1938). JG

Browning, Tod (1882–1944)
Born in Louisville (Kentucky), USA. Director. A conscientious and painstaking craftsman, Browning was possessed of a strange and unique vision, perceiving a sort of beauty in horror. Having run away from school to join a circus, Browning was a vaudeville comic at the time he joined Biograph Studios as an actor. He acted in GRIFFITH's *The Mother and the Law*, was an assistant on *Intolerance*, and directed his own first film in 1918 (*The Brazen Beauty*). He discovered his true vocation in the series of bizarre films made for MGM and starring LON CHANEY: *The Unholy Three* (1925), *The Blackbird* and *The Road to Mandalay* (1926), *The Unknown* and *London After Midnight* (1927), *The Big City* and *West of Zanzibar* (1928), *Where East is East* (1929). His activity became more restricted with the coming of sound and after the death of Chaney in 1930, though the sound films include his masterpiece *Freaks* (1932) as well as *Dracula* (with BELA LUGOSI, 1931) and *Devil Doll* (1936). Browning's last film was *Miracles for Sale* (1939). DR

Brynner, Yul
Born 1916 on Sakhalin Island, USSR. Actor and television director, he started his show-business career by singing in Paris night-clubs at the age of 13. He then worked as a trapeze artist and acted in repertory before making his film début in *Port of New York* (1949). For many years he worked in television and on Broadway, and in 1956 won an Academy award for his acting in the film version of his stage success 'The King and I'. After this film, which established him as a romantic star in spite (or because) of his baldness, he made many films in Hollywood including: *The Ten Commandments* and *Anastasia* (1956), *The Brothers Karamazov* and *The Journey* (1958), *Solomon and Sheba* and *Once more with Feeling* (1959), *The Magnificent Seven* (1960), *Escape to Zahrain* (1962), *The Magic Christian* and *The Mad Woman of Chaillot* (1969).

Bulgaria
This small, mainly rural country of some $8\frac{1}{4}$ million people has approximately 3,000 cinemas. Bulgaria began the production of films early (1910), but comparatively few were completed before the Second World War and the post-war establishment of a communist régime. The film industry was nationalized in 1948, and the initial films represented the normal style of Russian-inspired, patriotic and ideologically dedicated production, the leading directors being Zahari Zhandov (born 1911), Anton Marinovitch (born 1907), and Boris Shariliev (born 1922). A less conformist cinema emerged during the 1960s with a recession in the number of films with primarily political content, and the establishment of more purely human, individual subjects, and the production of entertainment films as such. Documentary films were developed alongside, and animation (led by Todor Dinov, born 1919) has flourished. The more notable Bulgarian films include:

1958 *On the Little Island* (Rangel Vulchanov, born 1928)
1959 *Stars* (Konrad Wolf; Bulgarian-GDR co-production)
1960 *First Lesson* (Rangel Vulchanov)
1961 *We Were Young* (Binka Zheljazkova, born 1923)
1964 *The Peach Thief* (Vulo Radev, born 1923)
1965 *The She-Wolf* (Rangel Vulchanov)
The Troubled Road (Yakim Kakimov)
1966 *Knight without Armour* (Boris Shariliev)
Hot Noon (Zacco Heskia)
1967 *The Longest Night* (Vulo Radev)
Sidetrack (Todor Stoyanov, born 1930, and Grisha Ostrovski)
The Scent of Almonds (Ljubomir Sharlandgiev, born 1931)
The Attached Balloon (Binka Zheljazkova)
1968–9 *Black Angels* (Vulo Radev)
Five from Moby Dick (Todor Stoyanov and Grisha Ostrovski)
1970–1 *Gerlovo Event* (Grisha Ostrovski)
A Strange Duel (Todor Stoyanov)
Wrathful Journey (Nikolai Korabov)
Confession (Yanko Yankov, born 1924)

Bulgaria has a noted composer of film music in Simeon Pironkov, who wrote the scores for many of the above films. The industry has an output of some 14 features annually, produced mainly at the studios in Sofia, but many co-produced with socialist and non-socialist countries alike. RM

Above: Luis Buñuel
Below: Catherine Deneuve in 'Tristana' (Luis Buñuel, Spain, 1970)
Below left: Nevena Koxanova in 'Sidetrack' (Todor Stoyanov and Grisha Ostrovski, Bulgaria, 1967)

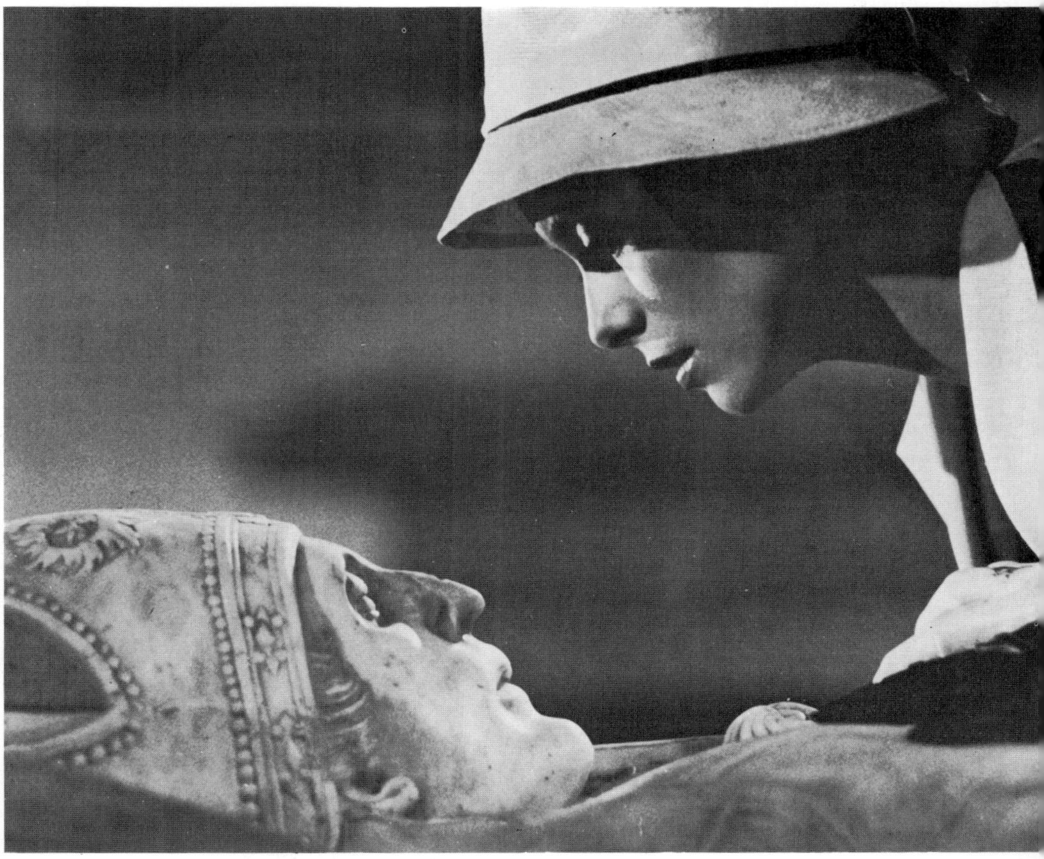

Bunny, John (1863–1915)
Born in New York, USA. America's first international comic star, Bunny had been a successful actor and manager before, shrewdly perceiving the potential of motion pictures, he offered his services to the Vitagraph Company in 1910. Rotund, genial and irresistibly comic, Bunny tended to be cast in stories which turned on social mix-ups and domestic embarrassments involving his plain and shrewish wife, played by Flora Finch. So successful were his films abroad that after his death the Russians created a series with an impersonator, V. Zimovoi, who adopted Bunny's Russian pseudonym of 'Poxon'. He made over 150 films, among which are included: *The New Stenographer* (1910), *Vanity Fair* (1911), *Bunny in Bunnyland* (1915).

Buñuel, Luis
Born 1900 in Calanda, Spain. Notwithstanding a virtually total interruption to his creative career during the 15 years between 1932 and

1947, Buñuel's work shows a continuity of interests and a consistency of achievement unmatched in the history of the cinema. Uncompromising, even when he has worked under the most constricting commercial conditions, he has remained faithful to his artistic origins in surrealism and the cultural heritage of his native Spain; and unchanging in his characteristic anarchic comedy and the anger which masks a deep, even sentimentally humanist affection.

After studying literature and philosophy at the University of Madrid, he went to Paris, and in 1923 became assistant to JEAN EPSTEIN. As a frequenter of the *surréaliste* group, he became associated with Salvador Dali on *Un chien andalou* (1928); and though their names appear jointly on the credits of this film – the most durable of all the works of the silent avant-garde – it now appears to bear the authentic signature of Buñuel himself. Next Buñuel made a full-length surrealist film, *L'Age d'or* (1930), financed by the Vicomte de Noailles, in which sound was used with the same scabrous wit as the images. The film, with its celebration of *l'amour fou* and its blasphemous equations of Christ and the Marquis de Sade, provoked enthusiasm and furious protest in fairly equal proportions. Returning to Spain Buñuel made *Tierra sin Pan* (1932), a bitter and satirical documentary about the plight of the Hurdes, a wretchedly poor and primitive rural community in Spain. From Paris Buñuel was recruited to Warner Brothers in a production capacity. In 1935–6 he was director of production for Filmofono of Madrid, for whom he supervised a few documentaries. In 1939 he returned to Hollywood, worked on Spanish dubbed versions for Warners and briefly at the Museum of Modern Art in New York. Only in 1946–7 did he resume feature film direction, in Mexico. Following *Gran Casino* (1947) and *El Gran Calavero* (1949), the enormous success of *Los Olvidados* (1950) and the Grand Prix which it won at Cannes in 1951 restored Buñuel definitively to the first rank of film artists, although he continued to work within the context of the Mexican commercial cinema, producing a long series of brilliant and characteristic films with very small budgets and shooting schedules: *Susana* (1950), *Don Quintin el Amargado, Una Mujer sin Amor* and *Subida al cielo* (1951), *El Bruto, Robinson Crusoe* and *El* (1952), *Abismos de Pasión* (adapted from 'Wuthering Heights'), *La ilusion viaja en tranvia* (1953), *El rio y la muerte* (1954), *Ensayo de un crimen* (1955). Later he made *Cela s'appelle l'aurore* and *La Mort en ce Jardin* (1956) and *La Fièvre monte à El Pao* (1959). There seemed no end to Buñuel's capacity for renewal, and after his return to Mexico in 1959 it was to make the first of the series of masterpieces of his mature years, *Nazarin*, which relates the difficulties of leading the truly Christian life in an imperfect world. After *The Young One* (1960) he made his first feature in his native Spain – *Viridiana* (1961), which resumed the theme of *Nazarin* with a carefree blasphemy and indecency which took the Spanish authorities somewhat by surprise. From this time Buñuel's career has been peripatetic. In Mexico he made *El Angel Exterminador* (1962), a return to purely surrealist themes; in France *Le Journal d'une Femme de Chambre* (1964), in striking contrast to RENOIR's adaptation of the same Mirbeau novel; in Mexico again the short feature *Simon del Desierto*; in France the masterly *Belle de Jour* (1967), his greatest popular success, and *La Voie Lactée* (1968), which turned a surrealist's eyes upon the heresies of the Catholic church. In 1970 Buñuel returned once more to Spain, whose culture has always been so formative to his work, to adapt a novel by Perez Galdos as *Tristana*. DR

Burel, Léonce-Henri

Born 1892 in Indret, France. Cinematographer. Became the great pioneering French cameraman of the silent period, his work including several collaborations with ABEL GANCE – *J'Accuse* (1918), *La Roue* (1922), *Napoléon* (1927) – whose grandiose imagination encouraged Burel to achieve many photographic innovations. His lighting style is one of the most distinctive in all cinema – with its precise manipulation of light and shade and extreme clarity in location scenes – and this highly refined plastic sense was most discernible in his later work for BRESSON, including *Le Journal d'un curé de campagne* (1951), *Un condamné à mort s'est échappé* (1956), *Pickpocket* (1959), *Procès de Jeanne d'Arc* (1962). He was, in fact, the unique instrument through which Gance, FEYDER and Bresson, among others, were able to express their vision. JG

Burks, Robert (1910–1968)

Born in USA. Cinematographer. Began in special effects and then became famous as HITCHCOCK's lighting cameraman on about 12 films including: *Strangers on a Train* (1951), *The Trouble with Harry* (1955), *The Wrong Man* (1957), *Vertigo* (1958), *North by Northwest* (1959), *The Birds* (1963), *Marnie* (1964). He developed a beautiful plastic sense, especially in the use of colour, and helped to build up the Hitchcockian atmosphere of mystery and suspense. Outstanding work for other directors includes: *The Unsuspected* (1947), *Key Largo* (1948), *Beyond the Forest* (1949), *The Enforcer* (*Murder Inc*, 1951), *The Spirit of St Louis* (1957).

Burnett, W. R.

Born 1899 in Ohio, USA. Prolific American writer of strong crime novels and screenplays which helped shape the gangster film trend of the 1930s and 1940s, as well as influence its revival in the 1960s. His work as novelist and/or screenwriter includes: *Little Caesar* (1930), *Scarface* (1932), *High Sierra* (1940), *This Gun for Hire* (1942), *The Asphalt Jungle* (1950), *The Racket* (1951), *Illegal* (1955).

Burton, Richard

Born 1925 in Pontrhyfen, Wales. Actor, at first on the stage. Made his film début in 1948 in *The Last Days of Dolwyn*; British films include *Waterfront* (1950), *Green Grow the Rushes* (1951) and *Look Back in Anger* (1959). He went to Hollywood in 1952 and made *My Cousin Rachel, The Robe* and *The Desert Rats* (1953) and *Alexander the Great* (1956). He then appeared in several films with ELIZABETH TAYLOR whom he married in 1964, including *Cleopatra* (1962), *The V.I.P.s* (1963), *Who's Afraid of Virginia Woolf?* (1966), *The Taming of the Shrew* (1967), *Dr Faustus* (which he co-directed and produced, 1967) and *Boom* (1968). His other films include: *Becket* (1964), *The Spy Who Came in from the Cold* (1965), *The Night of the Iguana* (1966), *Anne of the Thousand Days* (1970), *Villain* and *Under Milk Wood* (1971), *The Assassination of Trotsky* (1972).

Bute, Mary Ellen

Born period First World War in Houston, Texas, USA. Experimental film-maker. Began her career working with LEWIS JACOBS, and later concentrated with her husband, the cinematographer Ted Nemeth, on a series of abstract films using three-dimensional objects, linking light, colour and music. In black-and-white she made *Anitra's Dance* (1936), *Evening Star* (1937), and *Parabola* (1938), followed by the colour films *Toccata and Fugue* (1940), *Tarantella* and *Sport Spools* (1941). Her later films in this style include *Polka-Graph* (1953), *Color Rhapsody* (1954). Her live-action films include a feature based on sections of Joyce's 'Finnegan's Wake' (1964–5) and a version of WILDER's 'The Skin of our Teeth', which she began in 1966.

Elizabeth Taylor and Richard Burton in 'The Taming of the Shrew' (Franco Zeffirelli, USA, 1967)

C

Cabanne, William Christie (1888–1950)
Born in St Louis, USA. Director. An actor and assistant to D. W. GRIFFITH, Cabanne directed his first film (*The Sisters*, starring LILLIAN and DOROTHY GISH) in 1914, though he enjoyed his first real successes with the series of films which launched DOUGLAS FAIRBANKS, at Triangle. A capable but never inspired craftsman, Cabanne declined into second feature direction, lasting into the late 1940s.

Cacoyannis, Michael
Born 1922 in Limassol, Cyprus. London-trained Greek director and sometime actor who has not lived up to his early promise as a film-maker with a sensitive flair for indigenous Greek themes. During the Second World War he worked in radio with the BBC Greek Service in London, afterwards studying drama at the Central School of Dramatic Arts. He returned to Greece, where he moved into feature film production with the highly acclaimed *Windfall in Athens* (1953), *Stella* (1954), *A Girl in Black* (1955). In 1965 he scored a large success internationally with *Zorba the Greek*, followed by the embarrassingly bizarre *The Day the Fish Came Out* (1967). Latest film: *The Trojan Women* (1971).

Cagney, James
Born 1904 in New York, USA. One of the principal star personalities originating in the Hollywood heyday of the 1930s and a versatile actor overshadowed by his own distinctive tough-talking, fast-moving 'image'. Vaudevillian, dancer and chorus boy on Broadway, he eventually made a hit on the stage in 1930 in 'Sinner's Holiday', which was later filmed. He made his film début early in 1930 in *Doorway to Hell*, but it wasn't until *Public Enemy* (1931) that he registered with the public. His ruthless, irrepressible heroes (on either side of the law) who made up in vitality what they lacked in size were featured in countless Warner films. An urban Depression hero, he was one of the few Hollywood actors who could never come to terms with Westerns. In 1943 he won an Academy Award for his portrayal of George M. Cohan in the patriotic musical, *Yankee Doodle Dandy*. He directed one film, *Short Cut to Hell* (1958), and has been in retirement since the early 1960s. Other notable films: *A Midsummer Night's Dream* (in which he played a creditable Bottom, 1935), *The Roaring Twenties* (1939), *The Time of Your Life* (1948), *White Heat* (1949), *Mister Roberts* (1955), *Man of a Thousand Faces* (1957, a 'life' of Lon Chaney), *Shake Hands with the Devil* (1959), *One, Two, Three* (1961). MH

Above: Vivien Merchant and Michael Caine in 'Alfie' (Lewis Gilbert, GB, 1966)
Below: James Cagney in 'Public Enemy' (William Wellman, USA, 1931)

Caine, Michael
Born 1933 in London, England. Popular British 'working-class' actor whose underrated skills as a versatile player have been allied to an adroit personal flair for career-building. Enjoying only a mild success in the theatre and on television, he made his film début inauspiciously in *A Hill in Korea* (1956). In 1963 his uncharacteristic portrayal of an effete Army officer in *Zulu* made him a star. But the character that most firmly established him was his dry, laconic Cockney spy in *The Ipcress File* (1965) and lady-killer in *Alfie* (1966).

Other notable films: *Gambit* (1966), *Hurry Sundown*, *Deadfall*, *Play Dirty* and *The Magus* (1968), *The Italian Job* and *Too Late the Hero* (1969), *The Last Valley* and *Get Carter* (1970), *Zee and Co.* (1971). MH

Camera Angle
The angle of view of a camera when set up to shoot. The qualifying terms 'high', 'low', 'wide', are related to an imaginary norm rougly corresponding to a 35 mm camera with a 2-inch (50·8 mm) lens pointed at a scene from shoulder height.

Camera Track
Movement of the camera towards, away from, or alongside an object

Camera Viewpoint
The position of the camera in relation to the subject being photographed

Camerini, Mario
Born 1895 in Rome, Italy. Director. Together with Augusto Genina, he belongs to the generation of Italian directors who began in the 1920s with costume and adventure dramas. He later developed a pleasant, if relatively impersonal, comic style in such films as *Men are Such Rascals* (with an early acting performance by DE SICA, who appeared in several other Camerini films of this period, 1932). After more costume films during the Second World War, his post-war activities range from conventional neo-realism (*Molti Sogni per le Strade*, 1948) to overblown epics (*Ulysses*, 1954) and a script collaboration with KING VIDOR on *War and Peace* (1956).

Canada
Film production in Canada is largely in documentary and short films, though features have increased in numbers during the later 1960s, reaching upwards of 12 productions annually. The most important centre for Canadian film-making is the National Film Board produces some 200 subjects annually, largely of a documentary and educational nature, together with films for children. The Board is well-known as the sponsor over a period of a quarter-century of NORMAN MCLAREN's magnificent animated and experimental films. The Board's films are distributed world-wide, and shown nationally alike in the theatres, on television, and non-theatrically through more than 750 film libraries. [See DOCUMENTARY.] There are also several independent units, the most notable being the long-established Crawley Productions. Latterly the Board has assisted in the production of feature films, and a Canadian Film Finance Corporation was established in 1967 to encourage the production of films thought commercially viable.

Among notable productions from Canada in recent years are: *The Luck of Ginger Coffey* (IRVIN KERSHNER, a Canadian-US co-production, 1964). *Warrendale* (Allan King for CBC, 1968). *The Ernie Game* (Don Owen, a CBC-NFB co-production, 1968). *Isabel* (Paul Almond, 1968). *Act of the Heart* (Paul Almond, with Geneviève Bujold). *Le Viol d'une Fille Douce* (Gilles Carle). *Fortune and Men's Eyes* (Harvey Hart, 1971). *Don't Let the Angels Fall* (George Kaczender, with Sharon Acker and Arthur Hill). *Pinter People* (Gerald Potterton). *The Best Damn Fiddler from Calabogie to Kaladar* (Peter Pearson).

In the experimental field the films of JEAN-PIERRE LEFÈBRE and Gilles Groux and David Cronenberg's *Stereo* and *Crimes of the Future* have attracted most attention. Christopher Chapman's multiple-image 70 mm short, *A Place to Stand*, was made for Expo 1967. Canada sent over 20 features at the 1971 Cannes Film Festival, revealing a wide variety of styles; most notable were Donald Shebib's pleasant study of two young men in the big city, *Goin' Down the Road*, and Claude Jutra's *Mon Oncle Antoine*, a Truffaut-like account of a young boy's emotional awakening. RM

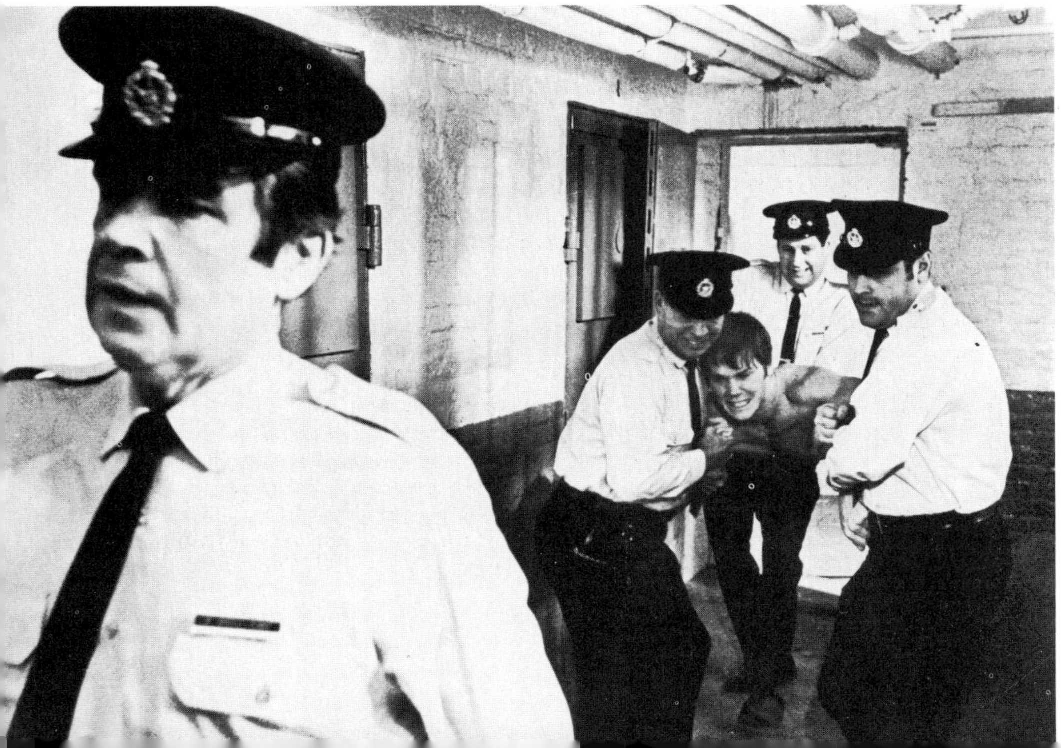

Above: Hattie, Issat and Pork, Eskimoes in 'Peoples of Canada' (National Film Board of Canada, G. Spasling, 1941)
Below left: Wendell Burton in 'Fortune and Men's Eyes' (Harvey Hart, 1971)
Below right: 'Drug Addict' (Robert Anderson)

Capellani, Albert (1870–1931)
Pioneer French director, coming to films in 1905 from the theatre. From 1907 supervised for CHARLES PATHÉ and his associates at Vincennes the films produced by La Société Cinématographique des Auteurs et Gens de Lettres (SCAGL), having specialized previously in short legendary and fantasy films. He made a sombre melodrama, *The Man with the White Gloves* (1908), and then, working with his colleagues at the rate of a film a week, adapted the works of such authors as Racine, Hugo, Balzac, and Sue. Teams of writers and directors were set up, and the films featured stars of the stage in these adaptations. Capellani prided himself on the accuracy of his locations, sets,

and costumes. In 1909 he pioneered the feature-length film with Zola's *L'Assommoir*, followed in 1912 by *Les Misérables*, made in a series of nine episodes totalling five hours. The success of this and subsequent films took him to Hollywood in 1917, where he directed ALLA NAZIMOVA in such films as *Eye for an Eye* (1917), *Out of the Fog* and *The Red Lantern* (1919). He returned to France in 1920. RM

Capra, Frank

Born 1897 in Palermo, Sicily. Director. Emigrated to Los Angeles, USA, in 1903. Worked at odd jobs before winning a scholarship which enabled him to graduate in 1918 from the California Institute and become a chemical engineer and army officer-instructor. After a period of ill-health he became, among other odd things, a farm-worker and part-time film extra, finally working for small-time film companies in San Francisco and Los Angeles before being hired as a gagman by MACK SENNETT. He composed gags for HARRY LANGDON, helping him to form the screen character which brought him success. From 1926–7 he directed Langdon's features *The Strong Man* (1926), which was highly successful, and *Long Pants* (1927), showing his ease of comic invention and feeling for sentiment. Disagreement over Langdon's future development of his character led to a separation. After making romantic comedy 'quickies' for Columbia, he side-stepped to direct three sound films about the armed services – *Submarine*, *Flight*, and *Dirigible* (1928–31) – which proved his ability to direct successful action pictures with skill and speed. He was signed by Columbia as a contract director at $25,000 a year in 1929, and moved into a period of increasing distinction, developing the gift for sophisticated comedy which was to be his principal contribution to American film. He collaborated at first with Jo Swerling as scriptwriter, and made, among other films, *Ladies of Leisure* (1930) with BARBARA STANWYCK, and *Platinum Blonde* (1931) with Loretta Young and JEAN HARLOW. He reached the peak of his career with ROBERT RISKIN as scriptwriter in the part-sentimental,

part sharply critical 'fantasies of goodwill' which appeared to resolve the social problems with which the USA was faced in the 1930s. *American Madness* (1932) offered faith and good-heartedness as a solution to a run on the banks. *Lady for a Day* and the intriguing *The Bitter Tea of General Yen* (1933) were followed by *It Happened One Night* (1934), the celebrated 'screwball' comedy with CLARK GABLE and CLAUDETTE COLBERT, which won a crop of Oscars. *Mr Deeds goes to Town* (1936) and *Mr Smith Goes to Washington* (1939), both with JEAN ARTHUR, pressed wish-fulfilment on the public along with acute social criticism. *Lost Horizon* (1937) was perhaps something of an aberration as an idealistic fantasy, but *You Can't Take it With You* (1938, based on the Kaufman-Hart play) was in line with Capra's main style and won the 1938 Academy award.

During the war Capra supervised and in part directed the notable propaganda films, the *Why We Fight* series (1942–5). He attained the rank of colonel and took charge of the whole Army film operation, working with such directors in uniform as JOHN HUSTON, GEORGE STEVENS, and WILLIAM WYLER. After the war, Capra tried with less success to recapture his old style in such films as *It's a Wonderful Life* (1946), *A Hole in the Head* (1959), and *Pocketful of Miracles* (1961). Capra was always proud of the independence he achieved from studio interference in the 1930s; he was one of the few directors to do so at this time. A celebrated letter he published in 1939 in the 'New York Times' emphasized the need for more directors to have full charge of their work. See his autobiography 'The Name Above the Title', New York: Macmillan, 1971. RM

Cardiff, Jack

Born 1914 in England. Director, who was first a child actor and then a cameraman. Worked on silent version of *The Informer* (1928), then as assistant cameraman in Hollywood. Photographed first English Technicolor film, *Wings of the Morning* (1936); worked with MOI Crown Film Unit on War Department films in Second World War. Films include: *Western Approaches* (1944), *Caesar and Cleopatra* (1945), *Black Narcissus* (1946), *The Red Shoes* (1948), and *War and Peace* (1956) as director of photography. Films as director include: *Sons and Lovers* (1960), *The Long Ships* (1964), *Girl on a Motorcycle* (which he also produced and co-wrote, 1968).

Cardinale, Claudia

Born 1939 in Tunis, North Africa. Effervescent Italian actress, successor to GINA LOLLOBRIGIDA and SOPHIA LOREN as a symbol of voluptuous Latin womanhood on the international screen. Over the years she has gained a reputation as a talented, versatile actress – as well as a comely pin-up – and has appeared most strikingly in three VISCONTI films, *Rocco and his Brothers* (1960), *The Leopard* (1963) and *Vaghe Stelle dell'Orsa* (1965). Despite some attractive performances, her spell in Hollywood was undistinguished. Other films include: *Persons Unknown* (1958), *Il Bell'Antonio* (1959), *The Trial* (1962), *Eight and a Half* and *The Pink Panther* (1963), *Blindfold* (1965), *The Professionals* and *Una Rosa per Tutti* (1966), *Once Upon a Time in the West* (1969), *The Adventures of Gérard* (1970), *Les Petroleuses* (1971). MH

Carné, Marcel

Born 1909 in Paris, France. Director. At first a journalist and film-critic, Carné became an assistant to FEYDER and CLAIR (1929–35), gaining experience at first by working as assistant cameraman to GEORGES PÉRINAL on *Les Nouveaux Messieurs* (Feyder, 1928), by directing short advertising films, and by making a short, *Nogent – Eldorado du Dimanche* (1930). In 1936 he directed *Jenny*, beginning through this film his association with the writer, JACQUES PRÉVERT, who wrote the script: the film was successful largely because of the performance of FRANÇOISE ROSAY. With their next film *Drôle de Drame* (1937), Carné and Prévert finally established their great reputation in the joint creation of works of poetic fatalism coming at the close of the 1930s, *Quai des Brumes* (1938) and *Le Jour se Lève* (1939), both featuring JEAN GABIN: films in which beauty and love suffer an inevitable, symbolistic defeat in stories which matched the mood of the period. The films were made under the influence of MURNAU and VON STERNBERG, projecting an artificial underworld. The same haunting atmosphere filled their later period films, *Les Visiteurs du Soir* (1942) and *Les Enfants du Paradis* (1944–5), both featuring the beautiful actress ARLETTY, who had appeared in their earlier films, *Hôtel du Nord* (1938) and *Le Jour se lève*. The symbolism of the captive lovers in *Les Visiteurs du Soir* seemed to represent the plight of France under occupation, while *Les Enfants du Paradis*, Carné and Prévert's greatest film, projecting 19th-century Paris on a grand scale, kept many French film-makers in work during the final years of German rule. After the war, Carné and Prévert made the perhaps inevitable mistake of seeking to maintain the same melancholy, heavily symbolist approach in *Les Portes de la Nuit* (1946), Carné's last film with Prévert. Carné's many later films have been of variable quality, though made with technical proficiency. They include the adaptation from Simenon, *La Marie du Port* (1950); *Juliette ou la Clé des Songes* (1951), a not very successful return to the symbolist style; *Thérèse Raquin* (1953); *Les Tricheurs* (1958), an attempt to reflect the problems of post-war youth; another adaptation from Simenon, *Trois Chambres à Manhattan* (1965); *Les Jeunes Loups* (1968); *Les Assassins de L'Ordre* (1971). RM

Caron, Leslie

Born 1931 in Paris, France. Dancer and actress. Educated in a Paris convent, then trained as dancer; joined Ballet des Champs Elysées and

Above: Leslie Caron in 'The L-Shaped Room' (Bryan Forbes, GB, 1962)
Below left: Catherine Hessling in 'En Rade' (Alberto Cavalcanti, France, 1927)
Below right: Sybil Thorndike in 'Nicholas Nickleby' (Alberto Cavalcanti, GB, 1947)

danced in London and Paris. MGM signed her up in 1950 to play the lead in *An American in Paris* and she has since made films in Hollywood, France and Britain and acted with the Royal Shakespeare Company. Her first film appearance in Britain was in 1950 in *The Doctor's Dilemma*; she made her London Stage début in 'Gigi' and her films include *Lili* (1953), *Gigi* (1958), *Fanny* (1960), *The L-Shaped Room* (1962, which, like *Lili*, won her a British Film Academy Award), *Promise Her Anything* and *Is Paris Burning?* (1966).

Casarès, Maria
Born 1922. Actress, of Franco-Spanish parentage, whose dark beauty and dramatic performance as Death brought her fame in COCTEAU's *Orphée* (1950). Other films include: *Les Enfants du Paradis* (1944) and *Le Testament d'Orphée* (1959).

Cassavetes, John
Born 1929 in New York, USA. Established actor and highly acclaimed experimental director whose improvised *Shadows* (1958–9) set the style – and found the market – for American underground film-makers. With theatre, radio and television training behind him, he made his film début in *Taxi* (1954) and gave lean, intense portrayals in *A Man is Ten feet Tall* (1957), *The Killers* (1964), *The Dirty Dozen* (1967) and *Rosemary's Baby* (1968). He also starred in a television series, *Staccato*, during 1959. Using unknown actors, he made *Shadows* for $40,000, winning the Critics' Award at the Venice Film Festival. The film won him offers from the big studios to direct: but, though interesting, neither *Too Late Blues* (1961) for Paramount nor *A Child is Waiting* (1962) for STANLEY KRAMER matched the merit of his directorial début. Working on similar lines to *Shadows*, he made *Faces* in 1968 and followed this with *Husbands* (1969): both films on aspects of marital trial and error. He also acted in two Italian films, *Machine Gun McCain* and *Roma come Chicago* in 1968. MH

Castellani, Renato
Born 1913 at Finale Ligura, Italy. Director. One of the most progressive of Italian directors during the wartime period (*Un Colpo di Pistola* 1941), after the war Castellani was identified with the fast-moving, warmly comic aspect of neo-realism, in the films *Sotto il Sole di Roma* (1948), *E Primavera* (1949), *Due Soldi di Spèranza* (1951). After a decorative but rather ineffectual *Romeo and Juliet* (1951), his activity was mostly confined to fairly unambitious commercial films: *I Sogni nel Casetto* (1957), *Nella Città l'Inferno* (1958), *Il Brigante* (1961), *Mare Matto* (1963) and, recently, work for RAI.

Castle, William
Born 1914 in New York, USA. Flamboyant, publicity-minded American producer and director, previously screen actor in the late 1930s, who hit the jackpot with a series of crude horror films exploiting the audience's pleasure in being scared out of its wits. Main 'shockers' include: *Macabre* (1958), *The House on Haunted Hill* and *The Tingler* (1959), *Homicidal* (1961), a tired remake of *The Old Dark House* as a horror-comic (1963) and the genuinely eery *I Saw What You Did* (1965). In 1968 he produced ROMAN POLANSKI's prestigious spine-chiller *Rosemary's Baby*.

Cava, Gregory La
See LA CAVA

Cavalcanti, Alberto de Almeida
Born 1897 in Rio de Janeiro, Brazil, and educated in Switzerland. Director, set-designer, scriptwriter. From 1920 he lived in France, where he became a notable set-designer, working with Fernand Léger on *L'Inhumaine* (1923 and for MARCEL L'HERBIER on *Feu Mathias Pascal* (1925), for which his sets involved, most unusually, low ceilings. He directed a number of films, working marginally as an avant-garde director, with a dawn-to-dusk study of the Paris streets, *Rien que les Heures* (1927), a comedy inspired by American burlesque, *La P'tite Lili* (1928), starring Catherine Hessling, who also appeared in his other comedy, *Le Petit Chaperon Rouge* (1929). *En Rade*, also with Catherine Hessling, was possibly his best, though very slow-moving, French film; it concerns a woman's disillusion and her desire to escape from a drab life as waitress in a sailor's bar. After working with sound in *Le*

Capitaine Fracasse (1929), he was invited by JOHN GRIERSON to join the documentary GPO Film Unit in London as a producer with special interest in the experimental development of sound. His principal documentary films were *Coal Face* (1935), a film oratorio with verse by W. H. Auden and music by Benjamin Britten, *We Live in Two Worlds* (1937), and the British Film Institute's anthology of documentary, *Film and Reality* (1942). He then joined MICHAEL BALCON at Ealing Studios as an associate producer and director. His chief films for Ealing were *Dead of Night* (co-director, 1945) and *Nicholas Nickleby* (1947), both notable for their stylish production. His later independent films included *They Made me a Fugitive* (1947). In 1949 he returned to Brazil, where he directed several films, among them *O Canto do Mar*, and attempted to revive the national industry. He also directed in 1955 in East Germany *Herr Puntila und sein Knecht*, which Berthold Brecht co-scripted, and in Italy *Les Noces Vénitiennes* (1959). Cavalcanti was an important influence in the uphill battle to develop an increased aesthetic interest in the possibilities of sound in British films during the 1930s and 1940s. RM

Cayatte, André
Born 1909 in France. Director and screenwriter. Background includes legal training and journalism. He scripted, among other films, JEAN GRÉMILLON's *Remorques* (1941). After making several films during the Occupation, he directed a tender modern version of the Romeo and Juliet story, *Les Amants de Vérone* (1948). He used his legal knowledge in a series of fiercely dramatic films exposing the operation of the law courts in France – *Justice est Faite* (1950), revealing the fallacies in the jury system, *Nous Sommes tous des Assassins* (1952), on the horrors of capital punishment – and was to continue these dedicated attacks in such films as *Avant le Déluge* (1953) and *Le Dossier Noir* (1955). His other films include: *Le Passage du Rhin* (1960), *La Vie Conjugale* (a pair of films, 1963), *The Road to Katmandu* (1969), *Mourir d'Aimer* (1970). RM

Cecchi D'Amico, Suso
Born 1914 in Rome, Italy. Screenwriter. Together with CESARE ZAVATTINI, she is the most influential screenwriter to emerge from post-war Italy. Sometimes providing the idea or working in collaboration with other writers, she has ranged from the harsh realities of the early neo-realist style to the zany, petty criminal satire of MONICELLI's *I Soliti Ignoti* (1958). She has worked with all the major Italian directors, moving from early DE SICA (*Bicycle Thieves*, 1948; *Miracle in Milan*, 1951) to VISCONTI (*Bellissima*, 1952; *Senso*, 1954; *Le Notti Bianche*, 1957; *Rocco and his Brothers*, 1960; *The Leopard*, 1963; *Vaghe Stelle dell'Orsa*, 1965), ANTONIONI (*I Vinti*, 1952; *La Signora senza Camelie*, 1953; *Le Amiche*, 1955), and ROSI (notably *Salvatore Giuliano*, 1961). In her best work, she reveals a sharp probing intelligence and skill in swift character delineation and, in her Antonioni films, a feeling for female psychology ideally suited to that director's analytical methods. JG

Cel
Transparent sheet of celluloid on which animation drawings are traced

Cellulose Acetate
Slow combustible, flexible, transparent plastic used since 1950 in the manufacture of cinematograph film

Cellulose Nitrate
Highly inflammable flexible, transparent plastic used before 1951 in the manufacture of cinematograph film

Censorship of Film
Censorship restraints and codes affecting the production and public exhibition of films differ throughout the world, as do the kind of authorities administering them. Broadly speaking, the public censorship of films, and the pressures lying behind the various concepts of censorship, have originated from:
(i) governmental authority, whether national or regional, whose interests may well be more ideological or political than ethical;
(ii) organized religions, whose interests are almost entirely ethical, though they will also be concerned with such other matters as blasphemy and the maintenance of codes of conduct which the particular religious creed involved holds to be socially desirable;
(iii) the film industry itself, which is concerned with self-protection from interference from outside (primarily by government and organized religion), and which must take account of any kind of pressure group whose opposition to any film released might be bad for business.

At times, there may well be a dual system of censorship in operation; for example, the Catholic Church has for long been in the habit of publishing its own, specialized grading of films, and actively forbidding attendance by the faithful at cinemas showing films to which the Church has taken exception, though they have been allowed exhibition by the secular wing of censorship.

Thus the motivation behind censorship, whatever its origin, can be extremely complex. The outcome in the form of cuts ordered to be made before a certificate or grading is given to a film, or its total prohibition, may or may not be followed by argument in public, though it is obviously desirable that the reasons for cuts or the outright banning of a film should be debated in any community which values maintaining freedom of expression. Responsible public opinion should possess the right to know exactly what has been cut from a film, and indeed if a film has been totally banned, why this has happened. Authoritarian governments normally refuse to discuss the reasons for the prohibitions they order, and many censors elsewhere are loath to discuss the details of their work in public. A notable exception has been the censorship authority in Britain during the 1960s. Such open discussion can easily become the first stage in phasing out any form of censorship altogether, other than that occasioned by the law itself, such as libel, which takes strict forms in countries such as Britain.

In different countries, censorship has naturally been exercised in different forms. It may result from bureaucratic decree, which is promulgated without any reason being given, as is often the case, for example, in the Soviet Union. In fact, the general public may not even know the prohibited film exists. However, a ban imposed in one period may be rescinded in another, as in the celebrated case of the second part of *Ivan the Terrible*, which was banned as ideologically undesirable under Stalin in 1946, but finally released under Khrushchev in 1958. Alternatively, a film may be banned as socially undesirable by the industry-sponsored censorship (such as that operated by the Motion Picture Association of America since 1930, or by the British Board of Film Censors since 1912), as in the case of the American film, *The Wild One*, which was banned by the British Board of Film Censors at the time of its initial release in 1953, but later allowed a certificate. Yet again, a film may be banned by a regional or local authority, where these authorities exercise the final control through the licensing of theatres where the prohibited film might otherwise be exhibited. This was the case with JOSEPH STRICK's *Ulysses*, which, though refused a certificate by the British Board of Film Censors, was nevertheless permitted exhibition in cinemas by certain local authorities in Britain, notably in Central London, but forbidden by most others, who normally take their cue from the recommendations of the national Censor Board. But the Board itself, being industry-sponsored, enjoys no statutory basis. In countries where the religious authority exercises a powerful influence, its views will normally prevail with the censors – this is true, for example, in Ireland, in Spain, in India, and in certain Moslem countries, such as Iraq.

The actual machinery of censorship not only differs widely from place to place, it is also constantly subject to reform and change. For example, some countries have, or have at one time had, written codes of prohibition, defining item by item what may not be depicted on the screen, most notably in the United States,[1] but also in France, India, and West Germany; the terms of the codes, however, may be modified from time to time. The complete State control of censorship is only to be expected in countries with communist régimes, but the machinery of censor control originates with the State in many other countries as widely differing as Argentina, Australia (through the Ministry of Trade and Customs), Brazil, Burma (the Police Department), Egypt, France, Hong Kong (one of Britain's few surviving Crown Colonies), Iraq, Italy, Portugal, Spain (with strong Catholic powers of veto on films considered undesirable), Syria, Thailand, and South Africa (with strong racial supervision). On the other hand, industry self-regulation is the rule in the USA, Britain, West Germany, and Japan, although in Britain (as we have seen), the final arbiter is officially the local civic authority, which can (if it wishes) permit the showing of films without a censor's certificate (as in the case of *Ulysses*), or change the grading recommended by the censor. Finally, the censorship of films has either ceased altogether, or is in the final stages of phasing out, in Belgium, Denmark, Sweden, West Germany, and certain areas of Switzerland (such as Zurich and Basle).[2]

In many countries the pendulum of censorship swings in the direction of regulating the audience rather than the film, which means that the main interest lies in preventing children or younger adolescents from seeing films which, it is felt by those responsible, have elements in the action or behaviour of the characters that require the so-called mature judgment of the adult to view without potential moral damage. The whole movement of censorship in the 'advanced' countries has been in the direction of protecting the very young from potential harm – that is, in those countries free from other, ideological pre-occupations applying alike to adults and juniors; in the so-called underdeveloped countries, concern is felt by many of the censoring authorities for the possible effect of films generally accepted elsewhere but which might harm or confuse their 'immature' adult audiences, and they act accordingly by banning or ordering cuts in many of these films. In the days of the British Empire, the censorship of films shown in the Colonies was kept strictly under the control of the Governor's office; now that his administration has virtually passed (except in such rare instances as Hong Kong and certain of the Caribbean islands), the censorship of films in most, if not all, of the former colonies remains just as strict and paternalistic as before.

A further important distinction must be made between the public and private screenings of films. In many countries unlicensed or uncertificated films may be shown under club conditions, that is to audiences composed solely of bona-fide adult members. In Britain, for example, these clubs range in kind from the opposite extremes of the National Film Theatre 'circuit' – composed nation-wide of tens of thousands of film enthusiasts who join for those screenings which remain special, 'for members only' – or the thousand or more film societies which operate up and down the country. In contrast, however, are the little clubs in London's Soho area and in similar localities in other big cities which exist to show the 'bluer' films, pretending to 'go further' than the films appearing in the increasingly permissive public cinemas and showing films for adults only. This deliberate loophole in the regulations governing the public exhibition of films is, in the long run, a form of abolition, or at least of abrogation, of the censorship principle in the face of a form of guarantee that children and the younger adolescents will not be admitted as members.

Censorship of films is indeed in recession in many parts of the world, largely as concerns sexual behaviour on the screen. During the 1960s full frontal nudity for both sexes became broadly accepted by the authorities and film-going public in many countries, though in some, notably in Scandinavia and West Germany, rather earlier than in others. The relaxation in the regulations affecting sexual (including homosexual) subjects in films made in the USA and Britain, brought with it a general relaxation in the kind of language possible in film dialogue intended to be heard in the public cinemas. On the other hand, the censorship in certain countries, and notably Britain, has refused to give much ground on the question of what is held to be gratuitous violence occurring in films. Many film censors have complained to the film-makers that gratuitous violence is very much on the increase in films (especially American films) during the 1960s. In Britain and elsewhere scenes or moments of extreme violence have frequently been cut from, for example, American films, which have nonetheless been permitted viewing even for children in the USA.[3]

Writing in 1971, the Secretary of the British Board of Film Censors said, 'The word "pornography" is usually related to sex. Why then do I use it to relate to violence? When writing about pornography D. H. Lawrence defined it as making sex dirty for money. It is this that makes me use the word to describe the use of violence for commercial profit. The pornography of violence seems to me worse than the pornography of sex. . . . I want everyone to recognize violence for what it is, something that is horrible, that causes pain, suffering, even death: and not to regard it as fun to watch as entertainment.'

As we discuss elsewhere (page 86), when considering the avant-garde and underground film, ciné-clubs and other forms of specialized screening have for long offered a challenge to censorship and to authority which imposes bans on total freedom of expression. In particular, during the 1960s in the USA, the exhibition of underground films has completely bypassed the normal form of censorship, and films primarily on sexual subjects which would be considered as taboo, but also on political subjects which could be held to be 'subversive', have been shown in off-beat theatres, clubs, or in temporary premises. In certain cases these screenings have been raided by the police, and the films have been confiscated. Similar incidents have happened in Europe, where there have been cases in which underground film-makers and their supporters have invaded the film festivals, notably at Oberhausen, West Germany, and taken over the festival theatre for the showing of the kind of films they want to see. RM

[1] For example, the Code operated in the USA was changed in 1966 (for its terms, see 'the International Motion Picture Almanac' for 1967, p. 760).

[2] Early enquiries into censorship and its principles in the USA, and the effect of films more especially on youth, were the celebrated Payne Fund Studies published in New York between 1933 and 1935. These were followed by other studies, including J. E. Harley's 'World-Wide Influences of the Cinema: a Study of Official Censorship and the International Cultural Aspects of the Motion Pictures' (University of California Press, 1940), and Ruth A. Inglis's 'Freedom of the Movies: a Report on Self-Regulation' (Chicago University Press, 1947). In Britain, D. Knowles published an early study: 'The Censor, the Drama and the Film' (1934); a recent, authoritative international survey of the whole subject, with a comprehensive bibliography, is Neville March Hunnings 'Film Censors and the Law' (1967); a lawyer with a special interest in the legal aspects of censorship, Dr Hunnings examines in detail the differing backgrounds to censorship in Britain, the USA, India, Canada, Australia, Denmark, France and Soviet Russia. The British Film Academy, and its successor, the Society of Film and Television Arts, have published special issues of their Journal giving the film-makers' view on this subject, in Autumn 1955, Autumn 1966, and again in Summer 1971.

[3] In 1971 the British Film Institute published a translation of André Glucksmann's 'Violence on the Screen'. It presents in summary form the main findings of those social scientists who have attempted research on the effects of violence in motion pictures (and on television) on young people. The results are very non-committal.

Ceylon

See ASIAN FILM

Chabrol, Claude

Born 1930 in Sardent, France. One of the leading figures of the *nouvelle vague* which revolutionized the French cinema in the late 1950s and 1960s and influenced progressive film-making all over the world. In the last few years – and especially in his masterly trilogy *Les Biches*, *La Femme Infidèle* (1968) and *Que La Bête Meure* (1969) – he has shed the occasional flamboyance of his earlier work, and is acclaimed as a film technician of rare skill, in the traditional style.

With other even more celebrated *nouvelle vague* colleagues, FRANÇOIS TRUFFAUT and JEAN-LUC GODARD, Chabrol was a writer on the film magazine 'Cahiers du Cinéma'. With ERIC ROHMER, he co-authored a study of ALFRED HITCHCOCK, a director he much admires, whose work has obviously had an important effect on Chabrol's. He appeared briefly in JACQUES RIVETTE's *Le Coup du Berger* (1956) and directed his first film, *Le Beau Serge* (1958), the spearhead of the coming film revolution. He followed this with *Les Cousins* and *Les Bonnes Femmes* (1959), which coolly explored the indulgences and weaknesses of youth in modern society – though both films have episodes that at the time were regarded as extravagantly vulgar.

The emergence of Godard and Truffaut then tended to overshadow Chabrol, whose own precise talent was more in tune with the older school of film-making. His films of the early and middle 1960s reveal an exuberant versatility – a 'Hamlet' variation, *Ophélia* and, a study

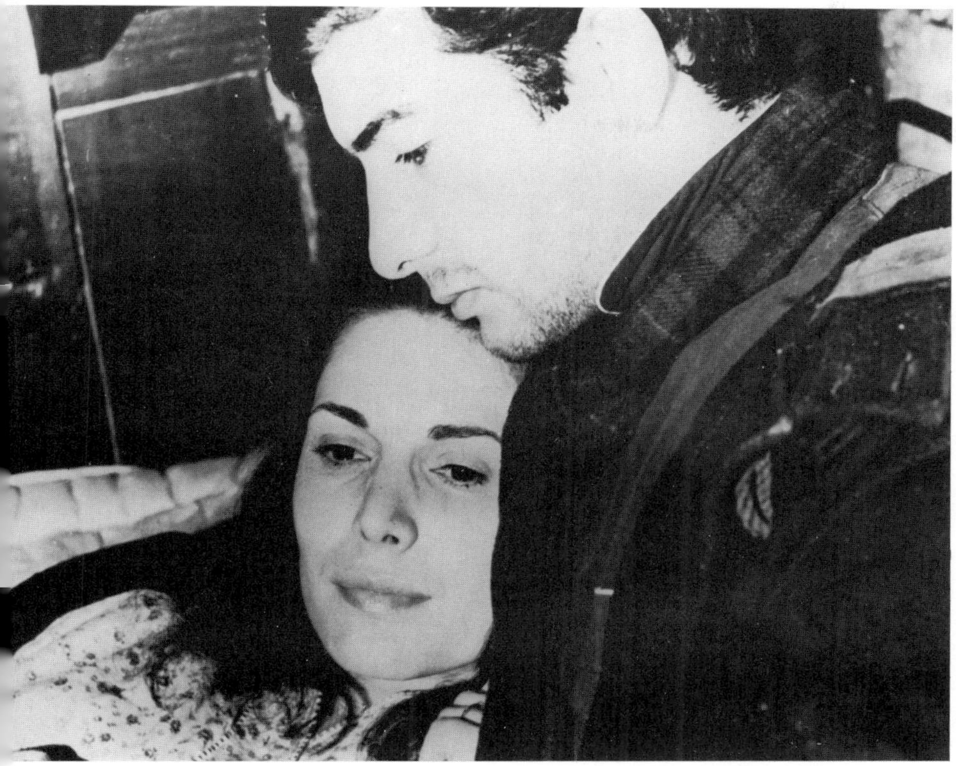

of the murderer *Landru* (1962), two spy fantasies based on the adventures of 'Le Tigre' (1964 and 1965), the thriller *Le Scandale* (1966).

In *Les Biches* his gift for examining complex relationships in great depth, together with his elegant visual style, re-established Chabrol as a superior film-maker. His wife Stéphane Audran has appeared in several of his recent films.

Other principal films: *A Double Tour* (1959), *Les Godelureaux* (1960), *L'Oeil du Malin* (1961), *La Route de Corinthe* (1967), *Le Boucher* and *La Rupture* (1970), *La Décade Prodigieuse* (1971).

See 'Claude Chabrol' by Robin Wood and Michael Walker (1970). MH

Above: Michelle Meritz and Jean-Claude Brialy in 'Le Beau Serge' (Claude Chabrol, France, 1958)
Below: Lon Chaney in 'The Hunchback of Notre Dame' (W. Worsley, USA, 1923)

Chaney, Lon (1883–1930)
Born in Colorado Springs, USA. Chaney's supremely expressive mime was generally attributed to the fact that his parents were both deaf-mutes. He was recruited from the theatre in 1912 by Universal, for whom he initially played in comedies and W. S. HART Westerns. Subsequently he directed a few films: *The Chimney's Secret, The Oyster Dredger* and *The Stool Pigeon* (1915). In 1919 he was first directed by TOD BROWNING in a horror film and from this point the direction of his subsequent career was decided. His most famous roles were as *The Hunchback of Notre Dame* (Wallace Worsley, 1923) and *The Phantom of the Opera* (Rupert Julian, 1925). The ideal collaboration however was with Tod Browning, with whom Chaney made *Outside the Law* (1921), *The Unholy Three* (1925), *The Blackbird* and *The Road to Mandalay* (1926), *The Unknown* and *London After Midnight* (1927), *The Big City* and *West of Zanzibar* (1928) and *Where East is East* (1929). His last film was a remake, by Jack Conway of *The Unholy Three* (1930). Chaney approached his horror films with the utmost seriousness, sparing himself no pains (often literally) to ensure their realism. DR

Change Over
Transistion from one reel on one projector to the next reel on another projector to enable a film to be run without a break.

Chaplin, Charles Spencer
Born 1889 in London, England. British director and actor. Chaplin's tramp is the single truly universal clown image: the little bowler, the too-small jacket and the too-large pants held up with string, the enormous boots on turned-out feet, the moustache and cane, are everywhere instantly recognizable and internationally comprehensible. The happy fact that Chaplin's genius found its medium and that this image was created within the first two decades of the cinema's history profoundly influenced and accelerated the whole subsequent progress of cinema history.

He was the child of struggling British music-hall performers – the father a wastrel and the mother mentally sick. His childhood in the poor streets and harsh charitable institutions of Victorian London gave him a vision of the world of the underprivileged that he was later able to romanticize and transmute into comedy. His apprenticeship on the music-halls trained and sharpened his natural gifts to a wonderful precision and versatility. He possessed natural grace and rhythmic sense, inexhaustible invention, a gift for observation which gave truth and belief to his mime and mimicry, impeccable timing and a genuine poetic instinct.

He was already a veteran performer, starring in Fred Karno's 'Mumming Birds' company, when MACK SENNETT recruited him in 1913. In his first film, *Making a Living*, Sennett dressed him as a broken-down swell, but already in his second film, *Kid Auto Races at Venice*, Chaplin had devised the costume that was to become famous. The broad lines of the character were already clear in the early shorts, but were constantly refined practically throughout the Tramp's career (Chaplin last used the character in *Modern Times*, 1936). As a comic character his uniqueness was the large range Chaplin was able to give him while remaining within the limits of total truth and credibility: his emotions ranged from callousness to high sentiment; his actions from nobility to larceny; and the resilience and fallibility of his nature were supremely human.

At Keystone Chaplin made 35 shorts, mostly one-reel broad slapsticks but already revealing a more deft and restrained comedy than was usual on the Sennett lot. In 1915 he made 15 films for the Essanay Company, of which the best were *The Tramp*, *The Woman* and *A Night in the Show*, a reminiscence of a Karno sketch 'A Night in an English Music Hall'. By now one of the highest paid and most popular stars in the world, Chaplin next went to Mutual. The 12 two-reelers made there were produced with greater care, which enabled him to create small masterpieces like the solo *One A.M.* and *The Pawnshop* (1916), *Easy Street* and *The Immigrant* (1917), in which an emotional element and serious satirical intentions first become evident in his work. A contract with First National gave him still greater financial rewards and still greater opportunity for careful planning and production. *A Dog's Life* (1918) showed sincere, albeit sentimental, social concerns. *Shoulder Arms* (1918), transmuting the horrors of trench life into comedy, remains one of the greatest films to be inspired by the First World War. *The Kid* (1920), his first full-length feature as a director (he had acted at Keystone in Sennett's six-reel *Tillie's Punctured Romance*), was rich in sentiment, and his greatest success, creating a world celebrity out of his infant co-star, JACKIE COOGAN.

After 1923 he was free of his First National contract and able to produce independently for release through United Artists, which he had formed in 1919 with FAIRBANKS, GRIFFITH and MARY PICKFORD. His first independent feature was *A Woman of Paris* (1923), which he directed, only acting in a tiny walk-on role. A brilliantly sophisticated treatment of a somewhat old-fashioned novelette story, it exemplifies Chaplin's extraordinary ability to visualize psychological action and had a profound effect on other film-makers, especially in Europe. After this Chaplin returned to his tramp character for *The Circus* (1918) and *The Gold Rush* (1925) and

Top: Charles Chaplin on the set of 'A Woman of Paris' (Chaplin, USA, 1923) Above: Maurice Chevalier and Margaret Lockwood in 'The Beloved Vagabond' (Kurt Bernhardt, GB, 1936)

his first sound films, *City Lights* (1931) and *Modern Times* (1936) – in which, while making ingenious and effective use of sound, he declined to use speech.

The Tramp was now finally abandoned, and in his next two films Chaplin exploited the penchant for grand, simplistic philosophical exposition already apparent in his commentary on modern urban and industrial life in *Modern Times*. *The Great Dictator* (1940) was a satire on Hitler, in which he played a dual role of the dictator himself and a Jewish barber who is mistaken for him. *Monsieur Verdoux* (1947) was a black comedy on a Bluebeard theme, with a strong pacifist message. Audiences seemed to regret the lost Tramp, and critics were inclined to dismiss Chaplin's simple but noble idealism as naive sentimentality. *Limelight* (1952) was a richly nostalgic return to the London and the music halls of Chaplin's childhood.

His two latest films, made in England, only intermittently reveal the old (but essentially undiminished) genius. Perhaps since losing his own studio (he left the USA at the height of anti-leftist feeling) he has not found really congenial conditions for his own kind of creation. *A King in New York* (1957) was a satire on the American way of life, seen through the eyes of an exiled European king. In *A Countess from Hong Kong* (1966) Chaplin once more directed other players (BRANDO and LOREN), this time in a mild romantic comedy which disappointed all but the most fervent Chaplin loyalists. These late films have perhaps obscured the historical perspective: even so, in my opinion, there can be no question that Chaplin is the greatest and the most important single artist in the first 75 years of the cinema.

He published 'My Autobiography' in 1964, and among the many books about him and his work the study by Theodore Huff, 'Charlie Chaplin' (1952) is outstanding. DR

Chayefsky, Paddy

Born 1923 in New York, USA. Playwright and screenwriter. Became a top television dramatist with realistic, sympathetic human studies which he subsequently re-scripted as films – notably *Marty* (1955) and *The Batchelor Party* (1956); *Marty* won him an Oscar for its screenplay. His stage play, 'Middle of the Night', was also adapted as a film in 1958. His later screenplays include: *The Goddess* (1957), *The Americanization of Emily* (1964), *Ice Station Zebra* (1967), *Paint Your Wagon* (1969).

Cherkassov, Nicolai (1903–1966)

Born in St Petersburg (Leningrad), Russia. Actor. At first a musician and dancer, working impartially in ballet, opera and the theatre, he eventually joined the Leningrad Pushkin Theatre. He made his name in films with the character of the eccentric, shrewd professor in the Lenfilm production by HEIFITZ and Zharkhi, *Baltic Deputy* (1936). He also appeared in Petrov's spectacular *Peter the Great* (1937) and in other films demanding naturalistic character roles, but he departed from this approach to acting in order to assume the heroic, larger-than-life stylization required of him by EISENSTEIN for the leading characters in *Alexander Nevsky* (1938) and the two parts which were completed of the trilogy, *Ivan the Terrible* (1943–6). Later he appeared in other films, such as ALEXANDROV's *Spring* and Heifitz's *In the Name of Life* (1947), Petrov's *Battle of Stalingrad* (1949), ROSHAL's *Moussorgsky* (1950) and *Rimsky-Korsakov* (1953), and KOZINTSEV's *Don Quixote* (1957). He wrote an autobiography available in English translation, 'Notes of a Soviet Actor' (*c.* 1957). RM

Chevalier, Maurice (1888–1972)

Born in France. Film star, stage actor, music-hall artist and singer. In 1911–4 he acted in shorts by MAX LINDER. His later American, British and French films include *The Love Parade* (1930), *One Hour With You* and *Love me Tonight* (1932), *The Merry Widow* (1934), *The Beloved Vagabond* (1936), *Pièges* (1939), *Le Silence est d'Or* (1947), *Love in the Afternoon* (1957), *Gigi* (1958), *Can-Can* and *Fanny* (1960) and *I'd Rather be Rich* (1964). He was given a Special Academy Award in 1958 for 'contributions to the world of entertainment for more than half a century'. See his autobiography 'With Love' (1960).

Chief

Head projectionist in a cinema

Children's Entertainment Films

Children form a substantial proportion of potential filmgoers, yet most films for adults, particularly those produced since the recession of censorship prohibitions in many countries during the 1960s, are very unsuitable for children. Just as books are produced exclusively for children, so it is obviously desirable there should be films specially made for child audiences. Efforts have been made in a number of countries not only to produce children's entertainment films but to organize exclusive screenings for them, attended by children only. This can rarely, if ever, be done without some form of subsidy, for the amount of money children as a potential audience can normally pay to see films bears no relation to their production costs if they are to be well made. And it is essential that children, whose tastes are in a highly formative stage, should be offered the best the medium can provide.

Countries as varied as the USSR, India, Japan, and Britain have, in one way or another, made special provision for children's entertainment through film. It is not easy to generalize about the age-groups into which children's films are divided. By the time they reach 15, most children want to share as much as they can in adult entertainment, and films made exclusively for children often cater for age groups rather younger than this. In Britain,

Above: John Aloisi in 'Toto and the Poachers' (made in East Africa for the Children's Film Foundation, Brian Salt, 1957)
Below: 'Runaway Railway' (made for the Children's Film Foundation, Ian Darnley-Smith, GB, 1964)

Lesley Roach and Anthony Sheppard in 'Mr Horatio Nibbles' (made for the Children's Film Foundation, Robert Hird, GB, 1971)

for example, the principal audience in the mind of the sponsoring organization, the Children's Film Foundation, lies within the age range of about 6 to 12, with an average around 8·5. In some other countries, such as Japan and Poland, this special branch of production is broken down to age-groups which differentiate between the younger and the older, going even as high as 18. In Western Europe and the USA, young people of 16 to 18 do not like to recognize their distinction from adults, though in certain countries (such as Britain) there are catagories of adult films they are not permitted to see.

What is understood, too, by the term 'children's film' differs considerably in different countries. Some are content to entertain their children with what they regard as suitably innocuous films selected from adult productions – Westerns, historical films and the like. In contrast, other countries have made a very careful study of the special problems involved in the choice of subject, scripting and direction of children's films, and the technique of presentation most proper to the evolving tastes and capacities of young audiences in the various age-groups. This represents true production for children's entertainment.

In the USSR and Japan, where production of children's films began as early as 1919 and 1924 respectively, special studios have been set up for the purpose. In Great Britain, a non-profit-making organization, the Children's Film Foundation, was established in 1951 by the film industry to sponsor and supervise productions commissioned from independent companies; prior to this all-industry sponsorship, the Rank Organization, as producers and exhibitors of adult entertainment, had from 1944 maintained a Children's Entertainment Division under the direction of Mary Field, who became the head of CFF when this was first set up. The continuous production of children's films has also existed for some time in Poland (since 1950), in the German Democratic Republic (since 1953) and in Czechoslovakia (since 1955). The Scandinavian countries, Norway, Sweden and Finland, have made occasional films for children. India founded the Children's Film Society, a non-official body, in 1955 on the recommendation of a Government Committee; it produces, distributes and arranges or encourages the exhibition of films for children. It receives financial aid from the Government, and has produced or acquired over 60 films since its establishment, of which about half are of feature-length.

The films which prove most successful with child audiences are naturally those in which children figure in the main parts, with adults for the most part kept well in the background. The audience likes to identify with child performers who are of a similar age to themselves. Dialogue is kept subsidiary to action, and the action must be swift, exciting, clearly motivated and credible to the children. The British child-feature seldom lasts longer than one hour, which is in fact more than long enough for the youngest patrons. They like best films which are strong in comedy and adventure, with plenty of thrills; they prefer these to adult-styled Westerns or war films. Makers of films for young children must avoid brutality or frightening misadventures for the child heroes. Nevertheless, child audiences are becoming tougher in their tastes each year.

The scale of production in a specimen year (1965) was as follows:

Japan	6 features and 4 shorts
USSR	14 features and 40 shorts
Great Britain	4 features and 2 serials
Czechoslovakia	5 features and 29 shorts
Germany (GDR)	4 features and 16 shorts
India	no features but 6 shorts
Poland	4 features and 34 shorts
Sweden	8 features and 13 shorts
Norway	1 feature but no shorts

There is also considerable interchange of production between countries making children's films, with the dialogue either dubbed or titled in the language of the country of exhibition. Britain in particular has sponsored production in many parts of the world, including Indonesia, Morocco, Tunisia, Canada and Australia.

Audiences recorded in 1965 were:

Great Britain	327,600
Czechoslovakia	128,185
Finland	16,100
Japan	372,676
Poland	168,309
Norway	26,908
USSR	4,260,000
India	1,180,682
Sweden	38,200

In many instances these figures represent a sharp decline parallel to the decline in cinema-going by adults. The child audience in Britain was only 27·7% of that in 1955; that in Japan was 42·9%. In contrast, the audience in the USSR represented an increase – 168·4% of the 1955 figure. Child audiences in India doubled between 1963, when the work of the Children's Film Society began, and 1967. Child audiences in Britain attend special Saturday morning matinées, held regularly in some 900 cinemas, with very low prices of admission; children's programmes in most countries take place at special times on either Saturday or Sunday, but there are also screenings in clubs, schools and camps. RM

China, People's Republic of

(See also ASIAN FILM: Hong Kong)

As with other non-industrialized countries, the first films seen in China were brought in by showmen from France and the USA. The earliest documented film programme was advertised in a Shanghai newspaper, 11 August 1896. Most of the foreign showmen were also equipped to film and send home 'views' of Chinese cities and landscapes that were shown widely in Europe and the Americas. The first Chinese production appears to have been filmed in 1908 – scenes of Peking opera (now lost).

In 1908 and 1909 Chinese films were more regularly seen, produced by the Asia Film Company, a collaborative venture in Hong Kong and Shanghai financed by an American, (Benjamin Polaski) with two Chinese theatre enthusiasts. Polaski failed in his efforts to export his Chinese productions. The next expansion was the opening of a film department in the prominent Shanghai publishing house, the Commercial Press, with more ambitious plots and better equipment. Their most important film was an adaptation (1920) of a short play as staged by Mei Lan-fang, the first of Mei's many efforts to find a method to film his art. (See Mei's 'The Filming of a Tradition', translated in 'Eastern Horizon' [Hong Kong], August–September 1965.)

The Commercial Press continued film production into 1925, but the most interesting and popular films of the early 1920s came from small companies that had less money to gamble with, and sometimes collapsed after one or two films, for lack of a distribution system. Among these successes were *Yen Rei-sun* (1921, China Film Research Society), *Sea Oath* (1921, Shanghai Film Co) and *Beauties and Skeletons* (1922, copied from a French or US serial, New Asia Film Co). Yet a few of the companies launched in this period survived: the Ming

Hsing Co established its leading position in Chinese cinema with *Orphan Rescues Grandfather* (1923); and in Canton they adroitly established firm ties in 1924 with the revolutionary Kuomintang government and followed them on the Great Northern Expedition to Hankow in 1926–7. Some independent companies found stability enough to last at least a decade – Great Wall, Tien Yi, White Lily. Many of the new companies formed in Shanghai after Chiang Kai-shek's *coup d'état* in 1927 changed their subjects from contemporary life to dimly historical adventure stories. Even the biggest of Asia's cigarette companies, the British-American Tobacco Co, used film advertisements, bought film theatres to show the advertisements, and finally produced fictional and fairy-tale films: the last of these was *Willow Tree and Butterfly Marriage* (William H. Jansen, 1925), shown in England as *Legend of the Willow Pattern Plate*.

In 1930 leading Shanghai companies raced to be the producer of China's first sound films, in spite of the commercial hazards of speaking a dialect, *pei hua*, that would not be understood by the many Chinese film-goers who could read the characters easily but could not understand the spoken (or sung) speech. To take advantage of this Shanghai problem the small companies in Canton and Hong Kong made quickly inexpensive sound films intended for Chinese audiences abroad. Most of these overseas Chinese came from South China and understood only Cantonese dialect.

For some years *any* sound coming from the screen satisfied the customers, and there were the same devices and advertisements as were used in Europe and the USA to give the impression of an 'all-talkie' film – though usually such synchronized speech was heard only in the last few minutes of the film. Even after sound and speech were no longer novelties, some studios were financially forced to continue to produce silent films.

It was at this time that several factors combined to change not only the Chinese film industry but also the whole political and cultural atmosphere. The Japanese army, already in control of North China, bombed Shanghai on 28 January 1932. Along with the ruin of several cinemas and studios some producers felt obliged to get the new patriotic attitudes into their films. At this same time the Chinese Communists (the party was founded 10 years before), in their programme to use the arts to increase the new patriotism, offered their writing and theatrical talents, first to the Ming Hsing Studio. The great success of their first year at Ming Hsing (*Wild Torrent, Outcry of Women, Spring Silk-worms, 24 Hours of Shanghai, Years of Plenty, Twin Sisters,* all released in 1933) was an astonishing record, and other studios wanted to win the new audience. The party's film committee (headed by Hsia Yen) worked for other Shanghai studios: Lien Hua (*Three Modern Girls, Dawn Over the Metropolis*), Yi Hua (*Existence of the Nation, Angry Tide of China's Sea*). Within a single year the whole picture of Chinese films and filmgoing changed radically. There were downs as well as ups, but by 1937, when the Japanese openly attacked Shanghai, the film industry's dependence on the leftist writers, directors, and actors influenced the propaganda apparatus of the fleeing government. First stop and studio, Hankow; next, Chungking to the end of the war: these were the new film bases. Some leftist film-makers decided that working in the South they would have more independence from government supervision. The film-studios of Canton and Hong Kong were active again, making patriotic films as much for overseas Chinese – in *their* Cantonese dialect – as for home distribution. Other film-makers, to escape the dawdling and bureaucracy of Chungking, found their way to Yenan; the new base in North China established to concentrate on political growth, a newly trained Red Army and guerrilla force, and a new definition of the intellectuals' role in the coming revolution. There, too, some newsreels and actuality films were made, but the constant obstacle was lack of film stock and apparatus (retreating Japanese forces supplied some of this but not enough). At least one film that stands out in the Yenan years is Wu Yin-hsien's record of the Canadian Dr Norman Bethune's field work in 1939.

Top: 'Sorrows Left at Spring River' (China-Japan, 1944)
Above: 'Daughters of China' (1949)
Below: 'The White-haired Girl' (Changchun Studios, 1950)

The Japanese invaders, with Japanese businessmen following close behind, did not hesitate to build or re-open film studios in captured territory. The studio they built in the 'Manchukuo capital' – now Changchun – is still workable. During its Japanese occupation, the studio issued a considerable number of 'Manchurian' films, usually featuring Shirley Yamaguchi, and usually directed by Japanese directors. When all of Shanghai was occupied, films were at once begun, using the Chinese artists and technicians who had chosen in 1937 to stay in Shanghai. Japanese and Chinese film-makers made co-productions to be distributed throughout Eastern Asia and the Pacific islands, wherever Japan's control had forced open cinemas to show their controlled programmes. The Japanese-Chinese staff of Shanghai studios made and circulated polished propaganda fictions, one on Lin Tse-hsu, the hero of the first Opium War, another on the Taiping Rebellion (*Sorrows Left at Spring River*, 1944) – in both the villains were clearly European and American.

In the period between the end of war and the founding of the Chinese People's Republic there was renewed struggle for control of the Chinese screens. The left film-makers were better prepared for this clash than the government companies, and the most popular films came from a left group that founded their own film company, Kun Lun. Most of Kun Lun's productions have been preserved until today to prove the excellence of *Spring River Flows East* (1947), *Lights of Ten Thousand Homes* (1948), and the realistic masterpiece of Chinese cinema – *Crows and Sparrows* (1949).

In the well-equipped Changchun Studio the first films of the Republic were made before the Chinese People's Republic was declared on 1 October 1949. *The Bridge*, *Light Spreads Everywhere*, and *Daughters of China* were the first productions, and in 1950 the same studio produced equally careful, effective films: *The White-Haired Girl*, *Chao Yi-man*, and *Steeled Fighter*.

The dedicated film people in Shanghai were not so lucky in these first two years. For a year after the happy event of *Crows and Sparrows* (in the cutting-room when the People's Liberation Army marched into Shanghai), the Kun Lun group was maintained as a private film producer, but then they made *The Life of Wu Hsun*. At the time of its release it was praised by everyone, critics and public alike. It was a few months later that Mao Tse-tung (who is not very interested in film) saw the *Wu Hsun* film, and the resulting explosions removed the film from all screens, removed its director, its author, with most of its cast, from film-making altogether, and ordered the merger of Kun Lun into one of Shanghai's government studios.

A Peking film-studio was opened for work in 1950 and one of its first releases, *New Heroes and Heroines*, written and directed by Shih Tung-shan, was sent to the Karlovy Vary festival in 1951. Aside from reportage filmed in Korea, this war was not intensively treated by the Film Bureau in the Ministry of Culture; the main themes of the 1950s were the anti-Japanese war and the victory over the USA-supported nationalist army.

The Hundred Flowers campaign, Mao Tse-tung's brief flirtation with free speech, may be responsible for the several surprising films that appeared in 1956. *Fifteen Strings of Cash*, adapted and directed by Tao Chin, is still the most stimulating use of Chinese opera in films. *Before the New Director Arrives* was a rare attempt at dangerous satire by Liu Pan, whose film career was ended in the following year. Although Lu Hsun, China's greatest 20th-century writer, refused to allow his work to be filmed, his death in 1936 freed film-makers to use his stories: the best of these, translated as *New Year Offering*, was adapted by Hsia Yen (the Vice-Minister of Culture in charge of film matters) and directed by Sang Hu; two of China's best film actors, Pai Yang and Wei Ho-ling, added to the value of this film.

Above: 'Girl Basketball Player No 5' (1957)
Below: 'La Chartreuse de Parme (Christian-Jaque, France, 1947–8)

Before 1959, the 10th anniversary of the People's Republic, Chinese films tried few experiments. Safe subjects, such as sport *(Girl Basketball Player No 5)*, women workers *(By the March 8 Canal* [March 8 is International Women's Day] and *Huang Pao-mei)*, spy warnings *(Case of Hsu Shou-lin)* were relied upon to fill the cinemas with offence to nobody.

For the anniversary year an extraordinary number of films were made, some of them worth serious attention: *Lin Tse-hsu* (on the first Opium War), *New Story of an Old Soldier*, *The Lin Family's Shop*, *Young People of Our Village*, and a completely original animation film based on Chi Pai-shih's paintings, *Where Is Mama?* (prize winner at Annecy in 1971). The most expressive film of China's film history was made this year with its author-director, Chin Shan, also playing a chief role – this was *Storm*, that might have occupied the place of *Strike* in Soviet film history if Chin Shan had continued to make films. Most of these films were shown at the first festival of Chinese films in the West, in the 1960 season of the National Film Theatre.

In 1960 the revolutionary veteran film director, Tsai Chu-sheng, opened the new Pearl River Studio with *Waves on the Southern Shore*. A lively period comedy came from the Haiyen Studio in Shanghai, *Master Chiao Mounts the Sedan*, with the skilful comedian Han Fei as Master Chiao. In 1961 came *Hurricane* (an adaptation of Chou Li-po's novel) and *Red Guards at Lake Hung* (a try at an outdoor opera). In 1962 an unusual number of 'light' films: the witty folk opera, *Third Sister Liu*, the stereoscopic comedy *Wondrous Encounters of a Magician*, and *Li Shuang-shuang*, the most popular film in China in its year. In 1963: Hsieh Tien's funny and pointed character comedy of a back-water railway station, *Better and Better*. The best and most passionate film of 1964 was *Serfs*, about the slaves and masters of Tibet. This was the first film to be offered abroad in two dubbed versions, English and French.

Meanwhile the Chinese film studios *outside* China continued to function without any perceptible advance over the Mainland films. Of these Hong Kong has the largest number of studios, with plenty of films to sell – often remakes of Shanghai's pre-1949 successes. The two film studios of Singapore and the studios of Taiwan tried to match the profits and styles of Hong Kong's easily saleable productions.

The beginning of the Great Proletarian Cultural Revolution marked a temporary end in 1966 of the Chinese fictional film. On the orders of Chiang Ching (Mme Mao) all film studios, except the Documentary (Peking) and Animation (Shanghai) studios, were closed, and remained closed in mid-1971. JL

Christensen, Benjamin (1879–1959)
Born in Viborg, Denmark. Director. From 1900–7 was an operatic singer and theatrical producer. With CARL DREYER, he was the most influential Danish director whose early work – *The Mysterious X* (1913), *Night of Revenge* (1915) and *Häxan*, or *Witchcraft through the Ages* (1921) – was technically far in advance of its time, with highly sophisticated lighting schemes, a subtle use of the moving camera, and a firm narrative sense. From the beginning, he was mainly concerned with bizarre, supernatural subjects (*Häxan* is a potted historical survey of diabolism), leavened with moments of sly, black humour. He retained these obsessions on going to America in the mid-1920s, where he made a series of fairly commercial fantasy films, the best known being *Seven Footprints to Satan* (1929), a 'haunted house' parody with echoes of FEUILLADE and a marvellous collection of screen monsters. He returned to intermittent film-making in Denmark in the 1930s and ended his career in relative obscurity. Also an actor of distinction, he can be seen as the obscene Devil in *Häxan* and as The Master in Dreyer's German-made *Mikael* (1924). JG

Christian-Jaque
Born 1904 in Paris, France. Director. Worked as journalist, art director and short-film maker until he entered features in 1932. Has made an enormous variety of films, mostly of a middlebrow, commercial nature. His technically slick, if somewhat monotonous style, is best seen in: *Les Disparus de Saint-Agil* (1938), a school fantasy with ERICH VON STROHEIM; *Symphonie Fantastique* (1942), a wild biography of Berlioz; *Boule de Suif* (1945); *La Chartreuse de Parme* (1948); *Fanfan la Tulipe* (1951), an exuberant period romp; *Nana* (1954); *La Tulipe Noire* (1963); and numerous comedies with such popular French stars as FERNANDEL, BRIGITTE BARDOT and Martine Carol. JG

Christie, Julie
Born 1941 in Chukua, Assam, India. Actress, who after drama school in England appeared on television in *A for Andromeda*. She acted with the Birmingham Repertory and the Royal Shakespeare Companies before working in films, which include: *Billy Liar* (1963), *Darling* (which won her an Academy Award, 1965), *Dr Zhivago* and *Fahrenheit 451* (1966), *Far from the Madding Crowd* and *Petulia* (1967), *In Search of Gregory* (1969), *The Go-Between* (1971).

Above: Julie Christie in 'Far From the Madding Crowd' (John Schlesinger, GB, 1967)
Below: Vera Kuznetsova and Ivan Marin in 'There Was Once an Old Man and an Old Woman' (Grigori Chukhrai, USSR, 1964)

Chukhrai, Grigori
Born 1921 in Melitopol, Ukraine, USSR. Director. The international success of Chukhrai's *The Forty-first* (1956), a remake of an old, silent PROTAZANOV film, and *Ballad of a Soldier* (1959) was of crucial importance to the renascence of the Soviet cinema in the second half of the 1950s. *Clear Skies* (1961) was the first Soviet film to make unambiguous reference to the Stalinist era and the impact of the thaw which followed Stalin's death and the Twentieth Party Congress. Subsequent films include: *There was an Old Man and an Old Woman* (1964) and an interesting *cinéma-vérité* story about Stalingrad, called *Memory* (1970). DR

CinemaScope
See ANAMORPHIC LENS

Cinematography
(See also COLOUR CINEMATOGRAPHY page 29)

The normal film is, plainly enough, a two-dimensional projected image, bounded by a frame. Whenever this basic form has been abandoned, it has been to achieve certain special effects, notably a three-dimensional image, or a deeply concave, large-scale picture (such as Cinerama, especially in its original triptych form), or a multi-screen group of images projected simultaneously (like the experiments at the Montreal and Osaka Expositions), or images which combine with the live performer (the Czechoslovak entertainment *Laterna Magica*). Normal film, however, projects on the screen

Above: R. W. Paul's Studio (GB, 1902)
Below: A combined cinecamera and projector designed by G. Demeny and manufactured by Louis Gaumont (France, 1896)

a two-dimensional photograph of a three-dimensional environment, whether derived from actuality or artificially simulated in a studio. Differences inevitably remain:

(i) It is a flat image, in many respects distorting both the perspective of the scene as we would perceive it in life, bi-focally, and the nature of any motion taking place, since this movement is occurring in a single plane;

(ii) it reproduces the image either in varying shades of grey lying within the scale of black-and-white photography, or in colour within the range reproducible through the colour process used;

(iii) its boundaries are artificially selected and restricted by the aspect ratio of the camera and screen frame;

(iv) the timing of the motion represented may be distorted by speeding up or slowing down the action, etc.

The history of film art is closely bound up with the kind of visual interpretation which the camera brings to the scene represented and the nature of the film stock used. The quality of both cameras and stock have varied greatly since filming was first undertaken, and the increasing sensitivity of the photographic image can best be realized by projecting, side by side if possible, films shot at ten-year intervals between 1895 and the present time. The early ORTHOCHROMATIC stock had a graininess which gave a combined sootiness and bleach-out effect to the camerawork, and demanded strongly contrasted lighting effects if, for example, facial expressions were to be seen with any kind of subtlety or detail (it should be remembered, also, that many of the early films we see have had their original photographic values diminished by being duped from old, used positive prints). However, once the lighting values necessary to obtain the best results from early stock were realized, remarkably good effects became possible, and this before the first major revolution which took place during the 1920s with the introduction of PANCHROMATIC stock. Consequently, the instinctive aesthetic understanding established between director and cameraman became crucially important: the cameraman had to be the photographic *alter ego* of the director, and the great team of GRIFFITH and BITZER, followed by EISENSTEIN and TISSE foreshadowed many similar close partnerships in various countries.

Above: Cineframe from the Lumières' shot of a train in their original demonstration film (France, 1895)
Below: 'Moana' (Robert Flaherty, USA, 1923–5)

Even during the fairly primitive early period of the cinema, Griffith and Bitzer were credited with many photographic innovations. These include the use of backlighting, or shooting into the sun to achieve luminous halation (1909); fireside lighting and 'morning light' effects (1909); and Rembrandt lighting, using pools of light amid shadows such as illuminate details in Rembrandt's paintings.

Griffith also experimented with a variety of different angles and camera placements which included:

(a) The dramatic use of CLOSE-UP, built into the editing along with MEDIUM and LONG SHOTS, from 1908 onwards and especially in *The Massacre* (1912);

(b) the long shot and panoramic action shot, (see PAN), as in *The Lonely Villa* (1909), and *Ramona* (1910);

(c) the dramatic use of panning shots and TRACKING with the action *(The Massacre)*, and of the mobile camera mounted on an automobile (*Home Sweet Home*, 1914);

(d) the dramatic use of the IRIS IN-AND-OUT, SPLIT-SCREEN with twin pictures, and the re-shaping of the frame image to produce upright panel shots and simulated wide-screen shapes (*Intolerance*, 1916);

(e) special shots, like the famous view of the Babylon set in *Intolerance* shot from an elaborate crane and pulley device.

Photography in the hands of Griffith and other directors favoured the conventional use of gauzes to achieve softly luminous images, especially for the female stars, who were backlit to give them an idealized appearance, with an almost Victorian touch of the halo. Landscapes, too, were filtered to give a lyrical, even unearthly, effect, and Griffith and Bitzer developed the convention of using clouds of smoke trailing laterally across the landscape, notably in the battle scenes in *Birth of a Nation* (1915), a device later adopted by the Russians for their war films.

Attempts to achieve colour effects by hand tinting and stencils were made as early as 1900, while the Englishman, George Smith, patented his two-tone Kinemacolor process in 1906. The universal practice of overall tinting added to the aesthetics of the screen image for some three decades. It was cheap and dramatically effective, like the beams of coloured limelight common in the theatre. The primary colours used were red, amber, green and blue and, according to the dramatic needs of the moment, whole sequences could be dyed in an appropriate colour. Tinting added another visual dimension to the artificial, melodramatic and theatrical conventions of the time, and when used by a great artist (*Birth of a Nation*, 1915, and *Intolerance*, 1916) added much to the overall visual and dramatic styling.

The introduction of panchromatic, in place of orthochromatic, stock in the mid-1920s crucially reshaped the techniques of cinematography. Orthochromatic emulsion, hitherto

Above: 'Birth of a Nation' (D. W. Griffith, cameraman Billy Bitzer, USA, 1915)
Below: Jean Hersholt (extreme left), Fanny Midgeley, Gibson Gowland, ZaSu Pitts and Frank Hayes in 'Greed' (Erich von Stroheim, cameramen Ben Reynolds and William Daniels, USA, 1923)

used universally, was insensitive to red and orange; panchromatic emulsion was sensitive to the whole visible spectrum. On the other hand, orthochromatic stock enabled a full depth of focus to be achieved as in Griffith's panoramic scenes and in the extraordinary contrasting details found in VON STROHEIM's *Greed* (1923), where scenes are viewed simultaneously indoors and, through a window, onto the street outside. Panchromatic film, with its greater sensitivity, had to be more narrowly focussed, emphasizing either foreground or background according to the requirements of the scene.[1] But panchromatic film gave the cameraman the chance to develop his own lighting and photographic methods, and the age of the great artist-cameramen began.

In America, particularly, with its quickly established tradition of the narrative film, a high degree of naturalism was sought, often allied to lighting which emphasized both the beauty of set design and the realism of locations – for example, John Seitz's work for REX INGRAM, and WILLIAM DANIELS's and Ben Reynolds's collaborations with von Stroheim (*Greed*, etc) – or highlighted the personality of a star (CHARLES ROSHER's work with MARY PICKFORD). In the early 1920s, directors tended to look at a scene from a fairly static viewpoint, obtaining movement and rhythm by cutting rather than by elaborate camera movements; as the 1920s progressed, however, increased mobility added to the cumulative comic or dramatic effect – much of KEATON's humour depends on the fast travelling shots used to climax a scene, and MURNAU's American films are notable for their slow, atmospheric movements as in *Sunrise* (1927), where the camera glides continually round both characters and settings.

[1] While making *Moana* (1923–4) in the South Seas, ROBERT FLAHERTY took with him a Prisma colour camera and the panchromatic stock used with it in order to experiment with colour cinematography. The colour camera broke down, and Flaherty was astonished by the beauty of the results obtained by using the panchromatic film in his black-and-white camera. It is often said that *Moana* was the first entirely panchromatic film.

The beauty of American silent film lighting reached such a peak of perfection (in films by such artists as GRIFFITH, VON STROHEIM, KING, VON STERNBERG, BROWN and the European émigrés, STILLER, CHRISTENSEN, LUBITSCH) that when sound came it inevitably brought stylistic changes and specialization within studios. Warner Brothers, for instance, favoured a raw, realistic style suited to the tough gangster, social dramas and back-stage musicals they produced (photographed by seasoned professionals like Sol Polito, Barney McGill, Tony Gaudio); whereas MGM, with their more glossy policy of historical dramas and star vehicles, developed a sumptuous, romanticized style involving elaborate craning and panning movements (executed by a star roster of cameramen including George Folsey, Joseph Ruttenberg, WILLIAM DANIELS, HARRY STRADLING). This was also the era of the love goddesses whose images were virtually created by the ornate lighting treatment conceived by director and cameraman (obvious examples are the

Above: Norma Shearer in 'Romeo and Juliet' (George Cukor, cameraman William Daniels, USA, 1936)
Below: Leslie Howard, Bette Davis and Olivia De Havilland in 'It's Love I'm After' (Archie Mayo, USA, 1937)

GARBO films lit by Daniels, and von Sternberg's projection of MARLENE DIETRICH in films shot by himself or talented associates like Bert Glennon and LEE GARMES).

A major innovation came in the early 1940s with WELLES's *Citizen Kane*, photographed by GREGG TOLAND, already known for his work with WYLER and FORD. In this case the style took in both European and American influences: heavy shadows, distortions and extreme deep-focus (which was common practice in the silent era but less favoured in the 1930s). Toland's experiments certainly influenced photographic methods during the succeeding decades; in America in the late 1940s, more realistic, documentary-style methods became the vogue, reflecting both the aftermath of the war and a rejection of the escapist, wish-fulfilment images of the 1930s.

Europe: Compared with America, the European silent cinema presents a picture of individual schools each with its own kind of pictorial signature. In France, for example, the serials of LOUIS FEUILLADE made during the First World War, with their audacious mixture of studio settings and real locations, contain images of deserted streets and shadowy buildings which look forward to ANTONIONI. The lighting is used to create sensations of mystery and suspense whereas, in Scandinavia, directors were seeking a luminous, open air lyricism and exploiting the light and shade of forest areas and snowy landscapes. DREYER's early work with the cameraman George Schneevoigt and

Top: Greta Garbo in 'Queen Christina' (Rouben Mamoulian, cameraman William Daniels, USA, 1933)
Above: Marlene Dietrich in 'Desire' (Frank Borzage, cameraman Charles Lang, USA, 1936)
Below: Dorothy Comingore in 'Citizen Kane' (Orson Welles, cameraman Gregg Toland, USA, 1940)

STILLER and SJÖSTRÖM with various collaborators produced some of the cinema's most painterly images.

The silent German cinema, on the other hand, was more studio-bound, emphasizing expressionist decor and tortured mental states and German cameramen like FRITZ ARNO WAGNER, KARL FREUND and Carl Hoffmann developed a suitably oppressive yet beautifully shaded lighting style full of magical, hallucinatory effects which pointed up both the intricately designed settings and the stylized movements of the actors.

In the USSR after the Revolution, the actual content of the subjects undertaken by the leading Soviet directors virtually dictated the visual style to be followed. Thus, Eisenstein with his revolutionary epics needed sharp, documentary-style shooting which his cameraman EDOUARD TISSÉ (beginning with *Strike*, with its great masses of crowds) brilliantly provided; likewise, DZIGA VERTOV, involved in the manipulation of raw newsreel material, drew on the resourcefulness of his numerous camera teams led by his brother MIKHAIL KAUFMAN; DOVZHENKO, with his highly personal, poetic vision full of stylized groupings and bizarre close-ups, found an ideal collaborator in Danilo Demutzky; and ANDREI MOSKVIN's more European-orientated, German-influenced interior lighting served KOZINTSEV and TRAUBERG in their semi-expressionist silent period.

In fact, the 1920s and 1930s were periods of intense photographic experimentation in both Europe and America during which a host of great cameramen emerged too numerous to mention in one article. Notable all-rounders (American cameramen seem the most versatile of all) like Ernest Haller, JAMES WONG HOWE, LEON SHAMROY, CHARLES LANG or Joseph MacDonald gave a distinctive visual style to subjects ranging from westerns to musicals; French cameramen like L.-H. BUREL (whose career stretches from GANCE to BRESSON) created all kinds of avant-garde, impressionist effects; GEORGES PÉRINAL moved from CLAIR's effervescent Parisian comedies to KORDA's cosmopolitan English empire; and MAX OPHÜLS took his delirious, continually tracking camera with him wherever he worked in Europe and America.

Asia: The photographic traditions of the main Asian film-producing countries (such as INDIA and JAPAN) have been formed from a fusion of Western technological influences and their own long cultural traditions in painting and sculpture. Although the West is only gradually discovering it, Japanese film history is both long and distinguished and has always concentrated on the beauty of the visual image. Years before KUROSAWA burst upon the West with his virtuoso, dynamic camera and cutting style, Japanese directors and cameramen were engaged in technical experimentation far in advance of their time: Ito's silent sword-play dramas with their rapid dolly shots and daring

Above left: Langhorn Burton and Joan Morgan in 'Two Little Wooden Shoes', a late example of the use of sunlight alone (Sidney Morgan, GB, 1920)
Above: Emil Jannings in 'The Last Laugh' (Friedrich Murnau, cameraman Karl Freund, Germany, 1924)
Below left: 'Kameradschaft' (G. W. Pabst, cameraman Fritz Arno Wagner, Germany, 1931)

pans; and Tasaka's sound films like *Five Scouts* (1938) with their audacious 'travellings' possibly inspired by ARTHUR EDESON's famous trench scenes in MILESTONE's *All Quiet on the Western Front* (1930). Among the other notable Japanese artists, MIYAGAWA stands out as one of the world's great poetic stylists (especially in his work with MIZOGUCHI), and Setsuo Kobayashi for his collaboration with ICHIKAWA, both in black-and-white and in the outstanding colour film, *An Actor's Revenge* (1963).

In India, where the emphasis until recent years was on studio-based dramas and extravaganzas, a more conservative tradition prevailed, but with the advent of the Bengali school led by SATYAJIT RAY in the early 1950s, location shooting and greater realism were introduced. This movement has produced at least two fine artists, Subrata Mitra (originally a stills photographer) whose work with Ray reveals a sensitive response to the Indian scene, with its rapidly changing seasons and dry, bare landscapes and Ray's subsequent cameraman Soumendu Roy.

Post-War Developments: The emphasis on location shooting and less glamourized imagery which became apparent in the post-war cinema all over the world can probably be traced back to the Italian neo-realist school led by ROSSELLINI, DE SICA and VISCONTI. Full of hard, grainy images (often caused by the enforced use of old film stock), these films introduced an air of freedom and improvisation into camera styles. And, in the hands of a considerable artist like G. R. ALDO, the neo-realist tenets were transformed in Visconti's *La Terra Trema* (1948) into a vast, painter-like fresco. Aldo's heir in the 1950s and 1960s was undoubtedly GIANNI DI VENANZO, whose fusion of documentary realism and soft-toned interiors served directors as disparate as ANTONIONI, LOSEY and ROSI.

As the 1950s progressed, the tendency towards 'filming on the spot' increased and it became necessary to introduce more mobile equipment suited to shooting in confined spaces and busy thoroughfares. Hand-held cameras and portable sound equipment (although not new inventions) provided the economy and, in a way, the artistic ethos for the French *nouvelle vague* (GODARD, TRUFFAUT, CHABROL, etc) whose favourite cameraman, RAOUL COUTARD, introduced a new fluidity and personal involvement into the concept of location filming. Young cameramen from other countries followed suit and we have seen a succession of virtuoso feats which would have been thought impossible 30 years ago. The post-war

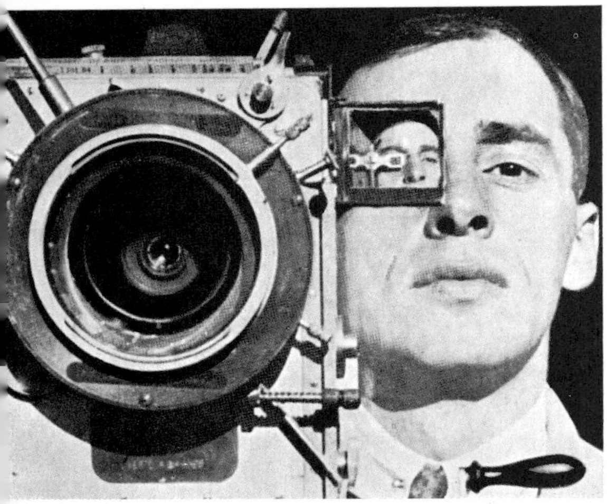

Above left: 'October' (Sergei Eisenstein, cameraman Edouard Tissé, USSR, 1927)
Above: 'Robinson Crusoe' in Semyon-Ivanov's three-dimensional system (USSR, 1945–6)
Left: Dziga Vertov in 'Man With a Movie Camera' (Vertov, cameraman Mikhail Kaufman, USSR, 1928)

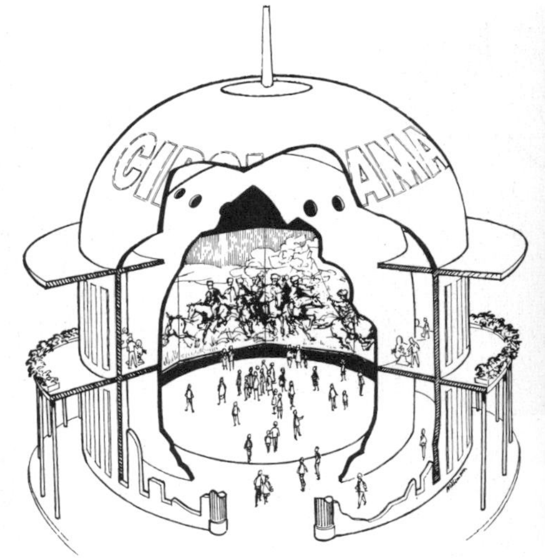

Top: The Russian 360° screen: Circlorama (invented by Gordovsky, 1960)
Above: 'Earth' (Alexander Dovzhenko, cameraman Danilo Demutsky, USSR, 1930)
Below: Jean Simmons, Jay Robinson and Richard Burton in 'The Robe', the first feature in CinemaScope (Henry Koster, cameraman Leon Shamroy, USA, 1953)

Soviet cinema, though still entrenched in rather academic directorial methods, has produced great photographic pyrotechnics in such films as *The Cranes are Flying* (1957, shot by Sergei Urusevsky), *The Story of the Flaming Years* (1961, with its 70 mm vistas of war-racked countryside) and *War and Peace* (1963–7, complete with helicopter-bird's-eye views and the cumulative weight of many cameramen shooting from every conceivable angle).

Colour: These new photographic methods, stemming from the introduction of wide-screen systems in the 1950s including CinemaScope, Cinerama and variations on the 70 mm process, have brought a new clarity and brilliance to modern cinematography, best seen perhaps in the big screen spectaculars from America, the USSR and certain European countries. Whatever their limitations in script, acting and direction, these films confirm the remarkable progress made in colour reproduction since the early Technicolor experiments of forty years ago. The 3D colour vogue of the 1950s has temporarily lapsed, due probably to the inconvenient spectacles required for viewing, but may well be revived when a non-spectacle system (like the Soviet invention of Semyon Ivanov) is fully developed.

The post-war period, in fact, has produced a whole school of cameramen specializing in colour photography, from Britain's JACK CARDIFF (*Pandora and the Flying Dutchman,* 1951, as well as much earlier work) to Italy's GIUSEPPE ROTUNNO (*The Leopard*, 1963, and *Fellini Satyricon*, 1969). During the last 10 years, the output of colour films has vastly increased (due partly to the demands of colour television), so that, in the 1970s, the black-and-white film is the exception rather than the rule. Among those artists using colour in a wholly creative

manner, Visconti in *Senso* (1954) and *The Leopard* showed how historical epochs could be almost palpably re-created by a sensitive response to colour textures; FORD's vision of the West in *The Searchers* (1956) and *Cheyenne Autumn* (1964) gained an extra dimension from the location colour; and French directors from CLAIR to OPHÜLS luxuriated in a flurry of period trappings and gorgeously coloured costumes.

Some of the most interesting colour experiments have come from the field of musicals, notably from the mid-1940s onwards, when FREED and MINNELLI began their great collaboration at MGM. Colour added a dimension to the song-and-dance film which artists like LUBITSCH and MAMOULIAN lacked in the 1930s; and MGM's musicals were conceived as a total synthesis of music, dance, light, colour, décor and rhythmic cutting. KELLY and DONEN took their subjects out of doors, incorporating the feel and bustle of city streets, while Minnelli developed a more interior, sophisticated style using rich décor and colour filters to give an edge and sheen to the numbers. And Mamoulian

Top: A triple-image from 'Napoléon' (Abel Gance, cameramen Léonce-Henri Burel and Roger Hubert, France, 1927)
Above: 'The Unvanquished' (Satyajit Ray, cameraman Subrata Mitra, India, 1956)
Right: Nicolai Cherkassov in 'Ivan the Terrible' (Sergei Eisenstein, cameraman Andrei Moskvin, USSR, 1944)
Below: Machiko Kyo and Masayuki Mori in 'Ugetsu Monogatari' (Kenji Mizoguchi, cameraman Kazuo Miyagawa, Japan, 1953)

showed how colour could be used in a lyrical relaxed way in *Summer Holiday* (1948), where the nostalgic lawns and exquisitely gowned dancers evoked an age of innocence paralleled in the silent cinema's rembrance of times past.

Despite the recent glut of theatrical adaptations, with their over-upholstered production numbers, an echo of the old MGM spirit can be found in such big-budget, widescreen extravaganzas as Kelly's *Hello Dolly!* (1969, photographed by HARRY STRADLING) and Fosse's *Sweet Charity* (1968, photographed by Robert Surtees).

The future of cinematography in the 1970s, then, seems to lie in colour, clarity and the big screen image. We also seem to be passing through a phase of chic, fashionable 'art' photography complete with misty filters, slow-motion, and arbitrary ZOOM LENS and focus-changing effects. These 'television-commercial' techniques hold a particular fascination for young film-makers all over the world, as do the technical facilities now available to all. It seems likely, however, that a reaction will eventually set in and we may see a return to the classical style formed by such artists as Renoir, Ford, Dreyer, Murnau and Mizoguchi in which the camera interpreted as well as recorded and meaningful movement became an integral part of the narrative style. JG and RM

Cinerama

Wide screen presentation, first devised in 1937, which originally used three separate 35 mm projectors to show the image on three slightly overlapping panels on a large deeply-curved screen. Later productions were photographed on 65 mm negative stock, using an ANAMORPHIC LENS. From this negative 70 mm prints were made by optical printing, during which changes of image geometry were introduced to make the print more suitable for projection on the deeply-curved screen.

Circuit

Group of cinemas owned by one distribution company

Circuit Release

The screening of a film by most, if not all the cinemas of a particular circuit

Clair, Mal St

See ST CLAIR

Clair, René

Born 1898 in Paris, France. Real name René Chomette. Director, screenwriter, author, and originally an actor. Son of a soap merchant, Clair showed a childhood interest in the theatre. After service as an ambulance-driver in 1917 he was invalided out of the service and suffered a religious crisis, as a result of which he retired for a while to a monastery when still under 20. He turned to journalism, writing for 'L'Intransigeant', and threw himself into the life of a Parisian artist, interested equally in literature, art, the theatre, ballet and, finally, the film, in which he first served as an actor, appearing in Loie Fuller's film, *Le Lys de la Vie* (1920), in PROTAZANOV's *Le Sens de la Mort* (1921) and in FEUILLADE's serials, *L'Orpheline* and *Parisette* (1921): he adopted the name René Clair during this period. Meanwhile, his brother Henri Chomette was studying film direction in Brussels as an assistant to Jacques de Baroncelli; René for a while joined them as Baroncelli's assistant, and then returned to Paris anxious himself to become a director, and accepting also to act as film editor to the journal, 'Le Théâtre et Comédie Illustré'. His interest in cinema thoroughly aroused, he rediscovered in particular the work of ZECCA and MÉLIÈS, and he joined for a while the group of avant-garde film-makers associated with EPSTEIN and L'HERBIER. His first films were *Paris qui Dort* (1923), a fantasy on which CLAUDE AUTANT-LARA acted as his assistant, and *Entr'acte* (1924), the latter made to be shown

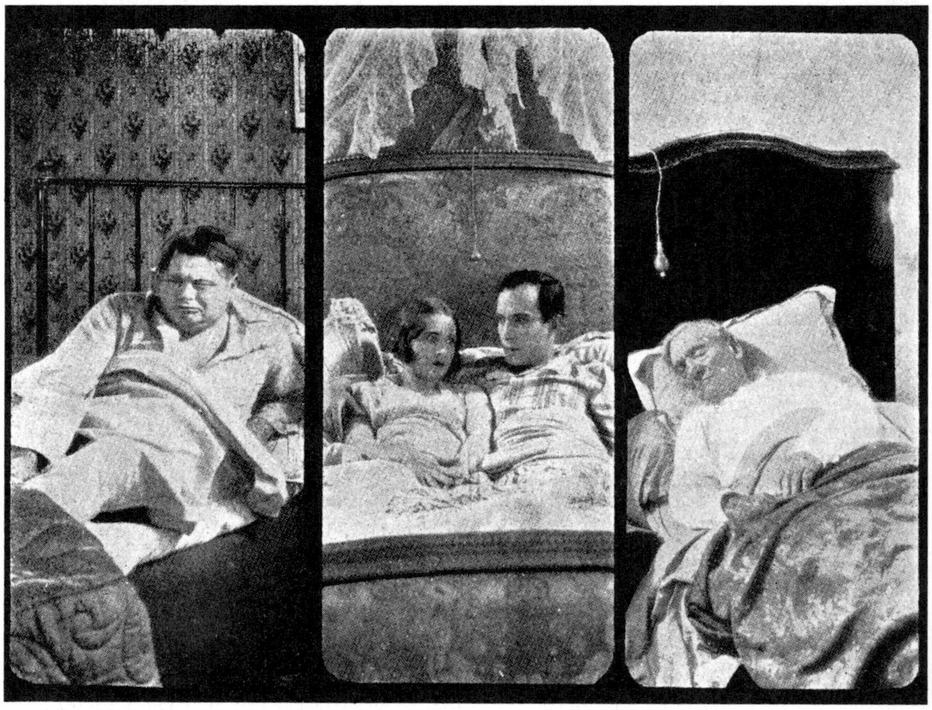

Top: 'La Proie du Vent' (René Clair, France, 1926)
Above: Jim Gerald, Vera Flory, Pierre Batcheff and Maurice de Feraudy in 'Les Deux Timides' (René Clair, France, 1928)

during the interval in the performance of the Ballet Relâche performed in the Dada manner by the Ballet Suédois; the treatment was by Francis Picabia, and this wholly delightful, surrealist film had many famous participants, including Marcel Duchamp. In the same year, Clair made *Le Fantôme du Moulin Rouge* (1924), in which he was able to carry much further his use of the camera's resources in a story involving a form of 'invisible man'. Fantasy appeared again in *Le Voyage Imaginaire* (1925), and Clair's technical precision was developed still further in *La Proie du Vent* (1926), in which he first worked with the designer, LAZARE MEERSON. Clair's first masterpiece was *Un Chapeau de Paille d'Italie* (*The Italian Straw Hat*, 1927), which he adopted from a farce by Labiche and Michel; this was the first of Clair's 'serious' comedies, with highly characterized comic performance and the careful development of gradually evolving humour rather than the quick laugh. Too advanced to be a commercial success, it nonetheless enhanced Clair's reputation as a director both at home and abroad. After making *La Tour* (1928), an example of *cinéma pur* in its presentation of the Eiffel Tower, using varied angles, speeds and cutting rhythms, Clair made *Les Deux Timides* (1928), another meticulous adaptation from Labiche and Michel.

Below: 'The Italian Straw Hat' (René Clair, France, 1927)
Bottom: René Clair and Maurice Chevalier on the set of 'Le Silence est d'Or' (Clair, France, 1947)

It is ironic that Clair came into his own with the arrival of sound, since he was violently opposed to 'talkies'; he recognized, however, the advantages natural sounds and music could bring to the cinema, and the succession of musical films he made were among the most creative produced anywhere at this time when the relationship of sound to the film had to be explored – *Sous les Toits de Paris* (1930), *Le Million* and *A Nous la Liberté* (1931) and *Quatorze Juillet* (1932), all the product of a brilliant production team comprising the cinematographer GEORGES PÉRINAL and the designer Meerson. *Le Dernier Milliardaire* (1934), made with another team, was less effective, and Clair came to England to work first of all with KORDA, for whom he directed *The Ghost Goes West* (1935). After making *Break the News* (1937) with Jack Buchanan, Clair, somewhat disappointed with the outcome of his work in England, returned to France to make a documentary about Montmartre, *Un Village dans Paris* (1939), and starting, with ROBERT BRESSON as his assistant, *Air Pur*, which remained unfinished with the onset of war.

In the spring of 1940, Clair left for Hollywood, where he made a series of enjoyable films, notably *The Flame of New Orleans* (with MARLENE DIETRICH, 1940), *I Married a Witch* (1942), which developed more fully his sense of visual fantasy, and *It Happened Tomorrow* (1943). He did not find it easy to work in Hollywood, and after the war he returned to France, where his later films, now he was entering his fifties, developed a more mellow charm along with their elegance of visual style and technical accomplishment: *Le Silence est d'Or* (1947), *La Beauté du Diable* (made in Italy, 1949), *Les Belles-de-Nuit* (1952), *Les Grandes Manœuvres* (1955), *Porte des Lilas* (1957), *Tout l'Or du Monde* (1961) and *Les Fêtes Galantes* (1965). Humour was now combined with irony and pathos.

Clair wrote virtually all his own screenplays, except during the period when he was working abroad. He was also a novelist, publishing 'Adams' (1926), 'De Film en Aguille' (1947) and 'La Princesse de Chine' (1951). In 1951 he also published 'Réflexion Faite', in which he collects a selection of his reviews and articles on the cinema written between 1920 and 1950, adding new comments upon the older pieces. An English translation appeared in 1953, 'Reflections on the Cinema'. There are many studies in French of Clair and his work, books by Jacques Bourgeois, by Georges Charensol and Roger Régent, by Jean Mitry, and by Barthélemy Amengual and, in English, an Index of his work by Catherine de la Roche (BFI, London, 1958). RM

Clapperboard
Pair of boards hinged at one end and banged

together in view of the camera at the start or end of a dialogue shot to enable picture and sound to be correctly synchronized.

Clarke, Shirley

Born 1925 in USA. *Cinéma-vérité* American director whose methods of working, subject matter and independence of the traditional Hollywood system has made her a key influence in the development of the American underground film. Principal films: *Bullfight* (1955), *The Connection* (1960), *Cool World* (1963), *Portrait of Jason* (1967). Appeared in *Lion's Love* (1969).

Clarke, T. E. B.

Born 1907 in Watford, England. Screenwriter. Formerly a journalist, he made a great reputation as an originator of comedy scripts at MICHAEL BALCON's Ealing Studios after the war. His principal credits include many of Ealing's best films – during the war period *For Those in Peril*, *Half-way House*, and *Johnny Frenchman* (all 1944–5): and after the war *Hue and Cry* (1946), *Passport to Pimlico* (1948), *The Blue Lamp* (1950), *The Lavender Hill Mob* (1951), and *The Titfield Thunderbolt* (1953). His post-Ealing credits include: *A Tale of Two Cities* (1957), *Gideon's Way* (1960), *Sons and Lovers* (collaborated), *The Horse without a Head* (1963).

Clayton, Jack

Born 1921, in London. After a long and traditional career as a technician, Clayton produced and directed a medium-length film, an adaptation from Gogol, retitled *The Bespoke Overcoat* (1955). He achieved commercial success with *Room at the Top* (1958), which, though it now looks somewhat conservative in style even for the period, nevertheless introduced the cinema to the new literature of the 1950s – specifically John Braine's best-selling novel about a small-time provincial careerist. Since then Clayton's output has been disappointingly restricted: an atmospheric adaptation of Henry James's 'Turn of the Screw' – *The Innocents* (1961) – a less happy adaptation of Penelope Mortimer's *The Pumpkin Eater* (1963) and *Our Mother's House* (1967).

Clément, René

Born 1913 in Bordeaux, France. Director. Originally he studied to be an architect, but entered films in 1934 to become a cameraman and assistant director. His early career was concentrated on documentary and short films (including *Soigne Ton Gauche* (1937) with JACQUES TATI), which developed the taste for realism shown in his admirable first feature film, *La Bataille du Rail* (1945), a study of the French Resistance, which had much in common with Italian neo-realism. His hatred of Nazism found further expression in *Les Maudits* (1947), a somewhat melodramatic story of mutual destruction among a group of Nazis escaping to South America by submarine.

Clément went to Italy for *Au Delà des Grilles*, which was originally scripted by the neo-realists CESARE ZAVATTINI and SUSO CECCHI D'AMICO, though the script was re-modelled in the direction of melodrama by JEAN AURENCHE and PIERRE BOST, who were to write many of his subsequent scripts; the film starred JEAN GABIN in his romantic, pre-war CARNÉ-like role of the doomed fugitive. Clément's initial passion for accuracy and eye for detail was better shown in *Jeux Interdits* (1952), a *film noir* about the effect of war on two small children, a country boy and an orphan refugee from Paris, who create their own secret world in a cemetery for animals. Clément draws his audience into this film which is strangely sympathetic in spite of its necrophiliac atmosphere.

Above: Georges Poujouly in 'Jeux Interdits' (René Clément, France, 1952)
Below: Montgomery Clift and Olivia De Havilland in 'The Heiress' (William Wyler, USA, 1949)

After making the ironic *The Knave of Hearts* (1954) in a two-language version in London, the story of an inconstant lover passing from woman to woman in which he used London locations brilliantly, Clément directed one of his darker masterpieces in *Gervaise* (1955), adapted from Zola's 'L'Assommoir'. Zola's detailed and unflinching realism attracted Clément to make a period film in the same spirit of exactness as a contemporary subject; 'Exactness must be a mania,' he said. FRANÇOIS PÉRIER, who played the alcoholic Coupeau, had to visit mental hospitals to study the behaviour of alcoholics. Clément does not hesitate to give reality to the degradation and filth of the period.

After this film Clément worked for some years abroad – making *Barrage contre le Pacifique* (1958) in Thailand, *Plein Soleil* (1959) in the Mediterranean, and *Quelle Joie de Vivre* (1961) in Rome; this work was less interesting, though often showing his characteristic technical brilliance. He returned to France to make two more films connected with the war years – *Le Jour et l'Heure* (1963), concerning a woman who becomes involved in resistance (and love) by harbouring an American airman, and the star-filled, epic-scale *Paris Brûle-t-il?* (*Is Paris Burning?* 1966) set in the liberation period. Latest films: *Passagers de la Pluie* (1969). Clément's recent films have aimed increasingly at being international in scope; in these glossier subjects he retains his skill as a craftsman but the sympathy, human understanding and authenticity of his earlier work have largely disappeared. RM

Clementi, Pierre

Born 1944 in Paris. After a number of minor roles in films and theatre, Clementi achieved sudden prominence with his interpretation of the young thug in BUÑUEL's *Belle de Jour* (1967). After this the participation of this handsome, impossibly lean young man with his haunted features seemed almost *de rigueur* in French or Italian films of progressive artistic or political tendency. Among the numerous films in which he was seen in the late 1960s and early 1970s were Peter Emmanuel Goldman's *Wheel of Ashes* and BERTOLUCCI's *Partner* (1968), PIER PAOLO PASOLINI's *Porcile*, Buñuel's *La Voie Lactée* (1969) and *La Pacifista* (JANSCÓ, 1970). He also directed the avant-garde short *Pontpoint* (1966).

Clift, Montgomery (1920–1966)
Born in Nebraska, USA. Hypersensitive American Method actor whose influence upon other actors far outweighed the range of screen roles he played. Overshadowed by MARLON BRANDO, he came to films via the theatre, making his screen début in *The Search* in 1948. His most popular performance was as a young Western hero in *Red River* in the same year. Despite a series of brilliant portrayals of intense, tormented heroes, he never quite achieved the promise of his early career which suffered after a serious car accident in 1957.

Notable films include: *The Heiress* (1949), *A Place in the Sun* (1951), *I Confess* and *From Here to Eternity* (1953), *Indiscretions of an American Wife* (1954), *Raintree County* (1957), *The Young Lions* (1958), *Lonelyhearts* and *Suddenly Last Summer* (1959), *Wild River*, *The Misfits* and *Judgment at Nuremberg* (1960), *Freud* (1963). He died soon after completing his last, disappointing film, *The Defector* (1966).

Cline, Edward F. (1892–1961)
Born in Wisconsin, USA. Director. Was a Keystone Cop in MACK SENNETT comedies, and made many Sennett Bathing Beauty shorts; from 1918, directed hundreds of comedy features and shorts including several collaborations with BUSTER KEATON. Cline is also likely to be remembered as director of some of the best W. C. FIELDS vehicles including *The Bank Dick* and *My Little Chickadee* (1940) and *Never Give a Sucker an Even Break* (1941). Fields's eccentric methods and reportedly cavalier treatment of directors must have made the tasks formidable ones, but Cline's training in the Sennett school and his concise film sense enabled him to enshrine some of Fields's most exuberant performances. JG

Clip
A short section from a complete film

Close-medium Shot
A shot between a close-up and a medium shot; in a human subject, from head to knees.

Close-up
A shot taken with the action or character close to the viewer; in relation to a human subject, a shot of the face only.

Clouzot, Henri-Georges
Born 1907 in Niort, France, Writer and director. He began his career in films as a scriptwriter and assistant director, but ill-health soon forced him to make writing plays and filmscripts his principal occupation. *Le Corbeau* (1943), his second feature film as a director and one of his most powerful, with anonymous poison-pen letters as its subject, was so virulent in its portrait of French provincial life that it was held to be anti-French, especially as it was produced by a Nazi-controlled company. As a result Clouzot faced a period of boycott after the war. In 1947, however, he was permitted to make *Quai des Orfèvres* (1947), a *roman policier* in which LOUIS JOUVET was magnificent as a detective whose approach to the investigation of a murder is governed by instinct; the film was unsparingly realistic, and brilliantly evoked the atmosphere of the Paris police headquarters and music-halls.

Manon (1949) was a more hybrid work, updating the Abbé Prévost's classic story and involving a complex post-war background, extending even to illegal Jewish immigration into Palestine. The 16-year-old Cécile Aubry played the amoral girl whose infatuation for her lover does not prevent her prostituting herself. *Manon* was a *film noir*, as was its successor, *The Wages of Fear* (1952) set in a community of degenerate European outcasts in Latin America but actually shot in an area near Nîmes. The film is, in effect, a fable about human relationships, in which four men team up to take two lorries of nitro-glycerine over a dangerous mountain route; Clouzot exacts the last drop of sweat from his actors and his audience. His next film, *Les Diaboliques* (1955), was even more sadistic, carrying horror to excess in a *grand guignol* study of murder which turns on a trick of plot.

More worthy of Clouzot's considerable talent was *Le Mystère Picasso* (1956) – one of the most remarkable films about art ever made. Picasso uses a translucent screen and special inks to create a gallery of paintings and drawings which also involve many different camera techniques, including stop-motion and reverse photography, and varied speed.

After the unsatisfactory hybrid *Les Espions* (1957), mixing violence with farce, Clouzot made *La Vérité* (1960) with BRIGITTE BARDOT, a study of another amoral girl, who stands trial for murder. The film shows the distortions which the evidence presented in court creates contrasted with the truth about the girl shown in flashback. Still held back by ill-health, Clouzot had to abandon his next film, *L'Enfer*, but managed to complete *La Prisonnière* (1968) – a study in perversion made with all his charac-

Michel Auclair and Cécile Aubry in 'Manon' (Henri-Georges Clouzot, France, 1949)

teristic ruthlessness and pessimism, but one of his finest technical achievements. RM

Cocteau, Jean (1889–1963)
Born in Maisons-Laffitte, France. Cocteau expressed his strong and distinctive artistic personality as naturally through the medium of film as he did in poetry, literature, theatre and painting. All his films are an integral part of the continuing intimate diary represented by his work, and characterized by his particular style of lyrical surrealism. In 1930 the Vicomte de Noaïlles financed two films by young avant-garde artists: one was BUÑUEL's *L'Age d'Or*; the other, Cocteau's *Le Sang d'un Poète*, in which he introduced the mythology and the symbols that were to recur throughout his later film work. During the war he scripted L'HERBIER's *La comédie de bonheur* (1940), de Poligny's *Le Baron Fantôme* (1942) and BRESSON's *Les Dames du Bois de Boulogne* (1945); but the first true Cocteau film was *L'Eternel Retour* (1943), directed by JEAN DELANNOY, yet uncompromisingly impressed by Cocteau's own personality. In the immediate post-war years many English-speaking critics, not realizing that the Tristran and Iseult legend was Breton in origin, criticized the film for its 'collaborationist' spirit.

Cocteau embarked on direction in his own right with the exquisite *La Belle et la Bête* (with RENÉ CLÉMENT, 1946) and *Les Parents Terribles* (1948). This, adapted from his play, is perhaps his best film: a concentrated psychological study of the mutual torments of a claustrophobic family group. *Les Enfants Terribles* (1949) was directed by JEAN-PIERRE MELVILLE, but remains, with its references to *Le Sang d'un Poète*, quintessentially a Cocteau picture. The mythology recurs again in the memorable *Orphée* (1950). Cocteau was to make two more short films, *La Villa Santo Sospir* (1951) and *Le rouge est mis* before deliberately creating his artistic testament, *Le Testament d'Orphée* (1960). Significantly this was in part financed by the new young generation of French directors, to whom Cocteau's uncompromising individuality had been an essential inspiration. DR

Cohl, Émile (1857–1963)
Born in Paris, France. Animation director. The father of the animated film, Cohl was a caricaturist before joining the Gaumont studios in 1907. He first directed trick films in the manner of MÉLIÈS, though rapidly developing his own elegant and individual style. His first experiments with animation, including *Fantasmagorie* and *Drame chez les fantôches*, were made in 1908. As well as technical expertise, Cohl's work was marked by a vivid visual invention, and his films retain all their life and vigour after more than 60 years. In 1913–5 Cohl worked in the USA, creating the *Snookums* series. His last film was *Les aventures des pieds-nickelés* (1918), made in collaboration with Benjamin Rabier. Cohl spent his last days in the same old people's home at Orly as Méliès, who died in the same month. A patriarchal figure, Cohl was killed when his long white beard was set alight by a candle.

Cohn, Harry (1891–1958)
Born in New York, USA. All-powerful and reputedly ruthless president of Columbia Pictures and head of production in Hollywood from 1932 until his death. A vaudeville performer and song-plugger, he, his brother Jack (with whom he waged constant war) and a friend Joe Brandt formed CBS Sales Company which became Columbia in 1924.

When Brandt retired, Cohn outwitted his brother's effort to oust him. A tough and often vulgar man who is supposed to have inspired the characterizations of the junk tycoon in *Born Yesterday* (filmed in 1950) and the movie mogul in *The Big Knife* (1955), he nevertheless created a tightly knit production company noted for such progressive and civilized films as the CAPRA comedies, the JUDY HOLLIDAY-JACK LEMMON satires, and *All the King's Men* (1949), *From Here to Eternity* (1953), *On the Waterfront* (1954). An enjoyable and perceptive biography of him, 'King Cohn' by Bob Thomas, was published in 1967. MH

Colbert, Claudette
Born 1905 in Paris, France. Sophisticated Hollywood star of the 1930s and 1940s who is equally adept at high comedy, domestic romance or heart-throbbing soap opera. Arriving in America as a child, she appeared in a number of successes on Broadway before making her film début in *For the Love o'Mike* (1927). Cast by CECIL B. DE MILLE as the sultry Poppea in *Sign of the Cross* (1932) and as *Cleopatra* (1934), she found her true *métier* in the smart, racy comedy of *It Happened one Night* (1934), for which she won an Academy Award and *Midnight* (1939). An infallibly attractive actress who made a graceful transition from *ingénue* to elegant mother-figure, she has not filmed since *Parrish* in 1961.

Above: Ronald Colman in 'A Tale of Two Cities' (Jack Conway, USA, 1936)
Below: Henri Crémieux and Jean Cocteau in 'Le Testament d'Orphée' (Cocteau, France, 1960)

Notable films: *Three-Cornered Moon* (1933), *Tovarich* (1938), *Arise My Love* (1940), *The Palm Beach Story* (1942), *Since you went Away* (1944), *Without Reservations* (1946), *Sleep my Love* (1948), *Let's Make it Legal* (1951), *The Planter's Wife* (1952). MH

Colman, Ronald (1891–1958)
Born in Surrey, England. Impeccably 'English' gentleman-star and leading purveyor of gallant, romantic heroism in the 1920s and 1930s. After First World War service and small parts in British silent films, he went to America, where he starred in *The White Sister* (1923). But his greatest success was achieved through the coming of sound and the need for actors with good diction together with the popularity of well-bred swashbuckling adventures such as *Clive of India* (1935), *A Tale of Two Cities* and *Under Two Flags* (1936), *The Prisoner of Zenda* (1937). His more subtle dramatic gifts were revealed in the comedy *Talk of the Town* (1942), *The Late George Apley* and *A Double Life* (both 1947), for which he won an Academy Award.
Notable films include: *Beau Geste* and *Bulldog Drummond* (1926), *Raffles* (1931), *Arrowsmith* (1932), *Cynara* (1933), *Lost Horizon* (1937), *Random Harvest* (1943), *Champagne for Caesar* (1950), *The Story of Mankind* (1957). MH

Colour Cinematography see p. 29

Colpi, Henri
Born 1921 in Switzerland. Director and writer, who had originally worked as a journalist. Films edited include three for RESNAIS, *Nuit et Brouillard* (1955), *Hiroshima mon Amour* (1959), and *L'Année Dernière à Marienbad* (1961). Films directed include *Une Aussi Longue Absence* (1961). *Codine* (1962), and *Mona, l'Étoile sans Nom* (1966). Colpi is also the author of a book on film music, 'Défense et Illustration de la Musique dans le Film' (1963) and he recently made several filmed concerts.

Comencini, Luigi
Born 1916 in Salo, Italy. Director and screenwriter. His first film was *Proibito Rubare* (1948). He is best known for his commercially successful light comedies, *Bread, Love and Dreams* (1953) and *Bread, Love and Jealousy* (1954), both with GINA LOLLOBRIGIDA and VITTORIO DE SICA. His other films include *La Valigia dei Sogni* (1952), *Mogli Pericolose* (1958), a film made in Berlin after a comedy by J. B. Priestley, *Und das am Montag morgen* (1959), and *Tutti a casa* (1960).

Conklin, Chester (1888–1971)
Born in Oskaloosa, Iowa, USA. Actor. 'A myopic and inebriated little walrus stumbling around in outsize pants' (James Agee). Originally a circus clown and vaudeville artist, Conklin joined MACK SENNETT at Keystone and made his début at the same time as CHAPLIN, in *Making a Living* (1914). He continued to appear as a supporting actor in numerous Chaplin films, right up to *Modern Times* (1936) and *The Great Dictator* (1941). A gifted, versatile and conscientious comedian, Conklin fulfilled his ambition of playing in legitimate roles when he appeared as ZASU PITTS's father in VON STROHEIM's *Greed* (1923). He continued to appear in films until 1960.

Connery, Sean
Born 1930 in Edinburgh, Scotland. Actor. Appeared on the stage and television and in minor film parts before becoming famous as James Bond in a series of films adapted from Ian Fleming's novels. Main films: *Dr No* (1962), *From Russia with Love* (1963), *Woman of Straw* and *Goldfinger* (1964), *The Hill* and *Thunderball* (1965), *You Only Live Twice* (1967), *Shalako* (1968), *The Molly Maguires* (1969), *Diamonds are Forever* and *The Anderson Tapes* (1971).

Console
A control panel used in sound recording and re-recording which enables the input from microphones or sound reproducers to be varied in amplitude and frequency.

Continuity
A form of swift construction which enables the story of a film to flow smoothly and without interruption from one shot to another.

Continuity Girl
Technician responsible for recording details of every take during shooting in order to ensure that no discrepancies occur to disturb continuity when the film is edited.

Continuity Sheet
A detailed report of each scene prepared at the time of filming, chiefly for the information of the editor.

Continuity Still
A still photograph taken during the course of film production with the object of assisting in the matching up of scenes taken at different times.

Continuity Title
A title used to preserve continuity by denoting a lapse of time, change of situation, not indicated clearly by the action of the film.

Contrast
The range of tones in a photographic negative

Sean Connery in 'Dr No' (Terence Young, GB, 1962)

Coogan, Jackie
Born 1914 in Los Angeles, California, USA. Actor, who made his celebrated début at the age of six opposite CHARLIE CHAPLIN in *The Kid* (1920). He then starred in many silent films, such as *Oliver Twist* (1921), *Daddy* (1923), *Old Clothes* (1925) and *The Bugle Call* (1927), and in early sound films including *Tom Sawyer* (1930) and *Huckleberry Finn* (1931). As an adult actor he has appeared in minor films and on television.

Cooper, Gary (1901–1961)
Born in Montana, USA. Prototype laconic Western star and sincere, if limited, actor. During the 1930s and 1940s his decent backwoods heroes spoke up for the values and standards of small-town rural America in direct opposition to the gabby, big city wise guys represented by JAMES CAGNEY, EDWARD G. ROBINSON, HUMPHREY BOGART. A cowboy and cartoonist, he became a film extra and made his début in a silent film, *Lightning Justice*, under his own name, Frank Cooper. He became a star in *The Winning of Barbara Worth* (1926) and thereafter made close to a hundred films, hardly ever deviating from his essential characterization. Although he played in period adventures, romances, gangster films, comedies (arguably his most disastrous casting was as a middle-aged Lothario in the comedy *Love in the Afternoon* in 1956), war films, he was most popular in Westerns. During his long career he won two Academy Awards, for *Sergeant York* (1941) and *High Noon* (1952). Other notable films: *Wings* (1927), *The Virginian* (1929), *Morocco* (1930), *A Farewell to Arms* and *City Streets* (1932), *Lives of a Bengal Lancer* (1935), *Mr Deeds goes to Town* (1936), *The Plainsman* (1937), *For whom the Bell Tolls* (1943), *The Fountainhead* (1949), *Friendly Persuasion* (1956), *The Hanging Tree* and *The Wreck of the Mary Deare* (1959), *The Naked Edge* (1961). MH

Corman, Roger
Born 1926 in Chicago, USA. Amazingly prolific and variously talented American writer, director and producer whose cheap (financially) and speedy output has earned him an honoured reputation with *cinéastes* and film distributors alike. A writer and rover before he became a director, he formed Roger Corman Productions in 1953, directed his first film *Five Guns West* (1954), followed by a series of action quickies, almost all made in less than three weeks: *Bucket of Blood* (1959) was made in five days. Averaging five films a year, he first attracted critical interest with his vividly atmospheric adaptations from Edgar Allen Poe, beginning with *The Fall of the House of Usher* (1960). While his horror films continued to be successful, he branched out with a deeply personal statement on race relations in the South, *The Intruder* (1961). Corman is an independent who does not suffer studio control gladly and his films have become increasingly uninhibited in their handling of violent themes. Most recent films: *The Mask of the Red Death* (1964), *The Wild Angels* and *The St Valentine Day's Massacre* (1966), *The Trip* (1967), *Bloody Mama* and *Gas!* (1969), *The Red Baron* (1971). MH

Above: Jackie Coogan in 'The Kid' (Charles Chaplin, USA, 1920)
Below: Gary Cooper and Barbara Stanwyck in 'Meet John Doe' (Frank Capra, USA, 1941)

Cornelius, Henry (1913–1958)
Born in South Africa. European-educated British director who caught the comic humours and idiosyncrasies of the English in two minor classics, *Passport to Pimlico* (1948) and *Genevieve* (1953), but failed to sustain that success. After studying under Max Reinhardt in Berlin, he went to France when Hitler came to power in Germany, and in 1935 arrived in England, where he worked as a cutter for ALEXANDER KORDA's company. Influenced by RENÉ CLAIR, for whom he worked on *The Ghost Goes West* (1935), he studied the French director's light comedy style; traces of CLAIR's technique were evident in his own films. After three years in the South African film propaganda service during the Second World War, he returned to Britain and joined Ealing Studios as associate producer and writer before making *Passport to Pimlico*. Other films: *The Galloping Major* (1951), *I am a Camera* (1955), *Next to no Time* (1957). MH

Cortez, Stanley
Born 1908 in New York, USA. Cinematographer. A brother of the actor Ricardo Cortez, he began as an assistant operator and shot several films in the 1930s, but it was WELLES's *The Magnificent Ambersons* (1942) which established his reputation as a cameraman particularly adept in manipulating black-and-white textures and conjuring up an uneasy, tense atmosphere. These qualities were again evident in DUVIVIER's *Flesh and Fantasy* (1943), LANG's *The Secret Beyond the Door* (1948), Fregonese's *Black Tuesday* (1954) and, especially *Night of the Hunter* (1955), CHARLES LAUGHTON's sole directorial work which gave Cortez a renewed chance for experimentation. In recent years he has worked less, or only on relatively off-beat films such as *Shock Corridor* (1963) and *Blue* (1968). JG

Costa-Gavras
Born 1933, of Russo-Greek origins. Director. Brought up in France, Costa-Gavras began his career as director with hard-hitting, American-styled films, *Compartiment Tueurs* (*The Sleeping-car Murders*, 1965) and *Un Homme de Trop* (1967). He then turned to political themes, attacking violence and oppression from whatever source

Top left: 'The St Valentine's Day Massacre' (Roger Corman, USA, 1966)
Top right: Tom Courtenay in 'The Loneliness of the Long-Distance Runner' (Tony Richardson, GB, 1963)
Above: Julie Harris and Laurence Harvey in 'I am a Camera' (Henry Cornelius, GB, 1955)
Right: Yves Montand (on poster) in 'Z' (Costa-Gavras, France-Algeria, 1968)

it came: from the Right in *Z* (1968), a French-Algerian film shot in Algiers but set in an unidentified Mediterranean country; and from the Left, in *L'Aveu* (*The Confession*, 1970), set in Prague in 1951. Both films were scripted by Jorge Semprun and shot with brilliant realistic effect by RAOUL COUTARD. Costa-Gavras has said that his aim is to expose contemporary political tensions to mass audiences in films of strong, dramatic-realist impact, but what emerges most clearly is his hatred of violence in all its manifestations.

Cotten, Joseph

Born 1905 in Virginia, USA. Impressive American actor in a minor key; initially celebrated as a member of ORSON WELLES's Mercury Theatre and leading actor in *Citizen Kane* (his screen début, 1940), *The Magnificent Ambersons* and *Journey Into Fear* (1942). His heroic good looks and quiet authority were later exploited by Hollywood in many sentimental romances, though, apart from WELLES's films, his most significant screen performances were in the thriller genre – HITCHCOCK's *Shadow of a Doubt* (1943) and CAROL REED's *The Third Man* (1949). Most recent films: *Jack of Diamonds* (1967), *Petulia* (1968), *Tora! Tora! Tora!* and *The Grasshopper* (1970), *White Comanche* and *The Abominable Dr Phibes* (1971).

Courtenay, Tom

Born 1937 in Yorkshire, England. Sensitive British actor who came to the fore during the 1960s along with ALBERT FINNEY, MICHAEL CAINE and TERENCE STAMP. Primarily a stage actor, he has appeared notably but intermittently in films, starring memorably in his first, *The Loneliness of the Long-Distance Runner* (1963), though the sullen, rebellious, working-class hero he played tended to type him on the

screen after that. Other main films: *Billy Liar* (1963), *King and Country* (1964), *King Rat* (1965), *The Day the Fish came out* (1967), *Otley* (1969), *One Day in the Life of Ivan Denisovich* and *Catch me a Spy* (1971).

Cousteau, Jacques-Yves
Born 1910 in Saint-André, Gironde, France. Director. While a naval officer in the 1930s, he became interested in underwater exploration and made numerous short films (from the early 1940s onwards) which opened up a new field of cinematography. Gathering together an experienced *équipe* (including, at one time, LOUIS MALLE), he travelled in many parts of the world, revealing aspects of the sea and oceanic life never seen before and shot in beautiful colour. Apart from the short films, he has made several features including *Le Monde du Silence* (1956) and *Le Monde Sans Soleil* (1964). In recent years, he has produced several underwater exploration series for television. JG

Coutard, Raoul
Born 1924 in Paris, France. Cinematographer. After working as a press photographer in the 1950s, he became associated with the rising French *nouvelle vague* school (GODARD, TRUFFAUT, DEMY), who favoured a hard, mobile, unromantic style which Coutard soon perfected. Apart from invariably being his own operator, he developed new methods of using hand-held cameras which has influenced cinematographers in many other countries. His work ranges from atmospheric black-and-white shooting in cities and countryside (*À Bout de Souffle*, 1959; *Tirez sur le Pianiste*, 1960; *Lola*, 1960) to the luscious colour photography of Godard's *Le Mépris* (1963) and *Pierrot le Fou* (1965). His long-term collaboration with Godard has produced consistently fine work to such an extent that one cannot easily separate Godard's ideas from Coutard's images. Truffaut, also, has worked creatively with him, notably in *Jules et Jim* (1961) and *La Mariée était en noir* (1967); indeed, Coutard seems able to adapt to a wide variety of directional temperaments. His considerable output has decreased somewhat in recent years; he spent many months directing a feature about Vietnam, *Hoa-Binh* (1970), whose avoidance of direct political comment caused controversy among his French colleagues. JG

Above left: 'Paysages du Silence' (Jacques-Yves Cousteau, France, 1946)
Above: Jacques-Yves Cousteau
Below: Noël Coward in 'Paris when it Sizzles' (Richard Quine, USA, 1963)

Coward, Noël
Born 1899 in Teddington, England. Knighted 1970. Distinguished British stage actor, writer, composer and director – intermittently involved in film-making. He made his first film appearance in *Hearts of the World* (1918) and in 1934 went to Hollywood to play a typically clipped, witty, ruthless hero in *The Scoundrel*. But his principal interest was – and is – the stage, although films have been made from many of his theatrically English plays including 'Cavalcade', 'Bitter Sweet', 'Private Lives', 'Blithe Spirit', 'Brief Encounter'. In 1942 he wrote, produced and co-directed with DAVID LEAN his gallant, sympathetic tribute to the Navy, *In Which We Serve*. He has frequently appeared in films playing characters which drew on his prototype pre-war 1930s charm – notably *The Astonished Heart* (1950), *Our Man in Havana* (1959), *Bunny Lake is Missing* (1965), *Boom* (1968), *The Italian Job* (1969). In the musical based on the life of his stage co-star Gertrude Lawrence, *Star* (1968), Daniel Massey gave a creditable impersonation of Noël Coward. His biography 'A Talent for Living' by Sheridan Morley was published in 1970. MH

Crane
A mobile device with a movable arm on which a camera is mounted permitting the camera to be tracked and at the same time moved in any direction during shooting. Both the tracking and arm movements may be either power driven or manually operated.

Crawford, Broderick
Born 1910 in Philadelphia, USA. Burly American stage and screen character actor whose portrayal of the megalomaniac grass-roots dictator in *All the King's Men* (1949) won him an Academy Award. His unsubtle but powerful presence has also been effective in comedy – notably as the crude tycoon in *Born Yesterday* (1950) – although his film and television career has suffered from stereotyping. The son of actress Helen Broderick, he came to films via the theatre, making his screen début in *Woman Chases Man* (1947). Principal films include: *The Time of Your Life* (1948), *New York Confidential*, FELLINI's *Il Bidone* and *Not as a Stranger* (1955), *Up from the Beach* (1965), *Red Tomahawk* (1966).

Crawford, Joan
Born 1904 in Texas, USA. Indomitable Hollywood *grande dame* and competent actress who spanned the circuit from chorine to 'horror' queen in 45 years of stardom. Born Lucille LeSeur, she won a local talent contest at 13 and danced on Broadway before being spotted by an MGM talent scout and brought to Hollywood. A bit part in *Pretty Ladies* (1925) led to a featured role in *Sally, Irene and Mary* (1925) and a name change – suggested by the winner of a movie magazine contest – to Joan Crawford. It was in *Our Dancing Daughters* (1928) that her frenetic flapper image caught on; but the astute actress has adapted her style to the demands of the times. In the 1930s as one of MGM's ranking stars she was the worldly-wise career girl – *Grand Hotel* (1932). She then switched to sophisticated comedy, *Forsaking all Others* (1934), and suffering womanhood, *A Woman's Face* (1941). A bleak period professionally was followed by her Academy Award winning portrayal of an ambitious mother in *Mildred*

Top: Broderick Crawford in 'All the King's Men' (Robert Rossen, USA, 1949)
Above: Joan Crawford and Bette Davis in 'Whatever Happened to Baby Jane?' (Robert Aldrich, USA, 1962)
Below: Bing Crosby in 'Riding High' (Frank Capra, USA, 1950)

Pierce (1945). Her most punishing change of pace was in the Gothic shocker *Whatever Happened to Baby Jane?* (1962) with her one-time rival, BETTE DAVIS. Since then her films have been generally sub-standard though often enjoyable. Selflessly devoted to the ideal of stardom and a particular idol of female fans in the 1930s, she published her autobiography 'A Portrait of Joan' in 1962. Other notable films: *Rain* (1932), *The Last of Mrs Cheyney* (1937), *The Women* (1939), *Humoresque* (1946), *Possessed* and *Daisy Kenyon* (1947), *Flamingo Road* (1949), *Sudden Fear* (1952), *Johnny Guitar* (1954), *Autumn Leaves* (1956), *The Story of Esther Costello* (1957), *I Saw What You Did* (1965), *Berserk* (1967), *Trog* (1970). MH

Credit Title
Titles included in a film containing a list of the cast, technicians and organizations concerned in its production

Creeping Title
Title which moves upwards on the screen as it is being read

Crichton, Charles
Born 1910 in Wallasey, England. Editor, later Director. Educated Oundle and Oxford. Entered the film industry in 1935 as editor, and cut among other films, *Sanders of the River*, *Elephant Boy*, *Things to Come* and *The Thief of Bagdad*. Joined MICHAEL BALCON's Ealing Studios in 1940, and was associate producer for HARRY WATT's *Nine Men*. His principal films as director for Ealing were *For Those in Peril* (1944), *Painted Boats* (1945), *Dead Of Night* (co-director, 1945), *Hue and Cry* (1947), *Against the Wind* (1948), *The Lavender Hill Mob* (1951), *The Titfield Thunderbolt* (1953), and *The Divided Heart* (1954). His later films include: *Battle of the Sexes* (1959), *The Boy Who Stole a Million* (1960), *He Who Rides a Tiger* (1965). He has also directed many films for television.

Cristaldi, Franco
Born 1924 in Turin, Italy. After getting a law degree at Turin University became involved immediately in film production. Produced his first film, a short on sports, at the age of 21. In 1953 he produced his first feature film, *La Pattuglia Sperduta*, directed by Piero Nelli, an unconventional interpretation of Risorgimento history. He was one of the first Italian producers to concentrate on quality production, and with his company Vides to launch new talents in acting and direction, including ROSI (*La Sfida*, 1958) and PETRI (*L'Assassino*, 1960). Among his most successful productions are *I Soliti Ignoti* (1958), *Salvatore Giuliano* and *Divorce Italian Style* (1961), *I compagni* (1963), *China is Near* (1967). In 1969, he produced the first official Italo-Soviet co-production, *The Red Tent*, directed by KALATAZOV. In 1968 Cristaldi was elected President of the Union of Italian Producers. MH

Cromwell, John
Born 1888 in Ohio, Toledo, USA. Director. Established himself as stage actor in early years of the century in parts ranging from *Little Women* to Shaw and Ibsen. Also acted in films before turning to direction in early 1930s with a variety of dramas and comedies. *Of Human Bondage* (1934), with BETTE DAVIS and LESLIE HOWARD, showed his sensitivity with players; later work included *The Prisoner of Zenda* (a richly enjoyable extravaganza, 1937), *Algiers* (the re-make of DUVIVIER's *Pépé-le-Moko*, 1938), *Made for Each Other* (1939), *Abe Lincoln in Illinois* (1940), *So Ends our Night* (1941), *Since You Went Away* (1944) and *The Enchanted Cottage* (1945) which confirmed his careful, professional approach to generally romantic material. His post-war output includes some lively thrillers and a version of CHAYEVSKY's *The Goddess* (1958) with Kim Stanley. In 1971, he was acting with touring companies. JG

Crosby, Bing
Born 1904 in Washington, USA. Durable singing idol and attractive light actor, who popularized the relaxed crooner image in the 1930s and 1940s, later supplanted in audience-appeal by FRANK SINATRA. A product of the big band era and training, he made his film début in *King of Jazz* (1930) and went on to star in a series of fly-weight musical comedies at Paramount. His box-office association with comedian BOB HOPE began with *The Road to Singapore* (1939) and journeyed through six other 'Road' films. In 1944 he won an Academy Award for his performance as the priest in *Going my Way*. Although he continued to make musicals, he played more frequently in dramatic roles, notably *Little Boy Lost* (1953), *The Country Girl* (1955), *Man on Fire* (1957). In 1953 he published his autobiography 'Call Me Lucky'. Other main films: *The Big Broadcast of 1932*, and *We're not Dressing* (1934), *Pennies from Heaven* and *Sing You Sinners* (1938), *Holiday Inn* (1942), *The Bells of St Mary* (1945), *Riding High* (1950),

White Christmas (1954), *High Society* (1956), *High Time* (1960), *Stagecoach* (1966). MH

Cross Cut
To alternate two or more scenes in editing

Cruze, James (1884–1942)
Born in Ogden, Utah, USA. In the space of 20 years Cruze made upwards of a hundred films and the bulk of his output, much of it commercial chores, has tended to obscure the real achievement of his best films. From the theatre, Cruze joined the Thanhouser company as an actor in 1908. In 1916 he moved to LASKY, and not until 1918 did he direct his first film, *Too Many Millions*. Immediately his versatility was evident, as he turned with facility from Wallace Reid romances to FATTY ARBUCKLE comedies. In 1923 Cruze made his biggest success with *The Covered Wagon*, whose spectacular and documentary qualities still outbalance its commonplace story. Later Cruze attempted to repeat the success with two other pioneer spectacles, the likeable *Pony Express* (1925) and the more pretentious (and less effective) *Old Ironsides* (1927). An element of the surreal and *avant-garde*, fairly unusual in twenties Hollywood, seems to have surfaced in *Hollywood* (1922) and *Beggar on Horseback* (1923) with their mad dream sequences and expressionist camera and design devices. After this Cruze tended to be assigned more conventional social comedy, which he was able to turn out with speed and glitter: *Ruggles of Red Gap* and *To the Ladies* (1923), *The Garden of Weeds*, *The City that Never Sleeps*, *The Enemy Sex* and *Merton of the Movies* (1924), *Welcome Home* and *The Goose Hangs High* (1925), *Marriage* and *Waiter from the Ritz* (1926), *On to Reno* and *The City Gone Wild* (1927). Cruze mistrusted sound films and his output was considerably reduced after 1928, although he continued to produce occasional films of interest, including *The Great Gabbo* (1930), with ERICH VON STROHEIM, and *Sutter's Gold* (1936). His last films, *Gangs of New York*, *Prison Nurse* and *Come on Leathernecks!*, were made in 1938. DR

Cuba
After the revolution in 1959 which saw the establishment of the Castro régime, the pattern of film production in Cuba naturally changed. Castro proclaimed: 'Cinema is an art'. Santiago Alvarez, head of newsreel production, also proclaimed: 'For me, there is no difference between art and politics'. The Cuban Institute of Cinematographic Art and Industry (founded in 1959) was charged with the task of both producing films itself and encouraging independent production, including documentary.

Films were used most immediately to deal with reform – for example, *This Land of Ours*, on land reform, and *Housing* – while the newsreels under Alvarez, *Actualida des Cubanas*, were kept lively and pungent. Mobile units carried the new films to the more remote parts of Cuba, which lacked cinemas. Two state-owned television channels were also established.

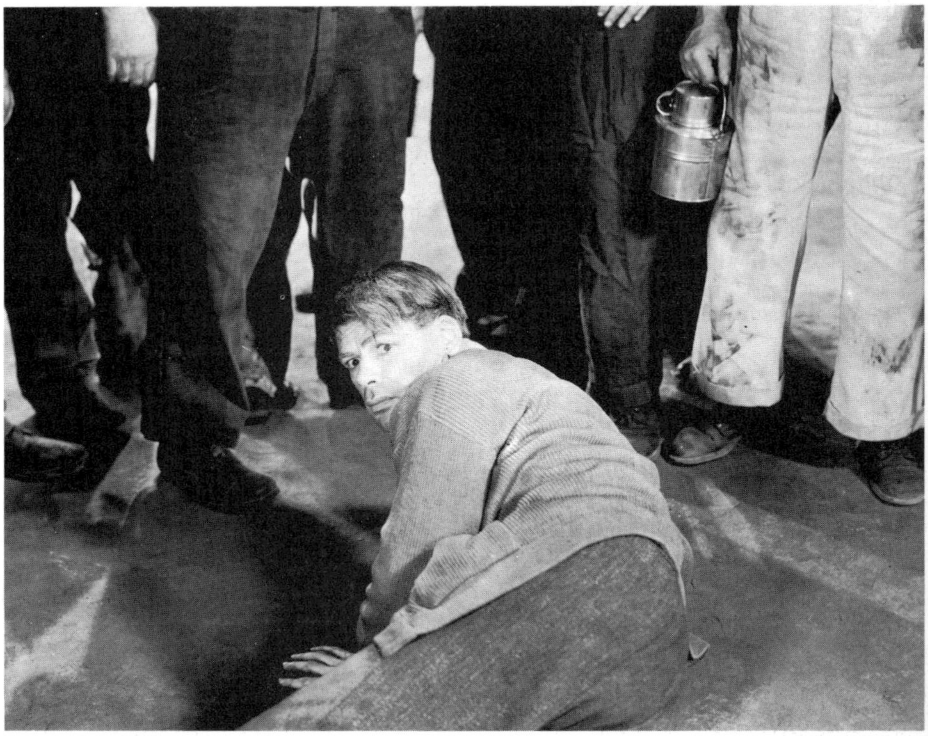

Above: 'The First Assault with Machetes' (Manuel Octavio Gomez, 1967)
Below: Paul Muni in 'Black Fury' (Michael Curtiz, USA, 1935)

By 1961 most of the films being shown were Russian or Czech; only three features were produced in that year in Cuba itself. But the style of Cuban film-making was beginning to emerge as youthfully excited and intensely political, but with an eye on artistic standards. Among the new Cuban film-makers who have developed during the 1960s are:

Manuel Octavio Gomez (journalist, film critic, documentary director), made *History of a Battle* (1962), dealing with the subject of illiteracy but with the Bay of Pigs invasion for background; *La Salacion* (1965), subject, marriage; *Tulipa*, dealing with the struggle of an artist under the previous régime; *La Primera Carga al Machete* (*The First Assault with Machetes*, 1967), a powerful film in the documentary style showing the rebellion against the Spanish in eastern Cuba in 1868 when the peasants used the machete as a weapon; *Days of Water* (1971), a study of miraculous phenomenon in the 1930s; many virulent anti-USA documentaries.

Julio Garcia Espinosa: *El joven rebele* (1961), the maturity of a boy guerilla; *Las Aventuras de Juan Quinquin* (1967), choir boy turned rebel told in impressionistic terms.

Humberto Solas: *Manuela*, the story of a girl guerilla, and *Lucia*, a study of women in Cuba.

Nicolas Guillen Landrian: *Ociel del Toa*, lyrical and impressionistic.

Santiago Alvarez: *The Forgotten War*, on the conflict in Laos, and *Hanoi, December 13*, on solidarity with North Vietnam.

Tomaas Gutiérrez Alea: *The Death of a Bureaucrat* (1966), a lively social-political satire and *Memories of Underdevelopment* (1969), a study of the revolution from the viewpoint of the bourgeoisie, perhaps the most intriguing of new Cuban films. RM

Cukor, George
Born 1899 in New York, USA. Major American director and craftsman whose best work has spanned three decades from the early 1930s to the 1960s; especially highly regarded for his sympathetic handling of feminine themes and for his ability to draw superior performances from leading actresses. Most comfortable with stylish comedy and elegant literary subjects, he seldom, if ever, has made a

film with a powerful personal statement, preferring the role of interpreter of the classics (Shakespeare, Dickens) as well as the moderns (GARSON KANIN and revamped Shaw).

He arrived in Hollywood from the theatre to work as dialogue director with LEWIS MILESTONE on *All Quiet on the Western Front* (1930), and with LUBITSCH – who obviously influenced his subsequent style – on *One Hour With You* (1932). In 1932 he directed KATHARINE HEPBURN in *A Bill of Divorcement*, beginning an association which produced over the years some of his handsomest social comedies, including *The Philadelphia Story* (1940) and several of the HEPBURN/TRACY sex-war comedies. Another partnership with JUDY HOLLIDAY – first in *Adam's Rib* (1949), followed by *Born Yesterday* (1950) – was almost equally productive.

Some other high points: his *Camille* (1936) with GARBO, *A Star is Born* (1954) with JUDY GARLAND, and the best of SOPHIA LOREN's Hollywood films, *Heller In Pink Tights* (1959). Less successful was his beautiful but over-ornate *My Fair Lady* (1964). His career has survived several controversies: notably his removal from *Gone with the Wind*, although he retained throughout the trust of the female stars. His sensitivity in finding the emotional pulse of a subject is sometimes wasted on inferior material, such as *The Chapman Report* (1961), but he remains one of the most civilized and consistently rewarding of Hollywood film-makers.

Other main films: *Little Women* (1933), *David Copperfield* (1934), *Romeo and Juliet* (1936), *Holiday* (1937), *The Women* (1939), *A Woman's Face* and *Two-Faced Woman* (1941), *A Double Life* (1947), *The Marrying Kind* and *Pat and Mike* (1952), *The Actress* (1953), *Les Girls* and *Written on the Wind* (1957), *Let's Make Love* (1961), *Justine* (1969), *Travels with my Aunt* (1972). MH

Curtiz, Michael (Mihály Kertész)
(1888–1962)

Born in Budapest, Hungary. Director. After training as an actor and serving during the First World War in the Austrian Army. Curtiz developed into a film director, working in Hungary, Scandinavia (assisting SJÖSTRÖM and STILLER), Germany, Italy, France and Austria, where he made *Sodom und Gomorrha* (1922) and *Samson und Dalila* (1923), and *Moon of Israel* (1924), the film which finally took him to the USA. In Hollywood he completed nine silent films between 1926 and 1929, including *Noah's Ark* (1929), which had synchronised sound. He was to become one of the most prolific directors in the history of American picture-making, working as a contract director for Warner Brothers. He was, potentially at least, one of the best directors of the 1930s and 1940s. He completed 44 films between 1930 and 1939, among them *The Strange Love of Molly Louvain* and *Cabin in the Cotton* (with RICHARD BARTHELMESS and BETTE DAVIS, 1932), *20,000 Years in Sing Sing* (with Bette Davis and SPENCER TRACY, 1933) and many films in a tough and cynical vein. Later he specialized in subjects for ERROL FLYNN, including *Captain Blood* (1935), *Charge of the Light Brigade* (1936) and *The Adventures of Robin Hood* (1938), as well as *Kid Galahad* (1937), *Angels with Dirty Faces* (1938), *Elizabeth and Essex*, with Bette Davis and *Dodge City* (1939). In the 1940s he became prolific in every kind of film, imposing where he could his own special, sombre, somewhat Germanic style with its finely controlled lighting and camerawork. His films included *The Sea Wolf* (1941), *Mission to Moscow*, *Yankee Doodle Dandy* and *Casablanca* (1942), the film which won him his Academy Award. His numerous later films included *Mildred Pierce* (1945), *The Breaking Point* (1950), *The Egyptian* and *White Christmas* (1954), *We're no Angels* (1955) and *The Comancheros* (1961). RM

Cut

1. A change of scene in successive frames
2. To trim and join shots together in editing
3. The order given by a director for action to stop together with the operation of any camera, sound recording equipment, or any other apparatus that may be running.

Cutting Print

The positive print of the complete film made up of separate scenes which have been assembled in the required order.

Cutts, Graham

Born in Brighton, England. Director. Was originally a marine engineer and then a film exhibitor. Became one of Britain's leading silent directors, specializing in thrillers, comedies and rich melodramas like *The Rat* series with IVOR NOVELLO, *The Passionate Adventure* (on which HITCHCOCK was assistant and designer, 1924) and *The Sea Urchin* (1926). Unlike many British directors of the period, Cutts had something of a personal style, often employing tracking camera movements around the characters instead of depending on montage. His sound films are mostly forgotten, with the exception of *The Sign of Four* (1931) and *Three Men in a Boat* (1933). JG

Cybulski, Zbigniew (1927–1967)

Born in Poland. Actor. Trained in Theatre School in Cracow, he left traditional theatrical work in the early 1950s to organize the student satirical theatre, Bim-bom, working as both director and actor. He had played small parts in films, including WAJDA's *A Generation* (1955), before being given the lead in *Ashes and Diamonds* (1958), the part which made him the symbol of Polish youth during the uneasy years of the search for cultural freedom. He was one of the first actors to embody the contemporary, 'dislocated' hero, searching for new values and the expression of his individuality. He appeared in many Polish films, including *Night Train* (1959), *Innocent Sorcerers* (1960), *The Saragossa Manuscript* (1964), and *Salto* (1966), as well as in films made outside

Zbigniew Cybulski and Adam Pawlikovsky in 'Ashes and Diamonds' (Andrzej Wajda, Poland, 1958)

Poland, Jacques Baratier's *La Poupée* (1962) and JORN DONNER's *To Love* (1964). He remained a well-known theatre and television actor, as well as appearing in satirical sketches. Apparently in the habit of leaping on and off moving trains (a feat he performed in *Salto*), he died doing just this in Wroclaw station in January 1967. Wajda's film *Everything for Sale* (1968) is, in effect, a highly personal elegy for the dead actor. RM

Cyclorama

An extended background in the studio or on a stage upon which light effects may be projected to give the impression of open air.

Czechoslovakia

Czechoslovakia has an important place in the prehistory of cinema, by reason of the work of the inventor J. E. Purkyne (1787–1869), who as early as 1818 wrote on the phenomenon of the persistence of vision; perfected his Phorolyty – a development of Stampfer's Stroboscope – in 1840–1; attempted to produce photographic moving images in his Kinesiscope (1850); may have projected animated drawings as early as 1853; and in 1861 used animated images to demonstrate the workings of the heart.

Above: Palo Bielik in 'Jánošík' (Martin Frič, 1936)
Below: 'A Blonde in Love' (Miloš Forman, 1965)

The first demonstrations of the cinema proper in Prague were, however, given by the LUMIÈRES's representative in 1896, and soon afterwards, by EDISON's agent; though the same year a Czech, H. Schächtel, appears also to have demonstrated motion pictures. The first recorded Czech productions were some actualities made with a Lumière apparatus in 1898 by an amateur photographer, J. Kříženeský, who in the same year made a few short comic films with a popular entertainer J. Šváb-Malostranský. By the turn of the century there were a number of itinerant Czech and Slovak cinema showmen; and in 1907 the first permanent theatre was opened in Prague by a magician, V. Ponrepo.

Native production began in earnest about 1910 with the formation of the Kinofa company, whose finest work was in nature and documentary films; and the Illusion company, specializing in films with popular actors. A third company, Asum, also attracted well-known stage performers, notably the actress A. Sedláčková.

European cinemas seemed to have had less difficulty than the Anglo-Saxon film industries in attracting a bourgeois audience and intellectual and literary collaborators. During and immediately after the First World War there was a notable cycle of literary subjects, often written by distinguished authors and played by actors from the principal theatres. The new firms which rose in the period were Pragafilm, Wetebfilm, Excelsiorfilm, Pojafilm and Favoritfilm; while the principal directors included M. Urban (who made the first version of *The Bartered Bride*), J. A. Pallausch, J. Kvapil and A. Fencl.

Until 1918 Czechoslovakia remained a part of the Austro-Hungarian Empire. Independence gave a new impetus to the native industry, which was however checked by the increase in foreign imports – notably from Germany and the USA. Legislation devised to protect the home industry had little effect, and a revival of production in the years immediately preceding the introduction of talking films was halted by the general economic crisis consequent on the American depression. Throughout the later silent period the most characteristic style of the Czech cinema remained literary adaptation. Among the Czech classics brought to the screen in silent versions was *The Good Soldier Schweik* (directed by K. Lamač). Among foreign works was *Werther* (directed by K. Lamač) and *The Kreutzer Sonata* (directed by Gustav Machatý). A few directors nevertheless were able to establish reputations with original subjects, among them Machatý with *Erotikon* and Mac Frič with *The Organist of St Vitus*.

With the coming of sound the Czechoslovak cinema found itself in the same situation as most of the smaller European producing countries. Talking pictures created a home market for Czech films but wholly cut off the foreign markets needed to make production economic. The tendency therefore was towards the most readily exportable *genres* – farces, operettas and so on. This did not prevent the production of a small but vigorous output of leftist orientated comic films and satires, especially the films of Vladislav Vančura (*Students*, 1932; *The Sunny Side*, 1933; *Father Marijko*, 1934) and the satirical comedies starring Voscovec and Werich (*Your Money or Your Life*, 1933; *Hej Rup!*, 1934).

A number of Czech films in the 1930s also achieved considerable international success, and earned both prestige and money. At the 1934 Venice Festival Machatý's sensational *Extase* (starring Hedy Kiesler, later LAMARR) and Karel Plicka's *The Earth Sings* both won prizes, and two years later Martin Frič's *Jánošík* was also shown at Venice. Other directors who came to the fore in the period included Otakar Vavra, J. Stallich and J. Revensky (*The River*). The best films of the early years of sound had developed beyond the successive influences of German Expressionism and the French avant-garde in the twenties, into a characteristic national style of realism. This feeling for realism was reflected also in the flowering of documentary in the thirties. Notable documentary directors of the period – most of them also feature directors – included Karel Plicka (*The Earth Sings*), A. Hackenschmied (*Record of Paradise*), V. Uhelila (*A Vanishing World*), J. Lekovec (*Faithful Stars*), Jiří Weiss (*Song of the Sad Earth*). Under the German occupation (1939–45) production diminished, though several of the leading pre-war directors, notably Frič and Vavra, continued to work. Wartime films tended to escapism rather than official propaganda.

On 11 August 1945 the Czech film industry was nationalized – the first industry in the country to be so brought under total state control. This was possible because even under Nazi occupation a progressive group within the industry had prepared a scheme for nationalization. The first significant works of the new state film industry were all concerned with the struggle to create a socialist state. Of a whole group of such films, the most notable remains Karel Stekly's *Strike*, from a novel by Marie Majerovic, describing workers' struggles in the 1880s; and Jiří Weiss's *New Warriors Shall Arise*. As in any cyclic production, the style developed its own stereotypes.

A Slovak cinema had always striven for survival alongside the Czech cinema. In 1947 the Czech director, Martin Frič, made the first Slovak feature film, *Warning*. Palo Bielik, an actor in Frič's prewar *Jánošík*, made himself the first true Slovak director, though his films belong to the arid period of Stalinist socialist realism. After this time the Slovak cinema tended to assert itself mostly in picturesque folk-lore films, until in the early 1960s a new generation emerged at the Studio in Bratislava: Stanislav Barabás (*Song of the Gray Dove*), Martin Hollý (*As the Crow Flies*), Eduard Grecher (*Seven Days of Every Week*), Štefan Uher (*Sunshine in a Net, The Miraculous Virgin*) and Peter Solan (*The Boxer and Death, The Face at the Window*).

In 1947 JIŘÍ TRNKA made his first puppet film (a puppeteer and cartoonist, he had begun to make drawn animated films in 1945). *The Czech Year*, a poetic evocation of national traditions, heralded the wide scope of his subsequent work, from folk-lore (*Old Czech Legends*) to national literature (*The Good Soldier Schweik*), from Shakespeare (*A Midsummer Night's Dream*) and Hans Andersen (*The Emperor's Nightingale*) to haunting visions of present and future (*Obsession, Cybernetic Grandma, The Hand*). Trnka made the puppet film into a new and independent screen genre, and maintained an international role for the Czech cinema at a time when feature production was not adequate to do so. Trnka's example was of inestimable advantage to a group of other fine puppet and cartoon film-makers – Eduard Hofman, Jiří Brdečka, Josef Kabrt, Václav Bedrich, Karel Zeman (*An Invention of Destruction, Baron Münchhausen*) and Hermina Tyrlová, whose films have generally been intended for children.

In common with much of the Eastern and socialist world, the early 1950s were a barren period for the cinema. Narrow ideological dogmas and insistence on the most restricted interpretations of 'socialist realism' led to a close dependence on committee-made scripts; and few films from this period have today more than passing curiosity.

Again following a pattern very similar to the other new socialist cinemas, with the thaw following the death of Stalin and the 20th Party Congress of the USSR, Czech film-makers became fascinated by the re-examination of history. The war, inevitably, provided a wide range of subjects, though – again following a familiar pattern – the treatment became more sophisticated and philosophical, progressing from adventure stories to ethical debate as the actual events receded into the perspective of history. A comparison between the approach of Jiří Weiss's *Stolen Frontiers* (1947) and the same director's *Romeo and Juliet in Darkness* (1960) demonstrates the developments of the decade between. Earlier periods of democratic activity also attracted film-makers: the Hussite movement (Vavra's *Jan Hus* trilogy) and the era of national revival (Václav Krška's series of biographies of Czech heroes; Milos Maakovec's *Three Men Missing*).

After 1956 directors were also freer to deal with contemporary subjects without retreating into 'socialist-realist' stereotypes. Vojtěch Jasný's first solo feature, *September Nights,* was a critical examination of abuses of the Stalinist era in the army; and his later films *Desire, Pilgrimage to the Virgin Mary* and the allegorical *That Cat* also dealt with human problems under socialism. Ladislav Helge's *School for Fathers* investigated the community status of the local schoolmaster, *Great Solitude* the role of the head of a collective farm, while *Spring Breeze* looked back to the events of February 1948. JÁN KÁDAR and Elmar Klos, from an older generation, also probed the experiences of the Stalinist years in *Three Wishes* (1958) and *The Accused* (1964) and later made *A Shop on the Highstreet* (1965).

Early in the 1960s – around the time that a new generation was arriving in Hungary, for the East seemed to have its New Wave a little later than the West of Europe – a new school of young film-makers emerged, drastically sep-

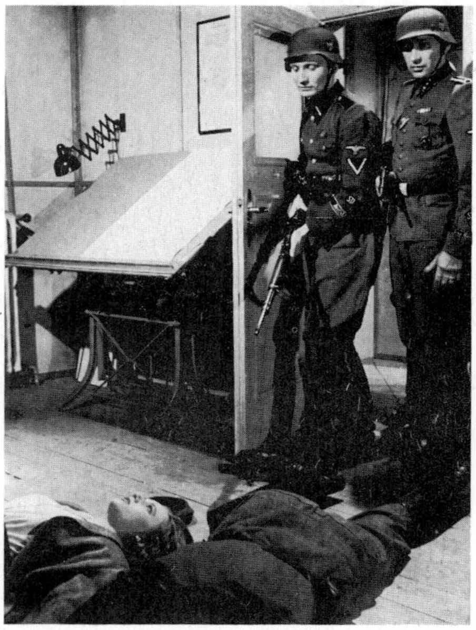

Above: 'The Heroes are Silent' (M. Cikán, 1946)
Below: 'Ballad of Seven Hanged Men' (Martin Hollý)

Above: Václav Neckář and Jitka Bendova in 'Closely Observed Trains' (Jiří Menzel, 1966)
Left: 'Josef Kilián' (Pavel Juráček and Jan Schmidt, 1963)
Below: Douglas Fairbanks Jr and Elisabeth Bergner in 'Catherine the Great' (Paul Czinner, GB, 1934)

arated from its predecessors in styles and preoccupations. No longer haunted like their elders by the old spectres of 'formalism' the new generation was characterized by technical assurance and innovation, and a frank, open outlook upon contemporary life and people.

The earliest of the group was Věra Chytilová, who graduated with *The Ceiling* in 1961 and the following year made *A Bag of Fleas*. Her sober contrast of the lives of two women, *Another Way of Life*, was more persuasive than her rather precious later work, *Daisies* and *The Fruits of Love* (1969; a co-production with Belgium). The dominant figure of the New Wave was MILOŠ FORMAN, whose unique gift of observing ordinary human beings, seeing at once their absurdity and dignity, was already evident in a short *Talent Competition* (1963) and was developed in the feature films *Peter and Pavla* (1964), *A Blonde in Love* (1965) and *The Firemen's Ball* (1967) – in which the comic observation of the elaborate arrangements for a village celebration took on more sombre allegorical meanings.

Forman's collaborator IVAN PASSER directed his first feature film *Intimate Lighting* in 1967. JIŘÍ MENZEL's *Closely Observed Trains* (1966) and PAVEL JURÁČEK's *Every Young Man* (1965) adopted approaches comparable to Forman's, though in *Capricious Summer* (1967) Menzel moved on to a pseudo-poetic style of fantasy, while JURÁČEK's first film, *Josef Kilián* (1963), had successfully aimed at a bizarre Kafkaesque fable. EWALD SCHÖRM, whose *Courage for Every Day* (1964) and *The Return of the Prodigal Son* (1966) adopted a more sober style of realism, was regarded as the ideologist of the new cinema.

In the early seventies the Czech cinema appeared not to have recovered from the events of 1968, with most of the New Wave directors apparently abroad or inactive. DR

Czinner, Paul

Born 1890 in Budapest, Hungary. After work in the Hungarian theatre, made films in Vienna and Germany from 1919. His principal silent film was *Nju* (1924), a *kammerspiel* drama which he scripted, and in which his wife ELISABETH BERGNER (born in Germany), starred, as she was to do subsequently in his other films, silent and sound, such as *Liebe* (1926), *Donna Juana* (1929), *Ariane* (1931) and *Dreaming Lips* (1932), the last two scripted by CARL MAYER, who joined Czinner when he and Elizabeth Bergner went to Paris; finally all three emigrated to England 1932–3. In England Czinner directed *Catherine the Great* (1934), *Escape Me Never* (1935), *As You Like It* (1936), the remake of *Dreaming Lips* in English (1937) and *Stolen Life* (1939). Since 1955 Czinner has developed a system of multi-camera coverage of live theatre performances of ballet and opera, producing such film-records as *Don Giovanni* (1955), *The Bolshoi Ballet* (1957), *The Royal Ballet* (1959), *Der Rosenkavalier* (1962) and, at the age of 76, *Romeo and Juliet* (1966). RM

D

Dahlbeck, Eva
Born 1920 in Stockholm, Sweden. Distinctive Swedish stage and screen actress, with a special gift for sophisticated comedy which has been usefully exploited by INGMAR BERGMAN in several of his lighter films. She was trained at the Royal Dramatic Theatre in Stockholm. Some principal films: *Waiting Women* (1952), *A Lesson in Love* (1954), *Smiles of a Summer Night* (1955), *So Close to Life* and *The Counterfeit Traitor* (1961), *Now About These Women* and *Loving Couples* (1964), *Les Créatures* (1965), *The Red Mantle* (1967), *People Meet* (1969).

Dailies
See RUSHES

D'Amico, Suso Cecchi
See CECCHI D'AMICO

Daniels, William (1895–1970)
Born in Cleveland, Ohio, USA. Cinematographer. Entered Triangle as an assistant operator in 1917; then created a detailed, realistic, yet luscious, lighting style in his work for VON STROHEIM – *Foolish Wives* (1922), *Greed* (1923), *The Merry Widow* (1925) – in collaboration with the cameraman Ben Reynolds. Then followed a remarkable series of GARBO films (Daniels was her favourite photographer), including: *The Flesh and the Devil* (1927), *The Kiss* (1929), *Mata Hari* and *Grand Hotel* (1932), *Camille* (1936), *Ninotchka* (1939). One of the greatest and most versatile of American camera artists, his long career has taken in musicals, post-war documentary thrillers, comedies and westerns; perhaps he will best be remembered for his celebrated, romantically-lit close-ups of stars like Garbo; for example, the long track forward at the end of *Queen Christina* (1933). JG

Daquin, Louis
Born 1908 in Calais, France. Director. Initially assistant to JEAN GRÉMILLON, he was a dedicated realist even at the time of the German Occupation, during which he directed an outstanding film about youth, *Nous les Gosses* (1941), and a film about mountaineering, *Premier de Cordée* (1944). A member with Grémillon, BECKER, PAINLEVÉ and others of the underground Comité de Libération du Cinéma Français, he helped to make with them a notable documentary of the final stages in the freeing of France, *Le Journal de la Résistance* (1945), shot during the fighting itself. He also made *Patrie* (1945), which, although derived from Sardou and set during the occupation of Flanders in the 17th century, managed to make a contemporary comment on the occupation of France. His most notable post-war film was *Le Point du Jour* (1949), a film about miners and mining. RM

D'Arrast, Harry D'Abbadie (1897–1968)
Born in Argentina. Director. Much travelled in his youth, he entered American films in 1922, and assisted CHAPLIN on *A Woman of Paris* (1923) and *The Gold Rush* (1925). He directed eight films between 1927 and 1934, then virtually disappeared, leading an obscure existence in Europe until his death. Influenced by LUBITSCH and MONTA BELL, his films have a polished, urbanely civilized tone, notably the three social comedies with ADOLPHE MENJOU – *Service for Ladies* and *Gentleman of Paris* (1927), *Serenade* (1928). His best known sound film, *Laughter* (1930), with its witty dialogue by DONALD OGDEN STEWART, anticipates many of the caustic, 'high-life' comedy romances of the 1930s; and its brilliant grasp of sound and camera techniques suggests that D'Arrast's other work is in urgent need of re-assessment. JG

Darrieux, Danielle
Born 1917 in Bordeaux, France. Actress, who first studied music; entered films in 1931, and won fame with *Mayerling* (1936). Subsequent films include: *The Rage of Paris* (made in Hollywood: 1938), *Occupe-toi d'Amélie* (1949) and three films by OPHÜLS: *La Ronde* (1950), *Le Plaisir* (1951) and *Madame de . . .* (1953). Also *Alexander the Great* (1955), *Lady Chatterley's Lover* (1959), *The Young Girls of Rochefort* and *L'Homme à la Buick* (1967).

Dassin, Jules
Born 1912 in the USA. Talented writer-director of savage, urban crime themes. His break with America during the McCarthy witch-hunt period changed the course of his career as well as the style of his work. A radio writer and actor, in 1941 he joined MGM in the shorts department, which served as a training ground for his later emergence as a fully-fledged director. He made one notable two-reeler: *The Tell-Tale Heart*. His first important feature film was *Brute Force* (1947), the tough, primitive urgency of which set the pattern for *Naked City* (1948), *Thieves' Highway* (1949) and his singularly unsuccessful attempt to do for London in *Night and the City* (1950) what he did for New York in *Naked City*. Exiled in France, he directed and acted in the successful study of the criminal underworld, *Rififi* (1954). Later his association with the Greek actress MELINA MERCOURI resulted in two amusing entertainments, *Never on Sunday* (1960) and *Topkapi* (1964), and two heavy soul-searchers *Phaedra* (1962) and *10.30 pm Summer* (1966). Returning to America, he directed a frenetic reworking of *The Informer* in Black Power terms, *Uptight* (1968). Latest film: *Promise at Dawn* (with Melina Mercouri, 1970). MH

Daves, Delmer
Born 1904 in San Francisco, USA. All-purpose American writer and director, more renowned for professionalism and fondness for crane shots than for creative originality. A versatile career as engineer, draughtsman, and commercial artist led him eventually into films. His first writer-director assignment was *Destination Tokyo* (1943), which caught the patriotic spirit of the times. Almost all his subsequent films reflect the prevailing public mood of the moment. Interesting on their own account are *The Red House* (1947), *To the Victor* (1948) and a series of

'Le Point du Jour' (Louis Daquin, France, 1949)

superior, off-beat Westerns – *Jubal* (1956), *3.10 to Yuma* (1957) and *Cowboy* (1958). His later films were superior glossy soap operas – *Parrish* (1961), *Youngblood Hawke* (1964), *The Battle of Villa Fiorita* (1965). Other main films: *Dark Passage* (1947), *Broken Arrow* (1950, which pioneered the idea of the sympathetic Red Indian), *Demetrius and the Gladiators* (1954), *The Hanging Tree* (1959), *Spencer's Mountain* (1962). MH

Davis, Bette

Born 1908 in Massachusetts, USA. Indestructible Hollywood star and rebel actress whose portrayal of the mettlesome female of the species achieved its peak of perfection in the 1930s and 1940s, side-tracking into comic-strip horror in *Whatever Happened to Baby Jane?* (1962).

Her indomitable characters, whether good or bad but never indifferent, owe a great deal to her own resourceful, no-nonsense background in New England, where as a girl of ten she took her first lessons in drama. A solid unusually wide experience in repertory and on Broadway led to her first film role in *Bad Sister* (1931). Untypical of the film actresses of the early 1930s, she was badly misjudged until GEORGE ARLISS picked her for the *ingénue* role in *The Man who Played God* (1932) and realized her potential.

She joined Warners as a contract artist where her tense, nervy style eventually found an ideal home in the bitchy Cockney heroine of Somerset Maugham's *Of Human Bondage* (1934). Her determined refusal to knuckle under to the rigid studio star system led to constant battles with the front office. She won an Academy Award for the best actress for *Dangerous* (1935): a sop, it was thought, for not winning the previous year.

In 1936, she challenged the Warners hierarchy, left Hollywood to film in Britain, was sued by the studio and lost. But she returned to a more respected status as a top Warner star and her battle against the contract 'life sentence' of never-ending suspensions for refusing unsuitable roles was eventually won by OLIVIA DE HAVILLAND in the 1940s. She received her second Academy Award for *Jezebel* (1938) and continued to bring great distinction to material that was basically romantic melodrama – notably *The Sisters* (1938), *Dark Victory* and *The Old Maid* (1939), *Now Voyager* (1942). She has twice played Queen Elizabeth I of England – in *The Private Lives of Elizabeth and Essex* (1939) and *The Virgin Queen* (1955).

In 1950 she created the role of the witty, flamboyant star Margo Channing in *All About Eve*. Her career declined after that and ten years later, partly in fun but partly in earnest, she put an ad for work in a trade paper. A cruder, more bizarre Davis found public favour again in *Whatever Happened to Baby Jane?*, as a venomous ex-child actress, with her star rival JOAN CRAWFORD, and she has tended to play similarly off-beat roles ever since. Several of her recent films – *The Nanny* (1965), *The Anniversary* (1967), *Connecting Rooms* (1969), *Madame Sin* (1971) – have been made in Britain.

Other principal films include: *Marked Woman* (1936), *Juarez* (1939), *The Little Foxes* (1941), *In This Our Life* (1942), *Winter Meeting* (1948), *Beyond the Forest* (1949), *Wedding Breakfast* (1956), *Hush Hush Sweet Charlotte* (1964), *Bunny O'Hare* (1970).

In 1962 she published her autobiography 'The Lonely Life'. MH

Above: Bette Davis in 'Elizabeth and Essex' (Michael Curtiz, USA, 1939)
Below: Doris Day and Brian Keith in 'With Six You Get Eggroll' (Howard Morris, USA, 1968)

Day, Doris

Born 1924 in Cincinnati, USA. Actress, singer, dancer and comedienne. Sang with a dance band and on radio before making her screen début in 1948 in *Romance on the High Seas*. Vivacious and popular, she has won awards as Best Money-Making Star and (in a radio poll) Best Female Vocalist. Main films: *Lullaby of Broadway* (1951), *April in Paris* and *Calamity Jane* (1953), *The Man Who Knew Too Much* (1955), *The Pajama Game* (1957), *Pillow Talk* (1959), *Move Over Darling* (1963), *The Glass Bottom Boat* (1966). In 1968–9 she had her own television series entitled *The Doris Day Show*.

Dean, James (1931–1955)

Born in Indiana, USA. Unique cult star of the 1950s whose three major performances and sudden death in a car crash combined to create a posthumous idol-image rivalled only by that of RUDOLPH VALENTINO. He became a prototype imitated by many other American and international actors who failed to recognize that the extraordinary appeal of his anguished, rebellious *persona* was a combination of the right hero at the right time in the right place. A trained stage and television actor, who had also played bit roles in films, he was chosen by ELIA KAZAN for the hero of *East of Eden* (1955). His only other film performances, in *Rebel Without a Cause* and *Giant* (1956), further identified him with the first doubts and protests of modern

American youth. After he died, a film biography was produced, *The James Dean Story* (1957). How talented he was as an actor is still open to question, but the hypnotic command of his screen presence cannot be doubted. His friend William Bast has published an interesting study of him, 'James Dean' (1956). MH

Dearden, Basil (1911–1971)
Born in Essex, England. Efficient British director whose association with writer and producer Michael Relph produced some notable indigenous Ealing films; later, they were responsible for several pioneer British 'problem' pictures, with the race-conscious *Sapphire* (1958) and the homosexual *Victim* (1962). A varied career in the theatre introduced Dearden to Ealing

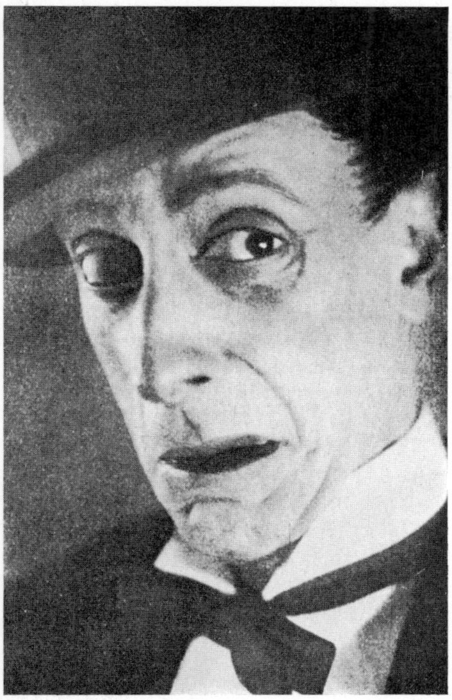

Above: André Deed as Cretinetti (Fool's-head)
Below: Elizabeth Taylor and James Dean in 'Giant' (George Stevens, USA, 1956)

Studios where he worked through several departments, emerging in 1940 as a director. He co-directed several WILL HAY comedies. His most important Ealing films were *The Bells go Down* (1942), an episode of *Dead of Night* (1945), *Frieda* (1947), *The Blue Lamp* (1950). In 1961 his attempt to make a jazz 'Othello', *All Night Long*, was a gallant failure; but a large-scale life of General Gordon, *Khartoum* (1967), was surprisingly successful. In the late 1960s the pressures of recurring British film crises limited his scope and – perhaps – his ambitions. Other notable films: *Halfway House* (1943), *The Gentle Gunman* (1952), *The Smallest Show on Earth* and *Violent Playground* (1957), *The League of Gentlemen* (1959), *Life for Ruth* (1962), *Assassination Bureau* (1968), *The Man who Haunted Himself* (1970). MH

Deed, André (1884–193?)
Born in Paris, France, as André Chapuis. The cinema's first true comic star, Deed was originally a music hall singer and acrobat. Though he had his first taste of the cinema as an actor in MÉLIÈS films, his career proper dates from 1906, when CHARLES PATHÉ recruited him from the Châtelet Theatre and put him in a chase film, *La Course à la perruque*. As Boireau ('Beoncelli' in Italy, 'Sanchez' in Spain and so on, for each country where his films were shown gave him a local name) he knew almost immediate popularity. In 1908 – perhaps feeling threatened by the growing popularity of MAX LINDER – Deed transferred to the Itala film company in Turin, where he became 'Cretinetti' ('Foolshead' in England, 'Toribio' in Spain, 'Glupishkin' in Russia, 'Gribouille' in France). Deed's screen character was never clearly defined in the way that Linder's was: his only constant characteristic was a pure and insuperable idiocy which generally resulted in a fine chaos of destruction. A good pupil of MÉLIÈS, Deed was the earliest comedian to make use of the trick possibilities of the medium. The Cretinetti series continued until 1915. Afterwards Deed appeared in one or two feature films, but finally drifted into obscurity, and at one period of his decline was reputed to be a doorman at the Pathé studios. His death was unremarked and unrecorded. DR

De Filippo, Eduardo
Born 1900 in Naples, Italy. His real name is Eduardo Passarelli. Eduardo, his brother Peppino and sister Titina were children of one of the great Neapolitan actor-dramatists, Scarpetta, with whose company of Neapolitan dialect comedians they acted from their early years. In 1932 the three De Filippos created their own company, which during the 1930s made them the most popular Italian comedians, in the Northern cities as well as in the South. Among Eduardo's early plays, 'Natale in casa Cupiello' is the most famous. Eduardo and Peppino made their film début in 1934 in CAMERINI's *Three Cornered Hat*. After the war, Eduardo and Peppino separated, each formed his own com-

Eduardo De Filippo

pany. Eduardo's greatest plays, *Napoli Milionaria*, *Filomena Marturano* and *Questi Fantasmi* were all filmed, directed by himself respectively in 1950, 1951 and 1954. The second and third plays have been re-filmed in English under the PONTI-LEVINE banner; *Filomena* as a vehicle for LOREN and MASTROIANNI (*Marriage Italian Style*, directed by DE SICA) and *Questi Fantasmi* with Loren and GASSMAN, directed by CASTELLANI. They lost all their original verve in the new versions. Similarly unsuccessful was an original script based on another of his plays, made for the same producers as a vehicle for Mastroianni and RAQUEL WELCH (*Shoot, Shoot Louder, I Can't Hear*). In 1958 Eduardo directed a film *Fortunella*, with GIULIETTA MASINA and a script by FELLINI. RM

De Havilland, Olivia
Born 1916 in Tokyo, Japan. Talented American actress and attractive Hollywood star whose sensitive performances are perhaps less interesting than her significant off-screen role in alleviating the bondage of the studio contract system in a celebrated court case of the 1940s. Brought up in California, she was chosen by Max Reinhardt to understudy the role of Hermia in his Rose Bowl production of 'A Midsummer Night's Dream' and inherited the role in his film version for Warners in 1935. A heroine of countless swashbuckling adventures, she established her claim as a serious actress as the long-suffering Melanie in *Gone with the Wind* (1939). She subsequently won two Academy Awards for her performances in *To Each His Own* (1946) and in *The Heiress* (1949). After a spell of more complex, sometimes mentally disturbed, heroines, she left Hollywood to live in Paris in the 1950s, returning to America to make two suspense films, *Hush, Hush, Sweet Charlotte* and *Lady in a Cage* (1964). Her sister is the actress JOAN FONTAINE. In 1960 she published a semi-autobiographical book, 'Every Frenchman Has One'. Other notable films: *The Charge of the Light Brigade* (1936), *Adventures of Robin Hood* (1938), *Eliza-*

beth and Essex (1939), *Hold Back the Dawn* (1941), *The Snake Pit* (1948), *That Lady* (1955), *The Light in the Piazza* (1962), *The Adventurers* (1970). MH

Dehn, Paul
Born 1912 in Manchester, England. Educated Shrewsbury and Oxford. Screenwriter, critic, poet, lyricist. Worked as a drama and film critic both before and after the war, most notably as film critic for 'The News Chronicle' (1954–60). Won a Hollywood Oscar for his first screenplay (collaboration), *Seven Days to Noon* (1950), and a British Film Academy Award for his screenplay of *Orders to Kill* (1958). Other screenplays include: *Goldfinger* (collaborator, 1964), *The Spy Who Came in from the Cold* (1965), *The Deadly Affair* (1966), *The Taming of the Shrew* (1967), *Beneath the Planet of the Apes* (collaborator, 1969) and *Escape from the Planet of the Apes* (1971). Wrote the scripts for BASIL WRIGHT's documentaries, *Waters of Time* (1952) and *A Place for Gold* (1960), and wrote the lyrics for the films *Moulin Rouge, I am a Camera,* and *The Innocents.* Also wrote many lyrics and sketches for revues. During the war he attained the rank of major in Special Forces, and has drawn on these experiences for many of his best screenplays.

Delannoy, Jean
Born 1908 in Noisy-le-Sec, Seine, France. Director. Began film career as editor and assistant director and began directing just before the Second World War. Although he belongs to the older generation of rather academic film-makers against whom the *nouvelle vague* revolted, his early work has a solid professionalism and narrative skill, especially when he worked with artists like COCTEAU in the legendary romance *L'Eternel Retour* (1943). Other literary adaptations (*La Symphonie Pastorale*, 1946; *Les Jeux sont faits*, 1947) have a genuine sensitivity as well. In the 1950s and 1960s, Delannoy alternated mainly between thrillers (like his notable version of Simenon, *Maigret tend un piège*, 1957) and grandiose, rather empty, historical spectacles (*La Princesse de Clèves*, 1960; *Vénus Impériale*, 1962). His recent work has been undistinguished and, like others of his generation, he has found it difficult to adapt himself to the requirements of the times. JG

De Laurentiis, Dino
Born 1919 in Naples, Italy. Italian producer and showman whose schedule of prestige productions and money-making hits placed him in the forefront of the Italian film revival after the Second World War. Later, he was a pioneer in the co-production field – with America and, more recently, with the USSR for *Waterloo* (1970). At the age of 16, he enrolled at the experimental centre of cinematography in Rome, took a course in acting but opted for producing. His first big box-office success was *Bitter Rice* (1949), the voluptuous star of which, Silvana Mangano, he married. Like Hollywood's HAL WALLIS he developed a flair for making his commercial successes pay for his critical gambles. He produced FELLINI's grim masterpiece *La Strada* (1954) and VADIM's science fiction pop-romp, *Barbarella* (1968). A judicious wheeler-dealer he is generally adept at sniffing out a screen trend in advance of the opposition. Other notable productions: the American-Italian *War and Peace* (1956), *Nights of Cabiria* (1957), *Barabbas* (1962), *The Bible* (1965). MH

Above: Michèle Morgan and Pierre Blanchar in 'La Symphonie Pastorale' (Jean Delannoy, France, 1946)
Below: Beata Tyszkiewicz and Senna Rouffaez in 'The Man who had his Hair Cut Short' (André Delvaux, Belgium, 1965)

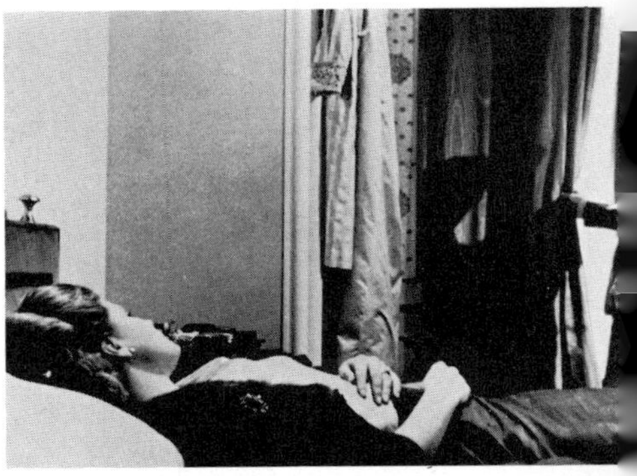

Del Giudice, Filippo (1892–1962)
Born in Trani, Italy. Producer, primarily in Britain. Educated in Rome University, where he received an LL.D., and qualified as an attorney-at-law. He eventually left Italy because of his distaste for fascism, and worked himself into the British film industry through his friendship with a wealthy Italian aristocrat who lived in London and helped finance films. He was a born impresario, and formed a company, Two Cities Films, to promote his productions. His first notable success was the film comedy by ANTHONY ASQUITH and Terence Rattigan, *French without Tears* (1939). He persuaded NOEL COWARD to make *In Which We Serve* (1942), a film only promoted with difficulty because its remarkable cast (Noël Coward, RICHARD ATTENBOROUGH, JOHN MILLS, BERNARD MILES, CELIA JOHNSON) were then virtually unknown to cinema audiences. This film was also DAVID LEAN's first work as an associate director, working with Coward, and it brought Del Giudice considerable financial success. He then promoted many of Britain's finest films of the period, including the Noël Coward-David Lean films *This Happy Breed, Blithe Spirit* and *Brief Encounter*; also CAROL REED's *The Way Ahead* and *Odd Man Out*, Asquith's *The Way to the Stars*, and LAURENCE OLIVIER's *Henry V* and *Hamlet*.

He left Two Cities, but after his next company, Pilgrim Pictures, had made only a few films he decided to leave England for the USA, where he had little success. He returned to Italy in 1952, and entered a Benedictine monastery. It was said he hoped he would be recalled to serve once again in the British film industry, but he had too many critics and opponents in power for this to happen. He died in hospital in Florence. His great service to British films has been insufficiently appreciated.

Delluc, Louis (1890–1924)
Born in Dordogne, France. Novelist, dramatist, scenarist, film theoretician and director. One of

the leading thinkers in the French cinema after the First World War, Delluc headed a group known as the Impressionists, which included GERMAINE DULAC, MARCEL L'HERBIER, ABEL GANCE, and JEAN EPSTEIN. He edited a journal, 'Cinéma', and especially admired certain American film-makers, INCE, CHAPLIN, GRIFFITH, as well as the Swedish and German expressionist directors. Nevertheless, he was a tireless advocate of the specific development of indigenous French cinema. He scripted *La Fête Espagnol* (Germaine Dulac, 1919), and wrote and directed several films, including *Le Silence* (1920), the study of an intending suicide, *Fièvre* (1921), perhaps his best film, set in Marseilles and remarkable for its creation of atmosphere, and *La Femme de Nulle Part* (1922), set in a town on the banks of the Rhône, an intimate psychological study of a woman. He died young, at the age of 34, after completing his last film, *L'Inondation* (1924). His books on the film include: 'Photogénie', 'Cinéma et Cie', 'Charlot', 'Drames du Cinéma', all published between 1919 and 1923. RM

Delon, Alain
Born 1936 in Paris, France. Popular French romantic actor whose colourful background and private life are no less exotic than the dashing exploits he performs on the screen. Chosen originally for his good looks and charm to play conventional French heroes in *Quand la Femme s'en Mêle* (1957), *Faibles Femmes* (1958), he developed an unexpectedly astringent acting talent, best displayed in *Plein Soleil* (1959), which brought him international recognition. He has divided his acting between prestigious films – such as VISCONTI's *Rocco and his Brothers* (1960), *The Leopard* (1962), MELVILLE's *Le Samourai* (1968) – and more trivial film entertainments such as *The Sicilian Clan* (1968). In 1970, he produced and starred in *Borsalino*. His latest project is to play Proust in a new Visconti film. Other main films include: *The Eclipse* (1961), *The Yellow Rolls-Royce* (1964), *The Love Cage* (1965), *The Last Adventure* and *Lost Command* (1966), *The Girl on a Motorcycle* (1967), *The Assassination of Trotsky* (1972). MH

Cecil B. De Mille (1942)

Delvaux, André
Born 1926 in Heverle, Louvain, Belgium. Director. Studied law, piano and composition and directed film education projects in Belgium. Works in both TV and film, making for the former several films on the directors FELLINI, ROUCH and DEMY. His three features for the cinema – *The Man who had his hair cut short* (1965), *Un Soir, un Train* (1968), *Rendez-vous à Bray* (1971) – reveal a highly distinctive, ambiguous, often difficult style (influenced by RESNAIS), and dealing with strange, semi-fantasy worlds in which illusion and reality are inextricably mixed and nothing is quite what it seems. The first and third films, in particular, have a slow, regularly controlled rhythm and precise visual styling which recall Delvaux's early musical preoccupations and training. JG

De Mille, Cecil Blount (1881–1959)
Born in Ashfield, Massachusetts, USA. American director. The paradox of De Mille was that the man who to such a significant extent shaped the image of the 1920s was essentially a Victorian. Every one of his films in one way or another is in direct line of descent from the theatre of David Belasco, the apogee of 19th-century spectacular drama. His work was founded on a wholly Victorian duality of values: the irresistible urge to succeed, combined with a comforting if preposterous certainty of his own concept of the Lord's will and the Christian ethic.

De Mille's father, a playwright and friend of Belasco, died when De Mille and his elder brother William were children. In 1900 at the age of 19, Cecil began to act; in 1906 he started to write plays. In 1912 he went into partnership with JESSE LASKY and Sam Goldfish (later GOLDWYN), and travelled to Hollywood to direct their first film, *The Squaw Man* (1913). The immediate success of this picture did as much to establish Hollywood as a new production centre as to found the fortunes of the Jesse L. Lasky Feature Play Co. In the numerous films De Mille made for the Lasky company in the course of the next few years, he always favoured adaptation to the screen of stage conventions. He was at the same time, however, a notable innovator. He did much to establish the pattern of feature-length films. He attracted to films notable stage players like Fannie Ward (*The Cheat*, 1915) and the opera star Geraldine Farrar (*Kindling* and *Carmen*, 1915; *Maria Rosa*, 1916; *Joan the Woman*, 1917). Some of his earlier films show considerable experimentation in their use of lighting and visual effects.

De Mille's greatest gift however was his intuitive ability to gauge and to anticipate the taste of the public – particularly the middle-class. His war films, *Joan the Woman*, *The Little American* (1917, with MARY PICKFORD) and *Till I Come Back to You* (1918) acutely reflect the changing mood of contemporary America. In 1918 he anticipated the new moral climate of the 1920s with the first of his socio-sexual comedies, *Old Wives For New*. This and the films that followed – including *Don't Change Your Husband* (1919), *Why Change Your Wife?* (1920), *Forbidden Fruit* (1921), *The Affairs of Anatol* (1921) and *Fool's Paradise* (1921) – were the wish-dreams of the 1920s. They depicted lives of luxury and leisure and moral freedom. They offered people models of manners and etiquette. De Mille shaped as much as he reflected the life of the 1920s.

At the moment when other directors (among them LUBITSCH) were coming along to eclipse him in sophistication and comedy, De Mille's career took a new turn. With *The Ten Commandments* (1924) he made the first of the long series of Biblical spectacles forever associated with his name. All De Mille's later films adopted a lofty moral tone (as he did himself in real life), though it was never permitted to detract from the display and sexuality. Condemning evil, De Mille believed in showing sin graphically and entertainingly. His most successful film in the later silent period, and his own lasting monument was *King of Kings* (1927), of which John Steinbeck commented tersely, 'Saw the picture, loved the book'.

De Mille remained eclectic. To the end of his life he continued to make spectacular Westerns like *The Plainsman* (1936) and *Union Pacific* (1938), problem pictures, social comedies and unclassifiable spectaculars like *The Greatest Show on Earth* (1952). Yet he always returned to the Biblical epic and his own unique extravagant, vulgar, sensual, high-toned style. His last film, appropriately, was a re-make of *The Ten Commandments* (1956). From the moment he began identifying and feeding the dreams and aspirations of the 1920s, De Mille made himself a being of legend, embodying for all time – with his megaphone, breeches and riding boots, his extravagance and autocracy and sense of the grandiose – the mythical image of the Hollywood film director. He published 'An Autobiography' in 1969, and appeared as himself in WILDER's film, *Sunset Boulevard* (1950). DR

Demy, Jacques
Born 1931 in Port Château, France. Director. After working on commercial cartoons and as an assistant to GEORGES ROUQUIER, he made several short films before entering features in 1960. Demy is the most tender and elegant of the younger French school, with a decorative charm (inspired by MINNELLI) and a very personal brand of bitter-sweet romanticism. *Lola* (1960), created by ANOUK AIMÉE, became his definitive female figure, vulnerable and fated,

and references to her occur in many of his subsequent films (she reappeared in Demy's American-made *Model Shop*, 1968). *La Baie des anges* (1963), a beautifully-concentrated study of a compulsive gambler played by JEANNE MOREAU, was followed by the two musicals *Les Parapluies de Cherbourg* (1964) with its sung dialogue, and *Les Demoiselles de Rochefort* (1966), a boisterous homage to the American musical which never quite equalled its models. MICHEL LEGRAND's wistful, rhythmic scores formed an integral part of all these films. *Peau d'âne* (1970) combines his usual decorative preoccupations with fairy-tale whimsy and acknowledgments to COCTEAU; enjoyable, of course, but this time the charm wears slightly thin. In Britain in 1971 he made *The Pied Piper of Hamelin*. JG

Deneuve, Catherine
Born 1943 in Paris, France. Glacially beautiful French actress, briefly under the star-building influence of ROGER VADIM, now generally acknowledged to be a flexible actress who can be as good – or as insensitive – as the direction she gets. Although she appeared in two films as a schoolgirl and later, she and her sister, Françoise Dorleac, played as sisters in *Ces Portes Claquent*, it was not until 1962 in VADIM's *Vice and Virtue* that she made an impact. She appeared successfully in the two musicals *Les Parapluies de Cherbourg* (1964) and *Les Desmoiselles de Rochefort* (1966) and made her American début in *The April Fools* (1969). Her most impressive performances have been in POLANSKI's *Repulsion* (1965), BUÑUEL's *Belle de Jour* (1967) and *Tristana* (1970). She also appeared in *La Chamade* (1968) and *Peau d'âne* (1970).

Denmark
See SCANDINAVIAN FILM

Depth of Field
The range of distances within which objects are in satisfactorily sharp focus

Depth of Focus
The range through which a photographic plate or film can be moved forward or backward with respect to the lens while maintaining satisfactory sharp focus on an object at a given distance.

Deren, Maya (1917–1961)
Born in Kiev, Russia. Avant-garde film-maker in the USA. Sometimes referred to as the 'mother of the underground film', she became a strong advocate in the 1940s for the personal film. She worked initially on the West Coast, but later transferred to New York, where she became a promoter of her own and other avant-garde film-makers' work, organizing public screenings. By initial training she was a dancer, and for a while she acted as secretary to the Katharine Dunham Dancers. Her interests also extended to Haitian voodoo. She made a series of influential symbolistic and symbolic films, which includes the study of psychological abnormality, *Meshes of the Afternoon* (1943), made with Alexander Hammid, and, after her removal to New York, *At Land* (1944), the story of a girl born of the sea. She appeared herself as the central figure in both these films. Her next film, *A Study in Choreography for Camera* (1945), presented the dancer Talley Beatty moving in camera space and camera time. After this she made *Ritual in Transfigured Time* (1946), a dance drama, *Meditation on Violence* (1948) and *The Very Eye of the Night* (1959), as well as unfinished films on Haitian voodoo and on Marcel Duchamp.

de Rochemont, Louis
Born 1899 in Boston, USA. American newsreel producer whose celebrated *March of Time* news magazines in the 1930s became the forerunners of the semi-documentary features which de Rochemont pioneered after the Second World War with *The House on 92nd Street* (1947). All de Rochemont's subsequent films – such as the tale of small town injustice. *Boomerang* (1947) and the Negro 'problem' picture *Lost Boundaries* (1949) – were based on genuine case histories. For a brief spell, he influenced the look of American films with his on-the-spot locations, non-professional and real life situations, which in the end was done to death by repetition and the zeal of the major studios in latching on to a winning genre. De Rochemont joined Fox Newsreel in 1923 and since his peak period in the 1930s and 1940s he has been involved in various cinematic experiments, including Cinerama. MH

De Santis, Giuseppe
Born 1917 in Fondi, Italy. Director and screenwriter. At first a film critic, he entered the industry through assisting on the scripts of such notable early realist and neo-realist films as VISCONTI's *Ossessione* (1942), ROSSELLINI's *Desiderio* (1943), and Aldo Vergano's *Il Sole Sorge Ancora* (1945). His first work as director was the war film *Caccia Tragica* (1947), but he made his name with the box-office success, *Bitter Rice* (1949), the lively and highly sexed study of women who tend rice-growing in Italy. Among his other films is *Roma ore Il* (1952), which some consider his best. Among his many script collaborators CARLO LIZZANI, Gianni Puccini, CESARE ZAVATTINI and ELIO PETRI have been most frequently credited.

De Sica, Vittorio
Born 1901 in Caserta, Italy. Key director in the Italian neo-realist revival after the Second World War and an actor of facile charm. Now demoted in critical estimation, his *Bicycle*

Above: Vittorio De Sica in 'Two Dozen Red Roses' (De Sica, Italy, 1940)
Below: Sandra Milo and Vittorio De Sica in 'Il Generale della Rovere' (Roberto Rossellini, Italy, 1959)

Thieves (1948) was a deeply compassionate study of hard working-class life in post-war Italy and if its sentimental 'natural' style is now outmoded, its commitment to its characters is still impressive.

Like much of the extravagantly acclaimed neo-realist work, De Sica's films have not worn well. But his significance in his time is historically important. His early career was devoted to acting. He made his professional stage début in 1922 and in the 1920s was celebrated as a popular matinée idol and singer. He made his first film in 1932, *What Rascals Men Are*, and continued to play light romantic roles in Italian films, graduating to directing in 1940 with *Two Dozen Red Roses*.

Later, he teamed with CESARE ZAVATTINI, one of the principal architects of Italian neo-realism. *I Bambini ci Guardano* (1942) marked a change of style for De Sica as a director and in 1946 he made *Shoe Shine*, which, less flashy than some neo-realist films, was no less concerned with the deprivation of a war-torn country. His use of non-professional actors – notably the leading man in *Bicycle Thieves*, Lamberto Maggiorani – was adopted by many film-makers. He turned to anarchist fantasy with *Miracle in Milan* (1950) and made his best, most austere film *Umberto D* in 1952. It was his last really significant work as a director: although his direction of SOPHIA LOREN in *Two Women* (1961) was impressive.

As an actor he is constantly in demand. But like ORSON WELLES he seems to act only to be financially able to direct. In 1959 he also starred in a television series, *The Four Just Men*, in Britain.

Other notable films, as director, *Indiscretion* (1952), *Gold of Naples* (1954), *Il Tetto* (1956), *The Condemned of Altona* (1963), *A Place For Lovers* and *Sunflowers* (1969), *The Garden of the Finzi-Contini* (1971); as actor, *Madame de . . .* (1952), *Il Generale della Rovere* (1959). MH

Design and Art Direction

Although EDISON employed a minimal sort of scenery for the little films shot in his Black Maria studio at West Orange, GEORGES MÉLIÈS was able to claim with justice that he was the true '*créateur du spectacle cinématographique*'. In 1897 he built a studio at Montreuil-sous-Bois. Its form was that of a large glass-house, at one end of which was a stage of theatrical form, 17 metres by 7 metres; at the other a camera, rigidly fixed in a special little cubicle. Basing his practice on his theatrical experience, Méliès to the end of his career worked almost exclusively with flat, painted décors. The baroque accoutrements of alchemists' laboratories, the weird landscapes of the moon, Fairyland, Westminster Abbey (for his recreation of the Coronation of Edward VII), the eruption of Mont Pelée, were all painted in *trompe-l'œil*, generally with a simple backdrop, occasionally with wings.

The other French companies of the early years, Pathé, Gaumont and the numerous minor firms, followed Méliès's practice, recruiting their decorators from the studios which habitually provided the scenery for the theatres: Colas, Vasseur, Gaston Dumesnil belonged to this early generation of painters of *trompe-l'œil* back-cloth décors, who nevertheless began to introduce, like Méliès, trick techniques from the theatre – 'practicable' waves or trains or painted cut-out cars.

But the cinema had found its first subjects in the streets and never really left them. In particular the English film-makers showed a preference (perhaps dictated in part by economy) for filming their brief, one-minute dramas and comedies in natural décors. André Heuze and the other directors who devoted themselves in France to the increasingly popular 'chase' films found that they needed a larger arena than a painted back-drop could provide; and their comic policemen, nursemaids or bumpkins cavorted down real Parisian streets. But this

Above: 'The Little Witness' (George Albert Smith, GB, c. 1900)
Below: 'L'Assassinat du Duc de Guise' (a 'Film d'Art' Production, Le Bargy and Calmettes, France, 1908)
Bottom: Sarah Bernhardt in 'Queen Elizabeth' (Louis Mercanton, France, 1912)

real-life Paris of pre-war years, with its boulevards and *terrains vagues* and horse-buses and motor cars, was used most consciously and brilliantly as décor by Victorien Jasset in the series of thriller-serials he made for Éclair between 1908 and 1914, and by LOUIS FEUILLADE. A period of economy at the Gaumont Studios led Feuillade to make his series of contemporary dramas, *La vie telle qu'elle est*, which saved the expense of elaborate period costumes or décors. Later, in his celebrated mystery thrillers, *Fantômas* (1914), *Les Vampires* (1915) and *Judex* (1916), he created poetic landscapes out of the every-day city scene by his instinct for the selection of locations. Meanwhile, however, the vogue of the *Film d'Art*, launched in 1908 by *L'Assassinat du Duc de Guise* had begun to encourage new attitudes to artificial décor. Although the inspiration of these films was essentially theatrical, it introduced the idea of a much more ambitious and spectacular style of staging, linked with the principles of Antoine's *Théâtre Libre*. From the heavy, elaborate, upholstered sets of *L'Assassinat du Duc de Guise*, furnished with real furniture and properties and not simply *trompe-l'œil* representations, it was not too great a step to the décor specifically contructed for a film. Already for a *Carmen* of 1910 the Pathé Studios had built a reproduction of the Square of Seville, 25 metres deep.

There were however profounder influences at work that were to take film from two to three dimensions, and to replace the painter by the architect. In the earliest years of the century Italy had begun a vogue for classical costume pictures. The films of ENRICO GUAZZONI, *Brutus* (1910), *I Maccabei* (1911), *Quo Vadis?* (1912) and so on, were at first played in the ready-made décors of classical ruins and formal gardens which were readily available under the Mediterranean sun. After this there was no possibility of the Italian cinema's regressing to the old restricted style; the constructional décors which were the logical outcome of the discovery of three-dimensional settings reached their apogee in GIOVANNI PASTRONE's magnificent *Cabiria* (1913), with its 40-foot high sets and the great naval battle which was convincingly staged with elaborate model work.

The influence of *Cabiria* on GRIFFITH has been disputed; but the American master emulated and surpassed *Cabiria's* architectural splendours in *Intolerance*. Earlier, *Birth of a Nation* (1915) had used the spectacle of natural scenery and locations, combining exteriors with studio interiors in a way that had been developed by the American western film since the time of PORTER's *Great Train Robbery* (1903), but particularly in the films produced by Thomas Harper Ince, one of Griffith's two partners in the Triangle Film Company (the third was MACK SENNETT, who also combined for his own brilliant and eccentric purposes location and studio work). Equally, the achievement of the great Swedish masters MAURITZ STILLER and VICTOR SJÖSTRÖM, was to weld the natural and the constructional elements of décor into a single plastic entity which played its own atmospheric role in the drama.

The classic German silent cinema returned the film quite firmly to the claustrophobia of the studio. Today the most memorable qualities of the monumental UFA costume pictures with which the name of ERNST LUBITSCH is most regularly associated are the spectacular designs of Karl Machus *(The Oyster Princess, Madame Dubarry)* and Ernst Stern, like Lubitsch himself an old alumnus of Max Reinhardt. Diametrically opposed to these films and to these designers was the work of the school of films whose vaunted Expressionism often went no further than their design. Expressionism, a uniquely and characteristically German phenomenon, had its origin in Munich in 1910; but its basic principle of 'isolating the most *expressive* expression of a fact or an object', though apparently ideally suited to film practice, did not in fact arrive in the cinema until 1919 and *The Cabinet of Dr Caligari*. Here the painted expressionist décors of HERMANN WARM and WALTHER RÖHRIG are paramount, defining the style of the costumes (Walther Reimann) and of the acting. Whether or not it is true that only shortage of materials and money in the immediate post-war period led the studio to impose the expressionist style on the director ROBERT WIENE, *Caligari* and its enormous success abroad had an influence upon the whole of German cinema during the succeeding decade. Directors sought out themes of menace and horror, ghost stories and science fiction which were not only traditionally dear to the German taste, but gave great scope for expressionist decoration.

Top: 'Cabiria' (Giovanni Pastrone, Italy, 1913)
Above: 'Dante's Inferno' (Italy, 1912)
Below: 'Herr Arne's Treasure' (Mauritz Stiller, Sweden, 1919)

For his next film, *Raskolnikov* (1923), Robert Wiene chose as art director the young designer Andrei Andreiev (1886–1966) who subsequently designed FEYDER's *Thérèse Raquin* (1928) and three films for PABST, *Lulu* (1928), *The Threepenny Opera* (1931) and *Don Quixote* (1933), all in the expressionist spirit. After *Caligari* Warm designed LANG's *Destiny* (1921), MURNAU's *Phantom* (1922) and Pabst's *The Love of Jeanne Ney* (1927); Walther Reimann designed *Genuine* (1920) and *Vanina* (1922); while RÖHRIG collaborated with Robert Herlth on several of the most opulent films of Murnau – *The Last Laugh* (1924), *Tartuffe* (1925) and *Faust* (1926). Among other important designers owing allegiance to the expressionist school were ALFRED JUNGE whose principal work was on *Waxworks, Moulin Rouge* (1928) and *Piccadilly*; Otto Hunte, who often collaborated with Karl Vollbrecht, and was particularly associated with the silent films of Fritz Lang – *Dr Mabuse* (1922), *Siegfried* (1923–4), *Metropolis* (1925–6), *Spione* and *Die Frau im Mond* (1928) – and PAUL LENI, with his singular expressionist designs for his own films *Hintertreppe* (1921) and *Wachsfigurenkabinett* (*Waxworks*, 1924).

Owing to its economic decline, the French cinema had fallen behind in its production methods. Right into the 1920s the canvas-flat spirit still to a large extent persisted: the big studios rarely thought of engaging designers for specific films. Normally it was enough to use the settings and props that lay ready-made in the studio stores. The first glimmerings of a more conscious and deliberate approach to design came from the Albatros Company, directed by Alexander Kamenka and formed largely of Russian émigrés – MOZHUKIN, Volkov, Tourjanski. Free of either the advantages or the embarrassments of a ready-made scenery stock, bringing with them the spectacular inclinations of the old Russian cinema and lessons learnt during their stop-over in Germany, the Russian artists of Albatros considerably improved on current French standards. Ivan Lochakov designed *Kean* (1922), *Le Brasier Ardent* (1923) and *Michel Strogoff* (1926); Boris Bilinksi decorated *Casanova* (1927) and *Monte Cristo* (1928), amongst other films.

Top: 'The Cabinet of Dr Caligari' (Robert Wiene, designers Hermann Warm, Walther Röhrig and Walther Reimann, Germany, 1919)
Above: 'Pandora's Box' (G. W. Pabst, designers Andrei Andreiev and Gottlieb Hesch, Germany, 1928)
Right: Lil Dagover and Emil Jannings in 'Tartuffe' (Friedrich Murnau, designers Walther Röhrig and Robert Herlth, Germany, 1925)
Below: 'The Love of Jeanne Ney' (G. W. Pabst, designer Hermann Warm, Germany, 1927)

The approach of the Albatros designers tended to be realist and spectacular. The Impressionists, or 'first avant-garde' which formed around LOUIS DELLUC was in reaction against such tendencies. 'If I have to say of a film that there are nice décors in it', wrote JEAN EPSTEIN, 'I think it's best not to speak of it at all: the film is bad. *The Cabinet of Dr Caligari* is the best example of the abuse of décor in the cinema. *Caligari* represents a grave malady in the cinema, hypertrophy of an accessory, the total importance credited to an accident, at the cost of the essential.'

The impressionists sought more than decoration: the setting had to contribute something to the whole atmosphere: thus the designs of Benois and Schildknecht for *Napoléon vu par Abel Gance* (1927), Pierre Kefer's neo-expressionist settings for Epstein's *Mauprat* (1927) and *La Chute de la Maison Usher* (1928), and MARCEL L'HERBIER's flirtation with every branch of modern art. Léger and Mallet-Stevens were commissioned to do sets for L'Herbier's *L'Inhumaine* (1922). Mallet-Stevens adapted his architectural approach to cinema design, also, for the films of RAYMOND BERNARD (*Le Miracle des Loups*, 1925; *Le Joueur d'Échecs*). In 1927 he wrote:

> In the theatre, just as in life, 'it is necessary to judge from appearances'. The actor, whose life is to interpret, to 'get into the skin' of someone else, must be that other being completely. It is just the same for the décor: without being real, it must be *true*, must have the appearance of truth.
>
> Décors destined to serve as a background for scenes taken from history must, it is generally believed, be absolutely realistic, excluding all imagination and all fantasy. A room in the castle

Top: Leslie Howard in 'Romeo and Juliet': a typically elaborate MGM period set and lighting (George Cukor, designers Cedric Gibbons, Oliver Messel and Adrian Messel, USA, 1936)
Above: 'Ben Hur' (Fred Niblo, designer Cedric Gibbons, USA, 1926)
Below: 'October' (Sergei Eisenstein, USSR, 1928)

of Pierrefonds or the *Galerie des Glaces* at Versailles must be reproduced scrupulously, servilely copied from the original, the smallest sculpted details being cast on the spot, the dimensions exactly measured. Such reproduction would be much less true than a décor which *interpreted reality*: 'Truth is sometimes not true-seeming'.

The classic Soviet cinema was born in a period of artistic ferment, when the USSR was still in the true avant-garde of plastic arts, with constructivism (and a host of rival 'isms'), with the work of Larionov, Malevitch, Tatlin. (Only one film, *Aelita*, 1924, had some purely constructional settings.) KOZINTSEV and YUTKEVITCH both exhibited paintings at the celebrated 1922 Left Stream Exhibition which included Tatlin's Black and White Square. Both youngsters (they were still teenagers at the time) belonged to the FEKS group ('Factory of the Eccentric Actor'), who made an expressionist version of Gogol's *The Overcoat* and a futurist lark, *The Adventures of Oktyabrina*; and generally followed a currently favourite path of absorbing into theatre and film practice all the traditions of circus, popular theatre, music hall, folk art, defining the whole tendency as eccentricism. (It is a pleasant instance of artistic continuity that Eugene Eine, the designer of *The Overcoat*, also was art director for Kozintsev's 1964 *Hamlet*.)

At the other militant extreme of the Soviet cinema were the practice and principles of DZIGA VERTOV, calling for reality quite unadorned; and the great achievement of the Soviet directors was to make the whole world their décor, just as they had made the people, the mass, their hero. The great Soviet directors could make locations violently dramatic like the Odessa steps in *Potemkin* (1925) or the Winter Palace in *October* (1928); or lyrical, like DOVZHENKO's Ukraine in *Earth* (1930).

The 1920s saw world domination of the cinema pass definitively to Hollywood. Inevitably to a very large extent *mise-en-scène* reflected opulence rather than artistic ambition. Vast, expensive, but often mindless or tasteless decoration was in vogue. There were exceptions of course. One of the earliest was ERICH VON STROHEIM with his reckless emphasis on realism, cost what it would (it cost, ultimately, his career as a director), which led to his constructing in Hollywood an imposing area of Nice for *Foolish Wives* (1921) and later, of Vienna for *The Wedding March* (1927). For *Greed* (1923) he shot in the tenement sectors of San Francisco. DOUGLAS FAIRBANKS equally went to enormous trouble with the accuracy and atmosphere of the setting and costumes of his period films; and for *Robin Hood* (1922) engaged CEDRIC GIBBONS, subsequently to design *Ben Hur* (1926) and to bring his flair and gifts for combining spectacle with good taste, to the direction of MGM's art department. Gibbons, who had begun work with Edison in 1914, is the doyen of art directors (though the term 'art director' itself seems to have been first applied to Winifred Buckland, recruited from the Belasco Theatre to Famous Players – Lasky).

Paramount was reckoned to have the strongest art department in the 1920s; and captured a considerable prize in HANS DREIER, brought from Germany (where he had been an assistant designer in the UFA Studios) by Universal. Dreier, whether as designer or organizer, had a large influence on American film design from *The Hunchback of Notre Dame* (1923) to *Sunset Boulevard* (1950). Van Nest Polglase joined Paramount in 1927, but was with RKO by 1940, the time of ORSON WELLES's *Citizen Kane* (*The Magnificent Ambersons*, in the following year, was designed by Mark Lee Kirk). Albert d'Agostino worked successively for MGM, Selznick, his own Tec-Art Studio; and in the 1930s for Universal and RKO. Lyle Wheeler became art director to Twentieth Century Fox in the early 1930s. Other notable designers of the golden Hollywood period were WILLIAM CAMERON MENZIES and Harry Horner.

The sound period ushered in the golden age of French cinema design; though already CLAUDE AUTANT-LARA's work on RENOIR's *Nana* (1926), Jean Hugo's on DREYER's *La Passion de Jeanne d'Arc* (1928) and above all the art direction of LAZARE MEERSON for the films of CLAIR and FEYDER brought the métier of the art director to its highest point. Meerson (1900–1938) was one of the Albatros designers; and first worked with Feyder in 1925 *(Gribouille)* and with Clair in 1926 *(La Proie du Vent)*. Whether he was recreating the Paris of *Sous*

Top: Falconetti in 'La Passion de Jeanne d'Arc' (Carl Dreyer, designers Jean Hugo and Hermann Warm, France, 1928)
Above: Vital Geymond, Olga Tschehowa and Albert Préjean in 'The Italian Straw Hat' (René Clair, designer Lazare Meerson, France, 1927)
Below: Josette Day in 'La Belle et la Bête' (Jean Cocteau, designer Christian Bérard, France, 1946)

les Toits de Paris (1930) or the 17th-century Flanders of *La Kermesse Héroïque* (1935), Meerson's images combined a painterly composition and brilliance of detail and lighting with a precise sense of the demands of the *mise-en-scène* and an ability to create décors which, however exquisite or magnificent, never obtruded or dominated. 'It is an art of abnegation', he wrote:

> The decorator must constantly efface himself, so as to leave in the foreground all the other elements of the realization: story, acting, *mise-en-scène*.
>
> The frame must never impinge upon or detract from the picture itself. The décor accompanies the film, harmonises with it; it is from the decoration as from the actors that the 'atmosphere', so precious to the director, comes.
>
> It is much more difficult to create an atmospheric setting which, unnoticed by the public, reinforces the action and confers on it its full value, rather than to execute a super-architecture which will make everyone's mouths drop open in admiration, but which altogether negates the sense and meaning of the scenario.

Meerson supremely fulfilled these essentials of the true art director: 'His productions seem to breathe in the same rhythm as the film', wrote Léon Barsacq, himself a distinguished designer. Meerson was also a thoroughly practical designer, and developed the use of new technical materials in the studios.

Meerson's habitual teaming with Clair and Feyder was characteristic of French practice. Thus the films of CARNÉ were generally designed by ALEXANDRE TRAUNER, a former assistant of Meerson; so that Trauner had a great influence upon the very characteristic look of the French poetic realism of immediate prewar years. Similarly the films of DUVIVIER were generally designed by Jacques Krauss; those of AUTANT-LARA by Max Douy; those of Renoir by Eugène Lourié, though Renoir used many other designers also during his long and prolific career, including a gifted pupil of Douy's, Jean André, on *Éléna et les Hommes* (1956). Jean d'Eaubonne designed most of the films of BECKER and OPHÜLS; and also COCTEAU's *Orphée* (1950), although Cocteau's favourite designer until his early death had been CHRISTIAN BÉRARD. Representative of a later generation – often trained as assistants of these directors who emerged in the 1920s and 1930s – are Paul Bertrand, often associated with RENÉ CLÉMENT, René Renoux, who frequently worked with DELANNOY, Robert Gys, associate of CHRISTIAN-JAQUE, and Maurice Colasson.

In Britain, where the cinema had languished sadly after its first triumphs at the end of the last century, the first considerable stimulus to more imaginative concepts of art direction came from ALEXANDER KORDA and his brother VINCENT, an exceedingly gifted, cultured and versatile designer. In 1936 Korda brought Meerson to London for *Fire Over England* (1936) and *Knight Without Armour* (1937) and Meerson's influence on British design was unmistakable. From about this time dates a tradition in design which has often proved more substantial and continuous than the progress of the British film itself. Laurence Irving, Paul Sherriff, Carmen Dillon, L. P. Williams, Michael Relph, John Bryan, Ralph Brinton, Roger Furse, Edward Carrick, Roy Oxley, John Box, Jim Morahan and others brought a distinctive and distinguished plastic quality to many British films of the 1940s and 1950s. Standing a little outside this group were ALFRED JUNGE, who left Germany in 1932 to work in England; Hein Heckroth, specializing in the spectacular and exotic qualities of the POWELL and Pressburger films; and Oliver Messel, who has occasionally essayed cinema design (*Caesar and Cleopatra*, 1945).

The neo-realist cinema suddenly presented Italian art directors with problems totally unlike those of the films of the Fascist period, which generally demanded the creation of a bourgeois never-never paradise of art-deco *telefono bianco*. The best of the designers met the challenge with a success which suggested that they had only been waiting such an opportunity as the demand for uncompromisingly realist settings, to free their talents. Gastone Medin, always an eclectic, turned with complete ease from creating opulent spectacles for Carmine Gallone (*La Traviata, Tosca, La Bohème*) in the 1940s to *L'Oro di Napoli* (1954) and *Il Tetto* (1956). Guido Fiorini – an architect and disciple of Le Corbusier – who had designed Gallone's *Giuseppe Verdi* in 1938, was art director on *Miracolo in Milano* (1950). The gifted Virgilio Marchi, who had designed costume spectacles like *Un' Avventura di Salvator Rosa* (1940) and *The Crown of Iron* (1941) for BLASETTI, progressed with Blasetti to *Quattri Passi fra le Nuvole* (1942), and subsequently (1952) designed DE SICA's *Umberto D.*

Above: A design by John Bryan for 'Brief Encounter' (David Lean, GB, 1945)
Below: Marius Goring in 'A Matter of Life and Death' (Michael Powell and Emeric Pressburger, designer Hein Heckroth, GB, 1946)

Chiari, designer of Renoir's *La Carozza d'Oro* (1952), Giannini's *Carosello Napolitano* (1954) and KING VIDOR's *War and Peace* (1956). VISCONTI's elegant *Senso* (1954) had as its designer Ottavio Scotti, generally best known as the art director of pseudo-historical spectacles like *Son of Spartacus*. *I Vitelloni* (1953) was designed by Chiari; but for his more aggressively decorative films – *Le notti di Cabiria* (1957), *La Dolce Vita* (1959), *8½* (1963) and *Giulietta degli spiriti* (1965) – FELLINI worked with PIERO GHERARDI, a former costume designer whose own highly imaginative vision contributed much to Fellini's creation. For *Fellini-Satyricon* the director changed his allegiance to Danilo Donati. MICHELANGELO ANTONIONI's art director on *L'Avventura* (1959), *L'Eclisse* (1962) and *Il Deserto Rosso* (1964), with their extraordinary poetic perceptions of the contemporary world, was Piero Poletto.

By the 1960s and 1970s the job of the art director, which for the first 20 years of the cinema's existence was left to hack scene painters, and was only dignified with a name after the First World War, was recognized as an integral part of the film's creation. Experience – the impact of neo-realism, the movement towards realism in Hollywood in the late 1940s when the old economics of production were already beginning to appear obsolete, the French *nouvelle vague*, the new tendencies of the British cinema in the 1950s, the shocks of *cinéma-vérité* – showed that there were many roads which led to the cinema, and that all of them made different demands on the powers and the strength of the art director. New generations grew up. In France Jacques Saulnier – designer of the films of RESNAIS, of *Les Amants* (1958), *Les Cousins* (1959), and *Landru* (1962) – and Bernard Evein (*Zazie dans le Métro*, 1960, *Viva Maria*, 1965) and the films of JACQUES DEMY and AGNÈS VARDA, helped give a distinctive look to the films of the *nouvelle vague* in France. Evein has written:

Whether filming in 'natural décors' or in the studio, our role is equally important. Except

Above: 'Rembrandt' (Alexander Korda, designer Vincent Korda, GB, 1936)
Below: Richard Burton and Elizabeth Taylor in 'Boom' (Joseph Losey, designer Richard MacDonald, GB, 1968)

The severe realism – to no slight extent dictated by economic necessity – had a far-reaching effect upon the cinema in many countries. The drama which the Italian film-makers extracted from the war-scarred streets and sun-baked countryside awakened other cinemas to visual materials at their disposal. It is possible only to hazard a guess how different the Polish renaissance of the mid-1950s would have been without the Italian example; and how different the development of other Eastern European cinemas would have been without the Polish example.

There was an inevitable if not always conscious reaction against neo-realism; and Italy's perennial predilection for historical and costume spectacles was not long forgotten. One of the best Italian designers in this *genre* was Mario

where the pure document is concerned, I do not believe in *cinéma vérité*. Reality must be modified in order to make it 'more true than the truth'.

If you show the public something, say your concierge's lodge, no one is going to believe that it is really a concierge's lodge; and if I show it my home, no one will believe that they are in a decorator's house.

To invent décors is to compose a universe. Of course, this universe must not be mine, but the director's.

In Britain Richard MacDonald's work with JOSEPH LOSEY has been notable in this sense of making a positive creative contribution to the *mise-en-scène* (though in his most recent films Losey has employed Carmen Dillon, whose design for *The Go-Between* (1971) was especially noteworthy). In a more aggressive style, Assheton Gorton, whose designs have included Antonioni's British film, *Blow-Up* (1966), gave the myth of swinging Britain in the early 1960s a visual definition. DR

Dialogue Track

In re-recording. The track which carries all the dialogue of a film, usually as synchronously recorded with the picture.

Diamond, I. A. L.

Born in Romania. Screenwriter. Educated in America, went into journalism and entered films as a studio staff writer, turning out fairly routine commercial pictures. BILLY WILDER saw several of Diamond's satirical sketches in the mid-1950s and teamed up with him for a writing partnership (Wilder had previously regularly collaborated with CHARLES BRACKETT) which produced a series of edgy, satirical comedies laced with romantic fantasy including: *Love in the Afternoon* (1956), *Some Like it Hot* (1959), *The Apartment* (1960), *One, Two, Three* (1961), *Irma la Douce* (1963), *Kiss Me, Stupid* (1964), *The Fortune Cookie* (*Meet Whiplash Willie*, 1966). Diamond also acted as co-producer on these films, and on the British production *The Private Life of Sherlock Holmes* (1970), a quirky, affectionate homage to Holmes and Conan Doyle. Recent solo credit: *Cactus Flower* (1969). JG

Dickinson, Thorold

Born 1903 in Bristol, England. Director and screenwriter. He entered films in 1925, working as an interpreter in Paris for the Welsh-Pearson company. After graduating from Oxford in 1926, he worked for a period as a supervising editor in several British studios, and finally at Ealing, where he directed his first film, *The High Command*, in 1936. He went to Spain in 1938 to co-direct with Sidney Cole *Spanish ABC* and *Behind the Spanish Lines*.

His many feature films, distinguished for their meticulous attention to technical detail and visual polish, have included *Gaslight* (1940), *The Next of Kin* (1941), *The Queen of Spades* (1948), *Men of Two Worlds* (1949) and *Secret People* (1951), about the making of which LINDSAY ANDERSON published the book, 'Making a Film' (1952). During the war he served from 1941 to 1945 in the Army Kinematograph Service, organizing the production of military training films. He directed *Hill 24 Doesn't Answer* in Israel in 1954. In 1956–60 he took charge of the United Nations Film Services in New York, producing many documentaries, including *Power among Men*. In 1960 he founded the Film Department at the Slade School of Fine Arts, University College, London, and became Britain's first Professor of Film in 1967. Author, with Catherine de la Roche, of 'Soviet Cinema' (1948) and 'A Discovery of Cinema' (1971). RM

Anton Walbrook and Yvonne Mitchell in 'The Queen of Spades' (Thorold Dickinson, GB, 1948)

Dieterle, William (Wilhelm)

Born 1893 in Germany. Technically accomplished German-American director whose ornate visual sense and teutonic attention to detail distinguished many Warner films of the 1930s. A one-time actor who served an apprenticeship under Max Reinhardt in Berlin, he went to Hollywood in 1930 under contract to Warners initially to act in and direct German versions of their films. With Reinhardt he co-directed the pictorially ravishing *A Midsummer Night's Dream* (1935), and became celebrated for his handling of somewhat heavy biographical subjects: *The Story of Louis Pasteur* (1935), *The Life of Émile Zola* (1937), *Juarez* (1939), *Dr Ehrlich's Magic Bullet* (1940), *This Man Reuter* (1941). During the 1940s and 1950s he tackled a wider variety of subjects – from the cloying romance of *Love Letters* (1945) to the taut, urban melodrama of *Dark City* (1950). In 1960 he returned to Germany as producer of a summer festival. Other notable films: *The Last Flight* (1932), *Fog Over 'Frisco* (1934), *The Hunchback of Notre Dame* (1940), *All that Money can Buy* (1941), *I'll be Seeing You* (1945), *Portrait of Jennie* (1948), *September Affair* (1950), *Salome* (1953), *Elephant Walk* (1954), *Magic Fire* (1955), *Omar Khayyam* (1957). MH

Dietrich, Marlene

Born (probably) 1901 in Berlin, Germany. Exotic super-star for 40 years, whose smouldering 'eternal woman' image was moulded by JOSEF VON STERNBERG in the 1930s with a series of tailor-made films: *The Blue Angel* and *Morocco* (1930), *Dishonoured* (1931), *Shanghai Express* and *Blonde Venus* (1932), *The Scarlet Empress* (1934) and *The Devil is a Woman* (1935), their last together. She was brought over from Germany, where she had been working in films unremarkably since 1922 until von Sternberg discovered her, as Paramount's rival to MGM's Garbo. Much imitated, her insolent, elegant, witty style matured, and after her separation from von Sternberg when the popularity of their films declined, a more approachable Dietrich emerged – in Lubitsch's *Angel* (1937), and the Western *Destry Rides Again* (1939). After the Second World War, during which she worked unsparingly entertaining troops fighting against the Nazis in her native Germany, whom she bitterly opposed, her most successful performance was in BILLY WILDER'S *A Foreign Affair* (1948). Since then she has filmed only intermittently, but has toured extensively in cabaret and on the stage giving one-woman shows.

Other notable films: *Song of Songs* (1933), *Desire* and *The Garden of Allah* (1936), *Knight without Armour* (1937), *Seven Sinners* (1940), *The Flame of New Orleans* (1941), *The Spoilers* (1942), *Stage Fright* (1950), *Rancho Notorious* (1952), *Witness for the Prosecution* (1957), *Judgement at Nuremberg* (1962).

Among many books about her are John Kobal's 'Marlene Dietrich' (1968) and Leslie Frewin's 'Dietrich – The Story of a Star'. MH

Diffuser

Screen made of silk, gelatin, frosted glass or other suitable material placed in front of a lamp to soften the light.

Di Palma, Carlo

Born 1925 in Rome, Italy. Cinematographer. After working as assistant and camera operator on several films (including *Ossessione*, 1943), he became a lighting cameraman in 1954, working at first on mainly commercial films. *L'Assassino* (1961) established his reputation and *The Red Desert* (1964) revealed him as a major colour artist. He continued his collaboration with ANTONIONI on *Blow-Up* (1966), with its brilliant dark-room scenes, and worked successfully with MONICELLI on *L'Armata Brancaleone* (1965), a witty period pastiche, and *La Ragazza con la Pistola* (1968) starring MONICA VITTI. *Nini Tirabuscio* (1970), also with Vitti, shows his colour control and lighting techniques at their most refined. Recent film: *La Pacifista* (1970). JG

Director

The person employed by the producer or maker of a film to be in charge of directing the performance of the actors and actresses portraying roles, and at the same time controlling the physical shooting of the film.

Disney, Walt (1901–1966)

Born in Chicago, USA. Doyen of American

Walt Disney (1951)

film animators, executive head of a studio whose name has become an international by-word for family entertainment and the major influence – for good or ill – in the field of screen animation. Although he was trained as a commercial artist, his own contribution to the art of animation was principally his ability to organize a brilliant team of artists and collaborators; in his businesslike flair for controlling, with his elder brother Roy, a company whose complex activities include television production, merchandising and the Californian showplace, Disneyland, which opened in 1955. All of these were mammoth offshoots from his cartoon and feature film products.

His most abiding talent was a primitive, grass-roots feeling for the passions and private thoughts of childhood, which informed his better live and animation films and which he never lost. Ironically, he was not a very inspired artist himself. When, after several false starts including a spell as an ambulance driver in the First World War, he set up shop in Hollywood in the 1920s, he produced a series of cartoon shorts called *Alice in Cartoonland* (which combined live figures with animation) and *Oswald the Rabbit*. But it was not until the invention of Mickey Mouse (initially christened Mortimer) in *Plane Crazy* and *Steamboat Willie* (1928) that Disney began his long love affair with film audiences. One of Disney's earliest collaborators was Ub Iwerks, who is credited with designing Mickey.

Other cartoon characters who have since became part of American folklore, emerged from the Disney studios starring in short films – Donald Duck, Goofy, Pluto. The *Silly Symphonies*, launched in 1933 with *Skeleton Dance*, developed a more sophisticated artistic technique and a noticeable moral tone. By 1936, Disney was being classed with Chaplin and Eisenstein as the only true geniuses films had produced (though his critical rating has fluctuated through the years, reaching its lowest point in the 1950s).

In 1938 he presented his first feature-length cartoon production, *Snow White and the Seven Dwarfs*. It won eight of Disney's thirty Academy Awards and was followed by *Pinocchio* (1939). A non-intellectual with a limited appreciation of the arts, Disney was persuaded to make *Fantasia* (1940). A mixture of animated sequences fitted to classical music pieces (conducted by Leopold Stokowski), it was intended to popularize culture but was only successful in part. In the 1970s, however, it has been rediscovered by a new generation.

Disney returned to the fairy-tale world he knew – and liked – best: *Dumbo* (1941), *Bambi* (1942). During the Second World War he made educational and propaganda films. After the war, the studio survived a bitter strike, the loss of some able Disney artists and the challenge of other American animators, notably the UPA organization. The critical mood was changing and Disney was accused of vulgarizing and sentimentalizing the classics: *Cinderella* (1950), *Alice in Wonderland* (1951), *Peter Pan* (1953).

In 1950, he went into live feature production with *Treasure Island* and a series of spirited adventure and animal films, many made in England. He branched out into full-length nature films which included *The Living Desert* (1953). He experimented with a new, less detailed and less homely style of animation in the short, *Toot Whistle Plunk and Boom* (1953), but reverted to type again with the full-length *Lady and the Tramp* (1956). A stream of live action trick comedies (such as *The Shaggy Dog*, 1959) and homespun period stories (*Pollyana*, 1960) poured out of the Disney Studios. In 1964 he produced his most successful live film-fantasy, *Mary Poppins*, and one of the best and least pretentious of his animated features films, *The Jungle Book*, was released in 1967 after his death. The studio still operates according to the Disney doctrine. A successor in the fantasy field of *Mary Poppins, Bedknobs and Broomsticks* was released in 1971, and in the same year the resort and entertainment attraction, which he had envisaged, Walt Disney World, was opened in Florida.

Books on Disney include 'The Art of Walt Disney' by Robert O. Feild (1944), a biography by his daughter Diane, and the critical 'Walt Disney' by Richard Schickel. MH

Dissolve (Lap Dissolve)

An optical effect in which the end of one shot gradually changes to another.

Di Venanzo, Gianni (1920–1966)

Born in Teramo, Italy. Cinematographer. Was assistant to various Italian cameramen, including Martelli and ALDO. Di Venanzo was one of the world's greatest cameramen capable of a wide variety of styles, from the harshest kind of location shooting to richly textured interiors and spectacular colour compositions. Greatly in demand by the leading Italian directors for his technical virtuosity and adaptability, his best work includes ANTONIONI's *Le Amiche* (1955), *Il Grido* (1957), *La Notte* (1960), *L'Eclisse* (1962), with their marvellous vistas of city streets and open spaces; FELLINI's *8½* (1963) and *Giulietta degli Spiriti* (1965), full of grandiose, dream-like imagery; and ROSI's *La Sfida* (1958), *Salvatore Giuliano* (1962), *Le Mani sulla Città* (1963), *Il Momento della Verità* (1964), all shot in his richest documentary style with a vibrant feeling for life and movement. Other work includes LOSEY's *Eve* (1962), with its evocative images of a wintry Venice, and films by MASELLI, MONICELLI and Wertmüller. He died whilst shooting MANKIEWICZ's *The Honey Pot* (1966), which was completed by his regular operator, Pasquale De Santis, now a prominent lighting cameraman. JG

Dmytryk, Edward

Born 1908 in Grand Forks, British Columbia, Canada. Independent American director who has tackled a wide range of subjects with uneven results. Working his way up in Hollywood from messenger boy to director of second features, he made several provocative early features, including *Hitler's Children* (1943), *Farewell my Lovely* (1944), and *Crossfire* (1947), before being caught up in the McCarthy witch-hunt investigations. A period of exile followed. Returning to Hollywood he made a number of prestigious films, notably *The Caine Mutiny* (1954), *Raintree County* (1957) and *The Young Lions* (1958), which lacked the forthright impact of his earlier, smaller films. Other main films include: *Give us this Day* (1949), *The Juggler* (1953), *The End of the Affair* (1954), *The Carpetbaggers* (1963), *Anzio* and *Shalako* (1968).

Documentary: the Factual and Specialized Film

The documentary, factual and specialized film, faces every country involved in its production with special problems alike of sponsorship and exhibition. Unlike feature films, the great majority of short films can never be expected to earn anything resembling their production costs through film rentals and box-office returns. In any case, only the smallest fraction of these films are intended for screening in movie theatre programmes. Though some, such as the American *March of Time* series, which started in 1934, or the Rank Organization's *Look at Life* series in post-war Britain, have been shown regularly to the film-going public – as indeed have many individual documentaries which appealed to the commercial distributors and exhibitors – their production costs are normally met in a manner quite different from those of feature-film entertainment.

The sponsor, whether a government agency, industry, or a private individual, usually underwrites the costs of production because, for one reason or another, the subject of the film is regarded as necessary for exposure to the public inside or outside the movie theatres. The public may be people in general, or some specialized group, such as engineers or farm-workers. The sponsor may represent, for example, some specific government department, an industrial combine, an educational or philanthropic organization, a propaganda pressure-group, an advertising agency or a public relations department, or even a film company or television corporation with screenspace to fill. The units promoting and making the films may be independent (there are a considerable number in many countries ready to accept commissions to produce such films), or they may be a built-in part of the promoting organization – such as the National Film Board of Canada, the international Shell Film Unit, British Transport Films or the permanent documentary units attached to the CBS or BBC Television organizations. BBC Television alone produces in footage the equivalent of some 300 feature films a year, a great part of it in the factual field.

In any modern State, the ramifications of short film production, like those of publishing, spread their roots wide and deep throughout the community. A technological age such as ours is one in which an increasing number of people have to be kept highly trained and informed. The motion picture, provided it is well made, has long proved an essential part of contemporary techniques of communication and instruction. In education, it is drawing closer to actual text-book publishing, as the work, for example, of the McGraw-Hill publishing house reveals, integrating books with 8 mm illustrative loops projected from cassettes.

Parallel with the problems of getting the necessary money to sponsor all the films on all the topics which would gain by being presented on film, there is the complementary problem of seeing that the films, once they are made, reach the right audiences in the right places. JOHN GRIERSON, the great pioneer in establishing the concept of the true documentary film in Britain and elsewhere during the 1930s and 1940s, has pointed out that there are vastly more seats outside the motion picture theatres than there are inside them, and with the gradual popularization of the 16 mm sound film projector during the past 40 years a solution was found – the system known as non-theatrical distribution, or inviting organizations with access to a 16 mm projector to hire the films they want or in some instances to borrow them free of charge. Sometimes sponsors went so far as to establish travelling projection units to take their films direct to audiences; in the Soviet Union during the 1920s State-sponsored news, information and propaganda films were transported and shown by 'agit-prop' trains, or by mobile units on trucks or even sledges. In the case of education, schools or colleges could acquire projectors and make constant use of the films they needed as they became available for hire. In the end, the problem has become to find adequate sponsorship to allow production to keep abreast of the demand from potential users for *good* documentary or specialized films.

The factual film, therefore, has grown up alongside the entertainment film, and forms the second great wing of film production. Made at first as a branch of entertainment to be enjoyed in much the same spirit as an illustrated article in a popular pictorial magazine, only later did it hive off, and seek outlets more appropriate to its serious use at a period, largely from the 1920s, when projection facilities became more readily available outside the 'theatrical' conditions of the cinema. 16 mm projectors suitable for use by the general public (as opposed to projectors showing the standard 35 mm width, and at that time highly imflammable film in the theatres) came into existence as early as 1923, and made the private or institutional projection of film possible; 16 mm projectors with optical sound were available from 1933. These so-called sub-standard, non-theatrical projectors facilitated a much wider screening of educational films, and by 1936 it was estimated, for example, that there were some 7,000 projectors in US schools, of which some 500 were equipped with sound.

History: the Factual Film during the Silent Period

The earliest factual, or 'interest' films as they were called, could be regarded as complementary to the news items [see NEWS AND RECORD FILM] without which no programme of short films was complete. The interest films dealt with more general factual subjects than the news pictures, which (real or faked) covered, or seemed to cover, real events, such as scenes from the Boer War. The comings and goings of Kings or Presidents, their elaborate obsequies, were supplemented by brief 'peeps' at industrial or agricultural subjects. Above all, travel sequences became the order of the time in lengths, during the first ten years or so, running up to five minutes or even longer. Typical are:

1898 *Cory* (British, R. W. PAUL) View of an enormous steam floating derrick, coaling several steamers at once. This is a panoramic picture taken from a tug which moves entirely round the vessels (40 or 80 feet).

1899 *Blacksmiths at Work – Tyring a Cartwheel* (British, J. Williamson) Shows three men hard at work at this operation. The red-hot rim is carried in and placed on the wooden framework and hammered on; afterwards water is poured on the hot rim to cool it. A busy scene, showing fine smoke and steam effects.

The latter was part of a 'Country Life' series. Other subjects in Britain were a 'Life in the Army' series, *A Collier's life, The Aliens' Invasion* (on immigration, 1905), and so forth. The phenomenon known as 'Hale's Tours' accompanied travel with its own form of special effects in the US at the turn of the century. They are described by the film historian, LEWIS JACOBS:

> 'At the St Louis Exposition, George C. Hale, ex-Chief of the Kansas City (Missouri) Fire Department, built as a sideshow a motion picture theatre in the shape of a railroad car, patterned inside and out after a typical coach of the day, with the ticket collector dressed as a train conductor. This attraction, 'Hale's Tours and Scenes of the World',

The growth of a pollen grain, from 'Secrets of Life' (cameraman Percy Smith, GB)

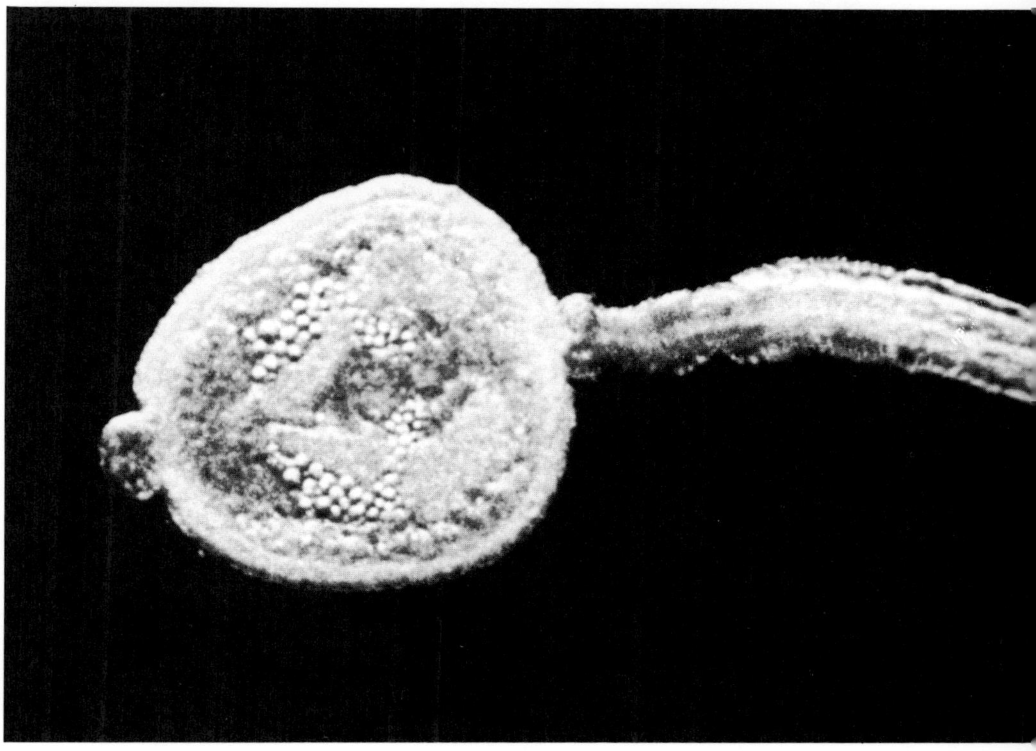

Above: 'Scott's Antarctic Expedition' (Herbert Ponting, GB, 1910–3)
Below: 'Nanook of the North' (Robert Flaherty, USA, 1922)

> began with a clanging of bells and a mechanical rocking of the theatre, simulating the motion of the train. The coach was darkened and motion pictures of landscapes, which had been taken from the rear platform of a speeding train, were flashed upon a screen . . . After the Exposition closed, Hale's Tours travelled the country triumphantly. Hale himself made about two million dollars in two years' time.'

On the whole, however, the taste of US audiences lay more in the direction of topical events, personal appearances by, for example, President McKinley, or disasters such as a film record of the Galveston Cyclone (1900), than the quieter 'interest' films made for British audiences.

Specialization in the production of actualities developed from the enthusiasm of individuals. Popular science is shown, for example, in the tinted Pathé film, *The Eruption of Mount Etna* (1909), filmed at close quarters to the lava flow. The phenomenon of the natural growth of flowers and plants filmed in accelerated motion with carefully predetermined timing was developed by PERCY SMITH, a British civil servant who later made this work his full-time profession. The first feature-length silent documentary was probably Herbert Ponting's 90-minute record film of Captain Scott's expedition to the Antarctic (1911–3), which was shown widely in the theatres; Shackleton's expedition two years earlier had also been covered on film. The Delhi Durbar of 1910 was filmed in the two-colour Kinemacolor process, and ranked above any newsreel recording as an 'interest' picture of more than ephemeral worth. No print survives, however.

There was, of course, considerable coverage of the First World War on film, largely in terms of newsreel records preserved in Britain at the Imperial War Museum and in the United States at The Library of Congress, Washington, D.C. War compilation films began to be developed – the first British feature-length documentary of the war was *The Battle of the Somme* (1916), specially shot by Geoffrey Malins and J. B. McDowell, both of whom were skilled cameramen who became official war photographers. A Department of Information with a Cinematograph Branch was established in 1917 after prolonged criticism that German propaganda was superior to British, and a War Office Cinematograph Committee was set up. This Committee agreed to back D. W. GRIFFITH's wartime location film in France, *Hearts of the World* (1918); VON STROHEIM as usual acted as his 'military adviser'. Griffith took 86,000 feet of film back to the US following his six months' work in France and (for some scenes) Britain. The unused footage became valuable archive material, eventually either given or sold to newsreel companies and government archives.

Germany acquired ownership of picture theatres in neutral countries such as Switzerland and Sweden for the purpose of ensuring that her propaganda films (and not those of Britain and, eventually, the USA) were shown regularly. America's films tended to side with the Allies during the period of neutrality, but her propaganda was expressed more through the fiction film (*War Brides*, for example, which, like *Civilisation* and *Intolerance*, was anti-war, or the pro-war films of J. Stuart Blackton, such as *The Battle Cry of Peace*). However, compilation films were made with titles such as *The Battling British* and *The Kaiser Challenges*. The USA, like Britain, set up a Federal Committee on Public Information with a Films Division after American entry into the war in April 1917. In adition to the endless propaganda trailers, the pro-war dramas began to pour out, showing horrible Huns ravishing and killing. The tone of the compilation 'documentaries' was little different in such films as *My Four Years in Germany*, based on a book by one of America's ambassadors, or *The German Curse in Russia*. Documentary had to be left to the authentic war record material from which the newsreels were made up. Post-war compilation studies of the war include the British series produced by H. Bruce Woolfe for British Instructional, *Zeebrugge* (A. V. Bramble, 1921), *Ypres* (Walter Summers, 1922), *The Attack on Zeebrugge* (1926), and *The Battles of the Falkland and Coronel Islands* (1927), which was feature-length and mainly reconstructed.

If Griffith is to be considered the father of the fiction film, ROBERT J. FLAHERTY was the father of documentary in its first, silent phase. If we accept Grierson's simple definition that documentary, as distinct from the record or interest film, is the 'creative treatment of actuality', then Robert Flaherty's *Nanook of the North* (1922) was the first film recording of actuality to make the significant advance of 'interpreting' it also. *Nanook* is the work of a man who used his camera among the Eskimos of the Hudson Bay as part of a process of coming to understand them and appreciating the manner in which they had adapted themselves to living and surviving in the harshest environment in which our species exists. Flaherty's camera watched the initiation, fufilment, and completion of traditional movements worn smooth with time and repetition, the economy with which Nanook builds his igloos or catches his seals. Nanook himself, his wife, his family became persons revealed by the director through a prolonged use of his camera, and through the final selection of shots, sequences, and economically worded explanatory titling. *Nanook of the North* was a great success throughout the world when it was finally 'road' shown as something of a special event in motion pictures

Above: 'The General Line' (Sergei Eisenstein, USSR, 1929)
Below: 'À Propos de Nice' (Jean Vigo, France, 1930)

and ethnography – the revelation of a way of life and a personality utterly foreign to the urbanized audiences to whom the film was shown. Creative documentary had been born.

The 1920s, a golden age alike for the fiction film and the film of fact, saw in the space of a very few years a sequence of silent films of a very high order from a number of countries – the USA, the USSR, France, Germany, Britain and elsewhere. Many of these, like *Nanook of the North*, were ethnographical, and many were of feature length. Flaherty, whose film had been sponsored by Réveillon Frères, the fur traders, found a sponsor in the film industry itself (Famous Players Lasky–Paramount) for *Moana* (1925), his study of life in the South Seas. Here existence was so lush and easy that man has had to invent artificial difficulties to overcome – the painful test of the tattoo applied at the dawn of manhood. Again Flaherty was responsible (helped now by his wife, Frances) for direction, script, and photography; these two films were completely personal creations. But Flaherty was no longer alone in the field. The same company had promoted Merian C. Cooper and Ernest B. Schoedsack's *Grass* (1925), a short-feature about the half-yearly migration of the remote Baktyaris of Persia. Other films which avoided the temptation to 'commercialize' ethnographical subjects (merely exploiting audience-curiosity about strange and remote peoples living in exotic, distant environments) included Cooper and Schoedsack's *Chang* (1927), LÉON POIRIER's *La Croisière Noire* (1925) and *Cain* (1929), and MARC ALLÉGRET's short, *Voyage au Congo* (1926): *Cain* introduced a story element, and represents the bridge between documentary and the story film which often exists, for example in the later work of Flaherty.

Along with *Nanook of the North* and *Moana*, the finest work in the silent period in ethnographical documentary is represented by the magnificent Russian documentary, *Turksib* (VIKTOR TURIN, 1929), concerning the building of the trans-Siberian railway and all that this meant to the development of a vast barren region and its irrigation. Sometimes a slight story element was introduced even when the primary interest lay in the people and their environment; as in F. W. MURNAU and Flaherty's *Tabu* (1929–31), made in the South Seas, and JEAN EPSTEIN's *Finis Terrae* (1928), on the island of Bannec off the coast of Brittany. Some of these bridge films were in effect wholly story pictures, but still possessed a marked documentary quality – for example, the epic Western, *The Covered Wagon* (JAMES CRUZE, 1923) or *The Iron Horse* (JOHN FORD, 1924), which showed the construction of North America's first trans-continental railway.

Turksib was intended as a propaganda film for Soviet enterprise and expansion, but it became far more than this; it was of outstanding visual beauty and edited with a slowly-evolving fluency and sense of form. More strictly propaganda was EISENSTEIN's *The General Line* (1929), in which he applied his wit and his practice of dynamic montage to the promotion of the idea of co-operative farming and mechanization in backward rural regions. The film developed its own artistic ritual in the attack it made on traditional feudalism, religious bigotry, and primitive farming methods in Czarist Russia. Similarly state-sponsored was *Man with a Movie Camera* (1928–9), key production of DZIGA VERTOV's Kino-Eye movement in Soviet factual film-making, which began with his researches and experiments of 1918–22, and flowered when he formed his own group of specialists, aided by his brother, MIKHAIL KAUFMAN. Their films deliberately exploited every technical resource of cinematography and cutting to present a multi-facet view of Soviet society, the man with the camera being the hero, the ever-resourceful Superman of the Cinema. The screen becomes a kaleidoscopic anthology of images presented with an aesthetic and at a time surrealistic wit, almost a textbook demonstration of what you can do with cinephotography and special processes.

Man with a Movie Camera was half aesthetic, half social; the intention of Western European documentary at this stage was more purely aesthetic, although JEAN VIGO's first, individually-financed film, *A Propos de Nice* (1930) was as much a study in death-wish imagery as a *cinéma-vérité* portrait of the society of Nice, and the contrast of rich and poor. It was made more in melancholy than in anger, but its visual poetry, again bordering on the surreal in the choice and concept of the images, made it a borderline film between a highly individualistic documentary and an avant-garde experiment. More impersonally aesthetic were JORIS IVENS's short study, *Rain* (1929), a flow of patterned images resulting from rain in Amsterdam, and the ambitious flow of 'city symphonies', beginning with CAVALCANTI's Parisian *Rien que les Heures* (1926–7) and RUTTMANN's *Berlin: Symphony of a City* (1927), both films sponsored within the film industry. *Berlin*, in particular, used cumulative, cross-cut montage reminiscent of the Russians, who became by far the most influential editors of the 1920s, just as the Germans were the most influential interior cinephotographers. Striking visual effects amounting to rhetoric became the order of the day, since their films had no special purpose but pictures-for-pictures'-sake. The movement within cities offered endless patterns and panoramas, displays of rhythm; given time and money and skilled camerawork, such films were relatively easy to make.

In an altogether harder school were the educational documentaries. Germany was one of the pioneers in this field during the silent period, UFA having a cultural and scientific film department. Russia, too, saw in the film a means of education as well as of wide-scale propaganda. In the United States educational films also began to appear during the silent period, a notable example the partly live-action, partly animated film, *Einstein's Theory of Relativity* (1923, MAX FLEISCHER). Coupled with education came the early research film, such as Dr R. G. Canti's studies in Britain of cell tissue culture in *Cancer* (1929) and PUDOVKIN's feature-length exposition of Pavlov's psychological theories, *Mechanics of the Brain* (1925). Nor was another form of instruction or persuasion overlooked – advertising from the screen.

The Coming of Sound: Grierson and Social Documentary Documentary acquired a second great master, later to become an influential figure on a world scale, in JOHN GRIERSON, whose only personally directed film, *Drifters* (1929), appeared just within the silent period. *Drifters* projected the Scottish herring-fishing industry in action, enhancing the effect with Russian-styled montage. The film was sponsored by the Empire Marketing Board, of which Grierson had become Film Officer, establishing a small but growing film unit in which much outstanding talent for the future was to be assembled during the early 1930s. Grierson's own film was a kind of manifesto addressed to the future, a first gesture towards demonstrating in practice what was to become a coherent theory of documentary film-making as part of society's means of acquiring self-knowledge and culture. Grierson's films were 'public relations' – emotive information rather than propaganda as such. Grierson, a Scottish academic, had studied public relations in the USA, and his mind became an inspired cross between these two seemingly divergent cultures.

The word 'documentary' was first used by Grierson in a review of *Moana* in the 'New York Sun' during February 1926; a new term was created which came to stand for a whole range of film-making (and later, television) – films which in one way or another offered a selective interpretation of man in his physical and social environment. In addition to becoming a documentary producer seeking out young, intelligent, socially-conscious men, mainly from the universities, who would share his point of view and help him establish a unit dedicated to making sponsored films of this kind, Grierson in his early thirties became a leading advocate in articles, lectures and other forms of promotion of the ideas he was evolving about the social film. He wrote ceaselessly for the intellectual magazines – the early 'Sight and Sound', the Scottish 'Cinema Quarterly', his own 'World Film News', and so forth, essays eventually collected in 'Grierson on Documentary'. The young men he gathered round him between 1929 and 1933 (when the Board ceased to function and the film unit passed as a going concern to the General Post Office with a mandate to make films on communications), burgeoned with ideas, alike social and aesthetic, about the new sound film. They included BASIL WRIGHT, ARTHUR ELTON, Stuart Legg, PAUL ROTHA, John Taylor, HARRY WATT, Donald Taylor, and EDGAR ANSTEY.

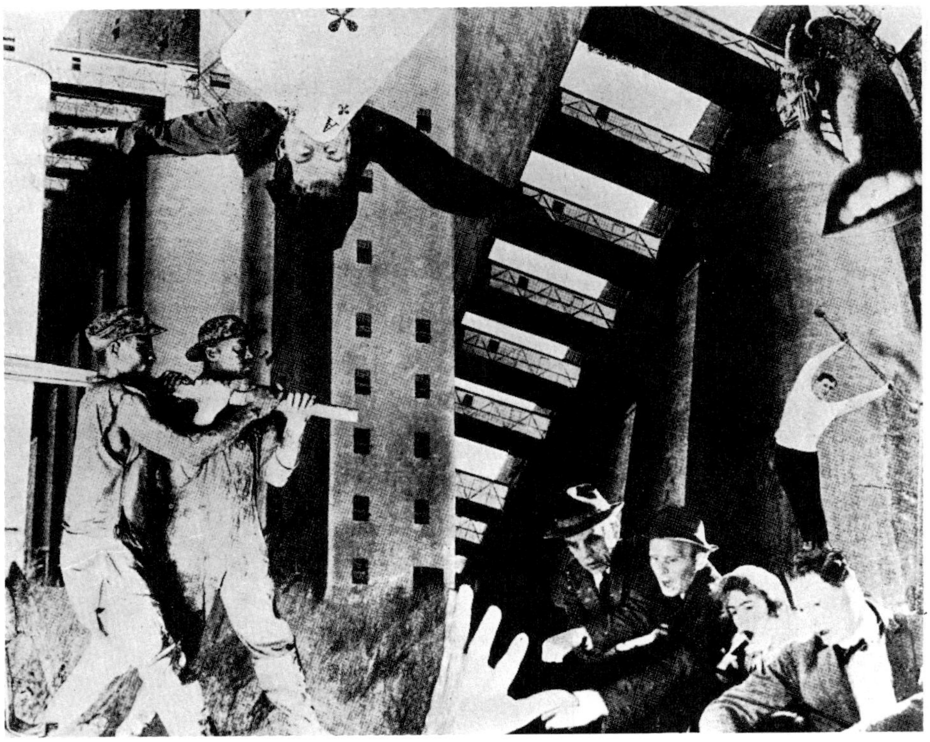

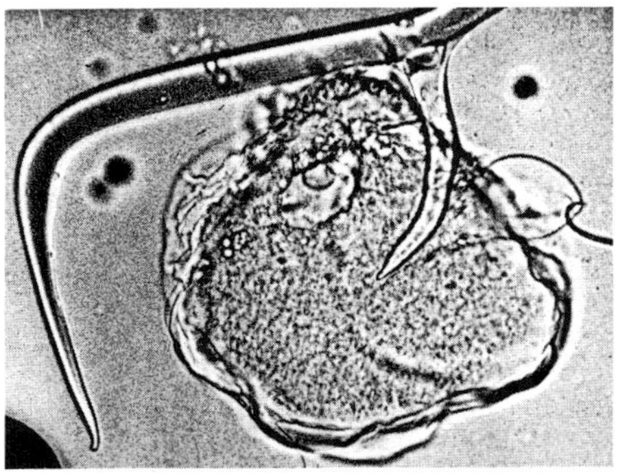

Above: 'Berlin: Symphony of a City' (Walter Ruttmann, Germany, 1927)
Below: Substituting nuclei (Jean Comandon and de Fontreux, France, 1929)

Grierson himself described what happened between 1930 and 1933, during which two and a half years some 100 subjects were made:

> The documentary film was, in spite of all foreign aids and instances, an essentially British development. Its characteristic was this idea of social use, and there, I believe, is the only reason why our British documentary persisted when other aesthetic or aestheticky movements in the same direction were either fitful or failed. The key to our persistence is that the documentary film was created to fill a need, and it has prospered because that need was not only real but wide. . . . It permitted the national talent for emotional understatement to operate in a medium not given to understatement. It allowed an adventure in the arts to assume the respectability of a public service. The third reason was the Empire Marketing Board and a man called Tallents.

Sir Stephen Tallents was the imaginative public servant who had chosen Grierson in the first place, and fostered this strange alliance between art and public service. Thus another coherent wing was added to factual film-making, which had first emerged as an art in its own right in the work of Flaherty and the Russians.

Alongside the EMB (later GPO) Film Unit others began to be formed during the decade before the Second World War. With the GPO as the pacemaker for British documentary, and Grierson's inspiring Scottish voice (with its colourful American nuances) loud alike in offices, pubs, locations and government departments, the movement developed until its work was known all over the world, and sponsors arose in many enlightened quarters, notably the oil industry. By the eve of the war, British social and industrial life, together with that of many parts of the then Empire, had been covered in some 300 films, many of which form a part of documentary film history:

> *Industrial Britain* (Robert Flaherty, 1932); *Contact* (Paul Rotha, 1933); *Aero-Engine* (Arthur Elton, 1934); *BBC, the Voice of Britain* (Stuart Legg, 1935); *Song of Ceylon* (Basil Wright, 1935); *Housing Problems* (Elton and Edgar Anstey, 1935); *The Face of Britain* (Rotha, 1935); *Shipyard* (Rotha, 1935); *Coalface* (Alberto Cavalcanti, 1935); *Enough to Eat* (Anstey, 1936); *Night Mail* (Wright, Cavalcanti, Harry Watt, 1935); *Four Faces* (Alexander

Top: 'Housing Problems' (Arthur Elton and Edgar Anstey, GB, 1935)
Above: 'Shipyard' (Paul Rotha, GB, 1935)
Below: 'Night Mail' (Basil Wright, Alberto Cavalcanti and Harry Watt, GB, 1935)

Shaw, 1938); *They Made the Land* (Mary Field, 1938); *The Londoners* (John Taylor, 1938); *North Sea* (Watt, 1938).

CAVALCANTI came from France to help with the artistry of the sound track; FLAHERTY came from the USA to film the traditional craftsmen of *Industrial Britain* (1932). Benjamin Britten, Walter Leigh, and others contributed music; W. H. Auden contributed verse. Films were made in every form from the audio-visual oratorio of *Coalface* (1936) to the spot interviews in the slums of London's Stepney for *Housing Problems* (1935). Grierson even invited LEN LYE to make his animated abstracts for GPO advertising trailers. Rotha's powerful visual sense and dynamic editing spanned the central period, from *Contact* (1933) to *Shipyard* (1935), while Wright's lyrical, poetic sensitivity was most finely expressed in *Song of Ceylon* (1935). Harry Watt's strength lay in handling non-professionals in films of action.

In 1937 Grierson, feeling the need for wider horizons, left the GPO Film Unit to assist establish an advisory centre for documentary production and sponsorship – Film Centre in London. The following year he visited Canada, as a direct result of which the National Film Board was set up in 1940, the first full year of the war, with Grierson at its head. It was to become the greatest unified centre for documentary production in the Western world, producing eventually between 200 and 300 films a year. A state-sponsored production centre, on a much smaller scale, was set up in Australia; after the war, one of Grierson's men, Stanley Hawes, left Canada to take charge. Canada was eventually to send its international series, *World in Action* (supervised by Stuart Legg) to some 7,000 theatres in Canada, the USA, and Britain. Its production programme extended during and after the war to every branch of the factual film.

In the USA, similar, though less centralized forms of production were developed, culminating in the Roosevelt government's sponsorship from 1935 of films with a strong social message – *The Plow that Broke the Plains* (1936) and *The River* (1937), both made by PARE LORENTZ, a former film critic. The cameramen included the photographers Paul Strand (whose film, *The Wave*, about fishermen in Mexico, had been sponsored by the Mexican government in 1935), Ralph Steiner and WILLARD VAN DYKE. The composer for both films was Virgil Thomson; other notable composers for US documentary were Marc Blitzstein and Aaron Copland. The style of Lorentz's films was rhetorical (both visually and aurally), but striking and emotive as film art. Before this centralized form of sponsorship, individual documentaries had been made with a social purpose – for example, Seymour Stern's unfinished *Imperial Valley* (1931) on the exploitation of labour in the Californian fruit fields.

JORIS IVENS was sent to Spain by Contemporary Historians Inc (a group comprising John dos Passos, Ernest Hemingway, Archibald MacLeish, Lillian Hellman, and others) to make *Spanish Earth* (1937) on the civil war, with a new-style, reporter-type commentary by Hemingway. Ivens – who had come to the USA after making *Borinage* (1933) with HENRI STORCK in Belgium and *New Earth* (1934) with John Fernhout (Ferno) and Helen van Dongen on land reclamation in Holland, using a fine score by HANNS EISLER – went to China to

Above: 'The Plow that Broke the Plains' (Pare Lorentz, USA, 1936)
Below: 'Spanish Earth' (Joris Ivens, USA, 1937)

Above: 'Zuyderzee' (Joris Ivens, Netherlands, 1930)
Below: 'Forgotten Village' (Herbert Kline, USA, 1941)

make *The 400,000,000* for CHI. The USA, prior to her entry into the war, produced a number of important films, including *The City* (1939, Ralph Steiner and Willard van Dyke), *Valley Town* (Willard van Dyke, 1940), and *The Land* (Robert Flaherty, 1940–2). In 1940 Ivens made *Power and the Land* for the newly-formed, official US Film Service, for which PARE LORENTZ, who was head of production, made *The Fight for Life* (1941) on maternity in the slums. To these should be added Herbert Kline and John Steinbeck's remarkable semi-feature on life and maternity in Mexico, *Forgotten Village* (1941). Unhappily, the films of the US Film Service proved too strong meat for reactionary tastes, and the project was voted out of existence. Another artistic tragedy was the loss of all but certain unedited material following Eisenstein's abortive, American-sponsored production *Que Viva Mexico!* (1931) following his dispute with Upton Sinclair.

Many of these American documentaries were propagandist-educational, in that they were, in one form or another, concerned with social welfare and advocated greater awareness with a view to achieving reforms. In the Soviet Union, Italy and Germany film was being used to inculcate the policies and outlook of authoritarian régimes. [See the general articles on films in these countries.] A distinctive contribution to the expansion of documentary was the Soviet use of the newsreel compilation for the grand-scale epic survey [see NEWS AND RECORD] as in Dziga Vertov's *Three Songs of Lenin* (1934), anticipated by ESTHER SHUB's silent films *The Fall of the Romanov Dynasty* (1927) and *The Russia of Nikolai II and Lev Tolstoy* (1928). PAUL ROTHA, one of the few historians of documentary as well as one of its most distinguished practitioners, finds the emotional, impressionistic film by Dziga Vertov 'obscure, romantic and bombastic', making no creative use of the sound track. He sees it as 'the first Soviet hymn' – much as the British film *Coalface* was the first film oratorio, serving up statistics to music and choral singing in a rich combination of Auden and Britten. The medium was being expanded, successfully or not so successfully, with much still to be learnt. In a similar, purely emotive vein, was LENI RIEFENSTAHL's hymn to Hitler, *Triumph of the Will* (1934), which incorporates a little existing material with much that was specially shot. A really extraordinary effusion was the pseudo-poetic Nazi 'Aryan' product, *The Eternal Forest* (Hans Springer, 1936), while Wilfried Basse made another Nazi film, *Deutschland von Gestern und Heute*. RUTTMANN left for Italy to make an undistinguished documentary on steel, *Acciaio* (1933), and Ivens had already before his career in the United States been to Russia to absorb communism and make *Komsomol* (1932), a film for the League of Youth.

All these films enjoyed substantial sponsorship grants. The film industry itself supported by widespread renting such magazine films as the American *March of Time* (1934, sponsored by the magazine 'Time', and shown in the USA and, from 1935, abroad), or the British films of Percy Smith in his *Secrets of Life* series. Outside the cinemas, the purely educational units, such as Gaumont-British Instructional, were sponsored by the industry to make films for hire to schools. The oil industry sponsored the Shell Film Unit (founded 1934), which produced admirable instructional films and documentaries in engineering and kindred subjects. The characteristics of such early Shell films as *Aero-engine* (ARTHUR ELTON, 1934), *Transfer of Power* (Geoffrey Bell, 1939), *Airscrew* (Grahame Tharpe, 1940) or *Distillation* (Peter Bayliss, 1940), are sheer clarity of exposition and the exact combination of picture (live action or animated diagram) with a precise but stylish commentary.

Outside these larger schools of documentary or propaganda film-making, notable examples of documentary promoted on a more individual basis had sprung up in Europe. We have already seen the example of the work of Joris Ivens before his departure to America. Belgium, Holland and France became modest centres of documentary output; Fernhout (Ferno) of Holland made EASTER ISLAND (1934); Henri Storck of Belgium made *Images d'Ostende* (1931). In France JEAN PAINLEVÉ became a distinguished successor to Percy Smith, bringing his own particular poetry to such films as *L'Hippocampe* (1934). Above all, BUÑUEL made an uncompromising study of the isolated community of retarded people, the Hurdes of North-East Spain, in *Land Without Bread* (1932).

The Period of the Second World War The planned use of the film in war was undertaken by British and Germans alike; the Canadians, who had Grierson at their head, made their own great film contribution. Later the Russians and the Americans were to follow suit. The result was an all-over superb record, often in depth, for which the future must for ever remain grateful. The war was covered from every aspect, strategically, technologically, ideologically, nationalistically – as a social and psychological cataclysm, as a visual spectacle, as an affair of blood, dust and rubble. By the end of it, the film archives were bursting.

While the German feature industry was solely concerned with dramatic films, German documentary (like the newsreels) was concerned directly with propaganda. The machinery of control set up by the Nazi régime is described elsewhere. [See NEWS AND RECORD FILM.] The newsreels, especially those for the occupied countries, were increased in length, sometimes reaching as long as 45 minutes, developing into propaganda magazines. Documentaries were made for specialized use, and all educational and instructional films for class or lecture-room were re-slanted to take in current ideology. Considerable use was made of the silent film, not only in the centres of education, but for army indoctrination. Teachers and instructors who were politically reliable spoke an appropriate commentary.

The newsreels and documentary shorts in the cinemas were supplemented from time to time by prestige feature-documentaries, as in Britain and elsewhere. Such films were *Baptism of Fire* (*Feuertaufe*, 1940) on the defeat of Poland, *Victory in the West* (1940, compiled from about a million feet of record material) on the collapse of Western Europe, and, most vicious of all, *The Eternal Jew* (1940), a 'black masterpiece' of virulent, anti-Semitic propaganda. Compilation films were also represented by *Campaign in Poland* and *Blitzkrieg im Westen* (both 1940). The Japanese made similar compilation films from their newsreels, such as *Malaya Taken, The Capture of Burma*, or *Occupation Sumatra* all resolutely put over to the accompaniment of Western symphonic music in the German style.

The Russians made many notable war films. There were severe losses of rich archive material through the German attacks on Moscow, and though the newsreel and documentary (as distinct from the feature) studios remained in Moscow, new resources of incoming material from the battle fronts had to replenish what little was left to draw on. ESTHER SHUB, the greatest of Russia's compilation editors, was among those evacuated, and the films she planned initially had to be abandoned. At later stages in the war, the Russian war documentaries began to appear, compiled from the work of such notable front-line cameramen as Arkadi Shafran. The films include:

In the Line of Fire (DZIGA VERTOV, 1941); *Defeat of the Germans near Moscow* (L. Varlamov and I. Kopalin, 1942); *Leningrad Fights* (R. KARMEN, 1942); *A Day of War* (edited from the work of one hundred cameramen from the Arctic to the Black Sea, 1942); *Stalingrad* (Varlamov and Karmen, 1943); *Peoples' Avengers* (V. Belyaev; partisan fighting, 1943); *Battle for the Ukraine* (supervised by ALEXANDER DOVZHENKO, 1943); *The Kharkov Trial* (Dovzhenko, 1945); *Berlin* (Y. RAISMAN, 1945); *Victory in Ukraine* (Dovzhenko, 1945); *Liberation France* (SERGEI YUTKEVICH, 1945).

The later documentaries were supervised by the feature director SERGEI GERASSIMOV. Many of the above films were of feature length. It is instructive to compare such magnificent wartime documentaries as *Stalingrad* (1943) with the pretentious, studio-made reconstructions of the post-war period, such as Vladimir Petrov's *Battle of Stalingrad* (1948) and Mikhail Chiaureli's film in praise of Stalin, *The Vow* (1946).

The outstanding series of American war documentaries involving compilation, the *Why We Fight* series, were supervised by such notable feature directors as FRANK CAPRA and ANATOLE LITVAK. These include: *Prelude to War, The Nazis Strike, Divide and Conquer*, covering the period 1918 to 1941; *The Battle of Britain, The Battle of Russia, The Battle of China.* Later official films added *Know Your Ally, Britain* and Samuel Spewack's *World at War* series (1943). Of the specially shot films, the outstanding titles included *Memphis Belle* (WILLIAM WYLER, 1944), *The Fighting Lady* (LOUIS DE ROCHEMONT, 1944), and JOHN HUSTON's *Report from the Aleutians* (1943) and *The Battle of San Pietro* (1944). Notable civilian documentaries of the war years were *A Place to Live* (IRVING LERNER, 1941), or the films sponsored by the Office of War Information (OWI), such as *War Town* (WILLARD VAN DYKE, 1943).

The British film effort was a large one – the combined output of the Government and Service film units and sponsored work from the best of the remaining independent documentary companies. Exhibition was through the movie theatres (also hired frequently for special screenings) and through the wartime Ministry of Information's mobile film unit scheme which at the height of the war maintained some 150 full-time travelling units to tour the towns and villages of Britain, turning over immediately to relief and public address work in any area under bombing. Programmes of varying length were shown to every kind of adult audience, from the general audience in the village institute to the ready-made, mass audience of workers in the war factory canteens. Films ranged from war record and information to instructional films relating to food, health and civil defence. The films themselves, at first uncertain and indifferent, soon began to achieve fire-power, led by the work of the Government Crown Film Unit (formerly the GPO Unit) and the Service units.

Above: 'Olympic Games' (Leni Riefenstahl, Germany, 1938)
Below: A mobile diagram by Francis Rodker from 'Airscrew' (Graham Thorpe, for Shell Film Unit, GB, 1940)
Bottom: 'Easter Island' (John Fernhout and Henri Storck, Netherlands, 1934)

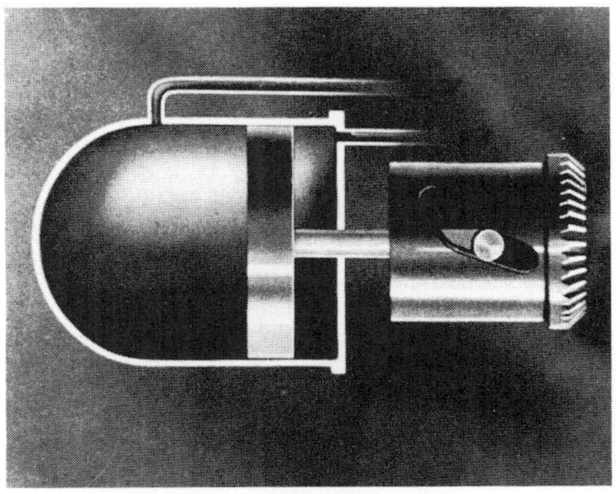

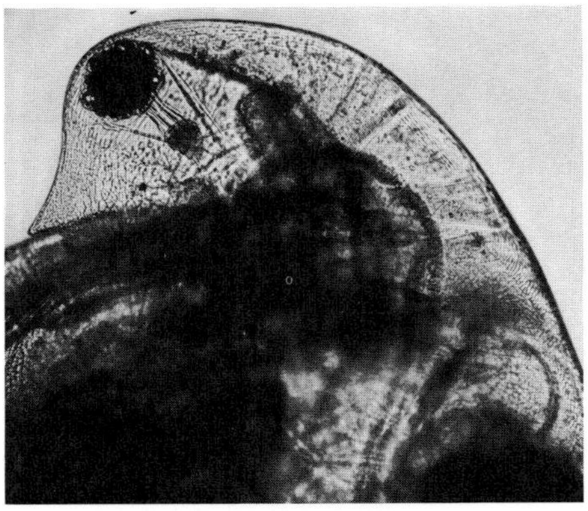

Top: 'Daphnia' (Jean Painlevé, France, 1926)
Above: 'Battle for the Ukraine' (Alexander Dovzhenko, USSR, 1943)
Below: 'Stalingrad' (Varlamov and Karmen, USSR, 1943)

Here are some:

Britain at Bay (Crown, with J. B. Priestley, 1940); *Merchant Seamen* (J. B. Holmes, 1941); *Kill or Be Killed* (LEN LYE, 1942); *Target for Tonight* (HARRY WATT, 1941); RALPH KEENE'S *Winter, Spring, Summer on the Farm* series, and *Crown of the Year*, (1941–2); *Listen to Britain* (HUMPHREY JENNINGS, (1941); *The World of Plenty* (PAUL ROTHA, 1942–3); *The Silent Village* and *Fires were Started* (Humphrey Jennings, 1943); *Desert Victory* (Service Film Units, 1943); *Western Approaches* (Pat Jackson, 1944); *Our Country* (John Eldridge and Dylan Thomas, 1945); *Cameraman at War* (edited by Len Lye, 1944); *Burma Victory* (Service Film Units, ROY BOULTING, 1945); *The True Glory* (Service Film Units, CAROL REED and GARSON KANIN, 1945); *The Land of Promise* (Paul Rotha, 1945).

The Post-War Period Post-war productions using resistance or otherwise hidden material were naturally comparatively rare; notable were *Le Journal de la Résistance* (1945), made in France by JEAN PAINLEVÉ, JEAN GRÉMILLON, LOUIS DAQUIN and PIERRE BLANCHAR, and an outstanding film, *Le Retour* (1945), on the liberation of concentration camp prisoners; assembled by Henri Cartier-Bresson and Richard Banks. In Denmark, Theodor Christensen did his best in *Your Freedom is at Stake* (1945) to use material shot during the occupation. The remarkable photographer, Julien Bryan smuggled out film covering the fall of Warsaw from which he made *Siege* (1939). A film never shown was *Effects of the Atom Bomb*, filmed by the Japanese cameramen in Hiroshima and Nagasaki three weeks after the holocaust.

Captured material shot by the Nazis, such as the record film of the Warsaw Ghetto, was

Above: 'The Fighting Lady' (Louis de Rochemont, USA, 1944)
Below: 'The Kharkov Trial' (Alexander Dovzhenko, USSR, 1945)

to be used in many compilation films after the war. One of the finest of these was the Polish *Requiem for 500 Thousand* (Jerzy Bossak and Waclav Kaźmierczak, 1962). Others were *Nuit et Brouillard* (ALAIN RESNAIS, 1955), *The Nuremberg Trial* (*Nazi Crimes and Punishment*, 1958), *Mein Kampf* (Erwin Leiser, 1960) and *The Life of Adolf Hitler* (1962), Rotha's film sponsored by Real Film in West Germany. The Russian retrospect on Nazism can be seen in *Ordinary Fascism* (MIKHAIL ROMM, 1964), and that of East Germany in the many compilation films of Andrew and Annelie Thorndike.

The vast proliferation of the factual film – the record and information film, the film for propaganda, education or advertising, the creative documentary, the film of personal statement – in the post-war world of the 1950s and 1960s defies analysis. The country barely exists which does not make some kind of short films, in addition to newsreels, for the projection of some kind of message for its own people or for use in foreign parts. These films may be seen in the local theatres, on television (where there is television), or non-theatrically at specialized screenings to audiences ranging from diplomatic or cultural gatherings to trade fairs, or in any place where films are needed – schools, colleges, conference centres, and so forth. Innumerable annual festivals have sprung up to celebrate the short film – over a hundred exist on a regular basis, commemorating general documentary production as well as the feature film, but some specializing in shorts and singling out films on certain themes; for example:

General Documentary and Short Film Festivals:
Venice, Tours, Oberhausen, Cracow, Edinburgh, Chicago, Leipzig, etc.

Specialized Festivals:
Belgrade, Bologna, Brussels, Budapest, Padua (Scientific, Technical, Medical, Educational), W. Berlin (Food, Agriculture), Cortina, Oberhausen (Sport), Toulon (Sea, Submarine Exploration), Trento (Mountaineering, and Mountain Exploration), Versailles (Military Films), etc.

Of the thousands of short and specialized films made in Britain since the war, it is impossible to indicate more than the general trends in contemporary production. Broadly speaking, the initiative passed around 1950 from Government sponsorship to that of industry, and the bias of subjects has therefore become increasingly technical, scientific, and commercial. Since the full national development of television (first by the BBC re-starting in 1946, and later by commercial television in competition with the BBC since 1954) the production of documentary and informational magazine items by the BBC and ITV film units has become an important part of British short film production, as in other countries with responsible television services.

What has happened in effect during the past quarter century is that short film-making in Britain has been forced increasingly in the direction of purely utilitarian production, following more or less exactly the needs of the sponsors. In specialized production (the scientific and technological film) standards can be remarkably high, and a few units, notably British Transport Films, the units of the Film Producers Guild, Shell, World Wide, and so forth aim to retain the former high standards of documentary production in the 1930s and 1940s. Apart from such units, it is to television that Britain has to turn for the permanent sponsorship of documentary in its widest sense. Television has become to a considerable extent the sponsor of the more advanced subjects and techniques in documentary, the BBC alone making 50 to 60 factual subjects a year during the 1960s. Lending libraries are maintained by the Government (the Central Film Library) and by industry (Shell, Ford, British Transport Films, UK Atomic Energy Authority, etc.), while abroad embassies, information service centres, or the offices of the British Council form a network of official distribution agencies for films sponsored by industry and adopted by the Government as suitable for distribution after negotiation with their sponsors. This is a pattern which other countries have also adopted; most embassies maintain film libraries abroad for the distribution of films which they think reflect credit on their countries' industrial and cultural life.

The principles which govern short film production in Britain reign elsewhere, except in those countries where the State itself remains the prime or only sponsor. In Britain, short film production comes under four main groupings according to the nature of the sponsorship: (i) *Government Departments or Public Authorities*, examples:

Children on Trial (Crown Film Unit, JACK LEE, 1946); *Daybreak in Udi* (Crown Film Unit, Terry Bishop, 1948); *Three Dawns to Sydney* (BOAC, John Eldridge, 1948); *Waters of Time* (Port of London Authority, BASIL WRIGHT, 1951); *World*

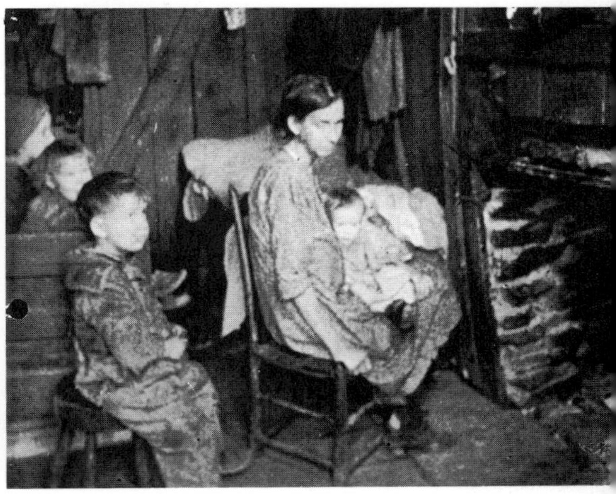

Top and above left: Two stills from 'Nuit et Brouillard' (Alain Resnais, France, 1955)
Above right: 'World of Plenty' (Paul Rotha, GB, 1942–3)
Below: 'The True Glory' (Service Film Units, GB, 1945)

without End (UNESCO, PAUL ROTHA and Basil Wright, 1953); *Seaward the Great Ships* (Films of Scotland, HILARY HARRIS, 1960).

(ii) *Industry*, examples:

Rig 20 (British Petroleum Company, 1952); *The Rival World* (Shell International, BERT HAANSTRA, 1955); *High Speed Flight* (Shell International, Peter de Normanville, Dennis Segaller, 1956–9); *Forming of Metals* (Shell International, Peter de Normanville, 1957); *Unseen Enemies* (Shell International, Michael Clarke, 1959); *The Revealing Eye* (Shell International, compilation film by Walter Storey of scientific phenomena which by reason of speed, slowness, or size escape the human eye, but can be observed through cinematography, 1960); *Electron Microscopy* (Associated Electrical Industries, Michael Crosfield, 1961); *We are the Lambeth Boys* (Ford Motor Company, KAREL REISZ, 1959).

(iii) *The Film Industry*, examples:

Look at Life series (Rank Organization), *Pathé Pictorial* series (Associated British Picture Corporation); *Atomic Physics* (Rank Organization, 1948); *Conquest of Everest* (Tom Stobart, 1953).

(iv) *Television*, examples:

BBC-TV Series on art and artists by John Read, made primarily during the 1950s.
BBC-TV *The Great War* series, made by Tony Essex.
The work of Denis Mitchell (*Chicago*, etc.), KEN RUSSELL (*Elgar, Delius*, and other composers), JOHN BOORMAN (*Citizen 63*, series), PETER WATKINS (*Culloden*, 1965; *The War Game*, 1966), Peter Morley (*Two Faces of Japan*, etc), JOHN SCHLESINGER (*The Class*, 1963)
BBC-TV. *Television and the World* (Richard Cawston, 1962)
Granada Zoological Series (1961–)
Anglia Survival Series (1961–).

The pattern of production in other countries varies. In India, for example, where there is virtually no television, State-sponsored documentary is dominant, much of it in travelogue form, well-made but conventional; more significant were the films made by the European documentary film-maker, Paul Zils (*Mother, Child, Community*, all 1948; the feature-length, *Our India*, 1950). Zils has devoted most of his career to work in India and Ceylon, while the British film-makers RALPH KEENE, Jack Holmes, Kay Mander, R. K. Neilson Baxter, and Tom Hodge have all worked for considerable periods in Asia. More recently Indian documentary is attempting to face the difficulties and problems of malnutrition and over-population; this newer school of film-making is represented by S. Sukhdev's *India 67*.

Canada, too, though there is much private and industrial sponsorship of independent units such as Crawley Films, retains its vast, state-sponsored production organization, the National Film Board of Canada, making factual films of every kind for information and education with planned distribution on a world scale. The emphasis is on use through television and non-theatrical outlets, as well as the movie theatres for those subjects which are suitable. Many exemplary films have come from Canada, such as the post-war psychological films starting

Above: 'The Rival World' (Bert Haanstra for Shell Film Unit, GB, 1955)
Below: Sidney Beadle filming close-ups of insects for 'The Rival World'

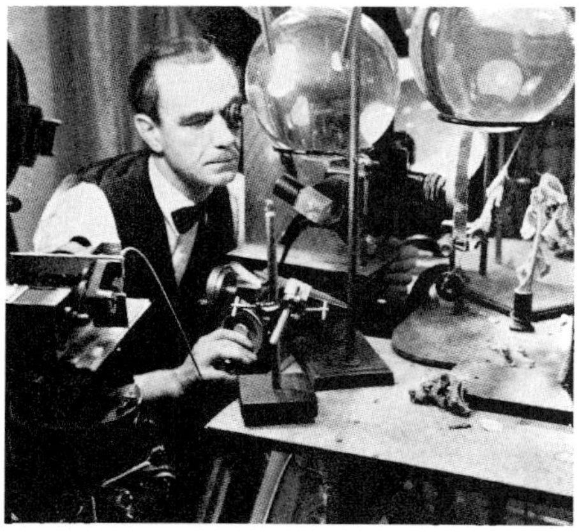

with *The Feeling of Rejection* (1947), such scientific films as *Man is a Universe* (1954), and the much-awarded film on space, *Universe* (1960). The Board's output during the 1960s reached as high as some 260 films annually, while the private sector of production adds a further 100 films a year in the non-theatrical field.

Australia's Commonwealth Film Unit, working until 1970 under Stanley Hawes, has also been responsible for Australia's main production in documentary, a notable example of which was *Great Barrier Reef* (1968).

Holland, too, has a tradition of sponsorship of films through public money, but the work is undertaken by independent units; apart from JORIS IVENS, whose work in Holland finished in the early 1930s, the principal Dutch film-makers in documentary are Herman van der Horst (nature films; *Houen Zo*, 1953, on the rebuilding of Rotterdam; *Shoot the Nets*, 1952; *Praise the Sea*, and more recently, *Fiery Love*, 1960, and *Symphony of the Tropics*, shot in Dutch Guiana, Amsterdam and Jakarta, John Ferno (*Broken Dykes, The Last Shot*, both 1945, and more recently, *Fortress of Peace*, 1964, and *Sky over Holland*, 1967, both shot in 70 mm), and BERT HAANSTRA (later films including *Rembrandt*, 1956; *Glass*, 1958; *The Voice of the Water*, 1966, which was feature-length).

In Italy and France short film production is more closely geared to theatrical release; incentives exist to encourage not only documentary production, with awards of cash prizes, but their exhibition. The average prizes given are relatively small (in France around $2,000), though substantially more (some $8,000) for those few reaching the top in the annual adjudications. In Italy some 200 short films are scheduled each year as compulsory for exhibitors to screen with a small rental to pay, and, as in France, modest sums can be won by film-makers in prize money – between $7,000 and $13,000 for each selected film. This prize money is shared in descending scale over about 100–120 films a year, all of which are distributed through a state enterprise, Istituto Nazionale Luce. In West Germany the Prädikat system offers incentives to exhibitors to show approved short films (as well as features) by reducing entertainments tax when they are screened, Germany has produced a single genius in post-war specialized production, Heinz Sielmann, whose wild-life films are celebrated all over the world.

Undoubtedly, the wide-scale uses of film, most notably in industry, but also on television and in the growing range of educational outlets, has encouraged sponsorship for the official, the industrial and the television units, as well as

Top: 'Isole nella Laguna' (Luciano Emmer and Enrico Gras, Italy, 1948)
Above: 'Native Earth' (John Heyer, Australia, 1946)
Below: 'Community' (Paul Zils, India, 1948)

for the independent units which rely on its steady flow from various sources. The resultant work, seen at festivals and elsewhere in cross-section, is seldom more than competently professional. However, the work of certain film-makers has come to the fore out of the annual production of thousands of films made for every conceivable purpose. In addition to the many well-established directors already mentioned, there are others whose films have been of importance in widening the scope of the medium. These include:

LINDSAY ANDERSON (*O Dreamland*, 1953; *Thursday's Children*, 1954; *Every day except Christmas*, 1957; *The Singing Lesson*, 1967).
SHIRLEY CLARKE (*The Connection*, 1960; *Portrait of Jason*, 1967).
HENRI-GEORGES CLOUZOT (*Le Mystère Picasso*, 1956).
LUCIANO EMMER and Enrico Gras (*Paradise Lost*, 1948; *The Drama of Christ*, 1948; *The Legend of St Ursula*, 1949, and other films about art).
GEORGES FRANJU (*Le Sang des Bêtes*, 1949; *Hôtel des Invalides*, etc.).
JEAN GRÉMILLON (*Le 6 Juin à l'Aube*, 1945; *Les Charmes de l'Existence*, with Pierre Kast, 1949).
John Heyer (*Native Earth*, 1946; *The Valley is Ours*, 1949; *Back of Beyond*, 1953).
Isaac Kleinerman (*The Twentieth Century* CBS television series; *Victory at Sea* television series).
RICHARD LEACOCK (cameraman on Flaherty's *Louisiana Story*, 1948; directs in *cinéma-vérité* style; *Primary*, 1960; *Nehru*, 1962; *The Chair* and *Quint City, USA* both 1963; *Igor Stravinsky*, 1966).
Jean Lods (*Maillol*, 1944; *Aubusson*, 1946).
CHRIS MARKER (at first assistant to ALAIN RESNAIS; *Dimanche à Pekin*, 1955; *Lettre de Sibérie*, 1957; *Description d'un Combat*, 1960, shot in Israel; *Cuba Si!*, 1961; *Le Joli Mai*, 1962; *Le Mystère Koumiko*, 1965, shot in Japan; moving spirit in composite film, *Loin du Viêtnam*, 1967. All these films representing, in one form or another, the cinéma-vérité style with which Marker's name, like Leacock's, is associated).
R. H. B. Mason (*Cornish Beam Engine*, 1949; *Grand Prix*, 1949; *Atomization*, 1949; *Le Mans*, 1952; *Mille Miglia*, 1953; *The Heroic Days* and others in the series on the history of motor racing, 1960–).
ALBERT and DAVID MAYSLES (*Showman*, 1963 on the cinema impresario, JOSEPH E. LEVINE, *The Salesman*, 1969, *The Beatles*, and other films for television illustrating the American wing of cinéma-vérité).
RICHARD MASSINGHAM (his highly personal films are difficult to classify, his humour is irresistible; his documentaries included *They Travel by Air*, 1948, for BOAC; *Brief City*, 1951, on the London South Bank Exhibition).
Sidney Meyers (*The Quiet One*, 1948; *The Savage Eye*, 1959, with Ben Maddow and JOSEPH STRICK).
SATYAJIT RAY (*Rabindranath Tagore*, 1961; a documentary on Sikkim, 1970).
John Read (*Henry Moore*, 1951; *Graham Sutherland*, 1954; *L. S. Lowry*, 1957; and many other films on art and artists for BBC television).
ALAIN RESNAIS (*Van Gogh*, 1948; *Guernica*, 1950; *Les Statues Meurent Aussi*, 1952; *Nuit et Brouillard*, 1955; *Toute la Mémoire du Monde*, 1956; etc.).
LIONEL ROGOSIN (*On the Bowery*, 1954; *Come Back, Africa*, 1958; *Good Times, Wonderful Times*, 1964).
GEORGES ROUQUIER (*Le Tonnelier*, 1942; *Le Charron*, 1943; *Farrebique*, 1947; *Le Sel de la Terre*. 1950; *Lourdes*, 1954; *Arthur Honegger*, 1955).
HENRI STORCK (*Rubens*, 1948, with Paul Haesaerts; *Le Monde de Paul Delvaux*, 1946).
ARNE SUCKSDORFF (*A Summer's Tale*, 1943; *Rhythm of a City*, 1947; *A Divided World*, 1948; *Indian Village*, 1951; *The Great Adventure*, 1953).
NICOLE VÉDRÈS (*Paris 1900*, 1946; *La Vie Commence Demain*, 1950; *Aux Frontières de l'Homme*, 1953).
Alexander Zguridi (*In the Depths of the Sea*, *The Power of Life*, *In the Sands of Central Asia*, made during the war period).

There are also brilliant technicians, such as J. V. Durden and Sidney Beadle of Britain and Canada, who use the camera as an instrument for scientific observation, allying the camera with the microscope through cinemicrography, as Jean Comandon has done at the Pasteur Institute at Garches. As we have seen, the camera can speed up long-term processes such as plant growth, reducing the time taken to minutes or seconds, or slow down quick motion to a phenomenal degree – 600 frames per second being possible with a 16 mm camera using intermittent action, but far greater speeds

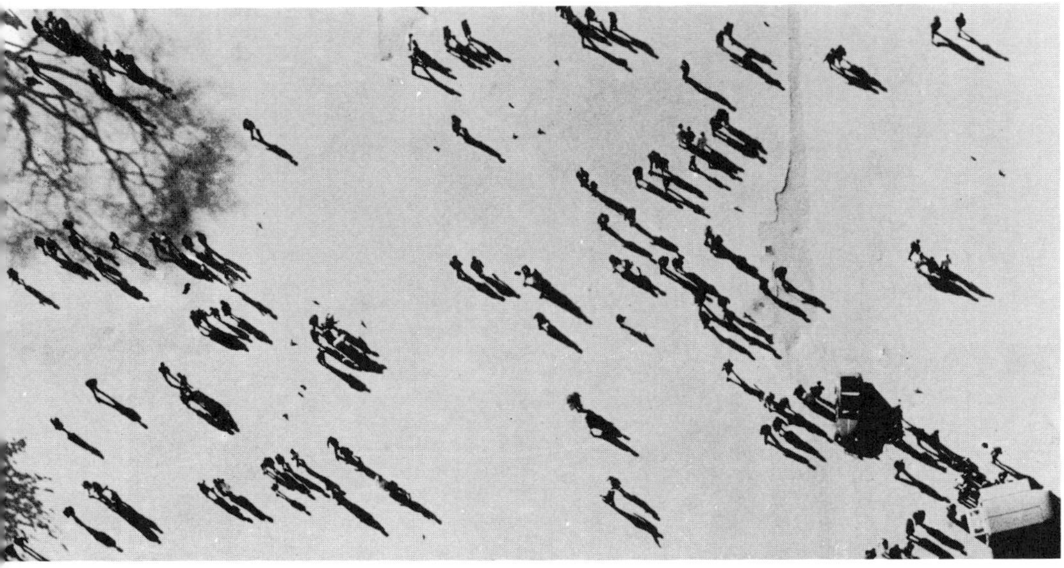

with other types of camera, reaching up to the millions of pictures per second with rotating mirror cameras. The Shell film *The Revealing Eye* assembles a fine selection of images achieved by the motion picture camera to aid scientific observation, while another Shell film, *Schlieren*, demonstrates special photographic technique which registers changes in air pressure in terms of changes of colour. The AEI film, *Electron Microscopy*, links the electron microscope with the film camera.

Another factor to keep in mind is the use of the film in developing countries. For example, films have been used since the 1930s to assist in the development of health and welfare in African territories. Britain's Colonial Film Unit was specially concerned, until its disbandment in 1952, in experiments with instructional films among people living in primitive or very simple conditions. Many of the former colonies of the British Empire still maintain document-

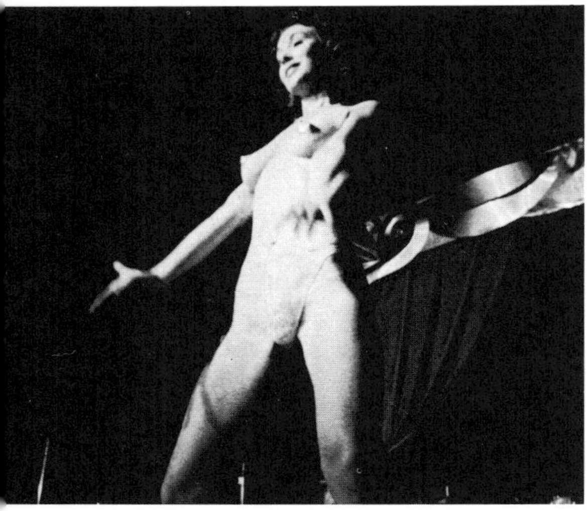

Top: 'Le Joli Mai' (Chris Marker, France, 1962)
Above: 'The Savage Eye' (Sidney Meyers, Ben Maddow and Joseph Strick, USA, 1959)
Above right: 'The War Game' (Peter Watkins for BBC Television, GB, 1966)
Below right: 'The Great Adventure' (Arne Sucksdorff, Sweden, 1953)
Below: 'High Speed Flight' (Peter de Normanville for Shell Film Unit, GB, 1956–9)

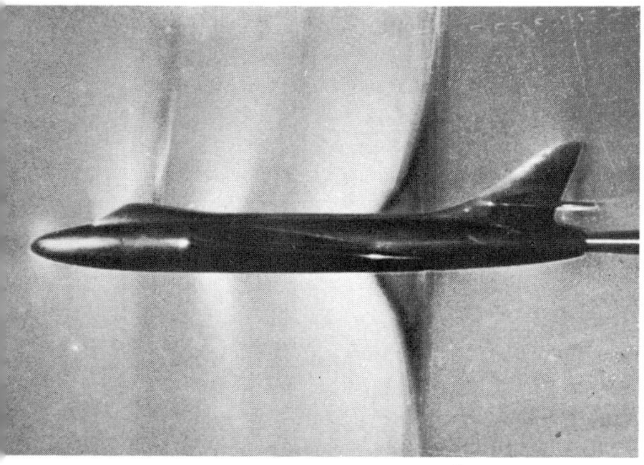

ary units to aid the development of their peoples. The films needed are simple and completely utilitarian, but none the worse for this.

In its more experimental forms, documentary joins both ANIMATION and the AVANT-GARDE AND UNDERGROUND FILM. No hard boundaries exist. Documentary tends to be the kind of film which, in one way or another, fulfils some evident public need; the underground or avant-garde film tends to be the more private expression of an individual or a group. These areas overlap, for example, in VIGO's *À Propos de Nice* (1930), in the lyricism combined with scientific observation in the films of PAINLEVÉ, in the philosophic viewpoint emerging from RESNAIS's *Toute la Mémoire du Monde*, or in the personal observation of a FLAHERTY, a SUCKSDORFF, or a ROUQUIER.

The documentary, factual and specialized film is at least the equal of the fiction film in its use of the medium to record our many societies and their problems in all their variant forms. Perhaps in the perspective of history the factual film, along with the newsreel, will be the more revealing of the two main branches of the cinema in the record it makes of our century, 'brought alive' since the 1930s in terms of sound and vision for the first time in history for future generations to wonder at. RM

Dolly
A wheeled chassis on which a camera is placed to give it greater mobility

Donat, Robert (1905–1958)
Born at Withington, Manchester, England. Actor, who trained for the stage and played in many theatres, including the Old Vic. He had an exceptionally fine voice in spite of suffering from chronic asthma. He entered films in 1932, and starred in *The Count of Monte Cristo* (1934), *The Thirty-nine Steps* (1935), *The Ghost goes West* (1936), *Goodbye Mr Chips* (1939), *The Young Mr Pitt* (1942), *The Winslow Boy* (1948), *The Cure for Love* (which he also directed: 1949), *The Magic Box* (1951) and *The Inn of the Sixth Happiness*, made shortly before his death in 1958.

Donen, Stanley
Born 1924 in South Carolina, USA. Inventive choreographer and director who, with GENE KELLY and VINCENTE MINNELLI, brought a fresh, intrinsically cinematic style and vigour to the film musical at MGM during the late 1940s and early 1950s. When the cumbersome screen versions of pre-sold stage musicals took over, he turned with less success to sophisticated thrillers and romantic comedies.

He started out in the stage chorus of 'Pal Joey' in New York where he met the star of the show Gene Kelly. In 1942 he went to Hollywood where he graduated from the chorus to assistant dance director. Renewing his acquaintance with Kelly, he collaborated with him on

Above: Frank Lawton and Robert Donat in 'The Thirty-Nine Steps' (Alfred Hitchcock, GB, 1935)
Below: John Raitt Jr and Doris Day in 'The Pajama Game' (Stanley Donen, USA, 1957)

Anchors Aweigh (1945) and they co-directed the two key musicals of this period *On the Town* (1949) and *Singin' in the Rain* (1952) – still unmatched for their zest, musical wit and originality.

He became a director in his own right on *Fearless Fagan* (1951) and scored an enormous popular success with *Seven Brides for Seven Brothers* (1954). He returned with Gene Kelly to an *On the Town* formula with the engaging *It's always Fair Weather* (1955). But his later musicals, lacking their overall originality, were based on stage shows; though *Funny Face* (1957) had some delightful sequences and *The Pajama Game* (1957) and *Damn Yankees* (1958) occasionally captured the spirit of his earlier work.

In the late 1950s he came to Europe where he has worked ever since on rather laboured frolics such as *Indiscreet* (1958), *Once More with Feeling* (1959), *Surprise Package* (1960). The best of his later films have been the crisp mystery comedy *Charade* (1963) and *Two for the Road* (1967). In 1969 he directed REX HARRISON and RICHARD BURTON in a disappointing screen version of the play 'Staircase' about a homosexual relationship.

Other notable films: *Wedding Bells* (1952), *The Grass is Greener* (1960), *Arabesque* (1966), *Bedazzled* (1967). MH

Doniol-Valcroze, Jacques
Born 1920 in Paris, France. Director, screenwriter, actor, critic. Co-founder with ANDRÉ BAZIN of 'Cahiers du Cinéma', to which he was a contributor. Director of several short films during the 1950s: *Bonjour M la Bruyère* (1956), *L'Oeil du Maître* (1957), *Les Surmenés* (1958). His first feature film, *L'Eau à la Bouche* (1959) showed something of the influence of RENOIR and BERGMAN in its study of a group of young people spending a weekend of love and luxury in a château. He has worked a great deal for television, and has scripted and acted in the films of other directors, notably those of Pierre Kast; he also appeared in ROBBE-GRILLET's *L'Immortelle*. His feature films include a comedy, *Le Cœur Battant* (1962), *Le Viol* (1968, made in Sweden), and *La Maison des Bouris* (1970), a sympathetic study of family relationships in a Renoir-like country setting.

Donner, Clive
Born 1926 in London, England. Director. Initially in the theatre, he became a film editor in 1942, working on many films, including

Genevieve (1953). His films as director include: *The Caretaker* (1963), *What's New, Pussycat?* (1965), *Here we go round the Mulberry Bush* (1967), *Alfred the Great* (1969).

Donner, Jörn

Born 1933 in Helsinki, Finland. Provocative Scandinavian writer and director who has worked a good deal in Sweden; was formerly film journalist and critic in Finland; has written many books including a study of INGMAR BERGMAN. Highly regarded among the younger contemporary film-makers, his films have gained fame – and censure – for their uninhibited approach to sex and the emotional problems of modern Scandinavian society. [See SCANDINAVIAN FILM]. Main feature films: *A Sunday in September* (1963), *To Love* (1964), *Adventure Starts Here* (1965), *Rooftree* (1967), *Black on White* (1968), *Sixty-Nine Portraits of Women* (1969) and *Anna* (1970).

Donskoi, Mark

Born 1901 in Odessa, Ukraine, Russia. Director. After a period of scriptwriting, he began directing in the late 1920s, but few of these early works have been seen in the West. He achieved international prominence with *The Maxim Gorki Trilogy* (1938–40), depicting the youth and early life of the great writer and realized with an immaculate period feeling: students gather by the river as a convict boat passes sadly by, children grow up and families part, the atmosphere of social change hangs heavily in the air. Apart from its evocation of times past, the films boast a rich gallery of character portraits, notably the wise, compassionate grandmother of Varvara Massalitinova. Donskoi's best-known war-time films – *The Rainbow* (1944) and *Unconquered* (1945) – are harsh, anti-Nazi statements, the former, in particular, showing the war's horrifying effect on children. The immediate post-war films (including *The Village Schoolteacher*, 1947) mark a return to the more intimate, poetic mood of the Gorki trilogy; then, like other major Soviet directors, Donskoi fell foul of Stalin's strict artistic policies and at least one film (*Alitet goes to the Hills*) was criticized, re-edited and apparently shelved. When he returned to active production with a re-make of *Mother* (1956), a good deal of the old passion and flair came through, tinged, however, with a rather calculated use of flashy camera effects. This attempt to be modern also flawed two exotic period dramas, *At a High Cost* (1957) and *Foma Gordeyev* (1959), but Donskoi's evident renewed enjoyment in film-making gave them a sweep and vitality missing from the more conservative Soviet films of the period. Two films about the Lenin family – *Heart of a Mother* and *A Mother's Devotion* (1966) – looked back once again to the period just prior to the Revolution and even repeated some of the Gorki images; though uneven and sentimentalized, they have much of the true Donskoi spirit, a more controlled camera style and splendid ensemble playing. During his long and eventful career, Donskoi has produced a body of work notable for its rich and varied characterizations and an almost palpable re-creation of a past era. Being a determinedly humanist director, he has failed mainly when he has forced his feelings too hard; but in moments like the grandmother's farewell to the young Gorki at the end of the trilogy's second part, *Out in the World*, a great artist is revealed. Latest project: *Chaliapin* (1972). JG

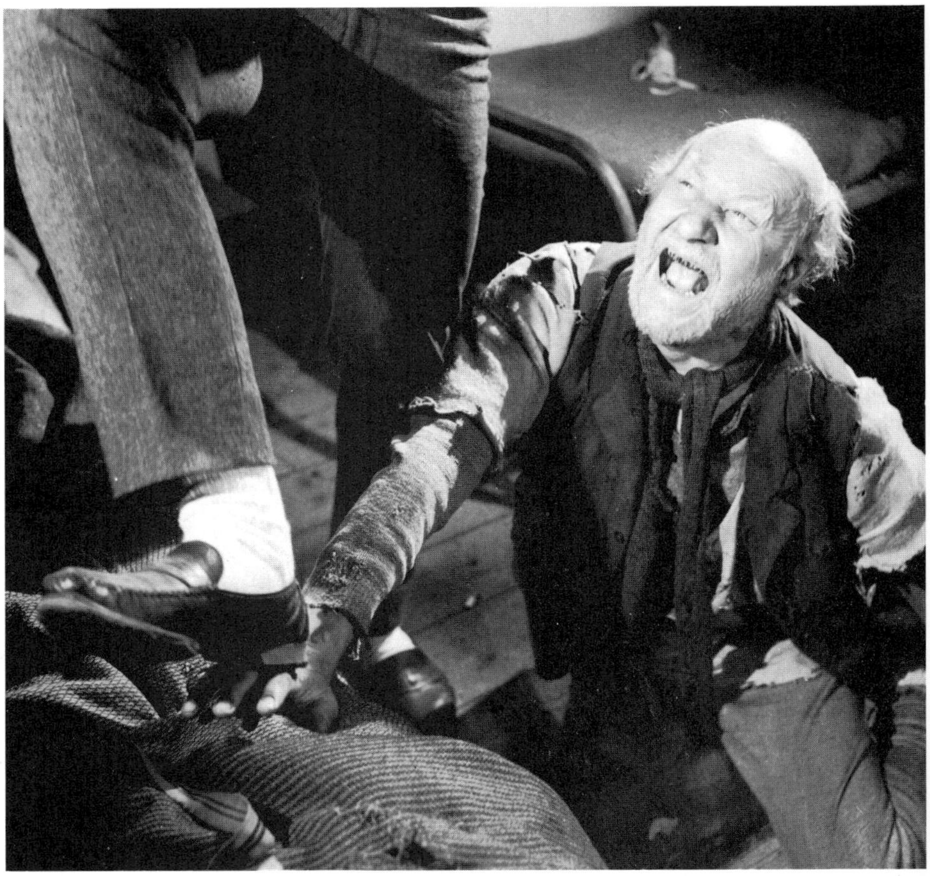

Above: Donald Pleasence in 'The Caretaker' (Clive Donner, GB, 1963)
Below: Alexander Dovzhenko (late 1940s)

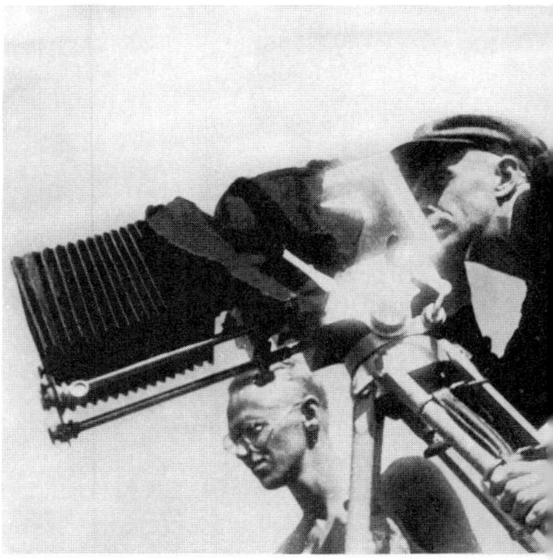

Dope Sheet

(1) An analysis of film material for purposes of classification.
(2) In animation. Frame by frame instructions to the cameraman as to cell levels, background movement and camera movement.

Double

One employed to take the place of an actor in scenes of risk or danger

Double Exposure

The exposure of sensitive material twice before development. See SUPERIMPOSE

Double Frame Animation

One animation drawing photographed for two frames instead of one

Double Head Projection

The synchronous projection of a picture track and a sound track

Douglas, Kirk

Born 1916 in Amsterdam, New York, USA. Actor, who made his stage début in New York in 'Spring Again'. During the Second World War he served in the US Navy. After the war he resumed stage work and did radio soap operas. He made his screen début in 1946 in *The Strange Love of Martha Ivers* and subsequently developed a tough neurotic image tinged with a vulnerable tenderness. He has also produced films. Main films as an actor include:

Mourning becomes Electra (1947), *The Bad and the Beautiful* (1952), *Ulisse* and *Twenty Thousand Leagues Under the Sea* (1954), *Lust for Life* (as Van Gogh, 1956), *Gunfight at the OK Corral* and *Paths of Glory* (1957), *Spartacus* (1960), *Lonely are the Brave* (1962), *Seven Days in May* (1963), *Is Paris Burning?* (1966), *There was a Crooked Man* and *The Arrangement* (1969), *Gunfight*, *The Light at the End of the World* and *Catch Me a Spy* (1971).

Dovzhenko, Alexander (1894–1956)
Born in Sosnichi, Ukraine, USSR. With EISENSTEIN, PUDOVKIN, KULESHOV and VERTOV, one of the great creators of the Soviet cinema. Originally a teacher, a painter and illustrator and a diplomat, Dovzhenko was already 32 – middle-aged in that era of Soviet art – when he joined the Odessa Studios in 1926. Improbably (although he always was drawn by comedy, and prided himself on his physical similarity to CHAPLIN) Dovzhenko's first solo film as director was a two-reel slapstick comedy, *The Little Fruits of Love*. After a foolish but stylish propaganda thriller, *The Diplomatic Pouch*, Dovzhenko revealed his rich lyrical gifts with *Zvenigora* (1928), a wild and wonderful *mélange* of legend and magic, which was only reluctantly recognized by the studio heads after it had the seal of approval of Eisenstein and Pudovkin.

Above: Marie Dressler and Charles Chaplin in 'Tillie's Punctured Romance' (Mack Sennett, USA, 1914)
Below: Carl Dreyer (1950s)

Arsenal (1929) was his most intense and concentrated film, assembling every kind of realist and fantastic element in its description of the revolutionary struggles of 1919. *Earth* (1930) remains his greatest film, a story of banal happenings and tragic drama on a collective farm, all invested with poetic and humane grandeur.

In *Ivan* (1932), the story of the great Dnieper-Petrovsk construction project, Dovzhenko showed that he could use sound and dialogue with the same fluidity and lyricism as images. *Aerograd* (1935) is no less brilliant, but compromised by the official doctrines of the Stalin era. *Shchors* (1939), a biography of the Ukrainian revolutionary hero, was made under still greater pressures, for Stalin took a personal interest in the film, requiring long periods of revision, which make the warmth and generosity of the film which eventually emerges all the more remarkable. After this Dovzhenko's career seems to have been clouded by official disapproval. A series of war-time documentaries, though bearing all the marks of his personality, appeared under the name of his wife, the former actress JULIA SOLNTSEVA. His last film, a biography of the botanist *Michurin* (1949), was subjected to severe pressures and revision, owing to changes in the official status of the scientist. The posthumous *Poem of the Sea* (1955–8) was completed by Solntseva, who thereafter dedicated herself to realizing other Dovzhenko projects: *Story of the Flaming Years* (1961), *The Enchanted Desna* (1965), *The Golden Gates* (1970). DR

Dreier, Hans (1885–1966)
Born in Bremen, Germany. Designer. After studying architecture, he went to UFA in Berlin (1919); moved to Hollywood four years later, becoming head designer at Paramount from the mid-1920s until 1952. He was as influential as CEDRIC GIBBONS was at MGM and his elegant, witty designs, which took in all forms of Americana as well as simulated foreign settings, were realized by a talented team of associate designers. Dreier had a special affinity with European-orientated directors, working notably with LUBITSCH over many years: *The Patriot* (1928), *Monte Carlo* (1930), *Trouble in Paradise* (1932), etc.; also MAMOULIAN (*Dr Jekyll and Mr Hyde*, 1932); STERNBERG (*The Devil is a Woman*, 1935). Other work includes several DE MILLE spectaculars (*Cleopatra*, with its fabulously decorated barge, 1934), *Lady in the Dark* (1944), *Sunset Boulevard* (whose dark, memory-filled mansion seems to evoke all of Dreier's Hollywood, 1950), and *A Place in the Sun* (1951). JG

Dressler, Marie (1869–1934)
Born in Cobourg, Canada. Actress. Real name Leila Kerber. The large, ferociously genial Marie Dressler made two incursions into films. As an established star of legitimate theatre and vaudeville, she filmed her stage success, *Tillie's Punctured Romance*, for MACK SENNETT in 1914. As a somewhat fallen star, she returned to Hollywood in 1929, established a new reputation with *Anna Christie* (1930), received an Oscar for *Min and Bill* (1931), and at her death had become Hollywood's best-loved star. Other films of this period were *Emma* (1932), *Dinner at Eight* and *Tugboat Annie* (1933).

Dreyer, Carl Theodor (1889–1968)
Born in Copenhagen, Denmark. Director. Brought up somewhat unhappily by foster-parents, Dreyer was forced at first to accept various clerical jobs. He adopted a radical, but never bohemian outlook, became a journalist and later, around 1912, dialogue writer and adapter for Nordisk. He graduated from script-writing and editing to directing his first film, *The President*, in 1919–20; it was a sentimental and somewhat moral melodrama. His second film, *Leaves from Satan's Book* (1919, released in 1921), began to reveal his style – austerely correct sets, careful casting and acting, 'advanced' cutting influenced at this stage by GRIFFITH, landscapes used for atmospheric effect. His next film, *The Parson's Widow* (1921), was shot in Norway and was more Swedish in style, ming-

ling ironic humour with a revelation of suffering. Before making his masterpiece in France, *The Passion of Joan of Arc* (1928), Dreyer made *Love One Another* (1921) and *Mikaël* (1924) in Berlin, *Once Upon a Time* (1922) and *Master of the House* (1925) in Denmark, and *The Bride of Glomdal* in Norway; these films are all concerned with some form of endurance, while *Mikaël* is held by Dreyer's admirers as a masterpiece of the current 'intimate drama', primarily concerned with psychological states. *Joan of Arc* cost some £50,000; its large, simple, stylized architectural set covered a considerable area of ground, but the film was concentrated upon Joan's trial. Stripped of all make-up, Maria Falconetti placed herself entirely in Dreyer's hands and gave a phenomenal performance, almost as if possessed; it was a close and at times tortured relationship, and the result was expressed in incessant close shot. The result justified Dreyer's belief that true acting should be naked, unmasked, a human revelation. *Vampyr* (1932), Dreyer's last film for over a decade, was a macabre fantasy based on 'Carmilla' by Sheridan Le Fanu; it was made on location and conjured up a remarkably eerie atmosphere by the simplest means.

After *Vampyr*, Dreyer made no further feature films for 12 years. Failing to get the contracts he wanted, he turned again to journalism in Copenhagen. In 1942, however, he made *Day of Wrath* with a budget of only £12,000; once again it dealt with a 'haunted' subject, witchcraft, and the persecution of woman. His Swedish film, *Two People* (1944), did not conform to his wishes. Dreyer's two final features were made at ten-year intervals – the impeccable *Ordet* (*The Word*, 1954), and *Gertrud* (1964), the latter unfortunately as much derided for its lack of overt action as it was admired by Dreyer's adherents. It proved to be the final expression of Dreyer's humane philosophy that life, which is in itself to be venerated, inevitably involves suffering and persecution for those who seek to live it positively. *Gertrud* concentrated entirely on the interplay of speaking characters, watched impassively by the camera which moved only when a narrative point needed to be stressed. Most of the principal characters in Dreyer's films were in one way or another lonely and persecuted. For all their outward austerity, Dreyer's films are made with deep feeling and sympathy, particularly towards women. He died without realizing the project he had had in mind for decades – a film on the life of Christ. A sympathetic and perceptive study of Dreyer's work can be found in Tom Milne's 'The Cinema of Carl Dreyer' (1971). RM

Above: Chico, Margaret Dumont and Harpo in 'Animal Crackers' (Victor Heerman, USA, 1930)
Below: Baard Owe and Nina Pens Rode in 'Gertrud' (Carl Dreyer, Denmark, 1964)

Dubbing

(1) The mixing of various sound tracks into a single track.
(2) The process of recording new dialogue to be substituted for the original dialogue of a film, generally in a different language.

Dulac, Germaine (1882–1942)

Born in Asnières, France, Director. Initially a writer and drama critic. Entered the cinema as scenarist around 1914. Her first film as director was *Sœurs Ennemies* (1915), her best-known *La Fête Espagnole* (1919), scripted by LOUIS DELLUC, and *La Souriante Madame Beudet* (1923), based on a play by André Obey. During the later 1920s she was primarily associated with the French avant-garde; her best-known film in this field was *La Coquille et le Clergyman* (*The Seashell and the Clergyman*, 1926), scripted by Antonin Artaud, a rather self-conscious, but to a certain extent effective essay in Freudian sexual symbolism, made at the Studio des Ursulines. Unfortunately it lacked the forceful performance Artaud could have given the role of the priest had he not been too unwell to play the part intended for him. Germaine Dulac made other experimental shorts during the period 1927–30: *L'Invitation au Voyage*, *Disque 927* (Chopin), *Arabesque* (Debussy), and *Theme and Variations*. In 1930–40 she was director of Pathé newsreels.

Dumont, Margaret (1890–1965)

American actress, closely associated with the MARX BROTHERS, in whose films she played the dignified matron who is the butt of their humour. Main films include: *The Coconuts* (1929), in which she gave a memorable performance, *A Night at the Opera* (1935), *Anything Goes* (1936), *A Day at the Races* (1937), *At the Circus* (1939), *Up in Arms* (1944), *What a Way to Go* (1964).

Dunne, Irene

Born 1904 in Louisville, USA. Actress, who made her screen début in 1931 after appearing on the stage in musical comedy. Soon established herself as a leading lady of the cool, well-bred type with a lively sense of humour and splendid comic timing. Main films: *Present Arms* (début) and *Cimarron* (1931), *Showboat* and *Theodora goes Wild* (1936), *The Awful Truth* (1937), *My Favourite Wife* (1940), *Penny Serenade* (1941), *The White Cliffs of Dover* (1944), *Anna and the King of Siam* (1946), *Life with Father* (1947), *I Remember Mama* (1948), *The Mudlark* (in which she appeared as Queen Victoria, 1951), *It grows on Trees* (1952).

Dunning, George

Born 1920 in Toronto, Canada. Animation director. Joined the National Film Board in

1943, and showed his originality in such films as *Cadet Rousselle* (1947), for which he used flat, jointed figures made of metal and animated to a traditional French folk-song. He came to England in 1956 and established Television Cartoons, making commercials and sponsored cartoons alongside his individual work, expressing his own quietist (but sometimes menacing) outlook: *The Wardrobe* (1960), *The Flying Man* and *The Apple* (1962), *The Ladder* (1967). He made a triple-screen cartoon, *Canada is my Piano*, in 1966 for the Montreal Exhibition, and he directed *Yellow Submarine* (1968), a cartoon feature sponsored by the Beatles and using pop-art graphics.

Dupont, Ewald Andreas (1891–1956)
Born in Zeitz, Saxony, Germany. One of the earliest German film critics, Dupont began his career as a director in 1918. A series of fairly mediocre films was followed by the enormously successful *Vaudeville* (1925), which brought Dupont an international celebrity to which his talent seemed unequal. After numerous films in Britain – including *Piccadilly* (1929), which had a striking visual and atmospheric quality, and *Atlantic* (1930) – and in the USA, Dupont settled quite happily to directing a Hollywood talent agency in the 1940s. He returned to direction in 1951 with a few films (*The Scarf, Problem Girls, The Neanderthal Man, The Steel Lady, Return to Treasure Island*) which added little to his lustre.

Duras, Marguerite
Born 1914 in France. Key French writer whose melancholy novels have formed the basis of several interesting contemporary films and one major influential script, *Hiroshima Mon Amour* (1959). Other films based on her writings: *The Sea Wall* (1957), *Moderato Cantabile* (1960), *Sailor from Gibraltar* (1966). The first film she both wrote and directed, *Destroy, she Says* (1969), was a study in suspended animation that almost verged on parody. Recent film: *Jaune le Soleil* (1971).

Durbin, Deanna
Born 1921 in Canada. Actress and singer. Made her first film *Three Smart Girls* (1936) at the age of 15 and won instant popularity. In 1938 she was given a special Academy Award 'for bringing to the screen the spirit and personification of youth'. Main films: *One Hundred Men and a Girl* (1937), *That Certain Age* and *Three Smart Girls Grow Up* (1938), *First Love* (1939), *Spring Parade* (1940), *It Started with Eve* (1941), *The Amazing Mrs Holliday* (1942), *Can't Help Singing* (1944), *For the Love of Mary* (1947).

Duvivier, Julien (1896–1967)
Born in Lille, France. Distinguished French director of elegant and nostalgic romances, who attained his peak period in the 1930s and made several high-toned melodramas in Hollywood just before and during the Second World War, although they lacked the quality of his French films. Trained in the theatre he entered films in 1919, writing and directing many silent productions, including *Poil de Carotte* (1925), which he remade in 1932. The quintessence of Duvivier's style is to be found in *Pépé Le Moko* and *Un Carnet de Bal* (1937); but it did not travel well and, in America, his *Great Waltz* (1938), *Tales of Manhattan* (1942), *Flesh and Fantasy* (1943) tended to be over-ornate and only passingly successful. After the Second World War, he made a disappointing *Anna Karenina* (1948) in Britain and *The Little World of Don Camillo* (1952), which launched a successful Franco-Italian series.

Above: Cary Grant and Irene Dunne in 'My Favourite Wife' (Garson Kanin, USA, 1940)
Below: William Bendix, Deanna Durbin in 'I'll Be Yours' (William Seiter, USA, 1946)

Other notable films: *Maria Chapdelaine* (1934), *Le Golem* (1935), *La Belle Équipe* (1936), *Lydia* (1941), *Panique* (1946), *Sous le Ciel de Paris* (1951), *Voici le Temps des Assassins* (1955), *Pot-Bouille* (1957), *La Grande Vie* (1961), *La Chambre Ardente* (1962), *Chair de Poule* (1963), *Diaboliquement Vôtre* (1967). MH

Dwan, Allan
Born 1885 in Toronto, Canada. Perhaps the most prolific director in the history of the cinema, some estimates of his output being as large as 1,500 films. In fact well over four hundred are firmly credited in his enormously long career. He went to the Essanay company as an electrical engineer in 1909, stayed on as a writer, and then joined a breakaway group which formed the American Film Company. In the spring of 1911 he went out to Arizona for the company, and directed his first films (a split reel), *Brandishing a Bad Man* and *A Western Dreamer*, in the spring of that year. He later moved to Universal (1913), to Famous Players (1914) and finally to the Triangle Company, where, between 1915 and 1917 he made some of DOUGLAS FAIRBANKS's earliest films. Later, for Fairbanks's own company, Dwan was to make two of the star's most successful features: *Robin Hood* (1922) and *The Iron Mask* (1929). He also directed GLORIA SWANSON in a series of brilliant comedies including *Zaza* (1923), *Manhandled* (1924) and *Stage Struck* (1925). With the coming of sound, Dwan's career became that of a prolific, reliable routine director, working by turns at Fox and 20th Century Fox, Small Productions, Republic and RKO. Dwan's last films – *Enchanted Island* and *Most Dangerous Man Alive* – were made in 1958. See 'Allan Dwan: the last pioneer', Peter Bogdanovich (1971).

E

Eames, Charles

Born 1907 in St Louis, USA. Architect, designer, and avant-garde film-maker. Together with his wife, Ray, who is a painter, Eames has made over 30 experimental films, mainly aesthetic in approach, some sponsored by industry. In the early 1950s, Charles and Ray Eames experimented in multi-screen techniques, starting with *Sample Lesson* (1951–3) and later in *Glimpses of the USA*, made for showing in the USSR, and *The House of Science* (1962), shown in the Science Pavilion at the Seattle World's Fair. Their other films include: *Blacktop* and *Parade* (1950); films of animated toys, *House* (1955) and *Toccata for Toy Trains*, *Kaleidoscope* (1961).

Eastwood, Clint

Born 1930 in California, USA. Sturdy American Western star, whose long, lean, laconic style in the low budget Spanish-Italian Western, *A Fistful of Dollars* (1966), made him a phenomenal, though hardly overnight, film success. He had previously made a hit in the long-running television series *Rawhide*. A gritty, interesting personality, he was featured in a series of unremarkable films before *Dollars*, after which he appeared in several repeat Westerns, registered as a disciplined, effective actor in *Coogan's Bluff* (1968), and co-starred attractively in the musical, *Paint Your Wagon* (1969). Other films: *Hang 'Em High* and *Where Eagles Dare* (1968), *Two Mules for Sister Sara* (1969), *Kelly's Heroes* (1970), *The Beguiled* (1971). Directed and acted in *Play Misty for Me* (1971).

Echo Chamber

A reverberant room in which is placed a loudspeaker and a microphone. The recording to which echo is to be added is played from the loudspeaker and picked up by the microphone with the addition of the echo produced in the room, and this is then re-recorded.

Edens, Roger (1905–1970)

Born in Hillsboro, Texas, USA. Producer and musical supervisor. Known for his vocal arrangements for singing stars like Ethel Merman and JUDY GARLAND. Went to Hollywood in 1933, joined MGM as musical supervisor and became associate producer to ARTHUR FREED on his great series of musicals beginning in the 1940s. Wrote famous songs for *Ziegfeld Follies* (1945), *On the Town* (1949), *Singin' in the Rain* (1952), *A Star is Born* (1954), *Funny Face* (1957), as well as staging some numbers. His sophisticated flair for song and dance sequences made him an essential part of the MGM team. More recently, he was associate producer on *The Unsinkable Molly Brown* (1964), *The Sound of Music* (1965), *Hello, Dolly!* (1969). JG

Edeson, Arthur (1891–1970)

Born in New York, USA. Cinematographer. Entered films during the First World War as an assistant operator. Began main career as lighting cameraman on DOUGLAS FAIRBANKS's films from 1917 onwards, including *The Three Musketeers* (1921), *Robin Hood* (1922) and *The Thief of Bagdad* (1924). These, together with HENRY KING's outstanding *Stella Dallas* (1925), reveal the beautifully balanced lighting style he perfected in the silent era. His skill in using the moving camera in sound films was best demonstrated in the trench scenes from MILESTONE's *All Quiet on the Western Front* (1930); and his expressive 'horror' lighting lent a special distinction to WHALE's *Frankenstein* (1931) and *The Old Dark House* (1932). In the late 1930s and early 1940s he turned to more realist dramas and thrillers – *They won't Forget* (1937), *Each Dawn I Die* (1939), *The Maltese Falcon* (1941) and *Casablanca* (1942) – where his subtle use of shadows, coolly lit interiors and mysterious close-ups helped to create a world of tense, suppressed violence. JG

Edison, Thomas Alva (1847–1931)

Born in Milan, Ohio, USA. Inventor and the

Clint Eastwood and Shirley MacLaine in 'Two Mules for Sister Sara' (Don Siegel, USA, 1969)

originator of the kinetoscope and of 35 mm film. Virtually self-educated, he began to experiment in mechanical invention at the age of ten. Devoting his whole time to invention from around 1870, he set up his first research laboratory to develop inventions in 1876, with research teams to work on any project he felt had possibilities. His inventions relating to the cinema developed at his second plant at West Orange, founded in 1887, by a senior assistant, W. K. L. Dickson. Dickson invented the kinetograph camera and kinetoscope individual peepshow viewer in 1891; these were exhibited in 1893 and commercialized. Edison also established the 35 mm standard-width film, perforated at the side to secure exact control of the movement and positioning of the film as it passes through camera and projector.

Edit

To assemble the scenes of a film in the required order and to the required lengths, with their accompanying sound tracks.

Editing Film

Editing, in the cinema, is the process of joining distinct and individual pieces of film in meaningful juxtaposition. At certain times in the cinema's history the editing process has seemed the whole basis of film art (PUDOVKIN wrote: 'Film art begins from the moment when the director begins to combine and join together the various pieces of the film'); at other times – and in much current film practice – this aspect of film technique has seemed less significant.

In the origins of the cinema, films were literally 'animated photographs'. The merit of the first EDISON and LUMIÈRE films, as far as their audiences were concerned, was that they *moved*. The motion picture film was an extension of the still photographer's art; and the first repertory of the film was very much that of the photographer: a portrait, a street scene, a simple action, a visual joke like *Watering the Gardener*, which might just as easily have been presented in a two-picture comic cartoon drawing. The possibility that the film might be a narrative or dramatic form suggested itself when film-makers began to present costume tableaux and to restage topical events – the natural film equivalent to the artists' impressions which appeared in the illustrated papers of the day.

From this it was not a great step – again given the example of series-illustrations in magazines, or of 'sets' of slides for the magic lantern, to assemble whole series of these *tableaux vivants*. As early as Easter 1898 two rival American firms presented *Passion of Our Lord*, each in a series of a dozen or so scenes whose resemblance to magic lantern lectures or series of slides for the stereoscope is immediately apparent. Soon afterwards GEORGES MÉLIÈS was using similar tableau techniques for his reconstruction of the Dreyfus affair, fairy tales like *Cinderella*, and a *Life of Joan of Arc*, in ten scenes. The method now became general for story films. Each individual shot represented a single and self-contained scene with its own setting and its own entrances and exits, rather as in the theatre. The only link between the shots was the same sort of chronological logic as connects the scenes of a stage play.

The first indication of the possibility of closer linkage of shot content came in Méliès's *Barbe Bleue*, in twelve tableaux, which appeared towards the end of 1901. One tableau ends with a character descending the stairs of a tower and exiting through a door; the succeeding scene shows the *outside* of the same tower, and begins with the same character emerging from the *outside* of the same door. This is a remarkable portent; but for the first sustained and significant effort towards a modern conception of editing we have to wait until the end of 1902 or the beginning of 1903, and EDWIN S. PORTER's *Life of an American Fireman*. Taking random scenes of fires and firemen (a favourite subject with the early film-makers as for the earlier magic lantern showmen), he assembled them together with newly shot material to form a dramatic film. The eight tableaux were:

1 A sleeping fireman dreams that a woman and child are in danger (conveyed by a double exposure); and wakes.
2 Close-up of an alarm signal. A hand comes into the frame and sets off the alarm.
3 Interior of the firehouse: the firemen respond to the alarm and slide down the pole from their dormitory into
4 Interior of firehouse, lower floor. The horses are harnessed and the fire-engine leaves.
5 Street: the fire-engine leaves the firehouse.
6 Street: fire-engine en route to the fire.
7 House interior: fireman rescues mother and child.

'Porter's decision to construct a story film from previously shot material was unprecedented', wrote KAREL REISZ in his 'Technique of Film Editing'. 'It implied that the meaning of a shot was not necessarily self-contained but could be modified by joining the shot to others . . .' Separate shots, from quite different sources, were joined together so as to give an illusion of a single continuous action.

At the end of 1903 Porter used his new-found editing technique with still greater freedom and flair, in *The Great Train Robbery*, in which he introduced the idea of parallel and overlapping action. One scene, for instance, shows the bandits making off towards the scene of their crime; the next shows the rescue of a telegraph operator whom they have left bound and gagged, by his little daughter; the next shows a dance hall, with an energetic barn-dance in progress, in the course of which the door bursts open and the exhausted but now freed operator suddenly appears with news of the impending robbery. Even today the action of this ten-minute film is still telling. For the audiences of 1903 it was a revelation, stirring them and exciting them more than anything they had previously seen on the screen.

Perhaps audiences were unaware to what extent the drama and emotional power of the film were due to Porter's new method of juxtaposing shots and images; but film-makers clearly did recognize the fact; and began to analyse Porter's discoveries. By 1905 CECIL HEPWORTH, in Britain, was able to edit his *Rescued by Rover* with notable sophistication and fluidity; and, though the tableau film was to survive to a degree for many more years, Porter's style of editing rapidly became general practice.

D. W. GRIFFITH's first job in films was as an actor in Porter's *Rescued from an Eagle's Nest* (1907). The following year he directed his first film, *The Adventures of Dollie*, at the American Biograph company, and from that moment set himself to achieve technical mastery of the medium. He rapidly developed all the possibilities indicated by Porter's discoveries and made new ones of his own. His fundamental advance over Porter was to split up a scene into small fragments, isolated elements incomplete in themselves, out of which he reassembled the whole. To quote Reisz again, 'Where Porter's camera had impartially recorded the action from a distance (i.e. in long-shot) Griffith demonstrated that the camera could play a positive part in telling the story. By splitting an event into short fragments and recording each from the most suitable camera position, he could vary the emphasis from shot to shot and thereby control the dramatic intensity of the events as the story progressed'.

Griffith's development of the principle of cutting within a scene seems to date from *After Many Years* (an adaptation of 'Enoch Arden', made in November 1908) only four months after his début as a director. Mrs Griffith recorded the difficulty her husband experienced in persuading the directors of Biograph that the audience would understand the juxtaposition of a shot showing Annie Lee waiting for her husband's return, and a scene of Enoch Arden cast away on a desert island: 'How can you tell a story jumping about like that? The people won't know what it's about'. Griffith defended his point with the analogy of the technique of the novelist; and his recognition of the similarity of montage to the methods of literature is especially interesting since it was to be taken up and developed much later by Eisenstein. By 1909 (*The Lonely Villa*) he was already employing the device of cross-cutting between parallel actions for the sake of suspense and drama – the celebrated 'Griffith Last-minute Rescue'. By 1912 (*The New York Hat*) he was freely using the flashback. The editing process had learned to control time as well as space. Griffith's methods and innovations were studied and adopted by practically every other American film-maker of the time. They reached their apogee however in his two great masterworks of 1915 and 1916, *Birth of a Nation* and *Intolerance*. These films were seen and studied all over the world, and had a profound influence on film-craft, establishing the styles of editing that were to be accepted for the next four decades.

In particular they were studied in the USSR, from which the next profound contributions to the art and conception of editing were to come. The special gift of the Russians was for rationalizing practice into theories. Even before the Revolution, LEV KULESHOV, then a designer and assistant to Yevgenii Bauer, had published a series of articles on film theory which were far ahead of his time. In 1920 he was given a studio, or 'Workshop', to study film methods with a group of students barely younger than his own 20 years. Research was interrupted by service at the front, and by the total unavailability of raw film stock; but by 1922 he was able to rake up enough film to make his experiments in montage which became famous as The Kuleshov Effect. In one experiment a series of shots taken at different times and at places as far apart as Red Square and the White House, was assembled to give the impression of a simple action in a single location. In another, images of different parts of the bodies of separate girls were assembled to give the spectator the impression that he was seeing only one girl, making up before a mirror. In the most famous of the experiments, the identical shot of the face of the actor MOZHUKIN was juxtaposed with shots of a plate of soup, a dead woman, a little girl playing with her toys. 'When we showed the three combinations to an audience which had not been let into the secret the result was terrific. The public raved about the acting of the artist... But we knew that in all three cases the face was exactly the same.' Griffith's discovery was to use editing to assemble individual elements into a continuous story. Kuleshov advanced further to show how the juxtaposition of shots can alter the intrinsic meaning of each shot. PUDOVKIN offered another example of the effect. To assemble shots of a smiling man, the close-up of a pistol and of the same man looking afraid, in that order, would indicate that the man was a coward; but if the same shots were placed in exactly the *reverse* order the audience would perceive the actor's reaction as bravery. A simple change in the order of the shots completely alters the emotional effect. Pudovkin's own films were the most notable vindication of Kuleshov's theories of montage.

EISENSTEIN, who had spent a very brief period as a Kuleshov student, developed theories of montage which diverged from the Kuleshov-Pudovkin view; and the contemporaries of Eisenstein and Pudovkin delighted in fanning the debate into angry partisanship. 'Pudovkin, in his theory of constructive editing, claimed that a scene is most effectively presented by linking together a series of especially chosen details of the scene's action. Eisenstein emphatically opposed this view. He believed that to build up an impression by simply adding together a series of details was only the most elementary application of film editing. Instead of linking shots in a smooth sequence, Eisenstein held that a proper film continuity should proceed by a series of shocks; that each cut should give rise to a conflict between the two shots being spliced and thereby create a fresh impression in the spectator's mind' (KAREL REISZ, op. cit.). The debate was purely theoretical. Essentially Eisenstein's most significant innovation was the use of editing to convey purely intellectual juxtapositions and impressions (as in *Battleship Potemkin*, 1925), rather than simple narrative continuities. The method (rapidly to be disapproved in the USSR as smacking of 'formalism' and dangerous 'intellectualism') was seen at its most highly developed in *October* (1928), for instance in the sequence in which Kerensky's ambitious rise to power is symbolized by shots of his mounting the stairway of the Winter Palace; and in another where symbols of religion are presented in a rapid and complex collage.

With modifications suggested by Eisenstein's intellectually more complex method, the Griffith method of film editing dominated the cinema for many years, though with the coming of sound and the increased technical complications of cutting, the fluidity and freedom the cinema had achieved in the best work of late silent days tended to be sacrificed. For 40 years there were only intermittent signs of revolt, as when Hitchcock introduced the celebrated ten-minute take into his adaptation of Patrick Hamilton's *Rope* (1948); and there were always directors whose independent styles stood apart from the post-Griffith conventions of unvaried rapid cutting: among them STROHEIM, RENOIR, KEATON, MURNAU and MIZOGUCHI.

It was not until the later 1950s that a concerted reaction against the old conventions became evident. Largely this was the result of the new screen shapes and sizes which were introduced in the course of the cinema's struggles against television. On the huge Cinerama or CinemaScope screen the old-style rapid rhythmic cutting appeared obtrusive and awkward, and sequences like Eisenstein's in *October* were unthinkable. The first fear was that the cinema had lost its basic tool. LEWIS MILESTONE mourned, in a questionnaire published in 'Sight and Sound', that 'the director is forced to throw away the "screen" for the "stage" technique. He loses the use of the close-up, the rhythmic cutting, and other advantages . . .'. But another veteran, Griffith's nearest American rival in the mastery of the old silent montage technique, HENRY KING, perceived that 'This lens enables the director . . . for the first time to show on the screen cause and effect in the same shot, whereas before we used to have to cut from cause to effect in a story, which in a great measure slowed down the pace and prevented the actors from playing long scenes and really feeling the characterizations, as they do on the stage. . . . We need fewer camera set-ups with this new lens and it brings to the screen a measure of three-dimensional illusion which adds tremendously to the realism of any story we are projecting.'

This statement was made in 1955. King's feeling was to be rationalized – as Eisenstein had rationalized Griffith's practice – by ANDRE BAZIN (1918–58), the most influential French critic of his time. He questioned the validity of the old forms of cinema in which the story was told in successions of small shots, and by the use of such devices as cross-cutting; and he laid down dogmatic principles of reform, such as: 'When the essence of an event is dependent on the simultaneous presence of two or more factors in the action, cutting is forbidden.' Among the directors he singled out for particular praise were Murnau and von Stroheim, in whose films 'reality admits its meaning like a suspect who is being grilled by the police. The principle of his direction, a simple one, is to look at the world from so close and with such insistence that it ends up by revealing its cruelty and its ugliness. One can well imagine, in theory, a Stroheim film composed of a single shot, which would be as long and as close-up as one liked.' He admired Renoir, who had developed the travelling camera and composition in depth to liberate himself from the necessity of cutting; and WELLES, who equally employed deep-focus compositions to produce dramatic effects within the shot.

Bazin's disciples and colleagues on the magazine 'Cahiers du Cinéma' figured most prominently in the young renaissance of the French cinema at the end of the 1950s which was popularly known as the *nouvelle vague*; and their work delivered a decisive blow to the slavish acceptance of the old Pudovkin notion that 'film art begins when the director begins to join together the various pieces of the film'. A still more extreme position was taken by the Hungarian director, MIKLÓS JANCSÓ, who composed whole feature films such as *The Confrontation* (1968) and *Silence and Cry* (1969), on the anti-montage principle, some in as few as twenty shots, running as long as ten minutes, and with the action and camera movement in them composed choreographically. With the 1970s, however, it seemed that the outcome of the editing debate would continue to be a compromise between the extreme positions of the montage and the total anti-montage principles. DR

Editing Machine

A machine that enables the editor to view the film and listen to the recorded sound, to facilitate editing.

Editola

Trade name for a make of editing machine

Edwards, Blake

Born 1922 in Oklahoma, USA. American film and television writer, producer and director whose gift for caustic story-telling has increasingly suffered under the strain of extrava-

Opposite: From top to bottom, frames from the Odessa Steps sequence in 'Battleship Potemkin' (Sergei Eisenstein, USSR, 1925)

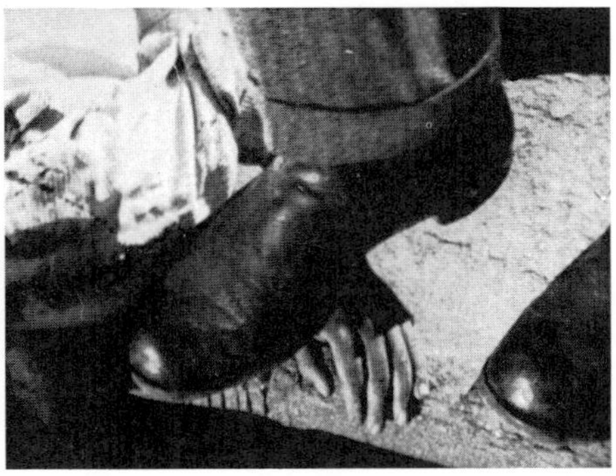

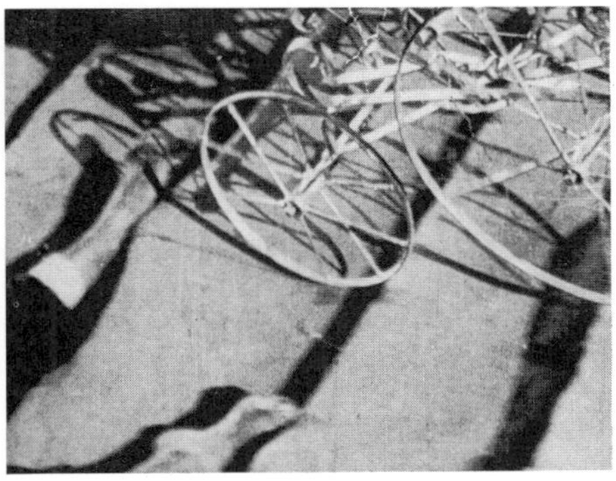

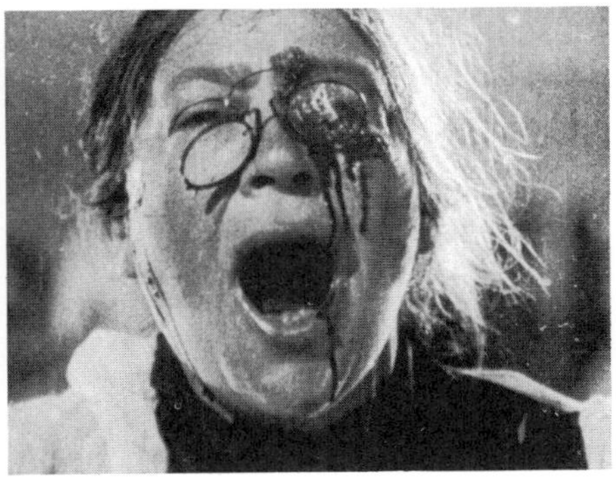

gant production and over-fussy technique. Starting out as a radio script-writer after the Second World War, he created several popular television series including *Peter Gunn*. Before making his début as a film director, he distinguished himself as a writer of sharp, lively screenplays – notably *Drive A Crooked Road* (1954) and *My Sister Eileen* (1955). A successful minor comedy-melodrama, *Mister Cory* (1958), which he wrote and directed for Universal, launched him as a popular modern film-maker with an elegant visual style and sophisticated comic sense.

Other main films: *Operation Petticoat* (1959), *Breakfast at Tiffany's* (1961), *The Pink Panther* (1963), *The Great Race* (1964), *The Party* (1968), *Darling Lili* (1969), *Wild Rovers* (1971).

Effects Track
In re-recording. The track on which the sound effects are carried.

Egypt
See ARAB FILM

Eisenstein, Sergei Mikhailovitch
(1898–1948)
Born in Riga, Russia. A director sometimes described as 'a modern Leonardo', Eisenstein was an artist bursting with creativity; and yet the circumstances of his career permitted him to complete only six films in the course of 25 years. Even so, his importance is out of all proportion to the slight bulk of his work. The intellectual and expressive possibilities revealed by *Strike*, *Battleship Potemkin* and *October* and the vast culture and intelligence he brought to film-making, film teaching and the problems of aesthetic theory in the cinema establish him firmly as one of the incontestable great masters of the art.

He was born into a middle-class Jewish family in Riga, and studied at the Institute of Civil Engineering in Petrograd. Following service in the Red Army, the greatest influence upon his career was the brief period he spent as a pupil of MEYERHOLD: although he rapidly became restive and struck out on his own, his own rational and analytical approach to art theory clearly reflects that of Meyerhold himself. After various essays as a designer, he worked from 1920 as a designer and director at the Proletkult Theatre; and it was during his production of Ostrovsky's 'Enough Simplicity in Every Wise Man' (1923) that he first tried his hand at film-making, devising the short fragment *Glumov's Diary* (a skit on DZIGA VERTOV's *Kino Pravda*) as an interlude in the stage production.

In 1924 Eisenstein was given a chance to direct a full-length film. *Strike* still bears clear evidence of his theatrical experiences and the influence of the then fashionable 'eccentricism'; but it was in every respect revolutionary, introducing for the first time on the screen the idea of the mass as hero. *Battleship Potemkin* (1925) was intended only as an episode in a spectacle

Above: Audrey Hepburn in 'Breakfast at Tiffany's' (Blake Edwards, USA, 1961)
Below and right: Sergei Eisenstein (late 1920s and mid-1940s)

to commemorate the anniversary of the 1905 revolution, but grew to be a full-length film – a totally new concept of revolutionary drama as well as film-editing techniques, which rapidly gained Eisenstein an international reputation, though it was less quickly accepted by the Soviet public for which it was intended. Work on *The General Line* was interrupted by a commission to make a film to commemorate the tenth anniversary of the October Revolution; and when it came out in 1929 it was retitled *The Old and the New* as a result of intermediate changes in official agrarian policy. The commemoration film, *October* (1928), took to extremes Eisenstein's experiments in using montage for intellectual, instead of simply narrative effect; and for this reason was somewhat criticized in the Soviet Union. Abroad however it only enhanced Eisenstein's reputation, which was at its peak when, along with ALEXANDROV and his cameraman, EDUARD TISSÉ, he embarked upon an extended tour of Europe and America, where the group was commissioned to prepare a film for Paramount. Two scripts – *Sutter's Gold* and *An American Tragedy* – were written, but all projects proved abortive and the trio moved on to Mexico to make a film with money raised by Upton Sinclair. Lack of funds and eventual disagreement with Sinclair's collaborators prevented Eisenstein from completing *Que Viva Mexico!* and in 1931 he returned home. For the remaining years of his life most of Eisenstein's creative energies were necessarily devoted to writing and teaching at the State Institute of Cinematography.

Two versions of a film on collectivization, *Bezhin Meadow* (1934–6), were begun but abandoned owing to accident and change in official agricultural policy; and not until 1938 did Eisenstein complete his first sound film, *Alexander Nevsky*, with a brilliantly integrated score by Prokofiev. Prokofiev also wrote the music for the monumental *Ivan the Terrible* (1943–6), which was halted by adverse criticism after only two of its three parts were completed. The second part was only released in 1958, ten years after the death of Eisenstein from a heart attack in 1948. In 1952 Marie Seton published a biography of Eisenstein, while translations of his own writings on film can be found in 'The Film Sense' (1943) and 'Film Form' (1949). DR

Eisler, Hanns (1898–1962)
Born in Leipzig, Germany. Composer. Trained under Arnold Schönberg in Vienna, later working in the theatre with Berthold Brecht and Slatan Dudow, who studied to become a film-maker under Eisenstein in the USSR. Eisler's initial scores for films included that for Dudow's left-wing German film, *Kuhle Wampe* (1932). In 1933 Eisler left Germany, composing notable scores in contemporary style for films made in a number of countries, especially JORIS IVENS' Russian *Komsomol* (1932), his Dutch documentary *New Earth* (1934), which integrated natural sound with music using strings and woodwind as well as jazz form, and Ivens' American-sponsored documentary shot in China, *The 400 Million* (1939). He also wrote the score for FEYDER's *Le Grand Jeu* (1934) in France. In 1939 he settled for a while in the United States, where he wrote scores for such films as LANG's *Hangmen also Die* (1942), CLIFFORD ODETS's *None but the Lonely Heart* (1944) and RENOIR's *The Woman on the Beach* (1947). After the war he went to work in East Germany, composing once again for Dudow on the film *Unser Täglich Brot* (1949), and also working on CAVALCANTI's film made with Brecht, *Herr Puntila und sein Knecht Matti* (1955). Apart from several other films in East Germany, Eisler composed a brilliant score for RESNAIS's *Nuit et Brouillard* (1955) and for DAQUIN's *Bel Ami* (1955). In 1947 his corruscating book on film music, 'Composing for the Films', was published in English translation. RM

Ekk, Nikolai
Born 1898 in Moscow, USSR. Director. Originally an actor with Meyerhold and subsequently a documentary director, Ekk is remembered for one film only – the still admirable *The Road to Life* (1931), one of the earliest Soviet sound films, which dealt with the plight of children abandoned after the Revolution. His subsequent films were *Nightingale, Little Nightingale* (1936, the first Soviet story colour film), *Sorochinski Fair* (after Gogol, 1939), *A May Night* (after Gogol, 1941).

Elton, Arthur
Born 1906 in England. Documentary director and producer. Educated Marlborough and Cambridge. Entered the film industry in the scenario department of Gainsborough in 1927; moved over to documentary films when he joined JOHN GRIERSON at the Empire Marketing Board Film Unit in 1930, and remaining when it became the GPO Film Unit in 1934. With JOHN GRIERSON and BASIL WRIGHT founded Film Centre in 1937. During the war, from 1941–4, he supervised production for the Ministry of Information, leaving to rejoin Film Centre, to which he was attached in 1945–57. Film Adviser to the Danish Government, 1946, and to the British Commission in Germany, 1947. Later worked for Shell International and for Associated Electrical Industries. His films include *Voice of the World, Upstream, Aero-Engine* (1934), *Housing Problems* (with EDGAR ANSTEY, 1935), and *Dawn of Iran* (1938). He has served on many bodies concerned with film interests, including the National Film Archive Committee, the British Film Institute, the Scientific Film Association. Joint author of UNESCO's 'Film Production in Six European Countries' (1951), author of 'Film as Source Material for History' (ASLIB, 1955).

Elvey, Maurice (1887–1967)
Born in Darlington, England. Real name William Folkard. The most prolific director in the history of the British cinema, Elvey began his career as an actor at the Theatre Royal, Nottingham. His first film was *Maria Marten* (1914) and in the course of the next 40 years he made some 300 features. His most admired silent films were *Nelson* (1918), *The Wandering Jew* (1923), *Mademoiselle from Armentières* (1926) and *Roses of Picardy* (1927). In the sound period he directed vehicles starring the British comediennes Gracie Fields (*Sally in Our Alley*, 1932) and Cicely Courtneidge (*Soldiers of the King*, 1933; *Under Your Hat*, 1941); he continued to specialize in comedy, his last films being *Fun at St Fanny's* (1955) and *Dry Rot* (1956).

Emmer, Luciano
Born 1918 in Milan, Italy. Director. After some political tension with the fascist régime, which disapproved of his attempts at documentary, Emmer moved for a while to Switzerland, but did not escape a period of confinement in a German prison camp. The initial phase of Emmer's career in films lay in the development, in collaboration with Enrico Gras, of short film studies of art and artists, with an emphasis on mood and dramatic narrative, notably where this could be built from a dynamically edited succession of details of action in the still paintings. Their films included *Paradise Lost* (1948, Bosch's altarpiece in the Escurial, Madrid), *The Drama of Christ* (1948, Giotto's frescoes in the Cappalla degli Scrovegni, Padua), *The Legend of St Ursula* (1948–9, Carpaccio's paintings in the Accademia, Venice), *The Legend of the True Cross* (1948–9, Piero della Francesca's paintings in the church of St Francis at Arezzo), *Goya* (1950), *Leonardo da Vinci* (1952), *Picasso* (1954). In addition, they made such sensitive, impressionistic documentaries on Venice and its surroundings as *Isole nella Laguna* and *Romantica a Venezia* (both 1948). In 1950 Emmer directed the first of his neo-realist feature films, *Domenica d'Agosto* (1950), an affectionate, comic portrait of Italian middle-class life. This was followed by *Parigi è sempre Parigi* (1951), *Ragazze di Piazza di Spagna* (1952), *Il Bigamo* (1956), *Il Momento più bello* (1957) and *La Ragazza in Vetrina* (1960). RM

Emulsion
A suspension of light-sensitive material, such as a silver halide, in a very finely divided state, in a medium such as gelatin.

Engel, Morris
Born 1918 in New York, USA. Director. Along with CASSAVETES, helped to set the fashion for making low-budget and off-beat independent feature films. He was a professional photographer, and working with Ruth Orkin he made *The Little Fugitive* (1953) and *Lovers and Lollipops* (1955); on the latter he acted as cameraman as well. His subsequent work includes *Weddings and Babies* (1958).

England
See GREAT BRITAIN

Epstein, Jean (1899–1953)
Born in Warsaw, Poland. Director and writer on film. He published an early study of the film, 'Bonjour Cinéma' in 1922, and the following year collaborated with JEAN BENOIT-LÉVY in the film *Pasteur* (1922), an official documentary study of the work of Pasteur. He then began a career which made him one of the leading imaginative directors of the French silent cinema, as well as a writer of influential essays and even poems in praise of the stars of the American screen. In 1923 he directed *L'Auberge Rouge* (from Balzac) and *Cœur Fidèle*, perhaps his best film, concerning rivalry in love between two men, and including a fairground sequence which became celebrated for its mobile camerawork. He also made in the same year *La Belle Nivernaise* (after Daudet) giving a picture of life on a canal barge. His later films showed some decline: they include *Le Lion des Moguls* (1924), featuring the exiled Russian actor, IVAN MOZHUKIN, *Robert Macaire* (1925), *The Fall of the House of Usher* (1928, after Poe), and other somewhat mannered productions. His documentary-style features – *Finis Terrae* (1928), followed by the sound films *Mor-Vran* (*The Sea of Crows*, 1930) and *L'Or des Mers* (1932), all set in the islands off Brittany, – represented a return to realism in their portrayal of a stark, natural environment. His later films included *Les Bâtisseurs* (1937) and *Le Tempestaire* (1947). RM

Ermler, Friedrich (1898–1969)
Born in Latvia, USSR. Director. A party member from the time of his youth, Ermler was the most dedicated Communist among all Soviet film-makers. But even during the period when he was most deeply committed to Stalinist and socialist-realist viewpoints, the hard-line didacticism of his films was offset by a personal warmth and an inescapable sense of reality. His early films all dealt with revolutionary situations or socio-economic problems of the new state: *Skarlatina* (1924), *Katka's Reinert Apples* and *Children of the Storm* (1926), *House on the Snow* and *The Parisian Cobbler* (1928). His masterpiece was *Fragment of an Empire* (1929), which showed a departure from the almost neo-realist styles of his earlier films. He collaborated with YUTKEVITCH on an early sound film, *Counterplan*, then went on to films of obvious propaganda utility: *Peasants* (1935), about the kulak problem, and *The Great Citizen* (1938–9), which presented the official version of the Kirov trials. Later films: *She Defends Her Country* (1943), *The Great Turning Point* (1945), *The Great Power* (1950), *Unfinished Story* (1955). Ermler's last film was perhaps his most interesting: *Before the Judgment of History* (1967) brought to the screen Shulgin, one of the survivors of the last Duma, to debate the events of the Revolution and the fall of the Russian empire. DR

Establishing Shot
The scene at the beginning of a sequence in a film, generally a long shot, which establishes to the audience the location of the action in time or place.

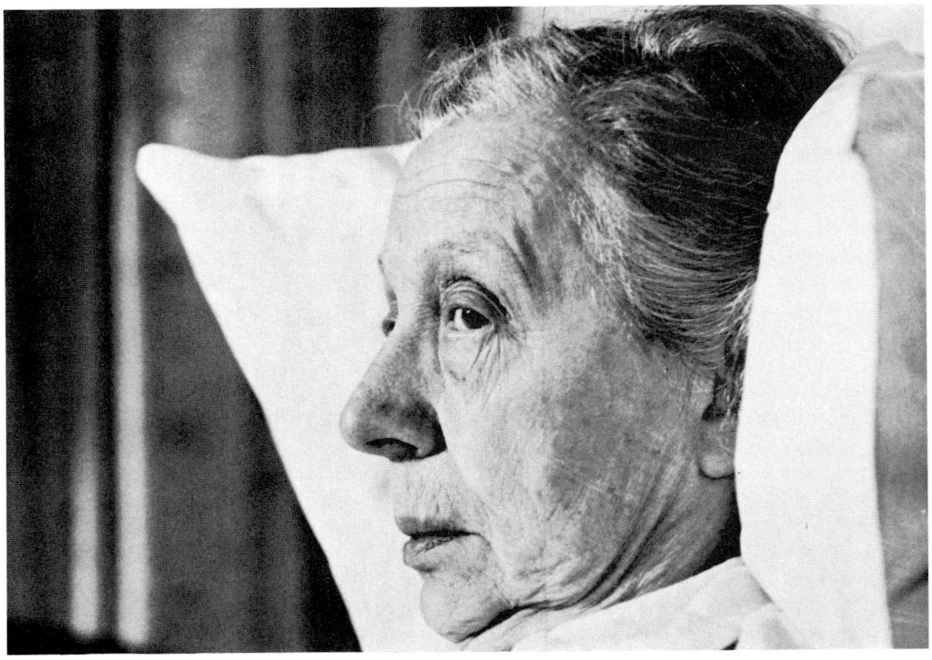

Above: Edith Evans in 'The Whisperers' (Bryan Forbes, GB, 1966)
Below: Pierre Étaix and Nicole Calfan in 'Le Grand Amour' (Étaix, France, 1969)

Etaix, Pierre
Born 1928 in Roanne, France. Piquant French comedian and director, reminiscent of KEATON and JACQUES TATI, who have obviously influenced his style of near-silent film humour. Trained in the circus and music hall, he acted in several dramatic films, including BRESSON's *Pickpocket* (1959), and made a number of short films before embarking on his first solo comedy feature, *Le Soupirant* (1962), which he directed, co-scripted and starred in. Although exceedingly elegant and beautifully designed, his comedies tend to lack variety and the personal fervour which distinguishes Tati's films. Other films: *Yoyo* (1965), *Tant qu'on a la Santé* (1966), *Le Grand Amour* (1969).

Exciter Lamp
Source of light in the sound head of a projector which shines through the sound track on to a photo-electric cell.

Expose
To produce a latent image in a photographic material by the action of light

Exposure
The product of the time of exposure and the intensity of illumination upon photographic material

Extra
An actor without lines to speak who is normally hired by the day to appear in crowd scenes.

Evans, Edith
Born 1888 in Pimlico, London, England. Actress, who performs primarily on the stage. Versatile and brilliant, she made her first stage appearance in 1912 as Cressida, afterwards touring with Ellen Terry in Shakespearean repertory. Since then she has given innumerable distinguished performances on the stage and in films. She was made a Dame of the British Empire in 1949. Main films: *The Queen of Spades* (in which she made her début, 1949), *The Importance of Being Earnest* (1953), *Look Back in Anger* and *The Nun's Story* (1959), *Tom Jones* (1963), *The Chalk Garden* (1964), *The Whisperers* (1967), *Prudence and the Pill* (1968), *David Copperfield* and *Scrooge* (1970).

F

Fábri, Zoltán
Born 1917 in Budapest, Hungary. Director. Originally trained as an artist, Fábri graduated from the Academy of Dramatic and Film Art of Budapest and began his professional career in the theatre. His first films – *The Storm* (1952) and *Fourteen Lives* (1954) – were made under the period of Rákosi's oppression; but with the thaw of the mid-1950s Fábri assumed a leading place in the Hungarian New Wave, with *Merry-Go-Round* (1955) and *Professor Hannibal* (1956). Fábri's best films in the 1960s were *Half Time in Hell* (1961) and *Twenty Hours* (1964), which looked back, with extreme frankness, to the problems of post-war collectivization of agriculture. Later films – *The Boys from Pál Street* (1968) and *The Toth Family* (1970) – have been disappointingly literary in manner. Other films: *Summer Clouds* (1957), *Sweet Anna* (1958), *The Brute* (1959), *Darkness in Daytime* (1963), *A Hard Summer* (made for television, 1965), *Late Season* (1967). DR

Factor, Max (1877–1938)
Born in Lodz, Poland. Doyen of Hollywood make-up experts, who emigrated to America in 1904, arrived in Los Angeles in 1908 and created the first special make-up for films. He worked with all the great silent artists. When he died his son took over as head of the business, which through its glamour association with Hollywood became one of the major commercial cosmetic companies throughout the world.

Factual Film
See DOCUMENTARY

Fade-In
(1) The gradual appearance of a projected screen image from total darkness to full screen brilliancy.
(2) To increase the level of sound gradually from inaudibility to the required volume.

Fade-Out
The reverse of Fade-In

Fairbanks Sr, Douglas (1883–1939)
Born in Colorado, USA. Swashbuckling idol of the 1920s and co-founder, with his wife MARY PICKFORD, CHARLES CHAPLIN and D. W. GRIFFITH, of United Artists Film Corporation in 1919. His extraordinary athletic grace and agility enhanced a restricted acting talent, which eventually forced him into retirement in the 1930s when he could no longer cope so energetically with the physical demands of his earlier adventure roles.

Born into a well-to-do middle-class family, Fairbanks enjoyed a restless youth, in which acting played a casual part until in 1915 he was signed by Harry Aitken to work for Triangle. But it was Anita Loos and director John Emerson who realized the potential of the boisterous young man. She wrote for him a series of comedies in which the extrovert Fairbanks debunked weaklings and current fads.

His greatest success, however, was in the field of costume adventure in *The Mark of Zorro* and *The Three Musketeers* (1921), the elaborately designed *Robin Hood* (1922), *The Thief of Bagdad* (1924) and *The Black Pirate* (1926). As his subsequent films grew more extravagant his performances tended to atrophy into a series of stunning daredevil stunts.

In 1929, he and his wife starred in a talking film (his first), a version of *The Taming of the Shrew*, and both revealed a pleasing aptitude for the Shakespearean roles which apparently were truer to life than Hollywood knew. Their marriage – the most glamorous, indeed regal, in Hollywood – broke up shortly after the film.

Fairbanks continued to make talking pictures. His last film was made in Britain, *The Private Life of Don Juan* (1934). In 1939 he was awarded a posthumous Academy Award

Douglas Fairbanks Snr in 'The Thief of Bagdad' (Raoul Walsh, USA, 1924)

for his 'unique and outstanding contribution to the international development of the motion picture'. His son Douglas Fairbanks Jr also became an actor of note.

Other principal films: his first, *The Lamb* (1914), *Manhattan Madness* (1916), *The Gaucho* (1927), *The Iron Mask* (1929), *Mr Robinson Crusoe* (1932). See 'Douglas Fairbanks: the Making of a Screen Character' by Alistair Cooke (1940). MH

Feature Film
Film at least 3,000 feet (910 metres) long, if 35 mm film is used

Fejös, Paul (1898–1963)
Born in Budapest, Hungary. Director and one of the most intriguing figures in the history of the cinema. Fejös's career constantly veered between films and a first love for science. He had made a few commercial films in Hungary before arriving in America to work in the bacteriological department of the Rockefeller Institution. The stage attracted him however, and he joined Theatre Guild for Molnar's 'Glass Slipper' (1924). Challenged by an offer of $5,000 to make an experimental film he made *The Last Moment* (1927) in four weeks and on the strength of it was offered a contract by Universal. The result was the brilliant *Lonesome* (1928) with its precocious *cinéma-vérité* techniques and its warm and human observation. After two more American films in 1929 *(Broadway* and *The Last Performance)* and French and German versions of Hill's *The Big House*, he returned to Europe to make *Fantômas* (1932) in France; *Maria, Hungarian Legend* and *Condemned Balaton* (1932) in Hungary; *Sonnenstrahl* (1933) in Austria; *Flight of Millions* (1933), *Prisoner No 1*, *The Outlaw* and *The Golden Smile* (1935) in Denmark; *A Handful of Rice* (1938) in Siam and several documentaries in Switzerland. Finally he returned to America and anthropology. DR

Fellini, Federico
Born 1920 in Rimini, Italy. Director. The son of a commercial traveller, he ran away at the age of 12 to join a circus and left home finally at 17. He worked in Rome as a cartoonist and illustrator for the *fumetti*, as sketch-writer for the theatre, and as ideas-man for film scripts, all of which culminated in his association with ROSSELLINI on *Rome, Open City* (1945) and *Paisa* (1946), and with other neo-realist directors. He was writer and assistant to LATTUADA and GERMI. His first important script was for *The Miracle*, the second part of Rossellini's *Amore* (1947), in which he also played the tramp who seduces the simple-minded peasant-woman who believes her seducer to be a saint; this was followed by the script for Rossellini's *Francesco Giullare di Dio* (1950). Both films showed something of Fellini's highly individual response to religion, a recurrent motif in his later films.

Above: Fernandel in 'Le Rosier de Madame Husson' (Bernard Deschamps, France, 1932)
Below: Federico Fellini (right) during the production of 'Ciao, Federico' (Gideon Bachmann, USA, 1970)

Fellini's first film as a director was *Luci del Varietà* (1950), made with Lattuada, which concerns the experiences of a girl who joins a destitute company of travelling players; the second, *Lo Sceicco Bianco* (*The White Sheik*, 1952), presents the infatuation of a recently-married middle-class woman for the absurd hero of a still-photograph strip production. Both films are ironic, at times gay, at times melancholy and both feature GIULIETTA MASINA, Fellini's wife. Fellini shows his extraordinary capacity to create a pervasive atmosphere out of a combination of strange people and strange places; his characters persist in indulging their illusions. *I Vitelloni* (*The Drifters*, 1953) is a semi-autobiographical study of young men living without purpose in a dead provincial town. Although disillusion is still the theme the film is coloured by the warmth which is an essential part of Fellini's work.

La Strada (1954) fully established Fellini's fame. Like the Franciscans in Rossellini's *Francesco Giullare di Dio*, its heroine Gelsomina, the vagabond performer, is innocent to the point of saintly imbecility. The film is a seemingly disparate flow of episodes, closely integrated by Fellini's command of atmosphere. Next came *Il Bidone* (1955), a powerful story of the destruction of a confidence-trickster; it is on the verge of being a moral tale. *Le Notti di Cabiria* (1957) is more baroque, the story of a saintly whore. Fellini does not want to preach; rather he is the wholly involved observer who draws no stated conclusions but is fascinated by the obsessions he finds around him.

Increasingly his films became projections of these stranger, more subjective worlds – *La Dolce Vita* (1959) was a study of that decadent branch of the cinema on which the *paparazzi* (and through them their public) feast like flies on a dunghill. With *8½* (1963, so-called because it enumerated his films so far, including a scarifyingly funny episode in the composite film, *Boccaccio '70*) he drew closer to the inner worlds of his characters, merging events which are actual and external to them with projections from their imaginings and subconscious memories. The central character of *8½*, played by MARCELLO MASTROIANNI, is a celebrated film director who breaks down under extreme pressure and refuses to face reality. *Giulietta degli Spiriti* (1965) went even further into the conjuration of the subconscious; he dedicated the film 'with affection' to his wife, who features in it. The film which followed – *Fellini–Satyricon* (1969) – is a return to the purely baroque, an extravagant projection of the decadent world of Petronius, and elicited some hostile criticism. Subsequent films include: *Clowns* (1970), *Roma* (1972). For studies of Fellini's work see Suzanne Budgen, 'Fellini', and John Russell Taylor, 'Cinema Eye Cinema Ear'. RM

Fernandel (1903–1971)
Born in Marseilles, France. Popular French comedian whose lugubrious features disguise a warm, folksy personality and an antic sense of the absurd in human behaviour. A vaudevillian and revue artist, he made several notable films in the 1930s, including *Le Rosier de Madame Husson* (*The Virtuous Isidore*, 1932), *Un Carnet de Bal* (1937) and *Fric Frac* (1939), but his greatest consistent success was as the Priest in the *Don Camillo* series of comedies in the 1950s. Other main films include: *La Fille du Puisatier* (1940), *L'auberge Rouge* (1951), *Mam'zelle Nitouche* (1953), *The Sheep has Five Legs* (1954), *The Cow and I* (1959), *L'Homme à la Buick* (1967).

Fernandez, Emilio
Born 1904 in Hondo (Coahuila), Mexico. Director and actor. After a period in America between 1924 and 1933, he established himself as a leading Mexican actor. His virile, Indian appearance made him particularly suitable for gaucho and bandit parts; when he took to direction in the early 1940s, his films explored similar territory taking in tragic, legendary and socially-orientated subjects – *Maria Candelaria* (1943), *The Pearl* (1946), *Rio Escondido* (1947), *Maclovia* (1948), *La Red* (1953). Many of these subjects were given a lush photographic sheen by the great cameraman, GABRIEL FIGUEROA and, in fact, he and Fernandez created the standard Mexican film image, with its vivid sunsets, ornate architecture and richly patterned exteriors. Fernandez has also appeared in several American-produced films, notably *The Wild Bunch* (1969), and assisted JOHN FORD on *The Fugitive* (1947). JG

Feuillade, Louis (1873–1925)
Born in Lunel, France. Director. Having worked as a journalist and playwright, Feuillade joined GAUMONT as a writer in 1906, and the following year succeeded ALICE GUY-BLACHÉ, the world's first woman director, as head of production at the Gaumont Studios. In the course of the next two decades he directed upwards of 800 films and produced hundreds more. When in 1911 Gaumont's finances demanded stringent economies, Feuillade issued a forceful manifesto in defence of cinema realism and launched his series *La Vie telle qu'elle est*, which dealt with real-life and contemporary subjects which could be shot in the streets without sets or special costumes. The gift thus revealed for observing the actual, contemporary scene, was what gave special quality to his mystery serials. The first, *Fantômas* (1913–4) was based on a popular pulp serial by Marcel Allain and Pierre Souvestre; and was followed by ten episodes of *Les Vampires* (1915). In response to objections by the Paris Prefect to unflattering depiction of the police, Feuillade launched *Judex* (1916), whose good and handsome hero was a defender of the law. After this came *La Nouvelle Mission de Judex* (1917), *Tih Minh* (1918) and *Barrabas* (1919). The quality of the serials, wrote a later film-maker, ALAIN RESNAIS, was their ability 'to create mystery and drama from the most everyday elements'; and it was this which so much commended them to the surrealists. Feuillade was in addition a superb director, working in a pre-GRIFFITH technique of long takes, which now looks surprisingly modern, and demanding high standards of photography and composition and of naturalistic acting. Feuillade's large output was not confined to mystery serials. He also directed numerous comedies, notably the *Bébé* series (1910–2) and the *Bout-de-Zan* series (1914–7). Later feature films included *L'Orpheline* and *Parisette* (1921), *Vindicta* and *Le gamin de Paris* (1923), *L'Orpheline de Paris* (1924), *Le Stigmate* (1925). DR

Feuillère, Edwige
Born 1907. French actress, on stage as well as screen. Distinguished member of the Comédie Française whose cool, striking presence and classical style are particularly suited to costume roles. Films include: *Topaze* (1932), *L'Idiot* (1946), *L'Aigle à Deux Têtes* (1947), *Woman Hater* (1948), *Olivia* (1950), *Le Blé en Herbe* (1953), *En Cas de Malheur* (1957), *Le Crime ne paie pas* (1962), *Do you like Women?* (1964).

Feyder, Jacques (1888–1948)
Born in Brussels, Belgium. Director. Feyder came to France in 1914 with ambitions to become an actor, but established himself as a director, his first considerable commercial success being *L'Atlantide* (1921) filmed in the Sahara. His artistic reputation was established with *Crainquebille* (1923), adapted from Anatole France, with touches of German expressionism in its style. He developed a tendency to combine the realistic with the poetic, not always with success. Moving restlessly from place to place for his films, he made the charming *Visages d'Enfants* in Switzerland in 1924 and *L'Image* (1926) in Hungary before directing his celebrated adaptation from Zola's story of a *crime passionel*, *Thérèse Raquin* (1928), in Berlin. This film, with its fine use of décor and magnificent performance by Gina Manès as Thérèse, became a classic of the French silent cinema. After the banning (for political reasons) of his lively satire *Les Nouveaux Messieurs* (1928), Feyder left for Hollywood. where he directed GRETA GARBO in a well-made, glossy silent film, *The Kiss* (1929). Returning to France in 1933, he collaborated with the noted script-writer CHARLES SPAAK on a series of successful films starring his wife, FRANÇOISE ROSAY, and assisted by MARCEL CARNÉ, whom he later helped to make his début as director. These were *Le Grand Jeu* (1934, filmed in N. Africa), *Pension Mimosas* and *La Kermesse Héroïque* (1935), set in 17th-century Flanders, with décor by LAZARE MEERSON. Restless again, Feyder made his next film in England, *Knight without Armour* (1937, with MARLENE DIETRICH). After this he made his last two notable films, *Les Gens du Voyage* (1938), in Munich, and *La Loi du Nord* (1939) in France and Norway. RM

Edwige Feuillère in 'L'Aigle à Deux Têtes' (Jean Cocteau, France, 1947)

Field, Mary (1896–1968)
Born in Wimbledon, England. Director and producer. At first a teacher, she held an M.A. degree of London University. She joined British Instructional Films in 1926, working with H. Bruce Woolfe and PERCY SMITH, with both of whom she transferred to GB Instructional in 1934. She worked on *The Secrets of Nature* series from 1928, *The Secrets of Life* series from 1934, and directed documentaries, including *The King's English* and *The Changing Year* (1932), *They Made the Land* (1938) and *The Medieval Village* (1940). J. ARTHUR RANK made her Executive Producer of Children's Entertainment Films (1944–50); from 1951–9 she served as Executive Officer of the Children's Film Foundation, the all-industry-sponsored organization in Britain responsible for producing entertainment films for children on a non-profit-making basis. [See CHILDREN'S FILMS.] In 1959–63 she was Children's Programme Consultant, ATV/ABC Television. She was the author of a number of books: 'Secrets of Life' (1934), 'Cine-Biology' (1941), 'Boys' and Girls' Book of the Film' (co-author), 'Good Company' (1952), 'See How They Grow' (1953). RM

Fields, William Claude (1897–1946)
Born in Philadelphia, USA. One of the most

original comedians ever to appear in films, Fields, after a hard childhood, doggedly set himself to become the world's greatest juggler, which soon after the turn of the century he was. Eventually the clowning which was integral to his stage act became dominant, and after starring in the Ziegfeld Follies he played the lead in the stage play 'Poppy': it was the character of Eustace McGargle which ultimately defined his comic *persona*. He was the most reprehensible clown ever to win the adoration of his audiences. He was mean, mendacious, larcenous, misanthropic, and generally anti-social. He had thin hair, a huge and unlovely tippler's nose, eyes screwed up in dreadful suspicion, a thin, unyieldingly mean mouth. He professed to hate children and animals. He also hated – and portrayed in all their nasty colours – wives, sons, mothers-in-law, daughters' fiancés, salesmen, bank managers, policemen, film producers, motorists. He first appeared in a short comedy film in 1915 and returned to Hollywood for half a dozen films between 1924 and 1927, including D. W. GRIFFITH's version of 'Poppy' – *Sally of the Sawdust*. Field's asides and unoiled creak of a voice were however an essential part of the character and his film career was only truly fulfilled in the 1930s. In his talking films, his mixture of guile and truculence gained him a degree of independence, and he generally wrote his own stories and dialogue, so as decisively to impose on works like *The Old-Fashioned Way* and *It's a Gift* (1934), *The Bank Dick* and *My Little Chickadee* (1940), *Never Give a Sucker an Even Break* (1941) one of the most individual personalities ever to work in films. A great Dickensian, Fields also played Micawber in GEORGE CUKOR's *David Copperfield* (1934) with great success. In private life a solitary, hard-drinking, mysterious man, Fields was happy to encourage legends that his private and screen persona were one and the same. DR

Figueroa, Gabriel

Born 1907 in Mexico. Outstanding cinematographer. After studying painting, he visited America in the mid-1930s to study photographic methods. Established himself as the leading Mexican cameraman from the 1940s onwards, often collaborating with EMILIO FERNANDEZ – *Maria Candelaria* (1943), *Enamorada* (1946), *Rio Escondido* (1947), *Maclovia* (1948), and others. He created a distinctively ornate, romantic style full of brightly lit exteriors, but significantly simplified his approach when working with BUÑUEL on *Los Olvidados* (1950), *El* (1952), *Nazarin* (1959), *The Exterminating Angel* (1962), *Simon of the Desert* (1965). Here, his lighting retained its rich luminosity (the village and desert exteriors in *Nazarin* and *Simon*) but without the earlier excessive ornamentation. Other films include: *The Fugitive* (1947), *Two Mules for Sister Sara* (1970). JG

Above: W. C. Fields in 'The Big Broadcast of 1938' (Mitchell Leisen, USA, 1938)
Below: Pedro Armendariz in 'Maria Candelaria' (Emilio Fernandez, cameraman Gabriel Figueroa, Mexico, 1943)

Filippo, Eduardo De

See DE FILIPPO

Finch, Peter

Born 1916 in London, England. Actor, who first appeared in Australia and later in London. He quickly gained popularity in England and the USA in films. Main films: *Rats of Tobruk* (made in Australia, 1944), *Robin Hood* (1951), *The Story of Gilbert and Sullivan* (1953), *Father Brown* (1954), *Simon and Laura* and *The Battle of the River Plate* (1955), *A Town Like Alice* and *The Shiralee* (1956), *The Nun's Story* (1958), *Kidnapped* and *The Trials of Oscar Wilde* (as Oscar Wilde; 1960), *No Love for Johnny* (1961), *Girl with Green Eyes* and *The Pumpkin Eater* (1964), *Far from the Madding Crowd* (1967), *Sunday, Bloody Sunday* (1971), *England Made Me* (1972). He brings a special sensitivity and maturity to his studies of vulnerable male characters.

Fine Cut

The version of a work print of a film following the rough cut stage. At each successive stage the cutting is refined as unnecessary footage is eliminated.

Finland

See SCANDINAVIAN FILM

First Run Cinema

Cinema which has the first showing of a film on its general release, the cost of film hire being greater than for a second or third run cinema.

Finney, Albert

Born 1936 in Salford, England. Actor, who made his début on the West End stage in 'The Party' in 1958. Afterwards played at Stratford-upon-Avon and in London in Shakespearean and other productions. His comparatively few films have given him rough-tongued, unconventional characters to play. They include: *The Entertainer* (1959), *Saturday Night and Sunday Morning* (1960), *Tom Jones* and *Night Must Fall* (1963), *Two For the Road* and *Charlie Bubbles* (which he also directed; 1968), *The Picasso Summer* (1969), *Scrooge* (1970), *Gumshoe* (1971).

Fischinger, Oskar (1900–1967)

Born in Gelnhausen, Germany. Animator. Conceived the idea of creating visual interpretations of poetry and music at the age of 19. His first film studies were shown at Düsseldorf in 1925. He entered the film industry to work on special effects, assisting FRITZ LANG on his space-fiction film *The Woman in the Moon*

Top: Albert Finney and Billie Whitelaw in 'Charlie Bubbles' (Finney, GB, 1968)
Above: Barbara Shelley and Christopher Lee in 'Dracula – Prince of Darkness' (Terence Fisher, GB, 1967)

(1928), and beginning in that year his own celebrated abstract, black-and-white designs animated to classical and other music, such as *Study No 5* (1928) choreographed to jazz, *Study No 7* (1931) to Brahms, and *Study No 11* (1932) to Mozart. In 1933 he began to explore colour, using the now obsolete Gaspar-color process he had helped to develop, in *Circles*, an advertising film designed to the music of Grieg and Wagner. In 1935 he won a prize at the Venice Film Festival for *Composition in Blue*, and as a result was invited to Hollywood by Paramount. He joined Disney to work on the semi-experimental *Fantasia* (1940), but his animation was considered too abstract to be included. After various projects for other sponsors, he continued his individual work with *Motion Painting No 1* (1947), an intricately evolving series of patterns in colour to the music of Bach's Brandenburg Concerto No 3, for which he won the Grand Prix at the Brussels Exhibition of 1949. He was one of the most stylish and witty artists to work in the field of abstract film. RM

Fisher, Terence
Born 1904 in London, England. Director. Was film editor from mid-1930s and worked on several WILL HAY comedies. Began directing in 1940s, mainly comedies and romantic dramas (*So Long at the Fair*, 1950), then specialized in horror subjects (mainly for Hammer Films) which earned him considerable reputation in France. Main titles include: *Dracula* (1957), *The Hound of the Baskervilles* (1958), *The Man who could Cheat Death* (1959), *The Phantom of the Opera* (1962), *The Gorgon* (1964), *Island of Terror* (1966), *The Devil Rides Out* (1968), *Frankenstein must be Destroyed* (1969). Fisher skilfully uses colour, design and graphic 'blood' effects to create atmosphere, although his films hardly rival the more reticent, slyly witty approach of JAMES WHALE and others in the 1930s. JG

Flaherty, Robert J. (1884–1951)
Born in Iron Mountain, Michigan, USA. After a romantic childhood as the son of a gold prospector and a voracious reader of Fennimore Cooper and Ballantyne, Flaherty developed a passion and talent for exploration in his teens. On one trip he took a film camera with him; and though the material he shot was all lost, he was encouraged to plan a film on Eskimo life. The result, sponsored by the Revillon Fur Company, was *Nanook of the North* (1922). Its critical and public reception were equivocal; but JESSE LASKY, who had a private passion for exploration, sent Flaherty to the South Seas to try to repeat the *Nanook* experiment. The South Sea islands were a disillusionment to Flaherty, and the film was shot under extreme difficulties; but Flaherty brought back *Moana* (1925), a poetic fantasy of the uncorrupted, traditional life of the islanders that might once have existed. Again the commercial results were not good, and Flaherty occupied himself with a couple of privately-sponsored shorts until MGM invited him to co-direct *White Shadows of the South Seas* with W. S. VAN DYKE; but disagreement with Van Dyke caused Flaherty to abandon the project. Another trip

to the South Seas was made with MURNAU, disillusioned, like Flaherty with the studios; but the result, *Tabu* (1929–31), seems more Murnau than Flaherty. In Britain Flaherty had more success, with a short *Industrial Britain* (1932) for JOHN GRIERSON, and *Man of Aran* (1934), produced by MICHAEL BALCON. *Elephant Boy* (1937) – the culmination of an old ambition to film Kipling, with whose romantic outlook Flaherty had much in common – was compromised by the spectacular elements imposed by his co-director ZOLTAN KORDA. In America Flaherty made *The Land* (1939–42) and his final, and perhaps most perfect feature, *Louisiana Story* (1948), about a child's parallel encounters with nature and an industrial society.

Flaherty was always most interested in the people living in remote communities, when pitting themselves against the natural harshness of their environment (as in *Nanook*) or inventing tests to assert their manhood (as in *Moana*). Flaherty's weakness was that where these conditions no longer existed, he was tempted to invent them (as in *Man of Aran*). As a documentary film-maker, Flaherty belongs to the romantic tradition, of which he was the first real exponent in the USA. DR

Flash Back

A sequence which takes the action or sound back into the past relative to the rest of the story.

Fleischer, Max

Born 1889 in Austria. Animator. Fleischer was brought up in the United States, where after studying art, he became a newspaper cartoonist. His animated cartoons of the early 1920s developed from his *Out of the Inkwell* series (from 1921), in which Koko the Clown emerged from a bottle of ink to gesticulate his way through the simple gags of the pioneer cartoons. Other characters created by Fleischer were Betty Boop, the screen vamp, and Popeye the Sailor (from 1933), whose phenomenal strength came from eating spinach which enabled him to overcome his huge and perennial enemy, Bluto. These cartoons were often very violent, and closely rivalled Disney's work in popularity.

Fleischer tried to develop feature-length work with *Popeye the Sailor meets Sinbad the Sailor* (1936), *Gulliver's Travels* (1939) and *Hoppity goes to Town* (*Mr Bug goes to Town*, 1941), which unfortunately failed. Later Popeye films included *Popeye for President* (1956). Fleischer's interests in animation included instructional films, some mixing live action with animation. The first of these date back to the First World War, when he was employed by the US Army to make films designed to achieve rapid training. Of more lasting interest are his instructional animated films, *Einstein's Theory of Relativity* (1923), made with the help of a team of Einstein's assistants, *Darwin's Theory of Evolution* and other pioneer scientific films. RM

Fleischer, Richard

Born 1916 in New York, USA. Capable American director whose best work is in the delineation of unusual crime themes, most notably *Violent Saturday* (1955), *Compulsion* (1958) and *The Boston Strangler* (1968). In 1970, he made *10 Rillington Place* in Britain, based on a nauseating crime case-history similar to *The Boston Strangler* and filmed in much the same factual style. The son of the animator MAX FLEISCHER, he worked on the stage before joining RKO in 1942. Among a series of unremarkable films, *So This is New York* (1949), a dry comedy for producer STANLEY KRAMER, stands out. Latterly, in between his more personal films, he has been used by Twentieth Century Fox as a reliable, all-purpose director on particularly awkward projects. Nevertheless, his elaborate and over-stuffed musical *Doctor Dolittle* (1967) was one of the company's major flops – mainly because of policy miscalculation rather than Fleischer's direction. Other principal films: *The Narrow Margin* (1951), *The Happy Time* (1952), *Twenty Thousand Leagues Under The Sea* (1954), *The Vikings* (1957), *These Thousand Hills* (1958), *Crack in the Mirror* (1960), *Barabbas* (1962), *Fantastic Voyage* (1966), *Che!* (1969), *Tora! Tora! Tora!* (1970), *Blind Terror* and *The Last Run* (1971), the latter begun by JOHN HUSTON. MH

Errol Flynn in 'The Sea Hawk' (Michael Curtiz, USA, 1940)

Fleming, Victor (1883–1949)

Born in California, USA. One of the most popular of Hollywood directors during the 1930s, with a flair for spectacular action and highly-charged atmosphere, plus the ability to harness important star images – notably CLARK GABLE, SPENCER TRACY – to suitable film vehicles. His most celebrated achievement was *Gone With the Wind* (1939), which he took over after GEORGE CUKOR left and for which he won an Academy Award. A stunt racing driver, he went into the film industry in 1910, working under ALLAN DWAN: he was cameraman on several of the elder Fairbanks films and also worked for D. W. GRIFFITH. After the First World War he was chief photographer for President Wilson at Versailles. He directed his first film – *When the Clouds Roll By* – in 1919. Other principal films: *Red Dust* (1932), *White Sister* (1933), *Treasure Island* (1934), *Captains Courageous* (1937), *Test Pilot* (1938), the record-breaking musical fantasy *The Wizard of Oz* (1939), *Dr Jekyll and Mr Hyde* (1941), *Tortilla Flat* (1942), *A Guy Named Joe* (1944), *Adventure* (1946), *Joan of Arc* (1949). MH

Florey, Robert

Born 1900 in Paris, France. Director and screenwriter. Began his career in France, but went early to the USA in 1921, and became an assistant to VON STERNBERG. Later, still in the silent period, he directed features for Columbia (such as *The Romantic Age*, 1927), and co-directed the first Marx Brothers comedy *The Coconuts* (1929). In the late 1920s he attempted experimental art films: *The Life and Death of 9413 – a Hollywood Extra* and *Johann the Coffinmaker* (1928), *The Loves of Zero* (1929). After a brief return to France, where he directed *Le Blanc et le Noir* in 1931 with MARC ALLÉGRET, he returned to Hollywood, where he scripted *Frankenstein* (1931), and resumed his career as a director of features, including *Murders in the Rue Morgue* (1932), with BELA LUGOSI, *King of the Gamblers* (1937) and *Dangerous to Know* (1938) with Akim Tamiroff, and *The Beast with Five Fingers* (1947). His films were to some extent influenced by romantic German Gothic conventions, and he co-directed with CHAPLIN *Monsieur Verdoux* (1947). He has made television films and written on technique.

Flynn, Errol (1909–1959)

Actor, born in Australia of Irish-American parentage, who led an adventurous life as a boxer and gold prospector before his film characterizations as a virile, handsome hero

(notably in the films of CURTIZ and WALSH) brought him popularity throughout the world. Main films: *Captain Blood* (1935), *The Charge of the Light Brigade* (1936), *The Prince and the Pauper* and *The Adventures of Robin Hood* (1937), *The Private Lives of Elizabeth and Essex* (1939), *They Died with Their Boots On* (1941), *Gentleman Jim* (1942), *Objective Burma* (which was much criticized, 1945), *Cry Wolf* (1947), *The New Adventures of Don Juan* (1948), *The Forsyte Saga* (in which he played Soames, 1949), *The Adventures of Captain Fabian* (which he wrote, 1951), *King's Rhapsody* (1956). He wrote two autobiographical books, 'Beam Ends' (1934) and 'My Wicked, Wicked Ways' (1959).

Focal Length
The distance from the optical centre of a lens to the point at which rays of light passing through it converge.

Focus
The point at which parallel rays converge after passing through a lens

Focusing
To adjust a lens so that it produces a sharply defined image

Fonda, Henry
Born 1905 in Nebraska, USA. Grass-roots Hollywood hero who best epitomized the American pioneer spirit and, later, the soul of the Depression in a series of perennial films, culminating in JOHN FORD's magnificent *Grapes of Wrath* (1940), principally during the late 1930s and 1940s. A versatile actor on Broadway, he was brought to Hollywood to make his screen début in *The Farmer Takes a Wife* (1935). Adept in sensitive romances and scatty comedies as well, he established his most enduring image of the victimized hero in *You Only Live Once* (1937). He was the ideal *Young Mr Lincoln* (1939), and returned again to the role of the victim in *The Ox-Bow Incident* (1943). Two of his most celebrated roles were in Ford's *My Darling Clementine* (1946) and *Fort Apache* (1948). With maturity he became regarded as the wise, thinking hero; the man who stood out against an unfair jury decision in *Twelve Angry Men* (1957); the troubled intellectual of *War and Peace* (1956); the US President in *Fail Safe* and a Presidential candidate in *The Best Man* (both in 1964). Latterly he has kicked over the traces, playing a particularly satisfying villain in *Once Upon a Time in the West* (1969). He is the father of JANE and PETER FONDA. Other notable films: *The Trail of the Lonesome Pine* (1936), *Jezebel* (1938), *The Lady Eve* (1941), *The Fugitive* (1947), *Mister Roberts* (1955), *The Wrong Man* (1956), *Advise and Consent* (1961), *Killer on a Horse* (1966), *Madigan* and *The Boston Strangler* (1968), *Too Late the Hero* (1969), *There was a Crooked Man* and *The Cheyenne Social Club* (1970). MH

Above: Henry Fonda in 'War and Peace' (King Vidor, USA, 1956)
Below: Jane Fonda in 'They Shoot Horses, Don't They?' (Sydney Pollack, USA, 1969)

Fonda, Jane
Born 1937 in USA. Increasingly impressive actress daughter of HENRY FONDA. A model and stage actress before making her film début in *Tall Story* (1960), she has recently devoted much time and energy to civil and women's rights. Main films: *Walk on the Wild Side* (1961), *The Chapman Report* and *Period of Adjustment* (1962), *La Ronde* (1964), *Cat Ballou* (1965), *Hurry Sundown* and *Barefoot in the Park* (1967), *Barbarella* (1968), *They Shoot Horses, Don't They?* (1969), *Klute* (1971).

Fonda, Peter
Born 1939 in USA. Actor and director. Son of HENRY FONDA he wrote and co-produced one of the key films of the 1960s, *Easy Rider*, and directed a flawed but arresting variation on the Western theme, *The Hired Hand* (1971). Main films: *The Victors* (1963), *Lilith* (1964), *The Wild Angels* (1966), *The Trip* (1967), *Easy Rider* (1969), and *Idaho Transfer* (directed, 1971).

Fontaine, Joan
Born 1917 in Britain, but lived in USA from childhood. Actress sister of OLIVIA DE HAVILLAND; on stage from 1935 to 1937, then appeared in films, often as a shy English-rose type, quiet and restrained. Main films: *A Damsel in Distress* (1938), *The Women* (1939), *Rebecca* (1940), *Suspicion* (1941), *The Constant Nymph* and *Jane Eyre* (1943), *Frenchman's Creek* (1944), *Letter from an Unknown Woman* (1948), *Ivanhoe* (1952), *Serenade* and *Island in the Sun* (1956), *A Certain Smile* (1958), *Voyage to the Bottom of the Sea* (1961).

Forbes, Bryan
Born 1926 in London, England. Live-wire British actor, writer and director, head of Production at EMI-ABPC Elstree Studios from 1969 to 1971. An ambitious small-part player, who made his screen début in *The Small Back Room* (1948), he doubled up as film journalist and graduated to filling out scripts for weary British action films. His first major screenplay credit was for *Cockleshell Heroes* (1955). In 1959, with actor RICHARD ATTENBOROUGH, he wrote and co-produced a good, gritty film about trade-union relations, *The Angry Silence* (1959), which became something of a landmark

in British films. He made his directorial début with *Whistle Down the Wind* (1961). His taut, clever writing and professional skill were most in evidence in *Seance on a Wet Afternoon* (1964) and *King Rat* (1965). His most personal and least glib film, about old age, *The Whisperers* (1966), however, was a critical but not a popular success. The more grandiose *Deadfall* (1967) and *Madwoman of Chaillot* (1969) failed to match the quality of his earlier work. In his two years' control of production at Elstree, he became a controversial figure and during this time he directed *The Raging Moon* (1971). MH

Ford, Aleksander
Born 1908 in Lódź, Poland. Director. A vital influence in the Polish cinema since the 1930s, Ford began his film career with two documentaries made in his native town: *To Morning* (1929) and *The Pulse of Poland's Manchester* (1930). He directed some of the most important Polish films of the 1930s including *Legion of the Streets* (1932), *Sabra* (1934), *People of the Vistula* (1937) and a documentary, *Street of the Young* (1936), which was banned for its too truthful picture of the Polish and Jewish poor. After working in the Soviet Union during the war, Ford returned as the organizing spirit of 'Film Polski' and directed *Border Street* (1948), *The Young Chopin* (1952), *Five Boys from Barska Street* (1953), *The Eighth Day of the Week* (1958), *Knights of the Teutonic Order* (1960), which, though rather traditional, contributed greatly to the reputation of Polish films abroad.

Ford, Glenn
Born 1916 in Quebec, Canada. All-purpose Hollywood hero for 30 years who has serviceably adapted himself to the demands of the role – whether as RITA HAYWORTH's male appendage in *Gilda* (1946), the grim victim of *The Big Heat* (1953) or the adventurer in several superior Westerns. He appears most relaxed in wry outdoor comedies such as *The Sheepman* (1958) and *The Rounders* (1965). Briefly in the theatre, he made his screen début in *Heaven with a Barbed Wire Fence* in 1939. Chief films include: *The Man from Colorado* (1948), *Undercover Man* (1949), *Human Desire* (1954), *The Blackboard Jungle* and *Trial* (1955), *The Teahouse of the August Moon* (1956), *Cowboy* and *3.10 to Yuma* (1957), *Pocketful of Miracles* (1961), *The Four Horsemen of the Apocalypse* (1962), *Dear Heart* (1965), *Is Paris Burning?* (1966), *Smith* (1969), *The Long Ride Home* (1970). MH

Ford, John
Born 1895 in Maine, USA. Pre-eminent Hollywood director and the chief architect of the pioneer (specifically, Western) tradition in American films. Although tethered to the Hollywood studio system for the greater part of his career, he has achieved a thematic consistency which informs even the unlikeliest of his films (for example, *Wee Willie Winkie* in 1937) and distinguishes his greatest (*The Grapes of Wrath* in 1940 and his classic Western series). His concern with the primary human virtues of loyalty, family or community pride, courage, the pioneer spirit, has produced a volume of work which is in essence a folk history of America from the birth of a nation to the Depression of the 1930s.

John Ford (1938)

His devotion to America and his own personal vision of its legendary qualities are deeply rooted in an immigrant background. The thirteenth child of Sean O'Feeney, who came to America from Galway, Ireland, Ford followed his elder brother Francis to Hollywood in 1913. His brother was a contract writer, director and actor at Universal and John (then known as Jack as he is listed in a 1916 issue of the 'Motion Picture News' Studio Directory) started his screen career as a labourer and prop man. He did stunts, played bit parts in many of his brother's films; also appeared as a Ku Klux Klans-man in GRIFFITH's *Birth of a Nation*.

Probably the first film he wrote and directed was the two-reeler *The Tornado* in 1917: Ford's own memory is apparently as vague as the official credits on the films prior to that. He worked thereafter at the rate of six or seven films a year. *The Iron Horse* (1924) established him as a director of more than usual merit. But his preoccupation with the West and the simple moral issues of right and wrong had set the pattern of his films before this. Switching from Universal to Twentieth Century Fox in 1921, he made one of his biggest money-makers *Four Sons* (1928) on which JOHN WAYNE was an assistant director. He later became a principal member of the Ford repertory company, which included VICTOR MCLAGLEN, Ward Bond, HENRY FONDA and many regular supporting actors. Ford also worked repeatedly with certain writers – most notably, DUDLEY NICHOLS.

His first talking picture was *Napoleon's Barber* (1928). During the 1930s his subject matter ranged from Sinclair Lewis's *Arrowsmith* (1931) to the prison comedy *Up The River* (1930), the moving First World War study of bereavement *Pilgrimage* (1933) and the aggressively masculine adventure *The Lost Patrol* (1934). He won his first Academy Award for *The Informer* (1935): Liam O'Flaherty's tale of the Sinn Fein rebellion, which some critics now rate less highly. Ford was to return several times to Irish themes, in earnest (*The Plough and the Stars* in 1936) or in fun (*The Quiet Man* in 1952). He subsequently won Academy Awards for *Grapes of Wrath*, *How Green was my Valley* (1940) and *The Quiet Man*.

In 1939, he directed possibly his most celebrated though by no means his best Western, *Stagecoach*. In the same year he produced the definitive screen portrait of the early Abraham Lincoln, *Young Mr Lincoln*. In between his epic Westerns – *My Darling Clementine* (1946), *Fort Apache* (1948), *She Wore a Yellow Ribbon* (1949), *Wagon Master* (1950), *The Searchers* (1956), *The Man who Shot Liberty Valance* (1962), and his last tribute to the exploited Red Indian he has come to respect, *Cheyenne Autumn* (1964) – he returned to the folksy small town sentiment of *The Sun Shines Bright* (a Ford favourite, 1953), and the knockabout male humour of *Donovan's Reef* (1963). In 1964 he started work on *Young Cassidy*, but was forced to withdraw through illness and in 1965 he made the remarkable *Seven Women*, in which he transferred masculine, Western values to a feminine, Oriental situation. His last credit was as executive producer on the much-delayed documentary *Vietnam! Vietnam!* (1971), a generally undistinguished contribution to the Vietnam war debate.

Tough, sentimental, brusque with admirers, he has sometimes been accused of being outmoded, racialist (in his paternal treatment of blacks) and reactionary. But his belief in, and poetic feeling for, the standards of an America now fast disappearing is constant, though his Westerns betray a progressively defeatist approach. His working methods have been conditioned by the hard school in which he learned. He brooks no nonsense, works quickly, dislikes the front-office men. A friend and honorary member of the Navajo tribe, he sticks invariably to the same location for his Westerns – Monument Valley in the Navajo Reservation between Arizona and Utah, which is identified exclusively as Ford country.

He has influenced such dissimilar directors as INGMAR BERGMAN, AKIRA KUROSAWA and ORSON WELLES, who paid Ford the ultimate tribute when, admitting he liked best the 'old masters', he added 'by which I mean John Ford, John Ford and John Ford'.

Other notable films include: *3 Bad Men* (1926), *Judge Priest* (1934), *Steamboat Round The Bend* (1935), *The Prisoner of Shark Island* and *Mary of Scotland* (1936), *Tobacco Road* (1941),

The Battle of Midway (his first war documentary, 1942), *They were Expendable* (1945), *The Fugitive* (1947), *Rio Grande* (1950), *The Long Gray Line* (1955), *The Last Hurrah* (1958), *The Horse Soldiers* (1959), the Civil War sequence of *How the West Was Won* (1962). See 'John Ford' by Peter Bogdanovich (1947) and 'John Ford' by Jean Mitry (1954). MH

Foreman, Carl
Born 1914 in Chicago, USA. Expatriate American writer, director and producer who left Hollywood at the time of the communist witch-hunt in the 1950s and is now settled in Britain. In 1948 he joined producer STANLEY KRAMER for whom he scripted some of Kramer's most successful films – *So This is New York* (1948), *Home of the Brave* and *Champion* (1949), *The Men* (1950) – most of which caught the prevailing contemporary feeling for tough, radical dramas based on real situations. He also wrote the classic Western, *High Noon* (1952), and a florid *Cyrano de Bergerac* (1950). His first major success in Britain was *The Bridge on the River Kwai* (1957) which certainly smoothed the course for his subsequent work. He wrote and produced the interesting romantic failure, *The Key* (1958), returning to block-busting heroics with *The Guns of Navarone* (1961). In 1963 he wrote, produced and directed a passionate but overheated anti-war film, *The Victors*. Since then he has been principally engaged in production – *Born Free* (1965), *MacKenna's Gold* (1968), *Living Free* (1971) and *Young Winston* (1972). He has also served as a Governor of the British Film Institute and a member of the Committee appointed to launch the first British National Film School in 1971.

Forman, Miloš
Born 1932 in Caslav, Czechoslovakia. Director. A leading member of the new, anti-conformist Czechoslovak cinema which emerged in the 1960s, Forman began as a script collaborator on several films and then made two shorts which were later combined into one film (1963). One of these, *Talent Competition*, already looked forward to his favourite themes and methods: a quizzical, sometimes bemused, analysis of human foibles and small-town ennui, using non-professionals wherever possible and shooting mainly on location. The three features which followed – *Peter and Pavla* (1964), *A Blonde in Love* (1965) and *The Firemen's Ball* (1967) – combined acute observation with a splendid sense of the ridiculous (marred, perhaps, by occasional touches of condescension) and, notably, in the last film, an undercurrent of political satire which upset the Czechoslovak authorities. Forman has now temporarily left Czechoslovakia to work in America; his first film in that country, *Taking Off* (1971), again returned to the theme of parents and children and, despite its alien setting, retained much of Forman's characteristic human sympathies and concern with the way people live as they do. JG

Fosco, Piero
See PASTRONE, GIOVANNI

Fox, William (1879–1952)
Born in Tulchva, Hungary. Traditional Hollywood immigrant film tycoon who started out in the garment trade, opened a nickelodeon in Brooklyn, developed a chain of film theatres, went into distribution and from there into film production in 1912 with the company that grew into the Fox Film Corporation. During the 1920s he experimented with sound on film and the wide screen. In the late 1920s and early 1930s he over-extended himself and was nudged out of his own company, which continued to use his name. In 1936 he filed a bankruptcy petition and in 1942 was sent to prison for attempting to bribe a judge.

Frame
An individual picture on a strip of film. When this is adjusted in the projector so as to be exactly in the projector aperture it is said to be In Frame.

France
The contribution of France to the film, unsurpassed by any country other than the United States, extends from the invention and commercial exploitation of the cinema in the 1890s, through the evolution of a film language, to the film's development as a medium of personal artistic expression. It is often forgotten that before 1914 it was France, not the USA, which dominated the world market. Indeed at one time the Pathé company distributed twice as many films in the United States as all the American companies put together. This pre-eminence was destroyed by the First World War, but even when France was no longer the dominant commercial power it continued to produce a succession of works of genuine artistic interest.

France made a full contribution to the invention of the various forms of film in the 1880s and 1890s. The French physiologist Étienne Marey (1830–1904), for example, developed a photographic gun which he used to study animal locomotion and which had all the basic elements of a successful film camera. In another sphere Emile Reynaud (1844–1918) created his optical theatre, with which, in the 1890s, he was able to anticipate the film cartoon with half-hour-long shows of hand-drawn and hand-coloured animated films. A Frenchman, too, has the distinction of having given the first commercial showing of films to a paying public. On 28 December 1895 a dozen or so films shot by LOUIS LUMIÈRE and his brother AUGUSTE were shown to an initial audience of 35 people in the basement of the Grand Café in the Boulevard des Capucines in Paris, and the film as we know it was born. It is interesting to note the varied backgrounds of these three precursors – a scientist, an artist and an industrialist – for film is the product of just such a mixture of 19th-century scientific curiosity, technology and artistic aspiration linked to commercial ambition.

The form which LOUIS LUMIÈRE gave the cinema was that of a recording device. His cinematograph recorded life as he could see it

Above: Drawing by Georges Méliès for 'Conquest of the Pole' (Méliès, 1912)
Below: Auguste Lumière feeding the baby in 'Baby's Breakfast' (Louis Lumière, 1896)

around him, a train entering a station or his brother feeding the baby in the garden. His camera-cum-projector was relatively easy to carry around and he used it with the same freedom that a contemporary still photographer would have used his apparatus. For him the novelty and interest lay in the simple fact of capturing movement. One of his early everyday scenes, *Watering the Gardener*, opened the path to the comic film but this was not Lumière's intention. Instead of developing the dramatic possibilities of the cinematograph he decided to maintain interest by the novelty of his shots, sending his cameramen all over the world to give film shows and to bring back shots of local scenes. The use of the camera was limited too in Lumière's films: only when mounted on a moving vehicle (tram, train or gondola) did it budge.

The man who first followed the theatrical possibilities of the film was another Frenchman, the conjuror GEORGES MÉLIÈS. The owner of an illusionist theatre, he tried to buy the cinematograph the moment he saw it. Refused, he turned to Lumière's rivals in England and set up on his own. Though he began in the Lumière manner, he soon used the camera to record his illusions and developed the trick potential of the film – stop action, multiple exposure and so on. Méliès built his own studio at Montreuil as an equivalent to his beloved Robert Houdin theatre. Though he made fake newsreels about the trial of Dreyfus and the coronation of Edward VII, Méliès is best known for his fantasies. Using all the powers of his abundant imagination, he filmed fairytales like *Cinderella* (1899) or *Bluebeard* (1901) and Jules Verne style stories like *A Trip to the Moon* (1902) and *The Conquest of the Pole* (1912). Humour, a touch of glamour (borrowed from the chorus lines of the Châtelet theatre) and a childlike delight in tricks and illusions are the characteristic feature of Méliès's art. The success of his Star Film company was, for a time, world-wide and his best films were much copied and imitated. Méliès aimed to bring together the film and the older traditions of the theatre; at much the same time ÉMILE COHL was helping to found the new art of animation with his cartoons about a family of matchstick men called Fantoche.

The cinema developed with incredible speed in France after Lumière's first projections and by 1896 the foundations of the two great production empires of pre-war France had been laid. LÉON GAUMONT was a manufacturer of photographic materials who dealt first in film cameras and projectors and then began to produce films of his own. The artistic responsibility for the latter he entrusted to his secretary, ALICE GUY-BLACHÉ, who in 1896 became probably the first woman director in the world. In 1900 she became head of production at what grew to be before 1914, the world's biggest film studio at Buttes-Chaumont in Paris. Gaumont attracted some of the best directors of the time (including Cohl and LOUIS FEUILLADE), experimented with

Top: 'Onésyme se Bat en Duel' (Jean Durand, 1913)
Above: Max Linder in one of the comedies he wrote and directed for Pathé

sound and colour and set up subsidiary companies in many foreign countries, including Britain, where his name is still preserved. Gaumont's great rival, CHARLES PATHÉ, came to hold an even more dominating position in world cinema. The son of a pork butcher, Pathé had tried his hand at many trades and had even emigrated temporarily to South America, before he made money by taking a phonograph around various rural fairs in France. From this it was a small step to another fairground amusement, the film. From a beginning selling kinetoscopes and projectors he moved on to film producing and turned a modest entertainment into a world industry. His organization, Pathé Frères, had a studio at Vincennes, where, by 1908, he employed 1,500 men. Like Gaumont, he did not limit himself to France but set up offices, production companies and laboratories all over Europe and in the USA. After the First World War, however, Pathé gave up film production and six years after his retirement in 1930 his firm, now Pathé-Nathan, was bankrupt.

Pathé's head of production was FERDINAND ZECCA, an ex-actor and prolific director who has acquired the reputation of being something of a plagiarist. He was very successful, however, and with films like *Histoire d'un Crime* (1901) and *Les Victimes de l'Alcoolisme* (1902) he helped to set the cinema on the path of realism and concern with everyday life and problems. A new direction was also given by the Film d'Art company which called on noted writers and actors from the Comédie Française for films like *L'Assassinat du Duc de Guise* (1908), directed by two actors, Le Bargy and André Calmettes, and with a score by Saint-Saëns. Film d'Art productions were often stilted and stagey, but they helped find new audiences for the film and attracted world famous actresses like Sarah Bernhardt to the studios. Among those who attempted to bridge the gap between realism and literature we might mention ALBERT CAPELLANI (1870–1931), who made adaptations of Dumas's *Les Misérables* (1912) and Zola's *Germinal* (1913). Capellani had been trained in the theatrical company of André Antoine (1858–1943), the advocate of stage naturalism, who himself directed several films between 1916 and 1922 in which he blended stage actors and real settings.

Gradually the French film industry began to develop its own distinctively cinematic forms. In particular the French established two of the staple elements of the popular silent cinema – slapstick comedy and the serial. One of the first of the screen comics was ANDRÉ DEED (1884–1931), who found fame with dozens of little comedies made for Pathé between 1906 and 1908, most of which starred him as Boireau. Then he spent two years in Italy (as Cretinetti) before returning to France. Like many of the other early comics he did not establish a single identity and relied simply on an abundance of gags, trick accessories and crude humour. While Deed was in Italy his place was taken by Charles Prince (1872–1933), better known as Rigardin, a clown with a superbly comic face whose films lacked, however, the verve of Deed. Gaumont too had his comics: the actor-director Léonce Perret (1880–1935), who made a series of films as Léonce before the war, and Jean Durand (1882–1946), who directed a group of films featuring a character called Onésyme in which everyday logic was turned upside down. But towering above Boireau, Rigardin and their imitators was the greatest precursor of CHAPLIN, MAX LINDER. Linder began his career in 1905 but it was not until five years later that he established his greatness. Having begun at a salary of 20 francs a day with a profound sense of shame (these were the days when serious actors looked down on the film), by 1913 Linder found himself earning a million francs a year from Pathé and being mobbed by crowds wherever he went. With him comedy entered a new phase. The elegant figure of Max, always impeccably dressed with hat, morning coat and stick, was far removed from the slapstick and simple chase formulas of the earlier comics. He remained at his best in his short films, mostly improvised in a single day's shooting. He extracted a wealth of humour from the simplest of actions – a duel or a boxing match, getting married or unwittingly getting drunk. Like several other noted French film makers (CAPELLANI, MAURICE TOURNEUR, etc.) he went to the USA around the time of the First World War and found the cinema in France much changed on his return. Beneath his laugh-provoking exterior was all the traditional clown's melancholy and Linder committed suicide with his young wife in 1925.

The development of American comedy with the advent of Chaplin and KEATON owes little directly to France, though Chaplin did hail Linder as 'the professor'. The serial on the other hand was a French idea and even the famous *Perils of Pauline* series of 1914 was produced by the American subsidiary of Pathé and directed by a Frenchman, LOUIS GASNIER. While none of the serials made in France had the same international impact, they did form an important part of the output of the film industry. The pioneer was Victorien Jasset (1862–1913), a man of multiple talents who began his *Nick Carter* series in 1908. After Jasset's early death his films were overshadowed by those of LOUIS FEUILLADE, who after years of neglect was rediscovered in the 1950s and had a profound influence on directors like FRANJU (who remade *Judex*) and RESNAIS. Feuillade, who succeeded ALICE GUY-BLACHÉ as head of production at the Gaumont studios, tried almost every kind of film in a career lasting almost 20 years. He made farces and biblical dramas, comic films with the child stars Bébé and Bout-de-Zan and a series of realist dramas in the Zecca tradition called *La Vie telle qu'elle est* (1912). Among his actors he numbered the future directors CLAIR and FEYDER as well as professionals like Marcel Levesque, Musidora, Renée Carl and René Navarre.

But Feuillade's current reputation is based almost exclusively on the serials he made between 1913 and 1920: *Fantômas*, *Les Vampires*, *Judex*, *Tih Minh* and *Barrabas*. The first two of these series set dogged heroes like Inspector Juve and the journalist Guérande in a life and death struggle against more picturesque villains, the arch-criminal Fantômas, Irma Vep or the band of Vampires. Then, yielding to censorship pressure, Feuillade created the figure of Judex, the caped avenger, who uses all the trappings of Fantômas but in the service of good. Feuillade's plots are full of fanciful and melodramatic devices – chases in cars and over roof-tops, kidnappings (even the lassoing of a woman from her bedroom window), bodies in trunks and hints of orgies in respectable-looking villas. A dead man seems to kill when Fantô-

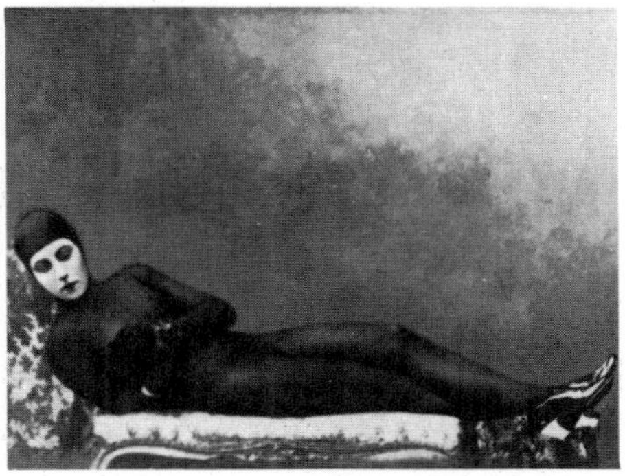

Above: Musidora in 'Les Vampires' (Louis Feuillade, 1915–6)
Below: 'Judex' (Louis Feuillade, 1916)

mas commits his crimes wearing gloves made from the skin of his hands. Elements of disguise and hypnotism, drugs and poison gas, snakes and secret passages occur again and again. Given the incoherences of the plot, which Feuillade usually made up as the shooting progressed, there emerged from these serials a strange nightmare vision of the world which attracted the surrealists, whose discovery of the cinema dates from about this time. Despite commercial pressures Feuillade worked with a freedom and spontaneity missing from the later French film until the days of GODARD.

In the 1920s with the scaling down of the industry the cinema took quite a new direction. As was to be the case 40 years later, the impetus for change came from critics, in this case the theoretician Riciotto Canudo (1879–1923) and the future director, LOUIS DELLUC. Delluc, who devoted his literary talent to the theatre until a viewing of CECIL B. DE MILLE's *The Cheat* converted him to the film, became a leading advocate of the American cinema. In the films which he wrote and directed, of which the best known are *Fièvre* (1921), *La Femme de Nulle Part* (1922) and *L'Inondation* (1924), he tried to create a new kind of cinema. He was interested less in dramatic conflicts of the Feuillade kind than in the conscious creation of atmosphere. All his films have plots that can be summarized in a sentence, yet create characters and situations in depth, benefiting from the performances of Eve Francis, his actress wife. Around Delluc it is convenient to group a number of other film-makers active in the early 1920s – GERMAINE DULAC, who directed Delluc's first scenario, *La Fête Espagnole* (1919), JEAN EPSTEIN, who was briefly his assistant, and MARCEL L'HERBIER, in several of whose films Eve Francis appeared. Dulac, whose career virtually ended with the coming of sound, was a prolific director, best remembered now for her direction of Antonin Artaud's *avant-garde* script, *La Coquille et le Clergyman* (1926). Epstein, like Delluc a theoretician of the film, ranged from the atmospheric study of *Cœur Fidèle* (1923) to the elaborate visual style of *La Chute de la Maison Usher* (1928) and the soberly realistic *Finis Terrae* (1928), filmed in the Ushant islands with non-professional actors. L'Herbier had a longer and more prolific career. In the 1920s he carried out various aesthetic experiments in films like *Eldorado* and *Don Juan et Faust* (1922) and *L'Inhumaine* (1923), the last with décor by Fernand Léger. Though with less freedom to choose his subjects, L'Herbier continued his career in the sound era, making his last film in 1953 before turning to television.

Towering above all these is the dynamic and forceful figure of ABEL GANCE, one of the great innovators of world cinema. Like most of this generation of directors, Gance had had literary ambitions in his youth and in fact wrote a verse tragedy for Sarah Bernhardt which would have been produced but for the outbreak of war. As early as 1909 he turned to the film, first writing scripts for Gaumont, then two years later becoming a director. But it was only after eighteen films that he really made his mark with melodramas like *Mater Dolorosa* (1917), in which Emmy Lynn appeared as a tormented wife, and *La Dixième Symphonie* (1918), in which Séverin-Mars portrayed a great composer creating art out of his sufferings. With *J'Accuse* (1918) such melodramatic elements were combined with a naive if strident pleading for peace. The hero (Séverin-Mars again) is a true Gance hero, a visionary who summons up the dead to reinforce his message. Gance's ambition was limitless – he dreamed of film dramas about the death of Christ and the end of the world – and he poured two years' work into *La Roue* (1922), which was eventually cut, like *Greed*, from over eight hours to two and a half. The director had already toyed with distorting

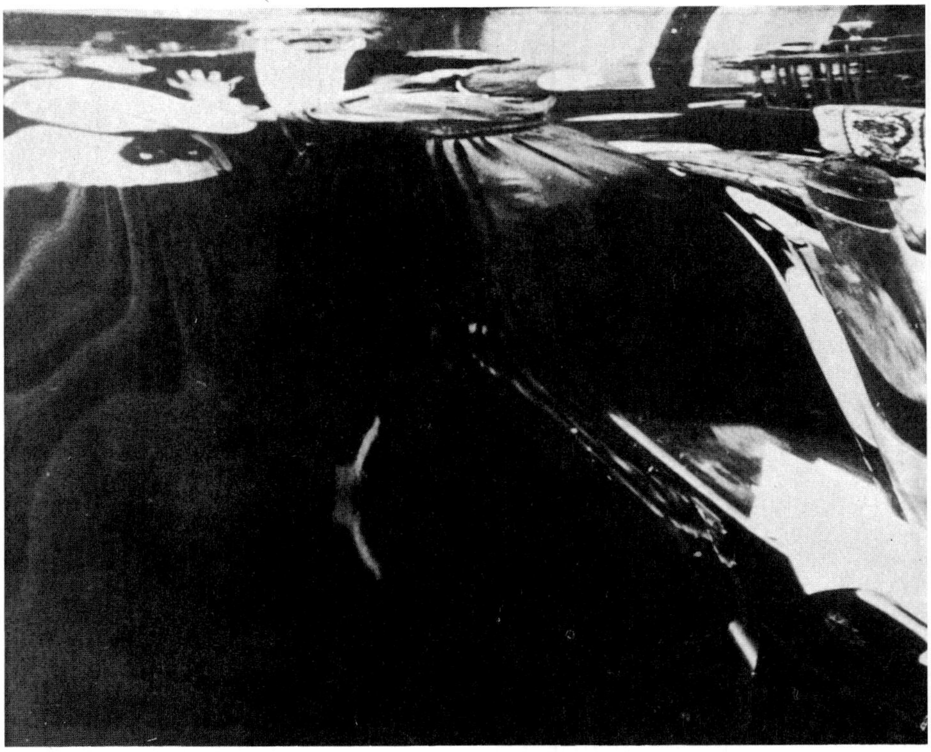

Above: Séverin-Mars in 'La Roue' (Abel Gance, 1922)
Above right: The use of a distorting lens in 'La Folie du Docteur Tube' (Abel Gance, 1916)
Below: 'Cœur Fidèle' (Jean Epstein, 1923)

mirrors in *La Folie du Docteur Tube* (1916) and here he obtained great effects with his photographic compositions and dynamic cutting. The poetry arises from the juxtaposition of contrasts: roses and railway engines, a joyful dance and a scene of death. Always Gance is diffuse, mixing sentiment and comedy, vision and melodrama and choosing as his hero a man who is Oedipus, Sisyphus and Lear rolled into one. It was inevitable that Gance should turn to Napoleon and the very title of his film, *Napoléon vu par Abel Gance* (1927) and his habit at this time of prefacing his films with a close-up of his own face give some idea of his pretensions. But Gance triumphantly lived up to them, using the camera as it had never been used before and building up great sequences like that of the storm (linking Bonaparte at sea with the Convention in Paris) and finally exploding the confines of the image with a triple screen climax. Gance, one of the great figures of the silent cinema, did not survive the 1930s with anything like the same success and after *Napoléon* his are no longer the decisive works of the French cinema. But his tenacity was enormous and as late as the 1960s he was able to continue his Napoleon saga with *Austerlitz* (1960) and pay a final homage to his mentor Edmond Rostand with *Cyrano et D'Artagnan* (1963).

It would be difficult to find a more striking contrast to Gance than RENÉ CLAIR, who like him was formed by literature. In Clair's case, however, the influence was that of the 17th-century classics (particularly Molière). As a result Clair was totally at home with the tight mechanics of farce and from the very first built his films around the notion he saw as basic to the cinema: movement. But in his films this was movement within the frame, not a Gance style camera movement. Clair's first film, *Paris Qui Dort* (1923), used a nicely cinematic notion of a handful of characters moving through a Paris suddenly frozen by a crazy professor's magic ray. His second, *Entr'acte* (1924), involved him with a dream world of a very different kind – the surrealist one of Francis Picabia (who wrote the script) and Erik Satie (who composed the musical accompaniment). The climax was a wild anarchic chase, which set the tone for his later work. Clair's comedy always arose from the creation of artificial fantasy worlds, as is clearly borne out by a film like *Le Voyage Imaginaire* (1925) in which the hero's dreams of winning his girl turn to a nightmare from which he only just escapes. In his first five films Clair mastered his craft, found valuable collaborators (notably LAZARE MEERSON, the designer who worked with him till 1932), and some of his favourite actors: Albert Préjean, Jim Gérald, Paul Olivier, etc. These elements were fused in the 1927 classic *Un Chapeau de Paille d'Italie*, adapted from a farce by Labiche and Michel. Here he treated the bourgeois world of 1895 with the same wit and irreverence he had previously applied to purely fantasy subjects. This film was the summit of his silent career; his next feature, *Les Deux Timides* (1928), looked forward to the tenderness and muted emotion of his early sound films while still creating a number of brilliant comic sequences.

Several of the directors who were to play such an important part in the 1930s film were active, like Clair, in the 1920s but failed to achieve a comparable success. JEAN RENOIR made an ambitious début with *La Fille de l'Eau* (1924) followed by *Nana* (1926) and *Tire-au-flanc* (1928), but such films as *Le Tournoi dans la Cité* and *Le Bled* (1929) were commercial undertakings that lacked the ambitions of his later work. JULIEN DUVIVIER had embarked on his prolific career in 1919 and his twenty or so silent films include pretentious religious dramas and mediocre literary adaptations. Far more interesting are the first films of JEAN GRÉMILLON, whose silent fiction films like *Maldone* (1927) and *Gardiens de Phare* (1929) mixed melodramatic plots with a rare gift for atmosphere and landscape. Grémillon's first full length film, *Un Tour au Large* (1926), had been a documentary on tuna fishing and towards the end of the silent era there emerged an interesting group of documentary works, among them the first films of MARCEL CARNÉ and JEAN VIGO. Carné's *Nogent – Eldorado du Dimanche* (1930) and Vigo's *À Propos de Nice* (1930) were atmospheric evocations of (very different) holiday resorts. The scientific documentary, too, made its appearance in France at this time with the first films of JEAN PAINLEVÉ.

Among the most interesting French silent films were those made by foreign directors. JACQUES FEYDER is often thought of as a Frenchman, but he was born in Brussels and remained all his life a traveller and a cosmopolitan. After establishing himself with *L'Atlantide* (1921), Feyder reinforced his reputation with an adaptation from Anatole France, *Crainquebille* (1923). Then his travels began. His sensitive study of childhood, *Visages d'Enfants* (1924), was made on location in Switzerland, *L'Image* (1926) was shot for a Viennese company and *Carmen* (1936) took him to Spain, while the unrealized *Le Roi Lépreux* was to have been made in Indo-China. The range of Feyder's work is shown by his last two European silent films, a version of Zola's *Thérèse Raquin* (1928), shot in Berlin, and a comedy in the style of René Clair, *Les Nouveaux Messieurs* (1928). Feyder's departure to Hollywood to direct GRETA GARBO seemed a natural development, but his Hollywood career did not work out satisfactorily and he did nothing of real interest till he returned to France in 1933. CARL DREYER is another director who did some of his best work in France. *La Passion de Jeanne d'Arc* (1928) is one of the classics of world cinema. In it Dreyer photographed the duel of Joan (played by Falconetti) and her judges in a series of close-ups set against a prison background and choreographed crowd scenes. By contrast, his French sound film, *Vampyr* (1932), was a horror film whose effect derived from the play of mists and shadows brilliantly photographed by RUDOLPH MATÉ (also responsible for *La Passion de Jeanne d'Arc*).

Above: Jean Angelo and Stacia Napierkowska (right) in 'L'Atlantide' (Jacques Feyder, 1921)
Below: Gina Manes and Wolfgang Zelzer in 'Thérèse Raquin' (Jacques Feyder, 1928)

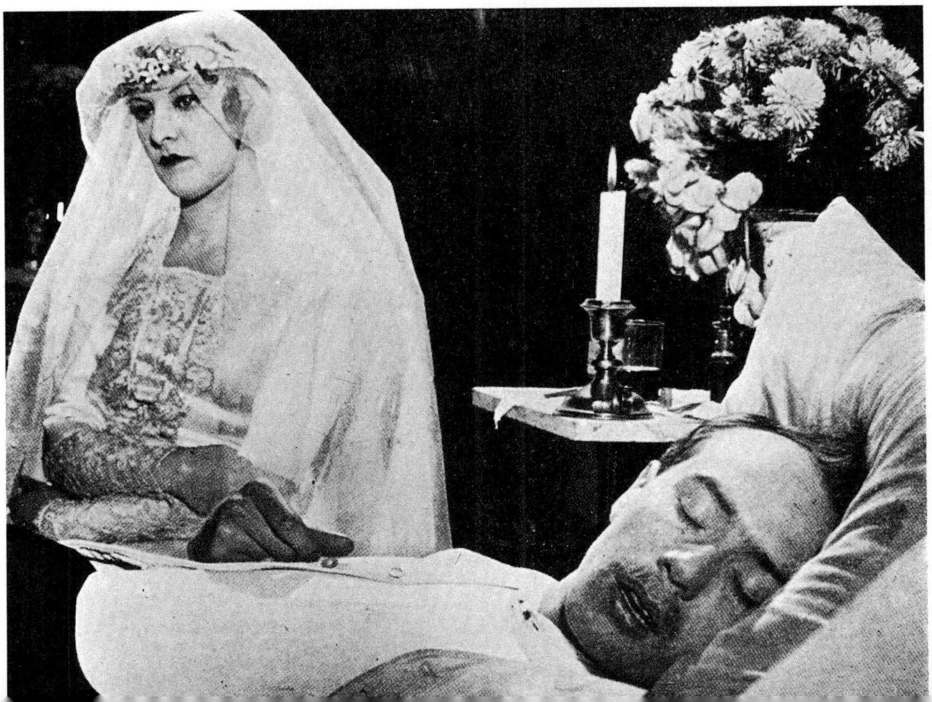

Aside from these two masters, there was a group of highly talented Russian *émigrés*, among them the producer Alexandre Kamenka, whose Albatros company was responsible for works like Epstein's *Le Lion des Mogols* (1924) and L'Herbier's *Feu Matthias Pascal* (1925) as well as Clair's last three silent films. The most characteristic products of the Russian school were the films starring the great actor IVAN MOZHUKIN. These included *Le Brasier Ardent* (1923) co-directed with Alexandre Volkov, *Kean* (1924), *Casanova* (1927), directed by Volkov, and Victor Tourjansky's *Michel Strogoff* (1926). In a very different vein are the atmospheric studies of another Russian-born director, DIMITRI KIRSANOV (1899–1957), author of *L'Ironie du Destin* (1924), *Ménilmontant* (1925), and *Brumes d' Automne* (1927). Even the avant-garde of the years of transition from silence to sound had an international flavour very different from the movement originated by Louis Delluc in the early 1920s. Its roots lay in the surrealist movement and its prime exponent was LUIS BUÑUEL, whose short *Un Chien Andalou*, made with Salvador Dali in 1928, is one of the purest of all examples of a non-narrative cinema. In the equally uncompromising *L'Age d'Or* (1930) the characteristic themes of the director – his social attack, his taste for blasphemy and passionate advocacy of human freedom – find expression. It is interesting to compare with these virulent works the first filmic experiment of JEAN COCTEAU, *Le Sang d'un Poète* (1930), in which the personal motifs of the later classic *Orphée* are to be seen. Apart from the films of Buñuel and Cocteau and the experiments of Dulac (*La Coquille et la Clergyman*) and Clair (*Entr'acte*), the best work of the avant-garde is the series of short rhythmic exercises in 'pure' cinema by men like Man Ray, Fernand Léger, Eugène Deslaw and Henri Chomette.

The major films of the early years of sound in France recapture something of the anarchic spirit of the avant-garde. The transition period was as chaotic in France as in other countries, but one man made his mark from the very first: René Clair. His comedies, *Sous les Toits de Paris* (1930) and *Le Million* (1931) earned him world fame and large audiences thanks to their inventive and subtle interweaving of action and music. The characteristic features of Clair's style are clearly apparent: the reliance on a chase pattern and a contrast of real and imaginary, a studio reconstruction of an affectionately viewed world of little people, a muting of emotions and a mild satire on pomposity and pretension. Clair was able to develop this style in two further films – treating the problems of automation with a carefree ease in *À Nous la Liberté* (1931) and deepening somewhat the portrayal of emotions in *Quatorze Juillet* (1932) – but by the time he came to make *Le Dernier Milliardaire* (1934) what had been innovation had become something of a formula. Clair went abroad, and a dozen years passed before he completed another feature in the French studios. It is worth mentioning *L'Affaire est dans le Sac* (1932), a film in a minor comic vein, directed by PIERRE PRÉVERT from a script by his brother the poet JACQUES PRÉVERT, who was later to work so successfully with Carné. But Pierre Prévert failed to establish himself as a feature director and over ten years passed before the brothers worked together on a feature again.

Above: Annabella in 'Quatorze Juillet' (René Clair, 1932)
Below: Dita Parlo and Jean Daste in 'L'Atalante' (Jean Vigo, 1934)

Another career cut short, in this case by a tragic death, was that of JEAN VIGO. When he died at the age of 29 one of his two major films was banned and the other was being mutilated by its distributors. Yet 25 years later his work, which amounts to little more than three hours' viewing, was seen to be decisive in the history of the French film. *Zéro de Conduite* (1933), a 45-minute evocation of Vigo's life at boarding school, is a unique blend of reality and fantasy, tenderness and caricature. Vigo's own character was strongly influenced by the social revolt of his father (an anarchist murdered in prison) yet his own temperament was basically happy and outgoing. As a result his poetic distillation of schoolboy life and revolt has a purity that recalls Alfred Jarry's 'Ubu' plays. Vigo was not limited to nostalgia, however, and his only feature film, *L'Atalante* (1934), was a study of married life set in the frustrating confines of a barge over which loomed the outsize personality of the eccentric mate, Père Jules, played by MICHEL SIMON. Poetic realism is the term often applied to the late 1930s in general and the doom-laden melodramas tailored to the personality of JEAN GABIN in particular, but no one blended the elements of reality and poetry, dream and obsession, more perfectly than Vigo.

One career that reveals most clearly the meanderings and contradictions of the period is that of JEAN RENOIR, who between 1931 and 1939 made no less than 15 films, culminating in the masterpiece *La Règle du Jeu*. After winning the confidence of producers by shooting a feature film, *On Purge Bébé* (1931), in a week, Renoir went on to find his own style with two films starring Michel Simon, *La Chienne* (1931) and *Boudu Sauvé des Eaux* (1932), both of which end with a happy sense of anarchy that recalls the contemporary work of Clair. Simon's portrayal of the artist turned tramp and the tramp almost (but not quite) turned bourgeois are performances to rank with his playing in *L'Atalante*. By contrast *Toni* (1934) is an early precursor of neo-realism, telling its tale of migrant workers and unhappy loves and filmed without stars in well chosen locations in the South of France. Throughout the 1930s Renoir was much concerned with issues raised by 19th-century literature and turned to Zola for *La Bête Humaine* (1938) and to Flaubert for *Madame Bovary* (1934). But the best of his adaptations is *Une Partie de Campagne* (1936), in which he combines a fidelity to Maupassant's tale of awakening passion with a response to landscape that recalls the painting of his own impressionist father. The director's involvement with social and political developments is particularly noticeable in the late 1930s. *Le Crime de Monsieur Lange* (1935) was scripted by JACQUES PRÉVERT and reflects an optimistic, Popular Front ideology. In 1936 Renoir also made *La Vie est à Nous* for the communist party, and *La Marseillaise* (1938), his patriotic film about the French Revolution, was planned as a rare example of genuine popular cinema to be financed by public subscription. But the atmosphere of France was moving against such optimism and Renoir's plea for international solidarity, *La Grande Illusion* (1937), scripted by CHARLES SPAAK, has more than a touch of hollowness and evasion. No such reservations need be made, however, about *La Règle du Jeu* (1939), the last film to be completed by Renoir before his departure to the USA and a masterly portrayal of the realities of a society which responds with frivolity to the threat to its values.

The advent of sound also attracted theatrical figures to the film. Foremost of these was MARCEL PAGNOL who turned to the cinema with the simple ambition of recording ideal performances of his plays and securing them wider distribution than the theatre could offer. In this way he began by producing his Marseilles trilogy, *Marius* (1931), *Fanny* (1932) and *César* (1936). While he continued adapting his own plays throughout the 1930s, his best films are those derived from Jean Giono novels – *Angèle* (1934), *Regain* (1937) and *La Femme du Boulanger* (1939). In all the films he directed Pagnol laid emphasis on the dialogue and actors at the expense of elegant photography or directorial fireworks. To actors like RAIMU, FERNANDEL and PIERRE FRESNAY he offered splendid opportunities, and his use of location shooting and his unique production methods (he had his own studio and his cast and crew lived as an extended family) gave him a rare impact. Another successful dramatist who had a brilliant career in the 1930s was SACHA GUITRY, author of over 100 plays and some 30 films. His conversation pieces (in which he usually played the leading role) were set in elegant interiors and acted with lively grace. Guitry had a particular taste for lightweight historical films such as *Les Perles de la Couronne* (1937) and *Remontons les Champs-Elysées* (1938), and though he was never an experimental artist his use of a first person commentary in *Le Roman d'un Tricheur* (1936) was a striking innovation. With remarkable facility Guitry continued to work right up to his death at the age of 72 in 1957.

Top: 'La Grande Illusion' (Jean Renoir, 1937)
Above: Carette (left) in 'La Règle du Jeu' (Jean Renoir, 1939)
Below: Jeanne Marken and Jacques Brunins in 'Une Partie de Campagne' (Jean Renoir, 1936)

The 1930s were very much a period of dialogued films in France, and novelists were less attracted to the cinema than dramatists, though André Malraux did make a notable film with *L'Espoir* (1939). The mid-1930s also saw the emergence of the professional script writer. When JACQUES FEYDER returned to France in 1933 it was to make a trio of films with the writer Charles Spaak: *Le Grand Jeu* (1934), a story of dual identity in a French Foreign legion setting, *Pension Mimosas* (1935), a tale of unhappy passion set this time on the Côte d'Azur, and *La Kermesse Héroïque* (1935). The last was a pacifist tale couched in the form of a farce, and lovingly recreated a painterly vision of 16th-century Flemish life. With these films Feyder gave a lesson in sheer professionalism in his handling of actors (particularly his wife FRANÇOISE ROSAY and LOUIS JOUVET in *La Kermesse Héroïque*) and his use of settings created by the designer LAZARE MEERSON. Spaak's wit and constructional skill contributed much to the success of all three and it was this writer too who helped the director JULIEN DUVIVIER to achieve some of his best results in the 1930s. Working with Spaak on *La Bandéra* (1935) and *La Belle Equipe* (1936) and with Henri Jeanson (born 1900) on *Pépé-le-Moko* (1936), Duvivier helped create the myth of romantic fatalism embodied in the figure of JEAN GABIN and later exploited in the films this actor made with Carné. Duvivier was always a gifted director of actors and his subsequent work shows frequent recourse to the episodic all-star film, such as *Un Carnet de Bal* (1937) or *La Fin du Jour* (1939).

The most celebrated writer-director team was that of MARCEL CARNÉ and JACQUES PRÉVERT. Carné, a former assistant of both Clair and Feyder, began his ten-year collaboration with Prévert in his first film, *Jenny* (1936). This was a fairly routine piece of work, but the

Above: Robert Vattier (left) in 'La Femme du Boulanger' (Marcel Pagnol, 1939)
Right: Raphael Medina, Raymond Aimos and Jean Gabin in 'La Belle Équipe' (Julien Duvivier, 1936)
Below: 'La Kermesse Héroïque (Jacques Feyder, 1935)

pair showed a more original touch with *Drôle de Drame* (1937), an all-star comedy with which Carné added two more indispensable members to his team, the designer ALEXANDRE TRAUNER and the composer MAURICE JAUBERT. With this team the director went on to create two of the most celebrated and characteristic works of the late 1930s: *Quai des Brumes* (1938) which starred Jean Gabin and MICHÈLE MORGAN and *Le Jour se Lève* (1939), in which Gabin was confronted by the villainous Jules Berry. Here Carné was at his best, creating in the studio an atmosphere of doom-laden urban gloom and finding poetry in the confrontation of the lovers and their fate. By completing these four films and the rather less successful *Hôtel du Nord* (1938) (from which the hand of Prévert was absent) before the age of 30, Carné proved himself one of the most gifted young film-makers in the history of film.

Carné's youthful achievements stand out especially if they are compared with the work of film-makers of an earlier generation. ABEL GANCE continued the struggle to maintain his independence but he was almost entirely limited to remaking such silent successes as *Mater Dolorosa* (1932), *J'Accuse* (1937) and a sound version of *Napoléon* (1934). MARCEL L'HERBIER, Jacques de Baroncelli and LÉON POIRIER, all of whom had made silent films of more than average interest, failed to achieve the same authority in their sound films. While some of the younger directors, most notably JEAN GRÉMILLON, found difficulty in obtaining backing for any but routine commercial projects, the French studios experienced a sudden influx of refugees from Nazi Germany: G. W. PABST, FRITZ LANG, ANATOLE LITVAK and ROBERT SIODMAK all made films in France on their way to Hollywood. But the only one of the *émigrés* to enhance his reputation was MAX OPHÜLS, who had been forced out of Germany immediately after his classic *Liebelei* (1933). In France between 1935 and 1940 he developed his characteristic themes centred on the tribulations of a beautiful woman, particularly in *Divine* (1935) and *La Tendre Ennemie* (1936) with the actress Simone Berriau, and *Sans Lendemain* (1939) and *De Mayerling à Sarajevo* (1940), both of which starred EDWIGE FEUILLÈRE. The interest of these films rests less on their intrinsic merits than on the ways in which they prepare the path for Ophüls's more brilliant successes in the 1940s and 1950s.

With the outbreak of war the whole pattern of French film-making changed. Ophüls, Duvivier, Clair and Renoir went to Hollywood, Feyder to Switzerland, and of the leading directors of the 1930s only Carné remained. With Prévert, Carné made two brilliant period spectacles which together stand as major works of the Occupation period. *Les Visiteurs du Soir* (1942) confronted pure-hearted lovers and a malicious but not omnipotent devil in an undefined medieval setting and was a direct extension of conflicts already treated in more realistic terms in the 1930s. *Les Enfants du Paradis* (1945) was more ambitious, an evocation of the 19th-century theatre peopled with startling figures embodying outsize passions. Around the beautiful heroine (ARLETTY) circle her lovers: a great actor, a brilliant mime and

an nihilistic murderer. The film marks the peak of the Carné-Prévert collaboration, its fatalistic message beautifully clothed in Carné's visuals and its meaning and ironies pointed by Prévert's witty dialogue.

In a very different vein Prévert also worked on the script of the film with which JEAN GRÉMILLON, after 20 years of film making, finally established his claim to greatness. *Lumière d'Été* (1943) had a more immediate sense of reality than *Les Enfants du Paradis* and was set in a world of work and social conflict. But it too contained a symbolic element in the use, for example, of costume in the masked ball at which the tensions of the characters finally reach breaking point. By contrast Grémillon's second major film of the Occupation years, *Le Ciel est à Vous* (1944), which was written by Charles Spaak, was a more sober piece, tracing the efforts of a family to set up a world aviation record. Grémillon had always had a marvellous gift for handling actors: Alcover in *La Petite Lise* (1930), RAIMU in *L'Étrange Monsieur Victor* (1938), GABIN and MICHÈLE MORGAN in *Remorques* (1939–40). In *Lumière d'Été* and *Le Ciel est à Vous* he was admirably served by his actors, led in each case by Madeleine Renaud.

Another director who came to the fore was CLAUDE AUTANT-LARA, who had entered the cinema as a designer at the age of 16 and worked as assistant on Clair's first film. After failing to impose himself with five films made in the 1930s Autant-Lara found his touch with a series of delicate films exploiting the beauty of Odette Joyeux, among them *Lettres d'Amour* (1942) and *Douce* (1943). Aside from the works of Carné, Grémillon and Autant-Lara the Occupation years are most remarkable for the emergence of a new generation of directors most of whom had already had a fairly long apprenticeship as writers and assistants. ROBERT BRESSON immediately established his personal style and authority with *Les Anges du Péché* (1943) written with Jean Giraudoux and *Les Dames du Bois du Boulogne* (1945), for which the dialogue was composed by JEAN COCTEAU. In a less intense fashion JEAN DELANNOY also made films with a strong literary content and is best known for his filming of Cocteau's version of the Tristan legend, *L'Éternel Retour* (1943). More down to earth were the early films of JACQUES BECKER and HENRI-GEORGES CLOUZOT. Clouzot's second film, *Le Corbeau* (1943), a sombre study of provincial life, received wide notoriety when, after the Liberation, its director was accused of producing anti-French propaganda.

Above: Jean Gabin in 'Le Jour se Lève' (Marcel Carné, 1939)
Below: Jean Brochard in 'Le Corbeau' (Henri-Georges Clouzot, 1943)

Though there was this general renewal, the year 1945 does constitute another abrupt break for several individual careers. Clouzot was prevented from working for four years, Grémillon never recovered the freedom he had enjoyed during the Occupation and made only three features, all of them crippled by commercial considerations, in the last 15 years of his life, while Bresson had to wait until 1951 before he could make a third film. The strongest current of the immediate postwar years was a realist trend which, however, owed more to the 1930s style of Carné and Renoir than to the kind of discovery of a totally contemporary reality that underlies Italian neo-realism. Carné and Prévert tried to continue as if nothing had changed but produced only a dated work, *Les Portes de la Nuit* (1946), which is a sad end to a brilliant partnership. Though the director's technical skill was still apparent in his later adaptations of Simenon (*La Marie du Port*, 1950) and Zola (*Thérèse Raquin*, 1953) he was no longer the dominant figure of the French realist school. Among younger directors there were, however, several contenders for the title. HENRI-GEORGES CLOUZOT followed an excellent thriller starring LOUIS JOUVET, *Quai des Orfèvres* (1947), with a more pretentious and uneven adaptation, *Manon* (1949). He achieved world fame with *Le Salaire de la Peur* (1952), which combined a gripping suspense plot with a realistic portrayal of a sordid South American township. YVES ALLÉGRET, who began directing during the war, produced a trio of black and defeatist films with the writer Jacques Sigurd, two of which starred SIMONE SIGNORET. *Dédée d'Anvers* (1947), *Une Si Jolie Petite Plage* (1948) and *Manèges* (1949) are brilliant works with a coherence and individuality which Allégret has never equalled.

To this same current of *film noir* belong the films of ANDRÉ CAYATTE, another wartime recruit to the ranks of director. His tenth film, *Les Amants de Vérone* (1948), was made from the last script of JACQUES PRÉVERT and contains a characterisitic mixture of star-crossed lovers (extras in a film *Romeo and Juliet*) and villainous grotesques. The best example of Cayatte's personal concerns is his judicial series: *Justice est Faite* (1950), *Nous Sommes Tous des Assassins* (1952), *Avant le Déluge* (1953) and *Le Dossier Noir* (1955). In these films, all scripted by Charles Spaak, the ex-lawyer Cayatte hammers home his arguments about the weaknesses of the French legal system with great honesty and passion, if little subtlety. By contrast the portrait of society drawn by JACQUES BECKER is tender and humorous. *Antoine et Antoinette* (1946), *Rendez-Vous de Juillet* (1949), *Édouard et Caroline* (1951) and *Rue de l'Estrapade* (1953) derive their impact from the authenticity and minute detail with which they reflect everyday life and problems. Against these modest and amusing domestic comedies one can set Becker's more violent films like *Casque d'Or* (1952), *Touchez pas au Grisbi* (1954) and his last work, *Le Trou* (1960), in which he deals with the themes of love and friendship in gangster or underworld settings. Less easily classifiable is RENÉ CLÉMENT whose first film *La Bataille du Rail* (1945) is a rare French example of the realistic handling of the problems of war. He went on, however, to make films that were either adventure melodramas (*Les Maudits*, 1947) or 1930s dramas uneasily set in a postwar world (his GABIN film, *Au delà des Grilles*, 1949).

Some of Clément's best works were written by the team of JEAN AURENCHE and PIERRE

Above left: 'Justice est Faite' (André Cayatte, 1950)
Above right: Daniel Gélin and Anne Vernon in 'Édouard et Caroline' (Jacques Becker, 1951)
Below: 'La Bataille du Rail' (René Clément, 1945)

BOST and belong to the tradition of tightly scripted films. Among these are Clément's study of children caught up unwittingly in war, *Jeux Interdits* (1952), and his adaptation of Zola's 'L'Assommoir' (*Gervaise*, 1956). The same writing team was responsible for CLAUDE AUTANT-LARA's adaptations of novels by Raymond Radiguet (*Le Diable au Corps*, 1947), Colette (*Le Blé en Herbe*) and Stendhal (*Le Rouge et le Noir*, 1954), as well as the original scenario, *L'Auberge Rouge* (1951), which starred FERNANDEL. In these films Autant-Lara showed his hatred of the Church, the military and the bourgeoisie and his advocacy of passion against the claims of society, but the impact still derives largely from the dialogue and the structure of the script. Aurenche and Bost were also responsible for some of the ambitious but academic productions of JEAN DELANNOY, for whom they wrote an adaptation of Gide's *La Symphonie Pastorale* (1946), *Dieu a Besoin des Hommes* (1950) and the GABIN film, *Chiens Perdus sans Colliers* (1955).

The trends of black drama and literary adaptation totally dominate the French cinema of the 1940s, though there are a few rare examples of comedy, most notably *Jour de Fête* (1947), JACQUES TATI's inimitable study of a French village postman, and two quirky films by the Prévert brothers, *Adieu Léonard* (1943) and *Voyage Surprise* (1946). Jacques Prévert was also concerned in the writing of some of the best French cartoons of the period, *Le Petit Soldat* (1947) and *La Bergère et le Ramoneur* (1953), made by PAUL GRIMAULT. A distinctive approach is shown by JEAN COCTEAU, who, after adapting a fairy tale (*La Belle et la Bête*, 1946) and two of his own plays (*L'Aigle à Deux Têtes*, 1947, and *Les Parents Terribles*, 1948), gave the French film one of its masterpieces in *Orphée* (1950). This work, a re-orchestration of the themes of *Le Sang d'un Poète* (1930) and itself echoed in *Le Testament d'Orphée* (1959), dealt with Cocteau's obsession with the myth of the poet, his love affair with death and his naive delight in the trick potential of the film. Two other resolutely independent figures were JEAN-PIERRE MELVILLE, director of *Le Silence de la Mer* (1947–9), *Les Enfants Terribles* (after Cocteau, 1949) and the gangster film, *Bob le Flambeur* (1955), and Roger Leenhardt, who in 1947 made an interesting study of adolescence, *Les Dernières Vacances* (1947). Leenhardt later turned to documentary film-making and this was a form in which much of the best work of the first post-war decade was done. Instances of work by the older generation are JEAN PAINLEVÉ's scientific films, the films on art by JEAN GRÉMILLON and the work of GEORGES ROUQUIER, particularly his feature-length study of farm life, *Farrebique* (1947), and his films on rural crafts. There were also many newcomers, including GEORGES FRANJU, author of the ferocious *Le Sang des Bêtes* (1949) and the splendidly ironic *Hôtel des Invalides* (1951), and ALAIN RESNAIS, well known for his art films, particularly *Guernica* (1950), and his masterly meditation on the concentration camps, *Nuit et Brouillard* (1955). Both Franju and Resnais eventually became masters of the fiction film too.

As the 1940s drew to a close many of the older generation of directors who had left France in 1939–40 returned. JACQUES FEYDER completed nothing of note, but RENÉ CLAIR made *Le Silence est d'Or* in 1947 to open a new phase of his career. Like the best work of his later years – *Les Grandes Manœuvres* (1955) and *Porte des Lilas* (1957) – it is a reflective work, filled with nostalgia for a world that will not return. Clair was not so successful in his version of Faust, *La Beauté du Diable* (1949), and his more farcical films – *Les Belles de Nuit* (1952), *Tout l'Or du Monde* (1961) and *Les Fêtes Galantes* (1965) – have an increasingly forced and artificial air. MAX OPHÜLS achieved some of his best work during the 1950s. In a quartet of films – *La Ronde* (1950), *Le Plaisir* (1952), *Madame de . . .* (1953) and *Lola Montès* (1955) – the director examined with mature insight and enormous technical polish his usual themes of love and pleasure, passion and frivolity. The films made in Europe by JEAN RENOIR after *The River* (1950) remain highly controversial. Using colour and spectacle he re-examined his 1930s themes: theatre and life (*Le Carrosse d'Or*, 1952, and *French Cancan*, 1954), the roundabout of love (*Eléna et les Hommes*, 1956), war and imprisonment (*Le Caporal Épinglé*, 1962). While it is possible to prefer Renoir's earlier handling of these themes, there is no denying his benign influence and technical innovation. In 1959, for instance, he was among the first directors to apply television methods to film, in *Le Testament du Docteur Cordelier* and *Le Déjeuner sur l'Herbe*.

Perhaps the major achievements of the early and middle 1950s (aside from the work in documentary) are due to ROBERT BRESSON and

JACQUES TATI. Resuming his career in 1950 Bresson made an austere adaptation of Georges Bernanos's novel, *Journal d'un Curé de Campagne*. He continued to pare down his style, reducing suspense even in his story of a prison escape, *Un Condamné à Mort s'est Échappé* (1956) and turning his non-professional actors into mere automata in *Pickpocket* (1959). With his totally uncomprising handling of *Procès de Jeanne d'Arc* (1962), filmed almost exclusively in medium shot without external drama or visual extravagance, Bresson reached the ultimate in this line of development. Bresson is too individual an artist to have exercised a direct influence, but his insistence on a non-theatrical cinema and concern to deal with forces and emotions outside the scope of a realist cinema are important contributions to the modern film. Equally individualistic is Jacques Tati, who, after *Jour de Fête* (1947), created a new comic figure, Monsieur Hulot, who gives scope to Tati's talents as a mime and embodies his basic philosophy of life. In *Les Vacances de Monsieur Hulot* (1952) it is Hulot's presence that pinpoints the absurdities of life by the sea. In *Mon Oncle* (1958), Tati's concern with realist comedy and involvement with the problems of modern living are clear, for Hulot's presence is balanced by the Arpels, who live in a gadget-ridden universe. Tati's films, all totally preplanned and the product of intense observation, and the subsequent *Playtime* and *Traffic*, constitute the only modern screen comedy that can be compared to the silent classics.

Most of those directors who had begun their careers during the 1940s found themselves caught up, a decade later, in commercially rather than artistically ambitious projects. Their works have a wider scope (often set outside France) and new technical resources such as colour and international casting. RENÉ CLÉMENT went to England for *Monsieur Ripois* (*Knave of Hearts*. 1954), shot *Barrage contre le Pacifique* (1958) in Thailand for an Italian company, and then worked for some years in Italy. His best films of late have been the thrillers *Plein Soleil* (1959) and *Les Félins* (1963) but he also directed the ponderous all-star epic about the Liberation, *Paris Brûle-t-il?* (1966). Another director to move away from purely French concerns was ANDRÉ CAYATTE, whose *Œil pour Œil* (1957) was set in the Lebanon and who dealt with Franco-German relations in *Le Passage du Rhin* (1960), then went to Nepal to make *Les Chemins de Katmandou* (1969), about the hippy generation. MARCEL CARNÉ remains very French despite a trip to New York for the locations of *Trois Chambres à Manhattan* (1965), but like Cayatte he has found the need to deal with the problems of the young. Unfortunately neither *Les Tricheurs* (1958) nor *Les Jeunes Loups* (1968) reveals more than a shadow of his old mastery.

It was the film-makers of this generation too who became most associated with the period spectacles that used colour and costumes to cover up a lack of real substance or originality. Thus CLAUDE AUTANT-LARA, despite an occasional courageous film like the anti-militaristic *Tu ne Tueras Point* (1961), made mostly films in the vein of *Vive Henri IV*, *Vive l'Amour* and *Le Comte de Monte Cristo* (both 1961). In this he followed the example set by JACQUES BECKER with works like *Ali Baba et les Quarante Voleurs* (1954) and *Les Aventures d'Arsène Lupin* (1957), and JEAN DELANNOY, whose period films *Marie Antoinette* and *Notre Dame de Paris* both appeared in 1956. By the mid 1950s it was clear that France needed a filmic renewal. No new director of the first rank had appeared since Tati in 1949 and even such brilliant short film-makers as FRANJU and RESNAIS found it impossible to make the transition to features (they spent, respectively, nine and eleven years as documentarists). At first the hints of novelty were rare and isolated, and there was little indication before 1958–9 of the united force and vigour that was to transform the French cinema with the advent of the so-called *nouvelle vague*.

When it came this renewal had various sources, principally film criticism and the documentary, but it was very much the product of individuals pursuing their own line of development and only incidentally forming a 'movement'. The magazine, 'Cahiers du Cinéma', founded by ANDRÉ BAZIN and JACQUES DONIOL-VALCROZE, became a focal point for young critics who dreamed of becoming

Above: Gérard Philipe in 'Le Diable au Corps' (Claude Autant-Lara, 1947)
Below left: Maria Casarès, Édouard Dhermittes, François Périer and Jean Marais in 'Orphée' (Jean Cocteau, 1950)
Below right: Serge Reggiani and Simone Simon in 'La Ronde' (Max Ophüls, France, 1950)

feature directors. Several of these made short films in the years 1956–8: JACQUES RIVETTE directed *Le Coup du Berger* (1956), FRANÇOIS TRUFFAUT made *Les Mistons* (1958) and JEAN-LUC GODARD *Tous les Garçons s'appellent Patrick* (1957) and *Charlotte et son Jules* (1958). Totally independently a young photographer from the Théâtre National Populaire, AGNÈS VARDA, made *La Pointe Courte* (1955), a feature-length film inspired by William Faulkner's novels which anticipated many of the stylistic methods of the 1960s. But before any real breakthrough could take place it was necessary for producers to feel confident that films by young directors could be commercially viable. The film-makers who first achieved this commercial respectability were men of diverse talents who shared at least a taste for technically polished film-making and an interest in exploiting the talents of actresses neglected by established directors. Many had been influenced by the American films shown by Langlois at the *La Cinémathèque Française*. The most superficial, but equally the most commercially successful was the former 'Paris Match' journalist ROGER VADIM, who starred his young wife BRIGITTE BARDOT in *Et Dieu Créa la Femme* (1956), a sympathetic study of amoral youth which launched its 28-year-old director on a successful and lucrative career. The even younger LOUIS MALLE made first the very competent thriller *Ascenseur pour l'Échafaud* (1957) and then the internationally successful *Les Amants* (1958). Both starred JEANNE MOREAU, who went on to become one of the most important actresses of the 1960s. In a similar vein, but without the same commercial success, the ex-novelist and critic ALEXANDRE ASTRUC directed two films with ANOUK AIMÉE, the elegant 45-minute *Le Rideau Cramoisi* (1952) and the feature-length *Les Mauvaises Rencontres* (1955).

It was in 1958, however, with the appearance of CLAUDE CHABROL's first film, *Le Beau Serge*, that the real breakthrough of youth began. Apart from some rather obvious religious symbolism of a kind totally absent from his later films, *Le Beau Serge* set the pattern for Chabrol's best work. With *Les Cousins* (1959) this pattern became clear: the sexual interaction of a handful of characters against a background of elegance, with delicate psychological insight interspersed with moments of farce. With his writer Paul Gegauff, Chabrol continued in this vein to produce *A Double Tour* and *Les Bonnes Femmes* (1959) and *Les Godelureaux* (1960). But after his initial success Chabrol's films were proving less and less popular and with his next few films – works like *L'Œil du Malin*, a tale of jealousy set in Germany, and *Ophélia* (1962), an idiosyncratic version of 'Hamlet' – he seemed to be losing his audience completely. As a result he was for some years constrained to make purely commercial films – thrillers, spy films and the like. Despite these later difficulties Chabrol's initial success opened the way for other 'Cahiers du Cinéma' critics. FRANÇOIS TRUFFAUT won international reputation with a sympathetic study of a young delinquent, *Les Quatre Cents Coups* (1959). He followed this with two films in a rather different vein – a parody gangster film, *Tirez sur le Pianiste* (1960), full of quirky humour, and *Jules et Jim* (1961), a lighthearted tale of two men linked by friendship and by their love of the same woman, the enigmatic Catherine (JEANNE MOREAU). With *La Peau Douce* (1964) Truffaut attempted to deepen his style with a more serious study of adultery. Though Truffaut's best works are his closely observed, sensitive and humorous studies of the young – *Les Quatre Cents Coups* and *Baisers Volés* (1968) and *L'Enfant Sauvage* (1970) – he himself nourishes an admiration for HITCHCOCK. This is apparent in his intelligent but unengaging adaptations of Anglo-Saxon novels: *Fahrenheit 451* (1966) from Ray Bradbury, *La Mariée était en Noir* (1967) and *La Sirène du Mississippi* (1969), both from William Irish.

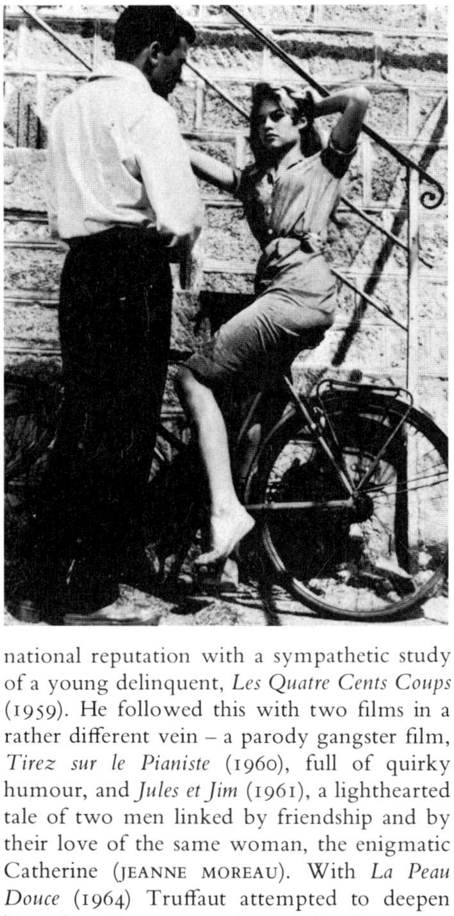

Above: Jacques Tati (holding rope) in 'Jour de Fête' (Tati, 1947)
Below: Jean-Louis Trintignant and Brigitte Bardot in 'Et Dieu Créa la Femme' (Roger Vadim, 1956)

Chabrol and Truffaut are, naturally enough for ex-film-critics, largely shaped by cinematic influences. Others of the 'Cahiers du Cinéma' group are more literary. ERIC ROHMER, after a sombre first feature, *Le Signe du Lion* (1959), embarked on a series of 'moral tales', some of them in 16 mm. The felicities of *La Collectionneuse* (1967), *Ma Nuit chez Maud* (1969) or *Le Genou de Claire* (1970) are as much verbal as visual. The rather austere JACQUES RIVETTE is likewise very literary, having adapted one film from Diderot (*Suzanne Simonin, la Religieuse de Diderot*, 1966) and set two others against a background of the production of a stage classic. Both *Paris Nous Appartient* (1961) and *L'Amour Fou* (1968) study the disintegration of human relationships, the one in the context of rehearsals for 'Pericles', the other during a production of Racine's 'Andromaque'.

But the figure who towers over all the 1960s in France is JEAN-LUC GODARD. With 18 features and numerous 'sketches' for collective films in the decade, Godard is the most prolific and influential of modern French film makers. Beginning with a jaggedly edited homage to the gangster film, *À Bout de Souffle* (1959), which established JEAN-PAUL BELMONDO as a star, Godard went on to paint a series of portraits of his wife, ANNA KARINA and to probe his relationship with her. The variety of these films is startling: *Le Petit Soldat* (1960) re-examined the gangster motifs in an Algerian Liberation context, while *Une Femme est une Femme* (1961) was a tribute to the American

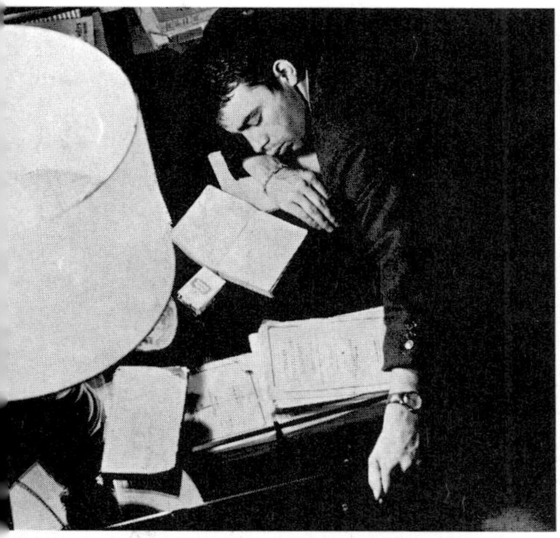

Top: Gérard Blain in 'Les Cousins' (Claude Chabrol, 1959)
Above: Jeanne Moreau and Oskar Werner in 'Jules et Jim' (François Truffaut, 1959)
Below: Albert Rémy, Claire Maurier and Jean-Pierre Léaud in 'Les Quatre Cents Coups' (François Truffaut, 1959)

Top: Giani Esposito in 'Paris nous Appartient' (Jacques Rivette, 1961)
Above: Jean-Paul Belmondo and Jean Seberg in 'À Bout de Souffle' (Jean-Luc Godard, 1959)
Below: Anna Karina in 'Bande à Part' (Jean-Luc Godard, 1964)

musical. In the pseudo-sociological *Vivre sa Vie* (1962) Karina appeared as a prostitute, while in *Bande à Part* (1964), a tender film set in the ugly Parisian suburbs, she appeared as a young girl full of romantic dreams. The climax of this phase of Godard's work was *Pierrot le Fou* (1965). By this time, however, Godard had also made an anti-war fable, *Les Carabiniers* (1963), analysed the nature of film with the aid of FRITZ LANG and an Alberto Moravia novel in *Le Mépris* (1963), and made films about adultery (*Une Femme Mariée*, 1964) and the dehumanized world of the future (*Alphaville*, 1965). After *Pierrot le Fou* Godard's films show new concerns. There is the analysis of society, evident in *Masculin-Féminin* (1965) and *Deux ou trois Choses que je sais d'elle* (1966), and Godard's particular concept of politics ('Walt Disney and Blood') is exemplified by *Made in USA* and *La Chinoise* (1967). With his bitter and in places horrific study of modern life, *Weekend* (1967), Godard paid a virtual farewell to the commercial cinema. Political ideas and action have come to be far more important to him than fictional film-making, and his more recent films – the British *Sympathy for the Devil* or the French television film *Le Gai Savoir* (1968) – have scarcely been designed for normal cinema audiences. Godard remains, however, a potent influence on young film-makers.

One film-maker who can stand comparison with Godard is the ex-documentarist ALAIN RESNAIS, a more austere figure who made only five films in his first ten years as a feature director. In each case Resnais worked with a novelist to produce a film of outstanding interest, probing such themes as time and memory, reality and imagination. With *Hiroshima Mon Amour* (1959), scripted by MARGUERITE DURAS, he made an audacious début with a film that linked two love stories fourteen years apart in time and dared to talk about the atomic bomb in a fictional context. Working with ALAIN ROBBE-GRILLET, Resnais then produced the most enigmatic of modern French films, *L'Année Dernière à Marienbad* (1961), perhaps best described as an attempt to tell the story of a love affair from the inside, as it is lived. The labyrinthine workings of Robbe-Grillet's plot were well matched by the beauty of Resnais's staging and lighting. By contrast to this timeless work, *Muriel* (1963), written by Jean Cayrol (who had previously scripted *Nuit et Brouillard*), was a strictly chronological study, set in Boulogne. Once more, as in Resnais's first film, the reawakened past swamped the present. Different sides of Resnais's character were apparent in his next two films. In *La Guerre est Finie* (1966), made from a script by Jorge Semprun, he dealt with left-wing refugees from Franco's Spain who endlessly and hopelessly plot revolution, while *Je t'aime, je t'aime* (1968), scripted by Jacques Sternberg, showed his sense of humour and interest in science fiction. One outcome of Resnais's work has been the increasing involvement of writers in the film. All the first three script-writers have subsequently directed films, the most important writer-turned-director being Alain Robbe-Grillet. In works like *L'Immortelle* (1963), *Trans-Europ-Express* (1967), *L'Homme qui Ment* (1968) and *L'Éden et Après* (1970) he explored the problem of film narrative, the clash of real and imaginary, and the erotic element in our lives.

Resnais's fellow documentarist GEORGES

Above: 'La Chinoise' (Jean-Luc Godard, 1967)
Below: 'L'Année Dernière à Marienbad' (Alain Resnais, France-Italy, 1961)

FRANJU made the transition to features in 1958 with a film about a young man condemned to a lunatic asylum, *La Tête Contre les Murs*. Unlike Resnais, Franju tends to use the accepted forms of film, his second feature, *Les Yeux Sans Visage* (1959), being a horror film and his third, *Pleins Feux sur l'Assassin* (1961), a murder mystery. To such subjects Franju brings a unique poetry, a lighting style deeply influenced by the German silent cinema and an anarchist sense of revolt. These qualities are also evident in his later films, two adaptations of literary works – *Thérèse Desqueyroux* (1962) from Mauriac and *Thomas l'Imposteur* (1965) from a JEAN COCTEAU novel – and his homage to the silent screen in the form of a remake of FEUILLADE's serial, *Judex* (1963). Another director of Franju's generation who made a masterly series of films in the 1960s was JEAN-PIERRE MELVILLE, who, after 14 years as a director, embarked on a new sort of career with *Léon Morin, Prêtre* (1961), an ambiguous tale about the love of a priest and a young widow. Then, in conscious emulation of the American cinema he admires so much, Melville made a series of gangster films: *Le Doulos* (1963) with JEAN-PAUL BELMONDO, *Le Deuxième Souffle* (1966) with Lino Ventura, and *Le Samourai* (1967) which starred ALAIN DELON. These, together with his Simenon adaptation, *L'Aîné des Ferchaux* (1963) and his Resistance film, *L'Armée des Ombres* (1969), are the best French action pictures of the period, classically constructed and edited. Melville's idol among French directors was JACQUES BECKER, whose last film, *Le Trou* (1960), was a brilliant study of prison loyalties and betrayal. The writer of this film and *Le Deuxième Souffle* was José Giovanni (born 1923), who directed his own films as well as providing scripts for many younger directors.

Generally speaking the work of the veteran directors in the 1960s is of less interest than that of the comparative newcomers. Renoir, Clair and Carné remained active but provided nothing to stand comparison with their earlier successes; but LUIS BUÑUEL, after a series of very uneven Franco-Mexican co-productions recovered his old verve with works like *Le Journal d'une Femme de Chambre* (1964), *La Voie Lactée* (1968) and, more especially, *Belle de Jour* (1967). JACQUES TATI made only one film in the 1960s, *Playtime* (1967), but this is a major work, the climax of a lifetime's concern with making comedy more realistic and bringing home to audiences the humour in the world around them. The most striking series of films was provided by ROBERT BRESSON, who in 1965 made *Au Hasard Balthazar*, a strange and enigmatic work which wove together the stories of a donkey and a young girl both vanquished by the world. He followed this with two other studies of victims, *Mouchette* (1967), adapted from Georges Bernanos, and *Une Femme Douce* (1969) from Dostoievsky. Bresson's personal style with its fastidious choice of detail and control of word and gesture is seen at its best in these works.

Those younger directors who had prepared the way for the new generation in 1958 and before had varying success in the 1960s. ALEXANDRE ASTRUC did little of real note after his beautiful adaptation of Maupassant, *Une Vie* (1957), and his film about a woman struggling to be free, *La Proie pour l'Ombre* (1960); of ROGER VADIM's prolific output only *Barbarella* (1968) deserves mention for its visual extravagance. By contrast, LOUIS MALLE steadily widened his range and deepened his approach with *Zazie dans le Métro* (1960), *Vie Privée* (1961) and, especially, his film about a man driven to suicide, *Le Feu Follet* (1963). Since then the scope of his work has been very wide: *Viva Maria* (1965), a colourful extravaganza set in South America, *Le Voleur* (1967), a further assault on bourgeois values, and *Calcutta* (1969), a documentary on India. AGNÈS VARDA too produced a series of outstanding works, in her case reflecting an interest in the interaction of reality and fantasy: *Cléo de Cinq à Sept* (1961), *Le Bonheur* (1965) and *Les Créatures* (1966). In 1969 she went to Hollywood and there produced one of her more engaging works, *Lions Love*. The late 1960s also saw the best films of CLAUDE CHABROL, who re-established himself as one of the leading directors of his generation with *Les Biches* (1968), which was followed by *La Femme Infidèle* (1968), *Que la Bête Meure* (1969) and *Le Boucher* (1970) among others. These films like his first works probed the sexual interaction of a small number of characters with great technical skill and sureness of touch.

Aside from the work of these major directors of the decade, the 1960s present a confused but lively picture. There was a shortlived vogue for *cinéma-vérité*, which stressed the importance of spontaneity and direct recording of reality. The leading exponent of this was the ethnographer JEAN ROUCH, who made several documentaries on black Africa before going on to mix documentary and fantasy in works like *Moi un Noir* (1958) and *La Pyramide Humaine* (1961). In 1961 too he applied his methods to Paris to make *Chronique d'un Été*, but his attempts at purely fiction films were less successful and he returned to documentary work: *La Chasse au Lion à l'Arc* (1965) and *Jaguar* (1968). CHRIS MARKER's *Le Joli Mai* (1962) is a companion

Monica Vitti in 'The Red Desert' (Michelangelo Antonioni, Italy, 1964)

piece to Rouch's *Chronique d'un Été* but Marker's range is much wider. He is a former poet and novelist, and his films are essays on the places he has visited. He uses witty, literary commentaries alongside the images to evoke Russia in *Lettre de Sibérie* (1957), Israel in *Description d'un Combat* (1960) or Cuba in *Cuba Si!* (1961). But he is not limited to travel documentaries and he has also made an animated cartoon, *Les Astronautes* (1959), with WALERIAN BOROWCZYK, a Resnais-style fictional short, *La Jetée* (1963) and was responsible for the collective anti-war film, *Loin du Viêtnam* (1967). Among more conventional film makers of the decade there were several who have been outstandingly successful in established genres on the Hollywood model. PIERRE ÉTAIX followed Jacques Tati in attempting to renew the style of silent comedy in several films, notably *Yoyo* (1965) and *Le Grand Amour* (1969), which showed him to possess the impassivity if not the genius of BUSTER KEATON. JACQUES DEMY, who made his début with the excellent *Lola* (1960), struggled to establish an authentic French musical-comedy style. His two films with the composer Michel Legrand, *Les Parapluies de Cherbourg* (1963) and *Les Demoiselles de Rochefort* (1966), were remarkable if hybrid works, but Demy was surprisingly unsuccessful when he went to work for Columbia in Hollywood (*The Model Shop*, 1968). CLAUDE LELOUCH after many struggles and setbacks found an audience with his sixth film, *Un Homme et une Femme* (1966), which had an international influence thanks to his masterly use of soft focus and the ZOOM LENS to convey a romantic mood. More promising for future developments are the studies of personal disintegration – like *La Vie à l'Envers* (1963) by Alain Jessua (born 1932) and *L'Une et l'Autre* (1967) and *Pierre et Paul* (1969) by René Allio (born 1924), a former stage designer – and the poetic vision of beauty and horror contained in *Goto, l'Île d'Amour* (1968), and *Blanche* (1971), directed by WALERIAN BOROWCZYK. The French cinema entered the 1970s without the flood of newcomers it had possessed ten years earlier but there is still an abundance of personal film-makers of this kind from whom major works can be confidently expected. RA

Top: Corinne Marchand in 'Cléo de Cinq à Sept' (Agnès Varda, 1961)
Above: Catherine Demongeot (back left) in 'Zazie dans le Métro' (Louis Malle, 1960)
Below: Edith Scob and Alida Valli in 'Eyes Without a Face' (Georges Franju, 1959)

Franju, Georges

Born 1912 in Fougères, France. Director. He was a theatre set designer for some time and in the mid-1930s founded, with Henri Langlois, one of the cinema's greatest archives, the *Cinémathèque Française*. Like other French directors in the post-war years, he used short films as a personal means of examining social ideas and attitudes: *Le Sang des Bêtes* (1949) takes an unflinching look at an abattoir; *Hôtel des Invalides* (1951) tours the French war museum and makes an anti-war statement at the same time; *Le Grand Méliès* (1951) is an affectionate harkback to the French cinema's age of innocence. These and other shorts contain an undercurrent of torment and fear which was to find further expression in the feature films which followed, notably *La Tête Contre les Murs* (1958), with its images of madness, real and imagined, and *Les Yeux sans visage* (1959), a kind of surrealist horror story whose macabre content was tempered with a strange pity. The spirit of COCTEAU is often evoked in Franju's work as well as that of FEUILLADE. Franju's remake of *Judex* (1963) sums up his thematic and visual preoccupations: loss of innocence, the sudden eruption of terror and violence, the use of doves as a poetic symbol. Two literary adaptations, Mauriac's *Thérèse Desqueyroux* (1962) and Cocteau's *Thomas l'Imposteur* (1965), illuminate their originals with highly charged images, although Franju's occasional falterings on a purely narrative level prevent their achieving total success. Following several minor projects and some work in television, Franju returned to the commercial cinema with an idiosyncratic adaptation of Zola's *La Faute de l'Abbé Mouret* (1970), turning it into a burning attack on religious dogma almost worthy of BUÑUEL. Its emphasis on ecstatic nature painting and the need for earthly as well as spiritual love, indicates that Franju, at least, has retained his own voice among the intellectual confusions of the contemporary French film scene. A study of his work, 'Franju', by Raymond Durgnat, appeared in 1967. JG

Frankenheimer, John

Born 1930 in New York, USA. With ARTHUR PENN, one of the most important of younger American directors to have come to films from television. From his first film, *The Young Stranger* (1957), his vivid studies of characters facing their moment of truth – whether political, physical or psychological – dominated the American screen until his work bogged down in the extravagant style of *Grand Prix* (1967) and the over-pretentiousness of *The Fixer* (1968). A welcome return to form was *The Gypsy Moths* (1969). Before going into films, he directed numerous television plays, for which he won several awards. A dynamic director on the set, he has an incomparable visual sense and cunning, qualities which especially distinguished his alarming political thrillers, *The Manchurian Candidate* (1962) and *Seven Days in May* (1964). His science fiction identity-drama, *Seconds* (1966), was a flawed but

'Fellini-Satyricon' (Federico Fellini, Italy, 1969)

impressive study of modern neuroses. Other films: *The Young Savages* and *All Fall Down* (1961), *Birdman of Alcatraz* (1962), *The Train* (1964), *The Extraordinary Seaman* (1968), *I Walk the Line* (1970), *The Horsemen* (1971). See 'The Cinema of John Frankenheimer' by Gerald Pratley (1969). MH

Franklin, Sidney Arnold

Born 1893 in San Francisco, USA. Producer and director. In films from 1915, beginning as assistant operator. During and after the First World War he made several films with his brother Chester, including sensitive versions of fairy-tales (*Jack and the Beanstalk*, 1917), and vehicles for NORMA SHEARER, MARY PICKFORD and the Talmadge Sisters. In the 1930s, he directed several successful films of stage plays, including *Private Lives* (1931) and *The Barretts of Wimpole Street* (1934, which he remade, less memorably, in 1957). After *The Good Earth* (1937), a lavish visualization of Pearl Buck's Chinese story, he turned to production at MGM, working on many prestige, 'inspirational' subjects: *Mrs Miniver* and *Random Harvest* (1942), *Madame Curie* (1943) and CLARENCE BROWN's charming *The Yearling* (1946). His post-war output has been more uneven and rather spasmodic. JG

Freed, Arthur

Born in 1894 in Charleston, USA. Producer. During 1920s and 1930s gained considerable reputation as a popular song writer and night-club contributor and was directing plays when IRVING THALBERG hired him for MGM. He subsequently produced the great series of MGM musicals which began in the 1940s with the first films of MINNELLI (whom he discovered and cultivated). Freed gathered together a unique collection of writers, directors, designers and arrangers as well as utilizing the talents of great performers like GARLAND, KELLY, ASTAIRE and Charisse, enabling them to make what was then considered to be experimental or way-out work – *Yolande and the Thief* (1946), *Summer Holiday* and *The Pirate* (1948). The innovatory musicals of Kelly and DONEN were produced under his aegis as were Minnelli's best films including *An American in Paris* (1951) and *The Band Wagon* (1953), and MAMOULIAN's *Silk Stockings* (1957). It is difficult to pinpoint Freed's precise contribution to all these films, apart from his obvious knowledge of all aspects of musical theatre. Clearly, he had faith in his projects (not all of which caught on at the box-office) and some, like *Singin' in the Rain* (1952), have now become classics of one of the cinema's most enjoyable genres. JG

Above: John Frankenheimer (1971)
Below: Pierre Fresnay in 'Monsieur Vincent' (Maurice Cloche, France, 1947)

Freeze Frame

A single frame which has been printed over and over again in an optical printer to the required footage.

Frend, Charles

Born 1909 in Pulborough, England. Editor and Director. Educated Kings School, Canterbury, and Oxford. Began his career in 1931 as editor at British International Pictures at Elstree, working subsequently for Gaumont-British and MGM-British. He cut many of HITCHCOCK's British films: *Waltzes from Vienna* (1933), *Secret Agent* (1936), *Sabotage* and *Young and Innocent* (1937). He also edited *A Yank at Oxford* and *The Citadel* (1938), *Goodbye Mr Chips* (1939) and *Major Barbara* (1940). He then joined MICHAEL BALCON at Ealing Studios as a director, largely of elaborately-staged, semi-documentary dramas including *The Big Blockade* (1941), *The Foreman went to France* (1942), *San Demetrio, London* (1943), *Johnny Frenchman* (1945), *The Loves of Joanna Godden* (1947), *Scott of the Antarctic* (1948), *The Cruel Sea* (1956). His later films include *Cone of Silence* (1960) and *Girl on Approval* (1962). He has also directed films for television.

Fresnay, Pierre

Born 1897 in Paris, France. Notable French stage and screen actor, who made his film début in the trilogy *Marius* (1931), *Fanny* (1932) and *César* (1934). Before that, however, he had established himself as a leading theatre actor in Paris and London. In England he played a small role in Hitchcock's *The Man who Knew too Much* (1934) and proved himself a considerable film actor in RENOIR's *La Grande Illusion* (1937). Probably his most popular role was as the suffering priest in *Monsieur Vincent* (1947), though the characterization tended to type him in subsequent works. Other films include: *Königsmark* (1936), *Mademoiselle Docteur* (1937),

Le Corbeau (1943), *Dieu a Besoin des Hommes* (1950), *The Fanatics* (1957).

Freund, Karl (1890–1969)
Born in Czechoslovakia. Cinematographer and director. Began his career as a newsreel cameraman, and became one of Germany's leading cinematographers during the silent period before going to Hollywood in 1929. He was responsible for luminous, stylized, often theatrical photography, using special effects, in such German films as the WEGENER-GALEEN production of *The Golem* (1920), MURNAU's films *The Last Laugh* (1924), *Tartuffe* (1925) and *Faust* (1926), DUPONT's *Vaudeville* (1925), and LANG's *Metropolis* (1926). He played a prime part in both the production and photography of RUTTMANN's documentary, *Berlin* (1927). In the USA he was responsible for the photography of such films as *Dr Jekyll and Mr Hyde* and *Dracula* (1931), *Camille* (1936), *The Good Earth* (1937, for which he won an Academy Award), *Marie Waleska* (1938), *Pride and Prejudice* (1940) and *Key Largo* (1948). He also directed a few films, including *The Mummy* (1933). Late in life he became a cameraman for television series, in particular *I Love Lucy*.

Fuller, Samuel
Born 1911 in Worcester, Massachusetts, USA. By a determined policy of sticking to low-budget production, often acting as his own producer, Fuller has remained the most personal and authoritative of recent American directors. This fact explains the great critical admiration he has received – especially from the 'Cahiers du Cinéma' schools of criticism – notwithstanding the crude though compelling melodrama of his subjects and his simplistic 'anti-Red' attitudinising. A deep admirer, Andrew Sarris, has called Fuller 'an authentic American primitive'. Films: *I Shot Jesse James* (1949), *The Baron of Arizona* and *The Steel Helmet* (1950), *Fixed Bayonets* (1951), *Park Row* (1952), *Pickup on South Street* (1953), *Hell and High Water* (1954), *House of Bamboo* (1955), *China Gate*, *Run of the Arrow* and *Forty Guns* (1957), *The Crimson Kimono* (1959), *Verboten!* (1960), *Underworld USA* (1961), *Merrill's Marauders* (1962), *Shock Corridor* (1963), *The Naked Kiss* (1964). He has also played small parts in *Pierrot le Fou* and *The Last Movie* (1971).

Furie, Sidney J.
Born 1933 in Toronto, Canada. Director, writer and producer for both television and films, who came to Britain in 1959. Films he has directed include: *The Young Ones* (1962), *The Leather Boys* (1963), *Wonderful Life* (1964), *The Ipcress File* (1965), *The Naked Runner* (1967), *The Lawyer* (1968). He also directed the *Hudson's Bay* television series.

Fusco, Giovanni
Born 1906 in Sant'Agata dei Goti, Benevento, Italy. Composer. Although he began writing film scores from 1936, his idiosyncratic, pared-down style did not really emerge until his work with ANTONIONI: *Cronaca di un Amore* (1950), *La Signora senza Camelie* (1953), *Le Amiche* (1955), *L'Avventura* (1960), *L'Eclisse* (1962), *Il Deserto Rosso* (1964); and RESNAIS: *Hiroshima mon Amour* (1959), *La Guerre est Finie* (1966). Scoring usually for chamber ensembles, Fusco lightly colours a scene with a sudden brassy interjection or a tantalizing whisp of melody, and is particularly adept in conjuring up a tense, disturbed atmosphere. JG

Above: 'Shock Corridor' (Samuel Fuller, USA, 1963)
Below: Will Fyffe and Graham Moffat in 'Owd Bob' (Robert Stevenson, GB, 1938)

Fyffe, Will (1885–1947)
Born in Dundee, Scotland. Comedian, music-hall singer and character actor. Son of John Fyffe, actor and producer, he was on the stage from childhood. After establishing his fame in stock and music-hall (making such songs as 'I belong to Glasgow' famous), he came comparatively late into films. His début was in *Elstree Calling* (1930); his principal films were *Rolling Home* (1935), *Owd Bob* (called *To the Victor* in USA, 1938), *The Mind of Mr Reeder* (one of a series of detective films), *Neutral Port* (1941) and *The Brothers* (1947). He went to Hollywood in 1939, where he made *Riders of the Sea*. He was in process of negotiating a contract to work in Hollywood at the time of his accidental death.

G

Gaál, István
Born 1933 in Salgatarjan, Hungary. Director. One of the most gifted of the young directors who came to the fore in Hungary after 1963. Gaál's work is marked by an uncompromising austerity, already evident in the short films he made after studies at the Rome Centro Sperimentale, where he also acquired marked influences from the neo-realist cinema and from Italian Renaissance painting. Feature films: *Current* (1964), *The Green Years* (1965), *Baptism* (1967), *The Falcons* (1970).

Gabin, Jean
Born 1904 in Paris, France. Durable French star whose tough, world-weary heroes most closely rivalled the image-making success of Hollywood's Gable and Tracy in the 1930s. A manual labourer before he burst into show business in the chorus of the Folies Bergères in 1923, he has retained the working class impudence and vitality which have played a great part in shaping the characters he portrays. He achieved film fame with *Les Bas-Fonds* and, above all, *Pépé Le Moko* (1936), followed by *La Grande Illusion* (1937), *Quai des Brumes* and *La Bête Humaine* (1938), *Le Jour se Lève* (1939). His success was not lost on Hollywood which subsequently remade many of his popular films in English. During the Second World War he made a few unsatisfactory films in Hollywood, returning to France in 1945 to make *Martin Roumagnac*. Since then he has continued to play heroes whose only difference from his early characters is that they are increasingly older. An impeccable actor in his field, whose underplaying matches that of the late SPENCER TRACY, whom he also resembles, he is much admired by younger French film players. Other notable films: *Le Plaisir* (1951), *Touchez Pas au Grisbi* (1953), *French Can Can* (1954), *Maigret Voit Rouge* (1963), *The Sicilian Clan* (1969), *Le Chat* (1971). MH

Gable, Clark (1901–1960)
Born in Oregon, USA. Supreme screen star of the 1930s and 1940s whose intensely masculine appeal reflected the feminine taste in film heroes of the period. Toward the end of his life he was able to display a genuine acting ability that had often been obscured earlier by his personal magnetism on the screen – most notably in his final film, *The Misfits* (1960). A stage actor, he played his first film role in *The Painted Desert* (1931). After a brief period of uncertainty about his 'type', his studio, MGM, found the formula in *A Free Soul* (1931) and allowed him to develop the treat-'em-rough male technique which was such a contrast to the graceful romanticism of the silent era.

In 1934 he was loaned to Columbia for the Capra comedy *It Happened one Night* and won an Academy Award for his performance. Apart from occasional disastrous miscasting, such as his *Parnell* (1937), his roles remained fairly consistent: the quintessential Gable emerging as Rhett Butler in *Gone with the Wind* (1939). After the Second World War his career lost steam, although he gave one of his most mature performances in *Command Decision* (1948). He left MGM after 25 years in 1955 and gave unexpectedly subtle comedy performances in *Teacher's Pet* (1958), *But not for Me* and *It Started in Naples* (1959). Other notable films: *Susan Lenox* and *Red Dust* (1932), *Night Flight* (1933), *Manhattan Melodrama* (1934), *Mutiny on the Bounty* and *China Seas* (1935), *Test Pilot* (1938), *Boom Town* (1940), *Adventure* (1945), *The Hucksters* (1947), *Across the Wide Missouri* (1951), *Mogambo* (1953), *Betrayed* (1954), *The Tall Men* (1955), *Run Silent, Run Deep* (1958). There are several biographies of him, including one by his widow. MH

Gaffer
Chief electrician

Gag
Joke or comic action or situation inserted into a film

Galeen, Henrik
Dates untraceable. Actor, screenwriter, director of Dutch origin. Early career in German and Swiss theatres before working as scriptwriter and actor in German films from about 1910. He appeared in the first version of *The Golem* (1914), which he co-scripted and co-directed with PAUL WEGENER; they returned to the subject in a new form in 1920. He became especially involved in the German experimental movement in the cinema, scripting F. W. MURNAU's *Nosferatu* (1922), and PAUL LENI's *Waxworks* (1924). Among the key expressionist films he himself directed were *The Student of Prague* (1926), which he also co-scripted with Hanns Heinz Severs, and *Alraune* (1927). During the 1920s he visited Britain, where he

Paul Wegener and Conrad Veidt in 'The Student of Prague' (Henrik Galeen, Germany, 1926)

directed *After the Verdict* (1928). There appears to be no trace of his subsequent career.

Gance, Abel

Born in 1889 in Paris, France. French director, author, actor, technical innovator in the cinema. Gance showed a precocious brilliance. He abandoned his job in a solicitor's office to become an actor; like GRIFFITH, he turned to films in their earliest days out of financial need, acting and selling scenarios. He overcame incipient tuberculosis, when his life was despaired of, and at the age of 20 set up as a theatre producer with little success. Sarah Bernhardt showed great interest in his play, 'Victoire de Samothrace', but the 1914 war ended hopes of production. During the war, however, Gance's film scripts brought him some success, and the producer Louis Nalpas gave him 5,000 francs to make a film, *Un Drame au Château d'Acre* (1915), which he shot in five days. Gance, already obsessed by the technical potential of the cinema, found the narrow studio conventions of the period increasingly frustrating although his work proved successful at the box-office. Audiences were not yet ready for the distorting lenses, the rapid travelling shots, the sudden, low-angled close-ups he used in his thrillers and fantasies of the period, such as *La Folie du Docteur Tube* and *Barberousse* (1916), in which he anticipated *Napoléon* (1927) by introducing a triptych shot (three connecting images put side by side on the screen).

Gance was consciously pushing the medium in the direction of psychological drama, and his success with *Mater Dolorosa* (1917) and *La Dixième Symphonie* (1918) established him, aided by his remarkable cameraman, LÉONCE-HENRI BUREL, as a great film-maker. He then went on to make the elaborate anti-war film, *J'Accuse* (1918), released shortly after the Armistice; it proved a brilliant and powerful film. Like its predecessor it featured the actor Séverin-Mars; the battle scenes offered an impressionistic sense of involvement, with quick-cut close-shots and rapid tracking; the parade of the Dead, enacted by soldiers on leave, was deeply moving. *La Roue* (1922), Gance's next film with Séverin-Mars (who was shortly to die from a heart condition) was cut by Gance from nine to three hours and was in many respects the most advanced film so far made. Its powerful psychological impact was achieved through elaborate, impressionistic editing, with very fast, highly calculated cutting in moments of climax.

The high-point of Gance's career was *Napoléon* (1927), originally intended as a six-part epic. Gance drew on every technical device he could to make the audience share in the psycho-physical experience of the action. Many sequences remain famous – for example, the snowball battle of Napoleon's boyhood, shot with the camera strapped to the cameraman's chest – thus forecasting modern *cinéma-vérité* techniques. The violent battle-scenes of Napoleon's maturity were uniquely impressive,

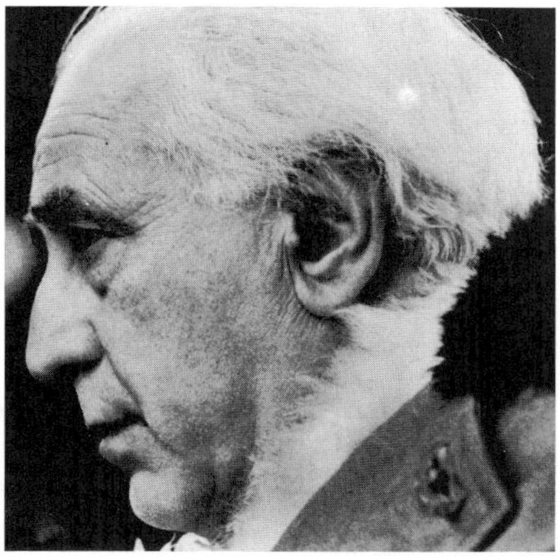

Above: 'J'Accuse' (Abel Gance, France, 1918)
Below: Abel Gance (early 1970s)

using split-screen images. The action finally opened up on to three screens (Polyvision, forecasting Cinerama) used sometimes compositely for panoramic scenes, sometimes with split-image, such as Napoleon seen in close-shot on the centre screen flanked by scenes of battle. Gance even shot some of the scenes experimentally in the third-dimension, and in colour. The film was sadly mutilated after its initial release in Paris and a few cities in Europe. It has rarely been shown since, and never in the form intended by Gance. Screened in its proper form, it was received with astonishment and acclamation. But the industry, faced with the coming of talkies, could not cope with Gance's elaborate inventiveness, which was later to involve stereophonic sound.

Gance has continued to make films, but never again on this scale. His later productions include: a second version of *Napoléon* (1934, a sonorisation), a sound version of *J'Accuse* (1937) *Un Grand Amour de Beethoven* (1936), *Paradis Perdu* (1939), *La Tour de Nesle* (1954), *The Battle of Austerlitz* (1960), *Cyrano et d'Artagnan* (1963). In 1971 at the age of 82, Gance was engaged in producing a sound version of his silent *Napoléon*. For an appreciation, see Kevin Brownlow's 'The Parade's Gone By'. RM

Garbo, Greta

Born 1906 in Stockholm, Sweden. Legendary film actress who, at the height of the Hollywood star system in the late 1920s and 1930s, embodied the essence of all that stardom then meant: the glamour, the mystery, the indefinable magnetism. She is popularly – and accurately – described as the face that launched a thousand imitators. Her extraordinary magic as an actress, in portraying the prototype doomed, destructive heroine who sacrifices all for love, has if anything increased its fascination for film enthusiasts since her retirement from the screen in 1941 and especially during the past ten years. Few of her films were outstanding in themselves, only as Garbo vehicles.

Christened Greta Gustafsson, she left school to earn a living after the death of her father when she was fourteen. She worked as a latherer in a barber's shop and as a clerk in a department store, where she was chosen to model hats for a millinery catalogue. She also appeared in a short publicity film for the store and its producer engaged her to star in another advertising film for a bakery. Unlike her later reputation in America, Garbo was then considered a jovial, outgoing girl inclined to chubbiness.

This led to a meeting with actor-director Erik Petschler and her first commercial film role in *Peter the Tramp* (1922). She studied at the Royal Dramatic Theatre in Stockholm for two years and met the leading Swedish film director MAURITZ STILLER who was to become her mentor, teacher and – to an extent – Svengali. She made her first full-length film for him: *The Atonement of Gösta Berling* (1924). After *The Joyless Street* (1925) in Germany for PABST, she and Stiller went to MGM in Hollywood. At first regarded as just another Continental actress, Garbo was exposed to the usual publicity treatment: her natural shyness and faulty English helped promote the impression of aloofness that was to become a Garbo trade-mark.

With her first Hollywood films, *The Torrent* (1926), *Flesh and the Devil* (1927), *Love* (1928), it was apparant that Garbo was no ordinary actress. As her fortunes rose, however, Stiller's declined and he returned to Sweden. The separation from the man who had shaped and guided her career drove Garbo even further into her shell. In 1930, Garbo made her first talking film, *Anna Christie*, adding greater glory to an already triumphant career. During the 1930s, she appeared in more opulent productions – *Mata Hari* and *Grand Hotel* (1932), *Queen Christina* (1933), *The Painted Veil* (1934), *Anna Karenina* (1935), *Camille* (1936), *Marie Walewska* (1938): despite the differences of period and setting, each role was tailored to the romantic ideal upon which the actress created delicate variations of character. In all but a few films her leading men were no match for her and she worked invariably with the same sympathetic cameraman, WILLIAM DANIELS, the same understanding directors, GEORGE CUKOR and CLARENCE BROWN.

Although there was always an element of deep humour in her performances, even in her most novelettish films, she was thought to be no comedienne until in 1939 she starred in *Ninotchka*. Another romantic comedy followed, *Two-Faced Woman* (1941), much ridiculed at the time of its first showing but since re-assessed as a fairly lively film and no disgrace for Garbo. But with the Second World War, Garbo's popularity (which had always been strongly European) began to wane. Voluntarily, she released herself from her contract with MGM. Since then it has often been rumoured that she is contemplating a screen come-back. In 1954 she received a belated Special Academy Award for her 'unforgettable screen performances'.

Other notable films: *A Women of Affairs*, *The Kiss* and *The Single Standard* (1929), *Susan Lenox* (1931), *As you Desire Me* (1932).

Opposite: Greta Garbo (1930s)
Below: Judy Garland and Ray Bolger in 'The Wizard of Oz' (Victor Fleming, USA, 1939)

Books about Garbo include: a biography by John Bainbridge, 'Great Garbo – the Authentic Life Story'; 'Garbo' by Fritiof Billquist; 'Greta Garbo' by Raymond Durgnat and John Kobal; 'The Films of Greta Garbo' by Michael Conway. MH

Gardner, Ava
Born 1922 in USA. Leading actress, who was once voted the world's most beautiful woman. Has been married to Artie Shaw, MICKEY ROONEY, and FRANK SINATRA; her biography 'Ava' by David Hanna was published in 1960. Main films: *We Were Dancing* (in which she made her début in 1940), *Whistle Stop* (1946), *East Side West Side* (1950), *Showboat* (1951), *The Snows of Kilimanjaro* (1952), *Mogambo* (1953), *The Barefoot Contessa* (1954), *The Little Hut* (1957), *On the Beach* (1959), *55 Days at Peking* (1962), *The Night of the Iguana* (1964), *The Bible* (1966), *Mayerling* (1968).

Garfield, John (1913–1952)
American actor, who first appeared on the stage with the Group Theatre, New York. He later became established as a film actor, whose speciality was the haunted, aggressive, hero of urban, post-Depression America. Main films: *Four Daughters* (1938), *They Made me a Criminal* and *Juarez* (1939), *Tortilla Flat* (1942), *Thank Your Lucky Stars* (1943), *Between Two Worlds* and *Destination Tokyo* (1944), *The Postman Always Rings Twice* (1946), *Body and Soul* (1947), *Gentlemen's Agreement* and *We Were Strangers* (1948), *Force of Evil* (1949), *The Breaking Point* (1950), *He Ran all the Way* (1951).

Garland, Judy (1922–1969)
Born in Minnesota, USA. Superbly gifted American singer and actress, who started out in vaudeville – as Frances Gumm – at the age of three and never let up as a performer from that time. A child star at MGM, she was constantly plagued by weight problems and personal crises. The image of her exuberant, vulnerable heroine in *The Wizard of Oz* (1939) endured throughout her life. An incomparable musical comedy actress during the peak period of MGM musicals, she later grew in stature as a serious actress, making a stunning comeback – after a spell of ill health – in *A Star is Born* (1954). But though she continued to be popular with the public, she made few films after this – the most notable were *Judgement at Nuremberg* (1961), *I Could Go on Singing* (1963). She continued to appear on the stage in solo acts. Her daughter Liza Minnelli is now a successful actress and singer. Main films: *Broadway Melody of 1938*, *Babes In Arms* (1939), *Strike Up the Band* (1940), *Meet Me in St Louis* (1944), *Under The Clock* (1945), *The Harvey Girls* (1946), *The Pirate* (1947), *Easter Parade* (1948), *In the Good Old Summertime* (1949), *If You Feel Like Singing* (1950), *A Child is Waiting* (1962). MH

Garmes, Lee
Born 1898 in Peoria, Illinois, USA. Cinemato-

grapher. After entering films in 1916 as an assistant cameraman, he worked on a number of comedy series before becoming a lighting cameraman in 1924 on MAL ST CLAIR comedies. An inventive black-and-white artist, he specializes in romantic, exotic subjects, his enormous output including early STERNBERG (*Morocco*, 1930; *Dishonored*, 1931; *Shanghai Express*, 1932), the impressionistic *Zoo in Budapest* (1933), and the experimental dramas of HECHT and MacArthur (*Crime Without Passion*, 1934; *The Scoundrel*, 1935, etc). He has worked with many other major directors – HAWKS's *Scarface* (1932), OPHÜLS's *Caught* (1948), RAY's *The Lusty Men* (1952) – and collaborated on several colour spectacles including *Duel in the Sun* (1946). Garmes has also acted as associate and co-director on several films, notably those by Hecht and MacArthur. JG

Garnett, Tay
Born 1892 in Los Angeles, USA. Director. Entering films as a screenwriter with PATHÉ in 1920, Garnett had by the end of the 1920s revealed himself as a commercial director of more than usual abilities. He continued to direct into the 1960s, when he did much work for television. His best-known films included *Her Man* (1930), *One-Way Passage* (1932), *China Seas* (1934), *My Favourite Spy* (1942), *Bataan* (1943), *Mrs Parkington* (1944), *The Postman Always Rings Twice* (1946). In Britain he made *The Black Knight* (1954) and *A Terrible Beauty* (1960).

Garson, Greer
Born 1908 in County Down, Northern Ireland. Red-haired actress, graduate of London University, who first appeared in repertory in Birmingham and continued her acting career on the London stage. Her screen début was as Mrs Chipping in *Goodbye Mr Chips* (1939) and her most famous period was during the 1940s in Hollywood when she was voted 'one of the ten best money-making stars in motion pictures'. Main films: *Pride and Prejudice* (1940), the famous *Mrs Miniver* (for which in 1942 she won an Academy Award as Best Actress), *Random Harvest* (1942), *Madame Curie* (1943), *The Valley of Decision* (1945), *The Forsyte Saga* (1949), *The Miniver Story* (1950), *Julius Caesar* (1953), *Sunrise at Campobello* (in which she played Eleanor Roosevelt, 1960), *The Singing Nun* (1966), *The Happiest Millionaire* (1967).

Gasnier, Louis
Born 1882 in Paris, France. After working as actor and director in the theatre, he began his film career as assistant to Lucien Nonguet of Pathé, later becoming director of films in which MAX LINDER appeared. In 1912 he left France for the USA, where he made his name as the director of serials, inspired initially by the success FEUILLADE had had in France with *Fantômas*. He directed *The Perils of Pauline* (1914), a serial in 20 episodes featuring PEARL WHITE, and backed financially by both Pathé and WILLIAM RANDOLPH HEARST, who gave great publicity to the venture in his press. It was made, like all Pearl White's serials, in New York. Gasnier also directed *The Exploits of Elaine* (36 episodes, also featuring Pearl White, 1915), and other serials, followed by a prolific output of normal box-office features, such as *The Corsican Brothers* (1919) and *The Beauty Shoppers* (1927). He returned to France in 1933, where he directed, among other films, *Topaze* (1933) with LOUIS JOUVET and EDWIGE FEUILLÈRE. From 1935 he continued to direct films in the USA. RM

Above: Vittorio Gassman and Helmut Dantine in 'Kean' (Gassman and Francesco Rosi, Italy, 1956)
Below: Greer Garson and Walter Pidgeon with Christopher Severn and Claire Sanders in 'Mrs Miniver' (William Wyler, USA, 1942)

Gassman, Vittorio
Born 1922 in Genoa, Italy. Handsome Italian stage and screen actor, who achieved superficial international fame as a romantic hero; though his career in the theatre and in several serious films is much more substantial. A notable actor-manager in the theatre, with his own stage company, he made some matinée idol appearances in Italian films before going to Hollywood to make *Sombrero* (1953) and *Rhapsody* (1954), in neither of which was he particularly impressive. Returning to Italy he became more involved with stage work. Main films include: *Bitter Rice* (1948), *War and Peace* (1956), *Barrabas* (1962), *Woman Times Seven* (1967)

Gate
The aperture unit in a camera or projector in which each frame is held momentarily during exposure or projection.

Gauge
The width of a film, normally expressed in millimetres

Gaumont, Léon (1863–1946)
Born in Paris, France. Pioneer inventor, producer, and exhibitor. In 1903 founded one of the two large, rival production companies in France, the other being Pathé. Gaumont originally planned to be a dealer in film equipment only, but was persuaded to enter production, with ALICE GUY as his initial director as early as 1898, the year in which he set up his British company, with Col A. C. Bromhead (born 1876) as managing-director. Production in France by Gaumont remained on a small scale until 1905, when he constructed his glass studios at Buttes-Chaumont. Early directors of note who worked for him included Victorien Jasset and LOUIS FEUILLADE, and it was Gaumont who sponsored in Britain Herbert G. Ponting's film record of the Scott Antarctic expedition (1910–3). In 1914 Gaumont opened his British studios at Shepherd's Bush, London, described as 'the first modern studio in Great Britain'. He followed this with further studios at Lime Grove in 1915; the latter were managed at first by Thomas Welsh and GEORGE PEARSON. Gaumont's interests in Britain were acquired in 1922 by Col Bromhead and his brother, Reginald Bromhead. In France, the Gaumont company passed under the control of combine-finance in 1928, but Gaumont produced *L'Eau du Nil* with synchronized phonograph discs following a system he claimed to have perfected before the war. Among key directors of the 1920s whose films he produced were RENÉ CLAIR, JACQUES FEYDER and MARCEL L'HERBIER. The trade name of Gaumont has remained in existence as a memory which stretches back to the earliest days of the cinema.

Gerassimov, Sergei
Born 1906 in Ural region, USSR. After a promising start with the youthful avant-garde Factory of the Eccentric Actor (FEKS) Gerassimov turned to films in 1930, co-directing *Twenty-two misfortunes* with Bartenev. His films rarely revealed his radical beginnings, but tended to become more and more conservative in approach. The best-known are the highly theatrical adaptations of Lermontov's *Maskerad* (1941) and *The Young Guard* (1948). Gerassimov also directed a spectacular version of *Quiet Flows the Don* (1957–8) and, more recently, a somewhat over-blown contemporary subject *The Journalist* (1967). As a professor at the All-Union State Film Institute (VGIK) in Moscow, Gerassimov directs the directors' faculty and also the actors' studio; and very many of the most significant post-war directors, including BONDARCHUK and Kulidjanov, have been trained under him.

Germany (with Austria)
Pioneers: the Industry Established The founding date in the history of the cinema in Germany is the Bioskop public screening given by Max and Emil Skladanowsky in the Wintergarten, Berlin, on 1 November 1895 – almost two months before the more celebrated public screening by the LUMIÈRES in Paris. Another founder of the industry was Oskar Messter, Germany's first major producer and a pioneer who, unlike EDISON, the Lumières and the Skladanowskys, believed in the future of motion pictures. He set up a studio in Berlin in 1897, and having, as an inventor, contributed the idea of the MALTESE CROSS to projection in his Kinematograph apparatus, which was on the market as early as 1896, stayed in the newly-born film industry to contribute many hundreds of short films of every kind to Germany's output in the earlier years of the century.

Like other producers of his time outside Germany, he made newsreels, 'interest' films, and films featuring famous music-hall artists of the day (such as Otto Reuter and Robert Steidl). When the cinema began to develop from the stage of the two- or three-minute movie 'squib' to the dramatic short, he introduced well-known actors from the theatre, such as Giampetro. His first long film, moving in the direction of feature-length entertainment, was *Andreas Hofer*, made in 1909; it concerned the Tyrolean folk-hero of the Napoleonic period. It was directed by Carl Froelich, later to become a prominent director under Hitler. Max Mack, a young and ambitious director, persuaded the great actor Albert Basserman to appear in one of his films, and this was symptomatic of a slackening in the opposition of the men of the theatre – managers, actors and dramatists – to their new rival. Max Reinhardt, Germany's greatest stage director, allowed his pantomime *Sumurun* to be recorded on film in 1910, and it was from Reinhardt's theatre that many of Germany's greatest screen actors and directors were to come, including PAUL WEGENER, ERNST LUBITSCH, EMIL JANNINGS, CONRAD VEIDT, WILLIAM DIETERLE and F. W. MURNAU.

Interest in films developed in Germany on a considerable scale in the years preceding the First World War; in 1908 some 300 cinemas opened. Not only were German producers making films, but French and American companies had their production and distribution outlets in Germany. Film exhibition had become highly international, and Germany an important centre for the rapidly growing industry. In production, new names began to appear. In 1913 the actor Paul Wegener made the first version of *The Student of Prague*, directed by Stellan Rye, who came from Denmark. The story of a poor student who sells his image in the mirror to a Satanic magician in return for wealth and love forecast what was to become an important vein of the macabre in German film-making of the 1920s. The star system began to establish itself in Germany, as elsewhere, with the films of HENNY PORTEN, a handsome blonde who was to feature in German films for decades from 1909, and another visitor from Denmark, the great stage actress ASTA NIELSEN, who was eventually to settle in Germany and become one of the outstanding stars of the silent period. She first made her reputation in the Danish *Afgrunden (The Abyss)* in 1910, and was to become the dark pin-up girl of not only the German but also the Allied forces during the war. She was introduced to German film-making by another ambitious film producer and exhibitor, Paul Davidson.

The war period saw the film industry fully established in Germany – some 2,000 cinemas (with a further 1,000 in Austria) were exhibiting German and foreign films; new studios were built near Berlin at Tempelhof and Neubabelsberg. Thrown on its own resources through the isolation caused by the war, home production had to increase to supply the wartime public with entertainment. Among the greater artists of the German cinema who made their initial films during the period 1914–8 were the actor-director ERNST LUBITSCH, who directed a comedy series for Davidson, the actor-producer Paul Wegener (whose second film, *The Golem*, was directed by the Dutchman, HENRIK GALEEN), the director FRITZ LANG, and the actor EMIL JANNINGS, as well as the established stars such as Henny Porten and Asta Nielsen. Lubitsch was so well established that in 1918 he was making *The Eyes of the Mummy* and *Carmen*, both featuring POLA NEGRI, a 20-year-old actress and dancer who had come from Warsaw. Both of these were made for the new production combine known by the initials UFA (Universum Film AG).

The Golden Age of the 1920s The end of the war saw the effects of a re-grouping of the German production companies under state influence. UFA was formed in November 1917, with capital of some £1·25 million, one-third coming from the Government and two-thirds from industry.[1] UFA embraced, among others, Davidson's and Messter's companies, and also Sascha-Film of Vienna, which brought into UFA's orbit a group of young Hungarians who were to contribute much to international cinema, including GUSTAV UCICKY. Mihály Kertész (MICHAEL CURTIZ in USA), and ALEXANDER KORDA. Set apart at this stage from UFA was Deulig, headed by the producer ERICH POMMER, who had brought the Austrian writer-director FRITZ LANG to work in Germany, and other companies, some of which merged with UFA during the difficult period of inflation in the early 1920s. UFA became the dominant production combine in Germany during the 1920s, the so-called Golden Age of German cinema, which began in 1919, and was heralded by the films of directors such as LUBITSCH (who went to Hollywood in 1922) and LANG.

[1] The idea of Government intervention in the film industry came from General Ludendorff, Chief of Staff to Hindenburg; his idea was that Germany should be able to match Allied propaganda, which was regarded as highly effective.

Lubitsch made *Madame Dubarry* (*Passion*, 1919, with POLA NEGRI), *Anna Boleyn* (1920, with HENNY PORTEN and JANNINGS) and *Sumurun* (1920), again with Pola Negri, who was in her mid-20s when she, like Lubitsch, went to Hollywood, leaving behind her last film with him, *The Flame*, which was shown in 1921. Lubitsch was still under thirty when he left Germany.

What Lubitsch contributed to the German cinema of the early 1920s as he moved between the spectacle of *Passion* or *The Loves of Pharaoh* (1921, with Emil Jannings) to the more intimate films he made, such as *The Oyster Princess* and *The Doll* (both 1919, with Ossi Oswalda), and *The Flame* (1921, with Pola Negri), was the famous 'touch', the small, closely observed and revealing action or gesture. This helped to establish a much-needed restraint in film acting, and the direction which brought it out. Much German acting of the 1920s, as elsewhere, is slow and heavily melodramatic, over-emphasizing the obvious in the effort to conquer silence by unmistakable dumb-show. Lubitsch was to achieve his greatest work in the USA.

Though she never appeared in Lubitsch's films, ASTA NIELSEN had a similar understanding of detail. From the beginning of her work in the cinema, she endeavoured to establish her characters through detailed study of costume and the handling of significant objects which would reveal thought and emotion. She used her striking face with marked restraint, where other actresses rolled their eyes and twisted their brows to emphasize emotion. Her later work included the strange film *Hamlet* (1920, in which Hamlet is a princess disguised as a man, and in love with Horatio); she appeared frequently as a woman suffering a dire fate in such films as *Downfall* (the prostitute in love with a youth, 1923), *Hedda Gabler* (1924), *The Lusts of Mankind* (1927), and also in PABST's celebrated film, *The Joyless Street* (1925).

Two other actresses who left their special mark on the films of the silent period were Brigitte Helm (born 1908), who appeared notably in Lang's *Metropolis* (1926), playing the opposing roles of the good leader of the oppressed people and her evil, robot double, and in Pabst's *The Love of Jeanne Ney* (1927); and Lil Dagover (born about 1897), famous for her appearances in *The Cabinet of Dr Caligari* (1919), *Destiny* (1921), *Tartuffe* (1925), *The Spy* (1928). Unlike Brigitte Helm, she was to enjoy a prolonged career in German sound films which extended to the 1960s.

One of the innovations the German cinema introduced to film art was Expressionism, which in one form or another, however slight, marked the work of several of Germany's prominent directors during the early 1920s. Expressionism had appeared in painting long before the war, and with various kinds of diffuseness penetrated the German theatre and cinema after the war. It was a form of symbolism and stylization designed to suggest 'phenomena of the soul' in an emotional, dramatic form, and it was peculiarly Germanic or Nordic in origin and feeling. It turned mind or emotion inside out, psychologically speaking, and when it was taken over by the designers of stage or film sets it hovered uneasily between mere decoration and rather over-obvious symbolism. In a difficult period – socially, politically, economically – it enabled German film-makers to become beautifully depressed and fatalistic, their characters caught up in the ruthless mesh of Fate, Destiny and the like.

Above: Henny Porten and Emil Jannings in 'Anna Boleyn' (Ernst Lubitsch, 1920)
Below: Pola Negri in 'Madame Dubarry' (Ernst Lubitsch, 1919)

The film which came to symbolize expressionism was *The Cabinet of Dr Caligari* (1919), a small production costing only some $18,000 and based on a script which POMMER bought from a young Austrian writer, CARL MAYER, and his anarchist friend, the poet Hans Janowitz. The story of the persecution of a young man of unstable mind by his psychiatrist was intended by them as an indictment of all authority; Pommer, however, had the story changed into a psychological melodrama in which this persecution becomes a delusion in the mind of the young madman, who sees his kindly psychiatrist as a homicidal maniac, a fairground showman using a hypnotized somnabulist to commit his murders for him. It was the remarkable expressionist sets and the striking acting of WERNER KRAUSS and CONRAD VEIDT respectively as the maniac and the somnambulist which brought this film success with the intellectuals both inside and outside Germany, and has done ever since. ROBERT WIENE, an uninspired director, could not kill the sense of fantasy and of the macabre which the constantly beautiful images (supposed to express the distortion of a madman's mind) and the intense acting of the two principals created. The principal designers, HERMANN WARM and WALTER RÖHRIG, were convinced expressionists.

Expressionism at once became a cult in the

'advanced' form of German cinema, and as a term came to include almost every form of the macabre or fantastic the studios had to offer between 1920 and 1925. Many of the films made were of lasting beauty, raising melodrama into poetry. Among the films claimed for expressionism are such widely divergent work as LANG's *Destiny* (*Weary Death*, 1921) and *Metropolis* (1926), Arthur von Gerlach's *Vanina* (1922, with Asta Nielsen and Paul Wegener, scripted by Mayer from Stendhal), ARTHUR ROBISON's *Warning Shadows* (1922, with FRITZ KORTNER and Fritz Rasp, a film of hallucination created by jealousy), F. W. MURNAU's *Nosferatu* (1922, adapted from Bram Stoker's 'Dracula'), GALEEN's *The Student of Prague* (1926, with Conrad Veidt) or, finally and very late, Alfred Abel's *Narcosis* (1929). More psychological than expressionistic, though projecting the images of hallucination, was the Austrian G. W. PABST's remarkable Freudian drama, *Secrets of a Soul.* Realism, or naturalism, is the enemy of expressionism, and the German cinema, led by Murnau and Pabst, was to turn in the direction of psychological realism in the middle 1920s, though because they frequently used simplified, densely shadowed studio sets, and expressed psychological reaction by means of images of mental phenomena, their work may appear to carry expressionist overtones. Rather, the two movements, hallucination and fatalistically inclined naturalism, reflected a state of mind typical of the troubled German society of the 1920s, with its spurious prosperity and political dangers. WIENE himself tried to make two wholly expressionist films, *Genuine* (scripted by Mayer, 1920) and, more notably, *Raskolnikov* (after Dostoevsky, with a cast from the Moscow Art Theatre, 1923). But the impulse for expressionism was passing.

Another branch of cinema popular in the earlier 1920s was the legendary, historical and folklore spectacle (pioneered by Lubitsch) which gave the magnificently equipped German studios an opportunity to show their technical prowess. Fritz Lang was responsible for the great legendary spectacle of *The Nibelung Saga* (1924), Murnau for *Tartuffe* scripted by Mayer from Molière (1925), and *Faust* with Emil Jannings (1926), Ludwig Berger for the exquisite *Cinderella* (1923), Arthur von Gerlach for *The Chronicle of the Grey House* (1923), and various directors for the series of films about Frederick the Great, whom Otto Gebühr devoted much of his life to impersonating on the screen. The great cameramen KARL FREUND (who shot *The Golem* of 1920, *The Last Laugh, Metropolis, Faust* and *Berlin* before going to USA in 1929, and FRITZ ARNO WAGNER (photographer of *Destiny, Nosferatu, Warning Shadows, The Love of Jeanne Ney* and many of Lang's and Pabst's later films) were both masters of lighting and the art of photographic illusion, model photography and the devices of the Schüftan and other processes designed to create the kind of images suggesting vast architectural sets, magic forests, landscapes bathed in mist and phosphorescent seas.

Germany, too, understood the importance of the screenwriter, even in the period of the silent film. For example, Fritz Lang's one-time wife, the popular novelist Thea von Harbou, wrote the scripts for most of his films, including: *Destiny* (1921), the macabre thriller *Dr Mabuse, the Gambler* (1922), *The Nibelung Saga* (1924), *Metropolis* (1926), *The Spy* (1928) – an excellent thriller – the space film *Woman on the Moon* (1928), as well as Lang's first sound films, *M* (1931), *The Last Will of Dr Mabuse* (1932). She wrote scripts for other directors, including Murnau. Thea von Harbou's scripts were often marred by over-emphasis and over-simplification, as in *Metropolis*, with its crass, pseudo-mystical social philosophy. But by far the most important and prolific of Germany's silent film writers was Carl Mayer, who was responsible for every kind of script from the expressionist *Caligari* and *Genuine*, or the decorative costume films like *Tartuffe*, to the important branch of German cinema of the mid-and later 1920s, the so-called *Kammerspiel* films (literally, chamber-dramas, or intimate screenplays). His skill lay in understanding the visual necessities of the screenplay with no spoken dialogue – 'light-plays', as he called them. Indeed, he experimented in his close association with LUPU PICK and Murnau in virtually ridding the silent film of dialogue,

Above: Pola Negri and Alfred Abel in 'The Flame' (Ernst Lubitsch. 1921)
Below: Conrad Veidt and Lil Dagover in 'The Cabinet of Dr Caligari' (Robert Wiene, 1919)

Above: Paul Richter in 'Siegfried' (Fritz Lang, 1924)
Right: 'Metropolis' (Fritz Lang, 1926)
Below: Brigitte Helm in 'Metropolis' (Fritz Lang, 1926)

as in such 'intimate' psychological films as Lupu Pick's *Shattered* (1921) and *Sylvester* (*New Year's Eve*, 1923) and the ironic film he wrote for Murnau, *Der letzte Mann* (*The Last Laugh*, 1924), the social and psychological catastrophe which faces a proud and elderly hotel doorman when he is deprived of his great-coat uniform.

Other significant *Kammerspiel* films include: PAUL CZINNER's *Nju* (1924) with ELISABETH BERGNER, Jannings and Veidt, which concerns a faithless wife; *Vaudeville* (DUPONT, 1925), which concerns a faithless husband, played by Jannings; the group of 'street films', including KARL GRUNE's *The Street* (with Eugen Kloepfer as the husband) and Pabst's *The Joyless Street*, concerned with prostitution. Pabst was to make a series of romantically disillusioned films of which *The Joyless Street* was one of the finest – set in Vienna with its post-war inflation, not only had it Asta Nielsen and WERNER KRAUSS (as the profiteering butcher who exploits the starving women around him) but it marked GRETA GARBO's brief entry into German cinema. After the psychological *Secrets of a Soul*, a Freudian study of impotence on which Pabst was advised by two of Freud's assistants, he made *The Love of Jeanne Ney* (1927); *Crisis* and *Pandora's Box*

(1928) both were romantically 'advanced' in their intimate concern with the sexual experiences of women, with fine performances by Brigitte Helm and LOUISE BROOKS, an actress who came from the United States, and played in another film about a sexually-obsessed woman, *The Diary of a Lost Girl* (1929). He also directed LENI RIEFENSTAHL in a mountain film, *The White Hell of Piz Palü* (1929), made in co-operation with the mountain film expert, Arnold Fanck.

These films represent the best and most unusual among a vast output, with its peak in the earlier 1920s of between 200 and 300 productions a year. German studios were mainly concerned to produce films for the box-office. But their record of good and interesting films was as high as anywhere else in the world, and this work was supplemented by that of short film production. Experiment in animation was carried out by HANS RICHTER, Viking Eggeling, OSKAR FISCHINGER and LOTTE REINIGER. The experimental shorts had a remarkable film-maker in ERNO METZNER. The documentary film-maker WALTHER RUTTMANN's *Berlin*, made in collaboration with KARL FREUND, the cameraman, was one of the first of the 'city symphonies', based on an idea by Mayer.

The Coming of Sound Messter had been among the pioneers who, notably in the USA, had endeavoured to establish sound on film. But it was the Germans Günther Vogt, Erich Engl and Josef Massolle who developed the reproduction of sound in terms of light as early as 1918; they called their system – pointing forward to the optical track which fully established sound-on-film – Tri-Ergon, the rights to which eventually passed to Tobis-Klangfilm in 1919. This company developed optical sound recording independently of the American interests in the hands of Warner Brothers and Fox, and by the end of 1930 virtually all German feature films were being made with sound.

A spate of popular musicals initiated the sound era – including *I Kiss Your Hand, Madame* (1929) with the cabaret artiste MARLENE DIETRICH, Wilhelm Thiele's *Three from the Petrol Pump* (1930), featuring the British actress LILIAN HARVEY – who also appeared with Willy Fritsch in Erik Charell's *Congress Dances* (1931) – and *The Private Secretary* (1931, with Renate Müller). It was Pommer who brought JOSEF VON STERNBERG from the USA to make *The Blue Angel* (1930), and Sternberg who insisted on casting Marlene Dietrich as the cabaret singer opposite the formidable EMIL JANNINGS, who played the stiff-necked schoolmaster who became obsessed by Dietrich's vamp. Music and singing were used to particular effect in this carefully stylized film, and Marlene Dietrich, who had so far appeared only indifferently in indifferent films, was, as she put it, 'made over' by Sternberg, who changed her screen image completely, and took her back with him to the USA.

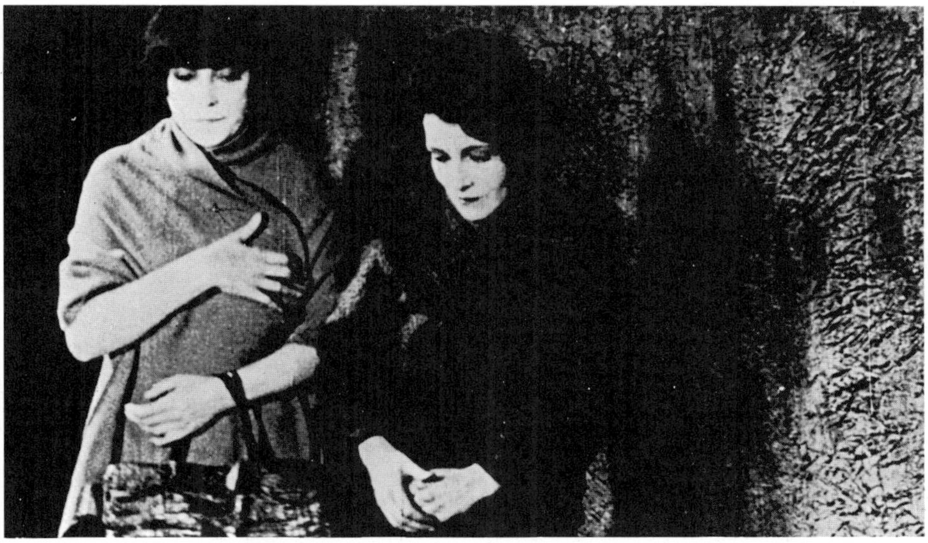

Top: Asta Nielsen and Herta von Walther in 'The Joyless Street' (G. W. Pabst, 1925)
Above: Marlene Dietrich in 'The Blue Angel' (Josef von Sternberg, 1930)
Below: Peter Lorre in 'M' (Fritz Lang, 1931)

They left a Germany deeply shaken economically after the withdrawal of American investments following the Wall Street crash. Unemployment rose phenomenally, and paved the way to the political stresses and disturbances which eventually gave Hitler his opportunity to come to power in January 1933.

Many of the principal films of the three years 1930–2 were either escapist, like the musicals with their rags to riches theme, or romantically melancholy, like PAUL CZINNER's *Dreaming Lips* (1932), which MAYER scripted for ELISABETH BERGNER, playing yet another married woman obsessed by love for a man not her husband – in this case a great violinist who could fill up the sound track. Some films were vaguely social, such as Alexis Granowski's *Song of Life*, about a young society girl who runs away with a worker and has his child. Less conventional were certain social films by the fatalistic Piel Jutzi, *Mother Krause's Journey to Happiness* (that is, suicide), made in 1929, and *Berlin-Alexanderplatz* (1931), while LANG made one of his most powerful social melodramas in *M* (1931), based on the Düsseldorf child-murders. PETER LORRE's *tour de force* performance as the compulsive murderer took him later to England and the USA. Lang went on to make *The Last Will of Dr Mabuse* (1932), which Goebbels immediately banned when the Nazis came to power the following year. Lang claimed that he had Hitler in mind in resurrecting his criminal lunatic with a craving for the destruction of mankind. PABST, working uneasily with Berthold Brecht, created a stylized underworld of the late 19th century in *The Threepenny Opera* (1931), his film version of Brecht's and Weill's adaptation of Gay's 'The Beggar's Opera'. GERHARD LAMPRECHT made a charming film of the chase of a criminal by a group of boys in *Emil and the Detectives* (1931). MAX OPHÜLS made *Liebelei* (1933), a stylish romance based on Schnitzler.

If there was any opposition revealed to what was to come politically for Germany, it found expression in the liberal films, in marked distinction from the right-wing, so-called nationalist productions. The chief of these liberal films were RICHARD OSWALD's *The Captain of Köpenick* (1931), which mocks militarism and the cult of the uniform, Leontine Sagan's *Girls in Uniform* (1931, an attack on ruthless authoritarianism rather than on strict discipline), Victor Trivas's *War is Hell* (1931, with its pacifist message), and Pabst's anti-war films, which are thought now to verge dangerously on the borders of sentimentality but which are superbly made – *Westfront 1918* (1930), with its remarkable sense of actuality and fluid camerawork achieved in the studio, and *Kameradschaft* (*Comradeship*, 1931), with its equally remarkable underground mining disaster reconstructed in the studio and its documentary style location scenes shot above ground. (Tribute should be paid to FRITZ ARNO WAGNER, who supervised the cameras for both films, and to ERNO METZNER, who achieved the miracle of the sets). This was, in effect, to mark the end of Pabst's career as an altogether outstanding film-maker. More strongly to the political Left was the Bulgarian Slatan Dudow's *Kuhle Wampe*, which exposes the suffering of life in the tent-colony of Kuhle Wampe which the homeless set up outside Berlin.

The rising tide of nationalism which helped sweep Hitler to power was reflected not only in the newsreels controlled by Hitler's ally, the right-wing nationalist Alfred Hugenberg, but also in certain films, relatively harmless in themselves, which in one way or another extolled the virtues of nationalist revolution and toughness. These included such period films as *Yorck* (1931), the Frederick films such as *The Flute Concert of Sanssouci* (1930), and Luis Trenker's *Rebel* (1932), set in the Austrian Tyrol. A strange film, *Eight Girls in a Boat* (1932), extols strength through physical discipline when an Amazonian sports coach champions a pregnant schoolgirl. LENI RIEFENSTAHL, later to be Hitler's great champion on the screen, continued her mountain films with Arnold Fanck, but also made *The Blue Light* (1932) independently, a film of considerable photographic beauty extolling the mystique of the mountains which appealed so much to her, as it did to Hitler.

The German Cinema under Hitler and Goebbels
Hitler became Chancellor of Germany on 30 January 1933, and absolute master of the nation the following May when the Enabling Act giving him autocratic power was passed by an enfeebled Reichstag. In March Hitler made his election campaign manager and head of Party propaganda, Joseph Goebbels, Minister of Propaganda and Public Enlightenment. Goebbels took immediate charge of all forms of public expression – the press, publishing, broadcasting, the film and the theatre. This propaganda policy was to impose as absolute a uniformity as possible. The Nazis had a word for it – *Gleichschaltung*, which meant putting everything into the same gear. Conformity was enforced by decree. On 28 March he summoned a representative cross-section of the industry to meet him at the Kaiserhof hotel; he told them that he held films to be of the greatest cultural importance, and painted a very pretty picture of the future to encourage them to conform.

The film industry was essentially conformist with Hugenberg already at the head of both UFA and Deulig. A considerable part of both production and exhibition was, as it were, on the path to being nationalized, and with some four-fifths of the newsreels under nationalist control since 1927, the nationalist viewpoint had been all but universal in screen-news. Nazi-sponsored films had been shown in hired cinemas. Immediately on the assumption of power by the Nazis, Goebbels banned all the films he had listed as undesirable, and started his campaign to outlaw the considerable Jewish element in the film industry. Among those who had to go – or who had already exiled themselves – were such great talents as LUBITSCH, DIETERLE, VEIDT, CZINNER, MAYER, LORRE, MARLENE DIETRICH, and Max Reinhardt, along with such great actors as Albert Basserman, OSCAR HOMOLKA and FRITZ KORTNER. Not all, of course, were Jewish; some, like Veidt, Dieterle and Dietrich, left because they were strongly anti-Nazi. However, many talented men remained, including the actors KRAUSS, HANS ALBERS, Gebühr, JANNINGS, Willy Fritsch, WEGENER, Heinrich George, and directors such as UCICKY, VEIT HARLAN, and (sadly) PABST from 1939.

During the summer of 1933, Goebbels set up his State Chambers of Culture, one for each medium, to handle decrees and directives at every level, national and regional. A provisional Film Chamber was established in July, and took its full official form in September. The Chamber exercised control over employer and employee alike, ordering dismissals for political or racial reasons; everyone had to belong to the single official State trade union, the *Deutsche Arbeitsfront*. Every film made had to be approved and was carefully censored.

Goebbels did not nationalize the industry until the war years, in 1942; he quite simply controlled it as it stood. He was not concerned, as the Russians were, that some sort of propaganda should be apparent in most films. He preferred to keep direct propaganda to a very few prestige features which would make their mark, while the rest should be escapist entertainment. He regarded the newsreels as sufficient for regular propaganda. He wanted the cinemas full. Goebbels extended his control by establishing a Film Bank in June 1933 to loan money to producers of the more highly desirable films; he also, very cleverly, established a state monopoly in the supply of film equipment. The Reich Film Law of 1934 ensured that all scripts should be scrutinized before production, and any changes thought desirable made. Censorship was organized at every stage. A system of 'marks of distinction' for films of special cultural or political worth – the so-called 'healthy' film – was set up, with entertainment tax exemption for the cinemas showing them. 'Unhealthy' films like *Westfront 1918* (1930), *Kameradschaft* and *Mädchen in Uniform* (1931), *M* (1932) were withdrawn. *Congress Dances*, innocuous politically, was withdrawn because Jews had participated in its production. Even before the seizure of power, Goebbels had had his own way of dealing with such undesirable imports as *All Quiet on the Western Front* (1930), adapted from the German pacifist novel by Remarque. He gave tickets to SA hooligans, who entered the cinema and caused a disturbance by releasing stink-bombs and white mice among the audience, and then left before the police arrived. The film was then banned as a potential cause of trouble. Such devices to hinder freedom of expression were no longer necessary. 'Undesirable' films were not imported; in fact, the ratio of home productions to importations changed radically – 42% German films in 1935, 79% in 1939. The emphasis in production was on comedy, but prewar attendance at Germany's 5,000 cinemas remained comparatively low – around 40% capacity, unless the films shown were exceptional. Production costs, however, rose steeply with the changing economy, and many films lost money. However, in a move towards nationalization, the State gradually acquired unprofitable production companies. UFA became state owned in 1937.

The effect was to lower the general standard of German film-making during the period of the régime, more especially, of course, in subject-matter. German films became mostly trivial. They remained, however, on the whole very well-made. A few, indeed, were to be technically outstanding, among them several which rank as prestige propaganda films. It is interesting that of some 1,100 feature films made under Hitler and examined after the war, barely 50 have powerful propaganda content. Nevertheless, Goebbels's Ministry did produce 96 feature films as directly sponsored product; these were known as *Staatsauftragsfilme* – that is,

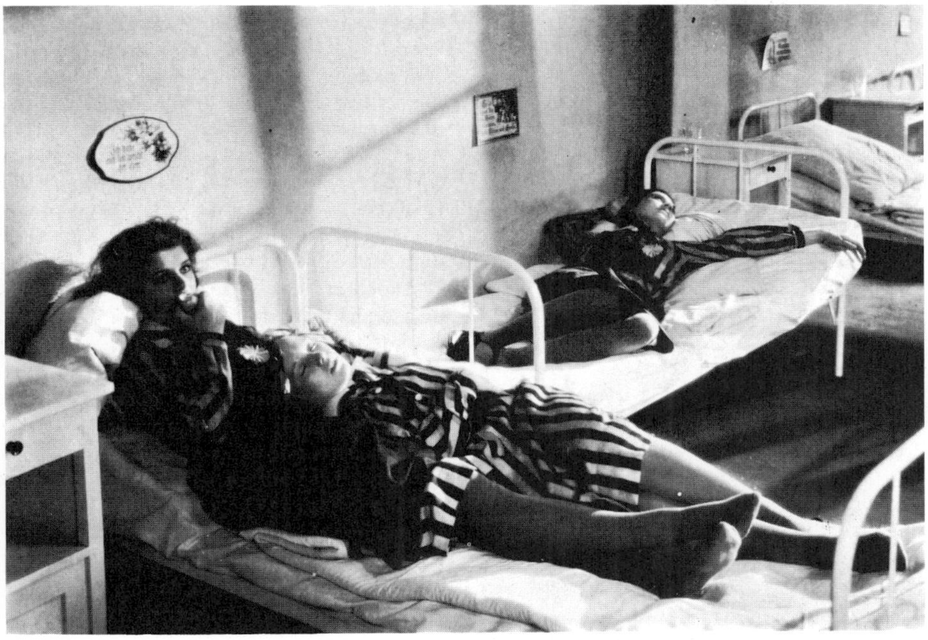

**Top: 'Kameradschaft' (G. W. Pabst, 1931)
Above: Hertha Thiele (centre) in 'Mädchen in Uniform' (Leontine Sagan, 1931)**

films produced and financed by order of the Reich. They did not all necessarily contain overt Nazi propaganda; rather they had nationalist or other content which was considered of special cultural value to the Nazi state. There were a few exceptions, such as *Amphitryon* (1935), directed by Reinhold Schünzel.

Among these more generally nationalist films were the continual flow of productions about Frederick the Great, for example *Der Alte und der Junge König* (1935), *Fridericus* (1936) and *Der Grosse König* (1942), the two latter with Otto Gebühr as the mature King, or *Bismarck* (1940), a film commemorating the statesman who was much admired by the Nazis. There was, indeed, considerable production of historical and biographical films, such as *Friedrich Schiller* (1940) and VEIT HARLAN's celebrated spectacular in colour, *Kolberg* (1944-5). This starred Heinrich George, PAUL WEGENER and Kristina Söderbaum (Veit Harlan's wife); it was in production for two years and only finished during the last weeks of the war. It enjoyed Goebbels's special patronage, partly because its scale was intended to show that Germany was still 'in business' in spite of the catastrophes on the war fronts, and because its theme, the determination of the mayor of Kolberg to lead civilian resistance against Napoleon during the war of 1806–7, was peculiarly appropriate to Germany anticipating eventual invasion of her territory in 1945. The army, too, is shown to be defeatist, and by this time Hitler was constantly at loggerheads with his general staff because his armies were giving ground to the enemy. The film, though completed, was never shown to the public; with a typical propaganda gesture, Goebbels dropped a print by parachute to the army besieged in Brest, where the film had its world première.

Other historical subjects favoured by the Nazis were those dealing from their point of view with the First World War – particularly UCICKY's *Dawn* (*Morgenrot*, 1933), made before Hitler came to power and dealing with the position of a German submarine crew whose vessel was rammed by a British destroyer when they were in fact rescuing British sailors from a ship they had torpedoed, or Wegener's *Ein Mann will nach Deutschland* (1934), about two Germans' hazardous wartime journey back to the Fatherland from South America. Ucicky even made a film about Lawrence of Arabia – *Aufruhr in Damaskus*. These films cannot be classed as hard-core propaganda; rather they represent the kind of nationalistic subjects any country produces, more especially in time of war.

But this period in German cinema will not be remembered for these films, or even for the occasional, non-political, entertainment film with high technical accomplishment – such as the fantasy *Münchhausen* (1943) with its remarkable special effects – but for its various levels of propaganda, some of which were to prove models of this insidious form of art. That they are comparatively few in number is due to Goebbels's deliberate policy that their effect would be enhanced by this scarcity. Each was to make its mark as it occurred. As we have seen, he wanted cinemas to be well attended, and realized that escapism, not propaganda, was the only means of achieving this. Nevertheless, propaganda films were at first rather more numerous. *Hans Westmar* was a largely fictitious biographical film of the pimp and street-fighter whom the Nazis chose to represent as a martyr because he wrote the words of the Nazi anthem, the 'Horst Wessel Lied'; *S.A. Mann Brandt* pitted a Nazi son against a Communist father, as did *Hitlerjunge Quex*. All these films appeared in 1933.

The more sentimental aspects of Nazi nationalism appeared in *The Eternal Forest* (1936), a documentary-feature which presents the strength and numbers of the German people through the image of the indestructible forests; the film is accompanied prominently by music, orchestral and choral, while a portentous voice speaking blank verse unfolds a legend-like history of the German race, emphasizing the importance of the soldier-peasant and the cultivation of the land. The Germans are shown

Top: Otto Gebühr (at table) in 'Der grosse König' (Veit Harlan, 1942)
Above: 'S.A. Mann Brandt' (Franz Seitz, 1933)
Below: 'Triumph of the Will' (Leni Riefenstahl, 1934)

to be an imperishable peasant-aristocracy – a *Herrenvolk* who cannot be destroyed by the threatening forces of the impure.

It was this lyrical strain which LENI RIEFENSTAHL caught in her celebrated *Triumph of the Will* (1934), in effect a paean to Hitler (who commissioned the film from her personally over the head of Goebbels, which did her little good in his eyes). With a large technical staff and 30 cameramen she moved into the 1934 Party Congress at Nuremberg. In spite of Goebbels's efforts to put difficulties in her way, she succeeded in expressing the overwhelming emotional response of great numbers of the German people to their Führer, who descends from the sky in his aircraft like a god come to meet them. The Wagnerian music, the Horst Wessel anthem played as Hitler's plane lands, the beauty of Nuremberg in the dawn, the massed crowds with arms extended to greet Hitler as he glides through them standing in his car, his arm stretched out above them, the great perspectives of people in the Congress Hall as the Nazi leaders pay respects to the Führer, the rhetoric, the rallies, the massed bands and singing which collectively made up Nazi display, have never been better projected. The spectacle was in many respects choreographed for the camera. The emphasis is on youthful fervour, and there can be no doubt the actress–director so signally favoured by the Führer had her heart in the job. *Triumph of the Will* remains a masterpiece of lyrical propaganda, excluding the dark side of Nazism already apparent by 1934 in the street violences, the vicious anti-Semitism, and the restrictions of the police-state and the abolition of civil liberties. This darker side was not to come openly on the screen until the war years. The feature films of the prewar years which reflected Nazism were comparatively mild – films such as *Der Herrscher* (1937), VEIT HARLAN's study of an authoritarian industrialist, with EMIL JANNINGS, or Carl Froelich's *Reifende Jugend*, about a virile, Nazi-minded headmaster. Such films were to intensify during the war, stressing discipline and self-sacrifice.

Far worse than these films were those which expressed anti-Semitism, such as Veit Harlan's *Jew Süss* (1940), which was not an adaptation of Feuchtwanger's novel (in a film version of which CONRAD VEIDT had starred in Britain in 1934), but an exposure from the Nazi viewpoint of the overweening financial grip which the Jew, Süss Oppenheimer, had exercised over the Duke Karl Alexander of Württemberg; another anti-Jewish film was *Die Rothschilds* (1940), which purported to show the vicious financial empire built up by this family of international financiers. The most vicious, and skilful, propaganda film made by the Nazis was probably *The Eternal Jew* (1940), directed by Franz Hippler. This was shot substantially in Poland in the ghettos where the Jews had been herded in various states of starvation and suffering. Hippler's cameraman, ruthlessly choosing the most degraded-looking of these victims, sought to expose the whole Jewish people as an inferior and parasitic race, feeding off the labour of honest and industrious 'Aryans' and infecting the life and art of every nation acting as host to them. Among the 'degraded' people exposed are LUBITSCH, KORTNER, LORRE, Reinhardt and even Einstein and CHARLES CHAPLIN. The climax of the film shows the Nuremberg race laws as a great act of cleansing, following terrible shots of the ritual killing of beasts to produce kosher meat. Nazi record films are shown at their worst in the appalling studies of life and death in the Warsaw ghetto, in the shots made in the concentration camps, or in the film records ordered by Hitler of the trial and executions of the officers and civilians involved in the attempt on his life in July 1944.

Nazi wartime films, naturally enough, attacked the enemy – for example, *Stukas* (1941) shows the French as demoralized and the British in chaos at the time of Dunkirk. Going back into the past, *Titanic* shows the fruitless struggle of an honest German ship's officer in his attempt to expose the President of the White Star Line, whose evil ambitions had led to the disaster from which both of them managed to survive. *Mein Leben für Irland* enjoys showing the British as oppressors in Ireland after the First World War. The best of the anti-British films is undoubtedly *Ohm Krüger* (1941), directed by Hans Steinhoff and featuring EMIL JANNINGS as Krüger, whom the Germans had always traditionally admired for the opposition he had put up to British 'guile'. Goebbels himself scripted some parts of this film, which represents Queen Victoria as a cunning alcoholic and Churchill as the overfed commandant of a concentration camp for starving Boer women. The film is lavishly,

Björn Andresen in 'Death in Venice' (Luchino Visconti, Italy, 1970)

CINÉMATOGRAPHE LUMIÈRE

ROBERT DORFMANN et BERTRAND JAVAL
L'aveu
YVES MONTAND
SIMONE SIGNORET
dans
réalisation de
COSTA-GAVRAS
d'après le récit de LISE
et ARTUR LONDON
adaptation et dialogue de
JORGE SEMPRUN
avec
GABRIELE FERZETTI
et
MICHEL VITOLD

even beautifully made, and displays the sardonic humour in which Goebbels delighted.

Most direct Nazi propaganda was, as we have seen, put over in Germany and the occupied countries in lengthy newsreels, as well as in certain of the instructional films used in schools, films used for indoctrination in the Army and elsewhere, and in the occasional prestige documentaries, such as *Baptism of Fire* (1940), a tribute to the Luftwaffe's part in the conquest of Poland, and *Victory in the West* (1940), on the conquest of Germany's western neighbours. German service cameramen were second to none in courageous coverage on the war fronts for documentaries and newsreels, and their casualty rate was high. The best documentary produced during the Third Reich was Leni Riefenstahl's *Olympiad* (1938), a record of the 1936 Olympic Games in Berlin, commissioned by neither Hitler nor Goebbels, but by the international committee controlling the Games. Once more, Goebbels was affronted, and Leni Riefenstahl's achievement, along with her team of cameramen, is all the greater for the official obstruction she endured. This film stands as the finest record of Olympic athletes and athletics, even in comparison with KON ICHIKAWA's formidable coverage in *Tokyo Olympiad* (1965) some 30 years later.

Post-War German Cinema 1946–8 Germany awoke from the final devastation of the war stunned and uncertain of the future. With their country divided into zones, and experiencing violent differences of policy and treatment as between East and West, the Germans were remarkably quick to re-establish their shattered economy, re-build their homes and get back to work in their rehabilitated industries. By 1946 the cinemas, mostly wrecked in 1945, were beginning to reopen in some numbers (considerable in Berlin), and audiences, tiring of the backlog of films made by the Allied nations, were soon anxious to see the product of the new Germany. Most of the key studios and equipment were under the control of the Russians in the Eastern Zone, where the state-sponsored DEFA (German Film Company) was established in 1946. The Western Allies began to licence individual German companies to make carefully supervised films, while old German films considered politically innocuous were permitted for exhibition.

There was to be a comparatively brief period from 1946 to 1948 when German film-makers were to distinguish themselves, producing films of great social and psychological interest directly reflecting the post-war mood in the various Zones, and the environment of rubble with which the Germans were surrounded. The more coherent group of social films came from the East – among them WOLFGANG STAUDTE's *The Murderers are Amongst Us*, GERHARD LAMPRECHT's *Somewhere in Berlin*, Milo Harbig's *Free Land*, all in 1946, and Kurt Maetzig's *Marriage in the Shadows* (1947). Most of these films were exported and gave the world outside occupied Germany its first direct contact with the German people for many years. These films came to be called 'rubble films', because they showed the appalling devastation of the German cities.

Above: Werner Krauss in 'Jew Süss' (Veit Harlan, 1940)
Below: Robert Forsch and Hildegard Knef in 'The Murderers are Amongst Us' (Wolfgang Staudte, 1946)

Staudte's *The Murderers are Amongst Us* (with HILDEGARD KNEF, or Neff as her name was to be spelled for her English-language films) introduced a new German director of evident talent. It dealt with one of the most difficult of Germany's post-war problems, the former war criminal who presents the innocent post-war face of a good citizen while avoiding detection. In this film two German victims of the Nazis join forces to bring to justice a man who once wiped out an entire Polish village; the ruins of Berlin made their own peculiarly effective setting, and the film was directed with restraint and imagination. While *Somewhere in Berlin* dealt with the special problems facing German soldiers returning after much suffering to their ruined homes, *Marriage in the Shadows* reflected another tragedy on the German conscience, the Nazi persecution of the racial German married to a Jew or Jewess; this film fictionalized the actual case of the actor Joachim Gottschalk, who had committed suicide along with his Jewish wife, the actress Meta Wolff, rather than face separation. *Free Land* had a more documentary approach about the redistribution of land to peasants and workers.

In the Western Zones some films dealt with contemporary problems – *Birds of Migration* showed the wandering German refugees who had no homes left, Wolfgang Liebeneiner's *Love '47* (1947) traced a woman's disillusion with Nazism, while Rudolph Jugert's and HELMUT KÄUTNER's *Film without Title* (1947) showed the reverse of fortune when a peasant-girl, once a servant in a wealthy man's house, marries her employer after he has been bombed out and made destitute – since she is now the one who is well-off, being a farmer's daughter. Arthur Brauner made *Morituri* (1946) with a

Opposite above: Yves Montand featured in a poster for 'L'Aveu' (Costa-Gavras, France, 1970)
Below: 1902 Poster for 'Watering the Gardener' at the Lumière Cinématographe (Louis Lumière, France, 1896-8)

concentration camp for setting. All these were made with British authorization. The Americans brought ERICH POMMER from the USA to supervise German production in their zone, where Robert Stemmle was to make one of the best of the 'rubble films', *The Ballad of Berlin* (1948), with Gert Fröbe as Otto Nobody in an ironic film-revue which satirized post-war German society and its occupiers alike, poking barbed fun at bureaucracy, hardship, black-marketeers, rationing, rubble, everything which characterized Germany at that time.

Few of these films escaped a touch of self-pity, understandable perhaps in the harsh circumstances of Germany during 1945–7. But the main problems were at least faced, as in the American-authorized subject, *Long is the Way* (1947), a Jewish-made film about the sufferings of Warsaw, Auschwitz and the post-war displaced persons' camps. FRITZ KORTNER returned to Germany to appear in *The Challenge*, about the disillusion of a German-Jewish professor who came back to Germany. Another film made in Germany and expressing deep disillusion (directed by the distinguished Italian director, ROBERTO ROSSELLINI) was *Germania Anno Zero* (1947), about the effects of starvation and the black market.

German production in the West was still sparse; only 26 films were made in 1948. But from 1949 a new, more aggressively commercial spirit was to enter the growing film industry. With the economic recovery, German audiences no longer wanted to see rubble films (the rubble was fast disappearing), and the industry turned in the direction of the gradually increasing output of box-office pictures of little merit beyond providing lightweight entertainment.

Decline With the first signs of recovery – following the currency reforms of 1949 – the number of films produced annually soon topped the hundred. The films were (broadly) escapist, many of them sentimental and rather fatalistic, with the traditional German emphasis on the beauty of nature and the evils of 'the street'. Nazism continued to be attacked in a few films, the more notable of which were HELMUTH KÄUTNER's *The Devil's General* (1955, with CURT JÜRGENS, soon to become one of Germany's international stars), about the dilemma of a Luftwaffe air-ace who is anti-Nazi, and Pabst's two films about Hitler, *Ten Days to Die* (*The Last Act*, 1954), a reconstruction of the last days in the Bunker, and *The Jackboot Mutiny* (*It Happened on 20 July*, 1955), about Count Stauffenberg's attempt on Hitler's life in 1944. LASLO BENEDEK came from the USA to make *Children, Mothers and a General* about the last weeks of the war, and Käutner, becoming one of Germany's best established directors of the 1950s, also made *The Last Bridge* (1954), with MARIA SCHELL as a German woman doctor in the hands of Yugoslav partisans. Bernhard Wicki, who had played Stauffenberg in *The Jackboot Mutiny*, and appeared in both *The Last Bridge* and *Children, Mothers and a General*, directed what is usually regarded as the most effective German-made, anti-Nazi film, *The Bridge* (1959), a study of seven boys during the last weeks of war in a small town; they receive their call-up and are left without any leadership to defend a bridge against American tanks. Six of them are killed. Another remarkable war film was Frank Wysbar's *Battle Inferno* (1959), reconstructing the collapse at Stalingrad.

In East Germany STAUDTE made *The Underdog* (1951): the story, derived from a novel by Heinrich Mann, concerned the creation of an authoritarian out of a weak youth. He next made, in the West, one of the best films of the 1950s, *Roses for the Prosecutor* (1959), in which a small-time thief is brought before an official prosecutor who, when holding the same position of authority during the Nazi régime, had condemned him to death just before the end of the war. The result was a sophisti-

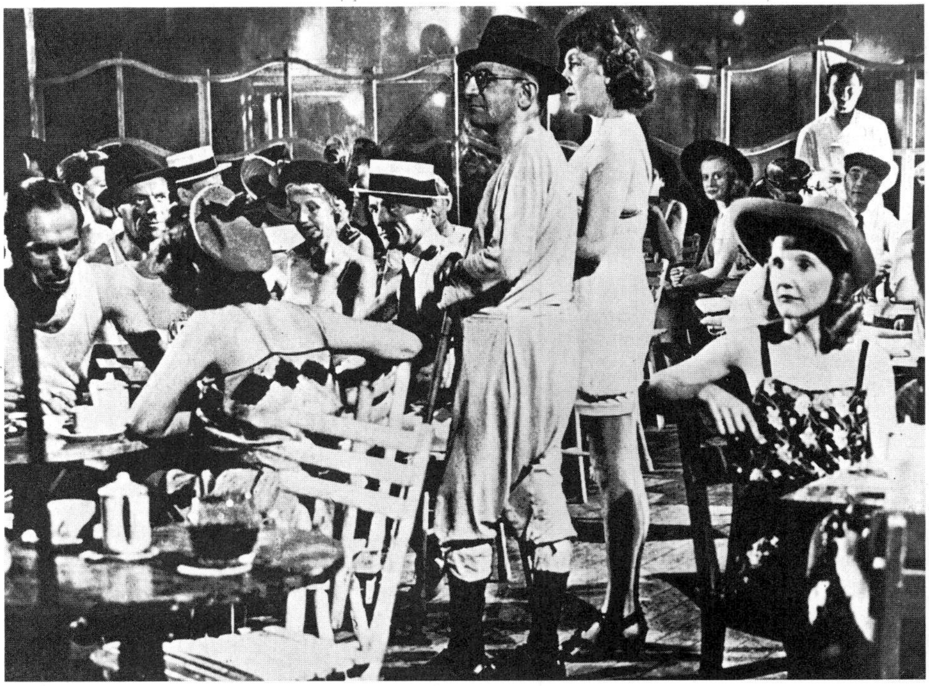

Top: 'The Ballad of Berlin' (Robert Stemmle, 1948)
Above: Curt Jürgens and Victor de Kowa in 'The Devil's General' (Helmut Käutner, 1955)
Below: 'The Bridge' (Bernhard Wicki, 1959)

cated and subtle comedy of political embarrassment. DEFA continued its violent attacks on the Nazis, preferably in a form likely to harry the West, such as Kurt Jung-Alsen's *Duped till Doomsday* (1957) and Kurt Maetzig's *Council of the Gods* (1950), an attack on armaments manufacturers who work alike for Hitler and, later, the Americans. The output from East Germany remained comparatively small and, in the main, ideologically slanted.

Particularly hard-hitting was the documentary, *The German Story* (1954–6), Andrew and Annelie Thorndike's study of the Government's struggle in Germany during the first half of the 20th century. The Thorndikes, and later Walter Heynowski and Gerhard Scheumann, have been unremitting in their production of documentaries using the film archives to attack what they claim to be the corruption of authority in West Germany and the survival in places of influence of former Nazi supporters. The archives have also been used to create a number of studies of the Hitler period made in West Germany, including PAUL ROTHA's *The Life of Adolf Hitler* (1962) and *The Nazi Crimes and Punishment* (*The Nuremberg Trial*, 1958) made by a group of journalists. (Other compilation films on the Third Reich, using German sources, have been made outside Germany – *Mein Kampf* (1960), by Erwin Leiser, a German living at the time in Sweden; and MIKHAIL ROMM's Russian film, *Ordinary Fascism* (1964).

Meanwhile, in the West, the reputation of entertainment films has rested until the mid-1960s in the hands of a very few established directors – Käutner, Staudte, Rolf Thiele (*The Girl Rosemarie*, 1958; *Labyrinth*, 1959; *Tonio Kröger*, 1964, all with Nadja Tiller, and highly erotic), and the specialist in romantic comedy, among other films, Kurt Hoffmann (*I Often Think of Piroschka*, 1956; *Felix Krull*, 1957; *Reinsberg*, 1967). New stars were established – CURT JÜRGENS, Horst Buchholz, MARIA SCHELL, Romy Schneider. HILDEGARD KNEF (Neff) went to work for a while in Hollywood, but she was more successful on the New York stage. Latterly in the 1960s, production has been enhanced by means of co-production with other Common Market countries, notably Italy and France, while the foundation of a Film Fund in 1967, to make grants to assist producers, and of a Film Institute in Berlin in 1968, to regulate the industry's affairs, has assisted at least the more conventional forms of production. Nevertheless quality in general has remained remarkably low. Interest has centred more recently on the younger group of directors, who rose to prominence during the later 1960s.

The New German Cinema It has taken a full generation since the end of the war for German cinema to show signs of true revival, apart from the best work of a very few directors. Perhaps this was to be expected. The young film-makers of today are without any but the most youthful experience of the Nazi régime. They are in sharp reaction against a German cinema which has taken wholly to money-making, including excessive indulgence in sexploitation films, sometimes presented under the mainly spurious guise of sex-instruction.

Leading personalities establishing the new generation are ALEXANDER KLUGE, EDGAR REITZ, Peter and Ulrich Schamoni, VOLKER SCHLÖNDORFF, JEAN-MARIE STRAUB, Roger Fritz, Hans-Jürgen Pohland, and Will Tremper. Their films date from 1966. Among those not aiming to belong specially to the avant-garde are Schlöndorff with *Young Törless* (1966), an anti-militarist, period study of a young boy in a military academy) and *A Degree of Murder* (1967), about a girl-murderess; Fritz with *Girls, Girls* and *Run, Rabbit, Run* (both featuring Helga Anders as a girl facing a sexual dilemma); and Edgar Reitz with *Lust for Love*, a study of the feminine mystique, and *Cardillac* (1969), about a master-jeweller who murders his clients in order to retrieve the masterpieces he has sold them.

Moving more in the direction of experiment are the Schamonis – Ulrich Schamoni with *It*, which concerns abortion and uses a very free camera style, and *Marriage Trouble*, and Peter Schamoni with *Schönheit für Füchse*, on the generation gap. In *Playgirl* Tremper experimented with improvisation in the story of a young girl living freely. But it was ALEXANDER KLUGE, in many respects the best-established spokesman for the generation out for experiment, who first gained an international reputation with the prize-winning films *Yesterday Girl* and *Artistes at the Top of the Big Top – Disorientated*. The first deals with a young Jewish girl disillusioned with life alike in East and West Germany, where she lives a drifting life, sexually and morally, hating to be judged by others, while the second film uses the circus as a symbol of contemporary society; a girl who inherits a circus finds its traditions so deeply embedded it is impossible to reform it as she wishes. Kluge is associated with the Munich group, the most alive centre of production in Germany, whereas Pohland, with *Brot der frühen Jahre*, adapted from a novel by Hein-

Above: Camilla Spira and Martin Held in 'Roses for the Prosecutor' (Wolfgang Staudte, 1959)
Below: Catana Cayetano and Hans Christian Blech in 'Cardillac' (Edgar Reitz, 1969)

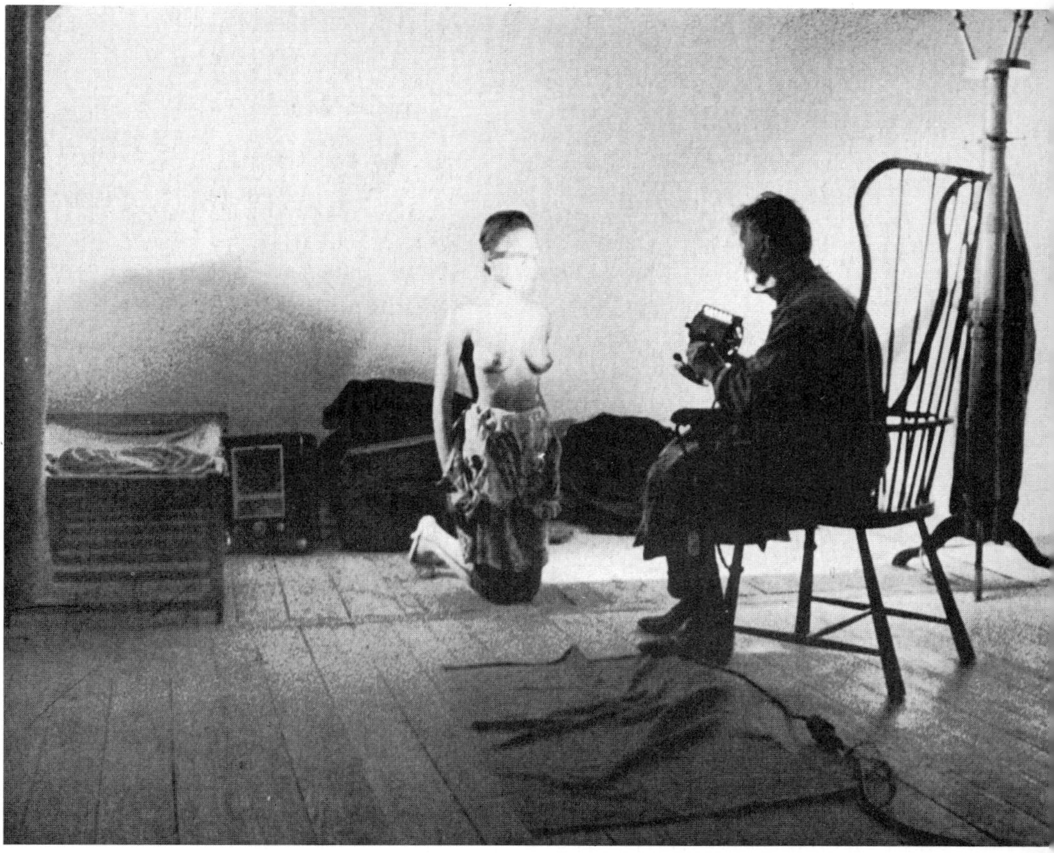

rich Böll, and Will Tremper both work in Berlin.

More austere than these film-makers, many of whom are based on Munich, not Berlin, is JEAN-MARIE STRAUB, a Frenchman. His films are quiet, cool, ironic studies of the authoritarian strain in right-wing society, whether in the distant past, as in *The Chronicle of Anna Magdalena Bach* (which he claims is a Marxist study of a composer working in an authoritarian atmosphere), or his adaptation of the stories of Heinrich Böll, such as *Machorka-Muff*.

Other directors of the newer school are Werner Herzog, Franz Josef Spieker, Peter Fleischmann, May Spils, Marvan Gosov, Johannes Schauf, Hans Rudolf Strobel and Heinz Tichawsky, Eckardt Schmidt, Ferdinand Khittl, all of Munich, and Hellmuth Costard of Hamburg, along with VLADO KRISTL, the cartoonist from Yugoslavia. May Spils's *Zur Sache, Schätzchen* (produced by Peter Schamoni in 1969) was one of Germany's outstanding box-office successes of the period.

The collective work of these directors, with all the faults and self-indulgence evident in some of their films, including the desire to shock, represents something quite new in German cinema, conceived on a scale which amounts to a movement. It remains to be seen if this movement can put German cinema once again into the forefront of international film-making. RM

Germi, Pietro
Born 1914 in Genoa, Italy. Director. A long career of conscientious, individualist but rarely inspired work was rewarded by the immense international success of the moral comedy *Divorzio all'Italiana* (1961). Main films: *Il testimone* (1946), *Gioventù perduta* (1947), *In nome della legge* (1949), *Il Camino Della Speranza* (1950), *La città si defende* (1951), *La presidentessa* and *Il Brigante di Tacca del Lupo* (1952), *Gelosia* (1953), *Il ferroviere* (1956), *L'uomo di paglia* (1957), *Un maledétto imbroglio* (1959), *Sedotta e abbandonata* (1964), *Signori e signore* (1966), *L'immorale* (1967).

Gershwin, George (1898–1937)
Gershwin, Ira (born 1896)
Both brothers were born in New York, USA. They collaborated in song-writing, George as the composer and Ira as the lyricist, and established themselves as probably the most distinguished team in American popular music. Their songs have invigorated screen musicals for many years from *Delicious* (1931), George Gershwin's first score written directly for the screen, to a few interpolated numbers in *Kiss Me, Stupid* (1964). The combination of Ira's wittily disenchanted lyrics and George's fund of memorable melody clearly attracted many film-makers. Particularly enjoyable use of the numbers (plus Ira's lyrics for other composers) were made in *Damsel in Distress* and *Shall We Dance?* (1937), *Goldwyn Follies* (1938), *Lady in the Dark* and *Cover Girl* (1944), *Rhapsody in Blue* (the Gershwin biography film, 1945), *The Barkleys of Broadway* (1949), *An American in Paris* (1950), *A Star is Born* (1954), *Funny Face* (1957), *Porgy and Bess* (1959). It is to be regretted that they never managed to make a really first-class original film musical of their own in the 1930s. JG

Gherardi, Piero (1909–1971)
Born in Poppi, Arezzo, Italy. Designer. One of the most inventive of Italian set and dress designers, his best work was probably with FELLINI on *Le Notti di Cabiria* (1957), *La Dolce Vita* (1959), *8½* (1963) and *Giulietta degli Spiriti* (1965), with their bizarre decorations and elegant, dream-like costuming. His other work ranged through comedies (*I Soliti Ignoti*, 1958), to realist dramas (*Kapo*, 1960) and period satire (*L'Armata Brancaleone*, 1965). Throughout his career, he maintained a marvellous style and wit, coupled with an awareness of colour values in relation to lighting and décor (as in the garden scenes in *Giulietta*).

Gibbons, Cedric (1895–1960)
Born in New York, USA. American art director who worked for MGM from 1924 and helped create the handsome, instantly recognizable Metro 'look' in films. Earlier, he worked at the Edison studios in New York. He received many Academy Awards, most notably for his art direction on *The Bridge of San Luis Rey* (1929), *Pride and Prejudice* (1940), *Blossoms in the Dust* (1941), *Gaslight* (1944), *Little Woman* (1949) and *An American in Paris* (1951). He is credited with designing the Oscar statuette and he co-directed one film in 1934, *Tarzan and his Mate*.

Gilbert, John (1895–1936)
Born John Pringle in USA. Actor, who came from a theatrical family and worked his way up from small parts to romantic leading roles, becoming for a period GRETA GARBO's leading man. He was most popular in the 1920s. Main films: *The Count of Monte Cristo* (1922), *Cameo Kirby* (1923), *The Merry Widow* and *The Big Parade* (1925), *La Bohème* (1926), *Love* and *Flesh and the Devil* (1927), *Man, Woman and Sin* and *The Cossacks* (1928), *Desert Nights* (1929), *Redemption* (1930), *Queen Christina* (1933).

Gilbert, Lewis
Born 1920 in London, England. Craftsmanlike British director, former child actor, who made his reputation with solid, if unimaginative, war films – *Albert RN* (1953), *The Sea shall not have Them* (1954), *Reach for the Sky* (1956), *Carve Her Name with Pride* (1958), *Sink the Bismarck* (1960), *HMS Defiant* (1962). But he revealed a sensitive feeling for the agonies of adolescence in *The Greengage Summer* (1961). In 1965 the success of the crude but currently trendy *Alfie* made him much sought after as a director, though his James Bond thriller *You only Live Twice* (1967) and turgid sex-adventure *The Adventurers* (1970) were unexceptional in all but sheer size and expenditure. Latest film: *Friends* (1970).

Alexandra Kluge in 'Yesterday Girl' (Alexander Kluge, Germany, 1967)

Gilliat, Sidney
Born 1908 in Edgeley, Cheshire, England. Writer, producer and director. Has always worked in close collaboration with FRANK LAUNDER (q.v.).

Girotti, Massimo
Born 1918 in Mogliano (Macerata), Italy. Actor. With no previous acting experience he was recommended in 1939 by his swimming instructor to director MARIO SOLDATI, who cast him in the juvenile lead in *Dora Nelson*. He then got the lead in BLASETTI's famous historical film *La Corona di Ferro* (1941). Next he went to drama school and made his stage début also under BLASETTI's direction. While playing a small part in RENOIR's unfinished *Tosca* he met LUCHINO VISCONTI, Renoir's assistant, who chose Girotti for the lead in *Ossessione* (1942). He then appeared on the stage under Visconti's direction in 'Anna Christie' and 'Tobacco Road' among other works. In 1950 he played the lead in the first film of ANTONIONI, *Cronaca di un amore*. In 1954 he played Alida Valli's cousin in Visconti's *Senso*. Under Visconti's direction he also returned to the stage in the 1960s, first in Strindberg's 'Miss Julie' and then as Trofimov in 'The Cherry Orchard', which inaugurated Rome's Stabile Theatre. Among his recent roles have been the father in PASOLINI's *Theorem* and the naval captain in *The Red Tent*. RM

Gish, Dorothy (1898–1968)
Born in Springfield, Ohio, USA. A stage actress

from four years old, when she played Little Willie in *East Lynne*, Dorothy Gish was brought to GRIFFITH at the Biograph Studios, along with her sister LILLIAN, in 1912. Her robust sense of comedy made her a less ideal Griffith heroine than Lillian; and her role as 'Lillian's little sister' tended sometimes to overshadow her own highly individual gifts. Her first film role was in Griffith's *An Unseen Enemy* (1912) and she continued to play regularly and successfully in films until 1929 (HERBERT WILCOX's *Wolves*). With sound she practically retired from the screen apart from appearances in *Our Hearts are Young and Gay* (1944), *Centennial Summer* (1946) and *The Whistle at Eton Falls* (1951). In later years she was constantly active on the New York stage.

Gish, Lillian

Born 1896 in Springfield, Ohio, USA. Perhaps the finest actress in the history of the silent cinema, Lillian Gish went on the stage at the age of six; and was brought to GRIFFITH, with her sister DOROTHY, in 1912, by MARY PICKFORD. Her fragile beauty made her the ideal Griffith heroine and she played leading roles in innumerable Griffith films from *An Unseen Enemy* (1912) to *Orphans of the Storm* (1922), but most notably in *Birth of a Nation* (1915), *Hearts of the World* (1917), *The Great Love* (1918), *The Greatest Thing in Life*, *The Romance of Happy Valley*, *Broken Blossoms*, *True Heart Susie* and *The Greatest Question* (1919), *The Love Flower* and *Way Down East* (1920). Later her Griffith training, her own conscientiousness and her rare spiritual vibrance was put at the service of other directors including KING (*Romola*, *The White Sister*), VIDOR (*La Bohème*) and SJÖSTRÖM (*The Scarlet Letter*, *The Wind*). After the advent of GARBO, MGM neglected Gish's talents and she returned to the theatre. In later years however she contributed some notable character performances. She directed one film, *Remodeling her Husband* (1920), starring Dorothy Gish.

Above: Felicity Young, Sarah Miles, Laurence Olivier, Thora Hird and Norman Bird in 'Term of Trial' (written and directed by Peter Glenville, GB, 1961)
Below: Jean-Luc Godard

Giudice, Filippo Del

See DEL GIUDICE

Glass Shot

A shot of part of a scene painted on a sheet of glass, where the painted part dovetails with the scene visible through the clear part of the glass. This glass is either photographed separately or superimposed on the main part of the scene during processing, or it is placed between the camera and the main set and filmed directly.

Glenville, Peter

Born 1913 in Hampstead, London, England. Director of highly polished films with good acting performances, he works mostly on stage adaptations. Films include: *The Prisoner* (1954), *Summer and Smoke* (1960), *Term of Trial* (1961), *Becket* (1964), *Hotel Paradiso* (1966).

Godard, Jean-Luc

Born 1930 in Paris, France. French director, actor and writer. Son of a doctor, he was educated in Switzerland and Paris. He studied at the Sorbonne and met BAZIN and TRUFFAUT in the Parisian ciné-clubs. During 1950, the year he helped found the journal 'Gazette du Cinéma', he contributed articles to the 'Cahiers du Cinéma'. After some three years travelling in North and South America he returned to Switzerland, where his mother was killed in a car accident. For a while he became a labourer on the construction of a dam, earning enough money to buy a 35 mm camera with which he made a film on the construction site. After returning to Paris he made a short film, *Une Femme Coquette* (1955), based on de Maupassant. While writing again for the 'Cahiers', he continued to make short films produced by Les Films de la Pléiade until in 1959 he directed his first feature film, *À Bout de Souffle* (*Breathless*). This was based on a subject suggested by Truffaut, whose recent award at Cannes secured finance for Godard's very modestly budgeted film featuring JEAN-PAUL BELMONDO and JEAN SEBERG. Photographed by RAOUL COUTARD, who has worked on most of Godard's films, it was shot in a month and won the director's award at Berlin the following year.

A leading exponent of the French new wave, Godard's output from 1960 was to be prolific; in 1967 his record was six films, together with collaboration in *Loin du Viêtnam*.

Breathless, a study of an amoral young criminal and his girl-friend in Paris, paid a tribute to the American gangster film which was almost a caricature. But characteristics of Godard's more mature style also appeared: the movement away from the story-film to the film of ideas; improvisation (creating directly through and by the camera and microphone); jump-cut editing; the presentation of social and moral concepts by adopting a dialectical approach which is partly visual, partly aural; the lengthy debates and monologues, with quotations from existentialist and other writers.

As Godard's films entered this social-political phase with *Le Petit Soldat* (1960) – shot in Geneva and banned until 1963 in France because of its references to Algeria – and *Les Carabiniers*

(1963), his techniques became increasingly expository and personal. The films are enacted social fables or essays. *Alphaville* (1965), Godard's horrific vision of a depersonalized, regimented city of the future, used the framework of science-fiction to expound the theme of the lack of humanity in contemporary Western culture.

Godard's coruscating techniques can be employed with melancholy, as in *Le Mépris* (1963), in which he appeared, or high spiritedly, as in *Bande à Part* (1964) or *Pierrot Le Fou* (1965), which in spite of their humour and charm sometimes appear merely self-indulgent and undisciplined. Godard is interested in the relations of the sexes, and the particular position of women in modern urban society dominated by the 'prostitution' of advertising, themes which are recurrently elaborated in *Une Femme est une Femme* (1961), *Vivre sa Vie* (an objective enquiry into prostitution, 1962), *Une Femme Mariée* (1964), and *Masculin-Féminin* (1965), films in which the situations of the characters are explored in debate and interview. ANNA KARINA whom he married in 1961, starred in most of his films made between 1960 and 1967.

Made in USA (1967) is a Brechtian demonstration that Godard's films promote ideas and are not to be taken as dramatic illusions. His players often speak in their own right. Films such as *Deux ou Trois Choses que je sais d'Elle* (1966), *La Chinoise* (1967), or *Sympathy for the Devil* (*One Plus One*, 1968) sometimes appear to be anthologies of quotations. *Weekend* (1967), one of his most brilliant and telling films, is in effect a fable of dehumanization, turning traffic-laden roads into an open battlefield. Recent films include *British Sounds* and *1 pm* (1969) and for television *Le Gai Savoir*.

Richard Roud, writing in his book, 'Godard', claims, 'Jean-Luc Godard is, of all contemporary directors, the most controversial. For many, he is the most important film-maker of his generation; for others, he is, if not the worst, then the most unbearable. However, as is often the case with controversial figures, he is admired and detested for the very same reasons.' Godard himself has said, 'Beauty and truth have two poles: documentary and fiction. You can start with either one. My starting-point is documentary to which I try to give the truth of fiction.' And also: 'I believe in dialectics'. He is deeply influenced by Existentialism, and his films project, often violently, as Roud points out, the extremes of contradiction – visual versus narrative, fiction versus documentary, reality versus abstraction. For good or ill, whether the implications of his work are understood or not, Godard's influence has been widespread on the film-makers of our time. RM

Godfrey, Bob

Born in Australia. Animation director. Made *Watch the Birdie* (1953) while in Australia. Came to Britain, and was for a while closely associated with the Biographic unit. Frequently concerned to satirize man's sexual pretensions and woman's predatory response, he made most notably in this vein *Polygamous Polonius* (1960) and *Henry 9 till 5* (1970). His other films include the wonderful *Do-it-Yourself Cartoon Kit* (1960), *The Rise and Fall of Emily Sprod* (1962) and the touching little tale of *Alf, Bill and Fred* (1964). Bob Godfrey has directed some of the most outrageously funny cartoons yet made.

Gold, Jack

Born 1930 in London, England. Television-trained British film director who scored a critical – though not commercial – success with his first feature film *The Bofors Gun* (1968). A carefully un-tricky director, he is particularly impressive exploring character and individuals' reaction to their environment. In 1969 he made *The Reckoning* with NICOL WILLIAMSON – a caustic comment on modern affluent society and the race for the top in Britain. His attempt to set up a new film version of 'Macbeth' failed and he has returned intermittently to television.

Goldwyn, Samuel

Born 1884 in Warsaw, Poland. Celebrated independent producer and one of the leading figures in the Hollywood power struggles of the 1920s and 1930s. A colourful personality, he changed his name from Goldfish after he joined the Selwyn brothers to form the Goldwyn Picture Corporation in 1918.

He arrived in America, via England, in 1899, worked in a glove factory and started his own glove-making business. In 1913 he co-produced *The Squaw Man* and teamed with his brother-in-law JESSE LASKY and CECIL B. DE MILLE to form Lasky Feature Plays. After the Famous Players-Lasky merger he left to join the Selwyns, taking the Goldwyn Picture Corporation to Culver City in Los Angeles. But the partnership did not last long. He was bought out when Metro-Goldwyn-Mayer merged, and he founded his own company.

From the middle 1920s Goldwyn emerged as the most important independent film-maker in Hollywood and continued to be so for thirty-five years. He owned his own studios, created his own stars, raised the finance for his films, and closely supervised their production. RONALD COLMAN, DAVID NIVEN and DANNY KAYE found fame with Goldwyn, whose films were noted for their elegance, craftsmanship and box office production values. His most distinguished period was marked by his association with director WILLIAM WYLER. Though his passion for commercial 'culture' and his largely invented Goldwynisms became something of a joke, his films were among the most stylish and sometimes unorthodox Hollywood had produced. At the other extreme, the comely Goldwyn Girls – in his musicals – became as famous as the Rockettes and Ziegfeld Girls.

After the trouble-prone *Porgy and Bess* (1959) he retired from active film-making. The most authoritative study of him is Richard Griffith's 'Samuel Goldwyn, The Producer and his Films'.

Principal films: *Arrowsmith* (1931), *Dead End* (1937), *Wuthering Heights* (1939), *The Little Foxes* (1941), *Up in Arms* (1944), *The Best Years of our Lives* (1946), *Hans Christian Anderson* (1952), *Guys and Dolls* (1955). MH

Gosho, Heinosuke

Born 1902 in Tokyo, Japan. Director. One of the most prolific of Japanese directors (about one hundred features), he entered the Shochiku Studios in 1923, became assistant to Yasujiro Shimazu, and made the first Japanese sound film *The Neighbour's Wife and Mine* (1931). Strongly influenced by American comedies, Gosho developed a naturalistic style (with an unusually sharp, quickly-paced tempo), building up detailed portraits of Japanese middle-class life and mixing sentimentality with comedy, laughter with tragedy. Some of the best examples of 'Gosho-ism' (as it was called) are *Four Chimneys* (1953), *The Valley Between Life and Death* and *An Inn at Osaka* (1954) and *Growing Up* (1955). Although not probing as deeply into human psychology as OZU, Gosho gives the impression of knowing his people well; he has a fine narrative grasp and a wry, typically Japanese humour. His films of the last decade have become somewhat novelettish and over-sentimental (a full-length puppet film about the Meiji period, made in 1968, has a good deal of nostalgic charm) and, like other artists of his generation, he has found it difficult to obtain finance for his kind of humanistic film-making, in an industry increasingly preoccupied with sensational and erotic subjects. JG

Gould, Elliott

Born 1939 in New York, USA. Trend-setting star actor of the 1970s, whose portrayal of the contemporary anxiety-ridden anti-hero shot him into the limelight in a brisk series of films starting with *Bob and Carol and Ted and Alice* (1969). A limitedly successful Broadway actor, he was overshadowed by his then wife, BARBRA STREISAND, until he made his film début in a supporting role in *The Night They Raided Minsky's* (1968). His talent for wry, neurotic comedy was consolidated in *M.A.S.H.* (1969) – the new look American anti-war film – *Getting Straight, Move, Little Murders* and *I Love my Wife* (all 1970). He is the first American actor to have been chosen to star in an INGMAR BERGMAN film, *The Touch* (1971), in which, however, he gave one of his least effective performances. MH

Goulding, Edmund (1891–1959)

Born in London, England. Director and writer. Was actor in London before the First World War, then transferred to USA, where his reputation as a theatrical writer led him to Hollywood and scriptwriting (including KING's *Tol'able David*, 1921). In the late 1920s, began directing and became renowned as an

Top: Elliott Gould and Yuko Hahn in 'M.A.S.H.' (Robert Altman, USA, 1970)
Above: Tyrone Power, Anne Baxter and Gene Tierney in 'The Razor's Edge' (Edmund Goulding, USA, 1946)
Below: Betty Grable in 'Mother Wore Tights' (Walter Lang, USA, 1947)

'actress' director – *Love* (1928) and *Grand Hotel* (1932) both with GARBO. During his Warner Brothers period, he specialized in sumptuously-staged melodramas full of strong situations and starring BETTE DAVIS in some of her richest performances: *Dark Victory* and *The Old Maid* (1939), *The Great Lie* (1941). Other notable titles include the charming *Claudia* (1943); *Of Human Bondage* and *The Razor's Edge* (1946). After the war, he turned to lighter material but will be remembered mainly for his solidly-built, meaty dramas of the 1940s. JG

Grable, Betty

Born 1916 in St Louis, USA. Actress, who first became famous as a singing and dancing star and as a US Army pin-up girl of the Second World War. In 1940 she was on the New York stage. Her film career started in the early 1930s; her first important part was in *The Gay Divorcee* (1934). Main films: *Million Dollar Legs* (1939), *Moon Over Miami* (1941), *Pin-Up Girl* (1943), *Mother Wore Tights* (1947), *How to Marry a Millionaire* (1953), *How to be Very, Very Popular* (1955). She was among the first ten money-making stars of the 1940s in the USA, was married to bandleader Henry James and appeared with him on television.

Grant, Cary

Born 1904 in Bristol, England. Impeccable British light comedy actor who has worked almost exclusively in Hollywood. His real name is Archibald Leach. After a varied career in the theatre, he landed in Hollywood to make his first film, *This is the Night*, in 1932 and quickly became a sought-after leading man. His first big impact was as MAE WEST's hero in *She Done Him Wrong* (1933), where under her influence he developed the nonchalant, quizzical style that he perfected in later films. During the 1930s and 1940s many of his films were serious dramas, but it was in crazy comedies such as *The Awful Truth* and *Topper* (1937) and *Bringing Up Baby* (1938) that he was most successful.

His easy style of acting concealed a highly professional sense of timing and there could be a touch of sinister shading in his charm, notably in his work for HAWKS and HITCHCOCK. If anything his popularity in this kind of role increased in his apparently ageless middle age, with such frivolous romps as *Indiscreet* (1958), *Operation Petticoat* (1959), *The Grass is Greener* (1960), *That Touch of Mink* (1962), *Charade* (1963) and *Father Goose* (1964). In 1966 he made a concession to his advancing years by playing a greying, but still devastating, match-maker in *Walk Don't Run* (1966). He has made few false moves in his career: one was the disastrous period spectacle, *The Pride and the Passion* (1957). Other notable films: *Sylvia Scarlett* (1935), *Holiday* (1938), *Gunga Din* and *Only Angels have Wings* (1939), *His Girl Friday* and *The Philadelphia Story* (1940), *Suspicion* (1941), *Notorious* (1946), *Mr Blandings Builds His Dream House* (1948), *I Was a Male War Bride* (1949), *Crisis* (1950), *Monkey Business* (1952), *To Catch a Thief* (1955), *North by Northwest* (1959). MH

Great Britain

Establishment of an Industry: The Pioneers
Britain was one of the 'founding fathers' of film. Amateur enthusiasts, as well as photographers and showmen, originated some part of the film medium, alongside others in the USA, France, Germany and some other countries, their pioneers working more in parallel than in conscious rivalry. Britain's pioneers included an optical instrument manufacturer, Birt Acres, who filmed the Derby and the opening of the Kiel Canal in 1895, and gave public and private demonstrations from August 1895 onwards; William Friese-Greene, a photographer whose imagination and inventive skills were stirred by the idea of movies in the 1880s, whose patents, at least, involved some of the principles of the movie, and who shot a pioneer film in 1889 in Hyde Park and claimed to have shown it to a passing policeman (a scene reconstructed in the feature film about him, *The Magic Box*); and R. W. PAUL, an instrument-maker, who constructed a peep-show device, like EDISON's Kinetoscope, which was in public use in 1895, and whose first public display of his films on a screen virtually coincided with that of the LUMIÈRES in Paris. But the successful international demonstration by the Lumières in Paris in December 1895, and in London and other cities in many parts of the world during 1896, overshadowed the efforts of pioneers elsewhere. Nevertheless, Robert Paul and the showman-inventor, CECIL HEPWORTH, who also began to make cameras and shoot films in 1896, went on to establish the first stages of the new film industry at the turn of the century. Another pioneer was Charles Urban, an American who settled in Britain and founded a production company in 1898.

From 1896, films of every kind, though very short at first, were to be manufactured, sold and shown in fairground booths (the first movie theatres, in effect), music-halls (as news and entertainment items), or in special temporary premises hired for the purpose – weekend shows in local halls, and the like. These films were poured out to meet the overwhelming public demand which showmen everywhere hastened to satisfy, and the first of the trade associations, the Kinematograph Manufacturers' Association, was founded as early as 1907. Paul specialized in comic trick films – cars which broke up and reassembled themselves, for example. Hepworth soon graduated from news and scenic sequences to brief dramatic and comedy films; he was more the artist by temperament than Paul, and made a film of considerable structural finesse in 1905, *Rescued by Rover*. A group of photographers and showmen in Brighton created the Brighton 'school', as it later came to be known: Esme Collings, G. A. Smith (who was to devise and patent the first photographic colour system, Kinemacolor, in 1908), and James Williamson. The invasion of film companies from abroad included two names famous in film history – LÉON GAUMONT, who perfected fireproof projection, and CHARLES PATHÉ, who established companies in Britain. The mass of imported foreign films even led to the first 'crisis' for British producers in 1909.

Only Hepworth among the British pioneers could be said to rank as an artist, albeit a minor one; as his films increased in length and to some extent sophistication, they tended to grow literary and slow in treatment. But until the entry of the former schoolmaster, GEORGE PEARSON, into the industry in 1909, Hepworth was the only real film-maker, as distinct from accomplished technicians in photography and trick effects, working in Britain.

By the time Pearson joined the industry it was expanding, at least from the distributors' and exhibitors' points of view. Distribution began as a branch of the industry with the hire, as distinct from the sale of films. Premises of every kind, from garages and restaurants to music-halls, were from around 1906 being converted to show films, to be followed soon by sedate and even luxurious 'picture palaces', with foyers, tea-lounges, and the like. Some of these were grouped in the form of circuits, under single managements. There were something over 3,000 cinemas in Britain by 1914.

The British Board of Film Censors was founded in 1912 to keep the foreign rather than the home product 'genteel', establishing a categorization of U for Universal, that is, suitable for children, and A, more suitable for Adults, which was to last until the 1950s. The Cinematograph Exhibitors' Association was founded the same year. A minor American 'invasion' began around 1913, when Dr Ralph Jupp's London Film Company and Florence Turner, the American star, both began to make films in Britain with American artists and technicians, though these were to withdraw after war began in August 1914, leaving the British fully active in feature-length film production operating from some 30 studios up and down the country. Among the leading film-makers were the producer-director CECIL HEPWORTH, and the exuberant Will Barker, whose spectaculars *Sixty Years a Queen* (1911) and *Jane Shore* (1915) were celebrated. For *Jane Shore* he used 5,000 extras, and he paid Herbert Beerbohm Tree £1,000 for a single day's work appearing as Wolsey in a film about Henry VIII. Others of importance were the producer G. B. Samuelson, inexhaustible and impetuous, MAURICE ELVEY, and the director who was to prove better than any of them, George Pearson.

Above: 'Rescued by Rover' (Cecil Hepworth, 1905)
Below: 'The ? Motorist' (R. W. Paul, 1905)

The fault with British production was that it stayed rigidly out-of-date in the face of the great advances made by American directors of the period up to 1920. Hepworth, Samuelson, and even Barker made literary and theatrical subjects. British films seemed tied to the popular novel, the popular play, and to popular stars of the theatre. But at first the output was prolific. Barker operated on the site which was to become that of the famous Ealing Studios; in 1915 Gaumont-British established the equally famous Lime Grove Studios at Shepherds Bush, West London (now occupied by BBC Television). Here George Pearson worked, with Thomas Welsh as manager, originating a series of macabre thrillers influenced by LOUIS FEUILLADE and called *Ultus, the Man from the Dead*. But what the vast wartime public for movies wanted were the American films, and by 1918 the money had dropped out of British-style production. Though the American film-makers had mostly returned to the USA during the war years, the greatest American of all, D. W. GRIFFITH, came to Britain in 1917 with his cameraman, BILLY BITZER, to make *Hearts of the World* (1918) for the Allied Governments. It was shot on location in France near the front lines and showed the effect of the war on a French village. Griffith's incursion proved a great inspiration to all those who met him.

The 1920s The remaining years of the silent film in Britain were like those in other countries, a period of transition and of new opportunity. Film-makers whose point of view belonged to the past were left behind in the competitive race to win the audiences. Barker retired; Hepworth (over-ambitious in his investments, and always the quiet artist rather than the businessman) went bankrupt; Samuelson faded; J. STUART

BLACKTON, from Vitagraph, and Oswald Stoll, the impresario, both failed with their prestige films. The new post-war generation of film-goers wanted new and far hotter blood, and they found it mostly in the more sophisticated film-making of the USA. Hepworth's *Alf's Button* (his last successful film) was no match for *The Four Horsemen of the Apocalypse* (with the new star RUDOLPH VALENTINO, 1921) or the new, highly pictorial German films, such as LUBITSCH's *Dubarry* (called *Passion* for the English-speaking public, 1919), with the seductive POLA NEGRI. FRITZ LANG's *Nibelung Saga* (1924) was shown at the Albert Hall for three weeks. At the end of 1924 British production actually ceased altogether.

It did not run down this far without a struggle. George Pearson's *Squibs* comedies with Betty Balfour as a Cockney *gamine* were popular from 1921; his war film *Reveille* (1924) as well as his later adaptation of John Buchan's *Huntingtower* (1927), with Harry Lauder, were well received. But J. Stuart Blackton's attempt to launch Lady Diana Manners as a star in *The Glorious Adventure* (1922) and *The Virgin Queen* failed. The older-style British films at least launched a number of important stars, including RONALD COLMAN, CLIVE BROOK, VICTOR MCLAGLEN, LESLIE HOWARD, CHARLES LAUGHTON and ELSA LANCHESTER. The last three appeared in some enterprising but unsuccessful burlesques directed by Adrian Brunel, including *Bluebottles* (1928), promoted by Ivor Montagu.

The British film industry was faced with unique problems. The American industry had been big business since before the war, and its films had no difficulty in penetrating Britain's 4,000 cinemas; the British production industry remained small business, and its films of the older school were unwanted in the USA, which had the enormously lucrative world market to draw on. The Americans have never wanted to see an independently successful British industry, with films distributed freely in the USA; this would be bad for the American film business. But for the British industry to be successful, then as now, it had to produce films which would appeal to the greater American and world markets. For this it needed a similar flair for audience taste both inside and outside Britain.

There were young men coming up who had this flair and were anxious to rebuild the British film industry, at least so far as their own work was concerned. One was a producer called HERBERT WILCOX, another a director called GRAHAM CUTTS, a third a film renter from Birmingham, MICHAEL BALCON, the fourth a director called VICTOR SAVILLE, and the fifth a man from the art title department at Islington Studios, ALFRED HITCHCOCK. Cutts was only 26 when he made *The Wonderful Lie* (1922) with Wilcox (aged 30) as producer. Its sentimental-sophistication made it the film of the year, and it featured a star internationally popular, in Europe at least, Lillian Hall-Davies. Cutts, Balcon, Saville and Hitchcock joined forces to make the outstandingly successful *Woman to Woman* (1923); it was directed by Cutts, and it fulfilled the magic formula of being as successful in the USA as it was in Britain. It starred the American actress Betty Compson, then at the height of her fame. It cost some £40,000 to make, the money coming mainly from entrepreneurs whose names were to be part of the story of the British film industry – C. M. Woolf and Oscar Deutsch, a metal merchant in Birmingham. Hitchcock was scriptwriter and assistant director, and the leading man was CLIVE BROOK.

But it was an uphill battle to re-establish a viable film industry in Britain. American films filled British screens, often available at cut-price rates because their costs had already been recovered in the States, let alone elsewhere in the world market.

There had been for some while growing pressures on the Government from industry in general, and not merely the film producers, to protect the nation's film industry by some kind of official 'quota' – though this was opposed by exhibitors on the grounds that they could then be forced by law to show unprofitable and badly made British products. Even some quality producers such as George Pearson, who was virtually out of production at the time, were dubious. But the first Cinematograph Trade Bill became law in December 1927, and enjoined the unwilling exhibitors to show 5% British registered product, rising to 20% by 1935–6. As a result, 52 British films were turned out in 1927 and 90 in 1928. But their overall quality was very poor. The Bill also legislated against the 'block' and 'blind' booking imposed on exhibitors mainly by the American distributors, who rented the less attractive along with the more attractive films in package deals, thus not only tying exhibitors to showing long successions of American films, but also robbing them of any real choice of subjects while doing so. This in turn encouraged the further development of cinema circuits, or chains of theatres under single ownerships, in order to increase the power of the circuit-owning exhibitor to bargain with the distributors. For example, the PCT group (originally founded by Jupp) owned 85 cinemas in 1927, while the Gaumont-British Corporation owned 21. The following year John Maxwell (producer and distributor) formed the ABC circuit with 40 theatres. But 87% of British cinemas were still independent, working outside circuit control, or owned in very small groups of under ten.

The sound film was soon to offer a further challenge in the economics of the industry. Meanwhile, during the silent period some notable films were made. In 1923–5 Hitchcock continued to work with Balcon as assistant and art director on Cutts's films, including *The White Shadow* (with Betty Compson and Clive Brook), *The Passionate Adventure* (with Clive Brook, Lillian Hall-Davies and VICTOR MCLAGLEN). Balcon (still under 30) very enterprisingly made an agreement with ERICH POMMER in Germany, as a result of which

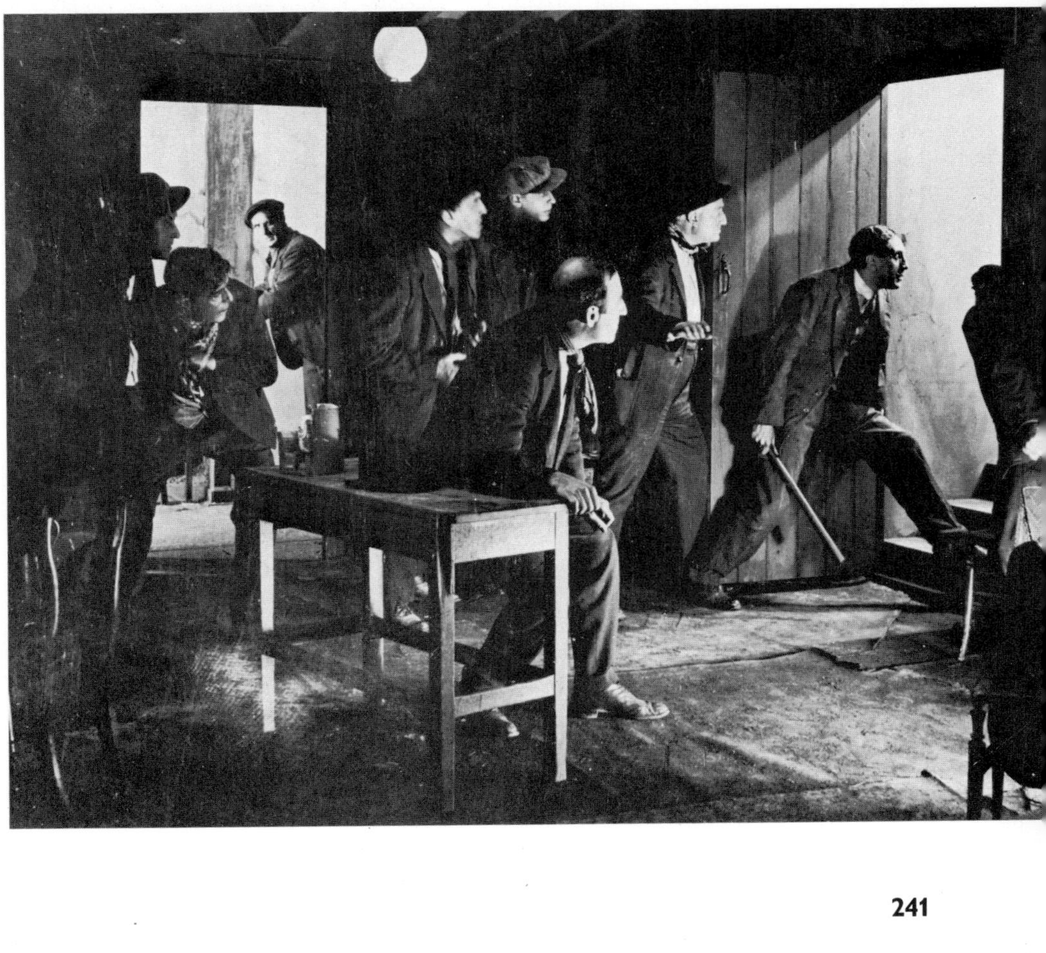

'Ultus, the Man from the Dead' (George Pearson, 1915)

Hitchcock made his first two individual films in Munich, not London, at the age of 25 – *The Pleasure Garden* and *The Mountain Eagle* (1926, also called *Fear O' God*), both with the Hollywood star, Nita Naldi. After this, Balcon brought Hitchcock back to London to make *The Lodger* (1926) and *Downhill* (1927), both with IVOR NOVELLO, and *Easy Virtue* (from NOËL COWARD's new play), before he went over to make a series of films for John Maxwell, culminating in *Blackmail* (1929), which was shot originally as a silent film and then remade with sound, with RONALD NEAME as clapper-boy and MICHAEL POWELL as still cameraman.

Hitchcock was the son of a shopkeeper; ANTHONY ASQUITH the son of a former Prime Minister. His silent films, all produced by H. Bruce Woolfe, were marked by their style; he assisted A. V. Bramble to direct *Shooting Stars* (1929), of which he had written the screenplay, while in 1928 he both wrote and directed *Underground*. Brian Aherne appeared in both films. After making *The Runaway Princess*, partly in Germany, he returned to England to make his last silent film *Cottage on Dartmoor* (1929), one of the most brilliant and atmospheric films of the silent period. (One version was put out with sound on disc.) Among the other films of the period were Herbert Wilcox's *The Only Way* (1926), Adrian Brunel's *The Constant Nymph* (1928), and VICTOR SAVILLE's ballet film, *Tesha* (with Maria Corda, ALEXANDER KORDA's first wife). But these few films did not make an industry, and apart from a handful of pictures in the 1930s, it was to be some while before British films established themselves sufficiently to contribute effectively to the mainstream of quality cinema. Britain, in fact, seemed to be turning to Germany for talent, as indeed Hollywood was doing. E. A. DUPONT took charge at Elstree; having made *Moulin Rouge* (1928) in Britain, he followed it by *Piccadilly* (1929) with Anna May Wong and CHARLES LAUGHTON in the cast. Britain was still hovering uneasily on the edge of sound, inserting a sound sequence here or a sound scene there, when Hitchcock, backed by Maxwell, took the plunge.

The Sound Film The consolidation of the larger, vertically integrated combines, which were to have such a grip on the British cinema, began at the turn of the 1930s. John Maxwell, the solicitor from Glasgow, became the prime mover, eventually founding ABPC (Associated British Picture Corporation), with cinema interests covering 147 theatres. The C. M. Woolfe-Ostrer Brothers combine owned the Gaumont-British circuit of some 287 theatres. A toughly-fighting union, the Association of Cine Technicians, was formed in 1931, providing a much-needed watch-dog to look after the interests of the film-makers and technicians.

By 1929 Britain was producing 138 films; by 1933, 159. But the quality of the early sound films was abysmal – filmed theatre and music-hall abounded, with a very few films rising above this. Exceptions were Hitchcock's versions for John Maxwell of O'Casey's *Juno and the Paycock* (1930), and of Galsworthy's *The Skin Game* (1931), or VICTOR SAVILLE's version of the north-country play *Hindle Wakes* (1931), and his re-make of the original German film, *Congress Dances*, as *Sunshine Susie* (1931), both produced by MICHAEL BALCON. The best film, as a film, of the period was Asquith's *Tell England* (1931), with the Gallipoli landings restaged in Malta and handled in the style of EISENSTEIN. The great success of 1932 was Walter Forde's *Rome Express* (produced by Michael Balcon, with Esther Ralston and CONRAD VEIDT, who had left Germany). Though in 1933 Asquith's film of the ballet, *Dance Pretty Lady*, adapted from Compton MacKenzie's novel 'Carnival' Victor Saville's *Friday the Thirteenth*, *The Good Companions* (from J. B. Priestley's novel), and *I Was a Spy* (with Madeleine Carroll, Conrad Veidt and HERBERT MARSHALL), set in Flanders, 1915, were all notable, the outstanding success was ALEXANDER KORDA's *The Private Life of Henry VIII*, with Charles Laughton.

Above: Alfred Hitchcock and John Longden in 'Blackmail' (Hitchcock, 1929)
Below: 'Blackmail'

Korda had come to settle in England after his failure to conquer Hollywood on his own terms in the year of the economic depression. He had made many films – in Budapest, in Vienna, in Berlin, in Paris. He came to London in 1931, made two successful light comedies, *Service for Ladies* (with LESLIE HOWARD) and *Wedding Rehearsal*, and founded his own company, London Films. For less than £50,000 he made the stylish, witty, and slightly bawdy film about Henry VIII, which featured a galaxy of beautiful women and good actors and made him the darling of the backers and the banks. He built what were reputed to be the finest studios in the world at Denham, which he wanted to make a centre for international production on a spectacular scale, using the exiled talent from Europe – particularly from his native Hungary and from Germany, which Hitler was purging of Jewish film-makers. He brought in PAUL CZINNER and his wife ELISABETH BERGNER to make *Catherine the Great* (1933), DOUGLAS FAIRBANKS SENIOR from Hollywood to appear under his own direction in *Don Juan* (1934), LESLIE HOWARD and Raymond Massey to appear in *The Scarlet Pimpernel* (1934), the designer-director WILLIAM CAMERON MENZIES to make the H. G. Wells spectacular *Things to Come* (1936), Lothar Mendes to direct Roland Young in another H. G. Wells story, *The Man who could work Miracles* (1936), MARLENE DIETRICH to appear in JACQUES FEYDER's *Knight without Armour* (1937), and RENÉ CLAIR to make *The Ghost Goes West* (1935). Korda himself directed Laughton once again in *Rembrandt* (1936), probably Korda's best film. His brother ZOLTAN KORDA directed PAUL ROBESON in *Sanders of the River* (1935), Sabu in *Elephant Boy* (1937, made with ROBERT FLAHERTY), *The Drum* (1938), and *Four Feathers* (1939). His second brother, VINCENT KORDA, was an outstanding film designer in his studios, and Merle Oberon, who became Korda's second wife, appeared in many of his films of this period. Korda spared no expense, now that the bit was between his teeth. He lost money on some of these films. But not all his films were spectacular; he sponsored Victor Saville's *South Riding* (1938). The whole programme represented a remarkable achievement.

Below: Charles Laughton (as King Henry), Robert Donat and Merle Oberon in 'The Private Life of Henry VIII' (Alexander Korda, 1933)
Bottom: 'Tell England' (Anthony Asquith, 1931)

John Maxwell's British International Studios, controlled by Walter Mycroft, aimed at box-office success with a miscellaneous programme, which started in the second period with *Blackmail* and DUPONT's *Atlantic* (1930). Many future British writers, directors and cameramen trained there, including SIDNEY GILLIAT, J. LEE THOMPSON, RONALD NEAME, JACK CARDIFF, and CHARLES FREND. Among the artists who also appeared in BIP pictures were Richard Tauber in *Blossom Time* (1934), Gertrude Lawrence and Douglas Fairbanks Junior in *La Bohème*, and the comedian WILL HAY (with a youthful JOHN MILLS) in *The Magistrate*. It was Gainsborough, however, at Lime Grove, who made the best of the many films of the character comedian WILL FYFFE, *Owd Bob* (1938), directed by ROBERT STEVENSON, as well as CAROL REED's best-known prewar film *Bank Holiday* (1937) and *The Stars Look Down* (1939).

J. ARTHUR RANK began his interest in the film industry in 1933, initially sponsoring religious films; he founded a production company, British National, which made an effective little film set in a Yorkshire fishing village and called *The Turn of the Tide* (1935), featuring another young player, Geraldine Fitzgerald. The only comparable film to this was MICHAEL POWELL's *The Edge of the World*, made on the Scottish island of Foula in 1937. Later Rank formed an association with C. M. Woolf, and took over the large new studios in Pinewood in 1935. At the same time Oscar Deutsch was building up his luxurious Odeon cinema chain, which by 1937 was some 250 cinemas. Rank joined the Odeon Board in 1939. Both Maxwell and Isidore Ostrer became less and less interested in making films, since far more money was to be made by showing them. Once again the old bogey raised its head: British films were doing little on the American market, since the greater part of them were too bad for any audience to tolerate.

The boom turned into a slump in 1937; the previous year to this, Britain over-produced, making 220 feature films. Studio space (at Denham, Pinewood, Elstree, Shepperton, Ealing, Teddington and elsewhere) had increased sevenfold in ten years. Production had led into world speculation, and the cheaply-made, so-called 'quota quickies' (which no-one wanted either to show or to see) were as disastrous as the expensive, spectacular failures – even good films could fail, like ERICH POMMER's *Farewell Again* (1937).

A new Cinematograph Film Act was due to come into operation in 1938, and in anticipation the Government appointed a Committee to investigate the affairs of the industry, only to find it in a state of deadlock. The exhibitors' quota for British feature films was reset at 12½% rising to 25%, and the production of expensive rather than cheaply-made films was encouraged by giving the expensive films a higher quota rating. As a result, the American companies moved into Britain with a view to making their own quality British film, which would qualify them for British quota. For a while Michael Balcon became producer for MGM-British. Warner, Radio, Twentieth Century-Fox all moved in, and the British entrepreneurs concentrated merely on exhibition. Among the films sponsored were KING VIDOR's *The Citadel* (with ROBERT DONAT and ROSALIND RUSSELL) and SAM WOOD's *Goodbye Mr Chips* (also with

Above: 'Things to Come' (William Cameron Menzies, 1936)
Below: 'The Stars Look Down' (Carol Reed, 1939)

Robert Donat). Among the foreigners making films were PAUL CZINNER, with *Dreaming Lips* and *As You Like It*, and Erich Pommer, whose *Vessel of Wrath* (1938) with CHARLES LAUGHTON and ELSA LANCHESTER, was humane, sophisticated and very funny. The Hungarian, GABRIEL PASCAL, persuaded Bernard Shaw to give him the film rights in his works, and made *Pygmalion* (1938) with Anthony Asquith, featuring LESLIE HOWARD and WENDY HILLER.

The successful films of the prewar years included Herbert Wilcox's *Victoria the Great* (with ANNA NEAGLE) and Harold Schuster's *Wings of the Morning* (a Technicolor feature which had HENRY FONDA in a large cast). Wilcox also made *Nell Gwynn* (1934) and *Sixty Glorious Years* (1938), both with Anna Neagle. Hitchcock, who had returned to Gaumont-British in 1934 to make *The Man who Knew too Much, The Thirty-Nine Steps* (1935), *The Secret Agent* and *Sabotage* for Michael Balcon in 1936, also made *Young and Innocent* (1937) and *The Lady Vanishes* (1938) for Balcon's successor at Lime Grove, Edward Black. He made his last British film of the period, *Jamaica Inn* (with Charles Laughton and Maureen O'Hara) in 1939 before taking up a new contract in the USA. Balcon, unhappy with MGM, made only *A Yank at Oxford* (1938, with ROBERT TAYLOR and a newcomer, VIVIEN LEIGH) before leaving to become head of production at Ealing Studios, where he was to remain for over 20 years. He was still only 44.

Ealing had had a rough passage financially after the construction of the new studios in 1941, backed by Courtauld money. It did well eventually with the series of films featuring the famous north-country singers, Gracie Fields and George Formby. Ealing also produced CAROL REED's first film, *Midshipman Easy* (1934). Their best achievements after the arrival of Balcon were two films directed by the youthful Pen Tennyson, *There Ain't No Justice*, a very indigenous film about boxing, and *The Proud Valley*, a film about Welsh miners, with PAUL ROBESON.

Britain had achieved one other valuable asset during the 1930s – the British Film Institute, officially founded in 1933, followed by the National Film Archive in 1935 (see ARCHIVES AND FILM PRESERVATION). This was the outcome of the increasing interest in the film as an art and as a form of record, and the need felt both to preserve films and make some study of them. This was linked with the growing film society movement, which had started with the London Film Society, founded in 1925, and had soon spread to the provinces, and with the few cinemas specializing in the showing of foreign-language and 'art' films, especially the Academy Cinema in London. The Institute's journal, 'Sight and Sound', began in 1932, and for three years the influential film society in Scotland, the Edinburgh Film Guild, published its own excellently produced journal, 'Cinema Quarterly' (1932–5).

The Film in Wartime It is unlikely that the British feature film would have been entirely eliminated in wartime. But the record of the 1930s was not encouraging as regards quality, and mere studio heroics could easily have been the ruination of the war film.

Instead, the miracle happened. British feature film-making was born of an entirely new spirit of austerity and strenuous work. The stupidities, extravagances and dishonesties of the passing decade were all but eliminated as if at a single stroke. Only about one third of the artists and technicians could be spared from the services or war work for film-making, and the number of studio stages left free was reduced to less than half. The rest were requisitioned. Quality began to emerge as if the industry had received shock therapy.

There were some guide-lines to hand, some films (of which too little notice had been taken) which had unpretentiously begun to create a truer portrait of the British people than the vast majority of the films of the 1930s – among them, as we have seen, were *The Turn of the Tide, The Edge of the World*, and *The Proud Valley*. And there had been that totally other world of film-making, the British documentary movement (see DOCUMENTARY) which, led by JOHN GRIERSON, had been making a world reputation in its own right for British factual films. The producer who had come nearest to recognition of its lessons for the feature film was MICHAEL BALCON, who was to play a leading part in establishing the new-style realism in British wartime productions. It was recognized that Britain at war was to be in great need of indigenous entertainment conceived from the British point of view, however much audiences continued to welcome films from the USA, which was still a country at peace. The sheer quantity of production, however, greatly decreased, and little more than between 50 and

60 feature films were to be made annually during wartime. The modest quota requirements were maintained without too much difficulty, standing at about one-seventh British film to the rest, which were almost entirely American, though there were Government restrictions in dollar expenditure for film imports. Jack Beddington, the vigorous and imaginative head of the Films Division of the Ministry of Information from 1940, advised by Sidney Bernstein, head of the Granada circuit of cinemas, pressed for good feature films as well as for good documentaries, for the production policy of which he was wholly responsible. British documentary, in any case, had had some ten years' experience to bring to its new task.

At the same time, a quiet revolution was taking place in the structure of the film industry. Both Maxwell and Deutsch died in 1941, and J. ARTHUR RANK became Chairman of the Gaumont-British and Odeon cinema circuits, representing over 600 theatres; at the same time Warner Brothers acquired a substantial holding in ABC, linked to the other great holding of over 400 British cinemas. In addition, the Rank Organization controlled some 50% of the studio space, with headquarters at Denham. By 1944 the two combines between them owned 1,061 of Britain's key cinemas, and the Government, even in wartime, appointed the Palache Committee to investigate the development of monopoly in the British film industry.

As the cinemas (closed initially because of the fear of air-raids) reopened, the public flooded in, searching for relief from hard work, companionship, release from tension, emotional indulgence, and, where they could find them, some reaffirmation of the values of humanity.

Above: Wendy Hiller in 'Pygmalion' (Anthony Asquith and Leslie Howard, 1938)
Below: Paul Robeson and Edward Rigby in 'The Proud Valley' (Pen Tennyson, 1940)

Cinema attendance rose from the prewar weekly average of 19 million to 30 million in 1945. The support for British films rose with their evident quality and their ability to meet the emotional needs of the growing cinema public.

A number of interesting films were in process of production and release during the bridge period of 1939–40. The films genuinely conceived in wartime barely began to emerge before 1941. These included several on the right lines for the future, for example the realist style of Reed's *The Stars Look Down* and John Baxter's *Love on the Dole*. Of the first films inspired by the war, MICHAEL POWELL's episodic *49th Parallel*, made principally in Canada and sponsored by government money, JOHN BOULTING's *Pastor Hall*, and Pen Tennyson's Ealing film, *Convoy*, began to offer effective replies to Nazi propaganda films, together with the enormously successfully short feature documentary about an RAF bombing raid, *Target for Tonight* (1941), made by HARRY WATT. *Target for Tonight* was the kind of government-sponsored documentary the public flocked to see, both in Britain and the USA.

During 1942–3 the good films began to be produced in some quantity, including *The Foreman went to France* (CHARLES FREND for Ealing), *One of our Aircraft is Missing* (Michael Powell), *Next of Kin* (THOROLD DICKINSON), *The First of the Few* (LESLIE HOWARD), *In Which We Serve* (NOËL COWARD and DAVID LEAN), *We Dive at Dawn* (ANTHONY ASQUITH), *San Demetrio, London* (CHARLES FREND), *The Lamp Still Burns* (MAURICE ELVEY), *Nine Men* (HARRY WATT), and the only film among these specifically about women in war work, *Millions Like Us* (FRANK LAUNDER and SIDNEY GILLIAT). Leslie Howard showed the lives of women in the Services in *The Gentle Sex*.

The new directors who were emerging had had long experience in film-making – David Lean, Charles Frend, Thorold Dickinson as editors, Frank Launder and Sidney Gilliat as screenwriters, Harry Watt and CAVALCANTI in documentary. As the war years dragged on, they turned to other subjects than war-action, dealing rather with the stories portraying the background and psychology of those at war: *The Way Ahead* (Carol Reed, with two scriptwriters, Eric Ambler and the youthful PETER USTINOV), Asquith's *The Demi-Paradise* (with LAURENCE OLIVIER) and *The Way to the Stars* with MICHAEL REDGRAVE, DEBORAH KERR and a rising actor, TREVOR HOWARD, *Waterloo Road* (Sidney Gilliat, with the coming star JOHN MILLS). 'Box-office' films began to reappear with *I Live in Grosvenor Square* (WILCOX) and *Perfect Strangers* (Alexander Korda). The realist style was maintained by Noël Coward and David Lean with *This Happy Breed* and, above all, *Brief Encounter*, the fantasy *Blithe Spirit* slipping in between. The feature documentaries were maintained by such outstanding films as *Desert Victory*, *Western Approaches* (Pat Jackson, taking Britain's only Technicolor camera to sea), *Fires were Started* (HUMPHREY JENNINGS, the poet of British documentary), and, finally, *The True Glory* (Reed and GARSON KANIN).

The great wartime impresario of films, FILIPPO DEL GIUDICE, enabled Laurence Olivier to direct *Henry V*, and other non-war films of note were made during the war years, including *Thunder Rock* (the BOULTINGS), *The Life and Death of Colonel Blimp* (POWELL), *Gaslight* (Dickinson), and *Kipps* (Reed). John Baxter's *The Common Touch* and *Shipbuilders* gave reality to working-class life in Britain. Ealing made the tension-ridden *Dead of Night* (Cavalcanti and others). JAMES MASON emerged as a star from a group of romantic costume films, including *The Wicked Lady* (with MARGARET LOCKWOOD) and *The Man in Grey*, and REX HARRISON established his skill in *The Rake's*

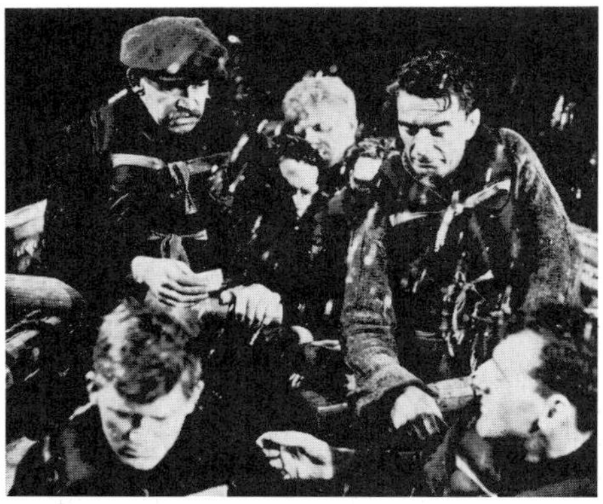

Top: 'San Demetrio, London' (Charles Frend, 1943)
Above: David Tomlinson and Trevor Howard in 'The Way to the Stars' (Anthony Asquith, 1945)
Right: James Mason and Margaret Lockwood in 'The Wicked Lady' (Leslie Arliss, 1945)
Below: Michael Redgrave and Hartley Power in 'Dead of Night' (Alberto Cavalcanti, Charles Crichton and Basil Dearden, 1945)

Progress (Launder and Gilliat). The new fully established stars included Michael Redgrave, RICHARD ATTENBOROUGH, DAVID NIVEN and Stewart Granger, while among the many newer actresses Deborah Kerr was to prove outstanding.

Prestige and Decline 1945–55 The film industry woke from the nightmare of war to find the massive, vertically integrated Rank Organization as the dominant force in British films. The quality producers, Michael Balcon and Filippo del Giudice, distributed their work through it, and John Davis was appointed Managing Director in 1946 at a period when its production policies were getting more and more out of hand and extravagant. In rivalry to Rank stood KORDA, whose London Films acquired control of British Lion Film Corporation in 1946, and Shepperton Studios in 1947 – the year in which an open dispute arose between the American distributors and the British Government over the 75% *ad valorem* duty imposed on imported films, with the result that for a while no American films reached Britain at all. The quota imposed by the new Cinematograph Film Act of 1948 shot the British proportion up to 45%. Hopes were high, and a British Film Academy was founded in 1947, with Roger

Manvell as director; its membership of established film-makers rapidly shot up to 400. Prestige British production was substantially stepped up, but only too soon with disastrous consequences, when American films began to flow in once more in 1948. The Government permitted a ceiling export of $17 million annually, the rest of the turnover for American product to be invested in American-sponsored British production. The Americans flooded the country with a back-log of films.

1949–50 was a bad year economically for British film production, though exhibition flourished with peak attendances of well over 30 million a week. Standing out clear above the mass of rubbish, the prestige films, inspired alike by wartime achievements and post-war euphoria, included *Hamlet* (Laurence Olivier), *The Red Shoes* (Powell and PRESSBURGER), *Odd Man Out*, *The Fallen Idol* and *The Third Man* (Carol Reed's brilliant trilogy), David Lean's *Great Expectations* and *Oliver Twist*, and Charles Frend's *Scott of the Antarctic*. Ealing, however, apart from *Scott*, kept to more modestly budgetted films, such as *Passport to Pimlico* (HENRY CORNELIUS), *Hue and Cry* (CHARLES

CRICHTON), *Whisky Galore* (ALEXANDER MACKENDRICK), and *The Overlanders* (made by Watt in Australia), as well as the comedy which helped to establish ALEC GUINNESS's great reputation, *Kind Hearts and Coronets* (ROBERT HAMER). The disastrous production by Gabriel Pascal of Shaw's *Caesar and Cleopatra* had done more than any other factor to put the Rank Organisation's production programme deeply in the red, while many expensive, slow-moving, literary films began to appear, which did nothing for the British cinema either at home or abroad but add to the losses incurred. It is symptomatic that in 1949 the Rank Organisation sold its Lime Grove studios to its rapidly-developing rival, BBC Television, and drastically reduced its investment in production, while in 1951 Denham Studios too were closed.

But good films continued to be made, in spite of the retrenchment. Korda, with a £3m loan from the Government's National Film Finance Corporation (established in 1948 to help independent producers with loans) became the continuing source for prestige productions, sponsoring (before Korda's unexpected death in 1956) such films as *The Fallen Idol*, *The Third Man*, the Boultings' *Seven Days to Noon* (1950), Lean's *The Sound Barrier* (1951) and *Hobson's Choice* (1954), and Olivier's *Richard III* (1954). But when Korda died, his losses were found to be in the nature of £2m. In 1950, the British Film Production Fund was set up to help active production with grants from a levy on most cinema admission prices; the levy was at first voluntary and later (1957) statutory. The succession of Government enquiries into the industry's affairs did little to resolve production problems, which were quite simply that a British film must earn at the box-office of its own country, plus its earnings in the rest of the world, six to seven times its initial costs, just to break even for the producers. British films had to continue to learn how to be exportable and welcome to audiences abroad.

Many were – the principal films of Lean and Reed, and the best of the Ealing comedies, for example. It was a matter of stars as well as stories, with important newcomers such as DIRK BOGARDE, JACK HAWKINS, KENNETH MORE, Richard Todd, LAURENCE HARVEY, RICHARD BURTON, PETER FINCH. But British actresses in the international star class remained scarce. Films such as *Genevieve* (HENRY CORNELIUS, 1953), *The Cruel Sea* (Charles Frend, 1952), *The Colditz Story* (GUY HAMILTON, 1955), *The Dam Busters* (MICHAEL ANDERSON, 1955), *The Ladykillers* (ALEXANDER MACKENDRICK, 1956) helped to keep the international reputation of British films high, while the box-office was kept healthy by such well-made popular vulgarities as the *Doctor* series (begun 1954) and the *Carry On* series (begun 1958).

The New British Cinema: the 1960s The British cinema, like many others in a modern industrialized State, had to face the inevitable competition of television. This had been started prewar by the BBC in 1936, but was closed down during the war before audiences had reached any significant numbers. Restarted by the BBC in 1946, and much enlivened by the competition offered it by commercial television, which started ten years later, the new medium for moving pictures began to make its great inroads into cinema attendance during the 1950s. The bare statistics make the point:

Television receivers in action		Cinema admissions (average per week)	
1945	nil	1945	31·4m
1955	4·5m	1955	22·7m
1965	13·56m	1965	6·3m

At the same time, the number of cinemas were reduced from over 4,000 to less than 2,000. The boom in other forms of public entertainment, dancing, jazz concerts, gambling, car and motor-cycle riding, and so forth, only added to

Top: Basil Sydney, Eileen Herlie, Felix Aylmer and Laurence Olivier in 'Hamlet' (Olivier, 1948)
Above: Joseph Cotten and Trevor Howard in 'The Third Man' (Carol Reed, 1949)
Below: Anthony Wager (as Pip), John Burch, Grace Denbigh-Russell, Hay Petrie, Freda Jackson and Bernard Miles in 'Great Expectations' (David Lean, 1946)

Above: 'Scott of the Antarctic' (Charles Frend, 1948)
Below: Stanley Holloway and Alec Guinness in 'The Lavender Hill Mob' (Charles Crichton, 1951)

the dislocations caused by television. Film-makers and exhibitors had to think afresh, and join the 'new society' which lacked many of the inhibitions of the old, inhibitions which film censorship had helped to maintain.

The answer lay, they found, in turning to the younger generation – in both film-makers and audiences. A middle-aged society in many respects tired of itself and decadent with self-doubt accepted almost gladly its exposure in the novels and plays of a new generation of writers and dramatists. The novels of John Braine ('Room at the Top') and Alan Sillitoe ('Saturday Night and Sunday Morning'), the plays of JOHN OSBORNE (notably 'Look Back in Anger') and Shelagh Delaney ('A Taste of Honey'), all challenging British society and convention in the late 1950s, were turned into films between 1958 and 1961 by a group of new directors, JACK CLAYTON, KAREL REISZ and TONY RICHARDSON.

The film censors wisely disregarded old prohibitions and permitted the far freer speech of these productions, with their unvarnished treatment of the problems of illegitimacy, homosexuality and abortion; censorship of the stage (under heavy fire for a decade) was finally abolished, to its own relief, in 1968. Film censorship, still concerned to protect the industry from the worst irresponsible or wholly corrupt film-makers might produce either at home or abroad in the way of open sadism and 'hard-core' pornography, was retained, though its recommendations did not apply to screenings conducted under club conditions, which greatly increased during the 1960s in face of the large production of 'underground' and avant-garde films in Europe and the USA. These off-beat films made the full-scale professional productions like *Saturday Night and Sunday Morning* and those that followed, such as JOHN SCHLESINGER's *A Kind of Loving* (1962) and *Billy Liar* (1963) or even LINDSAY ANDERSON's *This Sporting Life* (1963), seem relatively restrained. In any case, the rigours of censorship were considerably relaxed, the modifications in the categorization taking place in 1952 (the year of the introduction of the X certificate for films for adults only) and again in 1970.

These films were followed later in the 1960s by other work from directors both new and established, notably CLIVE DONNER's *Nothing but the Best* (1964) and *Here we go Round the Mulberry Bush* (1967), LEWIS GILBERT's *Alfie* (1966), TONY RICHARDSON's *Tom Jones* (1963), John Schlesinger's *Darling* (1965), KAREL REISZ's *Morgan, a Suitable Case for Treatment* (1966), RICHARD LESTER's *The Knack* (1965) and *How I Won the War* (1967), Lindsay Anderson's *If* (1968) and ALBERT FINNEY's *Charlie Bubbles* (1968), and the films of directors who came from television, such as PETER WATKINS's *The War Game* (1966) and *Privilege* (1967), KEN LOACH's *Poor Cow* (1967), Peter Collinson's *Up the Junction* (1967), KEN RUSSELL's *Women in Love* (1969), and JACK GOLD's *The Bofors Gun* (1968). Almost all these films portrayed working-class rather than middle-class characters, and brought many new acting talents to light, notably ALBERT FINNEY, RITA TUSHINGHAM, RACHEL ROBERTS, ALAN BATES, TOM COURTENAY, RICHARD HARRIS, DAVID WARNER, JULIE CHRISTIE and GLENDA JACKSON, while PETER SELLERS, TERENCE STAMP, James Fox, David Hemmings, DONALD PLEASENCE, PAUL SCOFIELD and VANESSA REDGRAVE had starred in other films. RICHARD ATTENBOROUGH, who had for long worked so successfully with the writer-director BRYAN FORBES in such films as *The Angry Silence* (1959) and *Séance on a Wet Afternoon* (1964), himself took to direction with the serious burlesque *Oh! What a Lovely War* (1969). Forbes, with many other films to his credit, was made head of production at the ABPC Studios in 1969, when the company was taken over by Bernard Delfont and EMI (Electrical and Musical Industries), though he subsequently resigned in 1971.

Ken Russell went on to direct two brilliant but much criticized films, *The Music Lovers* (1970) and *The Devils* (1971), which challenged the censorship radically with their phantasmagoria of sex, violence and the extravagant overspill of Russell's occasionally uncontrolled imagery.

Parallel with this newer wing of British cinema, work of the more traditional kind continued, bringing with many of the films just mentioned success to British cinema abroad as well as at home. To mention only a few, DAVID LEAN's *The Bridge on the River Kwai* (1957) and *Lawrence of Arabia* (1962), CAROL REED's *Oliver!* (1968), Jack Clayton's *The Pumpkin Eater* (1963), Karel Reisz's *Isadora* (1968), Tony Richardson's *The Charge of the Light Brigade* (1968), and the extraordinarily successful series of films about Ian Fleming's secret agent James Bond, which began with *Dr No* (1962).

Another factor in British films of the 1960s has been the American influence. First came the 'refugees' from the United States in the McCarthy period, of whom the chief were CARL FOREMAN (*The Guns of Navarone*, 1961, etc) and JOSEPH LOSEY; second came the wave of equally distinguished talents who preferred to make films in Britain – for example, SAM SPIEGEL in his association with David Lean, JOHN HUSTON, STANLEY KUBRICK (*Dr Strangelove*, 1963; *2001 – A Space Odyssey*, 1968), JOSEPH STRICK (*Ulysses*, 1967), and others; and finally, the producers and directors who came

Top: Alec Guinness in 'The Man in the White Suit' (Alexander Mackendrick, 1951)
Above: Yvonne Mitchell in 'The Divided Heart' (Charles Crichton, 1954)
Below: Rita Tushingham and Murray Melvin in 'A Taste of Honey' (Tony Richardson, 1961)

to Britain during the period when American financial investment virtually took over British production to the extent that 90 per cent of the capital tied up in production was American, sponsoring alike British creative talent and bringing in key American directors to work in British studios. As a result many distinguished directors such as BILLY WILDER, SIDNEY LUMET, DELBERT MANN, GEORGE SIDNEY, STANLEY DONEN, GEORGE STEVENS, MARTIN RITT, OTTO PREMINGER, ANTHONY MANN, RICHARD BROOKS, WILLIAM WYLER and FRED ZINNEMANN came to Britain for a film, or part of a film, in the later 1960s. Joseph Losey's record of production in Britain is remarkable, including *The Criminal* (1960), *The Servant* (1963), *Accident* (1967) and *The Go-Between* (1971). To the Americans who have worked in Britain should be added visiting directors from Europe, notably ROMAN POLANSKI with *Repulsion* (1965) and *Cul-de-Sac* (1966), FRANÇOIS TRUFFAUT (*Fahrenheit 451*, 1966), and MICHELANGELO ANTONIONI with *Blow-Up* (1967).

Owing to the economic recession in the USA and other factors, the amount of American investment in British films eased off suddenly in 1970, and the British industry was faced once again with the need to stand on its own feet. The industry has always been bred on crises, and is experienced in the art of getting round them. New kinds of production, made as much with television in mind as the big screen, were already emerging in the 1960s. Certain outstanding productions in the theatre were re-aligned (rather than re-created) for the camera: for example, the National Theatre's productions of *Othello* and *The Three Sisters*, the first featuring, and the latter directed by LAURENCE OLIVIER. The theatre inspired CLIVE DONNER's most effective, low-budget production of HAROLD PINTER's play, *The Caretaker* (1963), but this was wholly re-created for the cinema, as were several other plays ranging from JOHN OSBORNE's *Inadmissible Evidence* (with

Above: Shirley Anne Field and Albert Finney in 'Saturday Night and Sunday Morning' (Karel Reisz, 1960)
Below: Tom Courtenay and Rodney Bewes in 'Billy Liar' (John Schlesinger, 1963)

its star of the stage performance, NICOL WILLIAMSON) to PETER HALL's controversial version of his stage production of *A Midsummer Night's Dream*, originally produced at Stratford-upon-Avon, and PETER BROOK's remarkable *Marat-Sade* and *King Lear*, both transferred from his own stage productions. Directors are seeking new methods to achieve low-budget production, notably KEN LOACH with *Kes* (1970) and *Family Life* (1971).

But however versatile producers and directors may be in devising new means of getting their films made, they need distribution – opportunity in the home cinemas, opportunity through successful export, and subsequent distribution through television. This is the only way to keep British production economically viable. There is an increasing closeness between the former rivals, cinema and television; anticipating this very early, the British

Film Academy and the Guild of Television Producers and Directors merged in 1959 to form the Society of Film and Television Arts, their quarterly journal acting as the mouthpiece for representative views from their 600 membership of creative workers in film and television.

Meanwhile the study of film has spread in Britain with a powerful film society movement, the vastly increased activities of the British Film Institute (with 'Sight and Sound', the 'Monthly Film Bulletin' and other publications), the work of the National Film Archive, and of the Society for Education in Film and Television, which encourages film studies in schools. Training for film-making centres on the London Film School and in the Film Department of the Royal College of Art, while a new National Film School was constituted in 1969, and started work in 1971. The study of

Top left: Maggie Smith in 'Oh! What a Lovely War' (Richard Attenborough, 1969)
Above: Peter O'Toole in 'Lawrence of Arabia' (David Lean, 1962)
Below: Peter Finch and James Mason in 'The Pumpkin Eater' (Jack Clayton, 1963)

film takes place in certain universities and centres of further education, notably at the Slade School of Fine Art. The quality press and the weekly journals maintain, on the whole, a high level of regular film criticism. RM

Greece

The Greek film industry revived slowly after the difficult conditions following the war had for a while settled. Production, apart from the work of MICHAEL CACOYANNIS and of film-makers from abroad, notably the British director BASIL WRIGHT (*The Immortal Land*, 1958) and the American JULES DASSIN (*Never on Sunday*, 1960; *Phaedra*, 1962), has been of an entirely local character. Production has reached as many as 100 low-budget subjects in a year; the theatres in which they are shown number some 1,350, of which half are open-air. Censorship of imported films remains very strict. Greek actresses of note who have appeared in international productions include MELINA MERCOURI and the great stage actress, Katina Paxinou (born 1904), who appeared notably in *For Whom the Bell Tolls* (1943), *Mourning Becomes Electra* (1947),

Above: Dominic Guard, Margaret Leighton and Julie Christie in 'The Go-Between' (Joseph Losey, 1971)
Below: 'Marat-Sade' (Peter Brook, 1966)

and *Rocco and his Brothers* (1960).

During 1970 a new talent emerged – Theodor Angelopoulos, whose film *The Reconstruction*, a stark study of murder in a rural setting, caused considerable discussion at the 1971 Berlin festival. RM

Grémillon, Jean (1902–1959)

Born in Bayeux, Brittany, France. Director and composer. Started his career 1924–5 in documentary, working with the cameraman GEORGES PÉRINAL, and also making with him *Photogénie Mécanique*, which was avant-garde, and *Tour au Large* (1926), which was set in Brittany. He worked his way into feature production with *Maldone* (1927) and *La petite Lise* (1930), a naturalistically realized story of an escaped convict. These films were unsuccessful commercially, and Grémillon worked for a while in Spain and then in Germany, where he made French films such as *Gueule d'Amour* (1937) and *L'Étrange Monsieur Victor* (1938), which gave RAIMU a rich opportunity for character acting. Grémillon was always to be an exceptional director of actors. During the Occupation he made some of his best films – *Lumière d'Été* (1943) and *Le Ciel est à Vous* (1944), with its undercurrent of allusion to the condition of the French – and was a member of the underground Comité de Libération du Cinéma Français. Grémillon's true feelings were shown in the post-war documentary, *Le Six Juin à l'Aube* (1945), on the aftermath of war, in the delicate satire of his film about 19th-century popular upper-class art, *Les Charmes de l'Existence* (1949), and in his finest documentary, *André Masson et les Quatres Éléments* (1958). His later features were *Pattes Blanches* (1949), *L'Étrange Madame X* (1951) and *L'Amour d'une Femme* (1954). In most of Grémillon's films there is an expression of profound melancholy; though highly valued in France by critics and film-makers, his films met with little success with the public. RM

Grierson, John

Born 1898 at Kilmarnock, Scotland. Documentary producer. Served RNVR 1915–9; educated Glasgow and Chicago universities. His father was a schoolmaster, but he came of a line of lighthouse-keepers, and he has an inborn love of the sea and ships. In 1924 a Rockefeller Research Fellowship in Social Science took him to the USA, where he studied the press, cinema and other forms of mass communication. While in the USA he originated the word 'documentary' in a review written for the New York Sun in February 1926. His interest in the film was twofold, as a medium for public information and as an art form. On his return to Britain in 1927 he was appointed Films Officer at the Empire Marketing Board by Sir Stephen Tallents, himself a pioneer in public relations. The only film Grierson was personally to direct was *Drifters* (1929), a study of the North Sea herring catch, made much under the technical influence of EISENSTEIN. It was a silent film, but as Grierson entered films at the period of the coming of sound, his thinking was to be entirely geared to the sound film.

Grierson now became the combined impresario-gadfly-ideasman-critic-philosopher of British, and eventually world documentary, occupying a succession of key positions as producer, first of all at the EMB (1930–3, making over 100 films). During the 1930s many of the distinguished men of British documentary started their careers with him, including ROTHA, WRIGHT, ANSTEY, ELTON, WATT, Legg and JENNINGS. He was to encourage sponsorship of films by government departments and industry alike. He brought CAVALCANTI from France, FLAHERTY from the USA and introduced W. H. Auden and Benjamin Britten to film-making. He helped found the Empire Film Library (later Central Film Library), the monthly magazine 'World Film News', successor to the Edinburgh journal, 'Cinema Quarterly', to which he frequently contributed. He ceaselessly wrote and lectured about the film, more especially documentary. When the EMB ceased, he headed the GPO Film Unit (1933–7), specializing in communications subjects, resigning from this in 1937 when he was ready for wider activities promoting the documentary idea (film in the service of public information), which took him to Canada in 1938, and after this New Zealand and Australia. He became Film Commissioner in Canada in 1939, where his team at the National Film Board rose in six years to 800, and included such noted film-makers and assistants as Stuart Legg, Ross McLean, NORMAN MCLAREN and Tom Daly. Again with a widening of intention he resigned in 1945, his eye turning in the direction of the new medium of television, which was to offer the information film more immediate access to the public than the normal channels of film distribution. He became Director of UNESCO's Mass Communications (1946–8), and when this proved frustrating, Controller of Films at the Central Office of Information in London (1948–50). Increasingly he found that contact with post-war bureaucracy and cheese-paring economies held back the fulfilment of his ideas, and in 1951 he took charge (along with John Baxter) of the National Film Finance Corporation's Group 3, designed to develop the talents of young feature film-makers; his directors included WOLF RILLA, JOHN GUILLERMIN and PHILIP LEACOCK and he launched such stars as KENNETH MORE, PETER FINCH, and PETER SELLERS. After this operation failed through lack of adequate distribution for the films, Grierson finally turned to television in 1957, conducting for many years his own film programme for Scottish Television, *This Wonderful World*. Latterly he has returned to lecturing and teaching. He has never ceased to be a great teacher, creating a whole philosophy, sociology and aesthetic for film; he is often called 'the father of documentary', which he once defined as 'the creative treatment of actuality'. His essays, among the finest writing in existence on

Below: Irene Papas (centre) in 'Electra' (Michael Cacoyannis, Greece, 1961)
Bottom: Raimu in 'L'Etrange Monsieur Victor' (Jean Grémillon, France, 1938)

the subject, have been collected by his friend and colleague, H. Forsyth Hardy, in 'Grierson on Documentary' (1956; revised and enlarged 1966). He was awarded the CBE in 1961. RM

Griffith, David Wark (1875–1948)
Born in La Grange, Kentucky. The outstanding innovator in the whole history of the cinema, between 1908 and 1916 Griffith raised the medium to its maturity. With *Intolerance* (1916) the film came of age, aesthetically as well as chronologically. Griffith was the son of an impoverished Southern family; and had been an undistinguished actor and an unsuccessful writer when he sought work at the Edison studios in 1907. A scenario he submitted was turned down, but he stayed on to act in an EDWIN PORTER film, *Rescued from an Eagle's Nest*. Engaged by Biograph as a scenarist, he directed his first film, *The Adventures of Dollie*, in the summer of 1908. During the next five years he made some 500 short films for Biograph, in the course of which he established himself as America's leading director, saved the failing fortunes of Biograph, and explored and extended the whole creative range of the cinema.

Griffith's instinctive command of narrative technique and *mise-en-scène* was to a large extent the result of his familiarity with the techniques of the 19th-century novelists and the theatre of his youth. It was in the search for the most effective narrative techniques that he developed the means of the cinema. His love of Victorian painting also guided him forward from the stage-proscenium style of photography which predominated when he came to the cinema, to make use of composition, variety of shot-framing, depth of frame, light and shade, and other pictorial means to aid his narrative. His most profound contribution to film practice however was his development of the conception of film EDITING. Edwin Porter, in *The Life of an American Fireman* (1902) and *The Great Train Robbery* (1903), showed how a film could be composed out of short interdependent scenes. Griffith formularized the method of cutting *within* a scene, to divide a scene into short fragments, isolated elements incomplete in themselves, but capable of being reassembled as a total scene. He discovered that by the use of such fragments he could vary the emphasis from shot to shot, and so control the dramatic emphasis and intensity of his scene. Developing the idea of parallel action, and the use of the flashback, Griffith proved that editing could be used for the mastery of screen time as well as screen space.

As well as developing the cinema's language, Griffith significantly broadened its range of subjects, bringing to the screen the works of Tennyson, Browning, Hood and Poe; social problem films and philosophical essays like *Man's Genesis* (1912). When he insisted to the Biograph directors that a subject of the importance of *Enoch Arden* (1911) could not be adequately adapted within the one-reel film which was conventional at the time, and completed the film in two reels, he made a large contribution to the revolution which introduced the multi-reel 'feature' film to the American cinema.

After these formative years Griffith left Biograph; and in 1915 completed *Birth of a Nation*, perhaps the most influential picture in film history, a massive, torrential spectacle of the Civil War, only vitiated by the narrow racist attitudes which the film had taken over from the original novel on which it was based, Thomas Dixon's 'The Clansman'. Perhaps it was his sensitivity to the criticism the film received on this score – despite its huge commercial success – that stimulated the preparations for a film of still vaster scope, *Intolerance* (1916). The complex episodic structure of this film proved too difficult for audiences of the time, and the film failed to achieve the commercial success of *Birth of a Nation*. For much of the rest of his career Griffith was struggling to pay off the debts the film had incurred.

Despite this check however, Griffith was still at the peak of his career, with successes and masterpieces still to come: two war films, shot in Europe, *Hearts of the World* and *The Great Love* (1918); two rather hoary melodrama themes metamorphosed into art, *Broken Blossoms* (1919) and *Way Down East* (1920); a costume spectacle, *Orphans of the Storm*, a fine entertainment mystery, *One Exciting Night* (1922); and a remarkable portent of neo-realism, *Isn't Life Wonderful?* (1924), which dealt with the situation of ordinary people in defeated Germany.

But by the time that he attempted to repeat the success of *Birth of a Nation* with another historical spectacle, *America* (1924), Griffith's style was already out of mode. At 49 years of age he was *passé*: the Jazz Age had no time for his Victorian heroines and Victorian morality. Griffith had never lost his integrity or his narrative skill; but he found it harder and harder to find suitable work and his later films passed almost unnoticed: two W. C. FIELDS vehicles, *Sally of the Sawdust* (1925) and *That Royle Girl* (1926), a brilliant adaptation of Marie Corelli's *The Sorrows of Satan* (1926), a remake of his own old *Battle of the Sexes* (1928). An anachronism, Griffith lingered into the age of talking pictures, with *Abraham Lincoln* (1930) and *The Struggle* (1931). The last seventeen years of Griffith's life were spent in chafing inactivity, always planning films, or the dramatic masterpiece it had always been his ambition to write. Other films: *The Musketeers of Pig Alley* and *The Massacre* (1912), *Judith of Bethulia* (1913), *The Great Love* (1918), *The Romance of Happy Valley*, *The Greatest Thing in Life*, *The Girl Who Stayed at Home*, *True Heart Susie*, *Scarlet Days* and *The Greatest Question* (1919), *The Idol Dancer* and *The Love Flower* (1920), *Dream Street* (1921), *The White Rose* (1923), *Drums of Love* (1928), *Lady of the Pavements* (1929). DR

Griffith, Raymond (1895–1957)
Born in Boston, Massachusetts, USA. Actor. Perhaps Griffith's unjust neglect in later years is due to the extreme refinement of his slapstick which limited his appeal in his own lifetime. A short, rather chubby young man with a moustache and an unvarying sartorial elegance that recalled MAX LINDER, he always proved serenely superior to the catastrophes which he unwittingly invoked. Working in the cinema from 1914, he was a director for SENNETT from 1917 to 1921; then, at Paramount, became a star in his own right, his first film being *Fools First* (1922). His most notable films were *He's a Prince* (1925), a satire on the tours of the Prince of Wales, which was consequently not shown in Britain; *Hands Up!* and *Wet Paint* (1926), *You'd Be Surprised* (1927). He also played in D. W. GRIFFITH'S *The Sorrows of Satan* (1926). A vocal defect prevented him from continuing his career in the sound period, apart from a brief, mute but highly effective appearance as the dying French soldier in the shellhole in *All Quiet on the Western Front* (1930). In later years he worked in Hollywood as a writer and producer. DR

Grillet, Alain Robbe
See ROBBE-GRILLET

Grimault, Paul
Born 1905 at Neuilly-sur-Seine, France. Animation producer and director. Worked closely with André Sarrut – they called themselves *Les Gémeaux* – making commercials from the later 1930s. They developed their strongly drawn, almost puppet-like characters and highly decorative, solid-looking backgrounds to best effect in *L'Épouvantail* (1943) and the sad story of the animated toys, *Le Petit Soldat* (1947). Their work is characterized by well-developed storylines and the same prevailing romantic melancholy as that in the contemporary PRÉVERT-CARNÉ feature films. Their work culminated in the ill-fated feature-length cartoon, *La Bergère et le Ramoneur* (1953), scripted by Jacques Prévert from Hans Andersen, but adding its own post-war memories of what life was like under the Gestapo. Latterly Grimault has re-emerged as producer of cartoons by Jean-François Laguionie, such as *La Demoiselle et le Violoncelliste* (1964).

Grip
A stage hand delegated to a camera crew for handling and moving equipment

Grune, Karl (1890–1962)
Born in Vienna, Austria, but of Czech origin. Studied in the School of Dramatic Art, Vienna, and worked initially in the German theatre as actor and director, for a while with Max Reinhardt. He began scripting films and directing 1918–9. Among his many films of the 1920s his single outstanding production was *The Street* (1923), one of the silent films of 'disillusionment' made without narrative or dialogue captions and treated with stylized realism; he also made a moralizing pacifist film,

At the Edge of the World (1927), *The Schellenberg Brothers* (1926), featuring CONRAD VEIDT in a dual role, and the spectacular, over-theatrical *Waterloo* (1928). In 1931 he left Germany for France, and finally settled in England, where he directed *Abdul the Damned* (1935), *The Marriage of Corbal* (1936) and *Pagliacci* (1937), as well as producing *The Silver Darlings* (1947).

Guazzoni, Enrico (1876–1949)
Born in Rome, Italy. Pioneer Italian director and designer. Specialist in historical films – he directed *Agrippina* and *Brutus* in 1910 – Guazzoni completed his first outstanding Italian spectacular, *Quo Vadis?*, in 1912 at a cost of some £7,000, a large sum for the period. Although just preceded by two versions of *The Last Days of Pompeii*, made by ARTURO AMBROSIO and Ernesto Pasquali, Guazzoni designed and constructed large sets for his films and employed hundreds of extras, anticipating in spectacular production the even more celebrated *Cabiria* (1913) made by GIOVANNI PASTRONE. *Quo Vadis?* was in constant demand throughout the world, especially in the USA. Guazzoni continued to produce numerous films until well into the Second World War; his last production was *La Fornarina* (1943). Although he soon lost his position in the forefront of Italian directors, he was for a brief while the GRIFFITH of the Italian cinema, and one of the principal founders of the spectacle film which inspired Griffith. Among his other early productions were *Mark Antony and Cleopatra* (1913) and *Gaius Julius Caesar* (1914). RM

Guest, Val
Born 1911 in London, England. Competent British writer, producer and director, formerly a journalist on the Hollywood Reporter and an observer of the film industry in Hollywood during the 1930s. In Britain he wrote screenplays for many of the major native comedians, WILL HAY, Arthur Askey, the Crazy Gang. After writing and directing a number of small but serviceable comedies, principally for the home market, he turned to sterner subjects – *Quatermass II* (1956), *Hell is a City* (1959), *The Day the Earth Caught Fire* (1962) and *The Beauty Jungle* (1964). Particularly adroit with suspense thrillers such as *Where the Spies Are* (1965) and *Assignment K* (1967), he recently tried but failed to capture the new youthful spirit in *Toomorrow* (1970).

Guide Track
Sound track recorded during shooting not for use in the finished film but as a guide for post-synchronizing.

Guilaroff, Sidney
Born 1910 in Montreal, Canada. Flamboyant American hairdresser, at MGM for many years where he became a key craftsman in the studio's famous star-building system. Working in New York, he first attracted attention when he created a new hair-style for CLAUDETTE COLBERT which so impressed JOAN CRAWFORD that she persuaded MGM to bring him to Hollywood. He has dressed the hair of most of the leading female stars, adapting his more elaborate styles to the simpler post-Second World War fashions.

Guillermin, John
Born 1925 in London, England. British director, who started in films working on French documentaries and then went to Hollywood to study studio methods there. His first feature film was *Two on the Tiles* (1951). A succession of brisk, small-scale British films, including *Town on Trial* (1956) and *The Day they Robbed the Bank of England* (1960), were his *entrée* into the international film market. With *The Blue Max* (1966), *New Face in Hell* (1968), *The Bridge at Remagen* (1969), among others, he has established himself as a particularly adept action director, though his handling of the human element in his films suggests he may be more at home with machines and fast-moving violence than with actors.

Guinness, Alec
Born 1914 in London, England. Justly celebrated British character-actor and star whose film début in *Great Expectations* (1946) was the forerunner of many finely detailed screen performances through which few traces of the 'real' Guinness have ever filtered. The opposite of the personality Hollywood star, he started his career on the stage, to which he returns often. Playing eight roles in the Ealing black comedy, *Kind Hearts and Coronets* (1949), he achieved both popular success and critical acclaim. He won an Academy Award for his portrayal of the fanatical officer prisoner-of-war in *The Bridge on the River Kwai* (1957).

Memorable character studies include: Fagin in *Oliver Twist* (1947); assorted master criminals in *The Lavender Hill Mob* (1951) and *The Ladykillers* (1955); Disraeli in *The Mudlark* (1951); the reprobate artist in *The Horse's Mouth* (1959); King Feisal in *Lawrence of Arabia* (1962); Charles I in *Cromwell* (1970). His least effective portrayals are those that come closest to conventional romantic heroics, most disastrously in *The Malta Story* (1953). He was knighted in 1959. Other notable films: *A Run for Your Money* (1949), *The Man in the White Suit* (1951), *Father Brown* (1954), *The Swan* (1956), which he made in Hollywood, *Our Man in Havana* (1959), *Tunes of Glory* (1960), *Doctor Zhivago*, *Hotel Paradiso* and *The Quiller Memorandum* (1966), *The Comedians* (1967), *Scrooge* and *Cromwell* (1970). MH

Guitry, Sacha (1885–1957)
Born in St Petersburg, Russia. Distinguished French playwright, actor and director, who wrote as well as starred in his own films. His elegant, rather mannered style was particularly admired in films during the 1930s. After a period away from the screen, he was especially active in films during the 1950s. Main films: *Bonne Chance* (1935), *Le Roman d'un Tricheur* (1936), *Quadrille* (1938), *Ils Étaient Neuf Célibataires* (1939), *Le Poison* (1951), *Versailles* (1954), *Napoléon* (1955), *La Vie à Deux* (1957).

Above: 'La Bergère et le Ramoneur' (Paul Grimault, France, 1953)
Below: Peter Sellers, Alec Guinness and Herbert Lom in 'The Ladykillers' (Alexander Mackendrick, GB, 1955)

Guy-Blaché, Alice
Born 1873 in Paris, France. Director. The first woman director in the world, Alice Guy was secretary to LÉON GAUMONT when, in 1899, he asked her to make a film. Subsequently she began production in her own right, and in 1911 went to the USA with her husband Herbert Blaché where she made *Fra Diavolo* (1912), *Shadows of the Moulin Rouge* (1914), *Behind the Mask* (1917), *The Great Adventure* (1918) and *Tarnished Reputations* (1920). Her early films made in France include: *La Fée aux Choux* (1900), *Le Voleur Sacrilège* (1903), *Paris la Nuit* (1904), *La Vie du Christ* (1906). In her American studio at Fort Lee, New Jersey, the sign 'Be natural' was chalked up on notice boards, possibly under the influence of CAPELLANI, who worked with her. DR

H

Haanstra, Bert
Born 1916 in Holland. Documentary director and producer. After working as a painter and photographer and as film cameraman on the Anglo-Dutch feature, *Myrte and the Demons* (1949), he made the prize-winning documentary *Mirror of Holland* (1950), which won the Grand Prix for documentary at Cannes. He joined the Royal Dutch Shell Film Unit, for whom he began by making a series of instructional films in Indonesia. His best-known film for Shell (produced from Britain) was his international study of man's war on the insects, and notably the locust, in *The Rival World* (1955). Following this, his more outstanding documentaries were *Rembrandt* (1956), one of his many films on art, and *Glass* (1958), which uses superb photography and editing to reveal the rhythms in glass-making. In 1958 he turned, with less success, to feature film-making in *Fanfare*. His more recent documentary films have been *Bridges of Holland* (1968) and the feature-length *Voice of the Water* (1967), a study of the Dutch people's involvement with water. Haanstra has won over 50 international awards for his work. RM

Halas, John
Born in 1912 in Budapest, Hungary. Animation producer and director. Studied in Hungary and Paris before becoming assistant to GEORGE PAL in 1928–31. He began independent production in Hungary in 1934, coming to England in 1936 where he formed, with his future wife, Joy Batchelor, one of the longest-established and best-known animation units in the world. During some 30 years' continuous work, Halas and Batchelor have produced many officially-sponsored propaganda and instructional cartoons, including the first full-length British cartoon in Technicolor, *Handling Ships* (1946), an instructional film. Later they made the entertainment feature, *Animal Farm* (1954) – this was based on Orwell's political fable, and was the first entirely serious feature-cartoon to be made in the history of animation. The basic work of Halas and Batchelor tends towards the serious, such as the brilliantly designed and succinct *As Old as the Hills* (1950), on the geology of oil, *To Your Health* (directed by Philip Stapp, 1956), the satiric *History of the Cinema* (1956), and the alarming *Automania 2000* (1965), which won the unit more awards than any other short film. During the 1960s Halas and Batchelor have made a number of cartoon series, some for television, such as the Habatales, Foo-Foo, and the Hoffnung series. With the very successful *Snip and Snap* series the unit moved into paper-cut-out puppet film-making, but latterly they have worked increasingly in strictly educational film, especially in cassette form for 'instant' use in the classroom. They were the first unit in Britain to apply computerized animation techniques to mobile diagrammatic films for mathematical and science instruction. John Halas, with Roger Manvell, has written many books on animation: 'The Technique of Film Animation' (1959), 'Design in Motion' (1962), 'Art in Movement' (1970). John Halas also wrote 'Film and TV Graphics' (1967), and Roger Manvell's 'The Animated Film' (1954) gives a detailed and fully illustrated description of the making of *Animal Farm*. RM

Hall, Peter
Born 1930 in Suffolk, England. Prolific British stage director whose excursions into film-making have been less assured than his theatre work, though increasingly adept. Managing Director of the Royal Shakespeare Theatre at the age of twenty-nine, he is credited with revitalizing and enlarging the company and its repertory. In 1968 he made a film version of his stage production of *A Midsummer Night's Dream*, followed by an unsatisfactory treatment of the antic social comedy, *Work is a Four-Letter Word*. More successful was *Three Into Two Won't Go* (1969), and his cheeky crime comedy *Perfect Friday* (1970) revealed a flair missing from his previous films. He is still principally involved in the theatre and opera. MH

Hall, Willis
Born 1929 in Leeds, England. Playwright and film scriptwriter. Films (in collaboration with Keith Waterhouse) include: *The Long and Short and the Tall* and *Whistle Down the Wind* (1961), *A Kind of Loving* (1962), *Billy Liar* (1963).

Hamer, Robert (1911–1963)
Born in Worcestershire, England. Gifted British director who started in films in 1934 as a clapper boy and worked his way up to the position of editor and then director at MICHAEL BALCON's Ealing Studios. Although his work tended to be unpredictable, at his best his immaculate style produced several distinguished, indeed classic, examples of British film-making: notably a macabre sequence in *Dead of Night* (1945), the witty black comedy *Kind Hearts and Coronets* (1949), *Father Brown* (1954). Other films include: *Pink String and Sealing Wax* (1945), *It Always Rains on Sunday* (1947), *The Spider and the Fly* (1949), *His Excellency* (1952), *To Paris with Love* (1955), *The Scapegoat* (1959), *School for Scoundrels* (1960).

David Warner and Cilla Black in 'Work is a Four-Letter Word' (Peter Hall, GB, 1967)

Top: Googie Withers in 'It Always Rains on Sunday' (Robert Hamer, GB, 1947)
Above: Laurence Olivier, Ralph Richardson, Mary Kerridge, Cedric Hardwicke, Alec Clunes, Laurence Naismith and Helen Haye in 'Richard III' (Olivier, GB, 1954)

Hamilton, Guy
Born 1922 in Paris, France. Director; at first apprentice in Nice, then with British Paramount News. During the Second World War he served with the Royal Navy. Assistant director of *They Made me a Fugitive* (1947), and to CAROL REED in such films as *The Third Man* (1949). Films directed include: *The Ringer* (1952), *The Colditz Story* (1955), *The Devil's Disciple* (1958), *Goldfinger* (1964), *The Battle of Britain* (1969).

Hardwicke, Cedric (1893–1964)
British actor, born in Stourbridge, England. He studied with the Royal Academy of Dramatic Art, made his stage début in 1912 and served in the First World War. His film career did not begin until 1931 with *Dreyfus*, but from then on he appeared in many films in Britain and the USA. His American début was in *Becky Sharp* in 1935. Main films: *Nell Gwyn* (as Charles II) and *Jew Süss* (1934), *Things to Come*, *Peg of Old Drury* and *Les Misérables* (1935), *King Solomon's Mines* (1937), *Stanley and Livingstone* (he played Livingstone) and *Tom Brown's Schooldays* (1939), *The Hunchback of Notre Dame* (1940), *Suspicion* (1941), *Nicholas Nickleby* (1947), *The Winslow Boy* (1948), *Rope* (1949), *Richard III* (1954), *The Pumpkin Eater* (1964). He was knighted in 1934. His autobiography, 'A Victorian in Orbit', was published in 1961.

Hardy, Oliver
See LAUREL, STAN

Harlan, Veit (1889–1964)
Born in Berlin, Germany. Director and actor. Worked initially in the theatre under Max Reinhardt. Entered films as an actor, and began direction during the Nazi régime, becoming one of the most highly valued of Goebbels's exponents of Nazism and German nationalism. His main Nazi, or nationalist films, many of which he also scripted or co-scripted, included *Der Herrscher* (1937), the anti-Semitic *Jew Süss*, *Der Grosse König* (1942), and the spectacular *Kolberg* (1945), completed in the last weeks of the war. He was put on trial in Hamburg in 1950 on charges of crimes against humanity (with special reference to *Jew Süss*), but acquitted. Thereafter he resumed his career, making several films before his retirement in 1962. He died in Capri.

Harlow, Jean (1911–1937)
Born in Kansas City, USA. What CLARA BOW – the 'It' Girl – was to the 1920s, Jean Harlow – The Platinum Blonde – was to the 1930s. As it happened, one of her earliest film appearances was in a Clara Bow vehicle, *Saturday Night Kid* (1929). Her appearance in HUGHES's *Hell's Angels* (1930) and then WELLMAN's *Public Enemy* (1931) launched her to stardom; and FRANK CAPRA's *Platinum Blonde* (1931) consolidated both the myth and the quintessential Harlow character – the brash, wise-cracking, provocatively sexual, teasingly tarty girl with a figure and formation that were pure *art-deco*. Teaming her explosively with CLARK GABLE, in *Red Dust* (1932), *Hold Your Man* (1933), *China Seas* (1934) and *Saratoga* (completed posthumously, 1937), proved to be an inspiration on the part of the MGM executive. Like Bow, Harlow was constantly pursued by scandal, which reached a peak when her second husband, the MGM producer Paul Bern, committed suicide a few weeks after their marriage. She seems however to have been no worse than a good-natured, easy-going girl, whose last days were dogged by ill-health. Her MGM-staged funeral, marking the close of another era of Hollywood, was almost as extravagant as that of VALENTINO a decade earlier, with a vast bronze casket and Nelson Eddy and JEANETTE MACDONALD singing respectively, 'Ah Sweet Mystery of Life' and 'The Indian Love Song' from *Rose Marie*. DR

Harrington, Curtis
Born 1928 in Los Angeles, USA. Director.

Made various 8 mm and 16 mm films when young, studied film at the University of Southern California and became noted film critic with special reference to the American cinema. He was assistant to JERRY WALD and associate producer at Fox and worked for US Information Agency. He was known for his short avant-garde films before entering the commercial cinema as director with *Night Tide* (1961), a semi-surrealist film marred by rather pretentious working-out. After some other minor work, he made *Games* (1967), a Grand Guignol thriller influenced, perhaps, by CLOUZOT's *Les Diaboliques*. Probably his best film to date, *What's the matter with Helen?* (1971), continued his preoccupation with macabre subjects and was distinguished by a brilliant evocation of America in the 1930s and highly expert playing from Debbie Reynolds and SHELLEY WINTERS. Harrington (like Peter Bogdanovitch) belongs to the new generation of American directors whose work is closely integrated with their love and knowledge of the old American cinema. He has also made *The Gingerbread House* (1971) in Britain with Shelley Winters. JG

Harris, Hilary
Born 1929 in New York City, USA. Documentary and specialized film director. After studying at Columbia College, New York City, he became for a while assistant to MARY ELLEN BUTE. In 1953, after refusing to undertake military service, he was assigned to New York Hospital as a psychiatric aide. Meanwhile he was working on a succession of experimental films, *Longhorns* (1951), a study in movement, *Generation* (1956), an abstract film, and *Highway* (1958). At the invitation of JOHN GRIERSON, he came to Glasgow to make *Seaward the Great Ships* (1960) on shipbuilding in Scotland, a half-hour documentary which won many awards. Since 1961 he has been making sponsored documentaries and films for television in New York City; these include *The Walk* (1963), *The Squeeze* (1964), on over-population, a study of dance in terms of film called *9 Variations on a Dance Theme* (1966), and *The Nuer* (1970), a documentary feature on the Nilotes of Ethiopia and the Sudan.

Harris, Richard
Born 1933 in Ireland. Actor, who made his début in 1958 in *Alive and Kicking* – a film with a title appropriate to the gauche and rebellious character he usually portrays. Main films: *Shake Hands with the Devil* (1959), *The Long The Short and The Tall* and *Guns of Navarone* (1961), *Mutiny on the Bounty* (1962), *This Sporting Life* (1963), *The Red Desert* (1964), *The Bible* (1966), *The Molly Maguires*, *A Man called Horse*, *Cromwell* (in which he played the title role, 1970). Directed *Bloomfield* (1971).

Harrison, Rex
Born 1908 in Huyton, Cheshire. Actor, who first appeared on the stage in repertory in Liverpool and subsequently became well known as an urbane and well-spoken stage actor in London and on Broadway. His early films included *The School for Scandal* (1930), *The Citadel* (1938) and *Major Barbara* (1940). After serving in the RAF in World War II he returned to acting and appeared in such films as *Blithe Spirit* (1945), *The Rake's Progress* and *Anna and the King of Siam* (1946), *The Constant Husband* (1955), *The Reluctant Debutante* (1958), *Cleopatra* (1962), *My Fair Lady* and *The Yellow Rolls-Royce* (1964), *The Agony and the Ecstasy* (in which he appeared as the Pope, 1965), *Doctor Dolittle* (1967) and *Staircase* (1969). His deceptively easy and witty style is respected by many of his peers – notably David Niven, Dirk Bogarde – as the quintessence of light comedy artistry.

Opposite: Jean Harlow
Above: Richard Harris in 'Cromwell' (Ken Hughes, GB, 1970)
Below: Kurt Kreuger, Linda Darnell and Rex Harrison in 'Unfaithfully Yours' (Preston Sturges, USA, 1948)

Hart, William Surrey (1870–1946)
Born in Newburgh (New York), USA. For a decade, from 1915 to 1925, W. S. Hart was the supreme Western hero. Raised in the West, with a Sioux nurse, he became a stage actor in the 1890s and played roles as varied as Romeo, Armand (in 'Camille') and Messala (in 'Ben Hur') in Modjeska's and Belasco's companies. In 1905 he created 'The Squaw Man' and in 1907 'The Virginian' on the New York stage. Recruited to films in 1913 (his first film for the New York Motion Picture Company was *The Fugitive*), Hart achieved rapid and world-wide celebrity with the films he made for THOMAS INCE at Triangle after 1915. From 1917 Hart directed many of his own films, although his best work was generally directed by Lambert Hillyer (*The Toll Gate*, *The Testing Block*, *Three Word Brand*). His last, and perhaps his finest film, was King Baggott's *Tumbleweeds* (1925).

For all his lack of humour, his staccato movements, his mid-Victorian morality, Hart remains, on the screen, a commanding figure. He possesses an undeniable nobility and a quality of romanticism which is conveyed to the landscapes and the heroines and the horses (notably his own grey Fritz) with which he comes into contact. Above all he was a fine actor, in an archaic style, able to instil considerable subtlety into his creations of the good-bad man. DR

Harvey, Anthony
Born 1931 in London, England. Film editor and director. Films he has edited include: *Tread Softly, Stranger* (1958), *I'm All Right, Jack* (1959), *Lolita* (1961), and *Dr Strangelove* (1963). Films he has directed include *Dutchman* (1966) and *The Lion in Winter* (1968).

Harvey, Laurence
Born 1928 in Lithuania. Real name Larushka Skikne. Actor and producer-director. Began his career on stage in repertory and in British supporting films, and progressed to work in leading Hollywood productions. Main films: *Romeo and Juliet* (1954), *I Am a Camera* (1955), *Three Men in a Boat* (1956), *Room at the Top* (1958), *Expresso Bongo* (1959), *Butterfield 8* (1961), *The Manchurian Candidate* (1962), *The Ceremony* (of which he was also producer and director, 1963), *Of Human Bondage* (1964), *Darling* and *Life at the Top* (1965), *He and She* (which he also produced, 1969), *The Magic Christian*, *L'Absolute Naturale* and *Hall of Mirrors* (1970).

Harvey, Lilian (1907–1968)
Born in London, England. A dancer who, after appearing in ballet and revue, made her name in the German cinema following her discovery by the German director, Richard Eichberg. She appeared in a number of silent films, of which the first to be directed by Eichberg was *Die Kleine vom Bummel* (1925), but her reputation was more fully established when she appeared in the popular musical films which followed the introduction of sound, in particular *Die Drei von der Tankstelle* (1930) and *Der Kongress tanzt* (*Congress Dances*, 1931). Her sparkling good looks and vivacity made her one of the youthful symbols of her time. In 1933 she left Germany and attempted unsuccessfully to remake her career in the USA and France. She retired from films in 1939.

Hathaway, Henry
Born 1898 in California, USA. Versatile veteran American director whose films are always technically accomplished whatever their qualities as dramatic entertainment. His peak achievement was the launching, with producer LOUIS DE ROCHEMONT, of the semi-realist phase in Hollywood film-making after the Second World War, with *The House on 92nd Street* (1945) and *13 Rue Madeleine* (1946) although individual Hathaway films have been more interesting.

Above: Laurence Harvey and Heather Sears in 'Room at the Top' (Jack Clayton, GB, 1959)
Below: Lilian Harvey in 'Congress Dances' (Erik Charell, Germany, 1931)

He started his film career as a child actor at the age of ten and from 1914 to 1917 he worked at Universal as a property boy. Following service in the US Army he became property man to FRANK LLOYD in 1921. He started directing, at first a series of Westerns, in 1932 with *Wild Horse Mesa*. He quickly established a reputation for handling action films and large-scale adventures such as *The Lives of a Bengal Lancer* (1935), although he showed great sensitivity in dealing with a totally different, intimate subject, *Peter Ibbetson*, in the same year. In 1936 he directed the first outdoors American colour film, *The Trail of the Lonesome Pine*.

After the de Rochemont films he directed several taut thrillers based on fact, notably *Kiss of Death* and *Call Northside 777* (1947). Since then, in the tradition of the Hollywood craftsman-director he has accepted all kinds of subjects – from the comic-strip period piece *Prince Valiant* (1954) to the taut crime tale *Seven Thieves* (1960). His personal stamp only becomes apparent in his Westerns on which he lavishes great care and affection. His latest, *True Grit* (1969), won an Academy Award for its star JOHN WAYNE.

Other principal films: *Spawn of the North* (1938), *Johnny Apollo* and *Brigham Young* (1940), *The Dark Corner* (1946), *Niagara* (1952), *North to Alaska* (1960), *The Sons of Katie Elder* (1965), *Nevada Smith* (1966), *5 Card Stud* (1968). MH

Havilland, Olivia De
See DE HAVILLAND

Hawkins, Jack
Born 1910 in London, England. Distinguished actor, usually playing stalwart, British heroes, until a serious operation forced him to scale down his acting career. Stage début in 'St Joan' in 1924; screen début in *The Lodger* (1932). Has made a great number of films, both before and after service in Second World War; also television series *Four Just Men*. At height of popularity in 1950s, when he was three times voted top British star. Films include: *The Good Companions* (1932), *Peg of Old Drury* (1935), *The Small Back Room* (1948), *Mandy* (1952), *The Cruel Sea* (1953), *The Prisoner* (1955), *The Bridge on the River Kwai* (1957), *Ben Hur* (1959), *Lawrence of Arabia* (1962), *Lord Jim* (1965). He rested for a time after a throat operation, but returned (his voice being dubbed) in *Shalako* (1968), *Monte Carlo or Bust* (1969), *Waterloo*, *Jane Eyre*, and *The Adventures of Gérard* (all 1970).

Hawks, Howard
Born 1896 in Indiana, USA. Front-ranking American director whose films are a tribute to the Hollywood ideal of commercial entertainment. Spanning almost half a century as a film-maker, he has explored every popular *genre* – Westerns, gangster films, war films, who-dun-its, musicals, crazy comedies and every variety of action adventure. Although he dismisses the suggestion that his films are also art, underlying all his work there is a toughness, tension and honesty particularly in dealing with human relationships. The insolent, hard-crust America he depicts in many guises, is as personal to his viewpoint as JOHN FORD's legendary vision of the West.

Hawks was a flyer during the First World War and afterwards worked in an aircraft factory. His passion for flying and his awareness of the pressures it places on individuals have been responsible for some of his finest earlier films: *The Dawn Patrol* (1930), *Ceiling Zero* (1936) and, especially, *Only Angels Have Wings* (1939). He began his screen career as a prop man with the MARY PICKFORD Company; he later worked as an editor, in the script department and as assistant to M. NEILAN. He wrote, directed, financed two comic shorts and worked on several other films as a writer, until in 1926 he made his directorial début with *The Road to Glory*. By the 1930s he had established a flair for free-wheeling action though he seldom initiated new film trends. In 1932 he made the most notorious of the original gangster films, *Scarface*.

Perhaps the most intriguing feature of his essentially masculine films has been his image of the witty, go-getting, mettlesome heroine, most memorably portrayed by KATHARINE HEPBURN in *Bringing Up Baby* (1938), ROSALIND RUSSELL in *His Girl Friday* (1940), BARBARA STANWYCK in *Ball of Fire* (1941) and LAUREN BACALL in *To Have and Have Not* (1944) and *The Big Sleep* (1946). His Western *Red River* (1948) is a major contribution to American screen folklore. A later Western *Rio Bravo* (1959) was remade, less persuasively, by Hawks himself as *El Dorado* (1966). His direction is never flashy or obtrusive. Characteristically, he is quoted in Robin Wood's study of his work, 'Howard Hawks,' defining a good director as 'somebody who doesn't annoy you'.

Other principal films: *The Criminal Code* (1931), *The Crowd Roars* (1932), *Viva Villa!* (1934), *The Road to Glory* (1936), *Sergeant York* (1941), *A Song is Born* (1948), *I Was a Male War Bride (You Can't Sleep Here*, 1949), *Monkey Business* (1952), *Gentlemen Prefer Blondes* (1953), *Hatari!* (1962), *Man's Favourite Sport* (1963), *Red Line 7000* (1965), *Rio Lobo* (1970). MH

Below: Graham Moffatt, Will Hay and Moore Marriott in 'Oh! Mr Porter' (Marcel Varnel, GB, 1937)
Bottom: Jack Hawkins in 'The Cruel Sea' (Charles Frend, GB, 1952)

Hay, Will (1888–1949)
British actor, born in Scotland, who made his name on the music-halls in the role of a comic schoolmaster. Was equally successful on radio and in films, which he entered in 1934 in *Those Were the Days*. Main films: *Boys will be Boys* (1935), *Good Morning, Boys* (1936), *Oh! Mr Porter* and *Old Bones of the River* (1939), *Ask a Policeman* (1940), *The Black Sheep of Whitehall* (1941), *The Goose Steps Out* (1942), *My Learned Friend* (1944) – the last three being co-directed by him with BASIL DEARDEN. Will Hay

Above: Sessue Hayakawa
Below: Rita Hayworth

was also an enthusiastic amateur astronomer and discovered a spot on Saturn in 1933.

Hayakawa, Sessue
Born 1889. Japanese actor, popular in old silent films such as *The Typhoon* (1914), *The Cheat* (1915), *Forbidden Paths* (1917), and *Daughter of the Dragon* (1921). Later, he appeared in character roles; these more recent films include *The Bridge on the River Kwai* (1957) and *The Swiss Family Robinson* (1960).

Hayworth, Rita
Born 1918 in USA. Actress and dancer. Real name Marguerite Cansino. First appeared on the stage at the age of six. Made her film début in 1935 in *Dante's Inferno*. Main films: *Only Angels Have Wings* (1939), *Strawberry Blonde* (1941), *Cover Girl* (1944), *Gilda* (1946), *The Lady from Shanghai* (1947), *The Loves of Carmen* (1948), *Affair in Trinidad* (1952), *Salome* (1953), *Pal Joey* (1957), *Separate Tables* (1958), *The Money Trap* (1965) and *Sons of Satan* (1968). During the 1940s she and BETTY GRABLE were Hollywood's principal pin-up girls; but Rita Hayworth's charm, rhythmical grace and erotic glamour made her the more enduring star.

Head, Edith
Born 1907 in Los Angeles, USA. Influential Hollywood dress designer since the 1920s. For over twenty years chief designer at Paramount, she has dressed most of the major stars and won several Academy Awards, including awards for costume design on *The Heiress* (1949), *A Place in the Sun* (1952). Her first solo costume design credit was for *She Done Him Wrong* (1933). A personality as colourful as many of her more flamboyant designs, she has published her autobiography, 'The Dress Doctor,' and made an appearance on screen in *The Oscar* (1966).

Hearst, William Randolph (1863–1950)
Born in San Francisco, USA. Formidable millionaire newspaper-publisher, frustrated politician and film-making *dilettante*, who exercised a powerful influence in Hollywood during the 1920s and 1930s through his efforts to make a super-star of his mistress, Marion Davies. To this end, he set up Cosmopolitan Pictures, which operated chiefly within the MGM studios. At his bizarre mansion, San Simeon, he was a leading figure in Hollywood's high society, ruthlessly using his newspapers to publicize Miss Davies, and put down those who displeased him – most notably ORSON WELLES, whose *Citizen Kane* (1940) was reputedly based on Hearst. In the late 1930s, his fortune and extravagant life-style suffered a decline. In 1961 W. A. Swanberg published a superior biography of him, 'Citizen Hearst'. MH

Hecht, Ben (1894–1964)
Born in New York, USA. Prolific screenwriter, occasional director and producer and espouser of controversial causes, whose tough, gritty style and jaundiced view of society was most memorably contained in *The Front Page* (1931), *The Scoundrel* (1935) – for which he won an Academy Award – and *Nothing Sacred* (1937). After the Second World War, his extreme Zionist sentiments occupied much of his time and his later films – apart from *Kiss of Death* (1947) – were not up to his previous standard. Journalist and feature writer, he started in films in the late 1920s when he wrote the story for *Underworld* (1928). His more personal films, especially *Spectre of the Rose* (1946) and *Actors and Sin* (1952), both of which he produced and directed, betray a lack of selectivity in his work and, despite interesting elements, are for the most part floridly over-written. His published autobiography is entitled 'A Child of the Century'. Other notable films: *The Great Gabbo* (1930), *Viva Villa* and *Crime without Passion* (1934) which he also produced and directed, *Wuthering Heights* (1939), *Spellbound* (1945), *Notorious* (1946), *Miracle in the Rain* (1956), *Legend of the Lost* (1958). MH

Heflin, Van (1910–1971)
Born in Oklahoma, USA. Actor on stage and television as well as in films. Began his screen career in 1936 in *A Woman Rebels* and usually played serious-minded 'he-man' lead characters. Main films: *Santa Fé Trail* (1940), *Johnny Eager* (which won an Academy Award, 1942), *The Strange Love of Martha Ivers* (1946), *Acts of Violence* (1948), *Madame Bovary* (1949), *Shane* (1953), *3.10 to Yuma* (1957), *They Came to Cordura* (1959), *Stagecoach* (1966), *The Man Outside* (1967), *Airport* (1969).

Heifitz, Yosif
Born in 1905 in Russia. Director. Formed collaboration with director ALEXANDER ZARKHI in early 1930s and made several solid, theatrically-orientated political dramas including *Baltic Deputy* (1937) and *Member of the Government* (1940). Heifitz has never been a stylistic innovator; instead, he developed a quietly intimate narrative style which responded to a good story and rich characterization. His post-war work has been sadly intermittent and uneven – *The Big Family* (1954), with its saga-like construction, had more personal feeling than other Soviet productions of the time, but it was *The Lady with the Little Dog* (1959) which marked a creative renewal. Probably the cinema's best Chekhov adaptation, it is remarkable for its period reconstruction, beautifully shaded performances and romantic, melancholy tone. A further Chekhov film *In the Town of S* (1966) continued to explore a world of regret and lost opportunities but lacked the deeper poetic overtones of the earlier film. In 1970, Heifitz made *Salute Marya*, a study of a woman, set in the Revolutionary period of 1919. JG

Heller, Otto (1896–1970)
Born in Prague, Czechoslovakia. Cinematographer. From 1920, when he became a

lighting cameraman, he worked all over Europe, in Prague, Vienna, Berlin, Paris, Amsterdam and from 1942 in Britain. During the 1920s and 1930s, he worked with the Czech director Karel Lamac on many films and, most successfully, with MAX OPHÜLS on *De Mayerling à Sarajevo* (1940). In Britain, he brought a European sophistication and dark-toned atmosphere to many thrillers and dramas: *Temptation Harbour* and *They made me a Fugitive* (1947) and especially *The Queen of Spades* (1948). He also worked in many other genres from *The Crimson Pirate* (1952) to *The Ladykillers* and OLIVIER's *Richard III* (1954, with its impressive spatial and deep-focus effects).

Hellinger, Mark (1903–1947)
Born in New York, USA. American journalist turned screenwriter and producer whose handful of films in the 1940s captured precisely the raw, challenging, disillusioned mood of that period in the best Hollywood films. His gifts for incisive *reportage* was evident in his writings for such films as *The Roaring Twenties* (1940). As producer he worked on three key, trend-setting films, *The Killers* (1946), *Brute Force* and *Naked City* (1948), which opened up Hollywood film-making until it was temporarily suffocated by the communist witch-hunt trials.

Hellman, Lillian
Born 1905 in New Orleans, USA. Playwright, book reviewer and screenwriter. Her plays include 'The Children's Hour' and 'The Little Foxes'; and were characterized by their emphasis on difficult or challenging domestic or social relationships, such as lesbianism. Her principal films are: *The Little Foxes* (1941), *Watch on the Rhine* (1943), *Another Part of the Forest* (1948), *The Loudest Whisper* (*The Children's Hour*, 1962), *The Chase* (1966).

Hellman, Monte
Born 1932 in New York, USA. Director. Studied at the UCLA film school and worked in the theatre. Directed the beautiful exterior scenes in ROGER CORMAN's *The Terror* (1963) and his first films as director were sponsored by the Corman company. He first came to notice with two low-budget Westerns – *The Shooting* and *Ride the Whirlwind* (1965) – written and co-produced with JACK NICHOLSON which, although not fully worked out, brought a darkly nihilistic tone to the Western genre as well as a fresh visual eye for landscapes and figures. Though not widely shown, they undoubtedly influenced subsequent American independent production and, to some extent, Nicholson's own later work. Hellman's recent film *Two-Lane Blacktop* (1971) takes a theme akin to *Easy Rider* and gives it a hard, lean treatment as its four displaced characters speed across the American landscape. JG

Hepburn, Audrey
Born 1929 in Brussels, Belgium, of Irish-Dutch parentage. Stage and film actress, noted for her slim, gamine, elegant attractiveness. Acted on the stage in England, then went to USA where she appeared on Broadway and in films. After her début in *Laughter in Paradise* (1951) she rapidly rose to stardom in such films as *Roman Holiday* (1953), for which she won an Academy Award, *Sabrina Fair* (1954), *War and Peace* and *Funny Face* (1956), *The Nun's Story* (1958), *Breakfast at Tiffany's* (1961), *The Children's Hour* (*The Loudest Whisper*, 1962), *Charade* (1963), in which she was again voted Best Film Actress, *My Fair Lady* (1964), *How to Steal a Million* (1966), *Two for the Road* and *Wait Until Dark* (1967).

Above: Katharine Hepburn in 'The Madwoman of Chaillot' (Bryan Forbes, GB, 1969) Below: Shirley MacLaine and Audrey Hepburn in 'The Loudest Whisper' ('The Children's Hour' William Wyler, USA, 1962)

Hepburn, Katharine
Born 1909 in Connecticut, USA. Astringent star personality and gifted actress who survived the film fads of the past thirty years to achieve a reputation as one of the screen's indestructibles. Never a conventional 'type', she found her happiest *niche* in the celebrated series of battle-of-the-sexes comedies with SPENCER TRACY – though their last film together, *Guess Who's Coming to Dinner* (1967), was distinguished only by their presence.

A lady with strong New England principles (for promoting health, enjoying life and putting down 'phonies'), she was a star with her first film *A Bill of Divorcement* (1932), after a training in the theatre and a spell on Broadway. The next year in *Morning Glory* she won the first of her three Academy Awards: the other two were for *Guess Who's Coming to Dinner* and *The Lion In Winter* (1968).

Her angular beauty and forthright style flourished in a succession of roles, not all of them ideally suited to her talents: *Little Women* (1933), *The Little Minister* (1934), *Alice Adams* and *Sylvia Scarlett* (1935), *Mary of Scotland* (1936). Her comic qualities (a blend of upper-crust confidence and a sense of the absurd) were perfectly displayed in *Bringing Up Baby* (1938) and *The Philadelphia Story* (1940). Her first film with Tracy was *Woman of the Year* (1941); the best was *Adam's Rib* (1949). *The African Queen* (1951) with HUMPHREY BOGART launched her on a career as a screen spinster, who achieved an appropriate pathos in the brief romantic encounter of *Summer Madness* (1955).

Ironically, although much admired by fellow artists and critics, she was for a time regarded as 'box-office poison'.

Other principal films: *Stage Door* (1937), *The Rainmaker* (1956), *Suddenly Last Summer* (1959), *Long Day's Journey into Night* (1962), *The Madwoman of Chaillot* (1969), *The Trojan Women* (1971). With Tracy: *Keeper of the Flame* (1943), *State of the Union* (1948), *Pat and Mike* (1952), *The Desk Set* (1957). MH

Hepworth, Cecil (1874–1953)
Born in London, England. Pioneer inventor in cinematography, director and producer. Son of a famous lantern lecturer, T. C. Hepworth. Deeply interested in developing cinematographic equipment, he published in 1897 what is probably the first handbook on the subject, 'Animated Photography, or the ABC of the Cinematograph'. In the same year he patented an automatic developing plant, while the previous year he had designed a hand-feed electric arc lamp. He toured the country with his own cinematograph films, set up his own printing laboratory at Walton-on-Thames in 1898, and became a prolific producer of every kind of film during the earlier years of the present century, including the celebrated *Rescued by Rover* (1905), a six-minute film in which he evolved a neat structure and story continuity far in advance of its time. With studios as well as laboratory at Walton-on-Thames, his work developed along lines favoured by his more middle-class patrons. He reflected Edwardian culture in its most respectable form. He weathered the alternate slumps and booms which began to affect the film industry even before the First World War, building his fortunes not only on production but on the distribution of his own and other people's films. In spite of attempts at making social problem films, such as the short story-documentaries, *The Alien's Invasion* (1905) and *Rachel's Sin* (1911), his taste was for romantic and literary subjects, sentiment and polite comedy. He frequently sponsored films adapted from literature – *The Vicar of Wakefield* and *The Old Curiosity Shop* (1914), *Barnaby Rudge* (1915), for example – and was responsible as producer for the noted film version of *Hamlet* (1913), starring Johnston Forbes-Robertson. His leading directors were Henry Edwards and Tom Bentley, and he launched several stars, notably Alma Taylor, Chrissie White and Stewart Rome. After the war, his fortunes began to turn. He struggled to keep in production with such films as *Alf's Button* (1921) and *Sheba*, featuring a new young player, RONALD COLMAN. His final film, *Comin' Thro' the Rye* (1923), was perhaps his worst. He was declared bankrupt in 1924.

In his later years, the man who for long had been Britain's leading producer remained in the industry in a minor technical capacity, working as a contract director with National Screen Services, specialists in trailers and advertising films. RM

Herbier, Marcel L'
See L'HERBIER

Herrmann, Bernard
Born 1911 in New York, USA. Composer. Made name as conductor in early 1930s and was staff conductor at CBS from 1934. Began film career with WELLES' *Citizen Kane* (1941), a highly personal, evocative score whose qualities were also apparent in *The Magnificent Ambersons* (1942). Although he has collaborated with many distinguished directors, Herrmann's best work can be found in HITCHCOCK's films – *The Wrong Man* (1956), *Vertigo* (1958), *North by Northwest* (1959), *Psycho* (1960), *The Birds* (1963), *Marnie* (1964) – with their idiosyncratic style of orchestration, ranging from a chamber music delicacy to bold dissonant outbursts on brass and percussion. Other prominent scores include *Journey to the Centre of the Earth* (1959) and TRUFFAUT's *Fahrenheit 451* (1966). JG

Paul Newman and Robert Redford in 'Butch Cassidy and the Sundance Kid' (George Roy Hill, USA, 1969)

Heston, Charlton
Born 1923 in Illinois, USA. Actor on stage, radio and television as well as in films. After he had spent eight years in US Air Force he and his wife acted in and directed stage productions and appeared on Broadway. His screen début was in *Dark City* in 1950 and subsequently he played in a series of epic films creating larger-than-life, heroic characters of great romantic appeal. Main films: *The Ten Commandments* (1956), *The Big Country* (1958), *Ben Hur* (which won an Aacademy Award, 1959), *El Cid* (1961), *55 Days in Peking* (1962), *The Greatest Story Ever Told* and *The Agony and the Ecstasy* (1965), *Khartoum* (as General Gordon, 1967), *Planet of the Apes* (1967), *Beneath the Planet of the Apes* (1969), *Julius Caesar* and *Master of the Islands* (1970). In 1971 he directed *Antony and Cleopatra.*

Hill, George Roy
Born 1926 in Minneapolis, USA. Director. After considerable experience in the theatre, he began the direction of films in the 1960s with *Period of Adjustment* (1963). His later films included *Toys in the Attic* (1963), *The World of Henry Orient* (1964) and *Hawaii* (1966), but he achieved his greatest success with the strongly contrasting films *Thoroughly Modern Millie* (1967) and *Butch Cassidy and the Sundance*

Kid (1969), the outstanding award-winner of its year in Britain. Both were stylish, and the latter was in the van of contemporary American cinema in its oblique interest in violence.

Hiller, Wendy
Born 1912 in Stockport, England. Actress. Celebrated mostly for her work on the stage, she made her first appearance in films in *Lancashire Luck* (1937). Her capacity to give a character edge and to express emotional frustration, combined with a certain charmingly pawky awkwardness, soon brought her unusual and rewarding parts in films, including leads in *Pygmalion* (1938), *Major Barbara* (1940), and *I Know Where I'm Going* (1945). Her other films, both British and American, include *An Outcast of the Islands* (1951), *Separate Tables* (1958, for which she won an Academy Award), *Sons and Lovers* (1960), and *A Man for all Seasons* (1966). She has also worked extensively for television.

Hitchcock, Alfred
Born 1899 in London, England. Acknowledged screen master of suspense, who has devoted his forty-five years as a film director almost exclusively to the creation of ever more ingenious methods of chilling an audience's marrow. Much imitated professionally and over-analysed critically, he confesses to no motives more profound than a showman's desire to entertain. But his persistent pleasure in agitating the anxiety fantasies of audiences suggests a deeper compulsion.

According to Hitchcock, his strict Catholic upbringing and disciplinarian father led to religious fear and a dread of the police, though at a Jesuit boarding school in London he learned self-control and a capacity for organization. All these elements are evident in his work, both on the screen and behind the cameras. He trained to be an engineer, then joined the Famous-Players-Lasky office in London as a title designer. Graduating through the stages of art director, scenarist, assistant director in a then highly flexible film hierarchy, he directed his first film, *The Pleasure Garden*, in 1925 in Munich, sponsored by MICHAEL BALCON. In 1926 with *The Lodger*, he moved into the suspense-mystery field which he was to dominate, although he strayed from that area occasionally with typical society pieces of the period and an amusing boxing film, *The Ring* (1927).

In 1929, he was the first British director to appreciate the dramatic qualities of sound in *Blackmail*. After a fairly disastrous brush with Viennese musical romance, *Waltzes from Vienna* (1933), he made *The Man who Knew Too Much* (1934), which launched the British thrillers of the 1930s that made his name. In 1939 he went to the USA, where he has since made all his films except *Under Capricorn* (1949), *Stage Fright* (1950), his remake of *The Man Who Knew Too Much* (1956) and his latest, *Frenzy* (1972).

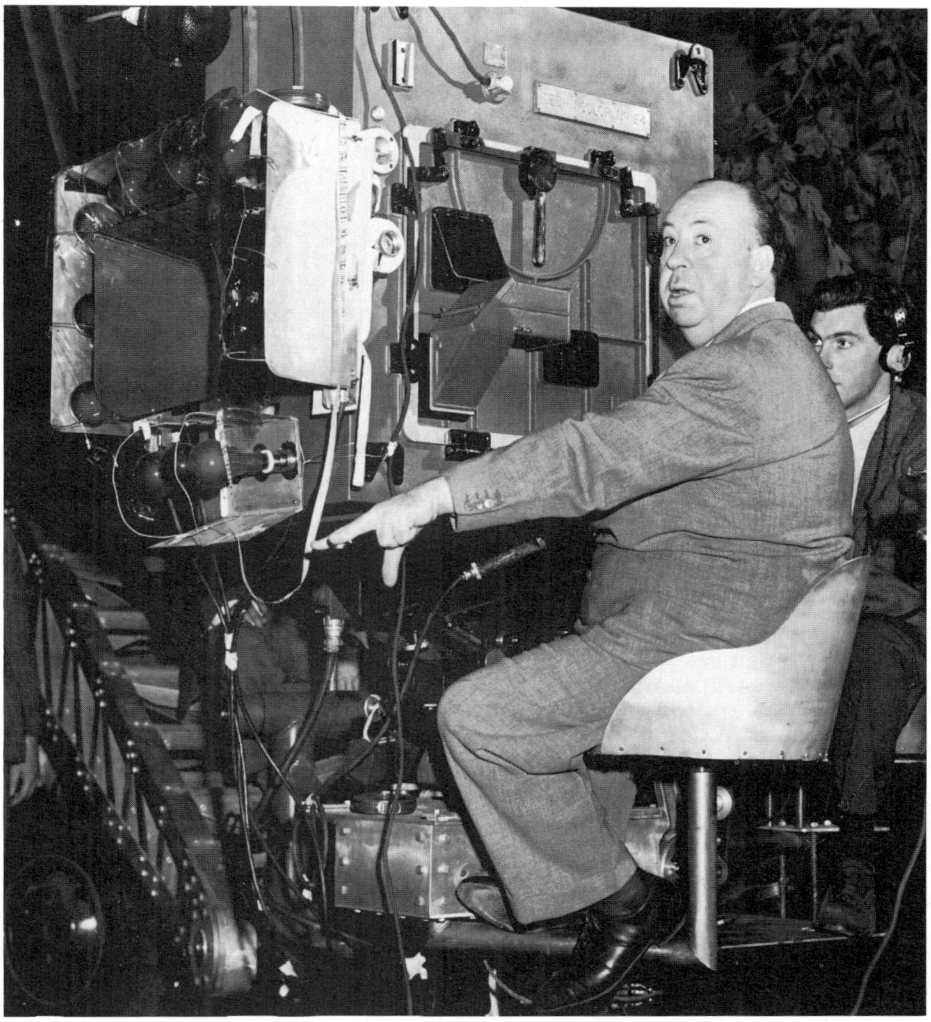

However in spite of his years in exile, Hitchcock has retained an English 'eye' and an English sense of the absurd, which among other things distinguishes his films from the thrillers of American film-makers. His obsession with

Top: Alfred Hitchcock with the camera while directing 'Under Capricorn' (GB, 1949)
Above: 'The Man who Knew Too Much' (Alfred Hitchcock, GB, 1934)

espionage – most intriguingly developed in the British *Thirty Nine Steps* (1935), *The Lady Vanishes* (1938) and the American *North by Northwest* (1959) – is, characteristically, directed towards the interplay of rival characters and the mechanics of the chase, rather than to the end product (the identity of the stolen secrets). He relishes bringing out the worst in his heroes: one of his most successful films was *Rear Window* (1954), in which JAMES STEWART played a peeping Tom trapped by his own *voyeurism*.

Alternatively, he concentrates on Kafka-esque situations where innocents are caught in a web of condemning circumstances: *Strangers on a Train* (1951), *I Confess* (1953), *The Wrong Man* (1957). Although they caused a stir at the time, his most overtly psychological thrillers, *Spellbound* (1945), *Rope* with its adventurous ten-minute takes (1948), *Vertigo* (1958) and *Marnie* (1964) seem contrived and less fluent than many Hitchcock films which in their period were dismissed as relatively routine. Critical hindsight has given, for example, *Sabotage* (1936) and *Saboteur* (1942), the second *The Man who Knew Too Much* (1956), pre-eminence over the melodramatic *Rebecca* (1940), *Notorious* (1946) and *The Paradine Case* (1947). Revealingly two of Hitchcock's own personal favourites are the wryly funny *The Trouble with Harry* (1956) and *Shadow of a Doubt* (1943): both set in small communities and both using the idiosyncratic qualities of their inhabitants, though for vastly different ends.

In 1960 Hitchcock directed his most daring film, *Psycho*, reviled at the time but since rehabilitated as the first truly contemporary thriller: he followed it with the not wholly successful *The Birds* (1963). After *Marnie*, he returned to his stand-by cloak-and-dagger theme; but neither *Torn Curtain* (1966) nor *Topaz* (1969) are vintage Hitchcock. He has also sponsored two long-running television series bearing his name.

Despite a reputation, which he encourages, for treating actors roughly, he constantly attracts the same artists, notably CARY GRANT and JAMES STEWART and has created a special kind of Hitchcock 'snow maiden', epitomized by GRACE KELLY and Tippi Hedren. Professing ignorance of the convoluted meanings attributed to him by, in particular, French writers and film-makers, he is sometimes guilty of a crudity in his films, best illustrated perhaps in the timing of his famous fleeting personal appearance on screen. His influence on younger, again particularly French, film-makers is immense and his meticulous pre-planned working methods have been much imitated.

Other notable films: *Juno and The Paycock* (1930), *Secret Agent* (1936), *Young And Innocent* (1937), *Foreign Correspondent* (1940), *Mr and Mrs Smith*, an untypical marital comedy (1941), *Lifeboat* (1943), *Dial M for Murder* (1954), *To Catch a Thief* (1955).

Of the many books about Hitchcock, including George Perry's 'The Films of Alfred Hitchcock' and Robin Wood's involved interpretations in 'Hitchcock's Films' (1965), 'Hitchcock' by FRANÇOIS TRUFFAUT (1965) is a unique and revealing analysis through interview, elaborately illustrated. For another French view, see CLAUDE CHABROL and ERIC ROHMER, 'Hitchcock' (1957). MH

Hoellering, Georg M.

Born 1900 in Baden, Austria. Producer, director, screenwriter and film editor; managing director of the Academy Cinemas, London. His early career was centred in Austria, Germany and Hungary, where he directed the most celebrated pre-war Hungarian film, *Hortobagy* (1936), made on location on the Hungarian plains. He also produced in Germany the left-wing film *Kuhle Wampe* (1932). After emigrating to Britain, he became involved primarily in the distribution and exhibition of Continental films centred on the most famous of London's specialized cinemas, the Academy. In 1951 he directed a film version of T. S. Eliot's play, *Murder in the Cathedral*.

Hoffman, Dustin

Born 1937 in Los Angeles, USA. Leading American actor who initiated the voguish anti-star image of the 1960s and 1970s. Achieved success in films with *The Graduate* (1967) and *Midnight Cowboy* (1969). Other films include *John and Mary* (1969), *Little Big Man* (1970), *Who is Harry Kellerman and Why is he Saying Those Terrible Things about Me?* and *Straw Dogs* (1971).

Holden, William

Born 1918 in Illinois, USA. Actor, who began his screen career in 1939 with *Golden Boy* and quickly became popular as a tough, reliable, romantic hero. By the 1950s he was playing leading parts in such films as *Sunset Boulevard* (1950), *Born Yesterday* (1951), *Stalag 17* (which won an Academy Award in 1953), *Sabrina Fair* (1954), *Love is a Many-Splendored Thing* (1955), *The Bridge on the River Kwai* and *The Key* (1957). In 1954, 1955 and 1957 he was voted 'one of the best money-making stars'. Films include *The World of Suzie Wong* (1961), *The Wild Bunch* (1969), *Wild Rovers* (1971).

Holland

See NETHERLANDS

Holliday, Judy (1923–1965)

Born in New York City, USA. Actress. At first worked in cabaret, music hall, and revue, writing and directing her own acts for night clubs. Acted on stage in supporting roles before becoming a leading lady. Began her screen career in the 1940s with such films as *Winged Victory* and *Something for the Boys* (1944), and *Adam's Rib* (1949). Her performance in *Born Yesterday* (1950), for which she won an Academy Award as Best Actress, brought her fame as a raucous but not-so-dumb blonde, and her later films include: *The Marrying Kind* (1952), *It Should Happen to You* and *Phffft* (1954), *The Solid Gold Cadillac* (1956), *The Bells are Ringing* (1959).

Holloway, Stanley

Born 1890 in London, England. Comic actor and singer, who has appeared on stage in musical comedy, revue and variety and on television as well as on the cinema screen. His career has been long; his stage début was in 1919, and his screen début in 1921, in *The Rotters*. He appeared in character roles in several of Ealing's post-war British comedies. His stage performances on Broadway and in London in 'My Fair Lady' brought him added fame. His main films include: *Sing as We Go* (1934), *Major Barbara* (1940), *This Happy Breed* (1944), *Caesar and Cleopatra* (1945), *Brief Encounter* (1946), *Nicholas Nickleby* (1947), *Hamlet* (1948), *The Lavender Hill Mob* (1951), *The Titfield Thunderbolt* (1953), *No Love for Johnnie* (1961), *My Fair Lady* (1964), *Ten Little Indians* (1965), *The Private Life of Sherlock Holmes* (1970).

Hong Kong

See ASIAN FILM

Homolka, Oscar

Born 1898 in Vienna, Austria. Powerful stage and screen actor whose strongly emphatic Central European style has made a distinctive impression in many films since his début in *Rhodes of Africa* in 1935. A prominent figure in the Austrian and German theatre after the First World War, he came to Britain in 1935. In 1936 he starred in HITCHCOCK's *Sabotage* and then left for America where he has worked fairly consistently since, returning to Europe for occasional films and stage appearances. Other chief films: *Ball of Fire* (1941), *Mission to Moscow* (1943), *I Remember Mama* (1948), *House of the Arrow* (1953), *War and Peace* (1956), *Mr Sardonicus* (1963), *Funeral in Berlin* (1966), *The Happening* (1967), *Billion Dollar Brain* (1968), *The Madwoman of Chaillot* (1970).

Hope, Bob

Born 1904 in London, England. American comedian and actor, who played for several years in vaudeville, radio, and musical comedy before his screen début in Hollywood. This was in *The Big Broadcast of 1938*, which started his long film career, consolidated by the famous 'Road' series, in which he appeared with BING CROSBY and DOROTHY LAMOUR. His main films include: *The Cat and The Canary* (1939), *Road to Singapore* (1940), *Road to Zanzibar* (1941), *Road to Morocco* (1942), *Road to Utopia* (1945), *Road to Rio* (1947) and *Road to Bali* (1952), *Paris Holiday* (1957), *The Facts of Life* (1960), *The Private Navy of Sergeant O'Farrell* (1968), and *How to Commit Marriage* (1969). He specialized in fast-spoken gags and elaborately-timed double-takes, and his hard work and meticulous professionalism has made him one of the richest men in show business. He was

Above: Oscar Homolka in 'The Billion Dollar Brain' (Ken Russell, GB, 1968)
Below: Bob Hope and Shirley Ross in 'The Big Broadcast of 1938' (Mitchell Leisen, USA, 1938)

given three special Academy Awards in the 1940s and early 1950s for entertaining US Forces and for charity appearances and has written two autobiographical books: 'Have Tux Will Travel (This is on me)' and 'I Owe Russia Two Thousand Dollars'.

Hopper, Dennis

Born in 1936 in Dodge City, Kansas, USA. Producer, director, actor, etc. Hopper's 'image' for contemporary youth as the universal anti-Establishment artist arose from the success of his film, *Easy Rider* (1969), made in association with PETER FONDA. His career as a young actor was consolidated by his close friendship with JAMES DEAN, formed when he appeared with him in both *Rebel without a Cause* (1955) and *Giant* (1956). Dean's personality was to have a deep influence upon him; he studied under LEE STRASBERG at the Actor's Studio and developed a parallel career as painter, sculptor and photographer. Among the films he appeared in were *The Sons of Katie Elder* (1965), *Cool Hand Luke* and *The Trip* (1967). But the phenomenal success of *Easy Rider*, his first feature as director – cost some $350,000; box-office takings, some $70 million – changed Hollywood's outlook on the small-budget picture overnight. He had an entirely free hand with *The Last Movie* (1971), a film shot in Peru, a serious subject overlaid by too many excesses due to seemingly uncontrolled improvisation and a desire never to stop going too far. Hopper has achieved considerable distinction as a still photographer, and maintains a much-publicized 'salon' in his house at Taos, New Mexico, which was once the home of D. H. Lawrence.

Houseman, John

Born 1902 in Romania. Writer, dramatist and producer. Educated at Clifton College, England, he emigrated to the USA in 1925, working at first as a journalist and translator. Later he became a director for Theatre Guild, and helped to found the Federal Theatre Project, a government-sponsored organization set up by the Roosevelt administration. Associated with ORSON WELLES in founding the Mercury Theatre in 1937, he became also for a period an associate professor in English at Vassar. During the war, he was for a while chief of overseas radio division of the OWI. After the war he became a film producer, concentrating on films of unusual quality, such as *The Blue Dahlia* (1946), *Letter from an Unknown Woman* and *They Live by Night* (1948), *The Bad and the Beautiful* (1952), *Julius Caesar* (1953), *Executive Suite* (1954), *All Fall Down* (1962), *Two Weeks in Another Town* (1964).

Howard, Leslie (1893–1943)

Born in London, England of Hungarian ancestry. British actor and, latterly, producer and director, whose sensitive cultivated heroes were much admired in the 1930s by audiences on both sides of the Atlantic. Wounded in the First World War, he had a distinguished career on the stage before making his film début in *Outward Bound* in 1930. For the next decade, dividing his time between British and Hollywood studios, he was romantically idealistic in *Smilin' Through* (1932), *Berkeley Square* (1933), *Of Human Bondage* (1934), *The Petrified Forest* (1936); a graceful, if rather elderly, Romeo in *Romeo and Juliet* (1936); an impressively wilting Ashley in *Gone with the Wind* (1939). In 1938, he acted in and co-directed *Pygmalion*.

The gallant victim even in his occasional crazy comedies such as *Stand In* (1937), his screen *persona* was beginning to lose its hold on audiences, who were turning to more aggressive film idols, when he was killed in a plane crash during the Second World War. His son Ronald is a notable actor, and his daughter Leslie Ruth wrote a biography of him entitled 'A Very Remarkable Father'. Other main films: *A Free Soul* (1931), *The Scarlet Pimpernel* (1934), *It's Love I'm After* (1937), *Escape to Happiness* (1939), *Pimpernel Smith* (which he directed, showing a sympathetic, civilized talent) and *49th Parallel* (1941), *The First of the Few* (which he also produced and directed, 1942). In 1943 he produced *The Gentle Sex* and *The Lamp Still Burns*, but did not appear in them. MH

Howard, Trevor
Born 1916 in Kent, England. Actor, who trained first for the stage and played in Shakespearean and other stage productions before serving in the Second World War. His screen début was in *The Way Ahead* in 1943, and since then he has given many memorable performances in films which include: *The Way to the Stars* (1945), *Brief Encounter* (1946), *The Third Man* (1949), *Odette* (1950), *An Outcast of the Islands* (1952), *The Heart of the Matter* (1953), *Cockleshell Heroes* (1955), *Around the World in 80 Days* (1956), *The Key* (1958), *Sons and Lovers* (1960), *Mutiny on the Bounty* (1962), *The Charge of the Light Brigade* (1968), *The Battle of Britain* and *Ryan's Daughter* (1970).

Howard, William K. (1899–1954)
Born in St Mary's, Ohio, USA. Director. Entered films through the INCE studios; the most distinctive of his silent work is *White Gold* (1927), a sombre, broodingly photographed outdoor drama. He seemingly found it difficult to direct actors and dialogue in the sound period (as in *Sherlock Holmes*, 1932); his most interesting work at this time was *The Power and the Glory* (1933), whose construction and lighting foreshadowed *Citizen Kane*, although it lacks a really consistent, developed style. Other films include *Transatlantic* and *Surrender* (1931), *Mary Burns, Fugitive* (1935) and *Fire over England* (1937), which again displayed his pictorial gifts and fondness for photographic set-pieces. JG

Howe, James Wong
Born 1899 in Kwanting Province, China. Moved to USA in 1904. Cinematographer. Entered industry in 1917 and has worked for all major American companies; since 1923, has made an enormous number of films of all types. Undoubtedly one of the greatest American camera artists, he combines great delicacy with a boldly dramatic use of light and shade. The lighting in *The Power and the Glory* (1933) anticipates *Citizen Kane*; VON STROHEIM's ill-fated *Walking Down Broadway (Hello, Sister!*, 1933) owes much to his feeling for seedy atmosphere; *The Prisoner of Zenda* (1937) has splendid romantic panache; and LANG's *Hangmen Also Die* (1943) is a symphony of sinister blacks. Apart from enlivening innumerable studio melodramas and thrillers, Howe is also a marvellous location cameraman: *The Brave Bulls* (1951) and *Sweet Smell of Success* (1957), with its vistas of glittering city streets. Recent work for newer directors includes *Seconds* (1966), *The Molly Maguires* (1969) and parts of *The Horsemen* (1971). JG

Hubley, John
Born 1914 in USA. Animation director. One of the leading break-away artists involved in the 1941 'strike' for individuality in the Disney Studios, he joined Stephen Bosustow and others in founding UPA in 1945. Perhaps the most purely original artist in the group, he designed many of their finest films: *Flathatting* (1945), *Ragtime Bear* (Magoo), and *Rooty Toot Toot* (1952). With his wife Faith he founded the unit, Storyboard, in 1952 to develop his work. He has made many striking commercials in addition to the personal films for which he is world-famous. Several of the latter have sprung from the imagination of his children, and are voiced by them; they include *The Tender Game* (1958), *Moonbird* (1960), *Children of the Sun* (1961, for UNICEF), *The Hole* (1962), *The Hat* (1964), and *Windy Day* (1968). His work, especially that done with his family, is tender and gentle, catching the natural fantasy of children in tinted, texturized sketches in which the bold outlines of most 'cleaned-up' animation is entirely discarded in favour of the unassertive lines and the soft colouration of animated watercolours. RM

Hudson, Rock
Born 1925 in Illinois, USA. Actor, who made his film début in *Fighter Squadron* (1948) after serving for two years in the US Navy. He quickly became popular as a tall, rugged hero, and in 1957 was voted 'No 1 Top Money-Making Star'. His films include: *Sea Devils* (1953), *Captain Lightfoot* (1954), *Giant* (1956), *A Farewell to Arms* (1958), *Pillow Talk* (1959), *Man's Favourite Sport* and *Send me no Flowers* (1964), *Tobruk* (1967), *Ice Station Zebra* (1968), *Darling Lili* (1969), *The Hornet's Nest* (1970), *Pretty Maids all in a Row* (1971).

Hughes, Howard
Born 1905 in Texas, USA. Industrial tycoon, aircraft designer, flyer and *dilettante* producer-director with a flair for creating headline films and trend-setting female stars. An intensely private and elusive person, he turned a useful inheritance – from the Hughes Tool Company – into a multi-million-dollar aircraft and electronics complex. An early interest in Hollywood led to his first important impact as an independent film-maker: the flying epic, *Hell's Angels* (1930), in which he introduced the new 'blonde bombshell' JEAN HARLOW. His other major star creation was Jane Russell in *The Outlaw* (1944), which he also part directed.

Despite his unorthodox working methods (hiring various directors and then dropping them) and a weakness for crude sensationalism on the screen, he has produced some films of enduring worth: *The Front Page* (1931), *Scarface* (1932). In the late 1940s he acquired RKO Studios, which had built up a post-war reputation for progressive and relatively radical productions. Under Hughes and the pressures of television the studio programme stagnated and Hughes sold out in 1957. Since then he has had little to do with the film industry.

Several biographies of him have been published including 'Howard Hughes' by John Keats and 'The Bashful Billionaire' by Albert B. Gerber. The hero, Jonas Cord Jr, in Harold Robbins's gross novel 'The Carpetbaggers' is reputed to have been based on Hughes.

Other notable productions: *Mad Wednesday* (1947), *Vendetta* (1950), *Jet Pilot* (1952–6). MH

Rock Hudson in 'A Gathering of Eagles' (Delbert Mann, USA, 1963)

Hughes, Ken
Born 1922 in Liverpool, England. Enterprising British writer-director with a solid grounding

in film and sound techniques from the age of 14 when he won an amateur film contest and a job in the industry. In 1952 he wrote and directed *Wide Boy*, followed by a series of brisk, superior second features which established his reputation as a fast, imaginative worker. He has been less successful with his major and much more costly productions, though his sensitive handling of a difficult homosexual theme in *The Trials of Oscar Wilde* (1960) was critically approved and *The Small World of Sammy Lee* (1963) was ahead of its time in analysing the seedy underside of London life. Other main films: *Joe Macbeth* (1955), *Town on Trial* (1957), *Arrivederci Baby* (1966), *Chitty Chitty Bang Bang* (1968), *Cromwell* (1970). MH

Hungary

The first Hungarian exhibitor appears to have been Arnold Sziklai, who in 1896 engaged a mechanic from Lyons, by the name of Mamoussen, to supply a machine and give projections at the 'Ikonograph', a converted hat-shop, which he opened on 13 June 1896. Sziklay and Mamoussen were also responsible for the first recorded actuality film to be shot in Hungary: a film of Franz Joseph at the Millennium Exhibition, looking at Munkacsy's painting 'Ecce Homo', which happened to be the property of Sziklai's brother Zsigmond. The film was a resounding failure, owing to the cameraman's grave difficulty in getting the Emperor's head in frame.

The Hungarian cinema proper however was born in the boulevard cafés which were so important a part of the life of Budapest, and whose proprietors offered moving pictures as an extra attraction. The LUMIÈRE Brothers gave their first showings in Budapest at the Royal Hotel, while the first established Hungarian producer-exhibitor was Mór Ungerleider, proprietor of the Velence Café. With József Neumann, Ungerleider founded the Projectorgraph Company which produced some of the earliest actualities, and ran the most ambitious theatre of early days, the Apollo Cinema.

Hungarians generally showed great enthusiasm for the cinema, which was christened *mozi*, the word having apparently been coined in a cabaret song by Jenö Heltai and Imre Kálmán in the late 1890s. By 1912 the country had a very high cinema population (in Budapest one cinema to every 10,000 inhabitants); yet at this late date no real national production had developed. Exhibitors were content with imported pictures and a few actuality films of local interest. The total failure of the Hunnia company with its ambitious studios on Pannónia Street (still in use today) – the result of professional inexperience, artistic incompetence and failure to appreciate the market – provided a marked discouragement to investment in Hungarian films.

Above: Puffy, a favourite comedian during the First World War. The inscription on the bomb reads 'Liège'.
Right: 'Romeo and Juliet' (1920)
Below: An early location shot on the Budapest Corso with the actor, Latabar

In 1912, however, production quite suddenly got under way with the formation of several companies; and between that year and the outbreak of the First World War more than fifty feature films had been made. Working at the Phönix company, Mihály Kertész (later to be better known as MICHAEL CURTIZ) rapidly established himself as the leading Hungarian director; and his trip to Denmark to study the methods of the Nordisk Studio, with their noted emphasis upon the actor's art, left its mark on the Hungarian cinema for the rest of the silent era. Other characteristics of the Hungarian cinema were formed at this time. From the beginning the studios of Budapest and Kolozsvár laid emphasis on the literary elements of the film. In general they seemed to prefer the predictable certainties of a formed screenplay to the more improvisational methods which prevailed in the Anglo-Saxon cinemas. They sought subjects in Hungarian literature. The theatrical epic *Bánk Bán* was filmed in 1914, and the works of Molnár, Petöfi and Herczeg were all adapted for the screen. This tendency in turn reflected upon the prestige of the cinema. Intellectuals in Hungary felt less of the scorn experienced elsewhere; and it was a highly intelligent radical journalist, Sándor Korda (later ALEXANDER KORDA), who founded Hungary's first serious film journal, 'Pesti Mozi', in 1912. Again, Hungarian actors experienced none of the Anglo-Saxon hesitance about working for the screen. The greatest Hungarian actress, Mari

Jászai, along with other members of the national theatre, felt no degradation in playing before the cameras for some of the very earliest Hungarian films.

By the end of the War, Hungary had developed a strongly national school of directors, among whom Sándor Korda had already taken a leading position. Starting his career with the director-producer Jenö Janovics in his Transylvanian studio, Korda soon bought the film and its name, Corvin, moved to Budapest, and went into partnership with the producer Mórics Miklós Pásztory. With characteristic flamboyance, he had built a studio, then razed it six months later to build a bigger one on a better site. He appointed Frigyes Karinthy as literary collaborator, and embarked on a programme of well-selected, carefully mounted films, always with a literary bias. Among these productions were *The Nightmare*, after Mihály Babits, *The Guardsman*, from the play by Molnár, and *The Woman With Two Souls* from Sándor Bródy's novel. Korda's dominant position was of course significantly fortified by his continuing proprietorship of the leading film magazine, now 'Mozihét'.

Practically nothing now survives of Kertész's considerable activity at this period, though it seems that in opposition to Korda's methods he tried to escape from literary domination, preferring to rely on original scenarios and the dynamic narrative style which was later to be evidenced in his American work.

Other significant directors of this period included Eugen Illés and Márton Garas, both German-trained and eclectic in output; Alfred Déesy and Janovics, both essentially producers; Ödön Uher, Antal Fórgács, founder of Gloria Studio, Károly Lajthay, founder of Rex, Lajos Lázár, founder of Lux. The doyen of the directors was Mórics Miklós Pásztory, who had begun life as a gardener, and always concentrated on rural subjects calculated to engage provincial audiences. Béla Balogh first appeared as a director in 1916, and made some of the most interesting films of the period, notably the first version (1917) of Molnár's perennially successful *The Boys from Pál Street*, *The Admirable Crichton* and a remarkable group of films of clear liberal protest – the first emergence of a political cinema in Hungary.

In 1919 Hungary witnessed one of the most extraordinary adventures in film history. In March of that year she was declared a Republic of Councils; and a decree of April 12 1919 – four months before the nationalization of the Soviet film industry – gave her the first nationalized, socialized film industry in history. This nationalized cinema was as strongly supported by the producers as it was resented by the distributors: a bitter conflict had been waging between the two ends of the business for some years before this, over the producers' complaints at the distributors' exploitation. The administrative board of the new film organization included such important creative figures as Sándor Korda, László Vajda and BÉLA LUGOSI. A central organization was set up; smaller studios were merged to provide six active studios. A central script department was established with Kertész and Vadja among its artistic advisers. There was a registry of actors which underwent considerable criticism for its hierarchic and bureaucratic methods. A grandiose programme of adaptations from world literature was, perhaps fortunately, abandoned. Nevertheless in the four months of its survival, this nationalized Hungarian cinema produced a remarkable record of thirty-one films.

Of these only *Yesterday* survives, and István Nemeskürty, the leading historian of Hungarian cinema, describes it as a film with a foolish, symbolist story, but a number of visual effects and editing styles uncommon in Hungarian films of the period. For the rest, although the majority were made by pre-Republican directors (Korda, Balogh, Garas, Deésy, Pál Sugár et al.) four young directors were able to direct their first films: Gyula Szöreghy, Béla Geröffy, Dessö Orbán and Sándor Pallos, who was tortured to death by Horthy's gendarmes, after making only a single film, *Chelkash*.

In August 1919 the Republic of Councils collapsed. Many of the directors and actors who did not rapidly emigrate (Korda, Kertész, and Béla Lugosi were among those who went to Vienna) were arrested. Geröffy committed suicide. The few who stayed behind included Antal Fórgács, PÁL FEJÖS and Béla Balogh. With her artists thus depleted, with grave economic difficulties, with the competition of cheap imported films, and with a political climate that encouraged nothing but the adaptation of pulp literature, Hungarian production slowly wound to a standstill. 'Those years were an irreparable loss, the effect of which – without exaggeration – may be said to be still felt in Hungarian film production. As if ten years had dropped from the history of a nation's literature, as if no books or periodicals had appeared for that long a time. The few films made in the second half of this barren decade provide a sad proof' (István Nemeskürty). By 1929 practically all the old studios had failed definitively. Perhaps symptomatic of the collapse of practical cinema activity, theoretical writing flourished, with László Moholy-Nagy's first idealistic projects for abstract films, with Iván Hevesy's 'Film Drama: Aesthetics and Structure' (1925) and BÉLA BALAZS' first writings on film theory, published in exile in Vienna and Berlin.

In September 1929 *The Singing Fool* was shown in Budapest; and in September 1931 the first Hungarian sound film, *The Blue Idol*, was released. A Hungarian film of any sort was by this time something of a rarity. Practically 100% of films shown in Hungarian cinemas were imported. Sound films did not immediately offer any impetus to home production, since the foreign companies simply ran off Hungarian-language versions of their successes, with Hollywood favouring Paris as her European production centre. The establishment of a modern state film studio – Hunnia – in the old Corvin studio, for use by independent producers, also attracted foreign producers rather than Hungarian enterprises. A further Government measure introduced special taxes and customs on imported films and imposed on cinemas a quota (one film in 20) of Hungarian products. Under pressure from Hollywood the quota was abandoned in favour of a financial levy to support Hungarian production. Out of this, subsidies were granted to scripts officially approved; which meant that the state was able to impose a rigorous precensorship (which Nemeskürty says even extended to the point of not permitting horses galloping off in clouds of dust, since this would be a reflection on the public highways).

The result was a production of innocuous, toothless films, catering to the lowest common denominator of taste in an audience which was, nevertheless, very ready to patronize any films shot in the Hungarian language.

The Blue Idol was quite overshadowed by the success of a much more modestly intended sound film which followed it: István Székely's *Hippolyte the Butler* (1931), a bourgeois comedy about the relationship of a likeable new-rich vulgarian with his tyrannical and patrician butler and aspiring wife. The title role was played by a distinguished legitimate actor, Gyula Csortos, but he was eclipsed by Gyula Kabos, who played the put-upon master. Kabos (1888–1941) had begun his career as a provincial actor. After this début in films he refined his interpretation of the burdened, bewildered, frightened petty-bourgeois clerk-class citizen to a degree which puts him among the great screen comedians. As the 1930s went on, his comedy took on a more tragic tone, which seemed to reflect political atmospheres. Finally, in 1939, anti-Semite pressures and fascist disapproval[1] of his increasingly realist portrayals of the lower middle class, drove him to emigrate to America, where he died, vainly struggling to win recognition in vaudeville theatres.

But during the first half of the 1930s the prosperity of the Hungarian cinema depended very largely upon the popularity of Kabos's films. The audience liked comedies; and the Film Industry Fund committee was reassured by the dream world of the sentimental romantic intrigues of the sub-plots. Székely and his writer Károlyi Nóti were required endlessly to reproduce the same formulas. The films were turned out with mechanical efficiency. The favourite romantic male stars were Pál Jávor and Antal Páger, who was to retain his leading position in the Hungarian cinema for four decades, up to the present day. The apogee of the style was reached with Béla Gaál's *The Dream Car* (1934), a clever combination of a cinderella story and petty-bourgeois comedy, which enjoyed an immense success and confirmed the style of the Hungarian cinema for

[1] Székely's *An Affair of Honour*, in which Kabos challenges an aristocrat to a duel, provoked demonstrations on account of its affront to the gentile and upper classes.

the rest of the decade. 'The extraordinary success of the film had a fatal effect on the Hungarian cinema. Everybody wanted to produce, to direct, to see such films, in the hope of sure success and first-class entertainment. . . . In the four years between 1934 and 1939, seventy-five film comedies were produced by the Hungarian film studios after the pattern of *The Dream Car*' (István Nemeskürty, 'Word and Image'). The films had nondescript yet immediately evocative titles like *Honeymoon at Half Price*, *Confectionery of Buda*, *Your Bill Madame*, *Room Wanted for Young Lady*. The formula was as predictable as Italian *commedia*, though as Nemeskürty points out it was not always entirely innocuous. The influence of the official Film Fund could result in the subtle injection of patriotic and political motifs.

There were exceptions to the *Hippolyte-Dream Car* style. Székely himself was versatile and facile. His *Rákócsi March* exploited a taste for romantic period films; and *Ball at the Savoy* failed to set a fashion for operetta films at that time only because its release alarmingly coincided with the collapse of the production firm that made it. Székely's most interesting and individual works were *Café Moskva*, and *Purple Acacia*, a more acid look at the world of *The Rákocsi March*, whose failure with the public who preferred the romantic view, drove him back to the inevitable bourgeois comedies.

One of the finest Hungarian directors, PÁL FEJÖS, who had emigrated to the USA in the mid-1920s, to achieve international celebrity with his brilliant *Lonesome*, was invited back by the French firm of Osso to make two films in his native country. *Spring Shower*, on folk themes, is said to have been technically advanced and of strongly progressive sympathies, but it was poorly received by Hungarian press and audiences. The failure also of *Verdict of Lake Balaton* – though it too was praised for its technical brilliance – was as discouraging to artistic ambition as to the return of other emigrés.

Apart from the profitability of the general run of production on the home market (films were made cheaply, with an average shooting schedule of two weeks) the prosperity of the Hungarian cinema in the 1930s was assisted by the discovery of a lucrative market in America (where there were practically as many Hungarians as in Hungary itself. Today there *are* perhaps as many); and also by Government interest, which resulted in the imposition of a quota requirement in Hungarian cinemas (10% of Hungarian product in 1935, raised to 15% the following year), and the provision of new studio facilities for feature production by the Hungarian Film Office. The Hungarian Film Office's studios gave greater opportunities for young directors (Viktor Gertler, László Vajda, Márton Keleti) than the Hunnia studios, which preferred to work with commercially proved directors like Székely, Béla Gaál, who specialized in 'scenic' films, and István György, given to overblown nationalistic subjects. The single survivor of the silent period, Béla Balogh, found the commercial value of old-fashioned sentimental melodramas, with titles like *Tommy the Frozen Child*.

By and large the cheap factory-production methods of Hungarian films of the 1930s dictated the style. Visually they permitted little enterprise either in décor, *mise-en-scène* or camerawork. In compensation, editing and montage styles were often showy. Dialogue acquired added importance, and the literary style of the American LUBITSCH comedies was a considerable influence on 1930s directors in Hungary. Other directors of the period were Emil Martonffy, who made some of the poorest comedies, Béla Pásztor, Ákos Ráthonyi, Sándor Szlatinay and Janos Vaszary.

The end of the period saw a further stage in the continual process of emigration from the Hungarian cinema. Székely went to Hollywood to become a producer and director of B-pictures, as Steve Sekely; László Vajda – son of Korda's scenarist of the same name – became a director in Spain, as Ladislao Vajda.

The war reduced foreign competition and opened up new markets in the Balkans, Italy and Scandinavia (though not in Germany). With an increased Hungarian film quota, production increased (from 28 features in 1939 to 53 in 1943) and new studios were built. State control now became explicit and official. The Film Industry Fund was reorganized as a National Film Committee which supervised every aspect of the industry, exerting strict censorship and tight political control. The anomaly of the arrangement was that films were still financed and produced privately, so that producers found the State strictly controlling every stage of their own personal expenditure. Inevitably the Film Committee fell under the control of bureaucrats who rejected all but safe conformist subjects, and slavishly followed the prevailing fascist and anti-semitic drift.

Projects like *The Abyss*, intended as the first film by László Ranódy, and *Song of the Cornfields*, written by Ranódy and to be directed by István Szöts, – both proposed by the progressive and intelligent producer István Erdelyi – were rejected almost automatically by the Committee. Small opportunist firms leapt in with militarist and propagandist films which were certain of approval. Hack writers were at a premium. The prevailing genre was still bourgeois comedy, though as the war went on tastes seemed to move towards sentimental, pseudo-tragic melodrama. The leading directors of the war years were Viktor Bánky, brother of Vilma Bánky and a declared fascist, Ákos Ráthonyi and Emil Martonffy.

A star cult developed around such artists as Klári Tolnay, Zita Szeleczky, Mária Tasnády, Margit Lukács, Bea Goll, Vali Hidvéghy and most spectacularly, the sensuous, 'almost provokingly vulgar', untalented Katalin Karády. The most popular male actors were István Nagy, László Szilassy, and Antal Páger. After Kabos's emigration, Kálmán Latabar attempted to take his place as the leading comic actor. From the general dross of the period, Nemeskürty singles out a few films of merit – Endre Toth's (in the USA, André de Toth) *Six Weeks' Happiness*, Arpád Horváth's comedy *White Tie*, László Cserépy's *We Two Alone*, Endre Rodriguez's *They Are Seven*.

The same historian perceives other tendencies,

'Hortobagy' (Georg Hoellering, 1936)

régime collapsed. BÉLA BALÁZS returned home from his long exile to teach at the newly founded Academy of Dramatic and Film Art. The classic Soviet films were shown for the first time. American distributors tried to recapture the market, with the result that a very large number of films from Hollywood were seen. A few films (including Márton Keleti's remake of Sándor Bródy's novel *The Schoolmistress* and Ákos Ráthonyi's *The Gold Watch*) were made by private enterprise; but from 1947 permits to produce films were given only to the leading parties. Out of this attempt to revive the industry came two notable films: István Szöts's *Song of the Cornfields* and Géza Radványi's *Somewhere in Europe*, one of the rare films scripted by Béla Balázs: a touching, idealistic fantasy about the reclamation of war orphans, clearly influenced by the Soviet film, NIKOLAI EKK's *The Road to Life*.

In March 1948 the Hungarian film industry – for the second time – was nationalized. The first film produced by the state film industry was auspicious: Frigyes Bán's *The Soil Beneath your Feet*, a realistic treatment of peasant life under the old régime. It set a pattern for historical films that was to be followed for some years. Another notable film was Imre Jeney's *A Woman Makes a New Start*, an interesting exami-

Top: 'Somewhere in Europe' (Géza Radványi, 1947)
Right: 'Late Season' (Zoltán Fábri, 1967)
Below: Antal Páger in 'Twenty Hours' (Zoltán Fábri, 1964)

however, hesitant, and other efforts, however feeble, to escape from the constrictions of the time: Lajos Zilahy turned to better literary models. Géza Radványi, returning from working in France, brought a more enterprising visual style to the three films he made during the war period. Imre Jeney's first film, *And The Blind Can See*, was unique in its attempt to depict a working class milieu. The genuine attempt at social criticism, and the technical ambition of László Cserépy's *The Thirtieth* were betrayed by its compromises to political demands.

The outstanding film of the whole period however was István Szöts's *People on the Alps* (1943), in plot a piece of Rousseauesque romanticism mingled with elements of melodrama; but which nevertheless succeeds, in a unique way, in linking the great traditions of the Soviet cinema with Italian neo-realism. Too little known in the West, this tender, indignant film about the exploitation of simple people, is perhaps the outstanding native film of the pre-nationalization cinema. (The best-known of all prewar Hungarian sound films, *Hortobagy*, recording the lives of dwellers on the Great Plains, was made by an Austrian, GEORG M. HOELLERING.)

The war ended, and with it the old Horthy

nation of the role of middle-class women in the immediate post-war period. FÉLIX MÁRIÁSSY's first film, *Anna Szabó*, also dealt humanely with problems of adjustment in the new socialist world. Máriássy was the only debutant of the generation. Bán and Jeney, like Viktor Gertler, Kálmán Nádasdy, Márton Keleti and Imre Apáthi had all begun their careers in the Horthy era. The period did however introduce new actors, some of whom – Téri Horváth, Adam Szirtes, Eva Ruttkai – were to retain their popularity for many years.

Towards the end of the 1940s Hungarian cinema began to suffer the pressures that forced

Top: Miklós Gábor, Philippe March, and Bernadette Laforet in 'Walls' ('Last Generation', András Kovács, 1968)
Above: Judit Halász in 'Love Film' (István Szabó, 1968)
Right: Zoltán Latinovits and Eva Ruttkai in 'Baptism' (István Gaál, 1967)

films, for two or three depressing years, into the worst schematic moulds of socialist realist film-making. In this period too Béla Balázs was removed from his post at the Academy of Dramatic and Film Art. The script became paramount, with any deviation from what was safely set down frowned on as opening the door to formalism. PUDOVKIN (whose own early works were currently disapproved of within the socialist camp) was sent from Moscow as 'adviser'. Significantly, the most successful films of the period were historical subjects, like Márton Keleti's *Erkel* or Frigyes Bán's *Semmelweis*.

From 1953, with the death of Stalin and Rákosi's loss of the premiership a new liberal feeling was reflected in the cinema. Historically the turning point seems to have been ZOLTÁN FÁBRI'S *Fourteen Lives Saved* (1954). New directors began to appear (FÁBRI having made his first film, *The Storm*, in 1952): KÁROLY MAKK with *Liliomfi*, László Ranódy with *Love Travels by Coach*, János Herskó with *Under the City*, Zoltán Várkonyi with *The Day of Wrath*, György Révézs with *Twice Two is sometimes Five*. The outstanding film of this new phase of liberalism however was Várkonyi's *The Birth of Menyhért Simon*, based on a script by Tibor Déry.

1955–6 represented a peak of artistic achievement, as Zoltán Fábri moved into a dominant place with *Merry-Go-Round* (1955) and *Professor Hannibal* (1956). Máriássy's *Spring Comes to Budapest* (1955) was a sober, gripping account of the events of the siege, while *A Glass of Beer* represented the contemporary working world in a style influenced by the neo-realists. László Ranódy at last made *Abyss*, the film which had previously been planned and rejected in 1942. Várkonyi made a film about the wartime struggle of communists: *Strange Mark of Identity*. Imre Féher made a striking début with the poetic and beautiful *Sunday Romance* (1956–7).

Despite emigrations and imprisonments (including István Dárvas, a fine actor and popular leading man of the period: he was to resume his career in the 1960s) the events of 1956 produced only a temporary hiatus in production and artistic evolution; and the conversion of the newsreel studio to a second feature film studio in 1957 was important not just for the possibility of increasing output (from five feature films in 1952 to six in 1953, eight in 1954, ten in 1955, ten in 1956 and fifteen in 1957) but also in the variety of approach encouraged by two competing production centres.

Two significant new names appeared in

Top: 'Sirocco' (Miklós Jancsó, Hungary-France, 1969)
Above and below: Two stills from 'The Confrontation' (Miklós Jancsó, 1968)

1960 when MIKLÓS JANCSÓ and ANDRÁS KOVÁCS directed their first feature films; but the real watershed which saw the decisive emergence of a new generation and a recognizably new Hungarian cinema was 1963. The key works of that year were Jancsó's *Cantata*, which was actually released just at the end of 1962, Herskó's *Dialogue* and ISTVÁN GAÁL's *Current*, followed early in 1964 by Kovács's *Difficult People*. There are clear historical reasons for the emergence from this time of a whole sizable generation of distinctive new talents. At the end of the 1950s the Government remarked a degree of stagnation in Hungarian films at a time when in other countries – France, Britain, East-coast America and even the Soviet Union – new waves of young directors were breaking resoundingly. In consequence the Academy of Dramatic and Film Art was reformed and younger teachers were appointed. The number of feature production groups was increased to four from January 1963, with young creative people put in charge of their artistic policy.

Alongside this reorganization was the creation in about 1961 of the Béla Balázs Studio. Begun by a group of new graduates from the Academy, the studio was formed to overcome the old situation in which new directors might wait years before they had a chance to direct their first films. The Béla Balázs Studio provided possibilities for the young to prove their abilities on short films; and their first productions clearly signalled a new wave when they were shown at international film festivals.

There were political and philosophical reasons for the phenomenon also. The treatment of history in films like *Dialogue* and subsequent films of the 1960s, and of contemporary issues in *Difficult People* and Kovács's later *Walls* (1968), presupposed liberalization of official attitudes to a degree which the Soviet Union, for instance, has never known. Alongside the liberalization went the great regard in which the young film-makers have tended to hold the Marxist philosopher György Lukacs, with his emphasis on the need for a frank self-criticism which has been rare in European communism.

The resulting New Cinema is sharply separated from the previous era. A leading characteristic has been an escape from the literary tradition which had dogged Hungarian cinema for better or worse since the days of KORDA. The new directors tend to be linked by strong mutual interest and admiration, helped by the fact that there are frequent close collaborations. Their films as a body have a remarkable cohesion. In contrast to the classic Soviet cinema, which was a cinema of political criticism and agitation, and Italian neo-realism which was a cinema of political criticism and comment, the new Hungarian film-makers endeavoured to use the film as a medium of socio-political debate. Their films are invariably open-ended and their rejection of schematic solutions marks a strong reaction against the bad old conventions of socialist cinema.

Among the themes of the films of the new generation have been re-examination of both old and recent Hungarian history (the films of Jancsó have ranged from the Austrian occupation in *The Round-up* to the Horthy régime in *Silence and Cry* and post-war socialization in *Confrontation*); socialist management and responsibility, (Kovács's *Difficult People*, and *Walls*; Ferenc Kardos's Pinteresque fable, *A Mad Night*); the maturing and social adjustment of young people against the background of the history of the past twenty-five years (István Gaál's *Current* and *The Green Years*; ISTVÁN SZABÓ's *Age of Illusions*, *The Father* and *Love*

Film); the social position of women (*Binding Sentiments*, directed by the wife of Jancsó, Márta Mészaros); the conflicts of town and country (*Cantata*; Herskó's *Hello Vera*; Mészaros's *The Girl*).

Despite a community of interests, the styles of the directors of the new generation are individual. Among the directors born in the 1920s, JANCSÓ (q.v.) is the most dramatically stylish, with his extremely long, balletically composed shots, while KOVÁCS, though he can apply himself to dramatic forms, as in *Cold Days*, experiments with informal styles like the reportage method of *Difficult People* or a film on pop music, *Ecstasy from 7 to 10*. Péter Bácso's work (*Summer on the Hill*, *The Fatal Shot*) tend to reveal his training as a script-writer. Of the younger generation – born in the 1930s and 1940s – the most obviously talented are ISTVÁN GAÁL, whose austerity and fine visual sense are best seen in *The Falcons* (1970), and ISTVÁN SZABÓ, whose use of sentiment does not efface a keen intelligence and feeling for metaphor. Ferenc Kósa's second film, *Judgment*, was disappointing after his début with the poetic *Ten Thousand Suns*. The cameraman, Sándor Sára in his first film *The Upthrown Stone* revealed a particular response to folklore and the peasant scene, as did Imre Gyöngyössy's highly inventive *Palm Sunday*. Other contemporaries – János Rózsa (*Grimaces*, with Kardos), Ferenc Kardos (*Red Letter Days*, *A Mad Night*), Pál Sándor (*Clowns on the Wall*), Sándor Simó (*Bespectacled*), Pál Gábor (*Forbidden Ground*) – all suggest in their débuts more urban orientations. Apart from Márta Mészaros, women directors of the new school of Hungarian cinema are Livia Gyarmathy (*Do You Know 'Sunday-Monday'?*) and Judit Elek, who made her début with the brilliant, understated *Lady From Constantinople*. DR

Hunter, Ross

Born 1921 in Ohio, USA. Exuberant American producer primarily of glossy tear-jerkers, portmanteau star vehicles and larky sex comedies made with wit and style. A teacher and actor (1944–6), he was appointed an associate producer at Universal in 1950 and has produced films there ever since. His first important popular success was *Magnificent Obsession* (1954), which set the tone for several subsequent 'weepies', notably *Imitation of Life* (1957), *Back Street* (1961) and *Madame X* (1966). In 1958 he produced the phenomenally successful DORIS DAY-ROCK HUDSON comedy, *Pillow Talk*. Well-dressed glamour has become his trademark whatever the subject matter of his films, and his one off-beat production – *The Pad* (1966) – failed. Latest films: *Thoroughly Modern Millie* (1967), *Airport* (1969).

Above: 'The Up-thrown Stone' (Sándor Sára, 1968)
Below: Lujza Orosz and Péter Fried in 'Horizont' (Pál Gábor, 1971)

Huston, John

Born 1906 in Missouri, USA. Highly individual American director, writer and occasional actor whose own muscular, roving life has influenced the themes of his films, which perpetuate the dilemmas of the 'loner', group loyalty and treachery. His flamboyance, both personally and professionally, has tended to obscure the integrity of his purpose and the tight-knit competence of his work. Technically, he has been responsible for several interesting experiments with the use of colour, notably in *Moby Dick* (1956) and *Reflections in a Golden Eye* (1967). A maverick within the Hollywood system, he has constantly been at odds with the front office and some of his films have suffered major surgery because of it, particularly *The Red Badge of Courage* (1951), the subject of Lillian Ross's incisive *exposé*, 'Picture', in which Huston appeared none too sympathetically.

The son of actor Walter Huston, who also starred in one of John's most characteristic films, *The Treasure of Sierre Madre* (1947), for which he received an Academy Award, Huston spent his childhood travelling with his mother: he briefly took up boxing, singing, the Cavalry in Mexico, short-story writing and painting. In London he worked for Gaumont-British as a writer, returning to New York where he acted on the stage.

In the late 1930s he went to Hollywood working as a scriptwriter on *Jezebel* (1938), *High Sierra* and *Sergeant York* (1941) among other films at Warners. In 1941, he directed his first film, *The Maltese Falcon*, the prototype hardshell private eye film which also launched his association with HUMPHREY BOGART, who starred later in Huston's *Key Largo* (1948), *The African Queen* (1951), *Beat The Devil* (1953). During the War, Huston made several official documentaries including *Report from the Aleutians*, *The Battle of San Pietro* and the controversial *Let There Be Light*.

Since 1951 Huston has worked almost exclusively away from Hollywood. He has made several expensive failures – *Moulin Rouge* (1953), *Roots of Heaven* (1958), and the undeservedly victimized *Freud* (1962). A biography, 'King Rebel', by W. F. Nolan was published in 1965. He has recently appeared as an actor in films, some of them notably sub-standard.

Other principal films: *We were Strangers* (1949), *The Asphalt Jungle* (1950), *Heaven Knows Mr Allison* (1957), *The Unforgiven* (1959), *The Misfits* (1960), *The List of Adrian Messenger* (1963), *Night of the Iguana* (1964), *The Bible* (1966), *Sinful Davey*, *A Walk with Love and Death* and *The Kremlin Letter* (1969); as an actor in *De Sade* (1969), *Myra Breckinridge* (1970) and *The Deserter* (1971). MH

Above: Frantisek Velecky in 'Palm Sunday' (Imre Gyöngyössy, 1969)
Below: John Huston and Mae West in 'Myra Breckinridge' (Michael Sarne, USA, 1970)

I

Ichikawa, Kon

Born 1915 in Mie Prefecture, Japan. Director. Began as an animator in 1933 and made a full-length puppet film at beginning of his career. Since the war, he has undertaken an astonishing variety of subjects (about 50 films), ranging from black comedy to stark tragedy, which has gained him a reputation as an eclectic artist with a formidable technical control, but no personal style. This is incorrect in that Ichikawa has stated that his main concern is with 'the pain of our age', which he expresses in varying forms including bitter laughter and satire. *The Burmese Harp* (1956), with its melancholy images of war tinged with pity and an anguished sentimentality, led to *Fires on the Plain* (1959), which depicted war as an unbearable modern Inferno. Other major dramas include *Conflagration* (1958), about a young man's obsessions which lead him to destroy a sacred temple, and *The Key* (1959), a quirky study of sexual obsessions and one of the few films to be shown commercially in the West. Ichikawa has the peculiar Japanese quality of being able to satirize even the most appalling subject (*The Billionaire*, 1954, includes a character who manufactures atom bombs in the attic), and even a relatively minor film like *Men of Tohoku* (1957) examines human frailties by thumbing its nose at them. This sly, debunking humour is best seen in *Alone on the Pacific* (1963), whose theme of personal heroism is never allowed to become facile or pompous. Likewise, in *Tokyo Olympiad* (1965), the coverage of the Japanese Olympic Games which nearly equals LENI RIEFENSTAHL's earlier German record, he manages to view the event with a bland, knowing eye which takes into account both its absurdities and its genuine human triumphs. In *An Actor's Revenge* (1963), an intriguing comic/serious study of a female impersonator in the Kabuki, Ichikawa's style is at its most eclectic and assured and this brilliantly realized film even surpasses his previous achievements in the use of colour and widescreen. Although he has made some distinguished shorts and a partly animated film in Italy, Ichikawa has produced only one feature since 1966 (he feels that the times are not ripe for the purely fictional film); unhappily *To Love Again* (1971) was only a slight syrupy love story. JG

'Tokyo Olympiad' (Kon Ichikawa, Japan, 1965)

In Between

In animation. The intermediate drawings between two key positions.

Ince, Thomas Harper (1882–1924)

Born Newport, Rhode Island, USA. Director. Belonging to a family associated with the theatre, he became an actor, appearing eventually on Broadway and marrying an actress, Alice Kershaw, who was to work for Biograph. He entered the film industry in 1910 and became a pioneer director of the period, for a while second only to GRIFFITH in importance. He directed MARY PICKFORD's films during her brief period with LAEMMLE at IMP, starting with *Their First Misunderstanding* (1911). Working the following year for Kessel and Bauman in Los Angeles, Ince raised the stature of the two-reel, half-hour Western with *War on the Plains* (1913), employing real Indians instead of made-up Whites. He built his own studio ('Inceville') on a 20,000-acre estate; starting from scratch, he developed his property as a complete self-sufficient workshop and landed estate. A series of successful films resulted from his careful planning, starting with the three-reeler, *Custer's Last Fight* (1912). Gradually Ince's films became more ambitious, such as *The Battle of Gettysburg* (1913) in which the battle scenes were covered by eight cameras; he was now beginning to rival Griffith, whose film *The Massacre* had appeared in 1912. In contrast to Griffith, Ince's films were all scripted and planned in detail with generally restrained acting and a leisurely romantic visual style. He preferred scripting and editing to directing, and assembled a team of directors to realize his scripts for him; the first was Francis Ford. He also signed WILLIAM S. HART, the distinguished theatre actor, as his first major star; Hart appeared in *The Bargain* and *Hell's Hinges* (both 1914) and other films, but he wanted to direct his own work, and resented what he regarded as Ince's interference. Ince was to introduce many important stage players to the screen, including H. B. Warner, Lew Cody, Lewis Stone, Mary Boland and Billie Burke, as well as newcomers, such as Charles Ray, who worked with him for some years. Ince's most celebrated production was *Civilization* (directed by Raymond B. West, 1916), an allegorical film conceived on the grand scale and advocating peace; like all Ince's mature films, it had its own music score, in this case composed by Victor Schertzinger, who became Ince's music director, and later directed films for him. (Schertzinger was later to direct *One Night of Love* and *The Road to Singapore*.) Another of his regular directors was Reginald Barker, who made some of the best westerns and dramas. In 1918 Ince built the famous Culver City Studios in California. His final productions were among his best, including notably *Human Wreckage* (1923) and the first film version of O'Neill's *Anna Christie* (1923), starring Blanche Sweet. His many other productions included *The Typhoon* (1914),

The Despoiler (1915), *The Aryan* (1916), and *Carmen of the Klondike* (1918). He died of a thrombosis in 1924 after spending a weekend on WILLIAM RANDOLPH HEARST's yacht. His brother, Ralph Ince the actor, also became a director, but died in a car accident in London in 1937. RM

India

The large output of Indian feature films, which stretches back well over half a century, must be understood in the light of certain overall pressures, problems and conditions governing Indian film-making. These are best taken into account at the outset, since they combine to create the restrictive framework within which the Indian cinema has been forced to develop, inhibiting progressive film-makers in ways not experienced in any other large-scale national film industry. These factors may be summarized as follows:

1 a vast existing, as well as potential market, but virtually entirely for films following traditional patterns of entertainment, and restricted by religious and social conventions which permit little or no development comparable in subject and treatment characteristic of film in the Western or the Japanese film industries;
2 problems arising from wide cultural and language differences in the various regions of India; the industry is divided mainly into Hindi, Bengali, Tamil, Gujarati, Malayalam, Marathi, and Telugu-speaking sections;
3 the industry has been for some decades financially corrupt, over-influenced by all-powerful stars who prefer to take huge sums in illegal 'black' money;
4 the industry suffers from severe import restrictions on raw stock, which can weigh heavily on the more progressive film-maker;
5 severe censorship restrictions have for long held back the more realistic treatment of Indian life (even if this were ever to be wanted by Indian audiences) apart from comparatively small, sophisticated groups in the metropolitan centres.

Indian film history can be divided into two periods, that up to Independence (August 1947) and that afterwards, when British rule ceased, and the territories of Pakistan were severed from those of India. Both periods represent troubled times politically, with the rising revolt against British rule led by Gandhi and the Congress Party from the 1920s, and the sad divisions (religious, cultural, economic) within Indian society which were further emphasized after Independence, together with the endemic poverty and starvation for the masses, and the phenomenal rise in the population, representing some 12 million a year. The population in 1969 was estimated to be some 500 million.

Motion pictures reached India in July 1896 when the LUMIÈRE agents began public showings in Bombay, with reserved boxes for ladies in purdah. Soon indigenous scenes began to be covered for Indian news and 'interest' films, and showmen began to provide popular entertainment in tents and booths. The pioneer producers Jamjetji Framji Madan of Calcutta and Abdulally Esoofally of Bombay set up rapidly expanding production-distribution-exhibition enterprises in the early years of the century, spreading over South-East Asia and showing, initially, imported films only.

Opposite: Tripti Bhaduri and Shobu Mitra in 'Children of the Earth' (K. A. Abbas, 1949)
Below: 'Two Acres of Land' (Bimal Roy, 1953)

The pioneer Indian film-maker, Dhundiraj Govind Phalke (1870–1944), was a highly educated man, working from 1912 in Bombay and making mythological feature films with male actors, at first, in women's roles. Phalke made India's first feature film, *Raja Harischandra* (1912), an hour long, and its success led him to set up a studio-estate at Nasik, north of Bombay, with an established company of players and assistants. Like his contemporary, MÉLIÈS, he was interested in magic, and introduced special effects into his films which number about 100. By the 1920s he was using actresses in his productions, but his ambitious enterprises finally foundered with the coming of sound in the late 1920s. Only fragments of his work survive; he retired from active film-making in 1937.

Other films, of course, were being produced during the same period, the work of innumerable mushroom companies. Notable films were few, but Dhiren Ganguly (born 1893) made a remarkable comedy, *England Returned* (1921) in Calcutta, satirizing Westernized Indians; however, he was temporarily banished by the ruling Nizam of Hyderabad for showing, in one of his cinemas, *Razia Begum*, a Bombay-produced film depicting love between a Muslim princess and a Hindu commoner. Other enterprising film-makers were Debaki Kumar Bose (born 1898) of Bengal, one of India's outstanding film directors, especially after the coming of sound, and Chandulal J. Shah (born 1898) of Bombay, whose film *Gun Sundari* (*Why Husbands Go Astray*, 1925), initiated the western-influenced 'social' film, and featured the beautiful star Gohar in a story challenging in terms of comedy women's servitude in marriage.

During the 1920s films were shown pan-nationally, with captions in up to three languages at a time, while those who could, read out loud for the benefit of their illiterate companions. Movie theatres in the big cities tended to divide between those showing all-Western programmes and those orientated as far as possible to the Indian product.

From the international point of view, the best-known Indian film of the 1920s was the Bengali, Himansu Rai's production *The Light of Asia* (1925), presenting the story of the life of the Buddha; it was co-produced with Emelka of Munich, and directed by the German, Franz Osten. Himansu Rai played the Buddha, and the film, though successful in the West, only brought losses to Rai; nevertheless, it was followed by two other silent, German-Indian productions: *Shiraz* (1926) and *A Throw of the Dice* (1929), with the same director and stars, Sita Devi playing the female lead in all three productions. In India, however, they were regarded as 'foreign' films.

By 1927 Indian cities had some 260 film theatres showing an overall 15% Indian and 85% foreign, mainly American, films. In the same year an Indian Cinema Committee was appointed by the British government in India to examine the industry. It reported in 1928, and revealed that most films were made on low budgets of some ten to twenty thousand rupees, that is, some $3,500 to $7,000 of the period. Many studios had their own, often primitive laboratories for processing. Provincial censor boards had operated from 1920 under the various British Commissioners of Police; the films were examined by paid inspectors, one British, one Indian. Acute problems arose from various Muslim and Hindu sensitivities, and, in a different context, from British political considerations. The report was highly critical of the alleged demoralizing effect of American films, and expressed general satisfaction with the strict censorship. It advocated increased Indian production and 'imperial preference' in imports. The Committee, however, only reflected the position in relation to the silent film, which was about to be replaced by the entirely new phenomenon of the sound film.

The arrival of sound immediately thrust the problem of the diverse languages of India into the foreground. The Indian film (up to now pan-national, as we have seen, with multilingual titling) found itself suddenly decentralized according to the language different metropolitan studios sought to serve. The main language groups were (with population statistics of 1930):

Hindi-speaking	140 million
Bengali-speaking (with centre Calcutta)	53 million
Marathi-speaking (with centre Bombay)	21 million
Tamil-speaking (with centre Madras, and additional outlets especially in Ceylon, Malaya, Africa)	20 million
Telugu-speaking (but with no metropolitan centre)	28 million
Punjabi-speaking	15 million
Gujarati-speaking	11 million
Kanada-speaking	11 million
Malayalam-speaking	9 million
Assamese-speaking etc.	2 million

The Madan theatre circuit in India led the way by introducing sound into key cinemas in 1929, using imported films. The company even set up sound studios in 1931 at Tollygunge, Calcutta – immediately known as 'Tollywood'. The Indian sound film was launched in 1931 with 23 productions in Hindi, three in Bengali, one in Tamil and one in Telugu, and the principle of including numerous songs and dances to attract an unlettered public was immediately established. Drama was traditionally linked with song and dance in Indian culture. Among the producers and directors of sound films (often made in two or more language versions) were Birendra Nath Sircar of Calcutta. He established studio and laboratory facilities and employed Debaki Bose (*Chandidas* 1932, *Puran Bhagast, The Devotee*, made in Hindi in 1933, and many other films with music, song and dance), and Pramathesh Chandra Barua (1903–1951), a prince and son of the Rajah of Gauripur in Assam. Chandra Barua produced and acted in social films of the period, such as *Devdas* (1935), in the Bengali version of which he played the lead; it was later remade in Hindi and Tamil. Its cameraman, BIMAL ROY, was to become an important director himself, and remake the story in Hindi in 1956. Although primarily romantic, the film was also 'social', since it dealt with the barrier against the love of a young nobleman and the daughter of an impoverished family. Barua's films dealt in romantic-tragic terms with certain of India's acute social divisions.

Another important director was Rajaram Vanakudre Shantaram (born 1901), who launched the Prabhat Studios based on Poona, where he made *Ayodhyecha Raja* (*The King of Ayodhya*, 1932) in Marathi and Hindi versions, introducing the high-caste actress, Durga Khote, later to become one of India's greatest and most highly respected stars. Shantaram also made 'social' films – *Duniya Na Mane* (*The Unexpected*, 1937) challenged the arranged marriage of a young girl to an old man, and *Admi* (*Life is for Living*, 1939) dealt with the idealized love of a police constable for a prostitute who wants to be freed from her profession. With the help of English capital the actor-producer Himansu Rai produced in English and Hindi *Karma* (*Fate*, 1933), which featured himself and his wife, the actress Devika Rani. The success of *Karma* in India led to the foundation of Bombay Talkies in 1934, where Rai employed a mixed staff of Indian, German and British technicians to undertake an ambitious programme of productions. Many noted Indian stars and film-makers learned their art at Bombay Talkies, including the actors Ashok Kumar and Raj Kapoor (who worked at first as a clapper-boy), and the screenwriter and director, K. A. ABBAS. Himansu Rai produced both mythological and social films, among the latter *Achhut Kanya* (*Untouchable Girl*, 1936), a Hindi film dealing with love between an Harijan outcaste girl and a Brahmin youth.

By the late 1930s the main centres of production had become Bombay, Madras and Calcutta, although companies mostly working in other language areas existed in nearly 20 cities. But the large Hindi market was by far the most profitable, and key film-makers, and if possible stars, were well advised to acquire Hindi if they spoke other languages. Among other films of the period were *Indira M.A.* (1934), featuring Sulochana (Ruby Myers), an Anglo-Indian star, in a film condemning the pretensions of the Western-educated girl, *Hunterwali* (*Girl Hunter*, 1935) – about, in effect, a female Robin Hood disguised as a man – and the spectacle *Sikander* (*Alexander the Great*, 1940).

In 1938 the industry celebrated its 25th anniversary. It had an air of prosperity; by now it boasted a year-book, and was supported by no less than 68 trade and fan journals, half of them in English. During the 1940s (including the war years) production gradually changed over to the mushroom independent producers, who hired studios rather than owned them.

Scene from a typical mythological film

Production lagged somewhat until 1946, when it picked up sharply with the end of the war (1940, 171 films; 1945, 99 films; 1947, 283 films). British censorship bore down heavily on references to Gandhi or the Indian Congress Party; war propaganda shorts had to be rented by the theatres, and a British-supervised newsreel (*Indian Movietone News,* becoming *Indian News Parade*) was dubbed into various Indian languages. Raw stock allocations to producers had to be rationed by the Government. During the inflationary war period, tax evasion (a patriotic gesture against the British Raj) was rife; the average star, for example, would receive Rs 20,000 in declarable fees for a film, plus Rs 30,000 in 'black', undeclared money, while top stars would demand in similar terms as much as Rs 100,000 or even 200,000 for appearing in films the total budgets of which would be Rs 400,000 to 500,000. Producers and their staffs suffered from these inflationary demands, and the technical grades were grossly underpaid. Unionization for studio staff did not begin until after the war, in 1946.

With the arrival of independence in 1947, the film industry had to pay its full toll to the new Government – faced as it was with the tragedies following on the division of the country, the massacres attendant on the interchange of refugees between India and Pakistan, and the endemic starvation. Tax piled on tax until 60% of the box-office was estimated to go to the State (it was still 40% to 50% in 1970). Other problems included the fierce impact of the new, centralized censorship on both foreign and Indian films – the kissing (occasional during the 1930s in Indian films) definitely had to stop, while foreign films were mutilated to the point of incoherence. Film production, though prolific on a low artistic level, was in a state of flux, with mushroom companies constantly rising and falling. Disenchantment soon set in, and a long-standing feud between the film industry and the Government began, especially when no action followed on the analysis of the industry's ills produced by the Government-appointed Film Enquiry Committee of 1949–50. Films became more and more set in the simple, money-making patterns of 'a star, six songs, and three dances', and the public responded; film music became hybrid, Westernized-Indian, and the songs were sold on disc and played ceaselessly on the radio – until the Government-sponsored All India Radio (unlike the commercial service from Ceylon, which also served India) launched a policy against broadcasting this Westernized music so universally popular with listeners.

Against these conventions a very few film-makers stood out – notably K. A. ABBAS, with his socially-conscious, neo-realist films, *Children of the Earth* (1949) and *The Lost Child* (1954), the latter the first Hindi sound film without song and dance in 23 years of Indian production. BIMAL ROY's *Two Acres of Land* (1953) and *Sujata* (*Untouchable Girl,* 1959) dealt with problems of poverty, debt, and the untouchables. Nimai

Top: 'Kalpana' (Uday Shankar, 1948)
Above: 'Aan' ('Savage Princess', Mehboob Khan, 1952)

Ghosh's *The Uprooted* (1950), a Bengali film, dared to deal with the tragedies following partition in a village on the borders with East Pakistan, and the refugee migrations to Calcutta. A gentle, poetic film by the documentary film-maker, Ezra Mir, *Pamposh* (1953), set in Kashmir, was also seen in Britain; *Two Acres of Land* won awards at the Cannes and Karlovy Vary film festivals; *The Lost Child* was shown at the Moscow and Edinburgh film festivals. Such films furthered the movement to show the real India on the screen, and helped pave the way towards international recognition for exceptional Indian films and, eventually, for the work of SATYAJIT RAY. The USSR in 1955 began to purchase films from India. Attempts to screen Shantaram's mythological film *Shakuntala* (1943) in the States were less successful.

Top, above and below: Three stills from a typical spectacular production

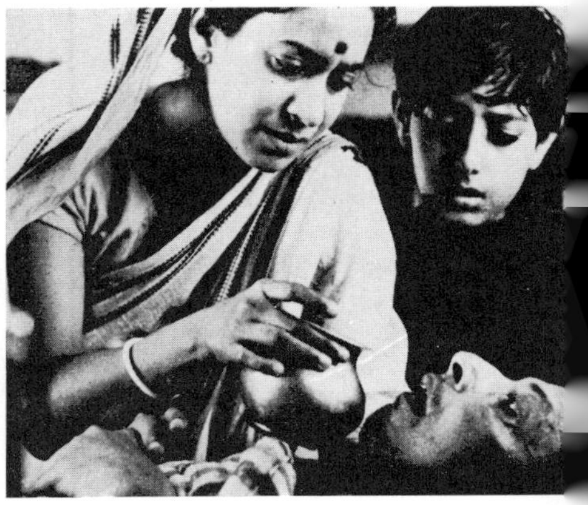

Top: Karuna Banerji in 'Pather Panchali' (Satyajit Ray, 1952-5)
Above: Sharmila Tagore and Sumitra Chatterjee in 'The World of Apu' (Satyajit Ray, 1959)
Below: Karuna Banerji, Pinaki Sen Gupta and Kanu Banerjee (front) in 'The Unvanquished' (Satyajit Ray, 1957)

Spectacular films began to emerge. *Chandralekha* (1948), a three million rupee production made by S. S. Vasan's Gemini Studios in Madras, appeared in Tamil and Hindi versions, while Uday Shankar's dance-spectacle, *Kalpana,* appeared the same year. Other spectacles seen in the West were Mehboob Khan's extravaganzas, *Aan* (1952) and *Mother India* (1957). By now Madras was beginning to rival Bombay as a commercial centre for film-making, and the bidding for the all-essential stars reached towards Rs 400,000 for top names, payable in white and 'black' money; the average projectionist received only Rs 100 a month. Certain prominent film stars became involved in politics and introduced political symbols into their films. But among the welter of self-indulgent and talentless stars were a few of merit, such as the popular actor-producer Raj Kapoor. But stars in demand normally chose to work in several films at once, indicating to worried producers when they would deign to work for them.

The studios in Calcutta, however, were faced with falling returns following partition; East Pakistan, an important region in the Bengali-speaking market, was closed to Indian films through the imposition of prohibitive customs duties, and finally complete embargo. Calcutta lost Bimal Roy and Bose to Bombay, and Barua had died. Nevertheless, it was to be Calcutta which produced India's single film director of world status – SATYAJIT RAY. While working in a British advertising agency in Calcutta, his long-standing love for films led him to start production out of his own resources on *Pather Panchali* (*The Song of the Road,* 1952–5); it was finally completed with financial help (Rs 200,000) from the West Bengal government, and won an award at the Cannes film festival. The film was successful alike in Europe and the USA and at least one part of India had been interpreted for the world by a master. The West Bengal government recouped Rs 800,000, and the idea of a Government-sponsored Film Finance Corporation, such as existed in Britain, was substantially furthered, and indeed finally set up in 1960. Henceforth, Ray had little difficulty in financing his succession of relatively low-budget films, including *The Unvanquished* (1957), *The Music Room* (1958), *The World of Apu* (1959), *Two Daughters* (from the Tagore stories, 1961), and other major works throughout the 1960s and 1970s, although outside West Bengal, with its limited market, they have to be projected with sub-titles. *The Unvanquished,* his second film, won him the 1957 Grand Prix at the Venice Film Festival.

Others who have attempted to follow in the footsteps of Ray have achieved some limited success: Asit Sen (*Chalalal,* and others), Tapan

Sinha (*The Merchant from Kabul, The Hungry Stones*, and others), Rajen Tarafdar (*Ganges*), and Ritwik Ghatak (*Meghe Dhaka Tara, Subarnarekha,* and *Komal Gandhar,* all dealing with contemporary problems, especially the refugee situation). Mrinal Sen, who is concerned more with individual, or domestic crises, with an interest in comedy, has made *Punashcha*, on the remarriage of a widow, and *Baishey Sravana* (*Wedding Day*), on the relations between an ugly man and his beautiful wife. Sen has been the most successful of the serious film-makers in Bengal alongside Ray. His *Bhuvan Shome,* a quietist film contrasting town and rural life, has won many awards in India and success at the box-office.

In addition to the wholly indigenous film, prominent co-productions and location films have been made in India, such as the Indian-Soviet *Pardesi* (*The Traveller*, 1957), the controversial American film, *Nine Hours to Rama* (MARK ROBSON, 1963), dealing with the events leading up to the assassination of Gandhi, and, genuinely indigenous, *Shakespeare Wallah* (1965), a wholly Indian production directed by the American JAMES IVORY with music by Satyajit Ray. Ivory's other films made in India include *The Householder* (1963) and *The Guru* (with RITA TUSHINGHAM and Michael York, 1969). Nor should JEAN RENOIR's exquisite film, *The River* (1950), be forgotten; Renoir's visit to Calcutta did much to inspire Ray during his formative years.

Meanwhile, in spite of its many difficulties, the Indian film industry keeps in production, producing annually over 300 films, 80–90 in Bombay (Hindi), 80–90 in Madras (Tamil), 30–40 in Calcutta (Bengali), and smaller numbers in other languages – principally Gujati, Malayalam, Telugu, and Marathi. India's film markets are far-flung, with exports in 1970 to 100 countries, including Britain, the East, West and North African countries with Indian populations, the West Indies, many Middle Eastern countries, the Persian Gulf, Iran, Ceylon, Burma, Afghanistan, Thailand, Singapore, Malaysia, and others. Export earnings amount to some 30 million rupees. Where there are Indian populations Indian films are always wanted. At the same time, India has some 6,000 home-based cinemas, patronized only by some 5 million of India's 500 millions, though still unaffected by the rival attractions of television, which only exists embryonically in India. In addition, the mobile cinemas, 'Touring Talkies', cater for some 350 million annual audiences in rural areas.

The conditions governing film-making in India are utterly against any kind of experiment except by those who are strongly placed, and 99% of them are not interested in anything but making money. The low budget, 'artistic' film comes almost entirely from Bengal.

However, interest in the art and technique of the film is widespread in intellectual circles in India, which is provided with a Film Institute, acting as a training centre since 1961 and occupying the former Prabhat film studios

Above: Mrinal Sen
Below: Chandana Banerji and Anil Chatterjee in 'Two Daughters' (Satyajit Ray, 1961)

Top: Gnanesh Mukerjee and Madhabi Mukerjee in 'Baishey Sravana' (Mrinal Sen, 1960)
Above: 'Bhuvan Shome' (Mrinal Sen, 1969)
Below: Shashi Kapoor and Felicity Kendal in 'Shakespeare Wallah' (James Ivory, 1965)

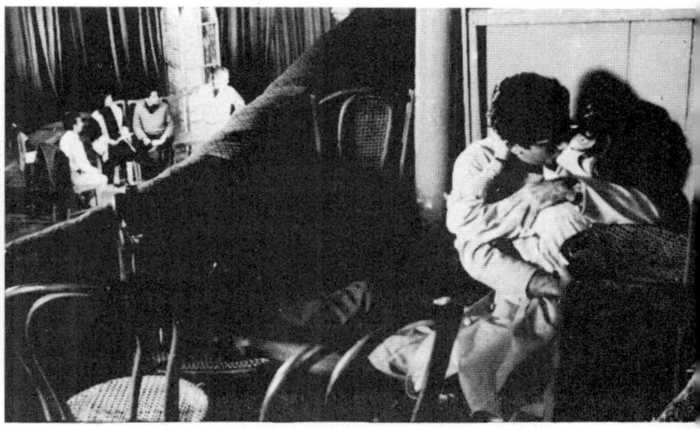

near Poona on a 21-acre estate. There is also a national film archive founded in 1964, and a rapidly expanding film society movement with over 100 affiliated societies belonging to the Federation of Film Societies, which has its headquarters in Calcutta and Satyajit Ray as President.

The hope for Indian film as an art lies with the film-makers in Calcutta, and with a new, younger generation whose work, helped by the Film Finance Corporation, can continue to establish a taste for less conventional subjects and treatments. Among the new generation are: Kantilal Rathod (*Kanku* in Gutarati and Hindi); Basu Chatterji (*Sara Akash*, in Hindi, shot in Agra); Mani Kaul (*Uski Roti*, shot in the Punjab); Rajendra Singh Bedi (*Dastak*, made in Bombay); Basu Bhattacharya (*Adhe Adhure*,

Above: Madhabi Mukerjee and Vasant Coudhury in 'Dibaratrir Kabya' (Bimal Bhowmick and Narayan Chakraborty, India, 1970)
Below: Helit Katmor in 'A Woman's Case' (Jacques Mory-Katmor, Israel, 1969)

shot at the Poona Film Institute); Tapan Sinha (*The Runaway*); Chetan Anand (*Neecha Nagar*); Yavar Abbas, who is based in England (*India, my India, Faces of India, India Called Them, Mother Ganges*); Bimal Bhowmick and Narayan Chakraborty (*Dibaratrir Kabya*). K. A. Abbas, a veteran film-maker now, but always concerned to make the unconventional subject if possible, has completed a film on the Goa liberation movement, *Saat Hindustani*. Together these films, and others being presented in script form by aspirant directors to the Film Finance Corporation, reveal a new life in the Indian film which needs support both inside and outside India. RM

Inflammable Film
A motion picture printed on a film base that fails to comply with the recommended standard for motion picture safety film.

Ingram, Rex (1892–1950)
Born in Dublin, Ireland. Noted silent screen director who came to Hollywood in 1911. Formerly an art student and actor, he made his first film, *The Great Problem* (1916), for Universal. Returning to Hollywood after serving in the Royal Flying Corps, he left Universal for Metro, where he made his reputation with *The Four Horsemen of the Apocalypse* (1921). Particularly marked in all his films is his sophisticated visual sense coupled with a flair for handling exotic romantic themes. In 1931, after making a final film, *Baroud,* he retired, apparently impatient with the size and ever more elaborate production requirements of the industry. Other main films: *The Prisoner of Zenda* (1922), *Scaramouche* (1923), *Mare Nostrum* (1926), *Belladonna* (1927), *The Garden of Allah* (1927), *The Three Passions* (1929) – all of which demand re-examination today.

Inking
In animation. The tracing of the outlines of the animated drawings on to the cells

Insert
A shot used to assist in explaining the action or to provide continuity

In Sync.
When the action is perfectly synchronized with the voices, sound effects, and music

Intercut
See CROSS-CUT

Interest Film
Film of a non-fictional subject in a popular manner

Iraq
See ARAB FILM

Iris
An adjustable diaphragm composed of thin plates commonly used before a lens, or between the components of a compound lens, so called because its action resembles that of the iris of the eye.

Iris-In
To open up an iris in front of the camera lens until the whole picture is revealed

Iris-Out
The converse of Iris-In

Israel
Israel has some 300 film theatres, and makes considerable use of 16 mm projection in the Kibbutzim and small settlements; television was only introduced in 1968. In addition to making documentaries and short films, Israel has always been ambitious to become a centre, however small, for feature production on Jewish subjects, or reflecting Jewish life in Israel, as well as a centre for directors from overseas. Standards were first set by inviting directors from outside Israel, such as THOROLD DICKINSON, to make films (*Hill 24 Doesn't Answer,* 1954). Feature production developed more fully during the 1960s, several films using the 1948 War of Liberation and the 1967 Six Day War for subjects, while others had an historical or literary basis.

The leading Israeli producer is Menahem Golan (a former assistant to ROGER CORMAN), who has produced and directed several films in Israel, among them *El Dorado* (starring Hayim Topol). He also produced *Salah,* directed by Ephraim Kishon with Topol, which was nominated for an Oscar, and *Tevye and his Seven Daughters,* a Ukrainian story which he directed himself. Golan has also directed the musical, *The Miracle,* a Venice award-winner, *My Love in Jerusalem, Eagles Attack at Dawn,* and *Lupo*. RM

Italy
Not surprisingly, at the origins of the Italian film one finds both realism and the historical spectacle. The two were in fact combined in what is generally considered the first Italian feature film, *La Presa di Roma* (*The Capture of Rome,* 1905), made in Rome by Filoteo Alberini and Dante Santoni. The historical subject was relatively close in time, the defeat of the Papal troops by the Piedmontese in 1870 which made Rome capital of a finally united Italy. The celebrated breach of the wall at Porta Pia by the

plumed-hatted Bersaglieri was reconstructed meticulously. Shortly after this film, in Turin, the first Italian pioneer of documentary, Rodolfo Omegna (1876–1948), began to film *dal vero*, from real life, and his films of the earthquake in Messina and of a leopard hunt obtained an enormous success and were much in demand in other countries.

Turin, the city which at the turn of the century was still basking in its patriotic and moral not to mention economic glory as having been the first capital of the unifying Italian state, had been the setting for the first film studios. The proximity to France and the familiarity of the Piedmontese with the French language had prompted an immediate reaction to the news of what had been happening *chez* LUMIÈRE in Paris. Between 1904 and 1905, ARTURO AMBROSIO, who had an optical business in Turin, had made his first films (with Omegna as cameraman) about the manoeuvres of Alpine troops and recorded motor races. In 1906 he built a studio where he started production of feature films. The first drama was *Romanzo di un derelitto* (1906, 470 ft), with Omegna photographing and directing, while the leading role was played by Luigi Maggi, a local amateur actor. In 1907 Ambrosio made *Il cane riconoscente* (*The Grateful Dog*), a precursor of the Rin-Tin-Tin type, while in 1908 Ambrosio's Turin studios made the first of a long line of *Last Days of Pompeii*. The director of this seven-reel pioneer colossal was Luigi Maggi and the cameraman was Omegna, while the leading roles were played by Lydia de Roberti and Mirra Principi.

But Turin was not alone in its industrialization of film production. In Rome, already in 1902, Filoteo Alberini had opened a cinema in Piazza Esedra, called like the cinema which stands there today, the Moderno. Together with Dante Santoni, he had in 1905 formed a production company Alberini-Santoni (which produced *La Presa di Roma*) and in 1906 the company became Cines, the most famous of all Italian production companies. The first important film produced by Cines, described as a 'féerie', was *La Malia dell'Oro* (*The Bewitchment of Gold*) from a story by Augusto Turchi and with music especially composed by Romolo Bacchini. By 1908, Cines had already produced a *Hamlet* and had launched its first director of note, Mario Caserini, who was to specialize in historical subjects such as *Marco Visconti* (1908), *Beatrice Cenci* and *Joan of Arc* (1909), *El Cid* and *Anita Garibaldi* (1910), as well as Shakespearian stories, *Romeo and Juliet* (1908), *Macbeth* (1909) and another *Hamlet* (1910), with Dante Cappelli in the title roles of these last two. Caserini then left Cines and was signed up by Ambrosio in Turin where his subjects became more and more grandiose, from *Siegfried* and *Parsifal* (1912) to the second Italian version of *The Last Days of Pompeii* (1913).

Many other companies were springing up in Rome, with high-falutin' names like Caesar, Tiber and Savoia, but none could rival Cines, who had built studios on the New Appian Way just outside the Gate of Saint John. In Naples, the pioneer was Gustavo Lombardo, founder of the company Titanus which was to be leader of the Italian industry until Gustavo's son Goffredo got lost in the murky finances of latter-day colossals in the 1960s. Milan, where after all the money was found, could not be left behind and attempts to establish a film industry were made there. But then, as now, they never succeeded, even if in that first period companies such as Armenia, Comerio and Bonetti were producing a large number of films.

By 1910, all companies were producing a large proportion of comics but it was not until Italia Film in Turin signed up ANDRÉ DEED and launched him with the name of Cretinetti that the Italian comic really attracted attention. Deed was already known in France by the name of Gribouille but it was as Cretinetti in a whole series of films made between 1909 and 1911 that he won a place among the great early screen comedians.

But it soon became clear that the real vocation of the Italians was for the spectacular with a touch of genuine culture thrown in. Between the two early versions of Pompeii's last days, there was the first *Quo Vadis?* (1912–3), directed by ENRICO GUAZZONI, who had directed two much-praised films of 1910, *Brutus* and *Agrippina*. Guazzoni was the first director in the world to reconstruct enormous sets (which he designed himself) and his film had a sensational success all over the world, with a gala première in New York in April 1913 which was probably the first real socialite film première. Guazzoni was not so good with his actors as he was on spectacle (also perhaps creating a precedent for costume pictures!) and the dramatics were very much in the tradition of Italian opera, as was only to be expected. At about the same time, a man calling himself Piero Fosco directed the first full-length Italian feature film, *La Caduta di Troia* (*The Fall of Troy*, 1912) at Itala's new studios in Turin. Fosco had written a screen treatment called *The Triumph of Love* set in Carthaginian times. He had the brilliant idea of calling in Italy's most exotic literary figure of the moment, Gabriele D'Annunzio, to 'write the script'. D'Annunzio had already ceded the rights of his literary works to Ambrosio and was an enthusiast of the new medium. Fosco's story set in 300 B.C. appealed to the poet and he gave it a new literary flavour, the resulting film being *Cabiria* (1913), with its innovatory use of gliding camera movements; it became the most celebrated film of the early Italian cinema and one that is much under-rated in cinema history for it preceded by several years GRIFFITH's *Intolerance* (1916).

'Gli Ultimi Giorni di Pompei' ('The Last Days of Pompeii', Mario Caserini, 1913)

D'Annunzio's main contribution to the script was in inventing names such as Cabiria and Maciste, while he wrote the titles in a prose that was certainly on a literary level far above those of Griffith's films. Because D'Annunzio was such a big name at the time, he was also credited with the direction (he was in fact described as author), but the imaginative and technical achievement of *Cabiria* was that of its real director, 'Piero Fosco', whose real name was GIOVANNI PASTRONE. Only later was the world to recognise Pastrone as the real author in film terms of *Cabiria*. At the time, Pastrone was acute enough – and modest enough! – to realise that the poet's name would be a bigger attraction at the box-office.

Not the least of the 'cultural' achievements of *Cabiria* was the musical score especially composed by Ildebrando Pizzetti, played by a full orchestra when the film was shown in important cinemas. 'The Fire Symphony' written for the scene of the Worship of Moloch (which was tinted red) is one of Pizzetti's best-known compositions. Music also played an important part in *Histoire d'un Pierrot* (1913) directed by Baldassare Negroni, an aristocrat who also claimed to have 'discovered' the close-up. His Pierrot film is considered by historians such as Barbaro and Lizzani as one of the best Italian films of the early years, using as it did the genuine Italian instincts for mime. It was also notable for its cast which included three of the top names of the period, FRANCESCA BERTINI, Leda Gys and Emilio Ghione. The last won great popularity with his character Za la Mort, a sentimental Apache. Ghione was one of the richest Italian stars of those years, having worked his way up from the early days as an extra in Turin to the years between 1915 and 1921 when he was earning 100,000 lire a month (£13,000). Yet he died, many years later, forgotten and impoverished, in a home for the aged.

Apart from Ghione (Za la Mort), the other popular idol was Maciste, who clung on to the name invented by D'Annunzio for his character in *Cabiria*. Pastrone had looked all over Italy for a man with the right muscles for his Maciste. He found him in the docks at Genoa, Bartolomeo Pagano. Maciste then became a star in his own rights and by flexing his muscles and saving damsels in distress in such pictures as *Maciste against Death* and *Maciste in the Lions' Den*, he inaugurated yet another trend that was to become a frequently re-occuring refrain in Italian films.

The star system had already been evident from the earliest days and the first popular Italian team had been Alberto A. Capozzi and Mary Cleo Talarani, while a young lady with the exotic name of Jeanne Terribili Gonzales was the Cleopatra of Guazzoni's impressive *Marcantonio e Cleopatra* (1913), which was rented for a year's exhibition in Britain alone for 300,000 lire, the exact cost of the production. Famous Italian stage stars appeared in many films of the time, the most notably successful being Amleto Novelli (who was in *Quo Vadis?*); only for historical reasons must we be grateful for the cinema appearances of Ermete Zacconi, whom Pastrone patiently directed in *The Father*. The great Eleonora Duse also starred in a film, after many years of hesitation. At the age of sixty she agreed to appear in an Ambrosio production of a novel by Grazia Deledda, *Cenere* (*Ashes*, 1916). La Duse had stipulated that she did not want close-ups, which was wise because though she gives us a spellbinding glimpse of her art in *Cenere*, her theatrical mannerisms show in the one or two close-ups which did in fact creep in. The close-up of her hands is however particularly moving. Strangely enough, in spite of her reputation, the film was not a box-office success. The top stars of the Italian silent screen were of course those who acted in cinematic terms, such as Francesca Bertini, who though born in Florence was of Neapolitan stock, as could be seen in her performance in films such as *Assunta Spina* (1914), a favourite war-horse for Italian actresses, based on the Neapolitan poet Salvatore di Giacomo's melodrama. Another great star was Lydia Borelli who was the first of many to build a villa on the Appian Way (and to marry a nobleman).

Top and above: Two stills from '1860' (Alessandro Blasetti, 1933)
Below: Eleonora Duse in 'Ashes' (Arturo Ambrosio, 1916)

But perhaps the film which most anticipated the other pole of the Italian cinema, the realistic vein, was *Sperduti nel buio* (*Lost in the Dark*, 1916), directed by Nino Martoglio, inspired by another famous Neapolitan drama of the time by Roberto Bracco, set in a well-off bourgeois home and in the slums.

However, the historical spectacles showed no signs of declining in popularity. Guazzoni continued from triumph to triumph, making a *Messalina* (1923) with a chariot race which was as good as that of the first *Ben Hur* (which was shot in Italy). Guazzoni's other titles range from *Fabiola* (1917) and a new version of *Gerusalemma Liberata* (1918) to *Il Sacco di Roma* (1920). But in 1922 there was a real 'sack of Rome' as the Fascists marched on the capital and forced the King to hand the government over to Mussolini. Some years were to pass before the Fascists got their grips on the cinema industry, but the decline of Italian films happened quickly during the 1920s. The last years of the silent film were dominated by the imported product, from America and Germany in particular. But the Italians could not let the film learn to speak without one last contribution to the costume spectacle cycle, and this could only be one subject: yet another version of Bulwer Lytton's *Last Days of Pompeii*, this time (1926) directed by Amleto Palermi (who in the same year in Germany made a film of Pirandello's *Henry IV* with CONRAD VEIDT in the title role). Co-director was Carmine Gallone, who was to become the leading specialist of the Italian spectaculars in the 1930s.

While the sound film was now arriving on the other side of the Atlantic, the two Italian directors who were to dominate the national cinema scene in the first decade of sound, ALESSANDRO BLASETTI and MARIO CAMERINI, were making their first important films – still silent however. Together with a group of friends who included Aldo Vergano, Umberto Barbaro and Mario Serandrei, Blasetti had founded a magazine in the late 1920s called 'Il Mondo dello Schermo' which aimed at encouraging an interest in the film as an art form. The same group of friends formed a film company, Augustus, which produced Blasetti's first film, *Sole (Sun)* (1929), with a script by Blasetti and Vergano, and Alessandrini as assistant director. It was a story about the reclamation of the marshes and waste lands south of Rome, one of the Fascist state's more successful achievements. But it was not yet a propaganda film and had some genuine qualities in the way it told how the reclamation was affecting life on the land. Visually the film had some beautiful sequences. Blasetti's first talkie was *Nerone* (1930), in which the most popular Italian stage comedian of the day, the Roman music hall artist and playwright Ettore

Petrolini, played the capricious emperor. The film was little more than a record of one of Petrolini's stage shows.

Blasetti then made what is still considered his greatest film, *1860* (1933), an astonishingly daring portrait of the Risorgimento period if one considers how fashionable the rhetorical vision of Italian history was then becoming. Lizzani has called *1860* 'the greatest Italian film made during the whole Fascist era'. But in the years that followed, Blasetti had to return to his 'professionalism', which included at least one film, *La Vecchia Guardia* (1934), which was blatantly apologetic for the régime. In his escapist pictures, such as *Ettore Fieramosca* (1938) Blasetti once again showed his worth. In 1941 he made *La Corona di Ferro*, set in mythological times. A Latin version of Germanic fables, the film is laughable today though it has a certain panache, and it is hard to find Blasetti's supposed 'pacifist message'. Perhaps its most notable achievement was that it launched a new star, the dazzlingly handsome young MASSIMO GIROTTI who a couple of years later (after some stage experience which improved his acting) was to play in *Ossessione*. Blasetti culminated this period with the film for which he is best known outside of Italy, *Four Steps in the Clouds* (1942), which some consider a precursor of neo-realism because it is a story of real people. Yet it belongs very much to the mood of the cinema of the 1930s. Gino Cervi's sensitive performance as the travelling salesman who is persuaded during a typical Italian bus journey to 'stand in' as lover for a country girl who has to explain her pregnancy to her simple-minded family, helped to make this survive as one of the most delightful Italian film comedies of all time.

The other director of the 1930s whose work can be considered as above average is MARIO CAMERINI. After working as a scriptwriter during the 'dark' 1920s and directing several insignificant films himself, the first of which was *Jolly* (1923), Camerini made a film on location in Africa, *Kiff Tebbi* (1927), which won him attention.

Camerini's first notable success was *Rotaie* (*Railway Tracks*, 1929), one of the last Italian silent films. While Blasetti was forming his group, Camerini had also been gathering around him a group of friends to form ADIA (Association of Italian Authors and Directors). Like the French film, *Hotel du Nord*, *Rotaie* begins with a couple entering a hotel with the intention of committing suicide, but the script by Corrado D'Errico was banal and the world depicted by Camerini was superficial and sentimentalized, with its Riviera life and casinos, the grand hotels and petit bourgeois dreams. However it had excellent photography by Ubaldo Arata, one of the top cameramen of Italian film history.

Talkies arrived in Italy in 1930, the first one entitled, appropriately enough, *La Canzone dell'Amore*, directed by Gennaro Righelli, a mediocre director who later in the 1930s will deserve mention only for having directed the first important films of MAGNANI. Camerini's first talkie was the Italian version of an international opus based on Conrad's *Dangerous Paradise: La Riva dei Bruti* (1930). The film which was really to establish Camerini's reputation and indeed to initiate a new school of Italian film-making, was *Uomini che mascalzoni!* (*What Rascals Men Are!*, 1932), a film which had the advantage of a script by Aldo de Benedetti and MARIO SOLDATI, two writers of considerable talent. Though the film is often cited as being the best of the 'white telephone' romantic comedies of the 1930s, perhaps because it was the first, it does not stand up so well to time. It did however introduce a new film star, a young stage actor named

Top: Clara Calamai and Massimo Girotti in 'Ossessione' (Luchino Visconti, 1942) Above: Adriana Benetti in 'Four Steps in the Clouds' (Alessandro Blasetti, 1942)

VITTORIO DE SICA. His acting was still that of an immature juvenile, though he was better here under Camerini's direction than in his next film, *Due Cuori Felici* (*Two Happy Hearts*, 1932), directed by Count Baldassare Negroni; in this De Sica played an American businessman visiting his Italian representative (complete with a phoney American accent and a musical number with an absurd English refrain, 'How Do You Do Mister Brown?').

De Sica was to find his happiest moment from the time when Camerini teamed him with Assia Norris in *Dariò un milione* (*I'll Give A Million*, 1935), with the first screen story written by CESARE ZAVATTINI. (Zavattini claims, however, that his story, *Buoni per un giorno*, got lost during the subsequent screenwriting and direction). That Camerini was no René Clair was proved by a rather un-funny costume comedy based on Alançon's 'Three-Cornered Hat': *Il Capello a Tre Punti* (1933), in which the great Neapolitan actor-playwright EDUARDO DE FILIPPO and his brother Peppino, in their first screen roles, seemed stiff and uncomfortable, obviously not guided by Camerini into developing their brilliant stage humour according to screen criteria.

Camerini's best film was *Il Signor Max* (1937), for which Soldati was assistant director and co-scriptwriter, and in which the couple De Sica-Norris were seen at their best. De Sica, in particular, here showed for the first time the real quality as an actor that makes it possible to believe the same man could later emerge as one of the world's greatest directors.

Most of the other films of the 1930s are best forgotten. Worth a mention however is *Acciaio* (*Steel*, 1933) made by the German documentarist WALTER RUTTMANN. In spite of a story by Pirandello scripted by Ruttmann with Soldati, and the casting of two real workers for important roles, the film is melodramatic. MARIO SOLDATI is one of the names most mentioned in the credit lists of the history of Italian films. He made 22 films between 1938 and 1958 but of these only one has survived in critical opinion, *Piccolo Mondo Antico* (1941), based on Fogazzaro's celebrated novel about the vicissitudes of a Lombard family during the last years of the hated Austrian rule in the mid-19th century. The film confirmed the promise of the young ALIDA VALLI who had made an impressive début as an ingenue in a mediocre film, *Mille lire al mese* (Max Neufeld, 1939) a typical product of the pseudo-Hungarian cinema which was the only real alternative permitted in these years of 'hot' fascism to grandiose war propaganda. Of the fascist films, the most famous is *Scipione l'Africano* (1937), which was angled at pointing a comparison between contemporary Italian conquests in Africa and those of Ancient Rome. The director was Carmine Gallone, 'official' director of the period, and needless to say the complicated system of state financing (which still survives today) found its ideal object for subsidy in films such as this, no matter how expensive they were.

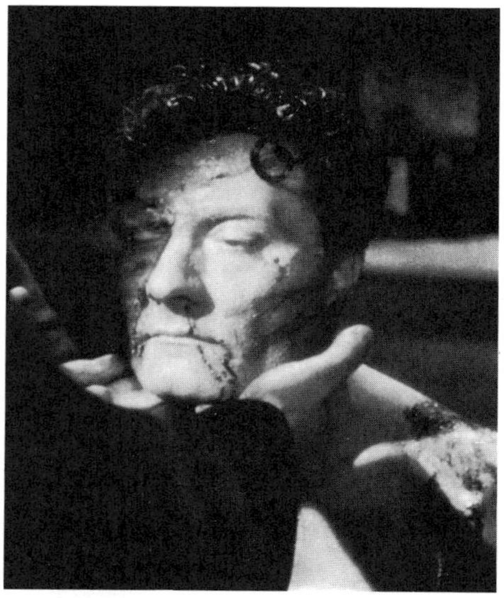

Above: Marcello Pagliero in 'Roma, Città Aperta' (Roberto Rossellini, 1945)
Below: Anna Magnani in the same film

The state film industry set up by Mussolini (whose son Vittorio took a personal interest in film-making) provided the basis of a system that has lasted till now. Unfortunately some of the political and bureaucratic catches, made for the convenience of the régime, have also survived. The showing of foreign films in their original language was forbidden, thus giving rise to the proliferous dubbing industry which, even if it has provided work for a whole category of actors who were not necessarily attractive or talented enough for the stage or screen, has also set a precedent which has made the Italians the laziest filmgoers in Europe.

Among some of the advantages that ensued from the Fascist concern for controlling what Lenin had prescribed for all totalitarian régimes as the most important of the arts, was the building of the Cine Città studios and the Istituto Luce (in whose vaults so much valuable footage has found refuge), as well as the film school, the Centro Sperimentale, where in addition to critics like Luigi Chiarini, its first director, and Umberto Barbaro, many of the important names of the Italian cinema were to find their first outlet, indeed their only one during the war-time period.

Another of the régime's notable inventions was the Venice Film Festival, the first of its kind. Founded by the Venetian nobleman Count Volpi, it was intended as a prestige tourist attraction for the Venice summer. But from the start it was called a *Mostra*, that is, an exhibition, and was essentially a feature of La Biennale. Naturally it soon became a showcase for the propaganda films of the Axis powers. At the first *Mostra*, in 1932, a blind eye was turned on such 'dangerous' foreign films as *A Nous la Liberté* (changed to *A Moi la Liberté* in Italy). But on the eve of Munich, while Britain sent *Pygmalion*, France *Quai des Brumes* and the USA *Snow White* and *The Prisoner of Zenda*, the Nazis showed off with LENI RIEFENSTAHL'S *Olympiad* and the Italians offered *Luciano Serra, Pilota*, an heroic air story directed by Goffredo Alessandrini and 'supervised' by Vittorio Mussolini himself.

With the Italian entry into the war in 1941, the patriotic mission of the Italian cinema became more accentuated, and the only alternative was the 'white telephone' comedy. And yet it was in the early 1940s that the first signs of a creative renaissance began to simmer underground. Names that were to become synonymous with a new kind of film-making were being heard. Count LUCHINO VISCONTI, the cousin of the Duke of Modrone, came from an aristocratic Milanese family. His mother was the heiress of an important pharmaceutical firm. He grew up in a Milan dominated by the social and artistic milieu of La Scala. In 1936 he had gone to France and by a stroke of luck managed to get a job working with JEAN RENOIR as assistant director on *Un Partie de Campagne* and *Les Bas Fonds*. Renoir then came to Italy to start a film of 'La Tosca', which he never finished (it was completed by Carl Koch). Visconti was again his assistant. Having moved to Rome, Visconti was mixing with the militant anti-fascist critics and film people who revolved around Barbaro at the Centro Sperimentale.

Visconti succeeded in setting up the production of *Ossessione* in 1942 even though its realistic treatment was not in line with the Fascist Ministry of Popular Culture. Cain's novel 'The Postman Always Rings Twice' seemed to the censors an ordinary enough story of adultery. In Visconti's hands it was transformed and became a story of real people in a particular social environment. Clara Calamai and GIROTTI as the lovers, Juan de Landa as the husband, and Elio Marcuzzo as the ambiguous Spagnuolo, all gave performances which already indicated that Visconti was a director who knew how to get the most from his performers.

The film was hardly seen in Italy in the years after it was made. On seeing the finished film, the censors realized that its undercurrent of individualism went against the strain of nationalistic sentiment which fascist cinema was supposed to promote. Stylistically influenced by RENOIR, Visconti nevertheless introduced a personal vision which was to become distinctive of his own brand of realism.

Vittorio De Sica's growing maturity as an actor now prompted him to try his hand behind the camera. Though producers were sceptical, they let him direct *Due Dozzine di Rose Scarlatte* (1940) on condition, of course, that he acted in it himself. It was a sophisticated comedy in the 1930s vein, scripted by De Benedetti from his successful stage play. Three other comedies followed, all however revealing De Sica's growing interest in the human condition. He played only a small part himself in his second film, *Un Garibaldino in Convento* (1942), and in the same year finally succeeded in convincing a production company, Scalera, to let him direct without acting in *I Bambini ci Guardano* (*The Children Are Watching Us*, 1942–3), in which he worked for the first time as director with ZAVATTINI. In order to make this picture De Sica had to agree to act in another film for Scalera. Anticipating the sensitivity with which he was to show the grown-up world in relation to the children of post-war Italy, in *I Bambini ci Guardano* he looks at the theme of an adulterous triangle through the eyes of the child of the married couple. His was not a moralistic attitude but simply one of human compassion.

While the Germans were in Rome, De Sica was in danger of being sent to Germany to make a film. Goebbels knew about his work and admired him. But in order to get out of accepting this 'compliment', he had let himself become involved in the making of a film which did not interest him, *La Porta del Cielo* (1944) about a pilgrimage to the Loreto sanctuary. He was thus able to inform Dr Goebbels that he could not move from Rome as he was 'making a film for the Vatican'.

The fall of Mussolini, the Nazi occupation of Rome, the establishment of Mussolini's short-lived Salo Republic in the North and the liberation of Rome by the Allies in 1944, inevitably interrupted normal film-making activity. But out of the moral and economic ruins of the film world, and not only the film world (the Cine Città studios were being used as a camp for displaced persons), a new phoenix was arising. The Italians themselves did not know it, but neo-realism was having its birth pains.

Though rumblings of the approach of a new age in film-making for Italians had been heard before Mussolini was forced from power, and though many critics have suggested that neo-realism is a mood of film-making if not a method, beginning with the films De Sica or VISCONTI or even BLASETTI made in the early 1940s, the facts are different. One film and one only can be credited with the birth of neo-realism, as Method and as Content, and that is *Roma, Città Aperta* (*Open City*, 1945) directed by ROBERTO ROSSELLINI.

Rossellini had collaborated with De Robertis on some of the pseudo-heroic war films and had directed one himself, *Un pilota ritorna* (1943). After Mussolini's fall and the occupation of Rome by the Nazis, he felt the urge to make a film about the experiences they were all living through at that moment in 1944. It was to have been a documentary about Don Morosini, a priest who had been shot by the Germans as being responsible for organizing a band of teenage saboteurs. A small sum of money was found to finance it but this soon ran out. The long winter of 1944–5, with the Allies still moving slowly up the peninsula towards Rome, left Rossellini in difficulties. Bits of film were found here and there. Scenes were shot secretly while the Germans were still in the streets outside.

Finally, after the Liberation, the film was completed. With the scriptwriter SERGIO AMIDEI, the other screenplay collaborator FEDERICO FELLINI (in his first film job) and the popular Roman players of the day ANNA MAGNANI and Aldo Fabrizi, Rossellini had made the first real co-operative film.

It was a way of making films which was to influence not only the post-war generation of film-makers in Italy and in many other countries, but also generations to come. Rossellini was to become Maestro of GODARD, TRUFFAUT and the French *nouvelle vague* in the 1960s. Rossellini's knack for improvisation (of which Italians are past masters) gave truth to the stories he was telling: the very crudeness of some of the technique was itself a guarantee of sincerity to audiences brought up on the polished Hollywood product of the type of *Mrs Miniver*.

'Paisà' (Roberto Rossellini, 1946)

In 1945 the film industry was in ruins, literally. In that same year as *Open City*, most of the films had titles like *O Sole Mio* or *Torna a Sorrento*. Camerini made a brave attempt to adapt himself to the new situation with a delightful little tale, *Due Lettere Anonime* (1945), with Clara Calamai, the actress of *Ossessione*. The film was in a sense a bridge between the cinema of the 1930s and that which was emerging in the late 1940s. Unfortunately, it was to remain an isolated example for Camerini, whose name subsequently disappears from the annals of serious film-making.

Rossellini followed up *Open City* with an equally important work, *Paisà* (1946), which for all the naivety of certain episodes (above all those set in Sicily and Florence, and the somewhat coy Fellini influence on the episode of the American priests) was a notable contribution to the development of the neo-realist movement, and an inspiration to the young directors who were groping their way to the surface. The final episode in the Po marshes is still one of Rossellini's greatest achievements.

1946 was to be the big year of neo-realism. De Sica made his *Sciuscià* (*Shoeshine*, 1946), a film which did scarcely any business in Italy, where the new American films – and those not seen during the war years – were flooding the market and satisfying the tastes of the escapist mood of the times. Later, after its success abroad, *Sciuscià* was to return to Italian cinemas.

At the same time Aldo Vergano made *Il Sole Sorge Ancora* (*The Sun Still Rises*, 1946). Though he had worked as a scriptwriter throughout the 1930s, starting with *Sole,* as a director Vergano is now remembered only for this impressive Resistance story in which he had DE SANTIS and LIZZANI as collaborators, while GILLO PONTECORVO was among the actors.

ALBERTO LATTUADA also emerged that year with *Il Bandito* (1946). Lattuada had made his first film during the war, *Giacomo l'Idealista* (1942), based on a 19th-century novel by De Marchi. After many other projects fell through, due to objections by the fascist ministry for either political or commercial reasons, Lattuada's second film was *La freccia nel fianco* (1944). *Il Bandito* put him immediately in the front rank with the directors of the new generation. During the years to follow, Lattuada will often be able to claim that he had been the first to tackle certain subjects or to launch new talent. In *Il Bandito* he was the first to deal with the problem of the rehabilitation of the men who had been educated to kill in wartime and, on finding that society had nothing positive to offer them in peacetime, decide to carry on killing as a full-time occupation. In this film, as in his next, *Senza Pietà* (1948), Lattuada revealed a sound professionalism which even if it went against the fashion of the time, was to prove a distinctive feature in his career. His sensitive handling of topical themes kept him within the neo-realist orbit, even if perhaps his most distinguished films remain historical subjects, beginning with his adaptation of Riccardo Bacchelli's rambling novel, *Il Mulino del Po* (1949).

Above: 'Shoeshine' (Vittorio De Sica, 1946)
Below: 'The Sun Still Rises' (Aldo Vergano, 1946)

Italian critics, especially those inspired by the Marxist thinkers from Barbaro to Aristarco, were inclined to be sceptical of formalistic film-making; directors such as Lattuada and RENATO CASTELLANI are not always given their just dues. Castellani had worked with Camerini, Soldati and Blasetti. After *Un colpo di pistola* (1941), a brilliant exercise in style almost *à la* Truffaut, he too found his mark in the hey-day of neo-realism with *Mio Figlio Professore* (1946), a sentimental but amusing vehicle for Fabrizi, and above all with *Sotto il sole di Roma* (1947). Because he showed the lighter side of human suffering, he was to be accused of contributing towards the decline of rigid neo-realist tradition, particularly for his subsequent film, *Due Soldi di Speranza* (1951).

LUIGI ZAMPA made three films between 1946 and 1948 which are among the most famous of the whole neo-realist movement. Two of these, *Vivere in pace* (*To Live In Peace*, 1946) and *L'onorevole, Angelina* (1947), are more appreciated outside Italy perhaps because their depiction of 'eternal Italian qualities' seems too familiar on home ground. The third film, *Anni Difficili (The Difficult Years*, 1948), for which Zampa had as script collaborator one of Italy's best contemporary writers, the Sicilian, Vitaliano Brancati, was indeed the first profound attempt to enquire into what had made the great mass of Italian people accept fascism. Some years later, Zampa was to make *Anni Facili* (*The Easy Years*, 1953), also scripted by Brancati, in which bureaucracy and the problems of making an honest living in a democratic society, were the themes that anticipated a whole school of Italian comedy (the GASSMAN genre of the 1960s).

Younger directors who were emerging in those first post-war years included GIUSEPPE DE SANTIS, who succeeded in combining a sincere left-wing approach to social problems with an inherent natural Italian flair for melodrama. This promised well in *Caccia Tragica* (1947) and found its most perfect expression in *Riso Amaro* (*Bitter Rice*, 1949) which is a landmark in the post-war Italian cinema for several reasons. On the one hand because it launched the first Italian female pin-up and international cover girl, Silvana Mangano, as well as two leading male stars, Raf Vallone and VITTORIO

Above: 'Sotto il Sole di Roma' (Renato Castellani, 1948)
Below: 'Il Mulino del Po' (Alberto Lattuada, 1949)

Above: Umberto Spadaro in 'Anni Difficili' (Luigi Zampa, 1948)
Below: Silvana Mangano (centre) in 'Bitter Rice' (Giuseppe De Santis, 1949)

GASSMAN; but no less important, though perhaps closely connected, was the fact that *Bitter Rice* was a box-office success, both at home and abroad, a rare event in those years for neo-realist films.

In the years to come, De Santis was to make many more films but he was certainly one of those directors who on a creative level did not survive the first impulses of neo-realism. PIETRO GERMI, on the other hand, whose early films, though always interesting, above all *In Nome della Legge* (1949), did not put him into the front rank, was to make his best films in his mature years. Politically less *engagé* than some of his colleagues, Germi nevertheless touched on social problems, even if *Il Camino della Speranza* (*The Way of Hope*, 1950), his most famous film of the first period, dealt very sentimentally and superficially with the problem of the Sicilian emigrants looking for work in the North.

Rossellini's decline had meanwhile set in with two films, *Germania Anno Zero* (1947), in which he tried with only partial success to apply his method to the German scene, and *Amore* (1947). His improvised style of film-making began to show itself inadequate when the subject-matter required deeper psychological analysis rather than emotional spontaneous observation. De Sica, on the other hand, was achieving maturity and with *Ladri di biciclette* (*Bicycle Thieves*, 1948) he made a film which stands alongside *Open City* as a true masterpiece of neo-realist film-making. Now master of the medium, De Sica's only problem was finding finance for the abundance of post-war themes which he and Zavattini found glaring at them, waiting to be filmed.

Luchino Visconti, who had been silent in films since *Ossessione*, now embarked on a project which was intended to be a film trilogy embracing the three sides of Sicilian working-class life: fishing, zinc mining and farming. He only shot one episode, but this resulting film, *La Terra Trema* (1948), is a complete work in itself. It was laughed at and booed by the sophisticated audience at the 1948 Venice Film Festival (when OLIVIER's *Hamlet* won the Golden Lion) – partly for political reasons, but also because its meandering three hours of beautiful images photographed by G. R. ALDO and its Sicilian dialect language made it hard-going for the average film-goer. *La Terra Trema* nevertheless soon found its admirers and gradually came to be considered the film in which neo-realist content and formalistic qualities found their happiest encounter. In Italy the film was shown dubbed into Italian and cut. It had little commercial success. Only many years later did the full original version begin to circulate.

With the new affluence that began to show itself in Italy in the early 1950s and the Cold War which spread from the international scene to domestic politics, it became more and more difficult for the socialist-minded directors to continue their social battles. The decline of neo-realism was very rapid. Rossellini's *Stromboli* (1949) was a grotesquely naive attempt to return to his spontaneous nerve centre – INGRID BERGMAN was as uncomfortable in the Italian setting as the character she played in the film, a Swedish woman who had married a husky young Mediterranean fisherman. But shortly afterwards Rossellini did find another flash of inspiration: an unpretentious and sincere interpretation of some of Saint Francis's 'little flowers', *Francesco, Giullare di Dio* (*Francis, God's Jester*, 1950). BLASETTI, who had challenged the trends of the time but at least been coherent to himself by making the historical extravaganza *Fabiola* (1948) in the full climate of the 1940s, came late to neo-realism with *Prima Comunione* (1951), a not very successful attempt to return to the mood of his enchanting *Four Steps*. LUCIANO EMMER had made his name

Above: 'Bicycle Thieves' (Vittorio De Sica, 1948)
Below: 'La Terra Trema' (Luchino Visconti, 1948)

with a series of documentaries on art subjects, made in collaboration with Enrico Gras. His first feature was *Domenica d'Agosto* (1949), a charming comedy about Roman bank holiday trippers. Full of clichés about Roman noisiness and gluttony, it naturally had a great success abroad. It also introduced film-goers to a new star, MARCELLO MASTROIANNI. Subsequently, Emmer never really made his mark.

The Neapolitan actor-dramatist EDUARDO DE FILIPPO, the only true genius that the Italian stage has produced since Pirandello, brought to the screen one of his best plays of the post-war period which he had been acting in with his brother Peppino and his sister Titina. This was *Napoli Milionaria* (1950), in which he divided his own stage role in two so that one of the best scenes of the play could be given to the greatest Neapolitan comic of this century, TOTO (stage name for Antonio De Durtis. Perhaps only in this film and in his last roles – under PASOLINI's direction – did Toto find parts worthy of his great comic gifts; however, during the post-war years he appeared regularly in anything up to five films a year, usually parodies of topical themes.)

In the years of neo-realism isolated figures emerge and disappear. One such was Curzio Malaparte, an ambiguously iconoclastic author, whose one film, *Cristo Proibito* (1950), had certain formalistic qualities and managed to capture a certain atmosphere of Tuscan religious folklore. On the whole, though, it was pretentious and rang false. Important débuts were however already established before the last cries of neo-realism had died out. MICHELANGELO ANTONIONI had collaborated on the script of *Caccia Tragica*, among other feature films. After his documentaries, many of which (such as *Gente del Po*) certainly belong to the neo-realist mind, he made his feature début as director with *Cronaca di un amore* (1950), in which his own individualist traits were already apparent, in spite of the exterior background that might have seemed 'realistic' at first glance. Neo-realism was fixing its sights on the bourgeois world of the new, 'miraculous' Italy.

Meanwhile LATTUADA, unable to realize some of his cherished projects, joined forces with FELLINI and their respective actress wives, Carla del Poggio and GIULIETTA MASINA, to make a film about the world of provincial music-halls, with which Fellini in particular was familiar (having worked for a while on those stages with Fabrizi). The film was *Luci del varietà* (*Variety Lights*, 1950). Both directors must share equally the credit for this film, which was genuinely a co-operative effort, though Lattuada can put a feather in his cap for having helped to launch the man who was destined to become Italy's most famous director.

By 1951, when Castellani had made his *Due Soldi di Speranza*, the climate was such that very little serious film-making could now be envisaged. Fellini and Antonioni had made their first films, but they were going to suffer endless disappointments before making their next. The scriptwriter of Castellani's film, Ettore Margadonna, was in fact to write the script of *Pane, Amore e Fantasia* (1953) and its even more successful sequel, *Pane, Amore e Gelosia*, directed by LUIGI COMENCINI. These films starring the Lollobrigida-De Sica team were to take Italian films once again to the top of the box-office stakes. GINA LOLLOBRIGIDA was a symbol of the new Italy that was emerging, a product of the craze for covering up the country's poverty with a glamorous gloss. De Sica had no other choice but to reconcile himself to the idea that maybe his rebirth as a popular actor, now the mature lover, might help him to find finance for the films he still wanted to make. The film that he had made 'to please Zavattini', *Miracolo a Milano* (1950), had won a prize at Cannes, but in Italy it had once again been considered too Italian (*sic*). Leaving aside the perhaps not very successful trick shots in the last sequence, the film was however unusual for Italian film comedy, combining Zavattini's whimsical Emilian brand of humour with De Sica's joy in human observation. It was the closest that the Italians ever got to a RENÉ CLAIR genre. Zavattini returned the compliment to De Sica by writing *Umberto D.* (1952), the film which might safely be described as the closing chapter in the neo-realist movement. Derided in Italy (and not only by Ministers and the Establishment but also by many 'progressive' critics who found its individualistic, personal image of an old age pensioner too detached from the more general social problem raised by the theme), De Sica was certainly asking for trouble by insisting on casting an old university professor for the part of Umberto. Maybe he was seeking someone who resembled his own father, to whom the film is dedicated, but certainly the choice did not help to render the old man sympathetic to audiences. True however to the principles that had imbued the whole neo-realist idea, De Sica went ahead and made the film the way he wanted it. In a way it was to be his swan song, for many years were to pass, even decades, before he made a film with such sincerity. At the Italian Film Week in London in 1954, as the Italians proudly showed off Lollo's breast measurements and the 'happy face' of the new Italian commercial cinema (rags yes, but with a smile and a song), De Sica, who was present in London as Lollo's partner, slipped away and showed his *Umberto D.* to the critics, as he was later to show it privately in Hollywood to Chaplin and a group of the latter's friends. On both occasions, he found hard-faced, unmovable people dabbing their eyes and after recovering their breaths overwhelming him with praise. It was vindication against that government under-secretary who had accused him of

'washing Italy's dirty linen in public'. But it was going to have to last him a very long time.

The 1950s began with the first films of Antonioni (*Cronaca di un amore*) and of Fellini *Lo Sceicco Bianco* (1952). After the success of the film he had made in collaboration with Lattuada, Fellini was asked by the producer Luigi Rovere to direct a script which Antonioni was originally going to direct. The story of *The White Sheik,* a charming comedy about a young provincial married couple and their honeymoon in Rome where the bride becomes involved in the world of the *fumetti*, the Italian pulp magazine stories, was by Antonioni, Fellini and Pinelli. Tullio Pinelli and Ennio Flaiano then wrote the screen play with Fellini. They were to remain two of his most faithful collaborators until *Giulietta degli Spiriti*.

But for both Fellini and Antonioni, in spite of the praise they had received from the critics, finding a producer was not easy at a moment when, following the death of neo-realism, the industry was demanding box-office guarantees that might repeat the successes of the *Bread, Love* genre of 'rosy realism'. Indeed, after *I Vitelloni* (1953) Fellini had hoped to make a sequel in which he showed what happened to Moraldo-Fellini when he arrived in Rome. We had to wait until *La Dolce Vita* and *Roma* to follow that up. But he was lucky in one respect. He did find a producer who was prepared to let him film a story he had written for his wife, Giulietta Masina.

The producer was DINO DE LAURENTIIS and the film was *La Strada* (1954). De Laurentiis was then in partnership with CARLO PONTI, but each was soon to go his own way. After the success of *Bitter Rice* De Laurentiis had married its star, Mangano. Though orientated towards

Above: 'Nettezza Urbana' (Michelangelo Antonioni, 1948)
Below: Lina Gennari and Carlo Battisti in 'Umberto D' (Vittorio De Sica, 1952)

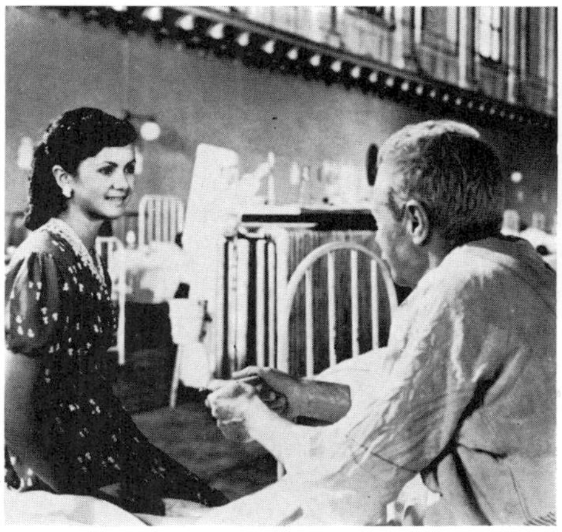

the big-time career as a tycoon in the Hollywood sense, De Laurentiis still liked to have the prestige of being associated with films of artistic commitment. As a sentimental Neapolitan he was acute enough to realize that *La Strada* would appeal to the tear-jerker public. The film was the centre of controversy at the 1954 Venice Festival when the Left took sides against Fellini in favour of Visconti, whose *Senso* (1954) was being derided by the Establishment. As so often happens in Italy, politics were taking precedence over creative criteria. In this particular case, it meant that *La Strada* was undervalued by the Italian critics, though it won a Silver Lion and *Senso* got nothing. As in 1948, Visconti had once again been beaten by a Shakespearean film, this time an Italian one, *Romeo and Juliet* (1954), made by RENATO CASTELLANI, with LAURENCE HARVEY as Romeo.

The way in which *Senso* was received was indicative of the local Cold War. After the hostile reception in Venice, the film was kept on ice for several months and then finally came out with further cuts and dialogue changes.

Making the film of one's choice became more and more difficult in those years. CARLO LIZZANI, a militant left-wing critic and scriptwriter, found one solution by forming a co-operative with workers' associations to make his first film as a director, a partisan story, *Achtung, Banditi!* (1951). ZAVATTINI meanwhile was trying to keep neo-realism alive, and founded what he called a 'cinematic newspaper'. The resulting film, *Amore in città* (1953), had episodes by Antonioni, Fellini, LATTUADA, Lizzani, DINO RISI, and Zavattini himself.

Meanwhile Rossellini was trying to explore the depths of incommunicability in advance of Antonioni, with *Viaggio in Italia* (1953), another clumsy film, with embarrassing English dialogue and bad acting by BERGMAN and GEORGE SANDERS. Antonioni himself was having

Above: Massimo Girotti and Lucia Bosé in 'Cronaca di un Amore' (Michelangelo Antonioni, 1950)
Below: Alberto Sordi in 'Lo Sceicco Bianco' ('The White Sheik', Federico Fellini, 1952)

a hard time finding backing. Two years after *Cronaca*, he succeeded in making a three-episode film, *I Vinti* (1952). Antonioni had difficulties with the French episode for reasons of libel, and with the Italian episode for reasons of censorship. But it was not for these reasons that he seemed more at home in England with the episode which featured Fay Compton and Peter Reynolds. Antonioni found an affinity with the British scene, which years later he was to turn to again so successfully.

Meanwhile, in addition to the episode *Attempted Suicide* of *Amore in città*, Antonioni then made *La Signora senza camelie* (1952–3), which was to be surrounded with controversy. He had originally wanted Lollobrigida to play the role of the beauty queen turned actress but La Lollo turned it down, finding the script offensive to her 'honour'. The part was played instead by Lucia Bosé.

De Sica, whose new come-back as an actor had in fact been inaugurated thanks to his appearances in the *Bread, Love* films and in BLASETTI's *Altri Tempi*, also with Lollobrigida (at her best, it must be said), seemed to be becoming a sort of Jekyll and Hyde at this point, for he still kept up his activity as a 'serious' director, even if his projects with Zavattini did not always see the light of day. For his next film he chose La Lollo's up and coming rival, SOPHIA LOREN, giving the young Neapolitan beauty discovered by Carlo Ponti her best role to date as the pizza-seller in *L'Oro di Napoli* (1954). The film itself was something of a compromise between the Zavattini-De Sica style of looking at reality and the more popular 'rags with a smile' genre that had been launched with the *Bread, Love* films. The most typically Zavattini-De Sica episode of the film, *The Little Funeral*, about the poor Neapolitan mother who wanted a first-class funeral for her dead baby, significantly enough, was cut from the version of the film which circulated in Italy. A year or so later, Loren was to be teamed with De Sica the actor in the third of the *Bread, Love* films, *Pane, Amore e . . .* (1956), this time directed by DINO RISI, a former doctor, who shortly afterwards launched a new genre of 'rosy realism' with the comedy *Poveri ma belli* (*Poor but Handsome*, 1956) in which Maurizio Arena and Renato Salvatori, two young men with good looks but little acting experience, were offered as beefcake alternatives to the Lorens and Lollos. The popularity of Arena was to last for only a few seasons, while Salvatori was wise enough to study acting and, thanks to working with Visconti and to his marriage with Annie Girardot, was later to win a niche for himself amongst the younger generation of Italian actors, even at times being allowed to dub his own voice in post-synchronization.

Above: Alida Valli and Farley Granger in 'Senso' (Luchino Visconti, 1954)

Below: Anthony Quinn in 'La Strada' (Federico Fellini, 1954)

Half way through the 1950s the industry really began to build the foundations of Hollywood-on-the-Tiber. Titanus had made a considerable profit on the home market with the *Bread, Love* films, as well as with a series of soap operas in the old Italian manner. The Titanus chief, Goffredo Lombardo, felt ready to launch out towards the international market and maintain a production of prestige pictures. Unfortunately, he was not always lucky. His backing of Fellini's *Il bidone* (1955) did not repeat the success of *La Strada*. De Laurentiis had started his big international programme with *Ulysses* (1954), starring KIRK DOUGLAS, and he was preparing the way for his first colossal, *War and Peace* (1956), directed by KING VIDOR with a predominantly international cast. In order to sign up AUDREY HEPBURN and Mel Ferrer, who were considering an offer to do the same film for MIKE TODD, De Laurentiis used all his instinctive Neapolitan flair for the imbroglio.

He also continued his prestige side-line support for the 'artistic' directors, backing a new Fellini film written for Giulietta Masina, *Le Notti di Cabiria* (1957), in which Fellini called in as script collaborator the poet PIER PAOLO PASOLINI, who was an expert on the life of the Rome underworld, its pimps and prostitutes.

New directors were emerging in rapid succession. VALERIO ZURLINI had made a promising first film based on a Pratolini novel, *Le Ragazze di San Frediano* (1954). The same author and setting (Florence) were to provide LIZZANI with the subject for his best film, *Cronache di Poveri Amanti* (1953). Franco Rossi, a director who has always been strictly a professional craftsman, did however make one film which won him recognition at home and abroad, *Amici per la pelle* (1955). MAURO BOLOGNINI had gone straight from the Centro Sperimentale to work as assistant to ZAMPA on several films, including this director's most interesting film of that period, *Processo alla civetta* (1957), *Giovanni Mariti* (1957) and *La* boiler, *Ci troviamo in galleria* (1953), but his first really interesting work was *Gli innamorati* (1955), a story of young Romans somewhat less glamorized than in RISI's 'Poor but Handsome' series. Later in the 1950s Bolognini was also to get a hand from Pasolini on the scripting of films set against the youth scene, in *Marisa la civetta* (1957), *Giovani Mariti* (1957) and *La Notte Brava* (1959), the latter being undoubtedly Bolognini's best film of the early period and one which anticipated the world of Pasolini imminent by now as a director. Others making their débuts at this time included FRANCESCO MASELLI, who made a very favourable impression at the Venice Festival with his first film *Gli Sbandati* (1955). Though Maselli's second film *La donna del giorno* (1956) also won him a festival prize (at Karlovy Vary) he never really lived up to the promise he had shown in that first work. Antonio Pietrangeli also made a promising first film *Il sole negli occhi* (1953); during a prolific career which included many strictly commercial chores, he made many films full of interesting observation, particularly on the Roman background. The best of his early films was *Lo Scapolo* (1956), which was one of the few serious films featuring ALBERTO SORDI. Sordi had given the best of himself in Fellini's first two films, but had become the most popular Italian male star on the home market of these years in films of purely local appeal.

PIETRO GERMI had meanwhile entered into his middle phase as a director, now also appearing in front of the camera. Both in *Il Ferroviere* (1954) and *L'Uomo di Paglia* (1957), Germi's impassive, unemotional physical presence lent an air of human reality to characters that were on paper very fictional. Perhaps his best film of this period was one in which he once again played the lead himself, *Un maledétto imbroglio* (1959), a thriller of unusually clever construction, adapted rather loosely from a classic of contemporary Italian literature, Gadda's 'That Ugly Mess on Via Merulano'. The film was to lead Germi towards new directions, the social satire of his third phase.

Antonioni meanwhile continued his exploration of a world in which feelings were gradually being crushed under the weight of modern society. From the elegant refinement of *Le Amiche* (1955), faithful to the spirit of Cesare Pavese's stories, he moved to *Il Grido* (1956–7), the hauntingly beautiful return to the world of the Po valley (which he had captured in his early documentary) in a story where for once he turned his eye from bourgeois society to that of a working class character. Then came the step which was to confirm him as one of the leading directors in the world – *L'Avventura* (1959). He and his cameraman Aldo Scavarda, his actress MONICA VITTI, and all the others associated with the enterprise truly made this film with the faith of people who believe that what they are doing is worth any sacrifice. Endless production difficulties, technical problems of shooting under hazardous and ever-changing weather conditions, the purely material problems of keeping alive as finance ran out again and again, produced *L'Avventura* which, with its concentration on atmosphere and emotion at the expense of conventional plotting, became a landmark in the history of the cinema.

Top: Anita Ekberg in 'La Dolce Vita' (Federico Fellini, 1959)
Above: Dominique Blanchar, Lelio Lutazzi, Gabriele Ferzetti and Esmeralda Ruspoli in 'L'Avventura' (Michelangelo Antonioni, 1959)
Below: 'Le Amiche' (Michelangelo Antonioni, 1955)

As the 1950s ended, Antonioni was fully launched and was already making his subsequent film, *La Notte* (1960). FELLINI had meanwhile turned once again to his sequel to Moraldo's adventures and the young man from the provinces turned into a Via Veneto journalist, impersonated, if not immortalized, by MASTROIANNI, whose sensitivity as an actor was at last beginning to be appreciated after years of being relegated to roles of the 'nice chap next door' in a series of Roman comedies. It had not been easy for Fellini to set up the production of *La Dolce Vita* (1959) and he had in fact come to the parting of the ways with De Laurentiis because the latter wanted an American star to play the lead, whereas Fellini could see only Mastroianni in the role. Finally, encouraged by Neapolitan producer Peppino Amato, whose one really great contribution to film history this was to prove, Angelo Rizzoli, the Milanese publisher and producer, was begrudgingly persuaded to back the film. Rizzoli's most successful productions till then had been the *Don Camillo* series. Needless to say he was never to regret his backing of Fellini as a business man though on a private level he often admitted that he never really understood what the film was about. Its enormous commercial success was certainly helped at the start by the air of scandal which was created around it, thanks also to a hasty condemnation by the editor of the Vatican newspaper. It was one of the great ironies of cinema history that whereas Fellini had set out to show how dull and empty was the *dolce vita*, the whole world was to believe that the film revealed a modern Rome more corrupt and orgy-ridden than that of Nero. The film is undoubtedly one of the most penetrating and authentic portraits of a particular historical moment that the medium is ever likely to produce.

The latest fad in Italian film-making at that time was a return to the muscle-man adventures of Maciste, launched by director Pietro Francisci with *Le fatiche di Ercole* (1957), in which an American named Steve Reeves flexed his muscles as Hercules. The first of these Hercules films were photographed by Mario Bava, who was later to direct some excellent spectaculars himself, as well as some thrillers. The Hercules films were bought very cheaply by the American producer JOE LEVINE. He then spent a million dollars to launch them in the States, with profitable results, thus prompting the Italians to overproduce a whole series of mediocre pictures on mythological themes with muscle boys picked up in gymnasiums on both sides of the Atlantic.

A more significant new genre was launched by MARIO MONICELLI, who after directing many comedies in collaboration with Steno, had started directing on his own with *Le Infedeli* (1953). The film which was to establish him as a master of Italian comedy was *I Soliti Ignoti* (1958) in which, in addition to Mastroianni and Toto, the comic gifts of VITTORIO GASSMAN were unleashed on a willing Italian public. Until then Gassman had been known either as a dramatic actor (his Hamlet was considered the best of the generation) or as a romantic lead (in several second-rate Hollywood films during the period when he was married to SHELLEY WINTERS). His comic versatility was even more evident in Monicelli's subsequent film, *La Grande Guerra* (1959), in which his Milanese soldier of World War One was matched by Alberto Sordi's now familiar Roman characterization. Monicelli's film caused the inevitable rumpus amongst the military establishment who once again felt that the honour of the Italian armed forces had been offended. There was also criticism of Rossellini, who, after a long and rather dull documentary about *India* (1959), had returned to the theme of war in *Il Generale della Rovere* (1959), in which DE SICA played the role of an actor imitating a general in order to carry out an imbroglio, and then accepting to die before a firing squad through an unexpected quirk of fate.

Producers were meanwhile encouraging the new directors. Titanus gave ZURLINI the chance to make one of his best films, *L'Estate Violenta* (1959), set like Maselli's *Sbandati* against the background of an Italian bourgeois family during the tragic summer of 1943. FRANCO CRISTALDI had founded a film company called Vides which was to distinguish itself by finding new names, both players and director. Among the actresses launched by Cristaldi were CLAUDIA CARDINALE, whom he was later to marry, and Rosanna Schiaffino, who was later to marry another producer, Alfredo Bini; among the actors was Giuliano Gemma, destined to become one of the most popular stars of Italian Westerns; among the directors launched by Cristaldi were ELIO PETRI with *L'Assassino* (1961) and FRANCESCO ROSI, who had been assistant to Visconti on *La Terra Trema, Senso* and *Bellissima*. Rosi had previously helped out Gassman on the film which the latter directed of his stage appearance in the Dumas-Sartre *Kean*, and had finished Alessandrini's not very fortunate film about Anita Garibaldi. His true début was with *La Sfida* (1958), a stunning film about the Neapolitan fruit market cammòrah, vaguely inspired by a real life story, with the 16-year-old Rosanna Schiaffino as the heroine. Rosi's film won him the award for the Best First Film at the 1959 Venice Festival. A somewhat less promising début was that of another of Visconti's former assistants, FRANCO ZEFFIRELLI, who at about the same time made his first film, *Camping* (1958), an artless little comedy in the 'rosy realism' manner. We were to have to wait another decade for Zeffirelli to make his 'official' début with more artistic potential.

The Maestro himself, VISCONTI, after the not altogether fortunate interlude of *Le Notti Bianche* (1957), notable only for its visual qualities and for Mastroianni's impressive acting, was now engaged in the making of his most significant contemporary film since *La Terra Trema*. This was *Rocco e i suoi fratelli*, (1960), the film which, alongside *La Dolce Vita*

Above: Sophia Loren in 'Two Women' (Vittorio De Sica, 1961)
Below: Marcello Mastroianni and Daniela Rocca in 'Divorzio all'Italiana' (Pietro Germi, 1961)

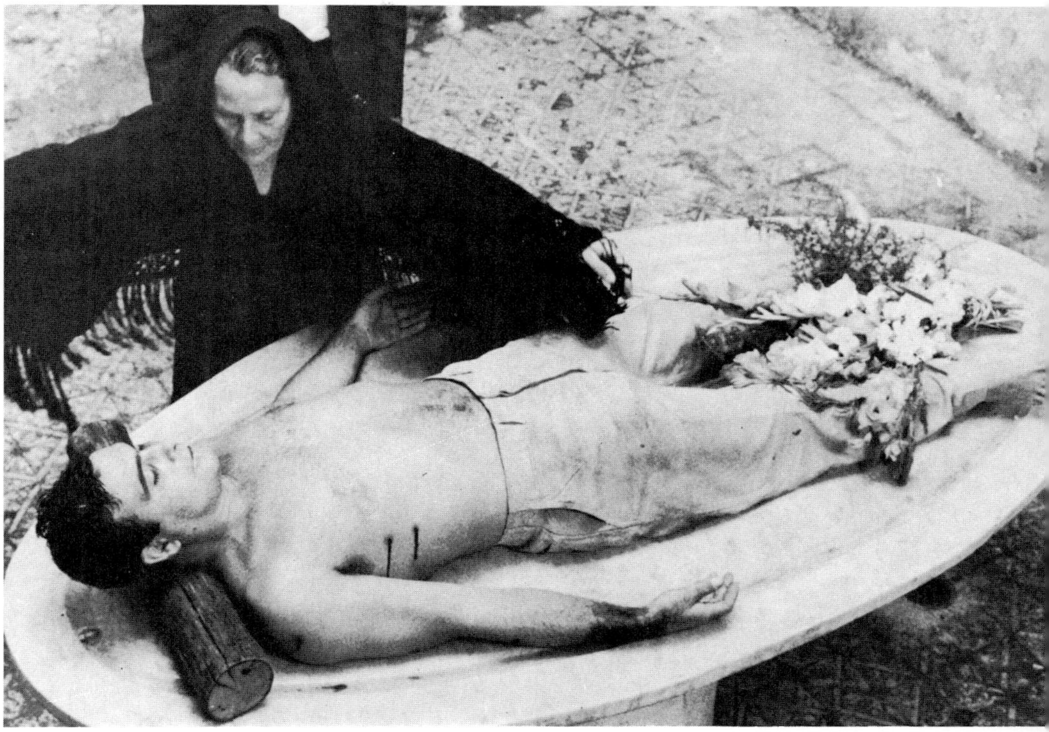

Above: Pietro Cammarata in 'Salvatore Giuliano' (Francesco Rosi, 1961)
Below: Alain Delon and Monica Vitti in 'L'Eclisse' (Michelangelo Antonioni, 1962)

and *L'Avventura,* was to indicate that even if Hollywood-on-the-Tiber was doing its best to crush creative impulses, the Italian Cinema could offer itself to the 1960s with an artistic face lift which was to inspire a whole new generation of film-makers, and not only in Italy.

The 1960–1 season was certainly the most fertile that the Italian cinema has seen in its history. Apart from the triumphs of the 'Big Three', Antonioni, Fellini and Visconti, there were many other achievements which were far from being secondary in importance. DE SICA found a momentary resurrection with his filming of Moravia's novel *La Ciociara (Two Women),* for which LOREN was to win an Academy Award (the second Italian actress to do so, after ANNA MAGNANI who won it for *The Rose Tattoo*). GERMI found a new lease of life with the beginning of his third phase, which was the internationally successful *Divorzio all'Italiana* (1960), in which Mastroianni doubled the reputation he was already winning for himself thanks to the Fellini film. Rosi more than fulfilled the promise shown with *La Sfida* and with the less interesting but still remarkable *I Magliari* (1959) by making his masterpiece, *Salvatore Giuliano* (1961), the best of the many films about Italian banditry and its political tie-ups. Antonioni had begun the season with the splendid *La Notte* (1960) and ended it with the controversial but fascinating *L'Eclisse* (1961). Here his exasperated slant on how the materialistic values of our society reduce feelings to objects, was given visual depth by the breathtaking cinematography of GIANNI DI VENANZO, also responsible for the camerawork of Rosi's *Salvatore Giuliano.* On the level of elegant direction of literary material, Bolognini was continuing his distinguished work, and came up with a version of Brancati's ironical parody of Sicilian sexual mores in *Il Bell'Antonio,* which he was to follow with no less refined adaptations of a Svevo novel, *Senilità* (*As A Man Grows Older*) and *La Viaccia* (*The Ugly Street*). These last recaptured period atmosphere respectively in Trieste and Florence. On a different level, though no less remarkable an achievement for the industry, was Jacopetti's harrowingly sinister *Mondo Cane* (1961), vile in the way it cheaply exploited human foibles or twisted facts for its own viewpoint, but nevertheless a gripping piece of film 'entertainment' as its world-wide box-office success proved.

But this was also the season of important débuts. At the Venice Festival in 1960, one found the first films of three directors of considerable talent: PIER PAOLO PASOLINI, who with *Accattone* (1960) transferred to the screen the Roman underworld that he had described so acutely in his novel 'Ragazzi di vita'. The haunting face of Franco Citti summed up centuries of human ignorance and suffering but without the sentimentality usual in films about Naples, even in De Sica's work. ERMANNO OLMI had already been noticed for a fascinating long documentary *Il Tempo si è fermato* (*Time Stood Still*). With *Il Posto* (1961), his first feature, he revealed unexpected traits of humour. But his vision of lower middle class drudgery was unlike that which a CASTELLANI or Germi had accustomed us to. It had an almost Russian flavour about it. The Italians were disconcerted by Olmi's film, and the Left objected to his inherent Catholicism; indeed *Il Posto,* like most of Olmi's subsequent work, was to find a more receptive audience abroad than at home. The other new director of 1960 was Vittorio De Seta, whose first film *Banditi a Orgosolo* was almost a return to the mood of neo-realism, spoiled perhaps by a dubbing into Italian which removed the genuine Sardinian atmosphere from the sound track.

One of Italy's leading stage actors, Salvo Randone, distinguished himself in ELIO PETRI's second film, *I Giorni Contati* (1961). Petri's *L'Assassino* (1961), has proved a skilfully-made thriller. Another director who made his début at this time was Damiano Damiani, with another thriller, *Il Rossetto* (*The Lipstick*, 1960). Alfredo Bini, the producer who had given Pasolini his first break, also produced Ugo Gregoretti's first film, *I Nuovi Angeli* (1962), an off-beat film in which a combination of documentary and reconstructed reality was used to give a portrait of the contradictions and absurdities of the younger generation. Bini also produced *Rogopag* (1961) with episodes by PASOLINI, GODARD, ROSSELLINI and Gregoretti. Only Pasolini's episode, *La Ricotta* with Orson Welles, was memorable.

The 'golden season' continued into 1962, with Titanus under Goffredo Lombardo's somewhat rash super-production policy. He embarked on costly adventures such as Visconti's *Il Gattopardo (The Leopard,* 1963), ALDRICH's *Sodom and Gomorrah* (1962), and DE SICA's version of Sartre's 'Altona'. All of these, though co-produced with Hollywood firms, left a financial burden on Lombardo's shoulders when they ran over budget disastrously, as with the Visconti and Aldrich films, or failed to make any impact on the box-office. This was the case with the unfortunate De Sica-Sartre fiasco, in which the personalities of LOREN, FREDRIC MARCH and MAXIMILIAN SCHELL proved incompatible. Another expensive Titanus film was *Cronaca Familiare* (1962), ZURLINI's elegant adaptation of Pratolini's leisurely story, which won half a Golden Lion in Venice, but failed at the box-office.

These colossal productions by Lombardo's company were supposed to cover the costs of a series of 'author's films' which he was producing simultaneously. Unfortunately, pictures such as OLMI's *I Fidanzati* (1962), Brunello Rondi's *Il Demonio* (1962), Franco Brusati's *Il Disordine* (1962, which was also very costly because of an all-star cast), only added further financial burdens. For Lombardo it was to be the end of his over-idealistic programme. In spite of the enormous box-office success of *The Leopard* in Italy, Titanus was destined to stop production shortly afterwards and to concentrate only on distribution. It was the beginning of the end of dreams of a Hollywood-on-the-Tiber.

A similar fate awaited another big company, Galatea, which had also been over-ambitious. Its intelligent and well-meaning producer, Nello Santi, was responsible for some interesting débuts, notably Lina Wertmüller's *I Basilischi* (1963) and Ginfranco De Bosio's *Il Terrorista* (1963), but not even the Golden Lion for Rosi's *Le Mani sulla Città* (1963), with one of ROD STEIGER's best performances, could guarantee it enough of an income at the box-office to save its producer from ruin.

Every producer's hopes that the phenomenal international success of *La Dolce Vita* could be repeated were soon dashed to the ground. Marco Ferreri had scored a similar *succès de scandale* with the first film he made in Italy after returning from several years in Spain. This was *L'Ape Regina* (*The Queen Bee,* 1963), which even had to have its title changed after its troubles with the censors. The aura of scandal around it helped to make it a box-office success and Ferreri was signed by PONTI to make several films. But the first one, *L'Uomo dei cinque palloni* (*The Man with Five Balloons,* 1964) so baffled Ponti that he refused to show it. He reduced it to one episode and brought it out a few years later with two others especially shot with MASTROIANNI.

The mid-1960s were characterized by the new panic which the collapse of Titanus and Galatea had provoked. Films had to be commercial at all costs. DE SICA had little difficulty in obliging Ponti, and came up with several films exploiting the Loren-Mastroianni formula. The authors could hardly get a word in. GIUSEPPE PATRONI GRIFFI, after the rejection of his first film *Il Mare* (1962) by both critics and audiences in Italy, returned to the theatre. The same happened to Franco Brusati. BERNARDO BERTOLUCCI, who had been assistant to PASOLINI on *Accattone*, made his first film on a Pasolini story, *La Commare Secca* (1962), and only made his second, *Prima della Rivoluzione* (1964), thanks to a shoestring budget and backing from friends and relatives. Eriprando Visconti, nephew of Luchino, also made a promising début with *Una Storia Milanese* (1962), but had to wait some years before making another. GILLO PONTECORVO had won much praise for his second film, *Kapo* with Susan Strasberg, but had to wait until 1966 to make *The Battle of Algiers*.

That Fellini was able to make *Otto e Mezzo* (*8½*, 1963) was due to the conscience of Rizzoli, who had made so much money out of *La Dolce Vita* that he felt obliged to let Fellini go ahead on a film which was a 'scriptless' script about a director who had no script – and with an ironic caricature of a film producer who gives his director a gold watch as compensation for all the millions made by the director's previous film, apparently a true anecdote.

'8½' (Federico Fellini, 1963)

The one producer who anyway for the moment always seemed to succeed in getting round the economic crisis was DE LAURENTIIS, who had even started building what were to be the most modern studios in Europe, if not in the world. Backed by government support and low interest loans, De Laurentiis went ahead planning his colossus of all time, which was to have been the whole of 'The Bible', or at least the first six books of the Old Testament, with directors such as WELLES, FELLINI, BRESSON and BERGMAN each realizing a book. In the end only Genesis appeared, with JOHN HUSTON directing and also playing Moses. When it looked as if De Laurentiis was losing the faith of his bankers, he announced the signing-up of Princess Soraya to appear in a film and his credit was immediately restored. The resulting film with the Princess, *Three Faces* (1964), has hardly ever been shown anywhere. The Introduction, a sort of secret screen-test covered by a journalist from a Rome left-wing afternoon paper, was done by ANTONIONI. Another episode was directed by Antonioni's former assistant, Franco Indovina.

New gimmicks were desperately needed. The craze for historical spectacles was over (and anyway they were too costly), the muscle boys were back in their gyms, and the fashion for trumped-up, round-the-world visits to Night Clubs (mostly shot in the Via Veneto or in the studios) launched by BLASETTI's *Europe by Night,* only lasted a season. It was at this point that the idea of the Italian Western was born. It was not expected to be accepted as 'Italian'. Indeed, the first of the kind, *Per Un Pugno di Dollari (A Fistful of Dollars)*, was credited to the director 'Bob Robertson', who was of course SERGIO LEONE. The leading man was authentically American, CLINT EASTWOOD, but the bad guy 'John Wells' was a pseudonym for Gian Maria Volonté, later to emerge as one of the best actors in the whole history of Italian films. The first Leone was blatantly cribbed from *Yojimbo*, but the second, *Per quàlche dollaro di più*, was definitely better. When United Artists bought up both films they commissioned Leone, scriptwriter Luciano Vincenzoni and producer Alberto Grimaldi to deliver them a third product, which was to be *The Good, The Bad and the Ugly* (1966). All three were to dominate the domestic market during those seasons.

Another popular trend which is likely to be eternal was set off by the success of DINO RISI's *Il Sorpasso* (*Easy Life,* 1962), certainly Risi's best film, with VITTORIO GASSMAN giving human depth to the stereotyped, bombastic Italian

Above: Clint Eastwood in 'The Good, the Bad and the Ugly' (Sergio Leone, 1966)
Below: Marco Bellocchio working on 'La Cina è Vicina' (Bellocchio, 1967)

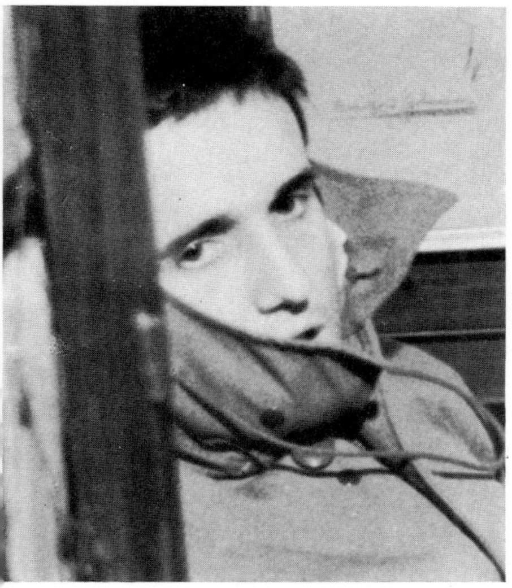

lounger. He was to repeat his performance, but with less subtlety and not always with Risi to control the situation, in many comedies in the years to come.

Antonioni made his first film in colour, *Deserto Rosso* (1964), making extraordinary use of the plastic possibilities which his new cameraman, CARLO DI PALMA, was to offer him. Fellini, who had used colour in the episode of *Boccaccio '70*, also sought for particular effects in *Giulietta degli Spiriti* (1965), though PIERO GHERARDI's exotic costumes and sets, so effective in the black and white of *8½*, tended to overwhelm the anyway slender theme which was not one of Fellini's happiest works. ROSI had two somewhat glamorous interludes: a bullfighting film in Spain, *Il Momento della verità* (1964), and a realistic Southern Italian fairy tale with SOPHIA LOREN as the rags-to-riches princess and OMAR SHARIFF as the prince, *C'era una volta Cinderella – Italian Style*, 1966). These two films disappointed some of Rosi's admirers and yet in spite of their occasional naivety within the context of the subjects treated, they were thoroughly consistant with the interest that Rosi has always shown for the myths of the underprivileged, lower Mediterranean peoples.

OLMI, the devout Catholic, slipped up, on his own admission, in a film about Pope John, with ROD STEIGER uncomfortably cast as a sort of narrator who incarnates the Pope in his earlier days, *E Venne un Uomo* (1964), while PASOLINI the agnostic made what is perhaps one of the most profoundly moving and aesthetically satisfying religious films of all time with his *Vangelo Secondo Matteo* (1964). The occasional return to the theme of the Resistance was not enough to bring back the mood of neo-realism, but Nanni Loi's *Le Quattro Giornate di Napoli* (1962) conveyed the feeling of a Neapolitan ballad and had something of the impact of Rossellini's early work.

The most outstanding individual talents who emerged during the mid-1960s in Italy were MARCO BELLOCCHIO and Carmelo Bene. Bellocchio won immediate fame in Italy and abroad with his tormented, almost Strindbergian *I Pugni in Tasca* (*Fists in the Pocket*, 1966) which he followed up with *La Cina è Vicina* (*China is Near*, 1968), a powerful satiric drama on the amorous connivances of Italy's Centre-Left politicians in the provinces. It was a film that heralded the advent of the years of *Contestazione* or Dissent, which were to take Bellocchio into extreme left political activity and keep him out of feature film-making until *In nome del padre* (1971), a return (to the intense autobiographical psychodrama. The work of Carmelo Bene, *enfant terrible* of Italian theatrical avant-garde, is equally autobiographical but less communicable to filmgoers uninitiated in his weird personal history. His first film, *Nostra signora dei turchi* (1968), based on a novel and stage production of his own and starring himself, as with all his films, won him the Jury's Special Prize at the much-contested Venice Festival in 1968 when Luigi Chiarini only managed to get the festival through to the end thanks to the massive intervention of the police. Bene's subsequent film *Capricci* (1969), vaguely inspired by the Elizabethan tragedy 'Arden of Feversham' and his stage production of it, was not so successful, though in his third film, *Don Giovanni* (1970), Bene seemed to be finally freeing himself from some of his theatrical self-consciousness.

BERTOLUCCI was another director much influenced by the events in Paris of 1968. After his somewhat esoteric *Partner* (1968), reflecting his almost blind adoration of GODARD, he returned to his own origins again in a fascinating film made for television, *Strategia del Ragno*

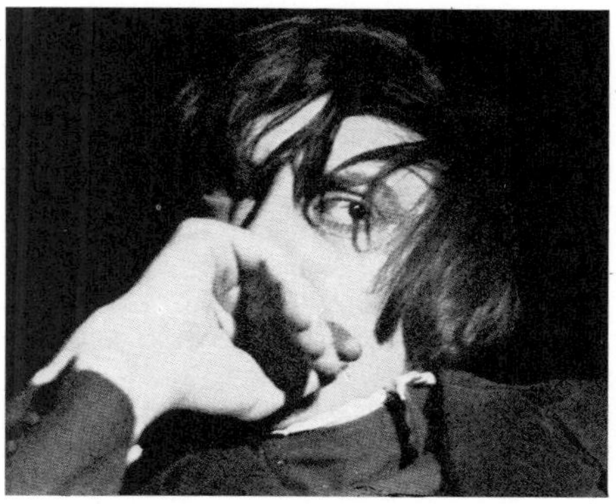

Above: Carmelo Bene in 'Don Giovanni' (Bene, 1970)
Below: Giulio Brogi and Alida Valli in 'The Spider's Strategy' (Bernardo Bertolucci, 1970)

(1970). In order to prove that he was not so esoteric as he had seemed, he then made *Il Conformista* (1970), a thoroughly professional piece of film-making without however making compromises or concessions.

The colour photography of Bertolucci's *Spider's Strategy*, by VITTORIO STORARO and Franco Di Giacomo, was inspired by the paintings of a half-mad Italian naif painter, Ligabue. It was a stunning example of the way in which Italian colour cinematography has been developing in recent years. Alongside the work of Pasquale De Santis, formerly cameraman to GIANNI DI VENANZO and his natural heir, responsible for ZEFFIRELLI's exquisite film version of *Romeo and Juliet* (1968), and for *Fellini-Satyricon* (1969), and GIUSEPPE ROTUNNO, responsible for *The Leopard*, new names have been emerging in recent years – CARLO DI PALMA, Antonioni's favourite cinematographer, and Ennio Guarnieri, who has filmed BOLOGNINI's *Metello* (1969) and DE SICA's *Il Giardino dei Finzi Contini* (1970).

Among the interesting newcomers of the late 1960s was Salvatore Samperi, who had been assistant to Bellocchio and made his first film, *Grazie Zia* (1967), which certainly had affinities with Bellocchio's own first film (as well as the same leading actor, the young Swede Lou Castel), but also revealed individual style. Samperi proclaimed himself publicly as a *contestatore,* which was fashionable at that time. His film had a big box-office success which was rare for first films. It enabled him to go ahead in making other pictures, but inevitably there was a certain disappointment in the follow-up, even if *Cuore di Mamma* (1969) was not without interest. At the same time as Samperi, another young director made a big impression with his first film which also had a great box-office success. This was Robert Faenza's *Escalation* (1968), which was a sort of compromise between the mood of 'swinging London' and its Milan version. But Faenza's second film, *H2S* (1969), had trouble with the censors and disappeared from circulation, persuading him to give up film-making for several years.

There were other interesting débuts or confirmations in the late 1960s and early 1970s. After *Trio* (1967), Gianfranco Mingozzi made *Sequestro di persona* (1968), a Sardinian bandit film with Franco Nero. Liliana Cavani, who had made an interesting television film about Saint Francis and a not so successful one about Galileo, made a strong impression with *I Cannibali* (1970). The Taviani brothers, now separated from Valentino Orsini, made a film that is under-rated, *I Sovversivi* (1967), set against the background of Togliatti's funeral, and later a disconcertingly esoteric philosphical fantasy, *Sotto il segno dello scorpione* (1970), set in prehistoric times. Enzo Muzii, a photographer turned director, made a curious love story, *Come l'amore* (1968), with British actor Alfred Lynch, and followed it up with a hauntingly beautiful film about a young Italian photographer who goes to India, *Una macchia Rosa* (1969), with Giancarlo Giannini, one of the best of the younger Italian actors of the new generation. Franco Brusati, after years writing for the theatre, returned to the cinema with a sophisticated comedy, *Tenderly* (1968), with Virna Lisi and George Segal, which was well above the average Italian comedy of the time. Naturally, it did not make a fortune. Neither did his subsequent film, *I Tulipani di Haarlem* (1970), with Frank Grimes and Carole André, shot in English and in excellent colour by Luciano Tovoli. A great box-office success, however, was obtained by another dramatist who returned after years to the cinema, Giuseppe Patroni Griffi, who filmed his own play *Metti, Una Sera a Cena* (1969), with great elegance, not succeeding however in making the empty social milieu seem any less superficial than it had on the stage. The film launched as a new Italian star the sultry Brazilian actress Florinda Bolkan, and also initiated an Italian career for Tony Musante.

Above: Gian Maria Volonté and Lucia Bene in 'Sotto il Segno dello Scorpione' (Paolo and Vittorio Taviani, 1970)
Below: Charlotte Rampling and Fabio Testi in an adaptation of John Ford's play 'Tis Pity She's a Whore' (Giuseppe Patroni Griffi, 1971)

CARLO LIZZANI, no longer quite as militant as in the old neo-realist days, continues a thoroughly efficient professional career, specializing for some years in real-life contemporary bandits, from *Svegliati e uccidi* (1966) and *Banditi a Milano* (1968) to *Barbagia* (1969). He then turned his attention to Rome's jet set in *Roma Bene* (1971). Other more or less politically militant directors remained. Ugo Gregoretti, who dedicates himself almost exclusively to trade union films such as *Contract* (1970), and Marco Ferreri, who after the excellent *Dillinger è Mòrto* (1969) seems to be searching for new ground.

But early in the 1970s, with a change in the political climate in Italy as the contrasts between Left and Right became more and more accentuated, mostly in favour of the Left, a new kind of political commitment began to appear in Italian films. Perhaps encouraged by the success of *Z*, Italian producers began to encourage directors who wanted to tackle 'hot' local political themes. PETRI, who had already made a good Mafia film, *A Ciascuno il suo* (1968) and followed it up with a not-too-successful pretentious study of a mad artist, *Un tranquillo posto in campagna* (1969), with VANESSA REDGRAVE and Franco Nero, really hit the bull's eye with *Indagine su un cittadino aldisopra di ogni sospetto* (1970), a film about a pathological policeman, but with scorching political overtones. It was the sort of film that nobody would have dared make even five years before. It was a big box-office success, an international hit and won for Petri the Hollywood Oscar as Best Foreign Film. He was able to follow it up with another scorching subject, *La classe operaia va in paradiso* (1971), about working-class problems. In both films, Petri had as actor Gian Maria Volonté, a militant Communist. Volonté had abandoned the cast of Patroni Griffi's *Metti, Una Sera a Cena* a week before shooting because he wanted to dedicate himself to political activity (it was May 1968, the hey-day of the French riots). He took part in *Vento dell'Est*, a rather silly Western cum-political-pamphlet made by GODARD in Italy, but returned to the commercial cinema to appear in *engagé* films such as *Indagine* and ROSI's *Uomini Contro*, an anti-heroic story of the First World War. Volonté also appeared in Giuliano Montaldo's *Sacco e Vanzetti* (1971), another hot political film containing the apparent miscarriage of justice in the United States of the 1920s which appealed to the anti-American 1970s scene.

As everywhere, the general cinema crisis of 1970 was felt deeply in Italy, particularly when the American companies began to withdraw their support for some rash Italian production adventures. CARLO PONTI had to abandon two projected spectaculars, a film of Malraux's 'La Condition Humaine' and a colossal reconstruction of the history of Tai-Pan. DE LAURENTIIS made *Waterloo* (1970) and risked it being as much a defeat for him as for Napoleon. The film was a co-production financed by Americans, Russians and British. He was to reap the Italian fruits, but the film was unsuccessful in Italy. He decided to close his studios and to try to induce the Government to buy them.

FRANCO CRISTALDI also made a colossal co-production with the Russians, *The Red Tent* (1969), but he sold it to Paramount and so could relax and return to producing more modestly budgeted films (BELLOCCHIO, Ferreri, MASELLI). The only company which could really keep its head above water was Euro International, whose indefatigible Venetian aristocrat producer, Countess Marina Cicogna, had proved her mettle with the success of the Petri film at a moment when the whole Italian film industry seemed on the verge of collapse.

The big directors, nevertheless, managed to keep on working. De Sica after the unfortunate experience of the Italo-Soviet co-production *Sunflower* (1969) – with LOREN and MASTROIANNI at their worst, though the film was a box-office hit – recovered his prestige with *Il giardíno dei Finzi Contini* (1970), a hauntingly beautiful adaptation of Giorgio Bassani's novel about Jews in the Ferrara of the fascist years. It was De Sica's best film since *La Ciociara*. ANTONIONI, nursing his wounds

Above: Dominique Sanda and Lino Capolicchio (centre) in 'Il Giardíno dei Finzi Contini' ('Tennis in a Garden in Ferrara', Vittorio De Sica, 1970)
Below: Pierre Clementi in 'Porcile' (Pier Paolo Pasolini, 1969)

after the American reaction to *Zabriskie Point*, consoled himself with the favourable Italian response (mostly politically inspired) but had to wait for the tide to change so that he could make a new film. VISCONTI, finding with *The Damned* (1969) that decadence pays off, attempted Mann's study of disintegration, *Death in Venice* (1970), which divided critics and audiences into 'loved' and 'hated' camps. FELLINI, after his *Satyricon* (1969), which equally divided opinion, took a respite to make a television film, *The Clowns* (1970), and then finally filmed his sequel to *I Vitelloni*, now called quite simply *Roma* (1971–2). PASOLINI pursued his own individual path as always, each of his new films proving a surprise. From the metaphysical *Theorem* (1968) and *Porcile* (1969), he moved to the pseudo-historical *Medea* (1969), with a plastically impressive Maria Callas, and then to the erotic splendours of *Decameron* (1971), in which Boccaccio's stories are given a Neapolitan slant, with Pasolini himself appearing as the painter Giotto. After this Pasolini came to England to make 'The Canterbury Tales'.

Nelo Risi, brother of Dino, made an interesting film based on a woman psychiatrist's experiences in a Lausanne clinic, *Diario di una Schizofrenica* (1969), and a film about Rimbaud: *Una Stagione all'Inferno* (*A Season in Hell*, 1971), with TERENCE STAMP as the poet. In the 1970–1 season there were two surprising directing débuts by popular actors, Nino Manfredi, who made a Fellini-like personal fantasy *Per Grazia Ricevuta,* and Enrico Maria Salerno, who made *Anonimo Veneziano,* a romantic story of a dying cellist, set against a melancholy Venice. Tony Musante, who played the cellist, became a top star in Italy thanks to this and to the first film of Dario Argento, *L'Uccello dal piumo di cristallo* (*The Bird with the Crystal Plumage*). The amazing success of this film in Italy and in the USA has ensured for Argento the role as inaugurator of a new trend, the 'erotic thriller', which took the place of the Westerns as the 1970s began.

The pattern for the 1970s seems to indicate that the Italian cinema has learned its lessons. Neo-Realism might be buried, but so are dreams of a Hollywood-on-the-Tiber. Directors such as FELLINI and VISCONTI will always be financed even for costly projects, even if they have to change producers every time. And Italian Television has stepped in to bolster up the industry, supporting both modest 'author's' films – OLMI made *I Recuperanti* (1970) and *Durante l'estate* (1971) for RAI-TV – and large-scale films of the kind which the cinema industry itself can no longer afford to make. In this field the most ambitious productions have been Franco Rossi's versions of *The Odyssey* (1969) and *The Aeneid* (1971), both made as television series and then reduced to feature-film length for cinema circuits, as was also the case with RENATO CASTELLANI's *Leonardo da Vinci* (1971). Italian Television also seem to have given *carte blanche* to ROSSELLINI with television series such as *Acts of the Apostles* (1969), *The Struggle for Survival* (1970–1) and the feature, *Socrates* (1971). As films, these works are not aesthetically noteworthy and disappoint after the brilliant *La Prise de la pouvoir par Louis XIV* (1966), made in France, which could be said to have inaugurated his new, so-called 'didactic' phase. Rossellini has declared that he is more interested in the educational than the aesthetic criteria for making films. Since he has remained perhaps the key figure of three decades of Italian film-making, through his personal influence, quite apart from the works he produces, one can only accept his judgement. JFL

Ivens, Joris

Born 1898 in Holland. Documentary director. Began film-making in Holland with *The Bridge* (1928) and *Rain* (1929), and an initial film on the reclamation of land in the *Zuyder-Zee* (1930). After other documentaries, he went to Russia where he developed his noted left-wing ideology and made *Komsomol* (1932) for the League of Youth movement. Back in the West, he made *Borinage* (1933) on the Belgian mining industry and his classic *New Earth* (1934), his second Zuyder-Zee subject. After this came *Spanish Earth* (1937), a dramatically conceived study of the Spanish Civil War made in association with Ernest Hemingway, John dos Passos and others, and, with the same associates, *The 400 Millions* (1939) in China.

In 1940 Ivens went to the USA to work briefly with PARE LORENTZ at the short-lived Government Film Service, making *Power and the Land* (1940) on the need for electrification on farms. After working in Canada, he was appointed Dutch Film Commissioner for the Dutch East Indies, based in Australia. However, he sided with the revolution in Indonesia, resigned, and made *Indonesia Calling* (1946).

In 1949 he went to Prague to make *The First Years* (1949), a feature-length propagandist documentary about the new Czechoslovakia, Poland and Bulgaria. After this, he made films in Poland, the USSR, East Germany, France, Mali, Cuba, China, Peru and North Vietnam. In France he worked on the episodic political film, *Loin du Viêtnam* (1967). Ivens has never compromised, and his peripatetic life has been spent almost wholly in making films which, however naively, sincerely promote the political views he has adopted. RM

Ivory, James

Born 1930 in Berkeley, California, USA. Director. Started career with three documentaries (one on Venice, two on India); then formed collaboration with writer Ruth Prawer Jhabvala and Indian producer Ismail Merchant, making films in India with a mixture of professionals and amateurs: *The Householder* (1963), *Shakespeare-Wallah* (1965), *The Guru* (1969), *Bombay Talkie* (1970). Apart from communicating the physical look of the country, Ivory's films present a sensitive outsider's comment on Indian life, emerging from the British Raj into the extrovert uncertainties of a Western-influenced society, and his flair (and that of his writer) is to pinpoint these ambiguities in a witty, humane manner. He often uses players associated with the films of SATYAJIT RAY (by whom he has been clearly influenced). Leaving India for a time, Merchant-Ivory Productions' latest film was made in America: *Savages* (1971). JG

Above: 'La Prise de la pouvoir par Louis XIV' (Roberto Rossellini, 1966)
Below: Renato Parracchi in 'Durante L'Estate' (Ermanno Olmi, 1971)

J

Jackson, Glenda

Born in Birkenhead, England. Actress. After leaving school at 16, she worked as a salesgirl at Boots the chemists, eventually, becoming an actress in provincial repertory. She appeared in the Royal Shakespeare Company under the direction of PETER BROOK, acting in both the stage and screen versions of the *Marat-Sade* (1966). It was her performance in KEN RUSSELL's *Women in Love* (1969) which brought her real prominence; for this she was awarded an Oscar in 1971. She appeared also in *Negatives* (1970), in Ken Russell's *The Music-Lovers* (1970), playing in both the mistress of a pervert, and in the universally-acclaimed film by JOHN SCHLESINGER, *Sunday, Bloody Sunday* (1971). Her success in the character of Queen Elizabeth I in a BBC television drama series led to her appearance in the same character in a film *Mary Queen of Scots* (1972). She also starred in RONALD NEAME's *Isabella of Spain* (1972). Her concern is primarily to present strong and, when called for, sensual women, uncluttered by any artificial feminine prettiness. RM

Jacobs, Lewis

Born 1909 in Philadelphia, Pennsylvania, USA. Director, film historian, and teacher in film studies. Trained initially as a painter, he gave his primary attention to the cinema, both as film-maker and critic. Founder of 'Experimental Cinema' in 1930, the first American magazine to be devoted to film as art and social force. He became a screenwriter in Hollywood, and directed a workshop for professional writers who wanted to learn about the medium. Since 1950 he has concentrated on directing short films, such as *The Raven, The Stylist, World that Nature Forgot, Another Time: Another Voice, Ages of Time, Mathew Brady, A Sculptor Speaks, The Hutterites.* He also lectures in film study courses at university level. His book 'The Rise of the American Film' (1939) set new standards in the writing of film history; later he edited a series of books: 'Introduction to the Art of the Movies' (1960), 'The Emergence of Film Art' (1968), 'The Movies as Medium' (1970), and 'The Documentary Tradition' (1971).

Jacubowska, Wanda

Born 1907 in Warsaw, Poland. Director and producer. Studied the history of Fine Art at Warsaw University. While still a student

Above: Miklós Jancsó (1969)
Below: Glenda Jackson in 'Sunday, Bloody Sunday' (John Schlesinger, GB, 1971)

she was one of the founders in 1920 of the radical Society of Devotees of the Artistic Film (START), which ALEKSANDER FORD, Jerzy Toeplitz and others joined around 1930. She became one of the earlier, prewar directors of documentary, including *Autumn Impressions* and *The Sea* (1932) and *We are Building* (1933). The negative of her film adaptation of the novel *On the Nieman* was lost in the burning of Warsaw in 1939. In 1942 she was confined in Auschwitz concentration camp, and later in Ravensbrück. After the war she made her award-winning film *The Last Stage* (1948) about life in Auschwitz. She was to be one of the key film-makers in the new, Socialist state, becoming artistic director of the Start Film Production group in 1955. Her other features include: *The Soldier of Victory* (1953), *The Atlantic Story* (1955), *Farewell to the Devil* (1957), *King Matthew I* (1958), and in 1960, *A Modern Story* and a co-production with East Germany, *Encounters in the Dark*. RM

Jancsó, Miklós

Born 1921 in Vac, Hungary. The most celebrated and one of the senior representatives of the Hungarian new wave which emerged significantly after 1963, Jancsó began his career as a director of newsreels. During the 1950s he made a number of documentaries, before embarking on his first feature film *The Bells Have Gone to Rome* in 1958. This was followed by the first part of *Three Stars. Cantata* (1962), dealing with very contemporary problems and situations, can be regarded as a formative film in the new Hungarian cinema. The characteristic technical style which contributed to Jancsó's international reputation – a style based on immensely long takes, of as much as ten minutes, with a choreographic planning of the movements of camera and performers – began to appear in *My Way Home* (1964) and *The Round-up* (1965). Other quintessential Jancsó films are *The Red and the White* (1967) and *Silence and Cry* (1969). Later, in *Sirocco* (1969) and *Agnus Dei* (1971), the director seemed sometimes to have fallen into self-parody. *The Confrontation* (1968) remains arguably Janscó's best film, an ideal blend of music and his characteristic choreographic style to illuminate a parable of the conflicts after the socialization of Hungary. Recent films: *La Pacifista* and *Young Attila* (both made in Italy, 1971). DR

Jannings, Emil (1884–1950)
Born in Rorschach, Switzerland. Actor. On the stage from the age of ten, he finally joined Max Reinhardt's company in 1914 at the Deutsches Theater, Berlin. He worked also for the cinema, and especially from 1917 for LUBITSCH, appearing in such early Lubitsch films as *The Eyes of the Mummy* (1918), *Madame Dubarry* (*Passion*, 1919), *Kohlhiesel's Daughters* (1920), *Anna Boleyn* (1921) and *The Loves of Pharaoh* (1922). During the 1920s he became one of Germany's most celebrated character actors, specializing in heavy, highly dramatic roles, and appearing in many of the best-known silent films, such as *Othello* (1922), PAUL LENI's *Waxworks* (1924), MURNAU's *The Last Laugh* and *Tartuffe* (1925) and *Faust* (1926), PAUL CZINNER's *Nju* (1924) and DUPONT's *Variété* (1925). He worked in Hollywood 1926–9; he won an Academy Award for his performance in STERNBERG's *The Last Command* (1928), and appeared also in Lubitsch's American film, *The Patriot* (1928). He had great trouble trying to learn English, and so returned to Germany after the arrival of sound; here he starred immediately in Sternberg's *The Blue Angel* (1930), and later in Hans Steinhoff's *The Young and the Old King* (1935) and many other films, including some made under Nazi influence, especially VEIT HARLAN's *Der Herrscher* (1937) and Steinhoff's *Ohm Krüger* (1941). Although far more interested in acting and earning good money than in politics, he was temporarily suspended from work by the Allied authorities after the war, but resumed his career when he was acquitted following enquiry into his work for the Nazi régime. After he had turned Catholic in later life, PABST intended to star him as Pope Boniface VIII in a biographical film, but he died before the film could be realized. Jannings was vain almost to the point of an amiable childishness, and enjoyed the conspicuous consumption of the good things of life along with his charming wife, the former cabaret *diseuse*, Gussy Holl. RM

Japan

The Japanese film industry is one of the most productive in the world. Since the 1920s the industry has been a large one, and even in the 1960s, with the impact of television very strong in Japan's highly commercialized urban areas, the average number of productions was kept high with over 400 features a year until recent years, when the total of orthodox films was reduced but the number of 'eroductions' (the so-called pornographic market) considerably increased. The Japanese have always been a film-going people from the time when films and movie theatres were universally available to them.

The periods into which Japanese film-making divides most naturally are three:
(i) the 'primitive' period, up to the mid 1920s
(ii) the 'illiberal' period, or time of imperialistic fascism leading up to the alignment with Hitler and Mussolini in Europe and involvement in the Second World War
(iii) the post-War period, from the American Occupation to the present time

During these three phases the Japanese cinema has been highly commercialized, with a vast turnover of films which aimed at providing mass entertainment through plentiful, cheap products made on stereotyped lines. In this respect, Japan, like India, has contributed nothing to the development of the art of the film. But, in pointed contrast, amid this great quantity of ephemeral entertainment, many films have appeared, especially since the Second World War, which are of the highest quality. A number of film-makers, among them OZU, KINOSHITA, MIZOGUCHI, KUROSAWA, ICHIKAWA, and, more recently, Hani, OSHIMA and Shinoda, have led to the Japanese film becoming well known to discriminating audiences throughout the world, and the best in Japanese cinema equals, if not surpasses, Europe's finest achievements.

Above: 'Collar-Shop, Kyoya' (Eiso Tanaka, 1922)
Below: 'Maid of the Deep Mountains' (Kyosei Kaeriyama, 1919)

The Early Period: 1896 to the mid 1920s
Like other countries, Japan first saw motion pictures demonstrated in 1896 when EDISON's individual 'peepshow' Kinetoscopes were imported, and from 1897 film exhibition began in the urban centres on a small scale after initial screenings by the LUMIÈRES's agents. Short films began to be made and shown alongside the imported ones from the United States and elsewhere, and film studios were established during 1908–9 in Tokyo and Kyoto, the ancient capital. Kyoto in particular specialized in the period, or costume, films which were to become a notable genre in Japanese production. Parallel with this, motion picture theatres began to be set up, the first appearing in Tokyo as early as 1903: there were 70 in the city by 1909. Films offered cheap mass entertainment for Japan's heavily urbanized and closely-packed population.

The Japanese film was held back initially in its development by the dominating position held by the *benshi*, story-telling narrators who became local stars in their own right in the cinemas up to the 1920s. The voices of the *benshi* took the place to some extent of film titling, and they worked with a dialogue script sent around with the film. Their presence discouraged any consistent developments in the art of the silent film in Japan, which produced fewer early stylistic innovations than, say the German, Russian or American cinemas.

Nevertheless, some attempts were made to oust the influence of the *benshi* and enable individual silent films to develop the potentialities of the medium. A pioneer at the turn of the 1920s was Norimasa Kaeriyama (born 1893) who, among other innovations, used actresses instead of the female impersonators normal in films (compare the position in India with this),

variable camera set-ups and distances, location instead of studio shots, and introduced a greater sense of realism in his approach to story-telling. He was utterly opposed to the *benshi*. He published a book, 'The Production and Philosophy of Moving Picture Drama'. His early films *The Glow of Life* (1918), *Maid of the Deep Mountains* (1919) and *Tale of the White Chrysanthemum* faced difficulties of distribution owing to his opposition to employing *benshi*. In the end Kaeriyama turned from artistic to technical matters concerned with projection. Other directors, however, attempted to force film technique forward, including Eiso Tanaka (whose film *The Living Corpse*, 1917, featured the future director TEINOSUKE KINUGASA in a woman's part) and the Hollywood-trained Thomas Kurihara (*Amateur Club*, 1920). A new company, Shochiku, had as its manager Kaoru Osanai, once a student at the Moscow Art Theatre, and aimed at introducing a more up-to-date occidental style into Japanese films and created one of the first female stars of Japanese films – Sumiko Kurishima. The vast majority of Japanese films, however, retained the *benshi*, in spite of the considerable counter-attack by film-makers who were American-influenced. Among the innovators was KENJI MIZOGUCHI, who made an atmospheric, if melodramatic, version of O'Neill's 'Anna Christie' called *Foggy Harbour* (1922). Mizoguchi dispensed entirely with the *benshi* and made a number of other important silent films.

In September 1923 came the cataclysmic earthquake which levelled both Tokyo and Yokohama, and virtually wiped out the principal studios and theatres on which the Japanese film industry depended. Within a year or so, a new industry was in the process of being created, and some companies moved to Kyoto. The earthquake also had the strange moral effect of enabling the industry, and the public, to adopt modern ideas more readily. Japanese films were consciously divided into *jidai-geki*, period drama, and *gendai-geki*, contemporary drama. Film in the contemporary vein appeared from Minoru Murata, whose films contained a realistic surface with certain allegorical significances not unlike certain German films of the period – for example, *Sersaku's Wife* (1924) and *The Street Juggler* (1925).

Advanced Japanese films began now to show their characteristic intense emotional feeling expended on some often minute cause in human relationships or failure in observation of social convention. In this sense, as Anderson and Richie have pointed out in their history of the Japanese film, the Japanese cinema can appear overwhelmingly sentimental to the Western mind. Murata's scriptwriter and fellow-director, Kiyohiko Ushihara, went to the United States to study film-making with CHAPLIN, which reinforced the sentimentality of such films as *Love of Life*. Chaplin's mixture of laughter and tears finds ready response in Japan. Other early directors of some importance were Yasujiro Shimazu (*Father*, a drama of ordinary people, which helped to establish another genre of cinema, the *shomin-geki*, films of the common people; *Sunday; A Village Teacher*) and a director who had worked in the USA, Yutaka Abe (*The Woman Who Touched the Legs*, and other comedies). In addition there were the period films of Daisuke Ito (*Sword Against Authority*, 1929) and others, shot with splendid camera virtuosity.

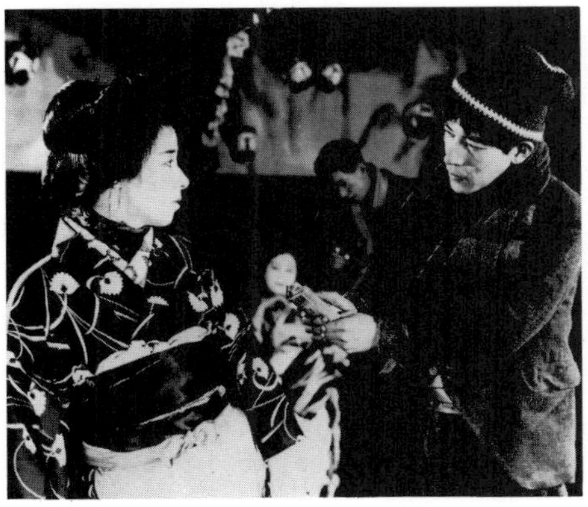

Above: 'Amateur Club' (Thomas Kurihara, 1920)
Below: 'The Street Juggler' (Minoru Murata, 1925)

Perhaps the outstanding Japanese film of the 1920s was TEINOSUKE KINUGASA's *Crossways* (*Shadows of the Yoshiwara*, 1928), a melodrama of a young brother and sister involved in an illusory murder which leads to a real one. Conceived in an impressionist style, with very deliberate use of hallucinatory flashback, the film is one of the most powerful to be made anywhere in the 1920s. Kinugasa subsequently went to study film with EISENSTEIN and with UFA in Berlin, where *Crossways* made a deep impression.

The Illiberal Period of Industrialization and War, 1926–45

The industry itself was tending in the later 1920s to become monolithic, a league of big companies (the Japan Motion Picture Producers' Association) being formed to squeeze out the independents. It was, in any case, a period of developing right-wing tendencies after the accession in 1926 of the new Emperor, Hirohito, with increasing dominance by the military and naval castes. Against this hardening came a genre termed the 'tendency film', with leftish leanings, established, for example, in Ito's period films such as *Servant* and *Diary of Chuji's Travels* (1927), *Ooka's Trial* (1928) and *Man-Slashing Horse-Piercing Sword* (1930), all films of revolution against established society set back in time. These were followed by his first sound film, *Sazen Tange* (1933). The 'tendency-film' also found expression in contemporary subjects, dealing with working-class or lower middle-class themes, as in MIZOGUCHI's *Street Sketches* (1925), *A Paper Doll's Whisper of Spring* (1926), and *Tokyo March* (1929), and GOSHO's *Tricky Girl* (1927) and *The Bride of the Village* (1927). Kinugasa's *Before Dawn* (1931), made after his return from Europe, was a period drama about women who revolt against being sold into prostitution. These and many other films with a strong left-wing feeling of protest behind them, led to a counter-movement by the censorship which imposed bans and cuts on films. The movement was remarkable for being spontaneous, of Japanese origin, and virtually uninfluenced by the work of directors such as EISENSTEIN, since the Russian films were not seen in Japan until much later. In one and the same year, 1931, Mizoguchi made another film of protest against enforced prostitution, *And Yet They Go On*, and a propaganda film for the government, *The Dawn of the Foundation of Manchukuo and Mongolia*.

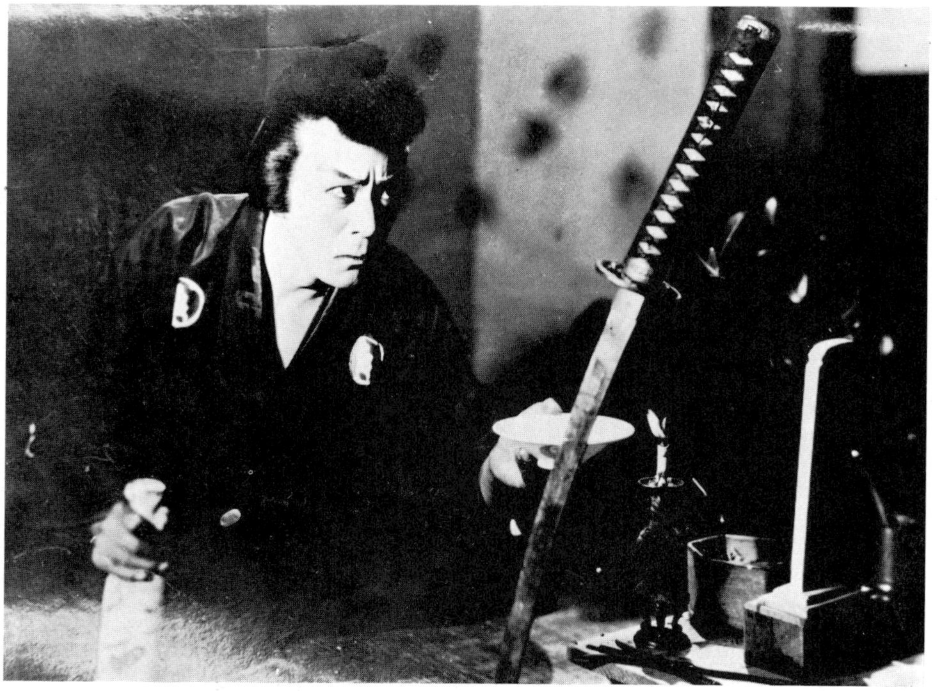

Top: 'Sword Against Authority' (Daisuke Ito, 1929)
Above: 'Slum of Ronin' (Masahiro Makino, 1928)
Left: 'The Bride of the Village' (Heinosuke Gosho, 1927)

Sound was introduced only very gradually into the Japanese cinema, finally suspending the tenacious *benshi*, who even resorted to violence to keep their employment. Gosho made the first successful talkie, *The Neighbour's Wife and Mine* (1931). In 1932 some 45 talkies only were made out of some 400 features, most of these made by the Shochiku company. Others who followed were Kinugasa with a period drama, *The Loyal Forty-seven Ronin* (1932), which featured, among others, the Kabuki actor Utaemon Ichikawa, *Two Stone Lanterns* (1933), and others. The 1930s were to see the rise of the great rival companies and an extension of the film industry from small to big business. One of these companies was Toho, which came to specialize in period films, with a strong roster of stars and directors.

The masters of the period film, in addition to Kinugasa, who had joined Toho, were Mansaku Itami (*Kakita Akanishi*, 1936), who later collaborated with Arnold Fanck of Germany to make *The New Earth* (*Daughter of the Samurai*), and Sadao Yamanaka, who used the past to comment pessimistically on the present in such films as *The Life of Bangoku* (1932), *The Elegant Swordsman* (1934), *The Village Tattooed Man* (1935) and, his most famous work, *Humanity and Paper Balloons* (1937), all films with a strong feeling for character. The last film so offended authority in the year of the capture of Shanghai, Soochaw and Nanking by the Japanese that Yamanaka was sent to China in the army, where he was shortly after killed in action. In contrast to the period films were the dramas and melodramas with a contemporary setting, such as the films of Yasujiro Shimazu, inventor of the term 'neo-realism' as applied to Japanese films: *Maiden in the Storm* (1933), *The Woman That Night* and *Our Neighbour Miss Yae* (1934), and *A Brother and His Younger Sister* (1939). GOSHO also worked in this *shomin-geki* genre. YASUJIRO OZU, one of Japan's greatest directors, began making contemporary silent comedies in the 1920s; he insisted on making silent films until 1936, among which was the Chaplinesque *I Was Born, But . . .* (1932), in which he continued his warmly humorous observations of middle-class life.

Another realistic director was Kajiro Yamamoto (*Composition Class*, 1938, and *Horse*, 1941), who employed AKIRA KUROSAWA as an assistant. *Horse*, shot on a mountain location, was near-documentary in its handling of horses and horse-breeding.

Social realism reached its height during the middle 1930s in such films as Ozu's *The Only Son* (his first sound film, 1936) or Mizoguchi's *Osaka Elegy* and *Sisters of the Gion* (1936), commonly considered the best pre-war sound films; the last-named tells the story of two geisha sisters, one hide-bound by tradition and the other destroying herself by too much license. Mizoguchi's output was prolific, with such films as *The Gorge Between Love and Hate* (1937) and *Ah, My Home Town* (1938). Other realist directors included Tomu Uchida (*Theatre of Life*, and *Unending Advance*, 1936; *The Naked Town*, 1937), whose best work was *Earth* (1939), a wholly dedicated film about a farmer and his problems. *Earth* was made from odd reels of film in semi-secret, its director constantly returning to the studio to complete money-making 'quickies'.

The undeclared war with China began in 1937. Japan's first considerable war film was Tomotaka Tasaka's *Five Scouts* and *Battle by the*

Top: Junosuke Bando and Masako Chihaya in 'Crossways' (Teinosuke Kinugasa, 1928)
Above: 'The Neighbour's Wife and Mine' (Heinosuke Gosho, 1931)
Below: Tatsno Saito as the father in 'I was Born, but . . .' (Yasujiro Ozu, 1932)

Above: 'Sisters of the Gion' (Kenji Mizoguchi, 1936)
Below: 'The Naked Town' (Tomu Uchida, 1937)

Wayside (1938), so essentially human a film that it is almost pacifist in its portrait of men under fire. His second war film, *Mud and Soldiers* (1939), was made on location in China. This was followed by Kimisaburo Yoshimura's *The Story of Tank Commander Nishizumi* (1940), considered to be the greatest war film of the period. Soon, however, the companies received instructions as to what films they should and should not make, what themes they should stress, and what to avoid in wartime Japan. By the early 1940s, regulations modelled on Goebbels's constitution for the industry in Nazi Germany were introduced. An Office of Public Information was set up to initiate propaganda subjects. A flood of conventional war films followed, especially after Pearl Harbour (December 1941). As Anderson and Richie point out, there was little caricature of Westerners in Japanese war films, since the Japanese were more familiar with men of the West, especially Americans, than Western audiences were familiar with Japanese. Westerners, however, were invariably played by Japanese actors, speaking unaccented Japanese. The films stressed not only 'hate-your-enemy' propaganda, but more than anything else the need for self-sacrifice and discipline. The 'quality' directors backed away into the past, avoiding the more jingoistic themes by making period films. Among these were MIZOGUCHI, whose *The Story of the Last Chrysanthemums* (1939), a beautifully made love story with a Kabuki setting, and *Woman of Osaka*, about the puppet drama, were the first of a wartime series. Others resorting to period drama included even the directors of contemporary subjects, Shimazu and KUROSAWA; in *There Was a Father* (1942), OZU made the scantiest of responses to war demands in a family story set in wartime, while KEISUKE KINOSHITA's *The Blossoming Port* (1943) was more about human nature than the war effort. Directors such as Ozu virtually ignored the war; Gosho tried his own particular brand of protest by turning all the militaristic subjects assigned him into love stories.

In 1941 the government imposed amalgamation on the major companies and threatened to withhold raw stock from any which did not fulfil its quota of films along the lines of national policy. The companies finally agreed to be redispersed into three main groups, each group rationed to the production of only two features a month. Theatres were grouped into two main circuits. By 1944, as a result of the bombing, many theatres were closed. Considerable co-production was developed with

Top: 'Earth' (Tomu Uchida, 1939)
Above: 'Five Scouts' (Tomotaka Tasaka, 1938)
Below: 'People by the Wayside' (Tomotaka Tasaka, 1938)

Korea, while the Japanese naturally dominated the Manchurian, Shanghai and Hong Kong industries.

The Post-War Period

When the Americans landed in Japan at the end of August, 1945, they found the Japanese surprisingly docile and, as it seemed, amenable to the policy of 'democratization' imposed by their conquerors. The dropping of the individual atom bombs on Hiroshima (6 August 1945) and at Nagasaki (9 August), coupled with the Soviet attack on Japan on 8 August led to the Emperor's decision to broadcast that, in effect, Japan must sue for peace. It was the first time in their national history that they had been defeated, much less occupied. Many Japanese cities, including Tokyo, were in ruins similar to the great cities in Germany occupied the previous Spring.

Soon the undamaged theatres were re-opened, though by October only 845 were functioning. Production, however, was slow to restart; it came eventually (March 1946) under the supervision of the Civil Information and Education Section of General MacArthur's headquarters, known as SCAP. Gradually, as the occupation authorities felt their way with a people so completely strange to them, the old wartime restrictions were cancelled, and new regulations came into force. Initially films reflecting the old feudal or imperialistic Japan, whether contemporary or period, were banned; the prints of films which met with disapproval were burnt or confiscated. SCAP then went so far in November 1945 as to announce what films the Japanese should undertake: 'In order to secure the objectives of the Occupation so that Japan will never in the future disturb the peace of the world, so that the freedom of religion, speech, and assembly will be encouraged and that Japanese militarism and military nationalism will be abolished, it is demanded that motion pictures of the following types will be made.' The themes desired were, in general, those showing a Japan at peace, with industry and agriculture developing productivity, with ex-soldiers being rehabilitated as industrious citizens, and the 'democratization' of Japanese customs, such as formal bowing, which the Americans found peculiarly distasteful and undemocratic. All scripts had to be vetted in advance, with much time wasted over misunderstanding of Japanese customs and intentions. Many leading members of the Japanese film industry found themselves in 1946 branded as 'war criminals'. The list was compiled for SCAP by the leftist Employees Union, but later had to be whittled down because it contained almost all the leading employers of the war and pre-war years. Recurrent trouble between the unions and the studios held back production during 1946. Toho, in particular, suffered from a succession of strikes. These troubles are directly dramatized in *Those Who Make Tomorrow* (1946), of which KUROSAWA was a co-director. Only 67 Japanese films were released during 1946, but American films were now being shown once again in Japanese cinemas. The Japanese, too, in order to get round the regulations which led to so much mutual misunderstanding, began to copy American-style pictures in Japanese terms. These included the introduction of kissing to the Japanese cinema – 'the first kiss scene in any Japanese film' was, however, obscured behind an open umbrella in 1946: it was soon to be followed by visible kissing, so creating a popular and lasting talking-point for critics and public alike. The Japanese were to remain shy of kissing in public for some time to come.

The occupation lasted from 1945–52; from around 1948 the policy of the American authorities moved in the direction of making Japan an ally firmly integrated into the anti-communist bloc. The Japanese enthusiasm for everything American began to wane as the years of occupation dragged on and more normal economic conditions returned. American aid in 1947 alone reached $400 million. The problem of assimilating new ideas, while at the same time discarding much of the authoritarianism of the immediate past, was difficult at least for the middle-aged; the young took more readily to the semi-Americanization of Japan. The mystique surrounding the Emperor had to be dissolved; leading war criminals had to be tried in the manner of the Nuremberg Trial in Germany; some 5,000 men of lesser rank were tried for murder and gross cruelty; some 200,000 officials were 'purged'; a new constitution for Japan was prepared by the Americans in 1946 to abolish all remnants of feudalism and establish certain basic human rights, including equality of husband and wife. Women received the vote and education was reformed. The Crown Prince married a commoner in 1959.

The departure of the Americans in 1952 as occupiers – though not as businessmen, diplomatic visitors, or tourists – left the Japanese to their own devices – whether or not to assimilate the ideas and customs of the West (in dress, social habits, political procedures etc.), whether or not to maintain the values of the past (in religion, again in dress and social habits, in resentment against intrusion by the 'foreigner'). This dichotomy in values is evident in many Japanese films of the 1950s and 1960s when production, like the rest of Japanese industry, reached the level of a boom. By January 1957, there were over 6,000 cinemas in operation.

The 'progressive' directors soon adjusted to the immediate post-war conditions and began to produce films of some note. Among them were films emphasizing the emancipation of women, such as KENJI MIZOGUCHI's *The Love of Actress Sumako* (1947) and Teinosuke Kinugasa's *Actress* (1947) on the same subject of an emancipated actress of the early 20th century. KINOSHITA made *Marriage* (1947), in which a young girl successfully opposes her family in choosing her husband. Post-war society and post-war problems reached the screen realistically, for example in KUROSAWA's *No Regrets for My Youth* (1946), on freedom of opinion, *Drunken Angel* (1948, with TOSHIRO MIFUNE), and *Stray Dog* (1949, also with Mifune), while the new 'intellectualism' appeared in GOSHO's *Once More* (1947). Mizoguchi made *Women of the Night* (1948) in

Top: 'Sea-Battle in Hawaii and Marei' (Kajiro Yamamoto, 1942)
Above: 'War and Peace' (Satsuo Yamamoto and Fumio Kamei, 1941)
Below: Takashi Shimura in 'Living' (Akira Kurosawa, 1952)

Osaka, exposing prostitution. The younger directors in the van of the modern movement were headed by Kurosawa (*Wonderful Sunday*, 1947), Kinoshita (*The Girl I Loved*, 1946, a light film with music), and Yoshimura (*The Fellows Who Ate the Elephant*, 1947). They were conscious of foreign models, and introduced what seemed to them relevant elements into Japanese film.

Fumio Kamei, who studied in Russia and had suffered some persecution during the war years and had had his post-war documentary, *A Japanese Tragedy*, burned because it supported the communist line, made *A Woman's Life* (1949), an attack on the feudal oppression of an over-worked, pregnant woman. Hideo Sekigawa was another left-wing director who in 1948 made *A Second Life*, a film about children.

During the initial period of readjustment, the principal directors and films in the social realist style included:

KUROSAWA: *Living* (1952)

KINOSHITA: *Apostasy* (1948), on the struggle of a young teacher who tries to convey the meaning of freedom;
Carmen Comes Home (1951), the reaction in her rural home to a strip-tease girl;
Carmen's Pure Love (1952), much influenced by RENÉ CLAIR;
A Japanese Tragedy (1953), the fall of the Japanese family system;
She Was Like a Wild Chrysanthemum (1955), an old man's recollection of the distant past when visiting his home town.

SHINDO: *A Woman's Life* (1953), a study covering the period 1927–53;
Epitome (1953), exposure of the geisha system.

Yoshimura: *Clothes of Deception* (1951), two contrasting sisters' behaviour as geishas.

MIZOGUCHI: *Picture of Mme Yuki* (1950), portrait of a nymphomaniac;
Gion Music (1953), a young and an older geisha;
Red Light District (*Street of Shame*, 1956), a study of the lives of women working in a Tokyo brothel.

Imai: *Until the Day We Meet Again* (1950), the post-war optimism of young people;
And Yet We Live (1951), the Japanese *Bicycle Thieves;*
The Tower of Lilies (1953), an anti-war film on the collective death of young High School nurses.

OZU: *The Record of a Tenement Gentleman* (1947), on homeless children, and his great genre of post-war family films starting with *Late Spring* (1949) and continuing until *An Autumn Afternoon* (1962).

Shimizu: *Children of the Beehive* (1948), also on homeless children with a non-professional cast of genuinely lost children.

Naruse: *Mother* (1952), the problems of a widow with three children to support;
Older Brother, Younger Sister (1953), a family problem film.

GOSHO: *An Inn at Osaka* (1954), an exposure of the influence of money in post-war Japanese society;
Where Chimneys are Seen (1953), life in the industrial section of Tokyo;
Growing Up (1955), a young girl doomed to prostitution.

ICHIKAWA: *Mr Pu* (1953), satire on contemporary Japan;
The Burmese Harp (1956), anti-war film; a Japanese soldier remains in Burma and becomes a priest wandering the countryside and burying the dead;
Conflagration (1958), the psychological study of a student-priest who sets fire to Kyoto's Golden Pavilion.

Sekigawa: *Listen to the Roar of the Ocean* (1950), first effective anti-war film, and anti-Imperial Army from a Leftist standpoint.

Satsuo Yamamoto: *Vacuum Zone* (1952), most powerful of all the early anti-war films.

There were also attempts at white-washing in such films as *Tomoyuki Yamashita* (with SESSUE HAYAKAWA), while resentment of the atom bomb appeared in Shindo's *Children of Hiroshima* (1953), with its excesses of sentimentality in an otherwise realistic presentation of the Hiroshima disaster. The climax of anti-

Top: 'She was Like a Wild Chrysanthemum' (Keisuke Kinoshita, 1955)
Above: Chishu Ryu, Haruko Sugimura and Setsuko Hara in 'Late Spring' (Yasujiro Ozu, 1949)

Americanism was Sekigawa's films, *Mixed-blood Children* and *Orgy*.

The period drama was soon revived, and led to the phenomenal success of Japanese films abroad during the 1950s. The most outstanding titles include:

Kurosawa: *Rashomon* (1950)
The Men Who Tread on the Tiger's Tail (1945/53), made in wartime, banned for a period as 'feudal', but actually a satire on feudalism.
Seven Samurai (1954)
Castle of the Spider's Web (*Throne of Blood*, 1957).
Kinugasa: *Gate of Hell* (1953), notable as a colour film
Kinoshita: *The Ballad of the Narayama* (1958)
Mizoguchi: *The Life of Oharu* (1952)
Ugetsu Monogatari (1953)
A Story from Chikamatsu (1954)
Sansho the Bailiff (1954)
Shin-Heike Monogatari (1955)
Yoshimura: *Tale of the Genji* (1952)
Imai: *Night Drum* (*The Adulteress*, 1958)
Kobayashi: *The Human Condition* (1959)

Rashomon's success at the 1951 Venice Film Festival opened up the possibilities of creating an export market for 'prestige' productions. Later awards consolidated this, especially those given to *Ugetsu Monogatari* in Venice and *Gate of Hell* in Cannes, both in 1954, and *The Burmese Harp* in Venice in 1956.

In fact, during the 1950s and early 1960s, the number of distinguished Japanese films available in Europe showed a substantial increase, though few equalled the commercial success of the big French and Italian productions of the period. The Japanese cinema certainly makes considerable demands on a European audience, in terms of tempo, stylistic conventions and sheer intensity, but it repays ample dividends. As the above survey suggests, a considerable number of major talents have worked in the industry during all its periods and some of the veteran directors turned out up to 100 features (far higher than most of their European and American contemporaries).

Visually, the Japanese cinema is one of the most refined in the world – an abundance of great cinematographers (working in both black-and-white and colour) have created marvellous poetic effects, notably in the depiction of country exteriors, the mysterious calm of temple interiors or the cluttered lived-in houses and tenements seen in so many contemporary subjects. Kurosawa revolutionized camera techniques in his perfection of the fast travelling shot and the quickly-cut battle scene (here the influence of Ito and his sword-play films is evident); Mizoguchi's period films have an exquisite sense of times past and a world of legend; Ozu perfected the family drama with its dense, deeply-felt characterizations and gentle delineation of life's joys and sorrows. In fact, at its best, the Japanese cinema has probed more deeply into the human condition than most national cinemas; the Japanese character, with its wide extremes of temperament and awareness, seems to have parallels with the Russian psyche – certainly, Kurosawa's adaptations from the Russian classics indicate this affinity.

It will take many years before the European critic can claim any kind of comprehensive knowledge of this multifarious cinema. So many of the key films (especially from the silent period) are lost, others are accessible only in Japan and there are about a dozen major directors who are scarcely known outside Japan itself. Retrospectives of individual directors held in London, Paris and New York are slowly filling in the gaps but, unfortunately, Europe discovered the Japanese cinema about 30 years too late, due mainly to the lack of exports to Europe in the 1930s and 1940s. Nevertheless, the door has now been opened and the voyage of discovery continues.

Consolidation of the Japanese Film Industry

The troubles at the studios characteristic of the late 1940s, with strikes, near bankrupt companies, and low productivity, were largely resolved by the early 1950s. Double-feature bills in the theatres pushed up the quantity of productions and the major companies (Shoch-

iku, Toei, Daiei, Toho, Shin Toho and later Nikkatsu) engaged in cut-throat competition with each other and any threatening newcomers. Co-production with other countries on the whole failed; but colour and widescreen soon succeeded, pioneered by Shochiku. Toho produced its own anamorphic system – Tohoscope. Television, beginning in Japan in 1953, was another threat to stability, with two million receivers by 1959.

The major companies, which collectively by the mid-1950s had a complete stranglehold on production, began to some extent to specialize – Shochiku in women's films, Toho in more sophisticated subjects, Daiei in the teenage audience (with a large output of teenage rebel films), Toei in thrillers, Shin Toho in ghost films. Other popular genres were the monster films (starting with *Godzilla*, 1954), science fiction, sex and war films. The teenage films included a great deal of sex and violence, including the Nikkatsu company's *Crazed Fruit*, which the industry's censor board ordered to be cut. But, on the whole, sex and nudity (as

Top: Shoji Yasui (centre) in 'The Burmese Harp' (Kon Ichikawa, 1956)
Below: Tatsuya Nakadai and Michiyo Aratama in 'The Human Condition' (Masaki Kobayashi, 1959)
Bottom: Masayuki Mori and Toshiro Mifune in 'Rashomon' (Akira Kurosawa, 1950)

Top: 'Ugetsu Monogatari' (Kenji Mizogushi, 1953)
Above: 'Boy' (Nagisa Oshima, 1969)
Below: Tadanori Yokoo and Rie Yokoyama in 'Diary of a Shinjuku Thief' (Nagisa Oshima, 1969)
Bottom: Shima Iwashita in 'Double Suicide' (Masahiro Shinoda, 1969)

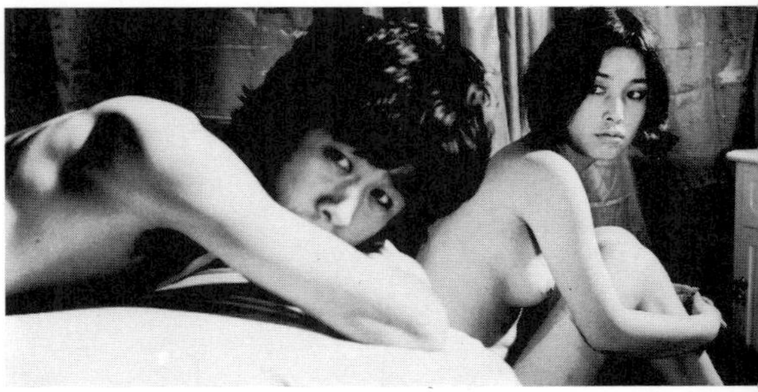

distinct from violence) offer little offence to the Japanese. But far worse than *Crazed Fruit* was to come in the late 1960s, with the proliferation of the 'eroductions' made by independent companies to bolster Japan's dwindling motion picture audiences in the face of colour television with multiple channels. Very few of these 'eroductions' have been seen commercially in the West, but those which which have reached us reveal the customary care and technical qualities associated with the Japanese cinema, allied to very novelettish scripts and an emphasis on explicit violence (close-up stabbings, people having their ears cut off), which give many of them a very disagreeable tone and reflect the least likeable aspect of the Japanese character.

During the last five years the number of truly significant Japanese productions has decreased: no true successors to MIZOGUCHI or OZU have appeared, KUROSAWA has produced only two features since 1965 – *Red Beard* and *Dodeska-Den* – and suffered a temporary set-back when he was employed to direct the Japanese sequences on the American sponsored *Tora! Tora! Tora!* but was removed owing to disagreements and ill-health. Other important figures like ICHIKAWA, KINOSHITA and KOBAYASHI have been relatively silent or have made films below their expected levels.

Some directors have, however, consolidated their reputations in the 1960s – NAGISA OSHIMA, Masahiro Shinoda, and HIROSHI TESHIGAHARA. Oshima, with his social awareness and rebellion against standard Japanese film traditions may be said to lead the New Wave movement; very eclectic in style, he ranges from hard-hitting studies of troubled youth to probing social dramas like *Death by Hanging* (1968) and *The Ceremony* (1970). Shinoda is a considerable visual stylist, whose recent work has been period films with a strong dramatic emphasis or satirical edge – *Double Suicide* (1969), *The New Adventures of Buraikan* (1970). Teshigahara has a bizarre, almost surrealist talent which was best expressed in *Woman of the Dunes* (1964) with its almost palpable sense of space, sand and flesh and feeling for claustrophobic detail.

It is difficult to foresee the immediate future development of the Japanese film – the inroads of commercialism and the ever-present television have taken their toll and it remains to be seen how the surviving veteran directors and the lively New Wave school will face up to the changing pattern of distribution and the new social demands of the 1970s. JG and RM

Jaque, Christian
See CHRISTIAN-JAQUE

Above: 'Woman of the Dunes' (Hiroshi Teshigahara, 1964)

Below: Kuniko Ishii and Akio Takahashi in 'Inferno of First Love' (Susumu Hani, 1968)

Top: Celia Johnson and Trevor Howard in 'Brief Encounter' (David Lean, GB, 1945)
Above: 'Fires were Started' (Humphrey Jennings, GB, 1943)
Below: Jennifer Jones in 'Gone to Earth' (Michael Powell and Emeric Pressburger, GB, 1950)

Jaubert, Maurice (1900–1940)
Born in Nice, France. The foremost French film composer of the 1930s. The complete antithesis of the Hollywood composer of the same period, Jaubert's style was essentially intimate and often scored with a chamber-music delicacy. He was very adept in using *leitmotivs* and individual instruments to create a mood – the solo flute in *Le Jour se lève* (1939) – and his music always made a strong atmospheric response to the narrative, whatever the subject might be. Jaubert's best work includes many collaborations with CLAIR, VIGO, DUVIVIER and CARNÉ, notably *Quatorze Juillet* (1932), *L'Atalante* (1934), *Un Carnet de bal* and *Drôle de Drame* (1937), *Quai des brumes* (1938). JG

Jennings, Humphrey (1907–1950)
Born in Suffolk, England. The most truly poetic of British directors, Jennings's major films were all made within a brief period of four years or so, and add up to barely three hours of screen time. An academic and intellectual, he painted ably and was identified with the British surrealist group, and also worked as a poet before being recruited to the GPO Film Unit where he worked with LEN LYE on *Birth of a Robot*. His first solo film as a director was *Spare Time* (1939), which already revealed the curiosity and the respect for the individuality of people which was to set such films as *The First Days* (in collaboration with CAVALCANTI, WATT and Pat Jackson, 1939), *London Can Take It* (1940) and *Heart of Britain* (1941) quite apart from conventional wartime film propaganda. Jennings had a unique ability – a poet's ability – to assemble sounds and images to produce unexpected and marvellous impressions, evocative and emotionally charged, building up to an unashamed elation of pride in Britain and the British people at war. *Words for Battle* (1941), which gave modern visual interpretations to great poetry of the past, *Listen to Britain* (1941) and *Diary for Timothy* (1944–5) were all such complex interweavings of connections and contrasts. Jennings's single feature film, *Fires Were Started* (1943), about a day-and-a-night's work in an Auxiliary Fire Station in Dockland was equally rich in mood and feeling. After the war, Jennings's work seemed to lose its impetus; and *A Defeated People* (1945), *The Cumberland Story* (1947), *Dim Little Island* (1949) and *Family Portrait* (1950) were conventional documentaries with little of the earlier inspiration. Perhaps, as LINDSAY ANDERSON, a deep admirer of his talent, has said, 'he wasn't able to see how traditions would have to be modified, adapted to a new Britain that could no longer accept the hierarchies of the past'. Jennings was killed in a cliff-fall while filming in Greece. DR

Johnson, Celia
Born 1908 in Richmond, Surrey, England. Actress, who trained at the Royal Academy of Dramatic Art, London, and made her London stage début in 1929 in 'A Hundred Years Old', and her New York stage début in 1931 as Ophelia in 'Hamlet'. Her roles are usually restrained but sensitive women; perhaps the most memorable was in *Brief Encounter* (1946). Her screen début was in *In Which We Serve* in 1942, and her other films include: *Dear Octopus* (1942), *This Happy Breed* (1944), *The Captain's Paradise* (1953), *A Kid for Two Farthings* (1956), *The Good Companions* (1957), *The Prime of Miss Jean Brodie* (1969).

Johnson, Nunnally
Born 1897 in Columbus, Georgia, USA. Screenwriter, producer, director. After work as an established journalist and fiction-writer, he became in 1933 a screenwriter, his wide range of scripts for others including *The House of Rothschild* (1934), *Cardinal Richelieu* (1935), *Jesse James* (1939), *The Grapes of Wrath* (1940) and *Tobacco Road* (1941). From 1942 he began to produce his own films, which he wrote himself; these included *The Moon is Down* (1943), *The Keys of the Kingdom* (1944), *The Gunfighter* (1950), *The Mudlark* and *Rommel, Desert Fox* (1951) and *How to Marry a Millionaire* (1953). During the 1950s he directed as well as produced and wrote his own films; among these were *Night People* (1954), *The Man in the Grey Flannel Suit* (1956), *The Three Faces of Eve* (1957), and *The Man Who Understood Women* (1959). After these, he continued to work as both writer and producer, one of Hollywood's most highly professional film-makers. RM

Jolson, Al (1880–1950)
Actor, singer and entertainer, of Jewish-American parentage. On stage, in vaudeville and eventually on Broadway, often as Negro singer, he became very popular, employing a loud, openly sentimental style. Starred in the pioneer sound film, *The Jazz Singer* (1927); other films include: *The Singing Fool* (1928), *Mammy* (1930), *Hallelujah, I'm a Bum* (1934), and *Swanee River* (1940), guest appearance in *Rhapsody in Blue* (1945). He dubbed for Larry Parks in two biographical films, *The Jolson Story* (1946) and *Jolson Sings Again* (1949).

Jones, Jennifer
Born 1919 in Tulsa, Oklahoma, USA. Actress

from childhood, when she toured with her parents' stock company. Began screen career under real name, Phyllis Isley. First major role as Jennifer Jones was in the part of Marie Soubirous in *The Song of Bernadette* (1943), for which she won an Academy Award as Best Actress. Mainly cast as a sultry temptress, she is also effective in sardonic comedy. Subsequent films include: *Cluny Brown* and *Duel in the Sun* (1946), *Madame Bovary* (1949), *Carrie* and *Gone to Earth* (1951), *Ruby Gentry* (1952), *Indiscretion* and *Beat the Devil* (1954), *Love is a Many-spendored Thing* (1955), *The Barretts of Wimpole Street* (1957), *A Farewell to Arms* (1958), *The Idol* (1966), *Angel, Angel Down We Go* (*Cult of the Damned*, 1969).

Journalism for Film

In 1889, the English journal, 'The Magic Lantern', commented on the development of a new invention: kinematography. It was one of the first ventures, if not the first, into that offshoot of film-making, film journalism, which was to exercise an important influence on the future of motion pictures.

The first entry was the introduction of trade film papers which had a firm basis in the various magazines already devoted to practical photography, such as 'The Camera'. Several still surviving trade papers grew out of these early magazines, including the British 'Kinematograph Weekly', which began publication in 1907 and was the successor to 'The Optical Lantern and Kinematograph Journal'. As its name suggests, the trade press services the trade – exhibitors, producers, distributors – and it can, if fearless enough and not over-dependent financially on film advertising, wield great power. In 1919, the influential British 'Bioscope' was predicting that the cinema and the Church would be legitimate competitors 'in moulding the character of the nation', as the film historian Rachael Low quoted in her book, 'The History of the British Film – 1918–29'. In the USA a similar service was performed by a number of early journals, notably from 1906 'The Moving Picture World', and from 1908, the 'Exhibitor's Times'.

The impact of the trade press has declined since the peak days of the studio networks in the 1930s and 1940s. By and large, its coverage of all aspects of the film industry and its often stringent, but necessarily box-office-orientated film reviews, are mainly of interest to people working within the industry. Among the most durable trade papers in Britain has been 'Kinematograph Weekly' (founded in 1907), which was taken over in 1971 by 'Today's Cinema' (which had in turn amalgamated with the 'Daily Film Renter' in 1958). The practical approach of the 'trades' has fulfilled a useful function in applying a realistic perspective to an art which, of economic necessity, must also be an industry.

In the USA there has been a wide range of trade journals; among the more influential have been:

Established	
1908–1914	'Exhibitor's Times'
1914–1918	'Motography'
1919–1929	'Film Daily'
	'Film Mercury'
	'Film Spectator'
	'Motion Picture News'
1930–1939	'Daily Variety'
	'Hollywood Reporter'
	'Hollywood Spectator'
	'Motion Picture Daily'
	'Motion Picture Herald'

Similarly other countries established their trade journals, such as the German 'Lichtbildbühne' and the French 'La Cinématographie Française'.

A second development in film journalism was the fan press. The fan magazine was born to feed the growing public interest in films and, more particularly, the stars who played in them. As film companies began to divulge the names of their leading actors and actresses, so the first movie columns in newspapers began to appear in 1909: according to Alexander Walker in his book 'Stardom', these columns were 'not yet criticism, of course, but interest-arousing news items and gossip'. The inevitable outcome of all this public interest was the publication soon after of Vitagraph's 'The Motion Picture Story Magazine' in America.

In 1911 the first issue of 'Pictures' was published in Britain and, in 1913, the weekly 'Picturegoer' was founded. Thereafter in every major filmgoing nation in the world, magazines sprung up which catered to the insatiable public appetite for news of the cinema and the stars. In Britain the 'big four' between the wars were 'Picturegoer', 'Picture Show' (published soon after 'Pictures'), 'Film Pictorial' and 'Film Weekly'; the last introducing a more serious and informed element into what still remained principally fan journalism.

In America the bland approach of 'Picture Play Magazine' (which flourished in 1915), with its stories of the films and the idealizing features on Francis X. Bushman and other big stars, gave way to the trenchant authority of 'Photoplay' (which in the 1920s was a power to be reckoned with in Hollywood), 'Motion Picture Classic', and 'Shadowland'.

The third and most significant development in film journalism was geared to the demands of the critical and intellectual audience which was tardier in declaring its allegiance to film. The history of film journalism, in fact, is reflected in the history of the film industry, which first attracted the showman and the, if not uneducated certainly under-educated public, before it impressed its potential qualities upon the artist and the intelligentsia.

The 1930s was the principal period for the emergence in Europe and the USA of these more serious film journals which discussed at some length the film as an art form. They were anticipated in Europe by 'Close Up', published in Switzerland from 1927 to 1933, and the first 'Revue du Cinéma', started in France in 1929. In Britain 'Cinema Quarterly' (1932–5) was published in Edinburgh, followed briefly by 'World Film News' in London and the wartime 'Documentary News Letter', while 'Sight and Sound', the journal of the British Film Institute, was founded in 1932 and 'The Monthly Film Bulletin' in 1934. Other journals of the period included, in the USA, 'Experimental Cinema', 'Educational Screen', 'Film Front', 'New Theatre' and 'The

Suzy Delair and Louis Jouvet in 'Quai des Orfèvres' (Henri Clouzot, France, 1947)

National Board of Review Magazine'; in Italy 'Bianco e Nero' (founded 1937); in the USSR, 'Iskusstvo Kino' (founded 1936). The second 'Revue du Cinéma' (founded by André Bazin in 1947) was succeeded in 1950 by 'Cahiers du Cinéma', which from 1952 was vigorously opposed ideologically by the left-wing 'Positif'. After the war, 'Penguin Film Review' was established in Britain, running from 1946 to 1949, when it was succeeded by the annual volume, the Pelican 'Cinema' (1950–52), while the professional quarterly of film art, the Journal of the British Film Academy, was started in 1947, and was succeeded in 1959 by the Journal of the Society of Film and Television Arts. All have been edited by Roger Manvell.

Regular film critics, as distinct from film gossip columnists, began to emerge after the First World War. By the early 1920s every major newspaper in Britain carried a film review feature and in this developing period for film art it is fairly certain that the opinions of such critics as C. A. Lejeune, Iris Barry (subsequently to work in the USA), Ernest Betts, Jympson Harman, Ivor Montagu, and, later, Richard Winnington, had a greater impact on the industry than even the most severe of contemporary critics.

The Russian revolutionary cinema of EISENSTEIN and PUDOVKIN, and the German cinema of the 1920s helped to win admiration from people with a wholly literary background. Arnold Bennett and G. K. Chesterton, for example, wrote serious essays on the art of film-making. Bernard Shaw was impressed later by the talking film. In the 1930s, Graham Greene served an apprenticeship as a film critic. Several people who subsequently moved into wider fields of creative activity spent significant periods as film critics, among then Alistair Cooke and BASIL WRIGHT.

In the USA the 1940s and 1950s saw the appearance of further serious film journals, including:

'Films'
'Film Comment'
'Film Culture'
'Hollywood Quarterly' (later, 'Film Quarterly')
'Cinema Journal'

On the technical side, in addition to the older established 'The American Cinematographer' and the SMPTE Journal, came 'Film World', 'Action' (a journal for film directors), and 'The Film Journal'.

After the Second World War, a fresh element in British film journalism was detectable; young writers whose passionately dedicated essays and reviews laid the foundation for their future involvement in the art and practice of film-making began as critics and commentators. From the editorial ranks of the quarterly 'Sequence' (founded in Britain in 1947) and 'Sight and Sound' under Gavin Lambert's editorship came the directors LINDSAY ANDERSON, KAREL REISZ, and TONY RICHARDSON, as well as Gavin Lambert himself as novelist-screenwriter. More recently the occasional magazine 'Movie' has reflected the views of younger French-orientated British writers.

Even more significantly 'Cahiers du Cinéma' offered an important outlet to the group of critics who in the late 1950s were to be among the film-makers who gave an entirely new impetus to the French cinema. It was a journalist who termed them *la nouvelle vague*. These critic-directors included CLAUDE CHABROL, JEAN-LUC GODARD, FRANÇOIS TRUFFAUT and ERIC ROHMER. Chabrol wrote: '. . . criticism helps. You end by discovering a method, an aesthetic. That is, your own personal aesthetic.' Godard was even more positive: 'All of us at the *Cahiers* considered ourselves to be future directors. Writing was already a way of participating in film-making . . .'

In Finland JÖRN DONNER is a noted critic turned film-director. Elsewhere, too, film criticism has fostered the talents of future film-makers, politically and sociologically aware, who have in common a respect for the film past (nurtured by their period as critics) combined with a desire to liberate the screen from the unnatural constrictions of that past (e.g. CURTIS HARRINGTON and Peter Bogdanovich in the USA).

Gradually the division between those who make, those who watch, and those who write about the film is disappearing, as the proliferation of underground, 'amateur' and student film-makers proves. In more ways than one, film journalism has promoted the concept of that popular art of, by and for the people which the early pioneers envisaged. Among other, serious journals to have appeared more recently than those named above are:

USA:
'Film Society Review' (New York)
'Cinema' (California)
'Film Heritage' (Dayton, Ohio)
'Cinéaste' (New York)

Great Britain:
'Films and Filming' (London)
'Film' (London). Journal of the Federation of Film Societies.
'The Silent Film' (London)
'Focus on Film' (London)

France:
'L'Avant-Scene du Cinéma' (Paris). Specializing in film scripts.
'Cinéma 70, 71,' etc. (Paris)
'Positif' (Paris)

Italy:
'Cinema Nuovo' (Genoa)

Sweden:
'Chaplin' (Stockholm)

Denmark:
'Kosmorama' (Copenhagen; Danish Film Museum). MH and RM

Jouvet, Louis (1887–1951)
Born in Crozon, France. Distinguished French stage director and screen actor who made an important impact in such characteristic French films of the 1930s as *La Kermesse Héroïque* (1935), *Drôle de Drame* and *Un Carnet de Bal* (1937), *Hôtel du Nord* and *La Fin du Jour* (1938). A power in the French theatre, he tended to be typed in films on the strength of his magnetic, rather menacing looks. His witty, sardonic performances were very much in the grandiose tradition of French character acting before the Second World War. His last films were a remake of *Doctor Knock* (1950) and *Une Histoire d'Amour* (1951).

Jump Cut
The elimination of a section from a scene in order to speed the action

Junge, Alfred (1886–1964)
Born in Görlitz, Germany. Production designer. After an early career as scenic artist at the Berlin State Opera and State Theatre studios, he entered German films as designer in 1931 for UFA, but had already worked in Britain on such films as *Moulin Rouge* and *Piccadilly*. He finally settled in Britain in 1932, and his innumerable productions as art director included *The Good Companions, I Was a Spy, The Constant Nymph, The Man who knew too much, Jew Süss, King Solomon's Mines, The Citadel, Goodbye Mr Chips,* and *Gaslight*. From 1942 he did especially distinguished work for MICHAEL POWELL and EMERIC PRESSBURGER on *The Life and Death of Colonel Blimp, A Canterbury Tale, A Matter of Life and Death,* and the superbly coloured Indian sets for *Black Narcissus* (1947), for which he received an Oscar. His later films included *Edward My Son, Mogambo, The Barretts of Wimpole Street,* and *A Farewell to Arms,* which he designed at the age of 72.

Juráček, Pavel
Born 1935. Originally a screenwriter, Juráček as director contributed two notable films to the Czech New Wave of the middle 1960s – *Josef Kilián* (co-directed with Jan Schmidt, 1963), a modern, Kafkaesque fable; and two episodes in *Every Young Man* (1965).

Jürgens, Curd (Curt)
Born 1912 in Munich. German stage and screen actor, scriptwriter and director. He co-scripted, directed and appeared in *Prämien auf den Tod* (1950), *Gangster-premiere* (1951), directed and appeared in *Ohne Dich wird es Nacht* (1956), and made his international reputation as an actor in *The Devil's General,* directed by HELMUT KAUTNER in 1955. His career as a gentlemanly seducer or villain can be traced in such films as *Les Héros sont Fatigués* (1955), *Et Dieu créa la Femme* (1956), *Inn of the Sixth Happiness* and the re-make of *The Blue Angel* (1958), *I aim at the Stars* (as Werner von Braun, 1959), *The Longest Day* (1962), *Lord Jim* (1964), *The Assassination Bureau, OSS 117, Murder for Sale* and *The Invisible Six* (1968), *The Battle of Neretva* and *Hello-Goodbye* (1970), *The Mephisto Waltz* (1971).

K

Kádar, Ján
Born 1918. A pre-war student of the Bratislava Film School, Kádar made several shorts and documentaries and one feature, *Katya* (1950), before joining forces with Elmar Klos with whom he has collaborated in all subsequent work: *Kidnapped* (1952), *Music from Mars* (1954), *Young Days* (1956), *House at the Terminus* (1957), *Three Wishes* (1958), *Spartakiade* and *Youth* (1960), *Death is called Engelchen* (1963), *The Defendant* (1964), *Shop on the High Street* (1965), *Adrift* (1969). He specializes in solidly built dramas on contemporary themes. Kádar and Klos also collaborated on the second programme of the multi-media *Magic Lantern*.

Kalatozov, Mikhail
Born 1903 in Tiflis. A brilliantly promising career was halted for several years when Kalatozov's first film *Salt for Svanetia* (1930) about a poor primitive community was criticized and his second *The Nail in the Boot* (1932) was prohibited on charges of negativism, formalism and distortion of history. For some years Kalatozov remained an administrator in the Tiflis Studios, and only returned to direction in 1939, with *Manhood*. In 1941 he made an aviation film, *Valeri Chkalov*, and thereafter was Soviet Consul in Los Angeles for four years. After the war he made *Conspiracy of the Doomed* (1950), *Firm Friends* (1954), and *The First Echelon* (1956), but enjoyed his biggest international success with *The Cranes Are Flying* (1957), one of the best of the post-Stalinist pictures. He failed to repeat the success with *The Letter That Was Not Sent* (1960). Recent co-productions: with Cuba (*I Am Cuba*, 1962); and with Italy (*The Red Tent*, 1969). DR

Kalmus, Herbert Thomas (1881–1963)
Born in Chelsea, Massachusetts, USA. Physicist, and after distinguished academic career, President of Technicolor Inc.

Kalmus, Natalie (1892–1965)
Born in Boston, USA. Wife of Dr Kalmus and colour director for Technicolor.

Dr Kalmus, in association with Dr D. F. Comstock and W. B. Westcott, developed first an additive colour motion picture process, later adopting for a while a two-colour subtractive process, using two separation negatives produced by a beam-splitting camera. The positive print consisted of two prints welded together for projection. This process was subsequently modified by introducing imbibition printing, which enabled the two subtractive images to be combined on a single film; later a three-colour printing process was introduced. To exploit their processes, Dr Kalmus and his associates founded Technicolor Motion Picture Corporation in 1915 and Technicolor Inc. in 1922, which later had a subsidiary plant in London. Natalie Kalmus, as the company's colour expert, was from 1915 associated with her husband's work, and credited as colour director on films using the Technicolor process.

Above: J. Kroner in 'The Shop on the High Street' (Ján Kádar and Elmar Klos, Czechoslovakia, 1965)
Opposite: Boris Karloff in 'Targets' (Peter Bogdanovich, USA, 1967)
Below: Anna Karina in 'Vivre sa Vie' (Jean-Luc Godard, France, 1962)

Kanin, Garson
Born 1912 in Rochester, NY, USA. Witty American writer, producer and director who has combined screenwriting with theatre work, often in partnership with his wife, Ruth Gordon. His major credits include the co-writing of two of the sharpest SPENCER TRACY–KATHARINE HEPBURN films, *Adam's Rib* (1949)

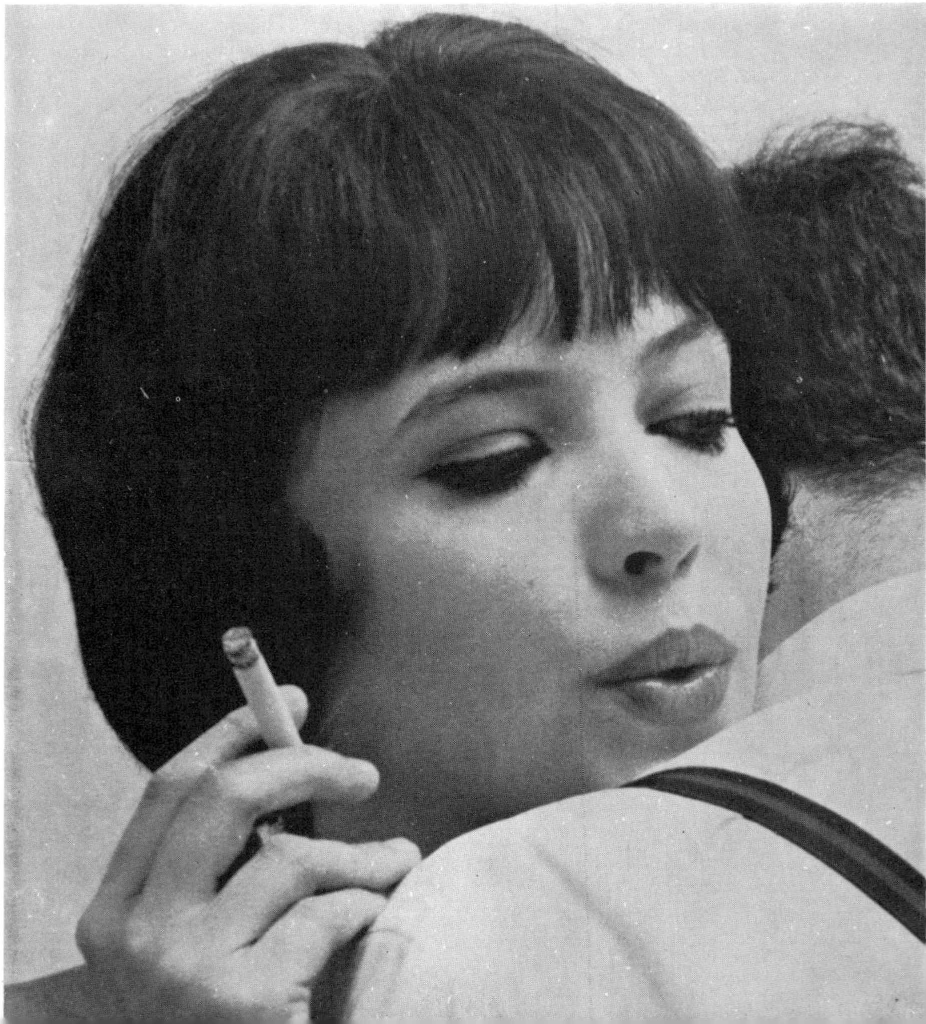

and *Pat and Mike* (1952). His acid, sophisticated Broadway humour was most memorably demonstrated in 'Born Yesterday', which was turned into a film in 1951. He has also created and produced a television series, *Mr Broadway*. Other films: *Bachelor Mother* (1939), *Tom, Dick and Harry* (1940), *A Double Life* (which he also wrote, 1947), *Some Kind of Nut* and *Where It's At* (which he also wrote, 1969).

Karina, Anna
Born 1940 in Copenhagen, Denmark. Actress, who was for a while a model, and went to France in 1958. Her striking appearance, with wide mouth and strong cheekbones, captivated GODARD when he saw her in an advertising film. She married Godard in 1961 and appeared in many of his films: *Le Petit Soldat* (1960), *Une Femme est une Femme* (1961), *Vivre sa Vie* (1962), *Bande à Part* (1964), *Alphaville* and *Pierrot le Fou* (1965), *Made in USA* (1966). Her later films for other directors include *Justine, The Oldest Profession* and *Laughter in the Dark* (all 1969), *Rendezvous à Bray* (DELVAUX, 1971).

Karloff, Boris (1887–1969)
Born in Dulwich, England. British character actor and prototype screen monster whose success as the man-made 'man' in *Frankenstein* (1931) typed his film career thereafter. Christened William Henry Pratt, he tried a variety of jobs prior to getting work as an extra at Universal Studios in Hollywood. He played several roles on stage and screen, before materializing as the *Frankenstein* Monster. He appeared in countless sequels and every variety of horror film and occasionally caricatured his own film image in comedies, with Abbott and Costello among others.

Although he played many straight dramatic roles, particularly on television, he continued to be associated with horror, but the compassion and sincerity he brought to his monster portrayals tended to be overlooked in favour of their spine-chilling effect. One of his last films, *Targets* (1968), gave him the opportunity to create a character – that of a horror film actor – very like himself. Throughout his life, his admirers were constantly surprised to discover that the most famous of film monsters was a gentle, cultivated man with a deep love of cricket.

Other notable films: *The Old Dark House* and *Scarface* (1932), *The Ghoul* (1933), *The Bride of Frankenstein* (1935), *The Walking Dead* (1936), *Tower of London* (1939), *The Body Snatcher* and *Isle of the Dead* (1945), *Bedlam* (1946), *Grip of the Strangler* (1957), *Frankenstein 1970* (1958), *The Raven* (1962), *The Terror* (1966), *The Sorcerers* (1967), *Curse of the Crimson Altar* and *Cauldron of Blood* (1968). MH

Karmen, Roman
Born 1906 in Odessa, Ukraine, USSR. Originally a stills photographer for the magazine 'Ogonyok' (from 1923), Karmen graduated as a cameraman from the Moscow Film Institute (GIK) in 1932. He shot distinguished newsreel compilations in Spain (1936–9) and China (1938–9) and at the front during the Second World War. Incontestably the USSR's finest documentarist, in the 1960s he made several films in and about Cuba.

Kaufman, Boris
Born in Bialystok, then Poland, now USSR. Cinematographer. Brother of MIKHAIL KAUFMAN and DZIGA VERTOV (Denis Kaufman), he entered films in France in the late 1920s, becoming famous for his work on VIGO's *À Propos de Nice* (with its experimental camera effects, 1930), *Zéro de Conduite* (1933), *L'Atalante* (1934). After coming to North America in 1942, he worked for the Canadian National Film Board and the OWI on various documentaries. After years of silence, he reappeared with *On the Waterfront* (1954); subsequent films like *Baby Doll* (1956), *Twelve Angry Men* (1957), *That Kind of Woman* (1959) and *Long Day's Journey into Night* (1962) confirmed him as an extremely sensitive black-and-white artist. Apart from *Splendour in the Grass* (1961), his colour work has been less inventive: *The Group* (1966), *Up Tight* (1968), *Tell Me that you Love Me, Junie Moon* (1970). JG

Kaufman, Mikhail
Born 1897 in Bialystok, then Poland, now USSR. Brother of BORIS KAUFMAN and DZIGA VERTOV (Denis Kaufman). Cinematographer and director. After an unsettled youth during the Civil War (including a spell in the Red Army), Kaufman became chief operator for Vertov on his famous *Kino-Eye* and *Kino-Pravda* series in the 1920s and subsequent full-length documentaries like *Man with a Movie Camera* (1929). Working with variable equipment, Kaufman and his colleagues created many novel effects (speeded-up and slow motion, split-screen juxtapositions), as well as shooting marvellous location material all over the USSR. In 1925 he made *Moscow*, whose style anticipates RUTTMANN's *Berlin*; and in 1929, filmed and directed *Spring*, a richly observed documentary study owing much to Vertov's theories of montage, but more openly relaxed and lyrical. Following the virtual demise of Vertov's group in the 1930s, Kaufman worked in various capacities at the Popular Science studios, but does not appear to have made any more personal films. JG

Käutner, Helmut
Born 1908 in Düsseldorf, Germany. Director, actor and screenwriter. Worked initially in the theatre as director and actor. Career in films began late 1930s as scriptwriter, but he began also to direct light and otherwise non-political films during the war period, including *Romance in a Minor Key* (1943) and *Grosse Freiheit Nr 7* (1944), in both of which he acted. After the war, he was one of the first directors to be given a licence to make films by the British authorities, and he was responsible for many of the best films during the post-war period: *In Former Days* (1947), *The Apple's 'Off'* (1948), two key films looking back on the Nazi period – *The Last Bridge* (1954) and *The Devil's General* (1955) – and *The Captain of Köpernick* (1956). He co-scripted most of these films, as well as many others he has directed, and he has scripted films for other directors, including Rudolf Jugert's *Film without Title* (1947), one of the more successful early post-war films. RM

Danny Kaye in 'Up in Arms' (Elliott Nugent, USA, 1944)

Kawalerowicz, Jerzy

Born 1922 in Gwozdziec (then Soviet Ukraine). Director. Began in Polish industry shortly after the Second World War as an assistant director, then scriptwriter. He is one of the Polish cinema's most serious artists who has never quite made the masterpiece which everyone expected. Social conditions as they affect individuals and war itself are important in several of his films, including *Under the Phrygian Star* (1953–4) and *The Real End of the Great War* (1957). The rather heavy symbolism he favours was less obvious in *The Shadow* (1956) and *Night Train* (1959), a thriller with a most convincing railway background and a typical performance from ZBIGNIEW CYBULSKI; these were followed by two elaborate period dramas, *Mother Joan of the Angels* (1961) and *Pharaoh* (1965), which, though powerfully realized, and full of gripping imagery, were marred by a certain inflexibility of style and narrative monotony. His recent film *The Game* (1969) was not received with much enthusiasm at home and it seems likely that he is marking time until a really conducive subject comes along. JG

Kaye, Danny

Born 1913 in Brooklyn, New York, USA. Actor, entertainer and dancer, he has won popularity on stage and in television as well as on the cinema screen. His main films include: *Up in Arms* (1944), *The Kid from Brooklyn* (1946), *The Secret Life of Walter Mitty* (1947), *A Song is Born* (1948), *Hans Christian Andersen* (1952), *Knock on Wood* (1953), *White Christmas* (1954), *The Court Jester* (1956), *The Man from the Diners' Club* (1963), *The Madwoman of Chaillot* (1969). In 1954 he was given a special Academy Award for his 'unique talents, his service to the industry and the American people'. He is a specialist in zany, mercurial comedy; his sympathetic personality is always a foil to his humour.

Kazan, Elia

Born 1909 in Istanbul, Turkey. Important American film and stage director, sometime actor and writer, of Greco-Turkish descent, identified with the advent of the Method school of acting and drama (especially that of Tennessee Williams) in American films during the 1940s and 1950s. His most personal films – *East of Eden* (1955), *Wild River* (1960), *America, America (The Anatolian Smile)* (1963) and *The Arrangement* (1969), the two last films based on his own semi-autobiographical novels – have a recognizable poetry and psychological insight that arise from Kazan's own immigrant background.

He is, however, principally noted for his films with MARLON BRANDO, *A Streetcar Named Desire* (1951), *Viva Zapata!* (1952) and *On the Waterfront* (1954), for which he won an Academy Award; and for a series of 'crusading' films in the 1940s, on the themes of corruption (*Boomerang*, 1947), anti-semitism (*Gentleman's Agreement*, 1947), for which he won his first Academy Award, and racial prejudice (*Pinky*, 1949), which, though competently made and in key with the times, have not survived well. He is particularly respected as an 'actors' director'.

Above: Elia Kazan (right) directing Karl Malden and Vivien Leigh in 'A Streetcar Named Desire' (USA, 1950)
Below: Buster Keaton in 'Sunset Boulevard' (Billy Wilder, USA, 1950)

Kazan (real name Elia Kazanjoglous) went to America in 1913 and in the 1930s joined the New York Group Theatre as an actor with JOHN GARFIELD and Lee J. Cobb. He began directing in the theatre and in 1947 organised the Actor's Studio with Lee Strasberg and Cheryl Crawford. He directed his first film in 1944, *A Tree Grows in Brooklyn*, although previously he had acted on the screen, most memorably as a cocky gangster in *City For Conquest* (1940).

He returns periodically to the theatre and has devoted much of his time in the last five years to writing.

Other principal films: *Sea of Grass* (1947), *Panic in the Streets* (1950), *Man on a Tightrope* (1953), *Baby Doll* (1956), *A Face in the Crowd* (1957), *Splendour in the Grass* (1960). MH

Keaton, Joseph Francis (Buster)

(1895–1966)

Born in Piqua, Kansas, USA. Buster Keaton's unique gifts and inimitable style as a performer have often tended to obscure the unobtrusive mastery and invention of his work as a film director – qualities which can perhaps in part be attributed to the fact that from his earliest infant consciousness he knew no other work than that of solving problems of *mise-en-scène*. His parents were vaudeville artists, and at the age of three Keaton joined the family knockabout comedy act. By 1917 when the family troupe broke up, Buster was already a star in his own right, and was offered lucrative engagement in Shuberts' *Passing Show of 1917*. With remarkable foresight, however, he chose instead to go into films, as a supporting player to FATTY ARBUCKLE, at a fraction of the salary he could have commanded on stage. His first film appearance was in *The Butcher Boy* (1917). During the next two years or so (allowing for a brief interruption during the last months of the war, when Keaton served in the 40th Infantry in Europe) he appeared in some fourteen Arbuckle films. As his own roles became larger, the subtlety and sophistication of the pictures increased noticeably.

In 1919 Joseph Schenck organized a company to produce shorts starring Keaton, which were from the start mostly written and directed by the star himself. After a slightly shaky beginning with *The High Sign* (1920), Keaton produced a score of two-reel shorts which represent one of the great peaks of Hollywood slapstick comedy, and include *The Goat*, *The Playhouse* and *The Boat* (1921), *Cops* (1922) and *The Balloonatic* (1923). In 1920 Keaton acted in a feature-length comedy for Metro, *The Saphead*, based on the stage success 'The New Henrietta'; but it was not until three years later that he embarked on feature production in his own right with *The Three Ages* (1923), in which he successfully overcame the disadvantages (for comedy) of an elaborate episodic structure which parodied *Intolerance*. The series of features which followed have a consistency of style and quality which confirms that though they often carried different directorial credits, Keaton was in total creative control. The films themselves were marked by fine visual quality, notably in their atmospheric period décor and flexible, often mobile, camera style, and classic structural form. The distinction of Keaton's comedy style was his ability to perform seemingly impossible acrobatic gags and to maintain his own so-called 'stone-face' personality – in fact it was a case rather of extreme economy of expression than in any respect inexpressiveness – without ever being inconsistent to the always clearly defined characters he was playing. The characteristic Keaton hero was always faced with apparently insuperable odds – which he ultimately triumphantly overcame. In *Our Hospitality* (1923) he is an innocent protagonist in a murderous Southern feud. In *Sherlock Junior* (1924), as a cinema projectionist, he dreams he is a detective single-handed against a gang of desperate criminals; in *The Navigator* (1924) he and his girl are adrift in an otherwise deserted ocean liner; in *Seven Chances* (1925) he finds himself caught between an avalanche and a gang of female furies bent on marrying him; in *Go West* (1925) he finds himself responsible for a cattle herd stampeding through an Eastern city; in *Battling Butler* (1926) he is obliged to pose as a prize fighter; in *The General* (1926) he is a spy, single-handed against the entire Northern armies; in *College* (1927) he is a weakling called upon to prove himself a pentathlon hero; in *Steamboat Bill Jr* (1928) he confronts a tornado and a flood. With the coming of sound, Keaton – who would undoubtedly have triumphed in the new medium – found himself caught up in the industrial reorganizations of the times, and producing through MGM. The big studio situation did not suit his methods of creation; and after two more lively, silent features, *The Cameraman* (1928) and *Spite Marriage* (1929), his career, though not his talent, began to decline. After one or two talkies he sought what work he could in indifferent shorts, and became a victim of alcoholism. Only towards the end of his life did the recognition of a new generation resuscitate both his spirits and his career, and at the time of his death he was overwhelmed with offers of work. His final appearance was in *A Funny Thing Happened on the Way to the Forum* (1966). DR

Keene, Ralph (1902–1963)

Born in Mysore, India. Documentary director and producer. Educated Marlborough College. Early career as painter and art-dealer. In 1934 he founded Strand Films with Donald Taylor, later in 1941 becoming principal producer for Greenpark. He was a specialist in films concerning nature and country life, and directed, among other films, the wartime *Power on the Land*, and the fine series of films, *Winter, Spring, Summer on the Farm*, followed by *The Crown of the Year*. After the war, he went to India for Greenpark, where he made the notable documentary *A String of Beads*; he also worked as a producer in Ceylon. Later he made two award-winning documentaries for British Transport films, *Between the Tides* and *Journey into Spring* (1957). For a short while he worked in feature film, and produced *A Boy, a Girl and a Bike* (1949).

Kelly, Gene

Born 1912 in Pittsburgh, USA. Versatile American dancer-choreographer-actor-director, who, in company with STANLEY DONEN, VINCENTE MINNELLI, ARTHUR FREED, helped launch a new concept of indigenous American film musicals at MGM during the late 1940s and 1950s. An attractive and technically consummate dancer, he came to Hollywood fresh from a Broadway and cabaret career, to make his screen début in *For Me and My Gal* (1942). But his vision extended beyond that of a performer. He co-directed the key musicals of the time, with Donen, *On the Town* (1949) and *Singin' in the Rain* (1952). The modern ballet in *An American in Paris* (1950) was revolutionary. His performance as D'Artagnan in *The Three Musketeers* (1948) was virtually ballet without music.

When the film mood moved away from original musicals in favour of cumbersome stage adaptations, Kelly appeared creditably in several straight roles; but his ambitious musical, *Invitation to the Dance* (1956), which he also directed, was only a limited popular and critical success. In television he starred in a series, *Going My Way* (1962). Since *The Young Girls of Rochefort* (1967), he has concentrated on screen directing: *A Guide for the Married Man* (1967), *Hello, Dolly!* (1969) and *The Cheyenne Social Club* (1970), in which he has managed to marry large-scale production values to an exuberant sense of period and fun.

Other notable films as performer: *Thousands Cheer* (1943), *Cover Girl* and *Christmas Holiday* (1944), *Anchors Aweigh* (1945), *The Pirate* (1947), *Summer Stock* (1950), *It's Always Fair Weather* (1955), which he also co-directed, *Les Girls* (1957), *Inherit the Wind* (1960), *What a Way to Go* (1964). Also as director: *The Tunnel of Love* (1958), *Gigot* (1963). MH

Kelly, Grace

Born 1928 in Philadelphia, USA. Actress, educated at the American Academy of Dramatic Arts. First played in amateur theatricals, and then on Broadway and television. Her film début was in *Fourteen Hours* in 1951, and her subsequent films include *High Noon* (1952), *Dial M for Murder* and *Rear Window* (1954), *The Country Girl* (1954), which won an Academy Award, and *High Society* (1956). She then retired from films to marry Prince Rainier III of Monaco; after the marriage a new constitution, hailed as a 'Coup de Grace', gave women full voting rights and eligibility to hold office in the National Council. Her screen personality was essentially cool and this aspect of her charm appealed especially to HITCHCOCK.

Kelly, Orry

See ORRY-KELLY

Kerr, Deborah

Born 1921 in Helensburgh, Scotland. An actress, educated at a ballet school, she began her career in repertory. Her screen début was in *Major Barbara* in 1940, and brought her immediate popularity. Usually playing poised, well-educated women, she made a number of films in Britain before going to Broadway and Hollywood. These include *Love on the Dole* and *Hatter's Castle* (1941), *The Life and Death of Colonel Blimp* (1943), *Perfect Strangers* (1945) and *Black Narcissus* (1947). Other British and American films include: *King Solomon's Mines* (1950), *Quo Vadis?* (1951), *Julius Caesar* (1953), *The End of the Affair* (1955), *The King and I* (1956), *The Innocents* (1961), *The Night of the Iguana* (1964), *Prudence and the Pill* (1968), *The Arrangement* (1969) and many more.

Kershner, Irvin

Born 1923 in Philadelphia, USA. American director, occasional television producer, who has made few but invariably off-beat and interesting films. In their attitude toward alienated American youth his first two films, *Stake Out on Dope Street* (1958) and *The Young Captives* (1959), were ahead of their time. Other main films include: *The Hoodlum Priest*

Above: Deborah Kerr and James Mason in 'Julius Caesar' (Joseph L. Mankiewicz, USA, 1953)
Below: Suzanne Bianchetti in 'Ménilmontant' (Dimitri Kirsanov, France, 1925)

(1961), *The Luck of Ginger Coffey* (1964), *A Fine Madness* (1966), *The Flim Flam Man* (1967), *Loving* (1970). MH

Key Light
The main light used for illuminating a subject.

Kidd, Michael
Born 1918 in Brooklyn, USA. Gifted American dancer-choreographer who contributed – with STANLEY DONEN and GENE KELLY – to the great MGM musical *renaissance* of the 1950s. After a career in ballet on the stage, he made his film début as a dancer and actor in *It's Always Fair Weather* (1955), and choreographed the free-wheeling dance routines in *Band Wagon* (1953), *Seven Brides For Seven Brothers* (1954), *Guys and Dolls* (1955). He directed DANNY KAYE in *Merry Andrew* (1958) and in 1969 he reunited with his former dancing colleague, now director, Gene Kelly, to do the choreography for *Hello, Dolly!*

Kinetoscope
A form of peep-show machine patented by Thomas Edison in 1889, for showing photographic moving pictures to one viewer at a time, the photographs being on an endless band of film, 50 ft (15·25 metres) in length.

King, Henry
Born 1892 in Virginia, USA. Traditionalist American director whose distinguished career during the silent 1920s has earned him the respect of many younger film-makers. His later work, with Twentieth Century Fox, during the 1930s, 40s and 50s has been mostly conventional family entertainment, though his range of subject-matter is remarkable by any standards.

An actor in vaudeville, burlesque, stock and films before he started working as an assistant director, he made a number of small films between 1915 and 1921 when he directed what some critics consider his finest silent film, *Tol'able David.* The freshness of his approach, coupled with an obvious affection for back-woods America, was particularly memorable. Subsequent silent films, *Sonny* (1922), *The White Sister* (1923), made in Italy, *Stella Dallas* (1925), *The Winning of Barbara Worth* (1926) established him as one of the great directors of the period. His later work failed to sustain this reputation, although he continued to be very successful and capable of key films, such as *The Gunfighter* and *Twelve O'Clock High* (1950) and *The Sun Also Rises* (1957).

Within the Fox set-up, he produced a perpetual stream of formula films, using the same contract stars (TYRONE POWER and GREGORY PECK, among them) and often adding a zest and subtlety that went beyond the rigid limitations of the plot. The unpopular biography of the American president *Wilson* (1944) was one of his more notable films of this period, and he brought an uncluttered rustic charm to the stuffy production of the musical *Carousel* (1956).

Other principal films: *State Fair* (1933), *Seventh Heaven* (1936), *Lloyds of London* (1937), *In Old Chicago* and *Alexander's Ragtime Band* (1938), *Jesse James* and *Stanley and Livingstone* (1939), *The Black Swan* (1942), *The Song of Bernadette* (1943), *Margie* (1946), *Prince of Foxes* (1949), *The Snows of Kilimanjaro* (1952), *Love is a Many Splendored Thing* (1955), *The Bravados* (1958), *Tender is the Night* (1961). MH

Kinoshita, Keisuke
Born 1912 in Hamamatsu, Japan. Director. Was assistant cameraman and assistant-director in the 1930s; began directing during the Second World War, including *Army* (1944), with its curiously ambivalent attitude towards the war. His post-1946 output has taken in various genres including satire (*Carmen Comes Home*, the first Japanese colour film, 1951), social drama (*A Japanese Tragedy*, 1953), love stories (*She Was Like a Wild Chrysanthemum*, with novel halo effects, 1955) and period legends (*The Ballad of the Narayama*, a stunning fusion of Kabuki and widescreen colour techniques, 1958). Kinoshita has considerable flair for unusual locations and fine ensemble playing, but he does not seem to have a strongly personal signature and his occasionally excessive sentimentality gives some of his work (like *Twenty Four Eyes*, 1954) a disconcertingly soft centre. JG

Kinugasa, Teinosuke
Born 1896 in Mie, Japan. Director. Was a female impersonator on stage and later on screen, having joined the Nikkatsu Company in 1917. Little of his considerable output as scriptwriter and director since the early 1920s has reached the West, which makes it difficult to assess his total contribution. His most famous silent film, *Crossways* (1928), has great dramatic power and is clearly influenced by German expressionism and Soviet montage (he later studied in both countries). Some of his many period films of the 1930s (notably *The Summer Battle of Osaka,* 1937) are reputedly interesting; but he only achieved international recognition in 1953 with *Gate of Hell,* a rather ordinary period melodrama but shot in outstanding colour, complete with complicated gauze effects and elaborately staged exteriors with multi-coloured flags, dashing horse-riding and colour-conscious décor. His subsequent output includes a number of competent, sentimentalized love stories. Clearly, Kinugasa should be a subject for further investigation, for his early work suggests that he was far more conscious of the European cinema than some of his contemporaries. JG

Kirsanov, Dimitri (1899–1957)
Born in Dorpat, Estonia, USSR. Director. With his wife, Nadia Sibirskaia, as his principal actress, Kirsanov made a group of stylish 'impressionist' silent films – *L'ironie du destin* (1923), *Ménilmontant* (1925), *Sylvie-Destin* (1926), *Sables* (1927), *Brumes d'automne* (1928) – which earned him a considerable critical reputation and were subsequently reckoned as harbingers of the 'poetic realist' mood of French films in the later 1930s. With the coming of sound, however, and particularly after his separation from Sibirskaia, Kirsanov's output declined into mediocre commercial work, though he continued to direct until 1956 (*Ce soir les jupons volent, Miss Catastrophe*).

Kluge, Alexander
Born 1932 in Halberstadt, Harz, Germany. Writer and director, qualified in law. Worked as an assistant to FRITZ LANG in Germany 1958–9. Deeply involved in the 'Junger deutscher' Film movement, he was one of the prime movers in promulgating the Oberhausen Manifesto of 1962, proclaiming the younger genera-

tion of German short-film makers' desire to make feature films in a new style, and develop a new German film industry. Responsible either as writer or director (or both) for many short films, he is best known abroad for his two striking feature films, prize-winners at the festivals, both films of ideas and discussion of social psychological and political issues, with symbolic situations and settings: *Yesterday Girl* (1967), featuring Alexandra Kluge, and *Artistes at the Top of the Big Top: Disorientated* (1968). Kluge remains one of the most influential of the younger German film-makers. Recent film: *The Big Mess* (1971).

Knef, Hildegard (Hildegarde Neff)
Born 1925 in Ulm, Germany. Trained in the post-war Berlin theatre. Her significant appearance in the notable film *The Murderers are Amongst Us* (1946) made her one of the key actresses to emerge after the war during the brief period of highly creative German cinema; she also appeared in *Film without Title* (1947). She went for a while to Hollywood and London to further her career, appearing in such films as *The Snows of Kilimanjaro* (1952) and *The Man Between* (1953). She returned to Germany, where she has appeared in many films, as well as developing a second career as a singer. See her autobiography 'A Gift Horse' (published by André Deutsch, 1971).

Knox, Alexander
Born 1907 in England. Actor and author, educated in Canada. First acted on British stage, making his début in 1930 and wrote the book 'Bride of Quietness'. His films (mainly British) include: *The Gaunt Stranger* (1938), *This Above All* (1942), *Wilson* (1944), *Sister Kenny* (1946), *The Sleeping Tiger* (1953), *The Divided Heart* (1954), *Reach for the Sky* (1956), *The Wreck of the Mary Deare* (1959), *The Psychopath* (1960), *The Damned* (1961), *Accident* (1966), *How I Won the War* (1967), *Shalako* (1968).

Kobayashi, Masaki
Born 1916 in Hokkaido, Japan. Director. Was assistant director from 1941 with Shochiku and then assistant to KINOSHITA in 1946. His theme, which is essentially one of revolt against corruption and inhuman codes of conduct in both past and present, was most completely seen in his 10-hour anti-war trilogy *No Greater Love* and *Road to Eternity* (1959), *A Soldier's Prayer* (1961). Later period films – *Harakiri* (1962), *Kwaidan* (1964), *Rebellion* (1967) – confirmed his dynamic style coupled with a real flair for colour and widescreen compositions. His main weakness is a tendency to over-emphasize and he has never quite achieved the lyrical tenderness for which he often strives. Recent work includes *Hymn to a Tired Man* (1968), an unusually muted study of post-war frustrations and memories which lacked overall conviction, and *Inn of Evil* (1970).

Alexander Korda (1947)

Korda, Alexander (1893–1956)
Born in Hungary. Dominant figure in British films during the 1930s and 40s. As producer, studio chief and star-builder, he is the only British-based film-maker to have rivalled the showmanship and grandiose flair of the Hollywood tycoons, though ironically he himself remained recognizably a Central European and he relied heavily on Continental talent to produce his British pictures.

In Budapest he worked as a journalist and schoolteacher to help support his younger brothers, ZOLTÁN and VINCENT KORDA, who subsequently joined his production team. He set up as an independent producer in Hungary, worked for UFA in Germany and went to Hollywood in 1926; there he directed several films before returning to Europe, where he formed an independent film company in Paris. He settled in London in 1930, directing his first British film, *Service For Ladies*, in 1931. In 1932 he founded London Films, started building Denham Studios and directed *The Private Life of Henry VIII* (1933) which, with constant showings on television, has since become arguably the most famous British film ever made.

The huge – and largely unexpected – success of this flamboyant and entertaining distortion of history led to *Catherine the Great* (1933), *The Scarlet Pimpernel* (1934), *Sanders of the River* and *Things to Come* (1936): all opulent productions which revealed Korda's gift for gauging public tastes. Korda spent lavishly and planned on a large scale, signing up important names in literature and the arts. He launched VIVIEN LEIGH, CHARLES LAUGHTON, ROBERT DONAT and ELISABETH BERGNER on international careers and put British films on the world map.

Eventually, his extravagance caught up with him and he found it difficult to get finance. For various reasons, an abortive production of *I, Claudius* with Charles Laughton and JOSEF VON STERNBERG directing was abandoned in 1937. Korda spent some years in Hollywood during the Second World War producing and directing one of his most patriotic films, *Lady Hamilton* (1941). He returned to Britain and continued to produce quality – if occasionally rather stuffy – films. He produced and directed *Perfect Strangers* (1945) and *An Ideal Husband* (1947), after which he became less involved in active production, though London Films survived until he died. Other principal films:

Above: Lionel Ngakane, Tom Enigboken and Barry Johnson in 'Cry the Beloved Country' (Zoltán Korda, GB, 1952)
Below: Fritz Kortner, Fritz Rasp and Ruth Weyher in 'Warning Shadows' (Arthur Robison, Germany, 1923)

The Ghost Goes West (1935), *Rembrandt* (also directed, 1936), *Knight Without Armour* and *Elephant Boy* (1937), *The Four Feathers* (1939), *Thief of Baghdad* (1940), *Anna Karenina* (1948). See 'Alexander Korda' by Paul Tabori (1959). MH

Korda, Vincent
Born 1896 in Turkeye, Hungary. Designer, working for his brother ALEXANDER. He created the sets for such notable films as *The Private Life of Henry VIII* (1933), *Catherine the Great* and *The Private Life of Don Juan* (1934), *The Scarlet Pimpernel* and *The Ghost Goes West* (1935), *Things to Come* and *Rembrandt* (1936) and *The Thief of Bagdad* (1940). After the war he was again production designer for London films, his credits including *An Ideal Husband*, *Bonnie Prince Charlie* and *The Fallen Idol* (1948) and *Summer Madness* (1955).

Korda, Zoltán (1895–1961)
Born in Turkeye, Hungary. Director, principally associated with his brother, ALEXANDER, at London Films. Started his career as a cameraman in Austria-Hungary; then editor for UFA in Germany. As a director, his interest lay mainly in spectacular films of action, and he directed *Sanders of the River* (1935), *Conquest of the Air* (co-director, 1936), *Elephant Boy* (co-director with FLAHERTY, 1937), *The Drum* (1938), and *The Four Feathers* (1939). In 1940–8 he worked in Hollywood, making such films as *The Jungle Book* and *Sahara* (1943), *The Macomber Affair* (1947), *A Woman's Vengeance* (1948). He rejoined his brother at London Films, to make what was probably his best film, *Cry the Beloved Country* (1952). He co-directed *Storm over the Nile* (1955).

Kortner, Fritz (1892–1970)
Born in Vienna, Austria. Actor and director. A theatre actor of wide experience in Austria and Germany, he joined Max Reinhardt in Berlin in 1911 and Leopold Jessner in 1919. His career as film actor began in 1916, and he became one of the most celebrated character actors of the German cinema, best remembered now for heavy and sinister parts in expressionist films. Among his many silent films were *Danton* (1921), Jessner's *Die Hintertreppe* (*Backstairs*, 1921), *Peter the Great* (1922), ROBISON's *Schatten* (*Warning Shadows*, 1922), WIENE's *The Hands of Orlac* (1925), and PABST's *Pandora's Box* (1928). He also directed a number of silent films, and starred in several sound films before the Hitler régime, including *Dreyfus* (1930). Since he was Jewish, he was forced to leave Germany for the United States, and it was difficult for his great talent (dependent on his handling of his own language) to find suitable outlet abroad. He appeared in Britain in GRUNE's *Abdul the Damned* (1935) and in the USA in *The Hitler Gang* (1944), *The Razor's Edge* (1946) and *The High Window* (1947); he also collaborated on screenplays. After the war he returned to Germany to appear in *Der Ruf* (*The Challenge*, 1949), which he co-scripted. His distinction as an actor and at times a highly controversial stage director was soon re-established in Berlin in productions of Shakespeare, Strindberg and Ibsen. He directed a few films, such as *Sarajevo* (1955), as well as working for television up to the time of his death. RM

Kosma, Joseph (1905–1969)
Born in Budapest, Hungary. Composer. After studying music in Budapest, he emigrated to France in 1933, establishing himself as a composer and song writer with JACQUES PRÉVERT. Long association with JEAN RENOIR on *Le Crime de Monsieur Lange* (1935), *Une Partie de Campagne* (1936), *La Grande Illusion* (1937), *La Marseillaise* (1938), *La Règle du Jeu* (1939), *Elena et les Hommes* (1955), *Dejeuner sur l'Herbe* (1959); and with CARNÉ – *Les Enfants du Paradis* (1944–5), *Les Portes de la Nuit* (1946), *La Marie du Port* (1949). Other work includes FRANJU's shorts *Le Sang des Bêtes* (1949) and *En Passant par la Lorraine* (1950); and BUÑUEL's *Cela s'appelle l'aurore* (1955). Kosma's essentially melodic style is tinged with a warm romantic melancholy ideally suited to Renoir (*vide* the masterly score for *Partie de Campagne*), coupled at times with a steely nervous energy most noticeable in his music for Franju and Buñuel. JG

Koster, Henry
Born 1905 in Berlin, Germany. Adaptable

director who has worked in Hollywood since 1936 when the first of his frothy DEANNA DURBIN musical romances, *Three Smart Girls,* salvaged the fortunes of Universal and made a name for its director. A commercial artist, cartoonist, film and drama critic, he graduated to screen-writing and directing in Germany: principal films, *Peter* (1933), *Marie Bashkirtzeff* (1936). Though his work has never been noticeably inspired, his occasionally wry sense of comedy has resulted in some attractive films – *It Started with Eve* (1941), *The Bishop's Wife* (1948), *Mr Hobbs Takes a Vacation* (1962). But he has tended to be weighed down by studio prestige pictures – including Twentieth Century Fox's first CinemaScope productions, *The Robe* (1953), *Desirée* (1954) and *A Man Called Peter* (1955) – to which he responded with ponderous sincerity. Other main films; *The Unfinished Dance* (1947), *The Inspector General* (1949), *Harvey* (1950), *No Highway* (1951), *My Cousin Rachel* (1952), *The Naked Maja* (1959), *Flower Drum Song* (1960), *Dear Brigitte* (1965), *The Singing Nun* (1966). MH

Kovács, András
Born 1925 in Budapest, Hungary. With JANCSÓ one of the two most prominent figures in Hungarian cinema today, Kovács's final years at the Budapest Academy of Dramatic and Film Art coincided with the peak of the Rákosi period, during which BELA BALAZS was 'voted' out of his post as rector of the Academy by a group of students. From 1951 to 1957 he worked in the unpopular script department of Hunnia Studios; and clearly his personal involvement in these difficult situations for the national cinema has resulted in the preoccupation of his films with problems of individual responsibility. After three years as an assistant, Kovács directed his first feature, *Summer Rain,* in 1960. Following two more unremarked films, he made *Difficult People* (1964), a *cinéma-vérité* reportage on five inventors frustrated by bureaucratic opposition to their work. *Cold Days* (1966) returned to more formal narrative style for a reconstruction of a wartime atrocity committed on Hungarians by Hungarians. *Walls* (1968) is a film dialogue on the same basic themes as *Difficult People.* Following a 90-minute reportage on pop music, for television, Kovács attempted in *The Relay* (1970) to combine *cinéma-vérité* and fictional narrative in furtherance of his attempt to create a cinema of philosophical dialogue. DR

Kozintsev, Grigori M.
Born 1905 in Kiev, USSR. Soviet director. One of the generation whom the 'heroic' days of Soviet art enabled to make their artistic débuts as adolescents. Kozintsev's career has spread over five decades; and his work in the 1960s has been in no way less important to the history of the Soviet cinema than his experimental efforts in the 1920s and the films of his maturity in the 1930s, which gave him and his collaborator LEONID TRAUBERG leading places in the Soviet film industry.

Kozintsev studied painting at the Academy of Fine Arts in Petrograd. In 1921, with SERGEI YUTKEVITCH, Trauberg and other teenagers, he established FEKS, 'The Factory of the Eccentric Actor'. This theatre company had as its aims the search for new forms of theatrical art which would overthrow the old traditional ways represented by the Moscow Art Theatre. They cultivated 'eccentricity', and managed to provoke a minor scandal in 1922 with a production of Gogol's 'Marriage' which introduced elements of music-hall and circus and ended with a new finale in which the author shot himself. Invited to make a film by Sevzapkino, the FEKS group made *The Adventures of Oktyabrina* (1924), at once a parody of American adventure films and 'a sort of propaganda film poster. . . . It was all rather disconnected but galloped along on the screen, abounding with dizzying abridgements of the story and shock cuts'. Two more adventures, *Mishka against Yudenich* (1925) and *The Devil's Wheel* (1926), were followed by a return to Gogol: a notable adaptation of *The Overcoat* (1926), with expressionist design and acting in vigorous reaction against the over-upholstered conventions of Russian costume pictures. After *Brothers* (1927) Kozintsev and Trauberg (the FEKS group proper having by now been dispersed) made two period films, *S.V.D.* (*Society of the Great Cause,* 1927), about the Decembrist Revolt; and *New Babylon* (1929), a glittering, sardonic reconstruction of the Paris Commune.

Alone (1931), one of the earliest Soviet sound films, was a contemporary realist drama which marked the final break with the FEKS 'eccentric' tendencies. The peak of the collaboration was the *Maxim* Trilogy. The three films, *Youth of Maxim* (1935), *Return of Maxim* (1937) and *The Vyborg Side* (1939) showed the development of a revolutionary out of the raw material of an irresponsible, carefree young worker. Films of enormous warmth, humour and humanity, undated after thirty years (though the earlier parts now plainly appear better than the later) the Maxim Trilogy provided an important model for ANDRZEJ WAJDA's *A Generation.* Maxim himself (played by Boris Chirkov) became a modern folk hero, and even reappeared in the films of other directors.

In 1944 Kozintsev and Trauberg made one of the few films of the war years about the home front – the story of the workers in an evacuated factory. This film, *Simple People,* fell foul of the growing Stalinist repression of the arts, was condemned for formalism and cosmopolitanism, and suppressed. Perhaps as a result of this the old partnership broke up; and Kozintsev has since directed alone. In 1948 he made a historical film, *Pigorov,* followed in 1953 by another, *Bilinski.* During the same period he was active in the theatre in Leningrad.

In 1957 Kozintsev directed the first of the major works of his latest period, *Don Quixote,* made in colour – a sensitive, melancholy interpretation of Cervantes, with NIKOLAI CHERKASSOV in the role to which he had many times returned in the course of his acting career. *Hamlet* (1964) was the realization of a very old ambition for Kozintsev. With its rich decoration always directly relevant to the intellectual content, this remains one of the finest film versions of Shakespeare. In 1970 Kozintsev completed *King Lear* which if it lacked the sustained brilliance of *Hamlet,* nevertheless grappled intelligently with the dramatic and psychological problems of the text. See

Grigori Kozintsev directing Valentina Chendrikova in 'King Lear' (USSR, 1970)

'Shakespeare – Time and Conscience' by Kozintsev (1967). DR

Kramer, Stanley
Born 1913 in New York, USA. Independent American producer and director who in the 1940s and 1950s helped consolidate the vogue for low budget, radical, hard-hitting melodramas based on contemporary problems: racial discrimination in *Home of the Brave* (1949), paraplegics in *The Men* (1950), motorcycle gangs in *The Wild One* (1954). After the McCarthy witch-hunt period and the separation from his partner, writer CARL FOREMAN, in the early 1950s, he turned to directing large-scale, star-studded films whose liberal sentiments were over-laid with glossy production values, notably *Not as a Stranger* (1954), *On The Beach* (1959), *Inherit the Wind* (1960), *Judgment at Nuremberg* (1961), *Ship of Fools* (1965), *Guess Who's Coming to Dinner* (1967).

After leaving University, he gained studio experience as a jack-of-all-trades, junior writer, prop man, cutter; worked for a while as a co-producer at MGM and, during the Second World War, on training and orientation films. Later he formed his own production company with Carl Foreman, producing, first, the light, dry comedy *So This is New York* (1948) and then the strikingly successful boxing film, *Champion* (1949). His biggest hit of this period was *High Noon* (1952), which Foreman wrote and FRED ZINNEMANN directed. When he took his company to Columbia, however, his programme of inexpensive, high quality films – including *Death of a Salesman* (1951), *Member of the Wedding* (1953) – failed at the box-office, a disappointment which probably influenced the more extravagant form and content of his later work.

Other principal films as director-producer: *The Pride and the Passion* (1957), *The Defiant Ones* (1958), *It's a Mad Mad Mad Mad World* (1963), *The Secret of Santa Vittoria* (1969), *RPM* (1970), *Bless the Beasts and Children* (1971). MH

Krauss, Werner (1884–1959)
Born near Koburg, Germany. Actor. He had lifelong experience in the German and Austrian theatre, and in films specially associated with the expressionist movement of the 1920s and, later, with certain of the more vicious propaganda films of the Hitler period, more especially the anti-Semitic *Jud Süss* (1940). He entered films in 1916, and his international fame was established by *The Cabinet of Dr Caligari* (1919). His other important silent films included *Scherben* (*Shattered*, 1921), *Fridericus Rex* (1922), Pilate in WIENE's *INRI* (1923), *Waxworks* (1924), *The Student of Prague*, *The Joyless Street* and *Tartuffe* (1925) and *Secrets of a Soul* (1926). In sound he appeared notably in *Yorck* (1931), *Robert Koch* (1939), *Die Entlassung* (1942) and *Paracelsus* (1943). After the war he was able to resume his career both on the stage and in films. RM

Kristl, Vlado
Born 1923 in Yugoslavia. Animation and live-action director. An outstanding artist, originally both actor and painter, who preferred at first to work with others in Zagreb. His rare, highly decorative films made there include *The Great Jewel Robbery* (1961) designed with Mladen Feman, and *La Peau de Chagrin* (1961), made with Ivo Urbanic, and his solo film, *Don Quixote* (1962), brilliantly designed and coloured. In West Germany, to which he emigrated in 1963, he has made a series of live-action short films, *Madeleine, Madeleine* (1963) and *Autorennen*, the live-action features, *The Dam* (1964) and *Der Brief* (1960), and the animated films, *Prometheus* (1964) and *Das Land des Überflusses* (1967).

Kubrick, Stanley
Born in 1928 in New York, USA. Producer, director, and screenwriter. His father, a doctor working in the Bronx, was a keen photographer, and passed his enthusiasm on to his son, who was later to be employed as a staff photographer for the magazine, 'Look'. In 1951 Kubrick produced, directed and wrote two documentaries, *Day of the Fight* and *Flying Padre*, and then, most unusually for beginners in the USA, Kubrick managed not only to direct, photograph and edit his first feature films, *Fear and Desire* (1953) and *Killer's Kiss* (1955), but raise the money for their production as well. At the start, therefore, he promoted his own work. Now fully launched, he wrote the screenplays as well as directing *The Killing* (1956) and the anti-war film, *Paths of Glory* (1958). After directing the period spectacle, *Spartacus* (1960), which had a much

Three stills from '2001 – a Space Odyssey' (Stanley Kubrick, GB, 1968)

more intelligent script than was common for this kind of film, Kubrick moved permanently to Britain, where his first film was *Lolita* (1962). He next turned to more wholly personal forms of film-making, writing the script as well as producing and directing *Dr Strangelove, or how I learned to stop worrying and love the bomb* (1963), and producing and directing *2001 – a Space Odyssey* (1968), which was scripted by Arthur C. Clarke, and was the most technically advanced and courageous film venture of the decade. Indeed, Kubrick is both fascinated by and exceptionally knowledgeable about film technology. Many of his films have explored violence in one form or another, culminating in the *reductio ad absurdum* of the nuclear threat in the black comedy-burlesque of *Dr Strangelove;* and the brilliantly visualized and savage burlesque of youthful violence matched by psychological persecution by the State in *A Clockwork Orange* (1971) derived from Anthony Burgess's novel. A study of him by Alexander Walker was published in the USA in 1971. RM

Kuleshov, Lev (1899–1970)
Born in Tambov, Russia. The first aesthetic theorist of film art and the true begetter of the Soviet cinema. Enrolled in the Moscow School of Painting, Architecture and Sculpture at fifteen, at seventeen Kuleshov was a set-designer for Yevgeni Bauer at the Khanzhonkov Studio; and also acted in Bauer's *After Happiness.* On Bauer's death Kuleshov completed this film, and went on to make *The Project of Engineer Prite*, which he described as the first Russian (or Soviet) film to be 'constructed dynamically, and editorially, with the use of close-ups'. About the same time Kuleshov published his first articles in a film magazine, defining, two years before *Caligari*, the key contribution of the designer in the expressive means of the cinema. After the Revolution he was despatched to the Eastern Front with a camera team. Returning to Moscow he was rapidly recruited to the teaching staff of the State Film School, and given his own 'Workshop'. With his group of students, who included young people who were to become the most significant creators of the new cinema, among them PUDOVKIN and, briefly, EISENSTEIN, Kuleshov conducted his famous experiments with montage, demonstrating theoretically for the first time the peculiar properties of film editing in making possible artificial dimensions of time and place. The Kuleshov group's first feature film was the witty parody, *The Extraordinary Adventures of Mr West in the Land of the Bolsheviks* (1924), which was followed by an adventure story, *The Death Ray* (1925), and his finest film, *Dura Lex* (1926), adapted from Jack London. *The Journalist* (1927), *The Gay Canary* and *The Great Buldis* (1929) met with little success, as did his first sound film *Horizon* (1932); and after his brilliant experiments with sound in *The Great Consoler* (1933) Kuleshov was criticized for 'Formalism'. After this he made only four conventional and anodyne films for children, his continuing importance lying in his inspired work as a teacher at the Film Institute, where he continued to work almost until his death from lung cancer. DR

Isuzu Yamada and Toshiro Mifune in 'Throne of Blood' (Akira Kurosawa, Japan, 1957)

Kuri, Yoji
Born 1928 in Japan. Animation producer and director. During the 1960s has made some of the most virulent cartoons yet, concerned especially with violence and the more predatory aspects of sex. His graphic style is grotesquely distorted, his humour black and surreal. In *Human Zoo* (1960) people are confined in cages, the women torturing their male victims. In *Love* (1963) a woman eats a man and excretes him, while on the track the single word *Ai* (love) is obsessively repeated. *The Button* and *The Window* both lead to destruction either by nuclear explosion or by fire. *Aos* (1964) is a cool paroxysm of sadism; *Samurai* (1965) a vortex of destructive sexuality. Kuri's films activate like lightning; his shortest lasts a minute, his longest half-an-hour. During the 1960s he has made some 80 subjects, and his work has become more popular in the West than in Japan. RM

Kurosawa, Akira
Born 1910 in Tokyo, Japan. Director. Probably the best-known of all Japanese directors, he first studied painting and entered films as assistant to Kajiro Yamamoto in the mid-1930s, writing numerous scripts for him and others. He began his directing career in 1943 with *Judo Saga* and subsequently alternated between modern and period subjects. Kurosawa brought an individual boldness to the Japanese cinema both technically and in terms of subject matter, and the Grand Prix award to *Rashomon* at Venice in 1951 marked a new phase for the Japanese cinema abroad. Notably in his period subjects, Kurosawa developed a truly virtuoso style, characterized by fast, complex travelling shots following horsemen pounding through forests, and extremely well-rehearsed, quickly-cut sword fights ending in a pile of toppled bodies (in which can be seen the influence of Daisuke Ito, a veteran director whom Kurosawa admires). These aspects are best seen in *Seven Samurai* (1954), *The Hidden Fortress* (1958), *Yojimbo* (1961), *Sanjuro* (1962), all featuring TOSHIRO MIFUNE, the most famous of Kurosawa's regular repertory company, as the resourceful, erratic, run-down samurai who invariably becomes involved with oppressed peasants fighting injustice. Parallels with the American Western hero who rides into town, despatches the villains and rides out again are obvious, particularly when one realises that JOHN FORD is another of Kurosawa's favourites. His modern stories develop the social awareness of the period films in a more calculated manner, introducing a vein of rather trite symbolism and drawn-out sentimentality which ultimately places Kurosawa on a slightly lower plane than MIZOGUCHI and OZU. Yet his achievements in the social drama are considerable when one remembers *Living* (1952), the story of a timid clerk who forces through a piece of useful legislation against an unfeeling bureaucracy, with its audacious construction and rich detail normally associated with the novel; and *Stray Dog* (1949), a HATHAWAY-like location thriller with the famous climax in which policeman and crook collapse together in a field after a cross-country chase. *Red Beard* (1965), a period hospital drama and *Dodeska-Den* (1970), a mosaic-like view of a slum community (and Kurosawa's first colour film) contain all of his strengths and weaknesses. Here, he explores again his favourite theme of the clash between illusion and reality and, notably in the latter, crystallizes the vein of ruthless, black humour which runs all through his work. His literary ventures – a version of Dostoievski's *The Idiot* (1951), the Macbeth adaptation *Throne of Blood* (1957) and Gorki's *The Lower Depths* (1957) – successfully translate the originals into a Japanese milieu and, at the same time, cast a new light on their authors' intentions. It has often been said that Kurosawa is the most 'Western' of Japanese directors due, probably, to his knowledge of and fondness for various American film genres, yet his work has an entirely personal feeling and control right down to the vertical wipes which he uses as a punctuation mark, and the rapid alternation of static dialogue scenes and sudden eruptions of action which constantly occur (as in *High and Low*, 1963). His concern for what ICHIKAWA has called 'the pain of our age' sometimes leads him into obvious, windy rhetoric (*Record of a Living Being*, 1955), yet his best films in all genres, with their gleaming camerawork and enthusiastic ensemble playing, belong to the essential fabric of cinema. JG

L

La Cava, Gregory (1892–1949)
Born in Pennsylvania, USA. Prolific American director, formerly a newspaper cartoonist, whose clever handling of social comedy in the 1930s revitalized many a soggy screenplay. He was particularly adept at coaxing superior performances from his actresses, notably CLAUDETTE COLBERT, CAROLE LOMBARD, GINGER ROGERS, KATHARINE HEPBURN. Main films: *The Half-Naked Truth* and *Gabriel over the White House* (1932), *What Every Woman Knows* (1934), *Private Worlds* and *She Married Her Boss* (1935), *My Man Godfrey* (1936), *Stage Door* (1937), *The Primrose Path* (1940), *Lady in a Jam* (1942), *Living in a Big Way* (1947).

Ladd, Alan (1913–1964)
Born at Hot Spring, Arkansas, USA. Actor. Short of stature, tough and versatile, he was a swimmer and diving champion, a reporter, and a salesman before he began his film career in 'bit' roles. He became one of the most popular stars of the late 1940s and early 1950s, often playing laconic, tough character parts. His main films include: *This Gun for Hire* (1942), *Two Years before the Mast* (1946), *The Great Gatsby* (1948), *Shane* (1953), *The Red Beret* (1954), *Boy on a Dolphin* (1957), *The Badlanders* (1958), *Duel of the Champions* (1961), *The Carpetbaggers* (1964).

Laemmle, Carl (1867–1939)
Born in Laupheim, Germany. Pioneer producer. Tenth child in an impoverished Jewish household. Emigrated at 17 to join his brother in Chicago. After working as a clerk and bookkeeper, he became manager of a clothing store in Oshkosh, Wisconsin, in 1898. He opened a nickelodeon, the Whitefront Theatre, in Chicago in 1906 after resigning from the store, and developed a chain of movie theatres together with a distribution company. He founded his Independent Motion Picture Company (IMP) to fight the patent war, in which he was a protagonist, producing his own films in the process and in 1912 establishing the Universal company with some of his allies. In 1915 he opened Universal City, California's largest studio at the time, in the San Fernando Valley. In 1929 his son, Carl Laemmle Jnr (born 1908), succeeded him as manager at Universal, until, in 1936, both father and son were forced out of the business by the declining fortunes of the company. Laemmle became a noted philanthropist. John Drinkwater, the English poet, wrote a commissioned, highly sympathetic biography, 'The Life and Adventures of Carl Laemmle' (1931). RM

Lake, Veronica
Born 1919 at Lake Placid, New York, USA. Actress, blonde and petite, with a cool 'smoochy' comedy style who was most popular in films of the 1940s. *I Wanted Wings* (1941) brought her immediate success, and her subsequent films include: *Sullivan's Travels* (1941), *This Gun for Hire* and *I Married a Witch* (1942), *Bring on the Girls* (1944), *The Blue Dahlia* (1946), *Ramrod* and *Saigon* (1947), *Stronghold* (1951). She then retired, but later made *Footsteps in the Snow* (1966), a Canadian film. She published her autobiography, 'Veronica', in 1968 and has recently appeared in British theatres.

Lamarr, Hedy
Born 1914 in Vienna, Austria. Actress, who began her film career in Europe in the early 1930s. *Extase* (1933), in which she appeared nude, won a top Italian film prize. She then went to Hollywood, where her name became a synonym for glamour and beauty. Amongst the films she made there are: *Comrade X* (1940), *Ziegfeld Girl* (1941), *Tortilla Flat* and *White Cargo* (1942), *The Conspirators* (1944), *Her Highness and the Bellboy* (1945), *The Female Animal* (1947), *Copper Canyon* (1949), *Samson and Delilah* (1950), *My Favourite Spy* (1951). Her autobiography, 'Ecstasy and Me', was published in 1967.

Lamorisse, Albert (1922–1970)
Born in Paris, France. Director. Best known for his medium-length films *Crin Blanc* (1952) and *Le Ballon rouge* (1956), with their mixture of child-like charm and rather cloying senti-

Alan Ladd and Deborah Kerr in 'Thunder in the East' (Charles Vidor, USA, 1951)

Above: Dorothy Lamour in 'A Miracle can Happen' (King Vidor and Leslie Fenton, USA, 1948)
Below: 'Somewhere in Berlin' (Gerhardt Lamprecht, 1946)

mentality. He had a highly developed camera eye (with a fondness for fast travelling shots) and the latter part of his career was devoted to perfecting a method of shooting from helicopters which achieved remarkable results in a feature, *Le Voyage en ballon* (1960), and several short films about France, full of breathtaking vistas of city and countryside seen from the air and shot in outstanding colour. His death in a helicopter accident deprived the cinema of a minor, yet distinctive, artist, whose camera innovations have influenced current photographic methods. JG

Lamour, Dorothy
Born 1914 in New Orleans, USA. Actress, who after becoming 'Miss New Orleans of 1931' began her career by singing on the radio. Her screen début was in *Jungle Princess* (1936); she was then type-cast for a number of years as a dusky, sarong-clad, exotic princess in the series of 'Road' films – *The Road to Singapore* (1939), *The Road to Utopia* (1945), etc, with BOB HOPE and BING CROSBY. She also appeared in such films as *Chad Hanna* (1940), *Beyond the Blue Horizon* (1942), *My Favourite Brunette* (1947), and *The Greatest Show on Earth* (1953). In 1953 she officially retired, but later made guest appearances in *Road to Hong Kong* (1961), *Donovan's Reef* (1963), and *Pajama Party* (1965).

Lamprecht, Gerhardt
Born 1897 in Berlin, Germany. Director, scenarist and film historian. Entered films as a scriptwriter, and became a prolific director from 1923, co-scripting most of his silent films with Louise Heilborn-Körbitz. His best-known films include the adaptations of Thomas Mann's *Buddenbrooks* (1928), his celebrated sound film, *Emil and the Detectives* (1931), and his excellent post-war 'rubble' film, *Somewhere in Berlin* (1946), which he also scripted. Certain of his films had a social interest, such as *Die Unehelichen* (1926). He continued in the regular production of films through the Nazi régime (though these were without political content) and into the 1950s.

Lancaster, Burt
Born 1913 in New York City, USA. Actor, at first circus acrobat; also producer, in partnership for some years with Harold Hecht. During the Second World War he acted and danced in Forces shows and also served with the US Army Special Service in Italy and North Africa. Although on the surface a tough and rugged man, his acting also involves a strong emotional, even sensitive, response and a capacity to measure up to the demands of unusual characterization. His screen début was in *The Killers* (1946), and since then he has appeared and starred in a great number of films, including: *Brute Force* (1947), *Sorry, Wrong Number* (1948), *Come back Little Sheba* and *From Here to Eternity* (1953), *Apache* (1954), *The Kentuckian* (which he also directed) and *The Rose Tattoo* (1955), *Gunfight at the OK Corral* and *Sweet Smell of Success* (1957), *The Devil's Disciple* (1958), *Elmer Gantry* (which won an Academy Award, 1960), *The Young Savages* and *Judgment at Nuremberg* (1961), *Birdman of Alcatraz* (1962), *The Leopard* (1963), *The Train* and *Seven Days in May* (1964), *The Professionals* (1966), *Castle Keep* and *Airport* (1969). RM

Lanchester, Elsa
Born 1902 in London, England. Actress, who was married to CHARLES LAUGHTON. She started at the Children's Theatre in London at the age of 16. Later she acted on the stage and screen, often with her husband, for example in the early experimental burlesque *Bluebottles* (1928). Her speciality lay in projecting an eccentric, even pathetic, charm. Her best

British film was the silent version of *The Constant Nymph*, and it was followed by *The Private Life of Henry VIII* (1933), *The Bride of Frankenstein* (1935), *The Ghost goes West* (1936), *Rembrandt* (1937) and *Vessel of Wrath* (1938). In 1940 she went to Hollywood, and her subsequent films include: *Ladies in Retirement* (1941), *Tales of Manhattan* (1942), *The Spiral Staircase* (1945), *Androcles and the Lion* (1953), *Witness for the Prosecution* (1957), *Mary Poppins* (1964), *Willard* (1970).

Lang, Jr Charles
Born 1902 in Bluff, Utah, USA. Cinematographer. Also a painter, he became a lighting cameraman in the late 1920s; established himself in the 1930s as a leading black-and-white artist, later becoming one of the world's major colour cinematographers with a distinctive lighting style full of soft contrasts, and a marvellous feeling for bare, sun-drenched locations. His most outstanding work includes *The Lives of a Bengal Lancer* and *Peter Ibbetson* (with its superb period recreation, 1935); *Angel* (1937) and *Zaza* (1939), two fine examples of his lighting methods with actresses; *Ace in the Hole* (1951); *The Big Heat* (1953); *The Man from Laramie* (1955); *Gunfight at the OK Corral* (1957); *Some Like It Hot* (1959, full of splendidly dark-toned interiors); *One-Eyed Jacks* (1961) and *Inside Daisy Clover* (1965), both typical of his painterly use of colour. Recent films include *Cactus Flower* (1969). JG

Lang, Fritz
Born 1890 in Vienna, Austria. Director. Trained for a career in architecture, at first he wandered about the world, especially to Munich and Paris, using his capacities as a graphic artist to earn a living. Serving in the Austrian army during the First World War, he was severely wounded and decorated for courage; he lost the sight of one eye. During his recuperation he began to write stories and screenplays for JOE MAY, and joined ERICH POMMER at Decla in 1919 as story editor. His first picture as director was *Halbblut* (*The Half-breed*, 1919), and only his commitment to the two-part serial *Die Spinnen* (*The Spiders*, 1919) prevented him from directing *The Cabinet of Dr Caligari*. He then collaborated on a number of indifferent films written by Thea von Harbou, whom he married in 1920: she was to work on the screenplays for all his films through to 1932. His first considerable film was *Der Müde Tod* (*The Weary Death*, or *Destiny*, 1921), a beautiful film responding fatalistically to the fashionable taste for expressionism, which suited the disillusioned post-war German mood. His taste was for melodrama, loosely linked to the expressionist style, but with meticulous care given to the design of grandiose architectural settings, as in the splendid décor for his two-part *Nibelung Saga* (1924); he lavished equal care on the visual qualities of his thrillers, *Dr Mabuse the Gambler* (1922) and *Spione* (*Spies*, or *The Spy*, 1928). Lang's German films are non-dynamic and slow-moving, visually always impressive, but often carrying melodrama to the verge of the absurd. His most important work artistically during the silent period was *Metropolis* (1926), the study of an authoritarian society of the future; once again, though pictorially impeccable, the social message involved in the film is absurd, as H. G. Wells was among the first to point out. Both *The Spies* and *Die Frau im Mond* (*The Woman on the Moon*, 1928), with its fine space ship and moon landscapes, were independent productions. Lang's first sound film, *M* (1932), was an impressive début, a serious attempt to face the psychological problems of a child-murderer, though still to some extent marred by melodrama. The film anticipates Lang's later move towards the powerful dramatic treatment of social problems involving victimization of the individual by society. However, his last work in Germany was his self-styled anti-Nazi film, the fantasy of a maniac who wants to rule the world, *The Last Will of Dr Mabuse* (1933), which Goebbels banned on the assumption of power by the Nazis in 1933. At the same time, he invited Lang to become a director of film for the Nazis, either ignorant of the fact or overlooking that Lang was a half-Jew. Lang left Germany the same night for Paris; he also left his wife, who was a supporter of Hitler.

After making *Liliom* (1933) in France, Lang went to Hollywood, where, after many projects and an intensive study of American small-town life, his first film was to be one of his most brilliant, *Fury* (1936), a violent attack on lynching. The film was successful, and he followed it with *You Only Live Once* (1937), another study of social injustice. His next film, *You and Me* (1938), lacked the same quality, and after this Lang's career moved more in the direction of producing quality box-office films. He made Westerns (*The Return of Frank James*, 1940, *Western Union*, 1941, and *Rancho Notorious*, 1952), the anti-Nazi films *Man Hunt* (1941) and *Hangmen also Die* (1943), thrillers such as Graham Greene's *Ministry of Fear* (1944), and the series of psychological mysteries including *The Woman at the Window* (1944) and *Scarlet Street* (1945). His best film of this later period was *The Big Heat* (1953), with its exposure of violence and corruption. In 1957 at the age of 67 Lang returned to Germany to remake the old stories he had once scripted for JOE MAY, *Das Indische Grabmal* and *Der Tiger von Eschnapur* (1958), and followed this with *Die 1000 Augen des Dr Mabuse* (1960). In spite of the commercial nature of a great part of his work, Lang's major films form a complete *œuvre* which proves him to be one of the masters of the medium. In 1963 he appeared in GODARD's film *Le Mépris* as himself. For studies of his work see Paul M. Jensen's 'The Cinema of Fritz Lang', Peter Bogdanovich's 'Fritz Lang in America', and the many critiques of his films written by his devoted admirer, Lotte Eisner. RM

Langdon, Harry (1884–1944)
Born in Council Bluffs, Iowa, USA. The child of Salvation Army officers, Langdon was a cartoonist, prop boy, barber, medicine-show performer and had toured for 20 years in vaudeville with an act called 'Jimmy's New Car' before being recruited to MACK SENNETT's Keystone lot in 1923. Despite long-standing

'Woman on the Moon' (Fritz Lang, Germany, 1928)

Above: Harry Langdon
Below: Graciela Borges and Alfredo Alcon in 'Summer Skin' (Leopoldo Torre Nilsson, Argentina, 1961)

legends, recent re-viewing of his early Sennett shorts reveal that his screen character was fairly clearly defined even before FRANK CAPRA, then a Sennett gag-writer, devised *Tramp Tramp Tramp* for him. From the start, Langdon was a mixture of pierrot and middle-aged baby. The baby character emerges in the odd, innocent, absorbed intentness of his foolishness; and at the same time gives an eerie edge to his moments of sexuality. The pierrot comes to the fore in his moments of frenzy as well as in the quiet and reflective passages in which his baby eyes and tiny LILLIAN GISH mouth acutely register, in the tiniest twitches, shock or disbelief or pleasure, or such other emotions as clowns are heir to. Langdon's best films were those in which he was directed by Capra – *The Strong Man* (1926) and *Long Pants* (1927). Like many silent comedians he found it harder to establish a niche in talking pictures, though he continued to work as a script collaborator and an actor in short films or supporting roles until his death. DR

Lap Dissolve
See DISSOLVE

Lara, Claude Autant
See AUTANT-LARA

Lasky, Jesse L. (1880–1958)
Born in San Francisco, USA. American film pioneer who, after a varied career in show business, formed Jesse Lasky Feature Plays in 1913 with his brother-in-law SAMUEL GOLDWYN, Arthur S. Friend and CECIL B. DE MILLE. In 1913 he produced *The Squaw Man* and later merged with ZUKOR's Famous Players, becoming Vice-President in charge of production of the studio that became known as Paramount. He supervised production there until he was forced out of the company in the early 1930s. Thereafter he worked intermittently at Fox, United Artists (as president of the Pickford-Lasky organization), RKO and MGM, returning to Paramount to prepare a film, *The Big Brass Band*, just before his death.

Although unable to equal his more formidable tycoon rivals, he played a major part in establishing Paramount as a major film company. His fall from grace was dogged by debt and disappointment, though his later work as a producer included some of the most successful films of the 1940s and 1950s – *Sergeant York* (1941) and *The Great Caruso* (1951) among them.

His son Jesse Jr achieved success as a screenwriter for Cecil B. De Mille. Lasky Senior published his autobiography 'I Blow My Own Horn' in 1958. MH

Lassally, Walter
Born 1926 in Berlin, Germany. Cinematographer. Came to Britain in his youth, worked his way up in the camera department and became known as lighting cameraman for the Free Cinema group of directors in the 1950s, working on *Thursday's Children* (1954), *Everyday Except Christmas* (1957), *We are the Lambeth Boys* (1959), etc. Collaborated with Greek director MICHAEL CACOYANNIS on *A Girl in Black* (1956), *A Matter of Dignity* (1958), *Electra* (1962), *Zorba the Greek* (1964); and TONY RICHARDSON on *A Taste of Honey* (1961), *Loneliness of the Long Distance Runner* (1962), *Tom Jones* (1963). Also worked with many new, younger directors: Sarne's *Joanna* (1968), Hall's *Three into Two won't Go* (1969). Lassally's versatility and knowledge of film make him much sought after for location pictures all over the world and those needing improvisatory techniques. Recent film: JAMES IVORY's *Savages* (1971). JG

Latin America
Latin-American film-making is led by Mexico, Brazil and Argentina. The current statistics are approximately as follows:

Mexico:	60 features a year; some 2,000 theatres for a 40-million population.
Brazil:	60 features a year; some 3,250 theatres for some 75-million population.
Argentina:	30 features a year; some 2,000 theatres for a 20-million population.

There is also a very limited production of feature films in Chile, Colombia, Peru and Venezuela. Both the Mexican and Argentinian accents are acceptable in the rest of Spanish-speaking Latin America.

Argentina The impetus first given to local Argentinian film-making came with the arrival of certain distinguished French film-makers,

Production stills from 'Samson and Delilah' (Cecil B. De Mille, USA, 1949)

who had left German-occupied France; these included the directors Pierre Chenal and Jacques Remy, and the actor LOUIS JOUVET. Quality was established sufficiently for Luis Saslavsky's film, *La Dama Duende*, to win a prize at the Cannes Film Festival after the war. The leading post-war director, however, was Hugo Fregonese, who had worked in Hollywood, and whose film *Donde Mueren las Palabras* (1946) was a poetic tragedy. Another director of the post-war period was Mario Soffici *(Celos; Martin Fierro)*. The films made at this time tended to have European literary sources for their inspiration.

The most important international figure to emerge during the 1950s and 1960s was LEOPOLDO TORRE NILSSON, whose baroque, socially-critical studies of bourgeois Argentinian society won many awards overseas, but were less popular in his own country. In recent years he has found it more difficult to make the kind of film on which his reputation was based, and he has moved into spectacular production with another version of *Martin Fierro* (1969), based on the legend of the gaucho hero of Argentina.

Brazil The Brazilian cinema, formerly associated with the name of ALBERTO CAVALCANTI, has undergone some change during the 1960s. This was due in part to the formation in 1966 of a National Institute of Cinema, to encourage with financial awards the production of features and shorts of merit, and to add a bonus system to the income derived by Brazilian producers from distribution. However, most of the films produced are aimed at popular entertainment and success at the box-office. A movement known as Cinema Nôvo, with an eye on bizarre treatments of social subjects, has been born, led by such directors of a new generation as GLAUBER ROCHA, Ruy Guerra, Nelson Pereira dos Santos, Roberto Santos, Julio Bressane, and others. Although Rocha's *Antonio-das-Mortes* won the prize for best direction in Cannes in 1969, this group of advanced directors has not yet achieved its aim in winning adequate sponsorship for its films. Also, censorship restrictions in Brazil are severe. Among the more interesting films are:

Glauber Rocha: *Barravento* (1961), *Deus e o diabo na terra do Sol* (1964), *Antonio-das-Mortes* (1969);

Ruy Guerra: *Os Cafajestes* (1962), *Os Fuzis* (1964); and outside Brazil, *Sweet Hunters* (1969) and *The Gods and the Devil* (1970);

Walter Hugo Khouri: *O Palacio des Anjos* (1970);

Joaquim Pedro de Andrade: *Macunaima* (1969);

Carlos Diégues: *The Big City* (1966), *The Resounding Cry* (1969), *Os Herdeiros* (1971);

Julio Bressane: *Matou a familia e foi ao Cinema* (1970), *Um Anjo Nasceu* (1970);

Nelson Pereira dos Santos: *Hungry for Love* (1969), *How Tasty was my Little Frenchman* (1971).

Mexico Mexico, like Argentina, established its national style in the post-war years. Its incomparable scenery, architecture and natural lighting led to the films by which it became best-known at this time (other than through American productions made on location in Mexico, such as Herbert Kline's *The Forgotten Village*, 1941) namely location-made dramas. A forerunner of these films had been Pancho Cabrera's *The Night of the Mayas*, filmed in Yucatan in the mid 1930s, and featuring Arturo de Cordova. The films which became best-known were those directed by EMILIO FERNANDEZ and photographed by the outstanding cameraman, GABRIEL FIGUEROA; these included *Las Abandonadas (The Abandoned)*, *Flor Silvestre (Wild Flower)*, and *Maria Candelaria* (1943), all starring Dolores del Rio, and *La Tierra del Fuego se Apaga* (1955). Fernandez also directed Maria Felix in *La Otra (The Others)* and *Enamorada*; the latter, like *Maria Candelaria*, featuring a new, young male star, Pedro Armendariz.

Top: 'Martin Fierro' (Leopoldo Torre Nilsson, Argentina, 1969)
Above: 'Los Inundados' ('The Floods', Fernando Birri, Argentina, 1962)

While the most popular star at the box-office was Jorge Negrete, the comedian Cantinflas (Mario Moreno) approached the world class. He produced a character out of Mexico's loafing street-boy which became popular throughout Spanish-speaking Latin America; he sensed a universal psychology in him which appealed everywhere and led to comparisons

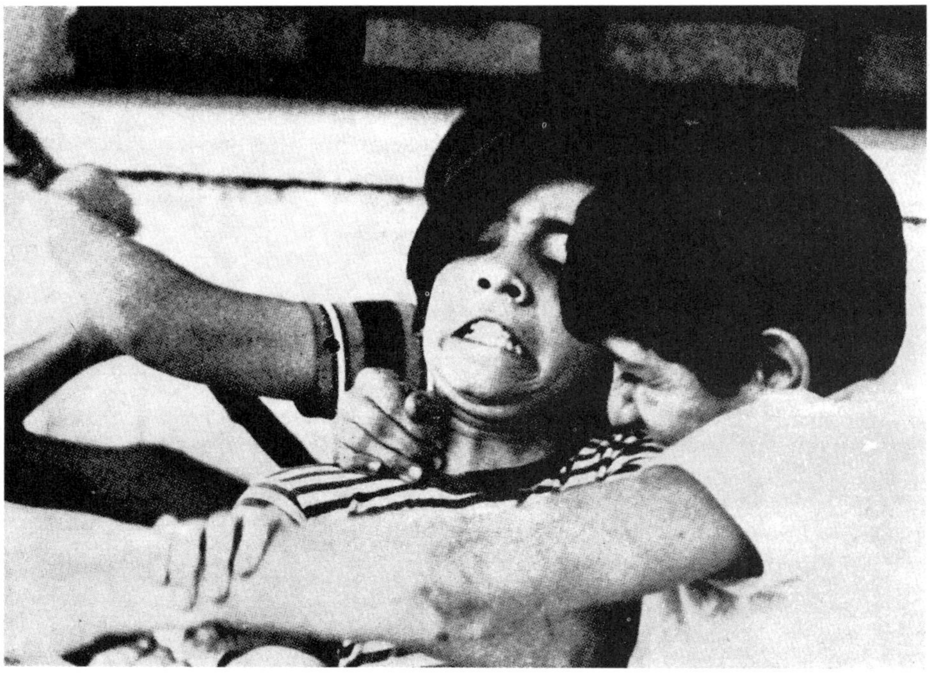

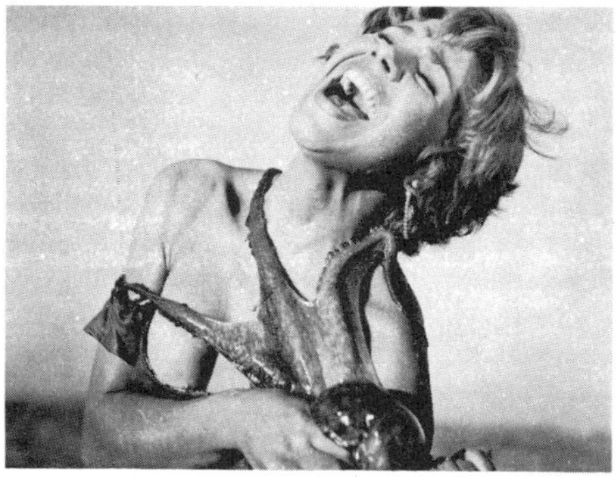

Top: 'La Soldadera' (José Bolanos, Mexico, 1966)
Above: 'El Rebozo de Soledad' (Roberto Gavaldon, cameraman Gabriel Figueroa, Mexico, 1952)
Below: Cantinflas and Maria Elena Marqués in 'Romeo and Juliet' (Mexico, 1943)
Bottom: Dolores del Rio in 'Maria Candelaria' (Emilio Fernandez, Mexico, 1943)

Top: 'Y que Patatin, y que Patatan' (Mario Sabato, Argentina, 1971)
Above: 'O Canto do Mar' (Alberto Cavalcanti, Brazil, 1953)
Below: 'A Grande Cidade' ('The Big City', Carlos Diégues, Brazil, 1966)

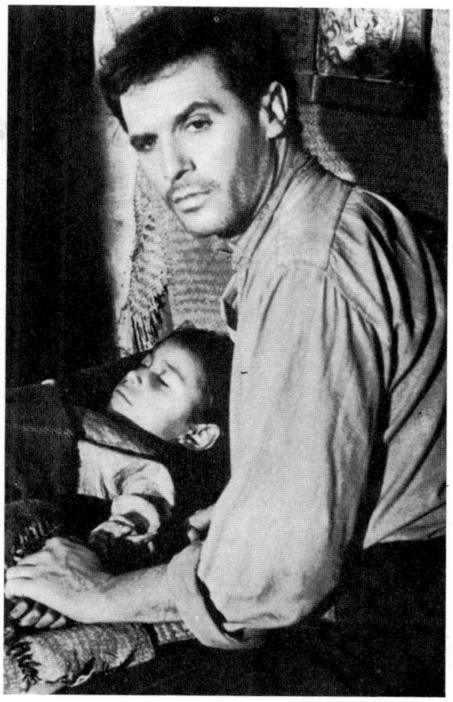

Above left: 'Antonio-das-Mortes' (Glauber Rocha, Mexico, 1969)
Above right: Francisco Rabal in 'Nazarin' (Luis Buñuel, Mexico, 1959)
Right: Dan O'Herlihy in 'Robinson Crusoe' (Luis Buñuel, Mexico, 1953)
Below: 'Simon of the Desert' (Luis Buñuel, Mexico, 1965)
Bottom: 'The Exterminating Angel' (Luis Buñuel, Mexico, 1962)

with CHAPLIN. In film after film he burlesqued in turn Romeo, D'Artagnan, a policeman in *The Unknown Soldier*, even a spiritualist medium in *I am a Fugitive*. His personality pervaded his pictures, which were in themselves simple enough. He became familiar to audiences across the world in MIKE TODD's production, *Around the World in Eighty Days*.

During the 1950s Mexican production expanded rapidly, including co-production with France, and especially Spain. Although the outstanding figure in Mexican cinema became inevitably LUIS BUÑUEL, who went to Mexico in 1947, Mexican films by other directors won occasional recognition abroad, such as Benito Alazraki's *Raices (Roots)* and Carlos Velo's documentary of bull-fighting, *Torero*. During the last few years Alexandro Jodorowsky has emerged as a bizarre talent, surrealistically violent and visually exciting, notably in *El Topo* (1970). See also CUBA. RM

Lattuada, Alberto

Born 1914 in Milan, Italy. As founder of the Milan Cineteca Italiana and an organizer of cineclubs, Lattuada had already become an influence on progressive Italian cinema even before the war. After working as a screenwriter (SOLDATI's *Piccolo mondo antico*; Poggioli's *Sissignora*), he made his first film as a director, *Giacomo l'idealista*, in 1942; but his most important work was done in the formative period of neo-realism (*Il Bandito*, 1946; *Il Delitto di Giovani Episcopo*, 1947; *Senza Pietà*, 1948; *Il Mulino del Po*, 1949). With *Luci del varietà* (co-directed with FEDERICO FELLINI, 1950) and *Il Cappotto* (1952) he developed new aspects of neo-realist expression. Later films include an episode of *Amore in città* (1953), *La Spiaggia* (1954), *La Tempesta* (1958), *L'Improvista* (1961), *La Mandragola* and *Don Giovanni in Sicilia* (1966), *Matchless* (1967), *Fräulein Doktor* (1968).

Laughton, Charles (1889–1963)
Born in Scarborough, England. Actor. After war service he succeeded, in spite of some opposition from his family of hoteliers, in fulfilling his ambition to become an actor, studying under Komisarjevsky at the Royal Academy of Dramatic Art in London in the early 1920s. After considerable success on the stage, he entered films tentatively in 1928 through the influence of the actress ELSA LANCHESTER (whom he married in 1929). He first appeared in a series of short, experimental comedies in which H. G. Wells, Ivor Montagu and Adrian Brunel were involved. After appearing in DUPONT's British film, *Piccadilly* (1929), he divided his time between the stage and films, working in the London and Broadway theatres with such marked success that Paramount offered him a contract which took both him and Elsa Lanchester to Hollywood. Here he gave initial outstanding performances in *The Devil and Deep* (1932) and as Nero in DE MILLE's *The Sign of the Cross* (1933). After creating an entertaining cameo performance in *If I had a Million* (1932), he won an Oscar for his work in ALEXANDER KORDA's celebrated *The Private Life of Henry VIII* (1933), made in England. After this his famous series of screen characterizations of the 1930s began to flow, including those in *The Barretts of Wimpole Street* (1934), *Ruggles of Red Gap* and, as Bligh, in *Mutiny on the Bounty* (1935). But Laughton, always uneasy and uncertain about his career, disliked being 'typed' as a villain, and returned to England to star in Korda's *Rembrandt* (1936). In 1937 he worked unhappily with VON STERNBERG on the abortive *I, Claudius*, achieving what was obviously the makings of a remarkable character performance, as the rushes shown in the BBC television documentary, *The Epic that Never Was* (1965), revealed. Next, in association with the exiled German producer, ERICH POMMER, Laughton founded the company called Mayflower, which from 1937 produced a number of films in which Laughton appeared, including *Vessel of Wrath* (1937) and *St Martin's Lane* (1938). But he found production as well as performance onerous, and returned to Hollywood, where throughout the rest of his screen career he was to appear in films of widely differing quality, many only too obviously below his high standard; the best included *The Hunchback of Notre Dame* (1940), *It Started with Eve* (1941), *The Canterville Ghost* (1944), *The Big Clock* (1947) and, in Britain, DAVID LEAN's *Hobson's Choice* (1954); he was also notable in WILDER's *Witness for the Prosecution* (1957) and in KUBRICK's *Spartacus* (1960). His last performance, before he died of cancer, was one of his most brilliant, the wily senator in *Advise and Consent* (1961). He also directed one memorable, if uneven film, *Night of the Hunter* (1955), which suggested that he could possibly have become a major screen director. Although primarily an actor of striking personality and with a theatrical love for the bravura effect, he was also capable of great delicacy of feeling; he was emotional and temperamental, with a keen sense of values, always striving to overcome what he held to be the physical disability of his appearance. He retained his connection with the stage, giving two remarkable and controversial seasons in Shakespeare at the Old Vic in 1933–4, and again at Stratford-on-Avon in 1959. Elsa Lanchester wrote a book of reminiscences, 'Charles Laughton and I', which was published in 1938. RM

Above: Charles Laughton as 'Rembrandt' (Alexander Korda, GB, 1936)
Below: 'Millions Like Us' (Frank Launder and Sidney Gilliat, GB, 1944)

Launder, Frank
Born in 1907 in Hitchin, England. Scriptwriter, director and producer, he entered the industry in 1930, and from 1937 was closely associated with SIDNEY GILLIAT. Together they were responsible for several of the best British scripts of the 1930s, including *A Yank at Oxford* (1938), *Tha Lady Vanishes* (1938) and *Night Train to Munich* (1940). Still in partnership with Gilliat, he co-scripted and directed *Millions Like Us* (1944), and directed *2,000 Women* (1944). He produced and co-scripted *The Rake's Progress* (1946). Either as producer, director or writer in the partnership, he has worked on many films, which include: *I See a Dark Stranger* (1945), *London Belongs to Me* (1949), *State Secret* (1950), *Only Two Can Play* (1962), as well as the series of girls' school farces starting with *The Belles of St Trinians* (1954). Both Launder and Gilliat have served for many years on the board of British Lion Films Ltd.

Laurel, Stan (1890–1965)
Born in Ulverston, Lancashire, England.
Hardy, Oliver (1892–1957)
Born in Harlem, Georgia, USA.
Laurel was a music-hall comedian who arrived in the USA with CHAPLIN and Fred Karno's Company; Hardy came from the deep South, and was a singer. Both had been with the HAL ROACH studios for years, and even played together, before they were definitively teamed in 1927 (*Putting Pants on Philip*). They provided the classic comic contrast of lean and fat, timorous and foolhardy, put-upon and bully. Although with their bowler hats and bow ties they seemed to aspire to respectable bourgeois values they were, wrote Charles Barr, 'supreme liberators from bourgeois inhibition'. The orgiastic destruction that they always managed to produce arrived despite their deference to

Top: Oliver Hardy, Jean Parker and Stan Laurel in 'The Flying Deuces' (A. Edward Sutherland, USA, 1939)
Above: David Lean directing 'Oliver Twist' (GB, 1947)

authority in the shape of policemen and virago wives. Throughout their films their archetypal enemy was the irascible James Finlayson, with whom they regularly played a game of mutual destruction. Each party would politely take turns to wreak horrible destruction upon the person of the other. Although a variety of good comic directors were assigned to their films, the creative genius behind them all was Laurel himself. They successfully survived the transition from silence to sound, and later from two-reel production to feature-length films. Only in their later films, when the big-studio system of the 1940s deprived them of the sort of creative freedom they needed, was there a falling-off in the quality of their pictures. Their last, regrettable film, *Atoll K*, was made in France in 1951 under difficult conditions and with both comedians in uncertain health. Even after that they continued to tour variety theatres with their stage act. Their best films included: *The Battle of the Century* (1927), *Liberty*, *Wrong Again* and *Big Business* (1929), *Helpmates* and *Laughing Gravy* (1931), *The Music Room* (1932). Books about them include those by William K. Everson, John McCabe and Charles Barr. DR

Laurentiis, Dino De
See DE LAURENTIIS

Lay Out
In animation, the design of a scene including background, characters in correct relative size, colours, cell levels and camera movements.

Leacock, Richard
Born 1921 in London, England. Cinematographer and director. Brother of director Philip Leacock. Photographed many semi-documentary films (notably FLAHERTY's feature, *Louisiana Story*, 1948); then became involved with American *cinéma-vérité* movement together with the directors Robert Drew, D. A. PENNEBAKER and the MAYSLES brothers. In collaboration, he has made many documentaries on social, sporting and political subjects, including *Primary* (1960), *Eddie Sachs in Indianapolis*, *Kenya* and *Football* (1961), *Nehru* (1962), *The Chair* (1963), *Happy Mother's Day* and *Republicans – The New Breed* (1964), *Stravinsky* (1966). Leacock's masterly use of portable camera equipment gives his shooting a raw, living quality which has influenced many other film-makers in this field. JG

Lean, David
Born 1908 in Surrey, England. Eminent British director whose supreme skill and long apprenticeship in the cutting room are the key to his work. Associated in his early directorial career with the literary trend in British films, through his adaptations from NOËL COWARD and Dickens, he has since become noted for mammoth international films (in scale, budget and production schedule).

He arrived at his profession via a rigidly disciplined Quaker childhood during which he was not officially allowed to see films, as his family considered it sinful. He nevertheless entered the industry as a clapper boy when he was 18, working his way up to third assistant director at the Gaumont Studios. In the 1930s he graduated to the cutting room and for a time cut, wrote and spoke the commentary for Gaumont British News.

As a film editor his first credit was *Escape me Never* (1935). Noël Coward picked him to co-direct *In Which We Serve* (1942) by the simple expedient of running through all the current British films and discovering that the best edited ones were those which Lean had cut. Further Coward films followed: *This Happy*

Breed (1943), *Blithe Spirit* (1944), *Brief Encounter* (1945), which set a new style in adult romance by sympathizing with two middle-aged, middle-class, married (but not to each other) lovers. The film established themes which in various ways were later to dominate Lean's work: the loneliness of a love 'out of true' and of those who challenge the accepted order.

The atmospheric mastery of his Dickens films, *Great Expectations* (1946) and *Oliver Twist* (1947), was followed by a period of re-orientation both for Lean and the British film industry. Two melodramatic conceits, *The Passionate Friends* (1948) and *Madeleine* (1949), were only partially successful. Lean's insistence on detail, preparation and sufficient time to do the job properly were almost pricing his films out of the British market. A story of the most important break-through in post-war flight, *The Sound Barrier* (1951), which he produced as well as directed, was a forerunner of the two 'superman' subjects that won him Academy Awards – *The Bridge on the River Kwai* (1957) and *Lawrence of Arabia* (1962).

Hobson's Choice (1954) was a return to a 19th-century world closer in spirit to Dickens, but still a triumph of indomitability over adversity; while *Summer Madness* (1955) echoed the bitter-sweet tones of illicit love from *Brief Encounter*, though rather more lushly orchestrated.

The later Lean style of working became apparent with *The Bridge on the River Kwai*, whose hero was a perversely brave and fanatical officer captured by the Japanese, and was significantly confirmed in *Lawrence of Arabia*. (Both films were produced by Hollywood's SAM SPIEGEL.) In 15 years he has completed only two other films: *Dr Zhivago* (1965) – again with a hero in opposition to his time – and *Ryan's Daughter* (1970), which was a near-record 12 months in actual production.

Unlike some equally prominent directors, Lean is disinclined to squander his thoughts about his work in interviews. Younger film-makers, coached in freer techniques, tend to down-grade him as an expensive perfectionist. Although actors admire him and seek to appear in his films, he admits he gets more satisfaction in the cutting room after the shooting is finished than from the filming. After *Dr Zhivago* he summed up his attitude to his work in terms that reveal a great deal about the film-maker: 'When I make a film I have the negative in my mind and what I am trying to do is make a print of it; so actors do tend to become puppets in the sense that I am trying to make them fit.' MH

Lebanon
See ARAB FILM

Lee, Jack
Born 1913 in Stroud, Gloucestershire, England. Director and producer, who entered films in 1938, working on documentaries. Assistant producer with Crown Film Unit during Second World War. Has written and directed many documentaries, including *Close Quarters* (1944) and *Children on Trial* (1946). Feature films include: *The Wooden Horse* (1950), *A Town Like Alice* (1956), *The Captain's Table* (1958), *Circle of Deception* (1961).

Lee, Rowland V.
Born 1891 in Findlay, Ohio, USA. Director. Long stage experience in stock companies and in New York. Entered films with the INCE company and began directing in 1921, tackling every kind of subject as did most directors of his generation. Few of his silent films are available today; the most distinctive work of his sound period is *Zoo in Budapest* (1933), a strange poetic fantasy set in a studio zoo and marvellously shot by LEE GARMES in a manner reminiscent of MURNAU. Lee also had a fondness for period adaptations – *The Count of Monte Cristo* (1934), *Cardinal Richelieu* and *The Three Musketeers* (1935) – and bizarre thrillers and horror films (including some of the early Fu Manchu pictures and the atmospheric *Son of Frankenstein*, (1939). JG

Lee Thompson, J.
See THOMPSON

Lefèbre, Jean-Pierre
Born 1942 in Canada. Director, screenwriter, and poet. Studied at the University of Montreal, and taught French at Loyola College, Montreal. His films are closely associated with Quebec, and with the 'liberation' movement in French Canada; they have been described as 'guerrilla cinema' and 'poetic dynamite'. He writes as well as directs his films. After making a short film, *L'Homoman* (1964), his first feature, *Le Révolutionnaire* (1965), shot in 16 mm and performed by non-professionals, concerned a body of revolutionaries in training at an isolated farm during winter. He wanted, he said, to 'demystify the mystique of revolution'. His other films include the feature length, *Il ne Faut pas Mourir pour Ca* (1968), two features for the National Film Board of Canada, *Mon Amie Pierrette* and *Jusqu'au Cœur* (both 1968), and *The House of Light*, shot in black-and-white Panavision in English and French language versions.

Legrand, Michel
Born 1931 in Paris, France. Composer. Originally a variety orchestra leader and song writer, he entered films in 1957 and soon established a personal (if American-influenced) style combining a fund of plaintive, romantic melody with a determinedly energetic rhythmic pulse. After working with REICHENBACH and GODARD (notably on *Bande à part*, 1964), he formed a collaboration with JACQUES DEMY in which the music played an integral part in the narrative: *Lola* (1960), *La Baie des Anges* (1962), *Les Parapluies de Cherbourg* (virtually a light opera, 1963), *Les Demoiselles de Rochefort* (1967), *Peau d'Âne* (1970). He also worked with AGNÈS VARDA (*Cléo de 5 à 7*, 1961) and several foreign directors including LOSEY on *Eva* (1962) and *The Go-Between* (1971). JG

Leigh, Vivien (1913–1967)
Born in Darjeeling, India. Elegant British stage and screen actress who achieved international stardom and the first of her two American Academy Awards with her playing of Scarlett O'Hara in *Gone with the Wind* (1939), the most fiercely coveted role in screen history. An actress of wit, integrity and cool charm, her reach sometimes exceeded her grasp. Her calm, collected playing in a sumptuous British film version of *Anna Karenina* (1948) and, later, in *The Deep Blue Sea* (1955) were particular failures.

But as a roguish temptress – *Caesar and Cleopatra* (1945) – and a neurotic misfit – *A Streetcar Named Desire* (1951), for which she won a second Academy Award, and *Ship of Fools* (1965) – few actresses could better her.

Settling in England as a schoolgirl, she studied at the Royal Academy of Dramatic Art in the early 1930s and made her film début in *Things are Looking up* (1934). A succession of British leading lady roles, notably her delightfully cool spy in SAVILLE's *Dark Journey* (1937), was followed, after *Gone with the Wind*, by a career on a far more elevated plane. Marrying LAURENCE OLIVIER, with whom she had previously acted on screen in *Fire over England* (1936), she starred with him in the morale-boosting *Lady Hamilton* (1941) during the Second World War. In the theatre together their achievements were less considerable, although she appeared in many stage successes independently.

Other notable films: *Storm in a Teacup* (1937), *St Martin's Lane* and *A Yank at Oxford* (1938), *Waterloo Bridge* (1940), *The Roman Spring of Mrs Stone* (1961). See 'The Oliviers' by Felix Barker (1953). MH

Leighton, Margaret
Born 1922 in Barnet Green, Worcestershire, England. Actress, who appears mostly on the stage. Her stage début was in 'Laugh with Me' in 1938, and her screen début in *The Winslow Boy* (1948). Her characterization is cool, elegant, sharp and often neurotic. Her comparatively rare films include *The Astonished Heart* (1950), *Carrington V.C.* (*Court Martial*, 1954), *The Constant Husband* (1955), *The Sound and The Fury* (1958), *The Waltz of the Toreadors* (1961), *Seven Women* (1965), *The Go-Between* (1971).

Leisen, Mitchell
Born 1898 in Michigan, USA. Director. After architectural training, he entered the cinema in 1919 as costume designer, then art director, working with DE MILLE (on ten films), DWAN and WALSH. Beginning as director in 1933, he developed a smoothly sophisticated ironic style taking in zany comedies like *Easy Living* (1937, scripted by PRESTON STURGES) and several collaborations with BILLY WILDER and

CHARLES BRACKETT, producing in *Midnight* (1939) a small masterpiece of 1930s social satire, as well as the romantic dramas *Arise, My Love* (1940) and *Hold Back the Dawn* (1941). Also in the 1940s, his work ranged from the Kurt Weill musical, *Lady in the Dark* (1944), to the decoratively charming *Kitty* (1945). His gentle, civilized talents received only intermittent opportunities after the war; in recent years, he has directed several television series, also managing a dance studio and nightclub in Hollywood. JG

Lelouch, Claude

Born 1937 in Paris, France. Contemporary young French director whose rather flashy visual style has had a doubtfully useful influence on film-makers in other countries. An ardent film enthusiast, he started making short films in his teens. His first – *Le Mal du Siècle* – was made when he was 13 and won an award at an amateur festival. Subsequent professional shorts, made in America, were banned from television and his left-wing politics have had a significant effect on his career and the responses to his films. His first film as writer, director and actor was *Le Propre de l'Homme* (1960) but he had to wait until 1966 for his major international success with the romantic *Un Homme et une Femme*. While still tending to be pictorially over-lush, later films have dealt with sterner social and political themes: *Vivre pour Vivre* (1967), part of *Loin du Viêt-Nam* (1967), *La Vie, L'Amour, La Mort* (1969), *Le Voyou* (1970); *Smic, Smac, Smoc,* (1971) was an uneasy essay in *cinéma-vérité* techniques. MH

Lemmon, Jack

Born 1925 in Boston, Massachusetts, USA.

Above: Laurence Olivier and Vivien Leigh on the set for 'Carrie' (William Wyler, USA, 1952)
Below: Jean-Louis Trintignant in 'Un Homme et une Femme' (Claude Lelouch, France, 1966)

Comedian and character actor, educated at Harvard, he made his début on the stage as a child. In later years he became popular on radio and television, and acted on Broadway. In the Second World War he served in the US Navy. Brilliantly expressive in both comedy and drama, his resilient, put-upon, 'loser' figure is best delineated in WILDER's films. His screen début was in *It Should Happen to You* (1953), and his other films include: *Phffft* (1954), *Mister Roberts* (1955), *Some Like it Hot* (1959), *The Apartment* (1960), *The Days of Wine and Roses* (1962), *Irma La Douce* (1963), *How to Murder Your Wife* (1965), *The Odd Couple* (1968), *The April Fools* (1969).

Leni, Paul (1885–1929)

Born in Stuttgart, Germany. Director and art director. Worked originally as set designer with both Max Reinhardt and Leopold Jessner. Influenced considerably by German expressionism, he designed sets for the two celebrated silent films, *Hintertreppe* (1921), a *Kammerspiel*, intimate drama which he co-directed with Jessner, and *Waxworks* (1924, directed with the help of ROBERT WIENE), a three-part story developed from the wax figures of Harun-al-Raschid, Ivan the Terrible, and Jack the Ripper. He also designed sets for several German silent films, including JOE MAY's *Veritas Vincit* (1918), RICHARD OSWALD's *Lady Hamilton* (1922), working in collaboration with HANS DREIER, and for Arthur Robison's *Manon Lescaut* (1925–6). In 1927 he went to the USA, where he directed highly atmospheric thrillers like *The Cat and the Canary* (1927) and *The Last Warning* (1929), before his sudden death. RM

Lenica, Jan

Born 1928 in Poznan, Poland. Animator. At first studied music and architecture, but later he took to art and became one of the founders of modern poster design, for which Poland is

Conrad Veidt in 'Waxworks' (Paul Leni, Germany, 1924)

now famous. He made his initial films in collaboration with WALERIAN BOROWCZYK (q.v.), and, like him, left Poland in 1958 to work in France, where he made *Monsieur Tête* (1959) with Henri Gruel; it concerns the spiritual life and death of an Everyman whose experiences represent those of contemporary society within the span of a day and a night. *Labyrinth* (1962) is more surrealist in its nightmare continuity of images representing man's destruction. Lenica's films usually represent fear, menace, and hallucination. In *Rhinoceros* (1963) he epitomizes

Above: John Welles in 'A Fistful of Dollars' (Sergio Leone, Italy, 1964)
Below: Roy Kinnear and Michael Crawford in 'How I Won the War' (Richard Lester, GB, 1967)

the spirit of Ionesco's play, while in *A* (1964) man is menaced by the intitial letter of the alphabet and, when he at last believes himself free, is faced by a looming letter B. Lenica's graphic style employs thick outlines and heavily stylized design, together with very simply choreographed movement. In 1963 he left France for West Germany; here he made *Adam II* (1969), a feature-length film which took three years to complete, needing 150,000 stop-frame exposures. Surrealist in conception, it has been described as a 'sad contour-face which reflects all its experiences in a poetic universe'. The characters move like cuckoo-clock figures, and computer-controlled man is shown living in some kind of electronic hell, while the sound-track is an amalgam of horrific sounds. Lenica has emerged as one of the great innovators in modern animation. RM

Leone, Sergio
Born 1926 in Italy. Director. Son of an Italian director, Roberto Roberti, he collaborated on many scripts after the Second World War and became obsessed with historical subjects and, latterly, the Western, of which he became the leading Italian practitioner. Leone's Westerns lovingly create the physical feel of frontier towns with their pioneering communities, outlaws and rough justice yet the tone is much more psychotically violent and sadistic (in a contemporary sense) than in their American counterparts. Great box-office successes like *A Fistful of Dollars* (1964), *For a Few Dollars More* (1965), *The Good, the Bad and the Ugly* (1966) were followed by *Once Upon a Time in the West* (1969, made partly in the USA), brilliantly staged and set, and with an added injection of 'significance' suggesting that Leone may be in danger of taking himself too seriously. Recent film: *Duck, You Sucker* with ROD STEIGER (1971). JG

Lerner, Irving
Born 1909 in New York, USA. Interesting individual director, former cameraman, with a disappointingly small output of films, among which *Murder by Contract* (1958) and *Studs Lonigan* (1960) are the most impressive. Previously worked on short documentaries, he co-directed *Muscle Beach* (1948), has also directed *Man Crazy* (1954) and *Cry of Battle* (1963) and co-produced *Custer of the West* (1967). Recent films: *The Royal Hunt of the Sun* (1969), *Darwin* (1972).

Le Roy, Mervyn
Born 1900 in San Francisco, USA. Prolific veteran producer-director and former actor, whose tough, racy Warners films of the 1930s have since become regarded as classic examples of a dynamic period *genre*. Although he insists his films never intentionally carried a message, the most memorable of them – *Little Caesar* (1930), *I am a Fugitive from a Chain Gang* (1932), *Gold Diggers of 1933*, *Hard to Handle* (1933), *They Won't Forget* (1937) – accurately captured the social climate of the Depression and the failure of the American dream. When he switched to MGM – where he produced *The Wizard of Oz* (1939) – he also changed his style, making for the most part glossy star romances and uplift melodramas. Despite occasional successes – notably a lively version of the musical, *Gypsy* (1962) – he has never achieved again the urgency of his 1930s films. Other principal films: *Five Star Final* and *Three on a Match* (1932), *Anthony Adverse* (1936), *Waterloo Bridge* (1940), *Johnny Eager* (1942), *Thirty Seconds Over Tokyo* (1944), *Little Women* (1949), *Quo Vadis?* (1951), *The Bad Seed* (1956), *Home Before Dark* (1959), *Moment to Moment* (1965). MH

Lester, Richard
Born 1932 in Philadelphia, USA. Director who has worked chiefly in Britain. His exuberant 'free' style was ideally suited to the vogueish personalities of the Beatles in the middle 1960s, when he made his first important impact with feature films starring the remarkable pop group, *A Hard Day's Night* (1964) and *Help!* (1965). These and subsequent films bore the stamp of his earlier association with the antic, surrealist comedy of the radio Goon Shows which featured PETER SELLERS, Spike Milligan and Harry Secombe.

After working in radio and television in the USA, Canada and Britain, he directed a Goon short comedy, *The Running, Jumping and Standing Still Film*, which was much admired and led to his feature film début, *It's Trad, Dad* (1961), a rollicking 'new look' pop musical. Between the Beatles films he made *The Knack* (1965), which again was perfectly tuned to the swinging, newly permissive times in Britain. But his film of *A Funny Thing Happened on the Way to the Forum* (1966) was an indulgent disappointment. Later he used his anarchic comedy techniques to condemn bitterly the glorification of war in *How I Won the War* (1967) and public apathy about the Bomb in *The Bed Sitting-Room* (1970). *Petulia* (1968), a complex marital drama, was a departure from his usual style and subject and the most deeply mature of all his films. MH

Levine, Joseph E.
Born 1905 in Boston, USA. Dynamic American film promoter-producer, formerly in

theatre ownership and distribution, who became a major figure in the film industry through his shrewd exploitation that transformed a utility Italian 'epic', *Hercules* (1959), into a phenomenal box-office success. Since then, through his company Embassy, he has helped set up the financing for prestige films, such as *Two Women* (1961) and *8½* (1963), and presented several more conventional English-speaking films, mostly with liberal lacings of sex and controversy, including *The Carpetbaggers* (1963), *Harlow* (1965), *The Oscar* (1966), *The Graduate* (1967). In 1968 Embassy amalgamated with Avco to produce, among other films, *The Lion in Winter* (1968), *Sunflower* and *Soldier Blue* (1970), *Promise at Dawn* (1971). MH

Lévy, Jean Benoît
See BENOÎT-LÉVY

Lewin, Albert (1895–1968)
Born in New York, USA. Highly individual writer, producer and director whose tastes ran to bizarre romantic themes – notably *The Picture of Dorian Gray* (1944), *The Private Affairs of Bel Ami* (1947), *Pandora and the Flying Dutchman* (1951). At their best his films were flamboyant in the grand manner; at their worst, they were naively vulgar. But in a grey decade for American film-making he was distinctly on his own. Other films: *The Moon and Sixpence* (1942), *The Living Idol* (1957), *Saadia* (1964).

Lewis, Jerry
Born 1926 in Newark, New Jersey, USA. Actor, singer, comedian; later producer and director. Began appearances in school theatricals; then played professionally in night-clubs with DEAN MARTIN. Gained many popularity awards in radio, television and films. Though often self-indulgent his comedies at best bear comparison with those of the great silent clowns and he is probably the most inventive and original screen comedian to have emerged in America in the last twenty years. Films with Dean Martin include *My Friend Irma* (1949), *Scared Stiff* (1953) and *Hollywood or Bust* (1957). He had directed and starred in many other films, including *The Bellboy* (1960), *The Nutty Professor* (1963) and *One More Time* (1970). His other films include: *Cinderfella* (1960), *Who's Minding the Store?* (1964), *The Patsy* and *The Disorderly Orderly* (1965), *Hook, Line and Sinker* (as actor, 1968), *Which Way to the Front?* (1970). RM

Lewton, Val (1904–1951)
Born in Yalta, Crimea, emigrated to USA. Producer. At first a script editor, he became in 1942 producer of low-budget horror films for RKO. These he built up with the director JACQUES TOURNEUR into a highly imaginative series; they include *The Cat People* (1942, with Simone Simon), *The Leopard Man* and *I Walked with a Zombie* (1943).

He also produced *The Curse of the Cat People* (ROBERT WISE, 1944), *Isle of the Dead* (MARK ROBSON, 1945), *The Body Snatchers* (Robert Wise, 1945), *Bedlam* (Mark Robson, 1946), the two latter starring BORIS KARLOFF. These films formed a genre of their own, as poetic in treatment as they were genuinely horrific.

L'Herbier, Marcel
Born 1890 in Paris, France. Director; also poet, playwright and scenarist; founder of the French film-training school, Institut des Hautes Études Cinématographiques (IDHEC), in Nice in 1943. Served during the First World War in the army cinematograph service. Poet and writer in the symbolist, impressionist school, he entered the cinema through writing scripts for Mercanton and Hergil, and produced an experimental film, *Phantasmes* (1917), which exploited soft-focus. His first significant films were *L'Homme du Large* (1920), after Balzac, and the decorative *Eldorado* (1922), set in Spain and photographed in a style approximating to French impressionism, while German expressionism influenced over-strongly his *Don Juan et Faust* (1922). *L'Inhumaine* (1923) was an elaborate visual experiment made with the help of CAVALCANTI, Fernand Léger, and the composer Darius Milhaud. One of his better films of the period was *Feu Mathias Pascal* (1925), after Pirandello. Subsequently he experimented still further (this time in the form of a restless portable camera) in his film *L'Argent* (1927), after Zola. After this he specialized in historical films, among which are *Le Mystère de la Chambre Jaune* (1931) and *La Citadelle du Silence* (1937). Among his later productions were *La Nuit Fantastique* (1942), one of his best films and intended as a tribute to MÉLIÈS and his theatre of magic, *Les Derniers Jours de Pompéi* (1949) and *Le Père de Mademoiselle* (1953). RM

Library Shot
Shot used in film that has been taken from a library or store of shots that has been kept for possible future use.

Light Box
An animation desk with registration pegs and glass drawing surface which can be illuminated either from above or through the glass.

Lindblom, Gunnel
Born 1931 in Göteborg, Sweden. Leading Scandinavian actress who built up an important reputation in the theatre before moving into films, where her quality of brooding femininity has been most significantly exploited in her work for INGMAR BERGMAN, including *The Seventh Seal* (1956), *Wild Strawberries* (1958), *The Virgin Spring* (1960), *Winter Light* (1961), *The Silence* (1963). Other films include: *Loving Couples* (1964), *Hunger* (1967), *The Girls* and *The Father* (1970).

Linder, Max (1883–1925)
Born in Saint-Loubès, France. The greatest clown of the pre-Chaplin era, Linder's prodigal invention devised a vocabulary of gags that was very little enlarged by subsequent film comedians, not excluding CHAPLIN himself. An only moderately successful stage actor from a well-to-do background, he changed his name from Gabriel Bourdeaux in 1905 to mitigate the shame of accepting work from the Pathé Studios. His big chance came when Pathé's comic star ANDRÉ DEED deserted to Italy in 1908. Linder's greatest innovation was to abandon the grotesque appearance and frenetic

Charles Chaplin and Max Linder (early 1920s in Hollywood)

antics of his predecessors. Handsome, elegantly dressed, ingenious and intelligent, the comedy of the Max character lay in the contrast between his self-possession and the ludicrous situations that befell him. Linder made over 400 films for Pathé, most of them exploiting his ability to create endless variations upon a single, simple situation. Remarkably, though they appear extremely polished in performance, structure and rhythm, his films were generally shot without retakes, after a single rehearsal. Two attempts to establish himself in the USA were unsuccessful despite the brilliance of the features he made on his second visit – *Seven Years' Bad Luck* and *Be My Wife* (1921) and *The Three Must-Get-Theres* (1922) – and Linder returned to France a prey to the comedian's occupational disease of melancholia. After starring in ABEL GANCE's *Au Secours!* and (in Austria) in Édouard-Émile Violet's *Le Roi du Cirque*, he took his own life, apparently in a suicide pact with his young wife, who was found dead alongside him in their hotel room. DR

Line Test
In animation, film of the pencil drawings which is projected, usually in negative to check the animation before proceeding with tracing on cells.

Lip Sync.
In animation, the animation of movements of the mouth to fit the recorded dialogue

Litvak, Anatole
Born 1902 in Kiev, Russia. European-trained director who has worked chiefly in America. His flair for handling flamboyant subjects – romantic, historical or psychological – was much in favour during the 1930s and 1940s, sparked off by his French film based on the Hapsburg tragedy, *Mayerling* (1936). From 1929 he had worked in films in Germany, Britain and France; and he left for America in 1937. His first Hollywood films included the rare (for Litvak) comedy, *Tovarich* (1938), and the pioneer American anti-Nazi film, *Confessions of a Nazi Spy* (1939); but his treatment of tough, indigenous American themes in *City for Conquest* (1940) and *Blues in the Night* (1941) was possibly more impressive.

After the Second World War, during which he served in the US Army, he achieved a fashionable success with *The Snake Pit* (1948), a harrowing study of the treatment of the mentally sick, followed by the tense thriller, *Sorry, Wrong Number* (1948). Since then he has been mostly associated with rather stuffy star vehicles based on theatrical and literary best-sellers and made in Britain or Europe.

Other principal films: *L'Équipage* (1935 in France), *The Amazing Dr Clitterhouse* and *The Sisters* (1938), *All This and Heaven Too* (1940), *The Long Night* (1947, a Hollywood remake of *Le Jour se Lève*), *Decision Before Dawn* (1951), *Act of Love* (1954), *The Deep Blue Sea* (1955), *Anastasia* (1956), *Goodbye Again* (1961), *The Night of the Generals* (1966), *The Lady in the Car* (1970). MH

Lizzani, Carlo
Born 1922 in Rome, Italy. Director. Began as a writer and film historian, later becoming screenwriter, collaborating with Vergano, DE SANTIS, ROSSELLINI, LATTUADA. Began directing in 1951 with *Achtung, Banditi!*, a Resistance drama with a strong political comment, and *Cronache di poveri amanti* (1954), a sensitive, solid adaptation of Pratolini's social novel. Since then he has tackled a variety of subjects from the long documentary *The Chinese Wall* (1958) to comedies and a Western. Lizzani's left-wing political allegiances have invariably coloured his work, which has a firm technical grasp but, apart from his first two or three films, his eclecticism makes it difficult to perceive a personal signature. JG

Above: Gina Lollobrigida in 'Bread, Love and Jealousy' (Luigi Comencini, Italy, 1954) Below: Harold Lloyd in 'Mad Wednesday' ('The Sin of Harold Diddlebock', Preston Sturges, USA, 1946)

Lloyd, Frank (1888–1960)
Born in Glasgow, Scotland. Prolific Hollywood director who generally specialized in grand-scale, spectacular adventures during the 1930s and 1940s, winning Academy Awards for *The Divine Lady* (1929) and *Cavalcade* (1933), although he is better remembered for *Mutiny on the Bounty* (1935). A performer in musical comedy and light opera from the age of 15, he went to Canada in 1913, then to Hollywood and, through a lucky accident, was pushed into filming a one-reel silent when the director became ill. Main films include: *Madame X* (1920), *The Sea Hawk* (1924), *Berkeley Square* (1933), *Under Two Flags* (1936), *Wells Fargo* (1937), *Rulers of the Sea* (1939), *Blood on the Sun* (1945), *The Last Command* (1955).

Lloyd, Harold (1893–1971)
Born in Burchard, Nebraska, USA. With CHAPLIN, KEATON, and LANGDON, Lloyd was one of the four great comedians of the American silent cinema. Unlike them his training was not in vaudeville but on the legitimate stage, where he made his first professional appearance as Macduff's child at the age of four. When HAL ROACH, a fellow extra at Universal Studios, inherited a small legacy and went into independent production, he hired Lloyd as a comic at three dollars a day, in 1916. Lloyd's screen character was only gradually worked out. At first he played a tramp figure, Willie Work;

then, after a brief and unsuccessful sojourn at the SENNETT Studios, he returned to Roach as Lonesome Luke. Only in 1917 in a film called *Over the Fence* did he have the inspiration of the lens-less horn-rim glasses which defined his famous screen *persona*. He was essentially the all-American boy, the 1920s go-getter – bold, brash, thick-skinned and bound for success despite the superficial diffidence and prissy manners. Whatever the immediate motive (generally the need to win a girl) his films are all built upon the hero's drive for social or economic betterment. Lloyd's own statements on his films indicate a sincere moral conviction in the Horatio Alger ideal and the American success story which in real life he classically embodied (he died a very rich man). He is best remembered for his unique style of comedy of thrills, awesome acrobatic feats performed on the tops of (apparent) skyscrapers, without the aid of camera tricks or doubles. Principal feature films: *Grandma's Boy* and *Doctor Jack* (1922), *Safety Last* and *Why Worry?* (1923), *Girl Shy* and *Hot Water* (1924), *The Freshman* (1925), *Kid Brother* (1927), *Welcome Danger* (1929), *Feet First* (1930), *The Cat's Paw* (1934), *The Milky Way* (1936), *Professor Beware* (1938), *The Sin of Harold Diddlebock* (1946). DR

Loach, Kenneth
Born 1936 in Warwickshire, England. Key British film director – a recruit from television, where his dramatized documentaries on social problems have been highly acclaimed. An extension of his television work, his first feature film *Poor Cow* (1967) presented a grimy and over-flamboyant view of life in the raw. His second film, *Kes* (1968), a far more restrained and deeply affecting indictment of authoritarian apathy and ignorance as they affect a deprived schoolboy, achieved some fame through being initially neglected by the film industry. His strong social commitment is also urgently displayed in *Family Life* (1971) about a girl driven into schizophrenia. JG

Location
Any place away from the studio where shooting takes place

Lockwood, Margaret
Born 1916 in Karachi, Pakistan. British actress. Trained at the Royal Academy of Dramatic Art, she is as well-known on the stage as on the screen. Her screen popularity was at its height in the 1940s in a series of ripely enjoyable period dramas.

Her films include: *Lorna Doone* (1935), *Bank Holiday* and *The Lady Vanishes* (1938), *The Stars Look Down* (1939), *Quiet Wedding* (1941), *Alibi* (1942), *The Man in Grey* (1943), *The Wicked Lady* (1945), *Hungry Hill*, her daughter Julia appeared as a child in this film, and *Jassy* (1947), *Cardboard Cavalier* (1948), *Trent's Last Case* (1952) and *Cast a Dark Shadow* (1955). Her autobiography, 'Lucky Star', was published in 1955.

Above: Carol White in 'Poor Cow' (Ken Loach, GB, 1967)
Below: Carole Lombard and Charles Laughton in 'They Knew What They Wanted' (Garson Kanin, USA, 1940)

Logan, Joshua
Born 1908 in Texas, USA. Respected stage and film director whose cumbersome musicals – *South Pacific* (1958), *Camelot* (1967), *Paint Your Wagon* (1969) – have been singularly successful, though, in the last case, ruinously expensive. Other films: *Picnic* (1955), *Bus Stop* (1956), *Sayonara* (1957), *Fanny* (1961), *Ensign Pulver* (1964).

Lollobrigida, Gina
Born 1927 in Subiaco, Italy. Actress, who trained in drama in Academy of Fine Arts in Rome, and made film début in Italy in *Love of a Clown*. Her physical charm and glamour won her outstanding international popularity, and she has since starred in such films as *Fanfan la Tulipe* (1951), *Les Belles de Nuit* (1952), *Bread, Love and Fantasy* (1953), *Trapeze* (1956), *Solomon and Sheba* (1959), *Woman of Straw* (1964), *Hotel Paradiso* (1966), *Stuntman* and *Buona Sera, Mrs Campbell* (1968) *King, Queen, Knave* (1972).

Lombard, Carole (1909–1942)
Born in Indiana, USA. American actress and comedienne, with a personality very much her own and an immaculate sophisticated comedy technique. She first appeared as child actress, and for a number of years was known as MACK SENNETT's 'bathing beauty'. Her main films include *A Perfect Crime* (1921), *Fast and Loose* (1930), *White Woman* (1933), *Twentieth Century* (1934), *My Man Godfrey* (1936), *Nothing Sacred* (1937), *They Knew what they Wanted* (1940), *Mr and Mrs Smith* (1941) and *To Be or Not to Be* (1942).

Long Shot
Scene staged with the camera actually or apparently at a distance from the action or characters.

Loop
(1) A slack section of film above and below the gate of a camera or projector to prevent the intermittent action damaging the film.
(2) A piece of film joined head to tail to allow for continuous running through a projector or reproducer in order to repeat the action or sound over and over again. Used in dubbing and as a means of providing continuous sound effects in re-recording.

Loren, Sophia
Born 1934 in Rome, Italy. Commanding Italian actress who has successfully survived the transition from pin-up starlet, during the heyday of 'Hollywood-on-the-Tiber', to versatile international star. Starting out in films as an extra in the early 1950s she became popular in Italy as a voluptuous screen spitfire. A spell in Hollywood produced some interesting star vehicles – notably *Black Orchid* and *That Kind of Woman* (1959), *Heller in Pink Tights* (1959) – but it was after her return to Italy that she achieved her major success in *Two Women* (1961), for which she won an Academy Award. Most recent films: *Arabesque* and *A Countess from Hong Kong* (1966), *C'Era Una Volta (Cinderella – Italian Style,* 1967), *Sunflower* (1969), *The Priest's Wife* (1970).

Lorentz, Pare
Born 1905 in Clarksburg, West Virginia, USA. Documentary director, originally a film critic. Became celebrated in the 1930s for his romantic, rhetorically poetic documentaries of social welfare – *The Plow that Broke the Plains* (1936), on the problems of the American Dustbowl, and *The River* (1937), dealing with the Mississippi floods. In 1940, as head of the short-lived US Film Service set up by the Roosevelt Administration, he made *The Fight for Life*, a courageous film on the problems of maternity in the Chicago slums, technically self-conscious but with a strong emotional drive. Congress killed the film project overnight, preventing further production on Lorentz's next film, *Ecce Homo*, dealing with unemployment. After producing for RKO-Radio, Lorentz worked for government agencies during the war, including control of the Air Transport Command's Overseas Technical Unit, while in 1946–7 he was chief of the Film Section of the Civil Affairs Division. RM

Lorre, Peter (1904–1964)
Born in Rosenberg, Hungary. Actor. He trained in drama in Vienna, and appeared on the German stage during the 1920s. He made his name as a film actor in FRITZ LANG's *M* (1931), in which he played a child-murderer who makes a passionate plea for psychological understanding. As a Jew, he left Hitler's Germany, working briefly in France and in Britain, where he appeared in HITCHCOCK's *The Man Who Knew Too Much* (1934) and *The Secret Agent* (1936). He finally settled in the USA, where he featured initially in the *Mr Moto* series (1937–9). He appeared with distinction in many American films, including *The Maltese Falcon* (1941), *Casablanca* (1942), *The Mask of Dimitrios* (1944). He specialized in roles which exploited his appearance, the ingratiating, cunning, but timid villain. He directed one quite personal film, *Die Verlorene* (1951), in post-war Germany. RM

Opposite: Joseph Losey (left foreground) with Julie Christie on the set for 'The Go-Between' (Losey, GB, 1971)

Losey, Joseph
Born 1909 in Wisconsin, USA. Expatriate American director who in 1952, during the McCarthy 'UnAmerican' hearings, settled in Britain where his most influential work – *The Criminal* (1960), *The Servant* (1963), *Accident* (1967) – has been produced, though most often under stress (due to insensitive censorship and intractable film industry attitudes). Acclaimed by 'Cahiers du Cinéma' as among the 'greatest of the great', he has until the late 1960s been a prophet without much honour in his own country. But his impact on European critics and young film-makers can hardly be overestimated.

An uncompromising individualist, Losey has been conditioned by a bitter history of political and artistic discrimination. Although he studied medicine at Dartmouth College, his interests were soon directed toward the theatre. In 1930 he was writing for the 'Theatre Arts Magazine'. He became an assistant stage manager, then stage director, much involved with the radical forces in the American theatre. In 1935 he went to Moscow with 'Waiting For Lefty'; in 1936 he collaborated on the Federal-backed theatre project, 'The Living Newspaper'; in 1947 he staged Brecht's 'Galileo' with CHARLES LAUGHTON. Since leaving America, he has produced two plays in London, 'The Wooden Dish' and 'The Night of the Ball', in 1954 and 1955.

The start of his career as a film-maker began in 1939 when he directed his first short film, *Pete Roleum and his Cousins*; before that he had supervised production of educational films for the Rockefeller Foundation. After the Second World War, during which he worked in radio and for the Army Signal Corps, he directed his first feature, *The Boy with Green Hair* (1948), for DORE SCHARY, then head of RKO-Radio. The film, an allegory about racial intolerance, ran into problems. The original producer, Adrian Scott, fell foul of the Unamerican Activities Committee; the substitute producer misunderstood what the film was about; and Schary was ousted when HOWARD HUGHES took over the RKO studios. The pattern of contention which was to harass the preparation and working conditions of many of Losey's films was set.

He went on to make several Hollywood films with powerful, direct social themes: *The Lawless* (known in England as *The Dividing Line*, 1949), *The Prowler*, a remake of *M* and *The Big Night* (1951). Here traces of the ambiguity and density of human relationships that distinguished his later films were detectable. Himself a victim of the communist witch-hunt, he arrived in Europe, but as a black-listed director he was forced to work under pseudonyms on films of little consequence: *Stranger on the Prowl* in Italy (1952), *The Sleeping Tiger* (1954) and *The Intimate Stranger* (1956) in Britain.

In 1957 he made his first British film under his own name, *Time without Pity* (1957), which interested him as an anti-capital-punishment subject. Ornate in texture, the film originated the criticism that Losey's treatments leaned to the baroque, though it was merely a phase in his experimentation with film style and form. The melodramatic *Gypsy and the Gentleman* (1957) was followed by the more successful *Blind Date* (1959) in which he sought to colour a trite mystery plot with the fascinating interplay of character and class tension.

The Losey 'feel' of a film was emerging. He became less interested in straightforward storytelling, more concerned with the underlying conflicts of hypocrisy – particularly in a class-conscious English context – and sexual ambivalence. After *The Criminal, The Damned* and the badly mangled *Eve* (1962), he embarked on the most significant period of his career in which he made *The Servant, King and Country* (1964), the erratic *Modesty Blaise* (1966) and his most impeccable film, HAROLD PINTER's screen adaptation of *Accident*. The leading player in each, DIRK BOGARDE, is an actor with whom he has a special *rapport*: others are STANLEY BAKER and ELIZABETH TAYLOR. The latter starred in his next two films, Tennessee Williams's *Boom*, and *Secret Ceremony* (1968) which, though brilliantly bizarre, tended to be over-stuffed with production values, including the richness of the international star casts.

After the predominantly masculine escape-adventure, *Figures in a Landscape* (1970) came his elegantly realized adaptation of L. P. Hartley's novel *The Go-Between* (1971), in which Losey – again in association with Harold Pinter, the screen author of the director's best work – examined in mature and leisurely detail the betrayal of a trusting innocent, caught in the middle of a reckless romance between the aristocratic daughter of a class-ridden Edwardian family and a tenant farmer. Latest film: *The Assassination of Trotsky* (1972). A major analysis is Tom Milne's 'Losey on Losey' (1967). See also 'The Cinema of Joseph Losey' by James Leahy (1967). MH

Lot
A piece of ground, generally attached to the studio, on which sets are erected and photographed.

Love, Bessie (real name: Juanita Horton)
Born 1898 in Texas, USA. The first appearance in her long and distinguished screen career was in D. W. GRIFFITH's *Intolerance*; and it was Griffith, inevitably, who renamed her. Soon afterwards a critic described her as 'the sweetest, demurest, tenderest, most plaintive little thing on the screen', but these qualities and her years as a Griffith heroine did not preclude a roguish humour which helped her hold her own as co-star to the ebullient FAIRBANKS in Triangle

days and also assisted the triumphant recovery of her career with talking pictures and her starring role in *Broadway Melody*. After settling in England, where she also worked as a writer and (during the war) as a technician, she returned to the screen as a resourceful character player, displaying the same qualities of impregnable sincerity which marked her early starring roles. Among many other films: *Atlantic Ferry* (1941), *Journey Together* (1944), *Isadora* (1968), *Sunday, Bloody Sunday* (1971). DR

Loy, Myrna
Born 1902 in USA. Actress, at first a dancer and then cast in oriental roles, acting in a Chinese theatre in Hollywood. Known for her slant-eyed beauty and impassive expression, she later featured and starred in many sophisticated, comedy roles. Her films include: *What Price Beauty?* (1925), *Ben Hur* (1927), *The Desert Song* (1929), *Arrowsmith*, *Love Me Tonight* and *Vanity Fair* as Becky Sharp, (1932), *The Thin Man* (1934) and its sequels, *The Great Ziegfeld* (1936), *Test Pilot* (1938), *The Rains Came* (1939), *The Best Years of our Lives* (1946), *Cheaper by the Dozen* (1950), *From the Terrace* (1960), and *The April Fools* (1969).

Lubitsch, Ernst (1892–1947)
Born in Berlin, Germany. Director. Studied acting while working in his father's clothing store, and left to join Max Reinhardt's company as a small-part player, while at the same time, from 1911, beginning his career in films by working as a technical apprentice at Bioscop. His early short film as a director, *Miss Lather* (*Fraülein Seifenschaum*, 1913), starred Ossi Oswalda; this was followed by the Pinkus comedy shorts (1913–8), in many of which he also appeared. After the war he made his first feature films, *The Eyes of the Mummy (Die Augen der Mumie Ma)* and *Carmen*, both in 1918 and both featuring POLA NEGRI; they were spectacular, dramatic subjects for UFA, and they started his long association with the screen-writer, Hanns Kraly. Their partnership continued with *Madame Dubarry* (*Passion*, 1919), *Anna Boleyn* and *Sumurun* (*One Arabian Night*, 1920), and *The Loves of Pharaoh* (*Das Weib des Pharao*, 1921), in many of which EMIL JANNINGS and POLA NEGRI starred. After this, Lubitsch turned to more intimate satirical subjects, in which he came to specialize, such as *The Oyster Princess (Die Austernprinzessin)*, *The Doll* (*Die Puppe*, 1919), both with Ossi Oswalda, and *The Wild Cat* (*Die Bergkatze*, 1921) and *The Flame* (*Die Flamme* or *Montmartre*, 1921), both with Pola Negri. It was the success of these films which took him and his scriptwriter Hanns Krähly to Hollywood in 1922.

By now he had developed what was termed the 'Lubitsch touch', the small revealing detail picked out in the action, such as the handling of significant or symbolic objects like the wedding-ring in *The Flame*, or some change in facial expression, presented in close, visual terms. He used a minimum of titles. Once in Hollywood, he directed some of the outstanding sophisticated and satiric sex comedies of the 1920s and 1930s, beginning with *The Marriage Circle*, *Three Women* and *Forbidden Paradise* (1924), *Kiss me Again* and *Lady Windermere's Fan* (1925), *So This is Paris* (1926) and *The Student Prince* (1927). In a serious vein he made *The Patriot* (1928) – Jannings's performance in this as the mad Czar was his most successful during his brief stay in Hollywood. But the film was to some extent spoilt by its clumsily synchronized music score, with sound and vocal effects.

Lubitsch made next a series of highly cinematic, fluidly moving musicals, beginning with an outstanding example, *The Love Parade* (1929), with JEANETTE MACDONALD and MAURICE CHEVALIER, and followed by *Monte Carlo* (1930), *The Smiling Lieutenant* (1931), and a film with musical interludes, *One Hour with You* (1932). These preceded one of his finest comedies, *Trouble in Paradise* (1932), which made a particularly witty use of music. The elegant sets for all these films were by the German designer, HANS DREIER. Parallel with some less successful lighter productions (except for the brilliant mime episode in 1932 in the composite film, *If I had a Million*, with CHARLES LAUGHTON), Lubitsch returned to drama with his anti-war film, *The Man I Killed* (1932) and directed Dietrich in one of her finest portrayals in *Angel* (1937). Comedy was always to be his strength, and appeared again in *Bluebeard's Eighth Wife* (1938) – with a screenplay by CHARLES BRACKETT and BILLY WILDER – *Ninotchka* (1939 – 'Garbo laughs'), the more uneven *To Be or Not to Be* (1942, an anti-Nazi burlesque set in Warsaw), and *Heaven Can Wait* (1943). His career ended with *Cluny Brown* (1946), which satirized British high society. He worked with many of Hollywood's greatest stars of the period, in particular Maurice Chevalier, Jeanette MacDonald, ZASU PITTS, GARY COOPER, MARLENE DIETRICH, Melvyn Douglas and Miriam Hopkins. Lubitsch was a master of screen comedy, and one of the originators of true screen acting. RM

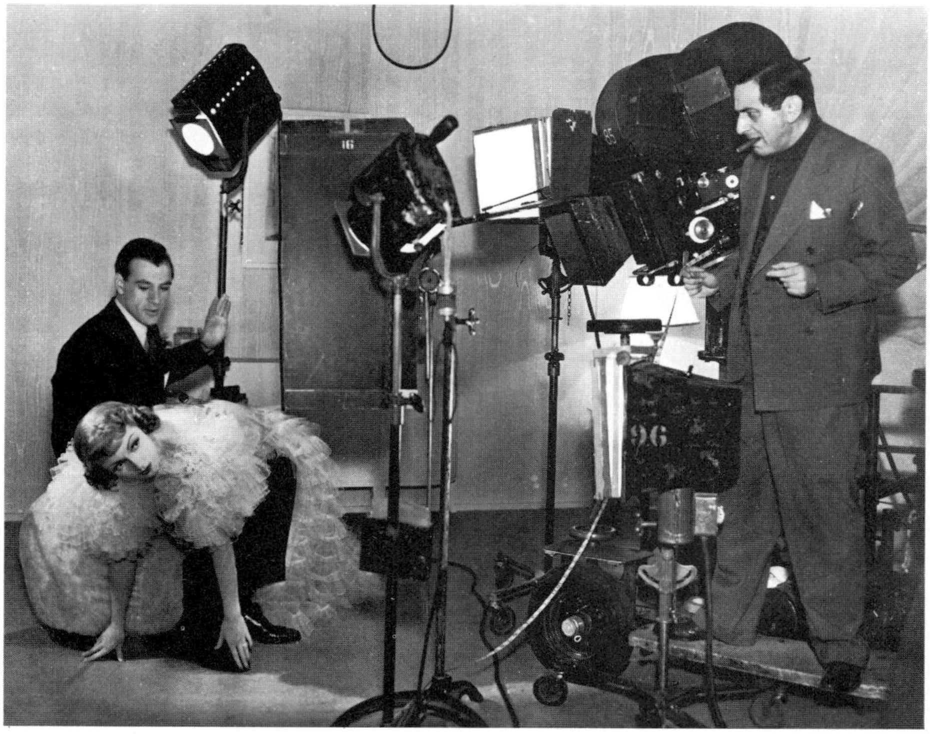

Above: Helen Chandler and Bela Lugosi in 'Dracula' (Tod Browning, USA, 1931)
Below: Ernst Lubitsch directing Claudette Colbert and Gary Cooper in 'Bluebeard's Eighth Wife' (USA, 1938)

Lugosi, Bela (1882–1956)
Born in Hungary. Actor, who trained for the stage in Budapest. His screen career began in Budapest in 1915; from 1921 he appeared on the US and European stage. He became famous

as Dracula (*Dracula*, 1931), and after that usually played horror roles, often in poor productions. His films include: *The Island of Lost Souls* (1933), *The Black Cat* (1934), *The Mark of the Vampire* (1935), *Son of Frankenstein* (1939) and several other Frankenstein films; *Return of the Vampire* (1943), *The Body Snatchers* (1945), *Mother Riley Meets the Vampires* (1952), and *The Black Sheep* (1956). He also appeared in a non-horror part in *Ninotchka* (1939).

Lumet, Sidney

Born 1924 in Philadelphia, USA. One of the 'young guard' of film directors who emerged from the ranks of television and revitalized the American screen in the late 1950s. A fairly prolific film-maker, he is at his best dealing with claustrophobic situations and characters at breaking point, very much in key with his television training.

A child actor whose father, Baruch Lumet, worked for the Yiddish Theatre, Lumet appeared in radio plays and on Broadway. After the Second World War he founded an off-Broadway theatre group and gave up acting for directing. During the 1950s he directed over 200 teleplays at a time when television was still a progressive launching pad for new talent. Lumet made the switch from television to films, along with JOHN FRANKENHEIMER, FRANKLIN SCHAFFNER and MARTIN RITT. His first film, based on a television play, was *Twelve Angry Men* (1957), in which he achieved an extremely cinematic drama entirely within the confines of one set, a jury conference room.

In *Stage Struck* (1958), *That Kind of Woman* (1959), *The Group* (1965) and *The Appointment* (1969), he displayed a feeling for romantic irony in his portrayal of women, His adaptations of famous plays, *The Fugitive Kind* (1960), based on Tennessee Williams's 'Orpheus Descending', Arthur Miller's *View from the Bridge* (1961), Eugene O'Neill's *Long Day's Journey into Night* (1962), Chekhov's *The Seagull* (1968) are at times less satisfying. But his handling of themes which pitch their characters into situations of gritty desperation – *Fail Safe* (1964), *The Deadly Affair* (1966) – has a strong atmospheric charge.

Other films: *The Pawnbroker* (1964), *The Hill* (1965), *Bye Bye, Braverman* and *The Anderson Tapes* (1970). MH

Lumière, Auguste (1862–1954)

Born in Besançon, France.

Lumière, Louis (1864–1948)

Born in Besançon, France.

Pioneer film-makers. The first show of projected, photographic motion pictures before a paying audience was given by the Lumière Cinématographe on 28 December 1895. A number of inventors in different countries had been competing to perfect a motion picture device; and if technically the Lumières won the race it was perhaps due in large part to their ability to call upon the resources of a soundly established industrial firm. In 1882, as young men, the brothers had gone into the photographic business established by their father Antoine (1840–1906) in Lyon; they had built up the fortunes of the firm through the success of a new brand of photographic plates. Somewhere about the end of 1894 their father suggested they might attempt the manufacture of films for the EDISON Kinetoscope peepshow; by February they were able to patent a device which would both photograph *and* project films. Throughout the rest of 1895 they gave carefully publicized demonstrations of their *Cinématographe* to photographic and other learned societies; and in December rented a room (the Salon Indien of the Grand Café, Boulevard des Capucines) for the first public shows. From 1896 Louis Lumière showed the same shrewdness in exploiting the invention, despatching agents to numerous different countries with the dual task of marketing films and machines and making new films to swell the repertoire. The films manufactured by the Lumières between 1896 and 1903, when they definitively abandoned production, are still astonishing for the clarity and quality of their photography. The Lumières also conducted influential experiments in colour and stereoscopic photography, in 70 mm film exhibited at the 1900 Universal Exposition and in Fotorama (1903), a method of projected panoramic still photographs. DR

Lupino, Ida

Born 1918 in London, England. Actress, producer and director; has also scripted all the films she has directed, as well as *Private Hell* (1936). The daughter of Stanley Lupino, stage comedian, she began acting in films in the early 1930s. After making a few films in Britain, such as *Her First Affaire* (1931), she went to Hollywood where she had a long career. Amongst the films in which she has acted are: *The Gay Desperado* (1936), *Artists and Models* (1937), *They Drive by Night* (1940), *High Sierra* (1941), *Devotion* (as Emily Brontë: 1943), *Deep Valley* (1947), *Woman in Hiding* (1949), *The Bigamist* (1953), *The Big Knife* (1955) and *While the City Sleeps* (1956): the films she has directed include *The Bigamist* and *The Hitch-Hiker* (1953), and *The Trouble with Angels* (1966). She has also starred in television series in the USA.

Lye, Len

Born 1901 in Christchurch, New Zealand. Animator and documentary director. Studied art in New Zealand and later Polynesian art in the South Seas. Began experimental animation in 1929; worked for JOHN GRIERSON in the GPO Film Unit, developing further the technique, originated by HANS RICHTER, of drawing and painting direct on to the celluloid reel, thus completing his work without the use of photography. His pre-war films were *Colour Box* (1935), *Rainbow Dance* (with Robert Helpmann dancing 'live', 1936) and *Trade Tattoo* (1937); in the last two he combined animation with live-action images, using an elaborate processing technique. In 1935 he worked in puppet animation for *Birth of a Robot*. During the war, in addition to making the cartoon *Musical Poster* (1941), he turned to documentary in *Kill or be Killed*, a realistic and ruthless study of the technique of street fighting, and the burlesque, *Swinging the Lambeth Walk*. After short film work in the USA – including collaboration with Ian Hugo on *Bells of Atlantis* (1952) – he withdrew from full-time film-making, concerning himself mainly with the fine arts, and latterly with kinetic art and electronic mobile sculpture. This has led to further abstract film studies such as *Rotational Harmonic* and *Black* (1961), and *Steel Fountain* (1963). For accounts of his experiments see Halas and Manvell, 'Design in Motion' (1962) and 'Art in Movement' (1970). RM

Ida Lupino and Jean Gabin in 'Moontide' (Archie Mayo, USA, 1942)

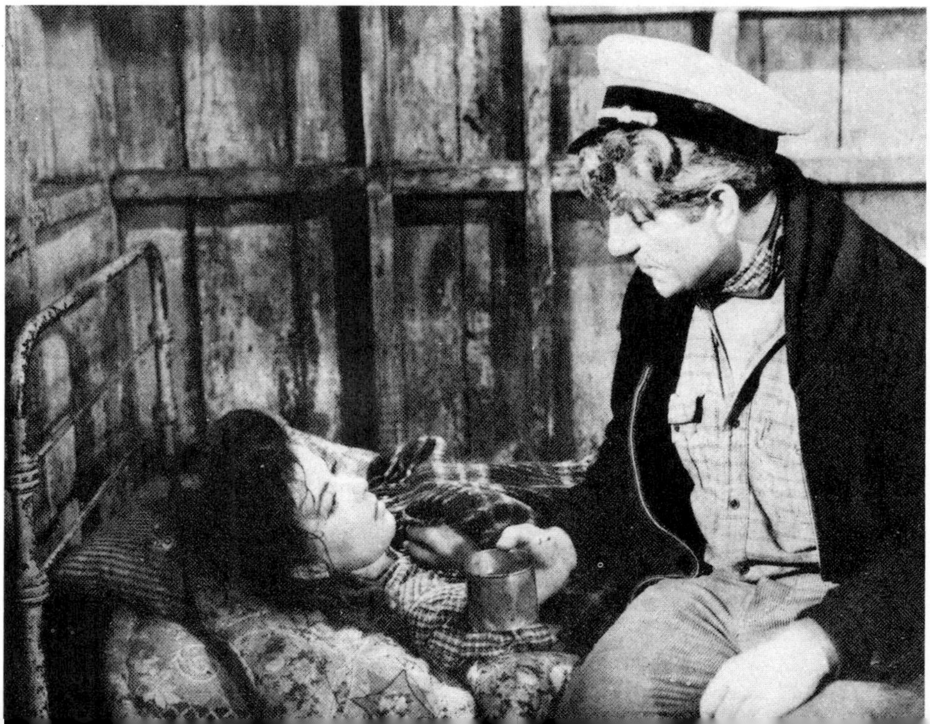

M

McCarey, Leo (1898–1969)
Born in Los Angeles, USA. Director. Worked in the 1920s under HAL ROACH, from whom he learned much about comedy timing and gag construction, which proved invaluable in the many comedies and LAUREL and HARDY shorts he wrote and supervised in the late silent/early sound periods, notably *Putting Pants on Philip*, *Battle of the Century* and *Big Business*. In the 1930s he worked with many celebrities including Eddie Cantor (*The Kid from Spain*, 1932), the MARX BROTHERS (*Duck Soup*, 1933) and MAE WEST (*Belle of the '90s*, 1934), but his more personal brand of zany, sophisticated comedy laced with nostalgic charm can be found in *Ruggles of Red Gap* (1934), *The Awful Truth* (1937), with superb playing from IRENE DUNNE, and *Love Affair* (1939). From the 1940s onwards, a rather sticky sentimentality gained the upper hand – *Going My Way* (1944), *The Bells of St Mary's* (1945) – and his post-war work has been very sporadic, although his technical control and flashes of the old debunking humour can still be found in *Good Sam* (1948), with its echoes of CAPRA, and the boisterous farce *Rally Round the Flag, Boys* (1958). JG

Harry Andrews and Peter McEnery in 'Entertaining Mr Sloane' (Douglas Hickox, GB, 1969)

McCrea, Joel
Born 1905 in Los Angeles, California, USA. Actor, who played in amateur dramatics and as an extra before becoming a leading man. Though generally typed as an agreeable and stalwart hero, he has achieved some interesting variations within that range. He also revealed an incisive gift for social comedy in *Sullivan's Travels* (1941) and *The Palm Beach Story* (1942). Films include: *The Jazz Age* (1929), *Wells Fargo* and *Dead End* (1937), *Union Pacific* (1938), *Foreign Correspondent* (1940), *The Great Man's Lady* (1941), *The More the Merrier* (1943), *Buffalo Bill* (1944), *The Virginian* (1946), *The Oklahoman* (1957), Sam Peckinpah's *Ride the High Country* (1961) in which he memorably played a resigned and ageing Westerner – the end-product of the life-style he had portrayed in Westerns throughout his career. RM

MacDonald, Jeanette (1902–1965)
Born in Philadelphia, USA. Actress and singer who began her career in the chorus in New York: later, with Nelson Eddy, she made a series of film operettas which were very popular in the 1930s. These included *Naughty Marietta* (1935), *Rose Marie* (1936), *Maytime* (1938), and *New Moon* (1940). Her most notable appearances were in musicals by LUBITSCH and MAMOULIAN including *The Love Parade* (1930), *One Hour with You* and *Love Me Tonight* (1932), and *The Merry Widow* (1934). She also starred in the spectacular film, *San Francisco* (1936).

McEnery, Peter
Born 1940 in Walsall, England. Young character actor, better known on the continent than Britain, who has appeared in several films including: *Tunes of Glory* (1960), *Victim* (1962), *The Moonspinners* (1964), *The Game is Over* (Paris, 1966). *Better a Widow* (Rome, 1967), *Negatives* (1968), *Entertaining Mr Sloane* (1969), *Rasputin* (France, 1969), *The Adventures of Gérard* (1970).

Machaty, Gustav (1901–1963)
Born in Prague, Czechoslovakia. Director. After entering the Czechoslovak industry, he studied for a time in America, assisting and observing several directors, including VON STROHEIM. He is remembered mainly for a handful of silent and early sound films: *The Kreutzer Sonata* (1926), *Erotikon* (1929), *From Saturday to Sunday* (1931), *Extase* (1934). Machaty's minor, but distinctive, talent (with its heavy lighting and moments of technical bravura) owes much to the German romantic tradition; his obsession with erotic imagery (a legacy from von Stroheim, perhaps) gives *Erotikon* and *Extase* an individual flavour – the latter, of course, gained notoriety for its nude scenes with a young HEDY LAMARR. He worked intermittently in various countries, including the United States, during his later years and collaborated on the script for PABST's German-made *Jackboot Mutiny* (1955). JG

Mackendrick, Alexander
Born 1912 in Boston, USA. Gifted director whose most characteristic film successes were achieved during his association with Britain's Ealing Studios, which specialized in indigenous,

'How the West was Won' (John Ford, Henry Hathaway and George Marshall, USA, 1962)

idiosyncratic comedies and social dramas. At the age of six he was taken to Scotland and he has lived in Britain ever since. An early career in advertising, cartoon illustration and screenwriting led to an assignment, during the Second World War, with the Ministry of Information; subsequently he became involved with the Psychological Warfare Branch, producing documentaries and newsreels. In 1945 he joined Ealing as a scriptwriter and directed his first film, the pawky Scottish comedy, *Whisky Galore* (*Tight Little Island* in America), in 1949.

His talent for dry, sly comedy with unusually alarming undertones was given ample play in the social satire *The Man in the White Suit* (1951) and the crime comedy *The Ladykillers* (1955). He also directed the touching story of a deaf child, *Mandy* (1952). Since leaving Ealing his fortunes have fluctuated. His brilliant study of Broadway megalomania, *Sweet Smell of Success* (1957), made in America, was a failure at the box-office. He started but did not finish *The Devil's Disciple* (1958). His subsequent films have revealed less of the wit and style that established him as an important director at Ealing.

Other films: *The Maggie* (1953), *Sammy Going South* (1962), *A High Wind in Jamaica* (1965), *Don't Make Waves* (1967). MH

McLaglen, Victor (1886–1959)
Born in Tunbridge Wells, England. Actor. Was a miner and heavyweight champion boxer in the army. One of six brothers, all in films, he became popular as a happy-go-lucky tough-guy character. He made several films directed by JOHN FORD, including *Hangman's House* (1928), *The Lost Patrol* (1934), *The Informer* (for which he won an Oscar, 1935), *She Wore a Yellow Ribbon* (1949), *Rio Grande* (1951), and *The Quiet Man* (1952). Among his other films are: *The Call of the Road* (1920), *Beau Geste* (1926), *Under Two Flags* (1936), *Sea Fury* (1958).

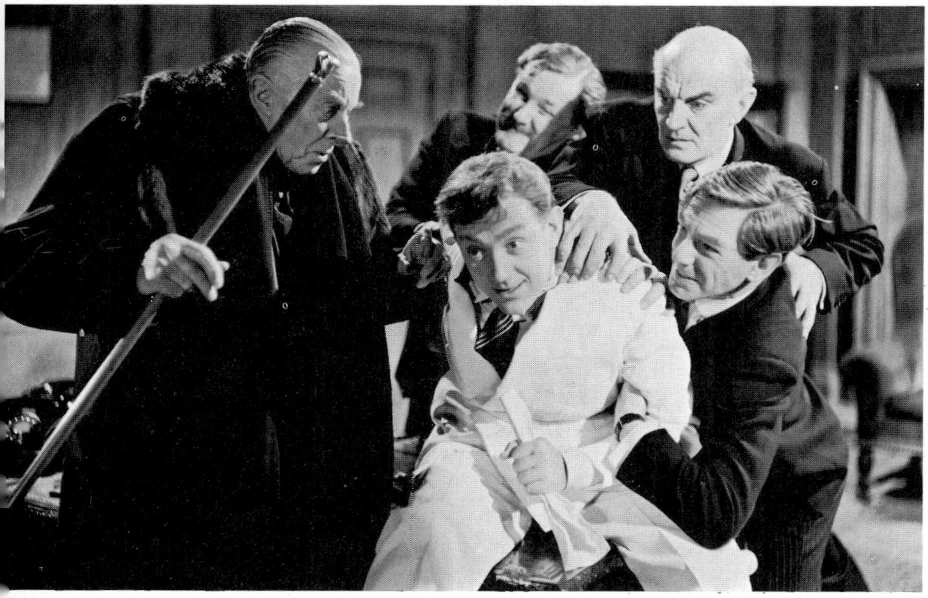

Above: Victor McLaglen in 'The Informer' (John Ford, USA, 1935)
Below: Alec Guinness (front), Ernest Thesiger, Howard Marion-Crawford, Desmond Roberts and Michael Gough in 'The Man in the White Suit' (Alexander Mackendrick, GB, 1951)

MacLaine, Shirley
Born 1934 in Richmond, USA. Actress sister of WARREN BEATTY. At first a stage dancer and singer, appearing on Broadway in the chorus before making her film début in *The Trouble with Harry* (1956). Her screen characters tend to be innocent and somewhat gamin, but with an underlying trend of commonsense and desire to preserve their own way of life. Other films include: *Artists and Models* and *Around the World in Eighty Days* (1956), *Some Came Running* (1958), *Can-Can* and *The Apartment* (1959), *The Children's Hour* (*The Loudest Whisper*, 1962), *Two for the Seesaw* and *Irma La Douce* (1963), *The Yellow Rolls-Royce* (1964), *Sweet Charity* (1968), *Two Mules for Sister Sara* (1969), *Desperate Characters* (1971). She came to Britain in 1971 to make a television series 'Shirley's World'. In the same year she published her autobiography 'Don't Fall off the Mountain'. MH

McLaren, Norman
Born 1914 in Scotland. Animator and documentary director. McLaren began live film-making while still at school. He made his first animated cartoon, *Camera Makes Whoopee*, in 1935, and was discovered by JOHN GRIERSON, who put him on the staff of the GPO Film Unit in 1937. He made in Britain between 1939 and 1942 over a dozen short films, some documentary, several cartoon. In animation he began to adopt the technique of working direct on the celluloid reel without the intervention of photography, following on the experimental work in this form begun by LEN LYE. Among these was *Love on the Wing* (1937). Again like Lye, he experimented with abstract mobile design in colour.

In 1939 Grierson went to Canada to head the newly established National Film Board and McLaren joined him in 1941 to concentrate on experimental animation. The results were *Dollar Dance* (1943), drawn direct on the reel with mobile backgrounds, *Alouette* (1944), using cut-out paper, *C'est l'Aviron* (1945), using a continual dipping and forward-tracking movement, as if from the prow of a boat, through a succession of cut-out landscapes, and *La Poulette Grise*, which experimented with an evolving pastel picture. McLaren used every kind of musical backing, including French-Canadian folksong.

With *Begone Dull Care* (1949) McLaren began to let his patterns evolve continuously along the roll of film, ignoring the frame boundaries, a technique to which he was to return repeatedly, for example in *Serenal* (1959), the patterns of which he etched with a vibra-drill, an instrument like a pneumatic drill, working to music from the West Indies. Similarly, *Short and Suite*, a 'colour cocktail' made the same year, was set to jazz. Music, of course, is of the highest importance in McLaren's work; examples are the march tune in *Stars and Stripes* (1943), to which the stars and stripes perform their acrobatics, the jazz of *Begone*

Opposite above: Charlton Heston in 'Ben Hur' (William Wyler, chariot race sequence by Andrew Marton, USA, 1959) Below: 'The Story of the Flaming Years' (Yulia Solntseva, USSR, 1960)

Dull Care, the steam-organ tune of *Hoppity-Pop* (1946), the American folk-song for the 'linear extravaganza' *Lines Horizontal* (1960) and the electronic piano for *Lines Vertical* (1960). McLaren has also devised a whole range of artificial sounds in purely graphic terms, as in *Dots and Loops* (1948); later he began to stencil carefully devised and card-indexed shapes on to the optical track, used notably in *Neighbours* (1953) and *Rhythmetic* (1956), while synthetic sound and music for the saxophone is mixed in the surrealistic film, *A Phantasy* (1952). The principles of this synthetic sound are demonstrated in *Pen Point Percussion* (1951).

McLaren has made extensive use of 'pixillation' (the animation of 'live' images of actors and objects) as in *Two Bagatelles* (1952) and *Neighbours*, and of animating cut-out shapes and objects, as in *Rhythmetic*, with its obstinately misbehaving numbers, or in the brilliantly conceived *Canon*, illustrating contrapuntal musical form. He has long been helped by his closest assistant, Evelyn Lambart, an animator originally trained in mathematics and physics, and possessing a scientific research worker's approach to the meticulous preparations necessary for the films of a perfectionist. McLaren has experimented, to take a further example, with visual effects dependent upon persistence of vision, as in *Mosaic* (1964) and *Blinkety Blank* (1955). He often uses what appear to be the most extraordinary techniques to achieve his graphic effects; for *Lines Horizontal* he engraved directly onto 35mm film with a penknife, a sewing needle and a razor-blade, applying the colours by hand with transparent cellulose dyes and a sable-hair brush. In *Fiddle-de-Dee* (1947) he exploited a phenomenon he discovered when particles of dust settle on freshly-painted material, creating a texture of their own. One of the greatest of his visual experiments is *Pas de Deux* (*Duo*, 1968), a magnificent demonstration of the use of staggered, synthesized multiple images derived from the live-action record of a dance movement. He has also experimented successfully with the abstract stereoscopic colour image in *Now is the Time* (1951), made for the Festival of Britain. Recent work includes *Spheres and Synchrony*.

Records of McLaren's techniques, sometimes described by himself, can be found in Halas and Manvell's 'The Technique of Film Animation' (1959; revised 1968), 'Design in Motion' (1962) and 'Art in Movement' (1970). He has also been the subject of an hour-long documentary made by BBC Television, *The Eye Hears, the Ear Sees*. RM

Above: Norman McLaren
Below: Steve McQueen in 'The Reivers' (Mark Rydell, USA, 1969)

McLeod, Norman Z. (1898–1964)
Born in Michigan, USA. Veteran Hollywood director from the early 1930s, previously a cartoonist, animator and screenwriter. He directed two of the MARX Brothers' most anarchic farces, *Monkey Business* (1931) and *Horse Feathers* (1932), and thereafter established a reputation for handling crazy comedy. Chief films include: *It's a Gift* (1934), *Topper* (1937), *The Kid from Brooklyn* (1946), *The Secret Life of Walter Mitty* and *The Paleface* (1948), *My Favourite Spy* (1951), *Casanova's Big Night* (1954).

MacMurray, Fred
Born 1908 in Kankakee, Illinois, USA. Versatile actor, who first sang and played in an orchestra to earn his tuition fees; he then went to Hollywood as member of a band, played as an extra on screen, went to New York with a comedy stage band and joined a revue company. An expert saxophonist, he has played in night clubs and performed on television. His film career really began in 1935 with *The Gilded Lily*. His many subsequent films include: *Double Indemnity* (1944), in which he gave one of his best screen performances, *The Caine Mutiny* (1954), *The Rains of Ranchipur* (1955), *The Apartment* (1960) and *The Happiest Millionaire* (1967).

McQueen, Steve
Born 1932 in Indianapolis, USA. Actor, who was at first a tank driver with US Marines. His screen career started after his television series *Wanted – Dead or Alive*. His films include: *Never Love a Stranger* (1958), *The Magnificent Seven* (1960), *The Great Escape* and *Love with the Proper Stranger* (1963), *Nevada Smith* (1965), *The Sand Pebbles* (1966), *Bullitt* and *The Thomas Crown Affair* (1968), *The Reivers* (1969), *Yucatan* and *Le Mans* (1971). His speciality lies in playing ruthless, intrepid characters, expecting and giving no quarter.

Magnani, Anna
Born 1909 in Rome, Italy. Stage and screen actress, whose variations on the intense and vital 'earth mother' characterization that made her internationally famous have won her many

prizes, including an American Academy Award for her performance in *The Rose Tattoo* (1955). She first achieved recognition outside Italy for her role in the pioneer neo-realist ROSSELLINI film, *Open City* (1945).

Brought up in Rome, she developed a talent for musical comedy which introduced her to a wide range of professional experience in cabaret, vaudeville and repertory. In 1934 she made her screen début in *The Blind Woman of Sorrento* which was followed by a number of unexceptional film performances. But the raging strength and sincerity of her heroine in *Open City* was repeated in many subsequent films – *The Miracle* (1948), *Volcano* (1951), *Bellissima* (1954). In Hollywood she was also type-cast as the free-living, exhibitionist virago in *The Rose Tattoo* and *Wild is the Wind* (1957), *The Fugitive Kind* (1959), her early flair for comedy being largely overlooked. Since her Hollywood period she has made only one film of note – PASOLINI's *Mamma Roma* (1962) – and her flamboyant style is no longer so fashionable even in Italy.

Other notable films: *The Golden Coach* (1954), *The Secret of Santa Vittoria* (1969). MH

Magnetic Tape

A plastic tape coated with ferric oxide powder, which, on being run through a variable magnetic field, can be made to register in a permanent form the impulses necessary for the reproduction of electronically produced sound and pictures.

Magnetic Track

The sound track of a film recorded on magnetic tape, either separate from the picture film, or (in the case of striped prints) on the picture itself.

Makavejev, Dusan

Born 1932 in Belgrade, Yugoslavia. The outstanding figure in the contemporary Yugoslav cinema, Makavejev graduated in philosophy and was a film critic and journalist before attracting attention with a satirical documentary, *Parade*, in 1962. His first feature film, *A Man is not a Bird*, appeared three years later. This and *The Switchboard Operator* (1967) were pertinent commentaries on life in a modern, socialist, urban society. *Innocence Unprotected* (1968) was a unique venture in which Makavejev revived, with a satirical documentary annotation, a strange, primitive film made during the war as a patriotic gesture by a professional strong man, Aleksić. WR – *Mysteries of the Organism* (1971) must be regarded as his masterpiece, a wise and hilarious exploration of the theories of Wilhelm Reich, subjecting politico-social doctrines of East and West alike to the searching test of Reich's combination of Marxist and Freudian thought.

Makk, Karoly

Born 1925 in Budapest, Hungary. Starting his career as an assistant director, notably on *Somewhere in Europe* (1947), Makk emerged as one of the outstanding Hungarian directors of the 1950s. In the 1960s, however, the promise of his short, *The Imaginary Invalid* (1952), and the excellent feature films *Liliomfi* (1954), *Ward No 9* (1955) and *House under the Rocks* (1958) seemed not to be fulfilled. In 1970 however Makk re-emerged as a director of first rank with his adaptation of two Tibor Déry stories, *Love*. Other films: *Tale on the Twelve Points* (1956), *Brigade No 39* (1959), *Don't Keep off the Grass* (1960), *The Fanatics* (1961), *The Lost Paradise* (1962), *The Last but One* (1963), *His Majesty's Dates* (1964), *Before God and Man* (1968).

Slobodan Aligrudic and Eva Ras in 'The Switchboard Operator' (Dusan Makavejev, Yugoslavia, 1967)

Malden, Karl

Born 1914 in USA. Actor, who first made his name on the stage, appearing in a number of Broadway productions. His films include: *They Knew What They Wanted* (1940), *Winged Victory* (1944), *Boomerang* (1947), *The Gunfighter* (1950), *A Streetcar Named Desire* (for which he won an award as best supporting actor; 1951), *Ruby Gentry* (1952), *I Confess* (1953), *On the Waterfront* (1954), *Baby Doll* (1956), *One-Eyed Jacks* (1959), *The Cincinnati Kid* (1965), *Nevada Smith* (1966), *Billion Dollar Brain* (1967), *Patton . . . Lust for Glory* (1969), *Cat O'Nine Tails* (1971). In 1957 he directed *Time Limit*.

Malle, Louis

Born 1932 at Thumeries (Nord), France. Director. Studied at the Paris film school, IDHEC, before becoming assistant to COUSTEAU, co-directing with him *Le Monde du Silence* (1956).

He also assisted BRESSON on *Un Condamné à Mort s'est échappé* (1956). Malle directed his first feature film, *L'Ascenseur pour l'Échafaud* (1957), when he was 25; it was a well-made thriller in which JEANNE MOREAU appeared to advantage, her achievement confirmed when she appeared as the dissatisfied society wife in Malle's next film, *Les Amants* (1958). *Zazie dans le Métro* (1960) was more experimental; Malle attempted to create a visual equivalent to Raymond Queneau's verbally witty novel; with its kaleidoscope of images, it is not entirely successful as crazy comedy. *Vie Privée* (1961), with BRIGITTE BARDOT, satirizes the life of a star of her kind, who can gain no privacy to conduct the one love affair which matters to her; Malle used jump cuts and frozen frames to objectify his narrative. *Le Feu Follet* (1963), on the other hand, is a deeply serious film concerning the last two days in the life of an alcoholic who has lost all contact with society. Then, as if reacting against the melancholy of this film, Malle broke away to make the lively *Viva Maria* (1965) in Mexico, pairing in it his two stars of the past, Jeanne Moreau and Brigitte Bardot. Together they create a revolution, combining striptease with love and politics. *Le Voleur* (1967), made in France, deals with another disillusioned man, played by JEAN-PAUL BELMONDO. Malle is an eclectic film-maker, anxious to extend his professionalism into many different genres of subject and treatment. His technical assurance has grown with the developing range of his work. He tends to favour strong, tense moments of human experience, which he handles in a highly disciplined way, and his best films are notable for their delicacy and restraint. After a series of controversial documentaries made in India, Malle returned to feature production with *Le Souffle au Cœur* (*Dearest Love*, 1971), a study of an adolescent and his incestuous relationship with his mother. RM

Maltese Cross
A component of the most commonly used device for producing the intermittent movement of film through a camera or projector.

Mamoulian, Reuben
Born 1898 in Tiflis, USSR. Director. Interest in theatre led him to a period of study with Stanislavsky; in his early years, he moved from Russia to Paris and London, studying theatre. In 1924 he went to America to direct the Rochester Theatre and subsequently became a distinguished theatrical producer (*Porgy and Bess*, *Oklahoma*, etc). He virtually taught himself film technique and with *Applause* (1929) made one of the most distinctive early sound films, with an audacious use of locations and a splendidly gritty theatrical atmosphere. During the next two decades, he experimented with all the standard genres: the gangster drama (*City Streets*, 1931), horror (*Dr Jekyll and Mr Hyde*, 1931, with its subjective camera techniques), period romance (*Queen Christina*, 1933, with GARBO at her most luminous), early colour (*Becky Sharp*, 1935, full of bold colour costuming and romantic set pieces), and adventure melodramas (*The Mark of Zorro*, 1940, and *Blood and Sand*, 1941, both staged with great panache and tongue-in-cheek humour). But perhaps his most significant (and enjoyable) achievements have been with musicals: *Love Me Tonight* (1932) is a goldmine of witty filmic inventions and infectious playing, integrating the songs with the narrative in a manner anticipating MINNELLI, DONEN and WALTERS. *High, Wide and Handsome* (1937) has fewer songs, but makes up with a brilliantly staged 'rush to the rescue' climax; and *Summer Holiday* (1948) takes O'Neill as a starting point and builds up an affectionate piece of Americana, with exquisite design and nostalgic numbers. Characteristically, one remembers *Silk Stockings* (1957) more for its music and the dancing of ASTAIRE and Charisse than as a re-make of *Ninotchka*. Apart from uncredited work on numerous features and preliminary shooting on *Cleopatra* (1962–3), Mamoulian has disappeared from the cinema in recent years, a fact greatly to be deplored as he has a civilized, innovatory talent which gives his best work a perennial freshness and vitality. JG

Helen Morgan in 'Applause' (Reuben Mamoulian, USA, 1929)

Mankiewicz, Herman (1897–1953)
Born in New York, USA. Celebrated American scriptwriter whose most enduring achievement was his collaboration with ORSON WELLES on *Citizen Kane* (1940). Previous work includes *Dinner at Eight* (1933). After *Kane*, he worked on fairly routine projects into which he injected some imagination and cool character appraisal: *Pride of the Yankees* (1942), *Christmas Holiday* (1943), *The Enchanted Cottage* (1945), *A Woman's Secret* (1948) among others.

Mankiewicz, Joseph L.
Born 1909 in Pennsylvania, USA. Leading American screenwriter, director and producer with a special talent for witty, sophisticated screenplays, ridiculing the manners of enclosed societies. Since his salvage operation on the costly and notorious *Cleopatra* (1963), he has worked only intermittently in films.

After leaving Columbia University he worked as a correspondent for the Chicago Tribune in Berlin, where he also translated film sub-titles into English for release in America and Britain. In 1929 he returned to the USA and joined his brother on the writing staff at Paramount. In the 1930s he became a producer. In this capacity his credits include *Three Godfathers* and *Fury* (1936), *The Philadelphia Story* (1940), *The Keys of the Kingdom* (1944). In 1945 he found a more congenial, creative role as writer-director: his first film was *Dragonwyck* (1945). But it was *A Letter to Three Wives* (1949), for which he won an Academy Award for the screenplay, that established his pre-eminence as an urbane, literate film-maker. His most memorable film of this period was *All About Eve* (1950), which won him two Academy Awards, for script and direction.

In 1953 he directed what many critics consider one of the finest of all Shakespearean adaptations, *Julius Caesar*; in 1955 he turned the musical *Guys and Dolls* into an infectiously enjoyable film. He followed this with a flawed version of Graham Greene's *The Quiet American* (1957) and a compelling adaptation of Tennessee Williams's *Suddenly Last Summer* (1960). But, despite some elegant writing, he could do little for the doomed *Cleopatra*; while *The Honey Pot* (1967) was more verbose than amusing. His achievement, though, in creating films which are both visually interesting and verbally engrossing cannot be over-estimated.

Other notable films (as director and writer): *No Way Out* (1950), *People Will Talk* (1951), *Five Fingers* (1952), *The Barefoot Contessa* (1954), *There Was a Crooked Man* (1970). MH

Mankowitz, Wolf
Born 1924 in England. Ebullient and versatile playwright, screenwriter, journalist, producer, impresario. Entered motion pictures in 1952 as screenwriter, adapting his own novels and plays: *Make Me an Offer* (1954), *A Kid for Two Farthings* (1955) and *Expresso Bongo* (1959). Also scripted *The Long and the Short and the Tall* and *The Millionairess* (1960), *Waltz of the Toreadors* (1962), *The Day the Earth Caught Fire* (1963), *Casino Royale* (1966), etc. His musical plays include 'Make me an Offer', 'Belle' and 'Pickwick'.

Mann, Anthony (1906–1967)
Born in California, USA. Often underrated director who introduced perceptive insights into his high, wide and handsome treatments of outdoor spectaculars, notably Westerns, war films and historical epics. During the 1960s period of box-office fascination with sheer size, his *El Cid* (1961) and *The Fall of the Roman Empire* (1963) rank as two of the most intelligent grand-scale spectacles ever made.

Arriving in Hollywood via Broadway and the theatre, he directed his first film, *Dr Broadway*, in 1942 for Paramount. In the 1950s he established the style that was apparent in all his subsequent work: the analysis of men of action under stress. His Westerns and film adventures with JAMES STEWART – plus a successful change of pace for both in *The Glenn Miller Story* (1954) – were especially notable. He died while directing the spy melodrama, *A Dandy in Aspic* (1968), which was completed by its leading actor LAURENCE HARVEY.

Other principal films: *Strange Impersonation* (1946), *Devil's Doorway* and *Winchester 73* (1950), *The Tall Target* and *Bend of the River* (1951), *The Far Country*, *Strategic Air Command* and *The Man from Laramie* (1955), *The Tin Star* (1957), *Man of the West* (1958), *Cimarron* (1960), *The Heroes of Telemark* (1965). MH

Mann, Daniel
Born 1912 in New York, USA. American stage and television director who came to films in 1953, directing the screen version of *Come Back Little Sheba*, which he had produced on the stage. Less original than other directors who had learned their film trade in television, he is particularly talented in his handling of gifted actresses – Shirley Booth in *Sheba* and *About Mrs Leslie* (1954) and *Hot Spell* (1957), ANNA MAGNANI in *The Rose Tattoo* and Susan Hayward in *I'll Cry Tomorrow* (1955). Other main films include: *The Teahouse of the August Moon* (1956), *The Last Angry Man* (1959), *Butterfield 8* (1960), *Five Finger Exercise* (1962), *Our Man Flint* and *Judith* (1965).

Above: Philip Abbott and Jack Warden in 'The Bachelor Party' (Delbert Mann, USA, 1957)
Below: Burt Lancaster and Anna Magnani in 'The Rose Tattoo' (Daniel Mann, USA, 1955)

Mann, Delbert
Born 1920 in Kansas, USA. American director whose work on over 100 television plays, during the peak experimental period for American television drama, influenced his early films including his first, *Marty* (1955), for which he won an Academy Award, and *Bachelor Party* (1957). The homespun urban realism of these two comedy-dramas, however, soon gave way to glossier commercial efforts – *Separate Tables*

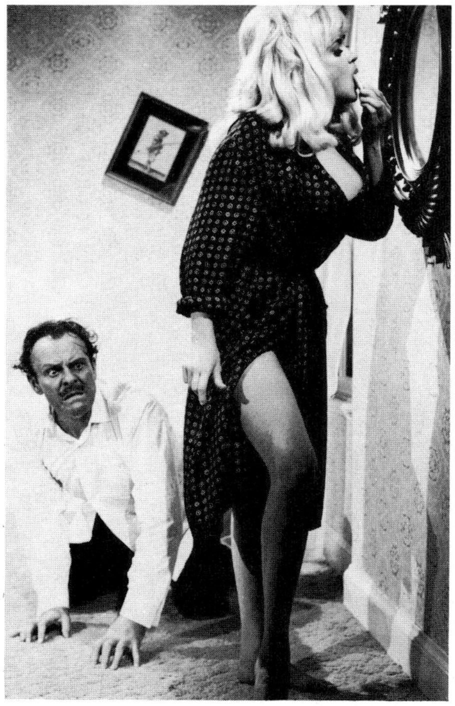

Terry Thomas and Jayne Mansfield in 'A Guide for the Married Man' (Gene Kelly, USA, 1967)

(1958), *Lover Come Back* (1961), *That Touch of Mink* (1962). The moving, low-keyed *Middle of the Night* (1959) and *The Dark at the Top of the Stairs* (1960) were more in keeping with his earlier work. Since the success of his *David Copperfield* (1969) he has filmed another literary classic, *Jane Eyre* (1970). MH

Mansfield, Jayne (1932–1967)
Born in USA. Actress, chiefly famous for her extremely well-developed bosom and an often lively comedy technique. After appearing in stage productions she entered films in 1955; her films include: *The Female Jungle* (1955), *The Sheriff of Fractured Jaw* (1959), *Too Hot to Handle* (1960), *It Happened in Athens* (1962), *A Guide for the Married Man* (1967).

Marais, Jean
Born 1913 in Cherbourg, France. Romantic French star whose heroic profile has tended to overshadow a more versatile dramatic talent than he is often given credit for. His association with JEAN COCTEAU, who gave him his first important stage role in 1937, resulted in several significant screen performances, in *L'Éternel Retour* (1943), *La Belle et la Bête* (1945), *Les Parents Terribles* (1948), *Orphée* (1949). Film début in *Le Pavillon Brule* (1942). His later post-Cocteau films have been mainly swashbuckling adventures and light-hearted thrillers; he made a Cocteau-like appearance in DEMY's *Peau d'Ane* (1970).

March, Fredric
Born 1897 in Wisconsin, USA. Respected American stage and screen actor, who in the 1930s and 1940s won film fame in a variety of roles, from romantic hero and light comedian to *Dr Jekyll and Mr Hyde* (1931), for which he won an Academy Award. His theatre-trained voice and commanding good looks made him a natural for period pieces such as *Smiling Through* (1932), *The Sign of the Cross* (1933), *The Barretts of Wimpole Street* (1934), *Les Misérables* and *Anna Karenina* (1935), *Mary of Scotland* and *Anthony Adverse* (1936), although his more memorable performances were as the has-been star in *A Star is Born* (1937) and as CAROLE LOMBARD's sparring partner in the black satire, *Nothing Sacred* (1937). In 1946 he won his second Academy Award for *The Best Years of Our Lives*, and went on to achieve great renown as a character actor in *Death of a Salesman* (1951), *Middle of the Night* (1959), *Inherit the Wind* (1960), *Seven Days in May* (1964), *Hombre* (1967), *tick . . . tick . . . tick . . .* (1969). MH

Máriássy, Félix
Born 1919 in Budapest, Hungary. In films since before the war, Máriássy was one of the first significant directors to emerge from the nationalized, post-war cinema. After collaborating with Geza Radványi on *Somewhere in Europe* (1947), he made his own admirable first film, *Madame Szabo*, in 1949. Subsequently he showed a special gift for intimate comedy. Other films: *The Marriage of Catharine Kis* (1949), *Full Steam Ahead* (1951), *Relatives* (1954), *A Glass of Beer* and *Spring in Budapest* (1955), *Smugglers* (1958), *Sleepless Years* and *A Simple Love* (1959), *It is a Long Way Home* and *Test Trip* (1960), *Every Day Sunday* (1962), *Goliath* (1964), *Fig Leaf* (1966), *Bondage* (1968), *The Impostors* (1970). RM

Marker, Chris
Born 1921 in Paris, France. Director and writer. Marker's literary upbringing (he is a critic and essayist) helped to develop his formidable analytical powers and when he began working in films in the mid-1950s as collaborator on some of RESNAIS's shorts, the French social cinema found an eloquent spokesman. Marker is an inveterate globe-trotter, looking at the world with a cool, sardonic eye, intolerant of received opinions and stupid prejudices. Although he is often classified with the *cinéma-vérité* movement, his best films have an entirely personal emphasis, both in the choice of images and in the literary, pointed commentaries. *Letter from Siberia* (1957), with its famous opening invocation, 'I am writing to you from a far-off country', is a synthesis of Marker's methods, full of little jokes and cartoons, parodies of documentary techniques and a use of film itself as an historical witness. *Description d'un Combat* (1960) and *Cuba si!* (1961) take similar, if less richly textured, looks at contemporary Israel and Cuba; and with *Le Joli Mai* (1962) Marker returned to a troubled Paris at the height of the Algerian crisis and recorded some startling, ironic interviews with worried and angry Parisians. *La Jetée* (1963) is his most original and certainly most haunting work – a bizarre science-fiction framework encloses an essay on time and memory (a harkback to his period with Resnais), using only still photographs to tell the story, except for one memorable moment when a sleeping girl suddenly opens her eyes. In recent years, he has written commentaries, assisted, edited and generally influenced a generation of French film-makers in a variety of projects, ranging from coverage of the May 1968 disturbances to supervision of the composite film *Loin du Viêtnam* (1967), in which several notable directors described their degree of involvement (or non-involvement) in the war. Marker's passion and commitment to causes occasionally leads him into the wordy rhetoric which besets French intellectual life, but his needle-sharp intellect and unwillingness to believe that two and two necessarily make four give his work a pungent eloquence; and in a film like *Letter from Siberia* he originated a form of visual essay which has produced several imitators but no peers. Recent work includes *The Battle of the 10 millions* (1970) and a short about MEDVEDKIN (1971). JG

Markopoulos, Gregory
Born 1928 in Toledo, Ohio, USA. Underground film-maker born of a family of Greek immigrants. His passion for film-making began at the age of 12, when he was working on 8 mm. His recurrent theme was homosexual love, beginning with a trilogy *Psyche, Lysis, Charmides* (1947–8). He was already experimenting with colour in these films, and establishing the style which was to become marked later of segmenting and combining images from different periods of time, often introduced through very rapid editing. His later films include *Swain* and *Flowers of Asphalt* (1951), *Eldora* (1952), a feature film, *Twice a Man* (1962–3), based on the Hippolytus legend, and *The Illiac Passion* (1964–6), which stars many members of the American underground, including ANDY WARHOL and JACK SMITH. RM

Married Print
A print containing pictures and sound records correctly synchronized for projection and reproduction.

Marsh, Mae (1895–1968)
Born in New Mexico, USA. Actress, who started in early films with D. W. GRIFFITH and became one of his most sensitive heroines. Her silent films include *Birth of a Nation* (1914), *Intolerance* (1915), *Polly of the Circus* (1917), and *The White Rose* (1923). She retired from the screen for several years, but returned to make sound films. Amongst these later films are: *Over the Hill* (1932), *Little Man What Now* (1934), *Jane Eyre* (1943), *A Tree Grows in Brooklyn* (1944), *The Robe* (1953), *Sergeant Rutledge* (1960).

Marshall, George
Born 1891 in Chicago, USA. Veteran American film director, who entered films as an extra in 1912, started directing Westerns in 1917 and has more than 400 films to his credit, plus several LAUREL and HARDY shorts. Though his work is noted more for its facility than for its artistic quality, he has proved himself especially adept at adapting to the spirit of the times and several of his films have a lively surface vigour, including *Destry Rides Again* (1939), *The Blue Dahlia* (1946), *Red Garters* (1954), *The Sheepman* (1958). Other films include: *A Message to Garcia* (1934), *You Can't Cheat an Honest Man* (1939), *The Ghost Breakers* (1940), *And the Angels Sing* (1943), *The Perils of Pauline* (1947), *Fancy Pants* (1950), a segment of *How the West Was Won* (1962), *Boy, Did I Get a Wrong Number* (1966), *Hook Line and Sinker* (1969).

Marshall, Herbert (1890–1966)
Born in London, England. Actor. An urbane, quiet performer, whose retiring manner concealed great accomplishment in the presentation of a very marked screen personality. After considerable stage experience in both Britain and the USA, his film career developed in Hollywood. His first considerable success was in *The Letter* (1929); the following year he appeared in HITCHCOCK's British film, *Murder*. His particular kind of romantic charm appealed to women, and he was a perfect foil to the many great women stars with whom he appeared, such as MARLENE DIETRICH (*Blonde Venus*, 1932), NORMA SHEARER (*Riptide*, 1933), and GARBO (*The Painted Veil*, 1934). He appeared to great advantage, too, in LUBITSCH's *Trouble in Paradise* (1932). Later his personality became too stereotyped and, in spite of appearing in many good films, he declined into the kind of actor whose familiar presence might turn up in any kind of film. His finest performances include those in *The Dark Angel* and *Forgotten Faces* (1936), Hitchcock's *Foreign Correspondent* (1940), *The Little Foxes* (1941), *The Moon and Sixpence* (1942), *The Razor's Edge* (1946), and *Stage Struck* (1958). RM

Martin, Dean
Born 1917 in Steubenville, Ohio, USA. Actor and singer. Was an amateur prize-fighter, and then tried many odd jobs such as petrol-station attendant before appearing in a night-club act with JERRY LEWIS as a straight singer. They remained together for some years, winning popularity polls in the early 1950s. His first films again teamed him with Jerry Lewis: *My Friend Irma* (1949), *At War with the Army* (1951), *Living it Up* and *Hollywood or Bust* (1956), and others. These brought him fame as a singer, and as an actor he has since made numerous other films, including: *The Young Lions* and *Rio Bravo* (1958), *Ocean's Eleven* (1960), *Kiss Me Stupid* and *The Sons of Katie Elder* (1965), *The Silencers* (1966), *How to Save a Marriage* (1967), *Bandolero* (1968), *Airport* (1969), *The Ravagers* (1970), *Something Big* (1971).

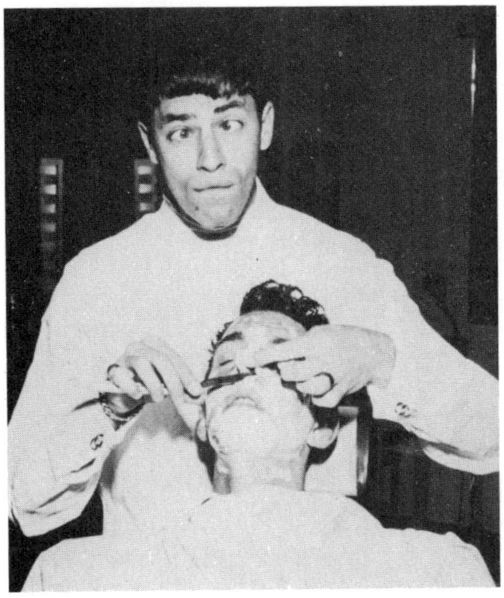

Above: Jerry Lewis and Dean Martin
Below: Chico, Harpo and Groucho Marx with Allan Jones in 'A Night at the Opera' (Sam Wood, USA, 1935)

Marvin, Lee
Born 1924 in New York, USA. Actor, who began his career in summer shows, graduating to Broadway, where he made his début in 'Billy Budd'. His first film was *You're in the Navy Now* (1951), and it was followed by several more in which he played aggressive characters, and in recent years he has developed a fine comic sense. Films include: *The Wild One* (1953), *The Caine Mutiny* and *Bad Day at Black Rock* (1954), *Attack* (1957), *The Man who shot Liberty Valance* (1962), *Donovan's Reef* (1963), *The Killers* (1964), *Cat Ballou* (1965), *The Dirty Dozen* and *The Professionals* (1966), *Point Blank* (1967), *Hell on the Pacific* (1968), *Paint Your Wagon* (1969), *Monte Walsh* (1970). He also made a television series, *M Squad*.

Marx Brothers:
Chico (real name Leonard, 1891–1961)
Harpo (real name Arthur, 1893–1964)
Groucho (real name Julius, born 1895)
Zeppo (born 1901)
Vaudeville and film comedians. Zeppo was the odd-man-out of the team, appearing only in their early films. The family were born and brought up in New York City, USA, and were of German-Jewish origin. They were on the stage from childhood, appearing initially in vaudeville with their mother, Minnie Marx, and subsequently on their own, first as 'The Four Nightingales' and later as 'The Four Marx Brothers'. All were accomplished musicians on more than one instrument, but it was Groucho who became the most formidable personality and delivered the ferocious wisecracks. Harpo was mute in the films, and Chico spoke with a broad Italian-style accent. Their surrealistic humour and ruthless burlesque, combined with their musical artistry, took them into films which grew out of their stage acts: *The Cocoanuts* (1929), *Animal Crackers* (1930), *Monkey Business* (the first to be made in Hollywood, 1931), *Horse Feathers* (1932) and *Duck Soup* (1933). After these Zeppo left the team, since he had merely acted as romantic relief, and had no gift for the highly creative destructiveness on which the others thrived, debunking every social pretension, particularly in the matronly form of MARGARET DUMONT. So far their films had not enjoyed box-office success, but IRVING THALBERG of MGM took them over and developed them into the big-time success of *A Night at the Opera* (1935) and *A Day at the Races* (1937), both well directed by SAM WOOD. Latter-day connoisseurs, however, tend to prefer the better of their

earlier films. *Room Service* (1938), made for RKO, again saw them in good form, but with Thalberg dead, MGM's poor scripts only contributed to their gradual decline in later films: *At the Circus* (1939), *Go West* (1940), *The Big Store* (1941), *A Night at Casablanca* (1946), and *Love Happy* (1950). They made occasional appearances in other films, and on television, Groucho even appearing as Koko in a television production of Gilbert and Sullivan's comic opera, 'The Mikado' (1960). Groucho co-scripted a film, *The King and the Chorus Girl* (1937), and wrote autobiographical works: 'Groucho and Me' (1959), 'Memoirs of a Mangy Lover' (1964). He is also a noted letter-writer, some of these being collected in 'The Groucho Letters' (1967). Harpo's autobiography appeared in 1961, 'Harpo Speaks'. See also Kyle Crichton, 'The Marx Brothers' (1950), Allen Eyles, 'The Marx Brothers, Their World of Comedy' (1966), and Paul D. Zimmerman and Burt Goldblatt, 'The Marx Brothers at the Movies' (1968). RM

Maselli, Francesco

Born 1930 in Rome, Italy. After he had worked as an assistant to Chiarini, ANTONIONI and VISCONTI, Maselli's directorial début was with an episode in *Amore in Città*. His first full feature was a notable study of the Resistance, *Gli sbandati* (1955). Later films: *La donna del giorno* (1956), *I delfini* (1960), *Gli indifferenti* (1963), *Fa in fretta a uccidermi . . . ho freddo* (1967).

Masina, Giulietta

Born 1926 in Giorgio di Piano, Italy. Piquant Italian actress with a Chaplinesque flair for blending comedy and pathos: her principal film performances have been in films directed by her husband FEDERICO FELLINI. Although the essence of her appeal is most completely captured in *Nights of Cabiria* (1957), in which she played a funny, waif-like prostitute, her most considered and significant portrayal is in Fellini's tormented study of a marriage, *Juliet of the Spirits* (1965).

From a family background with a high academic reputation, she went into the theatre after university, making her film début in *Senza Pietà* (1948). She became internationally known with *La Strada* (1954).

Other notable films: *Lights of Variety* (1950), *Il Bidone* (1955), *The Madwoman of Chaillot* (1969). MH

Mason, James

Born 1909 in Huddersfield, England. Distinctive, outspoken British character actor who has survived his early suavely sinister image to become an impeccable film player of great style and perception. Trained in the British theatre (including the Old Vic), he made his film début in *Late Extra* in 1935. In 1937 he collaborated on a play, 'Flying Blind', with Pamela Kellino whom he later married and divorced. He acted in a succession of serviceable roles but without making much impact until his portrayal of a Regency sadist in *The Man in Grey* (1944), which won him public adulation and stardom. Although less popular, his performance in *Odd Man Out* (1947) was a critical success.

In 1947 he went to Hollywood, appearing in many excellent films – including two for MAX OPHÜLS, *Caught* (1948) and *The Reckless Moment* (1949) – but invariably typecast. Since playing Brutus in *Julius Caesar* (1953) and the has-been star hero in *A Star is Born* (1954), he has given full range to his versatile talent, from Humbert-Humbert in *Lolita* (1962) to Chekhov's *The Seagull* (1968) and the blunt North Country comedy *Spring and Port Wine* (1969). In the past 10 years he has filmed outside America.

Other notable films: *The Bells Go Down* and *Thunder Rock* (1942), *Fanny by Gaslight* (1943), *The Wicked Lady* and *The Seventh Veil* (1945), *Pandora and the Flying Dutchman* (1951), *Five Fingers* and *North by Northwest* (1959), *A Touch of Larceny* (1960), *The Pumpkin Eater* (1964), *Georgy Girl* (1966), *The Deadly Affair* (1967), *Mayerling* (1968), *Age of Consent* (1969), *The Yin and the Yang* and *Die Boss, Die Quietly* (1970), *Bad Man's River* (1971). MH

Massingham, Richard (1898–1953)

As a practising doctor, Massingham made two amateur films of exceptional charm and cinematic wit: *Tell me if it Hurts* (1933–4) and *And so to Work* (1935–6). This led to his recruitment by the GPO Film Unit. Massingham found his niche with a long series of two- or three-minute trailers made for the Ministry of Information, in most of which Massingham himself – a large, genial character who was a cross between a latter-day JOHN BUNNY and a bewildered spaniel – personified the ordinary British citizen faced with wartime problems of conserving fuel, preventing colds and road accidents, scotching rumours and coping with gas masks and rationing. Later he produced and/or directed a number of longer documentaries including *Another Case of Poisoning* (1949), *The Cure* (1950), *Introducing the New Worker* (1951) and *The Blakes Slept Here* (completed by Jacques Brunius, 1953).

Giulietta Masina in 'Juliet of the Spirits' (Federico Fellini, Italy, 1965)

Master Shot

The main shot of a complete piece of dramatic action, which facilitates the assembly of the component shots of which it will finally be composed.

Mastroianni, Marcello

Born 1924 in Fontana Liri, Italy. One of the few Italian star actors to achieve as great an international success as the voluptuous female of the species – GINA LOLLOBRIGIDA, SOPHIA

LOREN, ANNA MAGNANI, CLAUDIA CARDINALE, etc. Discovered in the theatre by VISCONTI, he made his film début in *I Miserabili* in 1947 and won fame outside Italy for his portrayal of world-weary anti-heroic cynicism in FELLINI's *La Dolce Vita* (1959), although his most popular roles were those he played opposite Sophia Loren in *Yesterday, Today and Tomorrow* (1963) and *Marriage Italian Style* (1964). His very real talent as a character actor was amply demonstrated in *Divorce Italian Style* (1961) and *The Organizer* (1963). Main films include: *White Nights* (1957), *Il Bell'Antonio* (1960), *La Notte* (1961), *8½* (1963), *A Place for Lovers, Leo the Last* and *Sunflower* (1969), *Jealousy, Italian Style* and *The Priest's Wife* (1970). RM

Maté, Rudolph (1898–1964)
Born in Cracow, Poland. Cinematographer and director. During the 1920s he was assistant to KARL FREUND. He subsequently photographed DREYER's *La Passion de Jeanne d'Arc* (1928) and *Vampyr* (1932); also LANG's *Liliom* (1933). After going to America in the mid-1930s he never quite surpassed the masterly atmospheric lighting of these films, although he did much successful work: *Dodsworth* (1936), *The Adventures of Marco Polo* (1938), *Foreign Correspondent* and *Flame of New Orleans* (1940), *To Be or Not To Be* (1942), *Address Unknown* and *Cover Girl* (1944), *Gilda* (1946). On turning to direction after the war, he made several efficient thrillers – *The Dark Past* (1948), *Union Station* (1950), *Rough Company* (1955), *Three Violent People* (1956) – and period dramas, working in Italy as well as America. JG

Mathieson, Muir
Born 1911 in Stirling, Scotland. Conductor and director of film music. Began his almost lifelong career in film music as an assistant to ALEXANDER KORDA in 1931; in 1934 he became his full-time music director. In this capacity, working for Korda and later for J. ARTHUR RANK, he was mainly responsible for involving eminent composers with British films; not only did he guide them into learning the necessary techniques, creating a sympathetic liaison between them and the studios, but himself conducted literally hundreds of scores at recording sessions, using frequently the London Symphony Orchestra and the Philharmonia Orchestra. Among the composers he introduced very early to the cinema was Arthur Bliss, who composed his celebrated score for H. G. Wells's *Things to Come* (1936). Mathieson also continually interested himself in music for documentary films, working in particular for the Crown Film Unit during the war, and himself directed *Instruments of the Orchestra* (1946), the inspiring instructional film based on Benjamin Britten's 'A Young Person's Guide to the Orchestra' featuring the London Symphony Orchestra conducted by Malcolm Sargent. He also appeared on the screen himself as a conductor in *The Seventh Veil* and other films. Among the works of the more celebrated composers which he supervised and conducted are William Walton's scores for LAURENCE OLIVIER's Shakespearean films, Arnold Bax's score for *Oliver Twist*, and Vaughan Williams's score for *49th Parallel* (*The Invaders*, 1941). RM

Mathis, June (1881–1927)
Born in Leadville, Colorado, USA. June Mathis started her career as an actress and joined Metro in 1914–15, and wrote her first scenario, *The House of Tears*, in 1915. Very soon she had become one of the leading and most influential Hollywood writers and one of the first to stress the need for collaboration between director and writer. Her most important contribution to the screen was her discovery and development of the personality of VALENTINO in *The Four Horsemen of the Apocalypse* (1921) and later in *The Conquering Power* (1921), *Blood and Sand* and *The Young Rajah* (1922). Earlier, with equal intelligence, she had exploited the complex personality of NAZIMOVA in her scripts for *Toys of Fate* and *Eye for Eye* (1917), *Out of the Fog, The Red Lantern* and *The Brat* (1919). Mathis was also the first of the several successive writers of *Ben Hur* (1922–6).

Matras, Christian
Born 1903 in Valence, Drôme, France. Cinematographer. Started as newsreel cameraman and worked on many documentaries. Moved to feature films in 1930s as associate cameraman; finally established himself with RENOIR's *La Grande Illusion* (1937). His early work with DUVIVIER, CHRISTIAN-JAQUE and DELANNOY was precise yet relatively unexciting; but his films with MAX OPHÜLS – *La Ronde* (1950), *Madame de...* (1953), *Lola Montès* (1955) – gave him (and his skilful operator) splendid opportunities for luscious, sensual lighting and virtuoso camera movements. Other characteristic work includes *Fanfan la Tulipe* (1951), *Montparnasse 19* (1957), *Thérèse Desqueyroux* (1962), *Les Fêtes Galantes* (1965), *The Milky Way* (1968). JG

Matrices
Films made from three-colour separation negatives in which the photographic image is formed in relief in hardened gelatin.

Matte
A device for preventing the exposure of some part of a film in order to obtain a special effect during subsequent exposure.

Matthau, Walter
Born 1920 in USA. Actor who usually plays character parts involving a dry, twisted sense of humour. At first on the stage, he made his screen début in 1955 in *The Kentuckian*. This was followed by, amongst other films, *A Face in the Crowd* (1957), *King Creole* (1958), *Strangers when we Meet* (1960), *Lonely are the Brave* (1962), *Charade* (1963), *The Fortune Cookie* (*Meet Whiplash Willie*, 1966), *A Guide for the Married Man* (1967), *The Secret Life of an American Wife* (1968), *Hello Dolly* and *Cactus Flower* (1969), *A New Leaf* (1970), *Plaza Suite* (1971). He also made a television series, *Tallahassee 7000*.

Mattsson, Arne
Born 1919 in Uppsala, Sweden. Essentially a director of action films, and known as 'the Swedish Hitchcock', Mattsson began his career as assistant to Per Lindberg, directed a short, *The Regiment of Halland*, in 1942, and his successful first feature, *And All These Women*, two years later. *One Summer of Happiness* (1951) achieved an international reputation which Mattsson's later prolific output failed to sustain. Later films include: *Salka Valka* (1954), a remake of *The Phantom Carriage* (1958), *Bamse* (1968), *Ann and Eve* (1970).

May, Joe (1880–1954)
Born in Vienna, Austria. Producer and director in Germany. Turned from business, horse-racing and automobile racing to theatre and film before the First World War. Established himself as a maker of film serials with the American-influenced Joe Debbs and Stuart Webbs films of the mid-teens, and became a prolific director of thrillers and programme films up to 1933. His best known silent films were *Veritas Vincit* (1918), *Homecoming* (1928), and *Asphalt* (1929), but his general taste is better revealed by such titles as *The Hindu Tomb* (1921). In 1934 he went to Hollywood where he continued to produce a spate of secondary films during the 1930s, such as *The Invisible Man Returns* (1940). Married to the theatre and screen actress Mia May, who appeared in his films and went with him to Hollywood, where she managed a restaurant. RM

Mayer, Carl (1894–1944)
Born in Graz, Austria. Scriptwriter who was to become the most influential writer in the

Elaine Devry and Walter Matthau in 'A Guide for the Married Man' (Gene Kelly, USA, 1967)

German cinema during the silent period. He was much affected at first by expressionism (see page 224), and co-scripted *The Cabinet of Dr Caligari* (1919); Siegfried Kracauer has shown how the original subversive content in the script was modified at the desire of ERICH POMMER the producer and his director ROBERT WIENE; the ending was made conformist and the film (though still very striking with its expressionist sets symbolizing the mind of its mad hero under hypnosis) turned into a psychological thriller. Mayer's second expressionist film for Wiene, *Genuine* (1920), was less successful.

Mayer was a good writer and had a true instinct for the cinema; above everything else his scripts emphasized mood, preconceiving the story with the fluid continuity and strong visual atmosphere characteristic of the best German films of the period. He always wrote with the camera in mind. Mayer called his script for *Sylvester* (*New Year's Eve*, 1923), directed by LUPU PICK, a *Lichtspiel* (light-play) conceived in 54 'images', seeing the light and darkness in a man's soul through the chiaroscuro of photography. In 1921 he had already written for Lupu Pick *Der Dummkopf* and *Scherben*, a film without any printed titles, and in the same year he also wrote the script for *Hintertreppe* (*Backstairs*), directed by Leopold Jessner, once again dispensing with titles. His talent for the atmospheric film was further revealed in Arthur von Gerlach's *Vanina* (1922), a film featuring a sadistic tyrant's torture of his daughter and her lover, a rebel against his régime; ASTA NIELSEN gave one of her finest performances.

Mayer, who for a few years was to maintain a prolific output as an independent screenwriter, turned increasingly in the direction of the so-called *Kammerspiel* films, intimate psychological dramas. One of the outstanding films he wrote for MURNAU was *The Last Laugh* (1924), which used a form of stylized realism to project the inner experience of a hotel doorman whose whole existence turned on parading about in the uniform with which his work provided him, and what happened after he lost it when demoted through old age. This film remains the most celebrated of Mayer's titleless subjects. Mayer was to work closely with Murnau, one of Germany's most gifted directors. In 1925 he adopted Molière's *Tartuffe* for Murnau, and he also experimented in documentary, conceiving the original treatment for RUTTMANN's and FREUND's *Berlin*, the first of the city-symphony films.

Mayer had many offers to emigrate to Hollywood, but he preferred to remain in Europe. However, he wrote *Sunrise* for Murnau when the latter went to Hollywood in 1927. With the coming of Hitler, Mayer worked at first in Paris with PAUL CZINNER, acting as script adviser on Czinner's *Der Träumende Mund*. He finally settled in London, where his friendship with PAUL ROTHA led to his scripting Rotha's film about 'The Times', *The Fourth Estate*. Mayer's genius lay fundamentally in the art of the silent film, and he never achieved the same status with sound. RM

Mayer, Louis B. (1885–1957)
Born in Minsk, USSR. The archetypal figure of the Hollywood film producer of the golden era – crude, autocratic, insensitive – Mayer emigrated from Europe to Canada with his parents as a child, and began his career helping his father with a junk business which later grew into a ship salvage firm. In 1907 he bought a small movie theatre in Haverhill, Massachusetts and four years later opened a second theatre. From exhibition he moved to distribution and made a quarter of a million dollars out of the New England distribution rights to *Birth of a Nation*. He first became involved in production when Metro Pictures Corporation was formed in January 1915; and in 1918 established the Mayer Company. In 1924 Loews Inc. merged Metro, the Goldwyn Company and Mayer Productions to form MGM; and Mayer's appointment as vice-president and general manager of the firm, at a salary of $1,500 a week, established him in the powerful situation which he was to occupy for the next quarter of a century. For the first decade or so he had the important collaboration of IRVING THALBERG; and MGM's greatest years – the period of *Ben Hur*, GARBO, VIDOR, JEAN HARLOW – were certainly those in which artistic policy was guided by his younger colleague. It remains mysterious to what extent Thalberg's power was limited, in the years preceding his early death, by Mayer's intervention by intrigue. Certainly Mayer's disapproval brought about the end of many artistic careers, including that of BUSTER KEATON. In later years Mayer's own taste for All-American family entertainment was best reflected in the Andy Hardy series, which were his personal favourites among all the films his studio produced. In the 1950s his power was severely reduced by studio reorganization; and he is said to have died embittered, and feeling himself betrayed by his former colleagues – a fate which many would have seen as natural justice. DR

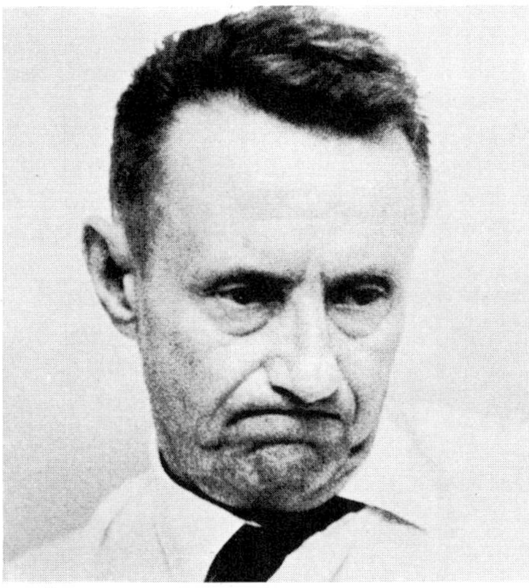

Above: Paul Brennan in 'Salesman' (Albert and David Maysles, USA, 1969)
Below: Leslie Howard, Dick Foran, Bette Davis and Humphrey Bogart in 'The Petrified Forest' (Archie Mayo, USA, 1936)

Georges Méliès's design for 'Indiarubber Head' (Méliès, France, 1902)

Mayo, Archie (1891–1968)

Born in New York, USA. Capable American director, ex-song-writer, gag man and onetime extra in films, who worked in Hollywood from 1916. In the early 1930s he made several dynamic films, typical of their depression-ridden time, including *Night After Night* (1932), *Bordertown* (1934), *The Petrified Forest* and *Black Legion* (1936), which during its production was a great source of controversy. After the Second World War he made few films – notably *A Night in Casablanca* (1945) and *Angel on my Shoulder* (1946). He produced *The Beast of Budapest* in 1957.

ʼlaysles, Albert

3orn 1933 in USA.

ʼlaysles, David

3orn 1931 in USA. Directors and cameramen. The Maysles Brothers have emerged in recent ʼears as two of the main exponents of a *cinéma-vérité* style concerned with capturing the sudden, unexpected aspects of their subjects. Using ʼortable camera and sound equipment (designed by themselves), they worked at first with ʼ)rew Associates and 'Time-Life', notably with ICHARD LEACOCK on *Primary*. Whereas the 'Time-Life' films were mainly journalistic and ʼramatic, the Maysles Brothers' work has been ʼore concerned with investigating character ʼraits. Main films (including some for television) ʼnclude, *Showman* (1963), a study of the American exhibitor JOE LEVINE; *What's Happening?* (1964), about the Beatles' tour in America; *Truman Capote* (1966); *Salesman* (1969), a lengthy reportage about a Bible salesman and his ʼerritory; and *Gimme Shelter* (1970), one of their most controversial works recording The Rolling Stones concert at Altamont, which ended in murder and chaos. JG

Medium Shot

A shot taken with the camera apparently closer than a long shot, but not so near as for a close-up; in relation to a human subject from knees upwards.

Medvedkin, Alexander Ivanovich

Born 1900 in USSR. Director and writer. Began in 1927 at Gosvoenkino Studios as scenarist and assistant director. He was in charge of the film-train which travelled round the big construction sites, developing new kinds of publicity involving shorts, posters, *film-feuilletons*, etc. He was a brilliant satirist taking in influences as disparate as MACK SENNETT, Gogol, Russian folk-lore and early DOVZHENKO; his best work includes the silent *Happiness* (1934), a grotesquely funny parody of farm life before and after the Revolution, full of rich visual invention and eccentricities, *Snatchers* (1935) and *Marvellous Girl* (1937, sound). During the Second World War he supervised front-line cameramen. Since the war, he has made several 'film-pamphlet' documentaries on contemporary issues which have not been seen in the West. A major talent, his early work is in need of revaluation. JG

Meerson, Lazare (1900–1938)

Born in Russia. Designer. From the mid-1920s was French cinema's most delicate designer, specializing in light, airy decorations and witty pastiches of various styles, including expressionism. After collaborating with CAVALCANTI (then also a designer), he worked mainly with directors JACQUES FEYDER (*Carmen*, 1926; *Les Nouveaux messieurs*, 1928; *La Kermesse Heroïque*, 1935) and RENÉ CLAIR, whose *Chapeau de paille d'Italie* (1927), *Les Deux Timides* (1928), *Sous les toits de Paris* (1930), *Le Million* (1931), *Quatorze Juillet* (1932) gave him full scope for period flummery and the creation of a poetic Parisian fantasy-world. Coming to England in the mid-1930s, he worked on *As You Like It* (1936), *Fire Over England* and *Knight Without Armour* (1937) and *Break the News* (1938), again with Feyder and Clair. JG

Mekas, Jonas

Born 1922 in Lithuania. Underground film-maker and promoter in New York. After enduring life in a concentration camp and then in a displaced persons' camp, arrived in the USA in 1950 and settled in New York. He began making a film diary from the year of his arrival, and has maintained this over the years. He made his first public film in 1953, *Grand Street*, a documentary about Brooklyn, followed after other work in shorts by the avant-garde feature, *Guns in the Trees* (1960–2), a film of protest. A protagonist for the underground film, in 1955 he became the publisher of the journal 'Film Culture' for the avant-garde and underground. From 1961 he began filming the artist Salvador Dali at work under the general title of *100 Glimpses of Salvador Dali*. In 1963 he assisted his brother Adolfas Mekas to make the feature, *Hallelujah the Hills*, and then went on to make what is probably his most famous film, *The Brig* (1964), assisted by Adolfas; this was a record of Kenneth Brown's play about a penal military camp as performed by the Living Theatre. It is described by Sheldon Renan as 'grindingly real'. *The Millbrook Report* (1966) presents a record of a raid on the headquarters of Dr Timothy Leary. He considers *Diaries, Notes and Sketches* (1966–9) his most important film. Jonas Mekas was the founder in 1960 of the New American Cinema Group dedicated to making uncensored films of personal experience, and of the Film-makers' Co-operative in 1962 for the distribution of underground films. In 1970 he established the 'Anthology Film Archives', a repository for selected films from Lumière to the present, that illustrate the development of movies as art. RM

Méliès, Georges (1861–1938)

Born in Paris, France. The cinema's first conscious artist and the *'créateur du spectacle cinématographique'*, i.e. the first to recognize that films were not simply a means of recording what was there, but could be artificially staged and controlled, like the theatre. Ultimately Méliès' cinema was too closely linked to the theatre, and by the time of the First World War was already archaic; but his contribution in

Above: Jean-Paul Belmondo and Emmanuèle Riva in 'Léon Morin, Prêtre' (Jean-Pierre Melville, France, 1961)
Below: Melina Mercouri in 'Promise at Dawn' (Jules Dassin, USA-France, 1970)

developing the fiction film, in exploring the entire range of cinematic trick work, and above all in leaving behind him a body of films of unique and unparalleled imagination, can never be over-estimated. The son of a well-to-do boot manufacturer, in 1884–5 he was sent to London to perfect his English: trying to avoid entertainments that placed too much strain on his verbal comprehension, he discovered the spectacular ballets of the Alhambra, and the magic theatre of Maskelyne and Cooke. His enthusiasm for these was formative; after a stint as a newspaper caricaturist, he headed the Théâtre Robert-Houdin and established himself as a magician. At first he saw moving pictures simply as an added attraction to his magic show. Launched into production, he at first filmed his stage tricks, then discovered, bit by bit, the cinema's own peculiar range of magic, in stop action, superimposition and so on. Some of his tricks have still not been surpassed or even explained. In 1897 he built the world's first true film studio at Montreuil-sous-Bois; and here he created an astonishing repertory of films and styles: *féeries*, like *Cendrillon* (1899) and *Le royaume des fées* (1903), Jules Verne science fiction fantasies like *Le Voyage dans la Lune* (1902), the film that brought him world fame and a world market; reconstructed actualities like *L'Affaire Dreyfus* (1899) and *The Coronation of Edward VII* (1902); above all hundreds of films of magic tricks and transformations. By 1913 however Méliès' style was outdated; he was obliged to release his last films through Pathé, and finally to give up production. He turned his studio into a theatre, and in 1923 destroyed all his negatives. In the 1930s he was found keeping a draughty kiosk on the Gare Montparnasse; and was eventually found a place in a home for cinema veterans where he died in 1938. FRANJU made a moving tribute to him in *Le Grand Méliès* (1953). DR

Melville, Jean-Pierre
Born 1917 in Paris, France. Director. Made amateur films throughout his adolescence and, after war service, founded his own production company. His first films, *Le Silence de la Mer* (1947), a war story after Vercors, and the admirable COCTEAU adaptation *Les Enfants Terribles* (1949), led to a series of gangster dramas which combined acknowledgments to the American cinema (notably HAWKS) with Melville's own acid depiction of relations between police and criminals who inhabit the same seedy, dimly-lit underworld where loyalties and manly friendships are often destroyed by last-minute betrayals and an implacable fate. *Bob le Flambeur* (1955), with its brilliant casino scene and vision of Paris by night, is probably Melville's most complete statement; *Deux Hommes dans Manhattan* (1958), *Le Doulos* (1963), *L'Aîné des Ferchaux* (1963), *Le Deuxième Souffle* (1966), *Le Samourai* (1967) and *Le Cercle Rouge* (1970) developed these themes with varying degrees of success. In the last-named, he achieved his biggest commercial success but, this time, some of the material seemed inflated and repetitious. Melville's brilliant control over camera and actors gives his work an entirely personal shading, even when he ventures into strange territory like *Léon Morin, Prêtre* (1961) about a girl who falls in love with a priest, and *L'Armée des ombres* (1969), an ambitious Resistance study which somehow over-reached itself. JG

Menjou, Adolphe (1890–1963)
Born in Pittsburgh, Pennsylvania, USA. Menjou's education took him from Culver Military Academy to Cornell University and thence to the theatre and vaudeville. He played in films as early as 1912, but first attracted notice in *The Three Musketeers* and *The Sheik* in 1921. The film which established Menjou as a star and defined his screen type was CHAPLIN's *A Woman of Paris* (1923), in which for the first time he personified the elegant, suave, witty, heartless man-about-town, a character he was frequently to repeat with variations, notably in LUBITSCH's *The Marriage Circle* (1923) and *Forbidden Paradise* (1924), ST CLAIR's *Are Parents People?* and *The Grand Duchess and the Waiter* (1925), *A Social Celebrity* (1926), D'ARRAST's *A Gentleman of Paris* and *Service for Ladies* (1927). He was altogether a versatile and intelligent actor and able to adapt to many roles in the course of his career, which extended to 1960 (*Pollyanna*). Other notable roles were in GRIFFITH's *Sorrows of Satan* (1926), FEYDER's *The Kiss* (1929), MILESTONE's *The Front Page* (1930), MAMOULIAN's *Golden Boy* (1939), CAPRA's *State of the Union* (1948) and KUBRICK's *Paths of Glory* (1958). DR

Menzel, Jiří
Born 1938 in Prague. An actor as well as a director, Menzel graduated with the short film *The Death of Mr Foerster* (1963). In 1965 he contributed episodes to two films, *Pearls of the Deep* and *Crime at a Girls' School* and made his first feature films, *Closely Observed Trains*, in 1966. This was very much in the style of the human and humorous observation of FORMAN and PASSER; but the succeeding *Capricious Summer* (1967), a whimsical period comedy, was more clearly to Menzel's personal taste. His subsequent films have been *Crime at the Night Club* (1969) and *Larks on a Thread*, from a story by Bohumil Hrabal about a collection of social misfits, which was disapproved by the regime and not released. Among Menzel's acting performances have been roles in SCHÖRM's *Courage for Every Day* and *Return of the Prodigal Son*.

Menzies, William Cameron (1896–1957)
Born in New Haven, Connecticut, USA. Designer, director and producer. Probably the most influential designer in the Anglo-American cinema (and virtually an *auteur* in his own right), Menzies became known in the 1920s with his elaborate fairy-tale settings in FAIRBANKS' *Thief of Bagdad* (1924), *Beloved Rogue* (1927), with its great vista of rooftops, and several other historical spectacles. He loved opulence and detailed building in depth, yet his most extravagant fancies always served the films' subjects, whether it was the amazing futuristic architecture of *Things to Come* (1936, which he also directed for KORDA, in England), the open-air Americana of *The Adventures of Tom Sawyer* (1938), the vast Civil War panoramas of *Gone with the Wind* (1939) or the Spanish backgrounds in *For Whom the Bell Tolls* (1943). Menzies officially directed about a dozen pictures – though his signature can be found on several others – including *Chandu the Magician* (1932) and *Address Unknown* (1944), an intriguing anti-Nazi story seemingly influenced by UFA and WELLES. His last major assignment was as associate producer on *Around the World in Eighty Days* (1956). JG

Mercouri, Melina
Born 1923. Greek actress, with considerable stage experience and a film career spanning comedy to social drama, often working with her husband JULES DASSIN. She began in 1954 with *Stella*, and subsequent films include: *He Who Must Die* (1956), *Never on Sunday* (1960), *Phaedra* (1961), *The Victors* (1963), *Topkapi* (1964), *A Man Could Get Killed* (1965), *10.30 pm Summer* (1966), *Chicago, Chicago* (1969), *Promise at Dawn* (1970).

Meredith, Burgess
Born 1909 in Ohio, USA. Highly-regarded stage and screen actor and director; a key figure in American theatre and, subsequently, films during the 1930s, when his characterization of disillusioned idealists caught the mood of the times. He made his film début in *Winterset* (1936), originally a play written for him by Maxwell Anderson, though possibly his most memorable performance was in *Of Mice and Men* (1939). Since the end of the 1950s he has played mainly character roles and enjoyed a reputation for bizarre comedy – notably as one of the weird villains in the television series, *Batman*. Other notable films: *Idiot's Delight* (1938), *The Story of G.I. Joe* and *Diary of a Chambermaid* (1945), *The Man on the Eiffel Tower* (1950), which he also directed, *Advise and Consent* (1962), *Madame X* (1965), *Hurry Sundown* (1967), *There Was a Crooked Man* (1969). Between films, he has continued to direct in the theatre.

Metzner, Erno (1892–1954)
Born in Hungary. Both set designer and director in the German cinema. As designer, or co-designer, he was responsible for the sets of some the more celebrated German films up to 1933, including LUBITSCH's *Sumurun* (1920) and *The Loves of Pharaoh* (1922, in collaboration with Ernst Stern and Max Gronau), *Fridericus Rex* (1922, with HANS DREIER), *The White Hell of Piz Palü* and PABST's *Diary of a Lost Girl* (1929), and, most remarkable of all his achievements as designer, the magnificently reconstructed realist sets for Pabst's *Westfront 1918* (1930) and *Kameradschaft* (1931); he also designed *L'Atlantide* for Pabst in 1932. In 1922 he co-directed *Salome* with Ludwig Kozma, and in 1927 co-scripted, designed and directed *Man Steigt Nach*. His most celebrated film as director is *Überfall* (*Accident*, 1929), an expressionist-styled short study of a man's hallucinations under anaesthetics in hospital following an attack by a thief. Metzner left Germany in 1933, and was associated with the British films *Chu Chin Chow* (Walter Forde, 1933) and *The Robber Symphony* (Friedrich Feher, 1935), Pabst's French film *De Haut en Bas* (1934), and, much later, RENÉ CLAIR's film made in the USA, *It Happened Tomorrow* (1943). RM

Mexico
See LATIN AMERICA

Meyerhold, Vsevolod Emilievitch (1874–1942)
Born in Penza, USSR. The great theatrical theorist and director made only two films, *The Picture of Dorian Gray* and *The Strong Man* (1915). Both are now lost; but their avant-garde techniques, brilliant use of décor and lighting, and intelligent use of actors (Meyerhold himself played Lord Henry) apparently made a great impression upon artists of the time. His greatest influence upon the Soviet cinema however was through his pupils, who included very many of the directors who were to come to the fore in the 1920s and 1930s, most notably EISENSTEIN, whose theoretical method owed an enormous debt to Meyerhold. It is more than likely also that KULESHOV's earliest theoretical articles, dating from 1917, were also written under the influence of Meyerhold's theatrical writings. DR

Mifune, Toshiro
Born 1920 in Tsingtao, China. Actor and producer. After his parents were repatriated to Japan, he spent five years in the Japanese Army and then entered films with Toho, achieving his first success in KUROSAWA's *Drunken Angel* (1948). Mifune has become the best-known Japanese actor in the West, due to his appearances in sixteen Kurosawa films including *Rashomon* (1950), *Seven Samurai* (1954), *Throne of Blood* (1957), *The Hidden Fortress* (1958), *Yojimbo* (1961), *Sanjuro* (1962), *Red Beard* (1965). His most popular screen image is that of the fearless, often run-down, samurai stalking through the countryside like some legendary Western hero. Equally at home in modern roles, he was particularly notable as the businessman in *High and Low* (1963). Mifune brings a brooding, banked-down intensity to these contemporary subjects, whereas the samurai films have a more extrovert physical bravura (complete with flashing swordplay) and a splendid feeling for the characters' comic eccentricities. Recently, he set up his own production company and has also appeared in several foreign films, notably as the Japanese soldier in BOORMAN's *Hell in the Pacific* (1968). JG

Mikhalkov-Konchalovsky, Andrei
Born 1937, in USSR. One of the most interesting younger talents working in the

Toshiro Mifune in 'Seven Samurai' (Akira Kurosawa, Japan, 1954)

Soviet cinema, Mikhalkov-Konchalovsky graduated from the Moscow Film Institute (VGIK) after a previous period at the Conservatoire. His first feature film, *The First Teacher* (1965), was one of the rare Soviet films in the 1960s to attract wide international attention. *The Story of Asya Klyachina, Who Loved But Did Not Marry* (1966) was considered controversial and was not released until 1969, the year of his exquisite Turgenev adaptation, *A Nest of Gentlefolk* followed by Chekhov's *Uncle Vanya* (1971).

Miles, Bernard
Born 1907 at Hillingdon, Middlesex, England. Actor, director and writer. Founder of the Mermaid Theatre in London. Made his stage début in 1930 in London in 'Richard III', and entered films in 1932 in *Channel Crossing*. He was knighted in 1969. His other films include: *Quiet Wedding* (1940), *In Which We Serve* (1942), *Tawny Pipit* (of which he was also co-author and director, 1944), *Great Expectations* (1946), *Nicholas Nickleby* (1947), *Chance of a Lifetime* (which he also wrote, produced and directed, 1949), *Moby Dick* (1956), *The Smallest Show on Earth* (1957), *Tom Thumb* (1958), *Sapphire* (1959), *Heavens Above* (1963), *Run Wild, Run Free* (1969).

Miles, Sarah
Born 1941 in Ingatestone, Essex, England. Actress, who entered films on leaving the Royal Academy of Dramatic Art, London. These include: *Term of Trial* (1962), *The Servant* (1963), *Those Magnificent Men in their Flying Machines* (1965), *I was Happy Here* and *Blow-Up* (1966), *Ryan's Daughter* (1970). She plays best young women with a sensual appeal they cannot or do not want to restrain. Latest project: *Lamb* (the first film to be directed by her husband, the screenwriter ROBERT BOLT).

Milestone, Lewis
Born 1895 in Odessa, Russia. Major American director of the old school who has too often wasted his great technical skills on unworthy subjects, although his place in film history is firmly based on the remarkable achievements of *All Quiet on the Western Front* (1930) and *A Walk in the Sun* (1945), the most memorable of American anti-war films.

Arriving in America when he was 17, he became interested in photography while serving in the Signal Corps during the First World War. After the war he went to Hollywood, working in the cutting rooms of various studios where he developed a gift for editing which is the most immediately noticeable distinction of all his films. He directed his first film, *Seven Sinners*, in 1925 and won an Academy Award for *Two Arabian Nights* (1927) and *All Quiet on the Western Front*.

Although the Hollywood system under which he worked required him to turn his hand to a great variety of films, he was happiest with predominantly masculine subjects, the closed shop *camaraderie* of men at work, in war, or in crime as in *The Front Page* (1931), *Of Mice and Men* (1939), *The Purple Heart* (1944), *Pork Chop Hill* (1959) and even the frivolous FRANK SINATRA thriller, *Ocean's Eleven* (1961).

In 1962 he took over the direction of *Mutiny on the Bounty*, a trouble-fraught production which was also the last film he made. Since then he has directed occasionally for television. A thorough-going professional with a professional's distrust of a dilettante approach to film-making, he sees himself as an interpreter of the author's work rather than as an artistic creator, although his war films in particular bear a recognizable personal stamp notably in their use of long travelling shots.

Other notable films: *Rain* (1932), *Hallelujah I'm a Bum* (1933), *Captain Hates the Sea* (1934), *The General Died at Dawn* (1936), *Edge of Darkness* and *North Star* (1943), *The Strange Love of Martha Ivers* (1946), *Arch of Triumph* and *The Red Pony* (1949), *Halls of Montezuma* (1951), *Melba* (1953), *They who Dare* (1954). MH

Above: Sarah Miles in 'Ryan's Daughter' (David Lean, GB, 1970)
Below: 'All Quiet on the Western Front' (Lewis Milestone, USA, 1930)

Milland, Ray
Born 1908 in Neath, South Wales. Engaging British actor who won stardom in the 1930s in Hollywood as a light romantic comedian much in the style of CARY GRANT, until his performance as the dipsomaniac in BILLY WILDER'S *The Lost Weekend* (1945) gained him an Academy Award and a new career as a respected dramatic actor. His screen début was in the British film, *The Plaything* (1929). In the 1960s he concentrated mainly on directing for television as well as for films, returning spectacularly to the screen as the balding and ageing patrician father in *Love Story* (1971). Some main films: *Payment Deferred* (1932), *The Gilded Lily* (1935), *Easy Living* (1937), *Her Jungle Love* (1938), *Beau Geste* (1939), *Arise My Love* (1940), *Skylark* (1941), *The Major and the Minor* (1942), *Lady in the Dark* (1943), *The Uninvited* (1944), *Golden Earrings* (1947), *So Evil, My Love* (1948), *The Thief* (1952), *Dial M for Murder* (1954), *The Premature Burial* (1961), *The Man with X-Ray Eyes* (1963), *Hostile Witness* (1968).

Mille, Cecil B. De
See DE MILLE

Miller, Arthur
Born 1895 in Roslyn, Long Island, USA. Cinematographer. Began as lighting cameraman in 1918 on a series of films directed by George Fitzmaurice. One of the most versatile of veteran cinematographers, his work encompasses spectacles (DE MILLE'S *The Volga Boatmen*, 1926) to comedies and dramas with WALSH (*Me*

and My Gal, 1932), MAMOULIAN (*The Mark of Zorro*, 1940), LANG (*Man Hunt*, 1941), FORD (*Tobacco Road* and *How Green was my Valley*, 1941). His skill in black-and-white textures was also demonstrated in *The Keys of the Kingdom* and *The Purple Heart* (1944), *A Letter to Three Wives* (1949), *The Gunfighter* (with its memorable images of Western streets and bars, 1950), *The Prowler* (1950). JG

Miller, David

Born 1909 in Paterson, New Jersey, USA. An editor at Columbia and Metro from 1930, he started direction with short subjects and made his first film, *Billy the Kid*, in 1941.

He subsequently remained with MGM as a useful, eclectic, essentially commercial director, his work ranging from the MARX Brothers' slapstick *Love Happy* (1950) to JOAN CRAWFORD vehicles such as *Sudden Fear* (1952), and *The Story of Esther Costello* (1957). Later films have included: *Midnight Lace* (1960), *Back Street* (1961), *Lonely are the Brave* (1962), *Captain Newman, MD* (1963), and, in Britain, *Hammerhead* (1968).

Above: Ray Milland in 'The Lost Weekend' (Billy Wilder, USA, 1945)
Below: Hayley Mills in 'The Family Way' (John and Roy Boulting, GB, 1966)
Bottom: John Mills in 'Oh! What a Lovely War' (Richard Attenborough, GB, 1969)

Mills, Hayley

Born 1946 in London, England. Actress, usually playing tomboyish parts; daughter of JOHN MILLS. Her screen début was in *Tiger Bay* (1959); her other films include *Pollyanna* (1960), *The Parent Trap* and *Whistle down the Wind* (1961), *The Chalk Garden* (1964), *The Family Way* (1966), *Take a Girl Like You* (1969).

Mills, John

Born 1908 in Suffolk, England. Popular British star, whose characterization of war and national heroes in the 1940s and 1950s tended to obscure his wider talents as a comedian and versatile actor. Starting his career in 1929 in musical comedy on the stage, he made his film début in *The Midshipmaid* (1933) and has worked regularly in films since then. Key performances, apart from his more conventional roles: the Dickens hero in DAVID LEAN's *Great Expectations* (1946), Scott in *Scott of the Antarctic* (1948), Mr Polly in H. G. Wells's *The History of Mr Polly* (1949), which he also produced, the simpleton hero of *Hobson's Choice* (1954), the rigid military man in *Tunes of Glory* (1960), the North Country working-class father in *The Family Way* (1966).

Other notable films: *In Which We Serve* (1942), *This Happy Breed* (1944), *The Way to the Stars* (1945), *The Colditz Story* (1953), *Ice Cold in Alex* (1958), *Summer of the Seventeenth Doll* (1959), *King Rat* (1965), *Oh! What a Lovely War* and *Run Wild, Run Free* (1969), *Return of The Boomerang* and *Ryan's Daughter* (for which he won an Academy Award, 1970), *Dulcima* (1971), *Lamb* (1972). He directed HAYLEY MILLS in *Sky West and Crooked* (1966). MH

Mimica, Vatroslav

Born 1923 in Yugoslavia. Animation, shorts and features director. He served in the Liberation Army, worked in journalism and studied medicine in Zagreb. He joined the film industry in 1949, and became one of the original members of the Zagreb group of animation directors. Among the best of his many cartoons are *At the Photographers* (1959), *The Inspector goes Home* and *The Egg* (1960), a satire on abstract sculpture, and the terrifying cartoon, *The Fly* (1967), in which a fly interchanges sizes with a man. Alexander Marks has worked with him as draughtsman on all his animated films. His short films are equally experimental in style, and include *The Telephone* (1962) and *The Wedding of Mr Marzipan* (1963). His best-known feature films include *Suleaman the Conqueror* (1961, made as a co-production with Italy), *Prometheus from the Island of Visevica* (1964), *Monday or Tuesday* (1966), *Kaya, I'll Kill You* (1967). Mimica's feature films helped to initiate a contemporary style of film-making into the Yugoslav cinema of the 1960s. RM

Minnelli, Vincente
Born 1913 in Chicago, USA. Director. Coming from a theatrical family, he became interested in theatre design and worked on many Broadway revues as designer and producer. Thanks mainly to producer ARTHUR FREED, he studied film-making at MGM and began directing with the Negro musical *Cabin in the Sky* (1943). Minnelli has divided his career fairly evenly between musicals, comedies and dramas with a recognizably American milieu. Together with DONEN, KELLY and WALTERS, he was responsible for the artistic revival of the film musical in the 1940s, giving it a new elegance in design and fresh rhythmic vitality in the staging, aided by the famous MGM technical team, musical arrangers and singing and dancing stars like GARLAND, KELLY and ASTAIRE. *Meet Me in St Louis* (1944) was a nostalgic, exuberantly sentimental flashback to America's past, whereas *Ziegfeld Girl* (1945), *Yolanda and the Thief* (1946), *The Pirate* (1948) and *An American in Paris* (1950) were more brash and modern with choreography designed for the camera and a painterly approach to colour. Other musicals followed (notably *The Band Wagon*, 1953, with its lively pairing of Astaire and BUCHANAN), but Minnelli was also turning to hard, satirical character dramas sometimes with film-making backgrounds – *The Bad and the Beautiful* (1952), *Two Weeks in Another Town* (1962) – and stylish modern comedies set against suitably lush décor, like *Designing Woman* (1957). His talent for comedies of domestic confusion is best represented in *Father of the Bride* (1950) and *The Long, Long Trailer* (1953). As a dramatic director, Minnelli occasionally overweights his material with hysteria and a rather risible portentousness, yet conveys a certain kind of abrasive relationship with uncommon skill (*Some Came Running*, 1959; *Home from the Hill*, 1960). During the past few year he seems to have experienced difficulty in finding congenial subjects (unhappily, the Minnelli kind of musical is no longer fashionable), and his most recent work *On a Clear Day You Can See Forever* (1969) has elegance and some nicely engineered numbers yet lacks the creative excitements of the earlier MGM period. JG

Mitchell, Thomas (1892–1962)
Born in New Jersey, USA. Character actor, of Irish-American descent. Was a reporter and a playwright who also appeared on Broadway. Extremely versatile, he acted a wide range of parts but specialized in wise, craggy old-timers. His films include: *Craig's Wife* and *Theodora Goes Wild* (1936), *Lost Horizon* (1937), *Mr Smith Goes to Washington*, *Stagecoach* and *Gone with the Wind* (1939), *The Hunchback of Notre Dame* (in

Above: Leslie Caron and Gene Kelly in 'An American in Paris' (Vincente Minnelli, USA, 1950)
Below: Robert Mitchum in 'Five Card Stud' (Henry Hathaway, USA, 1968)

which he played the king of the beggars), and *Our Town* (1940), *The Outlaw* (1943), *Buffalo Bill* and *The Sullivans* (1944), *High Noon* (1952), *The Secrets of the Incas* (1954), *Too Young for Love* (1959), and *A Pocketful of Miracles* (1961). He also appeared in several television series.

Mitchum, Robert
Born 1917 in Connecticut, USA. Actor, who first did odd jobs and then went to California. He acted in revues, and appeared with William Boyd in the *Hopalong Cassidy* series. His characteristic heavy-lidded, somewhat inscrutable manner sometimes obscures the fact that he has a fine instinctive acting style. Films include: *The Story of G.I. Joe* (1945), *Crossfire* and *Pursued* (1947), *One Minute to Zero* (1952), *Night of the Hunter* (1955), *Fire Down Below* (1957), *Thunder Road* (1958), *The Sundowners* (1960), *Two for the Seesaw* (1963), *El Dorado* (1966), *The Way West* (1967), *Anzio* (1968), *Ryan's Daughter* (1970).

Mix, Tom (1880–1940)
Born in Mix Run, Clearfield County, USA. Mix turned to films in 1910 after an adventurous youth with the Texas Rangers as a combatant in the Spanish-American war and the Mexican Revolution, and later as a US Marshal and circus performer. In the course of numerous low-budget Westerns, many directed by himself, he became second only to W. S. HART as the world's favourite Western hero. As famous as Mix himself, his horse Tony always played an active role in the melodramatic adventures in which Right (personified by Mix) triumphed in the end. The formulas of his films were so simple that it was difficult to tell one from another; but they brought him fame and riches. Mix found himself eclipsed however by the coming of sound, and by the time of his death in an automobile accident, the large fortune he had acquired was dissipated. His many films include several early FORD productions and *The Trouble Shooter* (1924), *Riders of the Purple Sage* and *Dick Turpin* (1925), *The Last Trail* (1927) and several small-scale sound westerns. DR

Mix
(1) Optical – The gradual transforming of one scene into another.
(2) Sound – The combining of the sounds from several sound tracks for the purpose of re-recording them on to a new track.

Mixer
(1) A panel or desk, equipped with various controls enabling sound from various sources to be mixed together and generally controlled.
(2) One who mixes sound tracks for purpose of re-recording.

Miyagawa, Kazuo
Born 1908 in Kyoto, Japan. Cinematographer. Although he began with the Kyoto Nikkatsu Studios in 1935 and shot a considerable number of films for mainly minor directors, his name was unknown in the West until KUROSAWA's *Rashomon* (1950). This brilliantly-photographed film, with its luminous forest scenes and grey, rainswept landscapes, was clearly the work of a master cameraman. His collaboration with MIZOGUCHI on such films as *Ugetsu Monogatari* (1953), *Chikamatsu Monogatari* and *Sansho Dayu* (1954) and *Shin-heike Monogatari* (1955) represented the peak of his career; here, his lighting superbly recreated the physical textures of a strange, barbaric past. His reputation as one of Japan's greatest camera artists in black-and-white and colour was confirmed when he turned to 'Scope, notably in ICHIKAWA's *Conflagration* (1958), *The Key* (1959) and *Tokyo Olympiad* (1965), where he helped supervise the many camera units. Other films include OZU's *Floating Weeds* (1959) and Kurosawa's *Yojimbo* (1961). Apart from his delicate plastic sense, Miyagawa is able to execute the most complex camera movements, whether craning high over the set or following action scenes in rapid travelling shots through forest and countryside. JG

Above: Tom Mix
Below: Thomas Mitchell, Claire Trevor and Louise Platt in 'Stagecoach' (John Ford, USA, 1939)

Mizoguchi, Kenji (1898–1956)
Born in Tokyo, Japan. Director. In his youth

he worked on a newspaper in Kobe and then became an actor at the Nikkatsu Studios. Began directing in 1922 and subsequently made nearly 100 features, including many literary adaptations from widely disparate sources, but hardly any of his silent films now survive. In the 1930s he continued with many social and politically-orientated subjects; then, in 1936, with *Osaka Elegy* and *Sisters of the Gion*, his fascination with the psychology of women and the sacrifices they are willing to make for love, family and honour crystallized. Of the extant films of the next decade, *The Story of the Last Chrysanthemums* (1939) creates a tragic love story from the lives of a group of travelling players and reveals Mizoguchi's preoccupation with long takes and precise, controlled playing; and *The Loyal Forty-Seven Ronin* (1942) takes a favourite Japanese film legend, characteristically cuts out most of the fighting, and turns it into an elegy of defeat and lost honour. His immediate post-war work often reflects the tragedies of a defeated people (*Women of the Night*, 1948) and served as a prelude to the marvellously productive last six years of his life. Mizoguchi had a rare and refined 'painter's eye'; his compositions have a rich complexity due partly to his fondness for viewing scenes in mid-long shot and he used close-ups very sparingly, so that when they do occur they carry the maximum emotional charge. His re-creation of legend and past historical epochs (the ravaging effects of war, the fate of fallen courtesans, the intrigues of a ruling class against lovers of a lower social order) reached an apotheosis in *The Life of O-Haru* (1952), *Ugetsu Monogatari* (1953), *Sansho Dayu* and *Chikamatsu Monogatari* (1954). Their superb amalgam of expressive camera-work, detailed settings and wholly committed acting transport one completely into their periods, almost as if one was watching a documentary reconstruction of the time. But Mizoguchi is not only concerned with literal reality: his compassion and involvement are essentially poetic in conception, as in the final scenes of *Sansho* with the camera craning round the seashore as the son finally discovers his lost mother, or the last shot of *Chikamatsu* with the condemned lovers being driven to their death, yet with their bound hands passionately entwined. When he turned to colour, Mizoguchi gained a dimension which, unhappily, was only explored in two films, *Yang-kwei-fei* and *New Tales of the Taira Clan* (both 1955); nevertheless, they suggest he might have become one of the cinema's supreme colourists. Mizoguchi was, in the best sense, the most aristocratic of directors; easy, facile effects played no part in his artistic make-up. He was continually exploring, refining and developing a cinematic language of which he alone held the key. He knew the secret of *communicating* through the camera (when to remain still and when to move) so that as the husband returns home, in *Ugetsu*, to find his dead wife apparently waiting for him, it is the slow panning camera movement which magically tells us that she is, in fact, a visitor from the spirit world. JG

Model Sheet

In animation, specifications defining the proportions of a character

Model Shot

A shot of a set containing small scale models which are generally required to appear full-size in the finished film.

Modot, Gaston (1888–1970)

Born in Paris, France. Trained as a painter, he made his début in films with Gaumont in 1909, and for practically half a century after that remained one of the best-known faces in the French cinema. He appeared in the primitive slapstick comedies of the *Onésime* series (1909–13); in GANCE's *La Zone de la Mort* (1919) and films of the first avant-garde such as DULAC's *La Fête Espagnole* (1919) and DELLUC's *Fièvre* (1921); in BUÑUEL's *L'Age d'Or* (1930), his most celebrated performance; and in CLAIR's *Sous les Toits de Paris* (1930) and *Le Quatorze Juillet* (1933). He was prominent in the period of fatalistic romanticism, in *Pépé-le-Moko* (1936), and appeared in two of RENOIR's finest films, *La Grande Illusion* (1937) and *La Règle du Jeu* (1939). He appeared in the most notable French film of the war period, *Les Enfants du Paradis*; and after the war in BECKER's *Antoine et Antoinette* (1947) and *Casque d'Or* (1952). By the time of Clair's *Le Silence est d'Or* (1947), Renoir's *French Can-Can* (1955) and *Eléna et les Hommes* (1956) and Buñuel's *Cela s'appelle l'aurore* (1956) he had come to seem a mascot of French films; and he survived to work for the *nouvelle vague*, in LOUIS MALLE's *Les Amants* (1958). DR

Molander, Gustav

Born 1888 in Helsinki, Finland. One of the most durable directors of the Swedish cinema, Molander made his first film, *King of Boda* (1920), at the peak of the classic era of Scandinavian films. The best work of his early period – *Thomas Graal's Ward* (1922), *The Pirates of Mälaren* (1923), *333,333* (1924), *Ingmar's Inheritance* (1925–6) were inevitably over- shadowed by the films of SJÖSTRÖM and STILLER. Among his numerous later films may be noted *Synd* (1928), *En Natt* (1931), *A Quiet Flirt* (1934), *Dollar* (1937) and remakes of *The Emperor of Portugal* (1944) and *Herr Arne's Treasure* (1954). The last film on which Molander worked was *Stimulantia* (1965–7), to which he contributed one episode.

Monicelli, Mario

Born 1915 in Rome, Italy. Director. After working on the scenarios for many post-war neo-realist films, he co-directed (with Steno) several comedies starring TOTO. In the late 1950s he developed his own style of satirical, often black comedy with *I Soliti Ignoti* (1958), alternating with more serious social dramas such as *I Compagni* (1963), and episodes in various sketch films. *L'Armata Brancaleone* (1965), a stylish, beautifully-judged take off on costume and epic dramas showed his humour at his best, and was followed by several sequels. He has guided many of Italy's top players, including VITTORIO GASSMAN and MARCELLO MASTROIANNI, into giving their best comedy performances. JG

Monroe, Marilyn (1926–1962)

Born in Los Angeles, USA. Prototype American sex symbol of the 1950s and the last of the great, wholly Hollywood-conceived star images. Her considerable talent for comedy and pathos was largely either unrecognized or belittled in her lifetime. But the impression of vulnerable innocence which stamped all her major portrayals made her unusual in appealing equally to women and to men.

Much has been made of her grim, disjointed childhood with an ailing, often absent mother and a succession of foster-parents. She arrived in Hollywood via a brief career as a photographer's model and made her film début in *Dangerous Years* (1948). But it was not until JOHN HUSTON chose her for *The Asphalt Jungle* (1950) that her potential became apparent. Under contract to Twentieth Century Fox, she graduated from conventionally blonde and frequently dumb super-girls in *We're Not Married* and *Monkey Business* (1952) to starring roles in heavy dramas, *Don't Bother to Knock*, *Niagara* (1952). Previously her stunning entrance in *All about Eve* (1950) had indicated a much shrewder talent than her studio credited her with. Non-stop filming and the revelation that she had posed in the nude for a calendar confirmed her success.

It was as a comedienne in *Gentlemen Prefer Blondes* and *How to Marry a Millionaire* (1953), *The Seven Year Itch* (1955) that she flourished. Meanwhile, her personal problems and insecurities made her ever more difficult to handle. Her ambition to be regarded as a serious actress led to intensive studies with the Strasberg's Actor's Studio, as well as a visit to Britain to make *The Prince and the Showgirl* (1957) with LAURENCE OLIVIER. Returning to America she made her most popular film, *Some Like It Hot* (1959), followed by the less successful *Let's Make Love* (1960). Her last film, *The Misfits* (1960), was written by her third husband, ARTHUR MILLER, and is regarded as an authentic portrait of Marilyn herself. After abortive tests and wrangles with Fox over a proposed new film, she died from an overdose of sleeping tablets. Some years later, a lamentable film compilation, *Marilyn*, was released by Fox.

Other principal films: *As Young as You Feel* (1951), *Clash by Night* (1952), *River of No Return* and *There's No Business Like Show Business* (1954), *Bus Stop* (1956).

Opposite: Marilyn Monroe in 'Bus Stop' (Joshua Logan, USA, 1956)

Several books have been published about her, the most notable being Maurice Zolotow's 'Marilyn Monroe' (1960) and Fred Lawrence Guiles's 'Norma Jean'. The latter title arises out of the actress's real name, Norma Jean Mortensen. MH

Montage
Quick cuts, dissolves, wipes or superimpositions used in a rapid succession of pictures to give a number of impressions in a short time.

Montand, Yves
Born 1921 in Tuscany, Italy. Seductive French singer-actor, protégé of Edith Piaf, he has for 20 years sustained parallel careers as a night-club and music-hall entertainer and as the star of increasingly dark and politically-motivated dramas – in particular *Z* (1968) and *L'Aveu* (1970). He made his film début in *Étoile sans Lumière* (1945) and achieved international acclaim in *The Wages of Fear* (1952), in which his rugged, Bogart-style personality was especially effective. His Hollywood career has been highly variable – *Let's Make Love* (1960), *Sanctuary* (1961), *My Geisha* (1962), *On a Clear Day You Can See Forever* (1969). Other main films: *The Witches of Salem* (1956), *Goodbye Again* (1961), *La Guerre est Finie* (1965), *Vivre Pour Vivre* and *Grand Prix* (1967), *Un Soir, Un Train* (1968).

Moorehead, Agnes
Born 1906. American actress, specializing in bitter or neurotic spinsters, sometimes flavoured with a sharp humour. First acted on Broadway; discovered by ORSON WELLES, with whom she worked on several films. Her films include: *Citizen Kane* (1940), *The Magnificent Ambersons* (1942), *Journey into Fear* and *Jane Eyre* (1943), *Dark Passage* (1947), *Johnny Belinda* (1948), *Fourteen Hours* (1951), *Magnificent Obsession* (1954), *How the West was Won* (1962), *Hush, Hush Sweet Charlotte* (1964) and *The Singing Nun* (1966), *What's the matter with Helen?* (1971). She also appears on television; her series, *Bewitched*, ran from 1964 to 1969.

More, Kenneth
Born 1914 at Gerrards Cross, England. Actor on stage and in television as well as in films. Made his theatrical début in vaudeville at the Windmill Theatre, London, in 1937, and his screen début in *Scott of the Antarctic* in 1948. Since then has made many films and was especially popular in the 1950s, playing breezy man-about-town types as well as more serious characters. Films include: *Appointment with Venus* and *Brandy for the Parson* (1951), *The Yellow Balloon* (1952), *Genevieve* (1953), *Doctor*

Above: Yves Montand in 'L'Aveu' (Costa-Gavras, France, 1970)
Below: George Coulouris, Harry Shannon, Buddy Swan and Agnes Moorehead in 'Citizen Kane' (Orson Welles, USA, 1940)

Above: Joan Morgan and Bryant Washburn in 'The Road to London' (Washburn, GB, 1920)
Below: Kenneth More and Susannah York in 'The Battle of Britain' (Guy Hamilton, GB, 1969)

in the House and *Raising a Riot* (1954), *The Deep Blue Sea* (1955), *Reach for the Sky* (1956), *The Admirable Crichton* (1957), *The Sheriff of Fractured Jaw* (1958) and *The Thirty-Nine Steps* (1959). His later films include: *Sink the Bismarck* (1960), *The Greengage Summer* (1961), *Fräulein Doktor* (1968), *Battle of Britain* (1969), *Scrooge* (1970). He published his autobiography, 'Happy Go Lucky', in 1959.

Moreau, Jeanne

Born 1928 in Paris, France. Luminous French actress with an international reputation. Her work with *nouvelle vague* directors LOUIS MALLE and FRANÇOIS TRUFFAUT established her as a highly contemporary actress who nevertheless could adapt to the traditional demands of Hollywood or British screen stardom. Theatre-trained, she made her film début in 1948 in *Dernier Amour*, but failed to achieve great success until *Lift to the Scaffold* (1957) and, more importantly, *Les Amants* (1958). She has been compared to BETTE DAVIS, but the melancholy sensuality she brings to her roles, plus a stinging sense of humour, is totally individual. Main films: *Moderato Cantabile* (1960), *La Notte* and *Jules et Jim* (1961), *Eve* (1962) *The Trial* (1963), *Diary of a Chambermaid*, *The Yellow Rolls-Royce* and *The Train* (1964), *Viva Maria* (1965), *Chimes at Midnight* (1966), *The Bride Wore Black* (1967), *Great Catherine* (1968), *The Immortal Story* (1969), *Monte Walsh* (1970).

Morgan, Michèle

Born 1920 in Paris, France. Actress, who trained at drama school, and at 17 appeared with CHARLES BOYER in 'Gribouille', which was later made into the film *The Lady in Question* (1940). Her cool somewhat mysterious sensuality enriched many films including: *Orage* and *Quai des Brumes* (1938), *Joan of Paris* (1941), *La Symphonie Pastorale* (1946), *The Fallen Idol* (1948), *The Seven Deadly Sins* (1951), *Les Grandes Manœuvres* (1955), *The Mirror has two Faces* (1960), *Landru* (1963).

Morgan, Sidney (1873–1946)

Born in London, England; he was a director and screenwriter: MORGAN, JOAN, born 1903, Britain's leading child screen actress towards the end of the First World War, and subsequently screenwriter, playwright and novelist. Like HEPWORTH, Sidney Morgan preferred to make serious, literary films which he both scripted and directed, adaptations of such subjects as Zola's *Drink* (1918), Dickens's *Little Dorrit* (1920) and Hardy's *The Mayor of Casterbridge* (1921) as well as *Bulldog Drummond's Third Round* (1925) and *The Flag Lieutenant* (1934). A number of his post-war films were made in a special glass studio built by a German company at Shoreham-on-Sea before 1914; the glass used allowed for an unusually effective use of sunlight with screens and reflectors. With the decline of British films in the 1920s, Morgan, as secretary of the British Association of Film Directors, did much to lobby the first (1928) Quota Act through Parliament. Joan Morgan, his daughter, appeared regularly on the stage and in films as a child actress between the ages of 8 and 16, including appearances in *Drink*, *Little Dorrit*, and Rider Haggard's *Swallow* (1921), made in South Africa. She also appeared in three American films made in New York in 1916. After appearing at the age of 15 in *The Road to London* with the American star Bryant Washburn, she was offered a five-year contract in Hollywood, which her father refused to accept. During the 1930s she acted as assistant director to her father, and by the close of the silent period had begun to script films. Among her many sound film scripts was that for *The Flag Lieutenant*, in which ANNA NEAGLE starred. She has more recently written several plays for theatre and television, including 'This was a Woman' (1944), which was later filmed. RM

Morocco

See ARAB FILM

Morricone, Ennio

Born 1928 in Rome, Italy. Composer. After a formal musical education (at one time with

Goffredo Petrassi) he became a concert composer, turning to films in 1961. Best known for his scores for Italian Westerns (notably those by LEONE), combining sweeping 'outdoor' melodies with rich, bizarre orchestrations and choral interpolations. He has also written music for other directors including BELLOCCHIO's *I Pugni in Tasca* (1965), *La Cina è Vicina* (1967); PONTECORVO's *Battle for Algiers*; and PASOLINI's *Uccellacci e Uccellini* (1966) and *Teorema* (1968). His extreme facility in recent years has led to a certain repetitious melodic monotony, although his orchestrations continue to surprise. JG

Moskvin, Andrei Nikolaievich
(1901–1961)
Born in St Petersburg, Russia. Cinematographer. Began in films with the experimental group FEKS. Absorbed much of their stylized expressionism, as visible in his lighting for films by KOZINTSEV and TRAUBERG – *The Overcoat* (1926), *S.V.D.* (1927), *New Babylon* (1929). Also worked with these directors on their Maxim trilogy (1935–8). Outstanding examples of his rich-toned lighting style, particularly suited to period subjects, are EISENSTEIN's *Ivan the Terrible* (1943–6), photographed in collaboration with EDUARD TISSÉ, *Don Quixote* (1957), and *Lady with the Little Dog* (1959), with its nostalgic images of Yalta, the sea and snow-filled city streets. JG

Moviola
Trade name of an American editing machine

Mozhukin (Mosjoukine), Ivan Ilyitch
(1889–1939)
Born in Penza, USSR. Recruited from the theatre to play the leading role in Chardinin's *The Kreutzer Sonata*, the first significant Russian story film, Mozhukin rapidly became the most popular romantic star in Russia, appearing in some 70 films of which the most notable was PROTAZANOV's *Father Sergius* (1918). Emigrating to France after the Revolution, he and his wife and partner, Nathalia Lissenko, became favourite actors of the avant-garde, Mozhukin (now restyled Mosjoukine) achieving his biggest successes in EPSTEIN's *Le Lion des Mogols* (1924), L'HERBIER's *Feu Mathias Pascal* (1925), and Alexander Volkoff's *Kean* (1922) and *Casanova* (1926). *Le Brasier Ardent* (1923), which he directed is a marvellously designed fantasy. Mozhukin's single American appearance, in Edward Sloman's *Surrender*, was a disaster. He returned to Europe to play in Germany, but his career rapidly declined. His final appearance was in Jacques de Baroncelli's *Nichevo* (1936). DR

Ivan Mozhukin in 'Kean' (Alexander Volkoff, France, 1924)

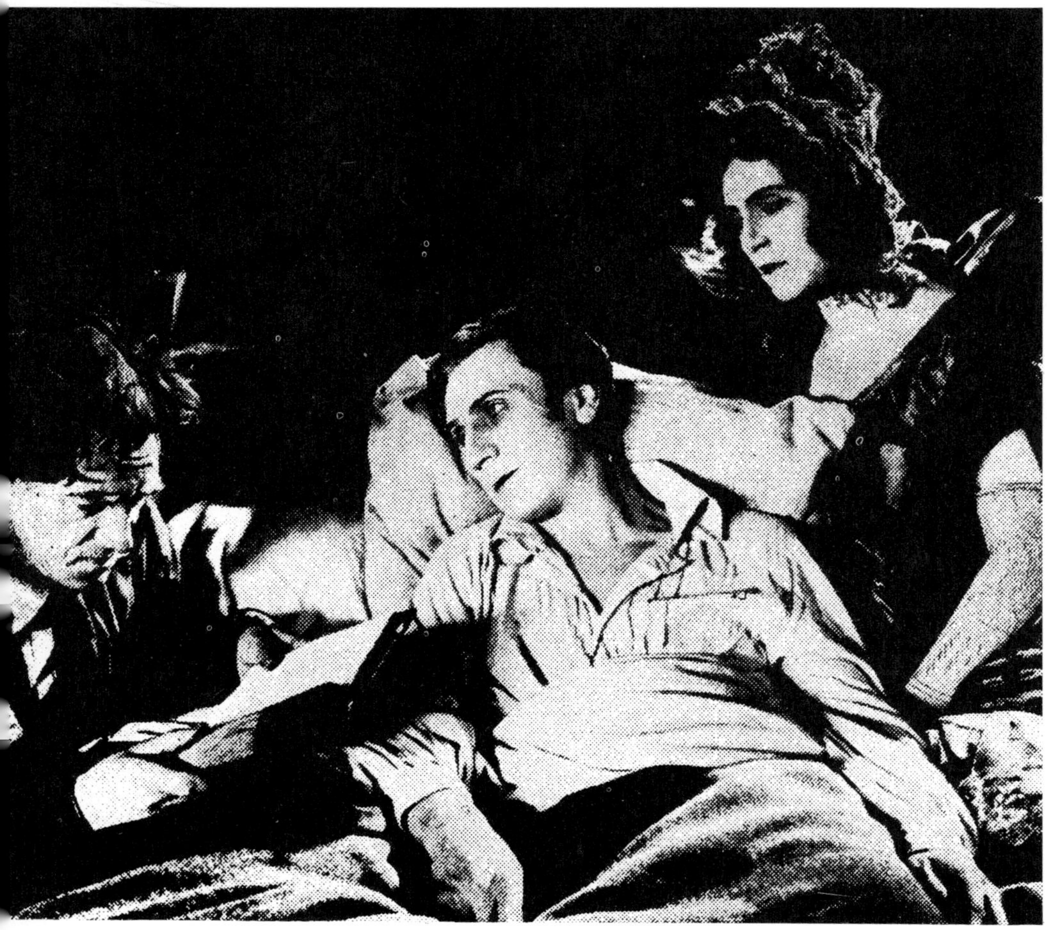

Mulligan, Robert
Born 1925 in The Bronx, New York, USA. Director, who first assisted with production and direction of radio opera and television shows. His films include: *The Rat Race* (1960), *The Great Impostor* (1961), *To Kill a Mockingbird* (1962), *Love with the Proper Stranger* (1964), *Baby the Rain Must Fall* and *Inside Daisy Clover* (1965), *Up the Down Staircase* (1967), *The Pursuit of Happiness* (1970), *Summer of 42* (1971). Mulligan's films show a humorous and sympathetic eye for the details of characterization.

Multiplane
Elaborated rostrum camera used in the making of animated films. In addition to the animation table a number of glass sheets are placed in tiers and operated independently, enabling a great many different planes of background perspective to be photographed simultaneously, giving an increased sense of perspective.

Multiple Exposure
Two or more exposures on the same series of film frames

Muni, Paul (1897–1967)
Born in Lemburg, Austria. Real name: Muni Weisenfreund. Highly esteemed stage and screen actor whose peak film period occurred during the 1930s with his characterizations of eminent historical figures: Pasteur in *The Story of Louis Pasteur* (1935), for which he won an Academy Award, Zola in *The Life of Émile Zola* (1937), *Juarez* (1939). But it was his earlier Central-European conception of particularly American heroes and anti-heroes that was most distinctive: in *Scarface* and *I am a Fugitive from a Chain Gang* (1932), *Hi Nellie* (1933), *Bordertown* (1934), *Black Fury* (1935).

Arriving in America as a child, he played in stock and vaudeville, before making his screen début in *The Valiant* in 1929. In retrospect some of his performances now appear heavy and consciously contrived. After the Second World War he made few films, although he appeared frequently on the Broadway and London stage.

Other notable films: *The Good Earth* (1937), *We are not Alone* (1939), *A Song to Remember* (1944), *Angel on My Shoulder* (1946), *The Last Angry Man* (1959). MH

Munk, Andrzej (1921–1961)
Born in Cracow, Poland. Director. After graduating from the Polish Film School in 1952, he made a series of excellent documentaries combining a sharp reporting style with a personal way of looking at past and present, as in *A Walk in the Old City of Warsaw* (1959). After a long documentary, *Men of the Blue Cross* (1955), he turned to fiction films with *Man on the Track* (1956), a particularly courageous project at the time as it dealt with an old railwayman who finds himself out of tune with the régime's ideals; *Eroica* (1957), a two-part film satirizing the concept of heroism; *Bad Luck* (1960), an ironic study of a would-be careerist;

and *Passenger* (1963), a disturbing look at concentration camp life. During its production, Munk was killed in a car crash and the uncompleted film was prepared for showing by his friend Witold Lesiewicz, in 1963. Munk's untimely death was a sad loss for the Polish cinema for he had a dry, persuasive humour, a deep concern for personal values and a less ornate shooting style than, say, WAJDA. His output was small but rich; had he lived, he would doubtless have had much to say about our times. JG

Murnau, Friedrich Wilhelm (1888–1931)
Born in Bielefeld, Westphalia, Germany. With FRITZ LANG one of the greatest directors of the classic period of silent films. After studying philosophy at Heidelberg, Murnau joined Max Reinhardt's company, was an assistant on *The Miracle*, and acted in a number of productions. After service in the First World War he worked in the theatre in Switzerland, and directed propaganda shorts for the German Embassy there. His first feature production, *Der Knabe in Blau*, with CONRAD VEIDT in the leading role, was made in 1919. *Satanas* (1919), *Der Bucklige und die Tänzerin* and *Der Januskopf* (1920) already showed him firmly aligned with the expressionists; the latter films were written respectively by CARL MAYER and Hans Janowitz, the writers of *Caligari*. A series of films which all paid tribute to a greater or lesser degree to expressionism – *Der Gang in die Nacht, Schloss Vogelöd* and *Sehnsucht* (1921), *Marizza, Genannt die Schmuggler* – *Madonna* and *Der Brennende Acker* (1922) – was followed by his masterpiece, *Nosferatu* (also 1922), loosely adapted from Bram Stoker's 'Dracula'; and *Phantom* (1922). After two comparatively minor works, *Austreibung* (1923) and the quite uncharacteristic *Die Finanzen des Grossherzogs*, *Der Letzte Mann* (1924) earned him an enormous international reputation, and enabled him to realize *Tartuffe* (1925) and *Faust* (1926) with greater opulence than any films he had previously made. Summoned to America by WILLIAM FOX, Murnau made the excellent and unmistakably expressionist *Sunrise* (1927); but the honeymoon with Hollywood was brief, and the production of *Four Devils* (1927), after the story by Herman Bang, and *City Girl* (*Our Daily Bread*, 1929) was hampered by producer interference, although the latter is wholly characteristic in its portrait of city and country *milieus*. With ROBERT FLAHERTY (who left the production before completion of the film), Murnau went to the South Seas to make *Tabu* (1931), whose success he did not live to see, being killed in an automobile accident on his return to Hollywood. Murnau's work in silent film has an almost hypnotic quality, due to the slowness and deliberation of his editing tempo, image following image with a stylized rhythm which induces a sense of inevitability. DR

Music and Effects Track
A sound track embodying a combination of music and effects sounds only, omitting dialogue, and generally used in foreign language dubbings.

Music and Film
It is obvious that the relationship between music and film is sharply divided between the silent and sound film periods. During the silent period the film, both as art and entertainment, was created in its own right, conceived without any form of mechanical sound accompaniment. The only exception to this lay in those tentative forms of sound film-making which experimented with phonograph recordings played in association with specific moving pictures, especially films of vaudeville artists, and the later efforts to record sound in other forms which finally produced optical sound recording in the public cinemas of the later 1920s. (See THE DEVELOPMENT OF THE FILM, page 57.)

The Silent Period
The early film-makers could for the most part rely on some form of live sound accompaniment at public performances. Asian cinemas specialized in narrators, such as the *benshi* in Japan; the narrator was not unknown in the West, but he achieved no status comparable to that of the Asian story-teller. In the West films were, for the most part, accompanied even in their fairground days by pianos and, where the nickelodeons and picture palaces flourished, by orchestral groups and combinations of the kind used to accompany plays and variety shows in the live theatre. So the history of musical accompaniment for silent films is the history of the special arrangements of established music and, in some cases, the special compositions which were developed to excite in the audience a greater emotional response to the films. In any case, it seemed (and still seems when viewing silent films today) 'unnatural' to sit for prolonged periods in utter silence when events of considerable humour or tension or excitement or grandeur were being performed on the screen. For centuries the theatre had used 'incidental' music during performances, and this had reached its height in the orchestral scores written by composers of note for the more spectacular productions of the 19th century theatre in Europe and the USA. It was just as natural for music to be introduced by the early exhibitors as an accompaniment to films as for story-tellers to be introduced in those countries in Asia where shadow theatres and other kinds of performances had been accustomed to use narrators in the past.

Four different forms of music developed to accompany films during the silent period. (1) Improvisations by pianists, who, with their eyes on the screen, followed the successive phases of the action with a kind of doodling or vamping on the piano reflecting the mood and tempo of the action. This doodling could vary from mere musical effects, chords, runs up and down the keyboard, 'hurry' music for chases and the like, to interludes derived from popular mood music, like 'Hearts and Flowers', so much used for sentimental scenes. Cinema pianists achieved great fluency and skill, responding to the action on their pianos after only a single rehearsal with the projectionist for each new film. This, however, was not so easy with orchestral groups, the cinema's music director (or 'fitter' as he was less respectfully called) in this case requiring band parts for his orchestras. Apart from certain pre-arranged musical or sound effects (drums, cymbals, horns, whistles, etc.), orchestras drew on a succession of popular numbers or light classical material which established a succession of moods or action sound effects as the conductor followed the film on the screen above the orchestra pit.

The needs of thousands of music directors accompanying perhaps up to 100 features a year in the movie theatres in towns and cities throughout the world led to the second form of movie music: (2) volumes of musical extracts classified for mood, atmospheric and dramatic effect. Among the earliest were the Sam Fox Moving Picture Music volumes compiled by J. S. Zamecnik and published in 1913; the most celebrated were Giuseppe Becce's Kinothek volumes published in Berlin in 1919. These volumes included not only extracts from established music but special compositions by Becce to meet all occasions. The pieces were timed for different requirements and throughout the accompaniments in the theatres you would constantly hear the conductor's baton signalling the switch from one selection to another as the cues came up from the screen.

From this far closer, less haphazard form of musical arrangement for a film developed the third branch of silent film music: (3) the score pre-arranged by the director himself, working with his own 'fitter', and derived, primarily at least, from well-known musical sources. The most celebrated of the early scores of this kind which survive is that assembled by D. W. GRIFFITH for *Birth of a Nation* (1915), working with the composer and orchestral leader, Joseph Carl Briel. Griffith himself had studied music and knew exactly the emotional effects he wanted to achieve; he dovetailed sequences from the compositions of Grieg, Wagner, Tchaikovsky, Rossini, Beethoven, Liszt, Verdi, along with traditional American airs such as 'Dixie' and 'The Star-Spangled Banner'. What they could not get from these sources, they composed themselves, such as the call of the Ku Klux Klan, an effect produced on reed-whistles and horns. Similar sound effects were introduced for the galloping horses, and above all recurrent themes and motifs associated with individual characters or repeated actions, such as the 'Ride of the Valkyries' accompanying certain of the Klan movements on horseback. The whole was assembled into a permanent score with band parts which circulated with the film, the score cued for the conductor within various frames reproduced from the film. The score contains 226 separate cues to guide the synchronisation of the music, for 165 minutes of screentime.

From such fixed arrangements as this, which

Griffith contrived for all his important films, developed: (4) the completely original scores created for specific films on occasion by eminent composers, of which the earliest was Camille Saint-Saëns's score for the French art-film subject, *L'Assassinat du Duc de Guise* (1908). This became Saint-Saëns's Opus 128 for strings, piano and harmonium which consists of an introduction and five tableaux, each part cued to the film, which featured Le Bargy and Calmettes, and came to the screen with the aura of the Comédie-Française.

Other films of note with specially composed scores, very few of which survive, include:

1919 *Broken Blossoms* (GRIFFITH) Largely original score by Louis F. Gottschalt (USA)

1922 *La Roue* (GANCE) Score by Arthur Honegger (France)
Foolish Wives (VON STROHEIM) Score by Sigmund Romberg (USA)

1923 *The Nibelung Saga* (LANG) Score by Gottfried Huppertz (Germany)
L'Inhumaine (L'HERBIER) Score by Darius Milhaud (France)

1924 *Le Ballet Mécanique* (Léger) Score by Georges Antheil (France)
Entr'acte (CLAIR) Score by Erik Satie (France)

1925 *Battleship Potemkin* (EISENSTEIN) Score by Edmund Meisel (composed in Germany)

1926 *The Adventures of Prince Achmed* (REINIGER) Score by Wolfgang Zeller (Germany)
Napoléon (GANCE) Score by Arthur Honegger (France)
Metropolis (LANG) Score by Gottfried Huppertz (Germany)

1927 *Berlin* (RUTTMANN) Score by Edmund Meisel (Germany) which survives as a piano score
The Italian Straw Hat (CLAIR) Score by Jacques Ibert (France) which survives as a piano score

1928 *October* (EISENSTEIN) Score by Edmund Meisel (composed in Germany)

1929 *The New Babylon* (KOZINTSEV and TRAUBERG) Score by Dimitri Shostakovich (USSR)

In the USA, original scores were not normally used, though compilation scores arranged for particular films of importance were common; among the principal composer-arrangers were Hugo Riesenfeld (*Gypsy Blood*, LUBITSCH's 'Carmen' of 1918 released 1921 in the USA; the MURNAU-FLAHERTY production, *Tabu*); Erno Rappé (for example, FORD's *The Iron Horse*, 1924); J. S. Zamecnik (VON STROHEIM's *The Wedding March*, 1927, with music on disc); and William Axt (VIDOR's *The Big Parade*, 1925, and the synchronized film directed by Alan Crosland, *Don Juan*, 1926).

Some theatres were equipped with organs capable of producing special sound effects, such as thunder, gunfire, or the musical siren of a locomotive. Sounds were also provided by an effects man in some theatres, working in the orchestra pit. Perhaps the most distinguished person to accompany films on the piano in the film theatre was Dimitri Shostakovich, who worked in a cinema during 1924 in order to earn the money needed to keep his family.

One other use of music in silent films should be noted – some directors favoured having music played in the studios themselves to induce artistes to give more emotional performances. It was by no means a universal practice. In Britain, GEORGE PEARSON, MAURICE ELVEY and ANTHONY ASQUITH had music played in the studio. In the USA, Griffith used music very sparingly on the set, though he introduced a brass band for the battle scenes in *Intolerance*. DE MILLE had Bizet played during the filming of *Carmen* (1915), and MARY PICKFORD was among the artistes who liked music as a background to her acting. Other directors who used music in this way included WILLIAM WELLMAN and KING VIDOR.

The Sound Period

The series of events leading up to the coming of optical sound (sound-on-film) are detailed elsewhere (see THE DEVELOPMENT OF THE FILM page 57 and UNITED STATES OF AMERICA page 476). There was an awkward interregnum with sound-on-disc running parallel with sound-on-film provided for those theatres which had installed the new equipment. The various film-making countries converted to universal sound-on-film in their own varied time, the USA and Britain very quickly, for example, and Japan relatively slowly.

The immediate temptation was simply to put a music-track on films shot substantially with silent technique: the second temptation was to make 100% theatrical-style talkies. Whether they resented the coming of sound or not, after Al Jolson's success in *The Jazz Singer* (1927), directors had to acknowledge that it was an established fact; in the early days it was difficult to achieve sound of high quality and to control the acoustics of recording dialogue 'live' on studio stages which were inadequately sound-proofed, using film equipment which itself produced extraneous sounds. Nevertheless, quite apart from the creative approach to the more restrained or naturalistic use of dialogue and sound effects (as, for example, HITCHCOCK in *Blackmail*, PABST in *Westfront 1918*, and MILESTONE in *All Quiet on the Western Front*), certain directors began to use music more creatively as an integral part of the dramatic or atmospheric structure of the films, and not as mere background noise. Among the more experimental scores prior to 1935, which was to be a key year for film music, were the following:

CLAIR in *Sous les Toits de Paris* (1930) with music by Raoul Moretti and Armand Bernard, and also in his other light musical films made 1931–4, with composers including Maurice Jaubert and Georges Auric.

VON STERNBERG in *The Blue Angel* (1930) Score by Friedrich Hollaender.

PABST in *The Threepenny Opera* (1931) Score by Kurt Weill, with Lotte Lenya singing.

COCTEAU in *Le Sang d'un Poète* (1930) Score by Georges Auric.

ERMLER and YUTKEVITCH in *Counterplan* (1932) Score by Dimitri Shostakovich.

DREYER in *Vampyr* (1932) Score by Wolfgang Zeller.

VIGO in *Zéro de Conduite* (1933) Score by Maurice Jaubert.

PUDOVKIN in *Deserter* (1933) Score by Yuri Shaporin.

ROTHA in *Contact* (1933) Score by Clarence Raybould.

IVENS in *New Earth* (1934) Score by HANNS EISLER.

PAINLEVÉ in *L'Hippocampe* (1934) Score by Darius Milhaud.

VERTOV in *The Three Songs of Lenin* (1934) Score by Yuri Shaporin.

WRIGHT in *Song of Ceylon* (1935) Score by Walter Leigh.

Alexander Feinzimmer in *Lieutenant Kizhe* (1934) Score by Sergei Prokofiev.

FLAHERTY in *Man of Aran* (1934) Score by John Greenwood.

VIGO in *L'Atalante* (1934) Score by Maurice Jaubert.

During the early period in the USA, CHAPLIN composed his own score for *City Lights* (1931), which was virtually a silent film set to music, MAX STEINER produced notable scores for *King Kong* (1933) and *The Lost Patrol* (1934), while an Academy Award was given to the Columbia Music Department in 1934 on account of the score for *One Night of Love*, with Grace Moore.

The USA's outstanding contribution at this stage to the sound track was in the musical itself, a form in which that country is in any case creatively outstanding on both stage and screen. The early musicals were mainly taken from stage-shows, but they added their own vigorous, visual continuity, with the pictorialization of their numbers. Most striking always was the highly patterned choreography of the show-girls. Some of the outstanding early American musicals were:

1929 *Sunny Side Up* (David Butler) Music by De Sylva, Brown and Henderson.
Broadway Melody (Harry Beaumont) Music by Nacio Herb Brown.

1930 *King of Jazz* (John Murray Anderson) Music by Paul Whiteman.

1932 *Love Me Tonight* (REUBEN MAMOULIAN) Music by Rodgers and Hart.

1933 *Forty-Second Street* (LLOYD BACON) Choreography by BUSBY BERKELEY.
Gold Diggers of 1933 (MERVYN LE ROY) Choreography by BUSBY BERKELEY.

1934 *The Gay Divorcée* (Mark Sandrich) With FRED ASTAIRE and GINGER ROGERS, choreography by HERMES PAN. The first of many intimate-style musicals lasting until the close of the 1930s.

Early musical films in other countries included Germany's *Congress Dances* (Erik Charell, 1931) and the USSR's *Jazz Comedy* (ALEXANDROV, 1934). To these musical films should be added the first animated films to combine sound and image with invention, including OSKAR FISCHINGER's German abstract compositions to popular classical music, the first sound films of HANS RICHTER and WALTER RUTTMANN, LOTTE REINIGER's silhouette films, especially *Papageno* (1935), Anthony Gross and Hector Hoppin's *Joie de Vivre* with a score by Tibor von Harsanyi, and the first Mickey Mouse and Silly Symphony series of WALT DISNEY. The most effective use of experimental music in early sound-film animation was Honegger's remarkable score for Bartosch's *L'Idée* (1934), using the electronic instrument, the Ondes Martenot.

By 1935, therefore, only six years after the first introduction of sound, a considerable measure of control and range of invention in the use of recorded music for films had been achieved, and a number of composers of distinction had begun to work for the cinema. The quality of sound recording had risen markedly owing to the skill of recording engineers in a number of countries, and there was a growing consciousness of the importance of music, and of its potentialities in film. From 1935 there was to be, if anything, an overuse of music because of its powerful emotional stimulus and its ability to give a sometimes spurious grandeur to the action on the screen. Small pictures would become inflated by the almost ceaseless activities of large symphony orchestras playing mainly nondescript scores.

In Britain, musical experiment was being developed in Grierson's documentaries under the guidance of CAVALCANTI. The rising young composer, Benjamin Britten, composed the first film oratorio in *Coalface* (1935) and another score for *Night Mail*, while the first 'opera' specially composed for the screen appeared in Britain, *The Robber Symphony* (director Friedrich Feher, 1935). The appointment by ALEXANDER KORDA of a young and enthusiastic music director, MUIR MATHIESON, to take charge of the scores for his productions resulted in Britain leading the way in bringing eminent composers into the studios to learn the craft of integrating their compositions to the requirements of the sound-track. Among the composers, some of them of advanced years, whom Mathieson was to introduce to the screen for Korda, and later for Rank, included between 1935 and 1945, Arthur Bliss (*Things to Come*, 1936), William Walton, WILLIAM ALWYN (who composed prolifically, including scores for many documentaries), Vaughan Williams, Arnold Bax and Alan Rawsthorne.

In the USA the more experimental scores contributed during the 1930s were those of Marc Blitzstein (*Spanish Earth*, 1937), Aaron Copland (*The City*, 1939; *Of Mice and Men* and *Our Town*, 1940) and Virgil Thomson (*The Plow that Broke the Plains*, 1936 and *The River*, 1937). In the feature film outstanding composers included Max Steiner (*King Kong*, 1933; *The Lost Patrol*, 1934; *The Informer*, a score which won him an Academy Award, 1935; and *Gone with the Wind*, 1939), Erich Wolfgang Korngold (*A Midsummer Night's Dream*, including music by Mendelssohn, and *Green Pastures*, 1935; *Robin Hood*, 1938), DMITRI TIOMKIN (*Lost Horizon*, 1937; *The Westerner*, 1940) and ALFRED NEWMAN (*Alexander's Ragtime Band*, 1938, Academy Award; *Tin Pan Alley*, 1940). In France, working with much smaller combinations than was fashionable in the USA and Britain, the outstanding pre-war composers were Georges Auric (*Entrée des Artistes*, 1938), Maurice Jaubert (*Le Quatorze Juillet*, and *L'Affaire est dans le Sac*, 1932; *Zéro de Conduite*, 1933; *Le Dernier Milliardaire* and *L'Atalante*, 1934; *Un Carnet de Bal*, 1937; *Quai des Brumes*, 1938; *Le Jour se Lève*, 1939), Darius Milhaud (*L'Hippocampe*, 1934; and other documentaries), and Arthur Honegger (*Crime et Châtiment*, 1935; *Mayerling*, 1936). In Russia one of the finest scores of the decade was that composed by Prokofiev for EISENSTEIN's *Alexander Nevsky* (1938).

By now, the theory of film music was being very fully discussed. The first notable book on film music was that by Leonid Sabaneev, 'Music and the Film' (1935), while the following year Kurt London's book 'Film Music', appeared in translation. Articles by composers and directors such as Raybould, Leigh, Milhaud, EISLER, CAVALCANTI, ROTHA, MATHIESON and HITCHCOCK had appeared in various film and music journals. PUDOVKIN had advocated his theory of contrapuntal music, which used underlying themes evocative of the 'inner' meaning of the action rather than themes directly related to the overt action on the screen; this theory was put forward in his book 'Film Technique' (translated 1933), and was demonstrated in his film *Deserter*. Later EISLER produced a key book, 'Composing for the films'. Few composers understood the potentialities better than Walter Leigh, who died shortly after composing his subtle and delicate score for BASIL WRIGHT's *Song of Ceylon* (1935).

Leigh wrote:

> 'The composer approaching the film problem for the first time will be struck by one especially important fact, namely, that in film-music more than in any other kind of music the greatest virtue is economy. A phrase of five bars lasting twenty seconds suitably fitted to thirty feet of picture may express as much as the whole slow movement of a symphony. One minute is quite a considerable length for a piece of music in a film. The academic principles of leisurely formal development are therefore of little use in the composition of film-music, though they may well be employed in the construction of the whole film and its sound-score. The same need for economy applies to the instrumentation; four instruments may well provide a better effect than forty, and a piece that sounds painfully thin and ridiculous in the concert-hall may be perfectly satisfactory over the microphone.
>
> It may be said without presumption that the peculiar powers of the microphone have, with the exception of one or two isolated experiments of which little notice has been taken, not been exploited to much advantage up to the present. The most obvious possibility is that of balancing, by placing at suitable distances from the microphone, those instruments whose normal volumes are entirely unequal. The film-composer has to recognize that the much-despised 'canned' quality of film-music is actually its most important characteristic and greatest virtue.'

In their books 'Film' (1933) and 'A Grammar of the Film' (1935) Rudolf Arnheim and Raymond Spottiswoode made initial attempts to understand the integration of music with natural sounds and speech on the composite sound-track. The craft of dubbing together various strands of sound, of balancing these to achieve specific effects and emphasis, grew out of the very nature of the manufacture of the sound-track during editing.

That the misuse of music in films has been far more apparent than its creative and imaginative use is evident to any film-goer of experience. Most films, even in the 1970s, pour endless streams of meaninglessly emotional sound into the ears of viewers during the credit-titles, establishing vague anticipation of the place and nature of the action. The opening of a film is intended to grip the audience, bringing them either violently or gently into relationship with the mood and action of the film. After this, according to the taste of the director and the degree of co-operation he receives from the composer, music appears or disappears from the track at intervals throughout the picture, adding its special dimension to the already powerful impact of the visuals. The films of the 1940s and 1950s on the whole overused music to, at times, a quite sickening degree, so that a rare film which used hardly any music or merely a linking theme song, such as MILESTONE's *A Walk in the Sun* (1945), seemed like an austere landmark, simply as a film which was content to let its somewhat stylized dialogue achieve its effects unaided. However, composers did emerge who were to use music fully but nonetheless well. A representative international list of such composers, chosen for range and difference of style, but excluding at this stage composers of musicals, might include, with examples of their scores:

WILLIAM ALWYN (GB)	*Desert Victory* (1943), *The Rake's Progress* (1946), *Odd Man Out* (1947).
MALCOLM ARNOLD (GB)	*The Sound Barrier* (1951), *Hobson's Choice* (1954), *The Bridge on the River Kwai* (1957).
Georges Auric (France)	*La Belle et la Bête* and *Hue and Cry* (1946), *Les Parents Terribles* (1948), *Orphée* (1950), *The Lavender Hill Mob* (1951), *Moulin Rouge* (1953), *Gervaise* (1955), *Le Mystère Picasso* (1956), *Bonjour Tristesse* (1957), *The Innocents* (1961).
Leonard Bernstein (USA)	*On the Waterfront* (1954).

Aaron Copland (USA)	*The Heiress* and *The Red Pony* (1949).
GIOVANNI FUSCO (Italy)	*Nettezza Urbana* (1948), *Cronaca di un Amore* (1950), *Le Amiche* (1955) (and many films by ANTONIONI), *Il Mare* (1962), *La Guerre est Finie* (1966), *Hiroshima Mon Amour* (1959).
BERNARD HERRMANN (USA)	*Citizen Kane* (1940), *The Magnificent Ambersons* (1942), *The Day the Earth Stood Still* (1951), *The Trouble with Harry* (1956), *Vertigo* (1958), *North by Northwest* (1959), *Psycho* (1960), *The Birds* (1963), *Marnie* (1964), *Fahrenheit 451* (1966).
Gail Kubick (USA)	*World at War* (1942), *The Memphis Belle* (1944), *Gerald McBoing Boing* (1950).
ALFRED NEWMAN (USA)	*Dead End* (1937), *Foreign Correspondent* (1940), *The Robe* (1953).
Alex North (USA)	*A Streetcar Named Desire* (1951), *Viva Zapata!* (1952).
Clifton Parker (GB)	*Western Approaches* (1944).
Sergei Prokofiev (USSR)	*Ivan the Terrible* (possibly the greatest score yet composed for film, 1943–6).
David Raksin (USA)	*Laura* (1944), *The Bad and the Beautiful* (1952).
Renzo Rossellini (Italy)	*Paisà* (1946), *Germany Year Zero* (1947).
Miklos Rozsa (USA)	*Double Indemnity* (1944), *The Lost Weekend* (1945).
Matyas Seiber (GB)	Many cartoon scores for HALAS and BATCHELOR, including *Animal Farm* (1954).
MAX STEINER (USA)	*The Big Sleep* (1946), *The Treasure of Sierra Madre* (1947).
Virgil Thomson (USA)	*Louisiana Story* (1948).
DMITRI TIOMKIN (USA)	*High Noon* (1952), *The High and the Mighty* (1954), *Giant* (1956), *Gunfight at the OK Corral* (1957), *Rio Bravo* (1959), *The Guns of Navarone* (1961), *The Fall of the Roman Empire* (1963).
Roman Vlad (Italy)	*Paradiso Perduto* (1948), *La Beauté du Diable* (1949), *Romeo et Juliet* (1954).
William Walton (GB)	*Henry V* (1944), *Hamlet* (1948), *Richard III* (1954).
Ralph Vaughan Williams (GB)	*Scott of the Antarctic* (1948).
Victor Young (USA)	*Shane* (1953).

Outstanding musicals since 1940 include:

1939	*The Wizard of Oz*	(VICTOR FLEMING)	JUDY GARLAND
1944	*Cover Girl*	(CHARLES VIDOR)	GENE KELLY, RITA HAYWORTH
	Meet Me in St Louis	(VINCENTE MINNELLI)	Judy Garland
1945	*Anchors Aweigh*	(GEORGE SIDNEY)	Gene Kelly and FRANK SINATRA
	Ziegfeld Follies	(Vincente Minnelli, etc)	WILLIAM POWELL, FRED ASTAIRE, etc
1946	*Yolanda and the Thief*	(Vincente Minnelli)	Fred Astaire, Lucille Bremer
1948	*The Red Shoes*	(MICHAEL POWELL and EMERIC PRESSBURGER)	Moira Shearer, Ludmilla Tcherina, Robert Helpmann, Leonide Massine
	Words and Music	(NORMAN TAUROG)	Gene Kelly, Vera Ellen, June Allyson
	Easter Parade	(CHARLES WALTERS)	Fred Astaire, Judy Garland
	Summer Holiday	(REUBEN MAMOULIAN)	Walter Huston, MICKEY ROONEY
	The Pirate	(Vincente Minnelli)	Judy Garland, Gene Kelly
1949	*The Barkleys of Broadway*	(Charles Walters)	Fred Astaire, GINGER ROGERS
	On the Town	(Kelly and DONEN)	Gene Kelly, Vera-Ellen, Frank Sinatra, Betty Garrett
1950	*Summer Stock (If You Feel Like Singing)*	(Charles Walters)	Judy Garland, Gene Kelly
	An American in Paris	(Vincente Minnelli)	Gene Kelly, LESLIE CARON
1952	*Call Me Madam*	(Walter Lang)	Ethel Merman, Donald O'Connor
	Singin' in the Rain	(Kelly and Donen)	Gene Kelly, Donald O'Connor, Debbie Reynolds
1953	*The Band Wagon*	(Vincente Minnelli)	Fred Astaire, Cyd Charisse
1954	*Seven Brides for Seven Brothers*	(Donen)	Howard Keel
	Carmen Jones	(OTTO PREMINGER)	Dorothy Dandridge
	A Star is Born	(GEORGE CUKOR)	Judy Garland
1955	*Guys and Dolls*	(JOSEPH MANKIEWICZ)	MARLON BRANDO, JEAN SIMMONS
1956	*Funny Face*	(Donen)	Fred Astaire, AUDREY HEPBURN
1957	*The Pajama Game*	(Donen and Abbott)	DORIS DAY, John Raitt
	Pal Joey	(GEORGE SIDNEY)	Frank Sinatra
	Silk Stockings	(REUBEN MAMOULIAN)	FRED ASTAIRE, Cyd Charisse
1958	*Orfeu Negro*	(Marcel Camus)	Luis Bonfa and Antonio Carlos Jobin
1959	*Porgy and Bess*	(Otto Preminger)	Dorothy Dandridge
1960	*Let's Make Love*	(George Cukor)	MARILYN MONROE, YVES MONTAND
1961	*West Side Story*	(ROBERT WISE and Jerome Robbins)	NATALIE WOOD, Richard Beymer
	Gypsy	(MERVYN LE ROY)	ROSALIND RUSSELL, Natalie Wood
1962	*I Could Go On Singing*	(RONALD NEAME)	Judy Garland
1963	*Les Parapluies de Cherbourg*	(JACQUES DEMY)	CATHERINE DENEUVE, Anne Vernon
1964	*A Hard Day's Night*	(RICHARD LESTER)	The Beatles
	My Fair Lady	(George Cukor)	REX HARRISON, Audrey Hepburn
1965	*Help!*	(Richard Lester)	The Beatles
1966	*Les Demoiselles de Rochefort*	(Jacques Demy)	Catherine Deneuve, George Chakiris
1968	*Finian's Rainbow*	(Francis Ford Coppola)	Fred Astaire, Petula Clark
	Funny Girl	(WILLIAM WYLER)	BARBRA STREISAND
	Sweet Charity	(Fosse)	SHIRLEY MACLAINE
1969	*Hello Dolly!*	(Kelly)	Barbra Streisand, WALTER MATTHAU
	Paint Your Wagon	(LOGAN)	LEE MARVIN, JEAN SEBERG
	On a Clear Day You Can See Forever	(Vincente Minnelli)	Barbra Streisand, Yves Montand
1971	*Fiddler on the Roof*	(Jewison)	Topol
1972	*Cabaret*	(Fosse)	Liza Minnelli, Michael York

Apart from Britain, the USA, France, Germany and the USSR, few other countries have a permanent tradition of film music, although interesting work has come from Eastern Europe, Japan (with its traditional music intermingled with Western harmonic schemes and orchestration as in KUROSAWA's films), and India (famed for its 'play-back' songs of popular Indian music and, more seriously, for the scores composed by the director, SATYAJIT RAY).

Since the war, the grandiose symphonic scores of the 1930s and 1940s have gradually lost ground to an intimate use of smaller ensembles as well as jazz and electronic experiments, while many of the younger directors in France and Italy have deliberately borrowed classical composers from the baroque period to the present day to add flavour and atmosphere to their films (Brahms in *Les Amants*, Satie in *Le Feu Follet*). Jazz and 'swing' were, of course, a staple diet in American musicals from the 1930s onwards, but with the appearance of musicians like André Previn and Elmer Bernstein (schooled in both jazz and serious music techniques), film scores now often use a form of symphonic jazz as a dramatic device (Elmer Bernstein's *The Man with the Golden Arm*, Ellington's *Anatomy of a Murder*). In Italy, a distinctive form of film music emerged in the 1960s centred round the composer ENNIO MORRICONE, who established a brilliant, highly melodic style, often with bizarre orchestrations, frequently heard in Italian Westerns.

Recent film music has also reflected contemporary tendencies in mixing national styles and instrumentation, so that many British and American films have soundtracks combining pop music with Indian instruments like the sitar, backed by exotic Eastern and Latin American percussion (the Beatles films). Serious jazz composers like John Dankworth also move between varying styles, sometimes composing in a jazz idiom and then turning to more conventional 'serious' writing (as in his collaborations with JOSEPH LOSEY).

In fact, the motto of the late 1960s and the early 1970s might be summed up as 'anything goes' – all styles and all combinations of instruments are favoured whenever the composer feels that the narrative demands a particular emphasis or sound. The increasing interest in electronic music, triggered off by the avant-garde, has also found its way into films, although so far its most frequent use has been to back up horror or mystery scenes where conventional instrumentation might have been less effective. A reckless use of these modern devices can lead to facile gimmickry, of course, and some contemporary film scoring tends to have the same monotonous sound. Yet the sheer range of resources available to composers today would have surprised and excited their colleagues of 30 years ago and, assuming the talent is available, the next decade may well produce its equivalents of Walton, Prokofiev, Steiner, Copland and Jaubert. JG and RM

Mute

A picture print or negative having no sound track on the same base

N

Natural Sound

Sound effects recorded directly from the real source as distinct from faked effects

Nazimova, Alla (1879–1945)

Born in Yalta, USSR. Educated in Montreux, Switzerland, she became an actress in her native Russia, and first appeared on the stage in New York in 1905. An exquisite dancer, with a diminutive figure and large, expressive eyes and mouth set in a pale face, she appeared early in George D. Baker's *Toys of Fate*, and consolidated her reputation in HERBERT BRENON's pacifist film *War Brides* (1916). Becoming a 'vogue' actress described as 'bizarre' and specializing in the interpretation of sensitive, passionate, neurotic women in 'advanced' post-war films, she earned in the 1920s as much as $13,000 a week. From 1917 her principal director was the French film-maker ALBERT CAPELLANI; together they made such films as *Eye for an Eye* (1917), *Out of the Fog* and *The Red Lantern* (1919). After this she appeared in inferior films directed by her husband, Charles Bryant, such as *Camille* (1921), *A Doll's House* (1922) and *Salome* (1923). Her later, sound film, appearances included *Escape* (*When the Door Opened*, 1940) and *The Bridge of San Luis Rey* (1944). RM

Anna Neagle and Trevor Howard in 'Odette' (Herbert Wilcox, GB, 1950)

Neagle, Anna

Born 1904 in London, England. Created Dame 1969. Actress, dancer and producer. Married to HERBERT WILCOX. At first taught dancing and was a world championship finalist; appeared in Cochran revues, and stage and screen musicals, as well as in straight plays. Her popularity was at its height during the 1940s and 1950s when she won several awards. In her early films she frequently played historical parts which she invested with a vigorous coyness. Her films include: *Goodnight Vienna* (1932), *Bitter Sweet* (1933), *Nell Gwyn* (1934), *Peg of Old Drury* (1935), *Limelight* (1936), *Victoria the Great* (1937), *Sixty Glorious Years* (1938), *Nurse Edith Cavell* (1939), *No No Nanette* (1940), *They Flew Alone* (as Amy Johnson, 1942), *Spring in Park Lane* (1948), *Odette* (1950), *The Lady with a Lamp* (1951), *King's Rhapsody* (1956), *The Lady is a Square* (1958). She also produced a series of films featuring Frankie Vaughan, and has continued her stage acting, notably in a five-year run of the musical 'Charlie Girl'.

Neame, Ronald

Born 1911 in London, England. Director and producer. Son of Ivy Close, a silent film actress well-known for her beauty, Neame possesses an in-born professionalism as a film-maker. Was assistant cameraman on first British full-length sound film, *Blackmail* (1929). Graduated to cameraman, his films including *In Which We Serve* (1942) and *Blithe Spirit* (1945). Then, still associated with DAVID LEAN, became a producer on such films as *Great Expectations* (1946) and *Oliver Twist* (1948). Became next a director: films include *Take My Life* (1948), *The Horse's Mouth* (1959), *Tunes of Glory* (1960), *I Could go on Singing* (1963), *The Chalk Garden* (1964), *Mister Moses* (1965), *A Man Could Get Killed* (co-directed, 1966), *The Prime of Miss Jean Brodie* (1969), *Scrooge* (1970).

Negri, Pola

Born 1897 in Poland. Actress, popular in silent films in which she created fiery, sexy heroines with a sense of humour. First acted in Germany in 1916, then went to Hollywood in 1922. Her films, initially made with LUBITSCH, include: *Die Bestie* (1915), *The Eyes of the Mummy* and *Carmen* (1918), *Madame du Barry* (1919), *The Flame* (1923), and in the USA, *Montmartre* (1923), *Forbidden Paradise* (1924), *Hotel Imperial* (1926), *Madame Bovary* (1935), and *Hi Diddle Diddle* (1943). Her later films include *The Moonspinners* (1964).

Negulesco, Jean

Born 1900 in Craiova, Romania. Cosmopolitan director, who previously worked as a painter in Paris and arrived in America in 1929. He soon established himself as a director of attractively decorated, romantic stories, proving himself particularly adept at getting sensitive performances from actresses, although he was also responsible for several tough 1940s melodramas the brilliant *Mask of Dimitrios* (1944) and *Roadhouse* (1948). Other main films include:

Above: Martin Stephens and Rossano Brazzi in 'Count your Blessings' (Jean Negulesco, USA, 1959)
Below: Peter Strauss and Candice Bergen in 'Soldier Blue' (Ralph Nelson, USA, 1970)

Kiss and Make Up (1934), *Three Strangers* and *Humoresque* (1946), *Johnny Belinda* (1948), *The Mudlark* (1951), *Phone Call From a Stranger* (1952), *How to Marry a Millionaire* (1953), *Three Coins in the Fountain* (1954), *Daddy Long Legs* (1955), *A Certain Smile* (1958), *The Best of Everything* (1959), *The Pleasure Seekers* and *The Invisible Six* (1965), *Hello, Goodbye* (1970). MH

Neilan, Marshall A. (1891–1958)
Born in San Bernardino, California, USA. Director/Actor. After period as stage actor, he joined various film companies (including Biograph, Kalem, Lasky) as character player, turning to direction in 1916 and becoming MARY PICKFORD's favourite director. His work with her has a superior visual sense (nostalgically evoking the American past) and a sensitive feeling for character: *Rebecca of Sunnybrook Farm* (1917), *Stella Maris* (1918), *Daddy Long Legs* (1919), *Dorothy Vernon of Haddon Hall* (1924). He also worked successfully with other favourite screen personalities of the time including Colleen Moore (*The Lotus Eaters*, 1921), Blanche Sweet (*Tess of the d'Urbervilles*, 1924; *The Sporting Venus*, 1925), Constance Talmadge (*Venus of Venice*, 1927). Neilan's obvious skill with actors was allied to an undemonstrative, yet acute, film sense. JG

Nelson, Ralph
Born 1916 in New York, USA. American film director, previously actor, playwright, stage and television director, who in the 1960s developed a reputation for tackling provocative themes in a thumpingly dramatic manner. Most recent subjects: mental retardation in *Charly* (1968), racial tension in *tick...tick...tick...* (1969), the US Cavalry's treatment of the Indians in *Soldier Blue* (1970). Other films include: *Blood Money* (1962), *Lilies of the Field* (1963), his most low-keyed and attractive film *Soldier in the Rain* and *Father Goose* (1964), *Duel at Diablo* (1966), *Flight of the Doves* (1971).

Němec, Jan
Born 1936 in Prague, Czechoslovakia. The controversial eccentric of the Czech New Wave of the early 1960s. Němec's first film was his diploma short, *A Bite to Eat*. Subsequently he made other shorts, *Memory of our Day* (1963), *Life After Ninety Minutes* (co-directed with Jan Schmidt, 1965) and *Mother and Son* (in Holland, 1967). His feature film début was the brilliant *Diamonds of the Night* (1964), followed by an episode in *Pearls on the Ground* (1965); a rather pretentious political allegory *The Party and the Guests*; and *Martyrs of Love* (1967), an essay in poetic fantasy. Even before the Soviet invasion of Czechoslovakia Němec's films had had difficulties with the authorities owing to their equivocal political satire. DR

Netherlands
The Netherlands have been noted in the past as a centre for excellent documentary film-making, producing several directors with a world-wide reputation, including JORIS IVENS, John Ferno, BERT HAANSTRA, and Herman van der Horst. [See DOCUMENTARY]. More recently feature production has been developed, assisted by the government-sponsored Film Production Fund, but the Dutch language tells against the achievement of world-wide distribution, and English may have to be adopted to make Dutch films economically viable. Support for documentary film-making, however, remains generous.

Among the fiction films produced recently:
What do I see? (Paul Verhowen)
Village on the River, The Knife, Mira (Fons Rademakers, the leading feature director)
The Rather Unhappy Return of Joszef Katus to the Land of Rembrandt (Wim Verstappen, born 1937)
Paranoia (Adriaan Detvoorst, born 1940)
Antenna (Adriaan Detvoorst)
Confession of Loving Couples (Wim Verstappen)
Drop-out (Wim Verstappen)
Illusion is a Gangster Girl (Frans Weisz, born 1938)
Made in Paradise (Frans Weisz)
Obsessions (Pim de la Parra, born 1940)
A Memory of Six Weeks, To Grab the Ring, 11.50 from Zürich (Nikolai van der Heyde, born 1935). RM

Newley, Anthony
Born 1931 in Hackney, London, England. Actor, composer, writer and singer. Has appeared on New York and West End stages and on television and was a child star on the screen. His films include: *Oliver Twist* (1948), *Cockleshell Heroes* (1956), *No Time to Die* (1958), *The Small World of Sammy Lee* (1963), *Dr Dolittle* (1967), and *Can Heironymus Merkin Ever Forget Mercy Humpe and Find True Happiness?* (which he also wrote and directed, 1969).

Newman, Alfred (1901–1970)
Born in New Haven, Connecticut, USA. Composer and Music Director. Studied piano

and composition and played with and conducted many American orchestras. Began film work from 1933 with United Artists, SAMUEL GOLDWYN and then Twentieth Century Fox, with whom he is usually associated. Almost as eclectic as MAX STEINER at Warners, his music has great melodic zest, a flair for musical pastiche and, at times, a somewhat soggy sentimentality. His best-known titles (often incorporating hit numbers) include *Dead End* (1937), *Wuthering Heights* and *Drums Along the Mohawk* (1939), *Foreign Correspondent* (1940), *Song of Bernadette* (1943), *The Robe* (1953), *Love is a Many Splendored Thing* (1955), *Bus Stop* (1956), *The Diary of Anne Frank* (1959), *How the West Was Won* (1962), *Nevada Smith* (1966), as well as arrangements for film musicals. JG

Newman, Paul

Born 1925 in Ohio, USA. Dynamic contemporary American stage and screen actor who, in films, best represents the fashion in anti-heroes which developed in the 1960s. A graduate of the Method school of acting and for some time hampered by his resemblance to MARLON BRANDO, he worked extensively in theatre and television before Warners brought him to Hollywood, where he made his film début in an abysmal epic, *The Silver Chalice* (1955).

His portrayal of the prize-fighter champion in *Somebody Up There Likes Me* (1957) established him as an actor of individuality and in subsequent films he has been particularly adept at catching the current mood – notably in *The Left-Handed Gun* (1958), an off-beat study of Billy the Kid, *Cat on a Hot Tin Roof* (1959), *The Hustler* (1962), *Hud* (1963), *Cool Hand Luke* (1967), *Butch Cassidy and the Sundance Kid* (1969). He has made several films with his wife, JOANNE WOODWARD, and he directed her in *Rachel, Rachel* (1968), a highly creditable directorial début. In 1971 he also made *Sometimes a Great Notion*, set in the West.

Other principal films as actor: *The Long Hot Summer* (1958), *Exodus* (1961), *Sweet Bird of Youth* (1962), *The Prize* and *The Outrage* (1964), *The Moving Target*, *Torn Curtain* and *Hombre* (1966), *Winning* (1969), *Hall of Mirrors* (1970), *WUSA* (1971). MH

News and Record Film

When the cinema came into being, in 1895, no-one had had an opportunity to decide what to do with it. The idea that it might be a medium for fictional narrative, for instance, only occurred much later. At first it seemed simply a novel extension of ordinary still photography; its first repertoire was essentially that of the professional photographer. The EDISON camera, fixed rigidly inside the tar-paper studio, the 'Black Maria' at West Orange, was very much the equivalent of the photographic studio; celebrities like Annie Oakley or Jim Corbett came there and posed for their photographs in characteristic attitudes. The LUMIÈRE camera however was a much lighter, more convenient and adaptable apparatus which could be set up

Top: New York Fire Brigade (1897)
Above: Admiral Dewey landing at Gibraltar (c. 1900)
Below: An American newsreel cameraman (c. 1910)

on a tripod anywhere in the open air. Thus the Lumière repertoire was much more like that of the snapshot photographer – waves on a high sea, the arrival of a train, baby being fed, workers leaving a factory.

But this was the period of the first illustrated magazines and newspapers, and the cinema also took its lead from them, filming not just the intimate and familiar (though in the early days it was the mere *fact* of movement and not the *nature* of the movement depicted which delighted the audience) but also the unusual and newsworthy event. In March 1895 the English inventor Birt Acres filmed the University Boat Race. In July of the same year the Lumière Brothers filmed their professional colleagues in the course of the Congress of French Photographic Societies. In 1896 ROBERT W. PAUL filmed the triumph of the Prince of Wales's horse, Persimmon, as it won the Derby; and brought off a notable coup by showing the film the same evening at the Alhambra, Leicester Square, thus establishing for the first time the topical possibilities and the topical compulsions of the newsreel.

Cinematographers now energetically recorded the great events of the closing years of the 19th century – the Coronation of Tsar Nikolas II of Russia (1896), the Inauguration of President McKinley (1897), Queen Victoria's Diamond Jubilee (1897), Gladstone's funeral (1898), the Boer War and the Boxer Rising.

Above: Arrest of a Suffragette in London (1911)
Below: Queen Victoria's Funeral (1901)

Such predictable events could be covered, but many great happenings eluded the cameras of the early film-makers, so that they were obliged to re-stage them. Thus in 1899 GEORGES MÉLIÈS re-enacted the Dreyfus affair on his little studio stage, and in 1902 he staged the eruption of Mont Pelée, the crash of the balloon Pad, and, more impressively, to the order of the Warwick Trading Company of London, he created the coronation ceremony of Edward VII, building a miniature Westminster Abbey in his studio and selecting a Châtelet chorus girl to play the Queen. The same year the English director James Williamson re-enacted an *Attack on a Chinese Mission* in the front garden of his London house. It is important to recognize that these staged actualities were not in any way regarded by the audiences of the time as fakes or deceptions. They were the precise equivalent of illustrating a news story in a magazine with drawings – a regular practice in the second half of the 19th century – instead of with photographs. (There were deliberate deceits all the same. In 1910 a Liverpool showman advertised the film of the funeral of Edward VII on the day of the event. The contented audience seemed not to notice that the deceased monarch might be glimpsed, stout and well and following his own supposed bier on horseback, for it was in fact a record of Queen Victoria's funeral, nine years before.)

In the period when programmes were made up of shorts of only a minute or so in length, these 'topicals' took their place quite naturally and easily alongside the rest of the repertoire. By 1910, however, when story films were well established and already reaching the marathon length of a whole 15-minute reel, the 50-foot news items were no longer so attractive either to showmen or audiences. Hence CHARLES PATHÉ took up an idea which had been suggested a little earlier by Leon Francini; and introduced a regular weekly reel made up of a collection of short news items. Very soon he was bringing out two editions each week. Pathé launched his *Animated Gazette* in France and England; and he was soon followed by his rivals: LÉON GAUMONT with his *Actualités* and the Éclair Company with a rather shorter-lived reel. In England the old native companies continued to make interest shorts, but began to package them into newsreels, and in 1911 the first issue of the durable *Topical Budget* made its appearance. The same year the Urban-Smith Kinemacolor Company began to include news subjects among its programmes of colour films, though their greatest triumph was the record of the Delhi Durbar of 1912. By the beginning of the 1920s most of the major American companies had their own newsreels which were distributed with their own programmes, and were often used with notable political aggressiveness – most notoriously in the 1930s, in the vicious campaign carried out by MGM through the HEARST newsreel against Upton Sinclair's candidacy for the Californian Governorship.

The largest bulk of surviving newsreel coverage of the First World War is very much behind-the-lines material, often shot with remarkable flair, and the war gave a great impetus to techniques of reporting; and events of the time like the suffragette movement and the Irish troubles were covered with a degree of skill and imagination which gives enormous value to the film documents left behind for posterity.

Throughout the 1920s and 1930s, as the reporting technique of the newsreels became more ambitious, the rivalry for scoops and exclusives became more and more vicious; and there is a hair-raising repertoire of stories about rank piracy, and the strong-arm gangs who would sabotage the efforts of rival firms.

In the summer of 1927 Fox Movietone cameras recorded the departure and return of Lindbergh; and interviewed Mussolini in Italy. By autumn of the same year Movietone News was appearing regularly each week; and by the end of 1929 Fox were producing no less than four weekly issues. They were rapidly followed into sound reporting techniques by Gaumont, Pathé and Paramount, though the major part of most newsreels continued for many years to be shot silent, and accompanied by post-synchronized sound effects and commentary. The latest newsreel to adopt synchronized sound was Universal, which seemed to be produced on a rather lower budget than the others.

Some early newsreels were hand-tinted; and the Kinemacolor experiment was followed in the late 1930s by a shortlived British colour reel, National. Subsequently colour was introduced from time to time for special items in the regular news reels; but it was perhaps only the stimulus of the Coronation of 1953, with the emphasis it gave to colour actuality film, together with the competition of television, which encouraged the development, in the late 1950s and early 1960s, of colour news films.

With the Second World War, Government regulations cut the average length of British newsreels from 850 or 900 feet to 730 feet per issue, encouraging greater economy and precision of technique. The rival companies were obliged by war conditions to pool their resources, since the Ministry of Information imposed a rota system, giving facilities to only one cameraman in each area of war operations,

and sharing the product of the Army and RAF camera units. At the same time an official censorship was imposed, although it was the proud boast that there had never been a *political* censorship upon newsreels.

In the widest sense this was illusory. Newsreels in Britain and the United States had gradually become and remained essentially trivial, escapist fantasies about society weddings and sporting events, which had totally ignored the immense portents of the 1930s. Hitler, Mussolini, Stalin and Gandhi, like all foreigners, remained figures of fun. The attitudes of the newsreels must not be blamed entirely on the men who made them. Audiences and exhibitors were vigorous in their resentment of anything which struck them as political; and as late as 1943 when Paramount News dealt with comparative seriousness with an item about the release of Oswald Mosley from internment, it caused a flurry of agitated Parliamentary questions which elicited from the Parliamentary Private Secretary to the Ministry of Information a statement that he 'shared my Noble Friend's dislike of the intrusion of politics into newsreels, which offer little scope for genuine discussion. In journalism there is always an opportunity to make a reply to polemics, but in newsreels there is not'.

In other countries actuality reportage was taken much more seriously; 'political' was not always considered a pejorative term. In the Soviet Union very soon after the Revolution, DZIGA VERTOV had begun to make newsfilms – *Kino-Pravda* and *Kino-Eye* – which introduced

Above: Geoffrey Malins, one of the official British cameramen, covering the First World War from the trenches
Below: Fashions at Ascot (1919)

Top: Lenin (c. 1920)
Above: Autoracer accident (Fox Movietone, USA)
Below: Japanese earthquake and tidal wave (Fox Movietone, 1923)

Above: Aerial stunt (USA, early 1930s)
Below: The 'Hindenburg' in flames in New York after its Atlantic crossing (1937)

a wholly new virility and political purpose into reporting. Later, in the Fascist countries as well as the USSR, newsreels became a potent propaganda force, used equally to stir up nationalist and militant spirit at home and to inspire alarm in potential victims.

The Anglo-Saxon myth of news as objective reporting (a myth, because the whole process of selection, the very devising of those trivial pots-pourris which passed in Britain and America for 'news', was a political act) was challenged in 1935 when the *March of Time* series made its first appearance in cinemas in America, to be followed later by an English series. Produced in association with Time and Fortune Magazines, and the 'March of Time' radio broadcasts, many issues dealt with a single topic, which was treated in depth and in a controversial interpretative style. It employed reconstructed and acted sequences alongside actuality material. '*March of Time* adapts from the newspaper a reporting purpose which claims to give the impartial inside story behind current events, and borrows from the fiction film a vivid method of presentation. . . . It tries to present an event in relation to its background, requiring a considered statement of facts over a period of time. Its visual images tend to illustrate the emotionally delivered commentary rather than the commentary serving as an explanation of the pictorial content. Like the newsreel, *March of Time* uses the personal interview, but fits the interview to an editorial purpose. *March of Time* can be compared to the column of a press commentator rather than to straightforward reporting of news events, although its sponsors claim to maintain a policy of impartiality.' (*The Factual Film*, 1947).

March of Time had a great influence upon wartime reportage; and with such films as the *Why We Fight* series, produced in America under the supervision of FRANK CAPRA, reportage begins to approximate to DOCUMENTARY FILM (q.v.).

The decline of the cinema newsreel after the late 1950s must ultimately be attributed to the competition of television. The earliest television news transmissions were ordinary cinema newsreels; when the full threat of television to the cinema was recognized, and these were no longer made available, television was for a time content with no more than a single news-reader delivering unillustrated reports. But gradually television developed its own style of film news coverage. Television made more and more use of its advantages over the cinema in the field of news reporting: it could use 16mm film, with no need for the production of large numbers of 35mm positive copies; and indeed could transmit from negative material directly, thus effecting a considerable saving of time between shooting and exhibition. The immediacy of television news coverage – soon enhanced by direct transmissions and the relaying of images by satellite – rendered the methods of the cinema sadly obsolete. Moreover the television audience became accustomed

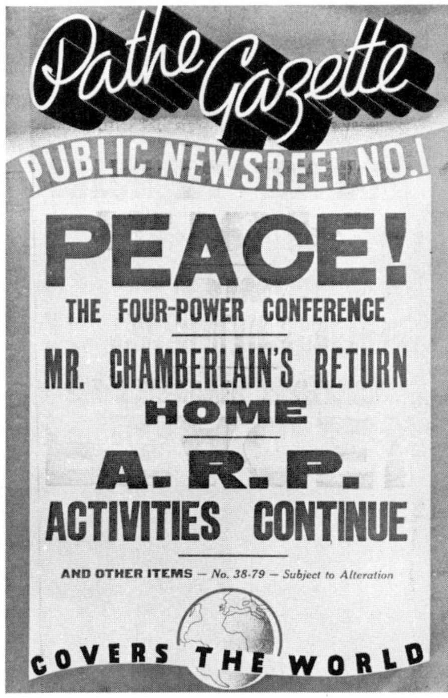

Above: Poster for the Pathé Gazette (GB, 1938)
Below: 'Uncle Sam – the Farmer' ('The March of Time' series, USA, 1939)

to a serious coverage of current events quite unlike the flip and superficial treatment of the old newsreels. No longer able to compete, the last gasps of the old cinema newsreels were efforts to stress the magazine, rather than the topical elements. But in Britain Paramount News ceased production in 1957, Gaumont British and Universal, which had combined, ended in 1959, Pathé ten years later. In 1971 only Movietone, the first sound newsreel, survived, thanks to its contracts to make overseas propaganda films for the Central Office of Information.

The fact that today's topicals are tomorrow's history was very soon recognized, and the first historical compilations were made within the first twenty years of the film's own history. The greatest exponent of the compilation film however remains ESTHER SHUB, whose series of films on Russian and Soviet history – *Fall of the Romanov Dynasty* and *The Great Road* (1927) and *The Russia of Nikolai II and Lev Tolstoy* (1928) – were of immense historical importance not only in establishing the genre in its own right, but also in rescuing and restoring thousands of feet of mouldering film of immense documentary value and in making apparent the need for film archives. There was a vogue for historical compilations in America in the 1930s: LOUIS DE ROCHEMONT's *Cry of the World* (1932), Gilbert Seldes and Frederick Ullman's *This is America* (1933), Max Eastman's *From Czar to Lenin* (1936). Later distinguished practitioners of the genre have included ALAIN RESNAIS (*Nuit et Brouillard*), Frederic Rossif (*Mourir à Madrid*, *The October Revolution*), MIKHAIL ROMM (*Ordinary Fascism*) and Albert Knobler (*Happiness in Twenty Years*); though television has made

Top: Pre-war shot of Hitler, later used in the 'Why we Fight' series produced in the USA
Above: London blitz (1941)
Below: 'One Day of War': a Russian wartime news shot

Above: Poster for 'The March of Time' (USA, 1945)
Below: 'Shadows of the Ruhr': post-war Germany

wide use of the historical compilation, notably in the extensive series on the life and times of Winston Churchill and *The Great War*.

Apart from its purposes as direct news reportage, the film's value as record has been recognized from the very earliest days. Even when the longest film ran no more than a minute, in 1896, Edison prophesied: 'I believe that in coming years by my work and that of Dickson, Muybridge, Marie (sic) and others who will doubtlessly enter the field, the grand opera can be given at the Metropolitan Opera House at New York without any material change from the original, and with artists and musicians long since dead.' During the First World War a special cinematographic committee was set up under the War Office; and the superb records made by official cameramen of, for instance, the campaigns of the Somme, Arras and Ancre, established a standard that has rarely been surpassed.

In the first decade of the film's existence Dr Jean Comandon in France and Dr Canti in Great Britain had already made extensive use of the cinema camera for purposes of medical and scientific record and research; while the natural history films of Percy Smith, *The Secrets of Nature* series and *The Secrets of Life* series were the first examples of films of reasonably serious scientific content which were able to attract a large popular audience. Since then the film has been used widely in scientific research, much of the work in Britain being co-ordinated by the Scientific Film Association. Again television has multiplied the possibility for scientific – especially anthropological – film records. DR

Above: Atom-bomb test at Bikini (Pathé News, USA official coverage, 1946)
Below: 'Crisis in Italy': the general strike

Niblo, Fred (1874–1948)
Born in York, Nebraska, USA. Brother-in-law of George M. Cohan, Niblo had a successful career in vaudeville and became a director in the legitimate theatre before joining the Ince Studios in 1917. There his first film was *The Marriage Ring* (1918), starring his future wife, Enid Bennett, with whom he made an extensive series of films. His work with DOUGLAS FAIRBANKS – *The Mark of Zoro* (1921) and *The Three Musketeers* (1921) – typed Niblo as a director of romantic costume spectacle; he directed VALENTINO in *Blood and Sand* and was given the formidable assignment of completing *Ben Hur* which had been begun by the Goldwyn company in 1922, but was later inherited by MGM. Recalling his costume vehicles for other stars, MGM assigned Niblo to two Garbo vehicles – *The Temptress* (1926), which had been begun by STILLER, and *The Mysterious Lady* (1928) – and two ambitious films designed to star Norma Talmadge, a modern version of *Camille* (1927), and an adaptation of 'Adrienne Lecouvreur', *Dream of Love* (1928). Niblo worked rarely after the coming of sound; his last film was *Three Sons o' Guns* (1941). DR

Nichols, Dudley (1895–1960)
Born in Ohio, USA. Screenwriter; later producer and director. After a career in journalism, he went to Hollywood in 1929, and became one of the most noted screenwriters during the earlier days of the sound film. He was President of the Screenwriters' Guild 1938–9. His many screenplays for JOHN FORD written during the 1930s include *Men without Women* and *Born Reckless* (1930), *The Informer* (1935), for which he received an Academy award, and *Stagecoach* (1939). Later he wrote, among other films, the scripts for *Scarlet Street* and *Pinky*. He wrote and directed *Sister Kenny* (1946) and wrote, produced and directed *Mourning becomes Electra* (1947).

Nichols, Mike
Born in 1931 in Berlin, Germany. One of the leading younger directors of the 1960s, he arrived in America as a child refugee from the Nazis. He came to films via cabaret (as a satirist with Elaine May) and the theatre. As a screen director he started at the top with *Who's Afraid of Virginia Woolf?* (1966), which won an Academy Award as did his next, *The Graduate* (1967). His rather flashy style spilled over into an otherwise persuasive film adaptation of *Catch 22* (1970). Most recent film: *Carnal Knowledge* (1971).

Nicholson, Jack
Born 1937 in New Jersey, USA. New-style American actor, writer and director, who, after working in Hollywood for over ten years more or less uneventfully, achieved sudden fame in the cult film *Easy Rider* (1969). Previously he had played bit parts in more than a dozen films, scripted *The Trip* (1967) and *Head* (1969), and worked as writer and producer with MONTE HELLMAN. After *Easy Rider*, he appeared in *On a Clear Day You Can See Forever* (1969), *Five Easy Pieces* and *Carnal Knowledge* (1971). In 1971 he also directed *Drive, He Said*.

Nielsen, Asta
Born 1883 in Copenhagen, Denmark. Actress, whose main career in films developed in Germany, where she eventually settled with her first director-husband, Urban Gad, whom she married in 1912. She achieved stardom in the Danish theatre before working for the Danish production company, Nordisk, which – largely through the films she made for them – achieved great success in France and Germany. Her first celebrated film for Nordisk was *The Abyss* (1910), written and directed by Urban Gad; this established her as an actress with a haunting, sphinx-like 'image', a feminine mystique all her own. She brought unusual intelligence to her work, which she took very seriously, realizing before any other star that silent film acting was a matter of detailed expression rather than the broad, theatrical effects which were generally characteristic of the time. She and Urban Gad were brought to Germany by the enterprising

producer, Paul Davidson, head of Projektions-A. G. Union, who offered her a contract of 40,000 marks a film, one of the first large fees to be offered a film star.

Asta Nielsen came to be known as the 'Duse of the screen'; her face could excite tragic emotions through the restraint of her expression and her large, passionate eyes. She used gesture sparingly, and understood the emotional significance which could be achieved through handling small, personal objects on the screen in close-shot. She soon became recognized as the leading screen tragedienne in Europe, as well as the 'pin-up' alike of the German and French forces, to whom her face became known through such Danish films as *The Black Dream*, *Gypsy Blood*, *Woman without Country* and *Youthful Folly*. The earlier films she made with Urban Gad in Germany included *Engelein* (1911), *Die Suffragette*, *Das Liebes A-B-C* and *Intoxication*.

Her post-war silent films made in Germany included *Hamlet* (1920) – based on the original Nordic story but with Hamlet as a woman disguised as a man, and directed by Sven Gade, who became her second husband – Arthur von Gerlach's *Vanina* (1922); *Downfall* (*Absturz*, 1923), in which she brought emotional characterization to the part of an elderly prostitute in love with a young boy; Leopold Jessner's *Erdgeist* (1923); *Hedda Gabler* (1924); PABST's *The Joyless Street* (1925); Bruno Rahn's *The Tragedy of the Street* and *The Lusts of Mankind* (1927). She specialized in playing, with almost obsessive sympathy, outcast women in the grip of misfortune.

Her career in effect ended with the silent film. Opposed to the Nazi régime, she finally left Germany and returned to Copenhagen in 1937, where she lives in retirement. RM

Nilsson, Leopoldo Torre
See TORRE NILSSON

Nitrate Film
Film of which the base is composed mainly of cellulose nitrate. Nitrate film is highly inflammable.

Niven, David
Born 1909 in Kirriemuir, Scotland. Actor, suave and debonair, who has a background of military training and has worked in Canada, Cuba, USA and England at a variety of jobs from lumberjack to newspaper reporter and Hollywood extra. Served in the British Army in the Second World War, becoming a colonel. His many films include: *Barbary Coast* (1935), *The Charge of the Light Brigade* (1936), *The Prisoner of Zenda* (1937), *Wuthering Heights* (1939), *The First of the Few* (1942), *A Matter of Life and Death* (1946), *The Elusive Pimpernel* (1950), *Carrington VC* (1955), *Around the World in Eighty Days* (1956), *Separate Tables* (1958), *The Guns of Navarone* (1962), *The Pink Panther* (1963), *The Extraordinary Seaman* and *Prudence and the Pill* (1968), *The Brain* (1969), *The Statue* (1970). His television series include *The David Niven Show* (1959) and *The Rogues* (1964).

Non Flam. Film
Slow burning film base made of cellulose acetate

Non Theatrical
An exhibition of films other than in a normal cinema, and films designed for such exhibition.

Normand, Mabel (1894–1930)
Born in Rhode Island, USA. Incomparable silent screen comedienne, whose dainty good looks belied a tough and witty talent. One of the earliest of MACK SENNETT's team of Keystone players, she had started out as an artist's model and made her first film in 1910. A perfect female foil for CHAPLIN, she starred individually in several comedies. Her main films include: *Fatty and Mabel Adrift* (1915), *Mickey* (1917), *Sis Hopkins* (1918), *Molly O* (1921), *Suzanna* (1922).

Norway
See SCANDINAVIAN FILM

Novak, Kim
Born 1933 in USA. Blonde actress who started as a model, won popularity awards and became not only a sex symbol but pliable material for such directors as HITCHCOCK and WILDER. Her films include: *Phffft* (1954), *The Man with the Golden Arm* (1956), *Jeanne Eagels* and *Pal Joey* (1957), *Vertigo* (1958), *Strangers when we Meet* (1961), *Kiss Me Stupid* and *Of Human Bondage* (1964), *Moll Flanders* (1965), *The Great Bank Robbery* (1969).

Novarro, Ramon (1899–1968)
Born in Mexico. Actor, whose education included singing, playing the violin, and dancing. He first appeared as a dancer, but soon became a Hollywood leading man specializing in suave Latin-type roles. He starred in both the silent and the sound versions of *Ben Hur* (1926 and 1959), and his other films include: *The Prisoner of Zenda* (1922), *The Midshipman* (1925), *The Student Prince* (1927), *Mata Hari* (1932), *The Big Steal* (1949), *Crisis* (1950), and *Heller in Pink Tights* (1960).

Novello, Ivor (1893–1951)
Born in Cardiff, Wales. Actor, dramatist and composer, best known for his First World War song, 'Keep the Homes Fires Burning' and his musical plays and light comedies. He became very popular as the romantic hero of his own productions, and in his silent films, which include: *Carnival* and *The Bohemian Girl* (1922), *The Rat* (1925), *The Lodger* (1926), *The Triumph of the Rat* and *The Constant Nymph* (1927); and in the sound period *Sleeping Car* (1933), and *Autumn Crocus* (1934). Later he returned to the stage and his musical comedies, of which *The Dancing Years* was filmed in 1950.

Number Board
A board on which are shown the name of the film, the scene and take number and sometimes other information. The number board is held in front of the camera and photographed before or after each scene is shot.

Ramon Novarro in 'Ben Hur' (Fred Niblo, USA, 1926)

OPQ

Odets, Clifford (1906–1963)
Born in Philadelphia, USA. Scriptwriter, playwright and stage actor associated with Theatre Guild Group Theatre productions. His scripts include: *The General Died at Dawn* (1936), *Golden Boy* (from his play, 1939), *None but the Lonely Heart* (also directed, 1944), *The Country Girl* (from his play, 1954), *The Big Knife* (from his play, 1955), *The Story on Page One* (also directed, 1960).

Olcott, Sidney (1873–1949)
Born in Toronto, Canada. An actor, Olcott went to work for Biograph in 1904; and by 1906 had moved to Kalem to become a director. The following year he made his celebrated one-reel adaptation of *Ben Hur* which was an innovation in the American cinema of the time both as a costume film and for its serious artistic pretensions. It was also the first film to raise the legal question of literary copyright. Olcott had a peculiar sensitivity to location; and his use of exotic locales as the setting for dramatic films was a major contribution to the discovery of the potential of the cinema. In 1908, for instance he took the Kalem Company to Florida to make a social study of the impoverished inhabitants of Jacksonville. In 1911 and 1912 the Kalem Company spent extended periods shooting in Ireland; and subsequently went to the Holy Land to make *From the Manger to the Cross* (1912). Olcott was one of the few prominent directors of the pre-1914 era to survive in the post-war cinema with notable success. He directed WILL ROGERS in *Scratch My Back* (1920), Marion Davies in *Little Old New York* and GEORGE ARLISS in *The Green Goddess* (1923), VALENTINO in *Monsieur Beaucaire* and SWANSON in *The Humming Bird* (1924), POLA NEGRI in *The Charmer* (1925) and RICHARD BARTHELMESS in *Ranson's Folly*, *The White Black Sheep* and *The Amateur Gentleman* (1926). In 1927 Olcott came to London to work for British Lion, against whom he was awarded judgement in a strange action brought because he refused to make films 'tending to glorify crime'. Evidently recognizing his inability to adjust to the new conditions of the talking film, Olcott retired definitively from the cinema at the age of 54. DR

Olivier, Laurence
Born 1907 in Dorking, England. Director of the National Theatre, London, from 1963. Knighted 1947; life peer 1970. Actor and director. After drama training, his career started in the Birmingham Repertory Theatre in 1926, and he had become a leading actor by 1930 in both London and New York. In 1931 he seemed destined for a star career in Hollywood, even being seriously considered as a leading man for GRETA GARBO. After a film début in Germany, he appeared in relatively undistinguished American films (*Westward Passage*, *Friends and Lovers*, *The Yellow Ticket*) until the economic depression in the USA led him to return to Britain. Here during the 1930s he consolidated his career both on the stage and in film; his films included *As You Like It* (1936), *Fire over England* (1937) and *Divorce of Lady X* (1938), before he returned to Hollywood in 1939 to appear in WYLER's *Wuthering Heights* (1939), HITCHCOCK's *Rebecca* (1940) and Robert Z. Leonard's *Pride and Prejudice* (1940), and, with KORDA as producer, *Lady Hamilton* (1941). He returned to England to serve in the Fleet Air Arm, but was given leave to appear in films, including MICHAEL POWELL's *49th Parallel* (1941) and ASQUITH's *Demi-Paradise* (1943), the latter sponsored by the impresario FILIPPO DEL GIUDICE, who then invited him to produce, direct and star in *Henry V* (1944–5) on the strength of the reputation he had made as a Shakespearean actor in the British theatre during the 1930s.

Henry V was a turning point in Olivier's career. He discovered his flair for film direction; *Henry V* was undoubtedly the most successful Shakespearean film so far made, and led to his *Hamlet* (1948). This caused some controversy on account of the considerable cuts which had been made in the play, but it is arguably the most imaginative of Olivier's Shakespearean films, the third of which, *Richard III*, was to come later, in 1954. Meanwhile, he had from 1944 to 1949 become co-director of the Old Vic, showing his incomparable sense of theatrical characterization in the parts of Oedipus, Lear, and Gloucester in 'Richard III', the performance which inspired Korda to invite him to adapt the play as a film.

Olivier has always valued range of performance in the theatre and film, and he has played far more contemporary and period parts than Shakespearean on the screen, working under the direction of others, and appearing in WYLER's *Carrie* (1952), BROOK's *The Beggar's Opera* (1953), KUBRICK's *Spartacus* (1960), RICHARDSON's *The Entertainer* (1960 – repeating his *tour de force* stage performance in JOHN OSBORNE's play), GLENVILLE's *Term of Trial* (1961) and DEARDEN's *Khartoum* (1966).

In 1957 he directed, rather improbably, MARILYN MONROE in Rattigan's *The Prince and the Showgirl*, playing opposite her, but eventually returned to Shakespeare in 1966 in a film-record of his celebrated stage performance as *Othello* for the National Theatre. More recently he has directed another film-record, the beautiful National Theatre production of Chekhov's *Three Sisters* (1970). RM

Olmi, Ermanno
Born 1931 in Bergamo, Italy. Perceptive Italian director in the Christian-humanist tradition, whose most celebrated films, *Il Posto* (1961) and *I Fidanzati* (1963), reveal a deep understanding of the pressures of lower-class Italian life and a rare sympathy for the human condition. Of peasant stock, he worked as a clerk within the Edison organization and then branched out into theatre and cinema. Between 1952 and 1959 he made some forty documentaries, but found himself more and more concerned with the human element in these films. His first feature film, *Il Posto*, about a young school-leaver's first humdrum job, established him as a director of international reputation, whose detailed, understated style was totally individual and timeless. Ironically, perhaps, his least satisfactory film was on a subject that affected him most deeply: the life of Pope John, *A Man Named John* (1965). He has also worked extensively in television.

Other notable films: *One Fine Day* (1969); *The Scavengers* (1970); *During the Summer* (1971) in which he has moved towards romantic fantasy. MH

Ophüls, Max (1902–1957)
Born in Saarbrücken, Germany. Director. Ophüls (real name: Max Oppenheimer) was an actor and stage producer, including a period at the Vienna Burgtheater, before entering films in 1930. He was an *auteur* in the fullest sense for, although he worked in various European countries and in America, his visual style was instantly recognizable, with its complex, swirling camera movements, deep-toned décor and its evocation of a romanticized Vienna, full of fashionable balls, aristocratic etiquette and doom-laden love affairs. Ophüls' most oft-repeated characters are women betrayed by an

impossible love or a looming fate, counterpointed by the music of Mozart or a Strauss waltz. *The Bartered Bride* (1932) is still the best opera film, often linking the narrative to a musical motif as in *Liebelei* (1933) and the Italian-made *La Signora di Tutti* (1934). After a productive period in France in the late 1930s, Ophüls moved to America but, apart from a few minor assignments, he was silent until 1947 when Douglas Fairbanks Jnr employed him to direct a swashbuckler, *The Exile*, which he did with all his former flair and camera panache. *Letter from an Unknown Woman* (1948), from Stefan Zweig's tragic love story, marvellously recaptured the mood of his European films, while his other American work, *Caught* (1948), and *The Reckless Moment* (1949) showed equal insight into the contemporary scene. Returning to France, he made *La Ronde* (1950), *Le Plaisir* (1952), *Madame de...* (1953) and *Lola Montès* (1955), all imbued with a knowing cynicism and world-weary awareness of life's foibles and the eternal 'game of love'. *Lola Montès* was his final testament, ornate, over-indulgent, superbly filmed in colour and 'Scope, ravaged by its distributors and a disastrous box-office failure. Like VON STROHEIM and LUBITSCH, Ophüls was both fascinated and revolted by the memories of an aristocratic Europe long since disappeared and, as his camera tracks and pans through fashionable ballrooms and misty Viennese streets, his vision of that world comes miraculously to life. JG

Above: Peter O'Toole in 'Murphy's War' (Peter Yates, GB, 1971)
Below: Laurence Olivier as 'Othello' (Stuart Burge, GB, 1966)

Optical
A special effect, such as a fade, dissolve, or wipe, obtained by the use of an optical printer

Optical Track
A photographic sound track produced by the action of a variable light source on light-sensitive photographic emulsion.

Orry-Kelly (1897–1964)
Born in Kiama, Australia. Leading Hollywood costume designer during the star-orientated 1930s and 1940s when world fashion was to an extent dictated by motion pictures. Less shackled to the idea of good taste fashion than his colleague at MGM, Adrian, he was a successful Broadway designer – designing KATHARINE HEPBURN's wardrobe for 'Death Takes a Holiday' – before arriving in Hollywood in 1931. Through his friend CARY GRANT, he was signed by Warners to design costumes for Ruth Chatterton and Kay Francis. A distinguished painter as well, he later excelled himself in the flamboyant costumes for *An American in Paris* (1950), which won him an Academy Award, and for *Les Girls* (1957), both at MGM.

Orthochromatic
A photographic material sensitive to all colours except red. The term is chiefly used to distinguish from the more sensitive panchromatic film.

Osborne, John
Born 1930 in London, England. Controversial trail-blazing British playwright, occasional screenwriter, actor and film executive, involved in the formation of Woodfall Films, which produced, among others, *Saturday Night and Sunday Morning* (1960). With varying success his plays, *Look Back in Anger* (1959), *The Entertainer* (1960), *Inadmissible Evidence* (1968), have been filmed and certainly the first of them helped to create the climate for the falsely dubbed 'kitchen sink' realism in British films of the 1960s. He wrote the screenplay for the successful *Tom Jones* (1963) and has acted in *First Love* and *Get Carter* (1970).

Oshima, Nagisa
Born 1932 in Kyoto, Japan. Director. After working as assistant director with the Shochiku company, he began directing in 1959, at first making fairly lurid studies of semi-delinquent youth. Later his work became more politically orientated, with biting attacks on bourgeois traditions and hypocrisy. Very eclectic in style (and sometimes influenced by GODARD), he leads the Japanese New Wave movement combining social comment with outbursts of violence and sex. His more recent films seen in Europe include *Death by Hanging* (1968), a stark examination of Japanese penal methods; *Diary of a Shinjuku Thief* and *The Boy* (1969), a complex study of a family's bizarre criminal activities; and *The Ceremony* (1970), a fascinating family saga taking in both Japan's past history and present preoccupations, shot in outstanding 'Scope and colour. JG

Oswald, Richard (1880–1963)
Born in Vienna, Austria. Director. Studied theatre production in Vienna, then formed his own film company in Germany during the First World War. Very prolific director of spectacular and historical subjects during silent period, with elaborate settings, famous stars like CONRAD VEIDT and Lya de Putti, and a rather heavy narrative style. Main films include *The Portrait of Dorian Gray* (1917), *Macbeth* (1921), *Lady Hamilton* and *Lukrezia Borgia* (1922), *Don Carlos and Elisabeth* (1924), *Cagliostro* (1928). His best sound work includes *Alraune* (1930); *The Captain of Köpernick* (1931), from Zuckmayer's famous satire which Oswald later re-made in America in 1941; and *Unheimliche Geschichten* (1932). His son, Gerd Oswald, is also a director in America. JG

O'Toole, Peter
Born 1932 in Britain. Actor and leading man, who began his career with the Bristol Old Vic and the Royal Shakespeare Company, and on television. His screen début was in *Kidnapped*

(1959), and he quickly became popular as a sensitive rather off-beat player; his subsequent films include: *The Day they Robbed the Bank of England* (1960), *Lawrence of Arabia* (1962), *Becket* (1964), *Lord Jim* (1965), *What's New, Pussycat?*, *How to Steal a Million Dollars* and *The Bible* (1966), *The Lion in Winter* (1968), *Goodbye Mr Chips* (1969), *Country Dance* (1970), *Murphy's War* (1971).

Ozep, Fedor (1895–1949)
Born in Moscow, Russia. A man of wide culture, Ozep first encountered the cinema as SANIN's co-director on *Polikushka* (1919). His next film was a collaboration with BORIS BARNET, *Miss Mend* (1926); and this and the succeeding *Yellow Passport* (1927) and *Earth in Chains* (1928; both films starring ANNA STEN who was to remain Ozep's favourite star) revealed the extent to which Ozep was committed to an older, more literary tradition of film-making which contrasted with the montage styles brought into current fashion by PUDOVKIN and EISENSTEIN. In 1929 Ozep went to Germany to direct the Soviet-German production of *The Living Corpse*; and stayed there to make his best film, *Die Mörder Dimitri Karamazov*. Ozep experienced little success with the succeeding sound films which he directed in France, Canada and Hollywood, and which included *Amok* (1934), *La dame de pique* (1937), *Tarakanova* (1938, with MARIO SOLDATI), *Gibraltar* (1938), *Three Russian Girls* (1944), *Whispering City* (1947). DR

Ozu, Yasujiro (1903–1963)
Born in Tokyo, Japan. Director. After studying at Waseda University, he entered Shochiku studios in 1923 as assistant to Tadamoto Okubo, from whom he learnt comedy technique, and also studied (one guesses) American directors, especially LUBITSCH. Ozu is known mainly in the West for his great post-war series of family studies (in which parent-child relationships and the problems of growing up and marriage are examined with a marvellous compassion and density), but much of his early silent work is lighter in tone and full of wry character observation which is both essentially Japanese and entirely universal. The harassed office workers of *Chorus of Tokyo* (1931), the rebellious children in *I Was Born, but...* (1932) are as essential a part of Ozu's world as the later studies with their mood of sad resignation and awareness of life's fleeting beauties. For a large part of his career, his script collaborator was Kogo Noda, who possessed an instinctive feeling for the kind of situations and dialogue Ozu needed. Technically, Ozu was the least demonstrative of directors; although, in his early period, he used travelling shots and some dissolves, he gradually pared down his style, eliminating most camera movement and concentrating on static set-ups, usually shot from near-floor level. Consequently, the main emphasis was laid on the editing rhythm, a fastidious use of 'lived-in' settings and a meticulous direction of the actors (over the years, he built up a brilliantly resourceful repertory, headed by Chishu Ryu as the perennial wise and lonely father). His first sound film, *The Only Son* (1936), introduced the elegiac note which was to become a constant factor in the post-war period. During the war itself, Ozu managed to avoid making any kind of military film – he continued with yet another family study, *Toda Brother and his Sisters* (1941), which is untypical only in that it deals with an upper-class milieu and makes a brief reference to Manchuria. With the success abroad of his best-known film, *Tokyo Story* (1953), Ozu emerged from relative obscurity and the subsequent films seen in Europe confirmed that he and MIZOGUCHI are the Japanese cinema's supreme artists. If Ozu's later work is virtually a series of variations on the same theme, he invariably found new facets in his gallery of favourite characters – the old men who constantly get drunk in bars, business colleagues recalling their youth and war experiences, young newly-weds leaving a father or mother alone in the painful emptiness of a darkened room... *Tokyo Story* (1953), *Early Spring* (1956), *Late Autumn* (1960), *Early Autumn* (1961) and *An Autumn Afternoon* (1962) are full of such scenes and characters, with Ozu's dry, insistent humour constantly pricking away at human fallibility and deflating pomposity with a subtle twist of the plot. Although it is possible to find Ozu's vision of the world over-sentimentalized and predictable, it is hardly possible to deny him his unique quality and flavour. He was an artist who did what he had to do. JG

Above: So Yamamura (extreme left), Chishu Ryu (centre), Setsuko Hara (back) and Chiyeko Higashiyama (extreme right) in 'Tokyo Story' (Yasujiro Ozu, Japan, 1953)
Below: 'The Threepenny Opera' (G. W. Pabst, Germany, 1931)

Pabst, Georg W. (1885–1967)
Born Vienna, Austria. Director. His career began with acting and directing in the theatre. He started film-making during the early 1920s, his first film of consequence being *The Joyless Street* (1925), a study of a middle-class family during the post-war inflation in Vienna, featuring WERNER KRAUSS, ASTA NIELSEN and GRETA GARBO. Though this film was praised at the time for its realism it can more justly be described as a brilliant example of the romantic pessimism fashionable at that time in Germany, with its emphasis on depravity and the sadistic exploitation of the unfortunate by those in a position to avoid the effects of inflation. This powerful, melodramatic film was succeeded by the equally striking *Secrets of a Soul* (1926) – the dramatization of a typical case for psycho-analysis, a professor rendered impotent through experiencing extreme jealousy in his youth.

The Love of Jeanne Ney (1927), interesting for its fine editing and for its almost 'free-style' camerawork by FRITZ ARNO WAGNER, also gives melodramatic treatment to a story by Ilya Ehrenburg about the machinations of a sadistic anti-Communist agent, played by Fritz Rasp.

After making *Crisis* (1928), the story of a woman's self-destruction through sexual excess, he turned to a similar theme in *Pandora's Box* (1928), which featured LOUISE BROOKS in the part of a prostitute who becomes a victim of Jack the Ripper. Another silent film about sexual obsession featuring Louise Brooks was *The Diary of a Lost Girl* (1929). Pabst also directed (with Arnold Fanck) the mountain location film, *The White Hell of Piz Palü* (1929), with LENI RIEFENSTAHL. This took him away from the melancholy world of extremes in light and shadow with which he had become preoccupied.

With the coming of sound Pabst's romantic fatalism remained uppermost in *The Threepenny Opera* (1931), derived from Brecht's and Weill's play with songs which reset Gay's *The Beggar's Opera* in a stylized underworld located in 19th-century Germany. In the years remaining before Hitler's seizure of power Pabst made among others his two pacifist films, *Westfront 1918* (1930) and *Kameradschaft* (1931); in these he exploited the new combination of sight and sound in order to achieve the maximum realism – the 'new objectivity' as it was called. Much of this was achieved through meticulous studio reconstruction (with the skilful help of the art director, ERNO METZNER) and the camera of Wagner, especially the scenes of no-man's-land in *Westfront 1918* and the shafts and galleries of the mine in *Kameradschaft*.

During his exile from Germany (1933–9) Pabst's work deteriorated. After making *Don Quixote* in France he produced a series of indifferent films in France and the USA before making his much criticized return to Hitler's Germany (in fact to Pabst's native Austria) on the eve of the war. It had been thought that his ostensibly left-wing views would have forbidden this, but it would appear that he was more of a romantic than a dedicated socialist. His films produced under the Nazis are relatively minor and virtually non-political, the best being the period film *Paracelsus* (1943), made in Prague with WERNER KRAUSS.

After the war he attempted when over 60 to come back to prominence with *The Trial* (1948), a study of anti-Semitism; a film about the last days of Hitler, *Ten Days to Die* (1954); and *The Jackboot Mutiny* (1955), an account of the attempt on Hitler's life in July 1944. These films, though presented in a semi-documentary style, are sober records rather than penetrating interpretations of these significant events in Nazi history. RM

Page, Geraldine

Born 1924 in USA. Actress, who performs mostly on the stage. Her films include *Hondo* (1954), *Sweet Bird of Youth* (1962), *The Happiest Millionaire* and *You're a Big Boy Now* (1967), and *Whatever Happened to Aunt Alice?* (1969), *The Beguiled* (1971).

Pagnol, Marcel

Born in 1895 in Marseilles, France. Playwright and director, who brought a storm of abuse on his head from the film aestheticians when, with the arrival of sound film, he proposed to have his successful stage plays filmed. His initial essays in film, *Marius* (ALEXANDER KORDA) and *Fanny* (MARC ALLÉGRET) both 1932, proved like their successors brilliant vehicles for the character acting of RAIMU, Charpin, FERNANDEL and others in stories located in Marseilles and the countryside in the south of France. Here he set up his own studio, drawing on the talent of the Marseilles music-hall, from which both Raimu and Fernandel came. Audiences were delighted by his films, all of which he scripted himself from various literary and dramatic sources, and in certain cases directed himself, such as *César* (1936), *Joffroi* (1934), *Merlusse* (1936), *Regain* (1937), *La Femme du Boulanger* (1939), *La Fille du Puisatier* (1940), *Naïs* (1945), *La Belle Meunière* (1948), *Topaze* (1951) and others. RM

Painlevé, Jean

Born 1902 in Paris, France. Scientific film director. The son of a mathematician, Painlevé has very varied interests. Motor-racing champion, underwater diver, biologist, he was first attracted to the avant-garde and surrealism in the cinema, and he brings his own form of poetry and fantasy to his meticulously made scientific films. His finest work has centred on underwater life, notably in *La Pieuvre* (1928), *Crevettes* (1930), *L'Hippocampe* (1934) and *Assassins d'Eau Douce* (1947). His other films include *Le Bernard-l'Hermite* (1930), *La Quatrième Dimension* and *Barbe-Bleue* (1937) and *Le Vampire* (1945). During the war he was a member of the underground Comité de Libération du Cinéma Français. After the war he was for a brief period appointed Commissioner to the Government Film Department, but soon resigned, though he was partly responsible for the official film *Le Journal de la Résistance* (1945). He collaborated with GEORGES ROUQUIER on *L'Oeuvre Scientifique de Pasteur* (1947). RM

Above: 'The Time Machine' (George Pal, USA, 1960)
Below: Geraldine Page and Paul Newman in 'Sweet Bird of Youth' (Richard Brooks, USA, 1962)

Pakistan

See ASIAN FILM

Pal, George

Born 1908 in Ceglad, Hungary. Animator, and later feature producer in Hollywood. During the 1930s he produced ingenious puppet advertising films in Holland and Britain, notably *On Parade* (1936), *What Ho! She Bumps* (1937) and *Sky Pirates* (1938), all for Horlicks. He used wire-jointed puppets with wooden heads, highly stylized in design, which were adjusted for pose and expression between the takes of stop-motion photography. He went to Hollywood in 1940, where he produced his Puppetoon series, including *Jasper goes Hunting* (1944), *Jasper's Close Shave (The Barber of Seville*, 1945). He received a special Academy Award in 1943 for discovering a new technique for animated films, which included combining animation with live action, and he also made instructional films for Shell Oil.

In Hollywood he developed a second career as the producer of feature films which involved special effects, for which many received Academy Awards. These included *Destination Moon* (1950), *When Worlds Collide* (1951), and *War of the Worlds* (1953), and he both produced and directed *tom thumb* (1958), *The Time Machine* (1960) and, for Cinerama, *The Wonderful World of the Brothers Grimm* (1963). RM

Palance, Jack
Born 1920 in Lattimer, Pennsylvania, USA. Actor, who has been a prize fighter and has served in the US Air Corps. His grimly gaunt features mainly type-cast him in villainous parts. His films include: *Shane* (1953), *The Big Knife* (1955), *Attack* (1956), *The Lonely Man* (1957), *The Mongols* (1960), *Barabbas* (1962), *Le Mépris* (1963), *Once a Thief* (1965), *The Professionals* (1966), *Che!* and *The Desperados* (1969), *Monte Walsh* (1970); also the television series *The Greatest Show on Earth*. He appeared on Broadway in 'A Streetcar named Desire'.

Palma, Carlo Di
See DI PALMA

Pan, Hermes
Born 1910 in USA. Greek-American dancer and choreographer, whose father was the Greek Consul-General in Washington, where his son first acquired an interest in dancing. In the 1930s in Hollywood he worked principally on the FRED ASTAIRE/GINGER ROGERS musicals and later arranged the dance routines for many of the major stage show film adaptations, including *Pal Joey* (1957), *Porgy and Bess* (1959), *My Fair Lady* (1964) and *Finian's Rainbow* (1968). He has also appeared as a dancer in several films including *My Gal Sal* (1942).

Pan (Panorama)
A sweeping panoramic shot accomplished by rotating the camera horizontally while shooting. In animation the effect is achieved by moving the background past the camera.

Panchromatic
Photographic material sensitive to the entire visible spectrum including red

Panning Shot
See PAN

Parallax
The difference between the image seen through the view finder and the image recorded by the lens, due to the lens and viewfinder being in different positions.

Parallel Development
The development of two pieces of action simultaneously, in which a fragment of one and then a fragment of the other are shown alternately.

Pascal, Gabriel (1894–1954)
Born in Transylvania, Romania. Central European producer and director who emigrated to Britain in the middle 1930s and cornered the market in film adaptations of Bernard Shaw's plays, after first building up an equable relationship with the unpredictable playwright. His first two Shaw films, *Pygmalion* (1938) – which he produced and ANTHONY ASQUITH directed – and *Major Barbara* (1940), which he both produced and directed himself, were fairly pedestrian but faithful to the originals. In 1946 *Caesar and Cleopatra* was, relative to the times, almost as costly a production as Fox's *Cleopatra* 16 years later. In 1952 he made *Androcles and the Lion* in Hollywood.

Above: Orson Welles (with cigar) in 'La Ricotta' (Pier Paolo Pasolini's episode of 'Rogopag', Italy, 1962)
Below: Jack Palance in 'The McMasters . . . Tougher than the West Itself' (Alf Kjellin, USA, 1969)

Pasolini, Pier Paolo
Born 1922 in Bologna, Italy. Most influential and original of the younger Italian writer-directors to have emerged since the demise of the neo-realist movement. A Marxist, he yet created the finest screen 'life' of Christ, *The Gospel According to St Matthew* (1964). His seemingly contradictory concern with Communist philosophy and religious enigma is very much in keeping with Italian intellectual thinking.

A contentious figure at odds with the Catholic Church, his films often celebrate peasant (i.e. primitive) standards to the detriment of the *petite bourgeoisie* which is Pasolini's *bête noire*. After the urban realism of his first two films as writer and director, *Accattone* (1961) and *Mamma Roma* (1962), he has become increasingly absorbed in the re-interpretation of significant myths, as in *Edipo Re* (1967) and *Medea* (1969), related to a contemporary viewpoint.

A prolific writer – of poetry and novels – before he became a director, Pasolini collaborated on the screenplays of many films, including *La Donna del Fiume* (1954), *Le Notti di Cabiria* (1957), *Morte Di Un Amico* (1960). With *Accattone*, he worked with a non-professional cast and prefers not to use actors or experienced extras unless absolutely necessary. In 1968, his *Theorem* – the first of his films to be placed in a *bourgeois* setting among affluent middle-class people – caused a scandal which brought upon him the wrath of the conservative wing of the Church, supposedly for equating religious experience with sex. In the ambiguous *Porcile* (1969) he delved deeply into the metaphysics of survival and political hypocrisy, through the shock tactics of cannibalism and bestiality.

Other films include: episodes in *Rogopag* (1962), *La Rabbia* (1963), *Comizi D'Amore* and *Sopraluoghi in Palestina* (1964), an episode in *Le Streghe* (1965), *Uccellacci e Uccellini* (1966), an episode in *Capriccio all'Italiana* (1967), an episode in *Love and Anger* (1967–9), *Decameron* (1971), *The Canterbury Tales* (made in England, 1972). See 'Pasolini' by the late Oswald Stack (1969). MH

Passer, Ivan
Born 1923 in Prague, Czechoslovakia. One of the most interesting young directors of the Czech *nouvelle vague* of the 1960s, Passer began his career as assistant to Brynych and Jasný, then co-scripted all MILOŠ FORMAN's films. His own *A Boring Afternoon* (short, 1964) and *Intimate Lighting* (1966) revealed that he shared Forman's gift for observing the absurd trivia of everyday life. Like Forman, he has recently moved to the United States, making *Born to Win* (1971), a characteristically quirky study of a drug addict.

Pasternak, Joe
Born 1901 in Szilagysomlyo, Hungary. Traditional Hollywood producer with a European background, who for over two decades unerringly judged the public taste for sentimental romances and exuberant musicals. He is credited with discovering DEANNA DURBIN, JUDY GARLAND and the temperamental, but phenomenally popular, actor-tenor Mario Lanza. Principal films: *Three Smart Girls* (1936), *Destry Rides Again* (1939), *Thousands Cheer* (1943), *Anchors Aweigh* (1945), *In the Good Old Summertime* (1948), *The Great Caruso* (1951), *The Merry Widow* (1952), *The Student Prince* (1954), *This Could Be The Night* (1957), *Jumbo* (1962), *Penelope* (1966).
He published his autobiography 'Easy The Hard Way' in 1956. MH

Pastrone, Giovanni (1882–1959)
Born in Italy. Pioneer Italian director, who worked under the professional name of Piero Fosco. He is remembered primarily as the director of the most celebrated of all the early Italian spectacular films, *Cabiria* (1913), which had a script by Gabriele d'Annunzio and a story set in the period of the Punic wars. He attempted to set standards of archaeological accuracy by conducting research for the film in the Louvre. He also made a star for the Italian cinema in this film, the former Genoese docker who came to be known as Maciste, the giant and strong man who featured under that name in the Maciste cycle of films of which Pastrone directed a number: *Maciste* (1915), *Maciste Alpino* (1916), *Maciste Atleta* (1918). Pastrone also directed *Il Fuoco*(*The Fire*, 1915), in which he made an early attempt to reduce the number of title cards for the audience to read, and *Hedda Gabler* (1919). He retired during the early 1920s.

Pathé, Charles (1863–1957)
Born in Chevry-Cossigny, France. The first great industrialist of the cinema, Pathé began his career exhibiting the EDISON phonograph in fairgrounds. From this he quickly moved on to counterfeiting phonographs and kinetoscopes; and in 1896 began the manufacture of a camera and projector devised by Henri Joly. By 1902 Pathé had built a large studio at Vincennes and embarked seriously on the production of films with a notable team of pioneer film directors, including Lorant Heilbronn, Georges Hatot, André Heuze, LOUIS GASNIER, ALBERT CAPELLANI, Gaston Velle, Charles Lepine, Segundo Chomon and FERDINAND ZECCA. By 1908 he had built up a massive industrial empire which extended vertically to comprehend every aspect of the manufacture of film stock and equipment, the production, distribution and exhibition of films; and horizontally to include agencies or filials in London, Moscow, Brussels, Berlin, St Petersburg, Amsterdam, Barcelona, Milan, Budapest, Calcutta and Singapore. In 1907–8, the year in which Pathé led the industry in abandoning totally the outright sale of films in favour of film hire, Pathé paid a 90% dividend and showed a profit of 8½ million francs. The monopolistic domination of the French cinema was already being threatened – notably from the USA – by the start of the First World War; and the War itself proved disastrous. Pathé began a gradual dismemberment of his empire from within; and the entire cinema suffered from the repercussions. With the coming of sound, Pathé, who had long ceased his production activities, went into partnership with Natan (Bernard Tannenzaft); and when Natan failed and faced criminal charges, Pathé suffered with him. Retired after 1930 to private life at Monaco, he lived to the ripe age of 94. DR

Paul, Robert W. (1870–1943)
Pioneer British cinematographer; the first Englishman to bring the film into commercial exhibition. A scientific instrument-maker, he is said to have projected motion pictures as early as February 1895 at his London workshop in Hatton Garden. On 20 February 1896 he demonstrated his Theatrograph at the Finsbury Technical College. (Birt Acres, another pioneer in Britain, had demonstrated his motion pictures to the Royal Photographic Society on 14 January 1896.) In March 1896, Paul gave commercial exhibitions of movies at Olympia, while in the same month Birt Acres did the same in Piccadilly. On 25 March, Paul's apparatus was moved to the Alhambra, London, to give further demonstrations. He established his celebrated glass studio at Sydney Road, New Southgate, London in 1899; it had a glass roof and sliding doors, and a well-equipped stage. His films were sold internationally and were very influential during the period in which the British film-making industry was being established. He filmed the Derby race-meeting in 1896, the Delhi Durbar in 1903, made comedies (such as *A Soldier's Courtship*, 1896), 'interest' films (see DOCUMENTARY), an *Army Life* series, travelogues, vaudeville films, and, from 1902, the trick films such as *The ? Motorist* (1905) for which he was most famous. Several of his films survive. He was essentially a technician in his approach; his interest lay in the techniques of cinematography, rather than in the art of the film. He retired from film-making around 1910. RM

Pearson, George
Born 1875 in London, England. Director. Originally a teacher, Pearson was 37 years old when he decided in 1912 to work in the cinema. After making a number of independent travel documentaries (*Through Fair Sussex*, 1912), he joined the Samuelson Studios as a director, his films including *Christmas Day in the Workhouse* (1914) and *John Halifax, Gentleman* (1915). Between 1915 and 1917 he made the *Ultus* serials, an English equivalent to the FEUILLADE mystery films. His greatest successes though were the many films he made with Betty Balfour as his star, most notably the *Squibs* series, about a London flower girl. Later films included *Huntingtower* (1927), *A Shot in the Dark* (1934), *Gentleman's Agreement* (1935) and *The Fatal Hour* (1937). Between 1940 and 1955 he directed numerous documentaries for the Colonial Film Unit. When the British cinema was at its lowest ebb in the 1920s and early 1930s the decent, uncompromised standards of Pearson's Welsh-Pearson company often seemed its only life-line. DR

Peck, Gregory
Born 1916 in California, USA. Actor, on stage from 1938 to 1944; since then his tall figure and reliable, if somewhat repetitious, characterizations of men under stress, have gained him much popularity. His many films include: *The Keys of the Kingdom* (1944), *Spellbound* (1945), *The Paradine Case* and *Duel in the Sun* (1947), *Gentleman's Agreement* (1948), *Twelve O'clock High* (1949), *The Gunfighter* (1950), *David and*

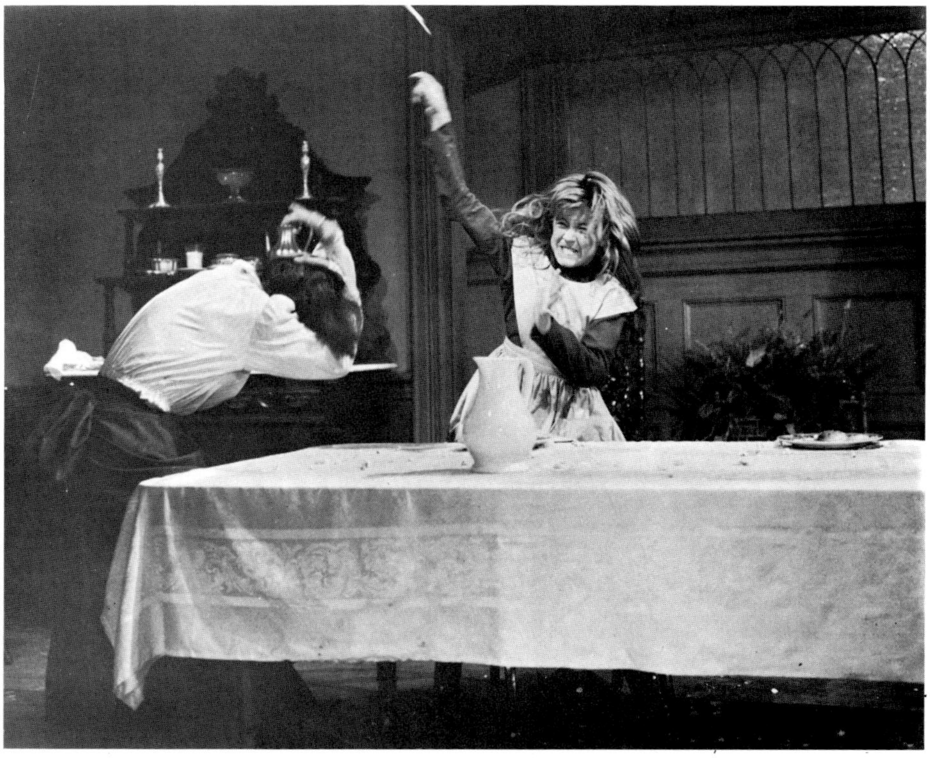

Above: Gregory Peck in 'Gentleman's Agreement' (Elia Kazan, USA, 1947)
Below: Anne Bancroft and Patty Duke in 'The Miracle Worker' (Arthur Penn, USA, 1962)

Bathsheba and *Captain Horatio Hornblower* (1951), *The Snows of Kilimanjaro* (1952), *Roman Holiday* (1953), *The Million Pound Note* (1954), *Moby Dick* (1956), *The Big Country* (1958), *Beloved Infidel* and *On the Beach* (1959), *The Guns of Navarone* (1961), *How the West was Won* (1962), *To Kill a Mockingbird* (1963), *Mirage* (1965), *Arabesque* (1966), *Marooned* (1969), *I Walk the Line* (1970).

Peckinpah, Sam
Born 1926 in California, USA. Leading American film and television writer and director whose ruthless, intelligent Western-type dramas introduced a fashionably neurotic undercurrent to the genre. Since he is part Indian and part pioneer Californian, his feeling for the West is rooted in memory and family background. A personal rebel often at odds with the studio-bound executives, he finally broke the back of the opposition with his bloody tribute to a dying breed of Western gunfighter in *The Wild Bunch* (1969), which was also a box-office success. But his most impeccable Western so far remains *Guns in the Afternoon* (1961) – titled *Ride the High Country* in America – in which he sympathetically portrayed the melancholy memories and dying fall of two veterans of the West, appropriately played by two real veterans, JOEL MCCREA and RANDOLPH SCOTT. He has also made several movies-for-television and scripted other director's projects, notably *The Glory Guys* (1965) and *Villa Rides* (1969).

Other principal films: *The Deadly Companions* (1962), *Major Dundee* (1965), *The Ballad of Cable Hogue* (1970). But his obsession with the urges that produce violence over-reached itself in *Straw Dogs* (1971) in which he disastrously attempted to place a Western theme in a Cornish setting. MH

Peg Bar
In animation. A flat metal bar from which protrude pegs which exactly fit the registration holes punched in all art work, and which are identical with the rostrum camera pegs, thus enabling them to be kept in proper relation to each other.

Penn, Arthur
Born 1922 in Philadelphia, USA. Television and theatre trained American director whose films most strikingly reflect the contemporary fascination with violence and anti-heroic myths. Previously a connoisseur's film-maker, Penn became a popular, as well as a critical, success with *Bonnie and Clyde* (1967), which re-created the traditional Hollywood gangster film as legend in the light of modern hindsight.

Yet the groundwork for *Bonnie and Clyde* had been laid in Penn's provocative portrait of Billy the Kid in *The Left-Handed Gun* (1958), which depicted the outlaw as an emotionally disturbed 'rebel' instead of a one-track ruthless killer, and in the ambiguous *Mickey One* (1964), a Kafka-esque tale of pursuit and destruction.

With no more than a handful of films, Penn has established himself in the forefront of international directors: although he has been severely criticized for gratuitous horror. In a documentary by Robert P. S. B. Hughes, *Arthur Penn, 1922— : Themes and Variants* (1970), Penn insisted that violence is part of the times and cannot be ignored.

In 1951, Penn went into television as a floor-manager and within a few years was directing a series of plays. When the creative urge went out of American television, Penn made *The Left-Handed Gun* for Warners. The experience, under the then still potent studio system, was unsatisfactory. He went into the theatre, where he directed many hit plays and it was a filmed play, *The Miracle Worker* (1962), the story of Helen Keller, which brought him back to films. Under SAM SPIEGEL he made *The Chase* (1966), and the film seems more Spiegel's than Penn's. Penn's association with WARREN BEATTY in *Mickey One* led to his most fully realized film, *Bonnie and Clyde*.

Penn followed this with a superficially different but fundamentally similar tale of youthful revolt in the 1960s, Arlo Guthrie's *Alice's Restaurant* (1969). And in *Little Big Man* (1971) he returned again to the 19th-century West for another study of an outsize legend, the American Indian and Custer's last stand.

See also 'Arthur Penn' by Robin Wood (1967). MH

Pennebaker, D. A.
Born in USA. Foremost American factual film-maker in the *cinéma-vérité* style, he worked originally with the MAYSLES and RICHARD LEACOCK. Beginning in 1953 with *Daybreak Express*, his characteristic technique became to take his chosen subjects as they came, recording them with camera and synchronized sound. His films include: *Opening in Moscow* (1959), *Primary* (1960, with Leacock, Al Maysles and others), *David* (1961, on the rehabilitation of a dope addict), *Susan Starr* (1962), *Jane* (1962, with Leacock and others; a film about JANE FONDA), *Don't Look Back* (1966, on Bob Dylan's tour of England), *Monterey Pop* (1968). In 1969 he edited and completed GODARD's film shot in the USA, *1 PM*, and made another large-scale coverage of a musical event, *Sweet Toronto* (1970). RM

Perforation
One of the holes punched in the film which are used for transporting the film through the apparatus in which it is intended to be used.

Périer, François
Born 1919 in Paris, France. Actor. His distinctive and expressive face, not conventionally handsome, became one of the more familiar in the French cinema from the late 1930s. His many films have included: *Hotel du Nord* (1938), *Le Silence est d'Or* (1948), *Orphée* (1949), *Gervaise* (1955), and the Italian *Nights of Cabiria* (1956).

Peries, Lester James
Born 1919 in Ceylon. Originally a journalist working in both Colombo and (1947–52) in London. Influenced by Lionel Wendt, the distinguished aesthete and photographer in Ceylon, Peries began film-making as an amateur while in London. His first film *Soliloquy* (1949), a short experimental film on the subconscious thoughts of a painter, was followed by others which won him awards in amateur competitions. He next joined RALPH KEENE as an assistant at the Ceylon Government Film Unit, directing documentaries, including *Conquest in the Dry Zone* (1954), on malaria. He continues to make documentaries alongside his feature films, the first of which, *Rekava* (1956), an evocative location film set in the villages of Ceylon, won international recognition and distribution; it represented for Peries and his cameraman, William Blake, a courageous challenge to the dead conventions of Sinhalese film-making. Peries's sensitive direction of actors, all virtually amateur in Ceylon, is seen in all his features: these include *Gamperalaia* (*The Changing Countryside*, 1964), which won the Grand Prix at New Delhi, *Delovak Athara* (*Between Two Worlds*, 1966), in which a wealthy young man is led to face certain moral issues in his life and conduct, *Ran Salu* (*The Yellow Robes*, 1961), *Golu Hadawatha* (*The Silence of the Heart*, 1968), his first box-office success, and *Akkara Paha* (*Five Acres*, 1969), a study of the relation of 'sophisticated' life in Ceylon to the less advanced life of the 'emergent' people. Peries is concerned to reveal always the thoughts of his characters; his films therefore move slowly, like the people he portrays. Though he has been termed by LINDSAY ANDERSON, 'that lonely artist in Ceylon', Peries's international status has enabled him to touch on (rather than face fully) subjects normally repressed by Ceylon's rigid censorship: caste, creed, and sex relations. Latest film *Nidhanaya* (1971). RM

Périnal, Georges (1897–1965)
Born in Paris, France. Cinematographer. His career divides into two main parts: in France with FEYDER (*Les Nouveaux Messieurs*, 1928), COCTEAU (*Le Sang d'un poète*, 1930) and CLAIR (*Sous les toits de Paris*, 1930; *Le Million*, 1931; *Quatorze Juillet*, 1932); and in England with KORDA's London Film Productions, including *The Private Life of Henry VIII* (1933), *The Private Life of Don Juan* (1934), *Things to Come* and *Rembrandt* (1936), *Under the Red Robe* (with JAMES WONG HOWE, 1937), *The Four Feathers* (1939), *The Thief of Bagdad* (1940). His airy, Gallic style perfectly set off Clair's comic fantasies as well as Korda's richly detailed period pieces. He worked with many other directors including MICHAEL POWELL and PRESSBURGER (*The Life and Death of Colonel Blimp*, 1943), REED (*The Fallen Idol*, 1948), PREMINGER (*Saint Joan*, 1957; *Bonjour Tristesse*, 1957) and MINNELLI (*The Four Horsemen of the Apocalypse*, 1961). JG

Top: Anthony Perkins in 'The Trial' (Orson Welles, France-Italy-W. Germany, 1962)
Above: Richard Benjamin and Carrie Snodgrass in 'Diary of a Mad Housewife' (Frank Perry, USA, 1970)
Below: Gamini Fonseka and Malini Fonseka in 'Nidhanaya' (Lester James Peries, Ceylon, 1971)

Perkins, Anthony
Born 1932 in New York City, USA. American actor, on stage, television and in films. Film début in *The Actress* (1953); subsequent films include: *Friendly Persuasion* (1956), *Desire under the Elms* (1957), *The Matchmaker* (1958), *On the Beach* (1959), *Psycho* (1960), *Phaedra* (1962), *The Trial* (1962), *Catch 22* and *Hall of Mirrors* (1969), *WUSA* and *La Decade Prodigieuse* (1971). His nervous, friendly yet slightly sinister acting-style was well used by HITCHCOCK and WELLES.

Perry, Frank
Born 1930 in USA. Fashionable American director, formerly theatre director, who with his writer-wife Eleanor Perry produced in 1963 a sincere film about a pair of mentally disturbed youngsters, *David and Lisa*, which was highly regarded as much for its small budget and independence of Hollywood as for its achievement. Since then his smart-serious treatment of contemporary American subjects has been increasingly slick but also increasingly entertaining. He is a leading member of the East Coast, as distinct from West Coast, school of

commercial film-makers. Main films include: *The Swimmer* (1968), *Last Summer* (1969), *Diary of a Mad Housewife* (1970), *Doc* (1971).

Persistence of Vision
The property possessed by the eye of retaining one image for a period of time after the light stimulus is removed, thus making it possible to eliminate visible discontinuity in the intermittent projection of film.

Petersen, Sidney
Born 1912 in Oakland, California, USA. Avant-garde film-maker. Based on San Francisco, Petersen began his career with *The Potted Psalm* (1946), a spill-over of images, beautiful individually but collectively incoherent. Working as a teacher of film-making at the California School of Fine Arts, Petersen produced a series of films including *The Lead Shoes*, a 16mm sound film – a surreal story accompanying two old English ballads set to jazz. Petersen gave up film-making in 1950 and is currently living in England.

Petri, Elio
Born 1929 in Rome, Italy. Following the outstanding success of his first two films, *L'Assassino* (1961) and *I giorni contati* (1962) much of Petri's work seemed compromised by commercial exigencies, although the intelligent *A ciascuno il suo* (1967) seemed to mark a return to his original form. Other films: *Il maestro di Vigevano* (1963), *La decima vittima* (*The Tenth Victim*, 1965), *Tre pistole contro Cesare* (1967), *A Quiet Place in the Country* (1968) and *Investigation of a Citizen above Suspicion* (1970), which was highly though of for its satirical look at the morality of justice.

Philipe, Gérard (1922–1959)
Born in Cannes, France. Archetypal sensitive French hero and imaginative stage and screen actor who sprang to prominence in films immediately after the Second World War, with his performance as the love-sick schoolboy in *Le Diable au Corps* (1947). Though he tended to be typed in similar roles, he also displayed an attractive sense of comedy in *La Beauté du Diable* (1949), *La Ronde* (1950) and *Fanfan la Tulipe* (1951). Other notable films: *Knave of Hearts* (1953), *Le Rouge et le Noir* (1954), *Les Grandes Manœuvres* (1955), *Les Liaisons Dangereuses* (1959).

Above: Werner Krauss and Edith Bosca in 'Scherben' (Lupu Pick, Germany, 1921)
Opposite: Douglas Fairbanks Sr and Mary Pickford in 'The Taming of the Shrew' (Sam Taylor, USA, 1929)
Below: Marcello Mastroianni in 'L' Assassino' (Elio Petri, Italy, 1961)

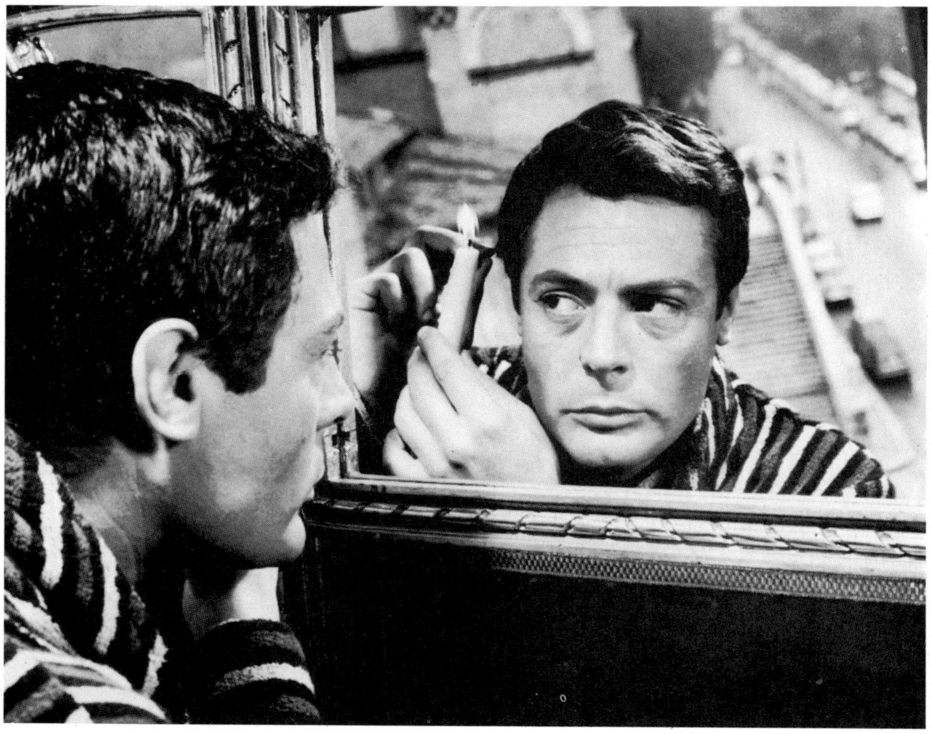

Photo-Electric-Cell (PEC)
A device for converting variations of light into corresponding variations of electrical current.

Pick, Lupu (1886–1931)
Born in Romania. Director, working largely in the German silent cinema. He began his career as an actor, appearing with Reinhardt's company; he acted notably in LENI's film *Waxworks* (1924) and LANG's *The Spy* (1928), as well as appearing in the film he directed himself, *Der Dummkopf* (1920). His best films as director were scripted by CARL MAYER: *Scherben* (*Shattered*, 1921) and *Sylvester* (*New Year's Eve*, 1923), in which he and Mayer experimented with using little or no titling. Mayer's other script in this series, known in English as *The Last Laugh*, was intended to complete a trilogy of the *Kammerspiel*, or intimate-style films depending on psychological issues, but he and Pick differed over the treatment, and MURNAU took the subject over, becoming, like Pick, a key exponent in this branch of German silent cinema. Pick's later films were less effective, and included *Napoleon auf St Helena* (1929), *One Night in London* (1928), and a sound film, *Gassenhauer* (1931). RM

Pickford, Mary
Born 1893 in Toronto. Real name: Gladys Mary Smith. After the death of her father when she was three, Mary Pickford became the family's principal breadwinner, working as a child actress. In 1907 she joined David Belasco, who changed her name and gave her work on Broadway. Only with some shame did she fill in with jobs in films, first acting for GRIFFITH at Biograph in 1909. She suited perfectly Griffith's taste for Victorian Cinderella figures; and her own sacrificed childhood and premature responsibilities gave a special poignancy to her portrayals in *The New York Hat* (1912), *Tess of the Storm Country* and *Cinderella* (1914), *Rags* (1915), *A Poor Little Rich Girl* and *Rebecca of Sunnybrook Farm* (1917) and innumerable other roles of the same genre, at first under Griffith's tutelage at Biograph; and later, after 1913, with other directors and producers (like the excellent MARSHALL NEILAN), but always with her own dominating supervision of her work. She was a conscious actress of fine instincts, highly developed intelligence and skill, a great fund of comedy and a unique and immediate appeal to the large popular audience of the time.

She was also – with the guidance of her mother – a formidable and astute business woman, who knew very well her value at the box office, and how to exploit it. In pursuit of ever higher salaries and greater independence she moved from company to company, with tough business men like ADOLPH ZUKOR helpless before her demands. The astronomical monetary value of her services revolutionized indus-

try economics. Finally in 1919, along with CHAPLIN, GRIFFITH and FAIRBANKS, likewise artists whom no company could afford to employ, she formed United Artists, through which all her subsequent films were distributed. She constantly tried to realize her full potential as an actress; but the public as constantly forced her back into the child roles in which they had first loved her: *Daddy Long Legs* and *Pollyanna* (1919), *Little Lord Fauntleroy* (1921), *Little Annie Rooney* (1925), *Sparrows* (1926) – rejecting her in more mature roles like *Rosita* (1923) and *Dorothy Vernon of Haddon Hall* (1924). By the time of talking pictures, threatened with the fate of becoming a monstrous phenomenon – a mature woman always playing child roles; a Victorian Cinderella lingering in the Jazz Age – she had little alternative but to retire, forever enshrined in her own legend, after making a few sound films like the lively Shakespearean adaptation *The Taming of the Shrew* (1929). DR

Piel, Harry
Born 1892 in Düsseldorf, Germany. Known as 'the German Douglas Fairbanks', Harry Piel entered the cinema in 1915, and starred in a long series of thrillers, many of which he directed himself. Despite the penny-dreadful level of their conception, Piel's films enjoyed enormous success throughout continental Europe in the immediate post-war era. Later Piel concentrated on directing, and was responsible for one of MARLENE DIETRICH's earliest films, *Sein grösster Bluff* (1927). His last film was *Der Tiger Akbar* (1951).

Pinter, Harold
Born 1930 in London, England. Gifted, contemporary writer and actor, whose plays and screenplays are particularly well suited to the modern screen. His spare plots, involving the interplay of a few characters, and deceptively uncommunicative word-play, (disguising undercurrents of alarming emotion), have established him as a key figure in the British theatre and film world. Son of a Jewish tailor in London's East End, he studied to be an actor, then concentrated on writing plays, two of which – *The Caretaker* (1963) and *The Birthday Party* (1969) – have been filmed and most of which have been seen on television. As a screenwriter he has worked most consistently and usefully with director JOSEPH LOSEY, providing the film adaptations for *The Servant* (1963), *Accident* (1967), and *The Go-Between* (1971). He also scripted *The Pumpkin-Eater* (1963). As a screen actor he appears, not very impressively, in *The Rise and Rise of Michael Rimmer* (1970).

A study of his work by Martin Esslin, 'The Peopled Wound', was published in 1970. MH

Pintoff, Ernest
Born 1931 in New York, USA. Animation, and latterly live action director. Created the character of *Flebus* (1956) for Terrytoons, the year he joined UPA. Later, as an independent animator, he made his uniquely funny series of cartoons with their entirely individual humour: *The Violinist* (1959), *The Interview* (1961), *The Critic* and *The Old Man and the Flower* (1962). Since these films, Pintoff has turned to live action film-making with the expressionist short, *The Shoes*, and the feature, *Harvey Middleman, Fireman* (1964), which he wrote and directed. Latest film *Dynamite Chicken* (1971).

Pitts, ZaSu (1900–1963)
Born in Parsons, Kansas, USA. Actress. Began in movies in small parts including several MARY PICKFORD films c. 1917. Equally adept in the silent and sound periods, she soon created her perennial screen image of the put-upon, slightly dowdy spinster with the strange sing-song voice, yet capable of a snappy reply when necessary. Her silent roles included BORZAGE's excellent *Lazybones* (1925), but it was ERICH VON STROHEIM who completely transformed her when he cast her as Trina in *Greed* (1923) and later as the crippled bride in *The Wedding March* (1927), performances which suggested a deeper, tragic gift. She also appeared in Stroheim's recently revived sound film, *Hello, Sister* (*Walking Down Broadway*, 1933). Her talents as a comedienne were intermittently used in

Top: ZaSu Pitts in 'Greed' (Erich von Stroheim, USA, 1923)
Above: Del Walker, Anne Gooding and Sam Shepherd in 'Bronco Bullfrog' (Barney Platts-Mills, GB, 1970)

the 1930s and 1940s as in *Mrs Wiggs of the Cabbage Patch* (1934) and *Ruggles of Red Gap* (1934). She played small parts up to her death, but it is the Stroheim performances which ensure her a firm place in film history. JG

Planer, Franz (1894–1963)
Born in Karlovy Vary, Czechoslovakia. Cinematographer. After becoming lighting cameraman in 1920 in Germany, he worked in many European countries before coming to America in 1937. A brilliant black-and-white artist with a very mobile style, he was especially attuned to MAX OPHÜLS with whom he worked on *Liebelei* (1933), *The Exile* (1947), *Letter from an Unknown Woman* (where he re-created his European-style lighting, 1948). Other work showing his fine atmospheric sense and, latterly, use of colour include *Maskerade* (1934), *Criss Cross* (1949), *711 Ocean Drive* (1950), *Death of a Salesman* (1951), *Decision Before Dawn* (1951), *Roman Holiday* (1953), *The Pride and the Passion* (1957), *Stage Struck* and *The Big Country* (1958), *King of Kings* and *Breakfast at Tiffany's* (1961). JG

Platts-Mills, Barney
Born 1944 in Colchester, England. Director. Started in films as an assistant editor on both theatrical and television subjects. Made two documentaries and, aided by a loan from a merchant bank, directed his first feature, *Bronco Bullfrog*, in 1970. This study of young people in the East End of London, alternately sad, wry and funny, caused much critical interest but received limited distribution. His second feature, *Private Road* (1971), this time in colour and with some professional players, was a sensitive warm-hearted study of a young couple's affair and their relationship with their 'drop-out' friends and non-comprehending parents. Platts-Mills is one of the most talented of the younger generation of British film-makers, seemingly unaffected by the flashy stylistic predilections of his colleagues. In an effort to overcome the inadequate distribution outlets for his kind of independent film, he and his company organized the exhibition of *Private Road* themselves. JG

Play back
The reproduction of a sound track on a set so that the picture can be synchronized with sound already recorded.

Pleasence, Donald
Born 1919 in Worksop, England. Actor, who was first in repertory and made his name on the stage before he appeared on the screen. Served with the RAF in the Second World War. Essentially a character actor, he can give highly introspective interpretations, which are intense and disturbing. His films include: *Manuela* (1957), *No Love for Johnnie* (1961), *The Caretaker* (*The Guest*) and *The Great Escape* (1963), *The Greatest Story Ever Told* (1965), *Cul de Sac* and *Matchless* (1966), *The Night of the Generals*, *You Only Live Twice* and *Eye of the Devil* (1967), *Mr. Freedom* (1968), *Outback* (1970), *The Pied Piper of Hamelin* (1972).

Plummer, Christopher
Born 1927 in Toronto, Canada. Actor, who first toured in repertory. Has acted in many Shakespearean productions and appeared in Shakespeare Festivals in USA and Canada. His film début was in 1958 in *Stage Struck*, and since then he has made *The Fall of the Roman Empire* (1964), *The Sound of Music* and *Inside Daisy Clover* (1965), *The Night of the Generals* and *Oedipus the King* (1967), *Lock up your Daughters*, *The Royal Hunt of the Sun*, *The Battle of Britain* and *Waterloo* (1969), and other films.

Poirier, Léon (1884–1968)
Born in Paris, France. Director. Coming from the theatre and the Parisian intellectual côteries, Poirier brought a totally new approach to film-making when he joined the Gaumont studios in 1913. Throughout his career he tended to express, in a highly individual manner, a preference for the literary and academic film, and a fascination with documentary and the exotic. Films include *Cadette* (1913), *Âmes d'Orient* (1919), *Narayana* (1920), *Geneviève* and *L'affaire du Courrier de Lyon* (1923), *La Brière* (1924), *La croisière noire* (1925), *Verdun, vision d'histoire* (1927), *Cain* (1929), *La folle nuit* (1932), *L'appel du silence* (1936), *Sœurs d'armes* (1937). Poirier's last film was *La route inconnue* (1948).

Poitier, Sidney
Born 1924 in USA. Negro actor. He first appeared in stage productions, including Broadway plays, and began his screen career in 1950 in *No Way Out*. He soon became well liked for his sympathetic, if consciously liberal, performances, and continued with such films as *Cry the Beloved Country* (1952), *The Blackboard Jungle* (1955), *A Man is Ten Feet Tall* (*The Edge of the City*, 1956), *The Defiant Ones* (1958), *Porgy and Bess* (1959), *A Raisin in the Sun* (1960), *Lilies of the Field* (1963), *The Long Ships* (1964),

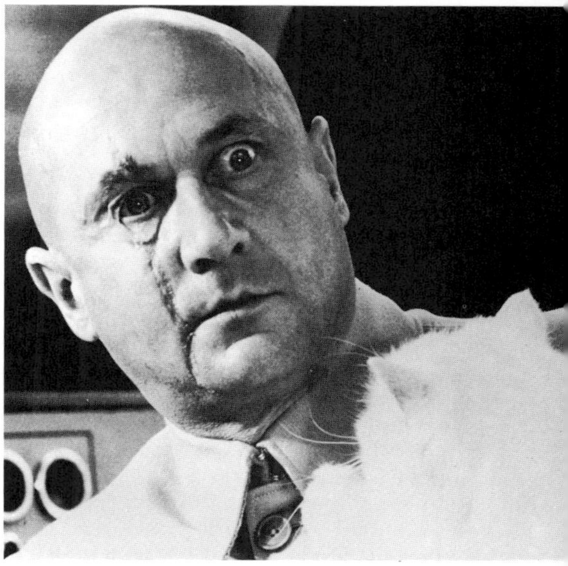

Top: Donald Pleasence in 'You Only Live Twice' (Lewis Gilbert, GB, 1967)
Above: Christopher Plummer in 'Oedipus the King' (Philip Saville, GB, 1967)
Below: Sidney Poitier in 'A Man is Ten Feet Tall' ('Edge of the City', Martin Ritt, USA, 1956)

To Sir with Love, In the Heat of the Night and *Guess Who's Coming to Dinner?* (1967), *The Lost Man* (1969), *They Call me Mister Tibbs* (1970), *King* and *The Organisation* (1971).

Poland

The first two names in Polish film history are Kazimierz Prószynski, who designed and developed his Pleograph apparatus during the period 1894 to 1902 to make and project films in Warsaw, and Boleslaw Matuszewski, a cinematographer from Warsaw who between 1896 and 1898 made many short films in different countries for the LUMIÈRE programmes. Matuszewski was also the author of two treatises about the cinema, published in Paris in 1898, 'Une Nouvelle Source de l'Histoire' and 'La Photographie Animée'.

Both film-making and exhibition developed gradually in Poland during the years preceding the First World War. What production took place was largely in the hands of stage actors, such as the Artists' Co-operative (a studio run by the actors of the leading Warsaw Variety theatre), and later, during the war years, the group which ran the Sfinks studio, of whom POLA NEGRI became one. After the war she, like her fellow star Mia-Mara, moved to Berlin to work in the German cinema.

Between the wars, film-making in Poland remained on a small scale, rising during the 1920s to about 20 feature films a year, with the number of film theatres rising to 827 in 1929. Films were made by small companies; among the more prominent directors were Ryszard Boleslawski (Richard Boleslavski), who went to Hollywood, Aleksander Hertz (discoverer of the prominent Polish actress of the period, Jadwiga Smosarska), and Wiktor Biegański, whose genuine flair for the film was seen in such productions as *Jealousy* and *Abyss of Repentance* (1922) and *Vampires of Warsaw* (1925). Another prominent actor was Adolf Dymska, a comedian of outstanding talent whose best work was to be in the sound period both before and after the war. Among other directors of the silent period were Józef Lejtes (*Hurricane*, 1928), together with Leonard Buczkowski and ALEKSANDER FORD, both directors of documentary. Ford made, for example, *The Pulse of Poland's Manchester* (1930), about Lodz, Poland's industrial centre.

The first film with sound to be made in Poland was *The Cult of Flesh* (Michal Waszynski, 1929); the sound was recorded on disc. Polish film-making lagged as the result of an economic slump during the early 1930s, but Józef Lejtes made *Wild Fields* (1932), a reasonably authentic picture of rural life, while Ford made the most notable of Poland's interwar features, *The Legion of the Streets* (1932), a film about the Warsaw newsboys. In 1934, after making *Sabra* in Palestine, he directed *Awakening*, the story of three adolescent girls who have just left school. Ford was among those who joined the radical movement known as START (the Society of Devotees of the Artistic Film), one of whose founders was the future woman director WANDA JACUBOWSKA. Her career began in documentary with such films as *The Sea* (1932) and *We are Building* (1933). Among the START group were Eugeniusz Cekalski, Tadeusz Kowalski, Stanislaw Wohl and Jerzy Zarzycki, as well as Jerzy Toeplitz, film critic and historian who was, after the war, to be rector of the influential film training school at Lodz. Members of START tended to work in documentary; *Three Études* (Cekalski and Wohl, 1937) won an award at the Venice Film Festival. START broke up in 1935, and was succeeded in 1937 by the Co-operative of Film Authors, formed to carry on the START tradition of study and practice of film art and technique. The first feature promoted by the group was *Ghosts* (Cekalski and Szolowski, 1938), based on a Polish novel. In Cracow a small avant-garde film movement began with Jalu Kurek, a poet and writer, as leader, while books on the art and technique of film were published by Boleslaw Wladyslaw Lewicki at his centre, Awangarda, in Lvov.

During the war, the Polish film industry was broken up. A few film-makers such as Antoni Bohdziewicz and Jerzy Zarzycki attempted to film underground record material. Many film-makers went into exile, some like Cekalski working in Britain and the USA, others like Ford, Jerzy Bossak, Stanislaw Wohl in the USSR, filming combat material. Ford, whose interwar films such as *The Road of Youth*, a film on Jewish orphans which was banned, and

Above: 'Unvanquished City' (Jerzy Zarzycki, 1950)
Below: 'The Last Stage' (Wanda Jacubowska, 1948)

People of the Vistula (both 1936) had shown more fully his radical views, organized in 1943 the Polish Army Film Command, producing the newsreel called *Fighting Poland*; he also made the first documentary report on a Nazi genocide camp, *Majdanek* (1944), when this area of Poland was liberated.

With the founding of the Socialist state in 1945 by the Provisional Government set up under the supervision of the Soviet Union, Poland began the task of establishing a new, state-controlled film industry, Film Polski. The 1947 elections were won by the Stalinist bloc, and from 1948 they took control of the country until 1956. One of the earliest films to be made was Leonard Buczkowski's *Forbidden Songs* (1947), a study of the war years with both tragic and lighter touches. 1948 was the year in which Wanda Jacubowska's important film, *The Last Stage*, appeared, a restrainedly realistic picture of life and death among the prisoners in Auschwitz Nazi Concentration camp; made in the documentary style, it had notable performances by the new actresses Barbara Drapińska and Wanda Bartówna, with Aleksandra Slaska and Alina Janowska in supporting roles. A whole new school of acting, as well as direction, was being developed. Parallel with this came Ford's *Border Street* (1948), showing the tragedy of the war as it affected the children of Warsaw and the Warsaw Ghetto; this film was an award winner at the Venice festival.

These were the films which set the pace for the new Polish cinema. Other films were *House of the Wastelands* (Jan Rybkowski, 1950), the story of an isolated girl during the occupation, *Unvanquished City* (Jerzy Zarzycki, 1950), a Warsaw story, and *Others Will Follow* (Antoni Bohdziewicz, 1949), a study of Warsaw society under the Occupation. Both production and exhibition remained on a very small scale during the first five post-war years; however, the film school was established at Lodz in 1948 with Jerzy Toeplitz as rector. The new films began to touch on post-war adjustments to a new ideology, for example, Jan Rybkowski's films *First Days* (1952) and *Hours of Hope* (1955). Ford's film on a post-war subject, *Five Boys from Barska Street* (1953), dealing with the problems of boys without home or discipline, won an award at Cannes. Other films, however, broke away from the war and post-war social problems – for example, Ford's *The Youth of Chopin* (1952) and JERZY KAWALEROWICZ's two-part film *A Night of Remembrance* and *Under the Phrygian Star* (1954), an award-winner at the Karlovy Vary festival.

The new Polish film-makers were, however, dissatisfied with the way in which the new state film industry was being run. In 1954–5 a reorganization resulted in the founding of the United Groups of Film Producers, splitting the creative workers into like-minded individual units desiring to establish their own group style of production. The state authorities consented to delegate to a considerable degree their former powers over choice of subject, budget, and so forth, leaving the groups reasonably autonomous to use their grants for film-making as they wished. Feature production rose in consequence from around four films a year to 16, reflecting a much greater variety of viewpoint as the younger generation of film-makers began to emerge from the Lodz Film School and were allocated, according to their bent, to one or another of the Units. The Warsaw Documentary Films Studio was also established to deal with social documentaries. Indeed, it was in documentary that one of the first major talents to emerge from the School shone; this was ANDRZEJ MUNK, who later, with W. Lesiewicz, made the fictionalized documentary *The Stars Must Shine* (1954), and the full-length documentary *Men of the Blue Cross* (1955) on the mountain rescue service; both were award-winners.

The Units into which the feature film-makers were grouped took different names: the following was their pattern at the beginning of the 1960s, a pattern which has enabled Poland's

Top: 'Kanal' (Andrzej Wajda, 1957)
Above: Zbigniew Cybulski in 'Ashes and Diamonds' (Andrzej Wajda, 1958)
Below: 'Five Boys from Barska Street' (Aleksander Ford, 1953)

greatest talents, such as ANDRZEJ WAJDA and ROMAN POLAŃSKI to flower during the initial years of its operation:

KADR Artistic director, Jerzy Kawalerowicz. Among the directors of this Unit, perhaps the most celebrated in Poland for the independence of its work from 1955, are Tadeusz Konwicki, Stanislaw Lenartowicz, Kazimierz Kutz, Janusz Morgenstern, and Andrzej Wajda.

STUDIO Artistic director, Aleksander Ford. Directors included Janusz Nasfeter, the husband and wife team Halina Bielinska and Wladislaw Haupe, Ewa and Czeslaw Petelski, Hubert Drapella and Zbigniew Kuzminski.

SYRENA Artistic director Jerzy Zarzycki; from 1961, Stanislaw Wohl. Directors included Jan Batory, Konrad Nalecki, Stanislaw Mozdenski, Jerzy Antczak, Adam Hanuszkiewicz, Josef Wyszomirski.

ILUZJON Artistic director, Ludwik Starski. Directors included Jerzy Passendorfer, Sylvester Checinski, Bohdan Poreba.

RYTM Artistic director, Jan Rybkowski. Directors included Stanislaw Różewicz, Stanislaw Lenartowicz, Stanislaw Jedryka.

DROGA Artistic director, Antoni Bohdziewicz. Developing production on more commercial lines.

START Artistic director, Wanda Jacubowska. Concentrating latterly on films for children.

KAMERA Artistic director, Jerzy Bossak. Directors included Witold Lesiewicz, Bohdan Poreba, Wojciech J. Has, Roman Polański (until he left Poland in 1964), Jerzy Hoffman.

Naturally, there has been some movement from one to another Unit, such as Ewa and Czeslaw Petelski from STUDIO to KAMERA, and Has from ILUZJON to KAMERA, when the latter Unit was set up 1957–8.

As a result of the establishment of the Units in the mid-1950s, a new individuality began to develop in Polish Cinema. It could be seen in the early films of the young directors Stanislaw Lenartowicz (*Winter Dusk* and *Encounters*, both 1957) and Wojciech Has (*The Noose*, 1958). These were carefully-styled films, the last an almost expressionist, Kafka-like subject. They dealt with more intimate human experience, *Encounters* dealing with love. Other films in the new, so-called 'aesthetic' style (that is, individual, artistic, nonconformist) were Chmielewski's comedy *Eve wants to Sleep* (with Barbara Kwiatkowska, 1958), and Tadeusz Konwicki and Jan Laskowski's *The Last Day of Summer* (1958), the story of two people on a deserted beach, which won the Grand Prix at the Venice Film Festival.

The mid-1950s, therefore, saw the arrival of the new generation of Polish directors, coming mostly from the Lodz School. They turned frequently to the period of the German occupation for subjects, but treated them with poetic vision and a fresh psychological understanding. In addition to Has and Lenartowicz, there were such new directors as Wajda, Munk, and Polański. Wajda in particular understood the tragic aspects of Polish wartime heroism; he and others were helped towards independence of viewpoint at this time by the establishment in 1956 of a government representing the anti-Stalinist wing of the Party under Gomulka, and the consequent, thorough 'de-Stalinization' in Poland. Wajda was at the head of the movement; his first film, *A Generation*, appeared as early as 1955, when Wajda was 29. It was a study of young people and their complex motivations during the Occupation; *Kanal* (1957) examined heroism and its motives during the Warsaw uprising; *Ashes and Diamonds* (1958), set during the troubled period immediately after the Liberation, saw Wajda's full development as a director of the first rank. A Polish critic has spoken of his 'feverish romanticism'; this could be found in his film *Lotna* (1959), oblique in its study of the impossible heroism of the Polish cavalry faced with the German Panzers in 1939. Wajda found an actor in ZBIGNIEW CYBULSKI, who understood the psychological ambivalence he was seeking to express in the leading character of *Ashes and Diamonds*, a young man lost in the political chaos of the post-war months.

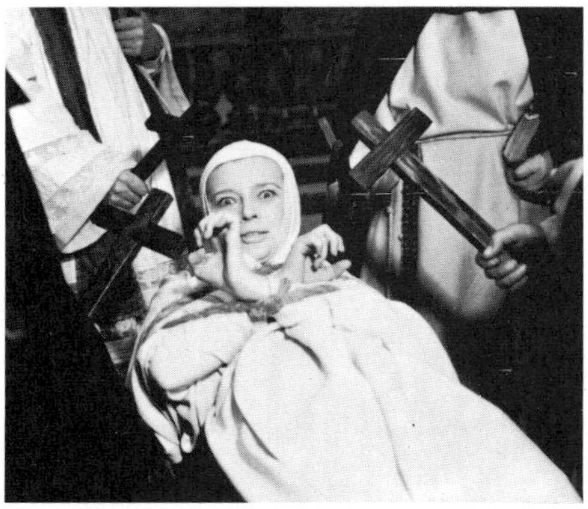

Top: 'Eroica' (Andrzej Munk, 1957)
Above: Lucyna Winnicka in 'Mother Joan of the Angels' (Jerzy Kawalerowicz, 1961)
Below: 'The Passenger' (Andrzej Munk, finished by Witold Lesiewicz, 1963)

Like Wajda, Munk also responded with sensitive vision to Polish psychological and political dilemmas in *Eroica* (1957), made when Munk was 37. It was an ironic study in disillusionment among those resisting the Germans, scripted by Stefan Stawiński, the writer of Wajda's *Kanal*. Munk's *Bad Luck* (1960) dealt with the sensitive subject of conformism and its failures. Another sympathetic study of the difficulties of the political transition was Has's *Farewells* (1958). Munk's last film, *Passenger* (completed after his tragic death in a car accident by Witold Lesiewicz, 1963), returned to the theme of the concentration camps.

A further widening of subjects came with Wajda's saucy comedy, *Innocent Sorcerers* (1960), with Kawalerowicz's thriller, *Night Train* (1959), another Venice prizewinner, and with his strange and powerful *Mother Joan of the Angels* (1961), a study of the 17th-century nuns possessed by the devil, and with the spectacular historical films, Kawalerowicz's *Pharaoh* (1964) and Ford's *The Knights of the Teutonic Order* (1960).

A talent of a different order was Roman Polański, whose experimental short film, *Two Men and a Wardrobe* (1958), excited much discussion – the tragi-comedy of two men who emerge from the sea carrying a two-door wardrobe, a burden from which they cannot get free. His first contact with feature films was as an actor; he appeared in several films, including *Innocent Sorcerers, Lotna,* and *Samson.* His first feature as director was *Knife in the Water* (1961), a subtle psychological study of a young man's momentary intrusion into an insecure marriage, a husband and wife both older than himself. This film, along with Wajda's *Innocent Sorcerers,* was singled out for attack by Gomulka in July 1964 at the debate of the 13th Plenum of the Polish Communist Party as lacking connection with the realities of everyday Polish life. 'Our cinematography,' he said, 'cannot be an instrument used entirely for experimental purposes by small groups of artists, but must serve the cultural and entertainment needs of the masses, always provided that they fulfil the ideological and educational purposes laid down by the Party. . . . Our film audiences expect from their film-makers, films whose action takes place, not somewhere in the world but here in their own country. They expect their heroes to be, not mannequins or flat figures devoid of life, which are the product of an over-stimulated and sick imagination, but live people of flesh and blood, people of labour. They are in favour of showing the true beauty of life and real heroism. We would like to hope that our creative artists will side with the forces of constructive effort and peace and use their creative ability to help the people to live, to work and to develop and to have their moral and emotional sensibilities touched by the true spirit of Socialism.'

The early 1960s, indeed, saw a 'crisis'. The many successes of the Poles at the international film festivals seemed now to be followed by a slump in creativity. Everything was blamed for this: the excessive influence of the Film School (since in 1964 four-fifths of 48 directors in the Polish cinema came from there); the excessive vanity of the swollen-headed young directors, who accepted too readily, it was alleged, the 'cult of the director'; or the fault was laid at the door of the Group system. In 1968 there appeared to be an anti-Semitic campaign which led to the removal of certain directors, including ALEKSANDER FORD, Jerzy Bossak, head of the State Documentary studio, and Jerzy Toeplitz, rector of the Film School. In addition, Cybulski, Poland's greatest international star, died in 1967, while such talented film-makers as Polański and later JERZY SKOLIMOWSKI (scriptwriter of *Innocent Sorcerers* and *Knife in the Water*; director of *Rysopis, Walkover* and other New Wave films like *Barrier* between 1964 and 1966) preferred to work abroad.

Wajda continued to make imaginative films, challenging alike in their allusiveness and their technical skill – *Everything for Sale* (1968), a meditation on the death of Cybulski; *Hunting Flies* (1969), a satire on contemporary life; *Landscape after a Battle* (1970), a return to the aftermath experience of war and the concentration camp; and *The Birch Tree* (1970). These films are deeply personal, and unlike his earlier films are not widely shown abroad. The Deputy Minister of Culture and Art announced at a press conference early in 1970 that the films of two promising young directors, *Toast* (Jan Lomnicki) and *From September to May* and *Sixty-Three Days* (Roman Wionczek), 'show normal people free of any complexes', and praised as 'badly needed' two new films which hark back to the war years, *Direction Berlin* (1968) and *The Last Days* (1969), both directed by Passendorfer, while *Angel's Face* (1970, Chmielewski) has for its setting the German camp for Polish children in Lodz. Spectacular historical films continue with *Colonel Wolodyjowski* (Jerzy Hoffman, 1969).

Cinema attendances have been dropping at the rate of 5% a year, largely owing to the growing popularity of television; nevertheless there are some 3,600 theatres, while the film society movement gains ground. There are some 20 art houses or specialized cinemas to show the more demanding kind of film programme. Short film output stands high at around 500 films a year; there are animation studios at Warsaw, Lodz, and in Silesia. Feature production, with studios at Warsaw, Lodz, and Wroclaw, remains at some 20 to 25 a year, with the objective of reaching 30.

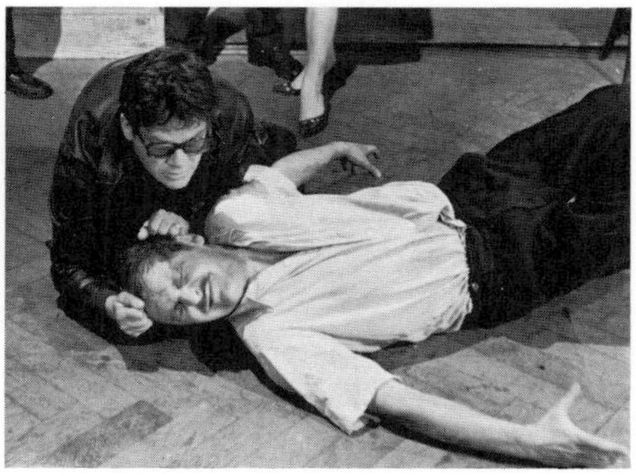

Above: Zygmunt Malanowicz, Jolante Umecka and Leon Niemczyk in 'Knife in the Water' (Roman Polański, 1962)
Below: Zbigniew Cybulski (left) in 'Salto' (Tadeusz Konwicki, 1965)

In 1969 certain administrative changes affecting the Groups were introduced to encourage greater development and creative enterprise among writers and directors. Apart from Wajda, Kawalerowicz and Polanski, as well as the directors of the older generation, the outstanding directors in Poland who have emerged or established themselves during the 1960s appear to be:

Tadeusz Chmielewski	*How I Started the Second World War* (war comedy) *Angel's Face* (war theme)
Wojciech Jerzy Has	*The Noose; Parting; How to be Loved; The Saragossa Manuscript*
Jerzy Hoffman	*By Fire and Sword; The Deluge; Colonel Wolodyjowski* (an historical trilogy, the last in particular on an epic scale)
Tadeusz Konwicki	*Salto* (a film of the New Wave)
Kazimierz Kutz	*Nobody Calls* *WhoeverKnows* *Salt of the Black Earth* (an historical film set in Upper Silesia)
Witold Lesiewicz	*Boleslaus the Courageous* (historical)

Witold Leszczynski	*The Life of Matthew*
Janusz Majewski	*The Criminal Who Stole the Crime* (crime film in documentary style) *Lokis* (period film)
Jerzy Passendorfer	*Scenes of Battle; Christened by Fire; Direction Berlin; The Last Days* (all Second World War themes); *Operation Brutus* (post-war political struggles)
Stanislaw Rózewicz	*Heaven and Hell* *Westerplatz* *The Prologue*
Jan Rybkowski	*When Love was a Crime* *Tonight a Town Dies* *The Return* (post-war problems) *Day of Purification* (wartime partisans) *The Polish Album* (post-war problems)
Jerzy Skolimowski	*Walkover; Barrier; Hands Up*
Wladyslaw Slesicki	*Shifting Sands*
Kryzsztof Zanussi	*Structure of Crystals* (problem film about scientists) *Family Life* (bizarre family relationship) RM

Polański, Roman

Born 1933 in Paris, France. Exciting international director and occasional actor whose handling of bizarre themes – black magic in *Rosemary's Baby* (1968), the progression of madness in *Repulsion* (1965) – reveal a Hitchcockian relish for shock treatment and a Bergmanian interest in natural evil. The son of Polish parents, he settled in Cracow as a child and was left to fend for himself during the war when his parents were taken to concentration camps by the Nazis. He started out as an actor in the theatre and, later, in films, among them *A Generation* (1954). He spent five years at the State Film College at Lodz, made several short films, and his surrealistic *Two Men and a Wardrobe* (1958) was acclaimed internationally. His major Polish film, a quiet neurotic study of three characters interacting on each other, *Knife in the Water* (1962), was a disturbing portent of his future work. In Britain, he made *Repulsion*, *Cul-de-sac* (1966) and a disastrous horror comic, *The Fearless Vampire Killers* (1967), in which he also acted. His most popular film, *Rosemary's Baby*, combined all the elements that had been separately evident in his previous films and was hideously echoed in life when his own wife, Sharon Tate, was killed in a ritual massacre in California in 1969. He appeared in *The Magic Christian* (1969) and his latest film is an elaborate personal version of *Macbeth* (1971). See 'The Cinema of Roman Polanski' by Ivan Butler (1970). MH

Top: 'Lokis' (Janusz Majewski)
Above: Marek Walezewski and Grzengorz Zuchowicz in 'Shifting Sands' (Wladyslaw Slesicki, 1968)
Below: 'Tonight a Town Dies' (Jan Rybkowski, 1961)

Polonsky, Abraham

Born 1910 in New York, USA. Liberal writer and director who was put out of business – at least under his own name – during the communist witch hunts of the McCarthy period in the 1950s. His tough-lyrical style was most evident in *Body and Soul* (1947), which he wrote, and *Force of Evil* (1948), which he wrote and directed. The long waiting period ended when he collaborated on the screenplay of *Madigan* in 1967 and then directed a striking parable of race discrimination, *Tell Them Willie Boy is Here* (1969). Latest film: *Romance of a Horse Thief* (1971).

Pommer, Erich (1889–1961)

Born in Hildesheim, Germany. Producer. One of the founding producers of German cinema, Pommer entered the service of GAUMONT in Paris in 1907, and later became Central European director successively for Gaumont and Éclair. Founded his own company Decla (Deutsche Éclair) in Berlin in 1915, later absorbed into UFA. His widespread influence as producer embraced such films as WIENE's *The Cabinet of Dr Caligari*, LANG's *Dr Mabuse the Gambler*, *The Nibelung Saga* and *Metropolis*, BERGER's *Cinderella*, MURNAU's *The Last Laugh* and, after the coming of sound, *The Blue Angel*, *Die Drei von der Tankstelle*, *Congress Dances* and many others. He left Germany in 1933 and became head of Fox-Europa in Paris, leaving in 1934 to produce from that year until 1950 in both the USA and Britain, where he formed a company, Mayflower Productions, with CHARLES LAUGHTON. Among his English-language productions were *Fire over England* (1936), *Farewell Again* (1937), *Vessel of Wrath* (which he directed, 1938), HITCHCOCK's *Jamaica Inn* (1939) and KANIN's *They Knew What They Wanted* (1940). In 1946 he returned to Germany as production supervisor for the US authorities, and in 1950 founded a new company, Intercontinental GmbH, which produced, among other films, Rudolf Jugert's *Illusion im Moll* and LASLO BENEDEK's *Children, Mothers and a General* (1955). Pommer returned to Hollywood in 1956. RM

Pontecorvo, Gillo
Born 1919 in Pisa, Italy. Director. Was film journalist for several years, working in Paris as Italian correspondent; then became directorial assistant to YVES ALLÉGRET. Returning to Italy, he worked on several documentaries and scripts before his first feature *La Grande Strada Azzura* in 1957. *Kapò* (1960), a strongly felt concentration camp drama with novelettish overtones, was followed by *The Battle of Algiers* (1966), his major work to date, dealing in a committed but dispassionate way with the French dilemma in Algiers, staged with remarkable realism and using real people and actual locations. He dealt with another revolutionary theme – this time set in the Caribbean – in *¡Queimada!* (1970), again with splendidly staged mass scenes and the mixed blessings of a starry professional cast. JG

Ponti, Carlo
Born 1913 in Milan, Italy. Producer. Educated in the University of Milan. Produced his first films in that city, and then became a producer for Lux in Rome, initiating a series of films featuring TOTO. After a period of association with DINO DE LAURENTIIS, he moved quite independently into the international class with such productions as *Attila the Hun* (1952), *Ulysses* (1954), *The Black Orchid* (1958), *Marriage Italian Style* and *Operation Crossbow* (1965), *Dr Zhivago* and *Blow-Up* (1966) and the disastrous *Sunflower* (1969). His marriage to SOPHIA LOREN, whose career he had fostered from its start, became one of the most publicized romantic attachments in Europe because of the difficulties arising out of the legal nature of Ponti's divorce. His production of DE SICA's film, *Two Women*, was an outstanding success in the USA, and won its star, Sophia Loren, an Oscar as best actress, the first time this distinction had ever been given to an actress appearing in a foreign language film. RM

Popesco-Gopo, Ion
Born 1923 in Romania. Animation and live-action film director. Studied art in Bucharest, and joined the family animation studio, making films for children such as *The Naughty Duck* and *The Bee and the Dove* (1951). In his films for adults his humour is original, if slightly didactic, featuring a little, nude 'everyman' in comic, generalized studies of human history, for example *A Short History* (1956), *The Seven Arts* (1958), *Homo Sapiens* (1960), *Hullo Hullo* (1961) and *Kiss Me Quick* (1969). He has also directed live-action films.

Porten, Henny (1890–1960)
Born in Magdeburg, Germany. Actress and producer. Daughter of an opera singer and early film director, Franz Porten. She made her first appearance in 1907, and from 1909 she became established as the 'Messter girl' in Oskar Messter's films at an initial salary of £10 a month. Her blonde, nordic beauty was much favoured, and she became one of the great stars of the German cinema up to 1933, appearing in innumerable productions, many of which were her own. Among her films were *Rose Bernd*, which she produced herself in 1919, LUBITSCH's *Anna Boleyn* and *Kohlhiesel's Daughters* (1920), Jessner's *Die Hintertreppe* (*Backstairs*, 1921), which she also produced, WIENE's *INRI* (1923), in which she played the Virgin Mary, *The Merchant of Venice* (1923), and many others both silent and sound. She was twice married, first to the director Kurt Stark, who was killed in the First World War, and later to Dr Wilhelm von Kaufmann, a Jew. It was on this account that her career was brought to a virtual standstill from 1933, though she appeared in a few films, including PABST's *Comedians* (1941). After the war she had little luck in her attempts to star once again though she appeared in two DEFA films, the second being *Carola Lamberti* (1955). RM

Above: 'Change in Life' (Paulo Rocha, Portugal, 1966)
Below: Robert Blake in 'Tell Them Willie Boy is Here' (Abraham Polonsky, USA, 1969)

Porter, Edwin S. (1869–1941)
Born in Scozia, Italy. Emigrated to USA in childhood. Pioneer director, having joined the staff of EDISON's studio. The first American film-maker of real note, whose early films, *The Life of an American Fireman* (1902) and, in particular, *The Great Train Robbery* (1903), made the first effective attempts at film narrative, breaking the story up into separate scenes with a more sophisticated continuity, including parallel action and camera pans to keep the protagonists centre-frame. Originally a maker of cameras and projectors, he joined Edison's studios in 1900. In 1907 Porter gave D. W. GRIFFITH his first experience of film acting in *Rescued from an Eagle's Nest*, in which he alternated studio with location shots. In 1909 he founded his own company, Rex, where he made, among other films, *Alice's Adventures in Wonderland* (1910). In 1912 he joined ZUKOR's newly formed Famous Players as production manager. He retired early from film-making after directing a film version of Hall Caine's novel, *The Eternal City*, in Rome in 1915.

Portugal
Portugal has a very small film industry, designed to satisfy the needs of her public of approximately ten million, and to export to Spain, Latin America, and possessions overseas, such as the Azores and Madeira. She has some 400 cinemas; television, introduced during the late 1950s, affects audiences to some extent.

Feature production stands at about seven films a year. The principal directors include:

António de Macedo (*Sunday in the Afternoon*, *Seven Bullets for Selma*)

Fernando Lopes (*Belarmino*, *Una Abelha na Chuva*)

Paulo Rocha (*The Green Years*, *A Change in Life*)

Manuel de Oliveira (*Douro Faina Fluvial*) There is also a considerable production of short films, especially for television. RM

Posters

The cinema – in the form of the Lumière Cinématographe – was born in Paris in 1895, at the very height of the golden age of the lithograph poster. One of the greatest masters of the form had indeed already applied his gifts to advertising projected moving pictures: in 1892 Jules Chéret had designed a poster, a characteristic creation showing a jolly, red-headed girl in a flurry of petticoats, to advertise Reynaud's 'Pantomimes Lumineuses'. Chéret also submitted a design to the LUMIÈRE Brothers, but it was apparently rejected, and only a sketch remains, now preserved in the Turin Film Museum. Three posters for the Lumière Cinématographe exist however: the first, by Brispot, showing a cheery *agent* controlling the crowds who jostle under a gas light, waiting their turn to get in to the show; another by M. Auzolle, depicting an audience laughing at the world's first film comedy, *L'Arroseur Arrosé* (see page 232); and a third by Abel Truchet, in which another audience is suitably startled by the onrush of the celebrated Arriving Train.

Only a small proportion of the French cinema posters of the succeeding decade equalled these. The best were those designed to advertise comedy, mostly in a broad caricature style, by artists of the calibre of Adrien Barrère and Auguste Leymarie. Posters for dramatic films tended to be less inventive, generally rather stiff representational impressions of the dramatic or tragic highspot of the story. Among the earliest poster designers was V. Lorant-Heilbronn, who had come from the theatre décor studios to be a director with PATHÉ. A large number of posters both for Gaumont and Pathé films were produced by the Atelier Faria. Italian posters of the period followed very much the same patterns as the French, the most successful comic artists being Marchetti and G. Grande. Some of the best Italian posters of the period were designed by Mauzan for the printing house of Ricordi: Mauzan was equally happy with broad comic effects or with the admirable atmospheric advertisements produced for the Italian releases of Gaumont's mystery serials directed by LOUIS FEUILLADE.

In England and USA, where the cinema had tended to stay in the music halls, the old music-hall style of letterpress advertising continued right to the end of the first decade of the century; and the pictorial poster only came into general and energetic use around 1910, as the bitter competition induced by the patents wars in the US industry made it vital to attract audiences at any cost. Based on the graphic style of contemporary theatre posters, crude but colourful and vivid in design, generally illustrating the most dramatic scene in the film, posters were produced for films that often ran for no more than four or five minutes. Cinema façades decorated with posters for each of the

Bills for two English cinemas: Albany Ward's Picturedrome (1911) and the Imperial Palace (1912)

eight or ten films that made up the programme must have presented an extremely colourful spectacle. This was, of course, before the days of identified film stars; and the story was evidently the main point of appeal to audiences. Not content with dramatic pictorial representation of the film's content, some companies included on their posters complete plot synopses of the films. A peculiar characteristic of the period was the marketing of films as factory product: many posters simply advertised the superior merits of the work of a particular company as a whole – 'So-and-so's pictures are the best'. From about 1912 actors and actresses began to be featured on posters with increasing prominence; and here again, in ominous foreboding of what the star system would eventually become, posters frequently advertised simply 'Asta Nielsen Pictures Are Shown at This Theatre'.

A very different approach was evident however in the posters which began to appear in Hungary about 1910, with the opening of sumptuous new theatres and the development of the Hungarian film industry. The cinema was held in altogether higher regard in Hungary than in the English-speaking countries, where it was reckoned a low-class and non-intellectual pastime; and just as the artists of the Budapest National Theatre were prepared to play in films, so graphic artists of a high order worked for the cinemas. Mihály Biró (1886–1948) and Imre Földes (born 1881) were producing striking graphic work for the Apollo and Projectorgraph cinemas some years before the First World War. The most striking and prolific artist of the period was however Lipot Sátori (1899–1943), who was only 18 years old when he began designing posters for the Urania Cinema in Budapest. Like Chéret, Sátori recognized the value to any poster of the figure of a beautiful woman; and the ladies of Sátori's posters must have been as familiar in the Budapest of the teens as Gibson Girls had been in America a decade or so before. Sátori and Földes frequently joined forces in a particularly happy combination of Sátori's elegant graphic mannerism and Földes' brilliant sense of form and tricks to seize the attention. Between 1917 and 1919 a whole generation of fine poster artists worked for the cinema, including Janos Bednar, Ekes, VINCE (VINCENT) KORDA, Jeno Pálla, Joszef Pan, Marton Tuszkay and the young Marcel Vértes.

The history of the cinema poster has seemed to follow lines quite independent from that of graphic work in other fields. Often it has seemed to be directly linked to the self-confidence and success of a national cinema at a particular moment. Thus in the immediate post-war period the high international prestige of the Scandinavian cinema was reflected in the exquisite posters of Hȯrde and Hȯkanssen for the films of SJÖSTRÖM and STILLER in Sweden; and in Denmark by Sven Brach, one of the rare artists already well known in other fields of poster work before he turned to designing film posters.

The great artistic developments of the 1920s were inevitably reflected in posters. The German Expressionist cinema produced a whole school of designers, in which the outstanding figure was Josef Fenneker (1895–1956). Fenneker's finest work dates from the period 1919–24 when he was designing posters for the Berlin Marmorhaus cinema. As with Sátori's work for the Urania cinema group, it was clear that work for a single, private (and necessarily imaginative) patron gave the artist more scope that his later work for distribution companies. who had perhaps to aim at a wider, more vaguely defined audience. Fenneker was not essentially an expressionist: like many of the best poster artists his work was eclectic and he was simply able to adapt the expressionist manner to graphic work with particular brilliance. Inevitably the powerful and prolific output of Fenneker tends to overshadow some of his contemporaries, notably Theo Matejko, Ludwig Kainer and Karl Michel, known for his striking poster for MURNAU's *Faust*, designed in the manner of an old German woodblock engraving.

Top: Poster for 'Leo the Widows' Friend' (Germany, c. 1911)
Above: Poster by Ludwig Kainer for 'The Private Secretary' (Joe May, Germany, 1917)
Below: British poster for 'The Ruling Passion' (D. W. Griffith, USA, 1911)

The great period of the Soviet cinema coincided with the era of Constructivism and associated artistic movements. Alexander Rodchenko designed forceful posters in the constructivist manner for DZIGA VERTOV's films. The Stenberg Brothers – like Fenneker, eclectics – were able to adapt their style to the character of any film while remaining totally individual and always recognizable. Their graphic styles look forward to (and even beyond) the best Polish film posters of the 1950s and 1960s.

The French avant-garde produced some remarkable and individual posters – Bilinsky's for *Le Lion des Mogols* (1924) and *Feu Mathias Pascal* (1925), Becan's for DELLUC's *La Femme de Nulle Part* (1922), Colin's for CLAIR's *Le Voyage Imaginaire* (1925) and Léger's for his own film (made in collaboration with Dudley Murphy) *Le Ballet Mécanique* (1924).

The arrival of sound saw an almost universal degeneration of the cinema poster, as US power and influence in the film industries of the entire world (excepting the USSR and those parts of Europe already dominated by Germany) resulted in a domination of US graphic styles. With very few exceptions (for instance the 'prestige' posters for the FAIRBANKS pictures, the comic posters commissioned by MGM from John Held Jr and some other attempts at more artistic work by the same company) American posters followed a monotonous pattern which had evolved out of the pre-1914 representational pictorial styles. The usual stereotype was to use gigantic heads of the stars or star superimposed upon a montage muddle of spectacular picture elements, all entangled with an excess of florid lettering, which had at once to fulfil contractual obligations of star and feature billing, and to make the most extravagant possible boasts and claims for the film's status and magnitude. American exhibitors, it seemed, could never escape the fairground origins of their industry. Exceptions to this all-pervading style, which swept the cinemas of almost the whole world, were few but singularly refreshing – the clean-cut posters of Clave and Blanco in Spain, and the work of a handful of independent-minded Swedish and French designers.

In Britain posters had practically been supplanted by plain letterpress announcements; but when they were revived in the late 1930s, they followed, by and large, prevailing trans-atlantic patterns. A significant effort to raise standards was launched by Ealing Films when Monja Danischewsky was placed in charge of publicity, and engaged S. John Woods to take over the graphic design department. In 1943 Morris Kestleman designed a singularly effective and attractive poster for *San Demetrio, London*; and subsequently many leading British artists of the day – John Piper, Edward Bawden, Edward Ardizzone, Leslie Hurry, John Minton and James Boswell – were commissioned to design posters. Not all the results were equally happy: there was a tendency for Ealing posters to remain first and foremost high class illustrations rather than truly effective publicity design. Among the notable successes however were a

bold bill for *Champagne Charlie*, designed by Woods in collaboration with Eric Fraser and Barnett Freedman, Rothhaltz's De Chirico-like landscape for *They Came to a City*, and Woods's vigorous design for *The Man in the White Suit*.

It is certain that the British example helped inspire the programme of high quality graphic work inaugurated in the Polish cinema in 1946, with Henryk Tomaszewski's *Black Narcissus* and Eryk Lipinski's *The Court of the Nation*. The object of the Polish posters was to offer a

Left: Danish poster by Sven Brach showing Thomas Meighan in 'The Man from Sing Sing' (USA, c. 1927)
Below left: Poster by Josef Fenneker for 'Hass' (Siegbert Goldsmidt, Germany, 1920)
Below right: Poster for 'Metropolis' (Fritz Land, Germany, 1926)

Above: Poster by Pedrza Blanco for 'España 1936' (Spain, 1936)
Below: Poster by Edward Bawden for 'The Titfield Thunderbolt' (Charles Crichton, GB, 1953)

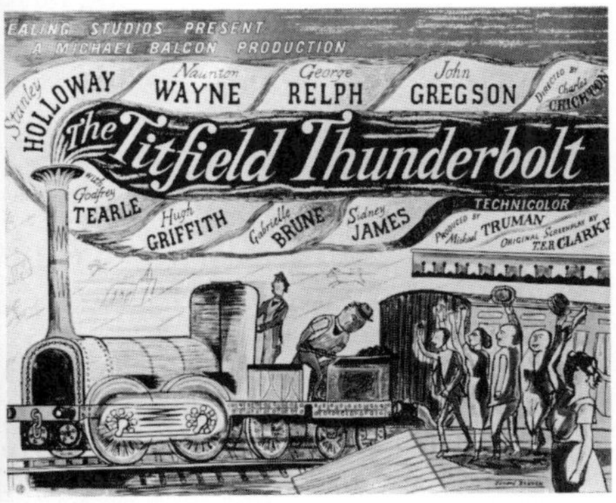

graphic abstract or synthesis of the film – as for instance in one of the most celebrated, Trepkowski's *The Last Stage*, which summarized the film's content simply by showing a broken carnation before the striped material of a prison-camp uniform. For a quarter of a century, with only slight fluctuation of quality, the Polish poster has maintained a remarkable level of graphic excellence in the work of designers like Lenica, Palka, Swierzy, Gorkà, Hibner and Starowieyski.

Other Socialist countries have been stimulated by the Polish example, the most successful being Hungary, where a more direct, less intellectual style has been involved in defining the essential theme or flavour of the film advertised. Notable Hungarian artists of recent years are Kass and Matè. Vyletal and Flejsar in Czechoslovakia; Bionov in Bulgaria, Berram and Segner in East Germany have been the most successful artists in the field in other Eastern European countries.

In the West the most sustained and influential effort at raising the standards of cinema graphics has been the work of Saul Bass, whose distinctive, economical style and ability precisely to define the character of a film in a simple graphic symbol makes his posters instantly recognizable and effective. In Western Germany an energetic revival of the film poster was effected by two independent distribution firms, Walther Kirchner, established in 1953, and Atlas Films,

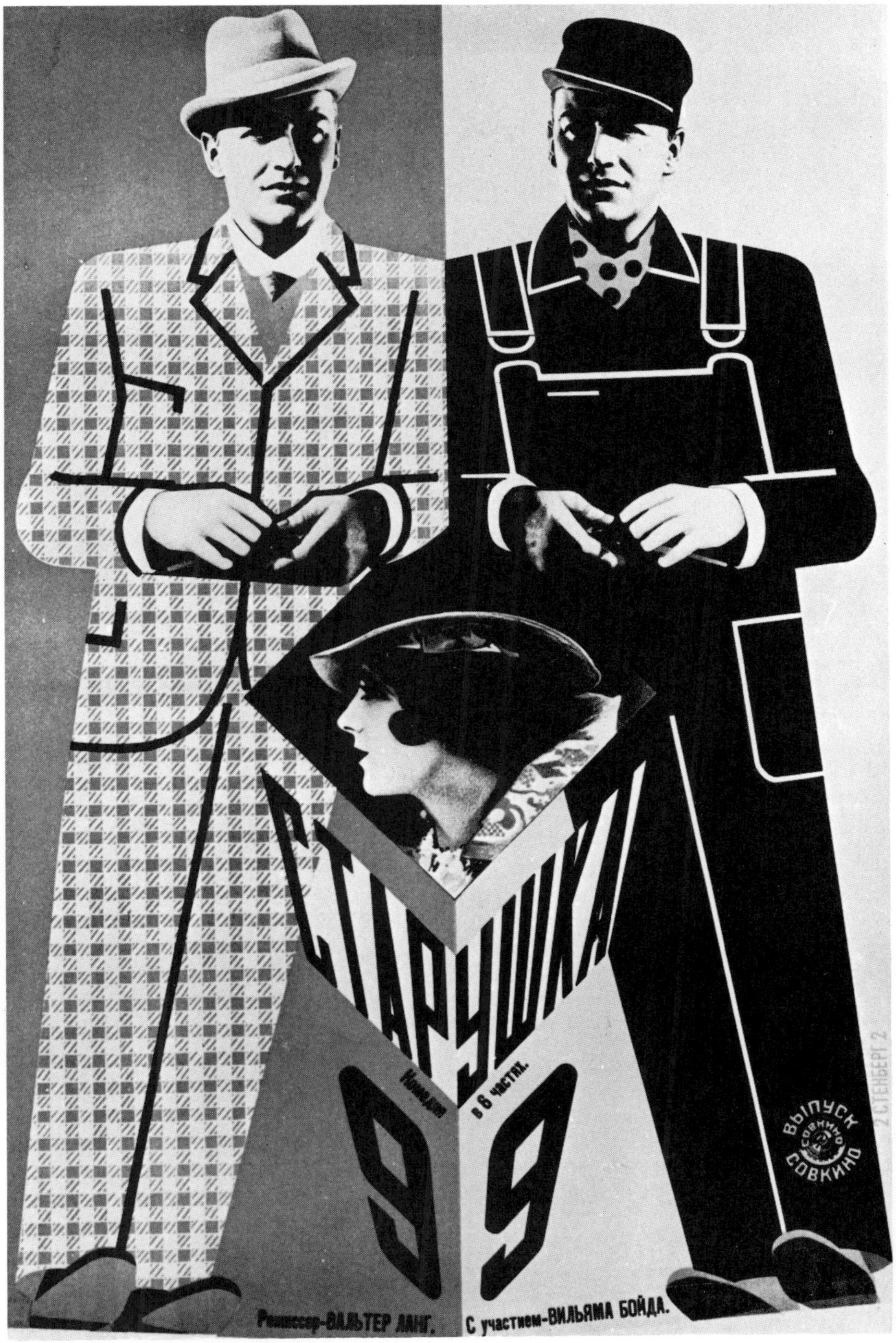

Above: Russian poster by the Stenberg Brothers showing William Boyd (twice) and Jobyna Ralston in 'Night Flyer' (Walter Lang, USA, 1928)
Left: Poster by Had Hadley for 'College' (J. Horne, USA, 1927)

established in 1960. Among many outstanding and mostly youthful artists commissioned by these two firms are Karl Blase, Hans Hillman and Isolde Baumgart.

The most remarkable recent revival of the art of the film poster has been in Cuba, where, as in early Soviet Russia, the poster has been recognized as a primary weapon of revolution. ICAIC, the official organization of the Cuban Film industry, has launched a programme of posters of remarkable graphic quality, designed by a small group of very young artists, and generally employing a silk-screen printing technique. The prevailing style of the Cuban posters is at once aggressively contemporary and rooted in national art forms. Newer designers – Nico and Dimas – are already however breaking away to develop styles distinct from those of the founders of the new school, Bachs, Rostgaard, Azcuy and Reboira.

If in the 1970s the style of cinema posters throughout much of the world is dominated by the tired old styles of American work of the 1930s, there is nevertheless enough activity, often isolated, but always energetic, to promise future revival. DR

Post-sync.
Recording sound to a picture after the picture itself has been shot

Powell, Dick (1904–1963)
Born Mount View, Arkansas, USA. Actor, producer, and director. At first acted on stage and played romantic singing roles notably in Warner's musicals; later, comedy and 'tough guy' parts. Became noted television producer and film producer and director. Films include: *Forty-Second Street* (1933), *A Midsummer Night's Dream* (1935), *Gold Diggers of 1935*, and other 'Gold Digger' films, *Christmas in July* (1940), *It Happened Tomorrow* and *Farewell My Lovely* (*Murder, My Sweet*, 1944), *The Bad and the Beautiful* (1952). Films as producer/director include: *The Conqueror* (1955), *You Can't Run Away from It* (1956), *The Enemy Below* (1957).

Powell, Michael
Born 1905 in Canterbury, England. Director. Joined REX INGRAM's company at 16 at the period when he was shooting *Mare Nostrum* in Europe. Later he became general assistant and stills cameraman for BIP at Elstree, and worked with HITCHCOCK on the sound version of *Blackmail* (1929). After directing two low-budget quickie thrillers, *Two Crowded Hours* and *Rynox* (1931), he made over 20 such short features between 1931 and 1936. Then, with American backing, he raised the necessary £20,000 to make his first individual picture, *The Edge of the World* (1937), a location story set in the Hebrides, the making of which he described in his book, '200,000 Feet on Foula' (1938). It was followed by *The Spy in Black* (1939) with CONRAD VEIDT, the film through which he came to meet his future partner, EMERIC PRESSBURGER. This atmospheric thriller of the First World War was successful, and ALEXANDER KORDA then invited him to work with LUDWIG BERGER on the colour spectacle, *The Thief of Bagdad* (1940). This opened his eyes to the possibilities afforded by the experimental use of colour, developed by VINCENT KORDA as designer and GEORGES PÉRINAL as photographer. Powell's respect for Continental techniques, especially German, grew out of his taste for unusual and sometimes bizarre themes, atmospheric treatment, and subjects offering a technical challenge. After a thriller, *Contraband*, Powell made his most ambitious film so far, *49th Parallel* (1941), an episodic story set in democratic Canada, as seen through the eyes of a Nazi German submarine crew who are forced to abandon their craft. The film was scripted by Pressburger and cut by DAVID LEAN. *One of our Aircraft is Missing* (1942) followed – the first film to carry the co-production credit of Powell and Pressburger. *The Life and Death of Colonel Blimp* (1943) was considered defeatist by the authorities, though Roger Livesey softened the character of the colonel, whom Powell had hoped LAURENCE OLIVIER would play. The German designer, ALFRED JUNGE, was

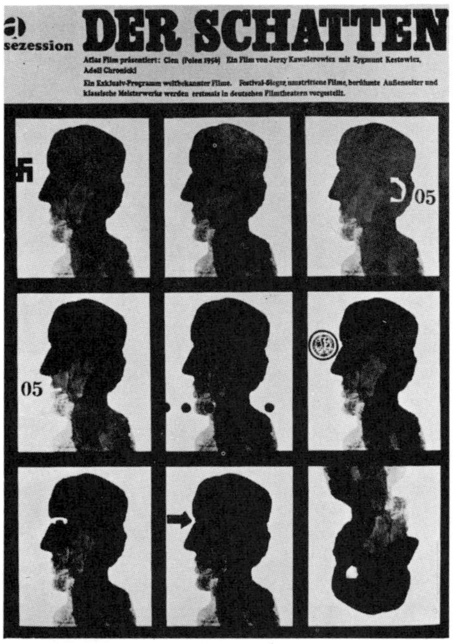

Above: German poster by Jan Lenica for 'The Shadow' (Jerzy Kawalerowicz, Poland, 1956)
Below: Poster by Rosalind Hoyt for 'Expresso Bongo' (Val Guest, GB, 1959)

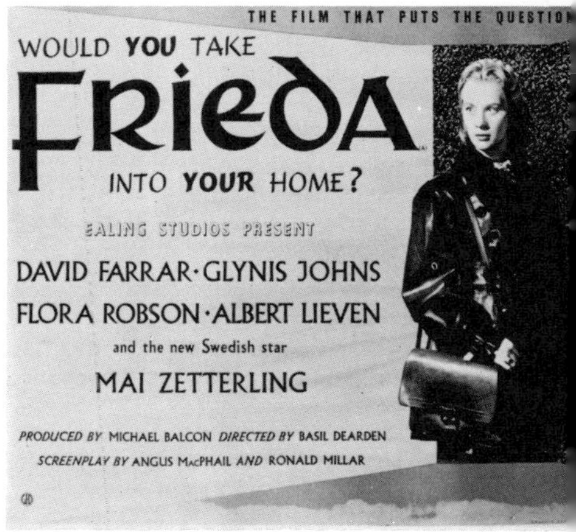

Above: Poster by S. John Woods showing Mai Zetterling in 'Frieda' (Basil Dearden, GB, 1947)
Below: Poster by Saul Bass for 'The Cardinal' (Otto Preminger, USA, 1963)

responsible for the art direction, and worked with Powell again on *Black Narcissus* (1947), which won an Oscar for its design and colour. Colour design by Hein Heckroth and choreography created for the cinema by Leonide Massine made *The Red Shoes* (1948) outstanding; Heckroth also designed *The Tales of Hoffmann* (1951), another film using colour beyond the narrow bounds of realism. This area had been explored earlier, in 1946, in *A Matter of Life and Death*, a romantic psychological extravaganza of great technical ingenuity and striking visual spectacle. *I Know where I'm Going* (1945) was another example of sensitive character exploration, set on location in Scotland. After the comparative failure of *Gone to Earth* and *The Elusive Pimpernel*, Powell's mainly romantic interest in psychologically disturbed characters (seen originally in *A Canterbury Tale* (1944) and the admirable *The Small Back Room* (1948) with its remarkable, prolonged scene on the beach covering the dismantling of a dangerous bomb) found its principal expression in *Peeping Tom* (1959), far ahead of its time in its exploration of the character of a sex murderer. After making two Service films, *The Battle of the River Plate* (1956), and *The Queen's Guard* (1960), Powell has concentrated mainly on production in Australia, including *They're a Weird Mob* (1966) and *Age of Consent* (1968), which have not, so far, equalled his earlier films in interest. Powell and Pressburger have been most remarkable for their ability to break away from the usual, rather pedestrian mould of British cinema, and if their films are on occasion over-extravagant and even self-indulgent, they represent both colour and imagination in a field where both are only too often absent. RM

Powell, William

Born 1892 in Pittsburgh, USA. Actor. Began his stage career in 1912 with 'The Ne'er-do-Well', and his screen career in 1920 with *Sherlock Holmes*. He played cowboy 'baddies', and graduated to the urbane character of the 'Thin Man' series, and other sophisticated man-about-town roles. His many films include: *Under the Red Robe* (1923), *Beau Geste* (1926), *The Four Feathers* (1929), *The Thin Man* (1934) and its five sequels, *The Great Ziegfeld* and *My Man Godfrey* (1936), *The Emperor's Candlesticks* (1938), *Ziegfeld Follies* (1946), *Life with Father* (1947), *How to Marry a Millionaire* (1953), and *Mister Roberts* (1955).

Power, Tyrone (1913–1958)

Born in Cincinnati, USA. American actor, whose film career began in 1932 with *Tom Brown of Culver*, and who gained a reputation as a handsome athletic, but usually gentle, hero. He died whilst *Solomon and Sheba* was being shot in 1958, and his part was taken over by YUL BRYNNER. His other films include: *Lloyds of London* (1937), *Alexander's Ragtime Band* and *Marie Antoinette* (1938), *Jesse James* and *The Rains Came* (1939), *Johnny Apollo* and *Brigham Young* (1940), *A Yank in the RAF* (1941), *This Above All* and *Crash Dive* (1942). After war service he continued his film career with, amongst others: *The Razor's Edge* (1946), *The Black Rose* (1950), *Rawhide* (1951), *King of the Khyber Rifles* (1953), *Witness for the Prosecution* (1957).

Above: Dick Powell in 'Farewell my Lovely' ('Murder, my Sweet', Edward Dmytryk, USA, 1944)
Below: Cécile Aubry, Tyrone Power and Jack Hawkins in 'The Black Rose' (Henry Hathaway, USA, 1950)

Preminger, Otto

Born 1906 in Vienna, Austria. Explosive director of the Hollywood-Central European school whose extreme skill in extracting the maximum tension out of bizarre crime themes – *Laura* (1944), *Where The Sidewalk Ends* (1950), *Anatomy of a Murder* (1959), *Bunny Lake is Missing* (1965) – is often overshadowed by his fondness for florid grand-scale projects such as *Saint Joan* (1957), *Exodus* (1960), *The Cardinal* (1963). He is also an actor – *Stalag 17* (1953) – with a relish for Teutonic villainy, although he made his stage début as Lysander in Max Reinhardt's production of 'A Midsummer Night's Dream' when he was 17. After a career in Europe in the theatre as actor-director, he went to America in 1935, directing his first films for Fox, *Under Your Spell* (1936) and *Danger, Love at Work* (1937). In 1953 he triumphed over the then rigid Hollywood Production Code with his 'adult' comedy *The Moon is Blue*. *The Man with the Golden Arm* (1956) was a pioneer film about drug addiction. Some of his other 'important' films – most recently *Advise and Consent* (1961), about presidential politics, and *Hurry Sundown* (1967), a race problem picture – have seemed heavy-handed and overstressed.

Other work includes: *Forever Amber* (1947), *River of no Return* and *Carmen Jones* (1954), *The Court Martial of Billy Mitchell* (1955), *Bonjour Tristesse* (1957), *In Harm's Way* (1965), *Skidoo* (1968), *Tell Me That You Love Me, Junie Moon* (1969), *Such Good Friends* (1972). MH

Pre-Release

The exhibition of a film to an audience paying admission to a cinema before the general release date.

Pre-Score

A recording of sound, usually music, made before the accompanying picture is photographed.

Preservation of Film

See ARCHIVES AND FILM PRESERVATION

Presley, Elvis

Born 1935 in Tupelo, USA. Pre-eminent, pop screen-star of the 1960s and – in his early days – musically an original. His characteristic 'hip-wiggle' earned him the nickname of

'Elvis the Pelvis', Some of his dramatic roles have indicated a likeable acting talent. His films include: *Love me Tender* (1956), *Loving You* (1957), *King Creole* (1958), *Flaming Star* (1960), *Frankie and Johnnie* (1965), *Double Trouble* (1967), *Charro* and *The Trouble with Girls* (1969), *Elvis – That's the Way It Is* (1970).

Pressburger, Emeric
Born 1902 in Miskosc, Hungary. Educated in Prague and Stuttgart. After working in Berlin as an author, journalist and screen writer, he settled in Britain, and finally joined the entourage surrounding ALEXANDER KORDA. After collaborating on the screenplay of *The Spy in Black* (1939), directed by MICHAEL POWELL, they formed a partnership after working together on *49th Parallel* (1941). For their work together, see MICHAEL POWELL.

Prévert, Jacques
Born 1900 in Paris, France. As the writer of films by RENOIR, CARNÉ, GRÉMILLON, GRIMAULT and his brother PIERRE PRÉVERT (q.v.) Prévert was a dominant influence in the French cinema of the 1930s and 1940s. In particular his scenarios for *Quai des Brumes* (1938) and *Le Jour se Lève* (1939) contributed largely to the definition of the 'poetic realist' school of the prewar period. Other Prévert-Carné scripts were *Drôle de Drame* (1937), *Les Visiteurs du Soir* (1942) and *Les Enfants du Paradis* (1944). For Renoir, Prévert scripted *Le Crime de Monsieur Lange*; for CAYATTE, *Les Amants de Vérone*; for Grémillon, *Lumière d'été* (1943), *L'Arche de Noé* (1946); for Grimault, *Le Petit Soldat*. Prévert's origins with the surrealists are most evident in the films he scripted for and with his brother Pierre: *L'Affaire est dans le sac* (1932), *Adieu Léonard* (1943), *Voyage Surprise* (1947) and *Paris mange son Pain* (1956).

Prévert, Pierre
Born 1906 in Paris, France. Writer and director, brother of JACQUES PRÉVERT. In the films on which they collaborated – *L'Affaire est dans le sac* (1932), *Adieu Leonard* (1943), *Voyage Surprise* (1947) and to a degree in the later short, *Paris mange son Pain* (1956) – the Prévert Brothers developed a style of satirical nonsense comedy that was altogether individual but, with the middle classes as its natural butt, remained a minority taste. In collaboration with BECKER, Prévert directed *Le commissaire est bon enfant* (1935). In 1959 the Prévert Brothers again collaborated on a short, *Paris la Belle*.

Preview
A special exhibition of a film to an audience, often non-paying, before the general release date, to test audience reaction.

Process Shot
A shot in which an illusion is created by the use of special effects

Properties (Props.)
Movable accessory articles, such as furniture, placed and photographed on a set.

Protazanov, Yakov (1881–1945)
Born in Moscow, Russia. Director. Entering the cinema as an actor with the Gloria Company in 1905, Protazanov made his début as a director in 1909 with *The Fountains of Bakhisarai*. In the course of the next few years he made a number of films for the firm of Thiemann and Reinhardt; but it was not until the war period and a series of literary adaptations – *War and Peace* (1915), *The Queen of Spades* (1916), *Father Sergius* (1917–18) – that he was able fully to exploit his gifts for psychological interpretation, clear narrative exposition and visual quality. With the Revolution, Protazanov emigrated to France where he made several films with other Russian émigrés, including IVAN MOZHUKIN, who starred in *L'Angoissante Aventure* (1919) and *Justice d'abord!* (1920). In 1924 Protazanov returned to the USSR and directed *Aelita*, a masterly experimental film after the story by Alexei Tolstoy, still interesting for the constructivist settings and costumes in which the dream sequences of a future world are staged. He subsequently directed: *His Call* (1925), *Trial of the Three Million* (1926), *The Man from the Restaurant* (1927), *The Forty-First* (1928), *The White Eagle* and *Don Diego and Pelagea* (1928), *Ranks and Men* (1929), *The Feast of Saint Jorgen* (1930), *Tommy* (1931), *Marionettes* (1934), *Without dowry* (1937), *Pupils of the Seventh Grade* (1938), *Salavat Julaev* (1941), *Nasreddin in Bokhara* (1943). DR

Below: Elvis Presley in 'Elvis . . . That's the Way it is' (Denis Sanders, USA, 1970)

Publicity
The role of publicity in the development of films as a mass entertainment is much greater than that of a decorative side-line. Certainly the motion picture could never have survived commerically without the staunch support of advertising and showmanship, the two prongs of any successful publicity campaign.

While working in conjunction, these are two distinct crafts: advertising is concerned with the fact, the finished film, as it is and as it can be sold; showmanship deals in something closer to fantasy, creating a dream world that must be open to public inspection and public adulation (which are, after all, the object of the exercise), but not to public participation.

Early on, the most dedicated publicity men realized that the very remoteness of films which distinguished them from live theatre, the invisible barrier set up between the filmgoers in the stalls and the awesomely large screen in front of them, could be utilized in promoting the product. Indeed it formed the basis of the Hollywood publicity system. Everything conspired to further the illusion of a separate, gifted breed of human beings who existed on an altogether more glamorous plane from that inhabited by Mr and Mrs John Public: particularly the fact that films were made and the stars lived in a self-contained Shangri-La called Hollywood, protected from the outside world.

Although every native film industry has of necessity found itself in the business of publicity, the history of showmanship-advertising is inevitably most closely linked with Hollywood, where, after the First World War, the greatest power (if not the greatest prestige) of the relatively young entertainment medium resided.

Before that publicity was largely a hit or miss affair, taking its cue from the tactics of Barnum and Bailey. The days of computerized efficiency of the studio publicity machine, under

A publicity device for Greta Garbo (1930s)

the guidance of such powers-behind-the-scenes as MGM's Howard Strickling, were yet to come.

The first example of salesmanship was the standard slogan of the 1890s – 'pictures that move'. Until the novelty of seeing just that – 'moving pictures' – had worn off, the pioneer exhibitors were not much bothered with finding a new approach to tempt the public in for the show. In the first decade of the 20th century, however, a selling technique promoting the thrills and excitement of *The Great Train Robbery* was devised and was found to pay off handsomely. In France, the public was responding to the lure of 'the magician of the screen', GEORGES MÉLIÈS, whose fantasy films were breaking new ground. Exhibitors advertised production companies, in lieu of personalities, organizing Pathé Weeks and Biograph Weeks.

But film publicity remained a fairly abstract art. An amazing and uncharacteristic lack of foresight prevented the film showmen from perceiving the limitless potential of the star system as a means of boosting the box-office. It was the public who forced the film-makers and exhibitors into creating stars. The lesson was not lost thereafter on the film industry, which, however frenziedly it sought to mould public taste, always acknowledged in the end that it was the public who made the stars.

The first American screen contract star to be billed was Florence Turner, who in 1910 was named as the 'Biograph Girl'. (Occasionally artists popular in other spheres – such as JOHN BUNNY from the music hall – were billed in their films.) The unveiling was brought about by popular demand. Filmgoers were beginning to write in, asking for the names of the regular heroes and heroines in the films they saw. Before that, production companies were most anxious to keep the identity of their artists a secret, fearing it would result in a demand for higher salaries. It is reported that a lady named Dot Davenport rashly revealed to the Press in 1909 that she was employed by Biograph and was promptly fired.

The response to the birth of the star system was immediate. Biograph's 'Little Mary', later to become the 'World's Sweetheart', MARY PICKFORD, emerged and discovered that fortune was the happy handmaiden of fame, provided the star had the shrewdness to exploit his or her supremacy.

Every major film-producing country created its own variation of the system. In Britain, film campaign sheets first appeared in 1910, to help cinema managers promote the films they were showing in their local districts.

The value in box-office publicity of a selling stunt began to be recognized. The public interest in stars and films was naturally seized upon by the Press. The first fan magazines appeared around 1910 and news stories about film favourites began to appear. Publicists realized that the Press could be a helpful ally. The success of a publicity stunt depended almost entirely on Press coverage; so the liaison between publicist and film journalist was established and has continued ever since.

One of the first major American stunts was staged by Bill Keefe, an ex-reporter working for D. W. GRIFFITH. In 1915, he organized a delegation of responsible-seeming citizens to the Los Angeles Chief of Police, complaining that *The Clansman* (later *The Birth of a Nation*) was likely to incite riots. Soon after a sign was displayed outside the theatre showing the film 'Closed by the Chief of Police', arousing public and Press curiosity about a film which they were convinced must be scandalous.

Some notable stunts misfired, but not before achieving their object, making the public aware of and avid for the film at the heart of the matter. In 1925, a stunt was staged in Britain which is still remembered for its sheer bravado. The Commanding Officer of a Royal Artillery Regiment was talked into providing full military escort for the film cans of *Phantom of the Opera*, taken from Southampton Docks to the film company's offices in Wardour Street in London. Irate questions were asked in the House by Members of Parliament and War Office censure of this calculated insult to His Majesty's uniform very nearly led to the hapless Commanding Officer being cashiered.

As time went on the public became increasingly *blasé* about the sensations dreamed up by the publicists: such stunts as Bebe Daniels getting herself arrested in 1921 for speeding and drawing a suspended ten-day prison sentence, all in the interest of a film called *The Speed Girl*, became almost commonplace. By the 1920s the superstar image was firmly established together with a superstar way of life in public that would ensure maximum coverage in the newspapers. At one Hollywood film première GLORIA SWANSON arrived seated on a throne built on the top of her car and TOM MIX drew up in a white stagecoach drawn by six white horses. When he first visited Britain in 1926, Mix created another sensation when he rode his trusty film steed, Tony, up the steps of the Mansion House to be welcomed by the Lord Mayor.

The greatest and possibly the first feat of star invention was lavished on a modest young lady known as Theodosia Goodman from Cincinnati. WILLIAM FOX put his publicity department to work on creating a screen siren from this unpromising material. Theodosia was physically re-vamped, given an exotic background and a new name, THEDA BARA, which is popularly believed to be an anagram of the provocative words 'Death' and 'Arab'; although in his book, 'Stardom', Alexander Walker believes the name had a more practical basis, Theda being a contraction of Theodosia and Bara a shortening of her mother's maiden name Baranger.

The manufacturing of screen personalities was standard procedure. But in most cases there was a certain substance to begin with in the fundamental characteristics of the actor or actress. Thus, the much-publicized aloofness of GARBO was inspired by the quality of the woman herself. The masculinity of GABLE was inherent; MGM merely capitalized on it. Labels were freely applied: CLARA BOW was the 'It' girl, JOHN GILBERT the 'Great Lover', Ann Sheridan the 'Oomph' girl, and so on. The danger of manufactured stars was that the public had an unerring instinct for detecting the phoney. For instance, SAM GOLDWYN's attempt to create a Continental temptress out of a gawky American-Norwegian girl renamed Sigrid Gurie, who spoke hardly any English, was singularly unsuccessful.

The publicity departments became a testing training scheme for enthusiastic young men who wanted to get into film production: HAL WALLIS worked as a publicist at Warners in the early 1920s.

During the 1930s, the star system was so well entrenched that the process of grooming a new arrival on the screen scene for public approval followed an almost routine pattern: press announcements in the gossip columns, a non-stop stream of 'cheesecake' or 'beefcake' photographs, romantic items in the fan magazines, 'at home' picture lay-outs in the quality magazines, personal interviews and, if the starlet grew into a star, refusals to do anything but the most prestigious publicity. But beneath the surface frippery, a solid career was often being built, from bit-parts to featured roles to star vehicles. When the Rank Organization in Britain in the 1940s and 1950s attempted to imitate the Hollywood star system it foundered precisely because it failed to provide the hopefuls it selected with the right film backing to support the personal appearances and frivolous publicity.

In other countries the star system was nothing like so calculatedly publicized as it was in Hollywood. Such international artists as Michèle Morgan, CONRAD VEIDT, DANIELLE DARRIEUX, EMIL JANNINGS, Lars Hanson, Renate Müller, CHARLES LAUGHTON, JEAN GABIN and FERNANDEL proved their popularity and ability in films before being acknowledged as stars.

The most systematic and successful star building technique outside Hollywood was promoted in post Second World War Italy. The combination of a desirable film environment and the provocative charms of young Italian women produced, via the traditional beauty contest route, a species of female stars, such as GINA LOLLOBRIGIDA, SOPHIA LOREN, Silvana Mangano, CLAUDIA CARDINALE, who were a publicist's dream. Not only did they look dazzling, but their fractured English knew no inhibitions in providing quotable quotes for the gossip columnist.

Film Festivals became useful settings for publicity: BRIGITTE BARDOT was a Cannes Festival 'discovery' in 1953.

Forty years after the first film stars were born, however, the publicizing of screen personalities had become a habit of which the public was beginning to weary. The emergence of boy-and-girl-next-door stars, such as Van Johnson, DORIS DAY and Debbie Reynolds, limited and eventually killed the grander flights of publicity fancy. By the 1960s the great days of star promotion were over, along with the elaborate studio star grooming schools. The newer stars (including ELIZABETH TAYLOR, MICHAEL CAINE, DUSTIN HOFFMAN, STEVE MCQUEEN, JEAN-PAUL BELMONDO, MARCELLO MASTROIANNI) created their own aura, either through their performances, their private lives or their nose for personal publicity.

But showmanship on behalf of the film flourished. In 1939 *Gone with the Wind* had perfected the cliff-hanging technique of film promotion, in which the casting of star parts achieved as much coverage as the territorial ambitions of Adolf Hitler. After the Second World War, several *entrepreneur* showmen moved into the field. JOSEPH LEVINE picked up an Italian sub-spectacle called *Hercules Unchained* and spent more on publicizing it than the film cost. It made a fortune. MICHAEL TODD's international drum-beating for his production, *Around the World in Eighty Days*, was certainly a major factor in the film's financial success.

Publicity relies increasingly heavily on allied promotions: DISNEY films are sold in conjunction with Disney toys, books, television programmes and, of course, Disneyland and Walt Disney World. Fashion plays a part – and indeed always has – in pushing a film: *Bonnie and Clyde* and *The Damned* clothes were fringe benefits that boosted the popularity of the films. The process of 'novelizing' a film script is not new. But in the last ten years the tie-up between films and paperback versions either of the screenplay or the book on which it is based has become routine.

The awe-inspiring instance in 1971 of *Love Story* – a screenplay which the author, Erich Segal, was persuaded to turn into a novel whose sales matched the box-office phenomenon of the film – suggests that the art of publicity is still very much alive. Purists may shudder, but the fact remains that the filmgoing public is just as susceptible to a selling proposition that catches its imagination as it was when it first responded to the call of 'pictures that move'. MH

Pudovkin, Vsevolod Ilarionovich

(1893–1953)

Born in Penza, USSR, of peasant stock. Russian director and film theorist, whose education included studying physics and chemistry at the University of Moscow, and who worked in a chemical plant after war service. His initial interests were the theatre and painting, and in 1920 at the age of 27 he abandoned his career for the cinema after seeing GRIFFITH's *Intolerance* and, later, CHAPLIN's *A Woman of Paris*. After study at the State Film School, acting in their productions and subsequently scripting and assisting in direction, he joined LEV KULESHOV's workshop studio, where he once more assisted in scripting, art direction and film direction, as well as giving excellent performances in *The Extraordinary Adventures of Mr West in the Land of the Bolsheviks* (1923–4) and *The Death Ray* (1924–5).

Pudovkin's first independent essay in direction was *Mechanics of the Brain* (1925), a feature-documentary presenting in detail experiments illustrating the key psychological theories propounded by the Pavlov Laboratory in Leningrad. It was photographed by Anatoli Golovnya, who was to become Pudovkin's regular cameraman. After a gay improvisation called *Chess Fever* (1925), Pudovkin made his first masterpiece, *Mother* (1926), freely adapted from Maxim Gorki's novel, given a spare and classic shape emphasizing the magnificent playing, as Mother and Son, of Vera Baranovskaya and Nikolai Batalov, both from the Moscow Art Theatre. The story is set in the period of the abortive revolution of 1905 and shows how a working woman learns the meaning of revolution through her love for her son, an underground revolutionary. The impressive crowd scenes culminating in the workers' procession in which the mother plays a leading part contrast with the utter simplicity with which the more intimate scenes are presented.

Pudovkin's skill as a film-maker stemmed partly from his understanding of detail in screen acting and partly from the fact that he did not let his consciousness of the developing technique of the film overcome the humanity of his work. In 1926 he published his initial ideas about the film in a book translated as 'Film Technique' (1929), in which he gives a clear exposition of Russian ideas of *montage*, or creative editing.

His next film, *The End of St Petersburg* (1927), in which Vera Baranovskaya also appeared, was made to commemorate the 10th anniversary of the October Revolution, and *The Descendant of Genghis-Khan* (also known as *Storm over Asia*, 1928) followed. It was a bitterly satirical story of the exploitation of a Mongolian hunter by the British Interventionist Army. Both these brilliant films used advanced forms of stylization to emphasize their themes.

After starring in FEDOR OZEP's film version of Leo Tolstoy's play *The Living Corpse* (1929), made in Berlin, Pudovkin directed *A Simple Case* (1929–32), which he had hoped would be a sound film; it is a study of marriage among revolutionary couples and was condemned for its excessive stylization in spite of substantial revision. Under Stalin, taste was increasingly turning to films involving only straight 'socialist realism'. With the coming of sound Pudovkin made *Deserter* (1931–3), a film about the struggle of Hamburg's dockers, in which he experimented with contrapuntal sound developed in *contrast* to the image in order to emphasize its underlying mood and content. Again he was condemned for his 'formalism'. Like EISENSTEIN, Pudovkin was established as one of Russia's principal teachers at the Moscow Cinema Institute, and he modified his original ideas to some extent in his second study, translated as 'Film Acting' (1935), in which he attempted to come to terms with the use of sound. With Eisenstein and ALEXANDROV he published a manifesto on sound in 1928.

Pudovkin's later films, *Victory* (1935–8) and *Minin and Pozharsky* (1939), and his biographical films *Suvorov* (1940) and *Admiral Nakhimov* (1944–6), though human in their detail, became far less experimental and more conformist in their treatment. He was deeply affected by the death (in a car accident in 1935, in which he was involved) of his constant collaborator, NATAN ZARKHI, the scenarist. For detailed studies of Pudovkin see 'Soviet Cinema' (1948) by Thorold Dickinson and Catherine de la Roche and 'Kino' (1960) by Jay Leyda. RM

Puppet Film
Film made by cinematographic animation of puppet figures

Purviance, Edna (1894–1958)
Born in Nevada, USA. Actress and leading lady, famous in silent films; her elegance, charm and wit, made her a perfect partner for CHAPLIN. She appeared in many of his films, including *A Night Out* (1915), *Easy Street* and *The Cure* (1916), *Shoulder Arms* (1918), *The Kid* (1920), *The Pilgrim* and *A Woman of Paris* (1923), *Limelight* (1952).

Quick Cutting
Any assembly of extremely short scenes so that they follow each other in rapid succession on the screen.

Quimby, Fred (1886–1965)
Born in USA. Head of MGM shorts and cartoon department from 1926 to 1956, where he was responsible for creating one of the most imaginative, if consistently violent, of cartoon series, *Tom and Jerry*. Among the best of his cartoons are *The Cat Concerto* (1946) and *Johann Mouse* (1952).

Quine, Richard
Born 1920 in Detroit, USA. Talented director and one-time film leading actor whose way with sharp thrillers – *Drive a Crooked Road* and *Pushover* (1954) – and sparkling comedies – *My Sister Eileen* (1955), *The Solid Gold Cadillac* (1956), *Operation Mad Ball* (1958) – established his high reputation at Columbia during the 1950s. But since then, as the films grew bigger and more expensive, he has not sustained the lively promise of his earlier work. Other chief films include: *Bell, Book and Candle* (1958), *The World of Suzie Wong* (1960), *The Notorious Landlady* (1962), *Paris When it Sizzles* (1963), *Hotel* (1967), *The Moonshine War* (1970).

Above: Vsevolod Pudovkin
Below: Anthony Quinn in 'La Strada' (Federico Fellini, Italy, 1954)

Quinn, Anthony
Born 1915 in Chihuahua, Mexico. Earthy Hollywood-trained Latin-style actor whose earlier promise has tended to dissipate itself in gutsy variations on the *Zorba the Greek* theme which won him his greatest success in 1964. After a varied and hardworking career, he started as an actor at Paramount in 1936, playing a gangster in *Parole* and an Indian in CECIL B. DE MILLE's *The Plainsman*. His association with De Mille, whose daughter he later married, ininfluenced his work, including the only film he has directed, *The Buccaneer* (1959). His rawboned portrayals in *Viva Zapata!* (1952) and *Lust for Life* (1956) led to two Academy Awards for best supporting actor. He also starred in FELLINI's *La Strada* (1954). Latest films: *The Shoes of the Fisherman* and *The Magus* (1968), *A Dream of Kings*, *The Secret of Santa Vittoria* and *A Walk in the Spring Rain* (1969), *The Last Warrior* and *RPM* (1970).

Quota
Minimum percentage of British films required by law to be exhibited by British cinemas

R

Rack
To adjust the position of a picture on a strip of film in relation to the gate of a projector. When the frame is exactly centred it is said to be In Rack or In Frame.

Raft, George
Born 1895 in New York. Actor. Was once a professional athlete; then a dancer, appearing in night-clubs all over Europe. Known mainly for his suave, underworld characters, his films include: *Scarface* (1932), *If I had a Million* (1933), *Limehouse Blues* (1935), *They Drive by Night* (1940), *Broadway* (1942), *Nob Hill* (1945), *Johnny Allegro* (1949), *A Bullet for Joey* (1955), *Some Like it Hot* (1959), *Rififi in Panama* (1966), *Skidoo* (1968).

Raimu, Jules Muraire (1883–1946)
Born in Toulon, France. Actor. His early days were spent in music-hall and revue as a comedian and singer and then as a theatre actor, particularly in the plays of Feydeau and Guitry. He first became known for his ebullient café proprietor in PAGNOL's trilogy *Marius, Fanny, César* (1931–6). Other notable roles were in ALLÉGRET's *Gribouille* and DUVIVIER's *Un Carnet de Bal* (1937), *L'Étrange Monsieur Victor* (1938), *La Femme du Boulanger* (one of his richest character parts, 1939), *Les Inconnus dans la Maison* (1942) and *L'Homme au Chapeau Rond* (1946). Although he never quite achieved the subtle intimacy of the greatest screen actors, Raimu belonged to that select band of French performers such as JOUVET and GABIN who were able to invest a variety of characters with a vital, living quality despite often inadequate material. JG

Rains, Claude (1889–1967)
Born in London, England. Actor. Worked as call-boy, stage prompter and assistant stage manager. First stage appearance at age of 11, in 'Nell of Old Drury'. His performance in *The Invisible Man* (1932) brought him fame, and he appeared regularly thereafter. His grave face and gift for dignified characterization led to frequent appearances as mature but slightly sinister professional men. Films include: *The Mystery of Edwin Drood* (1935), *Anthony Adverse* (1936), *They Won't Forget* (1937), *The Adventures of Robin Hood* (1938), *Juarez* and *Mr Smith Goes to Washington* (1939), *Lady with Red Hair* (1940), *Casablanca* (1942), *Caesar and Cleopatra* (1945), *Notorious* (1946), *The Passionate Friends* (1947), *The Man who Watched the Trains Go By* (1953), *Lawrence of Arabia* (1962). RM

Raisman, Yuli
Born 1903 in Moscow, USSR. One of the finest Soviet directors of the sound period, Raisman's work is less well known in the West than that of many of his contemporaries. Beginning his career in silent films as assistant to Eggert and PROTAZANOV, he directed his first feature film, *The Circle*, in collaboration with A. Gavronsky in 1927. This was followed by *Forced Labour* (1928), but Raisman's reputation was established with the documentary, *The Earth Thirsts* (1930). His masterpiece remains *The Last Night* (1937), an atmospheric Romeo and Juliet story of the first days of the October Revolution. During the war and immediate post-war era Raisman had great success with *Mashenka* (1942). *Moscow Sky* (1944) and a feature-length documentary on *Berlin* (1945). Later films, *The Lesson of Life* (1955) and *The Communist* (1958), showed him still able to infuse a human warmth into films that were clearly official chores. DR

Rank, Joseph Arthur
Born 1888 in Hull, England. Production executive, with considerable interests in the business world other than films. President of the Rank Organization. His initial interest in religious films brought him into the industry as both exhibitor and producer. He acquired control of both the Gaumont-British and Odeon theatre circuits and also of Denham, Pinewood, Lime Grove, Islington and other studios. Among the production companies he sustained were at one time Two Cities, Independent Producers, Gainsborough, Archers, Cineguild, Wessex, as well as G.B. Instructional and, for a while, Children's Entertainment Films. (See GREAT BRITAIN.) Among the films for which his companies took financial responsibility were: *In Which We Serve, The Way Ahead, This Happy Breed, Henry V, Caesar and Cleopatra* (one of the main causes of the company's considerable production losses at the close of the 1940s), *Brief Encounter, The Wicked Lady, A Matter of Life and Death, Odd Man Out, Hamlet, The Red Shoes, Great Expectations, Oliver Twist.* In 1953 he placed the control of the Organization in the hands of trustees in order that it should remain British. During the period of retrenchment in the 1950s the Organization's feature production was gradually narrowed down to Pinewood studios. He was awarded a peerage in 1957. A biography, 'Mr Rank', by Alan Wood, appeared in 1952. RM

Raw Stock
Unexposed and unprocessed negative or positive film

Ray, Nicholas
Born 1911 in Wisconsin, USA. Interesting American writer and director who never quite fulfilled the promise of his first, low-budget film, *They Live by Night* (1947), although even his most disappointing work has had some mark of quality to recommend it. Most notable films: the strange, Hollywood-atmospheric *In a Lonely Place* (1950), the bizarre feminine Western, *Johnny Guitar* (1954), the trend-setting 'generation gap' film, *Rebel without a Cause* (1955), *Wind across the Everglades* (1958). Other main films: *Knock on any Door* (1949), *Flying Leathernecks* (1951), *Run for Cover* (1955), *Bigger than Life* (1956), *Bitter Victory* (1957), *Party Girl* (1958), *Savage Innocents* (1959), *King of Kings* (1961), *55 Days at Peking* (1963). Unhappily in recent years he has failed to complete several projects, due to financial problems and personal difficulties. MH

Ray, Satyajit
Born 1921 in Calcutta, India. Director, screenwriter, composer. Son of Sukumar Ray, author, painter, musician, master-printer, photographer, friend of the poet Rabindranath Tagore, who died in 1923. Brought up by his maternal uncle while his mother earned a living by teaching. Graduate in economics at the age of 19 at Calcutta University. Then studied graphic art at Tagore's college, Santiniketan, working with Tagore until the latter's death in 1941. In 1943, Ray obtained employment in the Calcutta office of the London Keymer advertising agency, becoming art director in 1947, the year of Indian Independence and the year in which he became co-founder, with his colleague Chidananda Das Gupta, of the Calcutta Film Society. He had for sometime been a student of films, and as an exercise would prepare treatments of any literary work which he knew was being filmed so that he could compare his ideas with those of the adapters. In 1950 he was sent to London to study advertising methods, and

saw there the work of FLAHERTY and the Italian neo-realists. On his return he had discussions with RENOIR, then making *The River* on location near Calcutta; at the same time he acquired the film rights for Rs6,000 of the novel *Pather Panchali* (*Song of the Road*), and prepared a STORYBOARD treatment in sketch form for its adaptation.

While still working in the agency, Ray began to make the film in his spare time, using his own savings; he was encouraged to go on by JOHN HUSTON, then visiting Calcutta, and Monroe Wheeler of the New York Museum of Modern Art, who was preparing an exhibition of Indian art for the USA. It was the latter's enthusiasm which led to the government of West Bengal investing Rs200,000 in Ray's film, which became its property. The film, completed against time in 1955 for showing at the exhibition in New York, also won an award as the 'best human documentary' at the Cannes Film Festival. It was a modest financial success on the world market, and the W. Bengal government recouped four times its initial investment.

Ray never looked back; he gave up advertising, and concentrated upon producing low-budget films which fulfilled his own innate sensibility for Bengali subjects. His spirit is meditative, firm in understanding people and their problems, and greatly influenced by the compassionate wisdom of Tagore, whose life he presented with so much feeling in his documentary, *Rabindranath Tagore* (1961). His films deal alike with people in poverty (such as the Apu trilogy, *Pather Panchali, The Unvanquished, The World of Apu*, 1955–8, the story of a Brahmin youth), with the middle class (as in *Mahanagar, The Big Town*, 1963; and *Charulata*, 1964), and the wealthy (as in *The Music Room*, 1958, and *Kanchenjungha*, 1962). *Pather Panchali* accepts life in a Bengal village as it is, seen through the experience of a boy aged six and his adolescent sister, children of poverty-stricken but educated parents, who leave them free to live with little interference and to react with innocent curiosity to the traditional pattern of rural life. Universality is achieved through the perceptive simplicity of Ray's observation, a poetic sensitivity inherited from his response to the work of such film-makers as Flaherty and Renoir. His films have almost entirely drawn on the life and culture of Bengal, and he has normally preferred to use newcomers to the screen, mostly non-professionals, with whom he works patiently, slowly evolving interpretations of depth, revealing inner thoughts and emotions. He has, however, made deliberate use of stars, for example, Uttam Kumar in *Nayak* (*The Hero*, 1966), the story of a film star, and Waheeda Rehman in his Hindi/Bengali film *Abhijan* (*Expedition*, 1962). His desire is to work in as wide a field as possible, and he has even, with only fair success, attempted slapstick in *Parashpatar* (*The Touchstone*, 1958). Though seldom polemical, he attacked primitive superstition in *Devi* (*Goddess*, 1960), reactionary political views in *Kanchenjungha*, his

Above: Cedric Hardwicke and Claude Rains in 'The White Tower' (Ted Tetzlaff, USA, 1950)
Below: Satyajit Ray

first film in colour shot on location in Darjeeling, and the eclipse of tradition in *The Music Room*, with its many symbols of the past. More positively he is concerned with the freedom of a married woman to develop her own life and career in *Charulata*, a Tagore story set in the 1880s, and again in a contemporary setting in *Mahanagar*, in which a young married woman attempts, against her husband's will, to supplement the family income by working.

In the restrained style he has adopted, Ray has become a master of technique. He takes his timing from the nature of the people and their environment; his camera is the intent, unobtrusive observer of reactions; his editing the discreet, economical transition from one value to the next. His camera is composed constantly with the eye of a graphic artist, his sound track with the ear of a composer. The close observation of the human face remains the *leit-motif* of all his films.

More recently, since 1965, Ray has moved further away from the influence of Tagore and began to work with other themes in other styles in which he has yet to prove an equal mastery. His recent films include: *Chidiakhana* (*The Zoo*, with Uttam Kumar, a thriller); *The Adventures of Goopy and Bagha*, a fantasy based on a story written by his grandfather; a documentary on Sikkim; *Days and Nights in the Forest* (1970), *The Adversary* and *Company Limited* (1971). These last three investigate contemporary life and situations in Bengal, mixing Ray's former poetic style with modern social themes. In 1971 his friend, Marie Seton, published a highly informed and sympathetic biography, 'Portrait of a Director: Satyajit Ray'. RM

Reaction Shot

A shot which shows the reaction of a character to what has been said or done in the preceding shot.

Rear Projection

The projection of a moving film or slide onto the rear of a translucent screen

Record Film

See NEWS AND RECORD FILM

Redford, Robert

Born 1937 in Los Angeles, USA. Popular star actor of the 1970s, whose anti-heroic image was most effectively displayed in *Butch Cassidy and the Sundance Kid* (1969). A slow starter who has deliberately disassociated himself from the Hollywood star-promoting system, he came to the screen from the stage, appearing unspectacularly in a series of unsuitable roles in

Situation Hopeless, but not Serious and *Inside Daisy Clover* (1965), *The Chase* and *This Property is Condemned* (1966). He did, however, repeat the leading role he played on Broadway in the film of *Barefoot in the Park* (1967). Returning to films after two years, he chose his roles shrewdly and showed much talent as the Kid in *Butch Cassidy and the Sundance Kid* and *Tell Them Willie Boy is Here* (1969), and *Downhill Racer* (1970). Latest film: *Little Fauss and Big Halsy* (1971).

Redgrave, Lynn
Born 1943 in London, England. Daughter of MICHAEL REDGRAVE. Actress on stage and screen. Made her film début in *Tom Jones* (1963) and scored a particular success in *Georgy Girl* (1966), followed by *The Deadly Affair* (1967), *Smashing Time* (1968), *The Virgin Soldiers* (1969), *Blood Kin* (1970). Her characteristic type is that of the tom-boy in pursuit of men.

Redgrave, Michael
Born 1908 in Bristol, England. Knighted 1959. British stage and screen actor whose classical, theatrical training is perhaps less obtrusively apparent in his film performances than in those of his fellow knights, OLIVIER, RICHARDSON, Gielgud. His skill in portraying tight, introverted, upper-class characters – most notably in *The Loneliness of the Long-Distance Runner* (1963) – has tended to obscure his flair for stylish comedy, especially evident in *The Importance of Being Earnest* (1951). Early on in his film career he specialized in fairly conventional cheeky heroes, making his début in HITCHCOCK's *The Lady Vanishes* (1938). While remaining primarily a man of the theatre, he has made over 50 films including: *The Stars Look Down* (1939), *Kipps* (1941), *Thunder Rock* (1942), *The Way to the Stars* and *Dead of Night* (1945), *Fame is the Spur* and *Mourning Becomes Electra* (1947), *The Browning Version* (1951), *The Dam Busters* (1955), *The Quiet American* (1958), *Young Cassidy* (1964), *The Hill* (1965), *Goodbye Mr Chips* and *Connecting Rooms* (1969), *David Copperfield* (1970), *The Go-Between* (1971). MH

Redgrave, Vanessa
Born 1937 in London, England. Flamboyant British stage and screen actress, daughter of MICHAEL REDGRAVE. Her strong, radical views on politics and marriage, together with her deeply sensitive but rather mannered portrayals of free-willed women, have established her as a torch-bearer for the new style of anti-star actress. Despite her great success in the theatre, she did not achieve comparable distinction on the screen until *Morgan* (1966). Subsequent films: *Blow Up, Sailor from Gibraltar* and *A Man for All Seasons* (1966), *Red and Blue* and *Camelot* (1967), *The Charge of the Light Brigade* and *The Seagull* (1968), *Isadora, Oh! What a Lovely War* and *A Quiet Place in the Country* (1969), *The Drop Out, The Devils* and *The Trojan Women* (1971). In 1967 she was awarded the C.B.E. MH

Above: Michael Redgrave in 'The Way to the Stars' (Anthony Asquith, GB, 1945)
Below: Carol Reed directing Mark Lester in 'Oliver!' (GB, 1968)

Reed, Carol
Born 1906 in London, England. Knighted in 1952. Celebrated British director who, with DAVID LEAN, dominated the relatively thriving British film industry in the late 1940s. Since then he has made few films with only limited appeal until *Oliver!* (1968), for which he won an American Academy Award.

Unmistakably British in tone, although far-flung in setting, his work is noted for its graceful understatement, humanity and civilized sincerity. What emerges is less a creative passion for certain themes than a craftsman's respect for a good story. One idea, however, is consistent in his more personal films: the loner on the outside – of the law, the establishment, society. This, fundamentally, is the hero of *Odd Man Out* (1947), *The Third Man* (1949) – his most famous film, written by Graham Greene, set in occupied Vienna – *Outcast of the Islands* (1951), and *Our Man in Havana* (1959), also based on a novel by Graham Greene.

Reed started out as an actor in 1924 and became associated with the thriller-writer, Edgar Wallace. It was through Wallace that he went to British Lion Films. Later he joined Ealing Studios as dialogue director and directed his first film, *Midshipman Easy,* in 1934. For a while he became identified with realistic portrayals of working class life at work and play: *Bank Holiday* (1937), *The Stars Look Down* (1939) and *Kipps* (1941), which was a deft, inventive adaptation from Wells's novel. During the Second World War he was involved in directing two of the most influential war films, *The Way Ahead* (1943) and *The True Glory* (with GARSON KANIN 1945).

During the British film crisis of the 1950s, Reed moved into the international production market with *Trapeze* (1956) and *The Key* (1958). But it was in a field new to him – the film musical – that he scored his most solid box-office success with *Oliver!*

Other notable films: *Laburnum Grove* (1936), *Night Train to Munich* (1940), *The Young Mr Pitt* (1941), *The Fallen Idol* (1948), *A Kid for Two Farthings* (1955), *The Agony and the Ecstasy* (1965), *The Last Warrior* (1970). Latest project: *The Public Eye* (1972). MH

Reed, Oliver
Born 1939 in London, England. Tough British actor whose talent and reputation have developed significantly since his association in television and on film with director KEN RUSSELL. A nephew of CAROL REED, he made his film début in *The Bulldog Breed* (1959) and played a series of minor roles, graduating to broody heroes and young tearaways, notably in *The Damned* (1963) and *The System* (1964). In *The Jokers* (1966) he revealed a gift for comedy which he later exploited in *I'll Never Forget Whats 'is Name* (1967) and *The Assassination Bureau* (1968). He made his mark most dramatic

ally in Ken Russell's *Women in Love* (1969) and *The Devils* (1971). Films include: *Pirates of Blood River* (1962), *The Trap* and *The Shuttered Room* (1966), *Oliver!* and *Hannibal Brooks* (1968), *Sitting Target* and *The First of January* (1972).

Reel
A spool upon which film or tape is wound for use in projectors, cameras or tape machines

Register Pins
In animation, part of a camera gate designed to ensure that each frame of film is in exactly the same position as the preceding and following frames.

Registration Pegs
In animation. See PEG BAR

Reichenbach, François
Born 1922 in Paris, France. A documentary-maker with a keen and whimsical eye, Reichenbach has a lively, if occasionally vulgar approach to his subjects. The best of the numerous documentaries he has made since 1950 are *Les Marines* (1958), *L'Amérique insolite* (1960), *Rubinstein, l'Amour de la Vie* (1970). With *Un cœur gros comme ça* (1962) and *La Douceur du village* (1964) he attempted to develop a style of story film in *cinéma-vérité* style. Latest film: *Yehudi Menuhin – Chemin de la lumière* (1971).

Reiniger, Lotte
Born 1899 in Berlin, Germany. Adapting the centuries-old techniques of Chinese Shadows to the cinema, Lotte Reiniger, in collaboration with her husband Carl Koch, created a unique and inimitable style of animated cinema. Her first shadow films, created with articulated figures cut out of cardboard, tin and paper, were made at the *Berlin Institut für Kulturforschung* as early as 1919. After a series of short fairy-tales, she embarked on the first full-length animated film, *The Adventures of Prince Achmed* (1923–6), a work which still retains all its original freshness and charm. Throughout the 1930s she continued to create short films, with added sound – notably a series based on Hugh Lofting's *Doctor Dolittle* and the musical subjects *Harlequin* (based on 18th-century Italian music), *Carmen* (slightly parodying Bizet) and the exquisite *Papageno* (1935). From 1936–9 she worked in England; making among other films *Tochter*, with music by Benjamin Britten. At the start of the war she followed her husband to Italy, where they began *L'élisir d'amore* which remained unfinished. In 1944 she returned to Berlin to make *Die Goldene Gans*. Since 1949 Lotte Reiniger has worked in England making occasional films, operating a live shadow theatre, and sometimes working for television. DR

Reisz, Karel
Born 1926 in Czechoslovakia. One of the principal new directors to emerge during the British film *renaissance* of the 1960s. He has lived in England since the age of 12 and, after war service in the RAF and graduating from Cambridge, he joined the influential British film quarterly, 'Sequence', as critic and feature writer. He also worked for a while at both the British Film Academy, (for which he originally undertook his book 'The Technique of Film Editing'; 1953) and the British Film Institute, as well as serving as Film Officer for the Ford Motor Company. Toughly critical of the orthodox film industry, he went into the 'Free Cinema' movement, co-directing with TONY RICHARDSON *Momma Don't Allow* (1955), followed by *We are the Lambeth Boys* (1958).

His first feature, *Saturday Night and Sunday Morning* (1960) made a star of ALBERT FINNEY and set the style for many gritty, imitative, working-class films. Six years later, his sensitive instinct for the contemporary mood made *Morgan: a Suitable Case for Treatment* – with its antic, anarchic disrespect for the established order – set another film trend. He also produced *This Sporting Life* (1963), directed by his 'Sequence' and 'Free Cinema' colleague, LINDSAY ANDERSON. His other films, a remake of *Night Must Fall* (1963) and a grand-scale 'life' of *Isadora* (1968), failed to achieve the same impact. He would rather not make films at all than tackle subjects which do not appeal to him. MH

Above: David Warner in 'Morgan – a suitable case for treatment' (Karel Reisz, GB, 1966)
Below: Richard Attenborough and Lee Remick in 'A Severed Head' (Dick Clement, GB, 1970)

Reitz, Edgar
Born in 1932 in Morbach-Trier, Germany. Director, associated with the *Junger Deutscher Film* movement in Germany. Studied theatrical production in Munich. Entered films in 1953 as a production assistant on scripting, camera, and editing, and in 1962 became director of the experimental branch of Isel Film. He has scripted and directed many experimental short films, and two feature films (both presented in turn at the Venice Film Festival): *Mahlzeiten* (*Lust for Love*, 1967), about a girl who seeks freedom from the 'feminine mystique', and *Cardillac* (1968–9), a strikingly stylized film of great photographic beauty. In 1966 he acted as cameraman for ALEXANDER KLUGE's feature film, *Yesterday Girl*.

Release Print
A print made for general release

Release Script
Detailed record of the contents of a film produced after the completion of the film

Remick, Lee
Born 1937 in Boston, USA. Provocative American stage and screen actress who has successfully blended an air of well-bred respectability with a flair for smoulderingly sexy roles. She made a hit in her first film, ELIA KAZAN's *A Face in the Crowd* (1957), as a saucy drum-majorette, and went on to play various sultry heroines in *The Long Hot Summer* (1958), *Anatomy of a Murder* (1959) and *Sanctuary* (1961). Since 1969 she has worked in England, where her gift for crisp, bizarre comedy has been amply demonstrated in *A Severed Head* (1970) and *Loot* (1970). Other main films: *Wild River* (1960), *The Hallelujah Trail* (1963), *Days of Wine and Roses* and *Baby, the Rain must Fall* (1965), *The Detective* and *No Way to Treat a Lady* (1968), *Hard Contract* (1969).

Renoir, Jnr, Claude
Born 1914 in Paris, France. Cinematographer. Worked as camera operator and assistant director for his uncle JEAN RENOIR in the 1930s; also lighting cameraman on many of Renoir's films including *Toni* (1934), *Une Partie de Campagne* (1936), *The River* (1951), *Le Carrosse d'Or* (1952), *Eléna et les hommes* (1956). His black-and-white films have great lyrical feeling and his colour work has a superb range and density (especially in the period pieces): *Puccini* (1952), *Madama Butterfly* (1954), *Le Mystère Picasso* (1955), *Une Vie* (1957), *Et Mourir de plaisir* (1960), *La Curée* (1966), *Barbarella* (1968), *The Horsemen* (1971, in part only). JG

Renoir, Jean

Born 1894 in Paris, France. Director, actor, writer. Jean is second son of the painter, Auguste, brother of the actor, Pierre, and uncle of the cameraman, CLAUDE RENOIR. He served as a cavalry officer and pilot in the First World War and deserted his first occupation, ceramics, for the cinema after marrying Catherine Hessling, his first wife, an actress who was one of his father's models. He reveals his family background most warmly in the biography 'Renoir my Father' (1958). His earliest, silent films featured his wife, moving in subject between fantasy and realism, and included *La Fille de l'Eau* (1924), *Nana* (after Zola, 1926), *La Petite Marchande d'Allumettes* (1927), adapted from Hans Christian Andersen and the delightful Army farce, *Tire-au-Flanc* (1928). He acted in some of ALBERTO CAVALCANTI's silent films and later in his own.

With the coming of sound he distinguished himself as an artist. His films enjoyed considerable commercial success because of their strong and imaginatively handled stories. They included *La Chienne* (1931), *La Nuit du Carrefour* (after Simenon) and *Boudu sauvé des Eaux* (1932), *Madame Bovary* and *Toni* (1934), *Le Crime de M. Lange* (1935) and *Les Bas Fonds* (after Gorki, 1936) and *La Bête Humaine* (1938), in several of which JEAN GABIN and MICHEL SIMON appeared. ERICH VON STROHEIM, whose realistic silent films Renoir had greatly admired, starred in *La Grande Illusion* (1937), one of the films of the period exposing the futility of war. In 1936 Renoir made *La Vie est à Nous* for the French Communist Party, reflecting his own left-wing views of this period. *La Marseillaise* (1938), a documentary portrait of the French Revolution, was financed from public money; *Une Partie de Campagne* (1936) was a gay, lyrical film revealing a countryman's inborn response to nature. His crowning achievement of the 1930s was *La Règle du Jeu* (1939), a comedy of manners only appreciated much later for its subtle mixing of tragedy and farce, comedy and satire, exposing the underlying violence in human relationships symbolized by the destruction of wild life in the upper-class ritual of the shooting party. Renoir's work dominated French film-making in the mid-1930s; the economy, directness and simplicity of his style emphasized his innate and warm humanity.

Renoir's warmth (amounting, he would say, to love) in the handling of actors and actresses, and the humility with which he has always been prepared to abandon the established rules of film-making and permit improvisation, led him to anticipate post-war neo-realism and some of the technical freedoms adopted later by the French New Wave.

From 1939 to 1954 he made no films in France: in 1941 he went into self-imposed exile in the USA. There he made at least one film of note, *The Southerner* (1945), which owed much to its rural locations. In 1950 he made *The River* in Bengal, giving his encouragement, in passing, to an aspiring film-maker SATYAJIT RAY. In 1952 came *Le Carrosse d'Or*, made in Italy, and finally he returned to France to direct the highly successful *French Cancan* (1954); it re-created the Paris of the 1880s and the establishment of the Moulin Rouge. After the comparative failure of his next film, *Éléna et les Hommes* (1956), Renoir turned to the theatre and television, enjoying the opportunities for quick production which the latter offered. He directed a Jekyll and Hyde story for the small screen, *Le Testament du Dr Cordelier* (1959), in only ten days; there was a similar carefree style in *Le Déjeuner sur l'Herbe* (1959), a film which, like others before it, showed his lyrical response to the countryside, and in *Le Caporal Épinglé* (1961), a light-hearted story of prisoners of war and their attempts to escape. 'The only thing I can bring to this illogical, irresponsible and cruel universe is my love', Renoir has said. He takes the world as it is and interprets life with the generous humanity which is his greatest quality both as a man and an artist. His last film, *Le Théâtre de Jean Renoir* (1970) was made for French television. RM

Above: Jean Renoir and Carette in 'La Règle du Jeu' (Renoir, France, 1939)
Below: Delphine Seyrig in 'Muriel' (Alain Resnais, France, 1963)

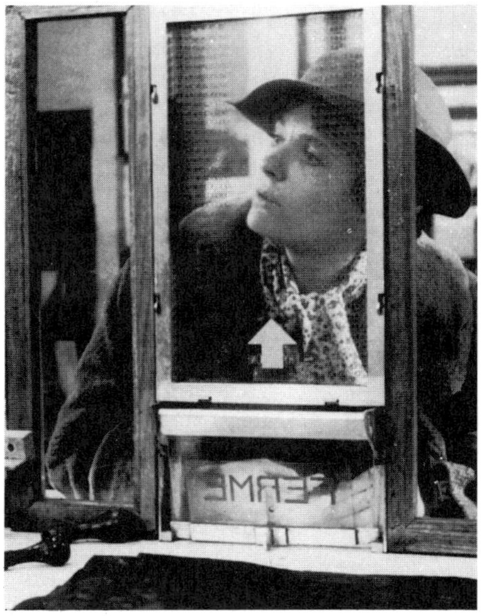

Renter

A company or person who hires a film to an exhibitor. Also known as a Distributor.

Re-recording

An electrical process of transferring sound recordings (such as dialogue, music, sound effects, etc.,) on to one sound track.

Resnais, Alain

Born 1922 in Vannes, France. After training as an actor during the Occupation period and for a year at IDHEC in Paris, he worked as a cameraman on documentary and acted as assistant director and editor on NICOLE VÉDRÈS's fine compilation film, *Paris 1900*. During the later 1950s Resnais acted as both editor and technical adviser for directors such as AGNÈS VARDA, JACQUES DONIOL-VALCROZE and HENRI COLPI. Meanwhile he had been experimenting with 8mm and 16mm short-film making, even making a 16mm feature, *Ouvert Pour Cause d'Inventaire* (1946), and a film using improvised techniques, *Un Dimanche tous Ensemble* (1956), which was abandoned. In 1947 he had also made a series of 16mm shorts on various painters, and other documentaries, culminating in his first professionally directed documentary, *Van Gogh* (1948). This was followed in 1950 by two films, *Gauguin* and *Guernica* – his most significant film on an art subject. He also made several other short films, *Nuit et Brouillard* (1955), arguably the best documentary on Auschwitz, and *Toute la Mémoire du Monde* (1956), a brilliant study of the *Bibliothèque Nationale* in Paris, which shows his absorption in the relationship of the present to the past and *Le Chant du Styrène* (1958), which turned industrial processes into an abstract kaleidoscope.

Resnais's first feature was one of his finest, *Hiroshima, Mon Amour* (1959), scripted closely with MARGUERITE DURAS. Resnais was always to do this with different writers – whose collaboration he recognized to be of the greatest importance to him provided they were prepared to integrate their creative talent with his. Resnais's prime concern is with human psychology, the drama of the mind, the integration of the personality present with that of the past. His characters become very real to him, though he prefers to leave the nature of their conduct open to speculation by the audience. In *Hiroshima, Mon Amour* a French actress's memory of a traumatic experience in the past (as a girl she had loved a German soldier, killed by the Resistance) is awakened while working in Hiroshima on a pacifist film; to some extent she comes to terms with this wound in her memory through a brief love affair with a Japanese, whose own trauma is linked with the bomb dropped on Hiroshima. The various themes, past and present, are subtly and beautifully intertwined, bound together by skilful editing and the musical themes of GIOVANNI FUSCO and Georges Delerue.

In varying ways Resnais's later films developed his key interest. *L'Année Dernière à Marienbad* (1961) operates entirely in the mind, leaving the audience to resolve the puzzle of what exactly were the past relationships of the three principals – a woman and two men who meet in a great baroque hotel and perform a wholly stylized action which is largely prompted by the illusion of what may have happened a year ago at Marienbad. *Muriel, ou le Temps d'un Retour* (1963) concerns the relation of Hélène, a gambler, to her past lover, the shady Alphonse. *La Guerre est Finie* (1966) is more political, a study of an exiled Spanish revolutionary's development in time, while in *Je t'aime, Je t'aime* (1968) a man is made to relive an old, difficult love affair. In 1967, Resnais contributed a striking episode to the composite film, *Loin du Viêt-Nam*, in which a left-wing intellectual pours out his feelings of guilt about the war in a monologue spoken to his girlfriend. His latest project is *Délivrez-nous du bien* (1971).

Resnais is a deeply thoughtful, seemingly rather detached, highly technical film-maker. Yet the themes of time, memory, the voluntary and involuntary nature of human behaviour are uppermost in his films, which should in perspective emerge as belonging to the most mature film-making of the second half of the century. See 'Alain Resnais, or The Theme of Time' by John Ward (1968) and 'The Cinema of Alain Resnais' by Roy Armes (1968). RM

Retake
The rephotographing of a scene, or the re-recording of a sound take

Rice, Ron (1935–1964)
Born in New York, USA. Underground film-maker. A remarkable talent, but unfulfilled, because of his early death. He came to film-making initially through his desire to record cycle-racing, in which he was involved. With his friends Vernon Zimmerman and Taylor Mead he made *The Flower Thief* (1960), a study of what Sheldon Renan calls 'a sort of beat saint'. His *Senseless* (1962), filmed in Mexico, has mainly aesthetic appeal. He followed this with the unfinished *The Queen of Sheba meets the Atom Man* (1963) and the aesthetic-erotic *Chumlum* (1964), the portrait of some sort of Arabian Nights brothel. A man of wild imagination, subject to drug-taking, he died impoverished but still full of plans in Acapulco.

Richardson, Ralph
Born 1902 in Cheltenham, England. Actor, who made his stage début in 1921 as Lorenzo in 'The Merchant of Venice'. He joined the Birmingham Repertory Company, and appeared in many plays. He has specialized in Shakespearean productions. He entered films in 1933, in *The Ghoul*. During the Second World War he was in the Fleet Air Arm; he was knighted in 1947. He is essentially a character actor with a sensitive command of emotion and a sharp eye for comedy and eccentric behaviour. His films include: *Things to Come* (1936), *The Citadel* (1938), *Anna Karenina* and *The Fallen Idol* (1948), *The Heiress* (1949), *An Outcast of the Islands* (1951), *Home at Seven* (which he also directed) and *The Sound Barrier* (1952), *Richard III* (1956), *Exodus* (1960), *Dr Zhivago* (1966), *The Battle of Britain*, *The Looking Glass War* and *The Bed-Sitting Room* (1969), *David Copperfield* (1970).

Richardson, Tony
Born 1928 in Yorkshire, England. One of the major younger British directors of the 1950s. Part of the 'angry young man' syndrome, he helped transfer the 'kitchen sink' drama of the theatre to the screen with *Look Back in Anger* (1958), *A Taste of Honey* (1961), *The Loneliness of the Long Distance Runner* (1963). Since the explosive – and unexpected – success of the period romp, *Tom Jones* (1963), his style has matched the extravagance of his subject matter; a cool, modern-orientated *Hamlet* (1969), based on his stage production with NICOL WILLIAMSON, is the exception.

A respected television and theatre director before he went into films (he began with amateur productions at Oxford), he first co-directed a 'Free Cinema' short with KAREL REISZ, *Momma Don't Allow* (1955), which was critically acclaimed. Drawing on his stage training and flair for directing and choosing actors, he made *Look Back in Anger* (1958) and *The Entertainer* (1960), both based on plays by JOHN OSBORNE, establishing a raw intensity and preference for on-the-spot locations still relatively unusual in British films.

With John Osborne he formed Woodfall Films, which sponsored the experimental work of other directors, including Karel Reisz's *Saturday Night and Sunday Morning* (1960). His Hollywood films – *Sanctuary* (1961), *The Loved One* (1965) – betrayed signs of studio pressures, and latterly he has exchanged the spartan spirit of his earlier work for provocative period themes, though he continues to be attracted to anti-establishment themes, notably in *The Charge of the Light Brigade* (1968) and *Ned Kelly* (1970).

Other films: *Sailor from Gibraltar* and *Mademoiselle* (1966), *Red and Blue* (1967), *Laughter in the Dark* (1969). MH

Richter, Hans
Born 1888 in Berlin, Germany. Avant-garde director, film theoretician and teacher, and also a distinguished painter. After art studies and war service he became involved in the Dada movement in Zürich. He formed a creative association with the Danish artist, Viking Eggeling (who died in 1925). As a result, from 1919, they developed an initial form of abstract film-making by painting directly on rolls of film, a technique to be adopted and carried further by LEN LYE and NORMAN MCLAREN during the 1930s. At this period he made *Rhythmus 21* (1921), *Rhythmus 25* (1925), *Filmstudy* (1926), *Inflation* (1926–7), *Vormittagsspuk* (1927–8), the latter with music by Paul Hindemith, and with appearances by Richter, Hindemith and Darius Milhaud; later he directed other experimental films, including *Everyday* (1929), made in London, and enjoying the distinction of showing EISENSTEIN dressed up as an English policeman. These and other films reveal an impish humour as well as a fine graphic sense. In the same year he took part in a congress on independent film-makers in Switzerland, where he made a short film, *Sturm über La Sarraz*, with Eisenstein and others, and published a book 'Filmgegner von heute – Filmfreunde von morgen'. In 1933–41 he worked variously in France, Switzerland and the Netherlands, making primarily sponsored and commercial films. In 1941 he emigrated to the USA, where he made many art films, including the celebrated composite feature, *Dreams That Money Can Buy* (1945–7, made with the artists Léger, Duchamp, Calder, Ernst, Man Ray, the composer Milhaud, and others). During the 1950s he was to make other films in Switzerland in association with these artists. In 1948–52 he was Professor of Film at the Film Institute of City College, New York. After this, he took up residence permanently in Switzerland. He has also worked throughout as a painter, holding international exhibitions from 1946. He contributed a detailed essay on his early work to

Roger Manvell's 'Experiment in the Film' (1949), and in 1967 published memoirs of the years 1915–33, 'Köpfe and Hinterköpfe'. RM

Riefenstahl, Leni
Born 1902 in Berlin, Germany. Actress and director. Trained as a dancer, she became a dance director in the theatre. Her career in cinema began with her appearance in Arnold Fanck's series of mountain films, *Der heilige Berg* (1926), *Der grosse Sprung* (1927), and the sound films *Der weisse Rausch* (*The White Hell of Piz Palü*, 1931) and *SOS Eisberg* (1933). She also directed and starred in her own mountain film, *Das blaue Licht* (*The Blue Light*, 1932). She then directed a series of Nazi documentaries: *Der Sieg des Glaubens* (*Victory of Faith*, 1933), based on the 1933 Party Congress; *Triumph of the Will* (*Triumph des Willens*, 1934), the record of the Nazi Rally at Nuremberg in 1934; *Tag der Freiheit – unsere Wehrmacht* (1935). She made her films at the direct request of Hitler, who was a great admirer of her talent, and as a result incurred the hostility of Goebbels. Her success with *Triumph of the Will* led to her being invited by the International Olympic Committee to make a record film of the 1936 Olympic Games, which were held in Germany. This film, *Olympiad* (*Fest der Völker* and *Fest der Schönheit*, 1936–8), remains in the estimate of many the finest record of the Olympics yet to have been made. (See also KON ICHIKAWA.) Both *Triumph of the Will* and *Olympiad* reveal complete mastery of editing; in the latter the vast body of material her cameramen recorded was edited with a tempo which not only matched but enhanced the natural movements of the athletes. Later Leni Riefenstahl directed another feature, *Tiefland* (1945), shot in the Italian Alps; it was based on Eugène d'Albert's opera, and she appeared in it as a gypsy girl. Later she was to attempt to make a documentary on the slave trade in East Africa, *Schwarze Fracht* (1956), which was not finished, and she also acted as camerawoman to an expedition in 1964 to the Sudan, Kenya and Tanganyika, during which she obtained some remarkable photographs of the little-known Nuba tribe. RM

Rilla, Walter;
Rilla, Wolf
Walter Rilla, born Saarbrücken, Germany, in 1899. After a long career as stage actor and producer in Berlin, he acted in several films in both France and Germany before coming to Britain in 1934, where he appeared in, among other films, *The Scarlet Pimpernel* (1934) and *Victoria the Great* (1937). After working during the war as a BBC radio drama producer, he returned to films as an actor, giving dignified, distinguished performances in such films as *The Lisbon Story* (1946) and *State Secret* (1950), and directing a religious film, *Behold the Man* (1951). His son Wolf Rilla (born 1920) has directed many British films, of which the best known are *Pacific Destiny* (1950), *Bachelor of Hearts* (1958) and *Village of the Damned* (1962). Wolf Rilla is the author of a textbook for students of professional film-making, 'A–Z of Movie-Making' (1970).

Risi, Dino
Born 1916 in Rome, Italy. An unpredictable director, Risi made a group of good documentaries *(Barboni, Cortili, Strade di Napoli)* in the early neo-realist period, contributed a creditable episode to *Amore in Città* (1953), and directed two satirical comedies of quality – *Una vita difficile* (1961) and *Il Sorpasso* (1962) – in between work of indifferent interest, with a preference for light farcical subjects. Other films: *Poveri ma belli; Belle ma povere* (1957), *Il Vedovo* and *Il Mattatore* (1959), *La Marcia su Roma* (1962), *I Mostri* (1963), *Il Tigre* and *Sissignore* (1967), *The Priest's Wife* (1970).

Riskin, Robert (1897–1955)
Born in New York, USA. Writer. Began writing original scripts for Paramount from age of 17 and later several plays. Very prolific screenwriter in the 1930s, developing a sophisticated, satirical style (with a fondness for innocent, oddball characters) which often reflected aspects of the New Deal ideology. Provided FRANK CAPRA with his best material, including *American Madness* (1932), *Lady for a Day* (1933), *It Happened One Night* (1934), *Mr Deeds Goes to Town* (1936), *You Can't Take it with you* (1938), *Meet John Doe* (1941) – in some cases adapted from notable stage originals. Also worked with Capra on his post-war remakes and turned producer on some features. Other films include *The Whole Town's Talking* (1935), written with Jo Swerling. JG

Ritt, Martin
Born 1919 in New York, USA. Meticulous American director, who entered films via the stage and television. His solid, fastidious craftsmanship occasionally makes for heavy-going

Below: Eiji Okada and Emmanuèle Riva in 'Hiroshima mon Amour' (Alain Resnais, France, 1959)
Bottom: Debbie Reynolds and Jason Robards Jnr in 'Divorce American Style' (Bud Yorkin, USA, 1967)

drama, but at his best – in *Hud* (1962), *Hombre* (1967), *The Molly Maguires* (1969) – he skilfully integrates commanding characters into credibly drawn backgrounds and situations. His sense of period (whether modern Western as in *Hud* or a 19th-century Irish immigrant setting in *The Molly Maguires*) is especially marked. Notable films include: *A Man is Ten Feet Tall* (1956), *No Down Payment* (1957), *The Long Hot Summer* (1958), *Paris Blues* (1961), *The Outrage* (1964), *The Spy who Came in from the Cold* (1965), *The Brotherhood* (1968), *The Great White Hope* (1970). MH

Riva, Emmanuèle
Born 1932 in North-East France. Graceful French stage and screen actress with a suggestion of Garboesque magnetism, whose performance in ALAIN RESNAIS's provocative *Hiroshima Mon Amour* (1959) established her as an important contemporary film personality. Her special gift for creating an atmosphere of uneasy quiet around her characters has been particularly effective in *Léon Morin, Prêtre* (1960), *Thérèse Desqueyroux* (1962), *Thomas L'Imposteur* (1965), *Soledad* (1966).

Rivette, Jacques
Born 1928 in Rouen, France. Director. Began as film journalist and assistant on films by BECKER and RENOIR. Shot several 16 mm shorts for other directors and made three himself. One of the most uncompromising of the new French school; his reputation over the last eleven years rests on three long features of which the first (and most stimulating) was *Paris nous appartient* (1961), a strange, hypnotic essay about a group of characters haunted by a vague, unseen menace and clearly influenced by LANG, but Rivette's brilliantly controlled narrative style and *angst*-ridden characterization seemed very much his own. *Suzanne Simonin, la Religieuse de Diderot* (1966) became the centre of a stupid controversy over its alleged anti-clericalism; a sensitive study based on the true story of an unwilling nun, it suffered from certain defects in casting. *L'Amour Fou* (1968), lasting over four hours, again contrasted the real world with private fantasies using a stage rehearsal as its starting point. Often over-intellectualized and tedious, it perhaps strained his talent too far, yet its best scenes confirmed Rivette's acute and fastidious intellect; unfortunately, until he finds a permanently sympathetic producer, it seems likely that he will only continue to work spasmodically. Recently he has worked for French television. JG

Roach, Hal
Born 1892 in Elmira, New York, USA. MACK SENNETT's nearest rival as a producer of slapstick comedy, Roach left home at 17 and went to Alaska, where, among other jobs, he was for a time a gold prospector. Drifting into movies in 1912, when he was signed as a screen cowboy by Universal, he entered production in his own right in 1914 when with HAROLD LLOYD he established Rolin Films. The success of Lloyd's *Lonesome Luke* series enabled Roach to expand his activities and remove from his small studio on Santa Monica Boulevard to a larger and better equipped one in Culver City (1919). In 1921 he initiated the *Our Gang* series of infant comedies which continued for more than two decades, with constant changes of personnel. The success of this series encouraged him also to the eccentric notion of a slapstick series employing only animal stars, the *Dippy-Doo-Dads* films. One of his greatest achievements however was to team STAN LAUREL and OLIVER HARDY, in *Putting Pants on Philip* (1927). Apart from innumerable two-reel comedies, including those of Harold Lloyd and Laurel and Hardy, Roach produced the *Topper* series – *Topper* (1937), *Topper Takes a Trip* (1939), *Topper Returns* (1941) and LEWIS MILESTONE's version of Steinbeck's *Of Mice and Men* (1940). Among the directors developed by Roach were GEORGE STEVENS, Gordon Douglas, Robert F. MacGowan, James W. Horne, James Parrott, Charles Parrott (Charley Chase), Edward Sedgwick, GEORGE SIDNEY, NORMAN Z. MCLEOD, Ray and LEO MCCAREY. In 1948 Roach formed Hal Roach Television Corporation. He was awarded an Oscar in 1937 as producer of the year's best short subject, *Bored of Education* (directed by Gordon Douglas). DR

Robards Jnr, Jason
Born 1922 in Chicago, USA. American stage and screen actor, son of a silent screen star, he made his film début in *The Journey* (1959). His rather Bogart-ish looks and sardonic style have not often been successfully used in films: though his performances in *A Thousand Clowns* and *Any Wednesday* (1966), *The St Valentine's Day Massacre* (1966), *The Night They Raided Minsky's* and *Isadora* (1968) were notable. In 1970 he starred disastrously as Brutus in *Julius Caesar*. Other main films: *Tender is the Night* (1961), *Long Day's Journey into Night* (1962), *Big Deal at Dodge City* (1966), *Divorce American Style* (1967), *Once Upon a Time in the West* (1969), *Tora! Tora! Tora!* and *The Ballad of Cable Hogne* (1970).

Robbe-Grillet, Alain
Born 1922 in Brest, France. Leading French novelist, and latterly screenwriter and director. His first link with the film came with ALAIN RESNAIS's invitation to script *L'Année Dernière à Marienbad* (1961); his introduction to the published script shows his sensitivity to the film medium. Since then he has directed films which develop themes established in his novels and in *Marienbad* – the search for identity and the nature of human relationships: *L'Immortelle* (1963), *Trans-Europe-Express* (1967) and *L'Homme qui Ment* (1968). The first reveals the erotic relationships within a tense triangle of people, investigating these relationships in stylized phases of contradiction and revelation; the second is a Pirandello-like immixture of the 'real' and the 'imagined'; while the third deals with a character who improvises his identity. *L'Éden et Après* (1970), a rather crude sexual fantasy, was followed by *Les Gommes* (1972). RM

Roberts, Rachael
Born 1927 in Llanelly, Wales. Actress, married for a period to REX HARRISON. Acts on stage and television as well as in films. At her best in strong, down-to-earth parts, women who suffer, but not gladly. Films include: *Valley of Song* (1952), *The Good Companions* (1957), *Our Man in Havana* (1959), *Saturday Night and Sunday Morning* (1960), *This Sporting Life* (1963), *A Flea in her Ear* (1968), *The Reckoning* (1969).

Robeson, Paul
Born 1898 in Princetown, New Jersey, USA. Singer and actor son of Negro minister who escaped from slavery. Graduated in, and at one time practised law; then turned to stage and concert singing. Notable for his massive physique and deep reverberant voice. Films: *The Emperor Jones* (1933), *Sanders of the River* (1935), *Showboat* (1936), *Song of Freedom* (1937), *Jericho* and *King Solomon's Mines* (1938), *The Proud Valley* (1939), *Tales of Manhattan* (1942).

Robinson, Edward G.
Born 1893 in Bucharest, Romania. One of the most important of the image-creating Hollywood stars of the 1930s and leading member of the Warner's gangster triumvirate which also included JAMES CAGNEY and HUMPHREY BOGART. His later, less type-cast portrayals reveal a powerful, if rather confined, talent. Emigrating to America with his family when he was ten, he studied at the American Academy of Dramatic Art, worked in vaudeville and stock and for the Theatre Guild. His first film was *The Bright Shawl* in 1923. But it was his ebullient, cocky gangster in *Little Caesar* (1931) that established his film 'type'. A critical as well as box-office success, *Little Caesar* cast him in a mould which dictated the style of his roles for many years. After the Second World War he demonstrated his greater versatility in such films as *The Woman in the Window* and *Our Vines have Tender Grapes* (1945), *All My Sons* (1948), *A Hole in the Head* (1959), *Sammy Going South* (1962) and *The Cincinnati Kid* (1965).

Other notable films: *Five Star Final* (1931), *The Whole Town's Talking* (1934), *Bullets or Ballots* (1936), *Kid Galahad* (1937), *A Slight Case of Murder* (1938), *Confessions of a Nazi Spy* (1939), *Dr Ehrlich's Magic Bullet* and *Brother Orchid* (1940), *The Sea Wolf* (1941), *Larceny Inc* (1942), *Double Indemnity* (1944), *Scarlet Street* and *The Stranger* (1946), *Key Largo* (1948), *Hell on Frisco Bay* (1956), *Two Weeks in Another Town* (1962), *The Outrage* (1964), *McKenna's Gold* (1969), *Song of Norway* (1970). MH

Robison, Arthur (1888–1935)
Born in Chicago, USA. Director in the German cinema. After studying at Munich university,

he became a Doctor of Medicine, but abandoned a medical career and entered the cinema in 1914, working initially as a scriptwriter and eventually as a director. His most celebrated films during the silent period were *Schatten* (*Warning Shadows*, 1922), an expressionist film of advanced technique and photography – one of the first to experiment with the omission of dialogue and narrative captions – and *Manon Lescaut* (1926), with its striking sets designed by PAUL LENI. In England he made a fine silent version of *The Informer* (1928). He worked in the sound period also, when his films included *Mordprozess, Mary Dugan* (1931) and a third version of the inescapable subject in the German cinema, *The Student of Prague* (1935).

Robson, Mark

Born 1913 in Montreal, Canada. American director who graduated from the cutting room on *Citizen Kane* (1941) and *The Magnificent Ambersons* (1942) and directed several of producer VAL LEWTON's much-admired horror films. A period with STANLEY KRAMER resulted in the excellent, hard-driving *Home of the Brave* and *Champion* (1949). His later work on conventional romantic subjects achieved a high technical gloss but little original style. Principal films include: *Isle of the Dead* (1945), *Bedlam* (1946), *My Foolish Heart* (1950), *The Bridges at Toko-Ri* (1954), *The Harder They Fall* (1956), *Peyton Place* and *The Inn of the Sixth Happiness* (1958), *Nine Hours to Rama* (1963), *Von Ryan's Express* (1965), *Valley of the Dolls* (1967), *Happy Birthday, Wanda June* (1972).

Rocha, Glauber

Born 1939 in Bahia, Brazil. As a critic Rocha was the principal architect of Brazil's *Cinema Nôvo*, and one of its best directors. His early feature films, *Barravento* (1961), *Deus e o Diabo na terra do sol* (1964), *Terra em Transca* (1967) and *Antonio das Mortes* (1969), created their own genre, associating anthropology, folklore, political agitation and an innate lyrical quality. A more recent film however, *Der Leone Have Sept Cabecas* (1970) has essayed a pretentious brand of political allegory, with dubious success. In 1971 he moved to Europe for political reasons.

Rochemont, Louis De

See DE ROCHEMONT

Rogers, Ginger

Born 1911 in USA. Actress, comedienne and dancer, and band singer; best known for her film musicals with FRED ASTAIRE in the 1930s and a series of subtle comedy performances in the 1940s and 1950s. These and other films include: *Gold Diggers of 1933* (1933), *The Gay Divorcée* and *Roberta* (1934), *Top Hat* (1935), *Follow the Fleet* (1936), *Shall We Dance?* (1937), *Stage Door* (1938), *Kitty Foyle* (for which she was given an Academy Award for Best Performance: 1940), *Tom, Dick and Harry* (a straight role, 1940), *The Major and the Minor* (1942), *Monkey Business* (1952). She made a successful stage come-back in London in the late 1960s in the musical 'Mame'.

Rogers, Peter

Born 1916 in Rochester, England. Prolific British producer whose record-breaking series of bawdy 'Carry On . . .' comedies has become one of the two most enduring, money-making successes in the post-war British film industry: the other is the Hammer 'Horror' series. A journalist, occasional playwright and radio scriptwriter, he entered the film business in 1942; but it was not until 1958, when he produced the first of more than twenty 'Carry Ons', *Carry On Sergeant*, that he found the crude but effective formula whose popularity is based on the British public's traditional fondness for music hall exuberance and vulgarity. While continuing to produce two 'Carry Ons' a year, he is now heading a film production programme of small budget entertainments.

Rogers, Will (1879–1935)

Born in Oklahoma, USA. Comedian and popular, home-spun philosopher, first in the Ziegfeld Follies. Films include: *Laughing Bill Hyde* (silent, 1918), *A Connecticut Yankee at the Court of King Arthur* (1930), *State Fair* (1933), *Judge Priest* and *Handy Andy* (1934), *Steamboat Round the Bend* (1935). A biographical film, *The Story of Will Rogers*, was made in 1952, with his son, Will Rogers Jnr, in the name part. His biography, 'Our Will Rogers', was published in 1953.

Rogosin, Lionel

Born 1924 in New York City, USA. Director. Rogosin made his reputation with *On the Bowery* (1954), a candid-camera study of alcoholism, and later *Come Back Africa* (1959), a film about Negro problems shot 'underground' in South Africa. Both films had a slight story element, though they were in the main documentaries. His later films include *Good Times, Wonderful Times* (1964).

Rohmer, Eric

Born 1920 in Nancy, France. Writer and director. Studied literature, became film critic for many French journals and, at one time, was chief editor of 'Cahiers du Cinéma'. With CHABROL, wrote major book on HITCHCOCK. Started in films as scriptwriter and director of shorts; then made feature *Le Signe du Lion* (1960) on Paris locations. His main literary work is the 'Six Contes Moraux', which he is now filming – two on 16 mm and, so far, three commercial productions: *La Collectionneuse* (1967), *Ma Nuit chez Maud* (1969), *Le Genou de Claire* (1970). Rohmer is a unique talent in the French cinema: a brilliant, epigrammatic writer, morally concerned with his characters' response to art, religion and life and quietly observing them as they try to work out old affairs or tentatively seek new ones. His film style has become more pared down over the years and *Maud* and *Claire*, in particular, concentrate on a series of cool, urbane conversations in which each scene makes its point and then stops. Rohmer's world has been criticized as being too cerebral and intellectualized but it is his *own* world and he continues to work precisely and enjoyably within it. JG

Röhrig, Walther

(Dates not known). Designer, at first working in Zürich for the theatre. He was closely associated with the expressionist movement in art and, like his colleagues HERMANN WARM (who began designing for the cinema in 1912) and Walther Reimann, was a member of the Berlin Sturm group. Like Reimann, he entered the film industry as a designer around 1918, and the three designers collaborated in creating the celebrated expressionist sets for *The Cabinet of Dr Caligari* (1919). Later Röhrig was to work, either alone or in association with Warm, and particularly with Robert Herlth, another member of the expressionist movement, on a great number of films, initially sustaining varied degrees of expressionism: LANG's *Destiny* (1921), MURNAU's *The Last Laugh* (1924), *Tartuffe* (1925), *Faust* (1926), as well as such films as *The Golem* (1920) and *The Chronicle of the Grieshaus* (1924–5). His partnership with Herlth lasted well into the 1930s, and their sound films together included *The Flute Concert of Sanssouci, Congress Dances, Morgenrot, Flüchtlinge, Das Mädchen Joanna,* and *Amphitryon*.

Romania

As in other Balkan countries, film-making before the Second World War had been sparse and difficult to establish. Under the new, post-war régime a nationalized industry was set up in 1948, and plans were laid down for the establishment of studios in Bucharest, along with film training and the development of cinema construction. The number of cinemas now stands at around 600. Production gradually took shape, and by the end of the 1950s was reasonably well developed. At the same time short-film production flourished, and Romania became an international centre for animation as a result of the outstanding work of the animator, POPESCO-GOPO. Every other year Mamaia stages the International Festival of Animated Film, alternating with Annecy.

The principal directors of features in Romania, with representative films are:

Mircea Drăgan (born 1932): *Golgotha* (1966); *The Column* (the struggle between the Dacians and the Romans; 1970)

Lucian Bratu (born 1924): *The Secret Code* (1959); *Tudor* (about the revolutionary hero Tudor Vladimirescu; 1964); *A Charming Girl* (1966)

Dinu-Constantin Cocea (born 1929): *The Revenge of the Outlaws* (a story of folk-heroes of the 19th century; 1967–8)

Sergiu Nicolaescu (born 1930): *The Dacians* (*The Immortals*, a Romanian-French co-

production; 1966); *Michael the Brave* (about a Romanian prince of the 16th century who unified Romania; 1969)
Mircea Muresan (born 1930): *Knock-out* (1967)
Julian Mihu (born 1926): *When the Mist is Lifting* (1957); *Sentimental Story* (1961)
Lucian Pintile (born 1933): *Sunday at Six o'Clock* (1965); *Reconstruction* (1968–70)
Victor Iliu (1912–68): *Mill of Luck and Plenty* (1956)
Andrei Blaier (born 1933): *He Was my Friend* (1961); *The Mornings of a Sensible Youth* (1966); *Then Came the Legend* (1968)
Savel Stiopul (born 1926): *The Last Night of Childhood* (1966)
Geo Saizescu (born 1932): *A Midsummer Day's Smile* (1963); *The Saturday Night Dance* (1968)
Livia Ciulei (born 1923): *The Eruption* (1959); *The Danube Waves* (1963); *The Forest of the Hanged* (1965)
Elisabeta Bostan (born 1932): *Youth without Old Age* (1968). RM

Above: Ginger Rogers and Fred Astaire in 'Top Hat' (Mark Sandrich, USA, 1935)
Below: Will Rogers and William V. Mong in 'A Connecticut Yankee at the Court of King Arthur' (David Butler, USA, 1930)

Romm, Mikhail (1901–1971)
Born in Irkutsk, USSR. A man of great culture, wit and intelligence, Romm made a notable début with his *Boule de Suif* (1934), one of the last silent films and a singularly elegant adaptation from Maupassant. In 1937 he was ordered to make a socialist equivalent of FORD's *Lost Patrol*, and delivered an excellent drama of a beleaguered patrol in the desert, *The Thirteen*. His official standing was assured by the success of the dignified hagiographies which for the first time presented the figure of Lenin in fiction films: *Lenin in October* (1937) and *Lenin in 1918* (1938). *Person No 217* (1945) was an often touching account of the plight of Russian women deported to German labour camps; but the films which followed – *The Russian Question* (1948), *Secret Mission* (1950), *Admiral Ushakov* and *Ships Storm the Bastion* (1953) and *Murder on Dante Street* (1956) – all seemed muted by the pressures of the late Stalinist era. Romm made a remarkable recovery, however, with *Nine Days of One Year* (1961) and the brilliant montage film, *Ordinary Fascism* (1964). DR

Room, Abram
Born 1894 in Vilna, Lithuania. Room had been a theatre director at the Vilnius Jewish Theatre and the Theatre of the Revolution in Moscow and had worked as a journalist before entering the cinema in 1924. His first films – a comedy short, *The Vodka Chase*, and two features, *Death Bay* and *The Traitor* (both 1926) – appear to have been made under the influence of the KULESHOV Studio and are said to have revealed already Room's care for psychological accuracy, despite the extreme formalism characteristic of the times. The following year he made his most famous film *Bed and Sofa*, a shrewd, witty and bitter satire on conditions in the NEP (1921–9) period of socialization. In 1929 Room adapted Barbusse's story *The Ghost That Never Returns*; and the following year made the first Soviet experimental sound film, *Plan for Great Works*. Later films (his most recent, *The Heart Beats Again*, was made in 1956) failed to match the achievements of his classic silent work. DR

Rooney, Mickey
Born 1922 in Brooklyn, New York, USA. Actor from early childhood; famous for his vitality and small stature. First appeared with his parents, who were vaudeville performers. Between the ages of 5 and 11 he played Mickey McQuire in shorts and later played in features. He was most popular in late 1930s and early 1940s and in 1940 won an Academy Award for his Andy Hardy characterization. Films include: *A Midsummer Night's Dream* (1935), *The Devil is a Sissy* (1936), *Boys' Town* (1938), *The Adventures of Huckleberry Finn* (1939), *Andy Hardy's Double Life* (1942) and other Andy Hardy films; later films include *Baby Face Nelson* (1958), *Breakfast at Tiffany's* (1961) and *It's a Mad Mad Mad Mad World* (1963). He directed and acted in *My True Story* (1951) and has also had television series. His autobiography, 'I.E.', was published in 1965.

Roos, Jorgen
Born 1922 in Gilleleje, Denmark. Gifted documentary-maker whose first short film, *Opus 1*, appeared in 1948. Among his numerous works may be mentioned: *Jean Cocteau* and *Tristan Tzara, Father of Dada* (1949), *Copenhagen* (1960), *Knud* (1965).

Rosay, Françoise
Born 1891. Actress. Was married to JACQUES FEYDER, director. She has had a long and distinguished career in films usually playing mature rather dignified women, but often with a strange sense of humour, which include: *Gribiche* (1925), *Le Grand Jeu* (1933), *La Kermesse Héroïque* and *Pension Mimosas* (1935), *Jenny* (1936), *Un Carnet de Bal* (1937), *Une Femme Disparaît* (1941), *Johnny Frenchman* (1945), *The Sound and the Fury* (1958), *The Full Treatment* (1960), *Up From the Beach* (1965).

Rose, William
Born 1918 in Missouri, USA. American screenwriter, for several key years based in Britain where he wrote one of the most celebrated of British film comedies, *Genevieve* (1953), about veteran car fanatics, and went on to write other comedies which exploited British idiosyncracies – *The Maggie* (1953), *The Lady Killers* (1955), *The Smallest Show on Earth* (1957). In America he continued to write comedies which

satirized the quirks in apparently normal human nature, the best being *The Russians are Coming, The Russians are Coming* (1966). But large-scale production values have tended to distort the small humours he celebrates in his work. His funny valentine to racial harmony, *Guess Who's Coming to Dinner* (1967), won him an Academy Award. Other main films include: *The Gift Horse* (1951), *It's a Mad Mad Mad Mad World* (1963), *The Flim Flam Man* (1967), *The Secret of Santa Vittoria* (1969). MH

Roshal, Grigori
Born 1899 in Moscow, USSR. A conscientious director with a penchant for literary adaptation and (latterly) biographical films, Roshal made his début as director with *The Skotinins* (1927). His best sound films were *White Nights of St Petersburg* (1934), *The Oppenheim Family* (an early anti-Nazi subject, 1939), *The Artamanov Affair* (1941), *Academician Pavlov* (1949), *Mussorgsky* (1950), *Rimsky-Korsakov* (1953), *The Sisters* (1957).

Rosher, Charles G.
Born 1885 in Britain. Noted cinematographer. After working in film laboratories in London, he moved to America around 1911, joining several small film companies and eventually United Artists in 1918. Became MARY PICKFORD's favourite cameraman, working with her on *Daddy Long Legs* and *Heart o'the Hills* (1919), *Pollyanna* (1920), *Tess of the Storm Country* (1922), *Rosita* (1923), *Dorothy Vernon of Haddon Hall* (1924), etc. His major silent achievement was MURNAU's *Sunrise* (shot with Karl Struss, 1927), a symphony of shadows, mists and long mysterious travelling shots. His technical mastery and skill in special effects and location shooting were only spasmodically used in the early sound period; then, in the 1940s, a new phase began with MGM musicals and costume romances, notable for their ravishing colour: *Yolanda and the Thief* (1945), *Ziegfeld Follies* (1946), *Words and Music* (1948), *Annie Get Your Gun* (1950), *Show Boat* (1951), *Scaramouche* (1952), *Kiss Me, Kate* (1953). JG

Rosi, Francesco
Born 1922 in Naples, Italy. Director. Began as assistant director to VISCONTI and ANTONIONI among others, and part-scripted several films for these and other directors. Co-directed *Kean* (1956) with VITTORIO GASSMAN, but started his career proper with *La Sfida* (1958), whose sharp, documentary fusion of fact and fiction set the tone for his later work. Rosi is one of the most socially-conscious of all Italian directors with a hard, precise, unsentimental style which, however, occasionally leads him into over-simplification. *Salvatore Giuliano* (1961), totally Italian in its feeling for local traditions and bandit lore; *Le Mani Sulla Città* (1963), a hard-hitting attack on building speculators; and *Il Momento della Verità* (1964), a critical analysis of bull-fighting mystique, have a dramatic photographic sweep and a profusion of documentary detail. A generally under-rated film, *C'era una Volta* (*Cinderella – Italian Style*, 1967), revealed an unexpected vein of charm and fantasy and made superb use of colour, costuming and natural settings. *Uomini Contro* (1970), a bitter anti-war study, suffered when compared with KUBRICK's *Paths of Glory* and lacked the vital creative excitement which informed his earlier work. JG

Rossellini, Roberto
Born 1906 in Rome, Italy. Director. Son of an architect, he showed interest in films from childhood. After making amateur films, he entered the industry to work in editing, dubbing and scriptwriting. He collaborated with Goffredo Alessandrini on *Luciano Serra Pilota* (1938) and Francesco De Robertis on *Uomini sul Fondo* (1940), and it was through De Robertis that he was commissioned to direct a documentary which developed into a feature, *La Nave Bianca* (1941). Its success led to two other films of Rossellini's so-called fascist period, *Un Pilota Ritorna* (1942) and *L'Uomo della Croce* (1943); both showed his inclination to give an 'actuality' treatment to conventional plots. After starting work on *Desiderio* (1943; completed by Marcello Pagliero, 1946), a realistic study of an unsettled girl which was to encounter censorship trouble on its completion after the war, Rossellini turned to planning *Rome, Open City* (1945). This evolved from a documentary about a priest serving in the Resistance to include also the pursuit and capture of a communist resistance worker – it became a strong film with a mixed cast of professional and non-professional players. It was this film which made Rossellini, in the eyes of the world, the leader of the Italian neo-realist movement. *Paisa* (1946), drained of all plotted drama, epitomized the fate of Italy at war in a series of episodes progressing in their setting from South to North. With *Germania Anno Zero* (1947) Rossellini moved to Germany, showing the breakdown of society through the story of a deprived child.

Rossellini turned away from war with *L'Amore* (1948), a tribute to the art of ANNA MAGNANI in two contrasted stories of sensual and spiritual (or superstitious) love, the second written by FELLINI, who had worked on *Rome, Open City* and *Paisà*. All these films reveal Rossellini's research into the resources of film in order to reflect the reality of people, their environment, their psychological condition. After an excursion into a burlesque with serious intentions, *La Macchina Ammazzacattivi* (1948), there followed another phase in Rossellini's career in the series of films he made with INGRID BERGMAN, mostly concerned with wo-

Above: Roberto Rossellini (1956)
Below: 'The World is Rich' (Paul Rotha, GB, 1948)

men isolated from society by some crisis in their lives; starting with *Stromboli, Terra di Dio* (1949). Increasingly obsessed by moral, social, and religious problems, Rossellini made *Francesco, Giullare di Dio* (1950), scripted in part by Fellini, showing St Francis as a man living in true and simple harmony with God and nature; *Europa '51* (1952) showed a woman persecuted because of her desire to do good, while *Dov'è la Libertà?* (1952) featured the comedian TOTO as a man who, released from prison, can only find happiness by returning there. *Viaggio in Italia* (1953) concerns the restoration of a threatened marriage, while *La Paura* (1954) shows a marriage in collapse. It was his last film with Ingrid Bergman, who had also featured in a film record of his stage production of Claudel and Honegger's *Jeanne au bûcher* (1954).

In 1957–8 Rossellini went to India, returning with sufficient material to make a series of films for television as well an episodic, feature-length documentary, *India* (1958), which reveals without comment his profound reaction to his discovery of India and her people. Returning to Italy, he had to make (to his regret) a purely commercial film, *Il Generale della Rovere* (1959). After compensating by making another war film in the tradition of *Rome, Open City* and *Paisà* – *Era Notte a Roma* (1960) – Rossellini made *Viva l'Italia* (1960) about Garibaldi. This started his series of austerely made historical studies, factual chronicles drained of all theatricality, and latterly made specifically for television: *Vanina Vanini* (1961), another study of the Risorgimento period; *La Prise de la Pouvoir par Louis XIV*, made for French television; *Atti degli Apostoli* (1968), five feature-length episodes, and *Socrate* (1970), both for RAI television. His last film at this time for the cinema was *Illibatezza* (1962).

After a post-war period when his world reputation as an innovating realist of the cinema was at its height, neither critics nor public seemed prepared to follow him in his subsequent attempts to make films which seemed to him right both in treatment and moral purpose. Latterly, however, there has been a considerable revival of interest in his work, largely initiated by a new generation of critics. For a highly sympathetic study of his work, see 'Roberto Rossellini' by José Luis Guarner (1970). RM

Rossen, Robert (1908–1966)

Born in New York, USA. Gifted American director and writer who, at his best, accurately mirrored the essential American need to succeed and the corruption that follows in its wake: most importantly in the study of political megalomania, *All the King's Men* (1949), for which he won an Academy Award, but equally vividly in *Body and Soul* (1947), which rejuvenated the *cliché* boxing film formula, and *The Hustler* (1961). He went to Hollywood in 1934, where he worked for Warners as a writer for seven years: among his screenplays are *Marked Woman* (1936), *They Won't Forget* (1937). He also wrote the classic screenplay for *A Walk in the Sun* (1945). In 1947 he directed his first film *Johnny O'Clock*. Thereafter his output was uneven, ranging from the masterly *The Brave Bulls* (1950) to the florid 'race problem' melodrama *Island in the Sun* (1957). His last film *Lilith*, made under difficult circumstances in 1964 and rarely screened, has since been reassessed as a disturbing and sensitive examination of relationships within a mental home.

Other notable films: *Alexander the Great* (1956), *They Came to Cordura* (1959). MH

Rostrum Camera

See ANIMATION CAMERA

Rota, Nino

Born 1911 in Milan, Italy. Composer. As well as enjoying a distinguished musical career in the concert hall and opera house, Rota established himself as a major film composer soon after the Second World War. His vein of lyrical, yearning melody tinged with a soft sadness was much in demand by all Italian directors for both comedy and drama. Main titles include: *Vivere in pace* (1946), *E Primavera* (1949), *I Vitelloni* (1953), *La Strada* (1954), *Le Notti di Cabiria* (1957), *La Grande Guerra* (1959), *La Dolce Vita* (one of his most elaborate scores, 1959), *Rocco and his Brothers* (1960), *Otto e mezzo* (1963), *Giulietta degli spiriti* (1965). Perhaps his most memorable film music is that for VISCONTI's *The Leopard* (1963), whose long flowing lines have an almost Brucknerian eloquence. JG

Rotascope

A piece of equipment for transferring a live-action shot to animated drawings

Rotha, Paul

Born 1907 in London, England. Producer, director, screenwriter and film historian. Trained in graphics at the Slade School of Fine Arts, he was commissioned at 20 to research and write 'The Film Till Now' (1930), which remains an early classic of silent film history, written when there were virtually no precedents to help establish a critical approach to film as a new art form. Rotha's perception as a writer on films was soon to be equalled by his brilliance as a film-maker. After working in 1931–3 with JOHN GRIERSON, Britain's greatest pioneer producer of social documentary, he directed a series of sponsored documentaries. In treatment, photography and calculated editing these represent the highest achievement in impressionistic documentary of the 1930s: *Contact* (1932–3), a film about Imperial Airways, its organization and air-routes; *Rising Tide* (1933–4), on Empire trade and the new docks at Southampton; *Shipyard* (1934–5), about the building of *S.S. Orion* and the men working on her; and *The Face of Britain* (1934–5), on planning in Britain for coal and electricity production. In 1936 Rotha published a critical, aesthetic and historical study of the medium, 'Documentary Film'.

Following a period in the USA (1937–8) he returned to Britain to make *New Worlds for Old* (1938) for the Gas Council and *The Fourth Estate* (1940) for 'The Times', before launching into regular wartime production. To this his outstanding personal contribution was *The World of Plenty* (1943), in which he used challenging technical innovations, derived in part from America's 'Living Newspaper' experiments, in order to jolt audiences into realization of the problems and needs of world food production and distribution. He used screen interviews, sharply integrated library and newsreel shots and Isotype statistical diagrams backed by a multi-voiced commentary, a technique developed further in *Land of Promise* (1945) and *The World is Rich* (1948). Rotha followed these films with *A City Speaks* (1947), a study of city administration in Manchester. Meanwhile Rotha's activities as a producer resulted in many important films, among them *Children of the City* (1944). He co-directed *World without End* with BASIL WRIGHT for UNESCO in 1952, the year after his first location-made feature, *No Resting Place*, a lively film about a tinker family in Ireland.

In 1953–5 Rotha acted as Head of Television Documentary for the BBC. After this he made further features in Germany and Holland: *Cat and Mouse* (1958), *The Silent Raid* and the important compilation film, *The Life of Adolf Hitler* (1962), arguably the best made on Nazi history. Rotha also wrote 'Movie Parade' (1936; revised with Roger Manvell, 1952), 'Rotha on the Film' (1958), and revisions with additions of 'The Film Till Now' (with Richard Griffith, 1949) and of 'Documentary Film' (with Richard Griffith and Sinclair Road, 1952). He also edited 'Television in the Making' (1956). RM

Rotunno, Giuseppe

Born 1923 in Rome, Italy. Cinematographer. Worked as operator with many famous Italian cameramen, including the great G. R. ALDO, becoming lighting cameraman in 1955. Superb in both black-and-white and colour, Rotunno, like DI VENANZO, is able to adapt to various directors' styles. For all, he produces a delicate plastic richness ranging from the operatic *verismo* of VISCONTI's *Le Notti Bianche* (1957), *Rocco and his Brothers* (1960), *The Leopard* (1963), to the baroque fancies of FELLINI's *Satyricon* (1969) and the social realism of MONICELLI's *I Compagni* (1963). He applied a more intimate, yet equally subtle, amalgam of light and colour to ZURLINI's beautiful *Cronaca Familiare* (1962). In recent years, he has worked on several international productions, including HUSTON's *The Bible* (1966) and, in the United States, *Carnal Knowledge* (1971). JG

Rouch, Jean

Born 1917 in Paris, France. Director. Trained as a civil engineer, he turned to ethnography, and, like ROBERT FLAHERTY some 30 years before in the Hudson Bay, shot his first film in 1947 in Africa for record purposes without any cinema-

'Chronique d'un Éte' (Jean Rouch, France, 1961)

tographic training, only to find the medium obtained a hold upon him. In his search for truth on the screen, he came to distrust the merely beautiful shot beloved by many documentary film-makers; what mattered, he thought, was to capture the live, unrepeatable image from the living subject, editing the final film from large quantities of relevant and irrelevant footage. He collected his first record films of African rites and customs in *Les Fils de l'Eau* (1955), showing also the resistance of the black peoples to white intrusion. *Moi un Noir* (1958) showed the life of a black stevedore in Abidjan, while in *La Pyramide Humaine* (1961) he attempted to mingle black and white schoolchildren living there.

For *Chronique d'un Été* (1961) Rouch, working with the sociologist and student of film, Edgar Morin, moved his venue to Paris, making a study of Parisians based largely on filmed interviews and discussions. Once again he attempted to mix people of diverse backgrounds, and the final film was edited from some 20 hours of material. His later attempts to apply his methods and improvisations to fictional situations were less successful; the principal was *La Punition* (1963), as he put it, 'an attempt to create fiction out of reality'. Recent film: *Petit à Petit* (1970). RM

Rough Cut
The initial version of an edited film in which the selected takes are joined in the order planned by the script. Later, this is trimmed and if necessary rearranged to produce the FINE CUT (q.v.).

Rouquier, Georges
Born 1909 in Lunel-Viel, Hérault, France. Director. At first a linotype operator, he was inspired largely by FLAHERTY's work to attempt film-making. In 1929 he had made a single documentary, *Vendanges*, but did not enter the profession until the years of the Occupation, when he started to make very simple studies of rural work and craftsmanship, such as *Le Tonnelier* (1942) and *Le Charron* (1943). His family lived on an isolated farm in the Massif Central, and from their life he created his masterpiece, *Farrebique* (1947), a feature-length documentary in which the passing of the seasons control the family's seemingly unchanging pattern of existence. Although he has attempted, unsuccessfully, to make commercial feature films, Rouquier's genius lies in documentary, such as *Le Sel de la Terre* (1950), set in the Camargue, *Malgovert* (1952), on the building of an hydro-electric station in the mountains of Savoie, and the objective examination of Lourdes, in *Lourdes et ses Miracles* (1954). In 1947 he collaborated with JEAN PAINLEVÉ to make *L'Œuvre Scientifique de Pasteur*. More recently he has been working in television. RM

Roy, Bimal
Born 1909 in Dacca, East Bengal. Cameraman, director, producer. Roy worked for Prince Barua as cameraman for *Devdas* (1935), *Mukti* (1937), and other films. He moved to Bombay to direct films in Hindi, launching his own company, Bimal Roy Productions, in 1952. His film *Two Acres of Land* (1953), dealing with the abortive struggle of a Bengali peasant, deep in debt, to retain his land by working as a rickshaw driver in Calcutta, won awards at both Cannes and Karlovy Vary and was an early example of Indian neo-realism. It was followed by *Sujata*, the story of an untouchable girl. His many other productions include *Gotama the Buddha* and *Bandini (Woman Prisoner)*.

Ruggles, Wesley (1889–1972)
Born in California, USA. Veteran American director, brother of actor Charles, who started in films in 1914, acting as a Keystone Cop. Capable of adapting to most Hollywood themes, he was happiest with romantic subjects with strong humorous or satirical undertones. In 1946 he came to Britain to make what is generally acknowledged to be one of the major disasters of British films – the musical, *London Town*. Principal films: *Cimarron* (1930), *No Man of her Own* (1932), *I'm no Angel* (1933), *Bolero* (1934), *The Gilded Lily* (1935), *I Met him in Paris* and *True Confession* (1937), *My Two Husbands* and *Arizona* (1940), *Somewhere I'll Find You* (1942), *See Here, Private Hargrove* (1944).

Rushes (Dailies)
The first prints made from sound and picture negatives separately for checking action, photographic quality and camera technique.

Russell, Ken
Born 1927 in Southampton, England. Flamboyant British television and film director whose often garish visual style and outrageous flights of dramatic fancy are sometimes impressively apt, sometimes alarmingly off-balance. His intensely personal television biographies have manipulated their real life characters to fit a well-defined 'line'. The best of them – on Isadora Duncan, Elgar, Delius – were possibly the most controlled. He made his first film, *French Dressing*, which he prefers to forget, in 1963. In 1967 he directed a singularly unsatisfactory 'Harry Palmer' spy thriller *Billion Dollar Brain*. But he scored a largely deserved success with his film version of D. H. Lawrence's *Women in Love* (1969), to be followed by a bizarre life of Tchaikovsky, *The Music Lovers* (1970), *The Devils* and *The Boy Friend* (1971). Odd man out among modern young film-makers, he seems to have a much closer affinity to JOSEF VON STERNBERG or MAX OPHÜLS, without, at the moment, their precise filmic judgement. RM

Russell, Rosalind
Born 1911 in Waterbury, Connecticut, USA. Actress on stage, including Broadway, and screen, who studied literature and theology as well as drama. On screen she often plays career women. Her wit and assurance, as well as her business-like good-looks, make her one of Hollywood's most agreeable stars. Films include: *Evelyn Prentice* (1934), *The Citadel* (1938), *The Women* (1939), *His Girl Friday* (1940), *My Sister Eileen* (1942), *Sister Kenny* (1946), *Mourning Becomes Electra* (1947), *Auntie Mame* (1957), *Five-Finger Exercise* (1952), *Rosie* (1967), *Mrs Pollifax – Spy!* (1970).

Russia and the USSR
Russia
Imperial Russia, like every other country of Europe, had its own pioneers of cinema invention. Early in 1896, some time after the LUMIÈRE Brothers in France, the inventors Alexei Sanarski and Ivan Akimov appear to have developed practical cinema apparatus along independent lines. But they were not quick enough to forestall the invasion of the French exploiters of the new craze, who correctly saw a vast market in Russia. It was to be more than a decade before the inception of a genuine native film production.

The Lumières, who had opened the world's first paying public performances in Paris on 28 December 1895, already had a representative in St Petersburg by May of 1896; and after some preliminary demonstrations at the Aquarium, the first film theatre in Russia opened on Nevsky Prospect. The Lumières were quickly followed by ROBERT W. PAUL from England, by EDISON's representatives, and, inevitably, by GAUMONT and PATHÉ.

For some years the cinema was itinerant. The intrepid pioneer showmen trekked the vast expanses of the Russian Empire, astonishing the peasantry at country fairs with their devilries. But from about 1903, following very much the same pattern as in other European countries, there was a rapid growth of static cinemas. The events of 1905 – the Russo-Japanese War and the abortive revolution – were a temporary check, but afterwards, as audiences renewed interest in the moving pictures, legislation was necessary to prevent proliferation of cinemas in the cities. The public's passion for the moving pictures was not shaken by the attacks of the censorship, the clergy, the worried managers of the legitimate theatres and music halls, the danger of fire, or the frequent possibility that the performances might be interrupted by harangues from revolutionaries, taking advantage of the anonymity afforded by the darkness of cinema halls.

The first serious moves towards national production began about 1907. In that year the first Russian studio was opened by Alexander Drankov, soon to be followed by a second, established by Alexander Khanzhonkov. The following year PATHÉ produced the first Russian feature film, *Cossacks of the Don*, acted by Russian actors, but directed by Maurice Maître, a Frenchman who had mastered no word of Russian. This was the period of the *film d'art* – the stagey, over-upholstered, elaborately costumed adaptations of theatrical or literary classics, played by eminent stage actors, which had the enormously important historical role of giving the infant (and formerly somewhat disreputable) cinema a new respectability and a new élite and intellectual audience. Khanzhonkov enjoyed considerable commercial success with importation of Pathé's *films d'art* – *L'Arlésienne* and *L'Assassinat du duc de Guise*; and the first notable Russian productions were all costume pictures in the *film d'art* manner. Drankov, after an abortive attempt at *Boris Godunov*, made the first true Russian film, *Stenka Razin*, in 1908. Appealing at once to national pride and the fashionable taste for costume pictures, the film enjoyed immense success, which stirred Drankov's dedicated rival, Khanzhonkov, to still more ambitious productions (*Song of the Merchant Kalashnikov*, *Queen of Spades*).

This was the period of massive investment of foreign capital in Russia; and alongside the establishment of authentic native production, foreign firms – with Pathé always in the lead – began large-scale production in Russia, using Russian talent. By 1910 the film industry was embarked upon a period of great prosperity, with ten active studios and an innumerable proliferation of cinemas throughout the Empire. Costume pictures remained supreme in Russia longer than anywhere else in Europe, partly because they were less hedged about by literary copyrights, but more because they were less vulnerable than contemporary themes to the neurotic censorship of the Tsarist police. Among the notable successes of the prewar years were Thieman and Reinhardt's *Death of Ivan the Terrible*, *Demon*, *Old Times in Kashira*; Pathé's *Peter the Great*, Khanzhonkov's *Evgeni Onegin* and *Defence of Sebastopol*, Drankov's *Crime and Punishment*, and *1812*, a spectacular production jointly made by Khanzhonkov and Pathé.

Another reasonably safe genre was comedy. Russian comics adopted the French patterns established by ANDRÉ DEED and his contemporaries, and refined by MAX LINDER. One of the most successful, Antonin Fertner, characterized a foolish, improvident gallant, closely based on the creations of Deed and Prince; and other comedians recruited from the circus brought the circus's internationality of style. But two pre-Revolutionary comedians established typical Slavic characters: V. Avdeyev, whose character was the fat bourgeois, Djadja Pud, and N. P. Nirov, *alias* Mitjukha, a peasant youth forever baffled by the mysteries of the big city. A little later, Arkady Boitler, influenced by Linder and CHAPLIN, introduced a more sophisticated style of clowning, with his Arkasha series. Throughout the period however the most popular comedian in Russia was the American JOHN BUNNY, nicknamed for Slav audiences 'Poxon'. His popularity was such that after his death in 1915 a Russian comic, V. Zimovoi, assumed the same identity as Bunny to make a further series of home-made 'Poxon' films.

Again in tune with movements elsewhere in the world, around 1912 cinema producers made a further bid for prestige by seeking to recruit important literary names. Artistically this generally proved a retrograde step: literary disciplines were not helpful to cinematic creation. The value of the tendency was to win the confidence of some elements of the legitimate theatre (though not Stanislavski or Meyerhold, the outstanding figures in the theatre at that time) and help recruit actors from the live stage – again not always an unmixed blessing. More crucial to the development of the cinema were other revolutions which the Russian film industry experienced at very much the same time as they were being experienced in the United States, Britain and most other countries where the cinema had established itself. The trickle of kopeks at the box-office windows combined to a torrent that none could ignore. Big business and businessmen were inspired to take an interest in this new entertainment medium. Businessmen looked for certainties in the lucrative but essentially uncertain world of the cinema; and one of the near-certainties they saw was the star system. For years ASTA NIELSEN, in her Danish films, remained the most popular star in Russia; but there were determined efforts to develop native stars: the romantic MOZHUKIN, Vera Kholodnaya, Vladimir Gaidarov, and Vera Coralli, recruited from the ballet. Star directors also began to arise, some of whose names were to remain famous after the revolution. The Thiemann and Reinhardt company, who had made a speciality and vogue of sentimental drama had Vladimir Gardin, YAKOV PROTAZANOV and Alexander Volkov. Khanzhonkov had Pyotr Chardinin, Yevgeni Bauer and Wladyslaw Starewicz, whose extraordinary animated films using models of beetles and other insects made him a kind of cinematic Grandville.

1913 was the Tercentenary of the Romanov dynasty, and the grandoise celebratory films of Khanzhonkov and Drankov added further to the prestige of the cinema, though perhaps not as much as the avowed interest of the Tsar, which brought a flood of fashionable patronage – a patronage which nevertheless tended to prefer the imported productions and scorn native films.

The War came, and with it still further impetus to Russian film production. Foreign competition was largely withdrawn, while the public packed the cinemas as never before, despite rising admission prices and a fuel shortage that often left theatres unheated in the winter. Even the February Revolution in 1917 did not for long affect admissions.

Nor – despite solemn meetings of cinema workers and protestations of loyalty to whoever at the moment offered the best prospects for the industry's future – did the repertoire of the cinemas change much. The war, it is true, brought a predictable crop of hate films and patriotic films. Under the Provisional Government, with the old censorship restrictions lifted, there were anti-Romanov films, Rasputin films and, later, anti-Bolshevik propaganda films put out by the Government itself. But by and large the public were still happy with their usual diet of sentimental dramas, costume pictures, clownish farces, guignols, detective stories, and a growing diet of 'decadent' pictures on mystical or satanic themes.

Yet even before the 1917 Revolution there were stirrings of a more creative use of the cinema's means. As early as 1913 a group of futurists made a bizarre *Drama in the Futurist Cabinet 13*; and though it did not have any lasting influence upon anything at all, its makers, young avant-gardists, were to become highly influential figures in early Soviet art: David Burliuck, Larionov, Goncharova, and above all Vladimir Mayakovski.

In 1915 MEYERHOLD, who as we shall see undoubtedly exerted the most important formative influence upon the later development of the Soviet cinema, recanted his initial vehement opposition to the cinema. His films of *Dorian Gray* (in which Dorian was played by the actress Varvara Yanova, while Meyerhold himself played Lord Henry) and *The Strong Man* are lost; but their reputation remains high, and their influence upon Meyerhold's artistic contemporaries was great. Meyerhold's importance was to bring to the cinema his capacity for fundamental analysis of the nature and the problems of a medium – the gift for asking the right questions; and this quality was to exert a powerful influence on the cinema, through Meyerhold's pupils, though most notably through SERGEI EISENSTEIN.

Other artists were finding their voices. Working within the context of the Khanzhonkov studios, Yevgeni Bauer's persistence in tackling contemporary themes instead of the costume and historical pieces in vogue, was a valuable initiative; and Bauer's sudden death in 1917 was a grave loss to the art. One of Bauer's assistants however was LEV KULESHOV, then a young designer barely eighteen years old. A series of articles on film theory which Kuleshov published in 'Vestnik Kinematografia' in 1917, startlingly ahead of their time, looked forward to Kuleshov's formative influence on the young Soviet cinema.

1917 also saw the production of the most important of all surviving pre-Revolutionary films, Yakov Protazanov's *Father Sergius*. Based on a story by Tolstoy which could only be filmed after the relaxation of censorship under the Provisional Government, the naturalism of acting, setting and psychology, the able narrative style, and the impressive performances of MOZHUKIN and Lissenko make it one of the most enduring films of its era, from any source.

USSR

Revolution and NEP The immediate effect of the October Revolution was a large-scale emigration of the old cinema people. From Odessa, the first line of retreat, where for a while they tried to set up a new film-producing centre, the old artists were scattered all over the world. Some (Ermoliev, Starewicz, Protazanov, Mozhukin) ended up in France; others (Khmara, Bukhowetski) in Germany. A few, like Boleslavski, were eventually to find their way to Hollywood.

Lenin at once gave practical support to his belief (apparently uttered to Lunacharski around 1920) that 'The cinema is for us the most important of the arts'. On 9 November 1917 a cinema sub-section was set up under the State Commission of Education, under Lenin's wife, Krupskaya. The reconstruction of the cinema was to be a hard fight however. The proprietors, who were actually experiencing a boom period in audience attendances, fought bitterly against any move towards nationalization. They boycotted state-run enterprises, concealed or exported their equipment and raw film stock. In March 1918 the Praesidium were obliged to bring in new regulations to check such sabotage. Cinema Committees were set up in Moscow and Petrograd. The Skobelev Committee – which had been formed under the Imperial Government to superintend the production of propaganda films – was nationalized; and a section of independent cultural and educational organizations, Proletkult, was set up.

The earliest Soviet productions were vague in ideological content, and dependent on commercial producers for their making. At the Neptune Company Mayakovski wrote three films, one apparently futurist in manner. The Petrograd Cinema Committee made an agit-comedy from a scenario by Lunacharski, the People's Commissar for Education: *Conquest*. The Moscow Cinema Committee, with the same partiality for single word titles, made *Signal* and *Underground*.

In 1918 the first 'agit-train' was despatched. The 'agit-trains' were fully self-contained propaganda centres, equipped to disseminate literature, present drama, and show and produce films. This first train had as its cameraman EDUARD TISSÉ who was later to be EISENSTEIN's most loyal collaborator. Later there was to be an 'agit-steamer' also, which plied the Volga under the direction of no less a person than Krupskaya. Of more permanent historical influence was the establishment of training establishments in both Moscow and Petrograd – the first cinema schools in the world.

Co-operation with the independent organizations worsened as the war drew to a close; and in July 1918 more severe decrees were issued to control cinema enterprises by registration, to control production by censorship, and to control all raw film stock. The immediate effect was the total disappearance of all raw film stock. In the face of this cheating and defection by the old film manufacturers, total nationalization of the film industry, which took place in August 1919, was inevitable.

This decision was partly encouraged by the recognition that the films produced by the Cinema Committees, however few and slight were, ideologically, immeasurably more effective than those produced by private enterprise. The Committees' productions consisted mainly of the 'agitki', tiny propaganda films furthering the revolutionary spirit by exhortation or entertainment. By Red Army Day, February 1919, thirteen of these had been made. One use of the 'agitki' was for recruitment, for the intervention wars had begun; and the development of the film had to be further delayed while young film-makers and potential film artists (including KULESHOV) were despatched to the front, either to fight or to film.

The real impetus needed however was provided by Lenin's New Economic Police (NEP) – partial return to private enterprise – which was introduced in 1921. Suddenly all the hidden film stock and equipment came mysteriously to light; and production shot from eleven features in 1921, to 157 in 1924. Stalin, as the powerful Commissar for Nationalities, valued the cinema no less highly than Lenin: 'The cinema is the greatest means of mass propaganda. We must take it in our hands'. The encouragement he gave to production in the National republics created healthy industries in the Ukraine and in Georgia, where Perestiani made one of the first really successful revolutionary films, *Little Red Devils*, about a group of children caught up with Red guerrilla fighters.

During the NEP period the economic bases of the Soviet film industry were laid down. In December 1922 the Council of People's Commissars reorganized the Cinema Committees into Goskino, a state cinema enterprise. The last private firm, Russ, was absorbed into Mezhrabpom, to become Mezhrabpom-Russ, which, like Leningradkino (formerly Sevzapkino) retained its autonomy after the setting up of the Sovkino Trust in 1925. In April 1923 Proletkino was founded to provide the ideological stimulus to production. During this period too the first programme of educational and scientific films was begun. Children's cinemas were established. In 1924, ARK – the Association of Revolutionary Cinema – published a manifesto laying down the principles of a revolutionary cinema. Among the signatories was EISENSTEIN.

The Creation of a Revolutionary Cinema 'They were astonishing and wonderful days', writes SERGEI YUTKEVITCH, who was thirteen at the time of the Revolution, 'the debut of a revolutionary art. When we talk about the years when we began to work, people are always surprised by the birth-dates of almost all the directors and the important artists of those times. We were incredibly young! We were sixteen- and seventeen-year-olds when we started into our artistic lives. The explanation is quite simple: the revolution had made way for the young. It has to be remembered that an entire generation had disappeared. Our elders had been dispersed throughout the country, or had perished in the civil war, or had even left Russia. Hence the Republic lacked a clear organization, lacked people; and our way in was easy – the country wanted us to work; the country needed people in every department of culture. That is why our generation, then so young, began its artistic life so early.

'This was a period of tumultuous expansion for Soviet art. It is difficult now to imagine it.' The young creators of revolutionary art were eager and aggressive. Old was bad and must be swept away. KOZINTSEV has described how the young artists of Kiev would ride about the streets of Kiev in lorries yelling the latest Mayakovski poems:

> Away with tuppeny truths!
> Sweep the rubbish out of your heads!
> The streets are our paint-brushes,
> The squares are our palettes!

A surprising number of the artists who made up the first generation of the Soviet cinema made their débuts in film in 1923–4; but others were already veterans. In 1920 Kuleshov was given a workshop. His activities there were interrupted when he went to the front to shoot actuality of the interventionist wars and on his return, raw film stock was so scarce that his group were obliged to exercise themselves on 'films without films' – études which proved useful when, by 1922, he was able to shoot the famous experiments which were the basis of Soviet theories of montage. He demonstrated the psychology of montage by juxtaposing the same close-up of the actor MOSKVIN with different shots of varied significance, showing that the audience interpreted the actor's reaction by relation to the next shot. He demonstrated synthetic chronology and geography by putting together shots made at different places and different times, but in such a way that they gave the impression of a single action. Among the members of Kuleshov's collective, apart from his wife and life-long collaborator Alexandra Khokhlova, was PUDOVKIN, who was to give his master's work its widest currency.

Later, in 1923, the collective was given a

chance to make a film; and the comedy, *The Extraordinary Adventures of Mr West in the Land of the Bolsheviks*, about the reactions of a nervous American to the country of which he has heard such horrific tales, justified all Kuleshov's theories. The reception of his next film, *The Death Ray*, was not so favourable; Jay Leyda, the most authoritative historian of Soviet films, says that 'the absence of emotion in this effort to condense all of PEARL WHITE, HARRY PIEL and Fantômas within one film . . . appears today as a danger signal in that youthful period of the Soviet film . . . *The Death Ray* is the ancestor of a technically proficient and emotionally empty tendency that was to emerge too often in the history of Soviet films.'

DZIGA VERTOV pointed quite a different way to a revolutionary cinema – a way which passed 'right over the heads of actors and over the roofs of the studios, directly into life and the true, multi-dramatic and multi-detective reality' (Vertov, 1923). His film activities in the Civil War had convinced him of the superiority of the film actuality over the dramatic film, which he condemned in aggressive articles in Mayakovski's journal, LEF. The first issue of his *Kino Pravda* went out in May 1922; and issue after issue of this newsreel showed his brilliant creative assemblies of real-life material. Inevitably he attracted the enmity of the feature film-makers; but audiences liked *Kino Pravda*. Vertov was put in charge of a studio and was able to make *Kino Eye*, a prototype of modern *cinéma-vérité* – 'the organization of the seen world'. There was a fallacy about Vertov's arguments about the superior value of unadulterated actuality. As a passionate revolutionary, Vertov could not help imposing his own powerful personality upon his material, giving his documents an extraordinary and invigorating power which, *as mere documents*, they did not necessarily possess. Films like *Leninist Film Truth* and *October Without Ilyich*, made to commemorate Lenin's death, betrayed a distinct emotional content.

The theatre, which had begun to find its revolutionary forms earlier, now began to contribute artists to the cinema. In the early 1920s, no extravagance was too great in the theatre, so long as it proclaimed strongly enough the overthrow of the traditional and old. The god of these times was VSEVOLOD MEYERHOLD; and his influence upon the cinema cannot be overstated. In 1936, Kozintsev referred to him as 'our teacher', from whose brilliant work, 'the Soviet cinema has learnt much more than the Soviet theatre'. His pupils included EISENSTEIN, EKK, Okhlopkov, YUTKEVITCH, ARNSHTAM, and the actors Ilinsky, Martinson and Straukh. Many other cinema artists had come more or less directly under his influence.

In particular Eisenstein's gifts for analysis of the fundamentals of an art seem to have been deeply influenced by Meyerhold's gifts as a theorist. Eisenstein joined Meyerhold's studio on the same day as Sergei Yutkevitch; and the two worked together on early theatrical projects. In 1923, directing a Proletkult Theatre production of Ostrovsky's 'Enough Simplicity in Every Wise Man', Eisenstein had his first taste of film-making, when he shot a short filmed insert, *Glumov's Diary*, a parody of *Kino Pravda*. He went on to direct *Gas Masks*, which (in a gesture characteristic of those times) he staged in an actual gas factory to which, unfortunately, audiences were disinclined to come. But the experiment evidently turned his attention to the cinema's larger potential; and in 1923 he began a film intended as one of a series to be produced by Proletkult Theatre. (Again it was typical of the times that the series never progressed beyond this first film.)

Strike was the turning point, the true beginning of the classic period of Soviet silent cinema. The theme of the film was the process of industrial oppression and of industrial revolution in the pre-Revolutionary days. The film broke completely with all previous patterns of narrative structure. The neat subject story was abandoned in favour of a dynamic chronicle form. Alongside eccentricities imported from the theatre, and Eisenstein's 'montage of attractions', was the construction of a dramatic narrative out of realist elements. For the first time the mass was seen as the hero.

Meanwhile Yutkevitch, Eisenstein's fellow pupil at the Meyerhold Studio, has joined up with two boys of his own age in Petrograd, Grigori Kozintsev and LEONID TRAUBERG, to form a theatre attractively called The Factory of the Eccentric Actor (FEKS). As Eisenstein had done, they aimed to refresh traditional dramatic forms with elements drawn from circus, vaudeville, puppets, and exotic theatrical traditions. In 1924 Sevzapkino invited the group to make a film. *The Adventures of Oktyabrina* appears to have been a wild, merry mess. *Mishka Against Yudenich*, which followed, was a more modest children's adventure story.

Above: 'Battleship Potemkin' (Sergei Eisenstein, 1925)
Below: Vera Baranovskaya in 'Mother' (Vsevolod Pudovkin, 1926)

Alongside all this youthful experimentalism a more conservative and traditional cinema co-existed. PROTAZANOV had returned from exile, to make a 'futurist' fantasy *Aelita* (1924), famous for the constructivist designs of Alexandra Exter and Alexander Rodchenko and a juggling with time decades before RESNAIS. Zheliabushki made a fine, traditional adaptation of *The Station Master*, which found a ready market abroad. Dmitri Bassaligo, an old Khanzhonkov actor, much honoured for his long Party membership, made an elaborate spectacle, *From Sparks – Flames*.

'The End of St Petersburg' (Vsevolod Pudovkin, 1927)

The USSR sets great store by its anniversaries; and anniversaries seem often to have provided important impetus for the cinema. For the 20th anniversary of the 1905 Revolution, Eisenstein was taken off a project for a film on Budyonny's Cavalry and given a massive historical script by Nina Agadjanova-Shutko, entitled *1905*. He was due to begin shooting in March 1925; but the weather in Petrograd drove him south to Odessa to shoot what was intended to be a single sequence in the finished film. Instead, the sequence grew to be the entire film, *Battleship Potemkin*. Edited in considerable haste, the film was nevertheless a triumphant demonstration of all Eisenstein's ideas of montage. From the experimental fireworks of *Strike* he had progressed at one leap to make one of the most perfectly formed and accomplished films in the history of the cinema. Its recognition at home however was slow: only after its acclamation abroad was Eisenstein acknowledged as the artistic leader of the Soviet cinema.

Potemkin ushered in the era which saw the zenith of the Soviet cinema, a period of brilliance perhaps unparalleled anywhere in the history of this art. The Kuleshov group, after the set-back of *The Death Ray*, made their greatest work, *Dura Lex* or *By the Law*, from a story by Jack London. Produced with minimal resources, the film achieved a maximum of expressive effect. Unhappily the group seemed never able to equal this effort, at least in silent days; and after a further set-back with *Your Acquaintance* Kuleshov went off to establish a studio in Tiflis.

Kuleshov's disciple PUDOVKIN, after a not very happy period as assistant to Konstantin Eggert, a traditionalist director, on *Marriage of the Bear*, was assigned the job of filming Pavlov's experiments in conditioned reflexes. In a break during this arduous but (to a scientific mind) congenial task, he filmed a short comedy *Chess Fever*, which combined actuality of a chess competition with fictional material, to demonstrate how well he had absorbed Kuleshov's principles of montage. On completing the Pavlov film, *Mechanics of the Brain*, he set to work with the scenarist NATHAN ZARKHI and the cameraman Anatoli Golovnya, to make what was to prove his finest work: an adaptation of Gorki's *Mother*. The perfectionism of his work with his actors, notably Baranovskaya as the mother and Batalov as her son, gave additional importance to the manuals on Film Technique and Film Acting which he wrote at this time and which were to become classic texts on cinema theory.

The FEKS group, after another adventure story, had gone on to *The Overcoat*, a richly pictorial and experimental adaptation of Gogol, whose expressionist design and acting demonstrated a strong reaction against the traditional Russian costume pictures, which were still being made: an example exactly contemporary with *The Overcoat* was Tarach's *Wings of the Serf*, an early film interpretation of the life of Ivan the Terrible.

Yutkevitch was now separated from the group, and associated as designer with the best film of ABRAM ROOM, who had come to the cinema from dentistry, *via* journalism and the theatre. In 1925–7 ROOM followed *Death Bay*, a stylish melodrama, and *Traitor*, about a Tsarist *provocateur*, with *Bed and Sofa*, a brilliant comedy drama about a *ménage à trois* produced by the housing shortage, full of social and psychological observation. Admiration of the film in the Soviet Union was, and remains, qualified: neither audiences nor officials much relished its anti-glamorous observation of its characters and of Soviet life.

The young cinema was invigorated by constant debates and theoretical battles. (Gerassimov recalls that when the FEKS boys were around 22 years old they overheard the 16-year-old-director of a newer studio declare that his group's aim was the overthrow of 'that academic institution, FEKS'.) In pursuance of one of these battles, FRIEDRICH ERMLER established the KEM group in opposition to FEKS, upholding the ideal of Revolutionary *content* as against Revolutionary *form*. He embarked on a series of honourable films which proclaimed his faith as an unswerving, but passionately humane Communist Party member. His first silent film, *Katka's Reinert Apples* (1926) was a bitter denunciation of certain aspects of the NEP mentality; while *The Parisian Cobbler* (1928) was a moral lesson for the Komsomols to demonstrate that the highest principles are not necessarily or automatically held by official Komsomol members.

The peak was reached in 1927: the Tenth anniversary of the Revolution again provided an important motive power. Eisenstein had to shelve temporarily his project for a film on agricultural collectivization, *The General Line*, to prepare *October*. Pudovkin was still finishing *Mother* when he and Zarkhi began work on *The End of St Petersburg*. The parallel preparation of these two films, on the same theme and shot on the same locations, greatly enlivened another heated public debate, between Eisenstein's theory of montage as 'collision' (i.e. the director works through the emotional or intellectual charges produced by the juxtaposition of two pieces of film) and Pudovkin's theory of montage as 'linkage'. Perhaps the debate was in the end fairly meaningless; but it maintained lively interest in film theory.

Both films turned out to be monumental. Eisenstein's came out some time later than Pudovkin's, and had its troubles. In the first place work on the film coincided with Trotsky's attempt to challenge Stalin's power. Trotsky's failure and disgrace made it necessary to revise scenes in the film in which his role in the Revolution was too graphically described. After its release Eisenstein began to suffer the charges of intellectualism and 'formalism' which were to be repeated, on and off, throughout the rest of his career.

Of the other commemorative films (they include a reconstruction, *Moscow in October*, by BORIS BARNET, a former boxer and Kuleshov pupil), the most important were the first two of a trio of works by ESTHER SHUB. Shub, trained as an editor, was the pioneer of creative compilation of old archive materials. For her

Opposite above: Vera Ellen and Gene Kelly in 'Les Girls' (George Cukor, USA, 1957)
Below: The chorus in 'Hello Dolly!' (Gene Kelly, USA 1968)

FRESH
BREAD-ROLLS-PIES
HOLLAND-DUTCH BAKERY
BREAD-ROLLS
BAKED DAILY
CAKES-PASTRY
CLOAK

films, *The Fall of the Romanov Dynasty* and *The Great Road* (1927) and *The Russia of Nikolai II and Lev Tolstoy* (1928), she brought to light thousands of feet of old actuality material which would otherwise have continued to rot in film vaults and cellars. Shub, more than anyone, first alerted people to the historic value of film, and of the need for film archives. Another of the comparatively rare women directors of this period was Olga Preobrazhenskaya, a veteran (she had directed a film as early as 1915) who made *The Peasant Women of Ryazan* in 1927.

The Republican cinemas, still benefiting from Stalin's personal interest, continued to develop. 1925 saw the first Uzbekh and Azerbaijan films; 1927 the first Byelorussian film. VUFKU, the Ukrainian film organization, had a well-rooted tradition of production; and it was in the VUFKU studios that the former Meyerhold actor Okhlopkov made the first of his three little-known films, *Mitya*, in 1927. In 1925, VUFKU began to publish a magazine, of avant-garde tendencies, to which ALEXANDER DOVZHENKO contributed some cartoons. Dovzhenko was a late starter in the cinema: he had been a teacher, diplomat and painter before joining the Odessa studios in 1926 at the age of 32. He wanted to direct comedy; and his first effort was a knockabout two-reeler, *The Little Fruits of Love*. Then he made a silly adventure film, *The Diplomatic Pouch*, distinguished, all the same, by visual style and noble romanticization of the proletariat. His real revelation however was *Zvenigora* (1928), a wild and wonderful *mélange* of legend, folklore and magic which alarmed the VUFKU bosses at the same time as it marked Dovzhenko out as a talent very much more than ordinary. *Arsenal* (1929), describing the revolutionary struggles of 1918, was his most intense and concentrated film, a fiery assembly of every kind of element of drama, caricature, folklore, all welded into a single lyrical vision. In 1930 he made his greatest film, *Earth*. It is a story of small, banal happenings: an old man dies, the collective buys a tractor; the young farm chairman is shot by a resentful Kulak and is buried. But Dovzhenko gives these events grandeur. The editing of the images generates its own energy and inevitability; the poetic effects of the juxtapositions, the moods, the characters, the drama all combine in one staggering effect.

By the end of the 1920s there were already forebodings of what the next decade might bring. Mayakovski thundered accusations after suffering various frustrations over scripts submitted to Sovkino; but even his voice seemed to have lost its force; and by 1930 he was dead by his own hand. Already, in 1928, Leyda tells us, a Congress on Film Matters, timed to coincide with the first Five-Year Plan, revealed a narrowing of the ideological outlook, a neurotic suspicion of all that smacked of 'formalism'. 'Film-makers began to cultivate a showy photographic manner, the sort of conspicuously handsome photography that has always won prizes. . . . Current and future attacks on "formalism" were not aimed at this evasive handsomeness (generally approved as another technical victory), but hit at elements of fantasy, unorthodoxies of structure or treatment, or almost any departure from the approved naturalistic norm.'

Above: 'Arsenal' (Alexander Dovzhenko, 1929)
Below: 'Earth' (Alexander Dovzhenko, 1930)

Pudovkin's *Storm Over Asia* (1928), for instance, was attacked for the fabulous elements introduced into the story of a Mongolian hunter who comes into unsought conflict with colonial powers.

The heroic period of Soviet art was over – for the theatre, for painting, for literature, as well as for the cinema. There were, nevertheless a few important silent works still to come. Dovzhenko, as we have said, made his two greatest films in *Arsenal* and *Earth*. ROOM adapted an Henri Barbusse story, *The Ghost That Never Returns*. Yutkevitch embarked on his first works as a director, *Lace* and *The Black Sail*. ERMLER's *Fragment of an Empire* ingeniously used the story of an amnesiac to contrast the old and the new Russia. Kozintsev and Trauberg made the finest of FEKS films, *The New Babylon*, one of the most sophisticated of silent films, a glittering and sardonic recreation of the Paris Commune, notable as having Shostakovich's first musical score. (The score was so novel that provincial audiences were inclined to write in and complain that the conductor of the orchestra was drunk!) BARNET made two excellent dramatic comedies, *The Girl With a Hat Box* and *The House on Trubnaia Square*. Barnet's collaborator on his first film, *Miss Mend*, FEDOR OZEP went to Germany to direct a co-production of *The Living Corpse*, and stayed there. Quite outside the general drift of Soviet production at these times were VIKTOR TURIN's *Turksib* and MIKHAIL KALATOZOV's *Salt for Svanetia*. *Turksib*, describing the construction of the Turkestan-Siberian railway, was a masterpiece of documentary, giving drama and narrative direction to the description of real facts. Kalatozov's film documented the life of a remote and deprived community. Both this and Kalatozov's next film, *The Nail in the Boot*, were severely critized for their 'negativism'; and he was prevented from directing again for several years.

Eisenstein made one more silent film – the last work that he was to complete for practically a decade. *The General Line*, about collectivization of agriculture, had been begun in 1926, but set aside in favour of *October*. Each of his films reveals a different approach: here the photography is much simpler in style, and the montage much less deliberately intellectual in its imagery. But after *October* every Eisenstein film seemed destined for difficulty. Stalin personally recommended changes to the ending of the film; but even after they were made the film was not officially approved, which is why the title was changed from *The General Line* to

Vivien Leigh in 'Gone with the Wind' (Victor Fleming, George Cukor and Sam Wood, USA, 1939)

the more non-committal (from the Party point of view) *The Old and the New*.

The end of the silent period (which in the USSR extended well into the 1930s) saw the rise of a second generation of Soviet film-makers. Practically all the directors who were to dominate the cinema in the course of the next two decades made their débuts around 1930: MIKHAIL ROMM, whose beautiful *Boule de Suif* (1934) was one of the very last silent films; YULI RAISMAN (*Katoroa*, 1928); MARK DONSKOI (*In The Big City*, with Michael Auerbach, 1929); ALEXANDER ZARKHI and YOSIF HEIFITZ (*Facing the World*, 1929); NIKOLAI EKK (*How and How Not to Do It*, 1929); Ivan Pyriev (*Strange Women*, 1929); the Georgian directors, Nikolai Shengelaya, Mikhail Chiaureli, Yefim Dzigan, and Mikhail Gelovani, best known as an actor and for the impersonation of Stalin in many films of the 1940s and 1950s.

Sound For the Soviet cinema the sound revolution was late and slow; and this delay had certain advantages in helping avoid the mistakes made elsewhere. Some of the real dangers, along with imaginary ones, were discussed in the celebrated manifesto issued by Eisenstein, Pudovkin and ALEXANDROV in 1928. Mezhrabpom-Russ, in Moscow, adopted the Tager sound system (variable density) demonstrated in Moscow as early as 1927: Sovkino adopted the Shorin system (variable area), first demonstrated in Leningrad in 1929. Ultimately the Tager system was adopted for general use.

Eisenstein, Alexandrov and Tissé were sent off to Europe and thence to America, primarily to investigate the development of sound film in other countries, but with various secondary motives like the research for one of Eisenstein's innumerable, never-to-be-fulfilled projects, an adaptation of 'Capital'. The trip was ultimately prolonged for more than 18 months, and ended tragically with the collapse of all Eisenstein's plans to make a film in Hollywood, and the abortion of the Mexican film promoted by Upton Sinclair. On his return he was to find himself maliciously thwarted in every project by Boris Shumyatski, appointed to the head of the film industry with the special task of building it up to support the Five-Year Plan's emphasis on heavy industry.

Meanwhile the directors who had stayed at home had made approaches, each in his own way, to the problems of sound. ROOM's *Plan For Great Works* (1930), a documentary with sound accompaniment, was accounted the first Soviet sound film. Kozintsev and Trauberg's *Alone* (1931) had a synchronized score and limited synchronized speech; but RAISMAN's *The Earth Thirsts* (1930), a perfectly conventional canal construction story, was reckoned the first true Soviet dramatic sound film. The value of sound to documentary and reportage was immediately obvious. There was a film record of a current trial of some industrial saboteurs, while another film quite simply recorded the daily activity (preferably noisy) of a

Top: 'Storm Over Asia' (Vsevolod Pudovkin, 1928)
Above: Vsevolod Pudovkin in 'The New Babylon' (Grigori Kozintsev and Leonid Trauberg, 1929)
Below: 'October' (Sergei Eisenstein, 1928)

collective farm. The veteran Protazanov adapted Ivanov's play 'Armoured Train 14–65', as *Tommy*.

More obviously creative approaches to sound were signalled however by Dziga Vertov's *Enthusiasm*, or *Donbas Symphony* (1931), in which he used montage of sound as creatively and vitally as he had always used pictures; by Yutkevitch's *The Golden Mountains* (1931), with its elegant use of its Shostakovich score; and by Nikolai Ekk's *The Road to Life* (1931), a beautiful, humane study of the abandoned children of the Revolution, in which free use of sound gave no sense of the strain or self-consciousness generally associated with an unaccustomed medium.

Pudovkin was obliged for technical reasons to abandon his idea of making *A Simple Case* with sound; and his first experiment with the medium was *Deserter* (1933). His elaborate editing and sound technique attracted charges of 'intellectualism'; and it is from this time, and especially after the death of his constant collaborator, the scenarist Nathan Zarkhi, that Pudovkin's work sensibly deteriorates into conventionality calculated to please the establishment.

Generally the best Soviet directors showed no nervousness in the face of the new medium – perhaps because of the reassurance given by the late start and the chance that had been given to observe the pitfalls and possibilities. Dovzhenko's *Ivan* (1932) uses sound and dialogue with complete fluidity. In this film Dovzhenko characteristically discovers lyrical exhilaration in so improbably concrete a theme as the Dnieper hydro-electric project. Montages of the construction work have a powerful sensuous effect, and the characterization of the workers – even the slacker of Stepan Shkurat – has a warmth and geniality notable even for Dovzhenko's work.

Kuleshov, after a disappointing melodrama, *Horizon*, made his brilliant *The Great Consoler* (1933), an elaborate interleaving of O. Henry's life story, his fictional creations and their originals, with use of sound as creatively original as his earlier work had been. Kuleshov's pupil, BARNET, made his best film in his first work with sound, *Okraina*, a tragi-comedy set in the war years. Shengelaya's *26 Commissars*, a subject once announced as a film project for Meyerhold, dealt with the Baku tragedy of 1918. Yutkevitch and ERMLER collaborated on *Counterplan*, a civilized didactic film designed to promote the industrial aims of the First Five-Year Plan.

Only Eisenstein, the man most equipped to seek fundamental approaches to the new medium, remained inactive. Project after project was frustrated, apparently by Shumyatski's personal disfavour. In fact Shumyatski, for all his dislike of artists – exceeded, according to report, only by his anti-Semitism – may have been the sympton of a deeper-seated repression of Soviet art. Symptomatic of a strengthened pressure upon artists, is the start of a retreat in this period from contemporary and social actuality. One line of escape was the musical. The first Soviet musical was Igor Savchenko's *Accordion*, a modestly intended comedy about komsomols, which enjoyed immense success. It was quickly followed by ALEXANDROV's more ambitious, Hollywood-influenced musicals, *Jazz Comedy* (1934), *Circus* (1936), and *Volga-Volga* (1938), variously retrieved by the gaiety of their star Lyuba Orlova (Mrs Alexandrov) and by Dunayevsky's admirable music; and by Pyriev's odiously hearty, more obviously indigenous musicals, such as *The Rich Bride* (1938), *Tractor Drivers* (1939), *The Swineherd and the Shepherd* (1941).

The vogue for big historical spectacles was revived by Ivanovsky's *Dubrovsky* and Petrov's *Peter the Great* (1937); while Chiaureli turned to themes from Georgian folk-lore, for *The Last Masquerade* and *Arsen*. The genre was neverthe-

Top: 'Circus' (Grigori Alexandrov, 1936)
Above: 'Volga, Volga' (Grigori Alexandrov, 1938)
Below: 'Peter the Great' Part 1 (Vladimir Petrov, 1937)

less to have a noble apotheosis in Eisenstein's *Alexander Nevsky* and *Ivan the Terrible*. *Chapaev* (1934), the one and only big success of the VASILIEV Brothers, started another vogue, for biographies of Revolutionary heroes. Few were as good as this original however, based on Furmanov's reminiscences of Chapaev (played by Boris Babochkin) and directed with great warmth, dash and humour. Later examples of the style included most notably Dovzhenko's *Shchors* (1939), which Stalin himself requested, asking the director for 'a Ukrainian *Chapaev*'. Stalin's continued keen interest, added to the fears of Ukrainian nationalism, made the film an unhappy experience for Dovzhenko.

Allied to this genre are reconstructions of Revolutionary incidents, like Dzigan's *We From Kronstadt* (1936), a stiff, overblown and generally over-estimated film and such a semi-fictional biography as Zarkhi and Heifitz's kindly *Baltic Deputy* (1937), in which NIKOLAI CHERKASSOV, later Eisenstein's Nevsky and Ivan, gave one of his greatest screen performances.

After ROMM's *Lenin in October* (1937) the door was opened for a whole cycle of historical films recreating the figures of Lenin and Stalin. Romm's Lenin in this film and in the succeeding *Lenin in 1918* (1938) was Boris Shchukin, who died shortly after completing the latter film. Maxim Straukh, the old Meyerhold actor and collaborator of Eisenstein, made the role his own in Yutkevitch's *The Man With the Gun* and *Yakov Sverdlov* (1938). Twenty and twenty-nine years later Straukh was still playing the role in Yutkevitch's *Stories About Lenin* (1958) and *Lenin in Poland* (1967). Meanwhile Mikhail Gelovani made himself the specialist impersonator of Stalin, appearing in this role in twenty films, right up to Stalin's and his own death.

Straukh also played Lenin in one of the most sympathetic film series of the period. In their 'Maxim Trilogy' (*The Youth of Maxim*, 1935; *Return of Maxim*, 1937; *The Vyborg Side*, 1939) Kozintsev and Trauberg pioneered the genre of the 'synthetic' revolutionary hero. The films

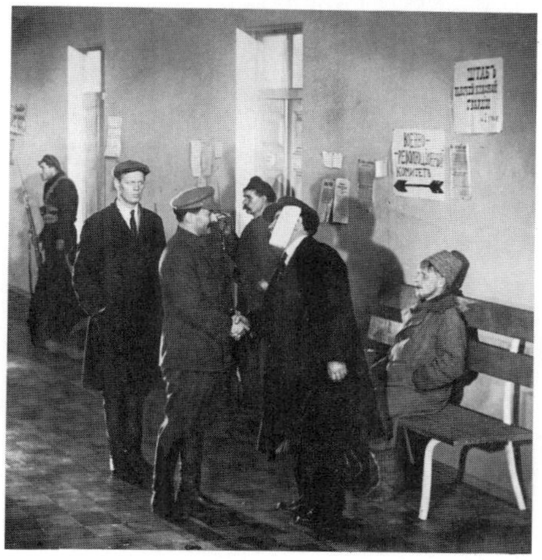

Top: 'Chapaev' (Sergei and Georgi Vasiliev, 1934)
Above: 'Lenin in October' (Mikhail Romm, 1937)
Below: Boris Shchukin in 'Lenin in 1918' (Mikhail Romm, 1938)

Above: 'Alexander Nevsky' (Sergei Eisenstein, 1938)
Below: 'Childhood of Maxim Gorki' (Mark Donskoi, 1938)

told with great (though progressively decreasing) humour and warmth, of the creation of a revolutionary. Their aim of getting away from the old conventions of disguising revolutionary themes in traditional adventure story forms was successful enough to be followed by others, notably Raisman in his fine *The Last Night* (1937).

To mark the tenth anniversary of Lenin's death, Vertov made his finest film, *Three Songs of Lenin* (1934), a brilliant, richly emotional association of actuality images with three folk-songs composed to the memory of Lenin.

Political situations were now weighing still more heavily upon film-makers. The 'liquidation' of the kulaks brought forth a number of films to discuss 'The Peasant Problem' and to justify official attitudes. Ermler's violent *Peasants* (1935) and Medvedkin's *Snatchers* which dealt with the comic aspects of the same situation, came out within a few weeks of one another. Leyda calls MEDVEDKIN's film 'one of the most original films in film history'. It is said to combine vaudeville, bawdy fun, expressionism and surrealism in much the same way as the series of short satirical comedies that Medvedkin is said to have made when he was in charge of a film-train – a latter-day equivalent of the agit-trains – around 1930.

The most interesting of the peasant films ought to have been Eisenstein's *Bezhin Meadow*; but this was foiled by Shumyatski like all the projects the director undertook during that official's regime. The story was a scenario by Rzheshevsky, then a fashionable film writer, and was based in part on Turgenev's 'Leaves From a Hunter's Notebook' and in part on the real life story of Pavel Morozov; a tale of a kulak father who kills his son when the child supports collectivization. The film was partly shot, but interrupted by Eisenstein's illness. By the time work was resumed, official attitudes had changed and the script had to be revised – this time by Isaac Babel in one of his rare encounters with the cinema. Shooting of the new version began, but was suddenly halted by Shumyatski. Eisenstein was charged with 'formalism' and worse crimes, and required to make expiation in a public recantation of his faults. All material from the film was accidentally destroyed during the war; and we can only guess what its splendours would have been from an assembly of stills made from reference off-cuts of the film by Naum Kleimann, with the supervision of Yutkevitch (1967).

The very darkest times of Stalinism had begun with the trials of 1934, resulting from the murder of Kirov; and the xenophobia encouraged by this event must to an extent explain the disagreeable tone of several films about interventionists, such as the Vasiliev's *Volochayevsky Days* (1938) and Dovzhenko's most brilliant and most dislikable film, *Aerograd* (1935). Its theme is socialist construction *versus* sabotage, arguing that even the best friend who is a possible enemy of the state must be ruthlessly liquidated (an idea only too topical). The film is all the more chilling since Dovzhenko's genius is still so persuasive, his visual effects so cruelly beautiful.

The repercussions of the trials were eventually to include the disappearance or death of a number of film personalities – along with Babel, Tretyakov and Meyerhold. Ermler's sober and much praised *The Great Citizen* (1938–9) presented the official version of the Kirov assassination.

Artistic creation had become a perilous profession; film-makers gingerly trod the narrow path between formalism and too candid realism. The hardening of official attitudes had at least the happy effect of encouraging Shumyatsky to overreach himself, in grandiose notions of a great Soviet Hollywood on the shores of the Black Sea. Apparently he was so enchanted by his plans that he neglected the efficiency of the production organization, and failed to produce anything to celebrate the next great Soviet Anniversary – the 20th of the October Revolution. In January 1938 he was sacked.

It seemed more than coincidence that Eisenstein was able to embark almost at once on a new film, *Alexander Nevsky* (1938), co-directed with Dmitri Vasiliev. His first association with Prokofiev achieved such remarkable use of music and symphonic structure of this (in other ways not altogether characteristic) Eisenstein film, as to make more tragic the years of enforced silence. The single consolation was that during the years since his return from Mexico he had developed his work as (from the evidence of former students and from Nizhni's record, 'Lessons With Eisenstein') the most remarkable teacher of the difficult subject of cinema.

There were other bright spots in these dark pre-war years. Alexander Ptushko's full-length animated film *The New Gulliver* (1935) was outstanding in the work of Soviet animation artists, who after a good start were already slipping into bad habits of sub-Disney realism.

Top: 'My Universities' (Mark Donskoi 1940)
Above: S. Meshinski as 'Professor Mamlock' (A. Minkin and J. Rappoport, 1938)
Below: 'The Rainbow' (Mark Donskoi, 1944)

Above all MARK DONSKOI's trilogy adapted from the life of Maxim Gorki (*Childhood*, 1938; *Out in the World*, 1939; *My Universities*, 1940) was a work of extraordinary humanity and optimism, which remains totally undated after more than thirty years.

War and Cold War In 1939 the USSR was reluctantly pushed into a non-aggression pact with her natural enemy, Nazi Germany, whereupon a cycle of anti-Nazi films – Minkin and Rappoport's *Professor Mamlock* (1938), GRIGORI ROSHAL's *The Oppenheim Family* (1939) and even *Alexander Nevsky* – were rapidly hidden away, to be replaced by a spate of pro-German films, to which Dovzhenko contributed *Liberation* (1940). The war gave a tremendous impetus to documentary, which despite the examples of Vertov and Shub had not had any notable successes for many years. (Documentary does not seem happily indigenous to the Soviet Union: despite, or perhaps because of, an opulently equipped documentary studio, the outside world has recently seen very little which rises above glossy journalism.) Not only were the war films made (best among them those of Belyaev, KARMEN, Troyanovsky, Dovzhenko) but Alexander Zguridi and Boris Dolin made their fine nature films, and Esther Shub completed *Spain* (1938) and *Twenty Years of Cinema* (1940). There were grandiose communal efforts like *A Day in the New World*, shot simultaneously in different parts of the Soviet Union by dozens of cameramen.

As the war progressed cameramen covered all the front lines and news film acquired an importance it had not known since Vertov's *Kino Pravda*. When Mosfilm was evacuated, the Newsreel studios took over the buildings. Among the most important newsreel coverages of the war years were ROMAN KARMEN's *Leningrad Fights*, L. Valamov's *Stalingrad* and another big co-operative affair made by 100 cameramen along the entire front, *A Day of War* (1942). Dovzhenko's *Battle For the Ukraine* (1943), though credited to his wife SOLNTSEVA, with Dovzhenko only as supervisor, proved to be the last of the director's great, personal films. The material was shot by 24 cameramen at various parts of the front; but Dovzhenko is said to have given each of them detailed advance instructions, and even drawings of what he wanted. In the finished film the images sweep along with the inevitability of a musical structure. The harrowing, factual images refer back in their forms and juxtapositions to the great fiction films – to *Arsenal* and *Earth*.

The feature film studios too were mobilized. Eisenstein – largely rehabilitated after a complimentary biography by Vishnevsky, but still seeking a project for his next film – was put in artistic control of the Moscow Studios; Ermler was put at the head of Lenfilm, Dovzhenko of the Kiev Studios and Yutkevitch of the Children's Film Studio, Soyuzdetfilm. With the German invasion of June 1941 the Cinema Committee was evacuated to Novosibirsk; and in October the Studios were also evacuated to Eastern republics – Mosfilm to Alma-Ata, the Ukrainian Studios to Ashkhabad and Tashkent, the Children's Studio to Stalinabad and the Cartoon Studio to Samarkand. Film-makers were set to directing quick, short sketch films which were assembled into monthly *Fighting Film Albums* aimed at propaganda or morale.

Feature films did not in the majority reflect the war directly. There were, it is true, films about the Finnish War (Eisimont's *The Girl from Leningrad*), about the role of women and children in the war (Donskoi's *The Rainbow*, Romm's *Girl No 217*), about the Resistance (Ermler's *She Defends Her Country*, Pudovkin's *In The Name of the Fatherland*), about the home front (Kozintsev and Trauberg's *Plain People*). But the output of musicals (Pyriev even made a war musical, *At 6 pm After the War*) and of historical films (Pudovkin's *Suvorov*, Petrov's *Kutuzov*) continued as before. The war also saw the perfection of a technical improvement unique to the USSR – Semyon Ivanov's stereoscopic process, which dispensed with the use of special glasses for the audience, was exhibited at a permanent special cinema from 1941.

The most distinguished of the historical films was Eisenstein's *Ivan the Terrible* (1943–6), a magnificent panorama of 16th-century Russia, of magnificent plastic textures and with Prokofiev's incomparable score. This was to be Eisenstein's last conflict with authority. The first part of the projected trilogy was released; but the second section was criticized and suppressed as historically, psychologically and artistically in error. Eisenstein collapsed with a heart attack on the day he finished editing this second part. The controversy went on throughout his illness; and he never recovered sufficiently to resume work on revision before his death two years later in 1948.

In 1944 the Studios were brought back from evacuation, and a new artistic council was set up to regulate the affairs of the industry. Vasiliev took over control at Lenfilm, Alexandrov at Mosfilm, Savchenko at Soyuzdetfilm. Ptushko was put in charge of the Animation Studios, while GERASSIMOV took over the documentary studios, where he tried the interesting experiment of giving documentary assignments to feature directors like Raisman (*Berlin*, 1945), Yutkevitch (*Liberation France*, 1945) and Zarkhi and Heifitz (*Defeat of Japan*, 1945). Eisenstein wrote: 'Documentary was once the leading branch of our cinema and feature films were influenced by it. Twenty years later we see the process reversed. Feature film-makers have renewed links with documentary. . . . The collaboration will be fruitful for both'.

The Soviet cinema however entered on the most unproductive era of its history, coinciding with the most negative period of communism. The mystique of socialist realism dominated all artistic activity; and there was a relentless witch-hunt for anything that smacked of 'formalism'. The second part of Lukov's *A Great Life* (1946) was condemned along with *Ivan the Terrible Part II*, Pudovkin's *Admiral Nakhimov* (1946) and Kozintsev and Trauberg's *Plain People* (1945). Pudovkin was allowed to revise *Nakhimov*, as Gerassimov was permitted to make changes to *The Young Guard*, an elegant, somewhat over-blown glorification of the Young Communists, which has historical interest for its introduction of a whole generation of new actors, including SERGEI BONDARCHUK. Yutkevitch's *Light Over Russia*, about Lenin's electrification scheme, was banned altogether. Dovzhenko had begun a film about Michurin when the scientist's career became a

Above: 'Suvorov' (Vsevolod Pudovkin and M. Doller, 1940)
Below: Nikolai Cherkassov in 'Ivan the Terrible' Part I (Sergei Eisenstein, 1945)

Above: 'The Vow' (Mikhail Chiaurely, 1946)
Below: 'Battle of Stalingrad' (Vladimir Petrov, 1950)

After 1953 Pudovkin died in 1953, the same year as Stalin's death; Dovzhenko died in 1956, the year of the Twentieth Party Congress; so that with Eisenstein gone, by the time a more liberal spirit came to the Soviet cinema the three greatest creators of that cinema were dead.

Even before 1956 there were signs of a more human approach, in films like Heifitz's *The Big Family* (1954) and *The Rumyantsev Case* (1955) and in Khutsiev's *Spring on Zarechnaya Street* (1956). GRIGORI CHUKHRAI's début with *The Forty-First* (1956) – a remake of a film which Protazanov had made almost thirty years before, about the brief, doomed passion of a Red girl partisan and her prisoner, a White officer – looked like a major breakthrough. The proof of a genuine *renaissance* came the following year, with a film by the veteran KALATOZOV. More than a quarter of a century after his *Salt For Svanetia, The Cranes Are Flying* (1957) used bravura without any fear of charges of formalism, and was the first of a series of films which saw the Second World War in terms that were not necessarily heroic, but realistic. Instead of Stalin in his white uniforms, audiences saw real people at war, shirkers and faithless wives as well as decent citizens and brave soldiers. This direction was pursued in BONDARCHUK's first film, *Destiny of a Man* (1959), and Chukhrai's *Ballad of a Soldier* (1959). The war continued to be a favoured subject for young directors, all of whom insisted more or less on the same realistic approach: Alov and Naumov's *Peace to the Newcomer* (1961), Tarkovsky's *Childhood of Ivan* (1962), Chkheidze's *A Soldier's Father* (1965). SAMSONOV's adaptation of *An Optimistic Tragedy*, however, adopted an ominously declamatory style.

Other directors treated intimate human and contemporary themes, such as Kulidjanov and Segel's *The House I Live In*, Revaz Chkheidze's *Our Yard* (1957) and Abuladze's *Somebody Else's Children*.

There was a revival of energy among the older generation, who nevertheless seemed disinclined to follow the lead of the young, apart

political issue, and three years' work and revision of the film left it with only few marks of Dovzhenko's personality. A campaign against 'cosmopolitanism' affected some distinguished artists, among them Yutkevitch, Kozintsev, Trauberg, Bleiman and Kapler.

The approved directors tended to dedicate themselves to approved official tasks, such as vicious Cold War propagandist subjects: Romm made *The Russian Question* (1948); Alexandrov, *Meeting on the Elbe* (1949); Room, *Court of Honour* (1948); Kalatozov, *Conspiracy of the Damned* (1950). Happily, Dovzhenko did not complete *Goodbye America!* The most that can be said in favour of these films is that they were generally less hysterical in tone than their American counterparts. Other directors sought refuge in filming theatrical productions – plays, ballets, operas. There was a spate, too of 'historical' films which brought the figure of Stalin – played by Gelovani or Dieki and generally in gleaming white – nearer and nearer apotheosis (*Battle of Stalingrad*, 1950; *The Unforgettable Year 1919*, 1951).

Top: Alexei Batalov in 'The Cranes are Flying' (Mikhail Kalatozov, 1957)
Above: Zinaida Kirienko and Sergei Bondarchuk in 'Destiny of a Man' (Bondarchuk, 1959)
Below: Shanna Prokhovenko and Vladimir Ivashov in 'Ballad of a Soldier' (Grigori Chukhrai, 1959)

from Romm, who made a fine film concerning the lives of atomic scientists, *Nine Days of One Year* (1961), and a highly personal compilation film about the Nazi period, *Ordinary Fascism* (1964). Donskoi returned to Gorki for the subjects of a rather flat remake of *Mother* (1956) and a baroque, Kalatozov-influenced *Foma Gordeyev* (1959). Later he made two films recreating Lenin's childhood and youth (*Heart of a Mother* and *A Mother's Devotion*, both 1966).

The FEKS group, apparently ageless in their enthusiasm, produced some of the outstanding works of the post-war period. Kozintsev followed a dazzling *Don Quixote* (1957) with a *Hamlet* (1964) which is arguably the most intelligent film adaptation of Shakespeare to date; and in 1971 he finished an equally personal version of *King Lear*. Yutkevitch was eclectic in his activities. In the 1950s his highly inventive theatrical revivals of Mayakovski's 'The Bed Bug' and 'The Bath House', made an important contribution to the revival of the Soviet stage. He embarked on animation with an inventive version of *The Bath House* (1962) for the cinema. Twice he returned, with Straukh, to the problems of recreating the figure of Lenin on the screen: *Three Stories of Lenin* (1958) was a quiet, gentle reconstruction of three episodes from Lenin's life, including the previously politically delicate subject of Lenin's last illness. *Lenin in Poland* (1967) covered an almost unknown period of Lenin's pre-Revolutionary activity. These films are the most human of all Soviet interpretations of the personality of Lenin. In 1969, *Subject For A Short Story* showed Yutkevitch as ready to experiment as in the old FEKS days, with an elegantly stylized examination of an episode in Chekhov's life at the time of the première of 'The Seagull'.

Heifitz, now permanently separated from Zarkhi, achieved enormous success with a Chekhov adaptation, *The Lady With the Little Dog* (1960), played by ALEXEI BATALOV, one of the most sensitive of the new Soviet actors, and photographed by ANDREI MOSKVIN, the veteran cameraman. The film seemed less the work of a veteran than a film for the time of *nouvelles vagues*. Heifitz did not quite repeat his success with another Chekhov story, *In the Town of S.* Gerassimov made big films: a showy adaptation of Mikhail Sholokhov's *Quiet Flows the Don* in 1958; *Men and Beasts* (1962) and then an extremely long, ultimately non-committal contemporary 'problem picture' nine years later, *The Journalist* (1967).

JULIA SOLNTSEVA, having completed *Poem of the Sea*, which Dovzhenko was preparing at his death, piously set herself to realizing other of his unrealized projects. The massive spectacle *Story of the Flaming Years*, though only a shadow of a Dovzhenko film, was successful enough to permit her to continue with other Dovzhenko scenarios: *The Enchanted Desna* and *The Golden Gates*. The last film of Friedrich Ermler, *Before the Judgment of History* (1967) is one of the most remarkable historical documents of the era; the story of the Revolution seen through the eyes of the old Duma member Shulgin.

A notable new talent of the 1960s was Sergei Paradjanov, a Georgian director working in the Kiev Studios whose *Shadows of Our Forgotten Ancestors* (1964), a wild, poetic, highly personal creation at least reminded audiences that DOVZHENKO once worked in Kiev.

But as the 1960s progressed there was a sense of new tightening of control. The release of films was often held up without explanation. Films on contemporary themes as apparently inoffensive as Khutsiev's *I Am Twenty* (1963) were regarded with official suspicion. Tarkovsky's massive panorama of *Andrei Roublev* was completed in 1966 but only released in the Soviet Union in 1971, on account of its 'negative' view of mediaeval Russia.

Along with these symptoms the late 1960s saw film-makers apparently less willing to

Top: Innokenty Smoktunovsky and V. Kolpakor in 'Hamlet' (Grigori Kozintsev, 1964)
Above: Yuri Yarvet and Valentina Chendrikova in 'King Lear' (Grigori Kozintsev, 1971)
Below: Iya Savina in 'The Lady with the Little Dog' (Yosif Heifitz, 1960)

Top: Vladislav Strzhelchik in 'War and Peace' (Sergei Bondarchuk, 1963–7)
Above: 'Waterloo' (Italy-USSR, Sergei Bondarchuk, 1970)
Below: Marianna Vertinskaya in 'I am Twenty' (Marlen Khutsiev, 1963)

experiment. Few Soviet films reached foreign festivals; and these tended to be on historical or literary themes, such as BONDARCHUK's opulent, heavy-handed *War and Peace* (1964–7) and (in co-production with DINO DE LAURENTIIS) *Waterloo* (1970), Pyriev's last film, *The Brothers Karamazov*, and Kulidjanov's *Crime and Punishment.* Not all were so bad as these: MIKHALKOV-KONCHALOVSKY made an extremely intelligent and sensitive adaptation of Turgenev's *A Nest of Gentlefolk* and Chekhov's *Uncle Vanya* Gleb Panfilov's two films, *The Début* and *No Ford through the Fire*, are also of high quality.

There were interesting historical films, too, like Konchalovsky's earlier *The First Teacher* (1965), about the difficulties of a teacher in a remote rural area in the early days of the Revolution; and Karasik's *The Sixth of July*, which told with fine historical reconstructions and creditable frankness the story of the July revolt of the Social Revolutionaries against the Bolsheviks. Often, though, historical 'frankness', as in *The Chairman* (directed by Saltikov, 1965), is illusory, convenient repetition of safe historical truisms.

There is said (1971) to be interesting activity in the national production centres of the Ukraine, Georgia, Armenia, Lithuania, Latvia, Estonia and Moldavia, which tend to recruit new graduates from the Cinema Institute; but little evidence of this activity has been allowed to reach the outside world. The most disturbing aspect of the Soviet cinema as it enters the 1970s is the difficulty in seeing the new controversial works by young directors who are, hopefully, forging new paths. See 'Kino' by Jay Leyda (Allen and Unwin, 1960). DR

Ruttmann, Walter (1887–1941)
Born in Frankfurt, Germany. Director and cinematographer. Early studies and interests, music, painting and architecture. Began work as an abstract film-maker in 1918, making *Die tönende Welle* (1921), a film experimenting with sound, *Opus I, II, III, IV* (1921–4), *Der Falkentraum* (an insertion for FRITZ LANG's *Nibelung Saga*, 1924), and collaborated with PUDOVKIN to make *Feind im Blut* (1931). After his feature-documentary *Berlin – Rhythm of a City* (1927) made with MAYER and FREUND, his career was largely devoted to sponsored documentaries, especially in the 'city-symphony' tradition which (although preceded by one year by CAVALCANTI in France with *Rien que les Heures*) he had done more than anyone to establish; he later made films about Düsseldorf, Stuttgart and Hamburg, one of the most famous being *Melodie der Welt* (1929). In other capacities than director he assisted LOTTE REINIGER with her feature-length silhouette film *The Adventures of Prince Achmed* (1923–6) and LENI RIEFENSTAHL with her *Olympiad* (1936–8), and in 1938 directed a feature film in Italy, *Acciaio (Steel)*, in which the industrial backgrounds at Terni were more important than the triangle drama provided in a script by Luigi Pirandello. He made documentaries for the Nazi régime, including *Deutsche Panzer* (1940). During the 1920s he also worked with the expressionist stage director, Erwin Piscator. RM

Above: Bolot Beishenaliev and Natalia Arinbasarova in 'The First Teacher' (Andrei Mikhalkov-Konchalovsky, 1965)
Below: Woody Strode and Robert Ryan in 'The Professionals' (Richard Brooks, USA, 1966)

Ryan, Robert
Born 1913 in Chicago, USA. Powerful American actor who has appeared in over 60 films during 30 years and survived more bad ones than almost any performer on the screen, creating many fine portraits of men-in-action, often under stress. Stage-trained, he made his film début in *Golden Gloves* (1940) and another boxing film gave him his finest role, *The Set Up* (1949). Principal films: *Bombardier* (1943), *Crossfire* (1947), *The Boy with Green Hair* (1948), *Act of Violence* (1949), *The Racket* (1951), *Clash by Night* and *Beware My Lovely* (1952), *The Naked Spur* (1953), *The Tall Men* and *Bad Day at Black Rock* (1955), *House of Bamboo* and *Men in War* (1956), *God's Little Acre* and *Lonely Hearts* (1959), *Odds Against Tomorrow* (1959), *King of Kings* (1961), *The Longest Day* and *Billy Budd* (1962), *The Professionals* (1966), *The Dirty Dozen*, *Custer of the West*, *Anzio* and *Hour of the Gun* (1967), *The Wild Bunch* and *Captain Nemo and the Underwater City* (1969), *Lawman* (1971).

S

Safety Film
See NON-FLAM FILM

Saint, Eva Marie
Born 1930 in Newark, New Jersey, USA. After theatre experience, she won an Academy Award as supporting actress in her first film, *On the Waterfront* (1954). She plays normally a girl of quiet, introspective character. Her films include several of distinction; among them are *Exodus* (1960), *All Fall Down* (1962), *36 Hours* (1964), *The Sandpiper* (1965), *The Russians are Coming, the Russians are Coming* and *Grand Prix* (1966), *The Stalking Moon* (1968) and *Loving* (1970).

St Clair, Mal (Malcolm) (1897–1952)
Born in Los Angeles, USA. Director. The son of an architect, St Clair was employed as a newspaper cartoonist before joining the SENNETT studios as a gagman in 1915. Making his début as a director in 1919 (*Rip and Stitch, Tailors*), he soon sought comedy styles of greater subtlety than were permitted at Keystone, and so went freelance, collaborating with BUSTER KEATON on two of his best shorts, *The Goat* and *The Blacksmith*. His first feature film was *George Washington* (1923). An unhappy period directing Rin-Tin-Tin dramas ended when St Clair had a singular success with the social comedy, *Are Parents People?* (1925), after which he was established as a director of sophisticated comedies, working with players of the calibre of ADOLPHE MENJOU, POLA NEGRI, Florence Vidor, CLIVE BROOK, LOUISE BROOKS and Constance Talmadge. In 1926, the year in which he made *The Show-Off* and *The Grand Duchess and the Waiter*, he was voted third – after LUBITSCH and STROHEIM – in the list of the best American directors. After *Gentlemen Prefer Blondes* (1928) St Clair's career seemed to lose its impetus; and though he continued to direct until 1948, most of his work in the sound period was on second features. Four features with Laurel and Hardy, *Jitterbugs* (1943), *Dancing Masters*, *The Big Noise* and *Street Angel* (1944) were among the comedians' least happy work. DR

Saltzman, Harry
Born 1915 in St John's, Canada. Entrepreneur film producer and promotion expert whose gamble on bringing Ian Fleming's spy hero, James Bond, to the screen was one of the most celebrated financial success stories in post Second World War films. After gaining experience in television, he set up the productions of *Look Back in Anger* (1959), the Bond series starting with *Dr No* (1962), *The Ipcress File* (1965) and *The Battle of Britain* (1969). A working producer, he tends to exercise more influence over the lavish style of his films than do the individual directors and writers engaged on them.

Samoilova, Tatiana
Born 1934 in Moscow, USSR. Actress. The daughter of a famous Soviet actor, Samoilova trained at the Vakhtangov and Mayakovski Theatres and achieved international fame with her role in KALATOZOV's *The Cranes Are Flying* (1957) and *The Letter that was not sent* (1960). Later appearances – for instance as *Anna Karenina* (1967) – revealed her as a trifle too chubby and cosy for the romantic sort of image the studios attempted to impose on her.

George Sanders in 'The Kremlin Letter' (John Huston, USA, 1969)

Samsonov, Samson
Born 1921 in Moscow, USSR. Director. A pupil of GERASSIMOV at the Moscow Film Institute, Samsonov was one of the many young people who began their careers on Gerassimov's *The Young Guard* (1948), on which he worked as an assistant. His first film as a director, *The Grasshopper* (1955), possessed a sensitivity and intimacy that was not recaptured in later films: a comedy, *Shop Window* (also 1955); a Revolutionary action adventure, *The Fiery Miles* (1957); *As Old as the Century*; an overblown adaptation of Vishnevsky's 'Optimistic Tragedy' (1964); and *The Arena* (1968).

Sanders, George
Born 1906 in St Petersburg, Russia; educated in England. Actor. In textile business before becoming actor in England. Appeared on stage, then on screen in *Strange Cargo* (1929). Has since made many films in Britain and America, often playing smooth or suavely crooked characters. Based himself in Hollywood in 1939. Films include: *The Man Who could Work Miracles* (1935), *Confessions of a Nazi Spy* (1939), *Rebecca*, *Foreign Correspondent* and *The Saint* (1940), *The Moon and Sixpence* (1942), *The Picture of Dorian Gray* (1944), *Samson and Delilah* (1949), *All About Eve* (1950), *Ivanhoe* (1952), *Moonfleet* (1955), *While the City Sleeps* (1956), *Solomon and Sheba* (1959), *Village of the Damned* (1962), *Moll Flanders* (1965), *The Quiller Memorandum* (1966), *The Kremlin Letter* (1969). Also television series. His autobiography, 'Memoirs of a Professional Cad', was published in 1960.

Sanin, Alexander
Real name: Schoenberg. A director at the Moscow Art Theatre, Sanin is mainly known as the co-director of *Polikushka* (1919), the first feature film made after the revolution and before the nationalization of the film industry. Sanin did however make other films: *Maids of the Mountain* (1918) and *Soroka-vorovka* (1920).

Santis, Giuseppe De
See DE SANTIS

Saura, Carlos

Born 1932 in Huesca, Spain. One of the most gifted of the younger school of Spanish directors, Saura first attracted attention with a striking neo-realist film about young delinquents in Madrid, *Los Golfos* (1960). *Llanto por un bandido* (1964), an adventure story, was less successful; but *La Caza* (1966), with its evident homages to BUÑUEL, was a highly intelligent and equivocal allegory on contemporary Spanish society, as were *Peppermint Frappé* (1968) and *The Garden of Delights* (1970).

Saville, Victor

Born 1897 in Birmingham, England. One of the key figures in the British cinema of the 1930s, Saville was a craftsmanlike director and a commercially intelligent producer. Originally a film salesman and exhibitor, he entered production with MICHAEL BALCON, his first work as a producer being GRAHAM CUTTS's *Woman to Woman* (1924). As director he initially collaborated on a number of MAURICE ELVEY's films, his first solo work being *Tesha* (1928), which he also wrote and produced. In 1931 he directed the English version of *Sunshine Susie*. Later films of note were *I was a Spy* and *The Good Companions* (1933), *Evergreen* (1934), *The Iron Duke* (1936), *Dark Journey* (1937), *South Riding* (1938). From 1940 Saville was producing and occasionally directing in the USA. Working on several notable musicals and thrillers, he continued to produce until 1961 (*The Greengage Summer*).

Scandinavia

The history of Scandinavian films is one of remarkable accomplishment. Taking into account the size, relatively limited resources and world outlets (because of language problems) of the countries involved, the far-reaching influence on international screen trends during various peak periods, especially from Sweden and Denmark, amply proves the power of a strongly indigenous film tradition; a tradition, admittedly, perpetuated by several massive talents and at least two creative geniuses (INGMAR BERGMAN and CARL DREYER).

Inevitably Sweden and, to a lesser extent, Denmark, figure most significantly in any study of Scandinavian films, although Norway and Finland have also made their contributions. While the Scandinavians have in general tried to maintain highly individual native film industries, they have also produced many artists – notably actresses, among them pre-eminently the greatest of screen stars, GRETA GARBO, and directors – who have made an impressive, if not wholly successful impact working in foreign film industries. Indeed the exodus of so much talent to Hollywood during the 1920s, including the key directors MAURITZ STILLER and VICTOR SJÖSTRÖM, handicapped Swedish film production, which, bedevilled by economic pressures, went into one of its periodic declines.

But in the earlier years of the 20th century, before sound depleted its international market, the revelation of the Scandinavian film for audiences and other burgeoning industries can hardly be over-estimated. Maurice Bardèche and Robert Brasillach in 'History of the Film' sum up the Scandinavian phenomenon: 'In the first years after the [First World] War the Scandinavian film and the Swedish film in particular attained such importance that there were many who believed that the northern countries had become the chosen land of motion pictures'.

The second golden age, since the late 1950s, has been dominated by one figure – Sweden's Ingmar Bergman – and its continuing impetus is fortified by the reactions for or against Bergman's influence among young Scandinavian directors.

Significantly, many of the best Scandinavian film-makers have drawn inspiration from the legends, culture, and religious and climatic conditions peculiar to these Nordic regions. To a large extent this source material dictated the identifiable style and look of Scandinavian films, which gained a reputation for great visual beauty and the celebration of nature, the countryside and the primitive instinct. In the last ten years, a wider international political awareness has changed the overall image of the hitherto rather enclosed Scandinavian film scene.

But it is unjust to discuss the Scandinavian film as an entity. Obviously there has been much interchange of ideas, artists and common interests between the four countries and it goes without saying that there is more recognizable affinity between a Swedish and, say, a Norwegian film than between a Swedish and Italian film. However, each nation prides itself on an individual film industry which should be studied separately.

Denmark This was the pioneer country. In 1898 a court photographer named P. Elfelt made a documentary film of the Danish royal family. This was followed by newsreel and interest shorts and, according to Forsyth Hardy's 'Scandinavian Film', the Danes claimed to have made their first dramatic film in 1903.

In 1906 Nordisk Films – one of the first major production companies in the world – was founded by Ole Olsen, who apparently arrived in films after a career as varied and unlikely as those of many early Hollywood film tycoons. His early films were mostly adaptations of novels and plays, but he quickly learned the value of shock appeal to audiences. In 1910 his company distributed *The White Slave Traffic* followed by other *risqué* titles. At the same time, though, the quality of Danish films (with their sophisticated lighting and camera techniques) contrasted with the cruder output from other countries, was being remarked upon internationally, where they were enjoying much success.

The exquisite actress ASTA NIELSEN, whose first film was *The Abyss* (1910), helped promote Danish films, though she scored her major successes in Germany. In 1913 BENJAMIN CHRISTENSEN, one of the great names of Danish films, made *The Mysterious X* and another pioneer, August Blom, made several large-scale dramas including *Atlantis*.

By the time the First World War broke out in 1914 Danish films were in a very strong position, but the hostilities cut down their markets drastically. By the time the war ended, the international situation had greatly changed. Denmark, like Britain, had lost ground. Hollywood had begun to stake its claim as the principal purveyor of screen entertainment. Sweden and particularly Germany were to become far more considerable film powers than tiny Denmark.

An attempt to claim its share of the English-speaking box-office resulted in several uninspired Danish adaptations of Dickens's novels. But a series of small-scale comedies featuring Carl Schenström and Harald Madsen were more successful. CARL DREYER made his first film, *The President*, in 1920, followed by *Leaves From Satan's Book*, although he had been engaged on scriptwriting as far back as 1912. Dreyer, however, was not to find total acclaim, or, indeed, complete sympathy with his methods of working in Scandinavia. Some eminent critics were to pronounce his unhurried, concentrated technique and use of close-ups 'uncinematic'. The intensity of the moral dilemmas that are the obsessive force in his films are perhaps more readily acceptable to modern audiences than to the audiences of 40 or so years ago. He went to France, where he was much admired, to create his masterpiece, *La Passion de Jeanne d'Arc* (1928).

The arrival of the talking picture posed a much more critical problem for Danish films than war-time restrictions. There was no retreat from sound and Danish was a very small minority language. The industry resigned itself for a while to catering for the home market with pretty but generally inferior comedies and romances, apart from occasional ambitious projects – *Palo's Wedding* (1934), for example, produced by the explorer Dr Knud Rasmussen, was a study of Eskimo life which was well received outside Denmark. In 1939 BENJAMIN CHRISTENSEN, who had made the remarkable *Witchcraft Through the Ages* (1921) in Sweden, returned to Denmark to direct *Children of Divorce* (1939), followed by *The Child* (1940), which dealt with important contemporary themes and influenced later Danish films.

In 1938 a Cinema Act was passed, which among other important points, made provision for a Film Fund to foster the production of educational and cultural films. This Government legislation had an effect more far-reaching than anyone at the time could have anticipated. The availability of money for production led to the making of several interesting pre-war documentaries and by the time Denmark was invaded by the Germans in 1940 a tradition of documentary film-making was too entrenched to be destroyed.

Under Dansk Kulturfilm, a series of documentaries were made which helped sustain the Danish spirit of resistance under the eyes of the Nazis. Together with the Government Film Committee, Dansk Kulturfilm sponsored over 100 documentaries during the five years of war-time occupation.

A common excellence in this type of film production led to a special *rapport* between the Danish and British documentary movements.

In 1943, Dreyer made his first feature film since *Vampyr* (1932), *Day of Wrath*, a magnificent study of witch-hunting hysteria in the 17th century, which, however, was not an immediate success in Denmark. Dreyer was to make three more films, *Two People* (1944) in Sweden, *Ordet* (1954) and *Gertrud* (1964) before he died in 1968.

After the war the documentary tradition found an outlet in the portrayal of realistic dramas, and several of the most noted documentary film-makers – including Johan Jacobsen, Bjarne and Astrid Henning-Jensen – utilized the techniques they had learned in the production of feature films. But as the war-time drive that encouraged the documentary growth receded Danish films lost stature, overshadowed by the achievements of Sweden.

Nevertheless, the later years of the 1960s and early 1970s have been especially interesting. The abolition of film censorship in 1969 brought forth a brief rash of 'blue' films mainly for the less liberated international market, but in general it had only a marginal effect on Danish production as a whole. With *Hunger* (1966), *People Meet* and *We are all Demons* (1969), Henning Carlsen has established himself as a stylish director. Other notable younger directors are Knud Leif Thomsen, Jens Rav and Jens Jorgen Thorsen, whose adaptation of Henry Miller's *Quiet Days in Clichy* (1969) was a notorious success. An attractive unforced maturity is evident in the new Danish films, particularly in their study of youth and the pressures of society, notably in Braad-Thomsen's *Dear Irene* (1971); however there still seems to be a popular market for the lamentably heavy-going comedies which have tended to be a feature of Danish film production. In common with all the other Scandinavian countries, Denmark favours interesting co-productions as a means of breaking through her own sound (i.e. language) barrier, such as Peter Brook's *King Lear* (1970).

Despite a decline in cinema attendance, a record 28 feature films were produced in Denmark in 1971, including the ambitious satire *Lost In The Sand* from a new TV-trained director Thomas Winding and Franz Ernst's semi-documentary on the inadequacies of the Welfare State, *Re: Lone*.

Sweden 'Probably no other nation of comparative population has matched the artistic success of Sweden in the cinema,' says Peter Cowie in his definitive 'Screen Series' on Sweden, 'but one man, Charles Magnusson, from Göteborg, was responsible for the foundations of this achievement'. In 1896 Magnusson started training as a cameraman and eventually became a newsreel photographer. In 1909 he joined Svenska Bio, which had been formed two years earlier and in 1919 was to be amalgamated into Svensk Filmindustri, the leading Swedish production company. Another newsreel cameraman, Julius Jaenzon, joined Magnusson in the company and their joint ambitions for a cinema that would be more than a fairground sideshow was to be the commanding influence on the future of Swedish films.

Above: Astrid Holm (above) and Mathilde Nielsen in 'Master of the House' (Carl Dreyer, 1925)
Below: Victor Sjöström and Edith Evastoff in 'Terje Vigen' ('A Man There Was', Sjöström, 1916)

In 1912, Magnusson signed up the men who were to be giants of the silent screen, VICTOR SJÖSTRÖM and Finnish-born MAURITZ STILLER. Both men, originally stage actors, played in the first films they directed – Stiller's *Mother and Daughter* (1912) and Sjöström's *The Gardener* (1912). They went on in the next decade to make over 40 films each. Hitherto Swedish films had leaned toward French and American film techniques. Stiller and Sjöström developed inherently Swedish themes (Selma Lagerlöf's stories were a notable source) which they adapted to their differing but uniquely Nordic styles of film-making. Of the two, Stiller was the more erratic; Sjöström was the greater directorial talent although he also continued to act throughout his film career – his last major performance was in INGMAR BERGMAN's *Wild Strawberries* (1957). Indeed Sjöström's examination of the interior conflicts of his characters have probably influenced the great trilogies of Bergman.

Apart from his conviction that films should be a social force as well as an absorbing entertainment, Magnusson's achievements at Svenska Bio are reputed to include the production of a stereoscopic film in 1910 and a reform of film censorship.

During the First World War Swedish films continued to prosper, unlike those of Denmark. But when it was over the shadow of American domination was as formidable for Sweden as it was for its smaller neighbour. To combat the

Above: Jenny Hasselvist and Mathias Taube in 'Johan' (Mauritz Stiller, 1921)
Below: Lars Hanson and Greta Garbo in 'The Saga of Gösta Berling' (Mauritz Stiller, 1924)

American threat, more lavish international productions were set in motion, with varying success, at the cost of that native individuality which had been the distinction of Swedish films. Two new talents – Olof Molander and Per Lindberg, who were to make their mark – emerged at this time.

As it has continued to do through the years, Hollywood began to attract many Continental film artists. After making *The Saga of Gösta Berling* (1924), in which he introduced his *protégée* GARBO, Stiller left for MGM, taking her with him. The leading actor, Lars Hanson, also responded to the American call; as did Victor Sjöström, although he was to return and pick up the threads of his Swedish film career in 1930. Stiller's contribution to Swedish cinema ended when he went to Hollywood. He, too, returned to Sweden in 1928, but died shortly afterwards. Neither director experienced the same freedom or the same sense of achievement in Hollywood that they had enjoyed in Sweden. Sjöström's Hollywood record increases in distinction as more films are rediscovered.

The American hold on the international public's preference in films weighed against the Swedish product and a series of co-productions were planned as a means of regaining a world market. An agreement was made with UFA to produce Swedish-German films. But most of these were as colourless as many of the co-productions of the 1960s and 1970s. An Anglo-Swedish co-production, *Sin* (1928), directed by GUSTAV MOLANDER (brother of Olof) from a Strindberg drama, was hardly more satisfactory. But a film made by the young director ALF SJÖBERG, *The Strongest* (1929), challenged the depressing triviality of Swedish films at the time. It was ten years before Sjöberg directed another film.

The climate of mediocrity continued through the 1930s, occasionally stimulated by a work of distinction, such as Molander's *One Night* (1931), which revealed a strong Russian influence, and his *Intermezzo* (1936), a polished, delicate romance that made a star of INGRID BERGMAN, who subsequently appeared in a remake of it in Hollywood.

By the end of the 1930s a fresh approach was detectable in Swedish films. New film companies were formed. A move toward original screenplays encouraged young writers to look to films for inspiration. Location shooting was to become the norm instead of the exception.

The figure of ARNE SUCKSDORFF emerged, first as a creator of short films which reflected a profound love for and awareness of nature. Among his later feature films *The Great Adventure* (1953) became an enduring classic, equally beloved by children and adults. But though Sucksdorff's influence is apparent in the pictorial quality of Swedish films, he remains a unique film artist set apart from Swedish cinema as a whole.

The Second World War years were especially productive for Swedish films, which tended to take their mood – though not necessarily their subjects – from the sense of grim reality experienced by the nations in conflict on the borders of neutral Sweden. Conversely, one of the few gifted Swedish comedians, Nils Poppe, came to the fore in *Money* (1945) and he was later to make an even more indelible impression in Bergman's *The Seventh Seal* (1956).

What is now considered the key film of the reinvigorated Swedish screen was Sjöberg's *Frenzy* (1944), a harrowing story of sexual torment for which Ingmar Bergman wrote his first screenplay. *Frenzy* became a popular as well as a critical success and Sjöberg confirmed his reputation as a major director in 1951 with a memorable film interpretation of Strindberg's *Miss Julie*.

Top: Nils Poppe and Inga Landgré in 'Soldat Bom' ('Private Bom', Lars-Eric Kjellgren, 1948)
Above: Ulf Palme and Anita Björk in 'Miss Julie' (Alf Sjöberg, 1951)
Below: Gunnel Lindblom and Georg Rydeberg in 'Fadern' ('The Father', Alf Sjöberg, 1969)

But from the 1950s onward the name that became synonymous with Swedish films was that of INGMAR BERGMAN. He directed his first film, *Crisis*, in 1945. By the middle 1950s, during which *The Seventh Seal* (1956) and *Wild Strawberries* (1957) had achieved wide popular appeal outside Sweden, the disturbing impact of his increasingly concentrated focus on the dark areas of the Swedish character, the religio-sexual obsessions and the torments of good versus evil, brought to international audiences a film vision so richly defined and personal that it could be measured only against the work of the masters in other media, painting, music, literature.

Like Dreyer's, however, Bergman's genius was not immediately recognized. Early critics spoke disapprovingly of his isolation, his concern with the abnormal and his restrictive philosophy: all of which was later to be repeated by younger politically-orientated Swedish film directors of the late 1960s and 1970s.

The luck (if that is the word) of Bergman was to emerge in a film industry which was small-scaled, indigenous and in which no production was ruinously expensive. In 1949, the average budget was between £20,000 and £30,000: this demanded a flair for planning and organization from the film-makers but it also encouraged experiment. In 1951 the effect of a ruinous entertainment tax was mitigated when a Government degree stipulated that part of the revenue should be returned to producers to aid future production.

The main change in the Swedish film industry since the dominant period of Bergman in the 1950s has been its political involvement, especially significant remembering the neutral tradition of Sweden even when its Scandinavian partners were invaded during the Second World War. Younger film-makers such as BO WIDERBERG – who later adapted the deceptively romantic texture of his *Elvira Madigan* (1967)

Top: Maj-Britt Nilsson and Birger Malmsten in 'Sommarlek' ('Summer Interlude', Ingmar Bergman, 1950)
Above: Eva Dahlbeck and Gunnar Björnstrand in 'Kvinnors Väntan' ('Waiting Women', Ingmar Bergman, 1952)
Below: Anders Ek in 'Gycklarnas af ton' ('Sawdust and Tinsel', Ingmar Bergman, 1953)

as a counterpoint to the severities of a local strike in *Adalen '31* (1969) and the tale of the worker-martyr *The Ballad of Joe Hill* (1971) which he made in America – and Vilgot Sjöman, have been increasingly concerned with themes of protest. Allied to this is a greater freedom in depicting sex – Sjöman's *I am Curious – Yellow* (1967) is perhaps the most striking, though by no means the best, example of this alliance.

Significantly, the centrepiece of a recent Bergman trilogy, *The Shame* (1968), revealed an awareness of doom on a world scale not previously apparent in his films.

Jan Troell is, perhaps, more obviously an heir to the great Swedish tradition of film-making, with a fine visual sensitivity, unhurried style and a deep feeling for the drives that mould his characters. His main films include *Here is your Life* (1966) and a massive work on Swedish migrants to America, *The Emigrants* (1970–1). A particularly engaging film from Stellan Olsson, *It's up to You* (1969), pilloried authority while admitting the weaknesses also of the radical artist who challenged it. Kjell Grede, Jonas Cornell and Jan Halldoff have also made important contributions to the new Swedish cinema.

A staunch feminist, actress MAI ZETTERLING, has become an important, if rather humourless, director, principally of themes directly concerned with women's place in society, either

Top: Ove Porath, Axel Düberg, Birgitta Petterson and Tor Isedal in 'The Virgin Spring' (Ingmar Bergman, 1959)
Above: Harriet Andersson and Max von Sydow in 'Through a Glass Darkly' (Ingmar Bergman, 1961)
Below: Liv Ullman and Max von Sydow in 'The Shame' (Ingmar Bergman, 1968)

Top: Pia Degermark and Thommy Berggren in 'Elvira Madigan' (Bo Widerberg, 1967)
Above: Per Oscarsson and Bibi Andersson in 'Syskonbädd 1782' ('My Sister, my Love', Vilgot Sjöman, 1965)
Below: Lena Nyman and Börje Ahlstedt in 'I am Curious – Yellow' (Vilgot Sjöman, 1967)

Above: Bengt Ekerot and Monica Ekman in 'Ola and Julia' (Jan Halldoff, 1967)
Below: Jörgen Lindström, Ingrid Thulin and Lauritz Falk in 'Nattlek' ('Night Games' Mai Zetterling, 1966)

past or present, as in *Loving Couples* (1964), *Night Games* (1966) and *The Girls* (1968); although her short film *The War Game* (1962) was a painful study of a predominantly masculine problem – violence.

The Swedish film industry has also sponsored films by unorthodox new directors from abroad – notably PETER WATKINS and Susan Sontag.

As in the 1920s and 1930s, Swedish players are highly regarded beyond their own shores: MAX VON SYDOW, Per Oscarsson, the Bergman 'repertory company' of actresses – INGRID THULIN, HARRIET and BIBI ANDERSSON and LIV ULLMAN.

In 1963, a Swedish Film Institute was founded to encourage and subsidize native production and in the four years after its organization, according to Peter Cowie's 'Sweden', more than 20 film directors made their début. Significantly, though, one of the biggest successes in Sweden in recent years was the sex 'information' film *The Language of Love*.

In 1971 the opening of the Film Institute's 'Film House' – an impressive complex of studios, cinemas, library and museum – fortifies the image of a lively and resilient industry, particularly receptive to young ideas and fresh, original talent.

Norway There has been a dogged film production programme in Norway since the end of the First World War, based on native Norwegian themes. A notable example of this was the film version of Knut Hamsun's *Growth of the Soil* (1920). A grandson of Ibsen, Tancred Ibsen, began to direct for Norsk Films in the 1930s. In general, though, Norwegian films were for Norwegians. This was especially true during the Second World War when the Ger-German occupation denied them access to American and British films.

After the war, film-makers made dramatic use of the themes of the Resistance. *Vi vil Leve* (*We will Live,* Olav Dalgard) was one of the first, in 1945. A certain amount of co-production followed: *The Battle for Heavy Water* was an ambitious Franco-Norwegian production directed by Titus Wibe Müller in 1947. By the 1950s, a steady output of three feature films a year and numerous documentaries was established. Local and national government is much involved in Norwegian production and exhibition.

Few Norwegian films have made a big impact outside Norway, but in the late 1960s and early 1970s there were signs of interesting new talents at work in the industry. Paul Lökkeberg's *Liv* was enthusiastically received at the Berlin Festival in 1968. R. Lasse Henriksen's film *Love is War* was selected for Berlin in 1971. Several significant co-productions – notably Casper Wrede's film of Solzhenitsyn's *One Day In The Life Of Ivan Denisovich* – reflect the desire of new Norwegian film-makers to work with artists from other countries where joint development of a theme could prove fruitful. Government subsidies in one form or another have been partly responsible for the high standard of enlightened production.

Finland In comparison the film industry of Finland – a country so small that it must depend on a sympathetic Government interest in film production – has in the past been hampered by limited State support. However in 1969, a Finnish Film Foundation was established which, along Swedish and Danish lines, promoted new Finnish film production. In 1970 a dozen films were made, though the difficulty of finding markets outside Finland remain. Among young Finnish directors, JÖRN DONNER is a notable talent who has made his mark internationally,

Above: Harriet Andersson and Zbigniew Cybulski in 'Att älska' ('To Love', Jörn Donner, 1964)
Below: 'The Battle for Heavy Water' (Titus Wibe Müller, France-Norway, 1947)

although working for the most part in Sweden. An ex-film critic and co-founder of the Finnish Film Archive, he has written several books, including a study of INGMAR BERGMAN. His wry erotic adventures, *To Love* (1964), *Black on White* (1968) and *Portraits of Women* (1970), have been highly praised, though not well received by Finland's relatively stringent censors.

On balance, though, the separate yet obviously similar drives of Scandinavian film-makers remain impressive examples of what can be achieved in small, thriving, and, above all, concerned film industries. MH

Scenario
See SCREENWRITING

Schaffner, Franklin J.
Born 1920 in Tokyo, Japan. Meticulous American director, trained in television, whose best work reveals a care for period detail and an overall intelligence whatever the subject matter may be. Principal films: *Woman of Summer* (1963), *The Best Man* (1964), *The War Lord* (1965), *Patton – Lust for Glory* (1969), for which he won an Academy Award, *Nicholas and Alexandra* (1971).

Schary, Dore
Born 1905 in Newark, USA. Influential producer among the liberal wave of American film-makers who made their mark during the 1940s. A one-time actor and journalist, he became a sought-after screenwriter during the 1930s and in 1942 headed a small-budget production unit at MGM with considerable success. A quarrel with MGM took him to RKO, where he was responsible for a number of strong, progressive films until HOWARD HUGHES took over. Back at MGM, in charge of production during the crucial period of change brought about by the impact of television on film-going habits, he fell victim to internal power politics as his production programme failed to remake the fortunes of the studio. He was forced to resign in 1956, since when he has written books, plays and set up occasional independent productions: *Lonelyhearts* (1959), *Sunrise at Campobello* (1960), *Act One* (1963). MH

Schell, Maria
Born 1926 in Vienna, Austria. Actress, sister of Maximilian Schell. Trained in Zürich she has worked equally in the theatre and in films, establishing a reputation for forthright and sincere character performances in international productions. Her films include: *The Magic Box* (1951), *The Heart of the Matter* (1952), *Die Ratten* (1955), *Gervaise* (1956), *Une Vie* and *The Brothers Karamazov* (1958), *Cimarron* (1961), *99 Women* (1969).

Schell, Maximilian
Born 1930 in Vienna, Austria. Brother of Maria Schell. Distinguished stage, television and screen actor who won an Academy Award for his performance in *Judgment at Nuremberg* (1961). He has worked internationally and favours strong character parts. His films include: *Kinder, Mütter und ein General* (1955), *The Young Lions* (1958), *Five-Finger Exercise* (1962), *The Deadly Affair* (1966), *The Castle* and *Krakatoa* (1968). He also wrote, produced and directed *First Love* (1970) and co-directed *The Castle*. Acted in *Paulina 1888* (1972).

Schlesinger, John
Born 1926 in London, England. British director who came to films via television and won an Academy Award in 1969 for his first American-based film, *Midnight Cowboy*. An early interest in theatre at Oxford encouraged him to become an actor and he appeared briefly in several films – notably *The Battle of the River Plate* (1956) – and on television. He quickly graduated to directing and won a prize at the Venice Film Festival for his documentary *Terminus* (1960). His feature film début was *A Kind of Loving* (1962), followed by *Billy Liar* (1963) and *Darling* (1965), in association with producer Joseph Janni; in all of which he revealed a sensitive feeling for the pressures, frustrations and excesses of modern society, coupled with an increasingly edgy film technique. Thomas Hardy's Victorian rural novel, *Far from the Madding Crowd* (1967), provided a complete change of pace and style for Schlesinger. His alien view of the human flotsam of New York City, *Midnight Cowboy*, captured the young mood of the moment and its vast audiences turned it into one of the surprise hits of its year.

Sunday, Bloody Sunday (1971), a sensitive emotional study of three lovers, is possibly his best film to date. MH

Schlöndorff, Volker
Born 1939 in Wiesbaden, Germany. Director. Studied at the French film school, IDHEC, in Paris, and worked as an assistant to LOUIS MALLE, ALAIN RESNAIS, and JEAN-PIERRE MELVILLE. Returned to Germany and worked initially for television, later becoming prominent in the 'Junger deutscher' Film movement. His feature films, which he also scripted, have been *Young Törless* (1966), a study of a sensitive boy's reaction to military training set in the period of the Austro-Hungarian empire; *A Degree of Murder* (1967), the analytical study of a murderess; and *Michal Kohlhaas – the Rebel* (1969), the story of an individual's fight for justice in the 16th century, featuring the British star, DAVID WARNER, and ANNA KARINA. Recent film: *The Sudden Fortune of the Poor People of Kombach* (1971).

Schörm, Ewald
Born 1931 in Prague, Czechoslovakia. First attracting attention with his graduation film, the documentary *Tourists* (1962), Schörm rapidly moved into a leading position in the Czech New Wave of the 1960s and is often regarded as its

Maximilian Schell in 'The Deadly Affair' (Sidney Lumet, GB, 1966)

philosophical leader. Subsequent documentaries included: *The Railwaymen* and *To Live One's Life* (1963), *Why?* (1964), *Reflections* (1965), *Carmen* (1966). Schörm's first feature was a brilliant examination of a man's malaise in contemporary urban and industrial socialism, *Courage for Every Day* (1964). Since then he has made *The Return of the Prodigal Son* (1966), *Five Girls Like a Millstone Round Your Neck* (1967) and episodes in *Pearls of the Deep* (1965), *Prague Nights* (1968) and *Pastor's End* (1969).

Schüfftan, Eugen
Born 1893 in Breslau, Germany. Cinematographer. One of the most influential of all cinematographers (both in Europe and America) and creator of the 'Schüfftan Process' (q.v.), a method of combing live-action with paintings or models utilizing a large silvered mirror, originally used in LANG's *Metropolis* (1926). Schüfftan was also an early experimenter in documentary techniques (SIODMAK's *Menschen am Sonntag*, 1929). He has collaborated with many notable directors including PABST (*L'Atlantide*, 1932, with its luminous desert scenes), Feher (*The Robber Symphony*, 1935, in England) and CARNÉ (*Drôle de drame*, 1937, full of subtly lit interiors; *Quai des brumes*, 1938, with its atmospheric low-key effects). After working on several films with OPHÜLS, he spent a period in America with CLAIR (*It Happened Tomorrow*, 1944) and SIODMAK (*The Dark Mirror*, 1946). During the post-war era, he has alternated between Europe and America, collaborating notably with FRANJU on *La Tête contre les murs* (1958) and *Les Yeux sans visage* (1959); and ROSSEN – *The Hustler* (1961) and *Lilith* (1964). Schüfftan's style combines great documentary realism with a luscious, glowing plasticity (he is essentially a black-and-white artist) and he has advised and assisted many of the directors he has worked with. JG

Schüfftan Process
A patented trick process in which a photograph of a small scale model is reflected into the camera lens off an inclined mirror, the full-size section of the set and actors being photographed through a clear area produced by the removal of the silvering in the remainder of the mirror.

Schulberg, Budd
Born 1914 in New York, USA. Provocative American author and screenwriter, son of studio executive and independent producer B. P. Schulberg. His novels 'The Disenchanted', based on the screenwriting experience of Scott Fitzgerald, and 'What Makes Sammy Run', have accurately limned the wheeling and dealing and creative pressures of Hollywood: while his hard-edged screen adaptations of his own writings, *On the Waterfront* (1954), for which he won an Academy Award, and *A Face in the Crowd* (1957), were ideally brought to the screen by director ELIA KAZAN. He also wrote the screenplay for *Wind Across the Everglades* (1959) and the novel of the fight-game exposé, *The Harder They Fall*, which was adapted for the screen in 1956.

Scofield, Paul
Born 1922 at Hurstpierpoint, Sussex, England. Distinguished actor who specializes in historical and Shakespearean parts, mostly on stage, less frequently on television and cinema screen. Particularly associated with The Royal Shakespeare Company and The National Theatre. First professional appearance in Westminster Theatre, London, in 'Desire Under the Elms'. Films include: *That Lady* (1955), *Carve Her Name with Pride* (1958), *The Train* (1964), *A Man for All Seasons* (1966), *Bartleby* and *King Lear* (1970).

Scott, George C.
Born 1926 in Virginia, USA. Outstanding American stage and screen actor, reluctant star and outspoken critic of the Academy Awards – which did not prevent him being voted the best actor of 1970 for his performance in *Patton – Lust for Glory*. Theatre-trained, he made his film début in *The Hanging Tree* (1959), was picked by OTTO PREMINGER to play the cameo role of the prosecuting attorney in *Anatomy of a Murder* (1959), and established himself as a character actor who could give weight and variety to a supporting but telling role: notably in *The Hustler* (1961), *Dr Strangelove* (1964). He also appeared in the television series *East Side, West Side* (1963). He achieved fully fledged stardom with *Patton*. Other main films: *The List of Adrian Messenger* (1963), *The Yellow Rolls-Royce* (1964), *The Bible* (1966), *The Flim Flam Man* (1967), *Jane Eyre* (1970), *The Last Run* (1971).

Scott, Randolph
Born 1903 in Virginia, USA. Stage actor before his film début in *Sky Bride* (1931). He soon became popular in stalwart, open-air type

Top: Paul Scofield as 'King Lear' (Peter Brook, GB, 1970)
Above: George C. Scott in 'Patton: Lust for Glory' (Franklin J. Schaffner, USA, 1969)
Below: Randolph Scott in 'Western Union' (Fritz Lang, USA, 1941)

roles. Other films include: *Home on the Range* (1933), *Go West, Young Man* (1936), *High, Wide and Handsome* (1937), *Jesse James* (1939), *My Favourite Wife* (1940), *Western Union* (1941), *Captain Kidd* (1945), *Guns in the Afternoon* (1962).

Scott, Zachary (1914–1965)
Born Austin, Texas, USA. Actor, on stage in London and New York, as well as screen. Often cast as a suave but likeable villain, 1940s-style, he made his film début in *The Mask of Dimitrios* (1944). Subsequent films include: *The Southerner* (1944), *Mildred Pierce* (1946), *Born to be Bad* (1951), *Appointment in Honduras* (1953), *The Young One* (1960), *It's Only Money* (1962).

Screenwriting
The Silent Period The earliest films were sometimes preceded by a few descriptive words scribbled down on paper, though many were simply improvised out of the heads of their makers. Films which related a single incident scarcely needed any schematized working-out in advance, but when the plots reached a sufficient degree of complexity that a breakdown of the action in a succession of scenes was needed, scenarios, as they came to be called, began to appear in the hands of the directors.

We begin to be aware of the existence of scripts, or scenarios, at the turn of the century; Biograph in the USA were in the forefront of companies which realized the importance of having good writers in their service, or story-editors in the sense that the term is used in television today, supervisors of the screenplays submitted by writers. According to Benjamin B. Hampton, one of the earliest of American screen historians, a young and enterprising journalist called Roy McCardell was hired in the 1900s at the considerable salary of $150 a week to create ten good scenarios weekly, while pressmen and story-writers could get from $10 to $25 for stories acceptable for shooting.

There is also, of course, the case of D. W. GRIFFITH, who while acting in EDWIN S. PORTER's early films began to turn over some extra dollars by presenting the company with written ideas for further one-reel films. These early scenarios composed by journalists, authors and actors would read much like the synopsis outlining the action which the companies published in their catalogues. For example, take this story by CECIL HEPWORTH, who himself originated, or adapted from other people's material, the earlier screenplays he used; the following is the opening scene of *Falsely Accused* (1906), the full outline of which amounts to some 1,200 words:

> 'Scene I: Interior of an Office in the City. Two or three clerks are larking together, when the Principal arrives, and serious work commences for the day. On opening his letters the Principal finds a number of banknotes, and hands them to one of the clerks, to place them immediately in the safe. The clerk turns over and checks the notes. As he does so the numbers are revealed to the audience by means of a short telescopic view. A fellow-clerk of forbidding aspect, looks over his shoulders meanwhile and observes the value of the notes. They are placed in the safe, but the clerk is called away for a moment before he has time to lock it. The sinister-looking man withdraws the key, and makes an impression on a piece of soap before he replaces it; the first clerk then locks the safe and hands the key back to his employer.'

GEORGE PEARSON, one of the most distinguished directors in the British silent cinema, relates how

Paul Newman and Elizabeth Taylor in 'Cat on a Hot Tin Roof' (Richard Brooks, USA, 1958)

his introduction to films came through scenarios: a schoolmaster fascinated by film, he wrote of his enthusiasm to the Managing Director of Pathé Frères and was invited to lunch:

> 'My . . . hosts suggested I might try my hand at writing a film "scenario", which they explained was nothing more than a simple pictorial statement of about a thousand words describing some novel and humorous incident that might make a pleasing film.'

He was successful, receiving cheques for three guineas for each of the subjects he sent in weekly, and finally left teaching and adopted the profession of film-making in 1912.

The silent film-makers, therefore, were well aware of the need for elementary scripts, and turned to the only work available to them as sources – plays, novels and stories by classical or contemporary writers of note. This began to happen comparatively early; for example, Gabriele d'Annunzio sold the screenrights in all his existing works to the Italian Ambrosio company in 1911 and tied himself to letting them have any of his future works they wanted for a flat rate of 40,000 lire (or £5,200 at that time). Work out of copyright, such as Shakespeare, became a normal plot-source for films. Some 300 Shakespearean plots (rather than plays) were produced as films during the silent period.

During the teens of the century the profession of scenarist began to develop more fully. Long films, which began during the period after 1910, obviously required fully developed screenplays, describing the action in scenes and sequences and suggesting something of the dialogue which had to be mimed, its essentials presented to the audience by means of title-cards. Many directors wrote their own screenplays if they had the time to do so. However, it is well-known that Griffith directed both *The Birth of a Nation* and *Intolerance* out of his head, without reference to any written script. Nevertheless, for some of his films even he used the services of screenwriters, as Seymour Stern has pointed out:

> 'If he did not actually write the scenarios of certain of his films, he supervised the scenarist so strictly, that the writing itself partook of his ideas, his style, even his expressive methods. He collaborated with many scenarists, of whom S. E. V. Taylor, Frank Woods, Anita Loos and Gerrit J. Lloyd were probably the most notable, but he never "had a writer", in the sense in which this expression is applied to modern directors. For while Griffith based his films on themes or stories, he seldom required more than a few pages of scenario; hardly ever consulted a written "treatment" or adaptation; and he never used a continuity or shooting script. He shot his films, as the saying goes, "off the cuff", and *Intolerance*, the most massive and complex film ever made, was directed and edited in its entirety, without recourse to scripts, "screenplays", treatments or any other kind of paperwork.'

But the profession was established and well paid. Hampton reports how Roy McCardell, as one of the most experienced of the full-time screenwriters, was given the princely sum of $30,000 for the story and editorial supervision of a serial, *The Diamond of the Sky*, at a time when $500 was the maximum normally paid for a screenplay, and $1,000 to a novelist or playwright for the screenrights in a work.

Anita Loos, one of the post-war 'sophisticates' and author of the celebrated burlesque novel, 'Gentlemen Prefer Blondes', was one of the earlier 'name' scenarists. Daughter of a newspaperman and showman, she had show-business in her blood, but sold the story of *The New York Hat* to Biograph when still a teenage actress. Anita Loos (born 1893) joined Griffith's studio as a staff-writer after *The Birth of a Nation*, and became, according to the pioneer historian Terry Ramsay, 'the founder of the modern art of screentitling'. She proved adept at writing witty captions, which were useless to Griffith, who liked to write his own somewhat heavy-handed or sentimental captions. Her name appears as scriptwriter for the films Griffith supervised (and often wrote) for Triangle before making *Intolerance*, the earliest being *His Picture in the Papers* (1916), followed by *The Half-Breed*, in which DOUGLAS FAIRBANKS appeared.

Another enterprising girl was Jeannie MacPherson, who worked with CECIL B. DE MILLE and, according to Hampton, discovered sophisticated sex appeal and introduced it to De Mille, by turning Barrie's play, 'The Admirable Crichton' into *Male and Female* (1919), in which he starred GLORIA SWANSON. Like Anita Loos, she had begun as a bright young actress selling stories to the studios, and was later to script such films as *The Ten Commandments* (1924).

In the boom-years of the 1920s the fees paid to scenarists rapidly surpassed those of the earlier period, and it has been claimed that screenrights also soared up to $10,000 for a well-known writer's short story, whereas best-selling novels or popular plays were bought for fees ranging between $25,000 to $100,000, or even $200,000. But these figures are probably publicity exaggeration. Terry Ramsay's story of the acquisition of Ibánez's *The Four Horsemen of the Apocalypse* (filmed 1921) is typical; the competitive bidding between companies ended with Ibánez accepting $20,000 and a 10% royalty from Metro. An expert screenwriter, JUNE MATHIS, was put on the work of scripting a film which some members of the company felt would flop because war-subjects were at this period supposed to be unpopular. When the film was discovered to be an outstanding success, the 10% royalty proved an embarrassment, and Ibánez was persuaded to sell his interest outright for a further $170,000. Had he stuck to his contract he would have earned $400,000.

June Mathis, who also scripted *Blood and Sand* (1922) and *Ben Hur* (1926), is celebrated as the expert called in to 'discipline' ERICH VON STROHEIM's ill-fated film *Greed* (1923), when MGM insisted on still further cutting after its original 42 reels (some 10½ hours) had been reduced to 18 (or 4½ hours). Stroheim, like many of the more celebrated directors of the silent period, preferred to write his own screenplays and adaptations. June Mathis (before her premature death in 1927) was made administrative head of the large scenario department of the Goldwyn Studios, but Hampton complains that she and Goldwyn came under the influence of 'sophisticates' and intellectuals when they hired smart critics and playwrights to advise them, with (he claims) no understanding of public taste.

Like Griffith and Stroheim, certain of the greater directors of the silent period preferred to script their own films, among them RENÉ CLAIR, ROBERT FLAHERTY, CARL DREYER, and CHARLES CHAPLIN, and, in certain instances KING VIDOR. EISENSTEIN wrote the scripts of all his silent films, aided by his assistant and friend, GRIGORI ALEXANDROV. Chaplin had been trained in the hard school of MACK SENNETT with his group of gagmen who had to come up with sure-fire comic ideas to feed into the action of the Keystone comedies. Many important film-makers started as gagmen, including such distinguished directors as GEORGE STEVENS, who was for a while gagman to HAL ROACH, producer of the LAUREL and HARDY pictures. This was another branch of screenwriting, as was scripting for cartoons, which was as much a visual as a verbal exercise. (See ANIMATION.) A few celebrated screenplays have even survived to be published, such as that for *Greed*.*

The screenplays of the silent cinema, in the more advanced style developed by June Mathis, took the form of a shot-by-shot shooting script, with considerable technical breakdown. They were not intended as works of literary art, but rather what came much later to be called a 'blue-print' for all those concerned in realizing the picture. They foresaw as far as was possible in words what the vision of the camera and screen would ultimately reveal in their own terms, a highly select succession of images. Observation guided through words is a wholly different experience from observation guided through pictures. It was, and still is, a difficult concept for writers to grasp, since they are by nature and training word-orientated. Words

* The script for *Greed* was first published by the Cinémathèque de Belgique. A distinction exists between the actual script as written before shooting, and the post-production scripts assembled by other hands than those of the film-maker or his writer and derived from the finished film. Shot-by-shot post-production scripts of *The Birth of a Nation* and *Intolerance* have been prepared by Theodore Huff and published in New York by the Museum of Modern Art. There are also available in published form the post-production scripts of *The Cabinet of Dr Caligari*, *The Golem*, and *Nosferatu* published in the USA by Richard B. Byrne (College Printing and Typing Co Inc), and of *The Battleship Potemkin* published in London by Lorrimer. In 1929 the Columbia University Press published a volume of post-production scenarios, which included Frances Marion's script for VICTOR SJÖSTRÖM's American film adaptation from Hawthorne's *The Scarlet Letter*, and Lajos Biro's and John Goodrich's scenario for VON STERNBERG's *The Last Command*.

Paul Newman in 'Butch Cassidy and the Sundance Kid' (George Roy Hill, USA, 1969)

are full of richly ambiguous suggestion; pictures are objective, actual, and ambiguity or suggestion have to be introduced into them imagistically. This is why it was far better for the directors themselves to create their scripts, using them purely as explanatory notes for the continuity of the film as they foresaw it developing in their mind's eye. Some directors, of course, worked with known and trusted writers – for example, LUBITSCH with Hanns Krähly and FRITZ LANG with his then wife, Thea von Harbou, a well-known writer of thrillers.

One outstanding writer of the silent period who was fully aware of the needs of scriptwriting was the German, CARL MAYER. He called his script for the film *Sylvester* (1923) a 'light play', meaning it in the double sense of a revelation through the light and shade of cinephotography of the light and shade of the characters he was portraying. He was more aware than most of the artistic dichotomy which occurred when the enacted scene (requiring an observer's visual concentration to appreciate) was constantly punctuated by printed titles which required, however modestly, a purely verbal appreciation to absorb. The audience was expected to switch now to one, now to another form of attention, often, in the case of snatches of dialogue interchange, seeing only momentary lip movements before being confronted with the dialogue caption blotting out the screen for as long as the less literate required to spell out the words. Most of the titles in any case were written by hacks with little or no feeling for words. Gradually the artists of the silent film, such as Mayer scripting *The Last Laugh* for MURNAU, drew away from the use of captions altogether or, like EISENSTEIN or DZIGA VERTOV, used them very sparingly, or for sudden, dramatic effects, like exclamatory, leaded headings to articles in the popular press. The art of scripting silent films, leaving just as much as possible to the images in the hands of the director, art director, cameraman and actors, was reaching its own specialized form when the whole perspective of the art was changed by the arrival of the sound film.

The Screenwriter and the Coming of Sound The natural reaction to the coming of sound-on-film was twofold: first, to retain the silent technique and add synchronized music throughout the picture with patches of song and spoken dialogue to show off the new medium, and, secondly, to turn wholeheartedly to 100% 'talkies', which were normally filmed stage-plays, or at best musicals with elaborately designed song-and-dance sequences, such as *Broadway Melody* (1929). A high proportion of stars disappeared completely because their voices or their accents were inappropriate to the kind of voiceless image they had built up. A few notable directors tried immediately to adjust to sound imaginatively – among them HITCHCOCK with *Blackmail*, CLAIR with *Sous les Toits de Paris*, MILESTONE with *All Quiet on the Western Front*, STERNBERG with *The Blue Angel*, and PABST with *Westfront 1918* and *Kameradschaft*. But of these only *Sous les Toits de Paris* was scripted by its director.

Both directors and actors realized that a new generation of writers would be needed who understood how to write dialogue suitable for the screen. The 'projected', often over-explicit dialogue of the box-office plays of the 1930s dogged the cinema for a decade or more. Screenwriters were needed who were sensitive to the special needs of dialogue to be spoken as a part of observed action and reaction and presented with the emphatic enlargement of the cinema-screen, and in a continuity of images which shifted the emphasis away from the speaker just as often threw him into the sudden magnification of close-up. The prolonged dialogue interchanges which were exciting and climax-making in the theatre became boring and intimidating in the enlarged, dynamic portraiture of movie.

Fortunately for the development of the sound film, photographed theatre receded in preference to screenplays which, whether as originals or adaptations, began to evolve a visual treatment and dialogue balance proper to the screen. Some of the notable American screenplays of the period 1933–42 were published under the editorship of John Gassner in 1943, and in an outstanding article DUDLEY NICHOLS, who by then had scripted over a dozen of JOHN FORD's films (including *Men without Women*, 1930; *The Lost Patrol*, 1934; *The Informer*, 1935; *Stagecoach*, 1939; and *The Long Voyage Home*, 1940), wrote of the writer's approach to screen dialogue:

> 'Writing for the screen, if long practised, also seduces one to write dialogue in a synoptic fashion, which may show itself to the eye when printed on a page, but should never reveal itself to the ear when spoken from the screen. Stage dialogue, no matter how wonderful in quality, cannot be directly shifted to the screen; it must be condensed, synopsized. The reason is obvious; on the stage the actor depends for projection upon the word; on the screen he relies upon visual projection. And it is hard to describe visual projection in a screenplay; that must be left to the director and cast.'

He also wrote about his approach to the script of *The Informer*, which won him an Oscar:

> 'At that time I had not yet clarified and formulated for myself the principles of screenwriting, and many of my ideas were arrived at instinctively. I had an able mentor as well as collaborator in the person of John Ford and I had begun to catch his instinctive feeling about film. I can see now that I sought and found a series of symbols to make visual the tragic psychology of the informer, in this case a primitive man of powerful hungers. The whole action was to be played out in one foggy night, for the fog was symbolic of the groping primitive mind; it is really a mental fog in which he moves and dies. A poster offering a reward for information concerning Gypo's friend became the symbol of the evil idea of betrayal, and it blows along the street, following Gypo; it will not leave him alone. It catches on his leg and he kicks it off. But it still follows him and he sees it like a phantom in the air when he unexpectedly comes upon his fugitive friend.'

Among the scripts included in this volume were those for FRANK CAPRA's *It Happened One Night* (ROBERT RISKIN), with its astringent, colloquial speech; GEORGE CUKOR's satiric film *The Women* (Anita Loos and Jane Murfin); HITCHCOCK's *Rebecca* (Robert E. Sherwood and Joan Harrison); WILLIAM WYLER's *Wuthering Heights* (BEN HECHT and Charles MacArthur); FORD's humane and moving social portrait of an uprooted family, *The Grapes of Wrath* (NUNNALLY JOHNSON); FRITZ LANG's realistic study of mob rule, *Fury* (Bartlett Cormack and Fritz Lang); Capra's bitter-sweet *Mr Smith Goes to Washington* (Sidney Buchman); and WILLIAM DIETERLE's *Juarez* (JOHN HUSTON, Wolfgang Reinhardt and Aeneas MacKenzie).

It will be seen from this list how small a part directors played in scripting (as distinct from the final screen treatment) of their films, and how heavily reliant the film became on its writers, many of whom were distinguished authors and dramatists coming to terms with a second profession. Comparatively few authors, however, actually adapted their own established work for the screen at this stage. Classics in plenty were turned over to the screen. Well-known writers working at this time in Hollywood were LILLIAN HELLMAN, S. N. Behrman, CLIFFORD ODETS, John Howard Lawson, Irwin Shaw, PRESTON STURGES, DORE SCHARY, JOSEPH L. MANKIEWICZ, JOHN HUSTON, and William Saroyan. Several, of course, were to become directors. The Screenwriters' Guild was established in 1933 to fight for the authors' right to due credit for their unique importance to the cinema, second only to that of the dramatist in the theatre. Argument abounded that with scripts such as the above, film had become now a writer-director-star medium and not, as usually propounded, a director's medium solely. The main problem in Hollywood was the only too frequent total divorce of writer and director. The producers hired the writer to complete the script, and then assigned it as a *fait accompli* to some director to realize on the studio floor.

In Britain, a parallel, if smaller-scale, movement of writers into the studios was to establish both up to and after the war years the talent of, among others, Eric Ambler, Nige Balchin, Bridget Boland, BASIL DEARDEN, LEWIS GILBERT, SIDNEY GILLIAT, Graham Greene, VAL GUEST, Noel Langley, Angus MacPhail, Ivor Montagu, FRANK LAUNDER, T. E. B. CLARKE Terence Rattigan, R. C. Sherriff, PETER USTINOV and Ted Willis. Again, many were to become producers and directors at a later stage, and some more eminent as playwrights for the stage. The Screenwriters' Association (later Guild) was established to serve the same ends as the Guild in the USA. Certain celebrated scripts were published, including that of Lajos Biro and Arthur Wimperis for ALEXANDER KORDA's *The Private Life of Henry VIII* and that of H. G. Wells for *Things to Come*. In France the most notable scriptwriters were in the 1930s CHARLES SPAAK, who worked with

FEYDER, RENOIR and DUVIVIER, and JACQUES PRÉVERT, who worked with CARNÉ.

Post-war screenwriting in Hollywood went through two phases. The first was the sorry business of the 'witch-hunt' period, starting in 1947 with the hearings in Washington involving such writers as John Howard Lawson, Albert Maltz, and DALTON TRUMBO, and spreading over into the McCarthy era in the early 1950s. For a period, initiative in the American cinema seemed to die, and began to recover again during the second phase, which brought fresh blood from the writers in the television studios into screenwriting (and into direction) – PADDY CHAYEFSKY, for example, with his television plays which became films (*Marty* and *The Bachelor Party*), Reginald Rose, creator of the television series, 'The Defenders', with *Twelve Angry Men*, and the notable playwright William Inge, with *Come Back Little Sheba* and *Picnic*. These writers were particularly associated with the revival of the American film in the hands of the independent producer-directors. Many of these producer–directors were also writers who scripted all, or most, of their work – JOHN HUSTON, JOSEPH L. MANKIEWICZ, DELMER DAVES, RICHARD BROOKS, ELIA KAZAN (in his recent films), and (working mainly in Europe) ORSON WELLES and CARL FOREMAN. It is common knowledge how closely ALFRED HITCHCOCK supervises his screenwriters, while BILLY WILDER has worked closely with CHARLES BRACKETT and, more recently I. A. L. DIAMOND. For the more recent generation of directors scripts are of the utmost importance, more especially to STANLEY KUBRICK and to Carl Foreman, who scripts himself most of the productions he sponsors. The scripts of some recent outstanding American films were written by the following:

SIDNEY LUMET's *The Group* (Sidney Buchman; source, novel by Mary McCarthy)

ARTHUR PENN's *Bonnie and Clyde* (David Newman and Robert Benton; original screenplay)

PAUL NEWMAN's *Rachel, Rachel* (Stewart Stern; source, novel by Margaret Laurence)

SAM PECKINPAH's *The Wild Bunch* (Walon Green and Sam Peckinpah; original screenplay)

DENNIS HOPPER's *Easy Rider* (Peter Fonda, Dennis Hopper, Terry Southern; original screenplay)

GEORGE ROY HILL's *Butch Cassidy and the Sundance Kid* (William Goldman; original screenplay)

ROBERT ALTMAN's *M.A.S.H.* (Ring Lardner; source, novel by Richard Hooker)

MIKE NICHOLS's *Catch 22* (Buck Henry; source, novel by Joseph Heller).

In Britain, the swing has also been towards close association between director and writer, usually in the adaptation of the work the writer has done previously in the form of a play or novel. ANTHONY ASQUITH, who was fond of working from theatrical sources, collaborated frequently with Terence Rattigan in film versions of his plays. DAVID LEAN has worked with ROBERT BOLT on three films – *Lawrence of Arabia*,

Peter Sellers in 'Only Two Can Play' (Sidney Gilliat, GB, 1962)

Doctor Zhivago, and *Ryan's Daughter*, the first and the last an original screenplay, a comparatively rare occurrence in post-war British films since the days of Ealing Studios, when T. E. B. CLARKE was notable for his original screen comedies. MICHAEL POWELL and EMERIC PRESSBURGER have co-scripted most of their films; so have the BOULTINGS, while the producer-director BRYAN FORBES has written most of his own screenplays. CAROL REED has worked on three films with Graham Greene (whose early career included perceptive film criticism): *The Fallen Idol*, *The Third Man* and *Our Man in Havana*, all among Reed's best films. Greene's novels reflect the strong influence of the film in their structure and visual detail, and approaching twenty of his novels and stories have provided material for films. There is no country which has kept so closely to successful novels and plays on the screen as Britain, and other well-known authors who have more recently become effective screenwriters include David Mercer, JOHN OSBORNE, Shelagh Delaney, PAUL DEHN (formerly a well-known film critic), the prolific writing-team Keith Waterhouse and WILLIS HALL, HAROLD PINTER, Alun Owen, Bill Naughton, Edna O'Brien, Charles Wood, John Mortimer, Wolf Mankowitz, and Frederick Raphael.

In contemporary European cinema a number of notable directors either write or closely collaborate on their scripts. Among these are: INGMAR BERGMAN, JEAN-LUC GODARD, ROBERT BRESSON (all his post-war films), JEAN-PIERRE MELVILLE, FEDERICO FELLINI (who worked originally as ideas-man and scriptwriter to ROBERTO ROSSELLINI and others), PIER PAOLO PASOLINI, and JEAN RENOIR (with occasional collaborators). ALAIN RESNAIS has worked as closely as HITCHCOCK with his series of distinguished script-collaborators. HENRI-GEORGES CLOUZOT has co-scripted his films, usually with either Jean Ferry or Jérôme Géronimi. CLAUDE CHABROL has scripted or co-scripted a high proportion of his films, as has LUIS BUÑUEL, AKIRA KUROSAWA, and FRANCESCO ROSI. ANTONIONI has, since *L'Avventura*, worked closely on his scripts with Tonino Guerra. Italy has established a tradition of employing (or crediting) teams of scriptwriters on many films; the celebrated screenwriter SUSO CECCHI D'AMICO invariably co-scripts with one or more colleagues the films on which she works; DE SICA, however, has worked for over 20 years with virtually the same screenwriter, CESARE ZAVATTINI, from *I Bambini ci Guardano* (1943) to *After the Fox* (1965). RM

Script

Written version of a film story in shooting sequence covering both picture and sound

Scriptwriting

See SCREENWRITING

Seberg, Jean

Born 1938 in Marshalltown, Iowa, USA. Actress; won State talent contest with 'outstanding performance'. Began professional career with summer-stock companies. At 17, chosen out of 18,000 contestants for leading part in OTTO PREMINGER's film, *Saint Joan* (1957). Subsequent films include: *Bonjour Tristesse* (1957), *The Mouse that Roared* (1959), *A Bout de Souffle* (1960), *La Recreation* (1961), *In the French Style* (1963), *Lilith* (1964), *Diamonds are Brittle* (1965), *Paint Your Wagon* and *Airport* (1969).

Sellers, Peter

Born 1925 in Southsea, England. Actor, who has graduated from variety and radio comedy to the 'Goon Show' and international film stardom. His brilliance as an actor lies in the wide range of his vocal imitations, which reveal an astonishing ear for character, accent and dialect. His personal style of acting tends to be easy-going, sometimes to a fault. Films include: *The Ladykillers* (1955), *The Smallest Show on Earth* (1957), *Up the Creek* and *Carlton-Browne of the F.O.* (1958), *I'm All Right Jack* and *The Mouse that Roared* (1959), *Two-Way Stretch* (1960), *Mr Topaze* (which he also directed, 1961), *Only Two Can Play*, *Lolita* and *Waltz of the Toreadors* (1962), *The Dock Brief* and *The Pink Panther* (1963), *Dr Strangelove* (1964), *What's New, Pussycat?* (1965), *The Party* (1968), *The Magic Christian* (1969), *There's a Girl in My Soup* and *Hoffman* (1970). He has also appeared on television.

Selznick, David O. (1902–1965)

Born in Pittsburg, USA. Second generation Hollywood producer, promoter and picture tycoon, whose prestigious independent company, Selznick International, was responsible for *Gone With the Wind* (1939) and many other significant films of the period.

Son of the film pioneer, Russian-born Lewis

Above: David O. Selznick (1941)
Below: Larry Semon in his last film 'Spuds' (USA, 1927)

J. Selznick, and at one time son-in-law to LOUIS B. MAYER, he was trained by his father and later branched out on his own as a producer of 'quickie' documentaries, after failing to make his way in publishing and property-selling. During the late 1920s and 1930s he worked for many of the major companies, including Paramount and RKO, before becoming Vice-President at MGM. In 1936 he founded Selznick International in the teeth of Louis Mayer's opposition. The company's success, and reputation for artistic quality which rivalled that of SAM GOLDWYN's independent organization, was based on *Gone With the Wind* (which Selznick released through MGM). This trouble-fraught production was master-minded by Selznick, revealing a pattern of producer-control which was to be repeated in most of his films and which exasperated several of his more individual directors; although HITCHCOCK and CAROL REED among others worked very productively with him.

But the financial success of *Gone With the Wind* was not repeated, though his baroque sex-Western, *Duel in the Sun* (1946), starring his second wife JENNIFER JONES, was highly profitable. Thereafter he devoted himself to promoting films for his wife, which had little box-office or critical success – *Gone to Earth* (1951), DE SICA's *Terminal Station* (1954), *A Farewell to Arms* (1958) for Twentieth Century Fox.

Before he died he had been planning some important productions, none of which materialized. Several films and novels have been at least partly based on his chequered career, including the MGM film, *The Bad and the Beautiful* (1952).

Other notable productions: the original *A Star is Born, Nothing Sacred* and *The Prisoner of Zenda* (1937), *Rebecca* (1940), *Since you Went Away* (1943), *Spellbound* (1945), *The Third Man* (1949), which he co-produced. MH

Semon, Larry (1889–1928)
Born in West Point, Missouri, USA. With his white mask of a face in which his eyes were set like little black sequins, Semon seemed a re-incarnation of Debureau's Pierrot Lunaire. He inhabited a world of violent and surreal gags with bombs and flour-sacks and other treacherous properties. As a child Semon had been trained on the vaudeville stage; later he was a newspaper cartoonist; and when in 1916 he joined Universal, it was as a director. Not until 1917 did he appear on the screen himself, in *Slips and Slackers*. Above all a gagman, he constantly declared that a comic was as good as his gags; and this belief may have hampered him from defining a consistent character. Between 1917 and 1924 Semon amassed a considerable fortune, which was largely dissipated in his effort to produce feature-length comedies – *The Girl in the Limousine* (1924), *The Wizard of Oz* (1925), *Stop, Look and Listen* and *The Perfect Clown* (1926), *Spuds* (1927). In 1927 – presumably in an effort to earn money to offset his losses – he made an appearance, playing a gangster, in VON STERNBERG's *Underworld*. When he died at the early age of 39, his friends said it was from worry. DR

Sennett, Mack (1880–1960)
Born in Richmond, Canada. Producer and director. Sennett began his life as a singer, then decided on a theatrical career and made his stage début in 1907 in 'The Boys of Company B'. After various theatrical experiences, including the formation of his own male voice quartet, The Happy Gondoliers, he joined Biograph as an actor around 1909. He began to write (*The Lonely Villa*, MARY PICKFORD's first film, was Sennett's work), and from 1910 also directed comedies for Biograph. Sennett himself related, in his autobiography, how he set himself to study GRIFFITH's methods, and used to hang about the studio doors at night so that he could walk home with The Master and glean some tips about their craft.

In 1912, with the backing of two bookmakers, Kessell and Bauman, he founded the Keystone Studios. At first he directed his own films; but as the studio acquired more player and directors, he assumed the role of a supervising producer. The style of comedy developed at Keystone under Sennett was an altogether new genre, with elements of vaudeville, circus, comic strip and pantomime, yet unique in its forms and conventions. Taking as its setting real-life America of the years surrounding the First World War, Keystone evolved a surreal and anarchic comic universe, peopled by curious creatures who were in every way larger and wilder and more vivid than life. The first Sennett stars were Ford Sterling, Fred Mace and MABEL NORMAND; later additions to the company included FATTY ARBUCKLE, Charley Chase, Billy Bevan, CHESTER CONKLIN, BEN TURPIN, Mack Swain, Edgar Kennedy, Polly Moran, Louise Fazenda and, albeit briefly, for Sennett's economy on salaries was not calculated to keep ambitious young stars for long – CHARLES CHAPLIN. Directors who emerged from the Sennett stable included MAL ST CLAIR, FRANK CAPRA, Eddie Sutherland and EDDIE CLINE.

Sennett's Keystone comedies not only enriched the world's comic folklore however. The needs of comedy resulted in important developments in technique – a new rhythm and fluidity of editing, a new freedom of camerawork. The enormous popularity of the films in every country of the world contributed very largely to the prosperity and international domination which the American cinema gained during and after the First World War.

Sennett's conception of comedy was essentially suited to the silent cinema, and he never seemed fully to recover from the impact of sound. His studios were reduced to routine work; and by 1935 he found himself out of business. His last films were a series of shorts, *Way Up Thar, Ye Old Saw Mill, Flicker Fever, The Timid Young Man* (all 1935), which he directed himself; and despite constant efforts to return, he made no film as producer or director during the remaining quarter of a century of his life. DR

Sequence
A section of a film consisting of a succession of edited scenes or shots, complete in themselves

Set-up
(1) An arrangement of the scenery, props, performers, lights, microphones, and cameras for a particular shot
(2) In animation, the field covered by the camera at a given distance from the drawings on the animation table

Shamroy, Leon
Born 1901 in New York, USA. Cinematographer. A technical innovator in his early days, he became lighting cameraman in 1927, working continually up to the present time. His expansive style is specially suited to musicals and large-scale productions in colour, although he has tackled every genre in his time. Best remembered for LANG's *You Only Live Once* (1937); several films with HENRY KING, including *The Black Swan* (1942), *Wilson* (1944), *Twelve O'Clock High* (1949), *The Snows of Kilimanjaro* (1952), *The Robe* (1953, the first film shot in CinemaScope), *Love is a Many Splendored Thing* (1955), *The King and I* (1956), *The Bravados* (1958), *Cleopatra* and *The Cardinal* (1963), *The Agony and the Ecstasy* (1965), *Planet of the Apes* (1968). JG

Above: Omar Sharif in 'Lawrence of Arabia' (David Lean, GB, 1962)
Below: Robert Shaw as 'Custer of the West' (Robert Siodmak, Spain, 1967)

Sharif, Omar
Born 1933. Egyptian actor, who has become an international leading man, especially in period film roles. He was perfectly cast as the arrogant prince in ROSI's *C'Era Una Volta* (1967). Films include: *Goha* (1959), *Lawrence of Arabia* (1962), *The Fall of the Roman Empire, Behold a Pale Horse* and *The Yellow Rolls-Royce* (1964), *Dr Zhivago* and *The Night of the Generals* (1966), *Funny Girl, Mayerling* and *Mackenna's Gold* (1968), *The Appointment* and *Che!* (1969), *The Last Valley* (1970), *The Horsemen* (1971).

Shaw, Robert
Born 1927 in Westhoughton, Lancashire, England. Actor, novelist and playwright. He has acted mainly on the British stage, including Stratford-upon-Avon and the Old Vic, and appeared in his own play 'Off the Mainland' at the Arts Theatre, London, in 1956. He has also starred on television, including the series *The Buccaneers*. He adapted his own novel 'The Hiding Place' for television and cinema. Usually he has played strong, reserved men, but his ebullience as Henry VIII revealed a new facet of his style. Films include: *The Dam Busters* (1955), *From Russia with Love* and *The Caretaker* (1963), *A Man for All Seasons* (as Henry VIII, 1966), *The Birthday Party* (1968), *The Battle of Britain* and *The Royal Hunt of the Sun* (1969), *A Town Called Bastard* (1971). He scripted as well as starred in JOSEPH LOSEY's film, *Figures in a Landscape* (1970).

Shearer, Norma
Born 1900 in USA. Actress, married to IRVING THALBERG, the MGM producer. She has a radiant, romantic personality and, when necessary, a refined comic sense. Films include *The Stealers* (1920), *The Student Prince* (1927), *The Divorcée* and *The Last of Mrs Cheyney* (1929), *A Free Soul, Private Lives* and *Strange Interval* (1931), *Smilin' Through* (1932), *The Barretts of Wimpole Street* (1934), *Romeo and Juliet* (1936), *Marie Antoinette* (1938), *Idiot's Delight* and *The Women* (1939), and *Escape* (1940).

Shindo, Kaneto
Born 1912 in Hiroshima, Japan. Director and

writer. Entered films in mid-1930s as an assistant designer and later became a scriptwriter, working regularly with the director Yoshimura and others. He formed an independent company with Yoshimura and has made a wide variety of films, ranging from social comedies to period 'horror' films. *Children of Hiroshima* (1952), a sincere, if rather sentimentalized, study of the aftermath of war, first brought him to the attention of the West. *The Island* (1961), an obsessive account of back-breaking working conditions, was remarkable for its lack of dialogue; and *Lost Sex* (1966) dealt with a man's impotence in a typically wry, knowing Japanese way. His period dramas *Onibaba* (1964) and *Kuroneko* (1968) combined extreme violence and sex with an expert, virtuoso camera style, though they lacked the poetic intensity Shindo always seems to be striving for. His other recent work, *Operation Négligé* (1968) and *Heat Wave Island* (1969), have flashes of interesting characterization and a professional gloss, but suggest that he may be entering a more obviously commercial period. Latest film: *Live Today, Die Tomorrow*, 1971. JG

Shooting Schedule
A list of all the set-ups in a film arranged in order of shooting, showing what scenes, characters, costumes and properties are required for each day.

Shooting Script
The final working script of a film with all details relating to picture and sound and with all necessary technical instructions for shooting.

Short
A film of a length of less than 3,000 ft (910 metres) when printed on 35 mm film

Shot List
Record of all shots in a completed film as well as any unused material, along with a description of their contents.

Shub, Esther or Esfir (1894–1959)
Born in the Ukraine, USSR. Originally at Goskino, where she worked with EISENSTEIN preparing the Soviet version of LANG's *Mabuse*, Shub was a pioneer in the creative editing of archive films. Her work on the triptych of 20th-century Russian and Soviet history – *The Fall of the Romanov Dynasty* and *The Great Road* (1927) and *The Russia of Nikolai II and Lev Tolstoy* (1928) – served several purposes: it inaugurated a totally new montage form; it salvaged thousands of feet of decomposing early film records; and it pointed out the need for film archives. Later documentaries: *Today* (1930), *Komsomol* (1932), *The Metro at Night* (1934), *Land of the Soviets* and *Spain* (1938), *Twenty Years of Cinema* (1940, with PUDOVKIN), *This Side of the Araks* (1947).

Above: Jean Simmons in 'The Happy Ending' (Richard Brooks, USA, 1969)
Below: Jane Fonda and Lee Marvin (front) in 'Cat Ballou' (Eliot Silverstein, USA, 1965)

Sica, Vittorio De
See DE SICA

Sidney, George
Born 1911 in New York, USA. Veteran all-purpose Hollywood director, child actor in films and vaudeville; occasional musician and director of 'Pete Smith' shorts at MGM in the 1930s. After arriving in Hollywood in 1932 and working his way up to feature director in 1941 with *Free and Easy*, he revealed a special flair for gaily likable musical-comedies – *Anchors Aweigh* (1945), *The Harvey Girls* (1946), *Annie get your Gun* (1950), *Showboat* (1951), *Kiss me Kate* (1953). More personal and genuinely exhilarating were the period adventures, *The Three Musketeers* (1948) and *Scaramouche* (1952). In 1956, he moved over from MGM to Columbia where he steered the reigning sex queen, KIM NOVAK, through her first major roles in *The Eddie Duchin Story* (1956), *Jeanne Eagels* and *Pal Joey* (1957). In the 1960s his films tended to become overloaded with production values, lacking the zest of his earlier MGM efforts.

Other main films: *Thousands Cheer* (1943), *Cass Timberlaine* (1947), *The Red Danube* (1949), *Young Bess* (1953), *Pepe* (1960), *Bye Bye Birdie* (1962), *Viva Las Vegas* (1963), *The Swinger* (1966), *Half a Sixpence* (1967). MH

Siegel, Don
Born 1912 in Chicago, USA. Recently-fashionable American director of lean, mean melodramas with powerful atmospheric effects and, invariably, a strong element of lawlessness. His short films – *Hitler Lives* and *Star in the Night* in 1945 – attracted attention. In 1946 he directed his first feature, *The Verdict*. After a succession of excellent second features, his hard-hitting *Riot in Cell Block Eleven* (1954) was notorious for its tough treatment of prison violence. Two years later, *Invasion of the Body-Snatchers*, despite front-office interference, was a significant addition to the science fiction rank as well as making an implicit political comment. Unwilling to compromise, he continued to work on small-scale projects which excited large-scale critical attention: notably *Baby Face Nelson* (1957), *Hell is for Heroes* (1962), *The Killers* and *The Hanged Man* (1964). In the past few years his films have increased in scope, budget and star values and have usually managed to retain his personal qualities, notably in *Coogan's Bluff* (1968) and the unexpected gothic of *The Beguiled* (1971).

Other main films: *Crime in the Streets* (1957) *The Line Up* and *The Gun Runners* (1958) *Flaming Star* (1960), *Madigan* (1967), *Two Mules for Sister Sara* (1969), *Dirty Harry* (1971). MH

Signoret, Simone
Born 1921 in Wiesbaden, Germany. French

actress, with stage experience. Married to YVES MONTAND. She has progressed from romantic heroines to the ravaged, sensitively observed character roles of her later years. Films include: *Dédée d'Anvers* (1947), *Manèges* (1949), *La Ronde* (1950), *Casque d'Or* (1951), *Les Diaboliques* (1954), *The Witches of Salem* (1956), *Room at the Top* (1959), *Term of Trial* (1962), *Is Paris Burning?* and *The Deadly Affair* (1966), *Games* (1967), *The Seagull* (1968), *Le Rose et le Noir* and *L'Aveu* (1970), *Le Chat* (1971).

Silverstein, Eliot
Director. After some years of directing for US television *(Dr Kildare, Route 66, Naked City, The Nurses)* Silverstein made his first cinema film, *Belle Sommers*, in 1962; and in 1965 enjoyed a big prestige and commercial success with *Cat Ballou*. The delicacy and humour which he revealed in that film seemed however somewhat to have eluded him in his subsequent work, *The Happening* (1967) and the somewhat pretentious *A Man Called Horse* (1969).

Simmons, Jean
Born 1929 at Crouch Hill, London, England. Actress, who made her début at age of 14 in *Give us the Moon* (1943). As an ingenue in British films, she had a touching innocent beauty; later she developed into a character actress of strength and passion. Has been married to Stewart Granger and RICHARD BROOKS, and has worked in USA since the early 1950s. Other films: *Great Expectations* (1946), *Black Narcissus* (1947), *Hamlet* and *The Blue Lagoon* (1948), *Androcles and the Lion, The Actress* and *The Robe* (1953), *Guys and Dolls* (1956), *The Big Country* (1957), *Spartacus* (1960), *Life at the Top* (1965), *Divorce, American Style* (1967), *The Happy Ending* (1969), *Say Hello to Yesterday* (1970).

Above: 'Riot in Cell Block 11' (Don Siegel, USA, 1954)
Below: Michel Simon in 'Panique' (Julien Duvivier, France, 1946)

Simon, Michel
Born 1895 in Geneva, Switzerland. Actor. At first a boxer and acrobat in music-hall, he became from 1920 a stage actor, appearing also in small parts in silent films, including *Feu Mathias Pascal* and *La Passion de Jeanne d'Arc*. He featured, however, in sound films, capitalizing on his sympathetic 'ugliness', which in fact gave him an exceptional expressiveness and charm. His appearance as the eccentric mate in VIGO's *L'Atalante* (1934) and in a succession of early films by RENOIR, *Tire au Flanc* (1929), *On Purge Bébé* and *La Chienne* (1931), and *Boudu Sauvé des Eaux* (1932) established him as a brilliant character actor. He also appeared in CARNÉ's films *Drôle de Drame* (1937) and *Quai des Brumes* (1938). Other films include: CHRISTIAN-JAQUE's *Les Disparus de Saint-Agil* (1938) and *Boule de Suif* (1945), DUVIVIER's *La Fin du Jour* (1939) and *Panique* (1946), CLAIR's *La Beauté du Diable* (1949), BLASETTI's Italian production *Fabiola* (1948) and FRANKENHEIMER's *The Train* (1964). His last major role in *Blanche* (1971) retained much of his old flair. RM

Sinatra, Frank
Born 1915 in New Jersey, USA. High-powered singer, actor and show-business tycoon. Was first a sports-writer, then a singer on radio and with Harry James's and Tommy Dorsey's orchestras and a 'pop' star of his time. Films include: *Higher and Higher* (1943), *Anchors Aweigh* (1945), *Words and Music* (1947), *On the Town* (1949), *From Here to Eternity* (1953), *The Tender Trap* (1955), *The Man with the Golden Arm, Guys and Dolls* and *High Society* (1956), *Pal Joey* (1957), *Some Came Running* (1958), *Ocean's Eleven* (1960), *The Manchurian Candidate* (1962), *None but the Brave* (which he also directed, 1965), *Cast a Giant Shadow* (1966), *The Naked Runner* and *Tony Rome* (1967), *Lady in Cement* and *The Detective* (1968). Progressing from musicals to dramatic parts, Sinatra has developed a strong, tough, screen personality, notably in his detective parts. In 1971 he announced his retirement. RM

Siodmak, Robert
Born 1900 in Tennessee, USA. Dynamic American director who trained in France and Germany (where he was taken at the age of one) and developed a masterly technique with powerful suspense melodramas such as *The Spiral Staircase* (1945) crime thrillers such as *The Killers* (1946), *Cry of the City* and *Criss Cross* (1949). He first directed *People on Sunday* (1929) in Germany, an experimental young man's film, on which BILLY WILDER and FRED ZINNEMANN collaborated. Leaving Europe when the Nazis came to power, he went to Hollywood where he quickly established a reputation much influenced by a Central European flair for bizarre, spine-chilling effects. His last notable personal film was *The Crimson Pirate* (1952). Returning to Europe, he made several films in France and Germany and *The Rough and the Smooth* (1959) in Britain. But nothing he has done since has equalled the skill and flair of his peak Hollywood period.

Other notable films: *Pièges* (1939), *Phantom Lady* and *The Suspect* (1944), *The Strange Affair of Uncle Harry* (1945), *The Dark Mirror* (1946), *The File on Thelma Jordan* and *The Great Sinner* (1949), *Le Grand Jeu* (1953), *Katja* (1959), *Escape from East Berlin* (1962), *Custer of the West* (1967). MH

Sirk, Douglas
Born 1900 in Germany. Real name: Detlef Sierck. Under-rated Hollywood director, with liberal European stage and screen experience,

who worked in America between 1940 and 1960 after making several lush romantic dramas in Germany. His first major success was at Universal with *Magnificent Obsession* (1954), after which he was in demand as a director who could give an original style to fairly routine properties, particularly 'weepies'. In *Written on the Wind* (1957) and *Tarnished Angels* (1957), however, he managed to circumvent the conveyor-belt expectations of the studio to introduce an astringent, disillusioned quality into the films which now look considerably more intriguing than many Universal productions of the period. Notable films include: *Summer Storm* (1944), *All That Heaven Allows* (1955), *Battle Hymn* (1956), *A Time to Love and a Time to Die* (1958), *Imitation of Life* (1959). MH

Sjöberg, Alf
Born 1903 in Stockholm, Sweden. Leading Swedish theatre and film director whose influence on Swedish films as a whole has been substantially larger than his screen output. A graduate of the Royal Dramatic Theatre in Stockholm, where he was subsequently to become a stage actor, producer and then director, he made his first film during a depressed period in the Swedish industry. Entitled *The Strongest* (1929), this was a tale of seal-hunters in the Greenland Sea and, in its near documentary portrayal of the primitive life of its main characters, it had an enormous impact.

Unaccountably, Sjöberg did not work in films again for ten years, during which the Swedish industry lavished its energies on trivial romantic melodramas and comedies. In 1939, just before Europe became involved in the Second World War, he returned to make the pacifist film, *They Staked Their Lives*, which suggested to some critics the fatalism of the films of MARCEL CARNÉ and the books of Graham Greene. He continued now to work in films, achieving other key works of the Swedish revival in *The Road to Heaven* (1942) and in *Frenzy* (1944), on which INGMAR BERGMAN worked as screenwriter; in 1951 his version of Strindberg's *Miss Julie* embodied many of his radical ideas about cinematic techniques. He followed this with the Biblical *Barabbas* (1953) and *Karin Mansdotter* (1954). After this Bergman became the international symbol of the Swedish cinema and Sjöberg emerges as the important link between the pioneer master, SJÖSTRÖM, and Bergman, though in retrospect a lesser force – but a necessary one – than either of them. (See SCANDINAVIA.)

Other main films: *The Royal Hunt* (1944), *Iris and the Lieutenant* (1946), *Only a Mother* (1949), *The Judge* (1960), *The Island* (1964), *The Father* (1969). MH

Sjöström, Victor (1879–1960)
Born in Värmland, Sweden. Dominant pioneer figure in Swedish films and one of the key film-makers in the international cinema; stage and screen actor and director, he illuminated the Scandinavian film scene during the silent period with his impressive use of landscape and understanding of the force of nature and mysticism in the Swedish character. He frequently used the works of Selma Lagerlöf and his themes often concentrated on man's struggle with nature – his own and the elements.

In a real sense he was instrumental in liberating the screen from the shackles of theatrical concepts, and his impact echoes still in the works of INGMAR BERGMAN and other younger Swedish film-makers. He continued to act almost up to his death, most memorably as the ageing, haunted hero of *Wild Strawberries* (1957). From 1943–9 he was the artistic director of Svensk Filmindustri.

Above: Alf Sjöberg
Below: Victor Sjöström in 'Wild Strawberries' (Ingmar Bergman, Sweden, 1957)

As a child he was taken by his parents to America where he lived for six years. He returned to Sweden and became a juvenile lead and stage manager of the Swedish theatre in Helsinki. In 1912 he joined Svenska Bio and made his film début in MAURITZ STILLER's *The Black Masks*. Together he and Stiller were to invigorate the Swedish film industry with their then revolutionary ideas of film-making, with Sjöström establishing himself as an expert comedy actor in Stiller's film satires. His passionate *rapport* with the Swedish scene was coupled with a concern for social problems, indicated in his first considerable film, *Ingeborg Holm* (1913), about the poor-law system. In 1921 he directed what is considered by some critics his masterpiece, *The Phantom Carriage*.

In the 1920s he went to Hollywood where (known as Victor Seastrom) he made several individual films, notably *He who gets Slapped* (1924), *The Scarlet Letter* (1926), *The Divine Woman* (1927), and particularly *The Wind* (1928), in which his personal, visual style was fused with outstanding American acting and technical talents. He later returned to Sweden and made a sound film, *Markurells i Wadköping*, which reinstated him as a vital Swedish director. He then retired from directing, though he went on acting and in 1937 he directed *Under the Red Robe* in Britain. (See SCANDINAVIA.)

Other films include: *The Clergyman* (1913), *The Miracle* (1914), *Terje Vigen* and *The Girl from Stormycroft* (1917), *The Outlaw and his Wife* and *The Sons of Ingmar* (1918), *Love's Crucible* (1922). MH

Skolimowski, Jerzy
Born 1938 in Warsaw, Poland. Director. In his early days, he was a boxer and a writer; studied at the Polish Film School in Lodz and collaborated on scripts of films by WAJDA and POLANSKI. His own early films – *Rysopis* (1964), *Walkover* (1965), *Barrier* (1966) – use autobiographical elements, very long takes and show the beginnings of his favourite theme of rebellion against a cynical authority. In *Le Départ* (1967, made in Belgium) the hero has a passion for fast cars and it is, in some ways, a homage to GODARD. After *Hands Up* (1967, an allegory whose strong social protest caused it to be banned in Poland), Skolimowski temporarily left his country to make *The Adventures of Gérard* (1968) in Italy, an enjoyable if rather disorganized historical romp. His quirky humour, economical shooting style and fondness for bizarre relationships found fuller expression in *Deep End* (1970), shot partly in London. Latest film: *King, Queen, Knave* (1972).

Skouras, Spyros P. (1895–1971)
Born in Skourohorian, Greece. Shrewd Holly-

wood immigrant President of Twentieth Century Fox in 1942–62, previously in cinema management with his two brothers who arrived with him from Greece in 1908. They opened their first cinema in 1914, developing powerful theatre chains allied to the major studios, Warners, Paramount, Fox. The two brothers remained in management when Spyros went into the production side at Fox, where his major technical achievement was the introduction of CinemaScope in 1953. When DARRYL ZANUCK returned to Fox in 1962, Skouras became merely the figurehead chairman of the company after a singularly unsuccessful financial period. He then sold his interest in the company and took to running oil tankers instead. A reputedly dubious 'life' of Skouras was published in 1967: 'Skouras: King of Fox Studios' by Carlo Curti. MH

Slate
See NUMBER BOARD

Slow Motion
Means by which movement in a shot is represented as taking place more slowly than it did in reality.

Smith, Jack
Born 1932, Columbus, Ohio, USA. Underground film-maker. Based on New York, he studied direction under LEE STRASBERG at the Actors' Studio. An artist in photography, an anarchist in outlook, he has made films which, meticulous in their craftsmanship, show details of sexuality which have led, when exhibited, to a record of banning and police raids. His films include *Overstimulated* (1960), *Scotch Tape* (1961), *Flaming Creatures* and *Normal Love* (1963). JONAS MEKAS has written of him: 'He has attained for the first time in motion pictures a high level of art which is absolutely lacking in decorum; and a treatment of sex which makes us aware of the restraint of all previous film-makers'. Jack Smith has written frequently for the journal 'Film Culture'.

Smith, Maggie
Born 1934 in Ilford, Essex, England. Actress, whose few, though distinctive, film roles have a high, theatrical intensity. Began with Oxford Playhouse and its School of Drama, then London and American stage. Films include: *Nowhere to Go* (1958), *The VIPs* (1963), *Young Cassidy* (1965), *Othello* (1966), *The Honey Pot* (1967), *Hot Millions* (1968), *The Prime of Miss Jean Brodie* and *Oh! What a Lovely War* (1969).

Smith, Percy (1880–1944)
English naturalist cinematographer. A clerk in the Ministry of Education, Smith gave himself up to spare-time biological photography, turning his small London home, with the help of his wife, into a combined laboratory and film studio. In 1908 he joined the pioneer English producer Charles Urban in order to develop the cinematography of the natural processes of growth, and made 54 films before the First World War in the series *The World before your Eye*, one of which, *Gladioli*, was shot in George Albert Smith's process, Kinemacolor. During the First World War he made technical research films for the Royal Air Force. He remained a lifelong and utterly dedicated enthusiast for nature photography; for most people his films were the initial revelation of the choreographic beauty of flowers turning and opening to the sun. He used and improved his own homemade devices (such as dripping water) to control the timing of camera-exposure and lighting. He developed the micro-cinematography of micro-organisms and marine life. In 1919 he was to work with the producer H. Bruce Woolfe in making the famous silent film series, *Secrets of Nature*; later his collaborators were to be MARY FIELD and the biologist H. V. Durden; collectively they developed a branch of scientific-record film-making called Cine-biology about which they wrote two books, 'Secrets of Nature' (1934) and the Pelican book 'Cinebiology' (1941). Smith's work on *Secrets of Nature* and later, during the sound period, on the *Secrets of Life* series, was to be familiar in the movie theatres for nearly a quarter of a century. In all he made some 200 films. RM

Smoktunovsky, Innokenty
Born 1925 in Krasnoyarsk, Siberia. Already established as a stage actor before he made his first significant film appearance in MIKHAIL ROMM's *Murder on the Rue Dante* (1956), Smoktunovsky subsequently played in many films including Romm's *Nine Days of One Year* and KALATOZOV's *The Letter that Was Not Sent*. He achieved major international success as Hamlet, in KOZINTSEV's adaptation (1964). For his next film, *Beware, Automobile!*, he undertook a broadly comic role, which emphasized his remarkable versatility. In 1969 he played in *Tchaikovsky* and, more notably, in *Uncle Vanya* (1971).

Sneak Preview
An unadvertised showing of a film before its general release

Soft Focus
Slightly hazy effect by shooting slightly out of focus

Soldati, Mario
Born 1906 in Turin, Italy. Originally a writer, Soldati started work for the cinema as a scenarist and the excellent scripts he wrote for CAMERINI and BLASETTI provided some of the brighter aspects of the Italian cinema of the immediate pre-war years. Soldati's first work as a director was a collaboration with FEDOR OZEP on *Princess Tarakanova*, though his career was only firmly established in 1940 with *Dora Nelson* and *Piccolo mondo antico*. Soldati only flirted briefly with neo-realism (*Fuga in Francia*, 1948); his preference for a more 'literary' cinema, and a particular *penchant* for costume and comedy made him a useful commercial director in the 1950s. He also directed the battle scenes for VIDOR's *War and Peace* and the second unit work on WYLER's *Ben Hur*.

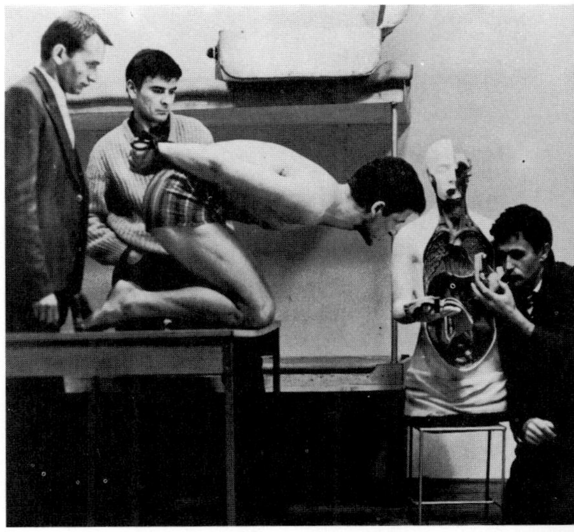

Tadeusz Lomnicki (centre) in 'Barrier' (Jerzy Skolimowski, Poland, 1966)

Solntseva, Julia
Born 1901. The statuesque and beautiful leading lady of PROTAZANOV's *Aelita* (1924) and Djeliabushky's *The Cigarette Girl from Mosselprom* (1924) later played in *Earth* (1930) and married its director, ALEXANDER DOVZHENKO. From then until Dovzhenko's death she was his loyal companion and artistic assistant. After his death she dedicated herself to making his unrealized projects: *Poem of the Sea* (1957), *Story of the Flaming Years* (1961), *The Enchanted Desna* (1965) and *The Golden Gates* (1970), which captured the general outline, if not the poetic insight, of his style.

Sordi, Alberto
Born 1920 in Rome, Italy. Popular Italian comedy-actor whose humour tends to have serious undertones. At the age of 13 he won a prize in an MGM contest to dub OLIVER HARDY's voice. Set on a career in some area of show-business, he became an amateur actor, then worked professionally on the stage. Main films include: *I Vitelloni* (1953), *A Farewell to Arms* (1957), *The Best of Enemies* (1960), *Those Magnificent Men in their Flying Machines* (1965).

Sound and Film
See THE DEVELOPMENT OF THE FILM p57; also pp227,450,476

Sound Camera
The machine through which the film passes and in which it is exposed during the process of recording sound on the film.

Above: 'Bienvenido Mr Marshall!' ('Welcome, Mr Marshall', Luis G. Berlanga, 1953)
Below: 'El Verdugo' ('The Executioner', Luis G. Berlanga, 1963)

Sound Effects
General term for sounds such as footsteps, crowd noises, etc, which are normally added to the sound track during re-recording

Sound Track
A longitudinal strip normally along one side of the frames of a sound film bearing a photographic sound record

Spaak, Charles
Born 1903 in Belgium. Scriptwriter, whose career has been spent in France. His work was prolific, variable, but highly professional, and he had a taste for naturalism which brought credible characterization and a sense of actuality to his best scripts. He became the writer of many of the best-known French films from the late 1930s, including specially the work of FEYDER, RENOIR, DUVIVIER, GRÉMILLON, and CAYATTE. His films include: for Feyder, *Thérèse Raquin* and *Les Nouveaux Messieurs* (1928), *Le Grand Jeu* (1934) and *La Kermesse Héroïque* (1935); for Grémillon, *La Petite Lise* (1930), *L'Étrange M. Victor* (1937) and *Le Ciel est à Vous* (1943); for Duvivier, *La Bandera* (1935), *La Belle Équipe* (1936), *La Fin du Jour* (1939), and *Panique* (1946); for Renoir, *Les Bas Fonds* (1936), *La Grande Illusion* (1937), and *The Vanishing Corporal* (1961); for Cayatte, *Justice est Faite* (1950) and *Nous Sommes Tous des Assassins* (1952). RM

Spain
Native Spanish production stretches back to the turn of the century, but little of distinction was made during the silent period. Nevertheless Spain produced one of the world's greatest directors, the Catalan LUIS BUÑUEL, who left Madrid to work in France, but returned to make *Land without Bread* (1932), his horrifying study of the mentally retarded inhabitants of Les Hurdes and, many years later, *Viridiana* and *Tristana*. Spain produced other directors of talent, including:

Benito Perojo: *My Husband, Boy, The Negro with the White Soul, World Crisis, Evasion*;
Florian Rey: *The Accursed Village, Augustina of Aragon, La Hermana San Sulpicio*;
Saenz de Heredia: *Patricia lifts her eyes to the Star*;
Francisco Elias: *Rataplan*.

After the Civil War and the establishment of the Franco régime, efforts were made around 1940 to redevelop film production, and during the 1950s the industry in Spain became productive, if largely uninspired. By this time Spain had some 4,500 cinemas, and production reached some 70 features a year. A new generation of directors, including Antonio del Amo and Nieves Conde, began to supersede the older established directors, such as Saenz de Heredia, the outstanding survivor from the 1930s. Conde, in particular, reflected something of the post-war neo-realism in such films as *El Inquilino*, which nevertheless suffered from melodrama in its study of the problems of tenants. Realism became known as 'calligraphism' and failed at this stage to achieve any real depth. Co-production (with Italy and Argentina) further diluted the quality of Spanish films.

It was the productions of BERLANGA and BARDEM which first attracted world interest to Spanish film, starting in the early 1950s. Neither, however, has been able to maintain his freshness and impact. More recently, during the 1960s, a number of films of some interest from new directors has been produced in Spain; among them are *Nueve cartas a Berta* (Basilo Martin Patino, 1965), *La Busca* (Angelino Fons, 1966), *Despues del Diluvio* (Jacinto Esteva Grewe, 1968), *Del Amor y otras Soledades* (Basilo Martin Patino, 1969), *El Hombre Oculto* (Alfonso Ungriá, 1970).

During the later 1960s, CARLOS SAURA has established himself as a director with some of Buñuel's predilections, combining sharp social satire with the black comedy beloved by so many Spanish directors. His main work includes: *La Caza, Peppermint Frappé, The Garden of Delights*. BUÑUEL himself made *Viridiana* (1961) in Spain, an anti-religious film causing repercussions with the administration. RM

Special Effects
A general term applied to many photographic

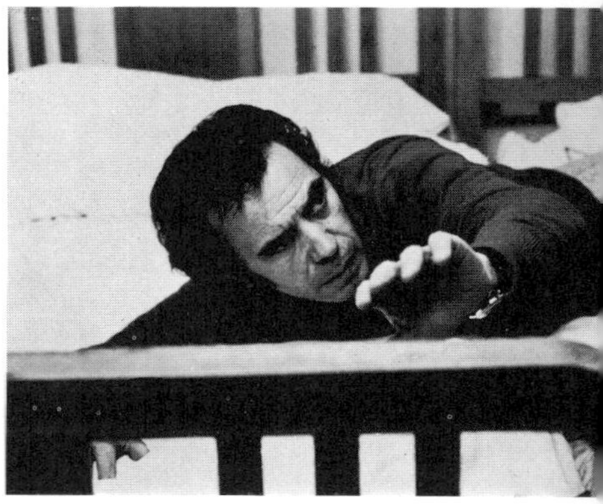

Top: 'The Wheelchair' (Marco Ferreri, 1959)
Above: 'El Hombre Oculto' (Alfonso Ungriá, 1970)
Below: Francisco Rabal in 'Despues del Diluvio' (J. Esteva Grewe, 1968)

mechanical, electrical and optical devices to produce a required effect.

Specialized Film
See DOCUMENTARY

Spiegel, Sam
Born 1903 in Jaroslau, then Austria, now Poland. Successful independent producer, who was involved in much behind-the-scenes film wheeling and dealing in Europe before settling in America in 1939. For a time he adopted the name of S. P. Eagle in order not to seem too Germanic. His shrewd choice of subjects and directors, often in the teeth of gloomy forecasts, paid off most notably – and commercially – with *The African Queen* (1951), *On the Waterfront* (1954), *The Bridge on the River Kwai* (1957) and *Lawrence of Arabia* (1962). Later gambles on *The Chase* and *The Night of the Generals* (1966), *The Swimmer* (1968) were less successful. Latest film: *Nicholas and Alexandra* (1971).

Splice
The join made between two pieces of film

Split Screen
A process shot in which only a part of the frame is exposed at one time

Sprocket Hole
Hole punched at regular intervals along the edge of cinematograph film which engages with the sprocket teeth of the camera or projector

Squeezed Print
A print of a film on which the pictures have been laterally compressed by the anamorphic process

Stage
That part of a film studio in which sets are built and action photographed and sometimes recorded

Stamp, Terence
Born 1940 in London, England. Actor. At first on stage, then in films, which include: *Billy Budd* and *Term of Trial* (1962), *The Collector* (1965), *Modesty Blaise* (1966), *Far from the Madding Crowd* and *Poor Cow* (1967), *Theorem* (1968), *The Mind of Mr Soames* (1970), *A Season in Hell* (1971). Though he made his name as the blond, angelically good Billy Budd, his dark good-looks are well suited to sulky, even malicious, moderns.

Standard Film
Cinematograph film 35 mm in width

Stand-in
One who takes the place of a star during the lengthy preparations preceding the rehearsal and taking of a shot (as opposed to 'stunt men' who perform actions too difficult or dangerous for the stars)

Above: Terence Stamp and Robert Ryan in 'Billy Budd' (Peter Ustinov, GB, 1962) Below: Barbara Stanwyck in 'Sorry, Wrong Number' (Anatole Litvak, USA, 1948)

Stanwyck, Barbara
Born 1907 in Brooklyn, New York, USA. Actress and dancer, on stage, in night clubs, and later in many television shows, brilliant creator of sulky villainesses, as well as a lively subtle comedienne. Films include: *The Locked Door* (1929), *So Big* (1931), *The Bitter Tea of General Yen* (1932) and other early CAPRA films, *Annie Oakley* (1935), *The Plough and the Stars* and *Stella Dallas* (1937), *Meet John Doe* and *The Lady Eve* (1941), *Double Indemnity* (1944), *The Strange Love of Martha Ivers* (1946), *The Two Mrs Carrolls* (1947), *Sorry, Wrong Number* (1948), *Clash by Night* (1952), *Jeopardy* (1953), *Executive Suite* (1954), *Crime of Passion* (1957), *A Walk on the Wild Side* (1962), *The Night Walker* (1965).

Staudte, Wolfgang
Born 1906 in Saarbrücken, Germany. Actor and director. Trained at first with Max Reinhardt and Erwin Piscator in the theatre, and entered films in 1933 as an actor. He appeared in many films during the Hitler period, including *Tannenberg, Pour le Mérite, Legion Condor, Jud Süss,* and *Friedemann Bach.* His earliest films as a director were advertising shorts, and he did not make his first feature film until 1943 *(Akrobat Schö-ö-ön).* His international reputation was established through his first post-war film both as screenwriter and director, *The Murderers are Amongst Us* (1946), made in East Berlin for DEFA. This stood out as a harbinger for post-war German film; it was of high quality and was also the first to deal with the problem of de-Nazification. For a while Staudte worked in both East and West sectors of Berlin, making such films in the East as *The Strange Adventure of Herr Fridolin B* (1948), *Rotation* (1949), *The Underdog* (1951), a study in authoritarianism, and the children's feature film, *Little Mook* (1953), made in Agfacolor. From 1955 he has worked exclusively in West Germany, making such films as *Roses for the Prosecutor* (1959), *Fairground* (1960), with its equal criticism of the governments of East and West, and a remake of *The Threepenny Opera* (1962). He also made *Herrenpartie* (1964) in Yugoslavia, and his recent films have been *The Lamb* (1964), *Ganovenehre* (1966) and *Heimlichkeiten* (1968). RM

Steiger, Rod
Born 1925 in New York, USA. Dominating American stage, television and screen actor in the distinctive Method style who has tackled an extraordinarily wide range of characters with more successes than failures. Theatre and television trained, after a versatile selection of manual jobs, he made his first big film impact in *On the Waterfront* (1954) and thereafter tended to be cast in the shadow of MARLON BRANDO, whose brother he played. A series of second-string character roles led to his portrayal of *Al Capone* (1958), which established him as a star in his own right. He won Academy Awards in America and Britain for his portrayal of the indolent Southern police chief in *In the Heat of the Night* (1967). Despite his 'interior' approach to a role, he is particularly adept at creating a credible external 'look' for his various characters. His most considerable

Rod Steiger in 'Waterloo' (Sergei Bondarchuk, Italy-USSR, 1970)

performance was in *The Pawnbroker* (1964) and in 1970 he added Napoleon to his portrait gallery in *Waterloo*.

Other notable films: *Teresa* (1951), *The Big Knife* and *Oklahoma!* (1955), *The Harder They Fall* (1956), *Run of the Arrow* (1957), *Seven Thieves* (1959), *Hands Over the City* (1963), *No Way to Treat a Lady* and *The Sergeant* (1968), *The Illustrated Man* and *Three Into Two Won't Go* (1969), *Duck, You Sucker* (1971). MH

Steiner, Max (1888–1971)
Born in Vienna, Austria. Famous composer. Showed musical talent at an early age and soon became composer/conductor in both concert hall and opera house. In 1914 he emigrated to America and, among other activities, organized pit orchestras for silent films. Worked initially for RKO in the 1930s, then moved to Warner Brothers, the home of many distinguished European musicians. His early 1930s work included musical direction on several ASTAIRE/ROGERS films and the scores for *King Kong* (1933) and *The Informer* (1935). During his rich period at Warners, he developed those qualities which make the best Steiner scores instantly recognisable: an ingenious use of leitmotifs; the deep, sinister orchestral sound; the unobtrusive knitting together of sequences. Particularly notable dramatic scores include *Jezebel* (1938) and other BETTE DAVIS vehicles, *They Died With Their Boots On* (1942), *Passage to Marseille* (1943), *Mildred Pierce* (1945), *The Big Sleep* (1946), *White Heat* (1949), *The Searchers* (1956). Steiner also had a high romantic style, full of memorable melodies, best demonstrated in *Gone With the Wind* (1939), *Casablanca* (1943), *The New Adventures of Don Juan* (1949), *A Summer Place* (1959). Although at times a skilful manipulator of high-class kitsch, he was unrivalled in the sheer technical skill of combining music with images. He is reputed to have written about 250 scores. JG

Sten, Anna
Born 1908. Russian actress, who went to Hollywood in 1933. She appeared in PUDOVKIN's *Storm over Asia* (1928) and more notably in *Die Mörder Dimitri Karamazov* (1931). An attempt to make her a romantic lead in the 1930s met with only moderate success. American films include: *Nana* (1934), *A Woman Alone* (1938), *Soldier of Fortune* (1955), *The Nun and the Sergeant* (1962).

Stereophonic
Sound system in which the sound comes from two or more loud speakers simultaneously to give the listener the impression of reality

Stereoscopic Film
Film which produces a three-dimensional effect when projected on a screen

Stevens, George
Born 1905 in California, USA. Major American director, who started in films at the age of 17 as a cameraman working on several LAUREL and HARDY comedies, also as gagman for HAL ROACH. During the 1930s and 1940s, his subtle, well-constructed light comedies, musicals and romances – notably *Alice Adams* (1935), *Swing Time* (1936), *A Damsel in Distress* and *Quality Street* (1937), *Vivacious Lady* (1938), *Woman of the Year* (1941), *Talk of the Town* (1942), *The More the Merrier* (1943) – put him in the front rank of adaptable Hollywood directors. After winning an Academy Award for *A Place in the Sun* (1951), he made one of the classic Westerns, *Shane* (1953), and won another Academy Award for *Giant* (1956). But his films tended to become more bloated as his prestige increased. *The Diary of Anne Frank* (1959) and *The Greatest Story Ever Told* (1964) were generally disappointing; although *The Only Game in Town* (1969) was a welcome return to the traditional comedy-satire form in which much of his early and most enjoyable work was cast. MH

Stevenson, Robert
Born 1905 in London, England. Reliable British director who has filmed in Hollywood since the 1940s. His competent work in Britain on *Tudor Rose* (1936), *King Solomon's Mines* (1937), though it lacked originality, ear-marked him as an efficient craftsman. His earlier films in America – particularly *Jane Eyre* (1943) and *To the Ends of the Earth* (1948) – revealed an entertaining feeling for atmosphere and mood. More recently he has worked exclusively for DISNEY and, within the limited Disney terms of popular reference, has produced some lively comedies – notably *The Absent-Minded Professor* (1960), *That Darn Cat* (1965), *Blackbeard's Ghost* (1967), *The Love Bug* (1969) – although his most prestigious assignment was *Mary Poppins* (1964).

Stewart, Donald Ogden
Born 1894 in Columbus, Ohio, USA. A distinguished writer and humorist whose career has taken in acting and playwriting. His first major film assignment was on the script and dialogue for D'ARRAST's *Laughter* (1930), one of the most literate of early sound films. Much of his subsequent work has consisted of adaptations and additional dialogue; he has a consistently witty, ironic approach alternating with more serious themes and in *Keeper of the Flame* (1942), made the strongest anti-fascist statement in any American film. Other notable scripts (sometimes in collaboration) include *The Barretts of Wimpole Street* (1934), *Holiday* (1938), *Love Affair* (1939), *Kitty Foyle* and *The Philadelphia Story* (1940), *Life with Father* (1947). He has lived in England during the past twenty years after a brush with the Un-American Activities Committee; although he has written no major scripts, he has acted as script 'doctor' for several European-based films. JG

Stewart, James
Born 1908 in Pennsylvania, USA. Durable, grass-roots American star who inherited the amusing, laconic Western style of GARY COOPER as well as the latter's dogged, small-town 'image' of heroism in the face of social injustice, most ingratiatingly expressed in the CAPRA comedies of the 1930s. Theatre-trained, he joined MGM in 1935, making his film début in *The Murder Man*. One of the most well-adjusted studio contract stars, he made 24 films in five years and won an Academy Award for his performance in *The Philadelphia Story* (1940). Other films include: *You Can't Take it with You* (1938), *Mr Smith Goes to Washington* and *Destry Rides Again* (1939), *It's a Wonderful Life* (1946), *Call Northside 777* (1948), *Winchester 73* (1950), *Harvey* (1951), *The Glenn Miller Story* (1953), *The Far Country* and *Rear Window* (1954), *The Man who Knew too Much* (1956), *Vertigo* (1958), *The Man who Shot Liberty Valance* and *How the West Was Won* (1962), *Cheyenne Autumn* (1964), *The Flight of the Phoenix* (1965), *Firecreek* (1967), *The Cheyenne Social Club* (1970), *Fool's Parade* and *Dynamite Man from Glory Jail* (1971).

Stiller, Mauritz (1883–1928)
Born in Helsinki, Finland. One of the two great directors, with VICTOR SJÖSTRÖM, of the silent era in Swedish films. Although his influence has been less lasting than Sjöström's, his personal brilliance played a major part in achieving international fame for Swedish film-making. Latterly, however, his own achievements have been overshadowed by his role as discoverer, mentor and moulder of the most luminous of stars, GRETA GARBO.

Descended from a family of Russian Jews, he emigrated to Sweden in his twenties. He joined Svenska Bio in 1912 and in his second film, *The Black Masks*, his leading actor was Sjöström. Although he became more involved with the particularly Swedish themes of man in conflict with mystical forces and the pull of nature, he revealed a sophistication rare in film-makers of the time together with a feeling for piquant social comedy, especially noticeable in *Love and Journalism* (1916).

In 1919 he made one of his best films,

Mauritz Stiller (1920s)

Herr Arne's Treasure, which, in his study of the Swedish cinema, Peter Cowie has compared to INGMAR BERGMAN's *The Virgin Spring*. In 1923 he starred Garbo in *The Atonement of Gösta Berling*, which so impressed LOUIS MAYER at MGM that he urged Stiller to come to Hollywood, reluctantly agreeing to welcome his *protégée*, Garbo, as well. His Hollywood period was a dismal failure, despite the box-office success of *Hotel Imperial* (1927) with POLA NEGRI. He worked intermittently on various projects while Garbo grew in screen stature. He returned to Sweden, where he died in 1928, attended by his friend Sjöström. (See SCANDINAVIA.)

Other notable films include: *Thomas Graal's Best Film* (1917), *Erotikon* (1920), *Gunnar Hede's Saga* (1923), in which his feeling for intimate drama is allied with an equally sensitive response to nature. MH

Stock-Shot
See LIBRARY SHOT

Stop Action Camera
Camera in which the successive frames of film can be exposed at regular but lengthy intervals

Stop Action Photography
Method of photography, in which the camera is stopped during shooting to allow some part of the scene to be rearranged before continuing with shooting

Stoppa, Paolo
Born 1906 in Rome, Italy. Actor. Began his career in films as early as 1932, and developed mainly as a wily comedy character actor, coming to the fore with his playing of the villain in DE SICA's fantasy, *Miracle in Milan* (1950). His other films include *La Beauté du Diable* (1949), *The Seven Deadly Sins* (1952) and *La Loi* (1959). His increasing international reputation enabled him to appear in a wider range of films, including *The Leopard* (1963) and *Becket* (1964). More recently he has appeared in *After the Fox* (1966), *C'era una Volta* (*Once Upon a Time in the West*, 1966) and *La Matriarca* (*The Libertine*, 1968).

Storck, Henri
Born in Belgium. Director. Began by making documentaries which came direct from the living scene, such as *Idylle à la Plage* (1930), in which two lovers are seen meeting on the seashore, and *Images d'Ostende* (1931), on both of which he worked as director and cameraman. After this, he turned to propaganda documentary, making *Borinage* (1933), about conditions in the Belgian mines, and *Les Maisons de la Misère* (1938), an exposure of slum conditions and the remedy of re-housing, with John Ferno as cameraman; in this field he later made *Les Carrefours de la Vie* (1949) on juvenile delinquency. He became Belgium's leading director and exponent of documentary subjects, with an especial interest in art and artists; he made two outstanding films on art, *Le Monde de Paul Delvaux* (1946) and *Rubens* (co-directed with Paul Haesaerts, 1948).

Storyboard
In animation. Board on which sketches of the action of a film are displayed in sequence

Stradling, Harry (1910–1970)
Born in Britain. Cinematographer. Began career in the French studios at Joinville in 1931, subsequently working in Britain and the USA with many notable directors. His French period includes FEYDER's *Le Grand Jeu* (1933) and *La Kermesse Héroïque* (1935); in Britain, among others, *Pygmalion* and *The Citadel* (1938), *Jamaica Inn* (1939). His American career from 1940 includes HITCHCOCK's *Suspicion* (1941), *The Picture of Dorian Gray* (1945), *A Streetcar Named Desire* (1951), *A Face in the Crowd* (1957). His enormous expertise and skill in complicated camera movements (especially crane shots) gave an extra bounce and rhythm to many musicals including *The Pirate* and *Easter Parade* (1948), *The Barkleys of Broadway* (1949), *Guys and Dolls* (1955), *The Pajama Game* (1957), *Gypsy* (1961), *My Fair Lady* (1964), *Funny Girl* (1968), *Hello Dolly!* (1969). His son is also a lighting cameraman. JG

Strasberg, Lee
Born 1901 in Austria. Director of acting, closely associated with ELIA KAZAN. Studied drama in the USA with Richard Boleslawsky and Marie Ouspenskaya. He was also influenced by the intense, naturalistic style of acting adopted by Eleanora Duse and by the Moscow Art Theatre company. He began his career in the theatre in 1925, founding the Group Theatre in 1930, and the Actors' Studio in 1948, where many of the future stars of the American cinema were trained, or returned for further exercise, including MARLON BRANDO, ROD STEIGER, MONTGOMERY CLIFT, PAUL NEWMAN, MARILYN MONROE, SHELLEY WINTERS, JAMES DEAN and EVA MARIE SAINT. The Studio is associated with the Method approach to acting, which encourages the actor to discover his own emotions, and draw on them to express emotion on the stage. It seeks to eliminate any hindrance the actor might harbour which prevents the full exploitation of his talent. An actor, Strasberg claims, must be extraordinarily conscious of himself before he can forget himself on the stage, perfecting the individual instruments of his talent – his personality, his voice, his body. Strasberg works on his artists almost in the manner of a psychiatrist, and the players who believe in him and the Method return to the Studio again and again for refreshment in their art; other players reject the Method as too constricting and formularized.

Straub, Jean-Marie
Born 1933 in Metz, France. Director. Organized various film clubs in his youth and worked as junior assistant in French studios, on films by GANCE, RENOIR, ASTRUC and BRESSON. Made several shorts and three features – *Nicht Versöhnt* (1965), *The Chronicle of Anna Magdalena Bach* (1967), *Othon* (1969) – in collaboration with Danièle Huillet. Despite his relatively small output, Straub has made himself the centre of a fierce critical controversy in Europe, his partisans hailing him as a new original force, his detractors claiming that his kind of minimal cinema (the Bach film consists largely of shots of musicians playing and Corneille's play 'Othon' is declaimed flatly against sundry traffic noises) is a tedious confidence trick. Straub's intellectual and political preoccupations make him a difficult artist to assess; *Anna Magdalena Bach*, his most approachable work, certainly works as a concert and has a compelling stylistic unity as well. JG

Streisand, Barbra
Born 1942 in New York, USA. Dynamic American musical comedy star who set a new style in 'plain' heroines with her persuasive stage, then screen performance in *Funny Girl* (1968), for which she won an Academy Award. Her intelligent use of a powerful singing voice (recalling JUDY GARLAND's) is particularly impressive, as are her theatrical timing and aura of glamour. A Brooklyn girl, she won a singing contest which led to nightclub engagements, television appearances, a Broadway show 'I Can Get It For You Wholesale' and then 'Funny Girl'. Other films: *Hello Dolly!* (1968), *On a Clear Day You Can See Forever* and *The Owl and the Pussycat* (1970) *What's Up, Doc?* (1972).

Strick, Joseph
Born 1923 in Philadelphia, USA. Fiercely independent American director whose controversial battles with censors and studios are almost as highly publicized as the resulting films. His subject matter – James Joyce's *Ulysses* (1967), Henry Miller's *Tropic of Cancer* (1970) – tends to be more remarkable than his rather pedestrian treatment of it. Other main films include: *The Savage Eye* (1959), *The Balcony* (1962) and a small portion of *Justine* (1969), which he relinquished to GEORGE CUKOR after disagreements with Fox. Recent film: *The Darwin Adventure* (1971).

Sturges, John
Born 1910 in Chicago, USA. Noted director of well-carpentered commercial films, distinguished by clever manipulation of suspense in action and deeper-than-average characterization of loner-heroes. A series of tense, moral Westerns – *Bad Day at Black Rock* (1954), *Gunfight at the OK Corral* (1957), *Last Train from Gun Hill* (1958), *The Magnificent Seven* (1960), based on *Seven Samurai* – are probably his most personal achievements.

He joined the film industry in the 1930s at RKO, assisted on the first Technicolor films including *The Garden of Allah* (1936) and became a cutter and editor. He worked with

WILLIAM WYLER on a combat documentary during the Second World War, returning to Hollywood where he directed his first feature film *The Man who Dared* (1946). In the 1960s his films tended to grow in size if not in stature. His ability in handling ferocious action was especially notable in *The Great Escape* (1963).

Other main films: *Mystery Street* (1950), *The People Against O'Hara* (1951), *Escape from Fort Bravo* (1953), *The Old Man and the Sea* (1958), *The Satan Bug* and *The Hallelujah Trail* (1965), *The Hour of the Gun* (1967), *Ice Station Zebra* (1968), *Marooned* (1969). MH

Sturges, Preston (1898–1959)
Born in Chicago, USA. American comedy-director supreme in the 1940s, who subsequently lost steam and purpose, leaving behind him one film classic – *The Lady Eve* (1941) – and several intriguing and off-beat satires – *Sullivan's Travels* (1941), *The Palm Beach Story* (1942), *Hail the Conquering Hero* (1944). With affiliations to the comedies of MITCHELL LEISEN and later BILLY WILDER, and produced under the same studio *aegis*, Paramount, Sturges's best work was in marked contrast to the saccharine entertainment of war-time. He mocked social conventions and pretensions, he was ruthless to 'suckers' and approving of attractive 'con' artists: his films subscribed to sophisticated, amoral standards and a dog-eat-dog code of ethics.

Overrated in his brief box-office time – from 1939 to 1946 – he has been undervalued since, largely on the basis of his last disappointing film, *The Diary of Major Thompson* (1955), which he made in voluntary exile in France. In 1958 he made a guest appearance in *Paris Holiday*.

After writing a hit Broadway play – 'Strictly Dishonourable' – he went to Paramount in the 1930s as a scriptwriter, persuading the studio to let him direct his first two films, *The Great McGinty* and *Christmas in July* in 1940 as inexpensive experiments. Both were modestly successful and the next year *The Lady Eve*, a ruthlessly funny social comedy with HENRY FONDA and BARBARA STANWYCK, achieved both popular and critical acclaim. Dependent on the quality of his actors, Sturges was notably less happy with standard contract Paramount players in the crude small town joke, *Miracle of Morgan's Creek* (1944). After *Hail the Conquering Hero*, an invigorating satire on the civilian adulation of war-time heroes, he made several laboured comedies, including one with HAROLD LLOYD, *Mad Wednesday* (1947), which was severely re-edited.

Other films: *The Great Moment* (1944), *Unfaithfully Yours* (1948) and *The Beautiful Blonde from Bashful Bend* (1949). MH

Substandard Film
Film less than 35 mm in width

Subtractive Process
A colour reproduction process in which a scene is recombined by subtracting (filtering out) from white light each of the three pairs of primaries, thus in each case transmitting the remaining primary.

Sucksdorff, Arne
Born 1917 in Stockholm, Sweden. Documentary director who turned later to feature film. His early interest in biology was equal to his interest in art, which he studied in Berlin. Working independently in Sweden, he developed his own kind of short nature films, 'parables' about the relationship of man and beast, and beast and beast. He showed the true balance between hunter and hunted which is maintained on every level of life. His early films included *A Summer's Tale* (1943), *The Gull* and *Dawn* (1944) and the celebrated *A Divided World* (1948), in all of which the struggle for existence is observed with a calmness and objectivity which possesses its own quiet poetry. He also made one urban documentary, *People of the City* (1947), viewing city life with similar objectivity, and two films made in 1951 in India, *Indian Village* and *The Wind and the River*, both quiet exposures of the need of an ancient civilization to understand nature and adapt itself to live.

Returning to Sweden, Sucksdorff made his first feature, *The Great Adventure* (1953), about the growing understanding of and sympathy for nature in two children brought up in countryside which is near a forest; it has a wonderful opening sequence of the forest waking to life at dawn, comparable in mood with FLAHERTY's opening to *Louisiana Story* (1948). There is much in common between these two great film-makers, especially in their restrained introduction of a story-line to their films. But Sucksdorff was now to embark on more ambitious but less artistically successful work. *The Flute and the Arrow* (1956–7), a study of remote tribal life in India, still has much of his quality of calm, compassionate observation, but also a certain straining for dramatic effect. *The Boy in the Tree* (1961), set in Sweden, was also overfictionalized. Sucksdorff was now to take charge of a film school in Rio de Janeiro, making at the same time *My Home is Copacabana* (1965), a study of impoverished children who live through petty thieving. Sucksdorff shot the Antarctic animal sequences in *Mr Forbush and the Penguins* (1971). RM

Sullivan, Pat (1887–1933)
Born in Australia; emigrated to the USA. Animation director. Newspaper cartoonist, who turned to animation. He originated Felix the Cat around 1916 – the idea, it has been said, coming from Kipling's story of the cat which walked by itself. Made *Felix gets it Wrong* (1916), etc., developing the character much later, during the 1920s, in an outstandingly popular cartoon series with its theme-tune known all over the world – 'Felix kept on Walking'. Felix was the most popular and versatile animal character on the cartoon screen before Mickey Mouse.

Superimpose
To print one scene on top of another so that it supersedes what is on the original film

Swanson, Gloria
Born 1898 in Chicago, USA. Actress and one of MACK SENNETT's Bathing Beauties in 1916–8. One of the great faces of the silent era, she developed a considerable range and made a memorable comeback in WILDER's *Sunset Boulevard* (1950). Films include: *The Meal Ticket* (1915), *Teddy at the Throttle* (1917), *Shifting Sands* (1918), *Male and Female* (1919), *The Affairs of Anatole* (1921), *Prodigal Daughters* (1923), *Madame Sans Gêne* (1925), *Untamed Lady* (1926), *Sadie Thompson* and *Queen Kelly* (1928), *Indiscreet* (1931), *Music in the Air* (1934), *Father Takes a Wife* (1941), *Nero's Mistress* (1956). Recently seen on tel evision. RM

Switzerland
The reputation of Swiss cinema was made initially by the films of Leopold Lindtberg (born 1902; *Marie Louise*, 1944; *The Last Chance*, 1945). Apart from production solely for local audiences, there has been little of note made in German-speaking Switzerland; Alain Tanner (remembered for his part in the British *cinéma-vérité* film, *Nice Time*) has emerged as the most original talent working in French-speaking Switzerland with *Charles Mort ou Vif* (1969) and *La Salamandre* (1970). Other directors in Switzerland include Henry Brandt (*Voyages chez les Vivants*), Jean-Louis Roy (*L'Inconnue de Shandigor*), Yves Versin (*Angèle*), and Mortiz de Heideln (*Burning Shadows*).

Sydow, Max von
See VON SYDOW

Synchronize
To match the sound track to the picture so that their relationship appears natural

Szabó, István
Born 1938 in Budapest, Hungary. One of the youngest of the new generation of Hungarian film-makers who came to the fore in and after 1963. Szabó's feature films have all dealt with aspects of the experiences and maturing of his own generation in the years since the end of the war; and have all been characterized by a sentimental surface which encloses a steely intelligence, and a streak of almost surreal whimsy. *Age of Illusions* (1964) dealt with the disillusionment of a group of young people graduating after 1956. *The Father* (1966) was a brilliant parable about a boy growing up and eventually breaking free of the myths of the past; *Love Film* (1970) presented a panorama of Hungary during and since the war, as a background to the maturing of a young couple who have grown up together but are separated when the girl leaves her native country in 1956. DR

Syria
See ARAB FILM

T

Table Top Animation
The moving of objects along a table top or similar surface and photographing them, usually by means of stop-action photography.

Take
A single continuous shot made by a camera. In filming, each take is numbered from one upwards and the number is recorded on the slate to assist identification in printing and cutting.

Tarkovsky, Andrei
Born 1932 in Moscow, USSR. Director. Son of the great poet Arseni Tarkovsky, he graduated from VGIK in 1961 and first came to notice with a semi-experimental short film. In 1962, he made *Ivan's Childhood*, a sympathetic study of a young boy involved in the Second World War, which was marred by over-calculated lyrical and 'filmic' effects. Then, between 1964 and 1967, he directed *Andrei Roublev* (co-scripted with MIKHALKOV-KONCHALOVSKY), an ambitious, allegorical study of the icon painter whose obvious allusions to the fate and condition of the contemporary artist (and its many religious references), caused it to be frowned upon by the Soviet authorities and it received only limited screenings. Although uneven, its epic feeling (the casting of the huge bell at the end) and passionate re-creation of an historical epoch suggested a major talent. In 1971–2, Tarkovsky was engaged on a massive 70 mm science-fiction project, *Solaris*, clearly intended to be Russia's answer to *2001–A Space Odyssey*. JG

Tashlin, Frank
Born 1913 in New Jersey, USA. Lately respected comedy writer and director, who started out as a cartoonist. His work with JERRY LEWIS has been especially highly regarded; while his exuberant style and ability to follow a gag through to its ultimate outrageous conclusion suggest an affinity more properly with silent comedy than with the sophisticated restrictions of sound. Main films: *The Paleface* (as writer only, 1948), *Artists and Models* (1955), *The Girl Can't Help It* and *Will Success Spoil Rock Hunter?* (1957), *Cinderfella* (1960), *It's only Money*, *The Man from the Diner's Club* and *Who's Minding the Store?* (1963), *The Disorderly Orderly* (1965), *The Glass Bottom Boat* (1966), *Caprice* (1967).

Tati, Jacques
Born 1908 in Seine-et-Oise, France. Austere, highly individual French comedy actor-director in the great silent tradition, whose rare, almost wordless, films – conceived, written and constructed by himself – are virtually one-man shows. Since his idiosyncratic *Jour de Fête* (1947), his films have shown an increasing concern with the conformity of contemporary, mechanized, electronic, pre-packaged life. With each film, the painstaking creative period grows longer, from *Monsieur Hulot's Holiday* (1952) to *Mon Oncle* (1958) to *Playtime* (1967) and *Traffic* (1971).

Before he started making his own films (beginning with shorts) his elegant balletic comedy style was nurtured in the music hall (where he made his show business début) and in cabaret. He also played roles in several French films notably *Sylvie et le Fantôme* (1945), and *Le Diable au Corps* (1947) – and wrote the scenarios for others before branching out into his own particular comedy format, which, though basically a string of sight jokes, is cleverly designed to imply, without actually making, a social comment. MH

Taurog, Norman
Born 1899 in Chicago, USA. Veteran Hollywood director and one-time actor who followed the traditional route from property man to director of two-reel comedies (with LARRY SEMON) to feature film-maker. He won an Academy Award for *Skippy* (1931) and most of his films in the 1930s and 1940s efficiently reflected the popular tastes of the time as dictated by the studios. Among his more personal films, however, were *If I had a Million* (1932), *The Adventures of Tom Sawyer* (1938), *Young Tom Edison* (1940), *Girl Crazy* (1942). His most recent films, including the PRESLEY musicals *Tickle Me* (1965), are forgettable. Other films include: *We're Not Dressing* (1934), *Mad about Music* and *Boys' Town* (1938), *Broadway Melody of 1940*, *Presenting Lily Mars* (1942), *Room for one More* (1952).

Taylor, Elizabeth
Born 1932 in London, England. Most glamorous of the highly-paid Hollywood-trained international stars to emerge since the Second World War and, until recently, a much underrated film actress. A war 'refugee' she was taken to California by her parents when she was seven and in 1942 was chosen to play the English heroine in *Lassie Come Home*. The film led to a long-term MGM contract. As early as 1944 her startling beauty was noted in *National Velvet*. A series of dull roles which simply exploited her looks followed, until *Father of the Bride* (1950) and, more importantly, *A Place in the Sun* (1951) confirmed the talent allied to the looks. Despite the inflated *Cleopatra* (1963), her gift for portraying neurotic beauties won her critical acclaim and two Academy Awards – for *Butterfield 8* (1960) and *Who's Afraid of Virginia Woolf?* (1966). Undoubtedly her crisis-ridden private life has helped, rather than handicapped, her popularity with the public. Since 1962 her most constant co-star has been her fifth husband, RICHARD BURTON.

Other notable films: *Little Women* (1949), *Elephant Walk* (1954), *The Last Time I Saw Paris* (1955), *Giant* (1956), *Raintree County* (1957), *Cat on a Hot Tin Roof* (1958), *Suddenly Last Summer* (1959), *The VIPs* (1963), *The Sandpiper* (1965), *The Taming of the Shrew* and *Reflections in a Golden Eye* (1967), *The Comedians* and *Boom* (1968), *Secret Ceremony* (1969), *The Only Game in Town* and *Under Milk Wood* (1970), *Zee and Co* (1971). See 'Elizabeth Taylor' by Ruth Waterbury. MH

Taylor, Robert (1911–1969)
Born in Nebraska, USA. Actor, who graduated at pre-medical college, where he acted and played 'cello; formed own trio for radio broadcasting. Film début in *Handy Andy* (1934), and many other films followed. He won popularity awards between 1936 and 1938. Lieutenant in US Navy in Second World War. Films include: *Magnificent Obsession* (1935), *Broadway Melody of 1936* (1936), *Camille* (1937), *A Yank at Oxford* and *The Crowd Roars* (1938), *Three Comrades* (1939), *Waterloo Bridge* (1940), *Song of Russia* (1943), *Quo Vadis?* (1951), *Ivanhoe* (1952), *Guns of Wyoming* (1962), and many others.

Tazieff, Haroun
Born 1914 in Warsaw, Poland. Director of specialized films. After childhood spent in Russia, he emigrated to Belgium, where he later became a lecturer in Mineralogy, Geology and Geophysics at Brussels University. After the war, during which he had served in the Resistance, he went to the Belgian Congo, working with the National Geological Service.

Here he began his study of volcanoes, to which he was to devote the rest of his life, travelling over the world to film them in eruption. The result of his unique and virtually unrepeatable work appears in *Volcano* (*Rendezvous du Diable*, 1958) and *The Forbidden Volcano* (1967). 'Once I start I do not know how to stop,' he has said. Clothed in asbestos, he and his assistants have made a record of the crust of the earth in exploding, molten disintegration, filming in colour surrealist landscapes of smoke, fire, and white-hot matter as if they were COUSTEAU filming underwater. RM

Technicolor
A proprietary colour process using a special camera which produces three separate negatives during shooting, registering the blue, green and red elements of the scene respectively. Colour prints are made from matrices produced from these three negatives. See COLOUR CINEMATOGRAPHY and HERBERT and NATALIE KALMUS.

Telecine Projector
Special projector which enables cinematograph film to be transmitted on television

Telephoto Lens
Lens of greater than normal focal length which produces enlarged photographs of distant objects

Temple, Shirley
Born 1928 in Santa Monica, USA. Most successful and extravagantly adored child star of the 1930s, whose blonde curls and ingratiating lisp still conjure up an instant image of cute baby charm for filmgoers who never even saw her on the screen. Genuinely talented, she was sympathetically managed by her parents, started filming at the age of three, and was a run-away hit from the time of *Stand Up and Cheer* (1934). Her success helped build the fortunes of Twentieth Century Fox. She made an uneasy transition into adolescence and young womanhood then retired from the screen after *Pride of Kentucky* (1950). Main films include: *Little Miss Marker* (1934), *Curly Top* and *The Littlest Rebel* (1935), *Wee Willie Winkie* (1937), *Rebecca of Sunnybrook Farm* (1938), *The Blue Bird* (1940), *Since you Went Away* (1944), *Fort Apache* (1948), *A Kiss for Corliss* (1949). In the late 1960s she became active in Californian politics. MH

Teshigahara, Hiroshi
Born 1927 in Tokyo, Japan. Director. Studied at Tokyo Art Institute and collaborated on several short films. His work reveals a fondness for bizarre subject matter, interlaced with elements of fantasy, even surrealism, all of which were evident in his first feature *The Pitfall* (1962), which combined social documentary with a ghost story. *Woman of the Dunes* (1964) is probably his best work, with its pervasive atmosphere of shifting sands, sultry

Above: George Murphy and Shirley Temple in 'Little Miss Broadway' (Irving Cummings, USA, 1938)
Below: Ingrid Thulin in 'The Silence' (Ingmar Bergman, Sweden, 1963)

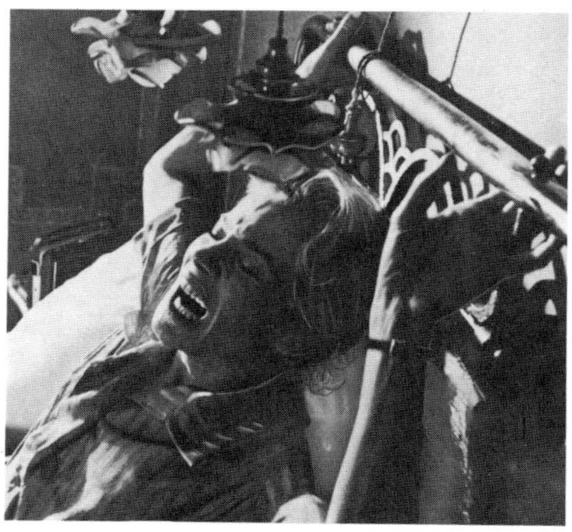

heat and a quirkily developed relationship between a scientist and a strange lady who lives in a sand-pit, all magnificently shot with that fastidious Japanese attention to physical detail. The succeeding films, *The Face of Another* (1966) and *The Man without a Map* (1968), continued his exploration of ambiguous relationships coupled with sinister undertones, but were marred by rather pretentious moralizing. His multi-screen film for one of the pavilions at the Osaka Exposition 1970 was certainly ingenious, yet suggested that futuristic slapstick comedy was not his real forte. JG

Thalberg, Irving (1899–1936)
Born in Brooklyn, USA. Thalberg's unparalleled reputation as Hollywood's production genius apparently comes from his possessing a degree of taste, self-assurance, decisiveness, a sense of honour and a freedom from pettiness in an environment in which the combination of these qualities (indeed the possession even of one or two of them) was exceedingly rare. His career was meteoric. A frail, middle-class Jewish boy, ill-health had made him a keen reader. A chance encounter with CARL LAEMMLE resulted in his leaving a post as a clerk in an importing firm to become a secretary at Universal's New York office. He made himself sufficiently useful to Laemmle to be taken out to California, and at 20 was put in virtual charge of Universal City. Thalberg was always driven by a passion for money; and in 1923 joined LOUIS B. MAYER at a better salary than Laemmle would raise. From the time of the consolidation of Metro-Goldwyn-Mayer Thalberg was in effective charge of production at the studios, until 1933, when he found himself ousted from control. During the last three years of his life he worked as an independent producer within MGM. In practical terms his quality as a producer lay in a sense of perfectionism, reckoning that money spent in achieving improvements to a project was ultimately an economy. His most famous productions include *The Big Parade*, *Ben-Hur*, *The Crowd*, *Broadway Melody*, *Anna Christie*, *Trader Horn*, *Grand Hotel*, *Mutiny on the Bounty* and *Camille*; and his most infamous *Merry-go-round* (Universal) from which he sacked VON STROHEIM; and *Greed*, which he cut to a bare fraction of the director's original version. Thalberg married NORMA SHEARER. DR

Thompson, J. Lee
Born 1914 in Bristol, England. Able British director, former actor and playwright, whose

attempt to introduce a more realistic tone into British films of the 1950s anticipated the successes of such directors as JACK CLAYTON, KAREL REISZ and LINDSAY ANDERSON some years later. His first film as director-writer was *Murder Without Crime* (1950), followed by *The Yellow Balloon* (1952), *The Weak and the Wicked* (1953). In 1956 he directed the impassioned anti-capital punishment drama, *Yield to the Night*. In the 1960s he worked mainly either in America or for American companies abroad. Despite the popularity of such extravagant adventures as *The Guns of Navarone* (1961), *Kings of the Sun* (1963), and *MacKenna's Gold* (1968), he has achieved more personal successes with tightly constructed suspense dramas such as *Cape Fear* (1962), *Return from the Ashes* (1965). Latest films: *Before Winter Comes* (1968), *The Most Dangerous Man in the World* (1969), *Brotherly Love* (1970). MH

Thulin, Ingrid
Born 1929 in Solleftea, Sweden. Authoritative Swedish stage and screen actress, most importantly associated with INGMAR BERGMAN as a member of his celebrated repertory company of actors. Her occasional English-speaking films have not used her to advantage, but her dominating munitions heiress in VISCONTI's *The Damned* (1969) was a *tour de force*. Main films: *Wild Strawberries* (1957), *So Close to Life* (1958), *The Face* (1959), *Four Horsemen of the Apocalypse* and *Winter Light* (1962), *The Silence* (1963), *Return from the Ashes* (1965), *La Guerre est Finie* and *Night Games* (1966), *The Hour of the Wolf* (1967), *The Rite* (1969).

Tilt
Upward or downward movement of a camera in a vertical plane

Time-Lapse Photography
Photographic method for accelerating the speed of movements of a slow-moving object, each frame of the film being exposed at a considerable time interval

Tint
To colour film with dye. Used in silent films to heighten the dramatic and emotional effect (see CINEMATOGRAPHY page 132).

Tiomkin, Dimitri
Born 1899 in St Petersburg, Russia. Composer and arranger. Studied music and piano under several famous teachers in early 1920s and became concert composer. Began working in American films from 1930, developing a lush symphonic style, often marred by excessive sentimentality, but which suited the climate of the times. His more distinctive scores include: *The Westerner* (1940), several notable war-time documentaries by HUSTON, LITVAK and CAPRA (*Why We Fight* Series), *Duel in the Sun* (1946), *Red River* (1948), *Strangers on a Train* and *The Thing* (1951), *High Noon* (1952), *I Confess* (1953), *The High and the Mighty* (1954), *Giant* (1956), *Gunfight at the OK Corral* (1957), *Rio Bravo* (1959), *The Alamo* (1960), *The Fall of the Roman Empire* (1964). He co-produced a Soviet-American biography of *Tchaikovsky* (1970). JG

Tissé, Edouard (1897–1961)
Born in Stockholm, Sweden. Cinematographer of Swedish-Russian parentage, he moved to Moscow from Sweden, where his parents lived, becoming a noted newsreel cameraman in the service of the Russian revolution. His initial work in feature films was seen in *Signal* (1918), the first Soviet-sponsored feature, directed by Alexander Arkatov, followed by others, including *Hunger, Hunger, Hunger* (1921), which PUDOVKIN co-directed. He was notable for his quick eye and brilliant choice of shot, especially in action photography on the warfronts. He became closely associated with EISENSTEIN, whose genius inspired his own; they worked together experimentally on Eisenstein's first film, *Strike* (1924, released 1925), and then during the silent period on *Battleship Potemkin* (1925), *October* (1928), and *Old and New* (*The General Line*, 1929). In 1929–31 Tissé accompanied Eisenstein and his assistant ALEXANDROV on their expedition to Western Europe, the USA and Mexico. During this period he shot for Alexandrov the short film, *Romance Sentimentale* (1931), and co-directed in Switzerland a feature of his own, *Woman Happy, Woman Unhappy* (1929), a distinctively personal comment on abortion and childbirth. He also created some of his finest work for Eisenstein's ill-fated Mexican study, *Que Viva Mexico!* (1931). Back in the Soviet Union, Tissé worked with ROMAN KARMEN on a documentary about the Kura-Kum expedition from Moscow to the desert regions. He also worked on DOVZHENKO's *Aerograd* (1935) and Eisenstein's *Alexander Nevsky* and the exteriors for *Ivan the Terrible* I and II (1943–6). His work was characterized by exactness of composition and a great understanding of photographic luminosity; he knew precisely which lens would bring the right degree of tone, while his filters turned summer into winter for the battle on the ice in *Alexander Nevsky*. Tissé's other films included Alexandrov's *Meeting on the Elbe* (1949) and *Glinka* (1952). RM

Todd-AO
A wide-screen process using a special film 65 mm in width

Todd, Mike (1907–1958)
Born in Minneapolis, USA. Indefatigable American stage and screen impresario with a flair for showmanship and a gambler's instinct which sustained him through a notoriously erratic career. His talent for theatrical spectacle, resulting in several Broadway shows, spilled over into the only film he personally produced, the star-studded *Around the World in Eighty Days* (1956), which won an Oscar and a vast amount of publicity coverage. He was also involved in the early days of Cinerama and gave his name to the Todd-AO wide-screen process. He died – in a plane crash – as spectacularly as he lived, and left ELIZABETH TAYLOR a widow. His son, Mike Jr, attempted to follow in his father's footsteps by producing the first movie with synchronised 'smells', *Scent of Mystery* (1959). A biography, 'The Nine Lives of Mike Todd', by Art Cohn, was published in 1959. MH

Toland, Gregg (1904–1948)
Born in Charleston, Illinois, USA. Cinematographer. One of the most influential American camera artists, he was assistant to George Barnes in the late 1920s; began his career proper with several Eddie Cantor sound musicals for GOLDWYN, then became known for his distinguished collaboration with WILLIAM WYLER – *These Three* (1936), *Dead End* (1937), *Wuthering Heights* (1939), *The Little Foxes* (1941), *The Best Years of our Lives* (1946). Toland's distinctive style, with its brilliant clarity, black-and-white shadings and deep-focus effects, was also seen to great effect in JOHN FORD's *The Grapes of Wrath* and *The Long Voyage Home* (1940), and, of course, WELLES's *Citizen Kane* (1940), which caused a major re-thinking of photographic techniques. It would be interesting to rediscover the long documentary Toland directed about Pearl Harbour, *December 7th* (1942), which was apparently mutilated by the military censorship of the time. JG

Torre Nilsson, Leopoldo
Born 1924 in Buenos Aires, Argentina. The son of a distinguished Argentine director, Leopoldo Torre-Rios (1899–1960), Torre Nilsson, with his highly original and baroque vision, occasionally revealing his admiration for BUÑUEL, is unquestionably the best director to have emerged from Spanish America. Most of his films have been scripted by his novelist wife, Beatriz Guido. Principal films: *El Muro* (short, 1950), *El Crimen de Oribe* (co-directed with Torre-Rios, 1950), *El hijo del crack* (co-directed with Torre-Rios, 1953), *Dias de odio* and *La Tigra* (1954), *Para vestir santos* and *Graciela* (1955), *El protegido* (1956), *La Casa del Angel* (1957), *El Secuestrador* (1958), *La Caida* (1959), *Fin de Fiesta* and *Un quapo del '900* (1960), *La mano en la trampa* and *Piel de verano* (1961), *Setenta veces siete* (1962), *Homenaje a la hora de la siesta* and *La terraza* (1963), *El ojo de la corradura* (1964), *Cavar un foso* and *Monday's Child* (1966), *The Traitors of San Anjel* (1967), *Martin Fierro* (1969), *El Santo de la Espada* (1970), *Guemes* (1971). DR

Totò (1895–1967)
Born in Naples. A lean, unsmiling, irresistibly comical man, Totò, of aristocratic birth, came to the cinema from music hall and revue, making his début in Gero Zambuto's *Fermo con le mani* (1936). In the course of the next 30 years, and dozens of films, he became Italy's best-loved screen comic. Later appearances included MARIO MONICELLI's *I Soliti ignoti*

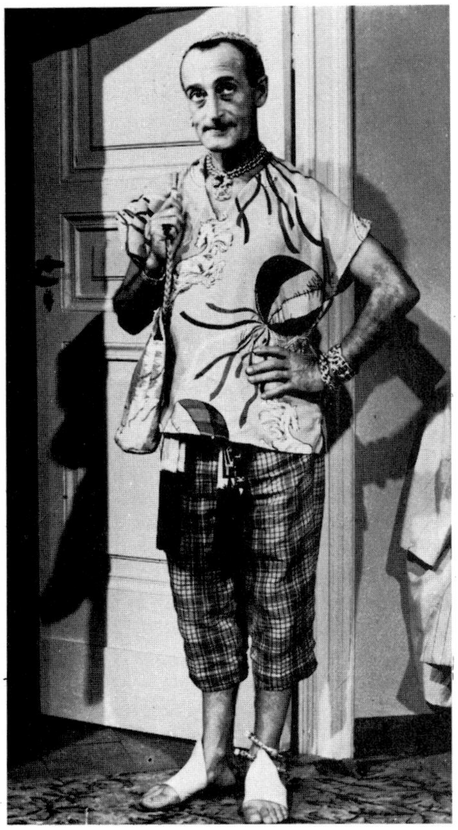

Above: Totò in 'L'Imperatore di Capri' (Luigi Comencini, Italy, 1950)
Below: Jean-Pierre Cargol and François Truffaut in 'L'Enfant Sauvage' (Truffaut, France, 1970)

(1958), LATTUADA's *La Mandragola* (1965), PASOLINI's *Uccellacci e Uccellini* (1966) and a whole series of 'Totò' comedies.

Tourneur, Jacques

Born 1904 in Paris, France. The son of MAURICE TOURNEUR. Essentially a small-budget director, with a penchant for the macabre. Tourneur's best work was done with the producer Val Lewton at RKO: *Cat People* (1942), *I Walked with a Zombie* and *The Leopard Man* (1943). Of his other films the most interesting were *Build my Gallows High* (1947), *Berlin Express* (1948), *Stars in my Crown* (1950), *Way of a Gaucho* (1952), *Wichita* (1955), *The Comedy of Terrors* (1964). Whatever the subject-matter, Tourneur brought a sharp camera eye and a vivid atmospheric sense to his work.

Tourneur, Maurice (1878–1961)

Born in Paris, France. A unique figure in the early days of film-making, Tourneur had begun his career as an artist and a student of Rodin. Later he had become an actor with Réjane, and for several years worked with Antoine. A quarrel with the great director of the *Théâtre Libre* drove Tourneur into films, as an actor. As a director for the Éclair company, he was sent to the USA in 1914 to run Éclair's Tucson studios. Within a year the pictorial quality of his films and the speed and clarity of their story-telling had put him in the front rank of American directors. 'We are not mere photographers,' he said about this time, 'we are artists'; and it was in this conviction that he made a series of prestige films including *The Blue Bird* and *A Doll's House* (1918), *Treasure Island* (1920), *The Last of the Mohicans* (1922), *The Christian* (1923), *Never the Twain Shall Meet* (1924), *Aloma of the South Seas* (1926). Finding his pictorial style of narrative outdated in the USA, Tourneur returned to France where his first film was *L'Équipage* (1927). Without ever really regaining the enormous prestige he had in America in the war and immediate post-war years, when he was rated the equal of GRIFFITH, Tourneur continued to direct films of notable quality, generally on literary subjects, until 1949 (*Impasse des deux anges*).

Tracking Shot

A shot made while moving the camera sideways, forwards or backwards

Tracy, Spencer (1900–1967)

Born in Wisconsin, USA. Impeccable stage-trained American film actor, acknowledged to be one of the greatest, if not the greatest, of screen technicians, whose incomparable talent won him two Academy Awards – for *Captains Courageous* (1937) and *Boys' Town* (1938) – and the enduring loyalty (despite his rather difficult temperament) of critics, film industry and public. Although less successful at the box-office than many of his films, his war-of-the-sexes social comedies with KATHARINE HEPBURN have become part of Hollywood history. He died soon after making his last film with Hepburn, *Guess Who's Coming to Dinner* (1967).

A liberal, all-American hero, he made his film début in *Up the River* (1930) and managed to avoid the intensive type-casting of the 1930s: though his humane, conscience-ridden characters, whose best friends were invariably CLARK GABLE, were the closest he came to establishing an 'image'. In the 1950s and 1960s, his performances as the characteristic seeker of justice. in *Bad Day at Black Rock* (1954), *Inherit the Wind* (1960) and *Judgment at Nuremberg* (1961) were especially memorable.

Other notable films: *Quick Millions* (1931), *Man's Castle* (1934), *Fury*, *San Francisco* and *Libelled Lady* (1936), *Test Pilot* (1937), *Stanley and Livingstone* (1939), *Boom Town* (1940), *Woman of the Year* (1942), *Keeper of the Flame* (1943), *The Seventh Cross* (1944), *Without Love* (1945), *The World and his Wife* (1948), *Edward, my Son* and *Adam's Rib* (1949), *Father of the Bride* (1950), *Pat and Mike* (1952), *The Actress* (1953), *The Mountain* and *The Desk Set* (1956), *The Old Man and the Sea* and *The Last Hurrah* (1958), *It's a Mad, Mad, Mad, Mad World* (1963).

A biography, 'Spencer Tracy', by Larry Swindell was published in 1969. MH

Trauberg, Ilya (1905–1948)

Born in Odessa, Ukraine, USSR. The younger brother of LEONID TRAUBERG, Ilya Trauberg entered the cinema as a writer in 1927. He is principally known for two pictures, *The Blue Express* (1929) and *Son of Mongolia* (1936), but also directed a documentary *Leningrad Today*

(1927) and the features *There will be work for you* (1932), *A Singular Affair* (1934), *The Year 1919* (1938) and *Waiting for Victory* (1941).

Trauberg, Leonid
Born 1902 in Odessa, Ukraine, USSR. Associated with KOZINTSEV in the experimental theatre FEKS. The two directors were constant collaborators until 1947 (for titles see under KOZINTSEV). During this period Trauberg made one solitary essay in direction with *The Actress* (1943). Since the partnership broke up Trauberg has written scenarios for other directors and directed *Soldiers on the March* (1958), *Dead Souls* and *Wind of Freedom* (1961).

Trauner, Alexandre
Born 1906 in Budapest, Hungary. Set designer. Worked in Paris as painter and assistant to LAZARE MEERSON on several CLAIR and FEYDER films in the 1930s. Developed his witty period style in CARNÉ's *Drôle de Drame* (1937), and his method of constructing detailed, lived-in interiors in *Le Jour se lève* (1939). After several other collaborations with Carné – the rich theatrical backgrounds for *Les Enfants du Paradis* (1943–5) – and other French directors, he teamed up with BILLY WILDER in the 1950s and absorbed the latter's harsh, dyspeptic world as completely as he had responded to the French scene, notably in the marvellously 'felt' city décor for *The Apartment* (1960). Other work for Wilder includes *The Private Life of Sherlock Holmes* (1970), with its nostalgic, delicate vision of Victorian England. JG

Travelling Matte
A film which is run through a film printer together with the film to be printed in order to mask a portion of it and prevent that section from being exposed.

Treatment
A stage in the development of a film story between the original synopsis and the final shooting script

Trick Film
Film of situations and events which would in reality be impossible, achieved by manipulation of the various production processes

Trnka, Jiří (1912–1970)
Born in Pilsen, Czechoslovakia. Animation director. Trained in art school, he later, in 1935, managed a puppet theatre, only turning to the film after the war. He began by making animated cartoons, notably the brilliant and violently savage anti-Nazi film, *The Devil on Springs* (also called *Spring-Heel Jack*, *The Chimney-Sweep*, or *The Springer and the SS*, 1946). Although returning to animated cartoons from time to time, Trnka preferred to work with puppets – as he once said, they have 'more presence' than drawings. He liked their slowness of movement (compared with the drawn figure), their solidity and stillness. Such early films as *The Czech Year* (1947); the Chinese legend, *The Emperor's Nightingale* (1949); the satire on Westerns, *Song of the Prairie* (1949); *Prince Bayaya* (1950); and *Old Czech Legends* (1953) established the outstanding artistry and variety of Trnka's work in the medium of the puppet film. His over-ornate, and in some respects far too traditional feature-length version of Shakespeare's *A Midsummer Night's Dream* (1959) nevertheless represents the height of Trnka's skill in puppet animation, of which for some two decades he became the acknowledged world master. Something of the force and bitterness of *The Devil on Springs* returned in certain of his later films, notably *The Hand* (1964) and *Archangel Gabriel and Mother Goose* (1965). Trnka's remarkable establishment of character in his puppets as well as control of significant movement gave his work its unparalleled distinction. RM

Troell, Jan
Born 1931 in Malmö, Sweden. Director and Cinematographer. Made amateur films in his youth; then met director BO WIDERBERG and photographed his first film *The Pram* (1963). As a director, Troell is known mainly for *Here is Your Life* (1966), an affectionate, detailed portrait of a young man's coming of age in First World War Sweden; *Who Saw him Die?* (1967), a painful study of a teacher's uneasy relationship with his pupils; and his most elaborate work to date, *The Emigrants* (1969–72), based on Vilhelm Moberg's epic novels about the perilous journey of a Swedish family to North America in the 19th century. This two-part film (photographed, as usual, by Troell himself), lasts about six hours and its warm, leisurely, chronicle style (plus the familiarity of the novels) made it the greatest Swedish box-office success for many years. JG

'The Devil on Springs' (Jiří Trnka, Czechoslovakia, 1945)

Trucking Shot
Shot taken with a camera mounted on a moving truck or trolley

Truffaut, François
Born 1932 in Paris, France. Director. Through contact with ANDRÉ BAZIN became a contributor to 'Cahiers du Cinéma', violently attacking in his articles conventional forms of French film-making. In 1956 he was for a while associated with ROSSELLINI. In 1957 he made a short fiction film, *Les Mistons*, about the adolescent reactions of a group of boys to Bernadette, a girl somewhat older than they. This film, with its charm and acute observation, was followed by the more celebrated *Les Quatre Cents Coups* (1959), which deals with a 13-year-old boy, half child, half adult, who ends up in a reformatory largely because of the lack of understanding he receives from the adult world. This initial feature film remains one of Truffaut's best, most perceptive and humane films; it was based to some extent on Truffaut's own youthful experience. In *Tirez sur le Pianiste* (1960) Truffaut experimented somewhat uncertainly with a form which was part-thriller, part comedy-burlesque; the film saw the beginning of Truffaut's use of the brilliant, free-style camerawork of COUTARD. *Jules et Jim* (1961) had greater assurance in its delicate handling of the triangle-relationship of two close friends and the woman they both love, played by JEANNE MOREAU. The film is successful in its simple suggestion of period, and contains much revealing discussion, as well as entertaining, seemingly inconsequent digressions. Its tragic end comes as a shock. After contributing an episode to the multi-national film *L'Amour à vingt ans* (1962), which he co-produced – the episode again featured Antoine Doinel (Jean-Pierre Léaud) of *Les Quatre Cents Coups* – Truffaut made a more nearly conventional film in *La Peau Douce* (1964), the study of an unsatisfactory love-affair between a middle-aged, married writer and an air-hostess; his skill in characterization saved the film from banality, but the end (when the wife shoots her unfaithful husband) is melodramatic. Truffaut's British film, *Fahrenheit 451* (1966) followed; it is a science-fiction parable derived from Ray Bradbury about an age in which the responsibility of firemen is to find and burn all books, Fahrenheit 451 being the combustion temperature for paper. The dénouement shows the emergence of an underground movement in the form of the so-called book people who attempt to save society by committing whole books to memory. *La Mariée était en Noir* (1967) links Truffaut to HITCHCOCK; it concerns the campaign of vengeance undertaken by a woman (Jeanne Moreau) against the men involved in the accidental killing of her husband on their wedding day. While *Baisers Volés* (1968) and *Domicile Conjugal* (1970) take up the later, troubled career of Antoine Doinel, *L'Enfant Sauvage* (1970) offered Truffaut entirely new territory – the minutely documented, drily narrated true story of the attempt by a humane doctor of the late 18th century (played by Truffaut himself) to educate a boy who has been discovered living wild in the forests of France. His latest film is *Les Deux Anglaises et le Continent* (1971). Truffaut's work moves, sometimes uncertainly, between the highly personal style of his best films (with their tendency towards episodic structure, diffident heroes, and suggestions of improvization), and those which seem to reflect American influences.

Truffaut's book, 'Hitchcock', made up from prolonged interviews with Hitchcock, published in 1967, shows the extent to which he is capable of a dedicated admiration for another, and very different film-maker. See 'The Cinema of François Truffaut' by Graham Petrie. RM

Trumbo, Dalton
Born 1905 in Colorado, USA. American reporter and then screenwriter blacklisted during the McCarthy period in the 1950s. In general his courageous reputation is more notable than his later tough-skinned, soft-centred scripts. Main films: *The Remarkable Andrew* (1942), *A Guy Named Joe* (1943), *Thirty Seconds over Tokyo* (1944), *Our Vines Have Tender Grapes* (1945), *Exodus* (1960), *Lonely are the Brave* (1962), *The Sandpiper* (1965), *Hawaii* (1966), *The Fixer* (1968). In 1970 he directed a harrowing, if uneven, version of his story *Johnny got his Gun.*

Tunisia
See ARAB FILM

Turin, Viktor (1895–1945)
Born in St Petersburg, Russia. Essentially an administrator, largely responsible for the development of the Ukrainian cinema, Turin is remembered for one film only, his masterly documentary on the construction of the Turkestan-Siberian railroad – *Turksib* (1929). Other films: *Order of the day* and *October 8* (1925), *Battle of Giants* (1926), *The Provocator* (1928), *The White Sea Canal* (1933), *Men of Baku* (1938).

Turkey
With a population of over 30 million, Turkey has some 1,000 theatres and has been active in the production of feature films for purely local distribution since 1914. Istanbul is the centre of production, which can reach as high as 200 films a year. Turkish films are seen occasionally abroad, and Metin Erksan's *The Dry Summer* (1964) won an award at the Berlin film festival. Other directors include Lütfu Ö. Akad, Memduh Ün, Atif Yilmaz, Halit Refiğ, and Turgut Demirağ. RM

Turpin, Ben (1874–1940)
Born in Louisiana, USA. Unique cross-eyed comic of the MACK SENNETT–CHARLES CHAPLIN school of silent comedy. Although he never achieved the status of Chaplin, LLOYD or KEATON, he developed an hilarious, unsubtle slapstick style which concentrated a good deal on his physical peculiarity and was – indeed still is – much appreciated by children. Vaudeville-trained, he joined Essanay first in 1907, later appeared in several Chaplin shorts. Sennett, recognizing his acrobatic skill and flair for caricature, cast him in several parodies: *East Lynne with Variations, Uncle Tom without the Cabin, The Shriek of Araby.* A genuine eccentric, he went on acting in films well into the 1930s. Main titles: *Small Town Idol* (1921), *The Prodigal Bridegroom* (1926), *Show of Shows* (1929), *The Love Parade* (1930), *Million Dollar Legs* (1939).

Ben Turpin

Tushingham, Rita
Born 1940 in Liverpool, England. Actress, who studied for the stage at Liverpool Playhouse, but gained immediate fame by her film acting in *A Taste of Honey* (1961). Her strength as an actress lies in her sincerity and directness, combined with a sympathetic but utterly unglamorous beauty of expression. Subsequent films include: *The Leather Boys* and *A Place to Go* (1963), *Girl with Green Eyes* (1964), *The Knack* (1965), *Dr Zhivago* and *The Trap* (1966), *Diamonds for Breakfast* and *Smashing Time* (1968), *The Guru* and *The Bed-Sitting Room* (1969).

Tuttle, Frank (1892–1963)
Born in New York, USA. Frank Tuttle came to Paramount from Yale and *Vanity Fair* to become one of Hollywood's most reliable directors of average pictures. The best of the fast-moving and witty films he made in the 1920s are *Lucky Devil* (1925), *Love 'Em and Leave 'Em, Second Fiddle* and *Kid Boots* (1926), in which CLARA BOW starred with Eddie Cantor whom Tuttle directed in his best sound film, *Roman Scandals* (1933). Of Tuttle's innumerable sound films the most interesting were *This Gun for Hire* (1942) and *The Magic Face* (1951). He continued to direct until 1958 *(Island of Lost Women).*

Two Shot
Shot of two persons taken with the camera as close as possible, while still keeping them both in the shot

U

Ucicky, Gustav (1898–1961)

Born in Vienna, Austria. Entered the cinema in Vienna as a cameraman at the Sascha studios, working with MICHAEL CURTIZ. He moved to Germany in 1928 and became well known mainly as a director of German nationalist-historical films, especially during the Hitler régime. Among his best-known films were *The Flute Concert of Sanssouci* (1930), *Yorck* (1931), *Men without Name* (1932), *Morgenrot* (*Dawn*, 1933), about German sailors trapped in a submarine during the First World War, the anti-Soviet film *Flüchtlinge* (1933), *Joan the Maid* (1935), *The Broken Jug* (1937), *Der Postmeister* (*Her Crime was Love*, 1940), and the anti-Polish film, *Heimkehr* (1941). Ucicky resumed his career after the war, working regularly from 1949 to the end of his life.

Ullman, Liv

Born 1940 in Tokyo, Japan, of Norwegian parents. Luminous Scandinavian actress and one of INGMAR BERGMAN's star protégées. A distinguished stage actress in her native Norway and Denmark, she was chosen by Bergman to co-star in *Persona* (1966) partly because of her resemblance to BIBI ANDERSSON. She acted in three subsequent Bergman films: *Hour of the Wolf* (1968), *The Shame* (1969), *A Passion* (1970). Latest films: JAN TROELL's *The Emigrants and The Settlers* (1971) with MAX VON SYDOW and *Pope Joan* (1972) in Britain.

Underground Film

See AVANT-GARDE AND UNDERGROUND FILM

United States of America

THE SILENT PERIOD

Although the LUMIÈRE Brothers must technically take the credit for presenting the first demonstration of projected moving photographs before a paying audience, on 28 December 1895 in the Salon Indien of the Grand Café, Boulevard des Capucines, America is also substantially responsible for the early development of the cinema. In the 1860s there were experiments in combining the magic lantern with devices for producing optical effects of movement and photographs: one such was Heyl's Phasmatrope, demonstrated in Philadelphia in 1870, which projected a rapid series of photographs so as to give an impression of motion. Heyl, however, had to pose each single photograph separately before an ordinary still camera. In 1873 an English-born photographer, Eadweard Muybridge, was commissioned by Governor Stanford of California to make instantaneous photographs of racehorses; and his experiments to this end led him to develop methods of taking rapid series of photographs. These he later re-drew on to discs which he projected in a machine called a Zoopraxiscope, producing an impression of a moving image on a screen, though with a cycle of movement limited to the number of separate images that could be placed around the edge of the disc.

In 1888 THOMAS ALVA EDISON met Muybridge, whose Zoopraxiscope evidently gave him the idea for a machine which would record and reproduce images as his phonograph already reproduced sound. He charged his English-born assistant, W. K. L. Dickson, to develop something on these lines. The following year in Paris Edison met Étienne Marey, who was pursuing similar lines of research to Muybridge, and from him derived the idea of using roll-film rather than glass discs or plates. By 1890 Dickson had perfected the Kinetograph, a moving picture camera; and by 1891 the Kinetoscope, a peepshow device for viewing the resulting images in movement. In 1893 the world's first film studio, 'The Black Maria' (so called from its tar-paper construction), was built in the grounds of Edison's laboratory at West Orange, to produce films for the Kinetoscopes, which were shortly afterwards put on the market by the Kinetoscope company, formed by Messrs Raff and Gammon.

Commercial exploitation proper began with the opening of the first Kinetoscope Parlour on Broadway in August 1894. The new toy was an immediate success; patrons enthusiastically dropped their nickels in the slots in the peepshow machines; and showmen at once perceived the advantages of projecting images on to a screen so that whole groups of people could watch them at once. Edison thereupon bought up the patents of Thomas Armat and Francis C. Jenikins who had devised a machine for projecting moving pictures, the Phantascope. Rechristening it the Vitascope, he gave the first demonstration of projected films in America in April 1896.

Meanwhile Dickson, having left the Edison factory, had developed a somewhat superior apparatus which was exploited by the American Mutoscope and Biograph Company. Other firms – Vitagraph, Kalem, Selig and Spoor and Lubin – rapidly entered the field, spurring Edison into launching a patents war in defence of his priority in film inventions. Despite this, the cinema took hold upon popular audiences, at first in the music halls, later in little closed-off spaces at the end of Kinetoscope Parlours and amusement arcades. The cinema had become an industry.

The earliest films ran for only a minute or so; and the repertoire was by and large confined to simple scenes of daily life (street scenes, fire engines and so on); glimpses of favourite stars or sportsmen (Annie Oakley, Buffalo Bill Cody and the prize-fighter Corbett all posed for Edison in the early days); topical news items, or more often re-enactments of them (which no-one thought any stranger or more fraudulent than drawings in the illustrated news magazines of the day); little jokes which were hardly more than animated versions of newspaper comic cartoons. At first films were bought outright by showmen at so many cents a foot; but from about 1903 the system of 'exchanges' grew up; showmen now rented films, thus introducing a third power in the industrial organization: to film manufacture and exhibition was added distribution. By 1907, over 100 such exchanges had taken place.

In 1905 the first 'nickelodeons' appeared: the name indicates the marriage of pretension and popularity. In America these permanent buildings set apart for the exclusive showing of films tended to arrive rather earlier than in Europe, where an intermediate period of fairground cinemas intervened between the music hall and

May Irwin and John C. Rice in 'The Kiss' (Thomas Edison, 1896)

'The Great Train Robbery' (Edwin S. Porter, 1903)

permanent cinema stages of exhibition. Films began to exceed the original one or two minutes; and as the story film developed audiences became only more enthusiastic and the film industry more prosperous.

The most significant early story films were two works by EDWIN S. PORTER. The earliest films had literally been animated photographs. It required little inventive effort, however, to *stage* scenes for the camera instead of simply photographing what was there; and only a short step further to assemble series of photographed scenes, like series of lantern slides or magazine pictures. Thus at Easter 1898 there were two rival versions of *The Passion of Our Lord* in which scenes from the life of Christ were illustrated, one scene following the next like Sunday School oleographs. As in the early films of MÉLIÈS, however, these stills resembled scenes in the theatre, each one independent, with its own beginning, middle and end. With *The Life of an American Fireman* (1902) Porter assembled a series of shots each one incomplete in itself but which combined with the rest to tell a story. Actuality shots of firemen and fire-engines were linked to staged shots of a bedroom rescue and (most remarkably) to a close-up of a hand sounding a fire alarm. Thus Porter proposed the basic idea of film editing. In 1903 *The Great Train Robbery* used his discoveries with still greater freedom, to tell a fairly elaborate Western story. Here Porter introduced the idea of parallel action. One group of characters was shown in one shot, a second group in the next shot; and the characters and action of the first were not taken up again until later in the film. This ambitious film, both as a result of its content and the newly exciting methods of its narrative, made a great impression upon audiences of the time and had an immediate effect upon film technique.

For some years more after this, however, films were regarded purely as industrial product, made in 'factories' at a regular production rate. Each producing firm affixed its trademark and publicized its films as a collective manufacture rather than individually. As the cinema industry continued to prosper, Edison became more aggressive in enforcing his patents. In 1909 the Edison, Biograph, Vitagraph, Lubin, Essanay, Selig, Pathé, Méliès and Kalem companies and the distributor Kleine banded together as the Motion Picture Patents Company, pooling their patents claims in exchange for licenses. Edison took royalties on all films sold. George Eastman, the major manufacturer of raw film stock, undertook to supply only members of this Trust. Levies were imposed on exhibitors in consideration of the right to use equipment, and there were sanctions to prevent them showing the product of non-Trust producers. In 1910, through the General Film Company, the Trust endeavoured to gain total monopoly of film exchanges.

Inevitably independent producers, distributors and exhibitors fought the Trust; and in 1913, WILLIAM FOX, a distributor who had been forced into production when the Trust refused to supply his film exchange, brought action under anti-trust legislation. By 1914 the Motion Picture Patents Company had become ineffectual. The struggle had had important side-effects however. Evading the pursuit of the Trust's strong-arm men, film manufacturers had discovered the advantages of California – proximity to the Mexican border in case of flight, reliable sunlight, cheap property and labour. The centre of production began to move from the Eastern towns – New York, Chicago, Philadelphia – and to drift to an area around Los Angeles and a small rural community called Hollywood.

The vital weapon in the Trust war was the competitive attractiveness of product. Producers were shaken out of the production-line mentality, and forced to try to make their films better and different from those of their rivals. One big attraction, it was realized, was the actors. Until now actors had not been identified by name. Stage-players were generally too ashamed of appearing in the 'galloping tintypes' to want publicity; while producers rightly feared that if they could be identified by the public, the actors would demand larger salaries. When growing numbers of picture-goers wrote to the studios asking for information about their favourites, they were ignored, and were obliged to identify them by made-up names – 'Little Mary', 'The Vitagraph Girl' and so on. Sometimes an artist would acquire as many names as the number of countries in which his films played. During the Trust war however one company after another began to identify their stars, in order to exploit their popularity. The first artist to be so identified was Florence Lawrence, 'The Biograph Girl', whose defection to the IMP Company was sensationally publicized.

One of the unwilling stage actors driven into films by unemployment was DAVID WARK GRIFFITH, whose first acting appearance in pictures was in an EDWIN S. PORTER film, *Rescued from an Eagle's Nest* (1907). Griffith's ambitions had always been to become a writer; and he was at least a little consoled when he began selling scenarios to the Biograph company instead of acting in films. In 1908 he was permitted to direct a film, *The Adventures of Dollie*; and even in this first effort he surprised his collaborators by the care he took over casting and staging. In the next five years he made over 500 short films, mostly less than a reel in length. 'David buckles to the job like a true sport', wrote his wife. 'It was *his job* and he would dignify it.' This was an understatement of the enthusiasm, energy and invention which Griffith brought to direction. His work during these years was to revolutionize the whole concept of film-making.

Striving quite simply to excel himself as a story-teller, Griffith explored all the means at his disposal. His literary ambitions and passion for 19th-century writers gave his films a much more sophisticated content than the cinema had known before: Griffith brought to the screen the works of Tennyson and Longfellow, Browning, Poe and Shakespeare. His love of Victorian painting also led him to enlarge the pictorial concepts of the screen, introducing composition, recognizing detail as well as grandeur, extreme close-ups as well as spectacular long-shots.

Most important, he developed Porter's discoveries to create a totally new artistic medium. Instead of just splitting up the action into small scenes, he sub-divided each scene into even briefer fragments, thus giving himself the possibility of varying viewpoint and emphasis from shot to shot. He discovered how to produce emphasis also through the composition and framing of shots, by the placing and the the movement of the camera, by the juxtaposition of the images and the speed and rhythm with which they followed one another. From 1909 (*The Lonely Villa*) Griffith developed his famous 'last-minute chases', using cross-cutting between two parallel actions in order to build up drama and suspense. He made dramatic use of the flash-back in *The New York Hat* (1912).

Griffith's ambitions became the aspirations of the American cinema. He could no longer be restrained by the limits of the one-reel film then in vogue; and against opposition from his employers he insisted that *Enoch Arden* (1911; the second of three versions he made of this subject) must be made in two reels. Two years later *Judith of Bethulia*, a grandiose historico-philosophical spectacle, reached the unprecedented length (for American films) of four reels, or one hour's running time. In this way, proving that audiences had the intellect and patience to follow a narrative of this length, Griffith made his own powerful contribution to the revolution in American cinema effected by the introduction of the 'feature' film – already becoming common in Europe by 1912, but for long resisted by the American industry. His total output was over 400 films.

Griffith's discoveries were not isolated experi-

Above: Blanche Sweet as 'Judith of Bethulia' (D. W. Griffith, 1913)
Below: Four scenes from 'Birth of a Nation' (D. W. Griffith, 1915): General Sherman's march to the sea; Lillian Gish, Vivian Cooper and the Ku Klux Klan; a battle scene showing smoke effects; Robert Harron

Top: Belshazzar's Palace in Babylon constructed by Huck Wortman for 'Intolerance' (D. W. Griffith, 1916)
Above and left: 3 shots of Mae Marsh in 'Intolerance'
Below: Lillian Gish in 'Way Down East' (D. W. Griffith, 1920)

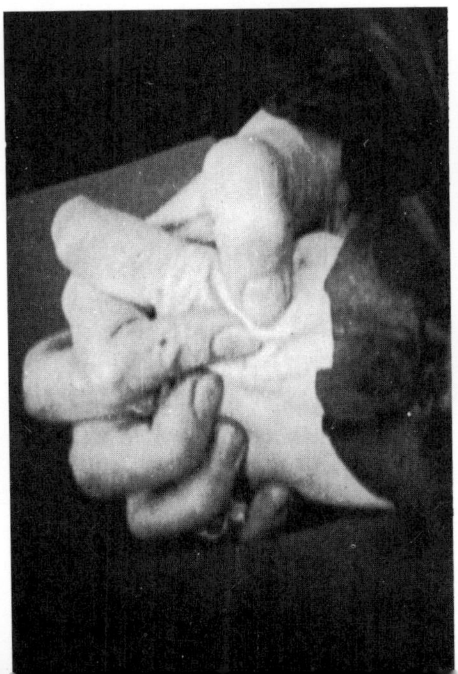

ments. The success of his films – which renewed the fortunes of the Biograph Company – made them famous; and every other director studied, adapted and imitated Griffith's innovations.

Thus the outbreak of the First World War found the USA suddenly in the creative forefront of world film production; while the abrupt cutting-off of foreign competition (though France's great cinematographic empire had already begun to crumble a year or two before) and her new, vast home market enabled America to lay the foundations for the domination of the world's cinema which she was to maintain for the next half century.

The characteristic monopolistic organization of the American cinema was already becoming evident; while the profitability of films had begun to attract investment, and with it increasing control by the financiers. Already, too, distribution as the means of access to exhibition outlets, had appeared as the crucial area of industrial organization. In 1915 the Motion Picture Patents Company was finally disbanded, though the General Film Company continued to distribute the productions of Biograph, Edison, Essanay, Kalem, Lubin, Selig, Vim and Vitagraph. Universal, established by CARL LAEMMLE, one of the most militant opponents of the Trust, grouped Universal, Bison, IMP, Joker, L-Ko, Nestor, Powers, Rex, Victor and the newsreel *Animated Weekly*. Mutual released the product of Broncho, Domino, Kay-Bee, Majestic, Reliance, Keystone, American, Beauty, Cub, Falstaff, Gaumont, Komic, Rialto, Thanhouser, North American and the newsreel *Mutual Weekly*. ADOLPH ZUKOR's Paramount, with a production tie-up with Famous Players – LASKY and Morosco, defied the more conservative elements of the industry to concentrate on the production of feature films. It very soon became clear that the future of the industry lay with features; and the survivors after the war was over were to be those producers who had embarked on this new production style – principally Universal, Fox, Paramount, World, Selznick, Metro, and a group of companies which had broken away from the General Film Company to form VLSE (the initial letters of Vitagraph, Lubin, Selig and Essanay).

In 1915 the three most powerful producer-directors in the industry were brought together in the Triangle Company, releasing through Mutual: Griffith, THOMAS INCE and MACK SENNETT. Griffith's two major works, *Birth of a Nation* (1915) and *Intolerance* (1916) were the culmination of his aesthetic and technical discoveries and altered the whole status of the cinema, giving it once and for all the dignity of an art but they were too big to be made within the Triangle organization. For Triangle Griffith produced a significant series of films, some directed by himself, others by directors of the calibre of John Emerson, W. CHRISTIE CABANNE, ALLAN DWAN and RAOUL WALSH. Ince was the ideal creative producer. The vanity which made him claim total credit for films directed by others has often obscured his real contribution in choosing and shaping material, in instituting the scenario as regular film practice; and demanding from his directors clear, direct and strong narrative values. Mack Sennett, an Irish-Canadian, who learned his craft by watching his senior D. W. Griffith in their Biograph days together, gave the cinema a fresh art form, the slapstick comedy – which derived variously from comic strips, circus, music hall, commedia dell'arte, and yet was unique and complete in itself. It was at once surreal, and a distorting mirror held up to the America of the 'teens and 'twenties. Sennett developed generations of clowns (his reluctance to raise their pay to star salaries ensured a rapid turnover), among whom the most illustrious was CHARLES CHAPLIN, the son of impoverished British music hall artists, who was recruited (unseen, it is said) by Sennett in the course of an American vaudeville tour in 1913.

Chaplin, along with MARY PICKFORD (a Griffith

Top: John Bunny in 'Father's Flirtation' (George D. Baker, 1914)
Above: Mabel Normand and Ford Sterling (centre) in 'Barney Oldfield's Race for Life' (Mack Sennett, 1913)
Right: Ford Sterling (left) and Fatty Arbuckle (right) as Keystone Cops (Mack Sennett, 1913)
Below: Warren William and Pearl White in 'The Perils of Pauline' (Louis Gasnier, 1914)

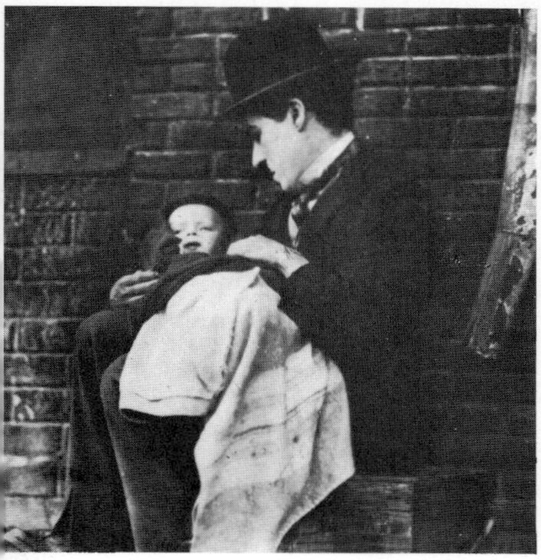

9 films directed by Charles Chaplin, who appeared himself in all but one, 'A Woman of Paris'.
Top: 'The Pawnshop' (1916)
Above: 'The Kid' (1920)
Below: Edna Purviance and Adolphe Men-jou in 'A Woman of Paris' (1923)

Top: 'The Gold Rush' (1925)
Above: 'The Circus' (1928)
Below: With Paulette Goddard in the closing shot of 'Modern Times' (1936)

Top: With Harry Myers in 'City Lights' (1931)
Above: With Paulette Goddard in 'The Great Dictator' (1940)
Below: With Margaret Hoffmann in 'Monsieur Verdoux' (1947)

actress from Biograph days) and DOUGLAS FAIRBANKS (recruited from Broadway to Triangle) acquired in the course of a year or two a world fame and popularity which enabled them to dominate the industry; and for several decades to come the star system would largely rule Hollywood economics. As the struggle to acquire monopolistic power over distribution grew more bitter, and Adolph Zukor's mighty Paramount organization was challenged, from 1917, by the First National Exhibitors' Circuit, the stars – including the star directors and producers, Griffith, Ince and Sennett – became vital pieces in the power game. In 1919 Chaplin, Pickford, Fairbanks and Griffith, having become too expensive for any producer to afford, founded their own distributing organization, United Artists.

The end of the war brought a short but sharp economic crisis. Audiences were reduced and cinemas closed by the influenza epidemic which took its toll of personnel in the cinema as well as in other industries. Such audiences as remained suddenly demanded quite different forms of entertainment; and many films already made to suit war needs had to be shelved. Many smaller firms were unable to survive this crisis; and the concentration of power in the hands of a few major firms, led by Paramount, Fox, Universal, Metro, First National and United Artists, was confirmed.

The end of the war reopened the American market to European producers, and the early 1920s revealed the strides that had been made elsewhere in cinema art: the naturalistic dramas of the Swedes with their fine pictorial qualities and psychological perception; the historical

Above: 'Civilisation' (Thomas Ince, 1916)
Below: Janet Gaynor and George O'Brien in 'Sunrise' (F. W. Murnau, 1927)

films of ERNST LUBITSCH and the new expressionist films from Germany. Hollywood embarked on a fresh policy, at once enriching the American cinema and despoiling her competitors by buying up foreign artists. Thus Lubitsch was brought to Hollywood, where, after an uncertain start, he inaugurated a totally new genre of light satirical comedy. FRIEDRICH MURNAU, E. A. DUPONT, PAUL LENI, ERICH POMMER, LUDWIG BERGER and Dmitri Buchowetski also came, to make less impression on the public than the stars they brought with them, such as POLA NEGRI and CONRAD VEIDT. From Hungary came fugitives from the collapse of the Republic of Councils of 1919: ALEXANDER KORDA, MICHAEL CURTIZ, PAUL FEJÖS. The Swedish cinema never survived the loss of its star directors VICTOR SJÖSTRÖM, who as Victor Seastrom did some of his most memorable work in the USA, and MAURITZ STILLER, whose American career had little result apart from the admirable *Hotel Imperial* (1927). MGM's most valuable Swedish investment, however, proved to be the actress GRETA GARBO, who surpassed all the other stars of the late silent period, gave the American cinema some of its finest acting performances and helped maintain European markets for over a decade.

The last decade of the silent cinema, between the Armistice and the Stock Market crash, was one of the most eventful in American history, an era of enormous technological and social revolution. The automobile, radio, cinema and advertising together changed the whole pattern of social and moral life. Returning servicemen and women newly emancipated – by war work as well as by the suffrage won in 1920 – demanded different social standards. America was fascinated by its own 'New Morality', propagated at one extreme by Scott Fitzgerald and at the other by the sensational evidences of the tabloid press. It was fascinated, too, by the nation's new economic and industrial self-confidence and prosperity. It was an era of unashamed materialism and get-rich-quick values and alongside the materialism went a vociferous and invigorating radical protest, most influential in the writings of Dreiser, Mencken, Lewis and Sherwood Anderson.

Prewar films had generally been characterized by the high moral tone of a Victorian, predominantly non-conformist, working-class and the setting of their stories had also tended to be the social milieu of the major part of the cinema's audience. The post-war films joyfully celebrated the relaxed moral atmospheres o the jazz age, and an imaginary society o beautiful, leisured, frivolous people. The Polly-anna ideal typified by the early Mary Pickfor and the other Griffith heroines – LILLIAN an DOROTHY GISH, Blanche Sweet, MAE MARSH BESSIE LOVE – already menaced by the lurid exotic sexuality of THEDA BARA, the *femme fatal* dreamed up by WILLIAM FOX and the directo Frank Powell in the years following 1915, nov gave way to the jazz babies and flappers and 'It girls: sportive, carefree, long-legged beautie like Colleen Moore, JOAN CRAWFORD and CLAR BOW.

The new values, the post-Freudian fascina tion with sex, the post-war woman, the dis carding of old codes of morality, the slackenin of marital ties, found their first clear expressio in a cycle of films made by CECIL B. DE MILL starting with *Old Wives For New* (1918). D Mille set off a vogue for films with pro vocative titles and ultra-modern content, whic

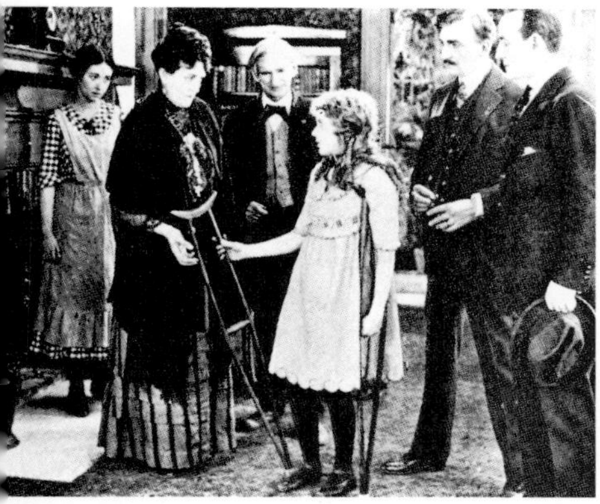

Top: Allan Jerome Eddy and Mary Pickford in 'Pollyanna' (Paul Powell, 1919)
Above: William S. Hart and Bessie Love in 'The Aryan' (Thomas Ince, 1916)
Below: Fritz Leiber and Theda Bara in 'Cleopatra' (J. Gordon Edwards, 1917)

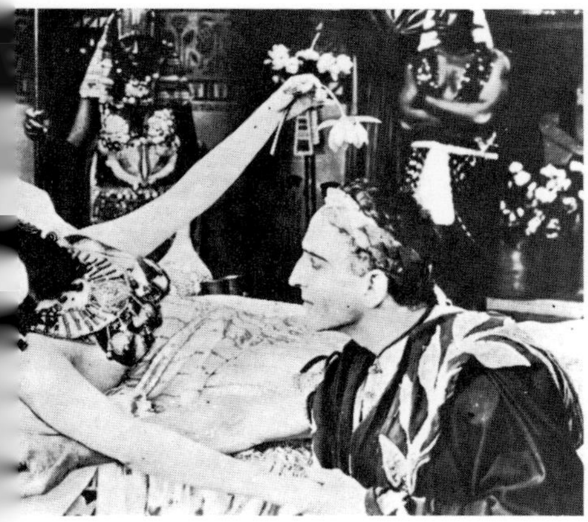

introduced backwoods America to the exciting new world of speakeasies, night-clubs, Eton crops, short skirts and batik gowns, and girls who smoked, drank, petted, and did not care. Sexual manners were handled with comedy and satire by Lubitsch, and with more brutal frankness and psychological truth by ERICH VON STROHEIM.

Nevertheless there was still clearly a place for the older values; indeed most of the jazz age dramas were in the end resolved with sentimental Old Morality denouements: erring wives returning to patient husbands, jazz babies marrying the boy next door. The success of Elinor Glyn, the middle-aged English novelist who became the arch-priestess of the New Morality, was due to her ability to reconcile new eroticism with old romanticism. Moreover two of the biggest successes of the immediate post-war period were Griffith's *Broken Blossoms* (1919) and *Way Down East* (1920), both firmly in the high-Victorian manner of sentimental tragedy.

Another sign of a degree of reaction against the cynical and materialistic standards of the day was the continuing romantic and nostalgic appeal of the Western, which reached its peak in this period with JOHN FORD's *The Iron Horse*

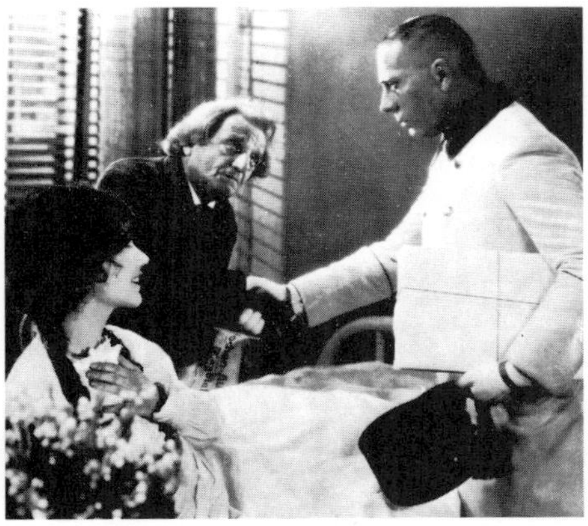

Top: 'The Covered Wagon' (James Cruze, 1923)
Above: Fay Wray, Cesare Gravina and Erich von Stroheim in 'The Wedding March' (von Stroheim, 1927)
Below: Clara Bow and Antonio Moreno in 'It' (Clarence Badger, 1927)

Top: Alla Nazimova and Rudolph Valentino in 'Camille' (Ray C. Smallwood, 1921)
Above: Rudolph Valentino as 'The Sheik' (George Melford, 1921)
Below: Douglas Fairbanks in 'The Black Pirate' (Alfred Parker, 1926)

(1924) and *Three Bad Men* (1926) and JAMES CRUZE's *The Covered Wagon* (1923). It was a period also of great Western stars, among them W. S. HART, TOM MIX, Ken Maynard, Hoot Gibson, and Harry Carey.

Another romantic escape was provided by the revival of the costume spectacle, whether in the richly decorative, urbanely satirical style of DOUGLAS FAIRBANKS, the erotic exoticism of RUDOLPH VALENTINO, or the florid mixtures of sex and sanctity which De Mille made his own speciality after *The Ten Commandments* (1924) and *King of Kings* (1927). A more touching romantic escape was indicated by the interest in anthropological or pseudo-anthropological films. The success of ROBERT FLAHERTY's *Nanook of the North* (1920–2) encouraged LASKY to send him to the South Seas to make *Moana* (1923–5). Merian C. Cooper and Ernest B. Schoedsack made *Grass* (1926) and *Chang* (1927); and meanwhile Tarzan and his 'never-never' forest maintained their popularity from generation to generation.

A new genre, born of the times, and not at all escapist, was the gangster film, which equivocally condemned and glorified the new race of criminals which was the joint bequest of war and prohibition. The best of these were JOSEF VON STERNBERG's trilogy *Underworld* (1927), *Dragnet* and, in *milieu* rather than plot, *The Docks of New York* (1928), and LEWIS MILESTONE's *The Racket* (1928).

Perhaps the greatest contribution made by this period of American cinema to screen art was the comedy. Apart from Chaplin, who during this period directed a brilliant comedy of manners in which he did not play, *A Woman of Paris* (1923), as well as some of his greatest films, including *Shoulder Arms* (1918) and *The Gold Rush* (1925), there were the incomparable BUSTER KEATON, a great director as well as a unique clown, HARRY LANGDON, HAROLD LLOYD (who alone among the great clowns had not had his early training in vaudeville), RAYMOND GRIFFITH, Marion Davies, and a galaxy of others whose gifts would have been outstanding in any period but one so rich.

James Murray, Eleanor Boardman, Estelle Clark and Bert Roach in 'The Crowd' (King Vodor, 1928)

Top: Betty Compson and George Bancroft in 'The Docks of New York' (Josef von Sternberg, 1928)
Above: Buster Keaton in 'The General' (Clyde Bruckman and Keaton, 1926)
Below: Harold Lloyd in 'The Freshman' (F. Newmeyer and S. Taylor, 1925)

In addition to the directors already cited, it is necessary to mention the veterans J. STUART BLACKTON and SIDNEY OLCOTT; ALLAN DWAN, a prolific director who made some fine comedies with GLORIA SWANSON as star; HERBERT BRENON, who specialized in glossy prestige pictures; HENRY KING, whose *Tol'able David* (1921) was a major influence on Soviet silent cinema; the variously gifted KING VIDOR, with *The Big Parade* (1925) and *The Crowd* (1928); CLARENCE BROWN, who created the most successful vehicles for such stars as Valentino and Garbo; MAURICE TOURNEUR, a French director with an outstanding visual sense; REX INGRAM, who first achieved success with the spectacular *Four Horsemen of the Apocalypse* (1921) and afterwards made a speciality of exotic and particularly oriental drama; TOD BROWNING, a master of the horrific and bizarre; MAL ST CLAIR, and FRANK CAPRA, both Sennett graduates who developed distinctive lines in comedy; and outstandingly professional directors like HOWARD HAWKS, WILLIAM WYLER, WILLIAM WELLMAN, SIDNEY FRANKLIN and FRANK BORZAGE, who were to produce major work in the next decade and sound films.

The 1920s were a golden era for American cinema. Yet already a degree of artistic decline could be discerned. The increasing control by large financial organizations inevitably tended to have a limiting effect. It is true that the producers' ever more urgent search for predictable box-office values, taken with the rise of the big studios and the great profitability of film production, served to raise technical standards of production. The crafts of SCREENWRITING, title writing, DESIGN AND ART DIRECTION and CINEMATOGRAPHY were all brought to standards as high as at any time or any place in the history of the cinema.

At the same time this demand for the predictable commercial values obliged producers to follow certain inhibiting policies: the star system; the practice of adapting known literary or stage successes, regardless of inherent suitability for film purposes; the 'cycle', following any successful film with countless stereotypes. More and more, too, films moved away from real life into escapist dreams which were by no means out of sympathy with the reactionary interests and policies of the controlling financiers. Though Hollywood's extraordinary line-up of outstanding cinema artists remained and produced an increasing number of remarkable individual films, the second half of the 1920s saw a stagnation in the general level of cinema production. The arrival of talking pictures was conveniently timed to save the industry, which even before the Stock Market crash had shown signs of the oncoming slump as audiences deserted the cinemas. DR

THE SOUND PERIOD

The Establishment of Sound: the 1930s and the Pre-War Film Sound had, of course, always been envisaged as an accompaniment to motion pictures. But until the 1920s the technical problems involved had proved insuperable – facilities for recording existed on disc, but failure lay in proper synchronization with the film, and in amplifying the sound adequately in theatre conditions. It was not until the 1920s that the amplification of sound-on-disc became practicable in the theatres, but by this time Lee De Forrest and others had developed independently the recording of sound-on-film by means of the photo-electric cell, registering sound impulses in terms of a continuous sound-track made up of fluctuating patterns of light and shade running alongside the picture track.

The two systems, sound-on-disc and sound-on-film, ran neck and neck. Warner Brothers used sound-on-disc with their Vitaphone system, while WILLIAM FOX turned to sound-on-film, using initially the German Tri-Ergon system. *What Price Glory?* (1927) had a music track so recorded in 1927, and Fox Movietone News, the first sound newsreel, appeared in April 1927. For a while silent films, disc-accompanied films, and films with sound-on-film ran in parallel as exhibitors hastened to equip themselves as best they could to meet the public demand for sound in one form or another, inspired by the success of the part-talking (and singing) picture with AL JOLSON, *The Jazz Singer* (first shown October 1927) and the first all-talking picture, *The Lights of New York* (first shown July 1928), both Warner productions with sound-on-disc. After such tentative beginnings, the sound film was fully established; in 1928, 1,300 of the 20,500 American movie theatres were wired for sound, and by 1929, 9,000. The industry had to adjust itself firmly to the new medium.

Al Jolson and May McAvoy in 'The Jazz Singer' (A. Crosland, 1927)

The great Hollywood companies of the 1930s built up an insurance policy based on safety in numbers – the product that succeeded sustained the product that failed. The interlocking of production, distribution and exhibition assured their product (good and bad) its regular outlets to the public. The ceaseless turn-over of films was what mattered, and after the first problems of conquering the effects of the Depression and the coming of sound and all that this entailed technically and financially, reliable turn-over was what Hollywood came to stand for. Its films represented a great success-story, and built their own legend alike in North America and in the rest of the world. The pressures on the world public of the constant recurrence of the familiar star images in a constant succession of films at their local theatres meant that they were prepared to accept as 'great' entertainment almost anything Hollywood had to offer, once they had adjusted their ears to the vagaries of the early sound tracks and (in English-speaking countries abroad) to American speech. Backed by incessant publicity and the joys of the 'fan' magazines, American films became virtually inescapable.

The cost at first was great; equipping the studios and the theatres for sound; finding new stars to replace the large numbers whose voices, or accents, or lack of English, made them unsuitable for the new medium; contracting new writers to provide the flow of dialogue on which the initial sound films became over-dependent. Among the established stars beaten by sound in Hollywood was, for example, POLA NEGRI; among those who survived was GARBO. Many new players, such as Ann Harding and FREDRIC MARCH, came from Broadway to replace those whose career in Hollywood was over. Salaries rose; but the companies became even more authoritarian in handling their creative staff, tying directors, actors, writers, and technicians alike with long-term contracts which could hinder as much as develop their careers.

Directors and stars were ordered, or pressured, into over-production – MICHAEL CURTIZ, for example, making no less than 44 films between 1930 and 1939, and JOHN FORD 26. Writers were kept in separate departments from directors, who were assigned scripts to shoot, often at short notice, which they had played no part in developing. The build-up of creative writer-director relationships was rare – like that, for example, between DUDLEY NICHOLS and John Ford. [See SCREENWRITING]. Yet the imaginative interplay between writer and director was of crucial importance for the sound film, and this was evident in some of the first effective films which used dialogue intelligently and not slavishly, such as MAMOULIAN's *Applause* (1929) and MILESTONE's *All Quiet on the Western Front*.

The industry ran into a second, and in fact deeper economic depression around 1933, with falling attendances at the theatres and labour problems in the studios. Producers were jolted into putting their houses in somewhat better order, regulating employment on fairer lines; distributors were forced to some extent to abandon block bookings, which forced exhibitors to take so many bad films along with the indifferent in order to get the plums in a package deal. 1934 saw the results in a recovery which was to show some 80,000,000 tickets a week sold at the American box-offices. The slump turned over for a while into a boom. 1938 proved, however, to be another year of stress, but by this time the film technicians had established their unions, while in 1938 the Screenwriters' Guild became the negotiating body for writers. The producers recognized the Directors and the Writers Guilds in 1939.

The Film Production Code, established by the Hays Office and adopted by producers in 1930 as technically an act of self-censorship of films by the industry, was frequently disregarded, and this led to the formation of the Catholic body, the National Legion of Decency, which classified films on moral grounds. The Hays Office, as administrative centre for the Code, appointed Joseph I. Breen to take charge of censorship, giving him power to impose fines on producers who released pictures without the Seal of Approval of the Production Code Administration. This proved for long an onerous burden for writers and directors, a barrier against the mature handling of sexual and other subjects.

The big companies whose trade marks were becoming so familiar on the screen, established certain 'house' styles. At the head stood the richly-endowed Metro-Goldwyn-Mayer studios, with product rising to over 40 films a year, controlled by LOUIS B. MAYER (the former junk dealer turned exhibitor and producer), who had been in charge since 1924 and was to stay in power until 1951. MGM's financial links were with the Chase National Bank, and its key style was set early by IRVING THALBERG (died 1936), a man of considerable if erratic taste, Mayer's second-in-command and husband of the MGM star, NORMA SHEARER. He was backed by the distinguished designer, CEDRIC GIBBONS, and the sound engineer, Douglas Shearer, brother of Norma. MGM's sets were magnificent, its photography (by WILLIAM DANIELS, Harold Rosson and others) bright and impeccable, its sound recording of the highest possible quality for the period. Its contract stars, in addition to NORMA SHEARER, included GRETA GARBO, JOAN CRAWFORD, JEAN HARLOW, MYRNA LOY, CLARK GABLE, SPENCER TRACY, WILLIAM POWELL and, later, MICKEY ROONEY; its directors included CLARENCE BROWN,

Top: William Powell and Myrna Loy in 'The Thin Man' (W. S. Van Dyke, 1934)
Above: Douglas Fairbanks Jnr (centre) and Edward G. Robinson in 'Little Caesar' (Mervyn Le Roy, 1931)
Below: Paul Muni and Erin O'Brien-Moore in 'The Life of Emile Zola' (William Dieterle, 1937)

who made many of Garbo's films, W. S. VAN DYKE II (*The Thin Man* series with Powell and Loy; the technically incomparable *San Francisco*, 1936), SIDNEY FRANKLIN (*The Good Earth*, 1937), Jack Conway (*Viva Villa!*, 1934, with HOWARD HAWKS; *A Tale of Two Cities*, 1935; the comedy *Too Hot to Handle*, 1938), and VICTOR FLEMING (*Gone with the Wind*, 1939; *The Wizard of Oz*, 1939). LUBITSCH also made some of his best films for MGM, including *The Merry Widow* (1934) and *Ninotchka* (1939).

In contrast with the lavish splendour of MGM was the penny-pinching at Warners, controlled in Hollywood by JACK L. WARNER, and by his brothers Harry and Albert in New York. They were the sons of a Polish immigrant pedlar and had left their various trades to become exhibitors and finally producers. Because of the financial straits of their company they had staked everything during the later 1920s on pushing sound onto the film industry. Warners was still unstable financially during the early 1930s, but their contract stars included (at low, long-term salaries) BETTE DAVIS, BARBARA STANWYCK, HUMPHREY BOGART, JAMES CAGNEY, ERROL FLYNN, and PAUL MUNI. The company was absolutely tied to quick turnover, at least up to 1935; they preferred punch to polish, and they caned their directors into high-speed production much of which had a journalistic verisimilitude and a liberal social conscience. They held great talent in thrall – the prolific Hungarian, MICHAEL CURTIZ (*20,000 Years in Sing Sing*, 1933); *Charge of the Light Brigade*, 1936; *Kid Galahad*, 1937; and very many others), MERVYN LE ROY (*Little Caesar*, 1931; *I am a Fugitive from a Chain Gang*, 1932; *Gold Diggers of 1933*; and *They won't Forget*, 1937), the German WILLIAM DIETERLE (*A Midsummer Night's Dream*, 1935; *The Story of Louis Pasteur*, 1935; *The Life of Emile Zola*, 1937; *Juarez*, 1939), and the Romanian JEAN NEGULESCO, whose work was to develop fully in the 1940s.

Paramount's strength lay in the field of sophistication. Like Warners, it had its financial difficulties, and was controlled by ADOLPH ZUKOR, who had been born in Hungary, traded as a furrier, and had been in the film industry as exhibitor and producer from the earliest years of the century. Paramount's films were remarkable for their visual beauty (HANS DREIER was their chief designer) and camerawork (by Victor Milner, and Theodore Sparkuhl), producing a more diffused image than MGM's electrifying clarity. Their key players included CLAUDETTE COLBERT, Miriam Hopkins, GARY COOPER and FREDRIC MARCH, while their principal directors were CECIL B. DE MILLE (from 1932, making such films as *The Sign of the Cross*, 1932; *Cleopatra*, 1934; *The Crusades*, 1935; *The Plainsman*, 1936; *Union Pacific*, 1939), ERNST LUBITSCH (*Trouble in Paradise*, 1932; *Bluebeard's Eighth Wife*, 1938), and REUBEN MAMOULIAN (*Applause*, 1929; *City Streets*, 1931; *Dr Jekyll and Mr Hyde*, 1932; *Love Me Tonight*, 1932). Mamoulian also made *Queen Christina* (1933) with GRETA GARBO for MGM. Later Paramount was to be joined by PRESTON STURGES, MITCHELL LEISEN and BILLY WILDER as writers and directors.

The other major companies were Twentieth Century Fox (following a merger in 1935), RKO, Universal, Columbia, and United Artists, which acted as distributor for independent producers. The aim of many of Hollywood's top directors was to become independent, working only on the subjects of their choice with various production companies. STERNBERG, originally contracted with his star MARLENE DIETRICH to Paramount – for whom he made *Morocco* (1930), *Dishonored* (1931), *Shanghai Express* and *Blonde Venus* (1932), *The Scarlet Empress* (1934) and *The Devil is a Woman* (1935), all with Dietrich – later worked for Columbia and MGM, as well as starting the abortive *I, Claudius* in England for KORDA. He proved too difficult, too intense and obsessive a director to suit Hollywood in the 1930s, with a central European sensuality of feeling for the pictorial image; his main cameraman at Paramount on later films was LEE GARMES, and his designer the German, HANS DREIER. Other directors of the 1930s who transcended the studios were CAPRA, FORD, CUKOR, WYLER, VIDOR, WELLMAN, and HAWKS, while directors as wholly independent as CHAPLIN worked only for themselves. KEATON, unhappily, gave up his independence and allowed himself to become stultified at MGM. His life and his art collapsed.

Ford in the early years of sound worked with Fox, Universal, Goldwyn, MGM, and RKO Radio. Among his many films of the period were: *Arrowsmith* (1931), *Pilgrimage* (1933), *The Informer* (1935), *Mary of Scotland* (1936) and *Stagecoach* (1939). Mostly he tailored his style to the studio sponsoring him, but gradually during the 1930s in association with his favourite scriptwriter, DUDLEY NICHOLS, he consolidated

Top: Gary Cooper in 'The Plainsman' (Cecil B. De Mille, 1936)
Above: 'Union Pacific' (Cecil B. De Mille, 1939)
Below: 'Stagecoach' (John Ford, 1939)

his own personal style. It is well known that to make *The Informer* Ford agreed with RKO Radio to take a share in any profits in lieu of salary. The film was shot in three weeks at a cost of little over $200,000; it won four Oscars (one each for Ford and Nichols) and established the importance of the writer-director principle, which Capra was also to establish with ROBERT RISKIN, initially at Columbia, with *American Madness* (1932), *Lady for a Day* (1933), and *It Happened One Night* (1934). By the time of *Mr Deeds Goes to Town* (1936), Capra could put on his films, 'A Frank Capra Production', Howard Hawks, another director slowly moving towards independence, took a co-production credit with HOWARD HUGHES on *Scarface* (*Shame of a Nation*, 1932), and sometimes claimed production and sometimes not, on his films of the 1930s such as *The Dawn Patrol* (1930), the comedy *Twentieth Century* (1934), the tragedy *The Road to Glory* (1936) as well as *Bringing Up Baby* (1938) and *Only Angels Have Wings* (1939). Hawks frequently worked with the writer BEN HECHT and later William Faulkner.

MILESTONE during the 1930s made some of the most important early American sound films – *All Quiet on the Western Front* (1930), *The General Died at Dawn* (1936), *Of Mice and Men* (1939). KING VIDOR, working for the studios on *Billy the Kid* (1930) and other films, financed *Our Daily Bread* (1934) himself, but its propaganda brought failure at the box-office and he was forced to return to commercial production. Wyler turned to Goldwyn to sponsor many of his films – *Dead End* (1937), *Wuthering Heights* (1939). Cukor moved from studio to studio, ending at MGM and making, with SELZNICK, *Dinner at Eight* and *Little Women* (1933), *David Copperfield* (1934), *Romeo and Juliet* and *Camille* with Garbo (1936). Wellman worked with Selznick when he made *A Star is Born* and *Nothing Sacred* (1937) before producing his own films, such as *Men with Wings* (1938).

Top: Gary Cooper (left) and Gustav von Seyffertitz (at the board) in 'Mr Deeds Goes to Town' (Frank Capra, 1936)
Above: Paul Muni and Henry Armetta in 'Scarface' (Howard Hughes, 1932)
Below: Joel McCrea and Humphrey Bogart in 'Dead End' (William Wyler, 1937)

For the standard turn-over of films and works of quality alike, certain main genres of film-making came to be recognized as 'Hollywood' entertainment in the eyes of both the film-makers and their audiences. The principal genres, with typical examples, might be listed as follows:

The Western, for example: *The Big Trail* (RAOUL WALSH, 1929), *The Virginian* (VICTOR FLEMING, 1929), *The Plainsman* (CECIL B. DE MILLE, 1936), *Stagecoach* (JOHN FORD, 1939), *Northwest Passage* (KING VIDOR, 1940; notable for its 18th-century setting).

First World War Films, for example: *Hell's Angels* (HOWARD HUGHES, Luther Reed and JAMES WHALE, 1930), *All Quiet on the Western Front* (LEWIS MILESTONE, 1930), *The Dawn Patrol* (HOWARD HAWKS, 1930).

Crime and Gangster Films, for example: *Little Caesar* (MERVYN LE ROY, 1931), *The Big House* (GEORGE ROY HILL, 1930), *The Public Enemy* (WILLIAM WELLMAN, 1931), *Scarface* (HOWARD HAWKS, 1932), *I Am a Fugitive from a Chain*

Greta Garbo and Robert Taylor in 'Camille' (George Cukor, USA, 1936)

Gang (MERVYN LE ROY, 1932), *Blood Money* (ROWLAND BROWN, 1934), *They Won't Forget* (MERVYN LE ROY, 1937).

Musicals, for example: *Broadway Melody* (Harry Beaumont, 1929), *King of Jazz* (John Murray Anderson, 1930), *Love Me Tonight* (REUBEN MAMOULIAN, 1932), *The Big Broadcast of 1932* (with BING CROSBY) and successors, *42nd Street* (LLOYD BACON and BUSBY BERKELEY, a choreographer originally brought from Broadway by SAM GOLDWYN, 1933), *Gold Diggers of 1933* (Mervyn LeRoy and Busby Berkeley) and successors, *The Gay Divorcée* (MARK SANDRICH, 1934, starring FRED ASTAIRE and GINGER ROGERS, who, with choreographer HERMES PAN, were established at RKO for their series of musicals), *One Hundred Men and a Girl* (HENRY KOSTER, 1937, with DEANNA DURBIN), *The Wizard of Oz* (Victor Fleming, 1939, with JUDY GARLAND).

The Social, Biographical and Literary Film, for example: *Ah Wilderness* (Clarence Brown, 1935), *Our Daily Bread* (King Vidor, 1934), *Fury* (FRITZ LANG, 1936), *Louis Pasteur* (WILLIAM DIETERLE, 1935), *You Only Live Once* (Fritz Land, 1937), *Émile Zola* (William Dieterle, 1937), *Of Mice and Men* (Lewis Milestone, 1939), *Confessions of a Nazi Spy* (ANATOLE LITVAK, 1939), *Mr Smith goes to Washington* (FRANK CAPRA, 1939), *The Grapes of Wrath* (John Ford, 1940), *Dr Ehrlich's Magic Bullet* (William Dieterle, 1940), *Meet John Doe* (Frank Capra, 1941), *Citizen Kane* (ORSON WELLES, 1940).

Romance and Drama, for example: *Grand Hotel* (EDMUND GOULDING, 1932), *Queen Christina* (Mamoulian, 1933), *A Star is Born* (Wellman, 1937), *Wuthering Heights* (Wyler, 1939), *Ninotchka* (Lubitsch, 1939), *The Letter* (Wyler, 1940), *Our Town* (SAM WOOD, 1940), *Kings Row* (Sam Wood, 1942), *The Little Foxes* (Wyler, 1941).

Top: Edward Woods and James Cagney in 'Public Enemy' (William Wellman, 1931)
Above: Bessie Love (right) and Charles King in 'Broadway Melody' (Harry Beaumont, 1929)
Below: Fred Astaire in 'Top Hat' (Mark Sandrich, 1935)

Top: Bruce Cabot in 'Fury' (Fritz Lang, 1936)
Above: Francis Lederer and Edward G. Robinson in 'Confessions of a Nazi Spy' (Anatole Litvak, 1939)
Opposite: The Marx Brothers in 'A Night at the Opera' (Sam Wood, 1935)
Below: Henry Fonda in 'The Grapes of Wrath' (John Ford, 1940)

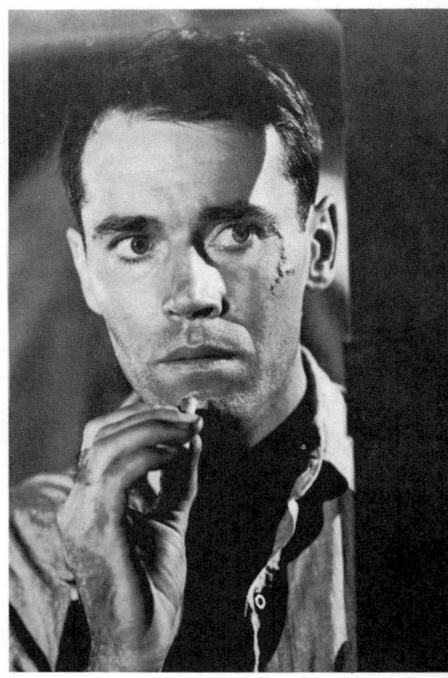

Macabre, Monster and Horror Films, for example: *Frankenstein* (JAMES WHALE, 1931, with BORIS KARLOFF), *Dr Jekyll and Mr Hyde* (Mamoulian, 1932), *Freaks* (TOD BROWNING, 1932), *King Kong* (Ernest B. Schoedsack and Merian C. Cooper, 1933), *The Invisible Man* (Whale, 1932), *The Black Cat* (Edgar G. Ulmer, 1934), *The Hunchback of Notre Dame* (Dieterle, 1939).
Epics and Period Spectacles, for example: *Cimarron* (WESLEY RUGGLES, 1930), *The Sign of the Cross* (De Mille, 1932), *Cleopatra* (De Mille, 1934), *San Francisco* (Van Dyke, 1936), *Lost Horizon* (Capra, 1937), *Gone with the Wind* (Fleming, 1939).
Burlesque, Slapstick and Farce, for example: *Animal Crackers* (V. Heerman, 1930) and other MARX BROTHERS films, the films of LAUREL and HARDY, *Road to Singapore* (V. Schertzinger, 1939, with BOB HOPE, BING CROSBY, and DOROTHY LAMOUR), *Hellzapoppin* (H. C. Potter, 1942).
Sophisticated Comedy and Satire, for example: *City Lights* (CHAPLIN, 1931), *She Done Him Wrong* (Lowell Sherman, 1933, with MAE WEST), *It Happened One Night* (Capra, 1934), *The Thin Man* series, beginning 1934, *Ruggles of Red Gap* (LEO MCCAREY, 1934), *Modern Times* (Chaplin, 1936), *Mr Deeds Goes to Town* (Capra, 1936), *The Women* (Cukor, 1939), *Midnight* (Leisen, 1939), *Tom, Dick and Harry* (GARSON KANIN, 1940), *The Great Dictator* (Chaplin, 1940).

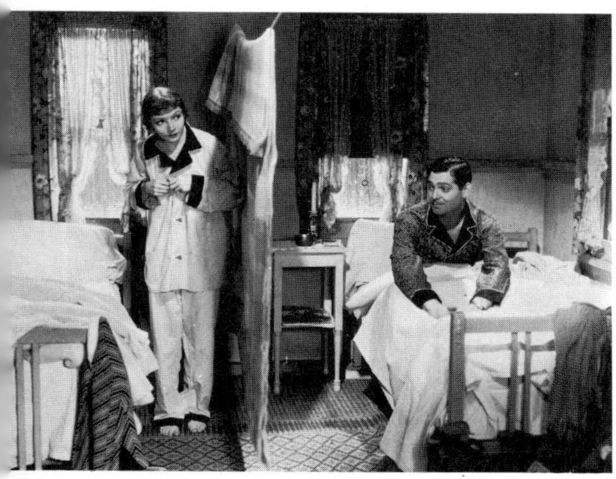

Above: 'The Sign of the Cross' (Cecil B. De Mille, 1932)
Below: Claudette Colbert and Clark Gable in 'It Happened One Night' (Frank Capra, 1934)

Top: Orson Welles in 'Citizen Kane' (Welles, 1940)
Above: Herbert Marshall, Teresa Wright and Bette Davis in 'The Little Foxes' (William Wyler, 1941)
Below: Fredric March in 'Dr Jekyll and Mr Hyde' (Reuben Mamoulian, 1932)

Hollywood has always represented a curious balance between harsh business dealing, keen artistry, foolish extravagance, and technical proficiency. Intellectuals abounded at all times, but they were kept in cages by their showmen-keepers, and normally let out only when they bartered their skills in a manner acceptable to their producers. Hollywood naturally became a place where unhappiness and frustrated ambition were matched by inflated fees and salaries, bringing success and affluence for those who emerged on top of the heap. The emphasis in entertainment was always on 'escape' – unreal romance and exciting melodrama, the spectacle of luxury and 'historical' flamboyance, the adventures of the outdoor rendered palatable to the city dweller, and the thrills of crime purveyed to the startled gaze of the law-abiding. A few films which were more socially aware came to be made, including the late 1930s type of biographical film. Such films were usually backed by the more up-and-coming individualist producers, with a more 'advanced' outlook than that of the now elderly heads of studios. The gangster, once a kind of hero in the eyes of the public, became recognized as a public enemy, and crime prevention and the exercise of the penal system (with *its* violences) were presented more realistically. Certain stars, EDWARD G. ROBINSON, JAMES CAGNEY and HUMPHREY BOGART, were associated with this significant branch of production. But if the Hollywood film was overwhelmingly in favour of the *status quo* in society, in the 1930s it nevertheless produced a splendid body of work by talented writers and directors, which, despite the studio system, now seems recognizably personal and consistent. Many of these once despised 'entertainment' films now seem fresher and more evocative than deliberately social 'significant' work in both the feature and the documentary field.

In spite of the censorship, sex was dealt with more explicitly in the films of JEAN HARLOW and the burlesques of MAE WEST, while women began to have far more edge to their characters on the screen with such stars as KATHARINE HEPBURN, CAROLE LOMBARD, BETTE DAVIS, MYRNA LOY and CLAUDETTE COLBERT. The men stopped being stuffed dummies, heroic in action and dreamy in love, and became more quirky and quicker-witted, like CARY GRANT, FRED MACMURRAY or CLARK GABLE. Men and women alike, theirs are the films which tend to survive best from the prewar product of Hollywood.

The War and its Aftermath
The USA entered on war following the Japanese attack on Pearl Harbour on 7 December 1941, and the American declaration of war on Germany on 11 December. The years of war led to the flood of war films – at first conditioned to the Hollywood treatment, since Hollywood, remote from all battlefronts, had no other rule than the codes of drama with which to measure these new excitements.

America's dislike of Nazism had already broken out in films made prewar. LITVAK's *Confessions of a Nazi Spy* (1939) heralded the anti-Nazi content in *The Mortal Storm* (FRANK BORZAGE, 1940), *Foreign Correspondent* (ALFRED HITCHCOCK, 1940), CHAPLIN's *The Great Dictator* (1940), *Man Hunt* (Lang, 1941) and others. The wartime films came somewhat nearer to reality in Lang's story of the assassination of Heydrich, *Hangmen also Die* (1943) and *The Hitler Gang* (John Farrow, 1944), a study of Hitler's rise to power, a difficult, almost impossible subject bravely tackled with a cast of refugee Germans. Uncertain in their understanding of the nature of Nazism, many films attempted ridicule and caricature of the Nazis – the cultured Germans appearing, for example as svelte and sadistic piano-players – or turned the situation into a vehicle for spy and resistance melodrama. An extravagant example of this was *Above Suspicion* (1943), with JOAN CRAWFORD and FRED MACMURRAY lurking in Southern Germany in pursuit of a magnetic mine formula: – 'Heil Hitler!' – 'Nuts to you, dope'. Far better was CURTIZ's memorably entertaining *Casablanca* (1942), with its wonderful cast including BOGART, CLAUDE RAINS, VEIDT, LORRE, Sidney Greenstreet, and INGRID BERGMAN. Hollywood developed a strange, pastiche Europe in its war films, as in the famous *Mrs Miniver* (1942) and *The White Cliffs of Dover* (1943), both of which impressed Dr Goebbels greatly when he screened his captured prints. Hitchcock made one of his more interesting films in *Lifeboat* (1943), a fable of Nazism versus a relatively unidealized democracy.

The war films were often embarrassing until a vein of true realism began to be discovered and worked. Of the artificial variety, Gregory Ratoff's *Song of Russia* (1944) with ROBERT TAYLOR, or RAOUL WALSH's *Objective Burma* (1945), with ERROL FLYNN conquering Burma without the British, are sufficient to remember what studio attitudes to war were like. Better, though still artificial, were Milestone's films, *North Star* and *Edge of Darkness* (both 1943) and *The Purple Heart* (1944). Among the best wartime fiction films were *The Story of G.I. Joe* (Wellman, 1945), Lewis Seiler's *Guadalcanal Diary* (1943) and Milestone's incomparable *A Walk in the Sun* (1945). Most of the good war films from the US came near the end of the war or were documentaries made by directors who donned uniform to make them – like Col. William Wyler's *Memphis Belle*, the *Why We Fight* series of documentaries made under the supervision of Col. Frank Capra and the imaginative reportage of JOHN HUSTON. [See DOCUMENTARY FILM.]

Generally Hollywood continued to make the kind of films on which its world reputation was based, though many actors and technicians were eventually to be drafted when war had

Henry Fonda and Cathy Downs in 'My Darling Clementine' (John Ford, 1946)

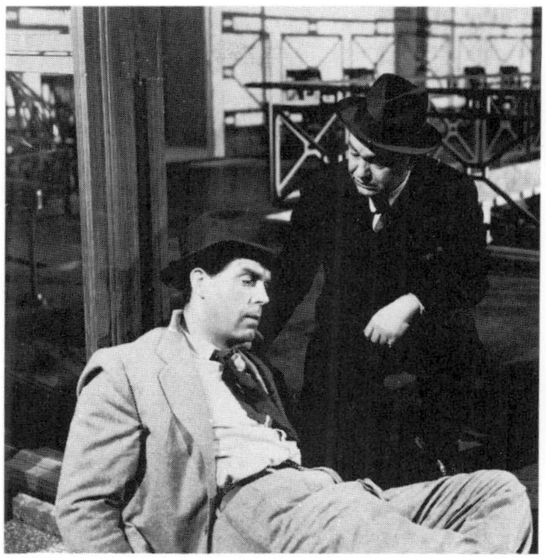

Above: Fred MacMurray and Edward G. Robinson in 'Double Indemnity' (Billy Wilder, 1944)
Below: Dana Andrews in 'A Walk in the Sun' (Lewis Milestone, 1945)

begun. But the war years (with the lead-in of 1941 included), saw many fine films including:

1941: *The Maltese Falcon* (JOHN HUSTON), *All That Money Can Buy* (Dieterle), *Lady Hamilton* (ALEXANDER KORDA), *The Lady Eve* (STURGES)

1942: *I Married a Witch* (RENÉ CLAIR), *Cat People* (JACQUES TOURNEUR), the first of a series of horror films produced by VAL LEWTON at RKO, *The Oxbow Incident* (Wellman), *The Magnificent Ambersons* (Welles), *The Moon and Sixpence* (ALBERT LEWIN), *The Palm Beach Story* and *Sullivan's Travels* (STURGES), *Keeper of the Flame* (CUKOR)

1943: *Shadow of a Doubt* (Hitchcock), *Flesh and Fantasy* (JULIEN DUVIVIER)

1944: *Phantom Lady* and *Christmas Holiday* (ROBERT SIODMAK), *Laura* (OTTO PREMINGER), *Double Indemnity* (BILLY WILDER), *The Lodger* (John Brahm), *The Mask of Dimitrios* (JEAN NEGULESCO), *It Happened Tomorrow* (Clair), *Wilson* (HENRY KING), *Jane Eyre* (ROBERT STEVENSON), *The Miracle of Morgan's Creek* and *Hail the Conquering Hero* (STURGES)

1945: *Scarlet Street* (Lang), *Mildred Pierce* (Curtiz), *Murder, My Sweet* (EDWARD DMYTRYK), *The Picture of Dorian Grey* (Lewin), *The Lost Weekend* (Wilder), *The Southerner* (JEAN RENOIR)

Top: Burgess Meredith in 'The Story of G.I. Joe' (William Wellman, 1945)
Above: Dana Andrews in 'The Best Years of Our Lives' (William Wyler, 1946)
Below: Humphrey Bogart, Sidney Greenstreet, Peter Lorre and Mary Astor in 'The Maltese Falcon' (John Huston, 1941)

1946: *The Spiral Staircase* (Siodmak), *The Big Sleep* (Hawks), *The Stranger* (Welles), *The Searching Wind* (Dieterle), *The Best Years of our Lives* (Goldwyn and Wyler), *The Diary of a Chambermaid* (Renoir), *My Darling Clementine* (Ford), *Duel in the Sun* (King Vidor and others; scripted by DAVID O. SELZNICK himself), *The Yearling* (CLARENCE BROWN).

During this period the more celebrated women stars included: BETTE DAVIS (*The Little Foxes, Now Voyager, Stolen Life*), JOAN CRAWFORD (*A Woman's Face, Mildred Pierce*), BARBARA STANWYCK (*The Lady Eve, Double*

Indemnity, *Cry Wolf*, and *Sorry, Wrong Number*), GREER GARSON (*Mrs Miniver*, *Random Harvest*). Some of their films constituted the powerful 'women's pictures' which were coming to the fore in place of the older-style romances. The age was growing tougher and darker, as many of the significant films of the period artistically testify.

The Post-War Phase: the Hollywood Shake-Up

The war undoubtedly hardened and up-dated the taste of both film-makers and film-goers. The war dislocated lives, severed relationships as well as creating new and unexpected ones, broke marriages, and enforced dangerous living on men and women in the armed services. Any remaining taste for the sweet and old-fashioned passed. The hard core of naturalism in the line of films to be traced through the pre-war *Fury*, *You Only Live Once* and *The Grapes of Wrath*, for example, to *The Lost Weekend* and *The Best Years of Our Lives* of 1945–6, as well as the new taste for a documentary touch in feature films generated by the outstanding war-record films, combined to produce an enthusiastic public for the 'new realism' characteristic of the post-war crime and social problem pictures which were made in some numbers from 1945–50. Many of these were produced by LOUIS DE ROCHEMONT, who had made his name as producer of the hard-hitting film magazine series, *The March of Time*, inaugurated in 1934 and still running after the war.

The 'new realism' was to be seen in such espionage, crime-detection, and social problem films as *The House on 92nd Street* (HENRY HATHAWAY, 1945), *Boomerang* (ELIA KAZAN, 1947), *The Naked City* (JULES DASSIN, 1948), and *Panic in the Streets* (Kazan, 1950). There were also honest films dealing with racial tensions, such as *Gentleman's Agreement* (Kazan, 1947), *Crossfire* (Dmytryk, 1947) – adapted from a novel by the future director, RICHARD BROOKS – *The Dividing Line* (JOSEPH LOSEY, 1949), *Pinky* (Kazan, 1949), and, above these even, Clarence Brown's admirably restrained racial picture, *Intruder in the Dust* (1949). Some films, like *The Snake Pit* (1948), over-dramatized or over-sentimentalized the problems – social, racial and psychological – which they put over with such energy and sincerity. Some even rose into large-scale productions, notably ROBERT ROSSEN's very striking film *All the King's Men* (1949), ostensibly about the corruption in regional politics generated by such figures as Huey Long. But most of these films were restrained, relatively modest in scale and budget, serious and effective. A new generation of film-makers was being born. Another film, *The Men* (1950), dealing with the problems of the paraplegic, brought together exciting new talent – STANLEY KRAMER as producer, CARL FOREMAN as writer, and MARLON BRANDO as actor with the more experienced FRED ZINNEMANN as director.

Top: Barry Fitzgerald in 'The Naked City' (Jules Dassin, 1948)
Above: Robert Ryan in 'Crossfire' (Edward Dmytryk, 1947)
Below: 'Intruder in the Dust' (Clarence Brown, 1949)

The immediate post-war period was a good one for quality films, but a bad one for the industry. The Americans had never felt at all happy in their wartime alliance with the Soviet Union, and the post-war spy scare and consequent 'witch-hunts' led to an early, pre-McCarthy investigation in October 1947 by the official House of Representatives Un-American Activities Committee into alleged communist infiltrations into the film production industry. During the years following a blacklist was drawn up which included many of the better writers and directors in Hollywood. By the early 1950s reaction in Hollywood to anything which hinted of being to the Left of Right was like that of a police-state; even the modest liberalism of sentiment shown in *The Best Years of Our Lives* became severely suspect. 'Liberal' was a dirty word. This led to the enforced retirement, or exodus elsewhere, of many talents. The 'Hollywood Ten' investigated by the Committee included EDWARD DMYTRYK, the writers Ring Lardner Jr, John Howard Lawson, Albert Maltz and DALTON TRUMBO, and the producer Adrian Scott. All ten received prison sentences for refusing to testify as to their political beliefs. Those who subsequently came to England included CARL FOREMAN and JOSEPH LOSEY, but it was long before they could put their name on a picture which would achieve American distribution.

This was the first great shake-up, taking much of the bounce and confidence out of post-war Hollywood. But even the Right itself was undermined by the Anti-Trust laws of 1950 which broke up the combined production, distribution and exhibition of movies by integrated companies. The great production companies lost their direct financial involvement in circuit exhibition, and with this their incentive to mass-produce films for exhibition in theatres they no longer controlled. Hollywood, which up to 1950 had prided itself in its great annual turn-over of features (between 350 and 500), let production slip back during the decade 1952–62 – production rate in 195 being 278 feature films, in 1960, 211 films, in 1962, 138 films.

The direct result of the Anti-Trust laws was the change-over of production into the hands of the independent producers, who took the initiative in setting up their personal productions and as often as not chose to work i foreign studios (in Britain, Italy, Spain, etc), where, for a while at least, production costs were much lower. The average costs for the Hollywood film rose threefold between pre-war 1941 and 1961, and costs continued to rise sharply during the 1960s. So many of the independents turned their backs, temporarily at least, on the States. The great Hollywood studios turned over more and more to the mass production of quickly and relatively cheaply-made series films and serials for television.

The third blow to the industry, with exhibition taking the brunt of it at first, was the accelerating popularity of television in American homes, especially during the 1950s (18 million receivers in 1952; 60 million receivers in 1960). The industry's reply was two-fold. Short-term, it was the introduction of wide-screen (the tryptych-screen of Cinerama in 1952; the revival of the anamorphic lens for CinemaScope in the same year), and the considerable enlargement of the standard size screens in the cinemas. All this, and also the increase in the production of the big-scale, colour spectaculars, starting with *The Robe* (1953). It was the most obvious answer possible to the little screen and the shaking, black-and-white image of early television.

But the most important factor by far was the rise of the independent producer, the one-picture-at-a-time man who chose his own subjects, often directed his own pictures, and raised his own finance – mostly from the familiar distribution companies as in the past, but taking the production initiative out of their hands. The companies even courted and promoted the independents. As STANLEY KUBRICK said in 1960: 'The source of the supremacy of the majors was their power to make money. When they stopped making money, they sent for the independent producers'.

A final element in the changing pattern of motion pictures during the 1950s and 1960s was the change in audience taste. Films became more youth-orientated and, especially in the 1960s, wider open in matters of sex, and frequently excessive in the portrayal of violence. The youthful audiences, even in the 1950s, did not like to think they had any inhibitions left about 'life', while the censorship administration found itself staggering along in the wake of the 'permissive' 1960s. The appointment in 1966 of a tough and wide-awake Texan, Jack Valenti, a former aide of President Johnson, to the important post of head of the Motion Picture Association of America, ensured a different policy in all matters, including censorship. Even the Legion of Decency (founded in 1934) felt outdated, and changed its identity, if not its principles, by re-naming itself the National Catholic Office for Motion Pictures.

The great spectaculars turned to multi-million dollar history on widescreen – *War and Peace* (Vidor, 1956), *Ben Hur* (Wyler, 1959), *Spartacus* (Kubrick, 1960), *El Cid* (ANTHONY MANN, 1961), *The Fall of the Roman Empire* (Anthony Mann, 1963), *Cleopatra* (salvaged finally from its many troubles by JOSEPH MANKIEWICZ, 1963) and many others. All of these were made outside the USA, mostly in Italy or in Spain. There were also war spectaculars, ranging from *The Battle of the Bulge* (KEN ANNAKIN, 1965) to *Patton: Lust for Glory* (FRANKLIN J. SCHAFFNER, 1969) and *Tora! Tora! Tora!* (RICHARD FLEISCHER, 1970). The later musicals went spectacular too – for example, *South Pacific* (JOSHUA LOGAN, 1958), *The Sound of Music* (ROBERT WISE, 1965), and *Camelot* (Logan, 1967), mostly replacing with sheer size the great, creative school of musicals of the later 1940s and earlier 1950s – which, starting on a new phase with VINCENTE MINNELLI's wartime *Meet Me in St Louis* (with JUDY GARLAND, 1944), flowered with the STANLEY DONEN-GENE KELLY films, *On the Town* (1949) and *Singin' in the Rain* (1952), and Minnelli's *An American in Paris* (with Gene Kelly, 1950). The USA is the world centre of the musical as it is the world centre of the Western, with directors such as Minnelli, Mamoulian, GEORGE SIDNEY and Stanley Donen and with dance-directors such as CHARLES WALTERS at the root of the creative choreography for the cinema. There was a revival of quality in the musical in the later 1960s with Wyler's *Funny Girl* (1968), Kelly's *Hello Dolly* (1968), both with BARBRA STREISAND, Coppola's *Finian's Rainbow* (1968) and Fosse's *Sweet Charity* (1968). Most of the film musicals, like these, originated on the stage.

Hollywood in some respects permitted the survival of the great conservatives – the traditional directors such as King, Cukor, Wellman, Hawks, Vidor, Curtiz, and, of course, Ford and Hitchcock. Curtiz, born in 1888, was still working in the 1960s; the others, born in the 1890s, were to remain staple directors in the mainstream of Hollywood production in bad days and good alike.

Milestone's post-war films, after *A Walk in the Sun* (1945), included *The Red Pony* (1949), the comedy-thriller *Ocean's Eleven* (1961), and *Mutiny on the Bounty* (1962). Michael Curtiz (with, it is said, some 400 films behind him in any list pretending to be complete) made *The Comancheros* in 1961 at the age of 73, the year before he died. ALLAN DWAN made *The Most Dangerous Man Alive* in 1961 at the age of 76. Hollywood, though dedicated to youth, does not necessarily let its masters retire at the so-called normal age. Henry Hathaway even launched into the new widescreen medium of Cinerama, making three episodes in the spectacular *How the West Was Won* (1962), and he was still directing at the age of 70. William Wellman, on the other hand, retired in his early 60s.

King Vidor made a number of notable post-war films, his largest the spectaculars *War and Peace* (1956) and *Solomon and Sheba* (1959), his most controversial, for its elementary sexuality, *Duel in the Sun* (1946) and later *Ruby Gentry* (1952); both starred JENNIFER JONES, a 'natural' exponent of sexual urge in women, as distinct from the old-style theatrical vamping and

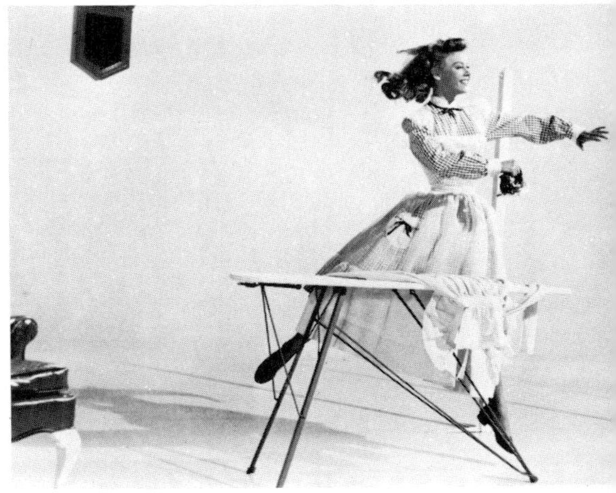

Top: Marlon Brando in 'The Men' (Fred Zinnemann, 1950)
Above: Vera-Ellen in 'On the Town' (Gene Kelly and Stanley Donen, 1949)
Below: Gene Kelly, Debbie Reynolds and Donald O'Connor in 'Singin' in the Rain' (Gene Kelly and Stanley Donen, 1952)

coquetry, Vidor, too, has chosen to be inactive in his later sixties. George Cukor, the director who likes to be thought of as highly sensitive to the performances of his stars, particularly women ('I achieve practically all my effects through the actors and actresses'), continued to make most kinds of film for which Hollywood is famous. He directed JUDY HOLLIDAY in *Born Yesterday* (1950), JEAN SIMMONS in *The Actress* (1953), JUDY GARLAND in *A Star is Born* (1954), ANNA MAGNANI in *Wild is the Wind* (1957), SOPHIA LOREN in *Heller in Pink Tights* (1959) and AUDREY HEPBURN in *My Fair Lady* (1964). He has maintained a very full output into his later 60s.

Such men have lived long for film-making, together with the two great professionals, the Anglo-American ALFRED HITCHCOCK and the Irish-American JOHN FORD. Hitchcock, the meticulous production planner of his films, is not so much concerned with large output (except in his role of television series producer) as he is with standards. If he makes a poor film (poor, that is, in comparison with his own high level) it is due to sheer miscalculation – and he is as likely to disapprove of it, in retrospect, as his critics. Everything in his films is the result of calculation of the effect he can achieve with an audience, and his style is as individual as it is in the long run inimitable. Hitchcock, therefore, left Britain after some 15 years' work there as a director, to become in effect a Hollywood institution. His best post-war films were to represent the highest level of his work – for example, *Rear Window* (1954), *The Trouble with Harry* (1956, not successful at the box-office), *North by Northwest* (1959), *Psycho* (1960, perhaps his most horrific film), *The Birds* (1963), serious thrillers which, while remaining in essence an extension of his calculated style and eye for a subject, respond also to the changing audience – becoming, for example, more concerned with psychopathology (in a dramatized form), or the off-beat (as in *The Birds*).

With FORD the impulse is different only in so far as film-making is so much part of his intuitive way of life that he approaches the work without any overt calculation, responding instinctively (and often sentimentally) to indigenous people (Whites or Indians), remote places, and strong situations, venerating the legend which they represent for him. He can therefore afford to be prolific, but he is mostly identified with the Western, seen as part of America's more legend-making history, because he had directed so many with a magnificent *panache* for atmosphere and heroic action set in the wonderful pictorial landscape of Monument Valley: *My Darling Clementine* (1946), *Fort Apache* (1948), *She Wore a Yellow Ribbon* (1949), *Wagonmaster* (1950), *The Horse Soldiers* (1959), *Two Rode Together* (1961), *The Man Who Shot Liberty Valance* (1962). He was 70 when he made *Seven Women* (1965). With all his other non-Westerns taken into account, it is a magnificent record for a man who claims his only interest in the medium is earning a living and being with the people he likes.

The men who were to show the first signs of disturbing the self-made moulds of the Hollywood film and strike out for themselves were born in the first years of this century. They include most notably PRESTON STURGES (died 1959), WILLIAM WYLER, GEORGE STEVENS, JOHN HUSTON, ANTHONY MANN (died 1967), DELMER DAVES, ANATOLE LITVAK, BILLY WILDER and FRED ZINNEMANN. The disturbing element several of these directors represented was not so much to change the established genres of entertainment, as to introduce their own forms of modernization. Their films became more challenging, more controversial, at times pushing aside the censorship restrictions, and introducing new twists and angles likely to intrigue audiences and make slightly more demand on their responses. Even the Western underwent certain radical changes.

Delmer Daves is a traditionalist in wholehearted acceptance of the standard Hollywood genres (he made a fine film of tension, *Dark Passage*, in 1947, and war films, such as *Task Force*, 1949), but his best work, like Ford's, lies in the Western genre – *Broken Arrow* (1950), *Jubal* (1956), *3.10 to Yuma* (1957), *Cowboy* (1958). But in *Broken Arrow* he made the Indians the heroes; in *3.10 to Yuma* he let the bad man (played by GLENN FORD) have as many if not more good lines than the good man (VAN HEFLIN). *3.10 to Yuma* was a restrained, humor-

Above: Cary Grant in 'North by Northwest' (Alfred Hitchcock, 1959)
Below: Anthony Perkins in 'Psycho' (Alfred Hitchcock, 1960)
Opposite: James Stewart in 'Rear Window' (Alfred Hitchcock, 1954)

Top: Van Heflin and Glenn Ford in '3.10 to Yuma' (Delmer Daves, 1957)
Above: 'Hallelujah Trail' (John Sturges, 1964)
Below: Alan Ladd and Van Heflin in 'Shane' (George Stevens, 1953)

ous Western, with refined characterization. The 1950s was a good period for Westerns from a variety of directors old enough to have sentiment for this kind of picture – JOHN STURGES with *Bad Day at Black Rock, Gunfight at the OK Corral*, and *Hallelujah Trail*, Anthony Mann with *The Man from Laramie*, George Stevens with the dour, magnificent *Shane*, Fred Zinnemann with *High Noon*, Wyler with *The Big Country* and ROBERT ALDRICH with *Apache*, which also sided with the Indians. The stars included GARY COOPER, VAN HEFLIN, ALAN LADD, GREGORY PECK, JAMES STEWART, JOHN WAYNE, JACK PALANCE, SPENCER TRACY, and BURT LANCASTER. These films all tended to be more than just great action pictures – they examined the motivations for moving west, for establishing isolated communities in the face of savage Indian counter-attack, and the struggle between the law-abiding and the lawless. But it was not until the 1960s that the Western went so far as to examine itself critically, as in *Lonely are the Brave* (DAVID MILLER, with KIRK DOUGLAS), or spoof itself as in Eliot Silverstein's burlesque *Cat Ballou* or create a *film noir*, as in MARLON BRANDO's *One-Eyed Jacks*, a sinister film of revenge set on the coast. The Western was to take on other, extreme forms in the later 1960s, as in the work of SAM PECKINPAH. But it also retained its traditional style in such films as RICHARD BROOKS's *The Professionals*, Howard Hawks's *El Dorado* and MARTIN RITT's *Hombre* (1967), John Sturges's *Hour of the Gun* (1967), and Henry Hathaway's *True Grit* (1969).

Preston Sturges was among the first to challenge convention in other fields of Hollywood entertainment; he began the process before the war was over with *Hail the Conquering Hero* and *The Miracle of Morgan's Creek* (1944), debunking in turn spurious heroism in war, and the romantic convention of the lightning marriage – with a pregnant heroine uncertain of the identity of her husband. Sturges anticipated another 'outrageous' director, BILLY WILDER, in those films which belonged in spirit to the future more than his post-war films, such as *The Beautiful Blonde from Bashful Bend* (1949), with BETTY GRABLE. Wilder, an Austrian scriptwriter who had to learn English in the States, was already going his own way with his astringent portraits of Hollywood in *Sunset Boulevard* (1950), of an amoral pressman in *Ace in the Hole* (1951), and of sexual fantasy in *The Seven Year Itch* (1955); he reached his top form in his association with the writer I. A. L. DIAMOND in such films as *Some Like It Hot* (1959), and their work of the 1960s, including *The Apartment* (1960), *Kiss Me Stupid* (1964), *Meet Whiplash Willie* (*The Fortune Cookie*, 1967), *The Private Life of Sherlock Holmes* (1970). Both situations and lines were a challenge to censorship in *The Apartment* and *Kiss Me Stupid*.

Others who leaned on the censor were, on occasion, RICHARD BROOKS and OTTO PREMINGER. Preminger who, like Wilder, came from Austria, made a film about drug addiction, *The Man with the Golden Arm* (1956, with FRANK SINATRA), and *Anatomy of a Murder* (1959, with LEE REMICK), in which detailed evidence concerning sexual matters was openly given. Preminger was also prepared, with an eye equally on showmanship and on intriguing social and political issues, to undertake films with a spectacular spread – such as *Exodus* (1960), *Advise and Consent* (1962), and *The Cardinal* (1963). His taste is catholic – he makes musicals (*Carmen Jones*; *Porgy and Bess*) and even recalls his earliest work now and then with a film like *Bunny Lake is Missing* (1965). His films have the individual touch and exploit fine acting, and his career illustrates one of Hollywood's principles – catholicity within the recognized genres of entertainment.

Top: Gary Cooper in 'High Noon' (Fred Zinnemann, 1952)
Above: Eddie Bracken and Betty Hutton in 'The Miracle of Morgan's Creek' (Preston Sturges, 1944)
Below: Gloria Swanson in 'Sunset Boulevard' (Billy Wilder, 1950)

Brooks's challenge to the censorship came with *The Blackboard Jungle* (1955), a film which exposed certain evils in education in tough city areas, and later again with *Elmer Gantry* (1960), which exposed corruption in revivalist religion. *Sweet Bird of Youth* (1962) offered a harsh picture of the corruption surrounding a predatory actress.

The chief films of this generation of directors – men who, like the century, were mostly in their 50s and 60s – dealt mainly with social corruption in the form of powerfully developed dramas. STANLEY KRAMER, another independent producer (of Fred Zinnemann's *The Men* and LASLO BENEDEK's *The Wild One*, on the terrorizing motor-cycle gangs) and producer-director, made *The Defiant Ones* (1958, on racial antipathies), *On the Beach* (1959, on the world destroyed by nuclear war – less effective than it might have been because of novelettish elements), *Inherit the Wind* (1960, on the so-called 'Monkey trial') and *Judgment at Nuremberg* (1961) – all films which dealt with, or attempted to deal with, major social issues, contemporary or period. 'I am a dealer in impact', Kramer has said, summing up the newer Hollywood philosophy of entertainment. ROBERT ROSSEN's *The Hustler* (with PAUL NEWMAN, 1961) was a study of gamblers; Newman, like Brando, has specialized in complex heroes who lived in and were part of a corrupt world. Union violence and racketeering were exposed in ELIA KAZAN's *On the Waterfront* (1954) and in ROBERT ALDRICH's *The Garment Jungle* (1956). American politics appeared once again in SCHAFFNER's *The Best Man* (1964), while STANLEY KUBRICK's startling bizarre premonitions of the future in *Dr Strangelove* (1963) and *2001: A Space Odyssey* (1968) were made in Britain.

On the level of individual and group psychology the films of the 1950s and especially the 1960s grew ever more uncompromising, as if humanity had to discover the worst about itself or burst in the process. These films probed into human relationships and failure in every kind of circumstance – in war (Aldrich's *Attack*; King's *Twelve O'Clock High*), in the family (Laslo Benedek's *Death of a Salesman* from Arthur Miller's play; NICHOLAS RAY's *Rebel without a Cause*, with the phenomenal JAMES DEAN as the disturbed adolescent), in the death cell itself (Wise's *I Want to Live*, 1958), and in many strange situations, such as Huston's and Arthur Miller's *The Misfits*, with MARILYN MONROE, and a last performance by CLARK GABLE. Huston invaded psychology itself in one of his most notable films, *Freud* (1962). Private relationships *in extremis* have been portrayed in MIKE NICHOLS's *Who's Afraid of Virginia Woolf?* and in his other film *The Graduate* (1967), while JOHN CASSAVETES's *Faces* was a derisive exposure of empty, materialist social life.

The Actors' Studio in New York founded by LEE STRASBERG in 1948 bred a new generation of actors and actresses for the 1950s who appeared in particular in the films of Elia Kazan – MARLON BRANDO, PAUL NEWMAN, MONTGOMERY CLIFT, KARL MALDEN, ROD STEIGER, EVA MARIE SAINT, SHELLEY WINTERS, Kim Hunter, LEE REMICK. Kazan's films were actors' films – from *A Streetcar named Desire* (1950) to *On the Waterfront* and *East of Eden* (1954), *Baby Doll* (1957), *Wild River* and *Splendor in the Grass* (1960). Kazan believed in photographed thought and emotional reaction as much as in speech – speech was a mere manifestation of thought and feeling. Lee Strasberg's so-called 'Method' style of

Top: Jack Lemmon and Marilyn Monroe in 'Some Like it Hot' (Billy Wilder, 1959)
Above: Jack Lemmon and Shirley MacLaine in 'The Apartment' (Billy Wilder, 1960)
Below: Charles Laughton in 'Advise and Consent' (Otto Preminger, 1962)

acting, stressing behavioural aspects of performance suggesting thought and emotion, suited the close observation of the actor usual in film, but led at times to exhibitionist performances. It was this emphasis on the actor, together with the new economics of the industry, which enticed actors themselves to become producers – including BURT LANCASTER, KIRK DOUGLAS, MARLON BRANDO, JOHN WAYNE, KARL MALDEN and, more recently, WARREN BEATTY.

A genre of American film-making which exists almost in a vacuum of its own is the school of horror and science fiction, which overlap to a considerable degree. The horror film in the traditional, 'gothic' style goes back to the earlier days of cinema, and particularly to the German cinema of the 1920s, though since the

Top: Paul Newman in 'The Hustler' (Robert Rossen, 1961)
Above: Richard Burton, Elizabeth Taylor, George Segal and Sandy Dennis in 'Who's Afraid of Virginia Woolf?' (Mike Nichols, 1966)
Below: Dustin Hoffman and Elizabeth Wilson in 'The Graduate' (Mike Nichols, 1967)

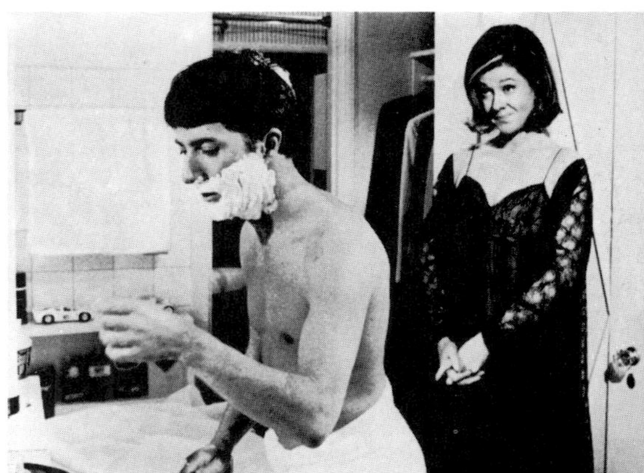

Second World War it has bred its own school in Britain with the great output of Hammer films. In the USA the horror film found a fine exponent in the productions of VAL LEWTON during the 1940s, and subsequently in ROGER CORMAN, while ROMAN POLANSKI's American production, *Rosemary's Baby* (1968), was a powerful exposé of witchcraft and its social implications. Leaving vampirism in the expert hands of the British, American horror films

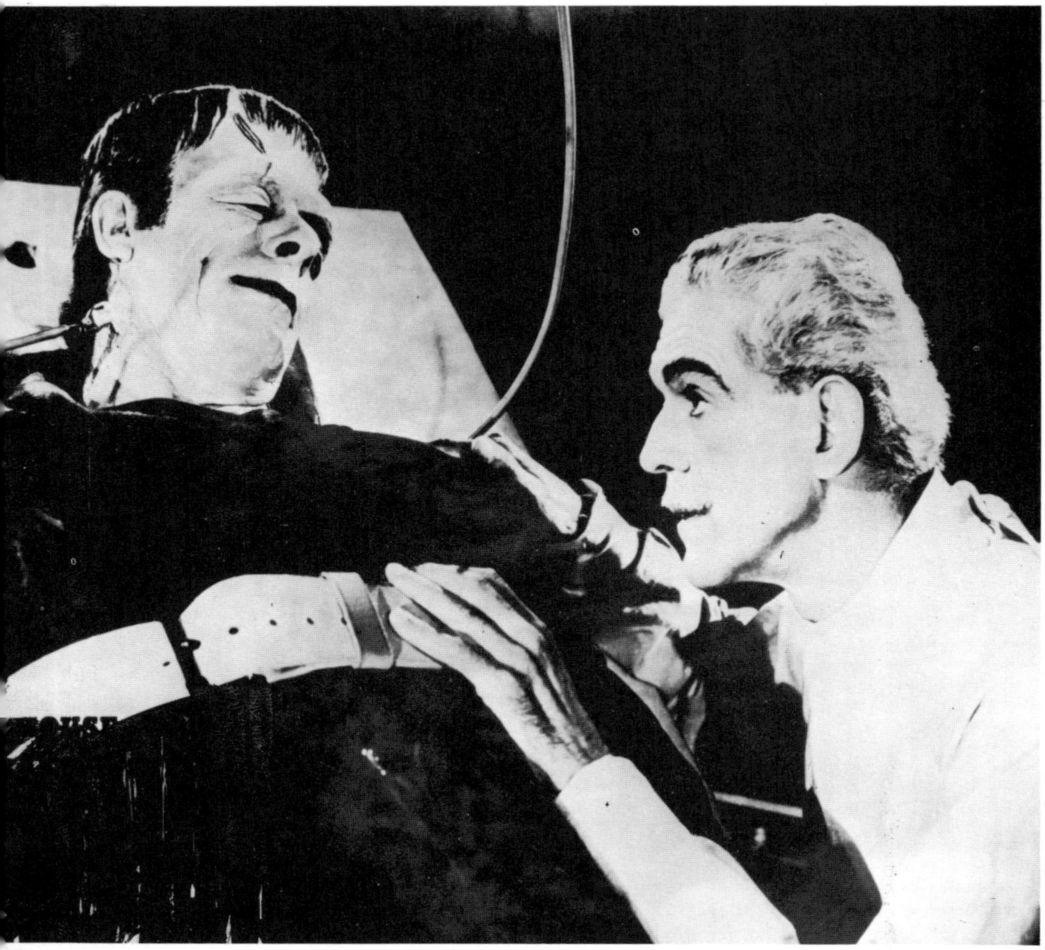

Above: Glenn Strange and Boris Karloff (right) in 'House of Frankenstein' (Erle C. Kenton, 1945)
Below: Mia Farrow and John Cassavetes in 'Rosemary's Baby' (Roman Polanski, 1968)

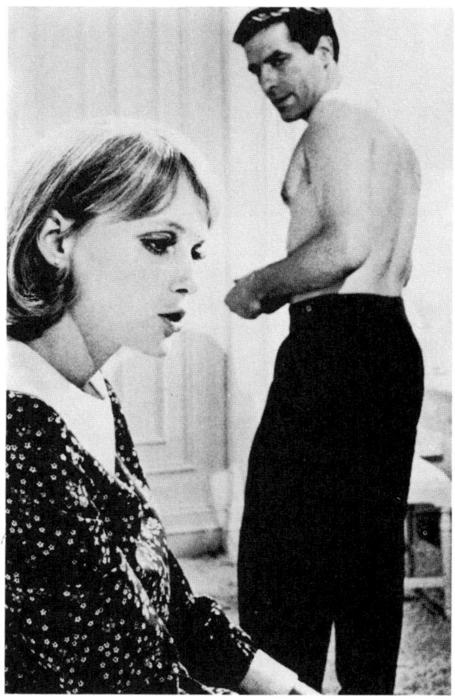

moved increasingly in the direction of science-fantasy, with the invasion of this entrenched planet by every kind of strange creature the Special Effects departments could devise – monsters conceived on every scale arising from the depths of land and sea, monsters from outer space, mummies from the grave, zombies and mutants: *The War of the Worlds* (Byron Haskin, 1953), *Them!* (Gordon Douglas, 1953), *Zombies of the Stratosphere* (Fred C. Brannon, 1953), *The Invasion of the Body Snatchers* (DON SIEGEL, 1956), *The Incredible Shrinking Man* (Jack Arnold, 1953), *The Fly* (Kurt Neumann, 1958).

RICHARD FLEISCHER's extraordinary 'travelogues' *20,000 Leagues under the Sea* (1954) and *Fantastic Voyage* (1966) remain unique as technical feats. But science fiction proper has tended to accept the hard facts which actual travel in space has introduced to the general public. Films of space travel to and from the Earth provide spectacular opportunities for displays of space ships and other equipment, reaching their climax in KUBRICK's *2001: A Space Odyssey* (1968), though this was in fact a British production by the American director. Notable American productions in this genre have been: *Destination Moon* (Irving Pichel, 1950), *The Day the Earth Stood Still* (ROBERT WISE, 1951), *When Worlds Collide* (RUDOLPH MATÉ, 1951), *It Came from Outer Space* (Jack Arnold, 1953), *The Conquest of Space* (Byron Haskin, 1954), *Forbidden Planet* (Fred McLeod Wilcox, 1956), *Robinson Crusoe on Mars* (Byron Haskin, 1964), and *Planet of the Apes* (FRANKLIN SCHAFFNER, 1967). Of all the above films, GEORGE PAL was producer of five, *The War of the Worlds, Destination Moon, When Worlds Collide, The Conquest of Space* and *Robinson Crusoe on Mars*. WALT DISNEY also contributed an excellent animated documentary on space travel, *Man in Space* (1956).

The newest generation of directors in the USA are not all in the same age-group since, for example, FRANK TASHLIN or BLAKE EDWARDS, directors of sophisticated comedy, are older than SIDNEY LUMET, JOHN FRANKENHEIMER and ROGER CORMAN. Corman is a prolific maker of horror films, and later such films as *The Wild Angels* (1966). Several of this new generation came, like the screenwriters PADDY CHAYEFSKY and Reginald Rose, from television – Lumet, Frankenheimer and Schaffner, for example. Some of their screenplays came from television – such as Lumet's *Twelve Angry Men* (1957) and DELBERT MANN's *Marty* (1955). Lumet (*The Pawnbroker*, 1964; *The Group* and *The Deadly Affair*, 1966), and Frankenheimer (*The Manchurian Candidate*, 1962; *Seconds*, 1966; *Grand Prix*, *The Extraordinary Seaman* and *The Fixer* 1968; *The Gypsy Moths*, 1969) have proved themselves among the more brilliant directors of the 1960s. A highly successful British invasion of the American scene was achieved late in the decade by JOHN SCHLESINGER with *Midnight Cowboy* (1969) and PETER YATES with *Bullitt* (1968).

Comedy has flourished with such satiric films as GENE KELLY's *A Guide for the Married Man* (1967), Bud Yorkin's *Divorce American Style* (1967), Francis Ford Coppola's *You're a Big Boy Now* (1966), GEORGE AXELROD's *The Secret Life of an American Wife* (1968), Paul Mazursky's *Bob and Carol and Ted and Alice* (1969) and, with its own peculiar brand of bad taste, Michael Sarne's *Myra Breckinridge* (1970). Black comedy with a background of war appeared in MIKE NICHOLS's *Catch-22* (1970) and ROBERT ALTMAN's *M.A.S.H.* (1969).

Other directors of growing importance came towards the close of the decade of the 1960s – for example, SAM PECKINPAH, ARTHUR PENN and GEORGE ROY HILL, whose *Butch Cassidy and the Sundance Kid* (1969) was one of the most successful and highly praised films of the period. The newest American cinema has achieved its own solid level of 'permissiveness'. Nudity is not only permitted – it has become a virtually obligatory commonplace. The sex act, as in Europe, is either shown or all-but shown. Homosexual and lesbian relations are presented as normally as heterosexual relations. Some films have contained appalling displays of gratuitous violence, while others have faced violence more responsibly by bringing home its reality, as in Arthur Penn's *Bonnie and Clyde* (1967) and Sam Peckinpah's *The Wild Bunch* (1969). The close of the 1960s saw also the phenomenal success of a low-budgeted, free-

Above: Dennis Hopper, Peter Fonda and Jack Nicholson in 'Easy Rider' (Hopper, 1969)
Below: Faye Dunaway and Warren Beatty in 'Bonnie and Clyde' (Arthur Penn, 1967)

style picture – DENNIS HOPPER and PETER FONDA's *Easy Rider* (1969), which readily appealed to young audiences and makes an interesting comparison with MONTE HELLMAN's more downbeat but less financially successful *Two-Lane Blacktop* (1971). It came at a time of increasing retrenchment in the film industry, which had faced heavy losses as a result of over-indulgence in films that, as in the past, had cost too much and failed to bring in commensurate returns.

The overall picture in the late 1960s and early 1970s, then, was of a great proliferation of films mainly by new directors – apart from those mentioned above, William Friedkin, William Fraker *(Monte Walsh)*, Peter Fonda *(The Hired Hand)*, Peter Bogdanovitch *(The Last Picture Show)* and the comedian Woody Allen all made notable, controversial work. Unhappily, not all these films reached the audiences which would most appreciate them. The industry in the United States (as well as in Great Britain) still seems geared mainly to the old, well-established patterns of distribution, so that films which cry out for individual, specialized handling (somewhat akin to that given to foreign imports) are subjected to all the hazards of bad, inadequate advertising and bookings in cinemas unsuited, both in size and locale, to their content. But in the United States (as in Europe), the potentialities of the film as a medium continues to excite young, would-be artists, and has taken over from literature and the theatre as the favourite form of personal expression. Despite all the current confusions and uncertainties, the 1970s could be one of the most exciting decades for the American film since halcyon days long ago. RM and JG

USSR

See RUSSIA AND THE USSR

Ustinov, Peter

Born 1921 in London, England. Enormously gifted and prolific cosmopolitan actor, writer, director and *raconteur* whose many-faceted talents have tended to be frittered away on unworthy projects. Of French, German, Italian and Russian descent, he wrote his first play in his teens and by the time he was twenty he had made a name for himself as a playwright, stage director and actor. He made his film début in the WILL HAY comedy, *The Goose Steps Out*, in 1941. His plays – notably 'The Love of Four Colonels' and 'Romanoff and Juliet' – are distinguished by their sly, deceptively gentle mockery of national characteristics. As an actor he won Academy Awards for his exuberant performances in *Spartacus* (1960) and *Topkapi* (1964). His first screenwriting was for the British war film, *The Way Ahead* (1943), in which he also acted. He wrote and directed *School for Secrets* (1946) and *Vice Versa* (1948). But in general his success as a director has been less pronounced than his popularity as an actor. His most considerable film, *Billy Budd* (1962), though flawed, is a deeply personal work and the most serious of all his screen productions. He usually finds a role for himself in the films he directs.

Other notable films: *Private Angelo* (1949), *Romanoff and Juliet* (1961), *Lady L* (1965). He also directed *Blackbeard's Ghost* (1969), *Viva Max* (1970). MH

Above: Rod Steiger in 'The Pawnbroker' (Sidney Lumet, 1964)
Below: Peter Ustinov in 'Billy Budd' (Ustinov, 1962)

VW

Vadim, Roger

Born 1928 in Paris, France. Celebrated French writer and director, sometime actor and journalist, whose films are on occasion less distinguished than his gift for re-moulding interesting actresses into sex symbols – BRIGITTE BARDOT, Annette Stroyberg, JANE FONDA – and then marrying them. He first worked in films as a scriptwriter for MARC ALLÉGRET on *Maria Chapdelaine* (1950). Discovering BARDOT in Italy, he directed most of her early image-making films, notably *And God Created Woman* (1956) and *Heaven Fell That Night* (1957). Apart from Bardot's, some of his films reveal a more than facile talent, especially *Les Liaisons Dangereuses* (1959), *Vice and Virtue* (1962) and *Barbarella* (1968), an exuberant comic strip spoof. But for the most part the plushy eroticism of his work is too overstressed to encourage serious appraisal.

Other main films: *Warrior's Rest* (1962), *La Ronde* and *Nutty Naughty Château* (1964), *The Game is Over* (1966), *Histoires Extraordinaires* (1968), *Pretty Maids All in a Row* (1970) and *Hellé* (1972). MH

Valcroze, Jacques Doniol

See DONIOL-VALCROZE

Valentino, Rudolph (1895–1926)

Born in Castellaneta, Taranto, Italy. One of the most strongly individual stars of the cinema, Valentino fulfilled all the fantasies of the romantic Latin lover which had been popularized for generations by cheap female literature. He offered dreams of escape and an exotic, thrilling eroticism. Having failed his course at the Venice Military Academy the young Rodolfo Guglielmi trained in agriculture and on his arrival in the USA in 1913 sought work as a gardener. Subsequently he worked as waiter, exhibition dancer and taxi-dance partner until he was given a bit-part in a dance-hall scene in Emmet Flynn's *Alimony* (1918). After this he was generally cast as a Latin villain until JUNE MATHIS recognized his attractions and arranged his casting in INGRAM's *The Four Horsemen of the Apocalypse* (1921). His success was immediate but his subsequent career uneven owing to the difficulties with producers fomented by his ambitious wife, Natacha Rambova. His subsequent films were *Uncharted Seas*, *Camille*, *The Conquering Power* and *The Sheik* (1921), *Moran of the Lady Latty*, *Beyond the Rocks*, *Blood and Sand* and *The Young Rajah* (1922), *Monsieur Beaucaire* (1923), *A Sainted Devil* (1924), *Cobra* and *The Eagle* (1925), *The Son of the Sheik* (1926). Shortly after finishing *The Son of the Sheik*, Valentino died – alone, weary, growing plump, and devastated by newspaper attacks on his 'degenerating influence' on American manhood. His lying-in-state and funeral were the signal for unprecedented scenes of hysteria and several suicides by inconsolable fans. It seemed almost irrelevant to his attraction that he was not only supremely photogenic (myopia gave his eyes a melancholy and mysterious look), but also a gifted performer, with a feeling for light comedy, a truth and restraint, and a sense of rhythm which was imparted to all the scenes in which he appeared. DR

Valli, Alida

Born 1921 in Pola, Italy. Actress, who studied drama at Rome Academy; married to Oscar de Mejo, pianist-composer. She has appeared in films since the 1930s, including the USA and Britain. Films include: *Piccolo Mondo Antico* (Venice Film Festival Award, 1941), *Eugénie Grandet* (1946), *The Paradine Case* (1948), *The Third Man* (1949), *Senso* (1954), *The Sea Wall* and *Il Grido* (1957), *Le Dialogue des Carmélites* (1959), *Ophélia* and *Une Aussi Longue Absence* (1961), *The Spider's Strategy* (1970).

VanDerBeek, Stanley

Born 1931 in New York, USA. Underground animation and experimental film-maker. After varying experience, in farming and television, VanDerBeek began making animated collage films, such as *What Who How* (1955) and 'time paintings' (evolving pictures) such as *Mankinda* (1956–7). His later films combined collage animation with live-action film, such as *Achoo Mr Kerrovchev* (1960), in which an animated cut-out of Khrushchev was superimposed on newsreels. His approach to film-making is largely technical, the resolving of visual feats and sleights of hand, like some modern Méliès, in such films as *Summit* (1963), on a meeting between Kennedy and Khrushchev, and his anti-war film, *Breathdeath* (1963–4), both elaborate trick films with political overtones. The basis of his work remained animation in ever more complex forms, including the use of distortion; his films of this period include *Fluids* (1965) and *The Life and Death of a Car* (1962). Later he developed his own Moviedrome, which enabled him to project multiple images, such as *Move-Movies*, a 'Choreography for projectors'. His work extends to videotape and computerized film-making, for example, *Collide-oscope* (1966). He is also a painter, sculptor, and calligrapher. RM

Van Dyke, Willard

Born 1906 in Denver, Colorado, USA. Influential documentary cinematographer, director and producer. His career began as a still photographer, among other occupations, and he helped as cameraman on one of the most celebrated American documentaries of the 1930s, PARE LORENTZ's *The River* (1937). With Ralph Steiner he founded American Documentary Films Inc, and co-directed with Steiner *The City* (1939), for which Aaron Copland provided a striking music score. His principal documentaries include *Valley Town* (1940), with a score by Marc Blitzstein, *The Children Must Learn* (1940), concerning life in a decaying town in the South, *Journey into Medicine* (1947), on the problems of medical training, *Years of Change* (1950), *Land of White Alice* (1959), *Search into Darkness* (1961), and *Frontline Cameras* (1965). In 1966 he succeeded Richard Griffith as director of the Department of Film, Museum of Modern Art, New York. RM

Van Dyke II, Woodbridge Strong (1887–1943)

Born in San Diego, California, USA. Director. After a period in vaudeville, he became an assistant director (with GRIFFITH, for a while) and also did scriptwriting and editing. His long directorial career stems from 1917, beginning with serials and many Westerns with Buck Jones and Tim McCoy. His interest in exploration and exotic settings was manifest in *White Shadows in the South Seas* (1927, a project started by FLAHERTY), *Trader Horn* (1931) and *Tarzan the Ape Man* (1932, with Johnny Weissmuller). In the 1930s, for MGM, he turned out a variety of entertaining comedies, family dramas and thrillers (notably *The Thin Man*, 1934, plus several sequels), musicals with Nelson Eddy and JEANETTE MACDONALD, and two MGM 'classics', the spectacular *San Francisco* (1936) and the historical biography *Marie Antoinette* (1938, with sensitive playing from NORMA SHEARER). He continued working in these various genres up till 1942. Van Dyke was a typical studio director of the 1930s, versatile and fast, who never really developed a recognizable signature, but who gathered together talented groups of writers, actors and designers capable of providing a high standard of entertainment movie which worked at the box-office. JG

Vanel, Charles
Born 1892 in Rennes, France. Powerful French stage and screen character actor whose magnetic, ravaged presence impressed international film audiences in the phenomenally successful *Wages of Fear* (1952). Other principal films include: *Les Misérables* (1933), *Le Grand Jeu* (1934), *Carrefour* (1939), *Les Diaboliques* (1955), *La Vérité* (1960), *Un Homme de Trop* (1967).

Varda, Agnès
Born 1928 in Brussels, Belgium. With *La Pointe Courte* (1955) and *Ô Saisons Ô Châteaux*, (1958), and other personal, perceptive and witty documentaries, Varda proved herself a harbinger of the French *nouvelle vague*, in which, after 1960, she assumed a dominant place. Other films: *Opera Mouffe* (1960), *Cléo de cinq à sept* (1961), *Salut les Cubains* (a short filmed in Cuba, 1964), *Le Bonheur* (1965), *Les Créatures* (1966), *Lion's Love* (made in USA, 1969).

Variable Area
A type of sound track in which the track is divided into two portions, one opaque and the other clear, the ratio of the area occupied by the two portions varying according to the signal imposed on the modulating device.

Variable Density
A type of sound track in which the density of the track is uniform across the width, but varies along its length according to the signals imposed by the modulating device.

Vasiliev, Sergei (1900–1959) **and Georgi** (1899–1946)
Russian directors who came to adopt the pseudonym the Vasiliev Brothers when they decided to work together, though in fact they were unrelated. Their early careers involved film editing, and they became students of SERGEI EISENSTEIN in the art of direction. As directors, their first film was the silent, *The Sleeping Beauty* (1930), with a script by GRIGORI ALEXANDROV, but their greatest success came with *Chapayev* (1934), their first sound film, which they wrote and directed, and which took two years to complete. It celebrated a highly individualistic Red Army commander, based on his own story as told by his political commissar, Dmitri Furmanov, with whom he established an edgy friendship. Chapayev was played by Boris Babochkin of the Leningrad Dramatic Theatre. The film combined lyricism with humour, an easy-seeing naturalism which was at the same time highly calculated. It won alike the approval of the State and of contemporary film-makers. It introduced what was termed the 'third phase' in Russian film history, in the words of Jay Leyda, 'synthesizing the mass film of the first period with the individual, naturalist stories of the second (or sound) period'. The Vasilievs' next film *Volochayevsk Days* (1938) was something of a self-imitation; they were never to equal again the fame of *Chapayev*. Their other films were *Defence of Tsaritsin* (1942) and *The Front* (1943). In 1944, Sergei became head of Lenfilm, and so became a producer during the sterile period of Stalin's post-war rule. Georgi having died, Sergei in the post-Stalin era made two technically-proficient, but otherwise uninteresting films, *The Heroes of Shipka* (1955) and *October Days* (1958). RM

Védrès, Nicole (1911–1955)
Born in France. Author, and director of outstanding documentaries, made with wit, irony and a strong social sense. She first of all supervised *Paris 1900* (1946–7) a feature-length compilation film recalling the city and the period; it remains one of the best of its kind, the result of 15 months' viewing and editing old newsreels at the Cinémathèque Francaise. RESNAIS acted as an assistant cutter on this film. Her later film, *La Vie Commence Demain* (1950), was an ambitious essay on the problems of the atomic age, including interviews with such personalities as Sartre, Picasso, and Gide. She followed this with another thematic film, *Aux Frontières de l'Hommes* (1953). She was the author of 'Images du Cinéma Français', an ingenious and imaginative collection of stills.

Veidt, Conrad (1892(3?)–1943)
Born in Potsdam, Germany. Veidt trained as an actor with Reinhardt at the Deutsches Theater in Berlin, and entered films in 1917. He played in innumerable silent films, including many of the most famous expressionist films of the 1920s: *The Cabinet of Dr Caligari* (1919), MURNAU's *Der Januskopf* and *Abend...Nacht...Morgen* (1920), *Lukrezia Borgia* (1922), *Waxworks* (1924), *The Student of Prague* and *The Hands of Orlac* (1925) and *The Man Who Laughs* (1927). A tall and handsome man, with a fine presence, his lean face could assume a darkly sinister or haunted appearance. Latterly he co-produced some of his silent films, and on one occasion, *Lord Byron* (1922), directed and scripted as well as appeared in a film. His career continued with the coming of sound: he starred, for example, in *Rasputin* (1930), *Congress Dances* (1931) and *Wilhelm Tell* (1934). From 1933 he began to appear in British films, and lived in England until moving finally to the USA. Among his British films are: *Rome Express* (1932), *I was a Spy* and *The Wandering Jew* (1933), *Jew Süss* (1934), *King of the Damned* (1935), *Under the Red Robe* and *Dark Journey* (1937), *The Spy in Black* (1939), *Contraband* and *The Thief of Bagdad* (1940), while in the USA he made several other notable films, including *A Woman's Face* (1941), *Nazi Agent* and *Casablanca* (1942), and *Above Suspicion* (1943). During the later phases of his career he often played Nazis, or German officers, investing them with steely intelligence and romantic charm. RM

Venanzo, Gianni Di
See DI VENANZO

Vertov, Dziga (1896–1943)
Born in Byalystok, Russia. Soviet director. Real name: Denis Arkadievich Kaufman. Vertov was the founder of Soviet documentary, though in his later years his methods were disapproved of officially. The full importance of his theories and ideas only became apparent after his death, when more adaptable technical equipment made possible their application and gave rise to the genre of *cinéma-vérité* – the direct successor and ultimate realization of Dziga Vertov's *kino-eye*.

Vertov studied at the Moscow Psycho-neurological Institute, but even before 1917 was conducting experiments in synthetic sound. After the Revolution he worked in the newsreel section of the cinema, and established, directed and edited a weekly newsreel, *Kinonedelya*, and later the periodical reportage *Kino-Pravda* (1922–4). Conducting a characteristically aggressive campaign against acted cinema, he headed a group of experimental documentary-makers who took the name of 'Kinoki' ('Kino-Eyes'). He constantly preached the supremacy of life *prise sur le fait*, though he could not help imposing his own personality upon the material, giving his documentaries an expressive and invigorating power which came from the director's own creative contribution more than their intrinsic force. This fact – in some respects contradictory to Vertov's own notions – became especially apparent in the fine films he made in honour of Lenin's death in 1924. His first full-length film was *Stride, Soviet* (1926); but the primary demonstration of all his theories was *Man with a Movie Camera* (made in collaboration with his brother, MIKHAIL KAUFMAN, the cameraman, 1928).

Vertov used sound as inventively and creatively as he used silent images. *Enthusiasm* (1931) was one of the first truly creative uses of sound *montage*; and *Three Songs of Lenin* (1934) remains his masterpiece. Dziga Vertov's individual and militant methods – strongly allied in their principles to constructivism – did not fit easily into the narrow restrictions of Soviet Realism; he was not prominently active after 1937. DR

Vidor, Charles (1900–1959)
Born in Budapest, Hungary. European-trained American director who worked in Hollywood from 1932. His lush decorative style was admirably suited to such star-orientated romances as *Cover Girl* (1944), *A Song to Remember* (1945), *Gilda* (1946), *Hans Christian Andersen* (1952), *Love Me or Leave Me* (1955) and he had a particular gift for blending music or musical numbers into basically dramatic material. He died while filming a 'life' of

Above: 'Hallelujah' (King Vidor, USA, 1929)
Below: Jean Vigo directing Jean Dasté and Dita Parlo in 'L'Atalante' (France, 1934)

Liszt, *Song without End*. Other main films: *The Mask of Fu Manchu* (1932), *The Tuttles of Tahiti* (1942), *Together Again* (1944), *The Swan* (1956), *The Joker is Wild* and *A Farewell to Arms* (1958). MH

Vidor, King

Born 1894 in Galveston, Texas, USA. One of the truly great directors of the silent cinema. Vidor succeeded during most of his long career in working within the context of the commercial studio establishment without ever compromising either the artistic quality or the strong social awareness of his films. ('I had always . . . the impulse', he wrote, 'to use the motion-picture screen as an expression of hope and faith, to make films presenting positive ideas and ideals rather than negative themes'.) He acquired a passion for films as a schoolboy when he worked as a projectionist in Galveston; and has recorded that he carefully studied the pictures that he showed at this period. Soon after 1910 he began to shoot local interest subjects for sale to the Pathé Exchange; and in 1915 trekked with his wife Florence Vidor (later one of the most graceful silent screen artists) to Hollywood. He directed a series of two-reelers for Universal, and improbably persuaded a consortium of ten doctors to put up the money for a film on Christian Science. The doctors also backed *Better Times* (1919), which introduced ZASU PITTS, whom Vidor had noticed on a bus. After half a dozen or so low-budget productions for his own studio, Vidor was recruited to Metro to direct Laurette Taylor in *Peg o' My Heart* (1923) and *Happiness* (1924). For many more years, he worked exclusively for Metro and later MGM. Vidor's gifts were an extraordinary sensitivity to character and relationships, a singularly expressive visual language, an ability to select images which precisely evoked a mood or an atmosphere. The film which finally established his reputation was *The Big Parade* (1925), a drama about the First World War made in defiance of the current belief that war subjects were out of favour, and brought to fruition with the personal support of IRVING THALBERG. He remained versatile, able to turn from a deeply pathetic *La Bohème* (1926) with LILLIAN GISH to brilliant and witty Marion Davies comedies – *Show People* and *The Patsy* (1928). His greatest silent film however was *The Crowd* (1928) which broke with every tradition of Hollywood to depict the petty tragedies of humble life, filmed in real-life locations and with a virtuosity of technique which after almost half a century is still dazzling. Vidor's success carried over into talking films, beginning with *Hallelujah!* (1928), an all-Negro film which introduced new concepts of the use of music in the cinema, the commercial and critical success of the sentimental *The Champ*, a vehicle for Jackie Cooper and WALLACE BEERY, and *Our Daily Bread* (1934). After this the innovatory fecundity of Vidor's work seemed to dwindle; and for the next quarter of a century he was principally recognized as a highly successful director of ambitious prestige subjects alternating with bizarre melodramas: *The Citadel* (1938), *North West Passage* (1940), *Duel in the Sun* (1946), *The Fountainhead* (1949), *Ruby Gentry* (1952), *War and Peace* (1956), *Solomon and Sheba* (1959). DR

Vierny, Sacha

Born 1919 in Bois-le-Roi, France. Cinematographer. Beginning as an assistant director, he turned to photography on a number of famous documentaries in the 1950s including RESNAIS's *Le Chant du Styrène* (1958, in which industrial processes are turned into a kind of surrealist landscape) and MARKER's *Lettre de Sibérie* (1957). Began collaboration with Resnais on *Hiroshima, mon amour* (1959), continuing with *L'Année dernière à Marienbad* (1961) and *Muriel* (1963). Other films include: *Le Bel Âge* (1958), *Aimez-vous les femmes?* (1964), *Belle de Jour* (1967, with its rich, Renoir-like exterior colour). Vierny has an unusually precise plastic sense, a keen eye for documentary material and a bravura technique when required by directors like Resnais and Marker. JG

Vigo, Jean (1905–1934)

Born in Paris, France, of Basque origins. Director. During the First World War his father, a journalist and outspoken pacifist, was imprisoned and died in mysterious circumstances. Vigo himself was educated in the kind of schools he was later to show in *Zéro de Conduite*. After a year's study, 1926–7, at the Faculté des Lettres, Paris, he developed tuberculosis and was finally sent to Nice for his health. Here he became a photographer's assistant, and in 1929 married Elizabeth Lazinska, who financed his first film, *À Propos de Nice* (silent, 1930), a ruthless exposé of the idle rich on the French Riviera and the contrast they made to the poor of Nice 'begging out of sheer laziness'; he felt death to be the resorts' ultimate symbol. Vigo called his film a *'point de vue documenté'*, often using a concealed 16 mm camera to capture his 'candid' portraits unnoticed, anticipating the later *cinéma-vérité* techniques. His cameraman was BORIS KAUFMAN (brother of DZIGA VERTOV), who was to photograph all his films. *À Propos de Nice* was shown at the Vieux Colombier, Paris, and Vigo's genius was recognized by the *cinéastes* of Paris; he became an enthusiastic supporter of the Ciné-Club movement for showing avant-garde films, an important development in France.

After making a highly stylized and witty short about the swimmer Jean Taris in 1932, Vigo made his two last and most significant films as a result of the financial sponsorship of an industrialist outside the film industry. *Zéro de Conduite* (1933) was an authentically surrealist study of the revolt of a group of children in a degraded kind of boarding-school. The staff and governors are shown as the children see them – tyrannical dwarfs, perverts and clowns who create a viciously ugly but also macabre and comic environment in which the children become their victims. The film, full of beautiful touches of revealing stylization and symbolism, was banned and suppressed as a travesty of the French educational system. *L'Atalante* (1934), which Vigo lived long enough to complete with the help of his many friends, was to some extent modified (mainly with cuts and additional music) for commercial distribution. Even so it remains one of the great imaginative films of the 1930s, with an outstanding performance by MICHEL SIMON as the crazy mate on a Seine barge, whose young captain is painfully separated from the peasant-girl he marries when she is swept away by the excitement of being in Paris for the first time. Again the extraordinary atmosphere, moving from a lyrical but austere actuality into psychologically motivated symbolic action and dream, was far in advance of its time. With Vigo's death in 1934 France lost one of her potentially greatest film-makers. See 'Jean Vigo' by

Joseph and Harry Feldman (British Film Institute, n.d.) and 'Jean Vigo' by Pierre Lherminier (1967, in French). RM

Vignette
The technique whereby the same subject is shown more than once in a frame, or the action in a number of distinctively separate locations is shown in different parts of the same frame. In filming, this effect is usually obtained by multiple exposure or multiple printing from suitably masked negatives.

Visconti, Luchino
Born 1906 in Milan, Italy. One of the most renowned Italian *auteur* directors (with FELLINI and ANTONIONI); regarded as the father of Italian neo-realism, although other directors, notably ROSSELLINI and DE SICA, became its more famous post-war exponents. Acclaimed also for his work in opera and for the theatre, he has made relatively few films and their rejection of currently fashionable trends has prompted criticism and even condemnation. Stylistically, his films are conceived in an operatic form which achieved its apotheosis in his Wagnerian indictment of Nazi Germany, *The Damned* (1969).

An aristocrat by birth (Count Luchino Visconti, Duke of Modrone) and a communist by inclination, he developed an early interest in music and drama through his parents. At military school, he found another life-long passion in the care and handling of horses. A meeting with JEAN RENOIR is credited with changing the direction of his life. After a spell in the theatre, he became Renoir's third assistant on *Une Partie de Campagne* in the 1930s. Under Renoir he became aware of the political and social scene in Europe.

During the war, in Rome, he wrote and directed *Ossessione* (1942), based on James Cain's harsh tale of self-destructive sexual passion 'The Postman Always Rings Twice'. Its impact on audiences and the docile Italian film industry under the Fascist régime was explosive. Banned by the censors, it was later reprieved (reputedly by Mussolini himself). But the film's troubles persisted and it has not been widely seen outside Italy. A similar fate attended his next film *La Terra Trema* (1948), which Visconti envisaged as a trilogy about the oppressed lives of the poor in Sicily. Only one part was made, however, the story of a fishing village, and this raw, majestic film, like *Ossessione*, has gained a reputation far greater than the range of its international distribution.

Thereafter, although he has returned often to the theatre (where he discovered the young MARCELLO MASTROIANNI and employed FRANCO ZEFFIRELLI as an assistant) and to opera (where his finest work has been with Maria Callas), it is on the screen that he has most fully realized his potential as an artist. The influence of his upbringing and his acute sense of history are apparent in the characterization in even his most desolate subjects (such as *La Terra Trema*), where the poverty-stricken protagonists have an inherent grandeur rooted in personal, primitive pride.

Above: Luchino Visconti during the filming of 'Death in Venice' (Italy, 1970)
Below: Jennifer Salt and Jon Voight in 'The Revolutionary' (Paul Williams, USA, 1970)

After the realist *Bellissima* (1951) with ANNA MAGNANI, Visconti made *Senso* (1954), a period drama about the Austro-Italian war of 1866, in which his use of colour confirmed his qualities as a director of unusual and meticulous visual sensibility. Again the film suffered from insensitive exploitation and brutal cutting. A smaller scale project, Dostoevsky's *White Nights* (1957) was pictorially as impressive, but less wholly successful.

It was with *Rocco and his Brothers* (1960), the story of a family of Sicilian migrants to Northern Italy, that Visconti at last achieved international fame. It was followed by Lampedusa's *The Leopard* (1963), set against a background of decaying feudalism in 19th-century Sicily and the third of Visconti's trio of Sicilian films, which was made under the American auspices of Twentieth Century Fox. Though a critical success, it was shown in the USA and Britain in a cut, dubbed version printed on inferior colour stock which destroyed many of Visconti's delicate colour effects and careful details.

The themes that predominate in his work are the solidarity and destructive power of family relationships, either corporate (as in *The Damned* and *Rocco*) or separate. Visconti's understanding of family as a dynastic entity is expanded in *The Leopard* and *Senso*, where he examines the substance of the old order, the challenge of the new. On the film scene he remains an unwavering individualist, as evidenced by his latest film, based on Thomas Mann's elegiac *Death in Venice* (1970).

Other films: *Vaghe Stelle dell'Orsa* (1965), *The Stranger* (1967), episodes in *Siamo Donne* (1953), *Boccaccio '70* (1962), *Le Streghe* (1965). Latest project: a film on Ludwig of Bavaria.

Notable initial study: Geoffrey Nowell-Smith's 'Visconti' (1967). MH

Vitti, Monica
Born 1933. Italian actress and leading lady who became internationally popular after her portrayals of neurotically disturbed women in Antonioni's films. She has however, a lively, infectious comic sense as well. Films include: *L'Avventura* (1959), *La Notte* (1960), *L'Eclisse* (1962), *The Red Desert* (1964), *Modesty Blaise* (1965), *The Chastity Belt* (1967), *Jealousy, Italian Style* and *Nini Tirabuscio* (1970), *La Pacifista* (1971).

Voight, Jon
Born 1939 in New York, USA. One of the leading younger American actors, theatre-and-television-trained, who made a spectacular impact as the pathetic would-be ladies' man in *Midnight Cowboy* (1969). Since then he has played successfully in *Catch 22* and *The Revolutionary* (1970) and *Deliverance* (1972).

von Sternberg, Josef (1894–1969)
Born in Vienna, Austria. Real name Jonas Sternberg. Director. Emigrated at an early age to the USA, and entered the industry as a film patcher in New York in 1914. He served during the war in the Signal Corps as a film technician and afterwards as technical assistant, until during 1924 he made, with the English actor, George K. Arthur, an experimental feature, *The Salvation Hunters*, costing only $4,800; this enjoyed some critical, but no commercial success when distributed by United Artists with the backing of CHAPLIN and FAIRBANKS. He made next *The Exquisite Sinner* (1925) for MGM, and *The Seagull* (from his own original screen-play, 1926) for Chaplin as a vehicle for EDNA PURVIANCE. These films (both at the moment lost) formed Sternberg's apprenticeship to the medium, and it was with the gangster

film, *Underworld* (1927), that he achieved his first outstanding success, establishing a new genre with this single masterpiece. The German designer, HANS DREIER, who worked with LUBITSCH, became closely associated with Sternberg's work, as did the ace cameramen, LEE GARMES, Bert Glennon, Harold Rosson, and Lucien Ballard. *Underworld* was followed by *The Dragnet* and *The Docks of New York* (1928), *The Case of Lena South* (1929), and the sound film, *Thunderbolt* (1929). He directed JANNINGS successfully in *The Last Command* (1927–8) and stressed the sensuality of women in the various performances he obtained from Evelyn Brent. It was on the strength of his work with Jannings that he was invited to Germany to make Jannings' first sound film, *The Blue Angel* (1930), in which he insisted on using MARLENE DIETRICH, whom he had seen on the stage, but whose initial films in Germany had been undistinguished. As she put it: 'He made me over', creating an entirely new screen image for her. Sternberg's meticulous screencraft, his insistence on exactitude in highlight and shadow in the camerawork, particularly his skill in deploying light on the human face, and his extraordinary taste in handling decor, were all by now apparent. He applied the same technical discipline to the use of sound. After *The Blue Angel* he formed a creative association with Dietrich, and took her back to Hollywood. She was the star of his films, *Morocco* (1930), *Dishonored* (1931), *Shanghai Express* and *Blonde Venus* (1932), *The Scarlet Empress* (1934), and *The Devil is a Woman* (1935); he also made a version of Dreiser's *An American Tragedy* (1931), but without Dietrich. *The Scarlet Empress* was the most advanced, bizarre film in the Dietrich cycle: its sets, which were designed by Dreier, were largely made up of distorted statuary placed against walls structured out of logs; while Glennon's luminous photography was unique at the time in its sensuality. Both *The Scarlet Empress* and *The Devil is a Woman* were coldly received; the Spanish government managed to secure the withdrawal of the latter on the grounds of the insult it was alleged to offer the Civil Guard. Sternberg moved from Paramount (with whom he had been since 1927) to Columbia, for whom he directed *Crime and Punishment* (1935) and *The King Steps Out* (1936), the latter a semi-musical with Grace Moore. This was followed by the abortive attempt to film *I, Claudius* (1937) for KORDA in London; fragments of the rushes for this film, in which CHARLES LAUGHTON sowed the seeds of a brilliant performance, were later salvaged and reconstructed as a programme for BBC Television. For a variety of reasons, the film was abandoned, partly owing to trouble between Laughton and Sternberg. Sternberg's late films included *Sergeant Madden* (1939); *The Shanghai Gesture* (a return to his sensual atmospheric style, 1941); *Macao* (partly reshot by other hands, 1952); *Jet Pilot* (also partly reshot, 1950–7); and *The Saga of Anatahan* (a strange war subject, shot in Japan, 1953). The chief outlet for Sternberg in his later years was film teaching. During the war he made one documentary, *The Town* (1943–4), for the Office of War Information. RM

Above: Erich von Stroheim in 'Mademoiselle Docteur' (Edmond Gréville, France, 1936)
Below: Marlene Dietrich in 'The Scarlet Empress' (Josef von Sternberg, USA, 1934)

von Stroheim, Erich (1885–1957)
Born in Vienna, Austria. American director and actor. One of the greatest directors in the history of the cinema, Stroheim was fated, largely by his own inability to compromise his art for commercial ends, to achieve only a very small output, and to see five of the nine films he made as director 'improved' by other hands. A certain mystery surrounds the early life of Stroheim: his own account of an impoverished but well-connected family and a career as a cavalry officer has been challenged in recent years. It is certain that about 1909 he emigrated to America, where he tried his hand at various jobs, including writing and acting, before being hired as an actor and assistant to GRIFFITH on *Birth of a Nation* (1915) and *Intolerance* (1916). In *Hearts of the World* (1918), as well as being Griffith's military adviser, he played one of the brutal Prussian officer roles which earned him the publicity slogan of 'The Man You Love to Hate'.

In 1918 Stroheim persuaded CARL LAEMMLE to let him direct his own script, *The Pinnacle* which was released as *Blind Husbands*. This was the first revelation of Stroheim's cynical realistically adult approach to sexual relationships, and was an immediate success. *The Devil's Passkey* (1920) has vanished without trace; but this film with the subsequent brilliant *Foolish Wives* (1921) completed the 'trilogy of adultery', which showed his ability to turn essentially novelettish material into harsh and powerful drama. It awoke American audiences to sophisticated European approaches to sex which they had until then innocently ignored. *Merry-Go-Round* (1923) was the first film in which Stroheim recreated the atmospheres – physical and moral – of old Hapsburg Vienna, and also marked his first conflict with producers. IRVING THALBERG, impatient with Stroheim's perfectionism and extravagance, handed the film over to Rupert Julian to complete.

SAMUEL GOLDWYN next invited Stroheim to make *Greed* (1923), in which the director wanted to adapt, word by word, Frank Norris's naturalist novel 'McTeague'. Before it was finished Goldwyn was merged with MGM and Stroheim again found himself confronted by Thalberg. Stroheim reduced his own final cut of the film from 42 reels to 18; MGM then cut it, without his collaboration, to ten. Even in this state it remains, in its expressive naturalism, one of the most remarkable and powerful works in the cinema. He approached *The Merry Widow* (1925) without much interest, but eventually turned Lehar's operetta into a mordant, brilliant, and entirely personal satire.

With *The Wedding March* (1927) he returned to the world of Old Vienna, and again exposed the haze of Ruritanian romance to the harsh light of his special kind of unsparing realism. One of his greatest achievements, the film was mutilated by Paramount, who re-edited the second half so as to show it as a self-contained film. When last seen, however, even this, *The Honeymoon*, still contained scenes of bitter satire that bore the unmistakable stamp of Stroheim's personality. *Queen Kelly* (1928), his last silent film, was abandoned with the coming of sound and the exhaustion of its budget; the parts already shot were assembled by the star, GLORIA SWANSON, into the (still remarkable) film that now remains.

Stroheim's final assignment as a director was a sound film, *Walking Down Broadway*, which fell victim to a dispute between producers, was revised, and reissued in a version not approved by the director as *Hello, Sister!* (1933); this version nevertheless has some typically mordant Stroheim touches. One more attempt to direct in France (*La Dame Blanche*) was frustrated by the outbreak of the Second World War; and for the rest of his life Stroheim, one of the most creative directors in the cinema, had to content himself with writing and with acting in other people's films, often equalling the impact he had made in silent films. His most notable performances were in *The Great Gabbo* (1930), *As You Desire Me* (1932), *La Grande Illusion* (1937), *Les Disparus de St Agil* (1938), *Five Graves to Cairo* (1943), *La Danse du Mort* (1948) and *Sunset Boulevard* (1950). There is a biography, 'Hollywood Scapegoat', by Peter Noble, 1954. See also 'Stroheim' by Joel W. Finler. DR

von Sydow, Max

Born 1929 in Lund, Sweden. Powerful Swedish stage and screen actor who has achieved his greatest success interpreting on film the anguished dilemmas of the soul devised by INGMAR BERGMAN. His impact in American and British films – most spectacularly playing Jesus Christ in GEORGE STEVENS's *The Greatest Story Ever Told* (1964) – has been less impressive. Working in the theatre in Sweden since 1948, he was ideally cast as the gaunt, tormented hero in Bergman's mediaeval morality, *The Seventh Seal* (1956): the role with which he is most enduringly identified. Main films include: *Wild Strawberries* (1957), *The Virgin Spring* (1960), *Hawaii* (1966), *Hour of the Wolf* and *The Shame* (1968), *The Kremlin Letter* (1969), *A Passion* (1970), *The Touch* and *The Emigrants and the Settlers* (1971).

Vukotić, Dušan

Born 1927 in Yugoslavia. Animation director. At first cartoonist on the satiric journal 'Kerempah'. The most prolific, and probably the most inventive, of the Yugoslav cartoonists who founded their studio at Zagreb in 1956. Vukotić's reputation was made with *Concerto for Sub-Machine Gun* (1959), though he had already won an award for *The Playful Robot* in 1956. Other striking cartoons included *Piccolo* (1960), *Ersatz* (the first non-American cartoon to win an Oscar, 1961). In 1961 he also made *1001 Drawings*, a documentary on cartoon film-making, and in 1966 a live-action feature, *The Seventh Continent*. More recently he has made the cartoons, *Opera Cordis* (1968) and *Ars Gratia Artis* (1969), as well as the strange, Kafka-like combination of animation and live-action, *A Stain on his Conscience* (1969). Vukotić believes that animation is a combination of science, poetry and philosophy 'suitable for avant-garde ideas and experiments'. RM

Wagner, Fritz Arno (1891–1958)

Born in Schmiedefeld am Rennsteig, Germany. Cinematographer. One of the founders (with KARL FREUND) of the great German photographic school, he travelled widely in his early days as a newsreel cameraman. Began work in features in 1919 with early films by LUBITSCH and MURNAU. With LANG's *Der Müde Tod* (1921) and Murnau's *Nosferatu* (1922) he established his famous atmospheric, low-key lighting style which was to become an integral part of the German silent cinema, notably in *Schatten* (1922), *Chronicles of the Greyhouse* (1924, with its splendid wind-swept exteriors), *The Love of Jeanne Ney* (1927) and *Spione* (1928). He moved easily into the sound period with PABST's *Westfront 1918* (1930), *Die Dreigroschenoper* and *Kameradschaft* (1931). Lang's *M* (1931) and *Testament of Dr Mabuse* (1932) were also remarkable for their claustrophobic lighting and design. The departure of so many major German directors in the mid-1930s meant that Wagner had to turn to more commercial projects (including some charming ones like Schünzel's *Amphitryon*, 1935). Although he continued working successfully in Germany throughout the Second World War and up to 1958, opportunities for the kind of rich visual styling with which he experimented in the earlier period were relatively infrequent. JG

Wajda, Andrzej

Born 1926 in Suwalki, Poland. Brought up in a traditional household (his father was an officer in the Polish Army), Wajda at the age of only 16 joined the Home Army, representing the Resistance as directed by the Polish government in exile. After the war he studied at the Cracow Academy of Fine Arts, and in 1950 went to the newly established school of cinema at Lodz, where he directed short films as part of his training. In 1953 he served as assistant to ALEKSANDER FORD on *Five Boys from Barska Street* (1953), before directing his first feature, *A Generation* (1954), a romantic film made in a realistic style about a boy's discovery of maturity through service in the left-wing Resistance. The film also reflected the newer cultural tendencies which followed on the still recent death of Stalin. His next film, *Kanal* (1957), also about the Resistance, was more assured and ambitious in technique, pointing forward to the full maturity of style achieved in *Ashes and Diamonds* (1957), which epitomized for the Poles of Wajda's generation the heart-searching and ambiguities of revolution. The action was compressed to the 24 hours of the day of the German surrender, and was concerned with a young man, Maciek, who, having fought the Germans in the Home Army, now fights the communists, in spite of some temptations to shift his allegiance to the Left. The film is filled with allusions to Poland's past; in its own way it is romantic, even nostalgic, while at the same time accepting Poland's newly orientated future.

The importance of Wajda's films – for himself, for Polish audiences, and as a contribution to film art – lies in their intensely personal use of the medium to resolve the troubled adjustment of a highly traditional and proud people to an entirely new and, for many, alien ideology. Most of Wajda's films, in one way or another, project this dilemma: for example, the white horse in *Lotna* (1959) is symbolic of Poland's ancient heroism, such heroism as led straight to death in 1939. 'This search for all the "coded" meanings is characteristic of us as Poles,' Wajda has said. 'We regard our work with seriousness as a type of psycho-therapy.' *Samson* (1961) also has the Occupation for background, with its story of a hunted man, a Jew, very much an alien, escaping from the ghetto.

Wajda's later work has varied more widely, moving away from the war. *Innocent Sorcerers* (scripted by JERZY SKOLIMOWSKI, 1960) was largely a dialogue picture, with a sexual basis. *Siberian Lady Macbeth* (1961), made in Yugoslavia from a script Wajda had written some years before, experiments with stylized melodrama, while the episode he contributed to the French film *Love at Twenty* (1962) adopts a more 'contemporary', fluid style. For many, Wajda's search for an idiom reached fruition in *Everything for Sale* (1968); a deeply personal and introspective work, it is structured round a film-within-a-film, the latter about the circumstances surrounding the death of an actor who dies as CYBULSKI had died. The two films, outer and inner, merge at many significant points as they seek to project the participant performers' own personal reactions to Cybulski's tragic death. *Landscape after the Battle* (1970) was another impressionistic, painful reaction to the war period, whereas *Hunting Flies* (1969) was a more intimate study in personal relationships made in a somewhat more controlled style than other of his more recent films. Wajda remains one of the most important film-makers of his generation, more especially as he has worked almost entirely within the bounds of a communist country. Latest work: *The Birch Tree* and a film made in West Germany (1970). RM

Wakhévich, Georges
Born 1907 in Odessa, USSR. Designer. Emigrated when young to France where he studied art and design. Entered cinema in 1929 as assistant to LAZARE MEERSON; became a major theatre and costume designer as well as film art director. His style is remarkable for its rich profusion of detail (notably in his costume pieces with COCTEAU), and its enjoyably wild grotesqueries. Films include *Madame Bovary* (1934), *La Grande Illusion* (1937), *Louise* and *La Marseillaise* (1938), *Les Visiteurs du Soir* (1942), *L'Éternel Retour* (1943), *Les Enfants du Paradis* (1944–5), *La Danse de Mort* (1946), *Ruy Blas* and *L'Aigle à deux têtes* (1947), *Ali Baba and the Forty Thieves* (1954), *Amours Célèbres* (1961), *Schéhérazade* (1962), *Le Journal d'une femme de chambre* (1964), *Les Fêtes Galantes* (1965). Many of these were collaborations with other designers. JG

Walbrook, Anton (1900–1968)
Born in Vienna, Austria. Stage and screen actor. On stage from 1920; London début in 1939 in 'Design for Living'. On screen from 1931, settling in Britain in the middle 1930s. With his distinctive manner and caressing voice, Walbrook swiftly established himself as the quintessential, Central European romantic figure. Films include: *Michael Strogoff* (1936), *Victoria the Great* (1937), *Sixty Glorious Years* (1938), *Gaslight* (1939), *Dangerous Moonlight* (1940), *49th Parallel* (1941), *The Life and Death of Colonel Blimp* (1943), *The Red Shoes* and *The Queen of Spades* (1948), *La Ronde* (1950), *Lola Montès* (1955), *Saint Joan* and *I Accuse* (1957).

Wald, Jerry (1911–1962)
Born in New York, USA. Live-wire American producer and screenwriter, popularly supposed to be the model for Budd Schulberg's hero in 'What Makes Sammy Run'. A former journalist, he came to Hollywood in the early 1930s, worked as writer, then producer, for Warners, Columbia and, finally, Fox, where he was responsible for many ambitious films, including *The Sound and the Fury* (1958) and *Sons and Lovers* (1960). He is perhaps better remembered for the dynamic series of films he promoted at Warners, including JOAN CRAWFORD's comeback film *Mildred Pierce* (1945), *The Breaking Point* (1950) and *Storm Warning* (1951). The last film he produced was *Woman of Summer* (1962).

Wallach, Eli
Born 1915 in New York, USA. American stage and screen character actor with a flair for comedy, frequently in partnership with his wife Anne Jackson. After a varied career in the theatre, he made his film début in ELIA KAZAN's *Baby Doll* (1956). Between films he has continued to work on the stage and on television and has lectured on the Method style of acting of which he is a leading exponent. Other main films: *The Magnificent Seven* (1960), *The Misfits* (1961), *The Victors* (1963), *Lord Jim* (1965), *How to Steal a Million* (1966), *The Tiger makes Out* (1967), *How to Save a Marriage* (1968), *MacKenna's Gold* (1968), *The Brain* (1970).

Wallis, Hal
Born 1899 in Chicago, USA. One of the most consistently successful independent producers, previously publicity man (for *The Jazz Singer* in 1927) and executive producer at Warners. Setting up Hal Wallis Productions, he moved to Paramount in 1947 where he created a remarkable 'schizophrenic' operating technique, making commercial films such as ELVIS PRESLEY musicals and MARTIN and LEWIS comedies (before the two split up) and prestige films with Shirley Booth, ANNA MAGNANI, BURT LANCASTER, and KATHERINE HEPBURN, based on notable stage plays.

He entered films on the exhibition side in 1922 and was involved at Warners on *Little Caesar* (1930), *The Story of Louis Pasteur* (1936), *Jezebel* (1938), *King's Row* and *Casablanca* (1942). The 'popular culture' of *Becket* (1964), a success which he made for Paramount, foreshadowed his first film after leaving them in 1969, *Anne of the Thousand Days*. More cinematically successful, though, was the hardy JOHN WAYNE Western *True Grit* (1969). Latest films: *Mary Queen of Scots* (1971), *The Public Eye* (1972). MH

Above: Joe Dallesandro in 'Flesh' (Andy Warhol, USA, 1968)
Below: Carroll Baker and Eli Wallach in 'Baby Doll' (Elia Kazan, USA, 1956)

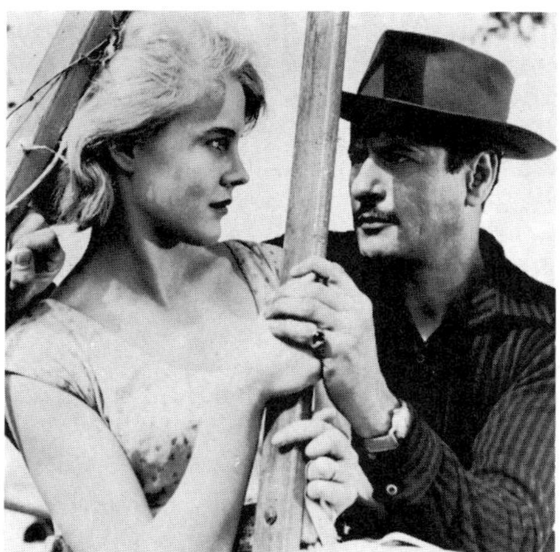

Walsh, Raoul
Born 1892 in New York, USA. Veteran American director whose skill in handling tough, masculine themes was much in demand during the 1930s and 1940s. A stage and screen actor before he became involved in the technical side of film-making, he played John Wilkes Booth in GRIFFITH's *Birth of a Nation* (1915) and was for a time assistant to the director. In 1923 he directed *Kindred of the Dust* and thereafter made more than 100 films, mostly on the Hollywood factory-belt system. Strong on free-wheeling action, his films (from gangster movies and Westerns to historical adventures) concentrate on fairly simple manly relationships, although several films, like *High Sierra* (1941) and *White Heat* (1949) combine more complex characterization with his usual technical prowess.

Other principal films: *Sadie Thompson* (1928), *The Bowery* (1933), *Klondike Annie* (1936), *St Louis Blues* and *The Roaring Twenties* (1940), *The Strawberry Blonde* (1941), *They Died with Their Boots On* and *Manpower* (1942), *Gentleman Jim* (1943), *Objective Burma* (1945), *Captain Horatio Hornblower R.N.* (1951), *Sea Devils* (1953), *The Tall Men* (1955), *The Naked and the Dead* and *The Sheriff of Fractured Jaw* (1958), *A Distant Trumpet* (1964). MH

Walters, Charles
Born 1911 in Pasadena, California, USA. Director and choreographer. After leaving Southern California University, he was actor and dancer in several New York shows in the 1930s. Became Broadway producer and choreographer before going to Hollywood in 1942, working almost entirely for MGM; was dance director on *Meet Me in St Louis* (1944), *Ziegfeld Follies* (1946, JUDY GARLAND's 'Interview' number), *Summer Holiday* (1948) among others. The early musicals he directed lacked the experimental stylization of MINNELLI, DONEN and KELLY but had a distinctive bounce and freshness and made enjoyable use of players such as ASTAIRE and GARLAND (*Good News*, 1947; *Easter Parade*, 1948; *The Barkleys of Broadway*, 1949; *Summer Stock*, 1950; *The Belle of New York*, 1952; and *High Society*, 1956). He also made several romantic comedies relying less on

music and dance, but with much decorative charm and a gentle sentimentality (*Lili*, 1953, with LESLIE CARON; *The Glass Slipper*, 1954; *Ask any Girl*, 1959; *Two Loves*, 1961). His more recent work has been less distinctive, although there are some witty inventions in *Billy Rose's Jumbo* (1962, a collaboration with BUSBY BERKELEY) and *The Unsinkable Molly Brown* (1964). JG

Wanger, Walter (1894–1968)
Born in San Francisco, USA. American independent producer and sometime studio power whose well-mannered background was reflected in the civilized breadth of most of his films, even the relatively tough ones such as *Riot in Cell Block 11* (1954) and *Invasion of the Body Snatchers* (1956) both directed by DON SIEGEL, when Wanger was fighting his way back into large-scale production. Brought to Hollywood by JESSE LASKY from the theatre in the early 1920s, he served time at Paramount, MGM and Columbia as producer and studio executive. He then went into independent production. After a domestic scandal involving an assault on the agent of his wife (Joan Bennett) and a brief prison sentence, Wanger signed up with Allied Artists to make small-scale quality pictures. Eventually he moved into big-budget production with *I Want to Live* (1958). His undoing was the trouble-prone, extravagant *Cleopatra* (1963), a traumatic experience from which his career never recovered and which he recorded in a book with Joe Hyams called 'My Life with Cleopatra'. A producer whose educated aspirations were never quite realized, he is reputed to be the model for the producer in Budd Schulberg's barely disguised novel about Scott Fitzgerald, 'The Disenchanted'.

Other notable films: *Queen Christina* (1933), *The Trail of the Lonesome Pine* (1936), *You Only Live Once* and *History is Made at Night* (1937), *Stand In* and *Blockade* (1938), *Stagecoach* (1939), *Foreign Correspondent* and *The Long Voyage Home* (1940), *Scarlet Street* (1945), *Joan of Arc* (1948). MH

Warhol, Andy
Born 1928, Newport, Rhode Island, USA. Underground film-maker, and the leading exhibitionist of this branch of the cinema. A fashion illustrator and 'pop' artist, Warhol took to film-making only in 1963. He immediately attracted widespread attention with his three-hour *Sleep* (1963), made up of one-reel segments recording a man sleeping. He followed this with a spate of movies in this static style, culminating in *Blow Job* (1964), a 40-minute head-and-shoulder study of a man in growing sexual ecstasy. These were all silent films. He moved next to a sound-film drama series, including *Life of Juanita Castro* and *Vinyl* (1965). These films were followed by a series which came near to *cinéma-vérité* documentaries, such as *Beauty Number Two* (1965), about a *ménage à trois*, and *My Hustler* (1965), about homosexual prostitutes. After this Warhol experimented in split-screen production, of which the best known is the three-and-a-half-hour film *The Chelsea Girls* (1966), projecting two sequences of film simultaneously, and shot at the Hotel Chelsea. His later films include *Bike Boy* (1967) and *Flesh* (1968). Not all his films are directed by himself; he is in effect the master-supervisor of a team of film-makers, notably Paul Morrissey on whose work he stamps his own very individual style and treatment. Other films include: *Lonesome Cowboys* (1968), *Trash* (1970), *Sex* (1971).

Warm, Hermann
Born 1889 in Berlin, Germany. Set designer. After work in the theatre, he entered the cinema in 1912 and became one of the great exponents of expressionist design in the German silent cinema, making his name with *The Cabinet of Dr Caligari* (1919), with its celebrated expressionist sets which he designed along with WALTHER RÖHRIG and Walter Reimann. He worked with FRITZ LANG on the two parts of *The Spiders* (1919–20) and *Destiny* (1921), with GALEEN on *The Student of Prague* (1925), and with PABST on *The Love of Jeanne Ney* (1927). He became a prolific designer for every kind of film, and from 1924 was more peripatetic, working as an architect as well as set designer in France, Hungary and Britain. His films of this period include CARL DREYER's *The Passion of Joan of Arc* (France, 1928) and the same director's *Vampyr* (Denmark, 1931); also in Germany, *Dreyfus* (1930), in France *Le Corbeau* (1943), and post-war in East Germany, *Wozzeck* (1947). In 1941–4 he worked in Switzerland, but returned to Germany in 1947 and continued to work on set designs for German films in the 1960s.

Warner, David
Born 1941 in Manchester, England. Actor, who made his name on stage with Royal Shakespeare Company. Essentially a character actor, he has specialized in vague, eccentric, but nevertheless astute, figures on the screen, with a strong vein of comedy. His films include: *Tom Jones* (1963), *Morgan–a Suitable Case for Treatment* (1966), *Work is a Four-Letter Word* (1967), *A Midsummer Night's Dream, The Bofors Gun, The Fixer* and *The Seagull* (1968), *Michael Kohlhass* (in Germany, 1969), *The Ballad of Cable Hogue, The Engagement, Perfect Friday* (1970), *Straw Dogs* (1971).

Warner, Jack L.
Born 1892 in Ontario, Canada. The best known of the four Warner Brothers – the others were Harry, Albert and Sam – who established and controlled the most resilient of the Hollywood major production companies. In 1904 the brothers ran a travelling film show, with Jack as a singing boy soprano. They moved into cinema management and film distribution and in 1912 Jack and Sam set up a film production company in California, but it was not until 1919 that the brothers were successful in the new medium. The company expanded and was the first in Hollywood to recognize the importance of sound, premiering the part-sound film, *The Jazz Singer*, on 6th October 1927. The Warner Brothers company absorbed other companies, notably First National, and after the death of Sam, Jack remained the Hollywood brother (Vice-President in charge of Production) and Harry and Albert were President and Treasurer in New York. Albert retired in 1956 and Harry died, but Jack stayed on in active control in Hollywood until the late 1960s, personally producing *My Fair Lady* (1964) and *Camelot* (1967), when Warner Brothers was amalgamated with Seven Arts. As tyrannical as most of his peers among the Hollywood tycoons between the wars, in his prime he had a shrewd feeling for the public fancy in entertainment. In 1965 he wrote, with Dean Jennings, his autobiography 'My First Hundred Years In Hollywood'. MH

Watkins, Peter
Born 1935 in Norbiton, Surrey, England. Director. Began as an amateur film-maker, with the award-winning films *Diary of an Unknown Soldier* (1959) and *The Forgotten Faces* (1960): the latter reconstructed the 1956 Hungarian uprising, and its impact on television led to Watkins joining the BBC, for whom he made *Culloden* (1964), an emphatically realistic documentary (with television-style interviews) about the destruction of the Scottish Highland clans after the Jacobite rising in 1746. His BBC-Television film *The War Game* (1966), using a similar style to reconstruct the aftermath of a nuclear attack on England, was sufficiently controversial for the BBC to reject it; it obtained limited release in the cinemas at home and abroad. Thereafter Watkins concentrated on the projection of large-scale controversial issues through feature films – *Privilege* (with Paul Jones, 1967), a combined attack on the Church, Authority and Pop culture, *The Peace Game* (*The Gladiators*, 1968), made in Sweden, and *Punishment Park* (1971), a forecast of an American society based on repressive violence. Watkins represents the highly individualistic contemporary film-maker, whose over-ambitious choice of subject tends to stretch his talents beyond their limits. RM

Watt, Harry
Born 1906 in Edinburgh, Scotland. Director. Educated at Edinburgh University. Joined JOHN GRIERSON at the Empire Marketing Board Film Unit in 1931. In 1934 became ROBERT FLAHERTY's assistant on *Man of Aran*, and was later director for *The March of Time* series. He directed some of the best, down-to-earth British documentaries before and during the war, including *Night Mail* (co-director, 1935), *North Sea* (1938), *Squadron 992* (1939), *London Can Take It* (1940), *Target for Tonight* (1941). He obtained excellent performances from non-professional actors, and carried this style of strongly marked, non-studio characterization

into the feature films he made for MICHAEL BALCON's Ealing Studios: *Nine Men* (1942), *The Overlanders* (1946), and *Eureka Stockade* (1948); the last two he scripted and directed in Australia for Balcon. He subsequently directed in Africa *Where No Vultures Fly* (1951) and *West of Zanzibar* (1954), and in Australia *The Siege of Pinchgut* (1959). Has also worked for a period in television. RM

Waxman, Franz (1906–1967)
Born in Königshütte, Germany. Composer. After musical studies in Germany and work in France, he came to the USA as composer and conductor. Worked with several major companies but is best known for his Warner Brothers scores characterized by brooding, deep-toned orchestrations, a subtle use of leit-motif and a close understanding of when music should appear in the narrative. Outstanding films from his enormous output include: *Fury* (1936), *Rebecca* (1940), *Dr Jekyll and Mr Hyde* (1941), *Woman of the Year* (1942), *Mr Skeffington* (1944), *Confidential Agent* (1945), *The Unsuspected* (1947), *The Paradine Case* (1948), *Sunset Boulevard* (1950), *A Place in the Sun* (1951), *Rear Window* (1954), *The Spirit of St Louis* (1956), *Peyton Place* (1957). During the latter stages of his career his music became over-bombastic and repetitive. JG

Wayne, John
Born 1907 in Iowa, USA. Real name: Marion Michael Morrison. Archetypal Western star in the individualistic tradition, echoed in his personal – and often stated – reactionary political principles. An actor of more merit than he is often credited with, he is a graduate of the JOHN FORD 'repertory school', although it was director RAOUL WALSH who gave him his first leading role in films, after a series of extra and bit parts, in *The Big Trail* (1929). He later played in a number of undistinguished Westerns until 1939, when John Ford presented him with the image-making role of 'the Ringo Kid' in *Stagecoach*. He has repeated that character, with subtle variations, in many Westerns (the best of them for Ford and HOWARD HAWKS) and has never been so successful in films outside his accepted genre. His fiercely anti-communist convictions spilled over into such rabid screen statements as *Big Jim McLain* (1953) and *The Green Berets* (1968). In 1969 he won a richly deserved Academy Award for his performance as the unorthodox law man in *True Grit*. Describing himself as a 'reactor' rather than an actor, he is one of the last of the Hollywood super-stars to hide their professional 'light' under a box-office 'bushel'.

Other notable films: *The Long Voyage Home* and *Seven Sinners* (1940), *Reap the Wild Wind* and *The Spoilers* (1942), *They Were Expendable* (1945), *Red River* and *Fort Apache* (1948), *Three Godfathers* and *She Wore a Yellow Ribbon* (1949), *Rio Grande* (1950), *The Quiet Man* and *Jet Pilot* (1952), *Hondo* (1954), *Rio Bravo* (1958), *The Horse Soldiers* (1959), *The Alamo* (which he also produced and directed, 1960), *The Man Who Shot Liberty Valance* (1962), *McLintock* (1963), *The Sons of Katie Elder* (1965), *The Undefeated* (1969), *Chisum* and *Rio Lobo* (1970), *Big Jake* (1971), *The Cowboys* (1972). MH

Above: George Bancroft, John Wayne and Claire Trevor in 'Stagecoach' (John Ford, USA, 1939)
Below: John Wayne in 'Chisum' (Andrew V. McLaglen, USA, 1970)

Wegener, Paul (1874–1948)
Born in East Prussia, Germany. Actor and director, he began his career on the stage in 1895, and in 1906–20 worked with Max Reinhardt in Berlin. He made a striking début in film with his performance in Stellan Rye's *The Student of Prague* (1913), which he co-scripted, and established his interest in macabre and period films with *The Golem* (co-directed and acted, 1914). After this he became a prolific director, normally appearing in his own films as well as directing or co-directing. Apart from his repeat of *The Golem* with a new story (directed by HENRIK GALEEN, 1920), the more interesting films in which he appeared were not his own: *The Loves of Pharaoh* (LUBITSCH, 1921), *Vanina* (1922), *Lucretia Borgia* (1927), and Galeen's *Alraune* (*Unholy Love*, 1927). After Hitler came to power he directed nationalist films such as *Ein Mann will nach Deutschland* (1934) and appeared in many others, among them *Hans Westmar* (the film about Horst Wessel, 1933), *Der Grosse König* (1941), VEIT HARLAN's *Kolberg* (1945), and PABST's non-nationalist *The Molander Affair* (1945–6), unfinished at the end of the war. RM

Welch, Raquel
Born 1942 in Chicago, USA. Contemporary screen 'sex symbol' and aspiring actress, whose jousts with comedy have been noticeably successful. A model and beauty contest winner, she decorated several unremarkable films until her appearance as a primeval temptress in Britain's *One Million Years B.C.* (1966) made her the principal candidate for the vacant role of Hollywood sex queen. Main films: *Fathom* (1967), *Bandolero* and *Lady in Cement* (1968), *Flare Up*, *The Magic Christian* and *100 Rifles* (1969), *The Beloved* and *Myra Breckinridge* (1970), *Hannah Caulder* (1971).

Welles, Orson
Born 1915 in Wisconsin, USA. Magnificent maverick among American film-makers; writer, director, actor, experimentalist and explosive life-force whose first Hollywood film

Citizen Kane (1941) has become a permanent fixture on almost every notable critic's 'top ten' film list. The dynamic ability that had earlier conceived the 'Invasion from Mars' broadcast, which panicked the American radio public in 1938, sustained him through *The Magnificent Ambersons* (1942), his next and, according to some *cinéastes*, better film. In later years he seemed to fritter away his talents in less satisfactory projects and flamboyant acting performances in inferior films (reportedly to pay for his own productions). But the revolutionary impact of Welles on the American and international film scene has firmly established him as one of the unique screen talents. No other film-maker has so searchingly examined and exposed the self-destructive complacency of the American Dream.

From childhood, Welles seemed destined to assume the role of *enfant terrible* which he was to play with such *panache* in his influential twenties. When his parents separated Welles was six years old. He spent two years with his mother from whom he inherited a feeling for poetry, painting and music. After she died, he stayed with his father, who introduced him to the world of actors and sportsmen and high society. By the time he was 11 he had travelled twice round the world and had become recognized for his precocity.

After the death of his father, he took off on a tour of Ireland, where at the age of 16 he was accepted by the Gate Theatre in Dublin, more for admiration of his nerve (he tried to convince them he was a famous New York star) than for any indication of rare dramatic gifts. In 1931 he made his stage début in 'Jew Süss' at the Gate. Returning to America, via Morocco and Spain, he joined Katharine Cornell's company, established himself in radio and became a leading force with JOHN HOUSEMAN in the Negro People's Theatre, producing the celebrated all-Black 'Macbeth'. Later he and Houseman launched the Mercury Theatre: to earn its keep Welles hired the company out to CBS radio to produce a series of plays adapted from famous novels. He also made, in New York, his first film, a farce *Too Much Johnson* (1938).

Top: Raquel Welch as 'Myra Breckinridge' (Michael Sarne, USA, 1970)
Above: Orson Welles as 'Macbeth' (Welles, USA, 1948)
Below: Orson Welles as Falstaff in 'Chimes at Midnight' (Welles, Spain-Switzerland, 1965)

Welles then took the Mercury company to RKO Radio in Hollywood where, after a couple of abortive starts, he wrote (with Herman Mankiewicz), directed and starred in *Citizen Kane* (1940), which was presumed to be modelled on the life of WILLIAM RANDOLPH HEARST, the newspaper magnate. Inexperienced in screen technique, Welles with his cameraman GREGG TOLAND and editor ROBERT WISE introduced many technical innovations that have since been admired and copied by film-makers all over the world. It was not, however, a conspicuous commercial success at the time. The ambiguous last word from the dying tycoon, 'rose-bud', has become one of the classic screen conundrums.

The film, however, made an enemy of Hearst. In 1942 Welles was asked to make *It's All True* in Latin America, a propaganda semi-documentary. During his absence, a change of 'government' at RKO occurred. When Welles went back to Hollywood he discovered that his second film, *The Magnificent Ambersons* (1942), had been savagely cut. He returned to broadcasting and the theatre and, though his services as a director were not greatly in demand (due to a largely unfounded reputation for being 'difficult'), he was much sought after as an actor. His most popular performances were possibly as Rochester in *Jane Eyre* (1943) and, even more memorably, as Harry Lime in *The Third Man* (1949).

In 1947 he directed his second wife, RITA HAYWORTH, in *Lady From Shanghai*, which did not find favour in Hollywood. Since his Gothic *Macbeth* (1947), Welles has done most of his work in Europe: the darkly sinister *Touch of Evil* (1958) was an exception. In between trite roles in triter films and occasional interesting stage productions ('Moby Dick' and 'Othello') he spent years obtaining finance for and preparing his major works: the film of *Othello* (1952), *The Trial* (1962), the Falstaff-Shakespeare masterpiece *Chimes at Midnight* (1966) and the long-delayed *Don Quixote* which Welles promised for release in 1972.

Other principal films as director and actor: *Journey into Fear* (1942), *The Stranger* (1946), *Confidential Report* (1955), *The Immortal Story* (1968); as actor: *Pay the Devil* (1957), *Compulsion* (1958), *A Man for All Seasons* (1966), *The Kremlin Letter* (1969), *Waterloo* and *Catch 22* (1970), *La Decade Prodigieuse* and *A Safe Place* (1971).

Many studies of Welles's work have been published, the latest being Charles Higham's disputed 'The Films of Orson Welles', Peter Bogdanovich's conversations with him and Pauline Kael's 'The Citizen Kane Book'. MH

Wellman, William

Born 1896 in Massachusetts, USA. Veteran Hollywood director whose films reflect box-office trends as well as his own artistic preference, although some outstanding productions reveal a shrewd, personal judgement of the current American scene: particularly *Wings*

(1927), *Public Enemy* (1931), *Nothing Sacred* (1937), *Roxie Hart* (1942), *The Ox Bow Incident* (1943), *The Story of G.I. Joe* (1945).

Experienced in handling any type of subject matter – including the original, graceful 'weepie', *A Star is Born* (1937), for which he won an Academy Award – he is undoubtedly at his best with the big, masculine, action film that, nevertheless, makes a valid point about social justice or standards. A former pilot, actor and Foreign Legionnaire, he flew with the Lafayette Escadrille in 1917: his film *Lafayette Escadrille* (1958), despite insensitive star casting, was a handsome memory of his own past, much underrated when it was released.

Arriving in Hollywood after the First World War to break into the acting profession, he started as a messenger boy and worked his way up to director on *The Man Who Won* (1923). His major silent work, *Wings* has a sturdy Hawks-like grandeur in its magnificently staged aerial scenes and honest sentimentality; and *Beggars of Life* (1928) featured LOUISE BROOKS in one of her best American roles. Although his Westerns, war and aerial films are principally remembered, *The Ox Bow Incident* – about a lynch mob – and the remarkable rural suspense melodrama, *The Track of the Cat* (1954), among other films testify to a fine creative talent that has never been fully stretched in his later period.

Other notable films: *Wild Boys of the Road* (1933), *Stingaree* (1934), *Call of the Wild* (1935), *Beau Geste* and *The Light that Failed* (1939), *The Great Man's Lady* (1941), *Yellow Sky* (1949), *The Next Voice You Hear* and *Across the Wide Missouri* (1951), *The High and the Mighty* (1954), *Blood Alley* (1956). MH

West, Mae

Born 1892 in Brooklyn, USA. Stage, screen and vaudeville actress and scriptwriter, the original larger-than-life sex symbol. Her films, most of which she scripted, are full of earthy humour and *double entendre*. They include: *She Done him Wrong* and *I'm No Angel* (1933), *Belle of the Nineties* (1934), *Klondike Annie* and *Go West Young Man* (1936), and *My Little Chikadee* (1940). Has recently made comeback in *Myra Breckinridge* (1970), and on television in *Mr Ed* series. Her autobiography, 'Goodness Had Nothing to do With It', was published in 1959.

West, Roland (1887–1952)

Born in Cleveland, Ohio, USA. Writer and director. Became actor-playwright in theatre and vaudeville and alternated in 1920s between film and theatre production. Silent films include *The Unknown Purple* (1924), *The Monster* (1925), *The Bat* (1926), *The Dove* (1927, starring Norma Talmadge, with whom he worked regularly) and the sound films *Alibi* (1929), *The Bat Whispers* (originally shot in 70 mm, 1930), *Corsair* (1931). West is a strange, shadowy figure in the early American cinema; obviously drawn to dramatic, semi-horror subjects, he had an off-beat style characterized by extreme camera mobility and great skill in lighting. Although his sound films suffer from awkward dialogue delivery, they are technically far in advance of their time; the Bat films, in particular, have a tongue-in-cheek humour somewhat akin to that of JAMES WHALE, also a recruit from the theatre. JG

Westmore, Perc (1905–1970)

Born in Canterbury, England. Eldest brother in the celebrated Westmore family of Hollywood make-up artists, he opened the first studio make-up department at First National, later to become Warners, where he remained for many years. His brother Bud became head of the Universal make-up department, where he specialized in 'horror' make-up; Wally was head at Paramount. Their father was a wigmaker who emigrated to America early in the century. The family founded the House of Westmore in 1935 and Perc was a founder of the Make-up Artists and Hair Stylists Guild in 1926.

Whale, James (1896–1957)

Born in Dudley, England. Director. After the First World War, he was a theatrical producer in London and became known for his production of R. C. Sherriff's 'Journey's End', later produced on Broadway. Its success brought him to Hollywood's attention and he became dialogue director on several early sound films, including *Hell's Angels*. His directorial career began with a version of *Journey's End* (1930), but it was not until *Frankenstein* (1931) that his film style really emerged – an urbane mixture of English 'Gothic' horror, parody and a civilized response to the absurd. *The Old Dark House* (1932) and *The Bride of Frankenstein* (1935) are masterpieces of the genre – economical and beautifully judged in tone; but he also took in social comedy, musicals and mock gangster dramas including *Kiss Before the Mirror* (1933), *One More River* (1934), *Remember Last Night?* (1935) and *Show Boat* (1936). *The Great Garrick* (1937), a wittily decorated period piece, is also a satire on the theatrical manners Whale knew so well and *By Candlelight* (1933) is a good humoured parody of LUBITSCH. Apart from *The Man in the Iron Mask* (1939), the films of his final period are less distinguished although his last film *Hello, Out There* (1949) has an interestingly experimental visual style. Unlike many directors who turned from theatre to film, Whale had a highly developed pictorial sense, a personal camera style (with a fondness for sudden, long tracking shots across the set), and a good-humoured way with actors. Seen today, his best work remains consistently fresh and lively. JG

White, Pearl (1889–1938)

Born in Green Ridge, near Springfield, Missouri, USA. American actress, who first appeared on stage at age of six, and later became a stunt woman. Silent film serials brought her fame the most famous of these being *The Perils of Pauline* (1914) and *The Exploits of Elaine* (1915). Her later feature films include: *House of Hate* (1918), *The White Moll* (1920), *Know Your Men*, *A Virgin Paradise* (1921). Betty Hutton later made a mock-biographical film of *The Perils of Pauline* (1947).

Whitelaw, Billie

Born c.1932 in Coventry, England. Actress. Came to London after experience in repertory and radio in the north of England. Has had an extensive career in television and on the stage, working in the National Theatre company 1964–5. She is an actress with a strong comic and dramatic personality, and has appeared in many films, including *Hell is a City* (1960), *No Love for Johnnie* and *Mr Topaze* (1961), *Charlie Bubbles* and *Twisted Nerve* (1968), *The Adding Machine, Leo the Last, Start the Revolution without Me* and *Gumshoe* (1969), *Frenzy* (1972).

Widerberg, Bo

Born 1930 in Malmö, Sweden. During the 1950s Widerberg became one of the best-known Swedish writers of his generation, and after four novels, two collections of short stories and a polemic book on the Swedish cinema, he directed his first feature film *The Pram* in 1962. This betrayed clear borrowings from the French *nouvelle vague*; but *Raven's End* (1963) revealed Widerberg's own distinctive personality: his visual sense and preoccupation with the history of the socialist movement. Two succeeding films, *Love '65* (1965) and *Thirty Times Your Money* (1966), dealt with contemporary themes, idealists faced with the welfare state and a commercial society. The romantic and exquisite *Elvira Madigan* (1967) was based on a real-life event, a tragic romance between an aristocrat and a tight-rope walker. Again in *Adalen '31* (1969) Widerberg reconstructed real events, a fatal clash between strikers and soldiers in Sweden in 1931. For many the essential seriousness of the subject was compromised by Widerberg's incorrigibly romantic outlook. The criticism was less valid in relation to *The Ballad of Joe Hill* (1971), which showed considerable restraint in its reconstruction of the life and death of Joel Häggstrom (Joe Hill), the Swedish immigrant who became the bard of the Industrial Workers of the World before becoming the victim of a judicial murder in 1915. DR

Wide Screen

A cinematograph picture with a ratio between the width and height of the projected image greater than that of a standard sound-film picture (1·37:1).

Opposite: Mae West in 'Every Day's a Holiday' (E. Sutherland, USA, 1938)

Widmark, Richard

Born 1915 in Sunrise, Minnesota, USA. Actor and producer, stage, radio and screen. At first often played psychopathic, sinister characters; then developed into Western and thriller character parts. Films include: *Kiss of Death* (1948), *Panic in the Streets* (1950), *Hell and High Water* (1954), *Time Limit* (which he also co-produced) and *Saint Joan* (1957), *The Alamo* (1960), *Judgement at Nuremberg* (1961), *How the West Was Won* (1963), *Cheyenne Autumn* (1964), *Alvarez Kelly* (1966), *Madigan* (1968), *The Moonshine War* (1970), *When the Legends Die* (1972).

Above: Judy Parfitt and Nicol Williamson in 'Hamlet' (Tony Richardson, GB, 1969) Billy Wilder directing 'The Private Life of Sherlock Holmes' (GB, 1970)

Wiene, Robert (1881–1938)

Director and actor. Born in Saska, Sachsen, Germany. Worked originally in the theatre, and entered films in 1914, serving as director and scriptwriter for films featuring HENNY PORTEN and EMIL JANNINGS. His almost accidental direction in 1919 of *The Cabinet of Dr Caligari* (the producer POMMER had offered the film to LANG) brought him international fame, which his later work failed to sustain – though *Genuine* (1920), *Raskolnikoff* (1923) and *The Hands of Orlac* (1925), despite variable merit, were interesting as expressionist films. His other films include *Salome* (1922), *INRI* (1923; also scripted), an elaborate spectacle film of the life of Christ in which WERNER KRAUSS played Pilate, Henny Porten Mary, and ASTA NIELSEN the Magdalen. Wiene continued his prolific output of films, silent and sound, until 1934.

Wilcox, Herbert

Born 1891 in Cork, Ireland. British independent producer-director whose peak popular period in the 1930s, 1940s and early 1950s coincided with the national film-going demand for frothy comedies and sturdy biographies of resolute ladies. He entered films as a salesman in 1919, starting a company with his brother. Later he went into film production, promoting such Hollywood names as DOROTHY GISH and LIONEL BARRYMORE in Britain. From 1932 his career was almost totally involved with that of the star he created, ANNA NEAGLE, whom he later married. Their first film together was *Goodnight Vienna*. Their *Nell Gwynn* (1934) was a commercial success and in 1937–8 they made two films based on the life of Queen Victoria, *Victoria the Great* and *Sixty Glorious Years*. Other joint 'lives' were *Nurse Edith Cavell* (1939), *Odette* (1951), *The Lady with the Lamp* (1952). His most enterprising touch, however, was to be found in the light comedies starring his wife and Michael Wilding, starting with *Piccadilly Incident* (1946). But attempts to break into the tougher, younger market after the arrival of commercial television in Britain were less successful. During the 1960s he announced several projects but none has reached the screen. MH

Wilder, Billy

Born 1906 in Vienna, Austria. Provocative writer and director with a *penchant* for strongly satirical themes, ribald sexual comedy and sardonic appraisals of the American scene. Much influenced by fellow expatriate ERNST LUBITSCH, Wilder has worked in Hollywood since 1934, first as screenwriter then as co-writer, director, producer. While working within the Hollywood system, he has enjoyed a greater degree of control over the finished product than many of his peers. His films bear the unmistakable Wilder stamp: thus while *Sunset Boulevard* (1950), *Ace in the Hole* (1951) and *The Seven Year Itch* (1955) may appear totally dissimilar, the nuances of Wilder's style and comment unite them.

He brings to his observations of American life an amused outsider's viewpoint. His most American film, which won him his second Academy Award, *The Apartment* (1960), examined the ethics and casualties of one-upmanship in business with a cynical compassion that is very Central European.

He started his career as a copy boy, then sports writer for a Viennese newspaper. In Berlin he became crime reporter. One detects the journalist's eye, too, in many of his films. On the fringes of Berlin café society, he started writing film scripts: he worked briefly on *Menschen am Sonntag* (1929) which had ROBERT SIODMAK as director and FRED ZINNEMANN as a member of the unit. In 1933 Wilder left Berlin for Paris: he continued to write scripts and co-directed *Mauvaise Graine* (1933). He eventually arrived in Hollywood and survived the hard times until he teamed up with writer CHARLES BRACKETT, an association which led to some of the most delightful films of the 1930s and early 1940s: *Bluebeard's Eighth Wife* (1938), *Ninotchka* and *Midnight* (1939) and *Ball of Fire* (1941) among them.

Wilder's first directorial assignment in Hollywood was *The Major and the Minor* (1942), followed by *Five Graves to Cairo* (1943). In particular Wilder's slyly funny handling of sex was becoming apparent. With the crime classic *Double Indemnity* (1944) and *The Lost Weekend* (1945), the Oscar-winning study of an alcoholic, Brackett and Wilder had established themselves as a seemingly infallible writer-director team. Wilder returned to Germany for his wicked satire on the impact of the vanquished Germans on the victorious Americans, *A Foreign Affair* (1948). After rending the Hollywood scene in *Sunset Boulevard* (1950), the team of Wilder and Brackett split up and Wilder made *Ace in the Hole* (1951) with other writers.

Of his subsequent films, those with particular actors and actresses share a common identity: the MARILYN MONROE sex comedies *The Seven Year Itch* and *Some Like It Hot* (1959); the AUDREY HEPBURN romances *Sabrina Fair* (1954) and *Love in the Afternoon* (1957); the JACK LEMMON social satires *The Apartment*, *Meet Whiplash Willie* (in the USA *The Fortune Cookie*, 1966). For the past 15 years he has collaborated most successfully and consistently with I. A. L. DIAMOND.

The record has not been unmarked by failure and contention. Wilder's Lindbergh tribute, *The Spirit of St Louis* (1957), was surprisingly dull except for its splendid airport scene. *One, Two, Three* (1961), a ruthlessly fast, furious and funny tale of East-West relations in Berlin is more highly regarded now than it was when it first came out. *Kiss Me, Stupid* (1964) was the ultimate in deliberate 'bad taste' Wilder; though in the permissive cinema of today it looks more honest than dishonourable. In *The Private Life of Sherlock Holmes* (made in England, 1970) his affection for Conan Doyle's fictional detective hero resulted in a gentle almost elegiacally humorous work which surprised admirers of his more typically sardonic style.

Other principal films: *The Emperor Waltz* (1947), *Stalag 17* (1953), *Witness for the Prosecution* (1957), *Irma La Douce* (1963).

See 'Billy Wilder' by Axel Madsen (1968). MH

Wild Track

A sound recording without simultaneous photography

Williams, Richard

Born 1933 in Canada. Animator, who worked with GEORGE DUNNING in Canada before coming to Britain in 1955. Here he worked on television commercials while making, in three years, his first individual film, *The Little Island* (1958), one of the most influential of modern cartoons. It is at once absurd and violent, madly serious and wildly funny. Three harmless little men (who have been described as like pear-drops in shape) representing Goodness, Truth and Beauty, develop into maniacal monsters in their efforts to prove to the others that they are right. The film is a virulent attack on the evils of blind idealism. Other of Williams's completed films are *Story of the Motor-car Engine* (1958) and *Love Me, Love Me, Love Me* (1962). Williams bursts with projects only partially realized, meanwhile supporting himself with commercials which are often brilliant in themselves, like *Guinness at the Albert Hall*, and titles and insets to such feature films as *What's New, Pussycat?* and *The Charge of the Light Brigade*. His films awaiting completion include *I. Vor Pittfalks*, *Circus Clowns* and *Diary of a Madman*. RM

Below: Marlon Brando and Stephanie Beauchamp in 'The Nightcomers' (Michael Winner, GB, 1971)
Bottom: Richard Beymer and George Chakiris in 'West Side Story' (Robert Wise, USA, 1961)

Williamson, Nicol

Born 1940 in Hamilton, Scotland. Stage and screen actor specializing in powerful, even desperate, character parts with a neurotic tendency. Films: *Inadmissible Evidence* and *The Bofors Gun* (1968), *Laughter in the Dark*, *The Reckoning* and *Hamlet* (1969), *The Jerusalem File* (1972).

Winner, Michael

Born 1935 in London, England. Energetic British writer, director and producer whose impudent disregard for the 'rules' of British film-making has resulted in a series of ambitious, variously interesting or awful screen surveys of the social scene: *West 11* (1963), *The System* (1964), *You Must Be Joking* (1965), *The Jokers* (1966), *I'll Never Forget What's 'is Name* (1967). Previously at the age of 20 he had talked his way into the business making nudist shorts and second features, after serving time as a film journalist and critic. In the last three years he has moved into the international market. Latest films: *The Games* (1970), *Lawman*, *The Nightcomers* and *Chato's Land* (1971).

Winters, Shelley

Born 1923 in Missouri, USA. Mettlesome American stage and screen actress who, after a routine spell as a traditional Hollywood leading lady, grew in professional stature as she gained in physical size. A model first, then a stage actress, she played many small parts in films after winning a contract with Columbia. But the first film in which she made a big impact was *A Double Life* (1947). Thereafter she was much in demand as a blonde bombshell, while managing to impress more intuitive directors with her wide range and talent. She has won two Academy Awards, for *The Diary of Anne Frank* (1959) and *A Patch of Blue* (1965), and lately has virtually cornered the market in over-voluptuous, tough-talking maneaters – *Alfie* and *The Moving Target* (1966), *Wild in the Streets* (1968), *How Do I Love Thee* (1970). Even more memorable was her blazing portrayal of Ma Barker in *Bloody Mama* (1970). Other notable films: *The Great Gatsby* (1949), *A Place in the Sun* (1951), *The Big Knife* and *Night of the Hunter* (1955), *Lolita* (1962), *The Balcony* (1964), *The Mad Room* (1969), *The Last Warrior* (1970), *What's the Matter With Helen*, *Whoever Slew Auntie Roo* and *Something To Hide* (1971). MH

Wipe

An optical effect for changing from one scene to the next in which the incoming scene appears and wipes the preceding shot off the screen along a visible line.

Wise, Robert

Born 1914 in Indiana, USA. Variable American director and former editor, notably with ORSON WELLES on *Citizen Kane* (1940) and *The Magnificent Ambersons* (1942). He joined RKO in the editing department in 1933, directed his first films, *The Curse of the Cat People* and *Mademoiselle Fifi* in 1944. In 1949 he directed what is certainly one of the finest, if not the finest, of boxing pictures, *The Set Up*. Although he has tackled every kind of subject, his best work is with intimate, almost claustrophobic themes – the business battles of *Executive Suite* (1954), the death-cell drama of *I Want to Live* (1958), the occult horror of *The Haunting* (1959). His success directing, with Jerome Robbins, his first musical, *West Side Story* (1961), won him an Academy Award and *carte blanche* for *The Sound of Music* (1965), another Academy Award winner which was also a huge commercial success. However, his third musical, *Star!* (1968), was an expensive box-office failure.

Other main films: *The House on Telegraph Hill* and *The Day the Earth Stood Still* (1951), *Captive City* and *Desert Rats* (1952), *Helen of Troy* (1955), *Somebody up There Likes Me* (1957), *This Could be the Night* (1957), *Two for the Seesaw* (1962), *The Sand Pebbles* (1966), *The Andromeda Strain* (1971). MH

Above: Joanne Woodward in 'Rachel, Rachel' (Paul Newman, USA, 1968)
Below: Natalie Wood in 'Inside Daisy Clover' (Robert Mulligan, USA, 1966)

Wood, Natalie

Born 1938 in San Francisco, USA. Actress, whose father was a Hollywood set designer and decorator, and whose mother was a ballet dancer. Appeared on screen as a child in, among others, *Happy Land* (1943), *Tomorrow is Forever* (1945) and *The Bride Wore Boots* (1946). She specializes in playing resilient yet vulnerable modern girls. Later films include: *Splendor in the Grass* (1960), *West Side Story* (1961), *Love with the Proper Stranger* and *Sex and the Single Girl* (1964), *Inside Daisy Clover* (1965), and *Bob and Carol and Ted and Alice* (1969).

Wood, Sam (1883–1949)

Born in Philadelphia, USA. Veteran American director whose polished, well-made films defy any thematic analysis, beyond a flair for survival (he directed two MARX BROTHERS films) and a gift for *schmaltz* (the best of the *Madame X*'s in 1937 and *Goodbye Mr Chips* in 1939). A buccaneering career in gold-mining and real-estate led him to Los Angeles where he became assistant to CECIL B. DE MILLE in 1915 and started directing films in 1920. He flourished under the studio system of the 1930s and 1940s, being particularly adept at framing the talents of the major stars. In 1942, he made *Kings Row* one of the most sumptuous of Warners dramas and in 1943 he produced and directed Hemingway's *For Whom the Bell Tolls*, but the rather ponderous production was only intermittently satisfying. In 1948 he made one of the pioneer Second World War reassessment films, *Command Decision*.

Other notable films: *Stamboul Quest* (1932), *The Late Christopher Bean* (1933), *A Night at the Opera* (1935), *A Day at the Races* (1937), *Our Town* and *Kitty Foyle* (1940), *Saratoga Trunk* (1943), *Casanova Brown* (1944), *Ivy* (1947), *Ambush* (1949). MH

Woodward, Joanne

Born 1931 in Georgia, USA. Sensitive American actress, whose intelligent portrayals of sensuous but usually deprived and frustrated heroines have made her one of the few female stars to survive the decline of the Hollywood film industry. Now married to actor PAUL NEWMAN, who directed her in a prototype Woodward role in *Rachel, Rachel* (1968), she trained for the theatre, appeared in more than 100 'live' television shows during the late 1940s and early 1950s and made her Hollywood début in 1955 in *Count Three and Pray*. Her first important role, as the schizophrenic heroine of *The Three Faces of Eve* (1957), won her an Academy Award in 1957. Other main films: *No Down Payment* (1958), *From the Terrace* (1959), *The Fugitive Kind* (1960), *Woman of Summer* (1962), *Big Deal at Dodge City* (1966), *Winning* (1969), *WUSA* (1971). MH

Workprint, Picture

A positive print usually consisting of intercut daily prints, prints of dissolved montages, library material etc., and which is in synchronism with the corresponding sound workprint.

Workprint, Sound

A sound print usually consisting of intercut sound daily prints and which may also include sound effects or music on the same or separate reels of film, synchronism with the corresponding picture workprint being constantly maintained.

Wright, Basil

Born 1907 in London, England. Documentary director and producer. Educated at Cambridge. In 1930, he became an assistant to JOHN GRIERSON, and one of the pioneers of documentary in Britain. His early films for the Empire Marketing Board (1931–3) included *Windmill in Barbados* (1930) and *O'er Hill and Dale* (1931), establishing his lyrical feeling for the short, landscape subject, and his command of both photography and editing. His reputation was finally established by the longer documentary, *Song of Ceylon* (1934–5), which won him the premier award at the Brussels Film Festival in 1935. With HARRY WATT he made the equally celebrated *Night Mail* (1935), assisted by W. H. Auden and Benjamin Britten, working for Grierson at the newly-founded GPO Film Unit. In 1937 he set up the Realist Film Unit, and his abilities as a producer were further consolidated through his work at Film Centre, a consultative organization for promoting documentary production, with which he was associated for many years. In 1945 he acted as producer in charge for the official wartime Crown Film Unit. He is an enlightened film critic and writer on film, working in this capacity on 'The Spectator' (1942–3) and at one

Above: 'Song of Ceylon' (Basil Wright, GB, 1935)
Below: William Wyler (1965)

time broadcasting regularly on film for the BBC. His executive work has made him widely travelled, and he is well-known as a lecturer in many countries, including especially the USA. Nevertheless, he had found time to direct many important films, including: *The Waters of Time* (1951) on the Thames; *World without End* (1953) with PAUL ROTHA; *The Immortal Land*, made in Greece in 1958; *A Place for Gold* (1961), all characterized by their humane and poetic approach. RM

Wyler, William

Born 1902 in Mulhouse, Alsace. Supreme example of the Hollywood craftsman-director, who flourished under the benign dictatorships of the studio régimes in the 1930s and 1940s. Enormously varied in both form and subject-matter, his work seems to have been much more significantly influenced by the quality of his co-workers (notably producer SAM GOLDWYN, cameraman GREGG TOLAND) than by any immediately identifiable Wyler style. Studying a list of his films prompts the conclusion that he is a greatly gifted story teller, with no particular theme to illustrate, who suits the treatment to the tale.

His European background – a Swiss father, German mother – and upbringing are hardly detectable in his films. CARL LAEMMLE, a relative of his mother's, persuaded him to come to America and try the movie business. Wyler left in 1920, discarding the prospect of a future in the family drapers. In the New York office of Universal, he created the company's foreign publicity department and in 1922 he went to Hollywood, where he started work as prop man, script clerk and cutter's assistant, mostly on two-reelers. When he was promoted to director he worked on 28 Westerns before attracting critical attention with *Hell's Heroes* (1929).

His first significant success was *Counsellor at Law* (1933). In 1935 he left Universal and later began the most productive phase of his career, with Sam Goldwyn. The films, based on best sellers, hit plays and the classics, reflect Goldwyn's taste for culture and flair for making it popularly acceptable: but Wyler's role as screen interpreter cannot be over-estimated. Between 1936 and 1941 they made: *These Three* and *Dodsworth* (1936), *Come and Get It*, which he co-directed with HOWARD HAWKS (1936), *Dead End* (1937), *Wuthering Heights* (1939), *The Westerner* (1940), *The Little Foxes* (1941). His association with Toland started with *These Three* and achieved its most distinguished work in *The Little Foxes*. In between the Goldwyn films, Wyler made two for Warners, starring BETTE DAVIS, in her archetypal role of the 1930s, *Jezebel* (1938) and *The Letter* (1940). After the Second World War, during which he directed a generous, if over-glamorous, tribute to British bravery, *Mrs Miniver* (1942), served in the US Air Force and made the magnificent documentary, *Memphis Belle* (1944), he renewed the partnership with Goldwyn for *The Best Years of our Lives* (1946). This tale of returning US servicemen was one of the most controversial and powerful films Wyler had made.

Through the late 1940s and 1950s, Wyler continued to create films of enduring entertainment value with professional cinematic skill – from the claustrophobic Henry James period piece *The Heiress* (1949) to the romantic comedy *Roman Holiday* (1953), the grim thriller *The Desperate Hours* (1955), the mammoth Western *The Big Country* (1958), and the Biblical epic *Ben Hur* (1959). He appeared equally at home in the great out-doors or in the confined staging of filmed plays, such as *Dead End* (1937) and *Detective Story* (1951).

During the 1960s the Wyler momentum slowed down. A remake of *These Three* (which in turn had been based on LILLIAN HELLMAN's 'The Children's Hour') with the Lesbian theme intact became the unsatisfactory *The Loudest Whisper* (1962). The critical failure of *The Collector* (1965) and *How to Steal a Million* (1966) was mitigated to an extent by his charming *Funny Girl* (1968). But *The Liberation of L. B. Jones* (1970) grossly overstated its racial case history, though flashes of the old Wyler flair break through.

Reluctant to talk about his work, he tends to let his record speak for itself: three Academy Awards for himself, 40 for other artists working on his films.

Other principal films: *The Good Fairy* (1935), *Carrie* (1952), *Friendly Persuasion* (1956).

Reference Work: British Film Institute Index on 'William Wyler'. MH

XYZ

Yates, Peter
Born 1929 in Aldershot, England. Highly competent British director whose craftsmanlike skill particularly in the handling of fast action took him to Hollywood where he made one of the most intrinsically 'American' thrillers of the 1960s, *Bullitt* (1968). Previously he had worked in the industry as cutter and assistant director and directed in the theatre, before directing his first film, a Hollywood-styled British musical, *Summer Holiday* (1962), followed by an off-beat black comedy, *One Way Pendulum* (1964). In 1967 his treatment of the British crime story *Robbery* led directly to *Bullitt*. Latest films: *John and Mary* (1969), *Murphy's War* (1971).

Young, Frederick A.
Born 1902 in London, England. Cinematographer. Started as a laboratory assistant in 1917, working his way up through the camera department until he became lighting cameraman in late 1920s. In the 1930s, he shot many films for HERBERT WILCOX and joined MGM British, working on *Goodbye, Mr Chips* (1939), etc. During the Second World War he was in the Army Film Unit and worked on features by POWELL and REED. With *Caesar and Cleopatra* (1945) he began his association with large-scale, spectacular productions: *Ivanhoe* (1952), *Invitation to the Dance* (1956), *Inn of the Sixth Happiness* (1958), *Solomon and Sheba* (1959), *Lawrence of Arabia* (1962), *Lord Jim* and *Doctor Zhivago* (1965), *You Only Live Twice* (1967), *Ryan's Daughter* (1970). Young has great technical expertise and flair, without the personal visual styling to be found among his great American contemporaries. JG

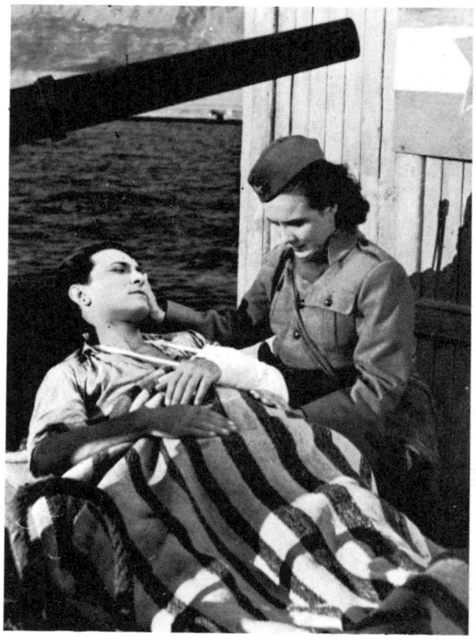

Above: Marian Lovric and Irena Kolesar in 'Slavitsa', the first Yugoslavian post-war feature (Vjekoslav Asric, 1947)
Below: 'Murphy's War' (Peter Yates, GB, 1971)

Yugoslavia
Film production in Yugoslavia is said to have been conceived during the war, when partisans in 1942 took possession of a German cine-camera and other equipment; the partisans began to produce their own newsreel records. There had, however, been an embryonic at-

Above: 'On Our Own Soil' (France Štigiic, 1948)
Below: 'The Prisoners' (Gustav Gavrin, 1949)

tempt at production before the war, including work by Mihailo-Mika Popović, of which *With Faith in God* (1932) was considered the best. In 1945 a Five Year Plan for film production was initiated in each of Yugoslavia's six constituent republics – Slovenia, Serbia, Croatia, Bosnia-and-Herzgovina, Macedonia, and Montenegro – under the control of a Federal Film Commission; artists and technicians alike were at first self-taught until in 1947 a Film Academy was established to give potential film-makers both a technical education and further studies in such subjects as literature, history, languages, social science and psychology. By 1948, 14 features and over 100 documentaries had been made, as well as the regular production of newsreels. At the same time an intensive programme of theatre construction had been undertaken. Only 300 cinemas existed in 1947, and even these were often closed through lack of anything to show; by 1967 there were some 1,700 theatres.

Problems facing producers included working in a country with five languages and four religions. Among the earlier films were, naturally enough, films of partisan warfare, such as *On Our Own Soil* (France Štigiic), *The Prisoners* (Gustav Gavrin, 1949), *The Sun is Far Away* (Radoš Novaković, 1953), *Two Peasants* (Zorž Skrigin, 1954), and 'period' films, of which the earliest was *Sofka* (Rade Novaković) and Fedor Hanžeković's *Brother Brne* (1951). Film production gradually consolidated during the 1950s, a time when the work of the 'Zagreb school' of animators became world-famous, more especially through the work of VUKOTIC, MIMICA, and KRISTL. [See ANIMATION.] Documentary was developed by the 'Belgrade school', led by the satirist Ante Babaja (*A Day in Rijeka*, 1955), Puriša Djord-

Top: 'Sofka' (Rade Novaković, 1950)
Above: Milan Ajvaz (centre) in 'Brother Brne' (Fedor Hanžeković, 1951)
Below: Neda Arnerić in 'Noon' (Puriša Djordjević, 1968)

Above: Jovan Milićević and Vera Gregović in 'Hanka' (Slavko Vorkapich, 1955)
Below: Milena Dravić (right) in 'The Role of my Family in the World Revolution' (Bata Cengić, 1971)

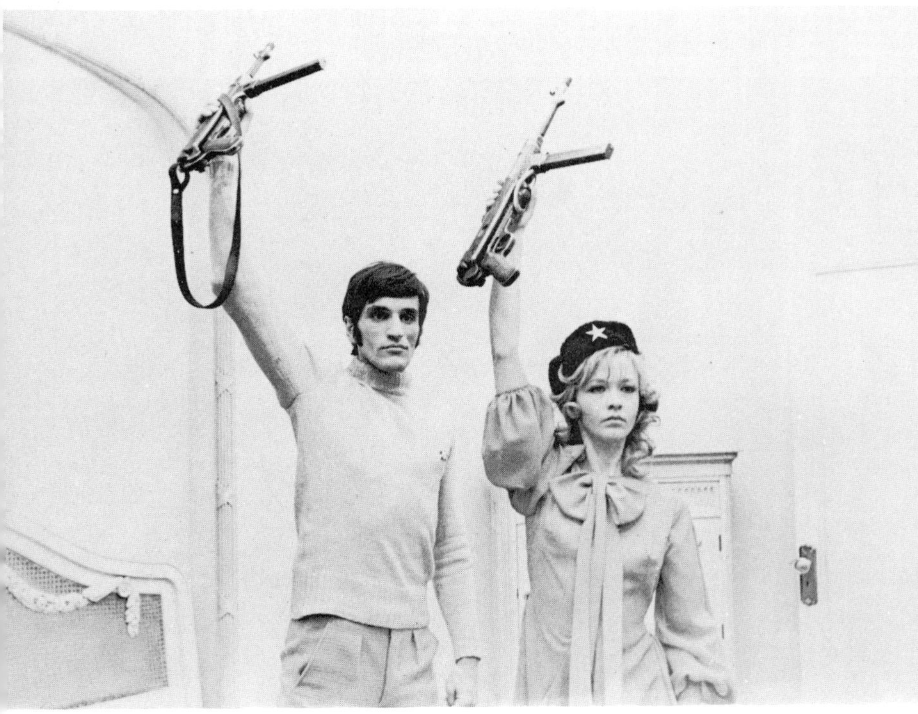

Above: Ljuba Tadić and Olivera Marković in 'Siberian Lady Macbeth' (Andrzej Wajda, 1961)
Below: 'The Protégé' (Vladan Slijepčević, 1966)

jević, whose style is lyrical, and Kristo Skanata, whose style is fiercely realist. Among the younger documentary directors of note is Zelimir Zilnik.

During the 1960s production rose to between 30 and 40 features a year, and a new, far more contemporary and less didactic style of film-making has developed. International awards at festivals have been frequent. Outstanding among the newer directors are the following, with a representative selection of their films:

Zvonimir Berković (born 1928): *Rondo* (1966)
Velko Bulajić (born 1928): *Train without a Timetable* (1958); *Skopje* (documentary, 1963)
Boštjan Hladnik (born 1929): *Dance in the Rain* (1961); *Sandcastle* (1962)
Bata Cengić (born 1931): *The Role of my Family in the World Revolution* (1971)
DUSAN MAKAVEJEV (born 1932): *A Man is not a Bird* (1965); *The Switchboard Operator* (1967), and *Innocence Unprotected* (1968); *WR-Mysteries of the Organism* (1971)
Zivojin Pavlović (born 1933): *The Enemy* (1965); *The Return* (1966); *The Rats Awake* (1967); *When I'm Dead and White* (1968)
Aleksandar Petrović (born 1929): *I even met some Happy Gypsies* (1967)
Puriša Djordjević (born 1924): the war trilogy, *The Girl, The Dream, Morning* (1965–67); *Noon* (1968)
Vatroslav Mimica (born 1923), as feature director: *Prometheus from the Island of Visevica* (1964), *Kaya, I'll Kill You* (1967), *Dogadaj* (*An Event*, 1969)
Ljubisa Kozomara (born 1935) and Gordon Mihic (born 1938), former scriptwriters: *Crows* (1970)
Zelimir Zilnik (born 1942): *On Wings of Paper* (1967) and *The Early Works* (1969)
Slavko Vorkapich: *Hanka* (1955)
Vladan Slijepčević: *The Protégé* (1966).

The last three are among those who represent the youngest generation of Yugoslav film-makers, whose work reveals the latest trends in style and approach. However, the director with the widest reputation outside Yugoslavia is undoubtedly DUSAN MAKAVEJEV, whose work has always reflected a satirical attitude towards the *status quo* (notably in *The Switchboard Operator*), and during the 1971 Cannes film festival, his *WR-Mysteries of the Organism* caused something of a *scandale* with its sardonic uncompromising attack on Stalinist doctrines and social and sexual repression in general. RM

Yutkevitch, Sergei Iosipovitch

Born 1905 in St Petersburg, Russia. One of the most attractive figures in the history of the

Neda Spasovejić and Boris Dvornik in 'Dogadaj' ('An Event', Vatroslav Mimica, 1969)

Soviet cinema, Yutkevitch belongs to the enchanted generation who began their artistic lives as boys in the optimistic years when the possibilities of creating a new art for the new society seemed boundless. At 17, having already trained in painting, he entered MEYERHOLD's Theatre Studio, where, from the day of the entrance examination he struck up a warm friendship with EISENSTEIN, a fellow-student; and together they collaborated on several stage productions. In 1922 Yutkevitch joined KOZINTSEV and TRAUBERG in forming 'The Factory of the Eccentric Actor' (FEKS), an avant-garde theatre from which Kozintsev and Trauberg went on immediately to co-direct films. After assisting ABRAM ROOM and acting as designer on Room's *Bed and Sofa* (1927) Yutkevitch directed his first feature film, *Lace*, in 1928. After one more silent picture, *The Black Veil* (1929), he made one of the earliest Soviet sound films, *The Golden Mountains* (1931) and collaborated with ERMLER and ARNSHTAM on *Counterplan*. After three documentaries, he made the first of the cycle of films in which he created, through the person of Maxim Straukh, the most famous screen representations of Lenin: *The Man With the Gun* and *Yakov Sverdlov* (1938). Later, still with Straukh, he was to make two gentle, reflective biographical studies of Lenin, *Stories About Lenin* (1958) and *Lenin in Poland* (1967), the most human and humorous study of Lenin the man. Yutkevitch's first important films after the war, during which he was mostly concerned with documentary and administrative work, were the spectacle *Skanderbeg* (1953) and a highly intelligent *Othello* (1955). In 1952 he made an animated film of Mayakovsky's *The Bathhouse*, which he had directed with great success on the stage. In 1969 he combined old FEKS experimental formalism with modern graphics in *Subject for a Short Story*, a series of impressions of Chekhov's life at the time of the disastrous first performance of *The Seagull*. DR

Zampa, Luigi
Born 1905 in Rome, Italy. Having made a short documentary in 1933, Zampa became one of the earliest students of the Centro Sperimentale in Rome, and afterwards a scriptwriter. His career as a feature director, initiated with *Fra Diavolo* (1941), experienced its greatest successes in the peak era of neo-realism, with *Vivere in Pace* (1946), *Anni Difficili* (1947) and above all *Processo alla città* (1952). Afterwards Zampa could never quite recapture the quality of the work of this period, though in the late 1950s and early 1960s he had some success with light satirical comedy. Films include: *La Romana* (1954), *Una questione d'amore* (1965), *Le dolci signore* (1967).

Zanuck, Darryl F.
Born 1902 in Nebraska, USA. Dynamic Hollywood writer-producer and studio tycoon of fluctuating fortunes and an awe-inspiring gift for survival, allied to an instinct for choosing commercial, marginally progressive subjects and talented film-makers. After a varied career in the First World War and as a jack-of-all-trades and story-writer, he went to Warners as a screenwriter (finding vehicles for Rin-Tin-Tin, the wonder dog), then as executive producer and later production chief. In 1933 he formed Twentieth Century with Joseph M. Schenck, which later amalgamated with Fox. As the vice-president in charge of production, he steered the company through two decades, concentrating on action-adventures, sentimental romances (many with his biggest box-office star SHIRLEY TEMPLE) and, after the Second World War, a series of explosive 'problem' pictures shrewdly stacked with star names – *Gentleman's Agreement* (1947), *Pinky* (1949), *No Way Out* (1950) – and literate, sophisticated comedies such as *All About Eve* (1950).

Under his sponsorship, too, JOHN FORD made *The Grapes of Wrath* (1940) and Zanuck's own personal project, *Wilson* (1944), was a worthy disappointment. In 1956 he left Fox, after several pretentious flops, but became an independent producer on *The Longest Day* (1962). After the *Cleopatra* crisis of 1962 he returned to Fox as President following a board-room power battle. His son Richard was, until ousted in 1971, head of production at the studio in Hollywood. A biography of Zanuck by Mel Gussow was published in 1971. MH

Zarkhi, Alexander
Born 1908 in St Petersburg, Russia. Between 1930 and 1946 Zarkhi was the constant collaborator of HEIFITZ. Subsequently he has directed alone *Pavlinka* (1952), *Nesterka* (1955), *The Heights* (1957), *Men on the Bridge* (1960), *My Younger Brother* (1962), *Anna Karenina* (1967).

Zarkhi, Nathan (1900–1935)
Already known as a playwright, Zarkhi wrote his first film script, for Gardin's *House of the Golubin Family*, in 1925. His most celebrated work, however, was his collaboration with PUDOVKIN on *Mother* (1926) and *The End of St Petersburg* (1927). He was killed in a car accident while being driven by Pudovkin, who was collaborating with him on the script of *Victory* and went on to finish it with Doller in 1938. Among other scripts which Zarkhi wrote was one for a film by EISENSTEIN, never realized, on the story of Moscow.

Zavattini, Cesare
Born 1902 in Luzzara, Italy. As a screenwriter – notably for the films of DE SICA – Zavattini was the principal architect and theorist of neo-realism. A dedicated Marxist, he wrote his first scenario for MARIO CAMERINI's *Dario un milione* (1935). He conceived an ideal of neo-realism as a cinema that would be total truth, abolishing the artificially plotted story, the deceit of the actor's performance, and transferring real life directly to the screen. Its subjects must be contemporary and must give people a sense of their own dignity and importance as human beings. In his ideal cinema, real people would play their own real life roles in their own real-life settings. Of the emergence of neo-realism, he wrote 'The reality buried under the myths slowly reflowered. The cinema began its creation of the world. Here was a tree; here an old man; here a house; here a man eating, a man sleeping, a man crying'. The idea was a chimaera; but in retrospect the films of the great neo-realist period did come nearer to a cinematic truth than the cinema had often known. Zavattini's scenarios for DE SICA include: *Tereša Venerdi* (1941), *I Bambini ci guardano* (1942), *La Porta del cielo* and *Sciuscia* (1946), *Ladri di Biciclette* (1948), *Miracolo a Milano* (1950), *Umberto D* (1952), *L'oro di Napoli* (1954), *Il Tetto* (1955), *La Ciociara* (1960). For BLASETTI: *Quatro passi tra le nuvole* (1942), *Un Giorno nella Vita* (1946). For EMMER: *Domenico d'Agosto* (1949). For VISCONTI: *Bellissima* (1951).

Zecca, Ferdinand (1864–1947)
Born in Paris, France. Originally a *café concert* monologuist, Zecca made his first films for GAUMONT in 1898. Initially employed by Pathé to record phonograph cylinders, on account of his excellent diction, Zecca rapidly passed to acting in and subsequently directing Pathé films. Among the early story-films created by Zecca was *L'enfant prodigue* (1901), *Les Victimes de l'Alcoolisme*, a five-minute adaptation of *L'Assommoir* (1902) and *La Passion* (1903). Zecca, though his fantasy and his films were much coarser than Méliès, was not without a degree of inventiveness, which he supplemented by some of the most blatant plagiarism in the history of the cinema, 'borrowing' freely from Méliès and from English competitors like PAUL and SMITH. During the First World War he was sent to the USA to take charge of the Pathé Exchange, and from 1920 was artistic director of the Pathé-Baby enterprise.

Zeffirelli, Franco
Born 1923 in Florence, Italy. Distinguished but controversial Italian stage director, whose career began in stage design, working on opera with LUCHINO VISCONTI, and himself directing opera, Shakespeare, etc in a specially striking manner, mostly in Italy and Britain. Has directed two highly successful Shakespearean films, with emphasis on action and location, *The Taming of the Shrew* (1967) and *Romeo and Juliet* (1968). Latest film: *Brother Sun and Sister Moon* (1972).

Zeman, Karel
Born 1910 in Czechoslovakia. Animation director. He began work on puppet films alongside JIŘÍ TRNKA with the *Mr Prokouk* series in 1947. His technical ingenuity has enabled him to animate Czech glass figures in *Inspiration* (1947); he combined puppet animation with graphics in *The Treasure of Bird Island* (1952), and created feature-length films which are an amalgam of animation forms and live action. His remarkable *A Journey into Primeval Times*

(1954) recreates prehistoric life, while both *Baron Münchhausen* (1962) and the medieval story *The Jester's Tale* (1964) excited his love for trick effects. He is particularly attracted by the works of Jules Verne, which he has adapted for animation in *The Invention of Destruction* (1956), *The Children of Captain Nemo* (1967) and *Hector Servadac* (1970).

Zetterling, Mai
Born 1925 in Västerås, Sweden. Swedish actress who scored a success in British films and since 1964 has turned director, mostly in her native Sweden. After a traditional stage training, she made several Swedish films, achieving international attention in *Frenzy* (1944). Her first British film was *Frieda* (1947), but her piquant style seldom found an ideal setting on the British screen. In 1962 she made the short film *The War Game* in Britain, then returned to Sweden where she directed her first feature, *Loving Couples* (1964), followed by *Night Games* (1966), and *The Girls* (1968). Passionately devoted to the cause of women's liberation she builds her films around this theme, although a certain humourlessness in the treatment tends to weigh against the undoubted skill she has developed as a film-maker. Main films as actress: *The Bad Lord Byron* (1948), *Knock on Wood* (1954), *Seven Waves Away* (1956), *Only Two can Play* (1961), *The Main Attraction* (1962).

Zinnemann, Fred
Born 1907 in Vienna, Austria. A leading director in the post Second World War American film industry whose humane and sensitive handling of acutely chosen and timely subjects won him a reputation which has not, latterly, been fully sustained. Trained in films in Paris and Berlin, he went to Hollywood where he played an extra in *All Quiet on the Western Front* (1930) and worked as a script clerk and director of shorts, including the Award winning *That Mothers Might Live* (1938) and several 'Crime Does Not Pay' episodes. The first film he directed was *Kid Glove Killer* (1942).

His courageous *The Seventh Cross* (1944), which proposed a tribute to the 'good' Germans in Nazi Germany at a time of rabid anti-German feeling, was typical of his concern for people as individuals later expressed in *The Search* (1948), *Act of Violence* (1949), *The Men* (1950), *Teresa* (1951) and, most spectacularly, in *High Noon* (1952). In 1953 he won an Academy Award for *From Here to Eternity*, after which his films grew ever more time-consuming and solid in scale, though the essential Zinnemann sympathy for the dilemmas of personal courage is just as apparent in *The Nun's Story* (1958) or *A Man for All Seasons* (1966). In 1970 his long-prepared film of Malraux's 'La Condition Humaine' ('Man's Fate') was cancelled just prior to production.

Other notable films: *The Member of the Wedding* (1953), *Oklahoma!* (1955), *A Hatful of Rain* (1957), *The Sundowners* (1960), *Behold a Pale Horse* (1964). Latest projects: *Day of the Jackal* and *Abelard and Heloise*. MH

Above: Michael York, Natasha Parry and John McEnery in 'Romeo and Juliet' (Franco Zeffirelli, GB-Italy, 1968)
Opposite: Mai Zetterling in 'Frenzy' (Alf Sjöberg, Sweden, 1944)

Zoom
Real or apparent rapid movement of the camera towards or away from an object

Zoom Lens
Lens of variable focal length which enables a camera to achieve a zoom effect without moving the camera towards its object.

Zukor, Adolph
Born 1873 in Ricse, Hungary. Among the earliest tycoons of the American cinema, he outlived all his rivals, and when well over ninety still went into his office in Paramount every working day. Emigrating to the USA in 1889, he went into the fur trade, but by 1903 had opened a Penny Arcade in partnership with Marcus Loew. Two years later he had a proper cinema, and a few years after that a whole chain. His success with the film of Bernhardt in *Queen Elizabeth* convinced him of the future of the feature film, and encouraged him to establish his Famous Players Company to produce 'famous plays with famous players'. Zukor early perceived that the two keys to power in the film industry were possession of the biggest stars and control of distribution outlets. In 1914, with W. W. Hodkinson, he formed a distribution company, Paramount Pictures, and until exhibitors finally rebelled and sought other sources of film product, imposed an onerous system of 'block booking'. This he was able to make effective by means of the immense popularity of the films of MARY PICKFORD whom he had under contract until 1918 when her financial demands exceeded even his need for her. Over the years Paramount's fortunes were built up through the films of the star directors DE MILLE and LUBITSCH and by a long succession of stars which included WILLIAM HART, Pauline Frederick, SESSUE HAYAKAWA, Charles Ray, Mae Murray, RUDOLPH VALENTINO, GLORIA SWANSON, CLARA BOW, MARLENE DIETRICH and MAE WEST. When Zukor wrote his autobiography in 1953 he called it, significantly, 'The Public is Never Wrong'.

Zurlini, Valerio
Born 1926 in Bologna, Italy. Director. Like many of his contemporaries, he worked as a documentarist for several years before entering features in 1954 with *Le Ragazze di San Frediano* based on a story by Pratolini. *Estate Violenta* (1959) and *La Ragazza con la valigia* (1961), sensitive studies of the war and mainly disillusioned love, were followed by his finest work to date: *Cronaca Familiare* (1962), a deeply felt account of family relationships and two brothers in particular, again based on Pratolini. His more recent works, *La Soldatesse* (1965) and *Seduto alla sua destra* (1968), were less fully realized. Zurlini's inward-looking, poetic temperament has made it difficult for him to maintain continuity in the commercialized Italian industry, but he could develop into a major talent. JG

BIBLIOGRAPHY

INTRODUCTION

Books on the art and technique of the film began to appear after the cinema had been in existence some 20 years. One of the earliest books to throw light on the potentialities of the new medium was Vachel Lindsay's 'Art of the Moving Picture' published in the USA in 1915. Other early commentators on film art were the Italian, Ricciotto Canudo (died 1923), and the French in a series of volumes published during the 1920s – LOUIS DELLUC's 'Cinéma et Cie' (1919), JEAN EPSTEIN's 'Bonjour Cinéma' (1921), Léon Moussinac's 'Naissance du Cinéma' (1925), and the series of volumes, 'L'Art Cinématographique' (1926–31). Canudo's essays were collected in a volume called 'L'Usine aux Images' (1927). PUDOVKIN's first book, 'Film Technique' (translated by Ivor Montagu, 1929) gave us an introduction to Soviet theories of montage. EISENSTEIN's essays on the cinema began to appear towards the end of the 1920s, but were not published in book form until Jay Leyda translated some of them for 'The Film Sense' (1943).

Film history might be said to have been initiated in book form by G.-Michel Coissac, whose largely technical 'Histoire du Cinématographe de ses Origines à nos Jours' was published in Paris in 1925 and Terry Ramsaye, whose 'A Million and One Nights' appeared in the USA in 1926; it provided a discursive, gossipy, fascinating, if at times unreliable background to the American silent cinema seen from the point of view of a man closely involved with the industry. The first independent, critical history of the international silent cinema was the work of a young man, PAUL ROTHA, whose 'The Film Till Now' (1930) appeared when Rotha was only 23. It was followed closely in the USA by Benjamin B. Hampton's 'A History of the Movies' (1931), which made a study of the American cinema from the point of view of business enterprise and in Czechoslovakia by Karel Smrz's 'Dajiny Filmu' (1933). Rotha followed with the first history of the factual film – 'Documentary Film' (1936). In France, Georges Charensol's brief 'Panorama du Cinéma' (1930) appeared in the same year as the longer historical study, 'Histoire du Cinéma' by Maurice Bardeche and Robert Brasillach. Three books appeared dealing with film aesthetics: Rudolf Arnheim's 'Film' (English translation, 1933), the work of an aesthetician. Raymond Spottiswoode's 'A Grammar of the Film' (1935), the work of a young film technician, and Kurt London's 'Film Music' (English translation, 1936), a study written by a music expert. JOHN GRIERSON's illuminating essays on the cinema, and more particularly documentary film, published during the 1930s, were not collected in book form until Forsyth Hardy's 'Grierson on Documentary' (1946).

The first fully comprehensive, analytical history of a national cinema was that by LEWIS JACOBS, 'The Rise of the American Film' (1939). This set entirely new, and scholarly standards for film studies; it was concerned alike with the aesthetic, the social, and the economic development of the American film industry.

After the war, film studies developed on a new, more comprehensive scale. In France, Georges Sadoul began to publish from 1946 his monumental historical studies, 'Histoire Générale du Cinéma'. His life's work (he died in 1967), remains the most extensive investigation into film history to be undertaken by a single research worker. René Jeanne and Charles Ford set high standards of scholarship in their massive 'Histoire du Cinéma' (1947–62). In Britain, Ernest Lindgren's careful and responsible book on film aesthetics, 'The Art of the Film' (1948) became the standard work on the subject for a whole generation. Roger Manvell, working first at the Ministry of Information, and later at the British Film Institute and the British Film Academy, began to write, edit and promote books on three different levels: (i) works of 'serious popularization'; (ii) research into film history; (iii) technical works primarily intended for those working in the film. On the first level appeared his first book, 'Film' (1944), and its successors in the Pelican and Penguin paperback series (1946–55); on the second Rachael Low's multi-volume history of the British film, covering so far the period 1895–1929, sponsored by the British Film Institute and the British Film Academy; and on the third level, the British Film Academy's series of books on different aspects of film art and technique, starting with KAREL REISZ's 'The Technique of Film Editing' (1953). In other countries large-scale research produced such general histories as Jerzy Toeplitz's 'Historia Sztuki Filmowej' (Warsaw, 1955–9) and Roberto Paolella's two volumes published in Naples – 'Storia del Cinema Muto' (1956) and 'Storia del Cinema Sonoro (1926–1939)' (1966) – and such major national histories as 'Historia del Cine Argentino' by Domingo Di Nubila (1959), 'Historie Ceskoslovenského Filmu, 1898–1945' by Jaroslav Broz and Myrtil Frida (1959–1965) and 'Historia Documental del Cine Mexicano' by Emilio Garcia Riera (begun in 1969).

The sociology of the cinema was approached tangentially, through government or other official reports on the alleged 'effects' of the cinema: for example, the British publication in 1917, 'The Cinema, its Present Position and Future Possibilities' (the Report of the Chief Evidence taken by the Cinema Commission of Inquiry instituted by the National Council of Public Morals). Endless speculation on this subject was hardened somewhat by J. P. Mayer's two books based on questionnaires and interviews, 'Sociology of the Film' (1946) and 'British Cinemas and their Audiences' (1949), supplemented in 1950 by the governmental 'Report of the Departmental Committee on Children and the Cinema'. In the USA the social investigators moved in before the war period with pioneer studies: Margaret Thorp's 'America at the Movies' (1939); Leo Calvin Rosten's 'Hollywood' (the result of a three-year investigation conducted by a team of enquirers); and, rather later, Hortense Powdermaker's 'Hollywood: the Dream Factory' (1951), an anthropologist's attack on the alleged obsessions of the American film-makers. Ruth Inglis in 'Freedom of the Moves' (1947) enquired into the anomolies of film censorship in the USA. A more recent study is 'Towards a Sociology of the Cinema' by I. C. Jarvie (1970).

Studies of the film industry from the economic standpoint began in Britain with a series of government reports published 1944–9[1], and, independently, 'The Factual Film' (1946), an enquiry into the position of documentary and 'The British Film Industry' (1952), a report sponsored by the organization known as Political and Economic Planning (P.E.P.), while the Swiss writer, Peter Bachlin, published 'Der Film als Ware' (1945) translated as

[1]These were preceded by a strongly polemical study of the British film industry and its economy by F. D. Klingender and Stuart Legg, 'Money Behind the Screen (1937), a report prepared on behalf of the Film Council.

'Histoire Economique du Cinéma' in 1947.

The period up to 1950, corresponding in effect to the first half-century of film, was a period of initial maturing. The post-war world produced during the 1950s and 1960s a great diversification in the cinema in all its branches – the fiction film, the factual film, and animation. This period has seen a rapidly developing second phase of maturity, in which the film has become more intimate, more immediate to the personal expression of the director, and far more variable and flexible as a medium for the artist/film-maker. Correspondingly, there has been a far greater range of work for the serious critic and historian to evaluate, and a new generation of critics has undertaken the task, at the best with an enthusiastic sense of dedication and scholarship. Helped by the growing number of archives, they have viewed and reviewed the work of individual directors, or separate genres of cinema, with the result that a large output of well-produced and illustrated original works in paperback have appeared, including Peter Wollen's 'Signs and Meaning in the Cinema', which reflects a growing interest in film theory largely stimulated by French theoretical writing, and a series of critical studies on directors by Robin Wood, who, with Raymond Durgnat, has been one of the most prolific writers in recent years. Other significant books include J. Leyda's comprehensive history of the Russian cinema, 'Kino' (1960), Joseph L. Anderson and Donald Richie's 'Japanese Film' (1959), Erik Barnouw and S. Krishnaswamy's 'Indian Film' (1963), Neville March Hunnings's 'Film Censors and the Law' (1967) and Kevin Brownlow's study of the American silent cinema, 'The Parade's Gone By' (1969). Substantial works of biography and autobiography have begun to appear, such as Marie Seton's studies of EISENSTEIN (1952) and SATYAJIT RAY (1971), CHAPLIN's 'Autobiography' (1965) and LILLIAN GISH and ANN PINCHOT's 'Lillian Gish: the Movies, Mr. Griffith and Me'. The 'sixties saw the development of the interview book, either devoted to a single director as in Tom Milne's 'Losey on Losey' and FRANÇOIS TRUFFAUT's 'Hitchcock' or containing a collection of interviews like Joseph Gelmis's 'The director as superstar' and it seems that the 'seventies will be marked by the reprinting of a large number of key writings on the film and the publication of a series of encyclopedias and dictionaries.

The following is a selected bibliography of film books of general interest, based on the holdings of the National Film Archive Book Library at the British Film Institute. Books have been included if they are useful and/or illuminating; if they are early examples of writing on the subject or of some other historic interest; or if they are the only documentation available at present on a particular topic. Most of the material is in English, but other languages are represented where there is no English alternative, or where a book is particularly important in its field. GH & RM

REFERENCE BOOKS

ACADEMY OF MOTION PICTURE ARTS AND SCIENCES and WRITERS GUILD OF AMERICA, WEST. 'Who Wrote the Movie and What Else Did He Write?: an Index of Screen Writers and Their Film Works, 1936–1969'. Los Angeles, the Academy and the Guild, 1970

'Annuaire Biographique du Cinéma', Paris, Contact Editions, 1953, 1957, 1962

BELLOUR, RAYMOND and BROCHIER, JEAN-JACQUES, editors. 'Dictionnaire du Cinéma'. Paris, Éditions Universitaires, 1966

BLUM, DANIEL. 'Screen World, 1949– '. New York, Greenberg, 1949– [annual]

CHARENSOL, GEORGES. 'Le Cinéma'. Paris, Larousse, 1966

COWIE, PETER, editor. 'International Film Guide, 1964– '. London, Tantivy Press; New York, A. S. Barnes, 1964– [annual]

'Filmlexicon degli Autori e delle Opere'. Rome, Edizioni di Bianco e Nero, 1958–

GRAHAM, PETER. 'A Dictionary of the Cinema'. London, Tantivy Press; New York, A. S. Barnes, 1964, 1968

HALLIWELL, LESLIE. 'The Filmgoer's Companion'. London, MacGibbon & Kee; New York, Hill & Wang, 1965, 1967, 1970

'International Film Annual Nos. 1–3'. London, John Calder, 1957–9

JEANNE, RENÉ and FORD, CHARLES. 'Dictionnaire du Cinéma Universel'. Paris, Robert Laffont, 1970

LIKENESS, GEORGE. 'The Oscar People: from Wings to My Fair Lady'. Mendota, The Wayside Press, 1965

MALTIN, LEONARD, editor. 'TV Movies'. New York, New American Library, 1969

MANVELL, ROGER, editor. 'Penguin Film Review nos 1–9'. Harmondsworth, Penguin Books, 1946–9

MICHAEL, PAUL. 'The Academy Awards: a Pictorial History'. Indianapolis, Bobbs-Merrill, 1965; London, Allen & Unwin, 1966

MILLER, MAUD M., editor. 'Winchester's Screen Encyclopedia'. London, Winchester Publications, 1948

NEW YORK CITY WORKS PROJECTS ADMINISTRATION. WRITERS PROGRAM. 'The Film index: a Bibliography. Vol. 1. The Film as Art'. New York, Museum of Modern Art, H. W. Wilson, 1941; New York, Arno Press, 1966

'The New York Times Film Reviews, 1913–68'. New York, New York Times; Arno Press, 1970

'The New York Times Film Reviews 1969–70'. New York, New York Times; Arno Press, 1971

NIVER, KEMP R. 'Motion Pictures from the Library of Congress Paper Print Collection, 1894–1912'. Berkeley, University of California Press, 1967

OSBORNE, ROBERT. 'Academy Awards Illustrated'. Hollywood, Marvin Miller Enterprises, 1965, 1969

'Picturegoer's Who's Who and Encyclopedia'. London, Odhams Press, 1933

RASMUSSEN, BJORN. 'Filmens hven, hvad, hvor'. Copenhagen, Politikens Forlag, 1968–9

SADOUL, GEORGES. 'Dictionnaire des Cinéastes'. Paris, Éditions du Seuil, 1965; 'Dictionnaire des Films'. Paris, Éditions du Seuil, 1965

SCHEUER, STEVEN H., editor. 'TV Key Movie Reviews and Ratings'. New York, Bantam Books, 1958, 1961, 1966; as 'Movies on TV'. London, Corgi Books, 1969

SCHUSTER, MEL, editor. 'Motion Picture Performers: a Bibliography of Magazine and Periodical Articles, 1900–69'. New York, Scarecrow Press, 1971

SPEED, F. MAURICE, editor. 'Film Review 1944– '. London, Macdonald, 1944– [annual]

'Variety Film Reviews, 1913–1970'. New York, Arno Press, 1972

WINCHESTER, CLARENCE, editor. 'The World Film Encyclopedia: a Universal Screen Guide'. London, Amalgamated Press, 1933

GENERAL INTRODUCTIONS

BARRY, IRIS. 'Let's Go to the Pictures'. London, Chatto & Windus, 1926; New York, Arno Press, 1972

BENOIT-LEVY, JEAN. 'The Art of the Motion Picture'; translated by Theodore R. Jaeckel. New York, Coward-McCann Inc., 1946

DAVY, CHARLES, editor. 'Footnotes to the Film'. London, Lovat Dickson, 1937; New York, Arno, 1970

GREY, ELIZABETH. 'Behind the Scenes in a Film Studio'. London, Phoenix House, 1966; New York, Roy, 1968

MANVELL, ROGER. 'Film'. Harmondsworth, Penguin Books, 1944, 1946, 1950; 'The Film and the Public'. Harmondsworth, Penguin Books, 1955; 'A Seat at the Cinema'. London, Evans Brothers, 1951; 'What is a Film?'. London, Macdonald, 1965

MARSHALL CAVENDISH BOOKS LTD. 'The Movies'. Marshall Cavendish Books Ltd., 1970

MONTAGU, IVOR. 'Film World: a Guide to Cinema'. Hammondsworth, Baltimore, Penguin Books, 1964

MOUSSINAC, LÉON. 'Naissance du Cinéma'. Paris, J. Povolozky, 1925

NAUMBURG, NANCY, editor. 'We Make the Movies'. New York, Norton, 1937; London, Faber, 1938

REED, STANLEY and HUNTLEY, JOHN. 'How Films are Made'. London, Educational Supply Association, 1955

STEWART, BRUCE. 'The World of Film'. London, Darton, Longman & Todd, 1971

WOLLENBERG, H. H. 'Anatomy of the Film: an Illustrated Guide to Film Appreciation'. London, Marsland Publications Ltd., 1947; New York, Arno Press, 1972

MISCELLANEOUS

AGEL, HENRI. 'Le Cinéma et le Sacré'. Paris, Les Éditions du Cerf, 1953, 1961

'L'Art Cinématographique'. Paris, Librarie

Felix Alcan, 1929–31; New York, Arno Press, 1970
AYFRE, AMÉDÉE. 'Conversion aux Images? les Images et Dieu: les Images et l'Homme'. Paris, Les Éditions du Cerf, 1964; 'Dieu au Cinéma: Problèmes Esthétiques du Film Religieux'. Paris, Presses Universitaires de France, 1953
BALL, ROBERT HAMILTON. 'Shakespeare on Silent Film: a Strange Eventful History'. London, Allen & Unwin; New York, Theatre Arts Books, 1968
BARNES, JOHN. 'Barnes Museum of Cinematography: Catalogue of the Collection'. Saint Ives, Barnes Museum, 1967
BARSACQ, LEON. 'Le Décor de Film'. Paris, Editions Seghers, 1970
BULTER, IVAN. 'Religion in the Cinema'. London, Tantivy Press; New York, A. S. Barnes, 1969
CAREY, GARY. 'Lost Films'. New York, Museum of Modern Art, 1970
COSTELLO, DONALD P. 'The Serpent's Eye: Shaw and the Cinema'. University of Notre Dame Press, 1965
CROSS, JOHN E. and RATTENBURY, ARNOLD, editors. 'Screen and Audience'. Saturn Press, 1948. (Film Today Books)
DURGNAT, RAYMOND. 'The Cinema of Sexual Alienation'. London, Studio Vista, 1972
DURGNAT, RAYMOND. 'Eros in the Cinema'. London, Calder & Boyars; New York, Fernhill House, 1966
ESSOE, GABE. 'Tarzan of the Movies: a Pictorial History'. New York, Citadel Press, 1968
EVERSON, WILLIAM K. 'The Bad Guys: a Pictorial History of the Movie Villain'. New York, Citadel Press, 1964
FENSCH, THOMAS. 'Films on the Campus'. New York, A. S. Barnes; London, Thomas Yoseloff, 1970
HALL, BEN M. 'The Best Remaining Seats: the Story of the Golden Age of the Movie Palace'. New York, Clarkson N. Potter, 1961
HOFMANN, CHARLES. 'Sounds for Silents'. With a foreword by Lillian Gish. New York, D.B.S. Publications, 1970
HUGHES, ROBERT, editor. 'Film Book 1: the Audience and the Film-maker'. New York, Grove Press, Inc., 1959
HUGHES, ROBERT, editor. 'Film Book 2: Films of Peace and War'. New York, Grove Press, Inc., 1962
KNIGHT, ARTHUR. 'The Hollywood Style'. New York, Macmillan, 1969
KYROU, ADO. 'Amour, érotisme et cinéma'. Paris, Le Terrain Vague, 1967; 'Le surréalisme au cinéma'. Paris, Arcanes, 1953, 1963
LAHUE, KALTON C. 'Collecting Classic Films'. New York, Amphoto, Hastings House, 1970
MANVELL, ROGER. 'Shakespeare and the Film'. London, J. M. Dent & Sons; New York, Praeger, 1971
MCARTHUR, COLIN. 'Underworld USA'. London, Secker & Warburg; New York, Viking, 1972
MORELLA, JOE and EPSTEIN, EDWARD Z. 'Rebels: the Rebel Hero in Films'. New York, Citadel Press, 1971
PARISH, JAMES ROBERT. 'The Great Movie Series'. New York, A. S. Barnes, 1972
RICHARDSON, ROBERT. 'Literature and Film'. Bloomington, London, Indiana University Press, 1969
SHARP, DENNIS. 'The Picture Palace, and Other Buildings for the Movies'. London, Hugh Evelyn; New York, Praeger, 1969
SPATZ, JONAS. 'Hollywood in Fiction: Some Versions of the American Myth'. The Hague, Mouton, 1969
TYLER, PARKER. 'Screening of the Sexes; Homosexuality in the Movies'. New York, Holt, Rinehart & Winston, 1972
WALKER, ALEXANDER. 'The Celluloid Sacrifice: Aspects of Sex in the Movies'. London, Michael Joseph; New York, Hawthorn, 1966

FILM-MAKING

ANDERSON, LINDSAY. 'Making a Film: the Story of "Secret People"'. London, Allen & Unwin, 1952
BADDELEY, W. HUGH. 'The Technique of Documentary Film Production'. London, Focal Press; New York, Hastings House, 1963, 1969
BRANSTON, BRIAN. 'A Film Maker's Guide to Planning, Directing and Shooting Films for Pleasure and Profit'. London, Allen & Unwin, 1967; New York, Hillary House, 1968
BRUNEL, ADRIAN. 'Film Script: the Technique of Writing for the Screen'. London, Burke Publishing Company, 1948
BURDER, JOHN. 'The Technique of Editing 16mm. Films'. London, Focal Press; New York, Hastings House, 1968
BUTLER, IVAN. 'The Making of Feature Films: a Guide'. Harmondsworth, Penguin Books, 1971
CALLAGHAN, BARRY. 'A Manual of Film-Making'. London, Thames & Hudson, 1972
CARLSON, VERNE and SYLVIA. 'Professional 16/35 mm Cameraman's Handbook'. New York, Amphoto, 1970
CARRICK, EDWARD. 'Art and Design in the British Film: a Pictorial Directory of British Art Directors and their Work'. London, Dennis Dobson, 1948; New York, Arno Press, 1972; 'Designing for Moving Pictures'. London, New York, Studio Publications, 1941, 1949
CLARK, FRANK P. 'Special Effects in Motion Pictures: Some Methods for Producing Mechanical Special Effects'. New York, SMPTE, 1966
CLARKE, CHARLES G. 'Professional Cinematography'. Hollywood, American Society of Cinematographers, 1964, 1968
COLPI, HENRI. 'Défense et Illustration de la Musique dans le Film'. Lyon, SERDOC, 1963
CORNWELL-CLYNE, ADRIAN. '3-D Kinematography and New Screen Techniques'. London, New York, Hutchinson, 1954
DEWHURST, H. 'Introduction to 3-D'. London, Chapman & Hall, 1954
EISENSTEIN, SERGEI MIKHAILOVICH. 'Notes of a Film Director'; translated by X. Danko. London, Lawrence & Wishart, 1959
EISLER, HANNS. 'Composing for the Films'. New York, Oxford University Press, 1947
FAULKNER, ROBERT R. 'Hollywood Studio Musicians: Their Work and Careers in the Recording Industry'. Chicago, Aldine/Atherton, 1971
FIELDING, RAYMOND. 'The Technique of Special-effects Cinematography'. London, Focal Press; New York, Hastings House, 1965
FISHER, DAVID. 'The Craft of Film'. London, Attic Publishing Ltd., 1970
HERMAN, LEWIS. 'A Practical Manual of Screen Playwriting for Theater and Television Films'. Cleveland, New York, The World Publishing Company, 1963
HUNTLEY, JOHN. 'British Film Music'. London, Skelton Robinson, 1948; New York, Arno Press, 1972
KLEIN, ADRIAN BERNARD (later Adrian CORNWELL-CLYNE). 'Colour Cinematography'. London, Chapman & Hall, 1936, 1939, 1951
LAWSON, JOHN HOWARD. 'Theory and Technique of Playwriting and Screenwriting'. New York, G. P. Putnam's, 1949
LEVITAN, ELI L. 'An Alphabetical Guide to Motion Picture, Television and Videotape Production'. New York, McGraw-Hill, 1970
LIVINGSTON, DON. 'Film and the Director'. New York, The Macmillan Company, 1953
LONDON, KURT. 'Film Music'. London, Faber, 1936; New York, Arno Press, 1970
MANVELL, ROGER and HUNTLEY, JOHN. 'The Technique of Film Music'. London, Focal Press; New York, Hastings House, 1957
MARNER, TERENCE. Editor. 'Directing Motion Pictures'. London, Tantivy Press; New York, A. S. Barnes, 1972
MASCELLI, JOSEPH V. Editor. 'American Cinematographer Manual'. Hollywood, American Society of Cinematographers, 1960, 1966
MERCER, JOHN. 'An Introduction to Cinematography'. Champaign (Ill.), Stripes Publishing Co., 1969
MILLERSON, GERALD. 'Technique of Lighting for Motion Pictures and Television'. London, Focal Press; New York, Hastings House, 1972
NILSEN, VLADIMIR. 'The Cinema as Graphic Art'. London, Newnes, 1936; New York, Hill & Wang, 1959
NIZHNY, VLADIMIR. 'Lessons with Eisenstein'; translated and edited by Ivor Montagu and Jay Leyda. London, Allen & Unwin, 1962; New York, Hill & Wang, 1969
PATE, MICHAEL. 'The Film Actor; Acting for Motion Pictures and Television'. New York, A. S. Barnes; London, Thomas Yoseloff, 1970
PINCUS, EDWARD. 'Guide to Film-making'. New York, New American Library, 1969
PORCILE, F. 'Présence de la Musique a l'Écran'. Paris, Éditions du Cerf, 1969
PUDOVKIN, V. L. 'Film Acting: a Course of Lectures Delivered at the State Institute of Cinematography, Moscow'; translated from the Russian by Ivor Montagu. London, George Newnes, 1935; 'On Film Technique: three essays and an address'; translated and annotated by Ivor Montagu. London, Victor Gollancz, 1929; as 'Film technique and film acting'.

London, Vision; Mayflower, 1958
QUIGLEY, MARTIN, JUNIOR, editor. 'New Screen Techniques'. New York, Quigley Publishing Co., 1953
REISZ, KAREL. 'The Technique of Film Editing'. London, Focal Press; New York, Hastings House, 1953, 1968
REYNERSTON, A. J. 'The Work of a Film Director'. London, Focal Press; New York, Hastings House, 1970
RILLA, WOLF. 'A–Z of Movie Making'. London, Studio Vista, 1970
SKINNER, FRANK. 'Underscore'. Hackensack, Wehman Bros., 1950, 1960
SMALLMAN, KIRK. 'Creative Film-making'. London, New York, Collier-Macmillan, 1969
SMPTE. 'Elements of Color in Professional Motion Pictures'. New York, SMPTE, 1957
SOUTO, H. MARIO RAIMONDO. 'The Technique of the Motion Picture Camera'. London, Focal Press; New York, Hastings House, 1967, 1969
SPOTTISWOODE, RAYMOND. 'Film and its Techniques'. London, Faber; Los Angeles, Berkeley, University of California Press, 1951; 'The Focal Encyclopedia of Film and Television Technique'. London, Focal Press; New York, Hastings House, 1969
TALBOT, FREDERICK A. 'Moving Pictures: How They are Made and Worked'. London, Heinemann, 1912, 1923; New York, Arno Press, 1970
WALTER, ERNEST. 'The Technique of the Film Cutting Room'. London, New York, Focal Press, 1969
WHEELER, LESLIE J. 'Principles of Cinematography; a Handbook of Motion Picture Technology'. London, Fountain Press; New York, Morgan & Morgan, 1953, 1958, 1963, 1969
WHITAKER, ROD. 'The Language of Film'. Englewood Cliffs (NJ), Prentice-Hall Inc., 1970
WYSOTSKY, MICHAEL Z. 'Wide-screen Cinema and Stereophonic Sound'. London, Focal Press; New York, Hastings House, 1971

FILM AND SOCIETY

ADLER, MORTIMER J. 'Art and Prudence: a Study in Practical Philosophy'. New York, Longmans Green, 1937
BACHLIN, PETER. 'Der Film als Ware'. Basle, Burg-Verlag, 1945; as 'Histoire économique du cinéma'. Paris, La Nouvelle Édition, 1947
CARMEN, IRA H. 'Movies, Censorship and the Law'. Ann Arbor, University of Michigan Press, 1966
CARTER, HUNTLEY. 'The New Spirit in the Cinema: an Analysis and Interpretation of the Parallel Paths of the Cinema Which Have Led to the Present Revolutionary Crisis, Forming a Study of the Cinema as an Instrument of Social Humanism'. London, Harold Shaylor, 1930; New York, Arno Press, 1970
CASTELLO, GUILIO CESARE. 'Il Divismo: Mitologia del Cinema'. Rome, Edizioni Radio Italiana, 1957
COGLEY, JOHN. 'Report on Blacklisting, I. Movies'. New York, Fund for the Republic, 1956; New York, Arno Press, 1972
COMMISSION ON EDUCATIONAL AND CULTURAL FILMS. 'The Film in National Life.' London, Allen & Unwin, 1932
FIELD, MARY. 'Good Company: the Story of the Children's Entertainment Film Movement in Great Britain, 1943–1950'. London, New York, Longmans Green, 1952
FORD, RICHARD. 'Children in the Cinema'. London, Allen & Unwin, 1939.
FURHAMMER, LEIF and ISAKSSON, FOLKE. 'Politics and Film'. London, Studio Vista; New York, Praeger, 1971
GLUCKSMANN, ANDRÉ. 'Violence on the Screen: a Report on Research into the Effects on Young People of Scenes of Violence in Films and Television'; translated from the French by Susan Bennett. London, British Film Institute Education Department, 1971
GREAT BRITAIN. 'Departmental Committee on Children and the Cinema: Report'. London, H.M.S.O., 1950
GUBACK, THOMAS H. 'The International Film Industry: Western Europe and America since 1945'. Bloomington, Indiana University Press, 1969
HANDEL, LEO A. 'Hollywood Looks at its Audience: a Report of Film Audience Research'. Urbana, University of Illinois Press, 1950
HUACO, GEORGE A. 'The Sociology of Film Art'. London, New York, Basic Books, 1965
HUNNINGS, NEVILLE MARCH. 'Film Censors and the Law'. London, Allen & Unwin; New York, Hillary House, 1967
INGLIS, RUTH. 'Freedom of the Movies: a Report on Self-regulation from the Commission on Freedom of the Press'. Chicago, University of Chicago Press, 1947
INTERNATIONAL EDUCATIONAL CINEMATOGRAPHIC INSTITUTE. 'The Social Aspects of the Cinema'. Rome, League of Nations, 1934
JARVIE, IAN C. 'Towards a Sociology of the Cinema'. London, Routledge & Kegan Paul, 1970; as 'Movies and Society'. New York, Basic Books, 1970
KAHN, GORDON. 'Hollywood on Trial: the Story of the Ten Who Were Indicted'. New York, Boni & Gaer, 1948; New York, Arno Press, 1972
KLINGENDER, F. D. and LEGG, STUART. 'Money behind the Screen'. London, Lawrence & Wishart, 1937
KNIGHT, DERRICK, and PORTER, VINCENT. 'A Long Look at Short Films'. London, New York, Pergamon Press for ACTT, 1967
KOENIGIL, MARK. 'Movies in Society (Sex, Crime and Censorship)'. New York, Robert Speller, 1962
LAWSON, JOHN HOWARD. 'Film in the Battle of Ideas'. New York, Masses and Mainstream, 1953
MAYER, J. P. 'British Cinemas and their Audiences: Sociological Studies'. London, Dennis Dobson, 1948; 'Sociology of Film: Studies and Documents'. London, Faber, 1946; New York, Arno Press, 1972
MORIN, EDGAR. 'Le Cinéma, ou l'Homme Imaginaire'. Paris, Editions de Minuit, 1956; 'The Stars'; translated from the French by Richard Howard. New York, Grove Press, 1960
NATIONAL COUNCIL OF PUBLIC MORALS. 'The Cinema: its Present Position and Future Possibilities, Being the Report and Chief Evidence taken by the Cinema Commission of Enquiry'. London, Williams & Norgate, 1917; New York, Arno Press, 1970
NOBLE, PETER. 'The Negro in Films'. London, Skelton Robinson, 1948; New York, Arno Press, 1970
PAYNE FUND STUDIES. 'Motion Pictures and Youth'. New York, Macmillan 1933–7; New York, Arno Press, 1970
PERLMAN, WILLIAM J., editor. 'The Movies on Trial: the Views and Opinions of Outstanding Personalities anent Screen Entertainment Past and Present'. New York, Macmillan, 1936
POLITICAL AND ECONOMIC PLANNING. 'The British Film Industry'. London, PEP, 1952. Supplement, 1958
RANDALL, RICHARDS. 'Censorship of the Movies: the Social and Political Control of a Mass Medium'. University of Wisconsin Press, 1968
ROBSON, E. W. and M. M. 'The Film Answers Back: an Historical Appreciation of the Cinema'. London, John Lane, The Bodley Head, 1939; New York, Arno Press, 1972
ROSTEN, LEO CALVIN. 'Hollywood: the Movie Colony, the Movie Maker'. New York, Harcourt, Brace, 1941; New York, Arno Press, 1970
SEABURY, WILLIAM MARSTON. 'Motion Picture Problems: the Cinema and the League of Nations'. New York, Avondale Press, 1929; 'The Public and the Motion Picture Industry'. New York, Macmillan, 1926
THORP, MARGARET FARRAND. 'America at the Movies'. New Haven, Yale University Press, 1939; London, Faber, 1946; New York, Arno Press, 1970
TYLER, PARKER. 'The Hollywood Hallucination'. New York, Simon & Schuster, 1944, 1970; 'Magic and Myth of the Movies'. New York, Henry Holt, 1947; London, Secker & Warburg, 1971
VIZZARD, JACK. 'See no Evil: Life inside a Hollywood Censor'. New York, Simon & Schuster, 1970
WALKER, ALEXANDER. 'Stardom: the Hollywood Phenomenon'. London, Michael Joseph; New York, Stein & Day, 1970
WHITE, DAVID MANNING and AVERSON, RICHARD, editors. 'Sight, Sound and Society: Motion Pictures and Television in America'. Boston, Beacon Press, 1968
WOLFENSTEIN, MARTHA and LEITES, NATHAN. 'Movies: a Psychological Study'. Glencoe, The Free Press, 1950; New York, Atheneum, 1970; London, Hafner, 1971

FILM THEORY AND AESTHETICS

ARNHEIM, RUDOLF. 'Film'; translated from the

German by L. M. Sieveking and Ian F. D. Morrow. London, Faber, 1933; 'Film as art'. London, Faber, 1958
BALAZS, BELA. 'Theory of the Film: Character and Growth of a New Art'; translated from the Hungarian by Edith Bone. London, Dennis Dobson, 1952; New York, Arno Press, 1972
BLOEM, WALTER S. 'The Soul of the Moving Picture'; translated from the German by Allen W. Porterfield. New York, E. P. Dutton, 1924
BOBKER, LEE R. 'Elements of Film'. New York, Harcourt Brace & World Inc., 1969
BURCH, NOEL. 'Praxis du Cinéma'. Paris, Gallimard, 1969; English edition. London, Secker & Warburg; New York, Praeger, 1972
CANUDO. 'L'Usine aux Images'. Geneva, Office Central, 1927
DURGNAT, RAYMOND. 'Films and Feelings'. London, Faber; Cambridge, Massachusetts, MIT Press, 1967
EISENSTEIN, SERGEI MIKHAILOVICH. 'Film Form'; edited and translated by Jay Leyda. London, Dennis Dobson, 1963; New York, Meridian Books, 1957; 'The Film Sense'; edited and translated by Jay Leyda. London, Faber, 1943; New York, Meridian Books, 1957
EPSTEIN, JEAN. 'Bonjour Cinéma: Collection des Tracts'. Paris, Éditions de la Sirène, 1921
FAURE, ELIE. 'The Art of Cineplastics'; translated from the French by Walter Pach. Boston, The Four Seas Company, 1923
FELDMAN, JOSEPH and HARRY. 'Dynamics of the Film'. New York, Hermitage House Inc., 1952
GESSNER, ROBERT, 'The Moving Image: a Guide to Cinematic Literacy'. New York, E. P. Dutton, 1968
HUSS, ROY, and SILVERSTEIN, NORMAN. 'The Film Experience: Elements of Motion Picture Art'. New York, Harper & Row, 1968
JACOBS, LEWIS. 'Introduction to the Art of the Movies: an Anthology of Ideas on the Nature of Movie Art'. New York, Noonday Press, 1960
JACOBS, LEWIS. 'The Movies as Medium'. New York, Farrar, Straus & Giroux, 1970
KRACAUER, SIEGFRIED. 'Theory of Film: the Redemption of Physical Reality'. New York, Oxford University Press, 1960; as 'Nature of Film', London, Dennis Dobson, 1961
LAWSON, JOHN HOWARD. 'Film the Creative Process: the Search for an Audio-Visual Language Structure'. New York, Hill & Wang, 1964
LEBEL, JEAN-PATRICK. 'Cinéma et Idéologie'. Paris, Editions Sociales, 1971
LINDEN, GEORGE W. 'Reflections on the Screen'. Belmong, California, Wadsworth Publishing Co., 1970
LINDGREN, ERNEST. 'The Art of the Film: an Introduction to Film Appreciation'. London, Allen & Unwin; New York, Macmillan, 1948, 1963
LINDSAY, VACHEL. 'Art of the Moving Picture'. New York, Macmillan, 1915, 1922; New York, Liveright, 1970
MARTIN, MARCEL. 'Le Language Cinématographique'. Paris, Éditions du Cerf, 1955, 1962
METZ, CHRISTIAN. 'Essais sur la Signification au Cinéma'. Paris, Éditions Kincksieck, 1968, 1971, 1972; English edition. New York, Praeger; London, Secker & Warburg, 1972 'Language et cinéma'. Paris, Larousse, 1971
MITRY, JEAN. 'Esthétique et Psychologie du Cinéma'. Paris, Éditions Universitaires, 1963–
NICOLL, ALLARDYCE. 'Film and Theatre'. London, George G. Harrap, 1936; New York, Arno Press, 1972
STEPHENSON, RALPH and DEBRIX, JEAN D. 'The Cinema as Art'. Harmondsworth, Penguin Books, 1965
SPOTTISWOODE, RAYMOND. 'A Grammar of the Film: an Analysis of Film Technique'. London, Faber, 1935; Berkeley, University of California, 1950
WOLLEN, PETER. 'Signs and Meaning in the Cinema'. London, Secker & Warburg; Bloomington, Indiana University Press, 1969

FILM CRITICISM

ADLER, RENATA. 'A Year in the Dark: Journal of a Film Critic, 1968–69'. New York, Random House, 1969
AGATE, JAMES. 'Around Cinemas'. London, Horne & Van Thal, 1946; New York, Arno Press, 1972; 'Around Cinemas (Second Series)'. London, Horne & Van Thal, 1948; New York, Arno Press, 1972
AGEE, JAMES. 'Agee on Film: Reviews and Comments'. New York, McDowell, 1958; London, Peter Owen, 1963
BAZIN, ANDRE. 'Qu'est-ce que le Cinéma? Volume 1: Ontologie et Language. Volume 2: Le Cinéma et les Autres Arts. Volume 3: Cinéma et Sociologie. Volume 4: Une Ésthetique de la Réalité, le Néo-réalisme'. Paris, Les Éditions du Cerf, 1958–62; 'What Is Cinema?'; essays selected and translated by Hugh Gray. Berkeley, University of California Press, 1967; 'What Is Cinema? Vol. 2'. Berkeley, University of California Press, 1972
BELLONE, JULIUS, editor. 'Renaissance of the Film'. New York, Macmillan Co.; London, Collier-Macmillan, 1970
BOWSER, EILEEN, editor. 'Film Notes'. Revised edition. New York, Museum of Modern Art, 1969
CLAIR, RENÉ. 'Reflections on the Cinema'; translated from the French by Vera Traill. London, William Kimber, 1953
COOKE, ALISTAIR, editor. 'Garbo and the Night Watchmen: a Selection from the Writings of British and American Film Critics'. London, Jonathan Cape, 1937; London, Secker & Warburg; New York, McGraw-Hill, 1971
CRIST, JUDITH. 'The Private Eye, the Cowboy and the Very Naked Girl'. New York, Holt, Rinehart & Winston, 1968
CROWTHER, BOSLEY. 'The Great Films: Fifty Years of Motion Pictures'. New York, G. P. Putnam's, 1967
EISENSTEIN, SERGEI MIKHAILOVICH. 'Film Essays, with a Lecture'; translated and edited by Jay Leyda, London, Dennis Dobson, 1968, New York, Praeger, 1970; 'Notes of a Film Director; translated from the Russian by X. Danko. London, Lawrence & Wishart, 1959; New York, Dover Publications, 1970
FARBER, MANNY. 'Negative Space'. New York, Praeger; London, Studio Vista, 1971
FULTON, A. R. 'Motion Pictures: the Development of an Art from Silent Films to the Age of Television'. Norman, Oklahoma, University of Oklahoma Press, 1960
GODARD, JEAN-LUC. 'Jean-Luc Godard: Articles, Essais, Entretiens; introductions et notes par Jean Narboni'. Paris, Pierre Belfond, 1968; as 'Godard on Godard'; edited and translated by Tom Milne. London, Secker & Warburg; New York, Viking, 1972
GRAHAM, PETER, editor. 'The New Wave: Critical Landmarks'. London, Secker & Warburg; New York, Doubleday, 1968
GREENE, GRAHAM. 'Film Criticism'; edited by John Russell Taylor. London, Secker & Warburg, 1972
HUNTER, WILLIAM. 'Scrutiny of Cinema'. London, Wishart and Co., 1932; New York, Arno Press, 1972
KAEL, PAULINE. 'Going Steady'. Boston, Little, Brown & Co.; London, Temple Smith, 1970; 'I Lost it at the Movies'. Boston, Little, Brown & Co., 1965; London, Jonathan Cape, 1966; 'Kiss Kiss Bang Bang'. Boston, Little, Brown & Co., 1968; London, Calder & Boyars, 1970
KAUFFMANN, STANLEY. 'A World on Film: Criticism and Comment'. New York, Harper & Row, 1966
LEJEUNE, CAROLINE ALICE. 'Cinema'. London, Alexander Maclehose and Co., 1931; 'Chestnuts in Her Lap, 1936–1946'. London, Phoenix House, 1947;
LENNIG, ARTHUR. 'The Silent Voice'. Albany, State University of New York, 1966
MACCANN, RICHARD DYER, editor. 'Film: a Montage of Theories'. New York, E. P. Dutton & Co., 1966
MACDONALD, DWIGHT. 'Dwight Macdonald on Movies'. Englewood Cliffs (N.J.), Prentice-Hall, 1969
MCBRIDE, JOSEPH, editor. 'Persistence of Vision: a Collection of Film Criticism'. Madison, Wisconsin Film Society Press, 1968
MANVELL, ROGER, and other editors. 'The Cinema 1950, 1951, 1952'. Harmondsworth, Penguin Books, 1950–2
MAURIAC, CLAUDE. 'Petite Littérature du Cinéma'. Paris, Éditions du Cerf, 1957
NATIONAL SOCIETY OF FILM CRITICS. 'Film 67/68: an Anthology'; edited by Richard Schickel and John Simon. New York, Simon & Schuster, 1968; 'Film 68/69'; edited by Hollis Alpert and Andrew Sarris. New York, Simon & Schuster, 1969; 'Film 69/70'; edited by Joseph Morgenstern and Stefan Kanfer. New York, Simon & Schuster, 1970; 'Film 1970/71'; edited by David Denby. New York, Simon & Schuster, 1971
RHODE, ERIC. 'Tower of Babel: Speculations on the Cinema'. London, Weidenfeld & Nicolson; Philadelphia, Chilton Book Company, 1966
ROTHA, PAUL. 'Celluloid: the Film Today'.

London, Longmans, 1931; 'Rotha on the Film: a Selection of Writings about the Cinema'. London, Faber, 1958
SARRIS, ANDREW, editor. 'The Film'. New York, Bobbs-Merrill, 1968
SITNEY, P. A., editor. 'Film Culture Reader'. New York, Praeger, 1970; as 'Film Culture: an Anthology'. London, Secker & Warburg, 1971
TAYLOR, JOHN RUSSELL. 'Cinema Eye, Cinema Ear: Some Key Film Makers of the Sixties'. London, Methuen; New York, Hill & Wang, 1964
THOMSON, DAVID. 'Movie Man'. London, Secker & Warburg; New York, Stein & Day, 1967
TYLER, PARKER. 'Classics of the Foreign Film: a Pictorial Treasury'. New York, The Citadel Press, 1962; London, Spring Books, 1966; 'Sex, Psyche Etcetera in the Film'. New York, Horizon Press, 1969; Harmondsworth, Penguin Books, 1971; 'The Three Faces of Film: the Art, the Dream, the Cult'. New York; London, Thomas Yoseloff, 1960
WARSHOW, ROBERT. 'The Immediate Experience: Movies, Comics, Theatre and Other Aspects of Popular Culture'. New York, Doubleday & Co. Inc., 1962
ZINMAN, DAVID. '50 Classic Motion Pictures: the Stuff that Dreams are Made of'. New York, Crown Publishers Inc., 1970

FILM GENRES

Animated films

BENAYOUN, ROBERT. 'Le Dessin Animé après Walt Disney'. Paris, Jean-Jacques Pauvert, 1961
BRYNE-DANIEL, J. 'Grafilm: an Approach to a New Medium'. London, Studio Vista; New York, Van Nostrand Reinhold, 1970
CHEVALIER, DENYS. 'J'Aime le Dessin Animé'. Paris, Éditions Denoël, 1962
HALAS, JOHN and MANVELL, ROGER. 'Art in Movement: New Directions in Animation'. London, Studio Vista; New York, Hastings House, 1970; 'Design in Motion'. London, Studio Vista, 1962; 'The Technique of Film Animation'. London, Focal Press; New York, Hastings House, 1959, 1968, 1971
HERDEG, WALTER, editor. 'Film and TV Graphics: an International Survey of Film and Television Graphics'. London, Studio Vista; New York, Hastings House, 1967
KINSEY, ANTHONY. 'Animated Film Making'. London, Studio Vista; New York, Viking Press, 1970
LEVITAN, ELI L. 'Animation Art in the Commercial Film'. New York, Reinhold, 1960; 'Animation Techniques and Commercial Film Production'. New York, Reinhold, 1962
MADSEN, ROY P. 'Animated Film: Concepts, Methods, Uses'. New York, Interland, 1969
MANVELL, ROGER. 'The Animated Film'. London, The Sylvan Press, 1954
REINIGER, LOTTE. 'Shadow Theatres and Shadow Films'. London, Batsford; New York, Watson-Guptill, 1970
STEPHENSON, RALPH. 'Animation in the Cinema'. London, Tantivy Press; New York, A. S. Barnes, 1967
THOMAS, BOB. 'The Art of Animation: the Story of the Disney Studio Contribution to a New Art'. New York, Simon & Schuster, 1958

Comedy

DURGNAT, RAYMOND. 'The Crazy Mirror: Hollywood Comedy and the American Image'. London, Faber, 1969; New York, Horizon, 1970
COURODON, JEAN-PIERRE. 'Keaton et Cie: les Burlesques Americains du Muet'. Paris, Seghers, 1964
LAHUE, KALTON C. and GILL, SAM. 'Clown Princes and Court Jesters'. South Brunswick, A. S. Barnes; London, Thomas Yoseloff, 1970
LAHUE, KALTON, C. and BREWER, TERRY. 'Kops and Custards: the Legends of Keystone Films'. Norman, University of Oklahoma Press, 1968
LAHUE, KALTON C. 'Mack Sennett's Keystone: the Man, the Myth and the Comedies'. New York, A. S. Barnes, 1971; 'World of Laughter: the Motion Picture Comedy Short, 1910–1930'. Norman, University of Oklahoma Press, 1966
MCCAFFREY, DONALD W. 'Four Great Comedians: Chaplin, Lloyd, Keaton, Langdon'. London, Tantivy Press; New York, A. S. Barnes, 1968
MALTIN, LEONARD. 'Movie Comedy Teams'. New York, New American Library, 1970
MONTGOMERY, JOHN. 'Comedy Films, 1894–1954'. London, Allen & Unwin, 1954, 1968
ROBINSON, DAVID. 'The Great Funnies: a History of Film Comedy'. London, Studio Vista, 1969; New York, E. P. Dutton, 1969

Documentary and Short Films

THE ARTS ENQUIRY. 'The Factual Film'. London, New York, Oxford University Press, 1947
GRIERSON, JOHN. 'Grierson on Documentary'; edited and compiled by Forsyth Hardy. London, Collins, 1946; London, Faber; New York, Praeger, 1966
JACOBS, LEWIS. 'The Documentary Tradition: from Nanook to Woodstock'. New York, Hopkinson & Blake, 1971
LEVIN, G. ROY. 'Documentary Explorations: 15 Interviews with Film-makers'. New York, Doubleday, 1971
LEYDA, JAY. 'Films Beget Films'. London, Allen & Unwin, 1964
LOVELL, ALAN and HILLIER, JIM. 'Studies in Documentary'. London, Secker & Warburg; New York, Viking, 1972
MALTIN, LEONARD. 'Classical Movie Shorts'. New York, Crown, 1971
MARCORELLES, LOUIS. 'Eléments pour un Nouveau Cinéma'. Paris, Unesco, 1970. English edition, 1972
PORCILLE, FRANÇOIS. 'Défense du Court Métrage Français'. Paris, Éditions du Cerf, 1965
ROSENTHAL, ALAN. 'Documentary in Action: a Casebook in Film-Making'. Berkeley, London, University of California, 1971
ROTHA, PAUL and others. 'Documentary Film: the Use of the Film Medium to Interpret Creatively and in Social Terms the Life of the People as It Exists in Reality'. London, Faber, 1936, 39, 52; New York, Hastings House, 1964

Experimental

BATTOCK, GREGORY, editor. 'The New American Cinema: a Critical Anthology'. New York, E. P. Dutton, 1967
CURTIS, DAVID. 'Experimental Cinema: a Fifty Year Evolution'. London, Studio Vista, New York, Universe Books, 1971
MANVELL, ROGER, editor. 'Experiment in the Film'. London, Grey Walls Press, 1949; New York, Arno Press, 1970
RENAN, SHELDON. 'An Introduction to the American Underground Film'. New York, E. P. Dutton, 1967; as 'The Underground Film'. London, Studio Vista, 1968
RICHTER, HANS. 'Filmgegner von Heute, Filmfreunde von Morgen'. Berlin, Verlag Hermann Reckendorf, 1929
STAUFFACHER, FRANK, editor. 'Art in Cinema: a Symposium on the Avant-garde Film'. San Francisco Museum of Art, 1947; New York, Arno Press, 1969
TYLER, PARKER. 'Underground Film: a Critical History'. New York, Grove Press, 1969; London, Secker & Warburg, 1971
VERDONE, MARIO. 'Cinema e Letteratura del Futurismo, con una Antologia di Testi'. Rome, Bianco & Nero, 1968
YOUNGBLOOD, GENE. 'Expanded Cinema'. London, Studio Vista; New York, E. P. Dutton, 1970

Horror and Science Fiction

BAXTER, JOHN. 'Science Fiction in the Cinema'. London, Tantivy Press; New York, A. S. Barnes, 1970
BUTLER, IVAN. 'The Horror Film'. London, Tantivy Press; New York, A. S. Barnes, 1967, 1970
CLARENS, CARLOS. 'An Illustrated History of the Horror Films'. New York, G. P. Putnam's Sons, 1967; as 'Horror Movies', London, Secker & Warburg, 1967
GASCA, LUIS. 'Cine y Ciencia-Ficción'. Barcelona, Llibres de Sinera, 1969
GIFFORD, DENIS. 'Movie Monsters'. London, Studio Vista, 1969; New York, E. P. Dutton, 1969; 'Science Fiction Film'. London, Studio Vista; New York, E. P. Dutton, 1971
LENNE, GERARD. 'Le Cinéma Fantastique et ses Mythologies'. Paris, Éditions du Cerf, 1970

Musicals

BURTON, JACK. 'The Blue Book of Hollywood Musicals'. New York, Century House, 1953
KOBAL, JOHN. 'Gotta Sing, Gotta Dance: a Pictorial History of Film Musicals'. London, New York, Hamlyn, 1971
MCVAY, DOUGLAS. 'The Musical Film'. London, Tantivy Press; New York, A. S. Barnes, 1967
SPRINGER, JOHN. 'All Talking! All Singing! All

Dancing!: a Pictorial History of the Movie Musical'. New York, Citadel Press, 1966
TAYLOR, JOHN RUSSELL and JACKSON, ARTHUR. 'The Hollywood Musical'. London, Secker & Warburg; New York, McGraw-Hill, 1971
VALLANCE, TOM. 'The American Musical'. London, Tantivy Press; New York, A. S. Barnes, 1970

Serials
BARBOUR, ALAN G. 'Days of Thrills and Adventure'. New York, Collier Books; London, Collier-Macmillan, 1970
FERNETT, GENE. 'Next Time Drive off the Cliff'. Cocoa, Florida, Cine-memories Publishing Co., 1968
LAHUE, KALTON C. 'Bound and Gagged: the Story of the Silent Serials'. New York, A. S. Barnes; London, Thomas Yoseloff, 1968; 'Continued Next Week: a History of the Moving Picture Serial'. Norman, University of Oklahoma Press, 1964

Westerns
BELLOUR, RAYMOND and BRION, PATRICK, editors. 'Le Western: Sources, Thèmes, Mythologies, Auteurs, Acteurs, Filmographies'. Paris, Union Générale d'Éditions, 1966
CORNEAU, ERNEST N. 'The Hall of Fame of Western Film Stars'. North Quincy, Massachusetts, Christopher Publishing House, 1969
EVERSON, WILLIAM K. 'A Pictorial History of the Western Film'. New York, Citadel Press, 1969
EYLES, ALLEN. 'The Western: an Illustrated Guide'. London, Tantivy Press; New York, A. S. Barnes, 1967
FENIN, GEORGE N. and EVERSON, WILLIAM K. 'The Western from Silents to Cinerama'. New York, The Orion Press, Inc., 1962
FORD, CHARLES. 'Histoire du Western'. Paris, Pierre Horay, 1964
KITSES, JIM. 'Horizons West: Anthony Mann, Budd Boetticher, Sam Peckinpah: Studies of Authorship within the Western'. London, Secker & Warburg, 1969; Bloomington, Indiana University Press, 1970
LAHUE, KALTON C. 'Winners of the West: the Sagebrush Heroes of the Silent Screen'. New York, A. S. Barnes; London, Thomas Yoseloff, 1970
RIEUPEYROUT, JEAN-LOUIS. 'Le Western, ou le Cinéma Américain par Excellence'. Paris, Éditions du Cerf, 1953

GENERAL HISTORIES

BARDÈCHE, MAURICE and BRASILLACH, ROBERT. 'History of the Film'; translated from the French by Iris Barry. Norton, Museum of Modern Art; London, Allen & Unwin, 1938; New York, Arno Press, 1970
BRUSENDORFF, OVE. 'Filmen: dens Navne og Historie'. Copenhagen, Universal Forlaget, 1939–41
CERAM, C. W. 'Archaeology of the Cinema'. London, Thames & Hudson; New York, Harcourt, Brace & World, 1965
CHARENSOL, GEORGES. 'Panorama du Cinéma'. Paris, Éditions KRA, 1930
COISSAC, G-MICHEL. 'Histoire du Cinématographe de ses Origines à nos Jours'. Paris, Éditions du Cinéopse, Gauthier-Villars, 1925
COOK, OLIVE. 'Movement in Two Dimensions: a Study of the Animated and Projected Pictures Which Preceded the Invention of Cinematography'. London, Hutchinson, 1963
COWIE, PETER, editor. 'A Concise History of the Cinema'. London, Tantivy Press; New York, A. S. Barnes, 1971; 'Seventy Years of Cinema'. London, Thomas Yoseloff; New York, A. S. Barnes, 1969
DESLANDES, JACQUES. 'Histoire Comparée du Cinéma'. Tournai, Casterman, 1966–
FERNANDEZ, CUENCA CARLOS. 'Historia del Cine'. Madrid, Afrodisio Aguado, 1948–50
FIELDING, RAYMOND, editor. 'A Technological History of the Motion Pictures and Television: an Anthology of the Journal of the SMPTE'. Berkeley, University of California Press; Cambridge U.P., 1967
FRAENKEL, HEINRICH. 'Unsterblicher Film: die grosse Chronik'. Munich, Kindler Verlag, 1956–7
GHIRARDINI, LINO LIONELLO. 'Storia Generale del Cinema (1895–1959)'. Milan, Carlo Marzorati, 1959
HOPWOOD, HENRY VAUX. 'Living Pictures: Their History, Photo-Production and Practical Working'. London, Optician and Photographic Trades Review, 1899, 1915
HOUSTON, PENELOPE. 'The Contemporary Cinema'. Harmondsworth, Penguin Books, 1963
JACOBS, LEWIS, editor. 'The Emergence of Film Art: the Evolution and Development of the Motion Picture as an Art, from 1900 to the Present'. New York, Hopkinson & Blake, 1969
JEANNE, RENÉ and FORD, CHARLES. 'Histoire Encyclopédique du Cinéma'. Paris, Robert Laffont, 1947–68
KNIGHT, ARTHUR. 'The Liveliest Art: a Panoramic History of the Movies'. New York, Macmillan, 1957
LEPROHON, PIERRE. 'Le Cinéma: Cette Aventure'. Paris, André Bonne, 1970
LEPROHON, PIERRE. 'Histoire du Cinéma'. Paris, Editions du Cerf, 1961–1963
LINDGREN, ERNEST. 'A Picture History of the Cinema'. London, Vista Books, 1960
MACGOWAN, KENNETH. 'Behind the Screen: the History and Techniques of the Motion Picture'. New York, Delacorte Press, 1965
MANVELL, ROGER. 'New Cinema in Europe'. London, Studio Vista; New York, E. P. Dutton, 1966
MITRY, JEAN. 'Histoire du Cinema: Art et Industrie'. Paris, Éditions Universitaires, 1967–
NIVER, KEMP R. 'The First Twenty Years: a Segment of Film History'. Los Angeles, Locare Research Group, 1968
O'LEARY, LIAM. 'The Silent Cinema'. London, Studio Vista; New York, E. P. Dutton, 1965
PAOLLELA, ROBERTO. 'Storia del Cinema Muto'. Naples, Giannini, 1956; 'Storia del Cinema Sonoro (1926–1939)'. Naples, Giannini, 1966
PASINETTI, FRANCESCO. 'Storia del Cinema dalle Origini ad Oggi'. Rome, Edizioni di Bianco e Nero, 1939
QUIGLEY, MARTIN, JR. 'Magic Shadows: the Story of the Origin of Motion Pictures'. Washington, Georgetown University Press, 1948
ROBINSON, DAVID. 'A Short History of World Cinema'. London, Methuen; New York, Stein & Day, 1972
ROTHA, PAUL. 'The Film Till Now: a Survey of the Cinema'. London, Jonathan Cape, 1930, 1949, 1960, 1967
SADOUL, GEORGES. 'Histoire Générale du Cinéma'. Paris, Éditions Denoël, 1946–54
SMRŽ, KAREL. 'Dajiny Filmu'. Prague, Družstevní Práce, 1933
THOMAS, DAVID B. 'The First Colour Motion Pictures'. London, HMSO, 1969
TOEPLITZ, JERZY. 'Histoire Sztuki Filmowej'. Warsaw, Filmowea Agencja Wydawnicza, 1955–9
VINCENT, CARL. 'Histoire de l'Art Cinématographique'. Brussels, Éditions du Trident, 1939
WISEMAN, THOMAS. 'Cinema'. London, Cassell, 1964; New York, A. S. Barnes, 1965
ZGUMICKI, FRIEDRICH VON. 'Der Weg des Films'. Berlin, Rembrandt, 1956
ZUNIGA, ANGEL. 'Una Historia del Cine'. Barcelona, Ediciones Destino, 1948

NATIONAL HISTORIES

National Cinemas

Africa
VIEYRA, PAULIN SOUMANOU. 'Le Cinéma et l'Afrique'. Paris, Présence Africaine, 1969

Arab Countries
LANDAU, JACOB M. 'Studies in the Arab Theater and Cinema'. Philadelphia University of Pennsylvania Press, 1958
SADOUL, GEORGES, editor. 'The Cinema in the Arab Countries'. Beirut, Interarab Centre of Cinema & Television, 1966

Argentina
DI NUBILA, DOMINGO. 'Historia del Cine Argentino'. Buenos Aires, Edicion Cruz de Malta, 1959

Australia
BAXTER, JOHN. 'The Australian Cinema'. London, Sydney, Angus & Robertson; San Francisco, Tri-Ocean, 1971

Austria
FRITZ, WALTER. 'Die Osterreichischen Spielfilme der Stummfilmzeit (1907–1930)'. Vienna, Osterreichischen Gesellschaft für Filmwissenschaft, for the Osterreichischen Filmarchivs, 1967
GESEK, LUDWIG, editor. 'Kleines Lexicon des Osterreichischen Films'. Vienna, Filmkunst, 1959

Brazil

GONZAGA, ADHEMAR and SALLES GOMES, P. E. '70 Anos de Cinema Brasileiro'. Rio de Janeiro, Editôra Expressao e Cultura, 1966

ROCHA, GLAUBER. 'Revisao Critica do Cinema Brasileiro'. Rio de Janeiro, Editôra Civilização Brasileira, 1963

Canada

CAHIERS SAINTE-MARIE. 'Le Cinéma Québécois: Tendances et Prolongements'. Montreal, Les Éditions Sainte-Marie, 1968

LIBERTE. 'Cinéma si'. Montreal, Liberté, 1966

MARSOLAIS, GILLES. 'Le Cinéma Canadien'. Montreal, Éditions du Jour, 1968

Cuba

AGRAMONTE, ARTURO. 'Cronologia de Cine Cubano'. Havana, Ediciones ICAIC, 1966

Czechoslovakia

BROZ, JAROSLAV and FRIDA, MYRTIL. 'Historie Ceskoslovenského Filmu 1898–1945'. Prague, Orbis, 1959–65

DEWEY, LANGDON. 'Outline of Czechoslovakian Cinema'. London, Informatics, 1971

ZALMAN, JAN. 'Films and Film-makers in Czechoslovakia'. Prague, Orbis, 1968.

ZVONICEK, STANISLAV, editor. 'Modern Czechoslovak Film, 1945–1965'; translated by Alico Denešovà. Prague, Artia, 1965

Denmark

HENDING, ARNOLD. 'Stjerner i Glashuse: et Causeri 40 Aars Film'. Copenhagen, Winkelmanns Forlag, 1936

NEERGAARD, EBBE. 'The Story of Danish Film'. Copenhagen, Danish Institute, 1962

SANDFELD, GUNNAR. 'Den Stumme Scene: Dansk Biografteater indtil Lydfilmens Gennembrud'. Copenhagen, Nyt Nordisk, Arnold Busck, 1966

Egypt

KHAN, M. 'An Introduction to the Egyptian Cinema'. London, Informatics, 1969

European Countries

HIBBIN, NINA. 'Eastern Europe: an Illustrated Guide'. London, Tantivy Press; New York, A. S. Barnes, 1969

LOVELL, ALAN, editor. 'Art of the Cinema in Ten European Countries'. Strasbourg, Council for Cultural Co-operation, Council of Europe, 1967

WHITE, ALASTAIR. 'New Cinema in Eastern Europe'. London, Studio Vista; New York, E. P. Dutton, 1971

France

AGEL, HENRI. 'Miroirs de l'Insolite dans le Cinéma Français'. Paris, Éditions du Cerf, 1958; With others. 'Sept Ans de Cinéma Français'. Paris, Éditions du Cerf, 1953

ARMES, ROY. 'French film'. London, Studio Vista; New York, E. P. Dutton, 1970; 'French Cinema since 1946'. London, Tantivy Press; New York, A. S. Barnes, 1966, 1970

DURGNAT, RAYMOND. 'Nouvelle Vague: the First Decade'. Loughton (Essex), Motion, 1963

JEANNE, RENÉ. 'Cinema 1900'. Paris, Flammarion, 1965

LEPROHON, PIERRE. 'Cinquante Ans de Cinéma Français (1895–1945)'. Paris, Éditions du Cerf, 1954

REGENT, ROGER. 'Cinéma de France'. Paris, Bellefaye, 1948

SADOUL, GEORGES. 'French Film'. London, Falcon Press, 1953; New York, Arno Press, 1972

Germany

BORDE, RAYMOND, and others. 'Le Cinéma Réaliste Allemand'. Lyon, Serdoc, 1965

BUCHER, FELIX. 'Germany'. London, Tantivy Press; New York, A. S. Barnes, 1970

COURTADE, FRANCIS. 'Jeune Cinéma Allemand'. Lyon, Serdoc, 1969

EISNER, LOTTE. 'The Haunted Screen: Expressionism in the German Cinema and the Influence of Max Reinhardt'; translated from the French by Roger Greaves. London, Secker & Warburg; Berkeley, California University Press, 1969

FURSTENAU, THEO. 'Wandlungen im Film: Junge Deutsche Produktion'. Wiesbaden, Deutschen Institut für Filmkunde, 1969

HULL, DAVID STEWART. 'Film in the Third Reich: a Study of the German Cinema, 1933–1945'. Berkeley & Los Angeles, University of California Press, 1969

KALBUS, OSKAR. 'Vom Werden Deutscher Filmkunst'. Bahvenseld, Bilderdienst Altona, 1935

KERSTEN, HEINZ. 'Das Filmwesen in der Sowjetischen Besatzungszone Deutschlands'. Bonn, Berlin, Bundesministerium für Gesamtdeutsche Fragen, 1963

KRACAUER, SIEGFRIED. 'From Caligari to Hitler: a Psychological History of the German Film'. Princeton, Princeton University Press; London, Dennis Dobson, 1947

LEISER, ERWIN. 'Deutschland erwache!: Propaganda im Film des Dritten Reiches'. Hamburg, Rowohlt, 1968; as 'Nazi Film'. London, Secker & Warburg, 1972

MANVELL, ROGER and FRAENKEL, HEINRICH. 'The German Cinema'. London, Dent; New York, Praeger, 1971

PLEYER, PETER. 'Deutscher Nachkriegsfilm, 1946–1948'. Münster, Verlag C. J. Fahle, 1965

WOLLENBERG, H. H. 'Fifty Years of German Film'. London, Falcon Press, 1948; New York, Arno Press, 1972

WULF, JOSEPH. 'Theater und Film im Dritten Reich: eine Dokumentation'. Gütersloh, Sigbert Mohn Verlag, 1964

Great Britain

BALCON, SIR MICHAEL and others. 'Twenty Years of British Film, 1925–1945'. London, Falcon Press, 1947; New York, Arno Press, 1972

DURGNAT, RAYMOND. 'A Mirror for England: British Movies from Austerity to Affluence'. London, Faber, 1970; New York, Praeger, 1971

FORMAN, DENIS. 'Films 1945–1950'. London, New York, Longmans, Green for the British Council, 1952

GIFFORD, DENNIS. 'British Cinema: an Illustrated Guide'. London, Tantivy Press; New York, A. S. Barnes, 1968

KELLY, TERENCE and others. 'A Competitive Cinema'. London, Institute of Economic Affairs; New York, International Publications Service, 1966

LOW, RACHAEL. 'The History of the British Film'. London, Allen & Unwin; New York, Fernhill House, 1948–

MANVELL, ROGER. 'New Cinema in Britain'. London, Studio Vista; New York, E. P. Dutton, 1969

POWELL, DILYS. 'Films Since 1939'. London, New York, Longmans Green for the British Council, 1947

Hungary

ESTÈVE, MICHEL, editor. 'Le Nouveau Cinéma Hongrois'. Paris, Lettres Modernes, 1969

LEVENSON, CLAUDE B. 'Jeune Cinéma Hongrois'. Lyon, SERDOC, 1966

NEMESKURTY, ISTVAN. 'Word and Image: History of the Hungarian Cinema'; translated by Zsuzsanna Horn. Budapest, Corvina Press, 1968

India

BARNOUW, ERIK and KRISHNASWAMY, S. 'Indian Film'. New York, London; Columbia University Press, 1963

PARRAIN, P. 'Regards sur le Cinéma Indien'. Paris, Éditions du Cerf, 1969

SHAH, PANNA. 'The Indian Film'. Bombay, Motion Picture Society of India, 1950

Ireland

REPUBLIC OF IRELAND. 'Film Industry Committee: report'. Dublin, Stationery Office, 1968

Italy

ARMES, ROY. 'Patterns of Realism: a Study of Italian Neo-realist Cinema'. London, Tantivy Press; New York, A. S. Barnes, 1972

BUCHER, FELIX. 'Italy'. London, Tantivy Press; New York, A. S. Barnes, 1972

FREDDI, LUIGI. 'Il Cinema'. Rome, L'Arnia, 1949

HOVALD, PATRICE G. 'Le Néo-Réalisme Italien et ses Créateurs'. Paris, Éditions du Cerf, 1959

JARRATT, VERNON. 'The Italian Cinema'. London, Falcon Press, 1951; New York, Arno Press, 1972

LEPROHON, PIERRE. 'Italian Cinema'; translated from the French by Oliver Stallybrass. London, Secker & Warburg; New York, Praeger, 1972

MALERBA, LUIGI and SINISCALCO, CARMINE, editors. 'Fifty Years of Italian Cinema'. Rome, Carlo Bestetti, 1954

MARINUCCI, VINICIO. 'Tendencies of the Italian Cinema'. Rome, Unitalia Film, 1959

RONDI, GIAN LUIGI. 'Italian Cinema Today, 1952–1965. London, Dennis Dobson, 1967

RONDOLINO, GIANNI. 'Catalogo Bolaffi del Cinema Italiano'. Turin, Bolaffi, 1967; 'Dizionario del Cinema Italiano, 1945–1969'. Turin, Giulio Einaudi, 1969

Japan

ANDERSON, JOSEPH L. and RICHIE, DONALD. 'The Japanese Film: Art and Industry'. Rutland, Vermont, Tokyo, Charles E. Tuttle, 1959

RICHIE, DONALD. 'The Japanese Movie: an Illustrated History'. London, Ward Lock & Co.; Tokyo, Kodansha International Ltd., 1966

SVENSSON, ARNE. 'Japan'. London, Tantivy Press; New York, A. S. Barnes, 1971

Mexico

AYALA BLANCO, JORGE. 'Aventura del Cine Mexicano'. Ciudad de Mexico, Era, 1968

GARCIA RIERA, EMILO. 'El Cine Mexicano'. Mexico, Ediciones Era, 1963

GARCIA RIERA, EMILIO. 'Historia Documental del Cine Mexicano'. Mexico, Ediciones Era, 1969–

Norway

EVENSMO, SIGURD. 'Det Store Tivoli: Film og Kino i Norge gjennom 70 Ar Oslo'. Gyldendal Norsk Forlag, 1967

Pakistan

KABIR, ALAMGIR. 'The Cinema in Pakistan'. Dacca, Sandhani Publications, 1969

Poland

BANASKIEWICZ, WLADYSLAW, and others. 'Contemporary Polish Cinematography'. Warsaw, Polania Publishing House, 1962

BANASKIEWICZ, WLADYSLAW and WITCZAK, WITOLD. 'Historia Filmu Polskiego'. Vol. 1 1895–1929. Warsaw, Wyddwnictwa Artystyczne i Filmowe, 1966

Portugal

DE AZEVEDO, MANUEL. 'Perspectiva do Cinema Português'. Porto, Clube Português de Cinematografia, 1951

Scandinavia

HARDY, FORSYTH. 'Scandinavian Film'. London, Falcon Press, 1952; New York, Arno Press, 1972

Soviet Union

AROSSEV, A., editor. 'Soviet Cinema'. Moscow, Voks, 1935

BABITSKY, PAUL and RIMBERG, JOHN. 'The Soviet Film Industry'. New York, Praeger, 1955

BRYHER. 'Film Problems of Soviet Russia'. Riant Chateau, Territet, 1929

DICKINSON, THOROLD and DE LA ROCHE, CATHERINE. 'Soviet Cinema'. London, Falcon Press, 1948; New York, Arno Press, 1972

KALASHNIKOV, Y. S. and others. 'Ocerki Istorii Sovetskogo Kino'. Moscow, Iskusstvo, 1956–9

LEYDA, JAY. 'Kino: a History of the Russian and Soviet Film'. London, Allen & Unwin; New York, Hillary House, 1960

LISAREVSKII, D. '100 Soviet Films'. Moscow, Iskusstvo, 1967

MACHERTA, A. V. and others, editors. 'Sovetskie Khudozhestvennie Filmy: Annotirovanni Katalog'. Moscow, Iskusstvo, 1961–8

SCHNITZER, LUDA and others, editors. 'Le Cinéma Soviétique par Ceux Qui l'Ont Fait'. Paris, Les Éditeurs Français Réunis, 1966; as 'The Cinema in Revolution: Twelve Witnesses of the Heroic Era of the Soviet Film'. London, Secker & Warburg, 1972

SCHNITZER, JEAN and LUDA. 'Vingt Ans de Cinéma Soviétique'. Paris, C.I.B., 1963

Spain

CABERO, JUAN ANTONIO. 'Historia de la Cinematografia Española'. Madrid, Graficas Cinema, 1949

CASAS, FERNANDO VIZCAINO. 'Diccionario del Cine Español, 1896–1965'. Madrid, Editora National, 1966

MENDEZ-LEITE, FERNANDO. 'Historia del Cine Español'. Madrid, Ediciones Rialp, 1965

Sweden

BERANGER, JEAN. 'La Grande Aventure du Cinéma Suédois'. Paris, Eric Losfeld, 1960

COWIE, PETER. 'Sweden 1'. 'Sweden 2'. London, Tantivy Press; New York, A. S. Barnes, 1970

IDESTAM-ALMQUIST, B. (Robin Hood). 'När Filmen Kom till Sverige: Charles Magnusson och Svenska Bio'. Stockholm, P. A. Norstedt, 1959

Switzerland

ALLGEMEINE KINEMATOGRAPHEN AKTIENGESELLSCHAFT. 'Film und Filmwirtschaft in der Schweiz: Fünfzig Jahre'. Zürich, Verlag Hans Rohr, 1968

United States of America

AGEL, HENRI. 'Romance Américaine'. Paris, Éditions du Cerf, 1963

ALLOWAY, LAWRENCE. 'Violent America: the Movies 1946–1964'. New York, Museum of Modern Art, 1972

BALSHOFER, FRED J. and MILLER, ARTHUR C. 'One Reel a Week'. Berkeley, University of California Press; Cambridge U.P., 1967

BAXTER, JOHN. 'Hollywood in the Thirties'. London, Tantivy Press; New York, A. S. Barnes, 1968

BILLINGS, PAT and EYLES, ALLEN. 'Hollywood Today'. London, Tantivy Press; New York, A. S. Barnes, 1971

BLUM, DANIEL. 'A Pictorial History of the Silent Screen'. New York, G. P. Putnam's, 1953; London, Hamish Hamilton, 1954; 'A Pictorial History of the Talkies'. New York, G. P. Putnam's, 1958; London, Spring Books, 1960, 1968

BROWNLOW, KEVIN. 'The Parade's Gone By'. New York, Knopf; London, Secker & Warburg, 1968

CONANT, MICHAEL. 'Anti-trust in the Motion Picture Industry: Economic and Legal Analysis'. Berkeley, University of California Press, 1960

COURSODON, JEAN-PIERRE and TAVERNIER, BERTRAND. 'Trente Ans de Cinéma Américain'. Paris, Éditions CIB, 1970

CROWTHER, BOSLEY. 'The Lion's Share: the Story of an Entertainment Empire'. New York, E. P. Dutton, 1957

DEMING, BARBARA. 'Running Away from Myself: a Dream Portrait of America Drawn from the Films of the Forties'. New York, Grossman, 1969

DUNNE, JOHN GREGORY. 'The Studio'. New York, Farrar, Straus & Giroux, 1969; London, W. H. Allen, 1970

FRANKLIN, JOE. 'Classics of the Silent Screen: a pictorial treasury'. New York, Citadel Press, 1959

FRENCH, PHILIP. 'The Movie Moguls: an Informal History of the Hollywood tycoons'. London, Weidenfeld & Nicholson, 1969; Chicago, Regnery, 1971

GOODMAN, EZRA. 'The Fifty-Year Decline and Fall of Hollywood'. New York, Simon & Schuster, 1961

GOW, GORDON. 'Hollywood in the Fifties'. London, Tantivy Press; New York, A. S. Barnes, 1971

GRIFFITH, RICHARD and MAYER, ARTHUR. 'The Movies: the Sixty-year Story of the World of Hollywood'. New York, Simon & Schuster, 1957, 1970; London, Spring Books, 1963, 1970

HAMPTON, BENJAMIN B. 'History of the Movies'. New York, Covici, Friede, 1931; London, Noel Douglas, 1932; New York, Arno Press, 1970; as 'History of the American Film Industry from its Beginnings to 1931'. New York, Dover, 1970

HENDRICKS, GORDON. 'The Edison Motion Picture Myth'. Berkeley and Los Angeles, University of California Press, 1961; 'The Kinetoscope: America's First Commercially Successful Motion Picture Exhibitor'. New York, The Beginnings of the American Film, 1966; as 'Origins of the American Film'. New York, Arno Press, 1972

HIGHAM, CHARLES and GREENBERG, JOEL. 'Hollywood in the Forties'. London, Tantivy Press; New York, A. S. Barnes, 1968

HUETTIG, MAE D. 'Economic Control of the Motion Picture Industry: a Study in Industrial Organization'. Philadelphia, University of Pennsylvania Press; London, Oxford University Press, 1944

JACOBS, LEWIS. 'The Rise of the American Film: a Critical History'. New York, Harcourt, Brace and Company, 1939; New York, Teachers College Press, Columbia University, 1968

JOBES, GERTRUDE. 'Motion Picture Empire'. Hamden (Conn.), Archon Books, 1966

KENNEDY, JOSEPH PATRICK, editor. 'The Story of the Films: as Told by Leaders of the Industry to the Students of the Graduate School of Business and Administration, Harvard'. A. W. Shaw, 1927

LAHUE, KALTON C. 'Dreams for Sale: the Rise and Fall of the Triangle Film Corporation'. New York, A. S. Barnes; London, Thomas Yoseloff, 1971

LEWIS, HOWARD T. 'The Motion Picture Industry'. New York, D. Van Nostrand, 1933

MACCANN, RICHARD DYER. 'Hollywood in Transition'. Boston, Houghton Mifflin Company, 1962

MANVELL, ROGER. 'New Cinema in the USA: the Feature Film since 1946'. London, Studio Vista; New York, Dutton, 1968

MAYER, ARTHUR LOEB. 'Merely Colossal: the Story of the Movies from the Long Chase to the Chaise Longue'. New York, Simon & Schuster, 1953

MAYERSBERG, PAUL. 'Hollywood: the Haunted House', London, Allen Lane, 1967; New York, Stein & Day, 1968

MICHAEL, PAUL, editor. 'The American Movies Reference Book: the Sound Era'. Englewood Cliffs, (N.J.), Prentice-Hall, 1969

POWDERMAKER, HORTENSE. 'Hollywood the Dream Factory: an Anthropologist Looks at the Movie-makers'. Boston, Little, Brown and Company, 1951

PRATT, GEORGE C. 'Spellbound in Darkness: Readings in the History and Criticism of the Silent Film'. Rochester, N.Y., University of Rochester, 1966

RAMSAYE, TERRY. 'A Million and One Nights: a History of the Motion Picture'. New York, Simon & Schuster, 1926; London, Frank Cass & Co., 1964

RIDEOUT, ERIC H. 'The American Film'. London, Mitre Press, 1937

RIGDON, WALTER. 'The Biographical Encyclopedia and Who's Who of the American Theatre'. New York, James H. Heinemann, 1966

ROBINSON, DAVID. 'Hollywood in the Twenties'. London, Tantivy Press; New York, A. S. Barnes, 1968

SARRIS, ANDREW. 'The American Cinema: Directors and Directions, 1929–1968'. New York, E. P. Dutton, 1968

SENNETT, TED. 'Warner Brothers Presents'. New York, Arlington House, 1971

SLIDE, ANTHONY. 'Early American Cinema'. London, Tantivy Press; New York, A. S. Barnes, 1970

THORPE, EDWARD. 'The Other Hollywood'. London, Michael Joseph, 1970

THRASHER, FREDERIC. 'Okay for Sound: How the Screen Found Its Voice'. New York, Duell, Sloan & Pearce, 1946

WAGENKNECHT, EDWARD. 'The Movies in the Age of Innocence'. University of Oklahoma Press, 1962

INDIVIDUAL STUDIES

Anderson

SUSSEX, ELIZABETH. 'Lindsay Anderson'. London, Studio Vista, 1969; New York, Praeger, 1970

Antonioni

CAMERON, IAN and WOOD, ROBIN. 'Antonioni'. London, Studio Vista, 1968; New York, Praeger, 1969

CARLO, CARLO DI. 'Michelangelo Antonioni'. Rome, Bianco e Nero, 1964

COWIE, PETER. 'Antonioni, Bergman, Resnais'. London, Tantivy Press; New York, A. S. Barnes, 1963

HUSS, ROY. 'Focus on Blow-Up'. Englewood Cliffs, Prentice-Hall, 1972

LEPROHON, PIERRE. 'Michelangelo Antonioni: an Introduction'; translated from the French by Scott Sullivan. New York, Simon & Schuster, 1963

Arletty

ARLETTY. 'La defense'. Paris, La Table Ronde, 1971

Asquith

NOBLE, PETER. 'Anthony Asquith'. London, British Film Institute, 1951

Astaire

ASTAIRE, FRED. 'Steps in Time'. New York, Harper, 1959; London, Heinemann, 1960

HACKL, ALFONS. 'Fred Astaire and his Work'. Vienna, Edition Austria International, 1970

Astor

ASTOR, MARY. 'A Life on Film'. New York, Delacorte Press, 1971

Astruc

BELLOUR, RAYMOND. 'Alexandre Astruc'. Paris, Éditions Seghers, 1963

Balcon

BALCON, MICHAEL. 'Michael Balcon Presents a Lifetime of Films'. London, Hutchinson, 1969

DANISCHEWSKY, M., editor. 'Michael Balcon's 25 Years in Films'. London, World Film Publications Ltd., 1947

Becker

QUEVAL, JEAN. 'Jacques Becker'. Paris, Éditions Seghers, 1962

Bennett

BENNETT, JOAN and KIBBEE, LOIS. 'The Bennett Playbill'. New York, Holt, Rinehart & Winston, 1970

Bergman, Ingmar

BJORKMAN, STIG and others. 'Bergman on Bergman'. London, Secker & Warburg, 1972

DONNER, JORN. 'The Personal Vision of Ingmar Bergman'; translated from the Swedish by Holger Lundbergh. Bloomington, Indiana University Press, 1964

GIBSON, ARTHUR. 'The Silence of God: Creative Response to the Films of Ingmar Bergman'. New York, Harper & Row, 1969

STEENE, BIRGITTA. 'Ingmar Bergman'. New York, Twayne Publishers, 1968

WOOD, ROBIN. 'Ingmar Bergman'. London, Studio Vista; New York, Praeger, 1969

YOUNG, VINCENT. 'Cinema Borealis'. New York, D. Lewis, 1971

Bergman, Ingrid

QUIRK, L. J. 'The Films of Ingrid Bergman'. New York, The Citadel Press, 1970

Bogart

MCCARTHY, CLIFFORD. 'Bogey: the Films of Humphrey Bogart'. New York, The Citadel Press, 1965

MICHAEL, PAUL. 'Humphrey Bogart: the Man and his Films'. New York, Bobbs-Merrill, 1965

Bresson

AYFRE, AMÉDÉE, and others. 'The Films of Robert Bresson'. London, Studio Vista, 1969; New York, Praeger, 1970

Bonomo

BONOMO, JOE. 'The Strongman'. New York, Bonomo Studios Inc., 1968

Brunel

BRUNEL, ADRIAN. 'Nice Work: the Story of Thirty Years in British Film Production'. London, Forbes Robertson Ltd., 1949

Buñuel

BUACHE, FREDDY. 'Luis Buñuel'. Lausanne, La Cité, 1970

DURGNAT, RAYMOND. 'Luis Buñuel'. London, Studio Vista, 1967; Berkeley, University of California Press, 1968

KYROU, ADO. 'Luis Buñuel: an Introduction'; translated from the French by Adrienne Foulke. New York, Simon & Schuster, 1963

Capra

CAPRA, FRANK. 'The Name Above the Title: an Autobiography'. New York, Macmillan, 1971

GRIFFITH, RICHARD. 'Frank Capra'. London, British Film Institute, 1951

Carné

CHAZAL, ROBERT. 'Marcel Carné'. Paris, Éditions Seghers, 1965

QUEVAL, JEAN. 'Marcel Carné'. London, British Film Institute, 1950

Carroll

NEMCEK, PAUL L. 'The Films of Nancy Carroll'. New York, Lyle Stuart, 1969

Cavalcanti

KLAUE, WOLFGANG, editor. 'Alberto Cavalcanti'. Berlin, Staatlichen Filmarchiv der Deutschen Demokratischen Republik, 1962

Chabrol

WOOD, ROBIN and WALKER, MICHAEL. 'Claude Chabrol'. London, Studio Vista; New York, Praeger, 1970

Chaney

ANDERSON, ROBERT G. 'Faces, Forms, Films: the Artistry of Lon Chaney'. New York, A. S. Barnes, 1972

Chaplin

CHAPLIN, CHARLES. 'My Autobiography'. London, The Bodley Head, 1964; New York, Pocket Books, 1966

HUFF, THEODORE. 'Charlie Chaplin'. New York, Henry Schuman, 1951; London, Cassell, 1952; New York, Arno Press, 1972

MCCAFFREY, DONALD W. 'Focus on Chaplin'. Englewood Cliffs, Prentice-Hall, 1972

MCDONALD, GERALD D. and others. 'The Films of Charlie Chaplin'. New York, Citadel Press, 1965

QUIGLY, ISABEL. 'Charlie Chaplin: Early Comedies'. London, Studio Vista; New York, E. P. Dutton, 1968

Cherkasov

CHERKASOV, NIKOLAI. 'Notes of a Soviet Actor'.

Moscow, Foreign Language Publishing House, 1957

Christensen

ERNEST, JOHN. 'Benjamin Christensen'. Copenhagen, Danske Filmmuseum, 1967

Clair

AMENGUAL, BARTHELEMY. 'René Clair'. Paris, Éditions Seghers, 1963

CHARENSOL, GEORGES. 'René Clair, et Les Belles de Nuit'. Paris, Éditions du Cerf, 1953

MITRY, JEAN. 'René Clair'. Paris, Éditions Universitaires, 1960

Clément

FARWAGI, ANDRE. 'René Clément'. Paris, Éditions Seghers, 1967

Clouzot

LACASSIN, FRANCIS and BELLOUR, RAYMOND. 'Le Procès Clouzot'. Paris, Le Terrain Vague, 1964

Cocteau

COCTEAU, JEAN. 'Cocteau on the Film: a Conversation Recorded by André Fraigneau'; translated from the French by Vera Traill. London, Denis Dobson, 1954

GILSON, RENÉ. 'Jean Cocteau'; translated from the French by Giba Vaughan. New York, Crown Publishers, 1969

Cohn

THOMAS, BOB. 'King Cohn: the Life and Times of Harry Cohn'. New York, Putnam, 1967

Cooper

DICKENS, HOMER. 'The Films of Gary Cooper'. New York, Citadel Press, 1970

Corman

WILLEMEN, PAUL and others. 'Roger Corman'. Edinburgh Film Festival; Cinema Magazine, 1970

Crawford

CRAWFORD, JOAN and ARDMORE, JANE KISNER. 'A Portrait of Joan: the Autobiography of Joan Crawford'. New York, Doubleday and Company, Inc., 1962; London, Frederick Muller Limited, 1963

QUIRK, LAWRENCE J. 'The Films of Joan Crawford'. New York, Citadel Press, 1968

Davis

DAVIS, BETTE. 'The Lonely Life: an Autobiography'. New York, G. P. Putnam's, 1962; London, Macdonald, 1963

GINGGOLD, GENE. 'The Films of Bette Davis'. New York, Citadel Press, 1966

Delluc

TARIOL, MARCEL. 'Louis Delluc'. Paris, Éditions Seghers, 1965

De Mille

DE MILLE, CECIL BLOUNT. 'The Autobiography of Cecil B. De Mille'; edited by Donald Hayne. New York, Prentice-Hall, 1959; London, W. H. Allen, 1960

RINGGOLD, GENE and DEWITT, BODEEN. 'The Films of Cecil B. De Mille'. New York, Citadel Press, 1969

De Sica

LEPROHON, PIERRE. 'Vittorio De Sica'. Paris, Éditions Seghers, 1966

Dietrich

DICKENS, HOMER. 'The Films of Marlene Dietrich'. New York, Citadel Press, 1968

KOBAL, JOHN. 'Marlene Dietrich'. London, Studio Vista; New York, E. P. Dutton, 1968

Disney

FEILD, ROBERT. 'The Art of Walt Disney'. New York, Macmillan, 1942; London, Collins, 1944

JUNGERSEN, FREDERICK. 'Disney'. Copenhagen, Danske Filmmuseum, 1968

SCHICKEL, RICHARD. 'The Disney version'. New York, Simon & Schuster, 1968; as 'Walt Disney'. London, Weidenfeld & Nicolson, 1968

Donskoi

CERVONI, ALBERT. 'Marc Donskoi'. Paris, Éditions Seghers, 1966

Dovzhenko

AMENGUAL, BARTHELEMY. 'Dovjenko'. Paris, Éditions Seghers, 1970

SCHNITZER, JEAN and LUDA. 'Dovjenko'. Paris, Éditions Universitaires, 1966

Dreyer

MILNE, TOM. 'The Cinema of Carl Dreyer'. London, Tantivy Press; New York, A. S. Barnes, 1971

PARRAIN, PHILIPPE. 'Dreyer: Cadres et Mouvements'. Paris, Lettres Modernes, 1967

PERRIN, CLAUDE. 'Carl Th. Dreyer'. Paris Éditions Seghers, 1969

Eisenstein

EISENSTEIN, SERGEI MIKHAILOVICH and SINCLAIR, UPTON. 'The Making and Unmaking of Que Viva Mexico!'; edited by Harry M. Geldud and Ronald Gottesman. Bloomington, Indiana University Press; London, Secker & Warburg, 1970

MONTAGU, IVOR. 'With Eisenstein in Hollywood: a Chapter of Autobiography'. Berlin, Seven Seas Publishers, 1968; New York, International Publications, 1969

MOUSSINAC, LEON. 'Serge Eisenstein'; translated from the French. New York, Crown Publishers, 1969

SETON, MARIE. 'Sergei M. Eisenstein: a Biography'. London, The Bodley Head, 1952; New York, Grove Press, 1960

Epstein

LEPROHON, PIERRE. 'Jean Epstein'. Paris, Éditions Seghers, 1964

Fairbanks

COOKE, ALISTAIR. 'Douglas Fairbanks: the Making of a Screen Character'. New York, Museum of Modern Art, 1940

Fellini

BUDGEN, SUZANNE. 'Fellini'. London, British Film Institute Education Department, 1966

SALACHAS, GILBERT. 'Federico Fellini'; translated from the French by Rosalie Siegel. New York, Crown, 1969

SOLMI, ANGELO. 'Fellini'; translated from the Italian by Elizabeth Greenwood. London, Merlin Press, 1967; New York, Humanities, 1968

Feuillade

LACASSIN, FRANCIS. 'Louis Feuillade'. Paris, Éditions Seghers, 1964

Feyder

BACHY, VICTOR. 'Jacques Feyder: Artisan du Cinéma'. Louvain, Librairie Universitaire, 1968

MICHA, RENÉ, editor. 'Jacques Feyder, ou, le Cinéma Concret'. Brussels, Comité National Jacques Feyder, 1949

Fields

DESCHNER, DONALD. 'The Films of W. C. Fields'. New York, Citadel Press, 1966

EVERSON, WILLIAM K. 'The Art of W. C. Fields'. New York, Bobbs-Merrill, 1967

TAYLOR, ROBERT LEWIS. 'W. C. Fields, his Follies and Fortunes'. New York, Doubleday, 1949

Fitzgerald

LATHAM, AARON. 'Crazy Sundays: F. Scott Fitzgerald in Hollywood'. New York, Viking Press, 1971

Flaherty

FLAHERTY, FRANCIS HUBBARD. 'The Odyssey of a Film-maker: Robert Flaherty's Story'. Urbane (Illinois), Beta Phi Mu, 1960; New York Arno Press, 1972

CALDER-MARSHALL, ARTHUR. 'The Innocent Eye: the Life of Robert Flaherty'. London W. H. Allen, 1963; New York, Harcourt, Brace, Jovanovich, 1966

GRIFFITH, RICHARD. 'The World of Robert Flaherty'. New York, Duell Sloan & Pearce Boston, Little Brown & Co., 1953

Flynn

THOMAS, TONY and others. 'The Films of Errol Flynn'. New York, Citadel Press, 1969

Fonda

SPRINGER, JOHN. 'The Fondas: the Films and Careers of Henry, Jane and Peter Fonda'. New York, Citadel Press, 1970

Ford

BAXTER, JOHN. 'The Cinema of John Ford'. London, Tantivy Press; New York, A. S. Barnes, 1972

BOGDANOVICH, PETER. 'John Ford'. London Studio Vista, 1967; Berkeley, University of California Press, 1968

Fox

ALLVINE, GLENDON. 'The Greatest Fox of Them All'. New York, Lyle Stuart, 1969

SINCLAIR, UPTON. 'Upton Sinclair Presents William Fox'. Los Angeles, published by the author, 1933; New York, Arno Press, 1970

Franju

DURGNAT, RAYMOND. 'Franju'. London, Studio Vista, 1968; Berkeley, University of California Press, 1969

Frankenheimer
PRATLEY, GERALD. 'The Cinema of John Frankenheimer'. London, Tantivy Press; New York, A. S. Barnes, 1970

Friese-Green
ALLISTER, RAY. 'Friese-Green: Close-up of an Inventor'. London, Marsland, 1948; New York, Arno Press, 1972

Fuller
GARNHAM, NICHOLAS. 'Samuel Fuller'. London, Secker & Warburg; New York, Viking, 1971
HARDY, PHIL. 'Samuel Fuller'. London, Studio Vista; New York, Praeger, 1970
WILL, DAVID and WOLLEN, PETER, editors. 'Samuel Fuller'. Edinburgh Film Festival, 1969

Gable
ESSOE, GABE. 'The Films of Clark Gable'. New York, Citadel Press, 1970

Gance
DARIA, SOPHIE. 'Abel Gance: Hier et Demain, avec un Texte Inédit par Abel Gance'. Paris, Éditions La Palatine, 1959

Garbo
BAINBRIDGE, JOHN. 'Garbo'. London, Frederick Muller, 1955; New York, Holt, Rinehart & Winston, 1971
CONWAY, MICHAEL and others. 'The Films of Greta Garbo'. New York, The Citadel Press, 1963
DURGNAT, RAYMOND and KOBAL, JOHN. 'Greta Garbo'. London, Studio Vista; New York, E. P. Dutton, 1965
ZIEROLD, NORMAN. 'Garbo'. New York, Stein & Day, 1969; London, W. H. Allen, 1970

Garland
MORELLA, JOE and EPSTEIN, EDWARD. 'Judy: the Films and Career of Judy Garland'. New York, Citadel Press; London, Leslie Frewin, 1969
TORMÉ, MEL. 'The Other Side of the Rainbow'. New York, William Morrow, 1970

Gish
GISH, LILLIAN and PINCHOT, ANN. 'Lillian Gish: the Movies, Mr Griffith and Me'. Englewood Cliffs, Prentice-Hall; London, W. H. Allen, 1969
PAINE, ALBERT BIGELOW. 'Life and Lillian Gish'. New York, Macmillan, 1932

Godard
CAMERON, IAN, editor. 'The Films of Jean-Luc Godard'. London, Studio Vista, 1967, 1969; New York, Praeger, 1969
MUSSMAN, TOBY, editor. 'Jean-Luc Godard: a Critical Anthology'. New York, E. P. Dutton, 1968
ROUD, RICHARD. 'Jean-Luc Godard'. London, Secker & Warburg, 1967; 1970; Garden City (N.Y.), Doubleday, 1968

Goldwyn
GOLDWYN, SAMUEL. 'Behind the Screen'. New York, George H. Doran Company, 1923

Grant
DESCHNER, DONALD. 'The Films of Cary Grant'. New York, Citadel Press, 1972

Grémillon
AGEL, HENRI. 'Jean Grémillon'. Paris, Éditions Seghers, 1969

Griffith
ARVIDSON, LINDA (MRS D. W. GRIFFITH). 'When the Movies Were Young'. New York, E. P. Dutton, 1925; New York, Dover Publications, 1969
BARRY, IRIS and BOWSER, EILEEN. 'D. W. Griffith: American Film Master', by Iris Barry, with an annotated list of films by Eileen Bowser. New York, Museum of Modern Art, 1965
GEDULD, HARRY M., editor. 'Focus on D. W. Griffith'. Englewood Cliffs, Prentice-Hall, 1971
HENDERSON, ROBERT M. 'D. W. Griffith: the Years at Biograph'. New York, Farrar, Straus & Giroux, 1970; London, Secker & Warburg, 1971
O'DELL, PAUL. 'Griffith and the Rise of Hollywood'. London, Tantivy Press; New York, A. S. Barnes, 1970
SILVA. 'Focus on Birth of a Nation'. Englewood Cliffs, Prentice-Hall, 1972

Harlow
CONWAY, MICHAEL and RICCI, MARK. 'The Films of Jean Harlow'. New York, Citadel Press, 1965

Hawks
WOOD, ROBIN. 'Howard Hawks'. London, Secker & Warburg; Garden City (N.Y.), Doubleday, 1968

Hepburn
DICKENS, HOMER. 'The Films of Katharine Hepburn'. New York, Citadel Press, 1971

Hepworth
HEPWORTH, CECIL MILTON. 'Come the Dawn: Memories of a Film Pioneer'. London, Phoenix House, Limited, 1951

Hitchcock
ROHMER, ERIC and CHABROL, CLAUDE. 'Hitchcock'. Paris, Éditions Universitaires, 1957
TRUFFAUT, FRANÇOIS and SCOTT, HELEN. 'Hitchcock'; translated from the French. New York, Simon & Schuster, 1967; London, Secker & Warburg, 1968
WOOD, ROBIN. 'Hitchcock's films'. London. Tantivy Press; New York, A. S. Barnes, 1965, 1969

Ivens
IVENS, JORIS. 'The Camera and I'. Berlin, Seven Seas Publishers; New York, International Publishers, 1969

Kazan
CIMENT, MICHEL. 'Kazan on Kazan'. London, Secker & Warburg; New York, Viking, 1972
TAILLEUR, ROGER. 'Elia Kazan'. Paris, Éditions Seghers, 1966

Kawalerowicz
ESTÈVE, MICHEL, editor. 'Jerzy Kawalerowicz' Paris, Lettres Modernes, 1967

Keaton
BLESH, RUDI. 'Keaton'. New York, Macmillan, 1966; London, Secker & Warburg, 1967
KEATON, BUSTER and SAMUELS, CHARLES. 'My Wonderful World of Slapstick'. New York, Doubleday 1960; London, Allen & Unwin, 1967
LEBEL, JEAN-PATRICK. 'Buster Keaton'; translated from the French. London, A. Zwemmer; New York, A. S. Barnes, 1967
ROBINSON, DAVID. 'Buster Keaton'. London, Secker & Warburg; Bloomington, Indiana University Press, 1969

Korda
TABORI, PAUL. 'Alexander Korda'. London, Oldbourne, 1959; New York, Living Books, 1966

Kubrick
WALKER, ALEXANDER. 'Stanley Kubrick Directs'. New York, Harcourt Brace Jovanovich, 1971; London, Denis Poynter, 1972

Kurosawa
RICHIE, DONALD. 'The Films of Akira Kurosawa'. Berkeley, University of California Press, 1965

Laemmle
DRINKWATER, JOHN. 'The Life and Adventures of Carl Laemmle'. London, William Heinemann Ltd, 1931

Lang
BOGDANOVICH, PETER. 'Fritz Lang in America'. London, Studio Vista, 1968; New York, Praeger, 1969
JENSEN, PAUL M. 'The Cinema of Fritz Lang'. London, Tantivy Press; New York, A. S. Barnes, 1969

Laughton
LANCHESTER, ELSA. 'Charles Laughton and I'. London, Faber, 1938

Laurel & Hardy
BARR, CHARLES. 'Laurel & Hardy'. London, Studio Vista, 1967; Berkeley, University of California Press, 1968
EVERSON, WILLIAM K. 'The Films of Laurel & Hardy'. New York, Citadel Press, 1967
MCCABE, JOHN. 'Mr Laurel and Mr Hardy'. New York, Doubleday & Co., 1961; London, Museum Press, 1962; New York, Grosset & Dunlop, 1966

Lefebvre
BERUBE, RENALD and PATRY, YVAN. 'Jean-Pierre Lefebvre'. Québec, Presses de l'Université du Québec, 1971

Lewis
LEUTRAT, JEAN-LOUIS and SIMONCI, PAUL. 'Jerry Lewis'. Lyon, SERDOC, 1965

Lewton
SIEGEL, JOEL. 'Val Lewton'. London, Secker & Warburg; New York, Viking, 1972

Linder
FORD, CHARLES. 'Max Linder'. Paris, Editions Seghers, 1966

Lloyd
CAHN, WILLIAM. 'Harold Lloyd's World of Comedy'. New York, Duell, Sloan & Pearce, 1964; London, Allen & Unwin, 1966
LLOYD, HAROLD and STOUT, WESLEY, W. 'An American Comedy'. New York, Longmans Green, 1928; New York, Blom, 1971

Lorentz
SNYDER, ROBERT L. 'Pare Lorentz and the Documentary Film'. Norman, University of Oklahoma Press, 1968

Losey
LEAHY, JAMES. 'The Cinema of Joseph Losey'. London, Tantivy Press; New York, A. S. Barnes, 1967
MILNE, TOM. 'Losey on Losey'. London, Secker & Warburg, 1967; Garden City (N.Y.), Doubleday, 1968

Lubitsch
WEINBERG, HERMAN G. 'The Lubitsch Touch: a Critical Study'. New York, E. P. Dutton, 1968

Malle
CHAPIER, HENRY. 'Louis Malle'. Paris, Éditions Seghers, 1964

Malraux
MARION, DENIS. 'André Malraux'. Paris, Éditions Seghers, 1970

Mamoulian
MILNE, TOM. 'Rouben Mamoulian'. London, Secker & Warburg, 1969; Bloomington, Indiana Press, 1970

March
QUIRK, LAWRENCE J. 'The Films of Fredric March'. New York, Citadel Press, 1971

Marx Brothers
CRIGHTON, KYLE. 'The Marx Brothers'. Garden City (N.Y.), Doubleday, 1950; London, William Heinemann, 1951
EYLES, ALLEN. 'The Marx Brothers: Their World of Comedy'. London, Tantivy Press; New York, A. S. Barnes, 1966, 1969
MARX, ARTHUR. 'Life with Groucho'. New York, Simon & Schuster, 1954; as 'Groucho'. London, Gollancz, 1954
MARX, GROUCHO. 'Groucho and Me'. New York, Bernard Geis; London, Gollancz, 1959
MARX, HARPO and BARBER, ROWLAND. 'Harpo Speaks!'. London, Gollancz, 1961
ZIMMERMAN, PAUL D. and GOLDBLATT, BURT. 'The Marx Brothers at the Movies'. New York, G. P. Putnam's, 1968

Mayer, Carl
HEMPEL, ROLF. 'Carl Mayer: ein Autor Schreibt mit der Kamera'. Berlin, Henschelverlag Kunst und Gesellschaft, 1968

Mayer, Louis B.
CROWTHER, BOSLEY. 'Hollywood Rajah: the Life and Times of Louis B. Mayer'. New York, Holt, Rinehart and Winston, 1960

Méliès
DESLANDES, JACQUES. 'Le Boulevard du Cinéma a l'Époque de Georges Méliès'. Paris, Éditions du Cerf, 1963

Melville
NOGUEIRA, RUI. 'Melville on Melville'. London, Secker & Warburg; New York, Viking, 1971

Minnelli
DE LA ROCHE, CATHERINE. 'Vincente Minnelli'. Wellington, New Zealand Film Institute; New York, Film Culture, 1959
TRUCHARD, FRANÇOIS. 'Vincente Minnelli'. Paris, Éditions Universitaires, 1966

Mizoguchi
MESNIL, MICHEL. 'Kenji Mizoguchi'. Paris, Éditions Seghers, 1965

Monroe
CONWAY, MICHAEL and RICCI, MARK. 'The Films of Marilyn Monroe'. New York, Citadel Press, 1964
GUILES, FRED LAWRENCE. 'Norma Jean: the Life of Marilyn Monroe'. New York, McGraw-Hill; London, W. H. Allen, 1969
HOYT, EDWIN P. 'Marilyn: the Tragic Venus'. New York, Duell, Sloan and Pearce, 1965; London, Robert Hale, 1967
WAGENKNECHT, EDWARD, editor. 'Marilyn Monroe: a Composite View'. Philadelphia, Chilton Book Company, 1969

Moore
MOORE, COLLEEN. 'Silent Star'. New York, Doubleday, 1968

Murnau
EISNER, LOTTE H. 'F. W. Murnau: Textes Additionnels de Robert Plumpe et Robert Herlith'. Paris, Le Terrain Vague, 1964. English edition, London, Secker & Warburg, 1972

Negri
NEGRI, POLA. 'Memoirs of a Star'. New York, Doubleday, 1970

Newman
QUIRK, LAWRENCE J. 'The films of Paul Newman'. New York, Citadel Press, 1971

Ophüls
OPHÜLS, MAX. 'Max Ophüls par Max Ophüls (Spiel im Dassein)'; translated from the German by Max Roth. Paris, Robert Laffont, 1963
ROUD, RICHARD. 'Max Ophüls: an index'. London, British Film Institute, 1958

Oswald
KAUL, WALTER and SCHEUER, ROBERT G., editors. 'Richard Oswald'. Berlin, Deutschen Kinemathek, 1970

Ozu
TESSIER, MAX. 'Yasujiro Ozu, 1903–1963'. Paris, Anthologie du Cinéma, 1971

Pabst
AMENGUAL, BARTHÉLEMY. 'G. W. Pabst'. Paris, Éditions Seghers, 1966

Pascal
PASCAL, VALERIE. 'The Disciple and his Devil: Gabriel Pascal, Bernard Shaw'. New York, McGraw-Hill, 1970; London, Michael Joseph, 1971

Pasolini
STACK, OSWALD. 'Pasolini on Pasolini: Interviews'. London, Secker & Warburg, 1969; Bloomington, Indiana University Press, 1970

Pathé
PATHÉ, CHARLES. 'De Pathé Frères à Pathé Cinéma'. Lyons, SERDOC, 1970

Pearson
PEARSON, GEORGE. 'Flashback: the Autobiography of a British Film-Maker'. London, George Allen & Unwin Ltd., 1957

Penn
WOOD, ROBIN. 'Arthur Penn'. London, Studio Vista, 1968; New York, Praeger, 1969

Peries
COOREY, PHILIP. 'The Lonely Artist: a Critical Introduction to the Films of Lester James Peries'. Colombo, Lake House Investments, 1970

Philipe
PÉRISSET, MAURICE. 'Gérard Philipe'. Paris, Fil d'Ariane, 1964

Pickford
NIVER, R. KEMP. 'Mary Pickford: Comedienne'; edited by Bebe Bergsten. Los Angeles, Locare Research Group, 1969
PICKFORD, MARY. 'Sunshine and Shadow'. New York, Doubleday, 1954; London, Heinemann, 1956

Polanski
BUTLER, IVAN. 'The Cinema of Roman Polanski'. London, Tantivy Press; New York, A. S. Barnes, 1970

Preminger
PRATLEY, GERALD. 'The Cinema of Otto Preminger'. London, Tantivy Press; New York, A. S. Barnes, 1971

Prévert
JACOB, GUY and others. 'Jacques Prévert'. Lyons, SERDOC, 1960
GUILLOT, GÉRARD. 'Les Préverts'. Paris, Éditions Seghers, 1966

Pudovkin
SCHNITZER, JEAN and LUDA. 'V. Pudovkin'. Paris, Éditions Seghers, 1966

Rank
WOOD, ALAN. 'Mr Rank'. London, Hodder & Stoughton, 1952

Ray, Nicholas
TRUCHARD, FRANÇOIS. 'Nicholas Ray'. Paris, Éditions Universitaires, 1965

Ray, Satyajit
SETON, MARIE. 'Portrait of a Director: Satyajit Ray'. London, Dennis Dobson, 1971
WOOD, ROBIN. 'The Apu Trilogy'. London, November Books; New York, Praeger, 1972

Renoir
BAZIN, ANDRÉ. 'Jean Renoir'; edited by Fran-

çois Truffaut. Paris, Éditions Champ Libre, 1971
CAULIEZ, ARMAND-JEAN. 'Jean Renoir'. Paris, Éditions Universitaires, 1962
DURGNAT, RAYMOND. 'The Works of Jean Renoir'. Berkeley, University of California Press; London, Studio Vista, 1972

Resnais
ARMES, ROY. 'The Cinema of Alain Resnais'. London, Tantivy Press; New York, A. S. Barnes, 1968
WARD, JOHN. 'Alain Resnais, or the Theme of Time'. London, Secker & Warburg, 1967; Garden City (N.Y.), Doubleday, 1968

Roach
EVERSON, WILLIAM K. 'The Films of Hal Roach'. New York, Museum of Modern Art, 1971.

Rogers, St Johns
ROGERS ST JOHNS, ADELA. 'The Honeycomb'. New York, Doubleday, 1969

Rossellini
GUARNER, JOSE LUIS. 'Roberto Rossellini'; translated by Elisabeth Cameron. London, Studio Vista; New York, Praeger, 1970

Rossen
CASTY, ALAN. 'The Films of Robert Rossen'. New York, Museum of Modern Art, 1969

Selznick
THOMAS, BOB. 'Selznick'. New York, Doubleday, 1970; London, W. H. Allen, 1971

Sennett
FOWLER, GENE. 'Father Goose: the story of Mack Sennett'. New York, Covici Friede Publishers, 1934
SENNETT, MACK. 'King of Comedy'. Garden City (N.Y.), Doubleday, 1954

Siegel
LOVELL, ALAN, editor. 'Don Siegel: American Cinema'. London, British Film Institute Education Department, 1968

Simon
FANSTEN, JACQUES. 'Michel Simon'. Paris, Éditions Seghers, 1970

Sinatra
RINGGOLD, GENE. 'The Films of Frank Sinatra'. New York, Citadel Press, 1971

Sirk
HALLIDAY, JON. 'Sirk on Sirk'. London, Secker & Warburg; New York, Viking Press, 1972

Sjöström
PENSEL, HANS. 'Seastrom and Stiller in Hollywood: Two Swedish Directors in Silent American Films, 1923–1930'. New York, Vantage Press, 1969
JEANNE, RENÉ and FORD, CHARLES. 'Victor Sjöström'. Paris, Éditions Universitaires, 1963

Stevens
RICHIE, DONALD. 'George Stevens: an American Romantic'. New York, Museum of Modern Art, 1970

Stiller
WERNER, GOSTA. 'Mauritz Stiller och hans Filmer, 1912–1916'. Stockholm, P. A. Norstedt, 1969

Straub
ROUD, RICHARD. 'Jean-Marie Straub'. London, Secker & Warburg; New York, Viking Press, 1972

Tati
CAULIEZ, ARMAND-J. 'Jacques Tati'. Paris, Éditions Seghers, 1962

Thalberg
THOMAS, BOB. 'Thalberg: the Life and the Legend'. New York, Doubleday, 1969; London, W. H. Allen, 1971

Tracy
DESCHNER, DONALD. 'The Films of Spencer Tracy'. New York, Citadel Press, 1968
SWINDELL, LARRY. 'Spencer Tracy: a Biography'. New York, World Publishing Co., 1969; London, W. H. Allen, 1970

Trnka
BOČEK, JAROSLAV. 'Jiří Trnka: Artist and Puppet Master'. Prague, Artia, 1965

Truffaut
CRISP, C. G. 'François Truffaut'. London, November Books; New York, Praeger, 1972
PETRIE, GRAHAM. 'The Cinema of François Truffaut'. London, Tantivy Press; New York, A. S. Barnes, 1970

Trumbo
TRUMBO, DALTON. 'Additional Dialogue: Letters of Dalton Trumbo, 1942–1962'; edited by Helen Manfull. New York, M. Evans, 1970

Turner
MORELLA, JOE and EPSTEIN, EDWARD Z. 'Lana Turner'. New York, Citadel Press, 1971

Ustinov
THOMAS, TONY. 'Ustinov in Focus'. London, Tantivy Press; New York, A. S. Barnes, 1971

Vertov
ABRAMOV, N. P. 'Dziga Vertov'; translated into French from the Russian. Lyon, SERDOC, 1965
SADOUL, GEORGES. 'Dziga Vertov'. Paris, Éditions Champ Libre, 1971

Vidor
VIDOR, KING. 'A Tree is a Tree'. New York, Harcourt, Brace, 1953

Viertel
VIERTEL, SALKA. 'The Kindness of Strangers'. New York, Holt, Rinehart and Winston, 1969

Vigo
FELDMAN, JOSEPH and HARRY, compilers. 'Jean Vigo'. London, British Film Institute, 1951
LHERMINIER, PIERRE. 'Jean Vigo'. Paris, Éditions Seghers, 1967
SALES GOMES, P. E. 'Jean Vigo'; translated from the French. London, Secker & Warburg; Berkeley, University of California Press, 1972
SMITH, JOHN M. 'Jean Vigo'. London, November Books; New York, Praeger, 1972

Visconti
NOWELL-SMITH, GEOFFREY. 'Luchino Visconti'. London, Secker & Warburg, 1967; Garden City (N.Y.), Doubleday, 1968

von Sternberg
SARRIS, ANDREW. 'The Films of Josef von Sternberg'. New York, Museum of Modern Art, 1966
VON STERNBERG, JOSEF. 'Fun in a Chinese Laundry'. New York, Macmillan, 1965; London, Secker & Warburg, 1966

von Stroheim
CURTISS, THOMAS QUINN. 'Von Stroheim'. New York, Farrar, Straus & Giroux, 1971
FINLER, JOEL. 'Stroheim'. London, Studio Vista, 1967; Berkeley, University of California Press, 1968
NOBLE, PETER. 'Hollywood Scapegoat: the Biography of Erich von Stroheim'. London, The Fortune Press, 1950; New York, Arno Press, 1972

Wajda
ESTÈVE, MICHEL, editor. 'Andrzej Wajda'. Paris, Lettres Modernes, 1968

Walsh
CANHAM, KINGSLEY. 'The Hollywood Professionals: Walsh, Hathaway and Curtiz'. London, Tantivy Press; New York, A. S. Barnes, 1972

Warhol
GIDAL, PETER. 'Andy Warhol: Films and Paintings'. London, Studio Vista; New York, E. P. Dutton, 1971

Warner
WARNER, JACK L. and JENNINGS, DEAN. 'My First Hundred Years in Hollywood'. New York, Random House, 1964

Wayne
FERNETT, GENE. 'Starring John Wayne'. Florida, Brevard Printing Co., 1969
RICCI, MARK and others. 'The Films of John Wayne'. New York, Citadel Press, 1970

Welles
COWIE, PETER. 'The Cinema of Orson Welles'. London, Tantivy Press, 1965, 1972
GOTTESMAN, RONALD, editor. 'Focus on Citizen Kane'. Englewood Cliffs, Prentice-Hall, 1971
HIGHAM, CHARLES. 'The Films of Orson Welles'. University of California Press, 1970
KAEL, PAULINE. 'The Citizen Kane Book'. New York, Little, Brown 1971; London, Secker & Warburg, 1972
MCBRIDE, JOSEPH. 'Orson Welles'. London, Secker & Warburg; New York, Viking Press, 1972
NOBLE, PETER. 'The Fabulous Orson Welles'. London, Hutchinson, 1956

White
WELTMAN, MANUEL and LEE, RAYMOND. 'Pearl White: the Peerless, Fearless Girl'. New York, A. S. Barnes; London, Thomas Yoseloff, 1969
WHITE, PEARL. 'Just Me'. New York, George H. Doran, 1919

Wilcox
WILCOX, HERBERT. 'Twenty-five Thousand Sunsets: the Autobiography of Herbert Wilcox'. London, Bodley Head, 1967; South Brunswick, A. S. Barnes, 1969

Wilder
MADSEN, AXEL. 'Billy Wilder'. London, Secker & Warburg, 1968; Bloomington, Indiana University Press, 1969
WOOD, TOM. 'The Bright Side of Billy Wilder, Primarily'. New York, Doubleday, 1970

Zanuck
GUSSOW, MEL. 'Don't Say Yes until I Finish Talking'. New York, Doubleday, 1971; as 'Zanuck : Don't Say Yes until I Finish Talking'. London, W. H. Allen, 1971

Zavattini
ZAVATTINI, CESARE. 'Zavattini: Scenes from a Cinematic Life'; translated by William Weaver. Englewood Cliffs, Prentice-Hall, 1970

Zukor
ZUKOR, ADOLPH and KRAMER, DALE. 'The Public Is Never Wrong: the Autobiography of Adolph Zukor'. New York, G. P. Putnam's, 1953

COLLECTED INDIVIDUAL STUDIES

ANTHOLOGIE DU CINÉMA. Each volume contains 10 separate studies, originally published separately on a subscription basis. Paris, C.I.B., 1966–
BULL, CLARENCE SINCLAIR and LEE, RAYMOND. 'The Faces of Hollywood'. New York, A. S. Barnes; London, Thomas Yoseloff, 1968
CAMERON, IAN and ELISABETH. 'Broads'. London, Studio Vista; New York, Praeger, 1969; 'The Heavies'. London, Studio Vista; New York, Praeger, 1969
CAMERON, IAN, editor. 'Second Wave'. London, Studio Vista; New York, Praeger, 1970
GELMIS, JOSEPH. 'The Director as Superstar'. New York, Doubleday, 1970; as 'The Film Director as Superstar'. London, Secker & Warburg, 1971
GRIFFITH, RICHARD. 'The Movie Stars'. New York, Doubleday, 1970
HIGHAM, CHARLES and GREENBERG, JOEL. 'The Celluloid Muse: Hollywood Directors Speak'. London, Angus & Robertson, 1969; Chicago, Regnery, 1971; 'Hollywood Cameramen: Sources of Light'. London, Secker & Warburg; Bloomington, Indiana University Press, 1970
MEYERS, WARREN B. Who is that?': the Late Late Viewers Guide to the Old Old Movie Players'. New York, Personality Posters Ltd., 1967
REBEL, ERIQUE J. and others. 'Great Cameramen'. London, Tantivy Press; New York, A. S. Barnes, 1972
ROSS, LILLIAN and HELEN. 'The Player: a Profile of an Art'. New York, Simon & Schuster, 1962
SARRIS, ANDREW, editor. 'Interviews with Film Directors'. New York, Bobbs-Merrill, 1967; part of the book as 'Hollywood Voices'. London, Secker & Warburg, 1972
SCHICKEL, RICHARD. 'The Stars'. New York, Dial Press, 1962
SHERMAN, ERIC and RUBIN, MARTIN. 'The Director's Event: Interviews with Five American Film-makers'. (Boetticher, Bogdanovich, Fuller, Penn, Polanski) New York, Atheneum, 1970
SHAY, DON. 'Conversations Vol. 1'. Albuquerque (New Mexico), Kaleidoscope Press, 1969
SHIPMAN, DAVID. 'The Great Movie Stars: the Golden Years'. London, Hamlyn; New York, Crown, 1970
TWOMEY, ALFRED E. and MCCLURE, ARTHUR. 'The Versatiles: a Study of Supporting Character Actors and Actresses in the American Motion Picture, 1930–1955'. New York, A. S. Barnes; London, Thomas Yoseloff, 1969
ZIEROLD, NORMAN. 'The Moguls'. New York, Coward-McCann, 1969: as 'The Hollywood Tycoons'. London, Hamish Hamilton, 1969

PUBLISHED FILM SCRIPTS

It is inappropriate to make a selection in this area since every title is of value provided that an accurate transcription has been made. The following simply indicates the main series and publishers.

France and Italy both have a well established tradition of film script publishing (publishers include Gallimard, Éditions de Minuit, and Éditions du Seuil in France and Garzanti, Einaudi and Marsilo in Italy) and provide the two oldest established series. 'L'Avant-Scène du Cinéma' is a monthly magazine entirely devoted to printing scripts of both feature and short films and began publication in 1961. Cappelli Editore in Bologna have published over 40 titles in the hardcover (now paperback) series *Dal Soggetto al Film* since 1955. They not only publish the final scripts, but also early drafts, interviews with the directors and other material.

Lorrimer Press in London have translated several 'L'Avant-Scène' scripts in their series (published since 1966 and handled by Simon & Schuster in America) which now includes over 40 titles. Other English publishers include Secker & Warburg (Eisenstein, Bergman and Dreyer), Studio Vista (Wilder), and Calder & Boyar, who have links with the Grove and Orion Presses in America, (Resnais, Bergman, Bellocchio etc).

Scripts have been published in America for many years, notably the volumes edited by John Gassner and Dudley Nichols for Crown in the 1940s, but, as in England, the main impetus has come in recent years, especially in paperback form. The best of these are the Grove Press Film Book series, which provide a large amount of relevant documentation in addition to the script (titles are *The 400 Blows, Rashomon, Masculine-Feminine* and *L'Avventura*). Grove Press have also published other books in this field (directors include Resnais and Sjöman). Orion Press have a growing list of scripts from the films of major European directors (Antonioni, Visconti, Cocteau, Buñuel and De Sica) and Ballantine Books produced translations of three Fellini volumes in the Cappelli series. Other publishers include Signet Books *(Easy Rider, Faces)*, Medallion Books *(The Married Woman)*, Bantam *(Butch Cassidy and the Sundance Kid)*, and Grossman *(Antonioni)*.

Scripts published in English up to and including early 1970 are listed in the following:-

MCCARTY, CLIFFORD. 'Published Screenplays a Checklist'. Kent State University Press, 197

INDEX OF TITLE CHANGES

The main entry for any film gives, first, its title in its country of origin, then its director and date, followed by alternative titles. Readers seeking a film under its alternative title are referred back to the main entry.

A

Aan (Mehboob Khan, INDIA, 1952). USA: *Savage Princess*

Abandon Ship. See: *Seven Waves Away*

Abbott and Costello Meet Frankenstein (Charles Barton, USA, 1948). GB: *(Abbott and Costello in) Meet the Ghosts*

Abdulla the Great (Gregory Ratoff, GB, 1954). USA: *Abdullah's Harem*

Abe Lincoln in Illinois (John Cromwell, USA, 1939). GB: *Spirit of the People*

Ace in the Hole. See: *The Big Carnival*

The Actress (Sidney Franklin, USA, 1928). GB: *Trelawney of the Wells*

Adios. See: *The Lash*

The Admirable Crichton. See: *Male and Female*

A Double Tour (Claude Chabrol, FRANCE, 1959). GB: *Web of Passion*. USA: *Leda*

Adventure in Baltimore (Richard Wallace, USA, 1949). GB: *Bachelor Bait*

Adventure in Hearts (James Cruze, USA, 1919). GB: *Captain Dieppe*

Adventure in Manhattan (Edward Ludwig, USA, 1936). GB: *Manhattan Madness*

Adventure in Washington (Alfred E. Green, USA, 1941). GB: *Female Correspondent*

Adventures of a Young Man (Martin Ritt, USA, 1962). GB: *Hemingway's Adventures of a Young Man*

The Adventures of Don Juan (Vincent Sherman, USA, 1948). GB: *The New Adventures of Don Juan*

The Adventures of (Ichabod and) Mr Toad. See: *Ichabod and Mr Toad*

Adventures of Sadie. See: *Our Girl Friday*

The Adventures of Sherlock Holmes (Alfred Werker, USA, 1939). GB: *Sherlock Holmes*

The Adventuress. See: *I See a Dark Stranger*

The Affairs of Sally. See: *The Fuller Brush Girl*

After Midnight. See: *Captain Carey, USA*

After Tonight (George Archainbaud, USA, 1933). GB: *Sealed Lips*

Agent 8¾. See: *Hot Enough for June*

Albert RN (Lewis Gilbert, GB, 1953). USA: *Break to Freedom*

Alias Nick Beal (John Farrow, USA, 1948). GB: *The Contact Man*

Alimony (James W. Horne, USA, 1924). GB: *When the Crash Came*

All American (Jesse Hibbs, USA, 1953). GB: *The Winning Way*

All at Sea. See: *Barnacle Bill*

Allegheny Uprising (William A. Seiter, USA, 1940). GB: *The First Rebel*

All for a Woman. See: *Danton*

All That Money Can Buy. See: *The Devil and Daniel Webster*

All This and Money Too. See: *Love is a Ball*

Along Came Sally. See: *Aunt Sally*

Altri Tempi (Alessandro Blasetti, ITALY, 1952). GB: *Infidelity*. USA: *In Olden Days*

The Amazing Mr Beecham. See: *The Chiltern Hundreds*

America, America (Elia Kazan, USA, 1963). GB: *The Anatolian Smile*

An American Dream (Robert Gist, USA, 1966). GB: *See You in Hell, Darling*

American Empire (William McGann, USA, 1942). GB: *My Son Alone*

An American Guerilla in the Philippines (Fritz Lang, USA, 1950). GB: *I Shall Return*

The Amorous Prawn (Anthony Kimmins, GB, 1962). USA: *The Playgirl and the War Minister*

The Anatolian Smile. See: *America, America*

And Then There Were None (René Clair, USA, 1945). GB: *Ten Little Niggers*

Angel Street. See: *Gaslight*

The Animal Kingdom (Edward H. Griffith, USA, 1932). GB: *The Woman in His House*

Anna Boleyn (Ernst Lubitsch, GERMANY, 1921). GB: *Anne Boleyn*. USA: *Deception*

Anni Difficili (Luigi Zampa, ITALY, 1948). GB: *The Little Man*

Anybody Here Seen Kelly? (William Wyler, USA, 1928). GB: *Has Anybody Here Seen Kelly?*

Any Wednesday (Robert Ellis Miller, USA, 1966). GB: *Bachelor Girl Apartment*

Annapolis Story (Don Siegel, USA, 1955). GB: *The Blue and the Gold*

The Ape Man (William Beaudine, USA, 1943). GB: *Lock Your Doors*

The Appaloosa (Sidney Furie, USA, 1966). GB: *Southwest to Sonora*

Appointment in Persia. See: *Teheran*

Appointment with a Soldier. See: *The Midnight Story*

Appointment with Venus (Ralph Thomas, GB, 1951). USA: *Island Rescue*

Are We all Murderers? See: *Nous Sommes Tous des Assassins*

Arms and the Girl. See: *Red Salute*

Arms and the Woman. See: *Mr Winkle Goes to War*

Army Capers. See: *The WAC from Walla Walla*

Arouse and Beware. See: *The Man from Dakota*

Arrivederci, Baby. See: *Drop Dead, Darling*

Artists and Models Abroad (Mitchell Leisen, USA, 1937). GB: *Stranded in Paris*

The Assassin. See: *Venetian Bird*

The Astounding She-Monster (Ronnie Ashcroft, USA, 1958). GB: *Mysterious Invader*

At Gunpoint (Alfred Werker, USA, 1955). GB: *Gunpoint!*

Atoll K (Léo Joannon, FRANCE, 1951). GB: *Robinson Crusoeland*

The Atomic Man. See: *Timeslip*

At Sword's Point (Lewis Allen, USA, 1951). GB: *Sons of the Musketeers*

Attack of the Giant Leeches (Bernard Kowalski, USA, 1958). GB: *Demons of the Swamp*

Attorney for the Defence. See: *Silent Witness*

Die Augen der Mumie Ma (Ernst Lubitsch, GERMANY, 1918). USA: *The Eyes of the Mummy*

August Week-end (Charles Lamont, USA, 1936). GB: *Week-end Madness*

Aunt Sally (Tim Whelan, GB, 1933). USA: *Along Came Sally*

Au Royaume des Cieux (Julien Duvivier, FRANCE, 1949). GB: *Woman Hunt*

The Avengers. See: *The Day Will Dawn*

B

Babes in Toyland (Gus Meins & Charles Rogers, USA, 1934). GB: *Wooden Soldiers* (1948), *Laurel and Hardy in Toyland* (1969)

The Bachelor and the Bobbysoxer (Irving Reis, USA, 1946). GB: *Bachelor Knight*

Bachelor Bait. See: *Adventure in Baltimore*

Bachelor Girl Apartment. See: *Any Wednesday*

Bachelor Girls. See: *The Bachelor's Daughters*

Bachelor Knight. See: *The Bachelor and the Bobbysoxer*

The Bachelor's Daughters (Andrew Stone, USA, 1946). GB: *Bachelor Girls*

Bachelor's Folly. See: *The Calendar*

Background (Dan Birt, GB, 1953). USA: *Edge of Divorce*

The Bad Man (Richard Thorpe, USA, 1941). GB: *Two-Gun Cupid*

The Bad One. See: *Sorority Girl*

Bad Sister. See: *The White Unicorn*

The Badge of Courage. See: *Turn Back the Hours*

The Baited Trap. See: *The Trap*

Ballad in Blue (Paul Henreid, GB, 1964). USA: *Blues for Lovers*

Bande à Part (Jean-Luc Godard, FRANCE, 1964). GB: *The Outsiders*
The Bank Dick (Edward Cline, USA, 1940). GB: *The Bank Detective*
The Barbarian (Sam Wood, USA, 1933). GB: *A Night in Cairo*
Barnacle Bill (Charles Frend, GB, 1957). USA: *All at Sea*
Les Bas Fonds (Jean Renoir, FRANCE, 1936). GB: *Lower Depths*. GB (reissue) & USA: *Underworld*
La Bataille (Nicolas Farkas, FRANCE, 1934). GB: *The Battle/Hara-Kiri*. USA: *The Battle/Thunder in the East*
Battle Hell. See: *Yangtse Incident*
Battle of the River Plate (Michael Powell & Emeric Pressburger, GB, 1956). USA: *Pursuit of the Graf Spee*
Battle of the V1 (Vernon Sewell, GB, 1958). USA: *V1/Unseen Heroes*
The Beachcomber. See: *Vessel of Wrath*
The Beasts of Marseilles. See: *Seven Thunders*
Beauties of the Night. See: *Belles de Nuit*
The Beautiful Cheat. See: *What a Woman*
The Beauty Jungle (Val Guest, GB, 1964). USA: *Contest Girl*
The Bed. See: *Secrets d'Alcove*
Behind Masks (Frank Reicher, USA, 1921). GB: *Jeanne of the Marshes*
Behold We Live. See: *If I Were Free*
Bela Lugosi Meets a Brooklyn Gorilla (William Beaudine, USA, 1952). GB: *Monster Meets Gorilla*
Belles de Nuit (René Clair, FRANCE, 1952). GB: *Night Beauties*. USA: *Beauties of the Night*
Bend of the River (Anthony Mann, USA, 1952). GB: *Where the River Bends*
Bengal Brigade (Laslo Benedek, USA, 1954). GB: *Bengal Rifles*
La Bête Humaine (Jean Renoir, FRANCE, 1938). GB (dubbed): *Judas Was a Woman*. USA: *The Human Beast*
Between Love and Desire. See: *Le Bois des Amants*
Beyond the River. See: *The Bottom of the Bottle*
B. F.'s Daughter (Robert Z. Leonard, USA, 1948). GB: *Polly Fulton*
The Bicycle Thief/Bicycle Thieves. See: *Ladri di Biciclette*
The Big Boodle (Richard Wilson, USA, 1956). GB: *Night in Havana*
The Big Carnival (originally *Ace in the Hole*). (Billy Wilder, USA, 1951). GB: *Ace in the Hole*
Big Deal at Dodge City. See: *A Big Hand for the Little Lady*
A Big Hand for the Little Lady (Fielder Cook, USA, 1966). GB: *Big Deal at Dodge City*
The Big Heart. See: *Miracle on 34th Street*
The Big Land (Gordon Douglas, USA, 1956). GB: *Stampeded*
Big Time Operators. See: *The Smallest Show on Earth*
Birds of Prey (Basil Dean, GB, 1930). USA: *The Perfect Alibi*
Blackout. See: *Contraband*
Black Sunday. See: *La Maschera del Demonio*
The Black Watch (John Ford, USA, 1929). GB: *King of the Khyber Rifles*
Blazing Sun. See: *Plein Soleil*
Blind Date (William Neill, USA, 1934). GB: *Her Sacrifice*
Blind Date (Joseph Losey, GB, 1959). USA: *Chance Meeting*
Blonde Crazy (Roy Del Ruth, USA, 1931). GB: *Larceny Lane*
The Blonde Reporter. See: *Sob Sister*
Blonde Sinner. See: *Yield to the Night*
Blood and Roses. See: *Et Mourir de Plaisir*
Blood is My Heritage. See: *Blood of Dracula*
Blood Money. See: *Requiem for a Heavyweight*
Blood of Dracula (Herbert L. Strock, USA, 1957). GB: *Blood is My Heritage*
Blood on His Lips. See: *The Hideous Sun Demon*
Blood on My Hands. See: *Kiss the Blood off My Hands*
The Blue and the Gold. See: *Annapolis Story*
Blues for Lovers. See: *Ballad in Blue*
The Bob Mathias Story (Francis Lyon, USA, 1954). GB: *The Flaming Torch*
Le Bois des Amants (Claude Autant-Lara, FRANCE, 1960). GB: *Between Love and Desire*
A Bomb for the Dictator. See: *Les Fanatiques*
Bonaventure. See: *Thunder on the Hill*
The Boob (William Wellman, USA, 1926). GB: *The Yokel*
Borderlines. See: *The Caretakers*
Born to Kill (Robert Wise, USA, 1947). GB: *Lady of Deceit*
Both Ends of the Candle. See: *The Helen Morgan Story*
The Bottom of the Bottle (Henry Hathaway, USA, 1955). GB: *Beyond the River*
The Boy from Barnardos. See: *Lord Jeff*
A Boy is Ten Feet Tall. See: *Sammy Going South*
Breaking the Sound Barrier. See: *The Sound Barrier*
Break to Freedom. See: *Albert RN*
Britannia Mews (Jean Negulesco, GB, 1948). USA: *Forbidden Street*
Brighton Rock (John Boulting, GB, 1947). USA: *Young Scarface*
Brink of Hell. See: *Toward the Unknown*
Brink of Life. See: *So Close to Life*
Broadway Bad (Sidney Lanfield, USA, 1933). GB: *Her Reputation*
Broadway Bill (Frank Capra, USA, 1934). GB: *Strictly Confidential*
Broadway Singer. See: *Torch Singer*
Broadway to Hollywood (Willard Mack, USA, 1933). GB: *Ring up the Curtain*
Bucking Broadway (John Ford, USA, 1917). GB: *Slumbering Fires*
Buck Privates (Arthur Lubin, USA, 1941). GB: *Rookies*
Buckskin Frontier (Lesley Selander, USA, 1943). GB: *The Iron Road*
The Bugler of Algiers (originally *We Are French*). (Rupert Julian, USA, 1916). GB: *Comrades*
Build My Gallows High. See: *Out of the Past*
Burning Arrows. See: *Captain John Smith and Pocahontas*
Burn, Witch, Burn. See: *Night of the Eagle*
Busman's Honey-Moon (Arthur B. Woods, GB, 1940). USA: *Haunted Honeymoon*
By Hook or by Crook. See: *I Dood It*
By Rocket to the Moon. See: *Frau im Mond*

C

Cadets on Parade. See: *Junior Army*
Cafe of Seven Sinners. See: *Seven Sinners*
The Calendar (T. Hayes Hunter, GB, 1931). USA: *Bachelor's Folly*
California Holiday. See: *Spinout*
Callaway Went Thataway (Norman Panama & Melvin Frank, USA, 1951). GB: *The Star Said No*
Call Me Genius. See: *The Rebel*
The Call of the North (Joseph Henabery, USA, 1921). GB: *The Conjuror's House*
Calypso. See: *Manfish*
Camels West. See: *Southwest Passage*
Canyon Pass. See *Raton Pass*
The Caper of the Golden Bulls (Russell Rouse, USA, 1966). GB: *Carnival of Thieves*
Captain Carey, USA (Mitchell Leisen, USA, 1950). GB: *After Midnight*
Captain Clegg (Peter Graham Scott, GB, 1962). USA: *Night Creatures*
Captain Dieppe. See: *Adventure in Hearts*
Captain John Smith and Pocahontas (Lew Landers, USA, 1953). GB: *Burning Arrows*
The Card (Ronald Neame, GB, 1952). USA: *The Promoter*
Cardigan's Last Case. See: *State's Attorney*
The Caretaker (Clive Donner, GB, 1963). USA: *The Guest*
The Caretakers (Hall Bartlett, USA, 1963). GB: *Borderlines*
Cargo of Innocents. See: *Stand by for Action*
Carmen (Ernst Lubitsch, GERMANY, 1918). USA: *Gypsy Blood*
Un Carnet de Bal (Julien Duvivier, FRANCE, 1937). GB (dubbed): *Christine*
Les Carnets du Major Thompson (Preston Sturges, FRANCE, 1955). GB: *The Diary of Major Thompson*. USA: *The French They Are a Funny Race*
Carnival (Walter Lang, USA, 1935). GB: *Carnival Nights*
Carnival in Flanders. See: *La Kermesse Héroïque*
Carnival Nights. See: *Carnival*
Carnival of Thieves. See: *The Caper of the Golden Bulls*
Carrington VC (Anthony Asquith, GB, 1954). USA: *Court Martial*
The Case of Mrs Pembroke. See: *Two Against the World*
The Case of the Missing Brides. See: *The Corpse Vanishes*
Cash (Zoltán Korda, GB, 1933). USA: *For Love or Money*
Cash and Carry. See: *Ringside Maisie*
Cash on Delivery. See: *To Dorothy a Son*
Casino de Paree. See: *Go into Your Dance*
Casque d'Or (Jacques Becker, FRANCE, 1952). GB: *Golden Marie*. USA: *Golden Helmet*
Cast Iron. See: *The Virtuous Sin*
Castle on the Hudson (Anatole Litvak, USA, 1940). GB: *Years Without Days*
Catch Us if You Can (John Boorman, GB, 1965). USA: *Having a Wild Weekend*
The Catered Affair (Richard Brooks, USA, 1956). GB: *Wedding Breakfast*
Cattle King (Tay Garnett, USA, 1963). GB: *Guns of Wyoming*
Caught by Television. See: *Trapped by Television*

The Cave Dwellers. See: *One Million BC*
The Chalice of Sorrow (Rex Ingram, USA, 1916). GB: *The Chalice of Remorse*
Chamber of Horrors. See: *The Door with Seven Locks*
Chance Meeting. See: *Blind Date*
The Charge is Murder. See: *Twilight of Honor*
The Cheat. See: *Le Roman d'un Tricheur*
Cheerless Lane. See: *Die freudlose Gasse*
Chicago, Chicago. See: *Gaily, Gaily*
Chicago Masquerade. See: *Little Egypt*
Chief Crazy Horse (George Sherman, USA, 1955). GB: *Valley of Fury*
The Children's Hour (William Wyler, USA, 1961). GB: *The Loudest Whisper*
The Chiltern Hundreds (John Paddy Carstairs, GB, 1949). USA: *The Amazing Mr Beecham*
Choose Your Partners. See: *Two Girls on Broadway*
Christine. See: *Un Carnet de Bal*
Christmas in Connecticut (Peter Godfrey, USA, 1945). GB: *Indiscretion*
Circus World (Henry Hathaway, USA, 1963). GB: *The Magnificent Showman*
City Girl. See: *Our Daily Bread*
The City Jungle. See: *The Young Philadelphians*
City of the Dead (John Moxey, GB, 1959). USA: *Horror Hotel*
Classmates (J. S. Robertson, USA, 1924). GB: *Winning Through*
Claudelle Inglish. (Gordon Douglas, USA, 1961). GB: *Young and Eager*
The Clock (William Worthington, USA, 1917). GB: *Time and Tide*
The Clock (Vincente Minnelli, USA, 1945). GB: *Under the Clock*
Clouds over Europe. See: *Q Planes*
Cobweb Castle. See: *Throne of Blood*
The Cockeyed Miracle (S. Sylvan Simon, USA, 1946). GB: *Mr Griggs Returns*
College Coach (William Wellman, USA, 1933). GB: *Football Coach*
College Days. See: *The Freshman*
College Swing (Raoul Walsh, USA, 1938). GB: *Swing, Teacher, Swing*
Colonel Blimp. See: *The Life and Death of Colonel Blimp*
Colt 45. See: *Thundercloud*
Comrades. See: *The Bugler of Algiers*
Concealment. See: *The Secret Bride*
The Concrete Jungle. See: *The Criminal*
Confession (Ken Hughes, GB, 1955). USA: *The Deadliest Sin*
Confessions of a Co-Ed (David Burton & Dudley Murphy, USA, 1931). GB: *Her Dilemma*
Confessions of an Opium Eater (Albert Zugsmith, USA, 1962). GB: *Evils of Chinatown*
Conflict of Wings (John Eldridge, GB, 1954). USA: *Fuss over Feathers*
The Conjuror's House. See: *The Call of the North*
The Conqueror Worm. See: *Witchfinder General*
Conquest (Clarence Brown, USA, 1937). GB: *Marie Walewska*
Consolation Marriage (Paul Sloane, USA, 1931). GB: *Married in Haste*
The Contact Man. See: *Alias Nick Beal*
Contest Girl. See: *The Beauty Jungle*
Contraband (Michael Powell, GB, 1940). USA: *Blackout*
Cop-Out. See: *Stranger in the House*
The Corpse Vanishes (Wallace Fox, USA, 1942). GB: *The Case of the Missing Brides*
The Corpse Vanished. See: *Revenge of the Zombies*
Cosh Boy (Lewis Gilbert, GB, 1952). USA: *The Slasher*
Counter Attack (Zoltan Korda, USA, 1945). GB: *One Against Seven*
Count the Hours (Don Siegel, USA, 1952). GB: *Every Minute Counts*
Court Martial. See: *Carrington VC*
The Court Martial of Billy Mitchell (Otto Preminger, USA, 1955). GB: *One Man Mutiny*
The Courtneys of Curzon Street (Herbert Wilcox GB, 1947). USA: *The Courtney Affair*
Cowboy from Brooklyn (Lloyd Bacon, USA, 1938). GB: *Romance and Rhythm*
The Crash of Silence. See: *Mandy*
The Crawling Eye. See: *The Trollenberg Terror*
The Creeping Unknown. See: *The Quatermass Experiment*
Crest of the Wave. See: *Seagulls over Sorrento*
Crime of the Century. See: *Walk East on Beacon*
The Crimes of Dr Mabuse. See: *Das Testament von Dr Mabuse*
The Criminal (Joseph Losey, GB, 1960). USA: *The Concrete Jungle*
Crooks in Clover. See: *Penthouse*
Cruising Casanovas. See: *Gobs and Gals*
Cry, the Beloved Country (Zoltan Korda, GB, 1952). USA: *African Fury*
Curse of the Allenbys. See: *She-Wolf of London*
Curse of the Demon. See: *Night of the Demon*
Cynthia (Robert Z. Leonard, USA, 1947). GB: *The Rich Full Life*
Czarina. See: *A Royal Scandal*

D

Damn the Defiant. See: *H.M.S. Defiant*
The Damned (Joseph Losey, GB, 1963). USA: *These are the Damned*
The Damned. See: *Les Maudits*
Damn Yankees (Stanley Donen, USA, 1958). GB: *What Lola Wants*
Dance of the Vampires (Roman Polanski, GB, 1967). USA: *The Fearless Vampire Killers*
Dancing Co-Ed (S. Sylvan Simon, USA, 1939). GB: *Every Other Inch a Lady*
Dangerous Cargo. See: *Forbidden Cargo*
Dangerous Days. See: *Wild Boys of the Road*
The Dangerous Flirt (Tod Browning, USA, 1924). GB: *A Dangerous Flirtation*
Dangerous Moonlight (Brian Desmond Hurst, GB, 1941). USA: *Suicide Squadron*
Danton (Dimitri Buchowetzki & Hans Dreier, GERMANY, 1920). GB: *Loves of the Mighty.* USA: *All for a Woman*
The Dark Avenger (Henry Levin, GB, 1955). USA: *The Warriors*
The Dark Eyes of London (Walter Summers, GB, 1939). USA: *The Human Monster*
Dark Sands. See: *Jericho*
Darling, How Could You (Mitchell Leisen, USA, 1951). GB: *Rendezvous*
Darlings of the Gods. See: *Sirens of the Sea*
A Date with Destiny. See: *The Mad Doctor*
Daughter of Luxury. See: *Five and Ten*
Daughter of Shanghai (Robert Florey, USA, 1937). GB: *Daughter of the Orient*
Daughters of Destiny. See: *Destinées*
The Day Will Dawn (Harold French, GB, 1942). USA: *The Avengers*
The Deadliest Sin. See: *Confession*
Dead Ringer (Paul Henreid, USA, 1964). GB: *Dead Image*
The Dead That Walk. See: *Zombies of Mora-Tau*
Deception. See: *Anna Boleyn*
Dementia 13 (Francis Coppola, USA, 1963). GB: *The Haunted and the Hunted*
Demons of the Swamp. See: *Attack of the Giant Leeches*
Demos (Denison Clift, GB, 1921). USA: *Why Men Forget*
Derby Day (Herbert Wilcox, GB, 1952). USA: *Four Against Fate*
Desk Set (Walter Lang, USA, 1957). GB: *His Other Woman*
Destinées (Jean Delannoy, ITALY-FRANCE, 1953). GB: *Love, Soldiers and Women.* USA: *Daughters of Destiny*
The Detective. See: *Father Brown*
The Devil and Daniel Webster (William Dieterle, USA, 1941). GB: *All That Money Can Buy*
The Devil is a Sissy (W. S. Van Dyke, USA, 1936). GB: *The Devil Takes the Count*
The Devil Never Sleeps (Leo McCarey, GB, 1961). USA: *Satan Never Sleeps*
Devil on Wheels. See: *Indianapolis Speedway*
The Devil's Envoys. See: *Les Visiteurs du Soir*
The Devil's Own. See: *The Witches*
The Devil Takes the Count. See: *The Devil is a Sissy*
Les Diaboliques (Henri-Georges Clouzot, FRANCE, 1954). GB: *The Fiends.* USA: *Diabolique*
Dial 999 (Montgomery Tully, GB, 1955). USA: *The Way Out*
Diary of a Bride. See: *I, Jane Doe*
The Diary of Major Thompson. See: *Les Carnets du Major Thompson*
Die! Die! My Darling. See: *Fanatic*
Die, Monster, Die (Daniel Haller, USA, 1965). GB: *Monster of Terror*
Dieu a besoin des hommes (Jean Delannoy, FRANCE, 1950). GB: *Isle of Sinners.* USA: *God Needs Man*
A Dispatch from Reuters (William Dieterle, USA, 1940). GB: *This Man Reuter*
The Dividing Line. See: *The Lawless*
The Dock Brief (James Hill, GB, 1962). USA: *Trial and Error*
Don't Bet on Women (William K. Howard, USA, 1931). GB: *More than a Kiss*
The Door with Seven Locks (Norman Lee, USA, 1940). GB: *Chamber of Horrors*
The Doolins of Oklahoma (Gordon Douglas, USA, 1949). GB: *The Great Manhunt*
The Dough Boys (Edward Sedgwick, USA, 1930). GB: *Forward March*
The Dover Road. See: *Where Sinners Meet*
Downhill (Alfred Hitchcock, GB, 1927). USA:

When Boys Leave Home
Dracula (Terence Fisher, GB, 1958). USA: *Horror of Dracula*
Drag (Frank Lloyd, USA, 1929). GB: *Parasites*
Dragées au poivre (Jacques Baratier, FRANCE, 1963). GB: *Sweet and Sour*
Dragstrip Riot (Felix A. Feist, USA, 1944). GB: *The Reckless Age*
Dreaded Mafia. See: *Salvatore Giuliano*.
Dressed to Kill (Roy William Neill, USA, 1946). GB: *Sherlock Holmes and the Secret Code*
Un Drôle de paroissien (Jean-Pierre Mocky, FRANCE, 1963). GB: *Heaven Sent*. USA: *Thank Heavens for Small Favors*
Drop Dead, Darling (Ken Hughes, GB, 1966). USA: *Arrivederci, Baby*
The Drum (Zoltan Korda, GB, 1937). USA: *Drums*
Duel of the Space Monsters (Robert Gaffney, USA, 1965). GB: *Frankenstein Meets the Space Monster*
Dulcimer Street. See: *London Belongs to Me*
Du Rififi chez des hommes (Jules Dassin, FRANCE, 1955). GB/USA: *Rififi*

E

The Earrings of Madame De. See: *Madame De . . .*
East of Java. See: *South Sea Sinner*
East of Shanghai. See: *Rich and Strange*
East of the Rising Sun. See: *Malaya*
L'École Buissonnière (Jean-Paul Le Chanois, FRANCE, 1948). GB: *I Have a New Master*
Edge of Divorce. See: *Background*
Edge of Doom (Mark Robson, USA, 1950). GB: *Stronger than Fear*
Edge of the City (Martin Ritt, USA, 1956). GB: *A Man is Ten Feet Tall*
Eight on the Lam (George Marshall, USA, 1966). GB: *Eight on the Run*
The Electric Man. See: *Man Made Monster*
The Electronic Monster. See: *Escapement*
Eléna et les hommes (Jean Renoir, FRANCE, 1956). GB: *The Night Does Strange Things*. USA: *Paris Does Strange Things*
Elephants Never Forget. See: *Zenobia*
Ellen. See: *The Second Woman*
Embassy Girl. See: *Hat Check Girl*
End as a Man. See: *The Strange One*
End of the Rainbow. See: *Northwest Outpost*
Enemies of the Public. See: *Public Enemy*
Enemy from Space. See: *Quatermass II*
Les Enfants Terribles (Jean-Pierre Melville, FRANCE, 1950). GB: *The Strange Ones*
The Enforcer (Raoul Walsh & Bretaigne Windust, USA, 1951). GB: *Murder Inc*
The Engagement. See: *I Fidanzati*
English Without Tears (Harold French, GB, 1944). USA: *Her Man Gilbey*
E'Primavera (Renato Castellani, ITALY, 1949). GB: *Springtime in Italy*
Escape from Yesterday. See: *Ride a Crooked Mile*
Escapement (Montgomery Tully, GB, 1957). USA: *The Electronic Monster*
Escape to Happiness. See: *Intermezzo*
Eskimo (W. S. Van Dyke, USA, 1933). GB: *Mala the Magnificent*
Eternal Youth. See: *West Point*
L'Éternel Retour (Jean Delannoy, FRANCE, 1943). GB: *Love Eternal*. USA: *The Eternal Return*
Et Mourir de Plaisir (Roger Vadim, FRANCE, 1960). GB/USA: *Blood and Roses*
Everybody's Cheering. See: *Take Me Out to the Ball Game*
Every Minute Counts. See: *Count the Hours*
Every Other Inch a Lady. See: *Dancing Co-Ed*
Every Woman's Man. See: *The Prizefighter and the Lady*
Evils of Chinatown. See: *Confessions of an Opium Eater*
Ex-Bad Boy (Vin Moore, USA, 1931). GB: *His Temporary Affair*
Experiment in Terror (Blake Edwards, USA, 1962). GB: *The Grip of Fear*
The Eyes of the Mummy. See: *Die Augen der Mumie Ma*
Eyes of the Skies. See: *Mission over Korea*
Eyes Without a Face. See: *Les Yeux sans visage*
Eye Witness. See: *Your Witness*

F

The Face (Ingmar Bergman, SWEDEN, 1958). USA: *The Magician*
The Falcon Takes Over (Irving Reis, USA, 1941). GB: *The Gay Falcon*
The False Madonna (Stuart Walker, USA, 1932). GB: *The False Idol*
The Fan (Otto Preminger, USA, 1949). GB: *Lady Windermere's Fan*
Fanatic (Silvio Narizzano, GB, 1965). USA: *Die! Die! My Darling*
Les Fanatiques (Alex Joffe, FRANCE, 1957). GB: *The Fanatics*. USA: *A Bomb for the Dictator*
Fanny by Gaslight (Anthony Asquith, GB, 1944). USA: *Man of Evil*
The Fantastic Disappearing Man. See: *The Return of Dracula*
Father Brown (Robert Hamer, GB, 1954). USA: *The Detective*
Father's Dilemma. See: *Prima Communione*
The Fearless Vampire Killers. See: *Dance of the Vampires*
Fear o'God. See: *The Mountain Eagle*
Les Félins (René Clément, FRANCE, 1964). GB: *The Love Cage*. USA: *The Joy House*
Female Correspondent. See: *Adventure in Washington*
Le Feu follet (Louis Malle, FRANCE, 1963). GB: *A Time to Live and a Time to Die*. USA: *Will o'the Wisp*
I Fidanzati (Ermanno Olmi, ITALY, 1963). GB: *The Engagement*
The Fiends. See: *Les Diaboliques*
The Fifth Chair. See: *It's in the Bag*
The Fighting Schoolmaster. See: *The Jucklins*
The Fighting Seventh. See: *Little Big Horn*
Fine and Dandy. See: *The West Point Story*
The First of the Few (Leslie Howard, GB, 1942). USA: *Spitfire*
The First Rebel. See: *Allegheny Uprising*
The First Time (James Nielson, USA, 1968). GB: *You Don't Need Pyjamas at Rosie's*
First Yank into Tokyo (Gordon Douglas, USA, 1945). GB: *Mask of Fury*
Fitzwilly (Delbert Mann, USA, 1967). GB: *Fitzwilly Strikes Back*
Five and Ten (Robert Z. Leonard, USA, 1931). GB: *Daughter of Luxury*
Five Angles on Murder. See: *The Woman in Question*
Five Million Years to Earth. See: *Quatermass and the Pit*
Flame Over India. See: *North West Frontier*
The Flaming Torch. See: *The Bob Mathias Story*
Die Flamme (Ernst Lubitsch, GERMANY, 1923). USA: *Montmartre*
Flap (originally *Nobody Loves Flapping Eagle*). (Carol Reed, USA, 1969). GB: *The Last Warrior*
The Flight of the White Stallions. See: *The Miracle of the White Stallions*
The Flim-Flam Man (Irvin Kershner, USA, 1967). GB: *One Born Every Minute*
The Flood. See: *The Johnstown Flood*
The Floradora Girl (Harry Beaumont, USA, 1930). GB: *The Gay Nineties*
Folies Bergere (Roy Del Ruth, USA, 1935). GB: *The Man from the Folies Bergere*
Football Coach. See: *College Coach*
Forbidden Cargo (Thomas Buckingham, USA, 1925). GB: *Dangerous Cargo*
Forbidden Games. See: *Jeux Interdits*
Forbidden Street. See: *Brittania Mews*
Forever (George Fitzmaurice, USA, 1922). GB: *Peter Ibbetson*
Forever in Love. See: *Pride of the Marines*
Forgotten Woman. See: *The Mad Parade*
For Love or Money. See: *Cash*
The Forsyte Saga. See *That Forsythe Woman*
The Fortune Cookie (Billy Wilder, USA, 1966). GB: *Meet Whiplash Willie*
The Fortune Hunter (William Whitney, USA, 1954). GB: *The Outcast*
Fortune is a Woman (Sidney Gilliat, GB, 1956). USA: *She Played with Fire*
49th Parallel (Michael Powell, GB, 1941). USA: *The Invaders*
Forward March. See: *The Doughboys*
For You Alone. See: *When You're in Love*
Four Against Fate. See: *Derby Day*
Françoise Steps Out. See: *Rue de l'Estrapade . .*
Frankenstein Meets the Space Monster. See: *Duel of the Space Monsters*
Fraternally Yours. See: *Sons of the Desert*
Frau in Mond (Fritz Lang, GERMANY, 1928). GB/USA: *Woman in the Moon/The Girl in the Moon/By Rocket to the Moon*
Free to Live. See: *Holiday*
The French They Are a Funny Race. See: *Les Carnets du Major Thompson*
Frenzy. See: *Latin Quarter*
The Freshman (Sam Taylor & Fred Newmeyer, USA, 1925). GB: *College Days*
Die freudlose Gasse (G. W. Pabst, GERMANY, 1925). GB: *The Joyless Street*. USA: *Cheerless Lane*
The Frightened City. See: *The Killer That Stalked New York*
Frou Frou. See: *Toy Wife*
The Fuller Brush Girl (Lloyd Bacon, USA, 1950). GB: *The Affairs of Sally*
Full House. See: *O. Henry's Full House*
The Full Treatment (Val Guest, GB, 1960). USA:

Stop Me Before I Kill
Fury Unleashed. See: *Hot Rod Gang*
Fuss over Feathers. See: *Conflict of Wings*

G
Gaily, Gaily (Norman Jewison, USA, 1969). GB: *Chicago, Chicago*
The Gang's All Here (Busby Berkeley, USA, 1943). GB: *The Girls He Left Behind*
Gang War. See: *Odd Man Out*
Gaslight (Thorold Dickinson, GB, 1940). USA: *Angel Street*
Gaslight (George Cukor, USA, 1944). GB: *The Murder in Thornton Square*
The Gay Divorcée (Mark Sandrichm USA, 1934). GB: *The Gay Divorce*
The Gay Falcon. See: *The Falcon Takes Over*
The Gay Lady. See: *Trottie True*
The Gay Mrs Trexal. See: *Susan and God*
The Gay Nineties. See: *The Floradora Girl*
Die Geiger von Florenz (Paul Czinner, GERMANY, 1925). GB: *Impetuous Youth/The Violinist of Florence*
A Genius in the Family. See: *So Goes My Love*
Gentleman for a Day. See: *Union Depot*
The Gentle Sergeant. See: *Three Stripes in the Sun*
The George Raft Story (Joseph M. Newman, USA, 1961). GB: *Spin of a Coin*
Get off My Back. See: *Synanon*
Gideon's Day (John Ford, GB, 1959). USA: *Gideon of Scotland Yard*
Gift Horse (Compton Bennett, GB, 1952). USA: *Glory at Sea*
A Girl, a Guy and a Gob (Richard Wallace, USA, 1941). GB: *The Navy Steps Out*
The Girl from Mexico. See: *Mexicali Rose*
The Girl from Missouri (Jack Conway, USA, 1934). GB: *One Hundred Per Cent Pure*
The Girl from Tenth Avenue (Alfred E. Green, USA, 1935). GB: *Men on Her Mind*
The Girl-Getters. See: *The System*
The Girl I Made. See: *Made on Broadway*
Girl in Distress. See: *Jeannie*
The Girl in Overalls. See: *Swing Shift Maisie*
The Girl in Pawn. See: *Little Miss Marker*
The Girl in Room 17. See: *Vice Squad*
The Girl in the Moon. See: *Frau im Mond*
The Girl in the Painting. See: *Portrait from Life*
Girl of the Year. See: *The Petty Girl*
The Girls he left Behind. See: *The Gang's All Here*
Girls in the Night (Jack Arnold, USA, 1953). GB: *Life after Dark*
A Girl was Young. See: *Young and Innocent*
Give Us this Day (Edward Dmytryk, GB, 1949). USA: *Salt to the Devil*
Le Glaive et la balance (André Cayatte, FRANCE, 1962). USA: *Two Are Guilty*
Glory at Sea. See: *Gift Horse*
G-Man's Wife. See: *Public Enemy's Wife*
Gobs and Gals (R. G. Springsteen, USA, 1952). GB: *Cruising Casanovas*
God Needs Man. See: *Dieu a besoin des hommes*
Go Into Your Dance (Archie Mayo, USA, 1935). GB: *Casino de Paree*
Golden Helmet. See: *Casque d'Or*
The Golden Hour. See: *Pot o'Gold*
Golden Marie. See: *Casque d'Or*
The Golden Virgin. See: *The Story of Esther Costello*
Golden Youth. See: *Just Suppose*
Der Golem (Paul Wegener, GERMANY, 1914). USA: *The Monster of Fate*
Le Golem (Julien Duvivier, FRANCE, 1936). GB: *The Legend of Prague*
Gone to Earth (Michael Powell & Emeric Pressburger, GB, 1950). USA: *The Wild Heart*
Good Dame (Marion Gering, USA, 1934). GB: *Good Girl*
Good Morning, Doctor. See: *You Belong to Me*
Goodnight Vienna (Herbert Wilcox, GB, 1932). USA: *Magic Night*
The Grace Moore Story. See: *So This is Love*
Grand National Night (Bob McNaught, GB, 1953). USA: *Wicked Wife*
The Grasp of Greed (Joseph DeGrasse, USA, 1916). GB: *Mr Meeson's Will*
The Great Barrier (Milton Rosmer, GB, 1937). USA: *The Silent Barrier*
Great Guy (John K. Blystone, USA, 1936). GB: *Pluck of the Irish*
The Great John L (Frank Tuttle, USA, 1944). GB: *A Man Called Sullivan*
The Great Manhunt. See: *The Doolins of Oklahoma*
Green-Eyed Woman. See: *Take a Letter, Darling*
The Greengage Summer (Lewis Gilbert, GB, 1961). USA: *Loss of Innocence*
The Grip of Fear. See: *Experiment in Terror*
The Guest. See: *The Caretaker*
Guilty as Hell (Erle Kenton, USA, 1932). GB: *Guilty as Charged*
The Guilty Secret. See: *The Intimate Stranger*
The Guinea Pig (Roy Boulting, GB, 1948). USA: *The Outsider*
Gunpoint! See: *At Gunpoint*
Guns in the Afternoon. See: *Ride the High Country*
Guns of Wyoming. See: *Cattle King*
The Guv'nor (Milton Rosmer, GB, 1935). USA: *Mr Hobo*
Gypsy Blood. See: *Carmen*

H
Hallelujah, I'm a Bum (Lewis Milestone, USA, 1933). GB: *Hallelujah, I'm a Tramp/Lazy Bones*
The Hammond Mystery. See: *The Undying Monster*
The Hands of Orlac. See: *Mad Love*
Happy Ever After (originally *O'Leary Night*). (Mario Zampi, GB, 1954). USA: *Tonight's the Night*
Hara-Kiri. See: *La Bataille*
Harmony Parade. See: *Pigskin Parade*
Harper (Jack Smight, USA, 1966). GB: *The Moving Target*
Has Anybody Here Seen Kelly? See: *Anybody Here Seen Kelly?*
Hat Check Girl (Sidney Lanfield, USA, 1932). GB: *Embassy Girl*
The Hatchet Man (William Wellman, USA, 1932). GB: *The Honourable Mr Wong*
The Haunted and the Hunted. See: *Dementia 13*
Haunted Honeymoon. See: *Busman's Honeymoon*
Having a Wild Weekend. See: *Catch Us if You Can*
The Hawaiians (Tom Gries, USA, 1970). GB: *Master of the Islands*
Hawthorne of the USA (James Cruze, USA, 1919). GB: *Hawthorne the Adventurer*
Head over Heels (Sonnie Hale, GB, 1937). USA: *Head over Heels in Love*
The Heart of an Actress. See: *Her Body in Bond*
Heart of a Nation. See: *Un tel Père et Fils*
Heaven Sent. See: *Un Drôle de paroissien*
The Helen Morgan Story (Michael Curtiz, USA, 1957). GB: *Both Ends of the Candle*
Hell Bent for Glory. See: *Lafayette's Escadrille*
Hello Sister. See: *Walking Down Broadway*
Hemingway's Adventures of a Young Man. See: *Adventures of a Young Man*
Her Body in Bond (Robert Z. Leonard, USA, 1918). GB: *The Heart of an Actress*
Her Dilemma. See: *Confessions of a Co-Ed*
Her Man Gilbey. See: *English Without Tears*
Her Reputation. See: *Broadway Bad*
Her Sacrifice. See: *Blind Date*
The Hidden Room. See: *Obsession*
Hidden Secret. See: *A Yank in Indo-China*
The Hideous Sun Demon (Robert Clarke, USA, 1959). GB: *Blood on His Lips*
The Hideout. See: *The Small Voice*
High and Dry. See: *The Maggie*
The High Bright Sun (Ralph Thomas, GB, 1965). USA: *McGuire Go Home*
High Fury. See: *White Cradle Inn*
The High Road. See: *The Lady of Scandal*
High Society. See: *Scandal*
His Affair. See: *This is My Affair*
His Lordship (Herbert Mason, GB, 1936). USA: *Man of Affairs*
His Majesty Mr Jones. See: *Prima Communione*
His Other Woman. See: *Desk Set*
His Temporary Affair. See: *Ex-Bad Boy*
Histoires extraordinaires (Roger Vadim, Federico Fellini & Louis Malle, FRANCE-ITALY, 1967). GB: *Spirits of the Dead*
Hitchin' Posts (John Ford, USA, 1920). GB: *The Land of Promise*
Hit Me Again. See *Smarty*
H.M.S. Defiant (Lewis Gilbert, GB, 1962). USA: *Damn the Defiant*
Hold 'Em Navy (Kurt Neumann, USA, 1937). GB: *That Navy Spirit*
Hold That Co-Ed (George Marshall, USA, 1938). GB: *Hold That Girl*
Holiday (George Cukor, USA, 1938). GB: *Free to Live/Unconventional Linda*
Holiday in Spain. See: *Scent of Mystery*
Home at Seven (Ralph Richardson, GB, 1952). USA: *Murder on Monday*
Honeymoon (William Keighley, USA, 1947). GB: *Two Men and a Girl*
Honeymoon in Bali (Edward H. Griffith, USA, 1939). GB: *Husbands or Lovers*
The Honourable Mr Wong. See: *The Hatchet Man*
The Horror Chamber of Dr Faustus. See: *Les Yeux sans visage*
Horror Hotel. See: *City of the Dead*
Horror of Dracula. See: *Dracula*

Hot Enough for June (Ralph Thomas, GB, 1963). USA: *Agent 8¾*
Hot Rod Gang (Lew Landers, USA, 1958). GB: *Fury Unleashed*
Hot Spot. See: *I Wake Up screaming*
House of Mystery. See: *The Night Monster*
Hounded. See: *Johnny Allegro*
The Hounds of Zaroff. See: *The Most Dangerous Game*
Hour of Glory. See: *The Small Back Room*
The Hours Between. See: *Twenty Four Hours*
The House Behind the Hedge. See: *Unknown Treasures*
The House in the Square. See: *I'll Never Forget You*
House of Horrors (Jean Yarbrough, USA, 1946). GB: *Joan Medford is Missing*
The Howards of Virginia (Frank Lloyd, USA, 1940). GB: *The Tree of Liberty*
Huddle (Sam Wood, USA, 1932). GB: *The Impossible Lover*
The Human Beast. See: *La Bête humaine*
The Human Condition. See: *No Greater Love*
The Human Monster. See: *The Dark Eyes of London*
Hunted (Charles Crichton, GB, 1952). USA: *The Stranger in Between*
Husbands or Lovers. See: *Honeymoon in Bali*
The Hypnotist. See: *London After Midnight*

I

I Can Get It for You Wholesale (Michael Gordon, USA, 1951). GB: *This is My Affair*
Ichabod and Mr Toad (Walt Disney, USA, 1949). GB: *The Adventures of Ichabod and Mr Toad/The Adventures of Mr Toad/Wind in the Willows*
I Dood It (Vincente Minnelli, USA, 1943). GB: *By Hook or by Crook*
If I Were Free (Elliott Nugent, USA, 1933). GB: *Behold We Live*
If You Feel Like Singing. See: *Summer Stock*
I Have a New Master. See: *L'École Buissonnière*
I, Jane Doe (John H. Auer, USA, 1948). GB: *Diary of a Bride*
I Like Money. See: *Mr Topaze*
I Live in Grosvenor Square (Herbert Wilcox, GB, 1945). USA: *A Yank in London*
I'll Get You for This (Joseph Newman, USA, 1951). GB: *Lucky Nick Cain*
Illicit Interlude. See: *Summer Interlude*
Ill Met by Moonlight (Michael Powell & Emeric Pressburger, GB, 1956). USA: *Night Ambush*
I'll Never Forget You (Roy Baker, USA, 1951). GB: *The House in the Square*
Imaginary Sweetheart. See: *Professional Sweetheart*
I Married a Communist (Robert Stevenson, USA, 1949). GB: *The Woman on Pier 13*
I Married a Werewolf. See: *Lycanthropus*
Immortal Batallion. See: *The Way Ahead*
Immortal France. See: *Un tel Père et Fils.*
I, Mobster (Roger Corman, USA, 1958). GB: *The Mobster*
The Imperfect Lady (Sidney Lanfield, USA, 1946). GB: *The Trouble with Women*
Impetuous Youth. See: *Die Geiger von Florenz*
The Impossible Lover. See: *Huddle*
Indianapolis Speedway (Lloyd Bacon, USA, 1939). GB: *Devil on Wheels*
Indiscretion. See: *Christmas in Connecticut*
Indiscretion. See: *Stazione Termini*
Indiscretion of an American Wife. See: *Stazione Termini*
Infidelity. See: *Altri Tempi*
The Informers (Ken Annakin, GB, 1963). USA: *Underworld Informers*
Innocence is Bliss. See: *Miss Grant Takes Richmond*
In Olden Days. See: *Altri Tempi*
The Intelligence Men (Robert Asher, GB, 1965). USA: *Spylarks*
Intermezzo (Gregory Ratoff, USA, 1939). GB: *Escape to Happiness*
Internes Can't Take Money (Alfred Santell, USA, 1937). GB: *You Can't Take Money*
Interpol (John Gilling, GB, 1957). USA: *Pickup Alley*
The Intimate Stranger (Joseph Walton, GB, 1956). USA: *The Guilty Secret*
Into the Night. See: *The Wise Guy*
The Intruder (Roger Corman, USA, 1961). GB: *The Stranger*
The Invaders. See: *49th Parallel*
The Iron Road. See: *Buckskin Frontier*
I See a Dark Stranger (Frank Launder, GB, 1946). USA: *The Adventuress*
I Shall Return. See: *An American Guerilla in the Philippines*
Island Escape. See: *No Man is an Island*
Island of Desire. See: *Saturday Island*
Island Rescue. See: *Appointment with Venus*
It Ain't Hay (Erle C. Kenton, USA, 1943). GB: *Money for Jam*
It Couldn't Have Happened (Phil Rosen, USA, 1936). GB: *One for All*
It Happened in Hollywood (Harry Lachman, USA, 1937). GB: *Once a Hero*
It Happened to Jane. See: *That Jane from Maine*
It Rains on Our Love (Ingmar Bergman, SWEDEN, 1946). USA: *The Man with an Umbrella*
It's in the Bag (Richard Wallace, USA, 1945). GB: *The Fifth Chair*
It's My Life. See: *Vivre sa Vie*
It Started in Tokyo. See: *Twenty Plus Two*
Ivory Hunter. See: *Where No Vultures Fly*
I Wake Up Screaming (H. Bruce Humberstone, USA, 1942). GB: *Hot Spot*
I Was a Male War Bride (Howard Hawks, USA, 1949). GB: *You Can't Sleep Here*

J

Jailbirds. See: *Pardon Us*
The James Brothers. See: *The True Story of Jesse James*
Janice Meredith (E. Mason Hopper, USA, 1924). GB: *The Merry Wives of Gotham*
Jeanne of the Marshes. See: *Behind Masks*
Jeannie (Harold French, GB, 1941). USA: *Girl in Distress*
Jericho (Thornton Freeland, GB, 1937). USA: *Dark Sands*
Jeux interdits (René Clément, FRANCE, 1952). GB: *The Secret Game*. USA: *Forbidden Games*
Jew Süss (Lothar Mendes, GB, 1934). USA: *Power*
Jim Thorpe – All American (Michael Curtiz, USA, 1951). GB: *Man of Bronze*
Joan Medford is Missing. See: *House of Horrors*
John Doe, Dynamite. See: *Meet John Doe*
Johnny Allegro (Ted Tetzlaff, USA, 1949). GB: *Hounded*
Johnny Come Lately (William K. Howard, USA, 1943). GB: *Johnny Vagabond*
Johnny in the Clouds. See: *The Way to the Stars*
Johnny Vagabond. See: *Johnny Come Lately*
The Johnstown Flood (Irving Cummings, USA, 1926). GB: *The Flood*
Jour de fête (Jacques Tati, FRANCE, 1949). GB: *The Village Fair*
Journey into Autumn (Ingmar Bergman, SWEDEN, 1954). USA: *Women's Dreams*
The Joy House. See: *Les Félins*
The Joyless Street. See: *Die freudlose Gasse*
The Jucklins (George Melford, USA, 1920). GB: *The Fighting Schoolmaster*
Judas Was a Woman. See: *La Bête humaine*
Jump for Glory (Raoul Walsh, USA, 1937). GB: *When Thief Meets Thief*
The Jungle Book. See: *Rudyard Kipling's Jungle Book*
Jungle Captive (Harold Young, USA, 1944). GB: *Wild Jungle Captive*
Junior Army (Lew Landers, USA, 1942). GB: *Cadets on Parade*
Justice est faite (André Cayatte, FRANCE, 1951). GB: *Let Justice Be Done*
Justice for Sale. See: *Night Court*
Just Suppose (Kenneth Webb, USA, 1926). GB: *Golden Youth*

K

The Kaiser (Rupert Julian, USA, 1918). GB: *The Kaiser, the Beast of Berlin*
Kansas City Confidential (Phil Carlson, USA, 1953). GB: *The Secret Four*
Keep an Eye on Amelia. See: *Occupe-toi d'Amélie*
The Keepers. See: *La Tête contre les murs*
Keep Smiling (Monty Banks, GB, 1938). USA: *Smiling Along*
La Kermesse Héroïque (Jacques Feyder, FRANCE, 1935). GB (dubbed): *Carnival in Flanders*
The Kid's Last Fight. See: *The Life of Jimmy Dolan*
Killer! See: *Que la béte meure*
Killer on a Horse. See: *Welcome to Hard Times*
The Killer that Stalked New York (Earl McEvoy, USA, 1950). GB: *The Frightened City*
King of the Khyber Rifles. See: *The Black Watch*
Kiss Me Again (William A. Seiter, USA, 1931). GB: *Toast of the Legion*
Kiss the Blood off My Hands (Norman Foster, USA, 1948). GB: *Blood on My Hands*
Knave of Hearts (Monsieur Ripois). (René Clément, GB, 1954). USA: *Lovers, Happy Lovers*

L

Ladri di Biciclette (Vittorio De Sica, ITALY, 1948). GB: *Bicycle Thieves*. USA: *The Bicycle Thief*
The Lady from Boston. See: *Pardon My French*
Lady Hamilton. See: *That Hamilton Woman*
Lady in Distress. See: *A Window in London*

Sunday
The Mask of Comedy. See: *Upstage*
Mask of Fury. See: *First Yank into Tokyo*
Master of the Islands. See: *The Hawaiians*
A Matter of Life and Death (Michael Powell & Emeric Pressburger, GB, 1946). USA: *Stairway to Heaven*
Maud. See: *Naked Hearts*
Les Maudits (René Clément, FRANCE, 1946). GB: *The Damned*
The McConnell Story (Gordon Douglas, USA, 1955). GB: *Tiger in the Sky*
McGuire Go Home. See: *The High Bright Sun*
Me and My Gal (Raoul Walsh, USA, 1932). GB: *Pier 13*
Medals. See: *Seven Days Leave*
Meet John Doe (Frank Capra, USA, 1941). GB (reissue): *John Doe, Dynamite*
Meet Me Tonight (Anthony Pelissier, GB, 1952). USA: *Tonight at 8.30*
Meet the Ghosts. See: *Abbott and Costello Meet Frankenstein*
Meet Whiplash Willie. See: *The Fortune Cookie*
Melody of Life. See: *Symphony of Six Million*
Melody of Youth. See: *They Shall Have Music*
Memory Expert. See: *The Man on the Flying Trapeze*
Men on Her Mind. See: *The Girl from Tenth Avenue*
Merrily We Go to Hell (Dorothy Arzner, USA, 1932). GB: *Merrily We Go to –*
The Merry Wives of Gotham. See: *Janice Meredith*
Mesa of Lost Women (Herbert Trevos & Ron Ormond, USA, 1953). GB: *Lost Women*
Mexicali Rose (Erle C. Kenton, USA, 1929). GB: *The Girl from Mexico*
Midas Run (Alf Kjellin, USA, 1969). GB: *A Run on Gold*
The Midnight Story (Joseph Pevney, USA, 1956). GB: *Appointment with a Soldier*
Military Policeman. See: *Off Limits*
Millionaire for a Day. See: *Let's Be Ritzy*
Million Dollar Mermaid (Mervyn LeRoy, USA, 1953). GB: *The One-Piece Bathing Suit*
Million Pound Note (Ronald Neame, GB, 1953). USA: *Man with a Million*
A Miracle Can Happen (King Vidor & Leslie Fenton, USA, 1948). GB: *On Our Merry Way*
The Miracle of the White Stallions (Arthur Hiller, USA, 1962). GB: *The Flight of the White Stallions*
Miracle on 34th Street (George Seaton, USA, 1946). GB: *The Big Heart*
Miss Grant Takes Richmond (Lloyd Bacon, USA, 1949). GB: *Innocence is Bliss*
Mission over Korea (Fred F. Sears, USA, 1953). GB: *Eyes of the Skies*
Mister Buddwing (Delbert Mann, USA, 1965). GB: *Woman Without a Face*
Mr Griggs Returns. See: *The Cockeyed Miracle*
Mr Hobo. See: *The Guv'nor*
Mr Imperium (Don Hartman, USA, 1951). GB: *You Belong to My Heart*
Mr Meeson's Will. See: *The Grasp of Greed*
Mr Potts Goes to Moscow. See: *Top Secret*
Mr Topaze (Peter Sellers, GB, 1961). USA: *I Like Money*
Mr V. See: *Pimpernel Smith*
Mr Winkle Goes to War (Alfred E. Green, USA, 1944). GB: *Arms and the Woman*
The Mobster. See: *I, Mobster*
Models Inc (Reginald LeBorg, USA, 1952). GB: *That Kind of Girl*
The Modern Miracle. See: *The Story of Alexander Graham Bell*
Money for Jam. See: *It Ain't Hay*
Monte Carlo or Bust (Ken Annakin, ITALY-FRANCE, 1969). USA: *Those Daring Young Men in their Flying Jalopies*
Monster Meets Gorilla. See: *Bela Lugosi Meets a Brooklyn Gorilla*
The Monster of Fate. See: *Der Golem*
Monster of Terror. See: *Die, Monster, Die*
Montmartre. See: *Die Flamme*
More than a Kiss. See: *Don't Bet on Women*
Morning Departure (Roy Baker, GB, 1949–50). USA: *Operation Disaster*
The Most Dangerous Game (Ernest B. Schoedsack, USA, 1932). GB: *The Hounds of Zaroff*
Mother is a Freshman (Lloyd Bacon, USA, 1949). GB: *Mother Knows Best*
Mother of Mine (Rupert Julian, USA, 1917). GB: *Mother Love*
Mother Riley Meets the Vampire (John Gilling, GB, 1952). USA: *My Son the Vampire*
Mother, Sir. See: *Navy Wife*
The Mountain Eagle (Alfred Hitchcock, GB, 1926). USA: *Fear o'God*
The Moving Target. See: *Harper*
Der Müde Tod (Fritz Lang, GERMANY, 1921). GB/USA: *Destiny*
Murder Inc. See: *The Enforcer*
The Murder in Thornton Square. See: *Gaslight*
Murder on Monday. See: *Home at Seven*
Murder Will Out. See: *The Voice of Merrill*
Music in Darkness. See: *Night is My Future*
Mutiny (Lynn F. Reynolds, USA, 1917). GB: *The Mutiny of the Alden Besse*
My Daughter Joy (Gregory Ratoff, GB, 1950). USA: *Operation X*
My Heart Goes Crazy. See: *London Town*
My Life to Live. See: *Vivre sa Vie*
My Son Alone. See: *American Empire*
My Son the Vampire. See: *Mother Riley Meets the Vampire*
Mysterious Invader. See: *The Astounding She-Monster*
My Teenage Daughter (Herbert Wilcox, GB, 1956). USA: *Teenager Bad Girl*
My Two Husbands. See: *Too Many Husbands*

N
Naked Hearts (Rupert Julian, USA, 1916). GB: *Maud*
Naked Light. See: *Sawdust and Tinsel*
The Naked Truth (Mario Zampi, GB, 1957). USA: *Your Past is Showing*
Nana (Dorothy Arzner, USA, 1934). GB: *Lady of the Boulevards*
Naughty Arlette. See: *The Romantic Age*
Naughty Baby (Mervyn LeRoy, USA, 1928). GB: *Reckless Rosie*
The Navy Steps Out. See: *A Girl, a Guy and a Gob*
Navy Wife (Edward Bernds, USA, 1956). GB: *Mother, Sir*
The Net (Anthony Asquith, GB, 1953). USA: *Project M.7*
Never Give a Sucker an Even Break (Edward Cline, USA, 1941). GB: *What a Man!*
Never Wave at a Wac (Norman Z. McLeod, USA, 1952). GB: *The Private Wore Skirts*
The New Adventures of Don Juan. See: *The Adventures of Don Juan*
Next Time We Love (Edward H. Griffith, USA, 1936). GB: *Next Time We Live*
Night Ambush. See: *Ill Met by Moonlight*
Night Beauties. See: *Belles de nuit*
Night Court (W. S. Van Dyke, USA, 1932). GB: *Justice for Sale*
Night Creatures. See: *Captain Clegg*
The Night Does Strange Things. See: *Eléna et les hommes*
The Night Fighter. See: *A Terrible Beauty*
A Night in Cairo. See: *The Barbarian*
Night in Havana. See: *The Big Boodle*
The Night is Ending. See: *Paris After Dark*
Night is My Future (Ingmar Bergman, SWEDEN, 1947). USA: *Music in Darkness*
The Night Monster (Ford Beebe, USA, 1943). GB: *House of Mystery*
Night of the Demon (Jacques Tourneur, GB, 1957). USA: *Curse of the Demon*
Night of the Eagle (Sidney Hayers, GB, 1961). USA: *Burn, Witch, Burn*
Nine Days a Queen. See: *Tudor Rose*
No Greater Love (Masaki Kobayashi, JAPAN, 1957). USA: *The Human Condition*
No Highway (Henry Koster, GB, 1951). USA: *No Highway in the Sky*
No Man is an Island (John Monks Jnr & Richard Goldstone, USA: 1962). GB: *Island Escape*
North West Frontier (J. Lee Thompson, GB, 1959). USA: *Flame over India*
Northwest Outpost (Allan Dwan, USA, 1947). GB: *End of the Rainbow*
Notorious Gentleman. See: *The Rake's Progress*
Nous sommes tous des assassins (André Cayatte, FRANCE, 1952). GB: *Are We All Murderers?*
Now I'll Tell (Edwin Burke, USA, 1934). GB: *When New York Sleeps*

O
Obssessed. See: *The Late Edwina Black*
Obsession (Edward Dmytryk, GB, 1948). USA: *The Hidden Room*
Occupe-toi d'Amélie (Claude Autant-Lara, FRANCE, 1949). GB: *Keep an Eye on Amelia*. USA: *Oh Amelia*
Odd Man Out (Carol Reed, GB, 1947). USA: *Gang War*
Off Limits (George Marshall, USA, 1952). GB: *Military Policemen*
Oh Amelia. See: *Occupe-toi d'Amélie*
O. Henry's Full House (Henry Koster, Henry Hathaway, Jean Negulesco, Howard Hawks, Henry King, USA, 1952). GB: *Full House*
Oh, for a Man! See: *Will Success Spoil Rock Hunter?*
Old Greatheart. See: *Way Back Home*

Old Ironsides (James Cruze, USA, 1926). GB: *Sons of the Sea*
O'Leary Night. See: *Happy Ever After*
Los Olvidados (Luis Buñuel, MEXICO, 1951). GB: *The Young and the Damned*
Once a Hero. See: *It Happened in Hollywood*
One Against Seven. See: *Counter Attack*
One Arabian Night. See: *Sumurun*
One Born Every Minute. See: *The Flim-Flam Man*
One for All. See: *It Couldn't Have Happened*
One Hundred Per Cent Pure. See: *The Girl from Missouri*
One Man Mutiny. See: *The Court Martial of Billy Mitchell*
One Million B.C. (Hal Roach & Hal Roach Jnr, USA, 1940). GB: *Man and His Mate/The Cave Dwellers*
One More River (James Whale, USA, 1934). GB: *Over the River*
The One-Piece Bathing Suit. See: *Million Dollar Mermaid*
One Woman's Story. See: *The Passionate Friends*
On the Carpet. See: *Little Giant*
On the Fiddle (Cyril Frankel, GB, 1961). USA: *Operation SNAFU*
Operation Disaster. See: *Morning Departure*
Operation SNAFU. See: *On the Fiddle*
Operation X. See: *My Daughter Joy*
Operator 13 (Richard Boleslavsky, USA, 1934). GB: *Spy 13*
O'Rourke of the Royal Mounted. See: *Saskatchewan*
Our Daily Bread (F. W. Murnau, USA, 1929). GB: *City Girl*
Our Girl Friday (Noel Langley, GB, 1953). USA: *Adventures of Sadie*
The Outcast. See: *The Fortune Hunter*
Outcast Lady (Robert Z. Leonard, USA, 1934). GB: *Woman of the World*
The Outlaw and the Lady. See: *Waco*
Out of the Darkness. See: *Teenage Caveman*
Out of the Past (Jacques Tourneur, USA, 1947). GB: *Build My Gallows High*
Outpost in Malaya. See: *The Planter's Wife*
The Outsider. See: *The Guinea Pig*
The Outsiders. See: *Bande à part*
Over the River. See: *One More River*
The Oxbow Incident (William Wellman, USA, 1943). GB: *Strange Incident*

P

Paid (Sam Wood, USA, 1930). GB: *Within the Law*
Panic in the Parlor. See: *Sailor Beware*
Panic on the Air See: *You May Be Next*
Panic on the Air (D. Ross Lederman, USA, 1936). GB: *Trapped by Wireless*
Paradise for Three (Edward Buzzell, USA, 1938). GB: *Romance for Three*
Parasites. See: *Drag*
Paratrooper. See: *The Red Beret*
Pardon My French (Bernard Vorhaus, USA-FRANCE, 1951). GB: *The Lady from Boston*
Pardon Us (James Parrott, USA, 1931). GB: *Jailbirds*
Paris After Dark (Leonide Moguy, USA, 1943). GB: *The Night is Ending*
Paris Does Strange Things. See: *Eléna et les hommes*
Paris Express. See: *The Man Who Watched Trains Go By*
Paris in the Spring (Lewis Milestone, USA, 1935). GB: *Paris Love Song*
Paris Underground (Gregory Ratoff, USA, 1945). GB: *Madame Pimpernel*
Parlor, Bedroom and Bath (Edward Sedgwick, USA, 1931). GB: *A Romeo in Pyjamas*
Passion. See: *Madame Dubarry*
The Passionate Friends (David Lean, GB, 1948). USA: *One Woman's Story*
The Passionate Sentry. See: *Who Goes There!*
Passport to Fame. See: *The Whole Town's Talking*
The Patsy (King Vidor, USA, 1928). GB: *The Politic Flapper*
Patterns (Fielder Cook, USA, 1956). GB: *Patterns of Power*
Paying the Penalty. See: *Underworld*
Pay the Devil. See: *Man in the Shadow*
Penthouse (W. S. Van Dyke, USA, 1933). GB: *Crooks in Clover*
Penthouse Party (William Nigh, USA, 1936). GB: *Without Children*
The Perfect Alibi. See: *Birds of Prey*
The Perfect Furlough (Blake Edwards, USA, 1958). GB: *Strictly for Pleasure*
Perfect Strangers (Bretaigne Windust, USA, 1949). GB: *Too Dangerous to Love*
Perfect Strangers (Alexander Korda, GB, 1950). USA: *Vacation from Marriage*
Perfect Week-end. See: *St Louis Kid*
Personal Column. See: *Lured*
Peter Ibbetson. See: *Forever*
The Petty Girl (Henry Levin, USA, 1950). GB: *Girl of the Year*
Pickup Alley. See: *Interpol*
Pier 13. See: *Me and My Gal*
Pigskin Parade (David Butler, USA, 1936). GB: *Harmony Parade*
Pillars of the Sky (George Marshall, USA, 1956). GB: *The Tomahawk and the Cross*
Pimpernel Smith (Leslie Howard, GB, 1941). USA: *Mr V*
The Planter's Wife (Ken Annakin, GB, 1952). USA: *Outpost in Malaya*
The Playgirl and the War Minister. See: *The Amorous Prawn*
Plein Soleil (Claude Chabrol, FRANCE, 1959). GB: *Blazing Sun/Purple Noon*
The Plot to Kill Roosevelt. See: *Teheran*
Pluck of the Irish. See: *Great Guy*
The Politic Flapper. See: *The Patsy*
Polly Fulton. See: *B.F.'s Daughter*
Pookie. See: *The Sterile Cuckoo*
Portrait from Life (Terence Fisher, GB, 1948). USA: *The Girl in the Painting*
Portrait of Alison (Guy Green, GB, 1955). USA: *Postmark for Danger*
Pot o'Gold (George Marshall, USA, 1941). GB: *The Golden Hour*
Power. See: *Jew Süss*
Present Arms. See: *Leathernecking*
The President Vanishes (William Wellman, USA, 1934). GB: *The Strange Conspiracy*
Pride of the Marines (Delmer Daves, USA, 1945). GB: *Forever in Love*
Prima Communione (Alessandro Blasetti, ITALY, 1950). GB: *His Majesty Mr Jones.* USA: *Father's Dilemma*
Private Number (Roy Del Ruth, USA, 1936). GB: *Secret Interlude*
The Private Wore Skirts. See: *Never Wave at a Wac*
The Prizefighter and the Lady (W. S. Van Dyke, USA, 1933). GB: *Everywoman's Man*
Professional Sweetheart (William A. Seiter, USA, 1933). GB: *Imaginary Sweetheart*
Project M.7. See: *The Net*
The Promoter. See: *The Card*
The Public Be Hanged. See: *The World Gone Mad*
Public Enemy (William Wellman, USA, 1931). GB: *Enemies of the Public*
Public Enemy's Wife (Nick Grinde, USA, 1936). GB: *G-Man's Wife*
Purple Noon. See: *Plein soleil*
Pursuit of the Graf Spee. See: *Battle of the River Plate*
Pussycat Alley. See: *The World Ten Times Over*
Pyro (Julio Coll, USA-SPAIN, 1964). GB: *Wheel of Fire*

Q

Q Planes (Tim Whelan, GB, 1939). USA: *Clouds over Europe*
Quatermass and the Pit (Roy Baker, GB, 1967). USA: *Five Million Years to Earth*
The Quatermass Experiment (Val Guest, GB, 1955). USA: *The Creeping Unknown*
Quatermass II (Val Guest, GB, 1956). USA: *Enemy from Space*
The Queen's Husband. See: *The Royal Bed*
Que la bête meure (Claude Chabrol, FRANCE 1969). GB: *Killer!.* USA: *This Man Must Die*

R

The Racers (Henry Hathaway, USA, 1955). GB: *Such Men Are Dangerous*
Racing Luck. See: *Red Hot Tires*
The Rake's Progress (Sidney Gilliat, GB, 1945). USA: *Notorious Gentleman*
Raton Pass (Edward L. Marin, USA, 1951). GB: *Canyon Pass*
The Rebel (Robert Day, USA, 1960). GB: *Call Me Genius*
The Reckless Age. See: *Dragstrip Riot*
Reckless Rosie. See: *Naughty Baby*
The Red Beret (Terence Young, GB, 1952). USA: *Paratrooper*
Red Hot Tires (Erle C. Kenton, USA, 1925). GB: *Racing Luck*
Red Salute (Sidney Lanfield, USA, 1935). GB: *Arms and the Girl*
Remorques (Jean Grémillon, FRANCE, 1939–41). GB: *Stormy Waters*
Rendezvous. See: *Darling, How Could You?*
Requiem for a Heavyweight (Ralph Nelson, USA, 1962). GB: *Blood Money*
Reserved for Ladies. See: *Service for Ladies*
Return of Dracula (Paul Landres, USA, 1958).

GB: *The Fantastic Disappearing Man*
Reunion in France (Jules Dassin, USA, 1942). GB: *Mademoiselle France*
Revenge of the Colossal Man (Bert I. Gordon, USA, 1958). GB: *The Terror Strikes*
Revenge of the Vampire. See: *La Maschera del Demonio*
Revenge of the Zombies (Steve Szekeley, USA, 1943). GB: *The Corpse Vanished*
Rich and Strange (Alfred Hitchcock, GB, 1932). USA: *East of Shanghai*
Richer than the Earth. See: *The Whistle at Eaton Falls*
The Rich Full Life. See: *Cynthia*
Ride a Crooked Mile (Alfred E. Green, USA, 1938). GB: *Escape from Yesterday*
Ride the High Country (Sam Peckinpah, USA, 1961). GB: *Guns in the Afternoon*
Rififi. See: *Du Rififi chez des hommes*
The Right to be Happy (Rupert Julian, USA, 1916). GB: *Scrooge the Skinflint*
Ringside Maisie (Edward L. Marin, USA, 1941). GB: *Cash and Carry*
Ring up the Curtain. See: *Broadway to Hollywood*
The Rise of Helga. See: *Susan Lenox, Her Fall and Rise*
Road to 'Frisco. See: *They Drive by Night*
Robinson Crusoeland. See: *Atoll K*
Rockets Galore (Michael Relph, GB, 1958). USA: *Mad Little Island*
Romance and Rhythm. See: *Cowboy from Brooklyn*
Romance for Three. See: *Paradise for Three*
Le Roman d'un tricheur (Sacha Guitry, FRANCE, 1936). GB: *The Cheat.* USA: *The Story of a Cheat*
The Romantic Age (Edmond T. Greville, GB, 1949). USA: *Naughty Arlette*
The Romantic Age. See: *Sisters under the Skin*
A Romeo in Pyjamas. See: *Parlor, Bedroom and Bath*
Rookies. See: *Buck Privates*
Rough Company. See: *The Violent Men*
Rough Riders (Victor Fleming, USA, 1927). GB: *The Trumpet Call*
Rough Shoot (Robert Parrish, GB, 1952). USA: *Shoot First*
The Royal Bed (Lowell Sherman, USA, 1931). GB: *The Queen's Husband*
A Royal Scandal (Otto Preminger, USA, 1945). GB: *Czarina*
Royal Wedding (Stanley Donen, USA, 1950). GB: *Wedding Bells*
Rudyard Kipling's Jungle Book (Zoltán Korda, USA, 1942). GB: *The Jungle Book*
Rue de l'Estrapade (Jacques Becker, FRANCE, 1953). GB: *Françoise Steps Out*
A Run on Gold. See: *Midas Run*

S
Sabotage (Alfred Hitchcock, GB, 1936). USA: *A Woman Alone*
The Sabre and the Arrow. See: *Last of the Comanches*
Sabrina (Billy Wilder, USA, 1954). GB: *Sabrina Fair*
Safe in Hell (William Wellman, USA, 1931). GB: *The Lost Lady*
Sailor Beware (Gordon Parry, GB, 1956). USA: *Panic in the Parlor*
Sailor of the King. See: *Single-handed*
St Louis Kid (Ray Enright, USA, 1934). GB: *Perfect Week-end*
St Martin's Lane (Tim Whelan, GB, 1938). USA: *Sidewalks of London*
Salomy Jane. See: *Wild Girl*
Salt to the Devil. See: *Give Us This Day*
Salvatore Giuliano (Francesco Rosi, ITALY, 1961). USA: *Dreaded Mafia*
Sammy Going South (Alexander Mackendrick, GB, 1962). USA: *A Boy is Ten Feet Tall*
The Sap from Syracuse (Edward Sutherland, USA, 1930). GB: *The Sap Abroad*
Saraband for Dead Lovers (Basil Dearden, GB, 1948). USA: *Saraband*
Saskatchewan (Raoul Walsh, USA, 1954). GB: *O'Rourke of the Royal Mounted*
Satan Never Sleeps. See: *The Devil Never Sleeps*
Saturday Island (Stuart Heisler, GB, 1951). USA: *Island of Desire*
Savage Princess. See: *Aan*
Savage Wilderness (Anthony Mann, USA, 1955). GB: *The Last Frontier*
Sawdust and Tinsel (Ingmar Bergman, SWEDEN, 1953). USA: *Naked Light*
Scandal (Wesley Ruggles, USA, 1929). GB: *High Society*
Scarface (Howard Hawks, USA, 1932). GB: *The Shame of a Nation*
Scent of Mystery (Jack Cardiff, USA, 1960). GB: *Holiday in Spain*
School for Secrets (Peter Ustinov, GB, 1946). USA: *Secret Flight*
Scrooge the Skinflint. See: *The Right to be Happy*
Scudda-Hoo, Scudda-Hay (F. Hugh Herbert, USA, 1948). GB: *Summer Lightning*
Seagulls over Sorrento (John & Roy Boulting, GB, 1954). USA: *Crest of the Wave*
Season of Passion. See: *Summer of the 17th Doll*
The Second Best Secret Agent in the Whole Wide World. See: *Licensed to Kill*
The Second Woman (James V. Kern, USA, 1949). GB: *Ellen*
Sealed Lips. See: *After Tonight*
The Secret Bride (William Dieterle, USA, 1934). GB: *Concealment*
Secret Flight. See: *School for Secrets*
The Secret Four. See: *Kansas City Confidential*
The Secret Game. See: *Jeux interdits*
Secret Interlude. See: *Private Number*
Secret Interlude. See: *The View from Pompey's Head*
Secrets d'Alcove (Henri Decoin, FRANCE-ITALY, 1954). GB/USA: *The Bed*
The Seekers (Ken Annakin, GB, 1954). USA: *Land of Fury*
See You in Hell, Darling. See: *An American Dream*
Separate Beds. See: *The Wheeler Dealers*
Serious Charge (Terence Young, GB, 1958). USA: *A Touch of Hell*
Service for Ladies (Alexander Korda, GB, 1931). USA: *Reserved for Ladies*
Seven Days Leave (Richard Wallace & John Cromwell, USA, 1930). GB: *Medals*
Seven Sinners (Tay Garnett, USA, 1940). GB (reissue): *Cafe of Seven Sinners*
Seven Thunders (Hugo Fregonese, GB, 1957). USA: *The Beasts of Marseilles*
Seven Waves Away (Richard Sale, GB, 1956). USA: *Abandon Ship*
The Shame of a Nation. See: *Scarface*
Shark Reef. See: *She Gods of Shark Reef*
She Couldn't Take It (Tay Garnett, USA, 1935). GB: *Woman Tamer*
She Gods of Shark Reef (Roger Corman, USA, 1956). GB: *Shark Reef*
Sherlock Holmes. See: *The Adventures of Sherlock Holmes*
Sherlock Holmes and Spider Woman (Roy William Neill, USA, 1944). GB: *Spider Woman*
Sherlock Holmes and the Secret Code. See: *Dressed to Kill*
She Played with Fire. See: *Fortune is a Woman*
She-Wolf of London (Jean Yarbrough, USA, 1946). GB: *The Curse of the Allenbys*
Shoot First. See: *Rough Shoot*
Should a Woman Tell? See: *Wandering Fires*
The Shulamite. See: *Under the Lash*
Sidewalks of London. See: *St Martin's Lane*
The Silent Barrier. See: *The Great Barrier*
The Silent Voice. See: *The Man Who Played God*
Silent Witness (Jean Yarbrough, USA, 1942). GB: *Attorney for the Defence*
Single-handed (Roy Boulting, GB, 1953). USA: *Sailor of the King*
Sinister House. See: *Who Killed Doc Robbin?*
The Sin of Harold Diddlebock (Preston Sturges, USA, 1940). GB: *Mad Wednesday*
Sirens of the Sea (Allen Holubar, USA, 1917). GB: *Darlings of the Gods*
Sisters under the Skin (David Burton, USA, 1934). GB: *The Romantic Age*
The Slasher. See: *Cosh Boy*
A Slice of Life. See: *Tempi Nostri*
Slumbering Fires. See: *Bucking Broadway*
The Small Back Room (Michael Powell & Emeric Pressburger, GB, 1948). USA: *Hour of Glory*
The Smallest Show on Earth (Basil Dearden, GB, 1956). USA: *Big Time Operators*
The Small Voice (Fergus McDonell, USA, 1948). GB: *The Hideout*
Smarty (Robert Florey, USA, 1934). GB: *Hit Me Again*
Smiling Along. See: *Keep Smiling*
The Smugglers. See: *The Man Within*
Sob Sister (Alfred Santell, USA, 1931). GB: *The Blonde Reporter*
So Close to Life (Ingmar Bergman, SWEDEN, 1958). USA: *Brink of Life*
So Goes My Love (Frank Ryan, USA, 1946). GB: *A Genius in the Family*
A Soldier's Plaything (Michael Curtiz, USA, 1931). GB: *A Soldier's Pay*
Sons of the Desert (William Seiter, USA, 1933). GB: *Fraternally Yours*
Sons of the Musketeers. See: *At Sword's Point*
Sons of the Sea. See: *Old Ironsides*
Sorority Girl (Roger Corman, USA, 1957). GB: *The Bad One*
Sorority House (John Farrow, USA, 1939). GB:

That Girl from College
So This is Love (Gordon Douglas, USA, 1953). GB: *The Grace Moore Story*
The Sound Barrier (David Lean, GB, 1952). USA: *Breaking the Sound Barrier*
South Sea Sinner (Bruce Humberstone, USA, 1949). GB: *East of Java*
Southwest Passage (Ray Nazarro, USA, 1954). GB: *Camels West*
Southwest to Sonora. See: *The Appaloosa*
Spider Woman. See: *Sherlock Holmes and Spider Woman*
Spin of a Coin. See: *The George Raft Story*
Spinout (Norman Taurog, USA, 1966). GB: *California Holiday*
Spinster. See: *Two Loves*
The Spirit of Culver (Joseph Santley, USA, 1939). GB: *Two Bright Boys*
Spirit of the People. See: *Abe Lincoln in Illinois*
Spirits of the Dead. See: *Histoires extraordinaires*
Spitfire. See: *The First of the Few*
Springtime in Italy. See: *E'Primavera*
The Spy in Black (Michael Powell, GB, 1939). USA: *U-Boat 29*
Spy in the Pantry. See: *Ten Days in Paris*
Spylarks. See: *The Intelligence Men*
Spy 13. See: *Operator 13*
The Squaw Man (Cecil B. De Mille, USA, 1918). GB: *The White Man*
Stairway to Heaven. See: *A Matter of Life and Death*
Stampeded. See: *The Big Land*
Stand by for Action (Robert Z. Leonard, USA, 1942). GB: *Cargo of Innocents*
Stars and Stripes Forever (Henry Koster, USA, 1952). GB: *Marching Along*
State of the Union (Frank Capra, USA, 1948). GB: *The World and his Wife*
State's Attorney (George Archainbaud, USA, 1932). GB: *Cardigan's Last Case*
Stazione Termini (Vittorio De Sica, ITALY-USA, 1953). GB: *Indiscretion.* USA: *Indiscretion of an American Wife*
The Sterile Cuckoo (Alan J. Pakula, USA, 1969). GB: *Pookie*
Stop Me Before I Kill. See: *The Full Treatment*
Stormy Waters. See: *Remorques*
The Story of a Cheat. See: *Le Roman d'un tricheur*
The Story of Alexander Graham Bell (Irving Cummings, USA, 1930). GB: *The Modern Miracle*
The Story of Dr Ehrlich's Magic Bullet (William Dieterle, USA, 1940). GB: *The Magic Bullet*
The Story of Esther Costello (David Miller, GB, 1957). USA: *The Golden Virgin*
The Story of Mandy. See: *Mandy*
Stranded in Paris. See: *Artists and Models Abroad*
The Strange Adventure(s) of David Gray. See: *Vampyr*
The Strange Conspiracy. See: *The President Vanishes*
Strange Incident. See: *The Oxbow Incident*
Strange Interlude (Robert Z. Leonard, USA, 1932). GB: *Strange Interval*
The Strange One (Jack Garfein, USA, 1957). GB: *End as a Man*
The Strange Ones. See: *Les Enfants terribles*
The Stranger. See: *The Intruder*
The Stranger Came Home (Terence Fisher, GB, 1954). USA: *The Unholy Four*
The Stranger in Between. See: *Hunted*
Stranger in the House (Pierre Rouve, GB, 1967). USA: *Cop-Out*
Strauss' Great Waltz. See: *Waltzes from Vienna*
Street Corner (Muriel Box, GB, 1953). USA: *Both Sides of the Law*
Strictly Confidential. See: *Broadway Bill*
Strictly for Pleasure. See: *The Perfect Furlough*
Strip-tease Lady. See: *Lady of Burlesque*
Stronger than Fear. See: *Edge of Doom*
Such Men are Dangerous. See: *The Racers*
Suicide Squadron. See: *Dangerous Moonlight*
Summer Interlude (Ingmar Bergman, SWEDEN, 1950). USA: *Illicit Interlude*
Summer Lightning. See: *Scudda-Hoo, Scudda-Hay*
Summer Madness (David Lean, GB, 1955). USA: *Summertime*
Summer of the 17th Doll (Leslie Norman, GB, 1959). USA: *Season of Passion*
Summer Stock (Charles Walters, USA, 1950). GB: *If You Feel Like Singing*
Summertime. See: *Summer Madness*
Sumurun (Ernst Lubitsch, GERMANY, 1920). USA: *One Arabian Night*
Susan and God (George Cukor, USA, 1940). GB: *The Gay Mrs Trexal*
Susan Lenox, Her Fall and Rise (Robert Z. Leonard, USA, 1931). GB: *The Rise of Helga*
Swamp Water (Jean Renoir, USA, 1941). GB: *The Man Who Came Back*
Sweet and Sour. See: *Dragées au poivre*
Swing Shift Maisie (Norman Z. McLeod, USA, 1943). GB: *The Girl in Overalls*
Swing, Teacher, Swing. See: *College Swing*
Symphony of Six Million (Gregory La Cava, USA, 1932). GB: *Melody of Life*
Synanon (Richard Quine, USA, 1965). GB: *Get Off My Back*
The System (Michael Winner, GB, 1963). USA: *The Girl-Getters*

T

Take a Letter, Darling (Mitchell Leisen, USA, 1942). GB: *Green-Eyed Woman*
Take Me Out to the Ball Game (Busby Berkeley, USA, 1948). GB: *Everybody's Cheering*
A Tale of Five Cities (Montgomery Tully, GB, 1951). USA: *A Tale of Five Women*
Target for Scandal. See: *Washington Story*
Tarzan's Peril (Byron Haskin, USA, 1951). GB: *Tarzan and the Jungle Queen*
Teenage Caveman (Roger Corman, USA, 1958). GB: *Out of the Darkness*
Teenager Bad Girl. See: *My Teenage Daughter*
Teheran (William Freshman, GB, 1947). USA: *The Plot to Kill Roosevelt;* GB (reissue): *Appointment in Persia*
Tempi Nostri (Alessandro Blasetti, ITALY-FRANCE, 1954). GB: *A Slice of Life*
Ten Days (Tim Whelan, GB, 1939). USA: *Spy in the Pantry*
Ten Little Niggers. See: *And Then There Were None*
Tennessee Johnson (William Dieterle, USA, 1943). GB: *The Man on America's Conscience*
A Terrible Beauty (Tay Garnett, GB, 1960). USA: *The Night Fighter*
Terror on a Train. See: *Time Bomb*
The Terror Strikes. See: *Revenge of the Colossal Man*
Das Testament von Dr Mabuse (Fritz Lang, GERMANY, 1932–3). GB: *The Last Will of Dr Mabuse/The Crimes of Dr Mabuse*
La Tête contre les murs (Georges Franju, FRANCE, 1958). GB: *The Keepers*
That Forsythe Woman (Compton Bennett, USA, 1949). GB: *The Forsyte Saga*
That Girl from College. See: *Sorority House*
That Hamilton Woman (Alexander Korda, USA, 1941). GB: *Lady Hamilton*
That Jane from Maine (Richard Quine, USA, 1959). GB: *It Happened to Jane*
That Man from Hong Kong. See: *Les Tribulations d'un Chinois en Chine*
That Navy Spirit. See: *Hold 'Em Navy*
That's My Man (Frank Borzage, USA, 1947). GB: *Will Tomorrow Ever Come?*
Their Secret Affair. See: *Top Secret Affair*
There is Another Sun (Lewis Gilbert, GB, 1950). USA: *Wall of Death*
Thérèse Raquin (Jacques Feyder, FRANCE-GERMANY, 1928). GB: *Thou Shalt Not*
These Are the Damned. See: *The Damned*
They Call It Sin (Thornton Freeland, USA, 1932). GB: *The Way of Life*
They Drive by Night (Raoul Walsh, USA, 1940). GB: *Road to 'Frisco*
They Flew Alone (Herbert Wilcox, GB, 1942). USA: *Wings and the Woman*
They Shall Have Music (Archie Mayo, USA, 1939). GB: *Melody of Youth*
Thin Ice (Sidney Lanfield, USA, 1937). GB: *Lovely to Look at*
The Third Key. See: *The Long Arm*
Thirst (Ingmar Bergman, SWEDEN, 1949). USA: *Three Strange Loves*
This is My Affair (William A. Seiter, USA, 1937). GB: *His Affair*
This is My Affair (1951). See: *I Can Get It for You Wholesale*
This Man Must Die. See: *Que la bête meure*
This Man Reuter. See: *A Dispatch from Reuters*
This Thing Called Love (Alexander Hall, USA, 1940). GB: *Married but Single*
Those Daring Young Men in Their Flying Jalopies. See: *Monte Carlo or Bust*
Thou Shalt Not. See: *Thérèse Raquin*
Three of a Kind. See: *Three Wise Crooks*
Three Strange Loves. See: *Thirst*
Three Stripes in the Sun (Richard Murphy, USA, 1955). GB: *The Gentle Sergeant*
Three Wise Crooks (Harmon Weight, USA, 1925). GB: *Three of a Kind*
Throne of Blood (Akira Kurosawa, JAPAN, 1957). USA: *Cobweb Castle*
Thundercloud (Edward L. Marin, USA, 1950). GB: *Colt 45*
Thunder in the East. See: *La Bataille*
Thunder on the Hill (Douglas Sirk, USA, 1951). GB: *Bonaventure*

Tiger in the Sky. See: *The McConnell Story*
Tight Little Island. See: *Whisky Galore*
Time and Tide. See: *The Clock*
Time Bomb (Ted Tetzlaff, GB, 1952). USA: *Terror on a Train*
A Time for Killing (Phil Harlson, USA, 1967). GB: *The Long Ride Home*
Timeslip (Ken Hughes, GB, 1955). USA: *The Atomic Man*
A Time to Live and a Time to Die. See: *Le Feu follet*
The Tip-off (Albert Rogell, USA, 1931). GB: *Looking for Trouble*
Toast of the Legion. See: *Kiss Me Again*
To Dorothy, a Son (Muriel Box, GB, 1954). USA: *Cash on Delivery*
The Tomahawk and the Cross. See: *Pillars of the Sky*
Tonight at 8.30. See: *Meet Me Tonight*
Tonight's the Night. See: *Happy Ever After*
Too Dangerous to Love. See: *Perfect Strangers*
Too Many Husbands (Wesley Ruggles, USA, 1940). GB: *My Two Husbands*
Top Secret (Mario Zampi, GB, 1952). USA: *Mr Potts Goes to Moscow*
Top Secret Affair (H. C. Potter, USA, 1956). GB: *Their Secret Affair*
Torch Singer (Alexander Hall & George Stevens, USA, 1933). GB: *Broadway Singer*
A Touch of Hell. See: *Serious Charge*
Toward the Unknown (Mervyn LeRoy, USA, 1956). GB: *Brink of Hell*
Toy Wife (Richard Thorpe, USA, 1938). GB: *Frou Frou*
Transatlantic Tunnel. See: *The Tunnel*
The Trap (Norman Panama, USA, 1958). GB: *The Baited Trap*
Trapped by Television (Del Lord, USA, 1936). GB: *Caught by Television*
Trapped by Wireless. See: *Panic on the Air*
The Tree of Liberty. See: *The Howards of Virginia*
Trelawney of the Wells. See: *The Actress*
Trial and Error. See: *The Dock Brief*
Les Tribulations d'un Chinois en Chine (Philippe de Broca, FRANCE-ITALY, 1965). GB: *Up to his Ears/That Man from Hong Kong*
The Trollenberg Terror (Quentin Lawrence, GB, 1957). USA: *The Crawling Eye*
Trottie True (Brian Desmond Hurst, GB, 1948). USA: *The Gay Lady*
The Trouble with Women. See: *The Imperfect Lady*
The True Story of Jesse James (Nicholas Ray, USA, 1956). GB: *The James Brothers*
The Trumpet Call. See: *Rough Riders*
Tudor Rose (Robert Stevenson, GB, 1936). USA: *Nine Days a Queen*
The Tunnel (Maurice Elvey, GB, 1935). USA: *Transatlantic Tunnel*
Turn Back the Hours (Howard Bretherton, USA, 1928). GB: *The Badge of Courage*
Twenty Dollars a Week (Harmon Weight, USA, 1924). GB: *The Man Maker*
Twenty Four Hours (Marion Gering, USA, 1931). GB: *The Hours Between*
Twenty One Days (Basil Dean, GB, 1939). USA: *Twenty One Days Together*
Twenty Plus Two (Joseph M. Newman, USA, 1961). GB: *It Started in Tokyo*
Twilight of Honor (Boris Sagal, USA, 1963). GB: *The Charge is Murder*
Two Against the World (William McGann, USA, 1936). GB: *The Case of Mrs Pembroke*
Two Are Guilty. See: *La Glaive et la balance*
Two Bright Boys. See: *The Spirit of Culver*
Two Can Play (Nat Ross, USA, 1926). GB: *The Love Test*
Two Girls on Broadway (S. Sylvan Simon, USA, 1940). GB: *Choose Your Partners*
Two-Gun Cupid. See: *The Bad Man*
Two Loves (Charles Walters, USA, 1961). GB: *Spinster*
Two Men and a Girl. See: *Honeymoon*

U
U-Boat 29. See: *The Spy in Black*
Unconventional Linda. See: *Holiday*
Undercover Maisie (Harry Beaumont, USA, 1946). GB: *Undercover Girl*
Under the Clock. See: *The Clock*
Under the Lash (Sam Wood, USA, 1921). GB: *The Shulamite*
Underworld (Josef von Sternberg, USA, 1927). GB: *Paying the Penalty*
Underworld. See: *Les Bas Fonds*
The Undying Monster (John Brahm, USA, 1942). GB: *The Hammond Mystery*
The Unholy Four. See: *The Stranger Came Home*
Union Depot (Alfred Green, USA, 1932). GB: *Gentleman for a Day*
Unknown Treasures (Archie Mayo, USA, 1926). GB: *The House Behind the Hedge*
Unseen Heroes. See: *Battle of the V1*
Un tel Père et Fils (Julien Duvivier, FRANCE, 1940). GB: *Heart of a Nation*. USA: *Immortal France*
Upstage (Monta Bell, USA, 1926). GB: *The Mask of Comedy*
Up to His Ears. See: *Les Tribulations d'un Chinois en Chine*

V
Valley of Fury. See: *Chief Crazy Horse*
Vampyr (Carl Dreyer, GERMANY, 1932). GB: *The Strange Adventure(s) of David Gray*
Venetian Bird (Ralph Thomas, GB, 1952). USA: *The Assassin*
Vessel of Wrath (Erich Pommer, GB, 1938). USA: *The Beachcomber*
Vice Squad (Arnold Laven, USA, 1953). GB: *The Girl in Room 17*
The View from Pompey's Head (Philip Dunne, USA, 1955). GB: *Secret Interlude*
Viking Women and the Sea Serpent (Roger Corman, USA, 1957). GB: *Viking Women*
The Village Fair. See: *Jour de fête*
The Violent Men (Rudolph Maté, USA, 1955). GB: *Rough Company*
The Violinist of Florence. See: *Die Geiger von Florenz*
V1. See: *Battle of the V1*
The Virtuous Husband (Vin Moore, USA, 1931). GB: *What Wives Don't Want*
The Virtuous Sin (Louis Gasnier & George Cukor, USA, 1930). GB: *Cast Iron*
Les Visiteurs du soir (Marcel Carné, FRANCE, 1942). USA: *The Devil's Envoys*
Viva Las Vegas (George Sidney, USA, 1963). GB: *Love in Las Vegas*
Vivre sa Vie (Jean-Luc Godard, FRANCE, 1962). GB: *It's My Life*. USA: *My Life to Live*
The Voice of Merrill (John Gilling, GB, 1952). USA: *Murder Will Out*

W
The WAC from Walla Walla (William Whitney, USA, 1952). GB: *Army Capers*
Waco (Lewis Collins, USA, 1951). GB: *The Outlaw and the Lady*
Walk East on Beacon (Alfred Werker, USA, 1952). GB: *Crime of the Century*
Walking Down Broadway (Erich von Stroheim, USA, 1932). GB: *Hello Sister*
Walk in the Shadow. See: *Life for Ruth*
Wall of Death. See: *There is Another Sun*
Waltzes from Vienna (Alfred Hitchcock, GB, 1933). USA: *Strauss' Great Waltz*
Wandering Fires (M. Campbell, USA, 1925). GB: *Should a Woman Tell?*
Wanderlust. See: *Mary Jane's Pa*
The Wanton. See: *Manèges*
The Warriors. See: *The Dark Avenger*
Washington Story (Robert Pirosh, USA, 1952). GB: *Target for Scandal*
Waterfront (Michael Anderson, GB, 1950). USA: *Waterfront Women*
The Way Ahead (Carol Reed, GB, 1944). USA: *Immortal Batallion*
Way Back Home (William A. Seiter, USA, 1931). GB: *Old Greatheart*
The Way of Life. See: *They Call It Sin*
The Way Out. See: *Dial 999*
The Way to the Stars (Anthony Asquith, GB, 1945). USA: *Johnny in the Clouds*
The Weak and the Wicked (J. Lee Thompson, GB, 1953). USA: *Young and Willing*
We Are French. See: *The Bugler of Algiers*
Web of Passion. See: *A Double Tour*
Wedding Bells. See: *Royal Wedding*
Wedding Breakfast. See: *The Catered Affair*
Week-end Madness. See: *August Week-end*
We Humans. See: *Young America*
Welcome to Hard Times (Burt Kennedy, USA, 1966). GB: *Killer on a Horse*
Werewolf in a Girls' Dormitory. See: *Lycanthropus*
West of Montana. See: *Mail Order Bride*
West Point (Edward Sedgwick, USA, 1928). GB: *Eternal Youth*
The West Point Story (Roy Del Ruth, USA, 1950). GB: *Fine and Dandy*
What a Man! See: *Never Give a Sucker an Even Break*
What a Woman (Irving Cummings, USA, 1943). GB: *The Beautiful Cheat*
What Lola Wants. See: *Damn Yankees*
What Wives Don't Want. See: *The Virtuous Husband*
The Wheeler Dealers (Arthur Hiller, USA, 1963). GB: *Separate Beds*

Wheel of Fire. See: *Pyro*
When Boys Leave Home. See: *Downhill*
When New York Sleeps. See: *Now I'll Tell*
When the Crash Came. See: *Alimony*
When Thief Meets Thief. See: *Jump for Glory*
When You're in Love (Robert Riskin, USA, 1936). GB: *For You Alone*
Where No Vultures Fly (Harry Watt, GB, 1951). USA: *Ivory Hunter*
Where Sinners Meet (J. Walter Ruben, USA, 1934). GB: *The Dover Road*
Where the River Bends. See: *Bend of the River*
Whisky Galore (Alexander Mackendrick, GB, 1948). USA: *Tight Little Island*
The Whistle at Eaton Falls (Robert Siodmak, USA, 1951). GB: *Richer Than the Earth*
White Captive. See: *White Savage*
White Cradle Inn (Harold French, GB, 1946). USA: *High Fury*
The White Man. See: *The Squaw Man*
White Savage (Arthur Lubin, USA, 1943). GB: *White Captive*
The White Unicorn (Bernard Knowles, GB, 1947). USA: *Bad Sister*
Who Goes There? (Anthony Kimmins, GB, 1952). USA: *The Passionate Sentry*
Who Killed Doc Robbin? (Bernard Carr, USA, 1948). GB: *Sinister House*
The Whole Town's Talking (John Ford, USA, 1935). GB: *Passport to Fame*
Why Men Forget. See: *Demos*
Wicked as They Come (Ken Hughes, GB, 1956). USA: *Portrait in Smoke*
Wicked Wife. See: *Grand National Night*
The Wife Takes a Flyer (Richard Wallace, USA, 1942). GB: *A Yank in Dutch*
Wild Boys of the Road (William Wellman, USA, 1933). GB: *Dangerous Days*
Wild Girl (Raoul Walsh, USA, 1932). GB: *Salomy Jane*
The Wild Heart. See: *Gone to Earth*
Wild Jungle Captive. See: *Jungle Captive*
Will o'the Wisp. See: *Le Feu follet*
Will Success Spoil Rock Hunter? (Frank Tashlin, USA, 1957). GB: *Oh, for a Man!*
Will Tomorrow Ever Come? See: *That's My Man*
A Window in London (Herbert Mason, GB, 1939). USA: *Lady in Distress*
Wings and the Woman. See: *They Flew Alone*
Winning Through. See: *Classmates*
The Winning Way. See: *All American*
The Wise Guy (Frank Lloyd, USA, 1926). GB: *Into the Night*
The Witches (Cyril Frankel, GB, 1966). USA: *The Devil's Own*
Witchfinder General (Michael Reeves, GB, 1968). USA: *The Conqueror Worm*
Within the Law. See: *Paid*
Without Children. See: *Penthouse Party*
A Woman Alone. See: *Sabotage*
The Woman Between. See: *The Woman I Love*
Woman Hunt. See: *Au Royaume des cieux*
The Woman I Love (Anatole Litvak, USA, 1937). GB: *The Woman Between*
The Woman in His House. See: *The Animal Kingdom*
The Woman in Question (Anthony Asquith, GB, 1950). USA: *Five Angles on Murder*
Woman in the Moon. See: *Frau im Mond*
Woman of the World. See: *Outcast Lady*
The Woman on Pier 13. See: *I Married a Communist*
Woman Tamer. See: *She Couldn't Take It*
Woman Without a Face. See: *Mister Buddwing*
Women's Dreams. See: *Journey into Autumn*
Wooden Soldiers. See: *Babes in Toyland*
The World and His Wife. See: *State of the Union*
The World Gone Mad (Christy Cabanne, USA, 1933). GB: *The Public Be Hanged*
The World Ten Times Over (Wolf Rilla, GB, 1963). USA: *Pussycat Alley*

Y

Yangtse Incident (Michael Anderson, GB, 1957). USA: *Battle Hell*
A Yank in Dutch. See: *The Wife Takes a Flyer*
A Yank in Indo-China (Wallace A. Grissell, USA, 1952). GB: *Hidden Secret*
A Yank in London. See: *I Live in Grosvenor Square*
Years Without Days. See: *Castle on the Hudson*
The Yellow Ticket (Raoul Walsh, USA, 1931). GB: *The Yellow Passport*
Les Yeux sans visage (Georges Franju, FRANCE, 1959). GB: *Eyes Without a Face*. USA: *The Horror Chamber of Dr Faustus*
Yield to the Night (J. Lee Thompson, GB, 1956). USA: *Blonde Sinner*
The Yokel. See: *The Boob*
You Belong to Me (Wesley Ruggles, USA, 1941). GB: *Good Morning, Doctor*
You Belong to My Heart. See: *Mr Imperium*
You Can't Sleep Here. See: *I Was a Male War Bride*
You Can't Take Money. See: *Internes Can't Take Money*
You Don't Need Pajamas at Rosie's. See: *The First Time*
You May Be Next (Albert S. Rogell, USA, 1935). GB: *Panic on the Air*
Young America (Frank Borzage, USA, 1932). GB: *We Humans*
Young and Innocent (Alfred Hitchcock, GB, 1937). USA: *A Girl Was Young*
The Young and the Damned. See: *Los Olvidados*
Young Man with a Horn (Michael Curtiz, USA, 1950). GB: *Young Man of Music*
Young and Willing. See: *The Weak and the Wicked*
The Young Philadelphians (Vincent Sherman, USA, 1958). See: *The City Jungle*
Young Scarface. See: *Brighton Rock*
Your Past is Showing. See: *The Naked Truth*
Your Witness (Robert Montgomery, GB, 1959). USA: *Eye Witness*

Z

Zenobia (Gordon Douglas, USA, 1939). GB: *Elephants Never Forget*
Zombies of Mora-Tau (Edward L. Cahn, USA, 1957). GB: *The Dead That Walk*
Zombies on Broadway (Gordon Douglas, USA, 1945). GB: *Loonies on Broadway*

KT

INDEX OF FILMS

This is a selective index. Biographies of directors and the longer articles, such as animation, the avant-garde, design and cinematography, have been fully indexed; significant references in the remainder of the text have also been included. Page numbers in roman type denote a textual reference, in *italics* a black-and-white illustration, in **bold** a colour illustration.

Index of Films

Index of Films

Index of Films

Index of Films

Index of Films

INDEX OF NAMES

This is essentially an index of those people mentioned in the Encyclopedia who are not the subject of an individual entry. However, those with an entry have been included and any significant reference to them elsewhere in the text has been indexed. Figures in *italics* denote an illustration either of an individual himself or of his work. Figures in **bold** type give the page number of the biographical entries.

Index of Names

Index of Names